THE BILLBOARD ILLUSTRATED ENCYCLOPEDIA *of* MUSIC

Publisher and Creative Director: Nick Wells
Commissioning Editor: Polly Willis
Managing Editor: Michelle Clare
Project Editor: Vicky Garrard
Editor and Picture Research: Julia Rolf
Picture Research: Melinda Révész

Chief Designer: Colin Rudderham
Designer: Jennifer Bishop
Design and Production: Chris Herbert
Production: Claire Walker

Proof readers: Marian Appellof, Anoushka Alexander, Howard Cooke,
Kevin Harley, Mariano Kalförs, Haydn Kirnon, Sonya Newland.

Engravers: Peter Dale, Steve Caine, Frances Gill,
Sara Loewenthal, Tim Williams

Special thanks to:
Frances Bodiam, Bob Nirkind, Graham Stride and Vanessa Nittoli

First published in 2003 by Billboard Books
An imprint of Watson-Guptill Publications
A Division of VNU Business Media, Inc.
770 Broadway,
New York, New York 1003
www.watsonguptill.com

Created and produced by
FLAME TREE PUBLISHING
Crabtree Hall, Crabtree Lane,
Fulham, London SW6 6TY
United Kingdom
www.flametreepublishing.com

Flame Tree Publishing is part of The Foundry Creative Media Co. Ltd

Library of Congress Control Number: 2003106299
ISBN: 0-8230-7869-8
Library of Congress Cataloging-in-Publication Data for this title can be
obtained from the Library of Congress.

First printing 2003

03 05 07 06 04

1 3 5 7 8 6 4 2

Printed in Italy

THE BILLBOARD ILLUSTRATED ENCYCLOPEDIA *of* MUSIC

Barry Alfonso, Bob Allen, Julian Beecroft, Lloyd Bradley, Keith Briggs,
Richard Brophy, Richard Buskin, Leila Cobo, Cliff Douse,
David Hutcheon, Colin Irwin, Nick Joy, Dave Ling, Carl Loben,
Bill Milkowski, Garry Mulholland, Steve Nallon, Douglas J Noble, Ed Potton

General Editor: Paul Du Noyer

Foreword by Sir George Martin

Consulting Editors
Ian Anderson, Geoff Brown, Richard Buskin, Paul Kingsbury,
Chrissie Murray, Michael Paoletta, Stanley Sadie,
Philip Van Vleck, John Wilson

Billboard Books
An imprint of Watson Guptill Publications, New York

How To Use This Book

The book is divided into the main categories of music, including rock, pop, classical, dance and jazz.

Album covers are often shown where they characterize the style of music.

Each category is divided into the main styles of music. For blues this list would include Delta blues, Chicago blues and British blues.

Cross-references throughout highlight the interplay of influences between musical styles and enable the reader to follow their interest into other parts of the book.

Each style is introduced at the head of the entry to enable the reader to sift through the book quickly to find specific areas of interest.

Quotes from artists, producers and commentators get to grips with the feel and passion of the music.

A list of leading exponents, supported by a comprehensive artists index at the end of each category, enables the reader to quickly locate their interest.

Four bars of music are provided for every style, teasing out the characteristic melodies or beats which differentiate one style from another. Guitar and percussion tabs are also shown where appropriate.

Contents

Foreword

I seem to have spent my entire life enjoying music: making it, writing it, orchestrating it, working with countless great musicians in performances of it and, of course, listening to it. Oh my word, have I *listened* to it! If you turned me upside down I am sure notes would tumble out of my ears!

Music has always been my friend and comfort in good times and bad, for it has a magic that will always give us what our heart desires. There is such an infinite variety of different forms of music that has evolved over the course of time, be it Bach or Mahler or Bacharach or McCartney, that there is something for everyone. Music, of all the arts, touches the human soul like nothing else: it is the most sublime, the most primeval, the very core of our beings. I believe our ancestors were able to make music before they could speak.

Music evolved and mutated fairly slowly over the years, but it was changed forever with the invention of the commercial recorder around a hundred years ago. This device immediately brought unknown types of music within reach of everyone in the Western world, and many new stars were born. Jazz thrived, once brilliant improvisations could be captured on disc, and along with radio, recorded music became a necessary part of our lives. Not only were we charmed and entertained, but we were able to learn from it, and I remember listening time and again to great jazz piano solos and copying them in my own way. Without the record, many of our greatest talents would still be doing their day jobs!

I had the good fortune to enter the music business at a crucial time. I began as a specialist in Baroque music in the 1950s, and part of my job was to advise the conductor where he should make a break in the score, so as to split the music into the different sections demanded of the shellac 78 rpm system, which only allowed four and a quarter minutes a side. My joy knew no bounds when the vinyl 33 $\frac{1}{3}$ rpm disc gave us up to half an hour a side, and later the introduction of the CD and digital recording which broke down all barriers on the road to perfection. Becoming head of a small record label, I found myself working alongside many fine artistes in all kinds of music, from folk and jazz to classical and pop, and I learned so much from them as my career advanced. It was an extraordinary plunge into the mainstream of good music, and I knew I was privileged indeed. You could say I was spoiled.

Nowadays, however, it is the consumer who is spoiled for choice. Music proliferates in every part of our lives, sometimes intrusively, and that may not be the best thing, either for us or for music. It is such a precious asset that is so easy to squander, most of us hearing a great deal by *listening* to little. Oscar Wilde spoke disparagingly of someone "who knew the cost of everything and the value of nothing." Well, have no fear: this book will give its readers the true value of music, exploring the incredible variety of evolving styles and explaining the importance of each genre. It will broaden their knowledge and point the way to a far deeper understanding and enjoyment of music. In an age where the visual image tends to dominate our minds, I hope this book will make us realise how very vital and precious is our sense of sound.

We all need to look less and listen more, which will make us all the more discerning. And we will find that the world *can* be a better place.

Sir George Martin
London, May 2003

Introduction

As I write this, playing in the background is music made by a pop singer from Uzbekistan. I scarcely know where that country is, but the effect of her voice is wonderful – curling and billowing through my house like the fragrance of flowers. Afterwards, I could turn to any of my other records: a compilation of classic Kinks singles, maybe, or the twenty-first-century hip hop of Missy "Misdemeanour" Elliott, and I know I would love it just as much. In another room is a TV set that offers a multiplicity of 24-hour music channels, and a radio that can supply even more. The Internet, of course, has become a resource to dwarf them all. And when I leave the house I can, thanks to my latest audio gadget, carry a pocket-sized jukebox of my favourite 4,000 tunes.

Music has never been as easily available as it is today. Actually, it is more than merely available: it is positively inescapable. I hear it on every city street, in every store I shop in and – notoriously – in every elevator I ride. No movie or TV ad is complete without it. And where the old-fashioned telephone would simply ring, its mobile descendants play anything from Robbie Williams to Beethoven. We all of us swim in a sea of entertainment nowadays, and the trick is to stop yourself getting swept along by the tide. That is where this book will prove invaluable.

When music is everywhere it is devalued. We hear so much we forget what it's like to listen. To appreciate the full beauty of music we need to become listeners again – active, curious, informed – not the passive recipients of whatever gets piped in our direction. We need to know what we're looking for and where we will find it. And once we have discovered that music, a little understanding of the circumstances that brought it into being will enrich and deepen our enjoyment.

This book is a wonderfully accessible way to make those discoveries and to acquire that understanding. You will find it divided into 16 sections, which between them cover just about any kind of music you are ever likely to encounter: rock and pop, R&B and hip hop, blues, jazz and folk, classical, futuristic and traditional styles from every corner of the planet. Within each section there are further divisions, examining the genre according to its various sub-genres. Each section will tell you about the origins of a particular category and introduce you to the most important artists – around 12,000 composers and performers in total – who have worked within that field. You will learn how any given style can be defined and what distinguishes it from other types of music. You will discover the influences it has absorbed and the influence it has exerted.

Thanks to the book's extensive use of lists and cross-references, it is possible to use the music you are familiar with as a route to whatever you want to discover. Be ready for surprises in the process. To my mind one of the chief delights of music is its inter-connectedness: you never know what may confront you at the next turning. Categories are essential to our mental map of music; they guide us through the infinity of available material. But, as our writers are quick to point out, categories were made to serve the music and not vice versa. Truly creative music has no boundaries. Every style shades into another: it will usually have its roots in earlier styles, evolving naturally from them; or it can be an instant synthesis of existing styles. Allow the book to lead wherever your inclination takes you.

As well as the text you will find an abundance of illustrations. Music has always had its visual dimension and has been a stimulus to fashion and the decorative arts. And, glamorous or not, images of performers bring us insight into their personalities. Whatever the area of music, I know the illustrations in this book will help bring you closer to its essence. In addition, there are many written examples of music: if you already read music you can use them to understand or even play a particular style, and if you do not – well, the book can teach you that as well. In fact, thanks to a glossary of instruments and terms, the non-musician need never feel excluded.

There is a wealth of knowledge within these pages, brought together by a diverse range of authors. What they have in common is expert understanding of their chosen fields and a real passion for the music. The latter is vital, because music is in the end about our emotions as much as our conscious understanding. It is a sensual pleasure, unrivalled in its power to uplift, excite or inspire, or simply to soothe and console. You could spend a lifetime exploring music. And you are now in the best possible company.

Paul Du Noyer
London, May 2003

Pop

Above

New York's Brill Building on Broadway was the hub of American pop music for many years.

"POP MUSIC IS THE MASS MEDIUM FOR CONDITIONING THE WAY PEOPLE THINK."

Graham Nash

Right

Perhaps the ultimate pop icon, Elvis Presley. Presley brought attitude and sexuality into the mainstream at a time when it was far from acceptable.

ACROSS the centuries and around the globe, many different forms of music have enjoyed mass appeal for a limited period of time. None, however, have been able to match the widespread influence of the popular music that erupted in America during the mid-1950s and, by the second half of the decade, was exerting its grip over much of the world.

Attaching doo-wop songs and soulful ballads to the main catalyst of rock'n'roll, this new youth-oriented pop, with its sometimes earthy lyrics and often grating beat, was the first to meld sexual energy with long-repressed feelings of teen angst and rebelliousness.

No longer prepared to do their parents' bidding by dressing and behaving like young adults, the postwar generation of kids demanded to be recognized on their own terms, and pop music was the vehicle that enabled them to achieve this. Forget those slick crooners, strict-tempo dances and sterile hits such as 'How Much Is That Doggie In The Window?'. The new music was all about

unleashing inhibitions and having unrestrained fun, not hanging out on street corners to kill time – and it was also about emphasizing the gulf between Mum, Dad and their over-sexed, under-compliant offspring.

Suddenly, teen emotions were being expressed in the words as well as in the rhythms, while the music was all the more accessible for the fact that vocal and instrumental virtuosity were not prerequisites for performing it yourself. Commencing in the mid-1950s, pop was, for the first time, truly music for the teen masses, to be enjoyed and even performed by teens. In the wake of Elvis Presley and Buddy Holly, guitar sales went through the roof, and it was not long before tens of thousands of juvenile bands began springing up on both sides of the Atlantic. Indeed, in cash-strapped Britain, which was still suffering from the ravages of the Second World War, R&B-based skiffle music served as a practical solution for kids who often did not have the funds to purchase decent instruments, while also providing them with a grounding in the basic skills that some would employ to great advantage just a few years later.

In the meantime, before pop's second big explosion could take place, its first phase had to run its course. As the 1950s segued into the 1960s, white adults were still running the show, and a combination of social pressure and self-destructive circumstances helped to spell the end for the black-derived rock'n'roll that some whites referred to as "jungle music". Chuck Berry was jailed for statutory rape, Jerry Lee Lewis was ostracized for marrying his 13-year-old cousin, Little Richard joined the Church, Buddy Holly and Eddie Cochran were killed in tragic accidents, and after Elvis emerged without sideburns from a two-year stint in the US Army, he threw

STYLES

Fifties Pop

Sixties Pop

Seventies Pop

Eighties Pop

Nineties Pop

Noughties Pop

POP STYLE

The pop music embraces a plethora of musical styles, catchy mid-range melodies combined with simple rhythms and light-hearted lyrics are staples of many hits.

Above
As Wham!, George Michael and Andrew Ridgeley went from having minor hits with cynical songs like 'Wham! Rap' to phenomenal commercial success with pop anthems such as 'Wake Me Up Before You Go Go'.

Right
The advent of the Beatles to the pop charts in 1962 changed the course of music history irrevocably. Their catchy songs, tuneful harmonies and loveable marketability opened the doors for a new era of British pop music.

dance material being written, produced and recorded inside Motown's Hitsville facility in Detroit; and about the surf-and-hot-rod sounds emanating from Californian outfits such as the Beach Boys.

In ironic contrast with the global tensions taking place during the nuclear age, pop music was espousing youthful optimism – serving as a welcome diversion from a troubled world, it was, for now, less a means of expression than a form of escapism. Nevertheless, although America had led the way with regard to popular music for much of the twentieth century, the status quo was about to change. Some British kids, whose lives had been irrevocably changed by rock'n'roll as well as by R&B, were stamping their own distinctive style and personality on the music. When they transported it back across the Atlantic, the shock waves reverberated throughout the industry, sweeping away virtually all before them.

In the vanguard of the mid-1960s "British Invasion" were the seemingly happy-go-lucky Beatles, whose guitar-and-drums-based sound infused the entire pop scene. Meanwhile, R&B-influenced rockers such as the Animals and the Rolling Stones, as well as mod outfits such as the Who, also provided contrast by way of their

himself head-first into a revamped scene that saw the old heavy brigade replaced by clean-cut, parent-approved smoothies: Fabian, Frankie Avalon, Connie Francis, Pat Boone, Bobby Vinton, Ricky Nelson. For now, the older generation had won the battle, even though the long term would see them forced to concede the war.

Still, the era that coincided with Cold War crises and President Kennedy's tenure in the White House was not just about soapy ballads and itsy bitsy teeny weeny yellow polka dot bikinis. It was also about the classic, three-minute pop songs that were being turned out by the brilliant young composing/production teams housed inside New York City's Brill Building, as recorded by artists ranging from the Drifters to the Shirelles; about a uniquely solo dance craze known as The Twist; about the innovative "Wall of Sound" hits produced by wunderkind Phil Spector; about the nonstop flow of pulsating

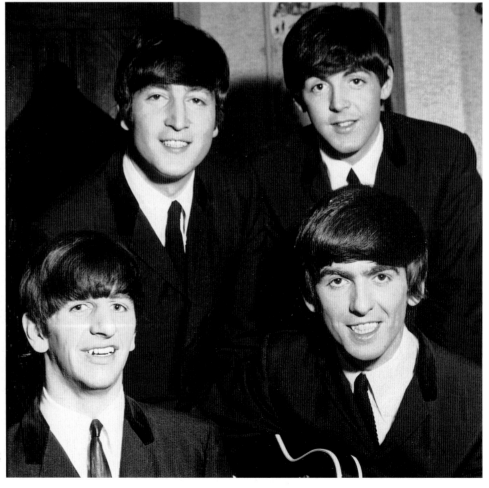

devil-may-care attitudes and slightly less clean-cut image. For a short time, many American artists found themselves in the unprecedented position of having to imitate their Brit counterparts in order to make the charts, although in the second half of the decade West Coast acts such as the Turtles and the Mamas & Papas helped to redress the balance.

By then, pop's fun and carefree attributes were charting a parallel but distinct course from the outspoken, introspective and experimental traits associated with the newly defined genre of rock music, as they were from the characteristics of numerous other musical categories that started to emerge. Largely appealing to pre-teens, early teens and middle-agers, pop would increasingly be associated with infectious commercialism at its best and crass exploitation at its worst.

While the emergence of reggae, rap and dance would see beat and rhythm jumping to the musical forefront during the ensuing decades, melody has continued to be at the centre of mainstream pop material. This has ranged from the teeny-bop product of The Osmonds and Bay City Rollers in the 1970s, Wham! and New Kids On The Block in the 1980s and Hanson and the Spice Girls in the 1990s, to the catchy Europop sounds of ABBA, the homogenous, production-line-type output of British songwriting/production team Stock,

Above
Fronted by Debbie Harry, Blondie had a unique sound combining a variety of influences from punk to disco and reggae. Their songs were easy to dance to, but retained a dark edge, with witty and often ironic lyrics.

Aitken & Waterman, the slick recordings of new romantics such as Duran Duran, and the even smoother product of boy bands such as Take That and the Backstreet Boys. Indeed, by tapping into other veins of music and infusing them with melody, sub-genres have fallen into the pop category – such as new wave (an offshoot of punk) and 2-tone (a by-product of ska).

Having split off from rock while incorporating anything from funk to Latin, pop music keeps evolving. Even so, its most consistent feature is its propensity for instant gratification. "If you can really get it together in three minutes," Blondie's lead singer Debbie Harry once observed, "that's what pop songs are all about."

Left
Without fans to buy the music and go to the concerts, pop music could not exist. This Cliff Richard fan, from the early 1960s, has covered her bedroom in pictures of her idol.

DURING THE MID-1950S, THE AMERICAN AND BRITISH POP SCENES EXPERIENCED A COMPLETE SHAKE-UP OF THE OLD ORDER. UP UNTIL THE DECADE'S HALFWAY POINT, THE AIRWAVES, RECORD STORES AND JUKEBOXES WERE FILLED WITH SENTIMENTAL BALLADS, NOVELTY SONGS AND INSTRUMENTALS THAT LARGELY REFLECTED THE TASTES OF WHITE ADULTS.

Fifties Pop

STYLES

Singer/Songwriters
Rock'n'Roll
Rockabilly
Doo-Wop
Skiffle

> "ROCK'N'ROLL... SMELLS PHONEY AND FALSE. IT IS SUNG, PLAYED AND WRITTEN FOR THE MOST PART BY CRETINOUS GOONS."
>
> *Frank Sinatra*

LEADING EXPONENTS

Paul Anka
Pat Boone
Lonnie Donegan
The Everly Brothers
Connie Francis
Bill Haley & his Comets
Buddy Holly
  & the Crickets
Jerry Lee Lewis
Frankie Lymon
  & the Teenagers
The Platters
Elvis Presley
Cliff Richard
Tommy Steele

AMERICAN artists such as Frankie Laine, Frank Sinatra, Dean Martin, Perry Como, Guy Mitchell, the McGuire Sisters, Eddie Fisher, Al Martino, Doris Day, Rosemary Clooney, Tony Bennett and Tennessee Ernie Ford dominated the charts on both sides of the Atlantic, while the British also enjoyed an array of homegrown acts, including pianist Winifred Atwell as well as singers such as Dickie Valentine, Ruby Murray, Alma Cogan, Anne Shelton, Jimmy Young and Vera Lynn. The one genuine teen heart-throb during this era was Johnnie Ray, a latter-day bobbysox idol whose early hits, 'Cry' and 'The Little White Cloud That Cried', coupled with a bawling style of singing that had his female fans in floods of tears, led to him being dubbed the "Prince of Wails" and, somewhat awkwardly, the "Nabob of Sob". Still, neither Ray nor any of his white contemporaries performed material that spoke to youthful vitality or rebellion. With his 1955 covers of Otis Williams & The Charms' 'Two Hearts' and Fats Domino's 'Ain't That A Shame', Pat Boone commenced his highly profitable enterprise of taking R&B songs originated by black artists, cleaning up their earthier lyrics, and crooning them in a style that, in line with his wholesome smile and white buck shoes, was deemed more acceptable to "moral" white audiences. Boone's sanitized covers of material by Domino, Little Richard, Ivory Joe Hunter, The Flamingos and The El Dorados would help him sell more records during the 1950s than any artist except Elvis Presley, yet it is debatable whether he helped push open the door for these innovative black artists or simply ensured that they continued to be marginalized.

Shake, Rattle And Rock'n'Roll

In 1954, Bill Haley did much the same when he covered Big Joe Turner's 'Shake, Rattle And Roll' and substituted many of composer Charles E. Calhoun's racier lyrics – "Get outta that bed, wash your face and hands" was transformed into "Get out from that kitchen and rattle those pots and pans", although the less explicit but actually more risqué "I'm like a one-eyed cat peepin' in a seafood store" remained, despite Haley assuring a reporter that "We stay clear of anything suggestive."

The previous year, blending country and western with R&B, Haley had introduced rock'n'roll to the charts by way of 'Crazy Man Crazy'. But it was his energetic recording of a song originally conceived as a "novelty foxtrot" by its veteran Tin Pan Alley composers that marked the first significant shift of power in the pop charts. 'Rock Around The Clock', tracked by Bill Haley & his Comets in 1954 and subsequently played over the title credits to juvenile delinquency film *The Blackboard Jungle*, displaced Pérez Prado's massively successful instrumental 'Cherry Pink And Apple Blossom White' atop the *Billboard* charts on 9 July 1955. After sharing pole position with Frank Sinatra's 'Learnin' The Blues' for a couple of weeks, it then occupied the summit all by itself. The old guard was giving way to a new era.

FIFTIES POP

The 6/8 time signature, giving a "smoochy" feel, was often a feature of 1950's pop ballads, as was the chord formation, going from the root to the minor, then the two and the five. Note also that the bass line carries quite a lot of melody.

The Soundtrack Of Youth

Those restless teens who had idolized Marlon Brando in *The Wild One* (a biker movie that was banned in Britain) and James Dean in *Rebel Without A Cause* were now lining up at the box office to see *The Blackboard Jungle* because of its theme song. Suddenly, youth had a soundtrack, and it was not long before numerous other artists began to jump on the bandwagon. In America, where *Billboard* magazine published three separate charts between 1955 and 1958 – "Bestsellers In Stores", "Most Played By Jockeys" and "Most Played In Jukeboxes" – before merging them into the "Hot 100", there was an almost immediate change in the record-buying demographic.

In addition to a string of definitive rock'n'roll hits by Elvis Presley, who represented the complete teen-friendly, parent-threatening package in terms of raw talent, good looks and a quasi-surly attitude, the upper regions of the charts were soon dominated by an assortment of rockers and pop-flavoured doo-woppers, ranging from Buddy Holly, Jerry Lee Lewis, Paul Anka and the Everly Brothers to the Platters and Frankie Lymon & the Teenagers. Indeed, if 1956 was a year of transition, 1957 was the year when the balance changed once and for all. This was also true for Britain, where the aforementioned American artists shared their success with a number of homegrown innovators and imitators. These included skiffle king Lonnie Donegan, Elvis-wannabe Cliff Richard and impresario Larry Parnes's stable of imaginatively named teen idols, such as Tommy Steele, Marty Wilde, Billy Fury, Dickie Pride, Duffy Power, Georgie Fame and Joe Brown (who refused to adopt the Parnes-suggested monicker of Elmer Twitch).

Both musically and culturally, young was in and old was square. Yet as the 1950s wound down, hardcore rock'n'roll was virtually dead, and a telling sign as to the short-term future arrived in the form of 'Venus', a sentimental, chart-topping ballad by clean-cut smoothie Frankie Avalon. For the time being, pop music was becoming acceptable once again.

Far Left

Johnnie Ray was one of the first white pop performers to really play the audience, taking the microphone from the stand, moving around the stage and emphasizing his songs with screams and real tears.

Above

Blind in his left eye since childhood, Bill Haley was self-conscious about his appearance. To draw attention away from his eye Haley wore his hair in a kiss curl, which became his trademark and sparked a kiss curl craze.

Left

Blackboard Jungle was a controversial film and was banned in some areas amidst fears that it would incite violence. However, the teenagers flocked to see it, above all for the theme song 'Rock Around the Clock'.

Fifties Pop Singer/Songwriters

UNTIL THE ADVENT OF ROCK'N'ROLL, POP SINGERS AND SONGWRITERS WERE, FOR THE MOST PART, DIVIDED INTO TWO SEPARATE CAMPS. THE SINGERS WERE TYPICALLY FACED WITH THE DAUNTING TASK OF UNEARTHING NEW HIT MATERIAL, UNLESS, LIKE FRANK SINATRA, THEY WERE SO ESTEEMED THAT THEY HAD THE BEST SONGWRITERS IN THE BUSINESS LINING UP TO WRITE FOR THEM.

Above

The Iowa plane crash in which Buddy Holly died also killed fellow singers J. P. Richardson (aka The Big Bopper) and Ritchie Valens. The tragic event was commemorated in Don McLean's 1972 single 'American Pie'.

> ## "A LOT OF SONGS I SANG TO CROWDS FIRST TO WATCH THEIR REACTION, THAT'S HOW I KNEW THEY'D HIT."
>
> *Little Richard*

Right

Sam Cooke's magnificent voice made an easy transition from gospel music to mainstream pop.

LEADING EXPONENTS

Paul Anka

Chuck Berry

Sam Cooke

Bobby Darin

Bo Diddley

Buddy Holly

Jerry Lee Lewis

Carl Perkins

Little Richard

Neil Sedaka

ALL of this began to change in the mid-1950s, however, as pop music commenced its evolution into a do-it-yourself art form in which, as with country and western and the blues, the performance of a song was often less about perfection than about feel.

Rockabilly singer/songwriter Carl Perkins secured his own place in pop history by way of his one major chart hit, 'Blue Suede Shoes', which became a rock'n'roll anthem when it was covered by Elvis Presley in 1956. At around the same time, the R&B field delivered the likes of Little Richard (real name Richard Penniman), an electrifying, gospel-rooted singer/pianist who co-wrote many of his biggest hits, including 'Tutti Frutti', 'Lucille', 'Long Tall Sally', 'She's Got It', 'Keep A Knockin' ', 'Slippin' And Slidin' ' and 'Jenny, Jenny'; and singer/guitarist Bo Diddley (born Otha Ellas Bates), innovator of the pounding, Latin-tinged rhythm and beat that infused not only self-referential compositions such as 'Bo Diddley' and 'Diddley Daddy', but also numerous classic songs by other artists down the years, such as The Strangeloves' 'I Want Candy', Buddy Holly's 'Not Fade Away', Johnny Otis's 'Willie And The Hand Jive', Shirley And Company's 'Shame, Shame, Shame', George Michael's 'Faith' and U2's 'Desire'.

Pure Poetry For A New Generation

Nevertheless, perhaps the single most influential singer/songwriter of the era was Chuck Berry, whose driving guitar licks and topical, witty and ingeniously quick-fire, poetic lyrics pretty much defined rock'n'roll. A native of St. Louis, Missouri, Charles Edward Anderson Berry threw country, R&B and boogie-woogie into the mix when concocting major chart hits such as 'Maybellene', 'Roll Over Beethoven', 'Rock And Roll Music', 'Sweet Little Sixteen', 'Carol' and 'Johnny B. Goode'.

FIFTIES POP SINGER/SONGWRITERS

Writers like Chuck Berry brought elements of blues into pop, using flattened notes (blue notes) in the melody, and keeping the tune the same when the chords changed under it. The bass line often used the same sequence of notes, changing key to suit the chords.

THE FIFTIES POP INTRO ➡ 12   POP PEOPLE A-Z ➡ 72   INSTRUMENTS A-Z ➡ 436   POP: ROCKABILLY ➡ 18   BLUES: BOOGIE-WOOGIE ➡ 165

The results were pure poetry for a new generation of car-cruising, guitar-strumming, record-playing, dancing and dating teens. As John Lennon once said, "If you tried to give rock'n'roll another name, you might call it Chuck Berry."

As attested to by his chart success and influence over 1960s superstars ranging from the Beach Boys and the Beatles to Bob Dylan and the Rolling Stones, Berry had little trouble appealing to white audiences. Meanwhile, another singer/songwriter who made a more concerted effort in that regard was Sam Cooke, who crossed over from his gospel origins as the lead singer with the Soul Stirrers to lend his sublime voice to self-penned mainstream white pop, flavoured with an assortment of soul, R&B and, on occasion, unadulterated kitsch. In 1957, Cooke enjoyed his first solo American number 1 with 'You Send Me', a romantic ballad complemented by white backing vocalists, and moved even further away from his roots with overtly commercial follow-ups such as 'Everybody Likes To *Cha Cha Cha*' and 'Only Sixteen' before really hitting his stride during the early part of the ensuing decade.

Inspiring The Composers Of Tomorrow

While Sam Cooke stood as a symbol of African-American achievement and prosperity, writing most of his hit material in addition to running his own management and publishing companies alongside an independent record label, several of his white contemporaries were also inspiring the composers of tomorrow by honing their skills as singer/songwriters. Bobby Darin (born Walden Robert Cassotto) enjoyed his first chart success in 1958 with the co-written novelty number 'Splish Splash', and he built on that the following year by penning the smash hit 'Dream Lover'. At the same time, while 'Words Of Love' was a Buddy Holly solo composition that would later be covered by the Beatles, Holly co-wrote several of his most memorable songs with members of his backing band The Crickets, as well as with producer Norman Petty; among them were 'That'll Be The Day', 'Peggy Sue', 'It's So Easy', 'Well … All Right', 'Think It Over' and 'True Love Ways'.

Shortly after his death in a plane crash in February 1959, Holly topped the UK charts with the posthumous (and ironically titled) single 'It Doesn't Matter Anymore'. This had been penned by Paul Anka, yet another multi-talented youngster who had enjoyed international success by recording his own material. A native of Ontario, Canada, Anka was only 16 when 'Diana', his 1957 paean to a girl four years his senior, made him an international star, and during the next couple of years he capitalized on this with a string of highly dramatic ballads focusing on teen romance (or the lack thereof), including 'You

Are My Destiny', 'Lonely Boy' and 'Put Your Head On My Shoulder'. He also wrote the lyrics to the big Sinatra hit, 'My Way'.

Unlike the veteran Tin Pan Alley composers, Anka was able to connect with teenagers and convey their emotions because he was one himself. This trend would pick up pace during the decades to follow.

Above

The ingenious songs of Chuck Berry combined clever and witty lyrics with fast-moving tunes and intricate guitar playing. Onstage, Chuck had a number of popular moves, including the famous "duck walk".

ALTHOUGH HE DID NOT COIN THE TERM "ROCK'N'ROLL" – WHICH WAS AN AFRICAN-AMERICAN SLANG TERM FOR SEX – NEW YORK DISK JOCKEY ALAN FREED DID POPULARIZE IT WHEN HE ATTACHED IT TO A TEEN-ORIENTED FORM OF MUSIC THAT EVOLVED FROM A FUSION OF ROCKABILLY, R&B AND, TO A LESSER EXTENT, GOSPEL AND BOOGIE-WOOGIE.

Rock'n'Roll

Above

Cobbled together by Specialty from outtakes and other leftover studio tracks, The Fabulous Little Richard presents the usually frenetic rock'n'roll star in a slightly more mellow mood.

Right

Being considered threatening and corruptive by the authorities only further ensured Elvis Presley's iconic status. In fact, despite his risqué onstage moves, Presley was really a sweet, home-loving boy.

> "LET'S FACE IT – ROCK'N'ROLL IS BIGGER THAN ALL OF US."
>
> *Alan Freed*

IN its early forms, rock'n'roll was often so similar to R&B (known as "race music" until *Billboard* journalist Jerry Wexler provided it with a more appropriate name) in terms of structure and feel that it is not easy to discern which of the categories certain records fell into or even to ascertain what was, in fact, the first true rock'n'roll record.

Jackie Brenston's 1951 classic, 'Rocket 88', which he cut as a member of Ike Turner and the Kings of Rhythm, is one of the most popular choices in this regard, but there are many, many other contenders, ranging from 1948 recordings such as Wynonie Harris's 'Good Rockin' Tonight' and Wild Bill Moore's 'We're Gonna Rock, We're Gonna Roll' to Jimmy Preston's 'Rock The Joint' in 1949 and Muddy Waters' 'Rollin' And Tumblin' ' in 1950. Waters' assertion that "the blues had a baby and they called it rock'n'roll" was only part of the story; other musical genres also played a major role in the evolutionary process.

A Hybrid Sound That Would Shake The World

'Rocket 88' was produced by the legendary Sam Phillips a year before he formed Sun Records, the small independent label which, along with his tiny Memphis Recording Service studio, soon became synonymous with the birth of rock'n'roll. Having opened up his facility to a number of R&B and blues performers, including Rosco Gordon and Howlin' Wolf, Phillips then began working with local country acts while searching for a white artist who could bring black music to the masses by conveying the true

feel and passion of the blues. As it turned out, that artist was Elvis Presley, who, through a process of trial and error, under guidance from Phillips, and in collaboration with guitarist Scotty Moore and bass player Bill Black, utilized his innate talent, steeped in country, gospel and the blues, to contrive a hybrid sound that would shake the world. In 13 months at Sun, from July 1954 to August 1955, Presley released five singles, each of which featured an R&B standard on one side and a souped-up country track on the other. While the latter

LEADING EXPONENTS

Chuck Berry
Eddie Cochran
Bill Haley
Buddy Holly
Jerry Lee Lewis
Little Richard
Elvis Presley
Gene Vincent

ROCK'N'ROLL

The pulsing chords in the top change from major to minor over the second two bars, creating the distinctive rock and roll feel. The bass line is "solid" playing a rolling up-and-down pattern that moves with the chords.

THE FIFTIES POP INTRO ➡ 12   POP PEOPLE A-Z ➡ 72   INSTRUMENTS A-Z ➡ 436   THE ROCK INTRO ➡ 410   THE BLUES INTRO ➡ 154

category helped to define rockabilly, the former held the key to rock'n'roll. When white Southerners heard the first of these R&B cuts, Elvis's feverish, yearning cover of Arthur "Big Boy" Crudup's 'That's All Right (Mama)', many of them assumed they were listening to a black singer; by the time of the second, a heavily suggestive version of 'Good Rockin' Tonight', they knew not only that he was white, but that it was time to lock up their daughters.

After Elvis's contract was sold to the huge RCA corporation in late 1955, he recorded the seminal 'Heartbreak Hotel', a sombre, haunting single that not only sustained its predecessors' blues feel and levels of sexual insinuation, but also gained him worldwide recognition. With its blues-laced piano, strident guitar solos and depressive, self-pitying lyrics, 'Heartbreak Hotel' served as a call to arms for disgruntled teenagers; from then on, Presley, whose youthful good looks and Brando-like sexuality stood in sharp and favourable contrast to the pudgy, kiss-curled visage of Bill Haley, pressed home his advantage with a series of blistering rock'n'roll recordings. 'Blue Suede Shoes', 'Hound Dog' and 'Jailhouse Rock' were just a few of the many classic tracks he laid down during a four-year period (along with the songs for the movie *King Creole*, which awkwardly merged rock with Dixieland jazz), yet while they epitomized the genre, some also smacked of manufactured pop rather than heartfelt R&B.

Energy And Attitude

Meanwhile, another Sam Phillips discovery was Jerry Lee Lewis, "The Killer" from Ferriday, Louisiana, whose arrogant, aggressive performances quickly established him as one of rock'n'roll's most inspirational figures during its halcyon period. Melding country and R&B with frenetic, boogie-style piano, Lewis turned out songs that would get the whole joint jumping: 'Whole Lotta Shakin' ', 'Great Balls Of Fire', 'Breathless' and 'High School Confidential'. If Elvis Presley was rock'n'roll's greatest sex symbol, Jerry Lee Lewis was certainly its wildest white performer.

Nevertheless, whereas Lewis belted out his songs' lyrics with manic intensity, and Presley traversed the musical boundaries to sound alternately raucous, gospel-tinged, crooner-like, countrified and bluesy, neither man could match Little Richard, another classic voice of rock'n'roll, for raw, throat-grating, lightning-quick delivery. Richard's exhaustingly energetic singing, punctuated with falsetto shrieks and breathless

asides, perfectly matched his flamboyant appearance and short-changed no one, least of all the kids for whom "awop-bop-a-loo-bop-a-lop-bam-boom" had complete meaning. Gibberish or not, it was a language they could instantly identify with, for it somehow encapsulated the energy and attitude prevalent in numbers such as 'Tutti Frutti', 'Long Tall Sally', 'Rip It Up', 'She's Got It', 'Lucille' and 'Good Golly Miss Molly'. What's more, it was a language that most parents could in no way understand, and that had to make it all the more pertinent.

Above
"The Killer" performs a storming rendition of the title track in the opening scenes of High School Confidential, *a film that involved a tongue-in-cheek exposé of drug abuse in American schools.*

A SLAPPED UPRIGHT BASS, TWANGING LEAD GUITAR AND ACOUSTIC RHYTHM GUITAR;
A BLUES STRUCTURE WITH COUNTRY AND BLUES INFLECTIONS; A STRONG BEAT AND
MODERATE-TO-FAST TEMPO; A WILD, YELPING, OFTEN STUTTERING VOCAL STYLE,
TOGETHER WITH PLENTY OF ECHO ON THE RECORDINGS ARE THE MAIN INGREDIENTS
OF ROCKABILLY.

Rockabilly

Above

Sam Phillips, owner of Sun Records and creator of the rockabilly style. Hearing Elvis Presley fooling around in the studio with Scotty Moore and Bill Black, Phillips recognized potential in the new sound.

THE rockabilly style was an eclectic hybrid of R&B, hillbilly music and country-boogie that emerged during the mid-1950s, and again owed much to Sam Phillips and his Sun Records label.

While country-boogie had drawn on jazz boogie-woogie rhythms during the previous decade, and been popularized by acts such as The Delmore Brothers, Webb Pierce, Red Foley and Moon Mullican, the acoustic bass and steel guitar prevalent in the hillbilly sound of Hank Williams exerted just as much influence on the likes of Bill Haley and, a little later on, Carl Perkins. When Perkins arrived at Sun, he was performing hillbilly honky-tonk infused with the rhythm of black blues music. With Phillips' guidance he then added some R&B touches by way of scatting his vocal phrases and completing them on guitar, resulting in cuts such as 'Gone, Gone, Gone', which appeared on the flip side of his first Sun single, and the seminal self-penned 'Blue Suede Shoes'.

> "I CAN HEAR ROCKABILLY IN THE MUSIC THAT THEY PLAY TODAY...BLUEGRASS AND THE COTTON-PATCH BLUES. THEY'RE STILL COPPIN' FROM THAT TODAY."
>
> *Charlie Feathers*

A More Commercial Sound

Complemented by Phillips' trademark use of slap-back echo and over-amplification, songs such as 'Gone, Gone, Gone' and 'Blue Suede Shoes' were quintessential rockabilly (or "hillbilly bop", as they were sometimes described), a style that the producer had largely concocted in collaboration with Elvis Presley. The B-side of Elvis's first single ('That's All Right',

issued in July 1954) was a total revamping of Bill Monroe's 1947 bluegrass waltz, 'Blue Moon Of Kentucky'. Searching for a more commercial sound that might appeal to a widespread audience, Phillips tried to encourage the young singer, as well as guitarist Scotty Moore and bass player Bill Black, to find a comfortable uptempo groove. This began to take shape over the course of several takes – "Hell, that's fine! That's different!" Phillips can be heard exclaiming at one point on the session tape: "That's a pop song now, nearly 'bout!" – until what finally emerged was a jumped-up, freewheeling, echo-bathed version, the feel of which was light years away from that of the Monroe original.

The process continued through subsequent Presley recordings such as 'I Don't Care If The Sun Don't Shine', 'Milkcow Blues Boogie' and, most supremely, an electrifying cover of Junior Parker's 'Mystery Train', which borrowed a guitar riff from Parker's earlier 'Love My Baby' to bridge the gap between country and R&B. Still, it was Carl Perkins' 1956 recording of the self-penned 'Blue Suede Shoes' that gained rockabilly worldwide recognition, encouraging major labels such as Capitol, Columbia, Decca,

ROCKABILLY

Rockabilly bands typically used an upright bass (contrabass), plucked on the note and slapped on the off-beats in between, here represented by the short notes alternating in the bass line. The guitar figure usually put in its own rhythmic counterpoint.

Mercury and RCA to jump on the bandwagon and exploit the genre. Coral signed the Johnny Burnette Rock'n'Roll Trio, Capitol signed Gene Vincent and RCA even signed "the female Elvis Presley", Janis Martin.

For its part, Sun served as the main rockabilly hub, and although only Presley and Perkins experienced large-scale success in this field, a number of other artists signed to the label did make some notable recordings. Prime among them was Charlie Feathers, who, with Stan Kesler, co-wrote 'I Forgot To Remember To Forget' – which Elvis subsequently recorded – before moving to other labels and recording classics of the genre such as 'Tongue-Tied Jill' and 'Get With It'. At a time when rock'n'roll was breaking big on both sides of the Atlantic, Feathers felt that he never got the record company support he deserved – a view shared by Billy Lee Riley, who was convinced that his own chances of success were compromised by Sam Phillips focusing his attention on the skyrocketing career of Jerry Lee Lewis.

Limited Chart Success

Riley's more memorable recordings at Sun included 'Rock With Me Baby' and 'Red Hot', but none made the chart inroads he hoped for and expected. A similar fate befell the

efforts of, among others, Sonny Burgess, Ray Harris, Hayden Thompson and Warren Smith. Rockabilly's place in the spotlight was limited and its time was short-lived; its performers came from a very specific background, too. Indeed, because only a handful of the artists were black, Sam Phillips wasn't even comfortable with the genre's name.

"I've always thought 'rock'n'roll' was the best term," he'd comment more than four decades later, "because it became all-inclusive of white, black and the whole thing, whereas 'rockabilly' tended to just want to lend itself so specifically to white. It also promoted the feeling that maybe we were stealing something from the blacks and wanted to put it in a white form, so I never did like 'rockabilly'."

Still, numerous people consider the golden era of rockabilly, which burned out towards the end of the 1950s, to be a shining period in the annals of popular music; a time when often basic instrumentation and primitive recording equipment combined with uninhibited energy to produce rough-edged music that was vital, honest and, to many minds, the purest form of rock'n'roll. It was also a musical form that encapsulated the feelgood party spirit of the mid-1950s: as Carl Perkins once said, "We shook the devil loose! We bopped those blues!"

Above

Carl Perkins, one of rockabilly's finest, sold two million copies of his song 'Blue Suede Shoes' before Elvis's cover version was released. A true country boy, Perkins originally wrote the song on a potato sack.

Left

Rockabilly enjoyed a revival in the 1970s and 1980s, with bands such as the Stray Cats playing down-home 1950s-style music with a punk-rock edge. There were also purist rockabilly revival bands who followed the original style more closely.

WHILE MANY HIT DOO-WOP RECORDS FEATURED FULL INSTRUMENTAL ACCOMPANIMENT, THE GROUPS THEMSELVES HAD USUALLY STARTED OUT SINGING A CAPPELLA. IT WAS, IN SHORT, A MUSIC THAT REQUIRED COLLABORATIVE EFFORT BUT NO INSTRUMENTAL OUTLAY OR EXPERTISE, TO BE PERFORMED ON STREET CORNERS AS A MEANS OF ESCAPE, PUBLIC ENTERTAINMENT, PERSONAL FULFILMENT AND PROFESSIONAL AMBITION.

Doo-Wop

Above

Doo-wop usually suggests sweet harmonies and tender ballads, but this was not always the case. This compilation contains a selection of more up-tempo doo-wop songs.

DERIVING its name from the nonsense backing vocals that often provided its rhythm, R&B-flavoured doo-wop was one of the most popular veins of music to attach itself to rock'n'roll during the second half of the 1950s. The most prominent characteristic of the emotive romantic ballads and jaunty, uptempo, sometimes comical numbers was their interweaving harmonies, whose roots lay not only in gospel but also in black American vocal outfits of the 1940s such as the Mills Brothers and the Ink Spots.

Arguably, the first doo-wop hit was the Orioles' 'It's Too Soon To Know' in 1948. Thereafter, a number of similar, bird-named groups emerged throughout the early 1950s, including the Cardinals, the Crows, the Larks, the Ravens, the Robins, the Wrens and the Penguins; the latter's 1954 hit, 'Earth Angel (Will You Be Mine)', was latched onto by white kids who could readily identify with lyrics concerning youthful romance. Consequently, a form of music that had initially been aimed at a predominantly adult, African-American audience began to cross over to a multiracial teenage market. In turn, this led to integrated doo-wop groups such as the Impalas and the Del-Vikings – whose 1957 hit 'Come Go With Me' was the first song that the adolescent Paul

> "WE SANG ON THE BEACHES, OR ON ROOFTOPS, OR IN HALLWAYS OF TENEMENT BUILDINGS. WE MUST HAVE BEEN SENSITIVE ARTISTS, EVEN BACK THEN, BECAUSE WE ALWAYS LOOKED FOR THE HALLWAY THAT HAD THE BEST SOUND."
>
> *Dion De Mucci*

McCartney ever saw John Lennon perform – as well as all-white outfits such as Dion & the Belmonts, the Mystics and the Skyliners.

The Doo-Wop Bandwagon

Doo-wop had made vast strides within a very short time, and many of the teens who were buying the records were also inspired to form their own a cappella groups. As singles by the Dominoes and Hank Ballard & the Midnighters made the transition from the R&B charts to the mainstream pop market, and as acts such as the Jewels, the Cadillacs, the Chords, the El Dorados and the Five Satins enjoyed short-lived success, so many of the record companies jumped on the

LEADING EXPONENTS

The Coasters
The Chords
The Clovers
Dion & the Belmonts
The Flamingos
Frankie Lymon & the
 Teenagers
Little Anthony & the
 Imperials
The Moonglows
The Platters
The Silhouettes

DOO-WOP

Doo-wop gets its name from the style of the harmony singing, typically a long note followed by a short one - the "doo" and the "wop" - which generally went on behind the lead vocals soaring over the top. The bass line is also sung and always hits the downbeat in every bar.

THE FIFTIES POP INTRO ➡ 12   POP PEOPLE A-Z ➡ 72   INSTRUMENTS A-Z ➡ 436   THE SOUL AND R&B INTRO ➡ 368

doo-wop bandwagon and hundreds of "new discoveries" were rushed into studios all over the US. Cities such as Los Angeles and Philadelphia produced a fair number of the acts, but the main hub was New York, where both African-Americans and Italian-Americans with little cash in their pockets, but with melody in their hearts, harmonized on teen-oriented songs that conveyed the innocence of a now long-gone era.

Thanks to the exploitative, cut-throat practices of the record industry at that time, many of the relatively small percentage of performers who did manage to have their efforts released still emerged without cash in their pockets. Still, some did profit from their endeavours, and others did enjoy an extended stay in the charts. These included the Clovers, the Moonglows, Little Anthony & the Imperials, and Frankie Lymon & the Teenagers, while the plateau was occupied by the Platters and the Coasters.

Crossover Success

One of the most pop-oriented of all the doo-wop groups, the Platters achieved crossover success in several regards, attracting not only a multiracial audience but also a worldwide, multigenerational one courtesy of such smash-hit ballads as 'Only You (And You Alone)' in 1955 and 'The Great Pretender', whose chart success peaked the following year, both composed by manager Buck Ram. While 'The Great Pretender' made the Platters the first black act of the rock era to top the pop charts, 'Twilight Time' and 'Smoke Gets In Your Eyes' also occupied pole position and helped the group defy the convention of white artists enjoying greater success with covers of R&B songs. The group's line-up would change over the years, but the most successful one comprised gospel-steeped lead singer Tony Williams, tenor David Lynch, bass Herb Reed, baritone Paul Robi and, unusually for a doo-wop outfit, female harmonizer Zola Taylor.

Meanwhile, the other massive doo-wop favourites of the late-1950s were the Coasters, whose wild, comedy-filled songs contrasted sharply with the Platters' plaintive, soul-stirring ballads. Thanks to the input of legendary composer-producers Jerry Leiber and Mike Stoller, as well as manager Lester Sill, the Coasters turned out a string of million-sellers such as 'Young Blood', 'Searchin' ', 'Yakety Yak', 'Charlie Brown' and 'Poison Ivy' that, in the case of the first two numbers, capitalized on the vocal and improvisational talents of bass lead Bobby Nunn and lead tenor Carl Gardner (both of whom had previously been part of the Leiber & Stoller-produced sextet the Robins). Tenor Leon Hughes and baritone Billy Guy completed the quartet. 'Young Blood' and 'Searchin'' were, in fact, released as a double-A-sided single, but by the time 'Yakety Yak' and 'Charlie Brown' were recorded for Atlantic's new Atco label, the group had relocated from Los Angeles to New York with a revamped line-up. This saw Nunn and Hughes replaced by bass lead Will "Dub" Jones and tenor Cornell Gunter, with Adolph Jacobs added on guitar, while among the choice session musicians were the likes of saxophone virtuoso King Curtis.

Thanks to the Coasters and their brilliant songwriting/production team, doo-wop was accorded an all-around brassier treatment in the form of strident sax solos and raucous vocal interplay. However, this only fuelled many people's tendency to not take the genre too seriously, and by the end of the decade it had run out of steam.

Left

Hank Ballard brought a mixture of gospel influences and raunchy R&B to the vocal group that he joined in 1953. Their big hit, 'Work With Me Annie', inspired answer records from various musical spheres.

Below

The winning combination of the Coasters' vocal talents, Leiber & Stoller's humorous lyrics and King Curtis's stonking saxophone solos led to a string of hits that reflected the light-hearted side of doo-wop.

A CHEAP ACOUSTIC GUITAR, A WASHBOARD, SOME THIMBLES, A TEA CHEST, A BROOM
HANDLE AND A LENGTH OF STRING, TOGETHER, WITH A MODICUM OF MUSICAL TALENT
– THESE WERE ALL THAT WAS REQUIRED FOR SKIFFLE, AN AMALGAM OF AMERICAN JAZZ,
BLUES AND FOLK THAT CAUGHT ON WITH BRITAIN'S LARGELY CASH-STRAPPED TEENAGERS
IN 1956 AND 1957, TEMPORARILY CHALLENGING THE SUPREMACY OF ROCK'N'ROLL.

Skiffle

Above

*Lonnie Donegan was the first
major star of British pop.*

RHYTHMIC and decidedly upbeat, skiffle was a white,
Anglicized extension of the black music that, drawing on
blues, jazz, rag and traditional country, had originated in
America during the late nineteenth century and been
performed all over the South during the 1920s and 1930s
by what were variously known as skiffle, skuffle, spasm,
hamfat, washboard, jook and, most popularly, jug bands.
These makeshift outfits usually consisted of a fiddle, a banjo,
a kazoo and, sometimes, a guitar, mandolin and/or harmonica,
together with percussive, rhythmic household items such
as spoons, tin cans and
washboards (upon which
thimbled fingers and
thumbs would be run up
and down). Nevertheless,
whereas the bass line was
provided by at least one
band member blowing into
or across the top of a jug,
when the 1950s skiffle
revival took place in
England, said jug was supplanted by a crude imitation of an
upright bass in the form of a broom handle poked through a
hole in an upturned tea chest, with a cord attached between
the two.

> ## "IT WAS A SIMPLE WAY INTO MUSIC BECAUSE A LOT OF THE SONGS HAD JUST TWO CHORDS, AND THE MAXIMUM WAS THREE.... EVERYONE WAS IN A SKIFFLE GROUP."
>
> *George Harrison*

Right

*The Vipers grew from the
vibrant music scene that
converged at the 21's Coffee
Bar in Soho, London, along
with countless other
performers, including Tommy
Steele, Joe Brown, Hank
Marvin and Adam Faith.*

LEADING EXPONENTS

Lonnie Donegan

Johnny Duncan

Tommy Steele

Sonny Stewart and his
  Skiffle Kings

The Vipers Skiffle Group

The Worried Men Skiffle
  Group

The Chas McDevitt
  Skiffle Group featuring
  Nancy Whiskey

folk standards in between sets by Ken Colyer's Jazzmen.
Playing banjo or acoustic guitar while backed by an upright
bass and drums, Donegan delivered the vocals in a raw,
American-accented style that quickly made him more popular
than the star attraction. When Colyer's outfit evolved into
Chris Barber's Jazz Band in 1954, Donegan took the lead on
what turned out to be a seminal track on the group's debut

A Raw, American-Accented Style

The king of British skiffle – and the only one of the artists
to earn international recognition – was Lonnie Donegan, who
introduced the music to concert audiences during the early
1950s when he performed his versions of blues, country and

SKIFFLE

*Skiffle was built around the
strumming of the acoustic
guitar, as represented by this
simplified part here. The
rhythm section was home-
made, with washboards and
saucepans for drums*

THE FIFTIES POP INTRO ➡ 12   POP PEOPLE A-Z ➡ 72   INSTRUMENTS A-Z ➡ 436   THE JAZZ INTRO ➡ 118   THE BLUES INTRO ➡ 154

album, *New Orleans Joys*. Featuring Barber on bass and Beryl Bryden on washboard, Lonnie Donegan's rendition of the old Huddie "Leadbelly" Ledbetter blues standard, 'Rock Island Line', was released as a single and sold a staggering three million copies, spending 22 weeks on the UK charts, where it peaked at number eight, while also making the American Top 10.

Still, although the sales figures were more than a little impressive, what made 'Rock Island Line' unique in the annals of British pop at that time was the fact that most of the people who bought the record were teenagers. Suddenly, like an oasis in a desert of staid formality, here was a raucous, bluesy, homegrown sound that not only caught the kids' attention but also inspired them to form their own bands in an attempt to duplicate the Lonnie Donegan formula. By the time Donegan's single 'Lost John' climbed to number two on the UK chart in early 1956, there was a full-scale skiffle boom taking place in Britain, with anywhere up to half a million teens forming their own bands while their idol was appearing on stage and nationwide television in America.

Donegan's first album, *Showcase*, sold in the hundreds of thousands, and he continued to make the Top 10 on the British singles chart with tracks such as 'Bring A Little Water Sylvie', 'Don't You Rock Me Daddy-O', 'Cumberland Gap' and 'Putting On The Style'. Meanwhile, a number of other acts were appearing on the scene. The Vipers Skiffle Group, whose sound was rougher than Donegan's, and more firmly steeped in folk and the blues, also enjoyed a Top 10 hit with 'Don't You Rock Me Daddy-O' (penned by Vipers singer/guitarist Wally Whyton). Courtesy of several subsequent releases, the Vipers were second only to Donegan in terms of their success. That of certain others, however, was altogether more brief: the Chas McDevitt Skiffle Group featuring Nancy Whiskey charted with 'Freight Train', and an American by the name of Johnny Duncan climbed to number 2 in the UK with 'Last Train To San Fernando'. Even Britain's first true rock'n'roll star, Tommy Steele, started out playing skiffle.

An Enduring Effect
On A Generation Of Teenagers

It was, of course, rock'n'roll that, by the end of 1957, put an end to the skiffle boom. However, although its time in the sun was short-lived, skiffle's invaluable contribution to popular music was the enduring effect that it had on a generation of teenagers who would be at the vanguard of the British – and subsequently international – rock scene of the 1960s: the Who, the Hollies, the Kinks, the Moody Blues, the Searchers, Procol Harum…. These and many more all had band members who cut their musical teeth on a skiffle-inspired acoustic guitar, washboard or tea-chest basis.

DICKIE VALENTINE

JIM DALE

LONNIE DONEGAN

PETULA CLARK

JOAN REGAN

RUSS HAMILTON

JUST SOME OF THE STARS in "6·5 SPECIAL"

ANGLO AMALGAMATED FILM DISTRIBUTORS LTD.

Above
The 6.5 Special, *launched by the BBC in 1957, featured live music including traditional folk and the latest craze, skiffle. Popular at first, the show went into decline when producer Jack Good defected to rival channel ITV.*

In fact, Lonnie Donegan's 'Putting On The Style' was sitting at the top of the UK chart when an outfit by the name of the Quarry Men performed the song at a church fête in Liverpool on 6 July 1957. The lead vocalist that day was a 16-year-old John Lennon; in the audience to see him for the first time was a 15-year-old Paul McCartney. Skiffle's role doesn't come any bigger than that.

AS THE 1960S APPROACHED, THE CONTROVERSY ASSOCIATED WITH ROCK'N'ROLL WAS SUPERSEDED BY AN ARRAY OF INOFFENSIVE SMOOTHIES ON BOTH SIDES OF THE ATLANTIC. HOWEVER, THE ONGOING POPULARITY OF ARTISTS SUCH AS ELVIS PRESLEY, BOBBY DARIN, RICKY NELSON, SAM COOKE, AND, IN THE UK, LONNIE DONEGAN, BILLY FURY AND CLIFF RICHARD, ENSURED A DEGREE OF CONTINUITY IN THE MUSIC SCENE.

Sixties Pop

LIKEWISE the success of singers such as Roy Orbison endured into the sixties, and the trend for pop instrumentals grew, courtesy of groups such as the Shadows in Britain and the Ventures in America, where Dick Dale & His Del-Tones were purveyors of the "surf guitar". The remains of white doo-wop could be heard in recordings by the Four Seasons and Dion (both with and without the Belmonts); and the last vestiges of Gene Vincent-style rock'n'roll was performed in Britain by Johnny Kidd & the Pirates.

Still, while the controversy associated with rock'n'roll had also been superseded by an array of parent-friendly smoothies on both sides of the Atlantic, there is little truth in the often-expressed notion that the US pop scene was uniformly bland before the Beatles came along. On the contrary, from 1960 to the end of 1963, there was a prevalence of material that epitomized the art of the perfectly crafted three-minute pop song.

Among the most successful exponents in this regard were Chubby Checker, whose renditions of 'The Twist' and 'Let's Twist Again' incited a new international dance craze; the teams of young composer/producers such as Gerry Goffin & Carole King and Jeff Barry & Ellie Greenwich housed

STYLE

Wall of Sound
Singer/Songwriters
The British Invasion
Surf
Merseybeat
Mod

"THIS GENERATION IS PRODUCING POETS WHO WRITE SONGS, AND NEVER BEFORE IN THE SIXTY-YEAR HISTORY OF AMERICAN POPULAR MUSIC HAS THIS BEEN TRUE."

Ralph J. Gleason

LEADING EXPONENTS

The Beach Boys
The Beatles
Chubby Checker
Sam Cooke
Bobby Darin
The Dave Clark Five
The Four Seasons
Gerry & the Pacemakers
Herman's Hermits
The Monkees
Roy Orbison
The Shadows
The Ventures
Phil Spector

SIXTIES POP

The rhythm of the bass part here was a staple ingredient of many 1960's hits, and there was also a move away from the root, four and five chords into more complex harmony and key modulations, as in the last chord here.

THE POP INTRO ➡ 8   POP PEOPLE A–Z ➡ 72   INSTRUMENTS A–Z ➡ 436   POP: THE WALL OF SOUND ➡ 26   POP: SURF MUSIC ➡ 32

inside New York City's Brill Building, who turned out hit after classic hit for artists such as the Shirelles, the Shangri-Las, the Chiffons, the Drifters, Little Eva, Connie Francis, the Crystals and the Ronettes; Phil Spector, whose slick, echo-bathed "Wall of Sound" creations added an entirely new dimension to record production; the in-house roster of songwriters, producers and artists assigned to Detroit's Motown label, whose dynamic soul- and R&B-based numbers were just starting to create waves; and, on the west coast, the surf-and-hot-rod bands led by the Beach Boys, whose brilliant singer/songwriter/arranger Brian Wilson was setting new pop standards by distinguishing fairly basic three- or four-chord songs with intricate four- and five-part harmonies.

In essence, although rock'n'roll had rebelled against the overt professionalism and sterility of the popular music that preceded it, the logical progression that took place during the early 1960s consisted of the aforementioned exponents, drawing on Tin Pan Alley's skilled and methodical approach towards songwriting in order to raise pop to the next level. What's more, while the likes of Brian Wilson helped set the precedent for artists writing and even producing their own songs, thanks to Wilson and Spector there was an increasing emphasis placed on the record's sound as well as its musical content. Not only was the studio evolving into the artist/producer's main instrument; in the case of Spector's productions, the artist's identity was often also peripheral.

Rock'n'roll had shaken things up by displacing most of the old brigade of artists at the top end of the charts. The early 1960s marked an end to the era of innocent lyrics prevailing in mainstream pop, as well as black acts feeling obliged to "dress white" – with the females straightening their hair or donning wigs – in order to broaden their appeal. Conformity had taken a temporary vacation when rock'n'roll was at its height; at this point it was about to disappear for good, even if it would be some time before black artists and producers (including those at Motown, where the label's slogan was "the sound of young America") felt sufficiently emboldened to create music more closely aligned with their ethnic roots.

Cynicism replaced optimism following Kennedy's assassination in 1963, and people began to look for a change. In musical terms, this need was answered by the glut of home-grown "beat groups" who swamped the UK charts throughout 1963 and invaded America the following year, sweeping away most of the previously established acts like so much dust.

Outfits such as the Beatles, Gerry & the Pacemakers, the Searchers, Freddie & the Dreamers, Billy J. Kramer & the

Dakotas, Herman's Hermits and the Dave Clark Five exuded youthful cheer and vitality by way of their vivacious guitar-and-drums-based music and well-groomed appearances. These, however, were counterbalanced by the relatively unkempt looks, surly demeanour and harsher, R&B-tinged sounds of fellow Brits such as the Rolling Stones and the Animals, not to mention the proto-heavy-metal riffs of the Kinks and, by 1965, the guitar-and-drums pyrotechnics of the Who.

Attitude had returned with a vengeance, and hereafter would remain the predominant characteristic of rock music as it branched away from the mainstream pop performed by American "answers to the Beatles" such as the Buckinghams, the Beau Brummels and even the Monkees. Add to that the folk-inspired protest lyrics that began to find their way into songs once Bob Dylan plugged his guitar into an amplifier, and, at a time when Western youth was becoming more concerned with the war in Vietnam than with carefree, fun-in-the-sun beach parties, popular music was suddenly shaping public opinion and inspiring social change instead of simply reflecting it.

Amid this acid-drenched, peace-and-love climate, the idea of young girls screaming hysterically during concerts was passé – and so, in an age of increasingly elaborate album projects, was the heyday of the three-minute single. Pop music would continue to evolve, but in many respects its halcyon years were now behind it.

Above

This photograph, staged by a national newspaper in the early 1960s, shows a selection of the myriad of Merseybeat bands that sprung up across Liverpool in the wake of the Beatles' phenomenal success.

Left

Chubby Checker, whose cover verrsion of Hank Ballard & the Midnighters' 'The Twist' was so close to the original that Ballard, upon hearing it, thought that it was his own recording.

Far Left

The fact that the Monkees were a fictional band put together by TV producers did not detract from their success – the "prefab four" were at one point outselling both the Beatles and the Rolling Stones.

The Wall Of Sound

NO ONE HAD EVER PRODUCED RECORDS LIKE PHIL SPECTOR.. THERE HAD BEEN LAVISH ORCHESTRATIONS AND RAUCOUS SOUNDS. BUT UNTIL THE EARLY 1960S. THE ELEMENTS WERE CLEARLY DEFINED IN RECORDINGS. WITH A FAIR AMOUNT OF SEPARATION ALLOTTED TO A LIMITED NUMBER OF RHYTHM AND PERCUSSION INSTRUMENTS WITHIN THE CONFINES OF A MAINLY MONAURAL MEDIUM. SPECTOR CHANGED ALL THAT.

Above

The rich arrangement of Ike & Tina Turner's Spector-produced single 'River Deep, Mountain High' seems to echo the landscape of the title, alternating flowing bassline passages and screeching climaxes.

APPLYING copious amounts of live and tape-delayed echo to layers of percussion, strings, brass, vocals and an R&B-derived rhythm section, comprising drums and multiple basses, keyboards and guitars, Spector, together with arranger Jack Nitzsche and engineer Larry Levine, fused the individual components into a unified "Wall of Sound", which, despite being monolithic, enriched the material to create timeless works of three-minute art.

Some of what Spector described as "little symphonies for the kiddies" made him more famous than the semi-anonymous artists – for example, although she was not a member of the Crystals, Darlene Love filled in for their regular lead singer, La La Brooks, on the group's US-chart-topping 1962 single, 'He's A Rebel'. Spector owned the band's name, so he could do as he pleased. However, rather than overwhelming the passionate lead vocals, his productions invariably glorified them. To this end, he employed the very best songwriters, as well as a wide array of the industry's foremost session musicians.

"THAT'S GOLD. THAT'S SOLID GOLD COMING OUT OF THAT SPEAKER."

Phil Spector to Sonny Bono after listening to the final playback of 'Da Doo Ron Ron'.

The Wrecking Crew

Right

Phil Spector infiltrated the LA music scene in the late 1950s and recorded his own composition 'To Know Him Is To Love Him', which was inspired by the inscription on his father's gravestone.

Working in LA's Goldstar Studios, Spector's "Wrecking Crew", as it came to be known, comprised a solid core of luminaries, including drummer Hal Blaine; bass player Carol Kaye; guitarists Glen Campbell, Barney Kessel, Tommy Tedesco and Billy Strange; keyboard players Larry Knechtel and Leon Russell; saxophonist Jay Migliori; and multi-instrumentalists Sonny Bono and Nino Tempo. Many, many others also

contributed to the sessions, ranging from King Curtis, Herb Alpert, Harry Nilsson and Lenny Bruce to Brian Wilson, Billy Preston, Cher and Dr. John. After running the musicians through each of their parts and rehearsing them incessantly, Spector would record countless takes until the sound approximated what he envisaged in his head; he would then complete the picture by way of the mixing process.

"Phil was notorious for never giving the band five because he didn't want anybody to move," recalled Bones

THE WALL OF SOUND

LEADING EXPONENTS

Bob B. Soxx & the Blue Jeans

The Crystals

Darlene Love

The Righteous Brothers

The Ronettes

Ike & Tina Turner

It's hard to express all of the wall of sound in a small musical sample, but some of the key characterisitics are a pulsing piano filling all of the beats, a rolling bass playing arpeggios around the chord, and an army of tambourines.

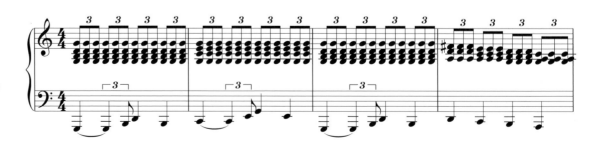

THE SIXTIES POP INTRO ➡ 24   POP PEOPLE A-Z ➡ 72   INSTRUMENTS A-Z ➡ 436   BLUES: RHYTHM & BLUES ➡ 173

Howe, who engineered a couple of Ike & Tina Turner and Ronnie Spector sessions. "He knew exactly where he wanted the instruments positioned, and it would take him such a long time to get the balance exactly the way he wanted. There'd be, say, a mandolin mixed in with the guitar section. … He had the band play the chart over and over and over again, like a tape loop. You know, the minute they reached the end they'd play it again, and he would go out and change people's parts. It would sometimes only be zillionths of an inch of change to make the difference that Phil wanted, but he'd know when it all fell into place. The amazing thing about it was, when that happened it did have an incredible sound, and I'm not sure that some of that wasn't just down to the musicians getting beat by playing it over and over and over again, so that the sound began to all melt together."

Multitalented And Autocratic

Whatever the formula, it certainly worked, as proven by a startling series of recordings between 1962 and 1966: 'He's A Rebel', 'Da Doo Ron Ron' and 'Then He Kissed Me' by the Crystals; the Ronettes' 'Be My Baby', 'Baby, I Love You', '(The Best Part of) Breakin' Up' and 'Walking In The Rain'; Darlene Love's '(Today I Met) The Boy I'm Gonna Marry'; 'Zip-a-Dee Doo-Dah' by Bob B. Soxx & the Blue Jeans; the 1963 all-star Christmas album, which included Darlene Love's majestic 'Christmas (Baby Please Come Home)'; 'You've Lost That Lovin' Feelin' ' and 'Unchained Melody' by the Righteous Brothers; and Ike & Tina Turner's 'River Deep, Mountain High'.

Multitalented and autocratic, Spector contributed to these and other recordings in numerous ways. Not only did he produce them; in many instances, he was also a co-composer (not least on 'Da Doo Ron Ron', 'Be My Baby', 'Then He Kissed Me', 'Baby, I Love You' and 'River Deep, Mountain High' with Ellie Greenwich and Jeff Barry; and 'Walking In The Rain' and 'You've Lost That Lovin' Feelin' ' with Barry Mann and Cynthia Weil). In addition, he played session guitar and owned the Phillies label, which he launched in late 1961 with Lester Sill. Not for nothing did the writer Tom Wolfe label him "The First Tycoon of Teen".

Suddenly Out Of Step

While girl-group classics such as 'Da Doo Ron Ron' and 'Be My Baby' stand as shining examples of pop perfection – the former an infectious expression of romantic joy, the latter an unforgettable anthem of teen desire – many cite 'You've Lost That Lovin' Feelin' ' and 'River Deep, Mountain High' as the apotheosis of the "Wall of Sound". Even so, and despite being a number 3 hit in the UK, 'River Deep' was a flop in the US upon its release in 1966. A dispirited Spector subsequently

folded his label and withdrew from a rapidly changing scene, one that was suddenly out of step with both his working methods and his preoccupation with producing singles instead of albums.

Spector resurfaced in the late 1960s but worked only sporadically during the next decade, bringing his "Wall of Sound" to records by, among others, George Harrison and The Ramones. Eccentric, egotistical and volatile, Spector enjoyed a relatively short halcyon period. And yet, during that time, he demonstrated a depth of artistic vision that forever changed the course of popular music.

Above

Spector was smitten with Veronica "Ronnie" Bennett, lead singer of the Ronettes, and reserved some of his best songs for the group, including 'Be My Baby' and 'Baby I Love You'. They later married.

Sixties Pop Singer/Songwriters

THE TERM "SINGER/SONGWRITER" TENDS TO BE APPLIED TO THE KIND OF INTROSPECTIVE, SOCIALLY CONSCIOUS ARTIST WHO – IN THE WAKE OF THE FOLK-INSPIRED MOVEMENT THAT WAS KICK-STARTED BY BOB DYLAN IN THE EARLY 1960S BEFORE PEAKING IN THE NEXT DECADE – PERFORMS IN A DIRECT YET REFLECTIVE MANNER, EMPHASIZING THE SONG'S MESSAGE OVER STYLE OR CALIBRE OF PRESENTATION.

Above
Leonard Cohen had been publishing his poems for over ten years by the time his debut album was released in 1967. A selection of his songs was used in the soundtrack to Robert Altman's film McCabe & Mrs Miller.

THIS is hardly an all-encompassing description, however. Following in the footsteps of 1950s luminaries ranging from Chuck Berry to Paul Anka, there have also been legions of more pop-oriented singer/songwriters, whose chief aim is to entertain rather than advocate ideas or indulge in self-analysis. Throughout the 1950s, singer/songwriters ranging from Paul Anka to Buddy Holly produced music whose primary aim was to entertain, and even if there was social commentary in the songs of Chuck Berry, self-analysis and radical ideas were never on the agenda. Accordingly, the early 1960s heralded yet another wave of pop-oriented singer/songwriters.

Having made the switch from writing 'Stupid Cupid' for Connie Francis to experiencing success in his own right with 'Oh Carol', Neil Sedaka started the decade with a string of solo hits, co-composed with Howard Greenfield: 'Stairway To Heaven', 'Calendar Girl', 'Little Devil', 'King Of Clowns', 'Happy Birthday Sweet Sixteen' and 'Breaking Up Is Hard To Do'. Among the most saccharine material created by the teams of young composers housed inside New York City's Brill Building, Sedaka's songs consisted of memorably catchy melodies constructed around lyrics relating to the ups and downs of teenage love. Such concerns were perfectly suited to the pop market of the era, as proven by smooth, self-penned numbers such as Sam Cooke's 'Cupid', 'Wonderful

> "TO BE A SINGER-SONGWRITER YOU MUST, FIRST AND FOREMOST, BE TOO SENSITIVE TO LIVE, TOO VAIN TO DIE."
> *David Dennum*

LEADING EXPONENTS
Sam Cooke
Ray Davies
Neil Diamond
Bob Dylan
Barry, Maurice and Robin Gibb
George Harrison
Mick Jagger and Keith Richards
John Lennon and Paul McCartney
Roy Orbison
Neil Sedaka
Paul Simon
Brian Wilson
Leonard Cohen

SIXTIES POP SINGER/SONGWRITERS

The light feel of the moving arpeggios in the midrange against the heavy pulsing of the bass provided a perfect background for bittersweet melodies of long held notes. The structure of the well-crafted 1960s pop song harked back to the values of the 1930s and 1940s, with often complex modulations and chord patterns, as well as the use of the "Intro", only happening once at the top of the song.

World', 'Another Saturday Night', 'Having A Party', 'Good Times', 'Twistin' The Night Away' and 'Shake', as well as the more melodramatic work of another 1950s carry-over, Roy Orbison.

Numbers That Were Carefully Crafted

In 1960, when the Orbison/Melson composition 'Only The Lonely' was rejected by Elvis Presley and the Everly Brothers (who had scored a hit with their rendition of 'Claudette', written by Orbison for his wife), the singer/guitarist who had struggled as a rockabilly artist decided to record the song himself. The result was a chart-topping single in the UK, which narrowly missed out on matching that feat in the US. Thereafter, "The Big O" demonstrated his remarkable vocal range in a succession of heavily produced, often doom-laden ballads and mid-tempo numbers, which were carefully crafted to suit his powerful voice and mysterious image. Distinguished by sweeping strings and striking crescendos at a time when much pop music was fairly lightweight, songs such as 'Running Scared', 'Crying', 'Blue Bayou', 'It's Over' and 'Oh, Pretty Woman' were Orbison co-writes, while 'Leah', 'Workin' For The Man' and 'In Dreams' were his own solo compositions.

In 1963, Roy Orbison toured Britain with the Beatles, whose self-contained writing team of John Lennon and Paul McCartney subsequently made the transition from the boy-loves-girl/boy-loses-girl innocence of 'Please Please Me', 'From Me To You', 'She Loves You' and 'I Want To Hold Your Hand' to the personally, socially and politically conscious numbers that would characterize rock music in the second half of the decade. Indeed, Lennon was composing introspective numbers such as 'There's A Place' as early as 1962; within a couple of years, too, he was taking a leaf out of Bob Dylan's book with 'I'm A Loser' and, in 1965, 'You've Got To Hide Your Love Away'.

Metaphors And Obscure Imagery

One of the great lyrical communicators of all time, John Lennon publicly acknowledged the influence of Bob Dylan on his writing. The incredibly talented and prolific team of Lennon and McCartney covered many musical styles, and inspired contemporaries such as the Kinks' Ray Davies and the Rolling Stones' Mick Jagger and Keith Richards to compose their own songs. Dylan's impact was to encourage a generation of artists whose roots were in folk, country, blues or rock'n'roll to infuse the pop canon with material that examined personal and social issues.

As Dylan kicked open the musical doors to protest social issues via the pop/rock scene, so he was joined by other folk contemporaries such as Joan Baez, Judy Collins, Joni Mitchell, Pete Seeger, Phil Ochs and Donovan. To an increasing extent, songs' poetic lyrics were steeped in metaphors and obscure imagery, while original material also began to take precedence over the time-honoured use of cover songs. Today, the savvy folk-pop numbers of Paul Simon; tomorrow, the darker, more rock-oriented compositions of Jim Morrison.

The Bee Gees' Barry Gibb was 19 years old and his twin brothers Maurice and Robin Gibb just 17, when, in 1967, they wrote and recorded timeless numbers such as 'New York Mining Disaster, 1941', 'To Love Somebody' and 'Massachusetts'. Not that Brian Wilson was any older than Barry Gibb when he began turning out hits for the Beach Boys in 1961. By the middle of the decade, Wilson was composing and arranging intricately structured music, while working with lyricists whose introspective themes were aeons away from those of the band's surf and hot-rod songs, written just a few years before.

The singer/songwriters were a rapidly expanding breed within the burgeoning rock field, and they would be far less the exception than the norm in years to come. In mainstream pop, on the other hand, the trend would not be quite so pronounced. Performing your own songs may have been cool, but for now it was not obligatory.

Left
The intensity of Bob Dylan's early songs introduced politics and social commentary to the pop charts, bombarding the saccharine music of the time with an explosion of words and sneering attitude.

Below
Together with Art Garfunkel, Paul Simon wrote some of the most enduring folk-based songs of the decade. The duo had little success until producer Tom Wilson added electric instrumentation to the acoustic 'Sound of Silence'.

The British Invasion

ON 1 FEBRUARY 1964, THE BEATLES' 'I WANT TO HOLD YOUR HAND' TOPPED AMERICA'S CASHBOX SINGLES CHART. SIX DAYS LATER, THEY ARRIVED IN NEW YORK FOR THEIR FIRST US VISIT, AND ON 9 FEBRUARY AN AUDIENCE OF AROUND 73 MILLION PEOPLE TUNED IN TO SEE THEM ON THE ED SULLIVAN SHOW, WHICH HAD BEEN BOOKED THE PREVIOUS NOVEMBER. THE TIMING COULD NOT HAVE BEEN BETTER.

ACCUSTOMED to leading the way in terms of pop culture but reeling from the recent assassination of President Kennedy, America was ready for change and in need of an uplifting diversion. With their infectious music, charismatic personalities and unconventional "moptop" appearance, the Beatles were able to deliver the goods. Even more remarkable than the Fab Four achieving the previously unimaginable feat of taking America by storm was the manner in which – with the doors to the States kicked wide open – a slew of other acts from across the Atlantic swamped the US charts. The shake-up quickly consumed all facets of American popular culture. In just less than 200 years after the War of Independence, a "British Invasion" was under way.

> **"MIDDLE-AGED AMERICA AT THAT TIME THOUGHT EVERYONE WITH LONG HAIR AND ENGLISH WAS A BEATLE."**
> *Peter Asher*

LEADING EXPONENTS

The Animals
The Beatles
Cilla Black
The Dave Clark Five
Petula Clark
Freddie & the Dreamers
Gerry & the Pacemakers
Herman's Hermits
The Hollies
The Kinks
Billy J. Kramer with the Dakotas
Manfred Mann
Peter & Gordon
The Rolling Stones
The Searchers
Dusty Springfield

Finally recovering from the ravages of the Second World War, Britain was in the thick of a particularly rich and creative period in all areas of the arts. With London about to "swing", it was in a prime condition to export its musicians, actors, writers and fashions to Americans who were, to an extraordinary and unprecedented degree, receptive to anyone with a Liverpudlian – make that English – accent. In 1963, while the UK pop charts were swamped by so-called Mersey sound acts such as the Beatles, Gerry & the Pacemakers, the Searchers, the Swinging Blue Jeans and Billy J. Kramer with the Dakotas, only three British singles managed to crack the US Top 40. In 1964, this paltry number rose to an astonishing 65. Previously, just two British singles – the 1962 instrumentals 'Stranger On The Shore' by Acker Bilk and 'Telstar' by The Tornados, written, produced and mixed by the legendary British producer Joe Meek – had topped *Billboard*'s "Hot 100". In 1964, nine of the 23 *Billboard* chart-toppers (for 26 out of 52 weeks) were by British acts.

Supposed Rivalry

Admittedly, six of those records were by the Beatles, who on 4 April held the top five positions on the "Hot 100" and another seven spots lower down the chart. However, others

THE BRITISH INVASION

The twanging riff leading into the beaty verse, with the guitar and bass bouncing off each other rhythmically and the drummer pounding the ride cymbal, was the hallmark of the first wave of the Brit invasion of America, and was the template for all the "Answer to the Beatles" bands.

THE SIXTIES POP INTRO ➡ 24   POP PEOPLE A–Z ➡ 72   INSTRUMENTS A–Z ➡ 436   POP: SKIFFLE ➡ 22   THE BLUES INTRO ➡ 154

were following fast behind them, and not only many of their aforementioned Liverpudlian compatriots. There was also the Animals from Newcastle, the Hollies from Manchester and the Dave Clark Five from Tottenham, North London. The DC5 had visited the US a month before the Beatles, having ended the six-week reign of 'I Want To Hold Your Hand' at the top of the British charts with 'Glad All Over' (composed by Clark and keyboardist/vocalist Mike Smith), prompting a national newspaper headline to ask, "Has The Five Jive Crushed The Beatles' Beat?" To help promote a supposed rivalry with the Beatles, the press described the combination of Smith's raw vocals and the band's loud, thumping beat as "The Tottenham Sound". However, despite making more appearances on *The Ed Sullivan Show* than anyone else, and scoring 17 *Billboard* Top 40 hits with numbers such as 'Bits And Pieces', 'Can't You See That She's Mine', 'Because', 'I Like It Like That', 'Catch Us If You Can' and 'Over And Over' (their sole US number 1), the DC5 were not a serious challenge to the Beatles' supremacy. No one was, although the Rolling Stones were the strongest contenders in that regard.

Throughout 1964, while the aforementioned British acts – in addition to newcomers such as Peter & Gordon, Herman's Hermits, Manfred Mann and the Kinks – all enjoyed Stateside success, the Stones struggled to establish themselves there. However, in the summer of 1965 their efforts finally paid off when '(I Can't Get No) Satisfaction' topped the *Billboard* "Hot 100", followed that November by 'Get Off Of My Cloud'. The Stones' breakthrough coincided with the second half of the British Invasion, which, in addition to lightweight acts such as Wayne Fontana & the Mindbenders, Freddie & the Dreamers (whose star had already faded in their home country) and Chad & Jeremy (who few people had even heard of in Britain), also included the folk singer Donovan ("Britain's answer to Bob Dylan") and the harder-edged sounds of the Who, the Yardbirds, the Zombies and the Moody Blues. In 1965, a total of 68 British singles cracked the US Top 40, with 11 of them again spending a combined 26 weeks at number one. And yet, although a number of American acts felt obliged to

adopt English-sounding names and even put on English-sounding accents, by 1966 the hysterical, all-encompassing Anglophilia was clearly on the slide, as evidenced by the abundance of home-grown artists who were redressing the balance on the pop charts.

Benefiting Both Sides

After a two-year onslaught, the "Invasion" started to come to an end. Yet aside from casting a number of previously successful American artists into the proverbial wilderness, it had served to benefit both sides. After struggling to come to terms with the virtual end of their Empire, the British had regained their self-esteem, while obliterating the invisible barrier that had traditionally prevented their pop acts from succeeding in the most prosperous market of all. The Americans, on the other hand, had not only been stirred out of their post-Kennedy blues; in addition, by being forced to respond, their own music scene had been greatly invigorated. There would be plenty of musical cross-pollination from here on, and the entire scene would be all the richer because of it.

Above
The Beatles arrive in New York in 1964. The group's reputation in the US was already established prior to their arrival, largely due to the support shown to them by influential New York DJ Murray "The K".

Centre Left
Ironically, many young Americans were introduced to their own country's musical heritage through England's Rolling Stones.

Far Left
The songs of the Kinks paired Ray Davies' quick-witted, observant lyrics with his brother Dave's powerful guitar style.

Left
A Guild guitar, similar to the one played by Dave Davies of the Kinks circa 1964.

CHARACTERIZED BY TWANGY, REVERBERATION-SOAKED GUITARS; PERCUSSIVE INSTRUMENTALS DESIGNED TO SIMULATE THE EFFECT OF CRASHING WAVES; VOCAL HARMONIES UNDERSCORED BY A SOARING FALSETTO – SURF MUSIC WAS PERFECTLY SUITED TO AN EARLY 1960S POP SCENE OF ESCAPISM AND INNOCENT FUN AND WAS TO HAVE A PROFOUND AND LASTING INFLUENCE ON THE SOUND OF THE ROCK GUITAR.

Surf Music

Above

The only surf act to graduate to the mainstream, the Beach Boys (and more specifically creative genius Brian Wilson) went on to record Pet Sounds in 1967, which many consider to be the most important album of all time.

WHEREAS chart-friendly instrumental recordings by bands such as the Ventures in the US and the Shadows in the UK helped to sustain the guitar's popularity in the period between the demise of rock'n'roll and the British Invasion, surf rock often featured the raunchiest and most expressive solos.

Leading the way in that regard was the justifiably self-proclaimed "King of the Surf Guitar", Dick Dale. A keen surfer, his musical endeavour to convey the excitement of the sport resulted in a rapid-fire style of single-note picking, coupled with an innovative use of portable reverb effects to help recreate the feel of the oceanic cascades. Born Richard Monsour to a Polish mother and Lebanese father, Dale further distinguished his music by infusing it with Eastern European and Middle Eastern melodies, all of which came to bear when Del-Tone released the first-ever surf instrumental, 'Let's Go Trippin' ', as a single in September 1961. This was only a regional hit in Southern California, but it single-handedly

"HEY, SURFING'S GETTING REALLY BIG. YOU GUYS OUGHT TO WRITE A SONG ABOUT IT."

Dennis Wilson to brother Brian and Mike Love, 1961

ignited a musical craze that saw the quick formation of dozens of local bands. Among the first of these were the Beach Boys, whose debut single, 'Surfin', was recorded the same month that 'Let's Go Trippin' ' was issued, prior to its own release on the tiny Candix label that December.

LEADING EXPONENTS	THE SURF STYLE
The Astronauts	*A string of single guitar notes*
The Beach Boys	*(like adrenalin), supporting*
The Chantays	*three part vocal harmonies (like*
Dick Dale	*gliding the waves), summing up*
Jan & Dean	*the sheer ecstasy of the sport*
The Pyramids	*and in a major key to promote*
The Surfaris	*the feel-good, good fun nature*
The Trashmen	*of the music.*

THE SIXTIES POP INTRO ➡ 24   POP PEOPLE A-Z ➡ 72   INSTRUMENTS A-Z ➡ 436   POP: THE WALL OF SOUND ➡ 26

A Flamboyant Performer

Dick Dale's influence was enormous. The 1962 *Surfer's Choice* was his and surf music's first album (released on Del-Tone before Capitol distributed it nationally). During the course of recording three further albums in 1965, he also helped develop, road test and popularize an array of equipment manufactured by the Fender Musical Instrument Company: amplifiers, reverb units and a custom-designed, left-handed, gold metalflake Stratocaster guitar. An accomplished musician and flamboyant performer, Dale played his guitars left-handed and upside-down in a style that made a significant impression on Jimi Hendrix, as well as on a subsequent generation of axe-wielding heavy-metal merchants.

In the meantime, while only a handful of surf instrumentals (such as the major 1963 chart hits 'Wipe Out' by the Surfaris and 'Pipeline' by the Chantays) enjoyed national success, the Beach Boys were bringing a new dimension to the genre. Under the guidance of songwriter/producer/arranger/musician Brian Wilson, the group blended Four Freshmen-inspired vocal harmonies, which conveyed a fun-in-the-sun California lifestyle, with lyrics describing the thrill of waxing down your surfboard, "loading up the Woody" and "walking the nose". After 'Surfin'' led to a contract with Capitol Records, the title track of the band's 1962 debut album, *Surfin' Safari*, made the national Top 20. That of its early 1963 follow-up, *Surfin' USA*, adapted pertinent lyrics to the tune of Chuck Berry's 'Sweet Little Sixteen' and catapulted the group into the Top 10, earning it nationwide recognition. Nevertheless, since surfing itself was still a growing fad, the first album's liner notes included a paragraph describing the activity. The notes to *Surfin' USA* then explained the meaning of expressions such as "a good set of heavies" and "toes-on-the-nose".

Tiring Of The Surfing Association

Later in 1963, the beautifully harmonized title ballad of the Beach Boys' third album, *Surfer Girl*, displayed a growing sophistication on the part of composer/producer Brian Wilson, who was already tiring of the surfing association. Although one of the record's other cuts, 'Surfers Rule', contained the competitive challenge "Four Seasons, you better believe it!" during the fade-out, following this album – and after Wilson handed Jan & Dean a chart-topper in the form of 'Surf City' – the band steered clear of the surfing theme with which its name would remain synonymous. The surf guitar and high harmonies

would be adapted increasingly to songs about hot rods and drag racing, before Wilson would rethink his approach in the wake of the Beatles, borrow from the production techniques of Phil Spector and, with the aid of mind-bending chemicals and new lyrical collaborators, focus on far more obscure topics. Landmark numbers such as 'Good Vibrations' and 'Heroes and Villains' would usher in a new era of increasingly sophisticated west coast music, even though drug abuse and emotional problems would subsequently force the chief Beach Boy to withdraw almost totally from the scene.

Surf music was another casualty of the British invasion, as was, eventually, the cycle of beach party movies that often featured cameo appearances and/or musical performances from luminaries of the genre: Brian Wilson in *Beach Party*, Dick Dale in *Muscle Beach Party*, the Surfaris in *The Lively Set*, the Astronauts in *Surf Party* and *Wild On The Beach* and the Beach Boys in *The Girls On The Beach*. The surfing craze would continue to flourish, but the music that popularized it was on the way out.

In early 1964, 'Surfin' Bird' by the Trashmen (who hailed from landlocked Minneapolis) was kept off the top of the charts by the Beatles, while the Pyramids' 'Penetration' would prove to be the last major instrumental surf hit. The following year, even Dick Dale was dropped by Capitol. Still, though its time in the sun was relatively short, the sound and influence of surf music lived on.

Left and Above
Dedicated surfer and influential musician Dick Dale was an inspiration to many, and his aggressive playing style led to the destruction of so many speakers that Fender was obliged to develop its existing amplifiers.

Below
Teen pop duo Jan & Dean were introduced to surf music when they shared a stage with the Beach Boys in 1963. Brian Wilson gave them his partially written 'Surf City' to record, to which he contributed guest vocals.

A BASIC LINE-UP OF DRUMS, BASS AND TWO GUITARS, SOMETIMES AUGMENTED BY A PIANO OR A SAXOPHONE – THIS WAS THE BLUEPRINT FOR THE 500 OR SO BANDS WHO, STAYING FAITHFUL TO THE SPIRIT AND MATERIAL OF CLASSIC ROCK'N'ROLL, AND TO MANY OBSCURE R&B SONGS, INVIGORATED THE POP SCENE IN AND AROUND LIVERPOOL BETWEEN 1958 AND 1964.

Merseybeat

Above

Meet the Searchers had a rather hurried release in order to cash in on the success of the Searchers' number one single 'Sweets for my Sweet'. The remaining eleven album tracks were recorded in the space of a day.

TAKING its name from the river that runs through the city, what came to be known as "Merseybeat", or the "Mersey Sound", was often built around guitars backed by a solid beat and fronted by an energetic lead vocal. However, because these characteristics weren't always shared or necessarily unique, it is debatable whether Merseybeat was anything other than a convenient, press-contrived pigeonhole assigned to bands hailing from the north-west of England.

Performed onstage at "jive hives" such as the Aintree Institute, Grosvenor Ballroom, Hambleton Hall, Litherland Town Hall, Knotty Ash Village Hall, New Clubmoor Hall and, most famously, the Cavern Club, the bright and melodic music was, largely, a throwback to the days of leather-clad rockers, both in terms of the material covered and, during an ultra-slick pop era, the groups' rough-and-ready appearances. Smart attire and smoother attitudes would only be adopted once the scene became known beyond Merseyside, for while British acts were virtual nonentities on the American pop charts throughout the early 1960s, much the same could be said about the UK recording scene for artists based anywhere but in London. All of the major British record labels and studios were located in the capital, and if the artists and/or their managers were not

> "BEAT CITY? A SPRAWLING AREA OF MURKY SLUMS AND MUDDY SEAS … EIGHTY THOUSAND CRUMBLING HOUSES AND 30,000 ON THE DOLE. AND YET, AT THE MOMENT, THERE'S MONEY TO BE MADE IN LIVERPOOL IF YOU SING OR PLAY WITH AN ACCENT."
>
> *Tom Spence, The Daily Worker, September 7, 1963*

LEADING EXPONENTS

The Beatles
The Big Three
The Fourmost
Gerry & the Pacemakers
Billy J. Kramer with the Dakotas
The Merseybeats
The Searchers
The Swinging Blue Jeans

MERSEYBEAT

A thick strumming guitar and a lyrical melody line was just one style of Merseybeat, as epitomized by the Searchers. More energetic styles took the songs at a faster tempo, and the rhythmic accents inside the guitar part became more staccato and punchy.

THE SIXTIES POP INTRO ➡ 24   POP PEOPLE A-Z ➡ 72   INSTRUMENTS A-Z ➡ 436   POP: SKIFFLE ➡ 22   BLUES: RHYTHM & BLUES ➡ 173

able to audition for them, it was equally unlikely that the A&R (Artists & Repertoire) people would venture north of Watford in search of new talent.

Ripe For Exploitation

All of that changed in 1963, however, after the manager Brian Epstein's tireless efforts to secure a recording contract for the Beatles reaped dividends in the form of their smash-hit singles 'Please Please Me' and 'From Me To You'. The latter's seven-week stay at number one was sandwiched between fellow Liverpudlians and Epstein stablemates Gerry & the Pacemakers' chart-topping 'How Do You Do It?' and 'I Like It'. As a result, it didn't take long for the record industry honchos to break with tradition and check out who else might be ripe for exploitation "up north". Liverpool was suddenly overrun with talent scouts, managers and booking agents, resulting in success for a few notable and not-so-notable acts. However, it also eluded many who, despite being highly popular on the local scene, fell between the cracks due to a fateful lack of luck and talent.

Rory Storm & the Hurricanes, whose line-up formerly included Ringo Starr on drums; Kingsize Taylor & the Dominoes, who claimed to have been Liverpool's first beat group; Derry Wilkie & the Seniors, who were the first Merseysiders to play a residency in the German rock'n'roll stomping ground of Hamburg; Faron's Flamingos – the raw-edged sounds and stage performances of these and other favourites may have excited the fans, but they did not translate well onto vinyl. Conversely, among the major local acts who did succeed in this respect, the band that best epitomized Merseybeat was, perhaps, the Searchers. Their well-arranged recordings of 'Sweets For My Sweet', 'Sugar And Spice' and 'Don't Throw Your Love Away' established the group as early rivals to The Beatles in the top region of the British charts, while the jangling sound of a 12-string Rickenbacker guitar distinguished both the superb 'Needles And Pins' (the band's US breakthrough, composed by Phil Spector associates Jack Nitzsche and Sonny Bono) and a cover of Jackie DeShannon's 'When You Walk In The Room'.

Blessed With Good Fortune

At the same time, certain lesser lights that were blessed with good fortune made a name for themselves on the domestic and international scenes. Having previously been backed by fellow Liverpudlians the Coasters, Billy J. Kramer was teamed with the Manchester-based Dakotas upon signing with Brian Epstein. Despite his vocal limitations, which the producer George Martin concealed by way of heavy double-tracking, Kramer scored a string of 1963 hits with songs penned by the

prolific team of John Lennon and Paul McCartney: 'Do You Want To Know A Secret?' as well as the previously unrecorded 'Bad To Me' and 'I'll Keep You Satisfied'. In 1964, he released 'From a Window' and then 'Little Children', written by the Americans Mort Shuman and John McFarland. The latter track became Kramer's third UK number one and first Top 10 hit in the States, where he was part of the British invasion. After a 1965 cover of the Bacharach-David composition 'Trains And Boats And Planes', however, the hits dried up.

The same applied to the equally clean-cut, lightweight and consequently outmoded Gerry & the Pacemakers, who, thanks to the compositional efforts of singer/guitarist Gerry Marsden, enjoyed international chart success until the tail end of 1965 with songs such as 'It's Gonna Be All Right', 'I'm The

One', 'Don't Let The Sun Catch You Cryin'' and 'Ferry 'Cross The Mersey' (the title of the group's only film). By then, with the Beatles having long since moved on to more progressive musical pastures, the Merseybeat explosion was over and, worse still for Liverpool, its incredible live scene had been decimated. Not only had most of the major acts been lured away by the prospect – real or imagined – of stardom elsewhere; so had many of the up-and-coming musicians who would have comprised the next generation. The city was now world-famous, but its musical glory days were at an end.

Above

Gerry & the Pacemakers' cheerful, chirpy sound embodied the more upbeat side of Merseybeat. The Ferry Cross the Mersey *film showcased the band, among other Liverpool acts, in the guise of a music contest.*

"ARE YOU A MOD OR A ROCKER?" A REPORTER ASKED RINGO STARR IN A HARD DAY'S
NIGHT. "UH, NO," HE ANSWERED, "I'M A MOCKER." THE QUESTION WAS A PERTINENT
ONE. ON 18 MAY 1964, JUST OVER THREE WEEKS AFTER THE FILM WAS COMPLETED, THE
ENGLISH SEASIDE TOWN OF MARGATE SAW A VIOLENT SHOWDOWN BETWEEN PACKS OF
FASHION-CONSCIOUS MODS AND LEATHER-JACKETED ROCKERS.

Mod

Above

The mod movement was carefully contrived and the style guidelines set by the mods were as sharp as the suits they wore. As well as clothes and hairstyles, mods had their own music, drugs and modes of transport.

THROUGHOUT that and the following year, there were further clashes at resorts such as Brighton, Hastings, Southend, Clacton and Bournemouth, resulting in chaos, destruction and plenty of arrests.

Little was resolved between the motorcycle gangs, who were still championing 1950s rock'n'roll, and the hedonistic "modernists" who lapped up American soul and R&B in addition to Jamaican ska. Indeed, up until the start of 1965, the mods belonged to a movement that was yet to spawn its own music. Even when that did take place, it was limited to just a couple of domestically well-known exponents and a handful of nearly-rans. Melding R&B with rock guitar and an idiosyncratic, British edge, they nevertheless defined a short-lived sub-genre that bridged the gap between the beat boom and psychedelia.

It was in 1963 that the working-class, male-dominated mod lifestyle really took off in Britain. Based in and around London, which was increasingly turning into a hub of high fashion and pop culture, this embraced a colourful, "New Dandy" dress-code of button-down shirts, narrow trousers, and sharp-looking mohair and two-tone suits, as well as the more casual parka, which was de rigueur for riding about town on economical Italian motor-scooters manufactured by Vespa and Lambretta. Attending any number of parties and clubs that catered to

their musical tastes, the mods bolstered their nightlife by way of amphetamines, anxiety suppressants and other drugs such as Dexedrine, "Black Bombers", "Purple Hearts" and "French Blues". It was this scene that gave rise to the Who.

Performances With Aggression

The Who started out as the Detours in the west London neighbourhood of Shepherd's Bush in 1963. The band's name was changed to the High Numbers by manager/publicist Peter Meaden, who dressed the quartet in mod attire and rewrote Slim Harpo's 'Got Live If You Want It' as 'I'm The Face'. (In mod slang, a "face" was a fashion leader.) The single flopped, but its target audience began attending the group's pub performances, featuring a set that consisted entirely of soul, Motown and R&B. Taking note of this growing fan following, the aspiring film directors Kit Lambert and Chris Stamp assumed the management reins, switched the band's name back to the Who, and encouraged the singer Roger Daltrey, composer/guitarist Pete Townshend, bass player John

> "WE WERE STILL A BUNCH
> OF ROTTEN, DIRTY-BOY
> ROCK'N'ROLLERS, BUT
> KIDS BEGAN IDENTIFYING
> WITH OUR SHORT HAIR
> AND IVY LEAGUE CLOTHES,
> AND IT JUST TOOK OFF
> FROM THERE."
>
> *Roger Daltrey*

Above Right

Although they later moved into rock territory, the Who were originally marketed as a mod band. Their status as mods was amplified by Pete Townshend's irreverent attitude and Keith Moon's diet of Purple Hearts.

LEADING EXPONENTS

The Action

The Creation

The Eyes

The Small Faces

The Smoke

The Who

MOD

Try to imagine the chords played on a guitar turned up full volume, with the drummer filling in every space with toms and cymbals; this kind of chord-based riffing was the genesis of rock and heavy metal.

THE SIXTIES POP INTRO ➡ 24   POP PEOPLE A–Z ➡ 72   INSTRUMENTS A–Z ➡ 436   BLUES: RHYTHM & BLUES ➡ 173

Entwistle and drummer Keith Moon to lace their performances with an aggression that would match that of the mods in their battles with the rockers.

So while Entwistle remained stoic onstage, Daltrey assumed the air of a brash thug, Townshend leaped into the air with his guitar while spinning his right hand in a windmill motion, and Moon played his drums like a crazy man. Echoing the painter Gustav Metzke's auto-destructive art, Townshend soon took to smashing his guitars against floors and amplifiers, prompting Moon to respond by virtually destroying his kit. It was this style of display that turned 'I Can't Explain' into the Who's first British Top 10 hit, after they performed the song on the landmark television pop show *Ready Steady Go!*.

Taking their lead from the Rolling Stones, the group had already courted publicity by way of a mod-friendly, anti-social attitude. This discouraged the major labels from signing them, despite a highly successful residency at London's Marquee Club. But on the strength of the Townshend-penned 'I Can't Explain', which clearly borrowed from the Kinks' 'You Really Got Me', the band secured a deal through Kinks producer Shel Talmy with American Decca (sub-contracted through Brunswick in the UK).

Adolescent Defiance

Sporting their target T-shirts and Union Jack blazers, the Who were the perfect embodiment of the mod movement and its affiliations to the whole "Swinging London", Carnaby Street fashion scene. Furthermore, although 'I Can't Explain' did not convey the band's more explosive attributes, this was rectified by its follow-up singles, 'Anyway, Anyhow, Anywhere' and 'My Generation'. The latter, a study in adolescent defiance armed with amphetamine-fuelled power-guitar chords and a stuttering lead vocal, was not only the mod anthem but also a pivotal number that helped turn pop into rock. At the end of 1965, the energy-pumped *My Generation* album further delineated the mod lifestyle, courtesy of Townshend originals such as 'Out In The Street' and 'The Kids Are Alright'. Before long, however, he and the band were looking towards other themes.

In August of that year, Decca issued 'What'cha Gonna Do About It', the debut single by the Who's East London contemporaries, the Small Faces. A stylish, R&B-oriented group fronted by the singer/guitarist Steve Marriott alongside bassist Ronnie Lane, keyboard player Jimmy Winston and drummer Kenny Jones, this was the only other major act to emerge from the mod scene. Soon after 'What'cha Gonna Do About It' climbed to number 14 on the British charts, Winston was replaced by Ian McLagan, and during 1966 the band enjoyed Top 10 UK hits with 'Sha-La-La-La-Lee', 'Hey

Girl' and 'All Or Nothing'. The last of these, a powerful slice of Anglo white soul, went all the way to number one, but although its cheery follow-up, 'My Mind's Eye', nearly matched that success, it also signalled a departure in style.

By the start of 1967, on the cusp of the peace-and-love "flower power" era, the mod scene was finished. At that point, neither the Who nor the Small Faces had broken through in the States, although that would subsequently change. The whole fad, then, remained an exclusively British phenomenon, to be revived with a vengeance by a new generation of musicians and fashionistas in the late 1970s.

Below
The Small Faces released some of the most commercially successful and durable music of the mod movement. They went on to fuse their cockney-mod style with psychedelia, resulting in their number one album Ogden's Nut Gone Flake.

THE EARLY 1970S MUSIC SCENE SAW ROCK AND POP CONTINUE TO SEPARATE, WITH THE LATTER USUALLY AIMING FOR NOT ONLY AN EVER-YOUNGER AUDIENCE, BUT ALSO AN INCREASINGLY MIDDLE-AGED ONE. THREE MAJOR STRANDS OF NEW POP DEFINED BOTH THIS PROCESS AND POP'S INCREASED PREOCCUPATION WITH DIFFERENT FORMS OF ESCAPISM.

Seventies Pop

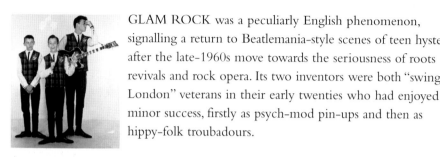

GLAM ROCK was a peculiarly English phenomenon, signalling a return to Beatlemania-style scenes of teen hysteria after the late-1960s move towards the seriousness of roots revivals and rock opera. Its two inventors were both "swinging London" veterans in their early twenties who had enjoyed minor success, firstly as psych-mod pin-ups and then as hippy-folk troubadours.

Above
In the early 1960s, the Bee Gees were child stars in Brisbane, Australia, where they released their first single. Their return to England set them on course for greater success.

Glamour Boys

Marc Bolan (born Mark Feld) became an overnight Britpop sensation at the tail end of 1970. His extraordinary blend of stomping rhythms, a pre-grunge guitar style, abstract sex lyrics, reverberant sound plucked from 1950s rock'n'roll, flamboyant glitter clothes and make-up, as well as androgynous beauty framed by a cascade of corkscrew hair, introduced British teenagers to the delights of both adolescent sexual confusion and joyously daft rock'n'roll fun. An inability to develop this trademark sound precipitated a fall from pop grace before the Electric Warrior died, tragically, at the age of 30, when his soul vocalist girlfriend Gloria Jones crashed their car into a tree near their home in south London.

As Bolan hit big in 1970-71, his south London friend and rival David Jones looked on in interest. Having already changed his name to David Bowie, the art-loving dance student transformed into an even more beautiful and sexually ambiguous figure than Bolan, teamed up with hard-rock guitarist Mick Ronson, and, influenced not by 1950s rock but by American cult-rockers Iggy Pop and Lou Reed, invented an iconic glam-rock character. His 1972 concept album, *The Rise And Fall Of Ziggy Stardust And The Spiders From Mars*, established Bowie as the pop phenomenon of the age. Of course, unlike Bolan, Bowie became a master of pop reinvention, switching from nihilistic rock to blue-eyed soul, to electronic introspection and mainstream pop, all the while remaining one of both pop and rock's most iconic and influential figures.

For the first four years of the 1970s, glam was the dominant language of UK pop. While Roxy Music further represented the intelligent side of this gender-bending exuberance, the likes of Gary Glitter, the Sweet, Mud and Suzi Quatro offered pure, infectious bubblegum and knowing slap-

> "FROM '72 TO '76 I WAS THE ULTIMATE ROCK STAR. I COULDN'T HAVE BEEN MORE A ROCK STAR. ANYTHING THAT HAD TO DO WITH BEING A ROCK'N'ROLL SINGER WAS WHAT I WAS GOING FOR."
>
> *David Bowie*

STYLES

Singer/Songwriters
Europop

LEADING EXPONENTS

David Bowie
Marc Bolan
Roxy Music
The Osmonds
The Jackson 5
Rod Stewart
The Carpenters
Fleetwood Mac
Queen
The Bee Gees

SEVENTIES POP

Pop of the early 1970s reached back to the days of rock'n'roll for its inspiration but mutated the chords and the arrangements, as here with a chord sequence alien to the likes of Chuck Berry. The high offbeat chops on the guitar were especially a feature of the music of T. Rex.

THE POP INTRO ➡ 8   POP PEOPLE A-Z ➡ 72   INSTRUMENTS A-Z ➡ 436

stick. The genre had less impact in the US, although satirical horror-rockers Alice Cooper and Kiss forged a more overtly theatrical connection. As the 1970s moved on, Scotland's Bay City Rollers took glam's three-minute anthems and sartorial madness (feather cuts and tartan flares, in this case) into the early boy-band genre, causing hysteria among teenage girls on both sides of the Atlantic. Meanwhile, Freddie Mercury's Queen fused the flamboyant androgyny of glam with the musical excesses of progressive rock. The epic meaninglessness of their 1975 number one hit, 'Bohemian Rhapsody', effectively brought a fitting end to glam's glorious mix of the daring and the deliciously daft.

Totty For Tots

Throughout all of this, a form of pop emerged for those too young and/or sensitive to deal with all this queerness and clowning. Teenybop – or Weenybop, to some appalled adults – struck with a three-pronged attack from America. The Osmonds, a family of Mormons from Ohio, purveyed a squeaky-clean kind of romantic schmaltz, centred on the toothy grin of their youngest member, Donny. The Osmonds' biggest competitors were the last great product of the Motown hit factory. Led by the sensational child prodigy Michael, Indiana's Jackson 5 were cooler and funkier – and, of course, blessed with a lead singer who would go on to change the course of pop history. Finally, the star of Monkees-lite US TV show *The Partridge Family*, the dreamily pretty David Cassidy, slayed a generation of pre-pubescent girls with a succession of sophisticated, breathy ballads. These three acts proved, once and for all, that you could market pop to small children without having to descend to novelty. Every subsequent manufactured pop act is sprinkled with a little of their stardust.

Be My Baby Boomer

But few of the above acts catered for the most significant new market. For those who were old enough to experience the cultural upheavals of the 1960s, but wanted a mellower pop soundtrack for their inevitable settling down, a classy and smooth kind of adult pop emerged. Yet another former mod from London, Rod Stewart moved from raucous roots-rock to a flashy yet restrained everyman style of pop, applying his white soul rasp to dramatic ballads and hilariously crass, disco-rock sexual come-ons. The Carpenters – again Mormons, again family, but this time the Californian duo Richard and Karen – produced the embodiment of anti-rock. Their Bacharach ballads and jolly versions of country classics appeared frothy and cynical, until you listened closely to the well of eerily detached sadness in Karen's clear, rich and

unique voice. She died of heart failure, brought on by a lifelong struggle with anorexia nervosa, in 1983, aged just 32.

Elsewhere, former 1960s rockers created a pop-rock hybrid based on high production values and lush, ambitious albums. The perfect FM radio soundtrack of 1977's *Rumours* marked Brit/US band Fleetwood Mac's transformation from blues-rock renegades to inventors of "divorce pop" – a smooth, dreamy sound smuggling bitter tales of broken marriages and lost ideals into the all-ages mainstream. California's Eagles used mellow country rock to detail the pain of growing old and the death of the hippy dream. But sly disillusion was not all there was. The Electric Light Orchestra, from Birmingham, England, took the Beatles' more pseudo-classical moments and carved an entire career out of them, making musical mountains out of lyrical molehills.

A rock theatre veteran from Texas formerly known as Marvin Lee Aday, Meatloaf teamed up in 1978 with producer/composer Jim Steinman for the magnificently overblown and massively successful *Bat Out Of Hell*, a loving pop pastiche of every teen-rock dream from Phil Spector to Springsteen's *Born To Run*. The decade ended with 1960s pop auteurs the Bee Gees applying their mastery of harmony pop to disco's dancefloor hedonism, the all-conquering soundtrack of *Saturday Night Fever* reinventing Manchester-via-Australia's Brothers Gibb as pioneers of the coming dance-pop crossover.

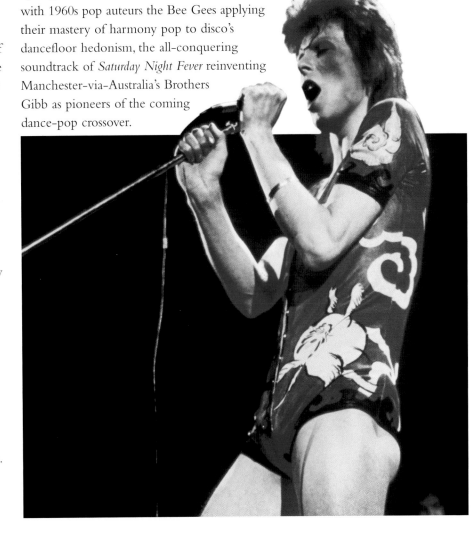

Left

Marc Bolan's love for rock'n'roll music was allegedly born out of a fortuitous mistake in which his father, trying to purchase a Bill Hayes record for Marc, accidentally picked up a Bill Haley single.

Below

David Bowie's foray into glam rock came in the form of his extraterrestrial alter ego, Ziggy Stardust. Bowie took the name Ziggy from a clothing boutique, while Stardust came from the inimitable Legendary Stardust Cowboy (a.k.a. Norman Carl Odam).

Seventies Pop Singer/Songwriters

THE 1970S REMAINS THE ERA MOST CLOSELY ASSOCIATED WITH THE ARTISTIC AND COMMERCIAL TRIUMPH OF THE SINGER/SONGWRITER. MATURE INTROSPECTION WAS THE ORDER OF THE DAY. THOUGH A YEARNING FOR SONGS THAT BOTH PONDERED YOUTHFUL NOSTALGIA AND THE CONCERNS OF ADULT LIVES LED TO THE EMERGENCE OF TWO DISTINCT CAMPS OF SINGER/SONGWRITERS.

Above

Carole King's 1971 album Tapestry proved that she was not only capable of writing successful hit songs but also of singing them in a gentle, emotive style that led the way for many other songwriters.

WHILE rock singer/songwriters dismissed hit singles and revealed their own state of mind through their art, pop singer/songwriters were more romantic and radio-friendly, less specific and challenging, and crossed over into what some sceptical critics labelled "hip easy listening". Although Carole King, the maker of the definitive 1970s pop singer/songwriter album, had only a short-lived superstardom, her biggest success neatly defines the key elements of the genre.

A Rich Tapestry

Formerly Carole Klein, New Yorker Carole King had formed one of the most successful songwriting partnerships of all time at the turn of the 1960s. Working out of the legendary New York hit factory The Brill Building, King and her future husband, Gerry Goffin, composed a host of pop anthems ('Will You Love Me Tomorrow' for the Shirelles, 'The Locomotion' for Little Eva and 'Pleasant Valley Sunday' for the Monkees, among many others) throughout the decade. Although King had a fitful career as an artist during the period – her only major success was 'It Might As Well Rain Until September' in 1962 – she suddenly re-emerged in early 1971 with *Tapestry*, a

> "GOOD SONGS SHOULD LAST. A GOOD ONE SHOULD LAST FOREVER. 'JUST THE WAY YOU ARE', BY BILLY JOEL, IS THAT SORT OF GREAT SONG."
>
> *Elton John.*

LEADING EXPONENTS

Carole King
Elton John
Billy Joel
Stevie Wonder
Paul Simon
Cat Stevens
Neil Diamond
Don McLean
Jim Croce
David Gates and Bread
Bob Dylan
Joni Mitchell
John Lennon

SEVENTIES POP SINGER/SONGWRITERS

The piano was the instrument of choice for the 1970s singer/songwriter, and it gave the songs a flavour that came partly from the instrument's ability to cover the whole musical range and to play several parts at once; they became more sophisticated and less reliant on sheer energy to carry them across to the listener.

THE SEVENTIES POP INTRO ➡ 38   POP PEOPLE A-Z ➡ 72   INSTRUMENTS A-Z ➡ 436   POP: SIXTIES POP SINGER/SONGWRITERS ➡ 28

complete break from tremulous teen pop. The album's deft blend of classic, Golden Age pop melody, white soul vocals and arrangements, combined with lyrics of sincere yet world-weary romance, made it the biggest-selling album ever at that point. King's subsequent career of typically Los Angeles adult pop never quite reached the same heights, but the former backroom girl had forged the template for all pop singer/songwriters to come.

Three Piano Men

A trio of ivory ticklers developed this budding pop tradition, and became commercial kings of the mainstream. The most unlikely, of course, was one Reg Dwight, a plump, bespectacled Englishman who changed his name to the more poetic Elton John and looked set for a journeyman career through British pop's backwaters until his second, self-titled album scored a surprise transatlantic hit in 1970. Although Elton never wrote his own lyrics (he forged a career-long partnership with wordsmith Bernie Taupin), and also gleefully embraced the comic end of glam rock's onstage sartorial flamboyance, his 30-years-and-counting success rate was, and is, based squarely upon classic singer/songwriterly values. Emotive, piano-led melodies, sad and introspective lyrical themes and an ever-present nostalgia for pop's past combine to make him the genre's most enduring superstar.

His American mirror figure was another plump and unprepossessing troubadour – Long Island's Billy Joel. Again, from his 1975 breakthrough album, *Piano Man*, to his eventual commercial slump in the 1990s, Joel's ability to blend lonely introspection with the nostalgia kick of, say, 1983's 'Uptown Girl' proved the key to him becoming one of the biggest-selling pop artists of all time. Joel was melancholy and musically articulate, but an ordinary guy – a description you couldn't apply to the third piano man, Stevie Wonder. The blind former Motown child prodigy Steveland Judkins broke away from his label's formula pop-soul with 1972's *Music Of My Mind*, embarking on a run of classic albums (through to 1980's *Hotter Than July*) that broke the R&B and pop mould with their blend of rock, funk, jazz, soul, romantic introspection and political protest. Black music was changed forever by the depth and breadth of Wonder's artistic vision.

The 1960s Revisited

Two particular artists refused to let hippy ideals lie – at least, within their music and for a short but significant period. Paul Simon split from Art Garfunkel and ploughed his own singular furrow of innocent 1960s pop, mature melodicism, wistful nostalgia and wry New York cynicism. His polished, post-graduate pop theorems threw everything from gospel and

doo-wop to jazz and reggae into the mix. In 1986, he delivered a unit-shifting fusion with African pop in *Graceland*, drawing praise and criticism when his insistence on recording and performing in South Africa broke the anti-apartheid cultural boycott.

Cat Stevens – a British/Greek/Swedish minor 1960s pop star – also went on to create controversy in later years. Having scored major success in the early 1970s with a folky brand of peace-loving acoustic pop, Stevens converted to Islam in 1979, changed his name to Yusef Islam and retired from music. The controversy arrived when he allegedly announced his support for the persecution of author Salman Rushdie in the 1980s.

MOR To Come

Elsewhere, various artists tugged the singer/songwriter impulse into increasingly shallow waters. In America, Tin Pan Alley veteran Neil Diamond, housewives' favourite Barry Manilow, 'Vincent' and 'American Pie' nostalgist Don McLean, died-young faux-country minstrel Jim Croce and one-man love-song factory David Gates (who hid behind the band name Bread) provided a mellow respite from rock's cultural domination. In the UK, even the MOR ("middle of the road") types needed a gimmick; hence Gilbert O'Sullivan's school uniform and Leo Sayer's clown suit in their early careers. Nevertheless, the sound was unmistakable: easy, catchy, introspective and nostalgic, with the guitars turned down to one. Both faded from view when they became typical, bouncy pop singers. But the singer/songwriter wave they were part of has never retreated and almost certainly never will.

CAMP. TRASHY. LIGHTWEIGHT. THROWAWAY. EXPLOITATIVE. FRAUDULENT. EUROPOP HAS DRAWN ALL THOSE INSULTS AND MORE. AND REMAINS, AFTER 30 YEARS, MOST POPULAR AMONG THOSE WITH A LOVE OF KITSCH. NEVERTHELESS, THE DANCEABLE POP OF EARLY 1970S MAINLAND EUROPE HAS HAD AN ENORMOUS INFLUENCE ON MANUFACTURED POP, AS WELL AS ALL HOUSE AND DISCO-DERIVED DANCE MUSIC.

Europop

Above
Boney M's 1978 single, 'Rivers of Babylon/Brown Girl in the Ring', became the biggest-selling single in UK chart history and secured a place for manufactured musicians in music history.

THROUGHOUT the 1950s and 1960s, America and Britain dominated global pop trends. Although Europe had already delivered some uniquely indigenous pop artists – most notably, the sophisticated, seductive pop suites of France's Serge Gainsbourg and Françoise Hardy, and the seminal electronic ruminations of Germany's Kraftwerk in the early 1970s – Europop as a universally recognized pop language was created in the mid-1970s by two very different artistic teams. One prioritized the song, while the other pioneered a new sound. All subsequent Europop blended the two on some level, but never with such artistry and impact.

Swede Soul Music

ABBA formed in 1971, after the four members had already become folk-pop stars in their native Sweden. It was 1974 before songwriters Benny Andersson and Björn Ulvaeus, and lead singers Agnetha Faltskog and Anni-Frid Lyngstad, achieved the international breakthrough they craved, winning the annual Euro trash-fest that is the Eurovision Song Contest with the arrestingly odd-but-irresistible 'Waterloo'. The two married couples (Björn and Agnetha, Benny and "Frida") went on to conquer the world (although

> "I REMEMBER THE DAY I CAME UP WITH THE PHRASE 'LOVE TO LOVE YOU BABY'. I HAD TO GO TO GIORGIO'S OFFICE AND I SAID TO HIM, 'LISTEN TO THIS LINE. ISN'T IT A CUTE LINE?'."
>
> *Donna Summer*

Britain and Europe favoured their innovations more than America) with an unbroken string of million-selling albums and singles, purveying an increasingly perfect and increasingly lovelorn blend of sweeping melody, glistening production and Beach Boys-meets-Mamas & the Papas-influenced harmony pop. Yet the sometimes surreal imagery produced by the Swedes' second-language English, and Benny and Björn's singular MOR-tinged songwriting style, created a pop language that transcended their US and UK influences.

The band fell apart in 1981 under the strain of both couples' divorces, with Benny and Björn scoring major successes as writers of stage musicals, and Agnetha and Frida drifting into reclusive retreat after lack of solo success. But, in seven short years, ABBA had become the biggest pop group since The Beatles, while simultaneously proving that you did not need a rock attitude – or good dress sense – to create affecting and original pop artistry.

Sex And Synths

Meanwhile, in Italy, a veteran Italian producer and a Boston-born star of German stage musicals were inventing what we now know as dance music. In 1975, Giorgio Moroder and Donna Summer caused a sensation with the 17-minute epic 'Love To Love You Baby', whereby Ms Summer moaned her way to orgasm over a low-tempo synthesized version of Philadelphian orchestral disco-soul. This was followed in 1977 by, arguably, the most influential dance record of the modern era, 'I Feel Love', a chugging, churning, futuristic disco machine based on one repetitious, but

LEADING EXPONENTS

ABBA
Donna Summer
Giorgio Moroder
Boney M
a-ha
Milli Vanilli
Aqua
Whigfield
Roxette
Ace Of Base

EUROPOP

As it is based around synthesizers and computer sequencers to play them, Europop uses complex syncopation and precise digital drumbeats to create it's infectious grooves. Try playing this example to see how hard it is for a human being.

THE SEVENTIES POP INTRO ➡38   POP PEOPLE A-Z ➡72   INSTRUMENTS A-Z ➡436   THE DANCE INTRO ➡310   DANCE: DISCO ➡314

subtly developing, electronic drone-riff. It made Summer a superstar – the first and biggest disco diva.

The pair went on to make hit after hit with synthetic takes on everything from hard rock ('Hot Stuff') to Spectoresque girl-group pop ('Love's Unkind'), all possessed of a camp sexual immediacy that somehow sounded entirely unique, entirely European. While Moroder was to enjoy even greater success as a soundtrack producer/composer (*American Gigolo* with Blondie, *Flashdance, Top Gun*), Summer headed towards a more overtly American kind of dance-pop, and then gospel as a born-again Christian. Her star waned when she made insensitive comments about people with HIV/AIDS (which she later insisted were misquotes), appalling her huge gay following. None of this, however, changes Summer and Moroder's invention of Eurodisco, key influence on house and techno, and guiding presence in every Europop and female vocal dance hit of the last 25 years.

Mime Doesn't Pay

The third great Europop progenitor was the German writer/producer Frank Farian, who formed a vocal quartet to front a string of strange novelty disco hit singles in the late 1970s. Comprising West Indian session singers Marcia Barrett, Bobby Farrell, Liz Mitchell and Maizie Williams, Boney M turned up on every European pop show of the period dressed in glitzy mutations of tribal or period costume, performing comic, catchy singalongs based on everything from historical drama ('Rasputin') to Christmas carols ('Mary's Boy Child') to Jamaican nursery rhymes ('Brown Girl In The Ring'). It had all petered out by the turn of the 1980s, predictably, but Farian's brand of manufactured pop genius was to return and provide a bizarre twist to the tale.

Milli Vanilli comprised two aspiring models, Rob Pilatus and Fabrice Morvan, who became an overnight transatlantic pop sensation in 1989 with a parade of massive, Farian-produced hits plucked from their 1989 *Girl You Know It's True* album. The problem was that their Grammy Award-winning songs had actually been recorded by singers Johnny Davis and Brad Howell, with rapper Charles Shaw. The pretty pair were simply mime artists. After Shaw almost blew the deal in an interview, and Pilatus and Morvan put pressure on Farian to let them sing on future recordings, Farian lost patience and revealed the truth in 1990. An embarrassed Grammy committee stripped Milli Vanilli of their award, and everyone involved in MV became pop pariahs. It all reached a grisly end when, after failed attempts to forge a new pop career, Pilatus slid into drug addiction followed by a public suicide attempt, various crimes (including assault), a jail sentence, stints in rehab, and, finally, his drugs- and alcohol-related death in 1998.

Euro Currency

Despite Milli Vanilli's tragic tale, Europop has continued to serve up light, frothy pop to those put off by the pretensions of "serious" rock and pop. Usually based on disco beats (Black Box, Technotronic, 2 Unlimited, Sash!, Livin' Joy); often applying "cheese" to various forms of black music soul food, such as rap (Snap!, Bomfunk MCs) and reggae (Ace Of Base); never, especially in the cases of Aqua, Whigfield and Roxette, taking itself too seriously. Europop artists generally score some huge hit singles before disappearing, having injected a little joy into the deliberately ephemeral side of chart pop. Classic Euro's happy, gay-friendly mix of repetition and catchiness directly influenced Madonna, Pet Shop Boys, Stock, Aitken & Waterman and the entire sweep of twenty-first-century boy- and girl-band pop.

Above
ABBA's popularity has endured to such an extent that a smash hit musical, Mamma Mia!, uses their timeless songs as its basis and draws in huge audiences from a wide range of ages and cultures.

Left
After contributing to the soundtrack of Top Gun in 1986, Giorgio Moroder steered away from dance music and focused on rock, producing the album Flaunt It by the short-lived band Sigue Sigue Sputnik.

ALTHOUGH MANY WOULD CONTEND THAT 1980S POP WAS TYPIFIED BY AN EMPTY, ASPIRATIONAL OVERLOAD OF BAD HAIRCUTS AND CYNICAL BLANDNESS, THE DECADE PRODUCED MANY OF POP'S MOST INDIVIDUAL ARTISTS. IN ADDITION, IT WAS ARGUABLY DEFINED BY 1985'S LIVE AID – A GLOBAL CHARITY EVENT UNMATCHABLE IN ITS REACH, AND DEFINITIVE IN ITS MARKING OF THE PERIOD.

Eighties Pop

STYLES

Singer/Songwriters

New Wave

New Romantics &
   Futurism

2-Tone

Manufactured Pop

THE pop of the 1980s was directly shaped by three developments, which significantly changed the musical marketplace. Firstly, the extraordinary technological leap that saw the humble synthesizer progress to the sampler, the sequencer, programmable drums and the practical, affordable means to replicate the sound of an entire orchestra at the touch of a button. Secondly, the advent of MTV and the success of the promo video meant that, as 1980s super-producer Trevor Horn's Buggles sang in 1979, 'Video Killed The Radio Star'. And, last but not least, the lines between "black" and "white" music became irrevocably blurred as, encouraged by the astonishing success of Michael Jackson's *Thriller*, everyone chased the ultimate crossover dollar by mixing soul, rock, pop and disco into an increasingly homogeneous whole.

> "I CAME HERE TO PLAY MUSIC, AND I DIDN'T REALLY REALISE THE FULL EXTENT AND MAGNITUDE OF WHAT IT IS ALL ABOUT. NOW I'M HERE. IT'S THE GREATEST EVENT EVER."
>
> *Ozzy Osbourne on Live Aid*

Pop's New Royalty

Former child star Michael Jackson became the self-proclaimed King Of Pop during the 1980s, with his Quincy Jones-produced albums *Off The Wall* (1979) and *Thriller* (1982). They defined the new commercial rules: sophisticated dance-pop combined with pop melody and occasional rock raucousness; lyrical themes that flitted between the self-referential and the more general pop languages of love, sex and dancing; and massively expensive and lavish video promotions, with the

television premiere of the 15-minute movie made for the 'Thriller' single synchronized into a global event. His sister Janet also threw off her teen-poppet image with the Jimmy Jam/Terry Lewis-produced *Control* in 1986 – a tough, feminist soul-pop album that took her immediately out of Michael's shadow.

LEADING EXPONENTS

Michael Jackson

Madonna

Prince

Pet Shop Boys

Whitney Houston

Janet Jackson

Trevor Horn/Frankie
   Goes To Hollywood

Wham!/George Michael

Eurythmics

Tina Turner

Duran Duran

Culture Club

EIGHTIES POP

The jumpy and intricate bassline is typical of 1980s pop where drums and bass were almost always computer-generated, allowing unheard-of precision in the rhythm section. Chord structures became less easily defined, with jazz-style triads creating the mood.

Jam and Lewis's Minneapolis funk band the Time numbered a pocket-sized but potent performer/singer/composer/multi-musician in their ranks by the name of Prince Rogers Nelson. His lascivious blend of funk, soul, pop and classic rock went supernova in 1984 with the soundtrack to his *Purple Rain* movie. His Hendrix-meets-Little-Richard-and-learns-James-Brown's-dance-moves image seduced the world, and saw him go on to be the decade's most talented and prolific pop prodigy.

Meanwhile, in New York, an ambitious ex-dancer was plotting her path to glory. The disco bounce of Madonna's first hit, 'Holiday', progressed into cheeky, smart and unforgettable dance-pop in 1984's 'Like A Virgin'. Ms Ciccone then embarked on almost two decades of unparalleled pop invention and reinvention, seamlessly staying one step ahead of each pop trend without breaking a sweat.

The soul-pop crossover continued apace in the shape of two contrasting divas. Tina Turner had been a rock'n'soul star since the 1960s, but had disappeared into obscurity until enjoying a comeback smash with the *Private Dancer* album in 1984, featuring songwriting credits from the likes of Dire Straits' Mark Knopfler and production work from the likes of British synth-popsters Heaven 17 and the ubiquitous Rupert Hine. Her blend of electro-AOR and ravaged soul vocals, coupled with revelations of abuse at the hands of former partner Ike Turner, transformed her into a survivor heroine.

At the other end of the age scale, the 22-year-old, gospel-trained session singer Whitney Houston released a self-titled album in 1985, which, with its glossy blend of carefree dance pop and overwrought balladry, became the most successful debut album of all time. Despite talent and beauty in abundance, the next 15 years saw decreasing sales and increasing public humiliation for the crossover diva, amid rumours of severe drug problems, rampant egomania and mysterious goings-on in her high-profile marriage to the R&B star Bobby Brown.

The New British Invasion

Eighties British pop and its success in America stemmed initially from its wave of pretty-boy acts crossing glam with synth-pop. But the key figure in 1980s Britpop was a producer, rather than an artist. Trevor Horn moved from being a member of Yes, as well as his own one-hit-wonder pop act the Buggles, to manning the desk for a slew of influential and successful Brit artists, including ABC, Spandau Ballet, Dollar, Frankie Goes To Hollywood, the Art Of Noise and the Pet Shop Boys. Despite differences between the acts, his sound was

immediately recognizable, as Horn pursued the sonic possibilities of the new Fairlight sampler and created an enormous wall of sound – crashing drums, cascading strings, fanfare brass, crunching bass, multi-layered vocals and sound effects which were either sugary sweet or speaker-blowing. This provided a high-concept contrast to the likes of George Michael, who moved away from the fun-poking dance-pop of Wham!, the band he formed with his school friend Andrew Ridgeley, into an increasingly personal, singer-songwriter style of pop, ending the 1980s as a major British pop star.

Electro-dance continued to be the major Britpop impulse, however, with bands as diverse as Eurythmics, former Depeche Mode leader Vince Clarke's Yazoo and Erasure, and punks-turned-electro-popsters the Cure and New Order producing successful, machine-driven pop containing varying degrees of light and shade. By the end of the 1980s, northern synth-pop duo the Pet Shop Boys had, in their deadpan, subtly political and strikingly intelligent way, combined all of the above Brit popsters' moods and methods into one cohesive, danceable, adult and enduringly popular whole.

Far Left

The successful soundtrack that accompanied Prince's 1984 Purple Rain *spawned such hits as 'When Doves Cry' and 'Let's Go Crazy', further increasing Prince's reputation for powerful lyrics and danceable guitar grooves.*

Left

Truly one of pop music's greatest icons, Madonna became one of the most commercially successful stars of her time, with an enormous following of dedicated fans who would follow her innumerable reinventions with great intrigue.

Below

Michael Jackson, renowned in the 1980s for his distinctive voice and fancy footwork, meets and greets his new waxwork at London's Madame Tussauds.

Eighties Pop
Singer/Songwriters

IN THE 1980S, THE CROSSOVER IDEAL – NOT JUST BETWEEN BLACK AND WHITE MUSIC, BUT BETWEEN ROCK AND POP, AND ADULTS AND KIDS – RULED THE AIRWAVES. EVEN THE PREVIOUSLY PERSONAL AND INTROSPECTIVE SINGER/SONGWRITERS WERE FORCED TO ADJUST, AND TO DILUTE THEIR PIANO-BASED ROMANTIC BALLADS WITH UPTEMPO, FULL-BAND, DANCE-FRIENDLY SONGS.

Above
Kate Bush's 1985 release
Hounds of Love *was produced and recorded in her very own home studio and spawned the single 'Running Up That Hill', which brought her to the attention of the US audience.*

THE brassy soul-pop nostalgia of New Yorker Billy Joel's 1983 hits, such as 'Uptown Girl' and 'Tell Her About It', were perhaps the ultimate examples of such crossover music. Nevertheless, those that managed to pull this balance off most successfully were an extremely varied bunch in style and approach, reminding us that, even in pop's most conservative periods, those artists with the most singular vision are those who tend to truly define their times.

English Eccentrics

Kent's Kate Bush became a superstar at the age of just 20 with her hysterical pop adaptation of 'Wuthering Heights' in 1978, and proceeded to illuminate the 1980s with a succession of increasingly adventurous and challenging pop concepts. On the one hand, her expressions of intense, freewheeling sexuality and gift for pseudo-classical melody made her a mainstream pin-up and hit-maker. On the other, her spooky, theatrical takes on subjects as wide-ranging as nuclear war ('Breathing') and the plight of aboriginal people ('The Dreaming') – plus her reclusive nature and often bizarre visual sense – gave her cult appeal and critical acclaim. Towards the end of the 1980s, she worked with the former Genesis frontman Peter Gabriel, a pioneer of globally attuned pop intellectualism. Gabriel's work incorporated elements of everything from synth-pop

> "THE CONTEMPORARY HIT RADIO FORMAT – THEY DON'T LIKE JAZZ, THEY DON'T LIKE HIP-HOP. IT IS AGAINST THEIR FORMULA. BUT BECAUSE IT IS MY RECORD THEY HAVE TO TAKE IT SERIOUSLY."
>
> *Sting*

to African tribal rhythms, was often vividly political (particularly on the anti-apartheid anthem 'Biko'), and achieved a perfect compromise with dance-rock and the video age in 1986's 'Sledgehammer'.

LEADING EXPONENTS
Kate Bush
Sting
George Michael
Elton John
Stevie Wonder
Phil Collins
Peter Gabriel
Suzanne Vega
Sade
Terence Trent D'Arby
Lionel Richie

EIGHTIES POP SINGER/SONGWRITERS
The lyrical ballads by Phil Collins that were a feature of 1980s songwriting derived some of their effect from two musical techniques demonstrated in this short piece: large intervals in the melody, and putting the 2nd note of the chord in the bass instead of the root (called the first inversion).

THE EIGHTIES POP INTRO ➡ 44   POP PEOPLE A–Z ➡ 72   INSTRUMENTS A–Z ➡ 436   POP: SEVENTIES SINGER/SONGWRITERS ➡ 40

No Band Required

The man who took over Gabriel's lead role in prog-rockers-turned-adult-popsters Genesis spearheaded a wave of singer/songwriters who easily transcended their roots in massively successful bands. Former child actor and drummer Phil Collins fused musicianly adult pop, the huge funky sound of Earth, Wind and Fire's brass section, the pop nostalgia pastiche typified by his cover of the Supremes' 'You Can't Hurry Love' and maudlin lyrics inspired by his marital problems to become one of the decade's most reliable unit-shifters. Collins's definitive brand of well-crafted divorce pop also made him a byword for blandness, according to the critics. A former member of the Motown funk band the Commodores, Lionel Richie was also critically dismissed while he delighted mature pop fans. This cardiganed creator of mawkish pop balladry and light dance-pop defined a particular brand of pop-soul crossover, influenced as much by mainstream country as by R&B.

Two other Englishmen who split era-defining pop groups before going on to even greater success were Gordon "Sting" Sumner and George Michael. The former Georgios Kyriacos Panayiotou had already left his north London Greek-Cypriot community far behind with teen-pop titans Wham!, in tandem with childhood friend Andrew Ridgeley. But 1987's *Faith* immediately redefined the pop prodigy as a more adult proposition, before *Listen Without Prejudice Vol. 1* matched a more Lennon/Elton John-derived introspection to the title's pretensions in 1990. Sting managed an equally seamless transition from new wave-meets-reggae Police pin-up in 1984, to self-consciously serious jazz-pop fusioneer in 1985. His high-profile association with various political and ecological causes exemplified what was expected from the mature rocker after the impact of 1985's Live Aid global charity event.

The Soul Side

As Lionel Richie exemplifies, the 1980s adult-pop crossover did cut both ways. Two extremely good-looking black artists working out of London blended the new singer/songwriter's high-concept craft with classic black music grooves and textures. Former US serviceman Terence Trent D'Arby was a native New Yorker, but put together his timely melange of old-school soul and modern pop production in England after a stint as a funk singer (and a boxer!) in Germany. His 1987 debut album, the hit-laden *Introducing The Hardline According To Terence Trent D'Arby*, melded his Sam Cooke-meets-Otis Redding soul scream with catchy pop-funk and ballads, appearing to herald the arrival of a pop genius. Sadly, D'Arby's sex-symbol impact and critical acclaim led to a loss of perspective, and his deliberately "weird" follow-up, *Neither Fish Nor Flesh*, became

Above
Suzanne Vega's serene a cappella vocals on her single 'Tom's Diner' morphed into an unlikely club hit once it was remixed by British DJs D.N.A. with electronic beats and sounds in 1993.

one of the most notorious "career suicide" albums in pop history, consigning him to subsequent near-obscurity. Meanwhile, a Nigerian/Brit female with equivalent model looks made no such mistakes. Sade (born Helen Folasade Adu) forged a smooth and effortless blend of mellow jazz and sleepily sensual pop romance, making a string of albums from 1984's massive *Diamond Life* onwards that not only sold, but had a profound influence on black music – largely through being the late-night seduction choice for many of the male artists who ruled the rap and R&B roost in the 1990s!

Old, New, Borrowed And Blue

Two of the best-loved singer/songwriters from the 1970s adapted easily to the next decade's commercial demands. While Elton John opened up about his sexuality and reinvented himself as a pop survivor with the single 'I'm Still Standing', the great Stevie Wonder left the gritty experiments of his peak years behind. He enjoyed his biggest hit singles with the MOR platitudes of 'Ebony and Ivory' (a duet with Paul McCartney) and that wedding-reception perennial, 'I Just Called To Say I Love You'.

Finally, one talented New Yorker continued and modernized the traditional female singer/songwriter lineage established by Joni Mitchell and Carole King. Suzanne Vega's cool, clever and melancholy ruminations on everything from bohemian cafés ('Tom's Diner') to domestic abuse ('Luka') ensured that the intelligent solo pop circle remained unbroken throughout the 1980s and beyond.

Left
George Michael's 'Faith' was a transatlantic smash, selling more than 10 million copies and topping the pop music charts. This single arrived at the peak of Michael's commercial success.

New Wave

FOR MANY VETERANS OF THE PUNK ERA, NEW WAVE IS NOT A GENRE AT ALL. THE TERM WAS COINED BY THE MUSIC PRESS TO ENCOMPASS ACTS WHO WERE INFLUENCED BY PUNK, BUT LESS OVERTLY REBELLIOUS AND WITH MORE TRADITIONALLY CRAFTED POP SKILLS. NEW WAVE ACTS TRADED LARGELY ON A BACK-TO-BASICS DESIRE TO REVIVE THE SHORT, SHARP THRILL OF THE CLASSIC, MID-1960S BEAT-POP SINGLE.

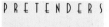

Above

The Pretenders released their self-titled debut album in 1980, which produced such sexually aggressive hits as 'Brass in Pocket' and a cover of the Kinks' 'Stop Your Sobbing'.

THEIR ethos was reflected in new wave's dress codes: tight, dark mod suits with skinny ties, short (or at least, shorter) hair, occasional biker-chic leather and Day-Glo pop-art dresses. The punk die-hards may have sneered, but new wave's legacy is one of the richest in pop history – a last blast of starkly produced, arty but direct, high-energy youth anthems, before the crossover hegemony of the 1980s swept it aside.

The Blank Generation

Like punk, new wave's mid-1970s origins can be traced to CBGB's, a small, smelly bar that became a gig venue on New York's Lower East Side. While Richard Hell, Television, the Ramones and Patti Smith were forging punk's template, fellow CBGB's regulars Blondie and Talking Heads were creating a punk-related, pop-styled sound that would conquer the world.

Former Andy Warhol acolyte Debbie Harry (Blondie's vocalist) became one of late-1970s/early 1980s pop's most adored icons, fusing classic girl-group pop with punk aggression and a disco groove. Her perfect look and cut-glass voice simultaneously reinvented and satirized the "blonde bombshell" image, while her (male) band's extraordinary run of pop anthems virtually defined female intelligence and sexuality in the late-1970s and early 1980s. Madonna cites her as a major influence. By stark contrast, Talking Heads were

> "IT WAS A POP THAT WAS VERY AGGRESSIVE AND WITH A FEMALE FRONT PERSON, AND THAT HAD NEVER REALLY BEEN DONE IN POP."
>
> *Debbie Harry on Blondie*

nerdy, nervy and deliberately asexual, purveying a unique brand of 1960s art-pop and white lo-fi funk. As the 1980s moved on, the Heads transformed themselves into a globally inspired, big-band funk outfit with the classic 'Once In A Lifetime' single, even managing to throw country-tinged Americana into the mix before the band's acrimonious split in 1991.

Stiff Upper Lips

Britain's new wave grew out of an independent record label. From 1977 onwards, London's Stiff Records cleverly mixed its roots in London's "pub rock" live scene with punk's eccentricity to introduce a number of unique alternative pop icons,

LEADING EXPONENTS

Blondie

Talking Heads

Elvis Costello

The Jam

The Police

The Pretenders

The Knack

The Stranglers

Buzzcocks

Devo

The Boomtown Rats

NEW WAVE

Reggae was a big influence on the new wave, with the chopping chord on alternate quavers and the pumping off-beat bassline. The new wavers, however, brought chordal complexity and pop melodies. Notice the underlying 12/8 feel.

including Nick Lowe, Ian Dury, Madness and the Pogues. But their key discovery was Declan McManus, an Irish-Liverpudlian from a musical family who changed his name to Elvis Costello and blended angry-young-man aggression with extraordinarily witty, literate songs and a strong US influence. Brit and Stateside hero worship followed, as his Buddy Holly look – tight office-worker suit, cheap spectacles, crew cut, skinny tie – established the dominant male imagery of new wave, and his increasingly sophisticated lyrical ruminations on love, sex and politics saw him graduate toward pop's top table, working with the likes of Paul McCartney and Burt Bacharach.

A group of other, equally striking Brit new wavers grafted pop craft onto various kinds of punk stance. The Jam injected youthful energy and anti-establishment bile into mod-era guitar pop, with young suburbanite Paul Weller crafting a string of sharp, relevant Who/Beatles-influenced UK chart-toppers while becoming a spokesman for a generation. The Stranglers added a sullen kind of London misanthropy to the Doors organ-dominated rock and became alternative pop icons throughout the late-1970s and early 1980s. Manchester's Buzzcocks made an early switch from scratchy punk to glorious pop love songs sung over a wall of guitars and thus laid the groundwork for every pop-punk act through to Blink 182 and Ash. Irishmen the Boomtown Rats mingled punk scruffiness with Stonesy rhythm and blues, Bowie-esque glam and even Springsteen-ish rock anthems, striking paydirt with the power ballad 'I Don't Like Mondays', which was inspired by a shooting in an American school. Their lead singer, Bob Geldof, went on to change the world with his Band Aid and Live Aid famine-relief campaigns. Finally, the Police pulled off the cleverest fusion, with Sting, Andy Summers and their American drummer, Stewart Copeland, channelling their jazz-level musicianship into a sparse, haunting blend of rock, pop and reggae. In their hands, new wave became a global commercial concern.

America Strikes Back

Although Akron, Ohio's Chrissie Hynde had served her rock apprenticeship as a musician in Paris and a journalist in London, her friendship with the Sex Pistols helped her form a UK band that perfectly blended the leather-chic end of

punk with her love of classic 1960s pop romance. The Pretenders were the ultimate transatlantic new wave band, seducing with Hynde's soulful, French-influenced vocals and songs that carried echoes of US radio rock as much as the Kinks (Hynde went on to marry and divorce the Kinks' frontman, Ray Davies). Meanwhile, the Cars and the Knack successfully married new wave pop's skinny-tie image and love of 1960s beat with familiar FM rock production, creating hits ('My Best Friend's Girl' and 'My Sharona' respectively) that succinctly summed up the times. Another Akron band, Devo, came up with a strange strand of new wave activity, moving from marvellously atonal covers of the Stones' 'Satisfaction' and the baffling concept of de-evolution, to smartly subversive dance-pop hits that ingeniously satirized the synthetic 1980s values they appeared to embody.

Above

Founded in 1975, the Stranglers were known for their dark lyrics, raucous sound and penchant for dressing fully in black, which earned them a loyal following throughout Europe and the US as the punk movement emerged.

Centre

Elvis Costello recorded and performed with the Attractions between 1977 and 1985, establishing himself as a prolific songwriter, with Johnny Cash and Roy Orbison among the artists who have performed his work.

New Romantics & Futurism

BORN OUT OF A REACTION TO BOTH PUNK AND 2-TONE'S POLITICS AND ANTI-STAR STANCE, THE BRITISH SYNTH-POP WAVE OF THE EARLY 1980S BROUGHT ALMOST INSTANT CHANGE TO THE UK POP SCENE. MOREOVER, THE US SUCCESS OF THE PRINCIPAL PROTAGONISTS SIGNALLED THE BIGGEST "BRITISH INVASION" SINCE THE BEATLES AND THE ROLLING STONES TRANSFORMED AMERICAN POP IN THE 1960S.

Above
With their self-titled 1981 release, Duran Duran became instant worldwide stars, renowned for their good looks as much as for their synthesized, neo-disco songs and innovative videos featured on MTV.

MIXING a heavily styled, fashion-conscious image, machine-dominated and danceable tunes and a return to narcissistic and aspirational lyrics with a little theatrical, existentialist misery, UK synth-pop essentially blended the three major phases of David Bowie's 1970s trailblazing – peacock glam, smooth, white funk and arty, electronic alienation. Roxy Music and Germany's Kraftwerk were the other major influences on the two complementary strands of the new romantics and futurism.

Pirates And Posers

When Londoner Stuart Goddard saw the Sex Pistols, he changed his name to Adam Ant and, after several punkish false starts, delivered a vibrant pop fusion that brought colour back to the cheeks of British pop. Adam And the Ants' *Kings Of The Wild Frontier* album heralded a new decade in 1980, mixing pirate and Native American costume, glam-rock guitars and chants with African tribal drumming and pure pop fun with original, even surreal noise. Adam's matinée-idol looks, yelping pop croon, joyfully silly pantomime imagery and theatrical promo videos enabled what would become the new romantic scene to blossom, opening the door for a number of former punks who wanted to dress up and embrace pop stardom.

The most cultish and influential of these were Japan, a London quintet led by David Sylvian, who was often referred to as "The World's Most Beautiful Man". Originally a rather limp copy of US glam-punks the New York Dolls, Japan reinvented themselves in 1979 with the electro-disco of *Quiet Life*, produced by electronic pioneer Giorgio Moroder. They went on to produce ever more subtle, atmospheric, Eastern-influenced art pop until their split in 1982, just as the shy, intellectual Sylvian was on the verge of a superstardom he did not want.

The quintessential new romantic group emerged from the trendiest end of London's club scene in 1980. Spandau Ballet mixed basic synth-disco, hilariously pretentious lyrics and the operatic vocals of Tony Hadley, before diminishing returns saw them become a showcase for Gary Kemp's increasingly

> "SUCH A PURITANISM HAS GROWN UP OF LATE. I'D RATHER DRESS UP LIKE LIBERACE."
>
> *Adam Ant*

Right
Gary Numan's experimental synth sounds led him to become reminiscent of royalty in the UK, where fans remain loyal to his innovative sounds that began with the groundbreaking hit 'Cars'.

LEADING EXPONENTS

Adam Ant
Gary Numan
Japan
Spandau Ballet
Duran Duran
Human League
Culture Club
Depeche Mode
Soft Cell
ABC
Visage

NEW ROMANTIC STYLE

Characterized by singable melodies, with every note of the main melody hitting the beats of the accompanying synthesizers and delivered by a male-dominated cast of good-looking, able singers. The tunes are catchy and easy to remember.

THE EIGHTIES POP INTRO ➥ 44 POP PEOPLE A–Z ➥ 72 INSTRUMENTS A–Z ➥ 436 ROCK: GLAM ROCK & GLITTER ➥ 84

smooth adult-pop songcraft, typified by the huge transatlantic hits 'True' and 'Gold'. Gary and his bass-playing brother, Martin, went on to star in the film *The Krays*, before Martin, after narrowly avoiding death by brain tumour, found more success in the 1990s as a star of the UK soap opera *EastEnders*.

Spandau's even more successful rivals were Duran Duran, who came out of the Birmingham club scene to purvey an aggressively rockish take on synthetic dance-pop that saw them become the embodiment of the big-in-America, model-dating, hedonistic pop group. Regional variants on the synth-dance-and-cheekbones formula sprang from every corner of the UK: the cheeky, camp, northern soul-influenced Soft Cell from Leeds; the funky, orchestral and wordy Trevor Horn-produced ABC from Sheffield; the grandiose Ultravox, led by Scotland's Midge Ure; and new romantic supergroup Visage, formed by London fashion faces and club promoters Steve Strange and Rusty Egan, and including Ure in its largely studio-based line-up.

Although he came directly from the same London club scene as Spandau and Visage, "Boy" George O'Dowd was a different kind of New Romantic icon. His extraordinary career took in the formation of Culture Club, flamboyant cross-dressing, a unique brand of white pop-soul that smoothly incorporated reggae ('Do You Really Want To Hurt Me') and MOR country (the ubiquitous 'Karma Chameleon'), a public fall from grace as a result of heroin addiction, America's rejection of his (surely always obvious?) homosexuality and a triumphant solo return as a DJ, raconteur and writer of the *Taboo* stage musical.

Synths And Sci-Fi

Like Adam Ant, Gary Webb was a London punk who rejected rebellion for glam reinvention. As Gary Numan, he produced an electronic kind of pop-rock that traded on images of a nightmarish, dystopian future while somehow seeming cosy, which was no mean feat given that they were delivered by a chubby-faced cockney wearing eyeliner. Heavily influenced by Bowie and cult figure John Foxx (who had led proto-futurists Ultravox before Midge Ure remade them as teen pop), Numan signalled the popular embrace of futurism, which had nothing to do with the Italian art movement and everything to do with noises and images that played with the mystery of a future dominated by machines.

The two most successful products of this school were Sheffield's Human League and Basildon's Depeche Mode. The League began as a superb, artful mix of synthetic throb, sly sci-fi imagery and arty slide shows, before the band split in two in 1980. Martyn Ware and Ian Craig-Marsh formed the British Electric Foundation in 1980, which then evolved into

Heaven 17 the following year; they went on to produce Tina Turner. Meanwhile, Philip Oakey hired pop tunesmiths Jo Callis and Ian Burden and girl backing singers/dancers Joanne Catherall and Susanne Sulley to form the new Human League line-up. Between them they created the magnificent *Dare*, the definitive synth-pop album of the decade and a huge transatlantic seller, courtesy of the ABBA-tributing anthem 'Don't You Want Me'.

Depeche Mode suffered similar personnel problems when Vince Clarke, the composer of their early, lovably cute synthetic ditties, left in 1981. While Clarke found long-term synth-pop success with various lead vocalists in the Assembly (the Undertones' Feargal Sharkey), Yazoo (Alison Moyet) and Erasure (Andy Bell), new songwriter Martin Gore and frontman Dave Gahan transformed the Mode into the ultimate stadium-friendly, synth-rock crossover, mingling sin, sadness, misery and mystery with globe-straddling appeal.

Above

Upon reaching number one in the charts with 'Do You Really Want to Hurt Me?', Boy George's Culture Club was transformed from a band that believed themselves to be anti-establishment to a major radio-friendly pop force that appealed to a diverse audience.

ONLY TWO RECORD LABELS IN POP HISTORY HAVE LENT THEIR NAME TO AN ENTIRE MUSICAL GENRE. THE FIRST IS DETROIT'S TAMLA MOTOWN. THE OTHER IS ENGLAND'S 2-TONE, A LATE-1970S/EARLY 1980S IMPRINT THAT STILL STANDS AS THE UK'S MOST POLITICALLY SIGNIFICANT POP PHENOMENON.

2-Tone

Above

Although popular in the UK, Madness's wild, ska/pop sound experienced only moderate success in the US, stemming from their single 'Our House' and its heavily played video on MTV.

2-TONE was set up in 1979 by the Special A.K.A., a multiracial ska- and reggae-inspired band from Coventry in England's Midlands. Comprising Jerry Dammers, Terry Hall, Neville Staples, Lynval Golding, John Bradbury, Roddy Radiation and Sir Horace Gentleman, this dynamic, working-class seven-piece revived the British/Jamaican Trojan label reggae of their childhoods, with the added extras of punk energy and angry, acerbic lyrics. Their songs of youth alienation, racism and working-class life were mostly sung by Hall with a blank, sneering sarcasm.

Black And White Unite

After building strong word-of-mouth supporting punk bands around Britain, the band set up their own independent label.

> "THE BASIC THING IS ANGLO-JAMAICAN MUSIC. IT'S TRYING TO INTEGRATE THOSE TWO."
>
> *Jerry Dammers*

Above Right

Inspired by the Specials and Madness, Bad Manners created a name for themselves with their outrageous stage performances and amusingly original ska covers of classic songs, such as 'Monster Mash'.

Again inspired by Motown and Trojan, 2-Tone aimed for a strong visual identity, encapsulated by the label itself – a cartoon of a well-dressed, racially ambiguous "rude boy" in pork-pie hat and mod suit (a rude boy is the term for a young ska/reggae fan), illustrated in sharp, chessboard black and white. The 2-Tone name applied equally to the band's attitude to racial politics, a crucial and courageous stance at a time when the overtly racist political party the National Front was, with some success, recruiting among white British urban youth.

Released in the UK in July 1979, the Special A.K.A.'s first single, 'Gangsters', promptly reached number six. This surprise

hit led to a licensing deal with the major label Chrysalis, a name change to the catchier the Specials and an almost instantaneous skinhead/mod revival among Britain's punk- and disco-fatigued youth.

Tales Of Everyday Madness

By the end of 1979, 2-Tone had released Top 10 singles by all the main players in the 2-Tone wave. North London septet Madness's 'The Prince' was, like 'Gangsters', a tribute to the Jamaican ska legend Prince Buster, but with the punk attack replaced by a cheeky, cheery, but occasionally wistful, cockney music-hall attitude. Graham "Suggs" McPherson and company soon left 2-Tone for Stiff Records and unleashed a string of hit singles and pioneering videos that established them as one of British pop's best-loved pop institutions until their split in 1986. The band still reform regularly for well-attended live shows.

Coventry's the Selecter, led by the charismatic female vocalist Pauline Black, made a big initial impact with their debut single, 'On My Radio' and first album *Too Much Pressure*. But although they possessed an even greater ska-punk raucousness than their friends the Specials, they quickly ran

LEADING EXPONENTS	2-TONE
The Specials	
Madness	
The Beat	
UB40	
Funboy Three	
The Selecter	
Bad Manners	

Ska music evolved with and from reggae, but was played with more pace; with a "rock steady" bass climbing up and down the triads and a double offbeat playing quick pairs either side of the normal reggae chop.

THE EIGHTIES POP INTRO ➡ 44   POP PEOPLE A-Z ➡ 72   INSTRUMENTS A-Z ➡ 436   REGGAE: SKA ➡ 350   REGGAE: ROOTS ➡ 354

out of steam. Finally, the Birmingham six-piece the Beat (called the English Beat in the US) emerged with a Christmas 1979 cover of Smokey Robinson's 'Tears Of A Clown' before forming their own Go-Feet label, again with the assistance of Chrysalis. Their strident punk-reggae protest songs, influenced by both Jamaican dub and classic 1960s pop, brought them transatlantic success before their split in 1983. Dave Wakeling and Ranking Roger went on to form General Public, while Andy Cox and David Steele found even greater success with Fine Young Cannibals.

Meanwhile, other, non-2-Tone-affiliated UK groups also contributed to the reggae- and mod-influenced spirit of the times. Birmingham's UB40 went for direct, albeit multiracial, dub and roots reggae, creating a mournful but infectious protest music that established them as the most successful non-Jamaican reggae act of all time. Of course, among all this protest and passion, someone had to come up with a lighter take. Step forward Bad Manners and their corpulent, skinhead frontman Buster Bloodvessel, with novelty ska revival hits such as 'Lip Up Fatty' and 'The Can-Can'.

Too Much Too Young

No matter how significant the achievements of these acts, the Specials remain the definitive 2-Tone band. But even as they were enjoying commercial and critical adulation for albums such as *Specials* and *More Specials*, and a UK number one single with a live version of the teen pregnancy-warning 'Too Much Too Young', the band were splitting under the pressure of musical and personal differences, as well as constant violence at their live shows from fascist skinheads who seemed unable (or unwilling) to accept the band's anti-racist stance. Immediately after their greatest achievement, the single 'Ghost Town' – which topped the UK singles chart as the anti-government riots it spoke so eloquently of raged through British inner cities – Hall, Golding and Staples quit to make excellent tribal pop with their own Funboy Three, while Radiation formed the short-lived Tearjerkers.

Reverting to the Special A.K.A. moniker, the bandleader Jerry Dammers recruited the vocalists Stan Campbell and Rhoda Dakar (the latter from a moderately successful 2-Tone act called the Bodysnatchers) to make a series of brave but less commercial political-issue singles, culminating in the Afro-pop anti-apartheid anthem 'Nelson Mandela'. The resulting album, *In The Studio*, was an undeserved flop, and a disillusioned Dammers split the band and the label in 1984, becoming a club DJ and full-time anti-apartheid activist.

Although a version of the Specials reformed in the 1990s without Dammers, Hall and Bradbury, largely to cash-in on 2-Tone's nostalgic popularity in the US, the legacy of 2-Tone resides, more appropriately, in American ska/pop/punk acts such as No Doubt, Save Ferris and the Mighty Mighty Bosstones, as well as multiracial British dance-pop adventurers such as Tricky, Massive Attack and the Streets – with the latter paying homage by including a snippet of the Specials' 'Ghost Town' in their live sets.

Below

Elvis Costello produced the 1979 self-titled debut release of the Specials, which launched their reputation as the forerunners of the 2-Tone ska movement and influenced countless other acts with their vibrant sound and stage performances.

Eighties Manufactured Pop

THE TERM "MANUFACTURED POP" IS, IN MANY WAYS, A RED HERRING. DESPITE THE CHANGES IN OUR PERCEPTION OF POP TALENT BROUGHT ABOUT BY THE BEATLES, MUCH MAINSTREAM POP HAS BEEN BASED ON THE "TIN PAN ALLEY" TRADITION, IN WHICH TEAMS OF PRODUCERS, COMPOSERS AND MUSIC-BUSINESS MOGULS FIND YOUNG, ATTRACTIVE PERFORMERS (MAINLY SINGERS) TO FRONT POTENTIAL HITS.

Above

Since splitting ways with S/A/W, Kylie Minogue has become one of the top pop stars in the world, with her hip, danceable grooves and supersexy looks, while Jason Donovan has gone on to a prosperous acting career.

THE term "manufactured pop" does not appear until the 1980s because of pop consumers' increasing knowledge of how pop is produced and presented. The Milli Vanilli scandal turned out to be the end of an era. From the late 1980s onwards, the pop Svengalis became more open about the lack of creative and musical input on the part of their performers. Therefore, consumers of heavily packaged pop product made an informed choice: who played and sang on the record was irrelevant so long as they enjoyed the song. In particular, two 1980s factory-pop providers were crucial in marking this change.

A S/A/W Point

Mike Stock, Matt Aitken and Pete Waterman (S/A/W) grew out of the north-western England soul, pop and disco tradition, a blend of light, soul-based melody and pumping dancefloor beats as pioneered by Waterman's fellow northern soul DJ and promoter, Ian Levine. Levine had virtually invented the gay club music Hi-NRG by blending his beloved Motown-derived soul with electronic Eurodisco. The S/A/W production team developed this into mainstream pop with their first major UK hit, 'You Spin Me Round (Like A Record)' by the Liverpool gay group Dead Or Alive in 1984. Using a true "hit factory" approach, S/A/W took the manufacture of pop one step further by stitching together songs out of computerized elements, taking a title out of a pre-written list, adding a numbered bassline, drum-pattern, melody line and so on, and then hiring a session singer to demo the song before

the 'star' added their own vocals. S/A/W went on to dominate the UK charts and crossover to the US Top Ten in the late 1980s, writing and producing a string of bouncy, unashamedly lightweight hits for Brits Rick Astley, Bananarama, Mel & Kim, Sonia, original Europop diva Donna Summer and, most famously, Australian soap opera stars Kylie Minogue and Jason Donovan.

As important as the impossibly catchy music and clean-cut appeal of the stars was Waterman's bullish, amused approach to the antipathy shown towards S/A/W by music critics. His

> ## "NOBODY GETS FANTASTICALLY RICH OFF POP RECORDS. THAT'S A MYTH."
>
> *Pete Waterman*

LEADING EXPONENTS

Stock, Aitken
  & Waterman
New Kids On The Block
Kylie Minogue
Jason Donovan
Rick Astley
Bananarama
Tiffany
Debbie Gibson
Bros
Five Star

EIGHTIES MANUFACTURED POP

The rhythm of the bass line is typical of the S/A/W formula, as are the lush, emotive chords over the top.

THE EIGHTIES POP INTRO ➡ 44   POP PEOPLE A–Z ➡ 72   INSTRUMENTS A–Z ➡ 436   SOUL AND R&B: NORTHERN SOUL ➡ 372

give-the-people-what-they-want attitude revealed a great deal of self-promotion at the expense of his artists, who – with the exception of the still hugely popular Kylie Minogue – usually attempted to forge careers without his factory formula, only to fail. The manufacturer had stepped in front of the performer and the process became more apparent, reaching its logical conclusion with the *Pop Stars* and *Pop Idol* TV shows of the early twenty-first century.

Stock and Aitken eventually split acrimoniously from Waterman in the 1990s, but it was the essentially non-musical Waterman who thrived, putting together the ABBA-for-toddlers outfit Steps and presiding over *Pop Idol*.

Starr Maker

When writer/producer Maurice Starr of Boston put together the Jackson 5-imitating African-American teen group New Edition, he could not have known how big an effect the quartet would have on future R&B after they "sacked" him in 1983. Starr recovered from losing his protégés, however, and put together a new five-piece, the oldest members of which were 16. New Kids On The Block were, effectively, the white New Edition, becoming global teen idols in 1988 with their *Hangin' Tough* album, which cleverly mixed clean-cut, teen-girl-oriented romance with a timely, but unthreatening, bad-boy stance lifted from hip hop. Despite writing much of their own material, the group's contrivance made them even more of a joke figure than the S/A/W acts and an attempt to break from Starr and make the leap into pop maturity flopped before they split in 1994. Nevertheless, the New Kids' blend of stage-school dance routines, heartthrob looks and diluted street style forged the template for what we now know as the "boy band".

Songs Of Innocents

S/A/W and Starr defined the future of manufactured pop in the late 1980s, but the decade had already brought plenty of more traditional teen-formula pop idols to short-lived prominence. Virginal US teen queens both, Tiffany and Debbie Gibson (discovered by moguls George Tobin and Doug Brethart respectively) became America's darlings in the late 1980s, performing classic radio bubblegum for nice kids. Their penchant for promoting themselves led to personal appearances at middle-American shopping malls, for which they earned the label "mallrats". Gibson became a symbol of toothy female conformity, too, inspiring satirical punk songs (Mojo Nixon and Skid Roper's wonderful 'Debbie Gibson Is Pregnant With My Two-Headed Love Child') and a hilarious Jimi Hendrix-meets-Debbie onstage skit by the controversial late comic Bill Hicks.

Meanwhile, the UK gave us Bros, fronted by the terrifyingly blonde, London-based brothers Luke and Matt Goss (plus Scottish brunette Craig Logan, who soon left their outfit for a successful A&R career). Bros reached their sub-Wham! peak in 1988-89 with eight consecutive UK Top 10 hits, before falling out of favour and slipping into solo obscurity. Like New Edition, Londoners Five Star favoured the Jackson 5 approach, with the black British Pearson family group notching up transatlantic pop-soul hits in a short but prolific career. They peaked with their 1986 album, *Silk And Steel*, before the inevitable drug problems and public fallings out took their toll.

Left
S/A/W helped to create more than 90 Top 40 hits, including 13 number ones, including Rick Astley's 'Never Gonna Give You Up' and Donna Summer's 'This Time I Know It's For Real'.

Below
Bros, England's heartthrobs between 1988 and 1989, topped the charts with 'I Owe You Nothing' and performed to throngs of screaming fans before their inevitable demise.

IF YOU ASK A YOUNG MUSIC CONSUMER WHAT KIND OF ACTS REPRESENT POP MUSIC, THEY WILL UNDOUBTEDLY REEL OFF A LIST OF TEEN-ORIENTATED, MANUFACTURED BANDS. POP HAS COME TO REPRESENT A NARROWLY FOCUSED GENRE, AS FAR AWAY FROM THE INITIAL, REVOLUTIONARY ROCK-MEETS-POP APPEAL OF ELVIS PRESLEY AND THE BEATLES AS CAN BE.

Nineties Pop

Above

The merchandising frenzy that erupted with the success of the Spice Girls signalled the beginnings of a growing trend in the music industry of creating and marketing music artists as personalities and entities, rather than musicians.

"I'M AN OLD-FASHIONED ENTERTAINER DOING IT IN A NINETIES STYLIE."

Robbie Williams

SINCE the 1950s, pop has been a catch-all term for almost all popular music made in the wake of rock'n'roll. But each generation has seen the development of more musical sub-genres, with the music business's increasing success at identifying these sub-genres, and marketing narrowly and heavily towards their fans, effecting a gradual change in the way the public views pop.

Nevertheless, the 1990s still boasted some artists who, in different ways, transcended the limitations of genre-specific forms of music. Before we look at some of these definitive 1990s pop artists, it is worth noting that the 1990s saw various completely manufactured acts achieving a credibility, longevity and unit-shifting power in the pop marketplace unanticipated even by the giants of 1960s Tamla Motown. Britain's Spice Girls, Australia's Kylie Minogue and America's Britney Spears attained a kind of commercial and critical success – based less on their music than on their extraordinary level of celebrity – that no one would have predicted when they emerged. Another UK teen band who pioneered this level of manufactured pop profile, the north-west England quintet Take That, produced one of the key 1990s pop stars, Robbie Williams, a former dancer who successfully mixed the sound and promotional devices of manufactured pop with a more individual vision, based on self-referential lyrics and videos as well as a great deal of charisma.

STYLES

Singer/Songwriters
Latin Pop
Britpop
Boy Bands

LEADING EXPONENTS

Madonna
Robbie Williams
Mariah Carey
Celine Dion
Spice Girls
Britney Spears
Kylie Minogue
Pet Shop Boys
Simply Red
M People
Michael Jackson

Singing While He's Winning

Stoke-On-Trent's Robbie Williams was just 21 when he stage-managed one of the most public band splits in pop history, rebelling against the boy-band strictures of Take That with a drunken offstage display at the 1995 Glastonbury Festival in the company of Britrock bad boys Oasis. Within two years, he established himself as Britain's biggest pop star with a heavily produced blend of Britpop and mature balladry on the *Life Thru A Lens* album. Since then, he has effectively rewritten the rules of pop, dance and rock crossover, jumping easily from the pseudo-rap and gory, banned video of the single 'Rock DJ' to the Sinatra-tributing, big-band standards of the *Swing When You're Winning* album. Although his ability

NINETIES POP

Pop in the 1990s borrowed heavily from the dance scene for its beats, especially the "loop" sound, where short pieces of drumming are sampled from records and mixed together to create a textured and complex groove, as here.

THE POP INTRO ➡ 8   POP PEOPLE A-Z ➡ 72   INSTRUMENTS A-Z ➡ 436   POP: 80S MANUFACTURED POP ➡ 54

to command inter-generational appeal, utilizing everything from mawkish sentiment to sexually explicit self-reference, has had difficulty translating to an American audience, he remains, at the time of writing, Britain's only truly transcendent pure pop star, overcoming musical limitations with his film-star good looks and boy-next-door cheek.

The Princesses Of Wails

Many of the biggest pop sales phenomena continue to derive from virtuoso vocalists who blend chart-oriented pop with mature MOR torch song. Two female singers who broke through in the early 1990s challenged the position of Whitney Houston as the FM radio, adult-pop queen of the divas.

Discovered by soul mogul Tommy Mottola (they married in 1993 and divorced in 1997), the New Yorker Mariah Carey made an immediate impact with her Olympian, five-octave voice and self-titled, largely self-written 1990 debut album. This definitive black/white crossover diva went on to become the first artist to top the US charts in each year of the 1990s and broke the Beatles' record for weeks spent in the Hot 100. The melodrama of her vocally self-indulgent songs turned out to be based on reality. After signing an $80m record deal with Virgin at the end of the 1990s and enduring disappointing sales and a critically savaged flop movie in *Glitter*, she posted sprawling suicidal messages on her website and spent time in rehab. Virgin dropped her in 2002, but it was not all bad news: the record company gave her a $28m pay-off.

Her Canadian rival Celine Dion also married her mentor, manager Rene Angelil, despite a 26-year age difference. The couple fell victim to a different kind of tragedy, though, as Angelil was diagnosed with throat cancer, prompting Dion's temporary retirement from music. Of course, the big-voiced chanteuse could afford the break, having achieved mega-lunged stardom with her brand of housewife-slaying MOR pop weepie. This was typified by her Grammy Award-winning songs for the movies *Beauty And The Beast* (with smooth soul man Peabo Bryson) and *Titanic* (the ubiquitous 'My Heart Will Go On', which, somewhat appropriately, became the Western world's most popular choice to be played at funerals).

In 2003, Dion returned from her sabbatical with a new album and a three-year deal to perform in a top Las Vegas hotel-casino.

Stars Old And New

Though most pop phenomena continued to rise and fall quickly, some 1980s icons remained relevant to the new decade. Madonna remains pop's biggest star, keeping one step ahead of dance-pop trends and changing image with each

release. Manchester's Mick Hucknall led Simply Red's blue-eyed pop soul to great success. And electro-popsters the Pet Shop Boys maintained their loyal fans as they became more overt about their bittersweet celebrations of gay life.

New, unmanufactured pop voices also rose to prominence. The Irish family group the Corrs mixed mainstream dance with Irish folk; Scotland's Texas struck with a glossy take on FM rock; Manchester and London's M People moved from pop-house to heroic, adult-oriented anthems; and California's No Doubt emerged from their local, 2-Tone-influenced scene with a smart blend of ska, pop and punk. All, of course, were led by women with strident singing voices and sex appeal, the likes of Sharleen Spiteri (Texas) and Gwen Stefani (No Doubt) further confusing the worlds of youth pop music and a very adult kind of pin-up.

Left
Increasingly featured in tabloid articles and notorious for his cheeky behaviour, Robbie Williams has continued to dominate the music world with his infectious mix of pop and rock and his good looks.

Above
Adopting the monikers Sporty, Baby, Posh, Scary and Ginger, the Spice Girls became a worldwide phenomenon with their professions of "Girl Power", sugary pop vocalizations and cutting-edge fashions.

Nineties Pop Singer/Songwriters

AFTER A DECADE THAT SAW THE ART OF THE SINGER/SONGWRITER BEING SOMEWHAT SUBMERGED BY THE DEMANDS OF ELECTRONIC OVER-PRODUCTION, DISCO CROSSOVER AND RELENTLESS FASHION HORRORS, THE 1990S SAW A REBIRTH OF THE SOLO ARTIST WITH A GENUINELY INDIVIDUAL STYLE.

Above

kd lang's 1992 release Ingénue *marked her foray into adult alternative/pop and spawned the beautiful and wrenching hit 'Constant Craving.'*

THIS proved to be of particular benefit to female artists who, while still having to conform to demands for feminine "sexiness", were at least able to broaden the scope of what that could mean, both in terms of looks and attitude. There were some new men on the block, but it was female artists, five women in particular, who achieved major success in the 1990s without having to make the compromises usually involved in aiming at a specific type of audience.

The Strange And The Strident

The Dubliner Sinéad O'Connor continues to pursue one of pop's most controversial careers. Emerging in the late 1980s with her angelic features hardened by a severe skinhead crop,

> "I SEE MY BODY AS AN INSTRUMENT RATHER THAN AN ORNAMENT."
>
> *Alanis Morissette*

her powerful, Celtic-influenced vocals became universally recognized in 1990 with her emotional, proto-trip-hop cover of Prince's 'Nothing Compares 2 U'. The accompanying album, *I Do Not Want What I Haven't Got*, was a global smash, but the strength of her opinions may have stolen some of its musical thunder. O'Connor followed her outspoken criticisms of the history of the British in Ireland with attacks on the anti-abortion stance of the Catholic church. In 1992, she tore up a picture of the Pope on American TV and refused to play at an American show that began with the US national anthem. Her music developed from strident, subtly dance-influenced AOR to a more tranquil and intimate fusion of pop, Celtic folk and ambient stylings, contrasting with increasingly graphic and gruelling

lyrics. Despite her commercial fall from grace, O'Connor's yelping, yodelling vocal style and angry woman stance have had a profound influence on female solo artists throughout the 1990s and beyond.

The equally questioning, but far less controversial, North Carolina native Tori (originally Myra Ellen) Amos became an overnight star with her 1992 debut album, *Little Earthquakes*. Although her rustic glamour, theatrical vocals and piano-led musical sophistication initially led to many comparisons with Kate Bush, Amos's new age, therapy-speak lyrics and kooky persona made her entirely unique, and the pure pop of her tunes led to an unlikely club hit with Armand Van Helden's hard-house reworking of 'Professional Widow' in 1996.

LEADING EXPONENTS

Alanis Morissette

Tori Amos

kd lang

Björk

Sinéad O'Connor

Paul Weller

Seal

Sheryl Crow

Elton John

George Michael

NINETIES POP SINGER/SONGWRITERS

A chord sequence of the type written here (using the 4th, 5th major and 2nd and 7th minor - and sometimes never the root) was popular with 1990s writers, as was the trick of repeating the same phrase over the shifting chords underneath.

Also finding a place in dance music, and also kooky, Iceland's Björk Gudmundsdottir split from the arty indie-goth band the Sugarcubes and released an astounding debut album (entitled *Debut*) in 1993. Unlike the previous decade's dance-rock crossovers, Björk possessed a genuine love and understanding of cutting-edge dance music in the post-techno era. Her blendings of rumbling beats with ambient textures, flights of romantic fancy with abstract electronic noise, and Asian melodies and motifs with deep and restless basslines, is made all the more striking by her baby-faced features, flamboyant visual sense and skyscraping vocals.

Perhaps the bravest stance of all belongs to Kathryn Dawn Lang, an androgynous Canadian who began her career as a camp alternative cabaret performer tapping into an almost unnoticed enthusiasm for country music among Stateside lesbians. But kd lang (her name is always kept lower case) had talent above and beyond ironic country and a truly gorgeous voice heavily influenced by her heroine, Patsy Cline. In 1992, the lush *Ingénue* album turned her into a unique star, with its erotically charged love songs, musical mix of country, soul and pop and a subtly gender-bending image that prompted Madonna, no less, to exclaim: "I've seen Elvis – and she's beautiful!" Along with the adult-rocker Melissa Etheridge, lang broke through the silence surrounding lesbianism in pop, building a loyal and large (and mainly female) following in supposedly conservative America.

Borrowing something from all of the above heroines, another Canadian, Alanis Morissette, completed a journey from manufactured Canadian pop poppet to Voice Of Modern Woman with the release of her massively successful debut album proper, 1995's *Jagged Little Pill*. Taking Amos's therapy-speak to a logical conclusion and applying O'Connor's kind of howling anger to the subject of inadequate and abusive males, Morissette's muse became so influential that it is now rare to hear a female artist without a yodel in her voice and righteous indignation at the expense of men in her lyrics. Her nouveau-hippy, just-got-of-bed image and catchy soft-rock anthems have made her the ultimate symbol of pop feminism, with the likes of Sheryl Crow, Fiona Apple and Jewel all benefiting directly from her breakthrough.

Male Survivors

While new female voices were defining the 1990s pop singer/songwriter art, veterans made the biggest impact among men. The likes of Sting and Elton John continued to enjoy success by doing exactly what they had always done, with the former Reg Dwight scoring his biggest-ever worldwide hit with his maudlin Princess Diana tribute, 'Candle In The Wind 97' and receiving a knighthood.

George Michael also continued to thrive, despite his notorious conviction for lewd behaviour in a Beverly Hills public toilet in 1998. Having previously moved away from the celebratory pure pop of *Faith* towards the self-consciously mature Elton John- and Lennon-influenced introspection of *Listen Without Prejudice Vol. 1* and *Older*, Michael responded to his humiliating outing by abandoning the heartfelt piano balladry and heading back towards light dance-pop and cover versions of standards.

There were no such personal confusions for ex-Jam leader Paul Weller, who became a harbinger of Britpop when the hit *Wildwood* album ended his solo wilderness years in 1993. Though his music is actually a gruff take on traditional late-1960s/early 1970s Britrock, the affection Weller continues to enjoy for his achievements with the Jam and the Style Council maintain his standing as a crossover between serious rock and chart pop.

The most striking new male singer/songwriter was the Nigerian/Brazilian Londoner Sealhenry Samuel, who, as Seal, used his vocals on dance artist Adamski's 1990 'Killer' hit (later covered by George Michael) as a stepping-stone to solo stardom. His slick blend of MOR pop and FM radio-friendly soul, typified by 1990's 'Crazy' and 1994's 'Kiss From A Rose', and unique physical presence (six-and-a-half foot, with childhood facial scarring) saw him enjoy global stardom throughout most of the decade.

Left

Controversial Irish singer Sinéad O'Connor has worked with such diverse artists as the Chieftains, Afro-Celt Sound System and The The.

Below

After the phenomenally popular Jagged Little Pill *took the world by storm in the mid-1990s, Alanis Morissette was awarded several Grammy Awards for her efforts, including Album of the Year.*

Nineties Latin Pop

LATIN POP HAS BEEN AROUND FOR AS LONG AS LATIN MUSIC ITSELF. AS FAR BACK AS THE 1920S, MEXICO, ARGENTINA AND SPAIN WERE VERITABLE FOUNTAINS OF POPULAR MUSIC, WHICH THEY EXPORTED TO ALL SPANISH-SPEAKING NATIONS. AN INTERNATIONAL AUDIENCE WAS FOUND IN THE UNITED STATES, ALONG WITH THE STEADY INFLUX OF LATINO IMMIGRANTS IN THE LATE TWENTIETH CENTURY.

Above
Enrique Iglesias' 2001 release Escape *spawned such hits as the title track and the ballad 'Hero', which was adopted as an unofficial tribute to those who perished in the World Trade Center attack.*

PRIOR to this, Latin music made its rounds through the decades via the boleros – traditional romantic songs – of composers such as Mexicans Agustín Lara ('Noche de Ronda', 'Granada') and Consuelo Velázquez ('Bésame Mucho'). Their songs were translated into English and popularized by various acts, ranging from Nat King Cole to Ray Charles.

Latin music also managed to supersede language barriers thanks to various Latin dance crazes criss-crossing the globe, primarily the Cuban mambo. Its best-known representative was Pérez Prado, a big-band leader and composer whose catchy compositions and simplified arrangements propelled the music to international renown in the 1950s.

The Pioneers

However, the rise of widely popular Latin acts remained relatively rare outside the Spanish-speaking world. Among the few exceptions are the Spanish balladeer Julio Iglesias, who crooned his way to fame in more than a dozen languages and Miami Sound Machine, the group created in the 1980s by the music mogul Emilio Estefan, who was a fledgling bongo player. With Estefan's wife Gloria as the lead singer, Miami Sound Machine brought to the table a dynamic mix of Latin percussion and heavy brass, blended with disco beats and performed in English. The combination, which the Cuban-born Estefans often described as rice and beans

> "I WILL NEVER STOP SINGING IN SPANISH ... THAT'S WHO I AM ... BUT THIS WAS ALWAYS PART OF THE PLAN."
>
> *Ricky Martin on making the transition with an English LP*

Right
Ricky Martin's enigmatic and talented stage performances and music videos complemented his songs and helped propel him into superstardom.

(Cuban staples) with hamburger, turned songs such as 'Conga' into international hits and paved the way for what many now refer to as the "Latin music explosion" of the late 1990s.

Ricky Martin

That explosion was spearheaded by Ricky Martin, a Puerto Rican singer whose hip-swivelling moves were reminiscent of Elvis Presley and whose generic, Western-world good looks

LEADING EXPONENTS

Ricky Martin
Marc Anthony
Luis Miguel
Maná
Gloria Estefan
Chayanne
Vicente Fernández
Alejandro Fernández
Soda Stereo

NINETIES LATIN POP

Built on the foundation of the highly detailed and formalized traditional Latin grooves, latin pop took some of these elements and mixed them up with dance beats, electric instruments and strong pop melodies.

THE NINETIES POP INTRO ➡ 56   POP PEOPLE A-Z ➡ 72   INSTRUMENTS A-Z ➡ 436   JAZZ: LATIN JAZZ ➡ 148

made him internationally appealing. Martin started out in show business with Menudo, a 1980s boy band who performed bubblegum Spanish-language pop. As a soloist, he became enormously popular throughout Latin America by singing Latin ballads, but gradually developed a parallel, upbeat style characterized by his use of Caribbean dance rhythms, percussion and brass.

That sound characterized 1998's 'La Copa De La Vida', or 'The Cup Of Life', a song conceived as the football World Cup anthem, which Martin recorded in several languages. Its worldwide success set the stage for Martin's self-titled English-language debut album in 1999, which featured 'Livin' La Vida Loca', a track that would become an international anthem in its English- and Spanish-language versions. 'Livin' ' was typical of Martin in its use of Latin rhythms, while its electric-guitar intro – reminiscent of 1960s California surf rock – gave it a far greater international feel. As well as propelling Martin to international superstardom, it opened the door for other Latin artists to embark on the crossover from Spanish to English.

The Latin Explosion

The late 1990s saw the international rise of Enrique Iglesias, the son of crooner Julio Iglesias, who, like his father, launched his career performing romantic ballads in Spanish. He ventured into English-language pop with 1999's *Enrique*, an album that featured romantic fare as well as more dance-oriented pop.

A more Latin direction was taken by Marc Anthony, a salsa singer born in New York to Puerto Rican parents. Anthony refused to sing salsa in English, something he once deemed a "sacrilege". But his 1999 English-language debut featured the single 'I Need To Know', whose rhythmic base was Latin and which featured Afro-Cuban percussion and hard-edged brass, culled from New York-style salsa.

Another New Yorker, the actress Jennifer López, launched her musical career after she played the leading role in *Selena*, a film based on the life of the Mexican-American singer who was tragically shot by a former employee in 1995. López's musical debut had more to do with urban and hip-hop beats than Latin music, but by virtue of her Hispanic name, she was thrown into the "Latin explosion" category. Equally importantly, her stature as a film star helped to raise awareness about the music performed by Selena. Called "Tejano", which is a Spanish word meaning a Texan of Mexican heritage, it is a hybrid of traditional Mexican cumbia, rancheras and polkas, with elements of American pop, blues and country.

Many other purveyors of Latin pop gained notoriety in the 1990s, among them the German singer Lou Bega, who revamped Pérez Prado's decades-old hit 'Mambo No. 5' with saucy English lyrics and renamed it 'Mambo No. 5 (A Little

Bit Of…)'. Within the broad Spanish-language marketplace, the Mexican crooner Luis Miguel was, by and large, the king of the decade with his successive recordings of boleros dating back to the 1940s, which he modernized with string orchestra and drums, and re-introduced to a new generation of listeners. At the same time, rock movements in Argentina and Mexico yielded major acts such as Maná, Latin rock's biggest-selling band to date.

Below
Since arriving on the music scene in 1999, Jennifer López has become the media's darling with her phenomenal fashion sense, high-profile relationships and frequent merchandising of products, such as a clothing line and a fragrance, eclipsing the imporatnce of her music.

BY THE EARLY 1990S BRITISH POP AND ALTERNATIVE FANS WERE CRYING OUT FOR HOMEGROWN POP THAT COMBINED OLD-FASHIONED ROCK CHARISMA WITH LYRICS AND A DEFINITIVELY BRITISH SOUND, TO COUNTERACT THE MANUFACTURED TEEN ACTS, EURO-DANCE NOVELTIES AND US IMPORTS. THIS ARRIVED IN THE MID-1990S IN THE SHAPE OF BRITPOP: A WAVE OF GUITAR BANDS WITH SHORT, SHARP POP SONGS.

Britpop

Above

The prolific Blur have continued to create innovative music since their 1991 entrance into the music scene, with lead singer Damon Albarn's spin-off cartoon group, Gorillaz also spawning a hit single in 2001.

THE heavily 1960s-influenced basis of Britpop was heralded in 1990, with the release of the self-titled debut album by Liverpool group the La's (a Merseyside slang word for "lads"). Led by the singer/songwriter prodigy Lee Mavers, the La's purveyed a deceptively simple guitar pop in the vein of the Beatles, the Who and the Hollies, but somehow made entirely fresh by Mavers's poetic flights and choirboy-thug vocals, typified by their beautiful hit 'There She Goes'. Sadly, the eccentric Mavers, after complaining bitterly in the press about the production on the released album, split the band up and went into hiding in his native Liverpool. While their bassist, John Power, enjoyed some mid-1990s success with the similar but far less exciting Cast, Mavers remains missing in action, obsessively perfecting the ultimate pop sound that only he can hear.

Meanwhile, Bowie-worshipping Londoner Brett Anderson formed Suede in 1989. By 1992, the quartet had released their *Suede* album to huge critical acclaim, with the mix of Anderson's Bowie-esque tales of seedy sex and squalid glamour, coupled with guitarist Bernard Butler's virtuoso riffs and squalls, delighting a UK press and public desperate for new guitar heroes. Although Butler left for a solo career in 1994, Suede continue to please their loyal following with unreconstructed glam rock.

"IF YOU GO BACK THROUGH 30 YEARS OF MUSIC WE'RE THE BEST BITS ALL ENCOMPASSED IN ONE BAND. WE'RE OASIS."

Noel Gallagher

LEADING EXPONENTS

Blur

Oasis

Pulp

The La's

Suede

Supergrass

The Verve

The Charlatans

Elastica

Catatonia

BRITPOP

Underlying the lighter side of Britpop were influnces going back to the 1960s, and this slightly jolly piano piece with its vamping style and modulating chords sets the mood.

THE NINETIES POP INTRO ➡ 56   POP PEOPLE A-Z ➡ 72   INSTRUMENTS A-Z ➡ 436   ROCK: MADCHESTER ➡ 99

The Britpop Wars

With Suede establishing a market for homegrown guitar pop, the three acts that define the Britpop era made their move. The superb London four-piece Blur summed up the mod-reviving, 1960s- and 1970s-quoting, anti-American mood on 1993's *Modern Life Is Rubbish* album and became a national obsession with 1994's *Parklife* – an irresistible blend of Kinks-ish English observational comedy, XTC- and Wire-influenced New Wave, and cockney singalong, with a sprinkling of glam and synth-disco. The album established Britpop as a UK commercial phenomenon overnight.

Hot on their heels were a Manchester band led by two confident and charismatic brothers. Noel and Liam Gallagher's Oasis were unashamed copyists, stealing riffs and melodies from Marc Bolan, the Sex Pistols and, most famously, the Beatles. But Liam's Lennon-meets-Johnny Rotten vocals and Noel's wall-of-sound guitar crunch made their first two albums, *Definitely Maybe* and *(What's The Story) Morning Glory*, almost universally popular in the UK, packed as they were with hard-rocking anthems and instantly classic power ballads.

Britpop reached its peak of homegrown national interest in August 1995, when Blur, arguably, contrived a popularity contest with intense rivals Oasis by releasing their long-awaited new single, 'Country House' on the same day as Oasis's 'Roll With It' in a race for the week's number one spot. Blur famously won the battle but lost the war, as *Morning Glory* outshone Blur's much-criticized follow-up to *Parklife, The Great Escape*, and the Gallaghers went on to become two of the most famous men on the planet.

Since then, Blur's reinvention of themselves as an eclectic, art-punk proposition has ensured long-term success and respect, while Oasis have simply continued to make less exciting versions of the same records, albeit with healthy sales. At the time of writing, though, what will become of Blur following the departure of their guitarist, Graham Coxon, remains to be seen.

The third Britpop kings were Pulp, a Sheffield group led by the geeky and witty former art student Jarvis Cocker. Although Pulp had been in existence since 1978, it was not until 1995, with the era-defining, class-warfare hit single 'Common People', that Cocker became the Morrissey of the 1990s. His own personal Britpop war was declared at the 1996 Brit Awards when, during a predictably self-aggrandizing cast-of-thousands guest performance from Michael Jackson, Cocker invaded the stage and started dancing before being bundled off by security. Cocker was arrested and Jackson's people accused him of assaulting the children onstage, before the threat of legal action forced them to withdraw the accusation. The accompanying tabloid furore turned Cocker into a symbol of plucky, rebellious England rejecting American celebrity excess.

Six-String Wonders

The Britpop market remained open until the end of the 1990s. A host of traditional British guitar bands made their mark: the 1960s retro of Ocean Colour Scene, Kula Shaker and funky Madchester veterans the Charlatans; the spiky post-punk anthems of Oxford trio Supergrass and London's Elastica, whose frontwoman, Justine Frischmann, began her career with Suede and had a very public relationship (and break-up) with Blur leader Damon Albarn; the catchy mainstream pop of Wales's Catatonia and Liverpool's Lightning Seeds; and the moody rock atmospherics of Wigan's the Verve, led by lips-and-cheekbones idol Richard Ashcroft. Britpop fell dramatically from favour at the end of the century, but it remains the last time that a pointedly English variety of pop/rock made a genuine impact on a wide range of music lovers.

Left

With nearly every action the Gallagher brothers creating a recipe for gossip fodder, the members of Oasis continue to enjoy success with their 2002 release, Heathen Chemistry.

Below

As the lead singer and lyricist of Pulp, Jarvis Cocker has become one of the most well-loved and admired musicians of the Britpop/alternative scene.

GROUPS OF FRESH-FACED YOUNG MEN SINGING CATCHY TUNES HAVE BEEN ONE OF THE MAINSTAYS OF COMMERCIAL POP SINCE THE BEATLES. IN THE LAST TWO DECADES, MANUFACTURED BOY BANDS SUCH AS NEW KIDS ON THE BLOCK AND TAKE THAT HAVE RULED THE ROOST. ALTHOUGH THEIR MUSICAL LEGACY BEARS NO COMPARISON TO THAT OF THE FAB FOUR'S, THE DEVOTION THEY INSPIRED WAS JUST AS FERVENT.

Boy Bands

Above

The surge of boy bands in the late 1990s saw legions of worshipping and swooning teenage fans in hysterics over seeing their idols perform.

MARKETING is everything for the modern boy band. Members are selected for characteristics that maximize their appeal to a fanbase largely made up of adolescent girls. Being youthful, squeaky clean and unthreateningly attractive are just as important as being able to sing in tune and dance in time.

Few contemporary boy bands play instruments and most purvey lightweight pop, divided between uptempo numbers and slushy ballads. Due to the disposable nature of their music, and fickle young audiences with rapidly evolving tastes, boy bands rarely survive for more than five years, although artists such as Take That's Robbie Williams and ★NSYNC's Justin Timberlake have been catapulted on to successful solo careers.

"IN THREE YEARS' TIME EVEN THOUGH THEY'LL BE FANS OF ANOTHER GROUP, THEY'LL NEVER FORGET TAKE THAT."

Howard Donald of Take That on fans

Right

In the first half of the 1990s, Take That became a global phenomenon with their good looks and catchy pop hits. Their released a mixture of covers – such as 'Could It Be Magic' and 'Relight My Fire' – and original material, which included 'Pray', 'Babe' and 'Back for Good'.

LEADING EXPONENTS

The Beatles

The Jackson 5

The Osmonds

New Kids On The Block

Take That

Boyzone

Backstreet Boys

Westlife

5ive

★NSYNC

Blue

From The Fab Four To The Fantastic Five

Although the boy band evolved into its familiar form in the late-1980s, its history stretches back to the early 1960s and is entwined in the origins of, arguably, pop's greatest group. The Beatles wrote their own songs from the outset and their longevity, artistic scope and degree of control over their careers remain unmatched by any of today's boy bands. But in the clean-cut appeal of their mop-top days, and in the bubblegum melodies of songs such as 1963's 'I Want To Hold Your Hand', they foreshadowed their less-esteemed successors.

The boy-band concept took its next evolutionary leap in the late-1960s, when Joseph Jackson realized the commercial viability of putting his sons Jermaine, Jackie, Marlon, Tito and Michael on the stage. One of the few post-Beatle boy bands whose music stands up well when revisited, the Jackson 5 combined pop, soul and disco to sublime effect. Their early sound was encapsulated by their breakthrough single, 'I Want You Back' (1970), a classic marriage of funky rhythms and sugary harmonies built around the sweet, expressive vocals of 12-year-old Michael.

BOY BANDS

Almost all boy bands have at some time recorded a song built around a riff like this, backed by a rhythm with an on-beat snare, motown-style.

THE NINETIES POP INTRO ➡ 56   POP PEOPLE A-Z ➡ 72   INSTRUMENTS A-Z ➡ 436   THE SIXTIES POP INTRO ➡ 24

The Jacksons' disciplinarian father, along with the legendary boss of their Motown record label, Berry Gordy, exerted tight control over their activities: they were not allowed to perform their own material until the mid-1970s. Every boy band since has been masterminded by similarly formidable figures, well-versed in the cut-throat whims of the music industry.

The 1970s saw several copycat groups appear, including the Osmonds, another sibling quintet with the focus on a talented younger brother – in this case, the cherub-faced Donny. Solo artists (including a liberated Michael Jackson) dominated the middle-ground of pop for much of the 1980s, but the boy band would be back with a vengeance by the end of the decade. With the increasing prevalence of synthesized backing tracks, acts abandoned live instrumentation in favour of choreographed dance routines and enlivened their music by diluting elements of hipper genres.

A Manufacturing Boom

The biggest of this new breed of boy band were New Kids On The Block, a quintet of Boston-based youngsters assembled by manager/songwriter Maurice Starr, who had considerable success earlier in the 1980s with New Edition. With brothers Jon and Jordan Knight, Donnie Wahlberg, Danny Wood and Joey McIntryre, Starr combined some of the macho posturing of hip hop with the tight harmonies of R&B and a heart that was pure pop. Their best-known hit, 'Hangin' Tough', was a frothy mix of faux-street style and singalong choruses, and a hit around the world in 1988. It kicked off three years of chart domination for the Kids, who eventually split in 1994.

NKOTB's success paved the way for Take That, composed of Gary Barlow, Robbie Williams, Mark Owen, Jason Orange and Howard Donald. The five-piece bestrode the European charts in the first half of the 1990s, shifting more records than any British act since the Beatles. Mega-selling singles such as 1993's 'Could It Be Magic' incorporated the hi-energy rhythms of the club music that was sweeping Britain at the time, while the members' toned physiques, combined with a fondness for covering disco classics such as Tavares' 'It Only Takes A Minute', endeared them to the gay community as well as teenage girls.

Take That disbanded in 1996, but not before inspiring a slew of British and Irish boy bands. These included Westlife, who scored a British record with 10 consecutive number one singles. At around the same time, Backstreet Boys, yet another five-piece, emerged with an eponymous album that became the second-largest seller of the decade, shifting 28-million copies. Their style picked up where that of the New Kids left off, but Kevin Richardson, Brian Littrell, Howie Dorough,

Nick Carter and A. J. McLean – all white, middle-class boys – borrowed even more heavily from black music than their predecessors. Monstrous hits such as 1999's 'Everybody (Backstreet's Back)' showcased their melodic synthesis of hip-hop, R&B, soul and pop, while Backstreet clones such as *NSYNC emerged throughout the late 1990s and early 2000s. Given the current popularity of R&B-infused acts such as the British band Blue, the public's appetite for boy bands shows no signs of being sated.

Above
The Backstreet Boys enjoyed phenomenal success during the mid-1990s, with their 1996 debut album landing in the Top 10 of nearly every European nation's music chart.

Noughties Pop

ALTHOUGH BOY BANDS AND GIRL BANDS HELD SWAY OVER ANGLO-AMERICAN POP FOR MUCH OF THE 1990S, THE END OF THE DECADE WITNESSED THE RETURN OF THE INDIVIDUAL ARTIST. WHILE THE LIKES OF *NSYNC, BLUE AND SUGABABES CONTINUED TO FLY THE FLAG FOR GROUPS, ARTISTS SUCH AS BRITNEY SPEARS, CHRISTINA AGUILERA AND PINK EMERGED AS ARENA-FILLING SOLOISTS.

Above

The phenomenal success of TV's Pop Idol in the UK resulted in runner-up Gareth Gates (left) also securing a record deal, along with the programme's winner, Will Young (right). Gates's subsequent success was such that his pop career swiftly eclipsed that of Young.

THE soaring popularity of R&B continued to leave its mark on the charts, with many pop acts making much use of tight harmonies, smooth melodies, streetwise beats and raunchy choreography.

The period also saw huge hits for a succession of performers who had found fame as members of groups. Take That's Robbie Williams, *NSYNC's Justin Timberlake, Destiny's Child's Beyoncé Knowles, the Spice Girls' Geri Halliwell and Boyzone's Ronan Keating were now stars in their own right. But perhaps the most significant development in early twenty-first-century pop was the increasingly powerful role of television in making and breaking stars.

The Small Screen Comes To The Fore

Having been an important player in the music business since Elvis's scandalous appearance on *The Ed Sullivan Show* in 1956, television widened its influence in the 1980s with the introduction of MTV and the subsequent rise of the music video. In 2001, however, the partnership entered a new era with the launch of *Popstars*.

Tapping into the British public's increasingly rabid obsession with both celebrity and reality TV, the show tracked thousands of young hopefuls as, through a merciless sequence of auditions, they were whittled down to a final line-up of five members. Myleene Klass, Kym Marsh, Suzanne Shaw, Danny Foster and Noel Sullivan adopted the name Hear'Say, and millions of viewers watched as they were groomed for stardom and recorded a debut single, 'Pure And Simple'. Crossing the identikit harmonies of Westlife with the bouncier grooves of S Club 7, it went straight to number one in 2001.

Critics accused *Popstars* of stifling creativity with unadventurous songs and formulaic marketing, as well as exploiting the power of television to line the pockets of its creators. Hear'Say certainly proved to be a short-lived

> "PEOPLE IN THE INDUSTRY ARE MUSICAL SNOBS: IT'S ALL ABOUT BEING COOL. THAT'S ALWAYS BAFFLED ME BECAUSE POP MUSIC IS POPULAR MUSIC."
>
> *Simon Fuller*

STYLES

Singer/Songwriters

Latin

LEADING EXPONENTS

Britney Spears

Justin Timberlake

Christina Aguilera

Pink

*NSYNC

Hear'Say

Will Young

Gareth Gates

Robbie Williams

Kylie Minogue

NOUGHTIES POP

Rhythms in Noughties pop have become less straight-forward, taking their cue from a dance culture that is ever more esoteric. As a result, a whole new language of grooves is emerging with less interesting chord structures.

THE POP INTRO ➡ 8   POP PEOPLE A-Z ➡ 72   INSTRUMENTS A-Z ➡ 436   POP: EIGHTIES MANUFACTURED POP ➡ 54

sensation. Marsh left the band in 2002 and they split later in the same year, having plunged from being media darlings to hate figures in the space of 12 months.

But the format remained a hugely popular one with the public. In 2002, *Popstars* was followed by *Pop Idol*, a series that shifted the focus from groups to solo performers and allowed viewers to vote on who should win. Fourteen million people saw the vote go to Will Young, whose popularity looks set to far outlast that of Hear'Say. Blessed with a muscular, soulful voice, he breathed life into 'Evergreen', the uninspiring Westlife ballad with which he made his (inevitably chart-topping) debut in 2002. Young also resisted efforts to package him as an anodyne pop clone, becoming one of the first pop stars to be openly gay from the start of his career.

The *Pop Idol* format was reproduced all over the world. *American Idol*, as it was known in the USA, launched a star in the huge-voiced Kelly Clarkson, whose debut single, 'A Moment Like This' (2002), sold a monstrous 236,000 copies in its first week of release. But it remains to be seen whether Clarkson, Young and Gareth Gates (Young's fellow *Pop Idol* alumnus), who all owe their fame to their familiarity with domestic audiences, will repeat the global success of three other former TV stars.

The Three Mouseketeers

Britney Spears, Christina Aguilera and Justin Timberlake began their careers in the early 1990s as Mouseketeers, youthful stars of Disney's *The Mickey Mouse Show*. A decade later, all three had swapped their over-sized ears for high-profile musical careers. The first to achieve supernova status was Spears, who debuted in 1999 with '…Baby One More Time', a huge-selling slice of commercial R&B laced with suggestive growls.

Spears' trump card was an ambiguous image that combined wide-eyed innocence with illicit sensuality. Although her publicity machine emphasized her wholesome upbringing and virginity, this contrasted with both the sado-masochistic undertones of the lyrics "hit me baby one more time" and the song's controversial video, in which Spears appeared dressed as a schoolgirl. Record buyers lapped it up and Spears became the most successful American teenager of all time.

She was followed into the charts by a succession of solo American females, including Aguilera, who became infamous for her skimpy outfits,

body piercings, raunchy videos and libidinous vocals. This direct marketing strategy began to pay rich dividends with the considerable success of her *Stripped* LP (2002) and 'Dirrty' single (2003).

Although Timberlake had been a mid-ranking star since the late 1990s through his involvement with *NSYNC, he was initially best known as Spears' boyfriend. But the couple split in 2002, Spears' career dipped, Timberlake made his solo debut in the same year with 'Like I Love You' and his star profile gradually eclipsed hers.

Timberlake's blend of commercial urban grooves and soulful pop hardly overflowed with originality. But he at least had the sense to work with respected producers such as the Neptunes and aim high by aping the sweet falsetto, high-pitched grunts and slick dance moves of Michael Jackson. By the beginning of 2003, on the back of his huge-selling *Justified* album, he looked poised to snatch the King of Pop's crown.

Left

Christina Aguilera (pictured), Pink, Mya and Lil' Kim received a Grammy Award for their song, 'Lady Marmalade,' from the Moulin Rouge *soundtrack. The hit denoted a transition in Christina's music from sugary pop ballads to a harder, sexier, more urban sound.*

Below

With a sex appeal that contradicts her squeaky clean image, Britney Spears has enjoyed phenomenal success both as a music artist and a major media fixture since her debut in 1999.

Noughties Pop Singer/Songwriters

WHILE MORE AND MORE OF THE MAINSTREAM IS OCCUPIED BY HEAVILY MANUFACTURED AND STYLIZED ROCK. POP AND R&B ACTS. THE EMERGENCE OF LESS-DEMONSTRATIVE ARTISTS – OFTEN FROM A SELF-FINANCING. SMALL-SCALE INDEPENDENT BACKGROUND – REPRESENTS A QUIET FORM OF REBELLION FROM THE POP NORM.

Above
David Gray's emotional music speaks of infidelity, pain and love highlighted by his powerfully unique voice and sincere guitar. His music has wowed thousands of fans, including Dave Matthews of the Dave Matthews Band, who helped secure Gray his American record deal.

THE success of mavericks such as Björk and Sinéad O'Connor in the 1990s continues to foster an independent spirit in the pop singer/songwriters of the new century. While the likes of Alanis Morissette, Sir Elton John, Paul Weller and Tori Amos remain relevant to a post-2000 audience, it is the new, low-key and rootsy pop singer/songwriters who are beginning to define the future of the genre.

Local Sounds From Local People

Although very different in musical style, six key artists have all grown from humble beginnings in specific locales, striving long and hard under difficult circumstances before hitting paydirt. The most striking example is David Gray, a Manchester-born multi-instrumentalist who grew up in Wales but found initial success in Ireland. His first album, *A Century Ends*, was released in 1993, but it took another six years of Irish support slots – and his entirely self-financed 1998 album, *White Ladder* – for his Van Morrison-goes-pop songcraft to achieve a crossover impact, along with friends in high places and a US release on Dave Matthews ATO label in 2000. Its 2002 follow-up, *A New Day At Midnight*, established him as a major adult pop star.

> ## "I'M AS MYSTIFIED NOW AS WHEN I STARTED. I'M NO CLOSER TO UNDERSTANDING THE DIFFERENCE BETWEEN THE INGREDIENTS OF A REALLY GREAT SONG AND A MEDIOCRE ONE."
> *David Gray*

Macy Gray, David's Ohio-born namesake, toiled for years on the Los Angeles jazz bar scene. She played piano and organized her own music and poetry club before establishing a highly individual blend of smoky and croaky vocals, eccentric performance, autobiographical lyrics and soul, rap, R&B, FM rock and pop stylings on her massive 1999 debut album, *On How Life Is*. Alaska's Jewel Kilcher worked as a waitress, strummed and sang in dives and lived in her car in San Diego before becoming an "overnight success" with the winsome folk-pop of 1995's *Pieces Of You*. Her blonde-sweetheart looks

LEADING EXPONENTS

Alanis Morissette
David Gray
Macy Gray
Badly Drawn Boy
Beth Orton
Sarah McLachlan
Jewel
Alicia Keys
Nelly Furtado
Tori Amos

NOUGHTIES POP SINGER/SONGWRITERS

Now the MTV generation are making their own records, there is always something happening, even in an introverted piano ballad. The chord form of: root, 5th, 2nd minor, and 4th is particularly popular, especially with the root and 5th note pedalling at the top of the chords.

THE NOUGHTIES POP INTRO ➡ 66   POP PEOPLE A–Z ➡ 72   INSTRUMENTS A–Z ➡ 436   POP: SIXTIES POP SINGER/SONGWRITERS ➡ 24

and intelligent songs have seen her build a transatlantic word-of-mouth following over subsequent years, even earning her an invite to a President Clinton inaugural ball in 1997.

On the British side, Norwich's Beth Orton spent time as a Buddhist nun before she was discovered by the dance producer William Orbit in 1991. By the mid-1990s, she was collaborating with dance acts the Chemical Brothers and Red Snapper, and her quietly funky 1996 debut album *Trailer Park* made her the queen of post-clubbing chill-out for Brits. The increasing sophistication of her Nick Drake- and Joni Mitchell-influenced bedsit melancholy has since seen her work with the likes of Beck and the Flaming Lips in the US. A gangly, shy six-footer, her appeal seems as as much due to her down-to-earth likability as it is to her American roots-influenced songs.

The same could be said for Manchester's Damon Gough, aka Badly Drawn Boy, who remained a hometown obscurity until he set up his own Twisted Nerve label with producer Andy Votel. He began recording and quickly caught people's attention with his lo-fi blend of songcraft, mischievous experiment and indie introspection. His 2000 debut album, *The Hour Of Bewilderbeast*, saw him win Britain's Mercury Music Prize, while his legendarily shambolic live shows and penchant for scruffy woollen hats have not prevented his rapid ascent to household name in the UK. In 2002, his soundtrack to Hugh Grant's *About A Boy* movie gained ubiquitous popularity, aided by the singles 'Silent Sigh' and 'Something To Talk About'.

But perhaps the most striking advert for organic growth is Nova Scotia's Sarah McLachlan. Eight years, three albums of Celtic folk-pop and much mind-expanding travel passed between her first album, *Touch*, and her central role in organizing Lilith Fair, a 1997 tour designed to promote marginalized female artists. The same year saw her *Surfacing* album hit big in America and Europe, while Lilith Fair has quickly become an essential stepping-stone for women attempting to break the charts without shedding their clothes.

Barely Out Of Diapers

Nevertheless, the impact of these mature artists was being mirrored and challenged by a wave of young female singer/songwriters. With the likes of Britney Spears establishing a new level of success and credibility for teen performers, the only thing better for a record company was finding equally young and visually appealing talent who could also write all their own material. Cue a slew of American singer/songwriter prodigies. Harlem's Alicia Keys, whose extraordinarily articulate and soulful R&B

debut album, *Songs In A Minor*, won the 21-year-old five Grammies. Canada's Nelly Furtado's career began with the rap duo Nelstar before success at 1999's Lilith Fair led to her hippy-chick mix of pop, Latin, folk, reggae and hip-hop on her 2000 album, *Whoa, Nelly!* The more traditional piano songcraft of Pennsylvania's Vanessa Carlton produced the global hit 'A Thousand Miles', as well as her precocious debut album, *Be Not Nobody*, in 2002. There is a never-ending demand for the emotional, intimate-yet-accessible material offered by singer/songwriters; if anyone discovers an introspective, angry but kooky piano-playing toddler in the next few years, they will have hit the jackpot.

Left

With a unique, growling voice and campy 1970s fashion style, Macy Gray has become renowned for her individual, funky sound and stage performances.

Below

Winner of Britain's prestigious Mercury Prize for Best Album in 2000, Damon Gough, or Badly Drawn Boy, has enjoyed increasing success outside of his home in the UK.

Noughties Latin Pop

BUOYED BY ITS UNPRECEDENTED INTERNATIONAL EXPOSURE IN THE 1990S, LATIN POP GREETED THE NEW CENTURY WITH THE FIRST-EVER LATIN GRAMMY AWARDS, WHICH TOOK PLACE IN THE UNITED STATES IN SEPTEMBER 2000.

CONCEIVED as an internationally minded award, clearly distinct from – although related to – the Grammys, one of the objectives of the Latin Grammys was to "promote the vitality of the many regional forms of Latin music". What emerged in much of the pop showcased from different countries was music that mixed folk elements from specific regions with more universal elements, as well as more sophisticated orchestrations and arrangements.

Bringing traditional music to the forefront remains a clear trend in Latin pop of this decade, with the Spaniard Alejandro Sanz, whose pop is based on flamenco harmonies and improvisations, being one of the clear leaders in the field. With his insightful songs, Sanz became a star in Spain in the 1990s before achieving prominence in the Latin market with Corazón Partío, a mix of flamenco and pop that included virtuoso flamenco guitar solos and gospel-like backing vocals. Thanks to two award-winning albums, *El Alma Al Aire* and *MTV Unplugged*, and to collaborations with artists as varied as the Irish pop-folk band the Corrs and flamenco guitarist Vicente Amigo, Sanz expanded his reach – notably to the United States and Europe – in the early 2000s.

But even as an increasingly broad-minded audience has embraced rootsy Latin pop, the crossover trend from Spanish to English with a more international sound shows no sign of abating. Indeed, artists are now passing back and forth between languages with considerable ease.

> "WRITING IN ENGLISH WAS A MAJOR CHALLENGE. I DIDN'T WANT OTHER SONGWRITERS TO WRITE FOR ME, I WANTED TO PRESERVE THE SPIRIT OF MY SONGS IN SPANISH."
>
> *Shakira*

Right

The infectious pop ditty, 'The Ketchup Song' by Spanish sisters Las Ketchup invaded the planet in 2002, earning the girls worldwide fame and notoriety.

LEADING EXPONENTS

Shakira
Christina Aguilera
Alejandro Sanz
Paulina Rubio
Carlos Vives
Juan Luis Guerra
Las Ketchup

NOUGHTIES LATIN POP

Melodies are flamboyant with their colourful syncopations where rhythmic stresses across the main beats are jovial and lilting.

Quite fast

THE NOUGHTIES POP INTRO ➡ 66   POP PEOPLE A-Z ➡ 72   INSTRUMENTS A-Z ➡ 436   POP: NINETIES LATIN POP ➡ 60   JAZZ: LATIN JAZZ ➡ 148

Christina Aguilera And R&B

The precursor for the decade was Christina Aguilera, a US teen act with a Latin surname, courtesy of an Ecuadorian father. After scoring a huge hit with her English-language debut in the late 1990s, Aguilera recorded a Spanish-language album, *Mi Reflejo*, in 2000, featuring translations from her English disc, original tracks and, in a move aimed to please traditional Latin audiences, a cover of a bolero standard, 'Contigo En la Distancia'.

Aside from this one track, there was nothing conspicuously Latin about Aguilera's sound. Instead, through songs such as 'Ven Conmigo', she introduced Latin pop laced with both an R&B vocal sensibility and hip-hop beats. The entire Aguilera package appealed to a younger Latin fan and in the ensuing years, R&B-tinged vocalizing has become a standard of Latin pop, particularly for a younger generation of acts, even as the more traditional renditions continued to hold court.

Aguilera's success in both languages also signalled that Latin audiences were open to a kind of linguistic passing back and forth. Enrique Iglesias furthered his English-language career with a generic pop sound (*Escape*) that he carried over to his return to Latin pop in 2002. Marc Anthony also recorded in Spanish in 2001, but put forth a full salsa album, *Libre*, whose strong sales suggest that it was also purchased by his pop fans.

Shakira

As of 2003, the most successful crossover of the decade is that of the Colombian pop-rock star Shakira, whose English-language debut, *Laundry Service*, became one of the top-selling albums worldwide for 2001 and 2002. Like other crossover stars before her, Shakira came from a solid foundation in the Latin world and was, arguably, already the most successful female Latin act of her generation. But she also co-wrote her material, an important asset when singer/songwriters seemed to be back in vogue worldwide.

In a move that has become standard for crossover acts, Shakira's first single, 'Wherever, Whenever', was recorded in both English- and Spanish-language versions. The track featured Andean flute, perhaps the only concession to the singer's Latin side, and was otherwise a bouncy pop song with a slight edge, drawing more from British and American rockers than from Latin balladeers or folklorists. (She has been covering Aerosmith's 'Dude (Looks Like A Lady)' and AC/DC's 'Back In Black' in her concerts.) This is in keeping with past crossover success stories. While acts retain their personal "exotic" characteristics, the music becomes largely generic in an attempt to please all. Instead, the task of showcasing the elements that are commonly associated with Latin pop – the Afro-Cuban beats, Latin rhythms and percussion and instrumentation that can veer from the sound of guitar trios to the brash brass of salsa – has fallen largely on acts who record in Spanish.

But the multiple trends also indicate that Latin pop is more open to variations than ever before, from the traditional crooner, still embodied by the Mexican Luis Miguel as well as country mates Alejandro Fernández and Cristian Castro, to Las Ketchup. In June 2002, the latter trio of Spanish sisters released 'Aserejé', a novelty track that has been compared to its 1990s precursor, 'Macarena'. A nonsensical song stemming from the 1980s hit 'Rapper's Delight', 'Aserejé (The Ketchup Song)' became a number one hit in 21 countries, which demonstrated that Latin pop in Spanish can be universal.

Far Left

With Latin mania sweeping the world, it is not surprising that Latin instruments, such as the maracas and bongos, would become incorporated into mainstream music to lend a pleasing sound.

Below

Colombian Shakira has become the largest Latin crossover artist since Jennifer López with her hit singles, 'Whenever, Wherever' and 'Underneath your Clothes'.

Artists: Pop

Entries appear in the following order: name, music style, year(s) of popularity, type of artist, country of origin

1910 Fruitgum Company, 1960s Pop, 1960s, Artist, American
20/20, 1970s Pop, 1970s–1990s, Artist, American
5th Dimension, 1960s Pop, 1960s–1970s, Artist, American
98 Degrees, 1990s Pop, 1990s–, Artist, American
ABBA, Europop, 1970s–1980s, Artist, Swedish
ABC, New Wave; 1980s Pop, 1980s–1990s, Artist, British
Abdul, Paula, 1980s Pop, 1980s–1990s, Artist, American
Ace of Base, Europop, 1990s–, Artist, Swedish
Ackles, David, 1960s Singer/Songwriters, 1960s–1970s, Artist; Songwriter, American
Action, The, Mod; British Invasion, 1960s, Artist, British
Adam and the Ants, New Wave, 1970s–1980s, Artist, British
Adams, Brian, 1980s Pop, 1980s–, Artist; Songwriter, American
Adkins, Hasil, Rockabilly, 1950s–1990s, Artist, American
Adventures in Stereo, 1990s Pop, 1990s–, Artist, British
Aerosmith, 1970s Pop, 1970s–, Artist, American
Aguilera, Christina, 1990s Pop, 1990s–, Artist, American
A-Ha, 1980s Pop, 1980s–, Artist, Norwegian
All Saints, 1990s Pop, 1990s–, Artist, British
Almond, Marc, New Wave; New Romantics, 1980s–, Artist, British
Alpert, Herb, 1960s Pop, 1960s–, Producer; Artist, American
Altered Images, New Wave, 1980s, Artist, British
Aluminum Group, 1990s Pop, 1990s–, Artist, American
Amen Corner, Mod; British Invasion, 1960s–1970s, Artist, British
America, 1970s Pop, 1970s–1990s, Artist, British
Amos, Tori, 1980s Pop, 1980s–, Artist, American
Andersen, Eric, 1960s Singer/Songwriters, 1960s–, Artist; Songwriter,
Andrews, Lee, Doo-Wop, 1950s–1960s, Artist, American
Andrews, Lee, and the Hearts, Doo-Wop, 1950s, Artist, American
Angels, The, 1960s Pop, 1960s, Artist, American
Animals, The, Rock'n'Roll; British Invasion, 1960s–1980s, Artist, British
Anka, Paul, 1950s Pop, 1950s–, Artist, Canadian
Ant, Adam, New Wave, 1970s–, Artist, British
Anthony, Marc, Latin, 1990s–, Artist, Puerto Rican
Apple, Fiona, 1990s Singer/Songwriters, 1990s, Artist; Songwriter, American
Apples in Stereo, The, 1990s Pop, 1990s–, Artist, American
Aqua, Europop, 1990s–, Artist, Danish
Arbors, The, 1960s Pop, 1960s, Artist, American
Archers of Loaf, 1990s Pop, 1990s–, Artist, American
Archies, The, 1960s Pop, 1960s–1970s, Artist, American
Armatrading, Joan, 1970s Singer/Songwriters, 1970s–1990s, Artist; Songwriter, British
Ash, Britpop; 1990s Pop, 1990s–, Artist, British
Associates, The, New Romantics, 1980s–1990s, Artist, British
Association, The, 1960s Pop; Wall of Sound, 1960s–1970s, Artist, American
Astley, Rick, 1980s Pop, 1980s, Artist, British
Astronauts, The, Surf, 1960s; 1980–1990s, Artist, American
Atlantics, The, Surf, 1960s–1970s, Artist, Australian
Atomic Kitten, Manufactured Pop; 1990s Pop, 1990s–, Artist, British
Auteurs, The, Britpop, 1990s, Artist, British
Avalon, Frankie, 1950s Pop, 1950s–1970s, Artist, American
Average White Band, Funk, 1970s–1980s, Artist, British
Axelrod, David, Wall of Sound; 1960s Pop, 1960s–, Producer, American
Aztec Camera, New Wave, 1980s–1990s, Artist, British
B*Witched, 1990s Pop; Manufactured Pop, 1990s–, Artist, British
B-52s, The, New Wave, 1970s–1990s, Artist, American
Bacharach, Burt, 1960s Pop; Wall of Sound, 1960s–1990s, Producer; Composer; Songwriter; Artist, American
Backstreet Boys, Boy Bands; 1990s Pop, 1990s–, Artist, American
Badfinger, 1960s Pop, 1960s–1980s, Artist, British
Baez, Joan, 1950s Singer/Songwriters, 1950s–, Artist; Songwriter, American
Baker, George, Europop, 1970s, Artist, Dutch
Banana Splits, 1960s Pop; Manufactured Pop, 1960s, Artist, American
Bananarama, New Wave; 1980s Pop, 1980s–1990s, Artist, British
Band, The, Rock n Roll, 1960s–1970s; 1990s, Artist, Canadian
Banda Machos, Latin, 1990s–, Artist, Mexican
Bangles, The, New Wave; 1980s Pop, 1980s, Artist, American
Barry and the Remains, Rock'n'Roll, 1960s, Artist, American
Barry, Claudja, Europop, 1970s–1980s, Artist, Jamaican
Barry, Jeff, 1960s Pop, 1960s–, Producer, American
Basia, 1980s Pop, 1980s–1990s, Artist, Polish
Bass, Fontella, 1960s Pop, 1960s–1970s; 1990s–, Artist, American
Bauhaus, Alternative Rock, 1970s–1990s, Artist, British
Bay City Rollers, 1970s Pop, 1970s–1980s, Artist, British
Beach Boys, The, Surf, 1960s–1990s, Artist, American
Beat, The, 1970s Pop; New Wave, 1970s–1980s, Artist, American
Beat Happening, 1980s Pop, 1980s–1990s, Artist, American
Beatles, The, Rock'n'Roll; British Invasion; Merseybeat, 1960s–1970s, Artist, British
Beau Brummels, The, 1960s Pop, 1960s–1970s, Artist, American
Beautiful South, The, 1980s Pop, 1980s–, Artist, British
Bee Gees, The, 1960s Pop, 1960s–, Artist, British
Beethoven, Camper Van, 1980s Pop, 1980s, Artist, American
Bega, Lou, Latin, 1990s–, Artist, German
Bell, Chris, 1970s Singer/Songwriters, 1970s, Artist; Songwriter, American
Belle and Sebastian, 1990s Pop, 1990s–, Artist, British
Belmonts, The, Doo-Wop, 1950s–1970s, Artist, American
Beltran, Graciela, Latin, 1990s–, Artist, Mexican
Berlin, New Wave, 1980s–, Artist, American
Berns, Bert, British Invasion; 1960s Pop, 1950s–1960s, Producer; Songwriter, American
Berry, Chuck, Rock'n'Roll, 1950s–1980s, Artist; Songwriter, American
Berry, Dave, British Invasion, 1960s–1980s, Artist, British
Berry, Heidi, 1980s Singer/Songwriters, 1980s–1990s, Artist, American
Biff Bang Pow!, 1980s Pop, 1980s–1990s, Artist, British
Big Country, New Wave; 1980s Pop, 1980s–1990s, Artist, British
Big Drill Car, 1980s Pop, 1980s–1990s, Artist, American
Big Star, 1970s Pop, 1970s, Artist, American
Birds, The, British Invasion; Mod, 1960s, Artist, British
Black, Cilla, 1960s Pop; British Invasion, 1960s–1990s, Artist, British
Blackbyrds, The, Funk, 1970s–1980s, Artist, American
Blades, Ruben, Latin, 1970s–, Artist, Panamanian
Blasters, The, Rock'n'Roll, 1980s, Artist, American
Blink-182, 1990s Pop, 1990s–, Artist, American
Blondie, New Wave; 1970s Pop, 1970s–1990s, Artist, American
Bloodstone, Funk, 1970s–1990s, Artist, American
Bloque, Latin, 1990s, Artist, Columbian
Blow Monkeys, The, New Romantics; New Wave, 1980s–1990s, Artist, British
Blue, Boy Bands; 2000s Pop, Artist, British,
Blue Ash, 1970s Pop, 1970s, Artist, American
Blue Nile, The, 1980s Pop, 1980s–1990s, Artist, British
Blueboy, 1990s Pop, 1990s, Artist, British
Blur, Britpop, 1990s–, Artist, British
BMX Bandits, 1980s Pop, 1980s–1990s, Artist, British
Bobettes, The, 1950s Pop, 1950s–1970s, Artist, American
Boettcher, Curt, 1960s Pop, 1960s–1970s, Artist, American
Bolan, Marc, Rock'n'Roll; 1960s Pop, 1960s–1970s, Artist; Songwriter, British
Bolton, Michael, 1960s Pop, 1960s–, Artist, American
Boo Radleys, The, Britpop, 1990s, Artist, British
Boone, Pat, 1950s Pop, 1950s–1990s, Artist, American
Bose, Michel, Latin, 1970s–, Artist, Panamanian
Bow Wow Wow, New Wave, 1980s–1990s, Artist, British
Bowery Electric, 1990s Pop, 1990s–, Artist, American
Bowie, David, 1960s Pop, 1960s–, Artist, British
Box Tops, The, 1960s Pop, 1960s, Artist, American
Boyz II Men, 1980s Pop, 1980s–, Artist, American
Boyzone, Boy Bands; Manufactured Pop; 1990s Pop, 1990s–2000s, Artist, Irish
Brady Bunch, The, 1970s Pop; Manufactured Pop, 1970s, Artist, American
Bragg, Billy, 1980s Singer/Songwriters, 1980s, Artist; Songwriter, British
Brass Construction, Funk, 1960s–1980s, Artist, American
Braxton, Toni, 1990s Pop, 1990s–, Artist, American
Brick, Funk, 1970s–1980s, Artist, American
Bronski Beat, 1980s Pop; New Wave, 1980s–1990s, Artist, British
Brooklyn Bridge, 1960s Pop, 1960s–1970s, Artist, American
Bros, 1980s Pop; Boy Bands, 1980s–1990s, Artist, British
Brown, Bobby, 1980s Pop, 1980s–, Artist, American
Brown, Maxine, 1960s Pop, 1960s–1970s, Artist, American
Browne, Jackson, 1960s Singer/Songwriters, 1960s–, Artist; Songwriter, American
Bruce and Terry, Surf; 1960s Pop, 1960s, Artist, American
Bryson, Peabo, 1970s Pop, 1970s–1990s, Artist, American
BT Express, Funk, 1970s–1980s, Artist, American
Buckinghams, The, 1960s Pop, 1960s; 1990s, Artist, American
Buckley, Jeff, 1990s Singer/Songwriters, 1990s, Artist; Songwriter, American
Buckley, Tim, 1960s Singer/Songwriters, 1960s–1970s, Artist; Songwriter, American
Buggles, The, 1980s Pop; New Wave, 1980s, Artist, British
Bunnygrunt, 1990s Pop, 1990s, Artist, American
Burgess, Sonny, Rockabilly, 1950s–1990s, Artist, American
Burlison, Paul, Rockabilly; Rock'n'Roll, 1990s, Artist, American
Burnette, Johnny, Rockabilly, 1950s–1960s, Artist; Songwriter, American
Burrows, Tony, 1970s Pop, 1970s, Artist, British
Burton, James, Rockabilly; Rock'n'Roll, 1960s–1970s, Artist, American
Butler, Jerry, 1950s Pop, 1950s–1990s, Artist, American
Byrd, Donald, Funk, 1950s–, Artist, American
C+C Music Factory, 1990s Pop, 1990s, Artist, American
Cadets, The, Doo-Wop, 1950s–1960s, Artist, American
Cadillacs, The, Doo-Wop, 1950s–1960s; 1990s, Artist, American
Cale, J. J., 1970s Singer/Songwriters, 1970s–1990s, Artist; Songwriter, American
Cannanes, 1990s Pop, 1990s–, Artist, Australian
Capris, The, Doo-Wop, 1950s; 1980s, Artist, American
Cardigans, The, 1990s Pop, 1990s–, Artist, Swedish
Cardinal, 1990s Pop, 1990s, Artist, American
Carey, Mariah, 1990s Pop, 1990s–, Artist, American
Carnes, Kim, 1970s Pop, 1970s–1980s, Artist, American
Carpenters, The, 1960s Pop, 1960s–1980s, Artist, American
Carr, Vicki, Latin, 1960s–, Artist, American
Carrack, Paul, 1970s Pop, 1970s–, Artist, British
Cars, The, New Wave; 1970s Pop, 1970s–1980s, Artist, American
Carter, Aaron, 1990s Pop, 1990s, Artist, American
Casey, Al, Surf; Rock'n'Roll, 1960s–1970s, Artist, American
Cash, Johnny, Rockabilly; Rock'n'Roll, 1950s–, Artist, American
Cash, Rosanne, 1970s Singer/Songwriters, 1970s–1990s, Artist; Songwriter, American
Cassidy, David, 1970s Pop, 1970s–, Artist, American
Cassidy, Shaun, 1970s Pop, 1970s–1980s, Artist, American
Cast, Britpop, 1990s–, Artist, British
Castro, Cristian, Latin, 1990s–, Artist, Mexican
Cat's Miaow, The, 1990s Pop, 1990s, Artist, Australian
Catatonia, Britpop, 1990s–2000s, Artist, British
Cellos, The, Doo-Wop, 1950s, Artist, American
Chad and Jeremy, British Invasion; 1960s Pop, 1960s; 1980s, Artist, British
Challengers, The, Surf, 1960s–1970s, Artist, American
Channels, The, Doo-Wop, 1950s, Artist, American
Chantays, The, Surf, 1960s; 1990s, Artist, American
Chantels, The, Doo-Wop, 1950s–1960s, Artist, American
Chapin, Harry, 1970s Singer/Songwriters, 1970s–1980s, Artist; Songwriter, American
Chapman, Tracy, 1980s Singer/Songwriters; 1980s Pop, 1980s–, Artist; Songwriter, American
Charlatans, The, Madchester; Britpop, 1980s–, Artist, British
Cheap Trick, New Wave; 1970s Pop, 1970s–, Artist, American
Cher, 1960s Pop, 1960s–, Artist, American
Cherry, Neneh, 1980s Pop, 1980s–1990s, Artist, Swedish
Chic, Funk, 1970s–1990s, Artist, American
Chicago, 1960s Pop, 1960s–, Artist, American
Chiffons, The, 1960s Pop, 1960s–1970s, Artist, American
Chords, The, Doo-Wop, 1950s–1960s, Artist, American
Christie, Lou, 1960s Pop, 1960s–1970s, Artist, American
Clark, Guy, 1970s Singer/Songwriters, 1970s–1990s, Artist; Songwriter, American
Clark, Petula, British Invasion; 1960s Pop, 1960s–, Artist, British
Clarke, Vince, 1980s Pop, 1980s–, Artist, British
Classics IV, 1960s Pop, 1960s–1970s, Artist, American
Clay, Joe, Rockabilly, 1980s, Artist, American
Clee-Shays, Surf, 1960s, Artist, American
Cleftones, The, Doo-Wop, 1950s–1960s, Artist, American
Cleopatra, 1990s Pop, 1990s–, Artist, British
Clique, The, 1960s Pop, 1960s, Artist, American
Clovers, The, Doo-Wop, 1940s–1950s, Artist, American
Coasters, The, Doo-Wop; Rock'n'Roll, 1950s–1970s, Artist, American
Cochran, Eddie, Rock'n'Roll; Rockabilly, 1950s, Artist, American
Cockburn, Bruce, 1960s Singer/Songwriters, 1960s–1990s, Artist; Songwriter, Canadian
Cocteau Twins, 1980s Pop, 1980s–1990s, Artist, British
Cohen, Leonard, 1960s Singer/Songwriters, 1960s–, Artist; Songwriter, Canadian
Cohn, Marc, 1990s Pop; 1990s Singer/Songwriters, 1990s, Artist; Songwriter, American
Cole, Jerry, Surf, 1960s, Artist, American
Cole, Natalie, 1970s Pop, 1970s, Artist, American
Cole, Paula, 1990s Singer/Songwriters, 1990s, Artist; Songwriter, American
Collins Kids, The, Rockabilly, 1950s–1960s, Artist, American
Collins, Edwyn, 1980s Pop, 1980s–1990s, Artist, British
Collins, Judy, 1950s Singer/Songwriters, 1950s–, Artist; Songwriter, American
Collins, Phil, 1970s Pop, 1970s–, Artist, British
Colvin, Shawn, 1980s Singer/Songwriters, 1980s–, Artist; Songwriter, American
Colyer, Ken, Skiffle, 1940s–1980s, Artist, British
Commodores, The, Funk, 1970s–1990s, Artist, American
Compulsion, 1990s Pop, 1990s, Artist, Irish
Cookies, The, 1950s Pop, 1950s–1960s, Artist, American
Corrs, The, 1990s Pop, 1990s–, Artist, Irish
Costello, Elvis, New Wave; 1970s Singer/Songwriters, 1970s–, Artist; Songwriter, British
Cowsills, The, 1960s Pop, 1960s–1990s, Artist, American
Cranberries, The, 1990s Pop, 1990s–, Artist, British
Crazy Elephant, 1960s Pop; Manufactured Pop, 1960s, Artist, American
Creation, The, Rock'n'Roll; British Invasion, 1960s, Artist, British
Creedence Clearwater Revisited, Rock'n'Roll, 1990s, Artist, American
Creedence Clearwater Revival, Rock'n'Roll, 1960s–1970s, Artist, American
Crenshaw, Marshall, New Wave; 1980s Pop, 1980s–, Artist, American
Crests, The, Doo-Wop, 1950s–1960s, Artist, American
Croce, Jim, 1960s Singer/Songwriters, 1960s–1970s, Artist; Songwriter, American
Crosby, David, 1970s Singer/Songwriters, 1970s–1990s, Artist; Songwriter, American
Crosby, Stills and Nash, 1960s Singer/Songwriters, 1960s–1990s, Artist; Songwriter, American
Crow, Sheryl, 1990s Singer/Songwriters, 1990s–, Artist, America
Crowded House, 1980s Pop, 1980s–1990s, Artist, New Zealander
Crows, The, Doo-Wop, 1950s, Artist, American
Cruz, Celia, Latin, 1950s–, Artist, Cuban
Crystals, The, 1960s Pop, 1960s, Artist, American
Cub, 1990s Pop, 1990s, Artist, American
Cuba, Joe, Latin, 1950s–1960s; 1990s, Artist, American
Cuff Links, The, 1960s Pop; Manufactured Pop, 1960s, Artist, American
Culture Club, New Wave; 1980s Pop, 1980s–1990s, Artist, British
Dale, Dick, Surf, 1960s–1990s, Artist, American
Damon and Naomi, 1990s Pop, 1990s–, Artist, American
Darin, Bobby, 1950s Pop, 1950s–1970s, Artist, American
Dave Clark Five, The, British Invasion, 1960s–1970s, Artist, British
David, Hal, 1960s Pop, 1960s–1980s, Producer; Songwriter; Artist, American
Davies, Richard, 1990s Pop, 1990s–, Artist, Australian
Dawn, 1970s Pop, 1970s, Artist, American
Dawson, Ronnie, Rockabilly, 1950s–1960s, Artist, American
Day, Bobby, Doo-Wop; Rock'n'Roll, 1950s, Artist, American
DBs, The, 1980s Pop, 1980s–1990s, Artist, American
De Burgh, Chris, 1970s Pop, 1970s–, Artist, British
Dead Can Dance, 1980s Pop, 1980s–, Artist, Australian
Deee-Lite, 1980s Pop, 1980s–1990s, Artist, American
Def Leppard, 1980s Pop, 1980s–, Artist, British
DeFranco Family, The, 1970s Pop, 1970s, Artist, Canadian
Delfonics, The, 1960s Pop, 1960s–1970s, Artist, American
Dells, The, 1950s Pop, 1950s–1990s, Artist, American
Del-Vikings, The, Doo-Wop, 1950s–1960s, Artist, American
Denver, John, 1960s Singer/Songwriters, 1960s–1990s, Artist, American
Depeche Mode, 1980s Pop, 1980s–, Artist, British
Descendents, 1980s Pop, 1980s–1990s, Artist, American
DeShannon, Jackie, 1960s Pop; 1960s Singer/Songwriters, 1960s–1980s, Artist; Songwriter, American
Destiny's Child, 1990s pop, 1990s–, Artist, American
Devo, New Wave, 1970s–1990s, Artist, American
Dexy's Midnight Runners, New Wave, 1980s, Artist, British
Diamond, Neil, 1960s Pop, 1960s–, Artist, American
Diamonds, The, Doo-Wop, 1950s–1970s, Artist, Canadian
Diddley, Bo, Rock'n'Roll, 1950s–, Artist, American
Dido, 1990s Singer/Songwriters, 1990s–, Artist; Songwriter, British
DiFranco, Ani, 1980s Singer/Songwriters, 1980s–, Artist; Songwriter, American
Dion, Doo-Wop; Rock'n'Roll, 1950s–, Artist, American
Dion, Celine, 1990s Pop, 1990s–, Artist, French-Canadian
Dodgy, Britpop, 1990s–, Artist, British
Dolby, Thomas, New Wave, 1980s–1990s, Artist, British
Domino, Fats, Rock'n'Roll, 1940s–1990s, Artist, American
Donegan, Lonnie, Skiffle; Rockabilly, 1950s–1990s, Artist, British
Donovan, British Invasion; 1960s Singer/Songwriters, 1960s–, Artist; Songwriter, British
Doobie Brothers, 1970s Pop, 1970s–, Artist, American
Downliners Sect, The, British Invasion, 1960s–1970s, Artist, British
Dr. Hook, 1960s Pop, 1960s–1970s, Artist, American
Drake, Nick, 1960s Singer/Songwriters, 1960s–1970s, Artist; Songwriter, British
Dream Syndicate, 1980s Pop, 1980s, Artist, American
Drifters, The, Doo-Wop, 1950s–1990s, Artist, American
Duncan, Johnny, Skiffle, 1950s–1970s, Artist, British
Duprees, The, Doo-Wop, 1960s, Artist, American
Duran Duran, New Wave; New Romantics; 1980s Pop, 1980s–1990s, Artist, British
Durcal, Rocio, Latin, 1960s–, Artist, Spanish
Duren, Van, 1970s Pop, 1970s, Artist, American
Dury, Ian, New Wave, 1970s–1990s, Artist; Songwriter, British
Dylan, Bob, Rock'n'Roll; 1960s Singer/Songwriters, 1960s–, Artist, American
E., Sheila, 1980s Pop, 1980s–, Artist, American
Eagles, The, 1970s Pop, 1970s–1990s, Artist, American
Earle, Steve, 1980s Singer/Songwriters, 1980s–, Artist; Songwriter, American
East 17, Boy Bands; 1990s Pop, 1990s–, Artist, British
East River Pipe, 1990s Singer/Songwriters; 1990s Pop, 1990s–, Artist; Songwriter, American
East Village, 1990s Pop, 1990s, Artist, British
Easter, Mitch, 1970s Pop, 1970s–, Artist; Producer, American
Easton, Sheena, 1980s Pop, 1980s–, Artist, British
Eddie and the Showmen, Surf; Rock'n'Roll, 1960s, Artist, American
Eddy, Duane, Rock'n'Roll, 1950s–1980s, Artist, American
Edison Lighthouse, 1960s Pop; Manufactured Pop, 1960s–1970s, Artist, British
Edmunds, Dave, Rock'n'Roll; New Wave, 1970s–, Artist, British
Edsels, The, Doo-Wop, 1950s–1960s, Artist, American
El Dorados, The, Doo-Wop, 1950s; 1990s, Artist, American
Elastica, Britpop, 1990s–, Artist, British
Electric Light Orchestra, 1970s Pop, 1970s–, Artist, British
Embrace, Britpop, 1990s–, Artist, British
Emilio, Latin, 1990s, Artist, American
Emmanuel, Latin, 1970s–, Artist, Mexican
English Beat, The, New Wave, 1980s, Artist, British
Enuff Znuff, 1980s Pop, 1980s–, Artist, American
Equals, The, 1960s Pop; Funk, 1960s–1980s, Artist, British
Erasure, 1980s Pop, 1980s–, Artist, British
Essex, David, 1970s Pop, 1970s–1990s, Artist, British
Essex, The, 1960s Pop, 1960s, Artist, American
Estefan, Gloria, 1980s Pop; Latin, 1980s–, Artist, American
Etheridge, Melissa, 1980s Singer/Songwriters, 1980s–, Artist; Songwriter, American
Eurythmics, New Wave; 1980s Pop, 1980s–1990s, Artist, British
Everly Brothers, The, Rock'n'Roll; Rockabilly, 1950s–1990s, Artist, American
Everything but the Girl, 1980s Pop, 1980s–, Artist, British
Exciters, The, 1960s Pop, 1960s–1970s, Artist, Jamaican
Eyes, The, Mod; British Invasion, 1960s, Artist, British
Fabares, Shelley, 1960s Pop, 1960s, Artist, American
Fabian, 1950s Pop, 1950s–1970s, Artist, American
Faces, Rock'n'Roll, 1970s, Artist, British
Faith, Adam, 1950s Pop, 1950s–1990s, Artist, British
Falkner, Jason, 1990s Pop, 1990s–, Artist, American
Fantastic Baggys, Surf; Rock'n'Roll, 1960s, Artist, American
Farmer, Mylene, Europop, 1980s–, Artist, French
Fastbacks, 1980s Pop, 1980s–1990s, Artist, American
Feathers, Charlie, Rockabilly, 1950s–1990s, Artist; Songwriter, American
Feelies, The, 1970s Pop, 1970s–1990s, Artist, American
Field Mice, The, 1980s Pop, 1980s–1990s, Artist, British
Figgs, The, 1990s Pop, 1990s–, Artist, American
Finn, Neil, 1970s Singer/Songwriters, 1970s–, Artist; Songwriter, New Zealander
First Class, The, 1970s Pop, 1970s, Artist, British
Fisher, Toni, 1990s Pop, 1990s, Artist, American
5ive, Boy Bands; 1990s Pop, 1990s–, Artist, British
Five Keys, The, Doo-Wop, 1950s–1960s, Artist, American
Five Man Electrical Band, 1960s Pop, 1960s–1970s, Artist, Canadian
Five Satins, The, Doo-Wop, 1950s–1960s, Artist, American
Flamin' Groovies, The, Rock'n'Roll, 1960s–1990s, Artist, American
Flamingos, The, Doo-Wop, 1950s–1960s, Artist, American
Flatmates, 1980s Pop, 1980s–1990s, Artist, British
Fleetwood Mac, 1960s Pop, 1960s–, Artist, British
Flock of Seagulls, A, New Romantics; New Wave, 1980s–1990s, Artist, British
Flower Pot Men, The, 1960s Pop, 1960s, Artist, British
Flying Machine, The, 1960s Pop, 1960s, Artist, British
Fogelberg, Dan, 1970s Singer/Songwriters, 1970s–, Artist; Songwriter, American
Folds, Ben, 1990s Pop, 1990s–, Artist, American
Fontana, Wayne, and the Mindbenders, British Invasion; Merseybeat, 1960s, Artist, British
Foundations, The, 1960s Pop, 1960s, Artist, British
Fountains of Wayne, 1990s Pop, 1990s, Artist, American
Four Seasons, The, 1960s Pop, 1960s–1990s, Artist, American
Fourmost, The, Merseybeat; British Invasion, 1960s, Artist, British
Frampton, Peter, 1970s Pop, 1970s–, Artist, British
Frankie Goes to Hollywood, New Wave; 1980s Pop, 1980s, Artist, British
Freddie and the Dreamers, British Invasion; Merseybeat, 1960s, Artist, British
Free Design, The, 1960s Pop; Wall of Sound, 1960s–1970s, Artist, American
Frida, Europop, 1970s–1990s, Artist, Swedish
Friends of Distinction, The, 1960s Pop, 1960s–1970s, Artist, American
Fuller, Bobby, Rock'n'Roll; Surf, 1960s, Artist, American
Funicello, Annette, 1950s Pop, 1950s–1980s, Artist, American
Further, 1990s Pop, 1990s, Artist, American
Fury, Billy, 1950s Pop; Rock'n'Roll, 1950s–1980s, Artist, British
G., Kenny, 1980s Pop, 1980s–, Artist, American
Gabriel, Juan, Latin, 1960s–, Producer; Artist, Mexican
Gabriel, Peter, 1970s Pop, 1970s–, Producer; Songwriter; Artist, British
Galaxie 500, 1980s Pop, 1980s–1990s, Artist, American
Game Theory, 1980s Pop, 1980s, Artist, American
Gang of Four, New Wave, 1970s–1990s, Artist, British
Gap Band, The, Funk, 1970s–1990s, Artist, American
Garrett, Leif, 1970s Pop, 1970s–1980s, Artist, American
Gates, Gareth, Manufactured Pop; 2000s Pop, 2000s–, Artist, British
Gene, Britpop, 1990s–, Artist, British
General Public, New Wave, 1980s–1990s, Artist, British
Genesis, 1960s Pop, 1960s–1990s, Artist, British
Germano, Lisa, 1990s Pop, 1990s–, Artist, American
Gerry and the Pacemakers, British Invasion; Merseybeat, 1960s; 1980s, Artist, British
Gibson, Debbie, 1980s Pop, 1980s–1990s, Artist, American
Gin Blossoms, 1990s Pop, 1990s, Artist, American
Go West, 1980s Pop, 1980s–1990s, Artist, British
Go-Betweens, The, 1980s Pop; New Wave, 1980s–, Artist, Australian
Goffin, Gerry, 1960s Pop, 1960s–1970s; 1990s, Songwriter; Artist, American
Go-Gos, The, New Wave; 1980s Pop, 1980s; 2000s, Artist, American
Goldsboro, Bobby, 1960s Pop, 1960s–1970s, Artist, American
Gomez, Britpop, 1990s, Artist, British
Gore, Lesley, 1960s Pop, 1960s–1970s, Artist, American
Gorky's Zygotic Mynci, Britpop, 1990s–, Artist, British
Grant, Amy, 1970s Pop, 1970s–, Artist, American
Grass Roots, The, 1960s Pop, 1960s–1970s, Artist, American
Gray, David, 1990s Singer/Songwriters; 2000s Pop, 1990s–, Artist; Songwriter, British
Gray, Dobie, 1960s Pop, 1960s–1970s, Artist, American
Gray, Macy, 2000s Singer/Songwriters, 1990s, Artist; Songwriter, American
Grays, The, 1990s Pop, 1990s, Artist, American
Green Day, 1980s Pop, 1980s–, Artist, American
Green on Red, 1980s Pop, 1980s–1990s, Artist, American
Greenbaum, Norman, 1960s Pop, 1960s–1970s, Artist, American
Greenfield, Howard, 1960s Pop, 1960s, Composer, American
Greenwich, Ellie, 1960s Pop, 1960s–1970s, Artist; Songwriter, American
Guadalcanal Diary, 1980s Pop, 1980s–1990s, Artist, American
Guess Who, The, 1960s Pop, 1960s–1970s, Artist, Canadian
Haley, Bill, Rock'n'Roll; Rockabilly, 1950s–1970s, Artist, American
Hall and Oates, 1970s Pop, 1970s–, Artist, American
Hancock, Herbie, Funk, 1960s–, Artist; Composer, American
Hanson, 1990s Pop, 1990s–, Artist, American
Harper, Ben, 1990s Singer/Songwriters, 1990s–, Artist; Songwriter, American
Harpers Bizarre, 1960s Pop; Wall of Sound, 1960s–1970s, Artist, American
Harptones, The, Doo-Wop, 1950s–1990s, Artist, American
Hawkins, Dale, Rockabilly; Rock'n'Roll, 1950s–1990s, Artist, American
Hawkins, Ronnie, Rockabilly; Rock'n'Roll, 1950s–1980s, Artist, American
Hayes, Isaac, Funk, 1960s–, Artist; Songwriter, American
Hazlewood, Lee, 1960s Pop; Wall of Sound, 1960s, Producer; Songwriter; Artist, American
Heaven 17, New Romantics; New Wave, 1980s–1990s, Artist, British
Heavenly, 1990s Pop, 1990s–, Artist, British
Henley, Don, 1980s Pop; 1980s Singer/Songwriters, 1980s–, Artist; Songwriter, American
Herman's Hermits, British Invasion; Merseybeat; 1960s Pop, 1960s–1970s, Artist, British
Hersh, Kristin, 1990s Singer/Songwriters, 1990s–, Artist; Songwriter, American
Heyman, Richard X., 1980s Pop, 1980s–, Artist, American
Hiatt, John, 1970s Singer/Songwriters, 1970s–, Artist; Songwriter, American
High Llamas, The, 1990s Pop, 1990s–, Artist, British
His Name Is Alive, 1990s Pop, 1990s–, Artist, American
Hitchcock, Robyn, 1980s Pop, 1980s–, Artist, British
Hollies, The, British Invasion; Merseybeat; 1960s Pop, 1960s–1980s, Artist, British
Holly, Buddy, Rock'n'Roll; Rockabilly, 1950s, Artist; Songwriter, American
Hollywood Flames, Doo-Wop, 1940s–1960s, Artist, American
Honeybunch, 1980s Pop, 1980s–1990s, Artist, American
Honeycombs, The, 1960s Pop; British Invasion, 1960s; 1980s, Artist, British
Honeys, The, Surf; 1960s Pop, 1960s; 1980s–1990s, Artist, American
Hopkin, Mary, 1960s Pop, 1960s–1970s, Artist, American
Hornets, The, Doo-Wop, 1950s, Artist, American
Hornsby, Bruce, 1980s Pop, 1980s–, Artist, American
Horton, Johnny, Rockabilly, 1950s–1960s, Artist, American
Hot Chocolate, Funk, 1970s, Artist, British
Housemartins, The, 1980s Pop, 1980s, Artist, British
Houston, Whitney, 1980s Pop, 1980s–, Artist, American
Human League, New Romantics; New Wave, 1970s–1990s, Artist, British
Hunter, Robert, 1970s Singer/Songwriters, 1970s–1990s, Artist; Songwriter, American
Hutchings, Ashley, Skiffle, 1960s–, Artist, British
Hyland, Brian, 1960s Pop, 1960s–1970s, Artist, American
Idha, 1990s Singer/Songwriters, 1990s, Artist; Songwriter, Swedish
Iglesias, Enrique, Latin; 2000s Pop, 1990s–, Artist, Spanish
Iglesias, Julio, Latin; 1970s Pop, 1970s–, Artist, Spanish
Imbruglia, Natalie, 1990s Pop; 1990s Singer/Songwriters, 1990s–, Artist; Songwriter, Australian
Impalas, The, Doo-Wop, 1950s, Artist, American
Impressions, The, 1950s Pop, 1950s–1970s, Artist, American
Indigo Girls, 1980s Singer/Songwriters, 1980s–, Artist; Songwriter, American
INXS, New Wave, 1980s–2000s, Artist, Australian
Isley Brothers, The, Funk, 1950s–, Artist, American
It's a Beautiful Day, 1960s Pop, 1960s–1970s, Artist, American
J Geils Band, Rock'n'Roll, 1970s–1980s, Artist, American
Jacks, The, Doo-Wop, 1950s–1960s, Artist, American
Jackson 5, The, 1960s Pop, 1960s–1980s, Artist, American
Jackson, Chuck, 1960s Pop, 1960s–1990s, Artist, American
Jackson, Janet, 1980s Pop, 1980s–, Artist, American
Jackson, Joe, New Wave; 1970s Pop, 1970s–, Artist, British
Jackson, Michael, 1970s Pop; Funk, 1970s–, Artist, American
Jackson, Wanda, Rockabilly, 1950s–1990s, Artist, American
Jam, The, Mod; New Wave, 1970s–1980s, Artist, British
James, Tommy, 1960s Pop, 1960s–, Artist, American
Jan and Dean, Surf; Doo-Wop; Rock'n'Roll, 1950s–1960s, Artist, American
Japan, New Romantics; New Wave, 1970s–1980s, Artist, British
Jara, Victor, Latin; 1960s Singer/Songwriters, 1960s–1970s, Artist; Songwriter, Chilean
Jaynetts, The, 1960s Pop, 1960s, Artist, American
JBs, The, Funk, 1960s–1990s, Artist, American
Jellybeans, The, 1960s Pop, 1960s, Artist, American
Jellyfish, 1990s Pop, 1990s , Artist, American
Jesus and Mary Chain, 1980s Pop, 1980s–1990s, Artist, British
Jesus Jones, 1980s Pop, 1980s–, Artist, British
JetSet, The, 1970s Pop, 1970s–1990s, Artist, British
Jetz, Jennifer Y los, Latin, 1990s–, Artist, American
Jewel, 1990s Singer/ Songwriters, 1990s–, Artist; Songwriter, American
Jive Five, The, Doo-Wop, 1950s–1990s, Artist, American
Joel, Billy, 1970s Pop, 1970s–, Artist; Songwriter, American
John, Elton, Rock'n'Roll; 1970s Singer/Songwriters; 1970s Pop, 1960s–, Artist; Songwriter, British
John's Children, Mod; British Invasion, 1960s, Artist, British
Johnston, Bruce, Surf; Rock'n'Roll, 1960s–1970s, Artist, American
Johnston, Freedy, 1990s Singer/Songwriters, 1990s–, Artist; Songwriter, American
Jones, Howard, 1980s Pop; New Wave, 1980s–, Artist, British
Jones, Marti, 1980s Pop, 1980s–, Artist, American
Jones, Tom, 1960s Pop, 1960s–, Artist, British
José José, Latin, 1970s–, Artist, Mexican
Journey, 1970s Pop, 1970s–, Artist, American
Kasenetz-Katz, 1960s Pop, 1960s–1970s, Artist, American
Keene, Tommy, 1980s Pop, 1980s–, Artist, American
Khan, Chaka, Funk, 1970s–, Artist, American
Kim, Andy, 1960s Pop, 1960s–1970s, Artist, Canadian
King, Ben E., 1960s Pop, 1960s–, Artist, American
King, Carole, 1960s Pop; 1960s Singer/Songwriters, 1960s–, Artist; Songwriter, American

THE FIFTIES POP INTRO ➡ 12 THE SIXTIES POP INTRO ➡ 24 THE SEVENTIES POP INTRO ➡ 38 THE EIGHTIES POP INTRO ➡ 44

Kinks, The, Rock'n'Roll; British Invasion, 1960s-1990s, Artist, British
Klaatu, 1970s Pop, 1970s-1980s, Artist, Canadian
Knack, The, New Wave, 1970s-, Artist, American
Knight, Gladys, 1960s Pop, 1960s-, Artist, American
Knox, Buddy, Rockabilly; Rock'n'Roll, 1950s-1980s, Artist, American
Kool and the Gang, Funk, 1960s-1990s, Artist, American
Kramer, Billy J. , Merseybeat; British Invasion, 1960s, Artist, British
Kula Shaker, Britpop, 1990s, Artist, British
La India, Latin, 1980s-, Artist, Puerto Rican
La Ley, Latin, 1990s-, Artist, Chilean
La's, The, Britpop, 1980s-, Artist, British
LaBelle, Funk, 1970s-1990s, Artist, American
Ladybug Transistor, 1990s Pop, 1990s-, Artist, American
Lagwagon, 1990s Pop, 1990s, Artist, American
Lambrettas, The, 1980s Pop; New Wave, 1980s, Artist, British
Lance, Major, 1960s Pop, 1960s-, Artist, American
Lancelot Link, 1970s Pop, 1970s, Artist, American
Lang, k. d. 1990s Singer/Songwriters, 1980s-, Artist; Songwriter, Candian
Lara, Agustin, Latin, 1920s-1960s, Artist, Mexican
Lara, Nils, Latin, 1990s, Artist, Cuban-American
Larks, The, Doo-Wop, 1950s-1970s, Artist, American
Latin Breed, Latin, 1990s, Artist, American
Lauper, Cyndi, 1980s Pop; New Wave, 1980s-1990s, Artist, American
Lecuona, Ernesto, Latin, 1920s-1960s, Artist, Cuban
Left Banke, The, 1960s Pop; Wall of Sound, 1960s-1970s, Artist, American
Lemon Pipers, The, 1960s Pop, 1960s, Artist, American
Lemonheads, The, 1980s Pop, 1980s-1990s, Artist, American
Lennon, John, Rock'n'Roll; 1960s Singer/Songwriters, 1960s-1980s, Artist; Songwriter, British
Lennox, Annie, 1980s Pop, 1980s-, Artist, British
Let's Active, 1980s Pop, 1980s, Artist, American
Level 42, 1980s Pop; 1980s Singer/Songwriters, 1980s, Artist; Songwriter, British
Lewis, Barbara, 1960s Pop, 1960s, Artist, American
Lewis, Gary, 1960s Pop, 1960s, Artist, American
Lewis, Huey, 1980s Pop, 1980s-, Artist, American
Lewis, Jerry Lee, Rock'n'Roll; Rockabilly, 1950s-, Artist, American
LFO, 1990s Pop; Boy Bands, 1990s-, Artist, American
Lightfoot, Gordon, 1960s Singer/Songwriters, 1960s-, Artist; Songwriter, Canadian
Lisa Lisa, 1980s Pop, 1980s-1990s, Artist, American
Little Anthony and the Imperials, Doo-Wop, 1950s-1970s, Artist, American
Little Casesar and the Romans, Doo-Wop, 1960s, Artist, American
Little Eva, 1960s Pop, 1960s-1980s, Artist, American
Little Richard, Rock'n'Roll, 1950s-1990s, Artist, American
Lively Ones, The, Surf, 1960s, Artist, American
Liverbirds, The, Merseybeat, 1960s, Artist, British
Loeb, Lisa, 1990s Singer/Songwriters, 1990s-, Artist; Songwriter, American
Lois, 1990s Singer/Songwriters, 1990s-, Artist; Songwriter, American
Long Riders, The, 1980s Pop, 1980s, Artist, American
Looking Glass, 1970s Pop, 1970s, Artist, American
López, Jennifer, Latin; 1990s Pop, 1990s-, Artist, American
Loud Family, 1990s Pop, 1990s-, Artist, American
Love, 1960s Pop; Wall of Sound, 1960s-1970s, Artist, American
Love, Darlene, 1950s Pop, 1950s-1970s, Artist, American
Lovin' Spoonful, The, 1960s Pop, 1960s-1970s, Artist, American
Lowe, John 'Duff', Skiffle; Rock'n'Roll, 1950s, Artist, British
Lowe, Nick, Rock'n'Roll; New Wave, 1970s-, Producer; Songwriter; Artist, British
Lulu, British Invasion; 1960s Pop, 1960s-, Artist, British
Luna, 1990s Pop, 1990s-, Artist, American
Lush, Britpop; 1980s Pop, 1980s-1990s, Artist, British
Lymon, Frankie, Doo-Wop, 1950s-1960s, Artist, American
Lymon, Frankie, and the Teenagers, Doo-Wop, 1950s-1960s, Artist, American
M People, 1990s Pop, 1990s-, Artist, British
Madness, New Wave; 1970s Pop, 1970s-, Artist, British
Madonna, 1980s Pop, 1980s-, Artist, American
Magic Hour, 1990s Pop, 1990s, Artist, American
Magnetic Fields, 1990s Pop, 1990s, Artist, American
Mamas and the Papas, The, 1960s Pop, 1960s, Artist, American
Mana, Latin, 1990s-, Artist, Spanish
Manchester, Melissa, 1970s Pop, 1970s-1990s, Artist, American
Manfred Mann, British Invasion, 1960s-, Artist, British
Manic Street Preachers, Britpop, 1990s-, Artist, British
Manilow, Barry, 1970s Pop, 1970s-, Artist, American
Mann, Aimee, 1980s Singer/Songwriters, 1980s-, Artist, American
Mann, Barry, 1960s Pop, 1960s-, Artist; Songwriter, American
Mann, Carl, Rock'n'Roll; Rockabilly, 1950s-1980s, Artist, American
Marcels, The, Doo-Wop, 1960s, Artist, American
March, Little Peggy, 1950s Pop, 1950s-1980s, Artist, American
Martha and the Vandellas, 1960s Pop, 1960s-1970s, Artist, American
Martin, George, British Invasion; Merseybeat, 1950s-1990s, Producer, British
Martin, Janis, Rockabilly; Rock'n'Roll, 1950s-1960s, Artist, American
Martin, Ricky, Latin; 1990s Pop, 1990s-, Artist, Puerto Rican
Marvellettes, The, 1960s Pop, 1960s-1970s, Artist, American
Marvelows, The, Doo-Wop, 1960s, Artist, American
Marx, Richard, 1980s Pop, 1980s-, Artist, American
Material Issue, 1980s Pop, 1980s-1990s, Artist, American
Matthews, Eric, 1990s Singer/Songwriters, 1990s, Artist; Songwriter, American
Mayfield, Curtis, Funk, 1950s-1990s, Artist, American
Mazz, Latin, 1970s-, Artist, Mexican
Mazzy Star, 1980s Pop, 1980s-1990s, Artist, American
McCartney, Paul, Rock'n'Roll; 1960s Pop, 1960s-, Artist, British
McDonald, Michael, 1970s Pop, 1970s-, Artist, American
McLachlan, Sarah, 1980s Singer/Songwriters, 1980s-, Artist; Songwriter, Canadian
Meat Loaf, 1970s Pop, 1970s-, Artist, American
Medicine, 1990s Pop, 1990s, Artist, American
Meek, Joe, 1960s Pop, 1960s, Artist, British
Melanie, 1960s Pop; 1960s Singer/Songwriters, 1960s-, Artist; Songwriter, American
Mellencamp, John Cougar, 1970s Pop, 1970s-, Artist, American
Men at Work, New Wave; 1980s Pop, 1980s-1990s, Artist, Australian
Menswear, Britpop, 1990s, Artist, British
Menudo, Latin, 1970s-, Artist, Puerto Rican
Mercury Rev, 1990s Pop, 1990s-, Artist, American
Merry-Go-Round, The, 1960s Pop, 1960s, Artist, American
Merseybeats, The, Merseybeat; British Invasion, 1960s; 1980s, Artist, British
Meters, The, Funk, 1960s-1990s, Artist, American
Michael, George, 1980s Pop, 1980s-, Artist, British
Michaels, Lee, 1970s Pop, 1970s, Artist, American
Miguel, Luis, Latin, 1980s-, Artist, Mexican
Millennium, The, 1960s Pop, 1960s, Artist, American
Miller, Steve, 1960s Pop, 1960s-1990s, Artist, American
Milli Vanilli, 1980s Pop; Europop, 1980s-1990s, Artist, German
Mindbenders, The, Merseybeat; British Invasion, 1960s, Artist, British
Minogue, Kylie, 1980s Pop; Manufactured Pop, 1980s-, Artist, Australian
Miracle Legion, 1980s Pop, 1980s-1990s, Artist, American
Modern Lovers, The, Rock'n'Roll, 1970s, Artist, American
Modest Mouse, 1990s Pop, 1990s-, Artist, American
Mojave 3, 1990s Pop, 1990s-, Artist, British
Momus, 1980s Pop, 1980s-, Artist, British
Monkees, The, 1960s Pop, 1960s-1990s, Artist, American
Monotones, The, Doo-Wop, 1950s, Artist, American
Moody Blues, The, British Invasion; Rock'n'Roll, 1960s-, Artist, British
Moonglows, The, Doo-Wop, 1950s, Artist, American
Moore, Mandy, 1990s Pop, Artist, American
Moore, Scotty, Rockabilly; Rock'n'Roll, 1950s-1990s, Artist, American
Moose, 1990s Pop, 199s-, Artist, British
Morissette, Alanis, 1990s Singer/Songwriters, 1990s-, Artist; Songwriter, Canadian
Morrison, Van, 1960s Pop, 1960s-, Artist, British
Morton, Shadow, 1950s Pop; 1950s Singer/Songwriter, 1950s-1960s, Producer, American
Motors, 1970s Pop; New Wave, 1970s-1980s, Artist, British
Move, The, Rock'n'Roll; British Invasion, 1960s-1970s, Artist, British
Muffs, The, 1990s Pop, 1990s-, Artist, American
Music Explosion, 1960s Pop, 1960s, Artist, American
MXPX, 1990s Pop, 1990s-, Artist, American
My Bloody Valentine, 1980s Pop, 1980s-1990s, Artist, Irish
Mystics, The, Doo-Wop, 1950s-1970s, Artist, American
Naked Eyes, New Romantics; New Wave, 1980s, Artist, British
Naked Raygun, 1980s Pop, 1980s-1990s, Artist, American
Nashville Teens, The, British Invasion; Rock'n'Roll, 1960s-1980s, Artist, British
Natalie Merchant, 1990s Singer/Songwriters, 1990s-, Artist; Songwriter, American
Nelson, Rick, Rock'n'Roll; Rockabilly, 1950s-1980s, Artist, American
Neon Philharmonic, The, 1960s Pop, 1960s, Artist, American
Nerves, The, 1970s Pop, 1970s-1980s, Artist, American
Neville Brothers, The, Funk, 1960s-, Artist, American
Neville, Aaron, 1960s Pop, 1960s-, Artist, American
New Edition, 1980s Pop, 1980s-1990s, Artist, American
New Kids on the Block, 1980s Pop, 1980s-1990s, Artist, American
New Order, 1980s Pop, 1980s-, Artist, British
New Radicals, The, 1990s Pop, 1990s, Artist, American
Newman, Randy, 1960s Singer/Songwriters, 1960s-, Artist; Songwriter, American
Nilsson, Harry, 1960s Pop; 1960s Singer/Songwriters, 1960s-1990s, Artist; Songwriter, American
Nomi, Klaus, Pop; New Wave, 1980s, Artist, German
NRBQ, Rock'n'Roll, 1960s-, Artist, American
***NSYNC,** 1990s Pop, 1990s-, Artist, American
Numan, Gary, New Wave; New Romantics, 1970s-, Artist, British
Nyro, Laura, 1960s Pop; 1960s Singer/Songwriters, 1960s-1990s, Artist; Songwriter, American
O'Connor, Sinéad, 1980s Pop, 1980s-, Artist, Irish
O'Jays, The, 1960s Pop, 1960s-, Artist, American
O'Sullivan, Gilbert, 1970s Pop; 1970s Singer/Songwriters, 1970s-, Artist; Songwriter, Irish
Oasis, Britpop, 1990s-, Artist, British
Ocean Colour Scene, Britpop, 1990s-, Artist, British
Ocean, Billy, 1970s Pop, 1970s-1990s, Artist, West Indian
Of Montreal, 1990s Pop, 1990s-, Artist, American
Off Broadway, 1970s Pop, 1970s-1990s, Artist, American
Offspring, The, 1980s Pop, 1980s-, Artist, American
Ohio Express, 1960s Pop, 1960s, Artist, American
Ohio Players, The, Funk, 1960s-1990s, Artist, American
Only Ones, The, New Wave, 1970s-1980s, Artist, British
Orange Juice, New Wave, 1970s-1980s, Artist, British
Orbison, Roy, 1950s Pop; Rockabilly; Rock'n'Roll, 1950s-1980s, Artist, American
Orchestral Manoeuvres in the Dark, New Wave; New Romantics, 1980s-1990s, Artist, British
Orchids, The, 1980s Pop, 1980s-1990s, Artist, British
Orioles, The, Doo-Wop, 1940s-1960s, Artist, American
Orton, Beth, 1990s Singer/Songwriters, 1990s-, Artist; Songwriter, British
Osmonds, The, 1960s Pop, 1960s-1970s, Artist, American
Pale Saints, 1980s Pop, 1980s-1990s, Artist, British
Palmer, Robert, 1970s Pop, 1970s-, Artist, British
Paper Lace, 1970s Pop, 1970s, Artist, British
Paragons, The, Doo-Wop, 1950s-1960s, Artist, American
Parker, Graham, New Wave; 1970s Singer/Songwriters, 1970s-, Artist; Songwriter, British
Parks, Van Dyke, 1960s Pop; Wall of Sound, 1960s-1990s, Artist; Producer, American
Parliament, Funk, 1970s-, Artist, American
Partridge Family, The, 1960s Pop, 1960s-1970s, Artist, American
Pastels, The, 1980s Pop, 1980s-, Artist, British
Paul Revere and the Raiders, Rock'n'Roll; 1960s Pop, 1960s, Artist, American
Pebbles, 1980s Pop, 1980s-1990s, Artist, American
Penguins, The, Doo-Wop, 1950s, Artist, American
Penn, Michael, 1980s Pop; 1980s Singer/Songwriters, 1980s-, Artist, American
Perkins, Carl, Rock'n'Roll; Rockabilly, 1950s-1990s, Artist, American
Pernice Brothers, The, 1990s Pop, 1990s-, Artist, American
Pet Shop Boys, 1980s Pop, 1980s-, Artist, British
Peter and Gordon, British Invasion; Merseybeat; 1960s Pop, 1960s, Artist, British
Petty, Tom, Rock'n'Roll, 1970s-, Artist, American
Pezband, New Wave, 1970s-1980s, Artist, American
Phillips, Esther, 1950s Pop, 1950s-1970s, Artist, American
Phillips, Sam, 1980s Pop, 1980s-, Artist, American
Pink, 1990s Pop, 1990s-, Artist, American
Pink Floyd, British Invasion, 1960s-, Artist, British
Pitney, Gene, 1960s Pop, 1960s-1980s, Artist, American
Pixies Three, The, 1960s Pop, 1960s, Artist, American
Pizzicato Five, 1980s Pop, 1980s-, Artist, Japanese
Platters, The, Doo-Wop, 1950s-1960s, Artist, American
Plimsouls, The, New Wave, 1980s-1990s, Artist, British
Police, The, New Wave, 1970s-1980s, Artist, British
Pomus, Doc, 1960s Pop, 1940s-1960s, Artist, American
Poni-Tails, The, 1950s Pop, 1950s, Artist, American
Pooh Sticks, The, 1980s Pop, 1980s-1990s, Artist, British
Poole, Brian, and the Tremeloes, British Invasion; 1950s Pop, 1950s-1980s, Artist, British
Posies, The, 1980s Pop, 1980s-, Artist, American
Powers, Johnny, Rockabilly; Rock'n'Roll, 1950s-1990s, Artist, American
Prefab Sprout, 1980s Pop, 1980s-, Artist, British
Presidents of the United States of America, 1990s Pop, 1990s-, Artist, American
Presley, Elvis, Rock'n'Roll; Rockabilly, 1950s-1970s, Artist, American
Pretenders, The, New Wave; 1970s Pop, 1970s-1990s, Artist, British
Pretty Things, The, Rock'n'Roll; British Invasion, 1960s-, Artist, British
Prewitt, Archer, 1990s Pop, 1990s-, Artist, American
Price, Lloyd, Rock'n'Roll, 1950s-1960s; 1980s, Artist, American
Prince, Funk; 1970s Pop, 1970s-, Artist, American
Psychedelic Furs, The, New Wave, 1980s-, Artist, British
Puckett, Gary, 1960s Pop, 1960s-1970s; 1990s-, Artist, American
Pulp, Britpop, 1980s-, Artist, British
Purify, James and Bobby, 1960s Pop, 1960s-1970s, Artist, American
Puya, Latin, 1990s-, Artist, Spanish
Queen, 1970s Pop, 1970s-1990s, Artist, British
Quickspace, 1990s Pop, 1990s-, Artist, British
Radiohead, Britpop, 1990s-, Artist, British
Rain Parade, 1980s Pop, 1980s, Artist, American
Raindrops, The, 1960s Pop; Doo-Wop; Rock'n'Roll, 1960s, Artist, American
Rainy Day, 1980s Pop, 1980s, Artist, American
Raitt, Bonnie, 1970s Singer/Songwriters, 1970s-, Artist, American
Ramazzotti, Eros, Latin, 1980s-, Artist, Italian
Rancid, 1990s Pop, 1990s-, Artist, American
Raparata and the Delrons, 1960s Pop, 1960s-1970s, Artist, American
Rascals, The, 1960s Pop, 1960s-1970s, Artist, American
Raspberries, The, 1970s Pop, 1970s, Artist, American
Ravens, The, Doo-Wop, 1940s-1950s, Artist, American
Razorcuts, The, 1980s Pop, 1980s-1990s, Artist, British
Records, The, 1970s Pop; New Wave, 1970s-1980s, Artist, British
Red House Painters, 1990s Pop; 1990s Singer/Songwriters, 1990s-, Artist; Songwriter, American
Redd Kross, 1980s Pop, 1980s-1990s, Artist, American
Reef, Britpop, 1990s, Artist, British
REM, 1980s Pop, 1980s-, Artist, American
Renay, Diane, 1960s Pop, 1960s, Artist, American
Replacements, The, 1980s Pop, 1980s-1990s, Artist, American
Rex, 1990s Pop, 1990s, Artist, American
Rhodes, Emitt, 1970s Singer/Songwriters; Wall of Sound; 1970s Pop, 1970s, Artist, American
Rich, Charlie, Rockabilly, 1950s-1990s, Artist, American
Richard, Cliff, 1950s Pop; Rock'n'Roll, 1950s-, Artist, British
Richie, Lionel, 1980s Pop, 1980s-, Artist, American
Ride, 1980s Pop, 1980s-, Artist, British
Righteous Brothers, The, 1960s Pop, 1960s-1990s, Artist, American
Riley, Billy Lee, Rockabilly, 1950s-1990s, Artist, American
Rip-Chords, The, Surf; Rockabilly, 1960s, Artist, American
Rivers, Johnny, 1960s Pop, 1960s-, Artist, American
Robins, The, Doo-Wop, 1940s-1950s, Artist, American
Robyn, Europop, 1990s-, Artist, Swedish
Rockpile, Rock'n'Roll; New Wave, 1970s-1980s, Artist, British
Roe, Tommy, 1960s Pop, 1960s-1970s, Artist, American
Rogers, Wayne, 1990s Pop, 1990s-, Artist, American
Rolling Stones, The, Rock'n'Roll; British Invasion, 1960s-, Artist, British
Romantics, The, 1980s Pop, 1980s-, Artist, American
Ronettes, The, 1960s Pop, 1960s, Artist, American
Ronstadt, Linda, 1960s Pop, 1960s-, Artist, American
Rooks, The, 1990s Pop, 1990s, Artist, American
Rosie and the Originals, Rock'n'Roll; 1960s Pop, 1960s, Artist, American
Ross, Diana, 1960s Pop, 1960s-, Artist, American
Roxette, Europop; 1980s Pop, 1980s-, Artist, Swedish
Rubinoos, The, 1970s Pop; New Wave, 1970s-1990s, Artist, American
Rundgren, Todd, 1970s Pop, 1970s-, Artist, American
Ryder, Mitch, Rock'n'Roll, 1960s-, Artist, American
S Club 7, 1990s Pop; Manufactured Pop, Artist, British,
Sade, 1980s Pop, 1980s-, Artist, British
Sagittarius, 1960s Pop; Wall of Sound, 1960s, Artist, American
St Christopher, 1990s Pop, 1990s-, Artist, British
Saint Etienne, Britpop, 1990s-, Artist, British
Santa Rosa, Gilberto, Latin, 1980s-, Artist, Puerto Rican
Scaggs, Boz, 1960s Pop, 1960s-, Artist, American
Schwarz, Brinsley, Rock'n'Roll, 1970s, Artist, British
Scott, Jack, Rockabilly; Rock'n'Roll, 1950s-1970s, Artist, American
Screeching Weasel, 1980s Pop, 1980s-, Artist, American
Scritti Politti, 1980s Pop; New Wave, 1980s-1990s, Artist, British
Scruffs, 1970s Pop, 1970s-1980s, Artist, American
Seal, 1990s Pop, 1990s-, Artist, British
Searchers, The, British Invasion; Merseybeat, 1960s-, Artist, British
Secada, Jon, Latin, 1990s-, Artist, Cuban
Secret Affair, New Wave, 1970s-1980s, Artist, British
Sedaka, Neil, 1950s Pop, 1950s-1990s, Artist, American
Seekers, The, 1960s Pop, 1960s-1970s, Artist, Australian
Seely, 1990s Pop, 1990s-, Artist, American
Seger, Bob, Rock'n'Roll; 1960s Singer/Songwriters, 1960s-1990s, Artist; Songwriter, American
Selena, Latin, 1980s-1990s, Artist, American
Self, Ronnie, Rockabilly, 1950s-1960s, Artist, American
Sexsmith, Ron, 1990s Singer/Songwriters, 1990s-, Artist; Songwriter, Canadian
Seymour, Phil, New Wave, 1970s-1980s, Artist, American
Shack, Britpop, 1980s-1990s, Artist, British
Shadows, The, 1960s Pop; British Invasion, 1960s-, Artist, British
Shakira, Latin; 1990s Pop, Artist, Colombian,
Shangri-Las, The, 1960s Pop; Rock'n'Roll, 1960s, Artist, American
Shannon, Del, 1960s Pop; Rock'n'Roll, 1960s-1980s, Artist, American
Shaw, Sandie, British Invasion; 1960s Pop, 1960s-1980s, Artist, British
Shear, Jules, 1980s Singer/Songwriters, 1980s-, Artist; Songwriter, American
Shed Seven, Britpop, 1990s-, Artist, British
Shep and the Limelites, Doo-Wop, 1960s, Artist, American
Sherman, Bobby, 1960s Pop, 1960s-1970s, Artist, American
Shirelles, The, 1950s Pop, 1950s-1970s, Artist, American
Shocked, Michelle, 1980s Singer/Songwriters, 1980s-1990s, Artist; Songwriter, American
Shoes, New Wave; 1970s Pop, 1970s-1990s, Artist, American
Shoestrings, 1990s Pop, 1990s, Artist, American
Shonen Knife, 1980s Pop, 1980s-, Artist, Japanese
Shop Assistants, 1980s Pop, 1980s-1990s, Artist, British
Silhouettes, The, Doo-Wop, 1950s-1960s, Artist, American
Simon and Garfunkel, 1960s Pop, 1960s-1980s, Artist, American
Simon, Carly, 1970s Singer/Songwriters, 1970s-, Artist; Songwriter, American
Simon, Paul, 1960s Singer/Songwriters, 1960s-, Artist, American
Simple Minds, New Wave; 1980s Pop, 1980s-, Artist, British
Simply Red, 1980s Pop, 1980s-, Artist, British
Simpson, Jessica, 1990s Pop, 1990s-, Artist, American
Sinatra, Nancy, 1960s Pop, 1960s-1970s; 1990s, Artist, American
Sir Douglas Quintet, The, Rock'n'Roll, 1960s-1990s, Artist, American
Skyliners, The, Doo-Wop, 1950s-1960s, Artist, American
Slave, Funk, 1970s-1990s, Artist, American
Sloan, 1990s Pop, 1990s-, Artist, Canadian
Sloan, P. F. , 1960s Pop; 1960s Singer/Songwriters, 1960s-1990s, Artist, American
Sly and the Family Stone, Funk, 1960s-1980s, Artist, American
Small Faces, The, British Invasion; Mod, 1960s-1970s, Artist, British
Smith, Warren, Rockabilly, 1950s-1980s, Artist, American
Smoke, The, Mod; British Invasion, 1960s, Artist, British
Sneakers, The, 1970s Pop, 1970s, Artist, American
Snow, Phoebe, 1970s Singer/Songwriters, 1970s-1990s, Artist; Songwriter, American
Soda Stereo, Latin, 1980s-, Artist, Spanish
Soft Boys, The, New Wave, 1970s-1980s, Artist, British
Soft Cell, New Wave; New Romantics, 1980s-1990s, Artist, British
Softies, 1990s Pop, 1990s-, Artist, American
Solis, Javier, Latin, 1940s-1960s, Artist, Mexican
Sonics, The, Rock'n'Roll, 1960s, Artist, American
Sonny and Cher, 1960s Pop, 1960s-1970s, Artist, American
Sopwith Camel, The, 1960s Pop, 1960s-1970s, Artist, American
Sorrows, The, Mod; British Invasion, 1960s, Artist, British
Soul II Soul, 1980s Pop, 1980s-1990s, Artist, British
Souther, J. D., 1970s Singer/Songwriters, 1970s-1990s, Artist; Songwriter, American
Spandau Ballet, New Romantics; New Wave; 1980s Pop, 1980s, Artist, British
Spaniels, The, Doo-Wop, 1950s-1970s, Artist, American
Spanky and Our Gang, 1960s Pop, 1960s-1970s, Artist, American
Sparklehorse, 1990s Pop, 1990s-, Artist, American
Spears, Britney, 1990s Pop; Manufactured Pop, 1990-, Artist, American
Specials, The, New Wave, 1970s-, Artist, British
Spector, Phil, Rock'n'Roll; 1960s Pop, 1960s-1970s, Producer; Songwriter; Artist, American
Spencer David Group, The, British Invasion, 1960s-1990s, Artist, British
Spice Girls, Europop; 1990s Pop, 1990s-, Artist, British
Spinanes, The, 1990s Pop, 1990s-, Artist, American
Spiritualized, 1990s Pop, 1990s-, Artist, British
Split Endz, New Wave; 1970s Pop, 1970s-1980s, Artist, New Zealander
Spongetones, The, 1980s Pop; New Wave, 1980s-, Artist, American
Springfield, Dusty, British Invasion, 1960s-1990s, Artist, British
Springfield, Rick, 1960s Pop, 1960s-1990s, Artist, Australian
Springsteen, Bruce, Rock'n'Roll; 1970s Singer/Songwriters, 1970s-, Artist; Songwriter, American
Squeeze, New Wave; 1970s Pop, 1970s-1990s, Artist, British
Squire, New Wave, 1970s-1980s, Artist, British
Stamey, Chris, 1970s Pop, 1970s-1990s, Producer; Artist, American
Stansfield, Lisa, 1980s Pop, 1980s-, Artist, British
Starr, Edwin, 1960s Pop, 1960s-1980s, Artist, American
Stealers Wheel, 1970s Pop, 1970s, Artist, British
Steampacket, Mod; British Invasion, 1960s, Artist, British
Steely Dan, 1970s Pop, 1970s-, Artist, American
Steps, 1990s Pop, 1990s-2000s, Artist, British
Stereolab, 1990s Pop, 1990s-, Artist, British
Stevens, Cat, 1960s Pop; 1960s Singer/Songwriters, 1960s-, Artist; Songwriter, British
Stevenson, B. W., 1970s Pop, 1970s-1980s, Artist, American
Stewart, Al, 1960s Singer/Songwriters, 1960s-, Artist; Songwriter, British
Stewart, Rod, Rock'n'Roll; 1960s Singer/Songwriters, 1960s-, Artist, British
Stills, Stephen, 1960s Singer/Songwriters, 1960s-1990s, Artist; Songwriter, American
Stone Poneys, 1960s Pop, 1960s-1970s, Artist, American
Stone Roses, The, Madchester; Britpop, 1980s-1990s, Artist, British
Straw, Syd, 1980s Pop, 1980s-1990s, Artist; Songwriter, American
Strawberry Alarm Clock, 1960s Pop, 1960s-1970s, Artist, American
Stray Cats, Rockabilly; New Wave, 1980s-1990s, Artist, American
Streisand, Barbra, 1960s Pop, 1960s-, Artist, American
Style Council, 1980s Pop, 1980s-, Artist, British
Suede, Britpop, 1990s-, Artist, British
Sundays, The, 1990s Pop, 1990s, Artist, British
Sunshine Company, 1960s Pop, 1960s, Artist, American
Super Friendz, The, 1990s Pop, 1990s, Artist, Canadian
Super Furry Animals, Britpop, 1990s-, Artist, British
Supergrass, Britpop; 1990s Pop, 1990s-, Artist, British
Supertramp, 1970s Pop, 1970s-, Artist, American
Supremes, The, 1960s Pop, 1960s-1970s, Artist, American
Surfaris, The, Surf, 1960s-1970s, Artist, American
Sweet, Matthew, 1980s Pop, 1980s-1990s, Artist, American
Swing Out Sister, 1980s Pop, 1980s-, Artist, British
Swinging Blue Jeans, The, British Invasion; Merseybeat, 1960s-1970s, Artist, British
Tages, The, Mod; Rock'n'Roll, 1960s, Artist, Swedish
Take That, Boy Bands; Europop, 1990s, Artist, British
Talk Talk, New Romantics; New Wave, Artist, British,
Talking Heads, New Wave; 1970s Pop, 1970s-1980s, Artist, American
Talulah Gosh, 1980s Pop, 1980s-1990s, Artist, British
Taylor, James, 1960s Singer/Songwriters, 1960s-, Artist, American
Tchaikovsky, Bram, New Wave, 1970s-1980s, Artist, British
Teenage Fanclub, 1980s Pop, 1980s-, Artist, British
Temptations, The, 1960s Pop, 1960s-1990s, Artist, American
Tex, Joe, Funk, 1960s-1980s, Artist, American
Texas, Britpop; 1980s Pop, 1980s-, Artist, British
They Might Be Giants, 1980s Pop, 1980s-, Artist, American
Thin White Rope, 1980s Pop, 1980s-1990s, Artist, American
Thompson Twins, New Wave; 1980s Pop, 1980s-1990s, Artist, British
Three Dog Night, 1960s Pop, 1960s-1980s, Artist, American
Three O'Clock, The, 1980s Pop, 1980s, Artist, American
Thunderclap Newman, 1960s Pop, 1960s, Artist, British
Tiger Trap, 1990s Pop, 1990s, Artist, American
Tigres del Norte, Los, Latin, 1970s-, Artist, Mexican
Til Tuesday, 1980s Pop; New Wave, 1980s, Artist, British
Tillotson, Johnny, 1950s Pop, 1950s-1960s, Artist, American
Tindersticks, 1990s Pop, 1990s-, Artist, British
TLC, 1990s Pop, 1990s-, Artist, American
Tokens, The, Doo-Wop, 1960s-1970s; 1990s, Artist, American
Tomorrow, 1960s Pop, 1960s, Artist, British
Toms, 1970s Pop, 1970s, Artist, American
Tornadoes, The, Surf; Rock'n'Roll, 1960s; 1990s, Artist, American
Toto, 1970s Pop, 1970s-1990s, Artist, American
Toys, The, 1960s Pop, 1960s, Artist, American
Trashmen, The, Rock'n'Roll; Surf, 1960s; 1990s, Artist, American
Travis, Britpop, 1990s-, Artist, British
Trembling Blue Stars, 1990s Pop, 1990s-, Artist, British
Tremeloes, The, British Invasion; Rock'n'Roll, 1960s-1980s, Artist, British
Troggs, The, British Invasion; Rock'n'Roll, 1960s-1980s; 1990s, Artist, British
True West, 1980s Pop, 1980s, Artist, American
Turner, Big Joe, Rock'n'Roll, 1930s-1980s, Artist, American
Turtles, The, 1960s Pop, 1960s, Artist, American
Tutone, Tommy, New Wave, 1980s-1990s, Artist, American
Twain, Shania, 1990s Pop, 1990s-, Artist, American
Twilley, Dwight, 1970s Pop, 1970s-, Artist, American
Twinkle, British Invasion, 1960s-1970s, Artist, British
Twitty, Conway, Rockabilly, 1950s-1990s, Artist, American
Ultravox, New Romantics; New Wave, 1980s-1990s, Artist, British
Undertakers, The, Merseybeat; British Invasion; Rock'n'Roll, 1960s, Artist, British
Usher, Gary, Surf, 1960s-1970s, Producer; Songwriter; Artist, American
Utopia, 1970s Pop; New Wave, 1970s-1990s, Artist, American
Vapors, The, New Wave, 1970s-1980s, Artist, American
Vaselines, The, 1980s Pop, 1980s, Artist, British
Vaughan, Ivan, Skiffle; Rock'n'Roll, 1950s, Artist, British
Vee, Bobby, 1950s Pop, 1950s-1990s, Artist, American
Vega, Suzanne, 1980s Singer/Songwriters, 1980s-, Artist; Songwriter, American
Velocity Girl, 1990s Pop, 1990s, Artist, American
Velvet Underground, The, Rock'n'Roll, 1960s-1970s; 1990s, Artist, American
Velvets, The, Doo-Wop, 1960s, Artist, American
Ventures, The, Surf; Rock'n'Roll, 1960s-, Artist, American
Verve, The, Britpop, 1990s, Artist, British
Vincent, Gene, Rock'n'Roll; Rockabilly, 1950s-1970s, Artist, American
Violent Femmes, New Wave, 1980s-, Artist, American
Vipers Skiffle Group, The, Skiffle, 1950s-1960s, Artist, British
Visage, New Romantics; New Wave, 1980s, Artist, British
Vitamin C, 1990s Pop, 1990s-, Artist, American
Vives, Carlos, Latin, 1990s-, Artist, Colombian
Wainright, Rufus, 1990s Singer/Songwriters, 1990s-, Artist; Songwriter, American
Walker Brothers, The, British Invasion; 1960s Pop, 1960s-1970s, Artist, British
Walker, Scott, 1960s Pop; Wall of Sound, 1960s-1990s, Artist, American
War, Funk, 1970s-1990s, Artist, American
Warwick, Dionne, 1960s Pop, 1960s-, Artist, American
Waterman, Pete, 1980s Pop; Manufactured Pop, 1980s-, Producer, British
Waters, Crystal, 1990s Pop, 1990s-, Artist, American
Watts 103rd Street Rhythm Band, Funk, 1960s-1970s, Artist, American
Webb, Jimmy, 1960s Singer/Songwriters; 1960sn Pop, 1960s-, Artist; Songwriter, American
Weezer, 1990s Pop, 1990s-, Artist, American
Weil, Cynthia, 1960s Pop, 1960s-, Artist, American
Weller, Paul, Britpop, 1980s-, Artist; Songwriter, British
Wells, Mary, 1960s Pop, 1960s-1980s, Artist, American
Westlife, Boy Bands; Manufactured Pop; 1990s Pop, 1990s-, Artist, Irish
Whalley, Nigel, Skiffle; Rock'n'Roll, 1950s, Artist, British
Wham!, Britpop; 1980s Pop, 1980s-1990s, Artist, British
Whigfield, Europop, 1990s-, Artist, Danish
Who, The, Rock'n'Roll; British Invasion; Mod, 1960s-, Artist, British
Wild Cherry, Funk, 1970s-1980s, Artist, American
Williams, Larry, Rock'n'Roll, 1950s-1970s, Artist, American
Williams, Maurice, Doo-Wop, 1960s-1980s, Artist, American
Williams, Otis, Doo-Wop, 1950s-1970s, Artist, American
Williams, Robbie, 1990s Pop; Britpop, 1990s-, Artist, British
Wilson, Brian, 1960s Pop, 1960s-, Artist; Songwriter; Producer, American
Wilson, Jackie, 1960s Pop, 1950s-1970s, Artist, American
Wolfie, 1990s Pop, 1990s-, Artist, American
Wonder, Stevie, Funk, 1960s-, Artist, American
Wondermints, The, 1990s Pop, 1990s-, Artist, American
Wood, Brenton, 1960s Pop, 1960s-1970s; 1990s, Artist, American
Wray, Link, Rock'n'Roll, 1950s-1990s, Artist, American
XTC, New Wave; 1970s Pop, 1970s-, Artist, British
Yardbirds, The, Rock'n'Roll; British Invasion, 1960s, Artist, British
Yaz, 1980s Pop; New Wave, 1980s, Artist, British
Yello, 1980s Pop, 1980s-, Artist, Swiss
Yellow Balloon, 1960s Pop, 1960s, Artist, American
Yellow Magic Orchestra, 1970s Pop, 1970s-1990s, Artist, Japanese
Yo La Tengo, 1980s Pop, 1980s-, Artist, American
Yonics, Los, Latin, 1980s-, Artist, Mexican
Young, Kathy, 1960s Pop, 1960s, Artist, American
Young, Will, Manufactured Pop; 2000s Pop, 2000s-, Artist, British
Youngbloods, The, 1960s Pop, 1960s-1970s, Artist, American
Yturbe, Victor, Latin, 1980s-1990s, Artist, Mexican
Yuro, Timi, 1960s Pop, 1960s-1970s, Artist, American
Zombies, The, British Invasion; 1960s Pop, 1960s, Artist, British
Zumpano, 1990s Pop, 1990s, Artist, Canadian

THE NINETIES POP INTRO ➡56 THE NOUGHTIES POP INTRO ➡66

Rock

Above

The Fender Stratocaster, first manufactured in 1954, is the quintessential rock guitar.

During the mid-1960s, America's military action in Vietnam was escalating out of control; students around the world were becoming more politically involved, civil rights and feminism were hot issues and the burgeoning youth movement was turning onto the effects of mind-bending drugs. Accordingly, certain strains of popular music melded attitude, experimentation and a social conscience, and the newly defined rock genre was the all-encompassing result.

"POP MUSIC OFTEN TELLS YOU EVERYTHING IS OK, WHILE ROCK MUSIC TELLS YOU THAT IT'S NOT OK, BUT YOU CAN CHANGE IT."

Bono

By the second half of the decade, many record buyers regarded pop as a tame and dated form of escapism for oldies and prepubescent teens. Rock, by comparison, diverted some of its listeners through psychedelic, acid-drenched terrain, yet it also provided

a heavy dose of realism, serving as an introspective outlet for a growing number of composer-performers, while expressing the concerns of those who were no longer prepared to look at the world through rose-tinted spectacles; Lennon-style granny glasses, perhaps, but ones whose lenses focussed on hard-hitting and sometimes controversial topics rather than the innocent themes of boy-loves-girl, boy-loses-girl.

Indeed, John Lennon and his fellow Beatles led the way among the handful of artists who made a successful transition from pop to rock. These included the Rolling Stones, the Yardbirds and the Who, who had already started out with a more aggressive rock sensibility. Add to them former folkies such as Bob Dylan and the Byrds, as well as emerging west coast acts like the Doors, Jefferson Airplane and the Grateful Dead, and it was clear that, echoing the musical revolution that had exploded on both sides of the Atlantic a decade earlier, rock was the new voice of youth.

STYLES

Hard Rock

Psychedelic Rock

Prog Rock

Glam Rock & Glitter

Pub Rock

Proto-Punk

British Punk

American Punk

Arena Rock

Melodic Rock

Goth Rock

Doom Metal

Heavy Metal

Speed & Thrash Metal

Death Metal & Grindcore

Madchester

Alternative/Indie Rock

Shoegazing

US Underground & Garage Rock

Progressive Metal

Black Metal

Southern Rock

Jam Bands

Grunge

Funk Metal

Riot Grrrl

Nu Metal

THE ROCK STYLE

Rock music is characterized by a heavy drum style, which provides a steady yet rhythmically varied base for the other musicians to play against, together with aggressive, riff-based guitar playing.

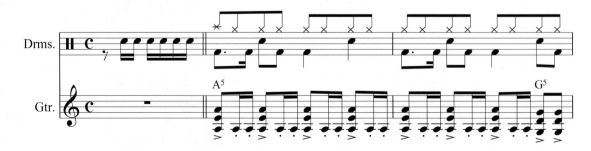

Kurt Cobain, frontman of grunge pioneers Nirvana.

Above

In the early 1970s, the Rolling Stones moved from their blues roots to a more polished rock sound. As a rock star, Mick Jagger's flamboyant stage persona became ever more exaggerated.

Page 74; Right

The most incredible – and noisiest – drummer who ever lived, Keith Moon's talents were further fuelled by his diet of pills and alcohol and his larger-than-life "Moon the Loon" personality.

Page 74; Left

Janis Joplin's incredible voice recalled the roaring blues vocals of Bessie Smith. Joplin was a big Bessie Smith fan and helped to buy her a gravestone in 1970, 33 years after she died in a car accident.

As the optimism of the Summer of Love gave way to late-1960s cynicism fueled by civil unrest, bloody anti-war riots and the hippy counterculture, so psychedelic and Eastern-tinged music were superseded by the vocal histrionics of Janis Joplin and Joe Cocker, as well as the blues-based hard rock of bands like Cream and the Jimi Hendrix Experience. Breaking with the pop tradition of producing catchy, radio- and juke-box-friendly three-minute songs, these acts indulged themselves and their followers with far lengthier numbers that were often distinguished by extended instrumental solos. In so doing, they paved the way for subsequent decades' purveyors of heavy metal, progressive, jam and arena rock. Yet even though this was largely touted as music for the mind rather than for the body, it wasn't long before the record companies tried to match the popularity of so-called supergroups like Pink Floyd and Led Zeppelin. This was attempted with what many among the press and public perceived as the formulaic, watered-down product of "corporate" acts such as Boston, Kansas and Foreigner.

In a world where Alice Cooper and David Bowie were displaying a thespian-like theatricality, innovative psychedelia transmogrified into razzle-dazzle glam rock, people were pushing for bigger sounds onstage and in the studio and concerts were being produced on an increasingly grand scale. It was as if excess was being equated with success and it was also evident that, just 20 years after the likes of Elvis Presley,

Little Richard and Jerry Lee Lewis had inspired teenagers, outraged parents and revolutionized Western culture, contemporary music had basically lost touch with its original *raison d'être*. No longer all that exciting, liberating or even controversial, it promoted an instrumental virtuosity that was completely at odds with the easy-to-play, do-it-yourself appeal of early rock'n'roll. Then along came punk rock, and for a brief time, the entire scene was treated to the shakeup that it so badly needed.

Between 1976 and 1978, the British punks in particular pumped up the aggression and devil-may-care attitude of their 1950s rock predecessors and quite literally spat in the face of authority, middle-class values and, just for the hell of it, one another. Drawing on often limited musical talents, outfits such as the Sex Pistols and the Clash channelled their anger and their energy into some blistering songs that once again helped to express the frustration and disenchantement of disaffected youth. The music was simply structured rock, and it had an invigorating effect on those who had grown tired of overblown, highly polished and, to their minds, soulless material. Nevertheless, almost as soon as the punk movement became an international phenomenon, it started to disintegrate, hijacked by kids from comfortable backgrounds who didn't have a clue about life on the streets, and undermined by some of the artists themselves, who embraced commercialism over independence when they signed with the major record labels.

Recalling how rock'n'roll had been usurped by parent-friendly pop at the start of the 1960s, the record companies attempted to broaden punk's appeal by associating numerous more mainstream acts with the genre, and the result was a watered-down hybrid that the media quickly dubbed "new wave". There were still traces of a surly attitude, and in the case of artists such as Elvis Costello there were clear musical skills, yet the spirit of punk had been laid to rest; for the next few years it would remain submerged while middle-of-the-road hard rockers and exotically-attired "new romantics" catered to the rapidly emerging MTV generation.

Once easy to categorize, rock music continued to fragment throughout the 1980s and 1990s, with heavy metal splitting off into subgenres ranging from thrash, speed and progressive to black, death and doom. At the same time, the alternative/indie tag served as a catch-all for a variety of styles, including

that whose aesthetic – if not its unmelodic structure – was closest to that of vintage rock'n'roll, and which consequently had the most far-reaching impact on the latter-day rock scene. Merging dissonant early 1970s heavy metal guitars with the hostile attitude, alienated lyrics and in-your-face music of punk, grunge first rose to prominence thanks to bands such as Soundgarden, Mudhoney and Green River, and then reached its apotheosis with the more melodic approach of Nirvana and Pearl Jam during the first half of the 1990s.

Still, history has a well-known habit of repeating itself, and in the case of the most successful rock music this is usually connected to financial considerations. For example thanks to astute marketing and the cooperation of the media, Nirvana's name became synonymous with grunge, and when the band went the way of so many others by joining the mainstream, the genre did likewise, trading in its punk sensibilities for more widespread popularity.

At the beginning of the twenty-first century, rock music keeps subdividing and reinventing itself, continually absorbing new influences from other musical spheres. Yet partly due to this mutation process, it also lacks freshness and vitality, and in the face of the cultural influence exerted by rap and hip hop, it no longer shapes opinions to the extent that it once did. Whether it can once again become the predominant force remains open to question.

Above
By the mid-1970s, rock had become sanitized and self-indulgent, as well as rather feminine. The punks stormed in and brought music back down to earth, with all the aggression and masculinity restored.

Left
For many, Queen were the epitome of rock, combining high camp with wailing guitars and over-the-top arrangements. The band's mini-opera 'Bohemian Rhapsody' is a unique piece that manages to transcend its pretensions.

HARD ROCK IS A CROSS BETWEEN ROCK'N'ROLL AND BLUES, BUT PLAYED LOUDER –
EVERYTHING ON "11" OR "ONE LOUDER", AS GUITARIST NIGEL TUFNELL IN SPOOF ROCK
BAND SPINAL TAP WOULD SAY. THE ELECTRIC GUITAR IS THE PROMINENT INSTRUMENT
IN HARD ROCK, AND MOST HARD ROCK SONGS ARE BASED ON A GUITAR "RIFF".

Hard Rock

Above
Steve Tyler of Aerosmith in
a classic image of the 1970s
rock star en route to the
next gig. Aerosmith's film
and soundtrack work has
helped to keep them in the
charts since their late-1980s
comeback.

THE classic example of a hard rock guitar riff
is the "dur, dur, dur..." beginning of Deep
Purple's 'Smoke On The Water' from *Machine
Head* (1972) – gloriously simple and yet
spectacularly effective and memorable. A "riff"
is a short series of notes, often in a low register,
repeated several times at the beginning of
a song and then repeated several times later
in the song.

The first hard rock bands such as the Jimi
Hendrix Experience, Cream and Led Zeppelin,
emerged at the end of the 1960s. It is
difficult to overestimate the contribution Jimi Hendrix made
to rock music in general and hard rock in particular by
revolutionizing the electric guitar, inventing a whole new
sonic vocabulary including harnessing distortion and feedback
for musical effect, as can be heard in 'Foxy Lady' from *Are You
Experienced?* (1967). Cream, featuring Eric Clapton on guitar
after he left John Mayall's Bluesbreakers, made onstage
jamming for rock musicians a viable proposition, as can be
heard in their rollercoaster ride through Robert Johnson's
'Crossroads' from *Wheels
Of Fire* (1968), and many
hard rock bands place an
importance on instrumental
prowess.

Formed by guitarist
Jimmy Page, Led Zeppelin
demonstrate that hard rock
is a broader arena than its
critics would have listeners

> "EVERY GREAT ROCK SONG
> HAS A GREAT RIFF, BE IT A
> SINGLE-NOTE MELODY OR
> A CHORDAL-BASED
> SEQUENCE, AND THAT'S
> PROBABLY WHAT MAKES
> IT A GREAT SONG."
>
> *Billy Corgan, Smashing Pumpkins*

believe. Their first album *Led Zeppelin* (1969) is heavily blues-
based, *Led Zeppelin II* (1969) includes the bombastic 'Whole
Lotta Love' which, along with Black Sabbath, was heavily

LEADING EXPONENTS

Deep Purple

Jimi Hendrix Experience

Cream

Led Zeppelin

Aerosmith

Queen

AC/DC

Guns 'n' Roses

HARD ROCK

The last two bars of this
hard rock chorus are followed
by one bar of riff. The guitar is
accompanied by an 8-to-the-bar
bass throughout.

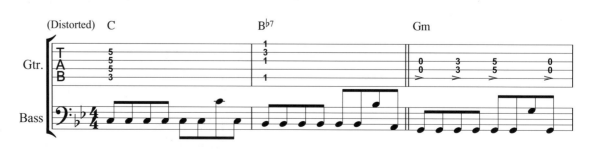

THE ROCK INTRO ➡ 74   ROCK PEOPLE A–Z ➡ 116   INSTRUMENTS A–Z ➡ 436   ROCK: PROG ROCK ➡ 82   BLUES: BLUES ROCK ➡ 175

influential on the heavy metal style. *Led Zeppelin III* (1970) shows a folky, acoustic side, and *Led Zeppelin IV* (1971) includes the famous 'Stairway To Heaven', one of the band's most ambitious and popular songs.

Swagger

Many listeners may regard hard rock and heavy metal as interchangeable, and while there is an overlap, there are also significant distinctions. Hard rock is generally blues-based and sometimes played with a swing feel or at least a certain blues-derived "swagger", whereas heavy metal, as inspired by the Zeppelin's 'Whole Lotta Love' and Black Sabbath, is far less blues-based and is more brutal.

British band Queen took hard rock to a new level of sophistication with the semi-operatic 'Bohemian Rhapsody' from *A Night At The Opera* (1975), which includes a long multi-tracked vocal section which the band were understandably unable to recreate live, followed by a pummelling riff section – contrast between delicate interludes and fortissimo ("as loud as possible") riffing is popular in hard rock bands. It certainly cannot be termed as subtle …

Interest in hard rock declined in the mid-70s as the scene became rather stale and punk rock and new wave captured listeners' attention, but was rejuvenated by American band Van Halen and their debut album *Van Halen I* (1978). Guitarist Eddie Van Halen, who played with an enthusiasm, aggression, energy and showbiz panache lacking in many hard rock bands, is credited with re-inventing the electric guitar vocabulary.

Sex And Drugs And Rock'n'Roll

Just as much of the music is bombastic and larger than life, many hard rock musicians enjoy a lifestyle of excesses – until it kills them that is. Ironically, AC/DC came back stronger than ever after the death of their singer Bon Scott, with *Back In Black* (1980). Aerosmith seemed destined for the "where are they now?" file after the ravages of drugs sidetracked their career – singer Steve Tyler survived being pronounced dead – but a collaboration with rappers Run-

DMC on Aerosmith's 'Walk This Way' in 1986 introduced them to a new generation, followed up by the highly successful *Pump* (1989). And speaking of mad, bad and dangerous to know, Guns 'n' Roses' *Appetite For Destruction* (1987) drew on 1970s rock but played with a punk attitude, making them an exciting proposition to younger listeners who had missed hard rock the first time around.

Partly because many hard rock musicians take their music and craft seriously, many hard rock bands and musicians have enjoyed long careers; at the turn of the millennium, Deep Purple, Eric Clapton from Cream, Jimmy Page and Robert Plant from Led Zeppelin, Aerosmith and AC/DC were still enjoying productive careers. This "old guard" of hard rock has been joined by newer bands such as Metallica and Pearl Jam, who made the crossover from thrash metal and grunge respectively.

Left

Eddie Van Halen started on drums, with his guitarist brother Alex, until they switched instruments. Their band, with David Lee Roth on vocals and Michael Anthony on bass, was spotted by Gene Simmons of KISS.

Below

Originally planning to call themselves the New Yardbirds, Led Zeppelin's name came from either Keith Moon or John Entwistle, who commented that the band's new, raw sound would go down like a "lead zeppelin".

Psychedelic Rock

SEVERAL MUSICAL MOVEMENTS ARE ASSOCIATED EITHER DIRECTLY OR INDIRECTLY WITH A SPECIFIC RECREATIONAL DRUG OR DRUGS; PSYCHEDELIC ROCK WENT A STEP FURTHER, AND WAS PRACTICALLY BORNE OUT OF LSD OR ACID, AS WELL AS OTHER HALLUCINOGENS INCLUDING PEYOTE, MESCALINE AND EVEN MARIJUANA.

Above

Love's Forever Changes *is a psychedelic masterpiece, with inspired arrangements and delicious, dark undertones.*

MUCH psychedelic rock attempts to recreate the mind expanding and awareness-enlarging sensations of an acid trip – the counter-culture of the 1960s put great emphasis on expanding one's mind through mind-altering drugs. So, musicians made use of the burgeoning new studio technology available and used effects such as the fuzzbox on guitars and exotic instruments such as the sitar, and broke away from traditional song structures of intro, verse, chorus, verse, chorus, middle eight, verse, final chorus. They also looked further afield for inspiration and forms of expression, to jazz or Indian music, for example. The Beatles' George Harrison became interested in the sitar that was used for an Indian restaurant scene in the Beatles film *Help!*, which led to the band becoming interested in Eastern culture.

The Yardbirds made a tentative exploration of this area with their 'Heartful Of Soul' single in 1965. In an effort to expand their sound and blend east and west in a kind of cross-cultural melting pot, the band drafted in a sitar player to play the song's instrumental hook. Unfortunately, the hapless sitar player was so used to playing complex eastern rhythms, that he couldn't get the hang of the basic rock beat, so guitarist Jeff Beck imitated the sound of the sitar with a fuzzbox.

> "THE PSYCHEDELIC ETHIC...RUNS THROUGH THE MUSICAL MAINSTREAM IN A STILL CURRENT. MUSICAL IDEAS ARE PASSED FROM GROUP TO GROUP LIKE A JOINT."
>
> *Richard Goldstein*

This anecdote neatly illustrates the problem with some psychedelic rock – mixing disparate musical elements may sound fine on paper, but in practice it might not work. Consequently, when it works psychedelic rock can represent

LEADING EXPONENTS

The Yardbirds
The Byrds
The Beatles
The Rolling Stones
The Doors
The Move
Jefferson Airplane
Love
Pink Floyd
The Moody Blues
Grateful Dead
Spaceman 3
Spiritualized
Country Joe McDonald
& Fish

PSYCHEDELIC ROCK

Psychedelic Rock is characterized by surreal lyrics and ethereal melodies that aspire to re-create the out-of-body experiences caused by psychedelic drugs.

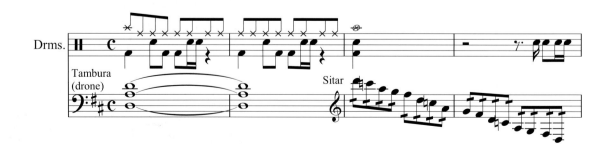

THE ROCK INTRO ➡ 74   ROCK PEOPLE A-Z ➡ 116   INSTRUMENTS A-Z ➡ 436   COUNTRY: COUNTRY ROCK ➡ 209   FOLK: FOLK ROCK ➡ 235

rock music at its most ambitious and breathtaking, but when it doesn't work it can appear incompetent, over-ambitious and foolhardy.

One of the first psychedelic records, the Byrds' 'Eight Miles High' single (1966), saw the band's guitarist Roger McGuinn attempting to emulate jazz saxophonist John Coltrane and also displaying an Indian influence in his rambling improvisation. The lyrics were assumed to be drug-inspired – an accusation often aimed at the psychedelic bands – although the Byrds denied this.

John Lennon attempted to recreate the mood of an LSD trip on the Beatles' 'Tomorrow Never Knows' from *Revolver* (1966), with multiple tape loops, a processed lead vocal, backwards guitar solo and lyrics inspired by LSD guru Timothy Leary and *The Tibetan Book of the Dead*; George Harrison contributed a sitar part. The Rolling Stones' 'Paint It Black' single (1966) used a sitar to great effect and their fleeting psychedelic incarnation culminated in *Their Satanic Majesties Request* (1967).

The Summer Of Love

1967, the so-called "Summer of Love", was an important year for psychedelic rock in America and Britain. In the US, the Doors released their self-titled debut album; singer Jim Morrison's highly poetic lyrics, keyboard player Ray Manzarek's hypnotic organ and the flamenco-trained guitarist Robbie Kreiger's improvizations proved an intoxicating mix. Fellow Americans Jefferson Airplane's *Surrealistic Pillow* featured 'White Rabbit' with its *Alice In Wonderland*-like lyrics and flamenco-influenced, moody introduction. Led by Arthur Lee, Love's *Forever Changes* included the classic 'Alone Again Or'; the album was not commercially successful, but it is regularly acclaimed by critics.

On the other side of the Atlantic, Pink Floyd's debut album, *The Piper At The Gates Of Dawn*, written mostly by Syd Barrett, revealed an English sense of whimsy on 'Bike', spacey, sci-fi rock on 'Astronomy Domine' and a taste for almost avant-garde experimentation on 'Interstellar Overdrive'. The Move captured the psychedelia of London's underground scene with 'I Can Hear the Green Grass Grow', conveying the experience of a marijuana high. The Beatles embraced the psychedelic spirit of the times on *Sgt Pepper's Lonely Hearts Club Band*, a loosely-themed concept album, as exemplified in 'Lucy in the Sky with Diamonds' – John Lennon denied that the song was about LSD, but the dreamy and surreal lyrics clearly reflect the LSD experience, whether intentional or not. For 'A Day In The Life' on the same album, a full symphony orchestra was asked to

start from each musician's lowest note, then play up to their highest note in a non-synchronized manner in an attempt to simulate the effect of a drug rush.

One of the longest lasting psychedelic bands was the Grateful Dead, whose free-form live shows earned them an obsessive cult following. Improvization was a big part of the Dead's musical make-up, as can be heard on the *Live/Dead* album (1969) which features 'Dark Star', a song never performed the same way twice.

Overall, psychedelic rock was a relatively short-lived phenomenon with bands either splitting up or moving onto new musical territory such as the Byrds, who moved onto country rock with *Sweetheart of the Rodeo* (1968), and Pink Floyd who succeeded in making progressive rock commercially successful with their best-selling *Dark Side Of The Moon* (1973).

Neopsychedelia

Psychedelic rock was largely a 1960s phenomenon, although in Britain Jason Pearce led a valiant one-man crusade for psychedelic rock in the late-1980s and 1990s, first with the ramshackle Spaceman 3, whose chaotic and overwhelming blend of neopsychedelia can be heard on *Playing With Fire* (1989), then as the leader of Spiritualized with the altogether more accomplished and critically acclaimed *Ladies And Gentlemen We Are Floating In Space* (1997). Psychedelic rock's most notable revival, however, occurred with the rise in popularity in the 1990s of trance, a style of dance music of which it is considered to be a forerunner.

WORLD: INDIA ➡ 284   DANCE: TRANCE ➡ 321

Left
Artwork played an important role in psychedelic rock, with record sleeves and concert posters becoming increasingly colourful and ornate. This example is a poster for the Monterey Pop Festival.

Below
George Harrison's forays into Indian music helped to popularize the psychedelic sound and look. He is shown here with Ravi Shankar, who taught Harrison the rudiments of sitar playing.

"TO BOLDLY GO WHERE NO BAND HAS GONE BEFORE ..." COULD HAVE BEEN THE MOTTO OF THE PROGRESSIVE ROCK BANDS, TAKING ROCK MUSIC TO PLACES IT HAD NEVER BEEN IN TERMS OF HARMONY AND STRUCTURE. THEY TEND TO FAVOUR LONG SONGS WITH LENGTHY INSTRUMENTALS, GUITAR AND KEYBOARDS BEING THE FOREMOST INSTRUMENTS, WITH AN EMPHASIS ON INSTRUMENTAL DEXTERITY AND VIRTUOSITY.

Prog Rock

Above

King Crimson, whose sound was described by one critic as "organized anarchy". Constant personnel changes within the band have left Robert Fripp as the only original member.

MANY prog rock songs have different sections or parts, like a classical symphony. For example, Yes's 'Starship Trooper' from *The Yes Album* (1971) has three different sections – Life Seeker, Disillusion and Würm. Essentially, prog rock is music of the mind rather than music of the body.

Inspired by the psychedelic scene of the late-1960s, bands such as the Nice, the Moody Blues and Procol Harum started writing a strain of music influenced by classical and symphonic sounds and musical structures, producing a form of symphonic rock which laid the foundation for progressive rock. This can be heard in Procul Harum's debut single and best-known song, 'A Whiter Shade of Pale' (1967) in which the chord progression was influenced by J. S. Bach.

The late-1960s saw the beginnings of two of the longest lasting progressive rock bands, King Crimson and Yes, who took instrumental virtuosity and songwriting structures to new levels. King Crimson's stunning debut *In The Court Of The Crimson King* (1969), which includes their trademark song '20th Century Schizoid Man', not only has the instrumental prowess associated with prog rock, but also

rocks harder than the other prog rockers. After distinctly psychedelic beginnings, Yes forged their unique identity on *Close To The Edge* (1972), with album side length "suites" enabling all five band members to flex their musical muscles.

Some prog rockers put on theatrical stage shows, and Genesis' then-lead singer Peter Gabriel would wear bizarre

"HISTORICALLY MUSICIANS HAVE FELT REAL HURT IF THE AUDIENCE EXPRESSED DISPLEASURE. WE DIDN'T DO THAT. WE TOLD THE AUDIENCE TO GET F****D."

Frank Zappa

LEADING EXPONENTS

Procol Harum

The Moody Blues

Yes

King Crimson

Genesis

Emerson, Lake & Palmer

Pink Floyd

Frank Zappa

Marillion

Dream Theatre

Soft Machine

PROG ROCK

Classical tunes played with rock instrumentation combine to produce the signature sound of progressive rock.

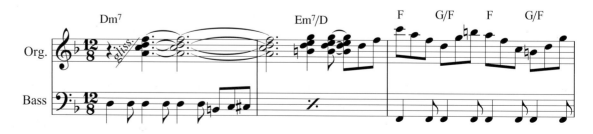

THE ROCK INTRO ➡ 74   ROCK PEOPLE A-Z ➡ 116   INSTRUMENTS A-Z ➡ 436   ROCK: PSYCHEDELIC ROCK ➡ 80

costumes as a visual extension of the music.
Genesis made the transition to mainstream
rock/pop band in the 1980s, but in the early
1970s they were a prog rock band, as can be
heard on *Foxtrot* (1972). Three already established
musicians, Emerson, Lake and Palmer formed the
first prog rock "supergroup" (a group formed by
members who had already made a name for
themselves in other groups) and their reworking
of Mussorgsky's *Pictures at an Exhibition* (1972)
took the combination of classical and rock to its
logical extreme with a band reworking a piece of
classical music.

Pink Floyd started their career as a psychedelic
band, then after songwriter Syd Barrett left they
moved more towards progressive rock, although
Barrett's replacement David Gilmour brought a
distinct blues influence, something rarely found in
progressive bands. Pink Floyd managed to make
prog rock more accessible with their best-selling
album *Dark Side of the Moon* (1973), curbing the
excesses of the genre.

To their critics, the prog rockers were
overblown and self-indulgent, as epitomized by
Yes's notorious triple concept album *Tales of
Topographic Oceans* (1974), or quite simply BOFs
("boring old farts"); they were also perceived as
being elitist since it required considerable musical
proficiency to play prog rock. And for every
action there's a reaction; running alongside prog
rock, pub rock took music back to its roots,
offering a more earthy alternative, then punk
rock spat in prog rock's face and attempted to
destroy it altogether.

Like Punk Never Happened

While punk gained all the headlines and sidelined
the prog rockers in the mid-1970s, it seems you
couldn't keep a prog rocker down, and many of
the progressive rock groups survived to enjoy
far longer careers than the punks. Despite almost ever-
changing line-ups, both King Crimson and Yes have continued
to record and tour, King Crimson's *THRAK* (1995) showing
that they are still a creative force with something to say.

Almost meriting a musical category of his own, Frank
Zappa started his musical career in the mid-1960s with *Freak
Out* (1966) and continued writing and recording until his
death in 1993. As with prog rock, Zappa's music drew from
a multitude of musical styles, often demanding the highest

instrumental standards from an ever-changing band of
musicians, but unlike the prog rockers his lyrics were often
humorous or highly sarcastic.

In the 1980s, UK band Marillion bravely flew the
prog rock flag, defiantly swimming against the tide, with
their *Misplaced Childhood* (1985) concept album even
spawning a couple of hit singles. In the 1990s, US band
Dream Theatre introduced prog rock to a new, younger
generation, played with impeccable musicianship by
highly-schooled instrumentalists.

Above

*Pink Floyd made some of the
most accessible prog rock
music. Their grandiose* The
Wall *(1979) provided them
with their first number one
single, a lavish tour and a
spin-off film.*

Left

*Yes's Rick Wakeman's trade-
mark sound came from the
Mellotron and MiniMoog.*

A LARGELY BRITISH MOVEMENT, GLAM ROCK AND GLITTER WERE HIGHLY POPULAR IN THE EARLY 1970S – SO POPULAR THAT ONE ARTIST, MARC BOLAN, WAS GIVEN HIS OWN TV SERIES. INSPIRED BY EARLY ROCK'N'ROLL AND BUBBLEGUM POP, GLAM ROCK WAS FUN, CATCHY AND MELODIC, PLAYED WITH CRUNCHY, DISTORTED GUITARS, WITH THE MUSICIANS DRESSING UP IN OUTRAGEOUS AND ANDROGYNOUS COSTUMES.

Glam Rock & Glitter

Above

Suzi Quatro was discovered in her native Detroit by British record producer Mickie Most, who was working there with Jeff Beck. Suzi's cool, leather-clad image landed her a role in the TV sitcom Happy Days.

WHILE Britain has a long history of pantomime dames and drag queens, America was slightly wary of glam rock's blurring of gender identity, which partly explains why it never took off as strongly in the US. Similarities can be found between the British glam rockers and American hard rockers KISS, especially in the dressing-up and make-up department. KISS started their career with flamboyant costumes and theatrical face-painting in the mid-1970s and famously didn't reveal their faces, at least not to the wider public, until the *Lick It Up* album in 1983. For the glam rockers, almost as much effort and creativity went into the appearance as the music, and while contemporary artists such as Elton John and Paul McCartney & Wings may not have been influenced by the music, they were certainly inspired by the fashion.

Starting out as folk rockers, T Rex, largely Marc Bolan's group, set the glam rock ball rolling with *Electric Warrior* (1971) and *The Slider* (1972) – fun, trashy rock'n'roll with catchy hooks and often inane lyrics, with T Rex refusing to take themselves too seriously. Although glam rock and glitter are essentially the same thing, the "glitter" bands are generally the more glitzy, trashy and throwaway bands, as inspired by T Rex – Slade, Sweet, Suzi Quatro and Gary Glitter.

After flirting briefly with a skinhead image, Slade's *Slayed?* (1972)

> ## "BOWIE HAS SOLD HIS TALENT FOR FAME, FORTUNE AND A WHITE FUR RUG; A ONCE CREATIVE ARTIST IS NOW SLIPPING ON WOOLWORTH'S GLITTER; SHAMELESS, BOWIE HAS BECOME A SHOWBIZ STAR."
>
> *Simon Frith*

established them as bona fide glam rockers, complete with foot-stomping beats and rousing, anthemic choruses. Slade's gimmick was to mis-spell song titles, such as 'Mama Weer All Crazee Now', thus endearing them to the nation's schoolkids, much to the horror of their teachers. For better or worse, Slade still get airplay in Britain every year by unimaginative DJs who insist on playing 'Merry Christmas Everybody' come Christmas time, their saving grace being singer Noddy Holder who possessed one of the classic British rock voices.

Grannie's Old Clothes

Sweet adopted the glam dressing up, but, with the possible exception of the singer, ended up looking like bricklayers dressed up in their granny's old clothes – not a pretty sight, it must be said. Fortunately, they sounded better than they looked and after ditching the songwriting team who penned their early hits, *Desolation Boulevard* (1974) is the band at their peak and includes the hit 'Ballroom Blitz'. Sweet were a significant influence on the New Wave Of British Heavy Metal band Def Leppard.

LEADING EXPONENTS

T Rex
Slade
Sweet
Suzi Quatro
Gary Glitter
David Bowie
Mott the Hoople
Roxy Music
Queen

GLAM ROCK & GLITTER

Glam rock's electronic sound is produced by playing a steady funk-style backing, with rock guitar riffs over the top.

THE ROCK INTRO ➡ 74   ROCK PEOPLE A-Z ➡ 116   INSTRUMENTS A-Z ➡ 436   THE SEVENTIES POP INTRO ➡ 38

Despite all the experimentation with sexual identity, glam rock was very much a male-dominated genre, with one notable exception – Suzi Quatro. Singer and bass player Quatro is seen by some admirers as a proto-riot grrrl, although her music has none of the sexual politics and feminism championed by the riot grrrl movement. Famously leather-clad and diminutive, Quatro's self-titled 1973 album includes the hit single 'Can the Can'.

Real name Paul Gadd, Gary Glitter's *Glitter* (1972) consolidated his position as one of the leaders of the era, although musically he was even more of more of a singles artist than the other glitter acts, and is thus best represented on *Rock'n'Roll: Gary Glitter's Greatest Hits* (1998). Glitter was backed by – who else? – the Glitter Band, who went on to have their own successful career. After suffering bankruptcy in the 1980s and 1990s, Gary Glitter revived his live act, although his musical career was brought to an abrupt halt after he was convicted for paedophile offences in the late-1990s.

Multi instrumentalist Roy Wood, one of the more eccentric and prolific British performers on the glam/glitter rock scene in the early 1970s, led the band Wizzard while also enjoying a solo career. Wood drew inspiration from a host of musical genres such as 1950s rock'n'roll, classical music and psychedelia. Wizzard had a hit with 'I Wish It Could Be Christmas Every Day' in 1973, which hasn't quite had the same longevity as Slade's Christmas hit, although it is not far behind.

Art School

Alongside the glitter bands, David Bowie and Roxy Music took a more arty perspective on glam rock. Bowie revelled in the theatrical aspect of glam rock and reinvented himself with a new persona, Ziggy Stardust, as heard on the album *The Rise And Fall Of Ziggy Stardust* (1972), with his backing band the Spiders From Mars. Bowie revived the career of hard rockers Mott the Hoople by giving them a glam rock makeover on *All The Young Dudes* (1972), producing the album and writing the well-known title track. Having lived through and weathered numerous rock movements, at the turn of the millennium rock chameleon David Bowie remains a creative force.

Roxy Music successfully combined their art-rock leanings with a glam rock setting, and showed that avant-garde and highly experimental ideas can work in a three minute pop song context, as on *For Your Pleasure* (1973). This album was the last to be made with Brian Eno, who represented the experimental side of the band, and thus subsequent albums had a more conventional feel to them. Roxy Music singer Bryan Ferry released solo albums while still in the band, then pursued a more sophisticated and adult-pop sound after the demise of Roxy Music in 1983.

Although not primarily thought of as a glam rock act, Queen's self-titled debut album (1973) has one platform-shod foot firmly in the glam rock school. Bombastic and camp, Queen also showed themselves to be far more versatile and multi-dimensional than any of the other glam acts. Although very much an early 1970s phenomenon, a glam rock influence can be seen in several 1990s British bands such as Gay Dad, Suede and Kenickie. Ex-Felt member Lawrence Hayward formed Denim in 1990 as a tribute to glam rock, their debut album *Back in Denim* (1992) including a song entitled 'The Osmonds' after the US pop-singing family who flirted with glam rock, and contributions from two ex-members of the Glitter Band.

Left
Marc Bolan and T Rex never made it big in America, but their runaway success in Britain, with songs such as 'Ride A White Swan' and 'Get It On' led to a wave of popularity termed "T Rextacy" by the press.

Below
With Noddy Holder's powerful vocals and guitarist Dave Hill's equally arresting dress sense, Slade were one of the most successful British chart bands of the 1970s, scoring seventeen consecutive Top Twenty hits.

A BRITISH PHENOMENON, PUB ROCK WAS A REACTION TO THE SELF-INDULGENCE OF THE PROGRESSIVE ROCKERS AND THE VAIN PREENING OF THE GLAM ROCKERS. THE PUB ROCK BANDS DREW FROM A VARIETY OF ROOTS-MUSIC STYLES, SUCH AS BLUES, FOLK AND COUNTRY, WITH THE FOLK INFLUENCE DATING BACK TO THE UK FOLK-ROCKERS OF THE LATE-1960S SUCH AS FAIRPORT CONVENTION.

Pub Rock

Above
Ian Dury's debut album New Boots And Panties!! *showcased his sharp, witty lyrics and funky pub rock sound, and contained character songs such as 'Billericay Dickie' and 'Clevor Trevor'.*

> "YOU DON'T HAVE TO BE A MUSICIAN TO PLAY ROCK'N'ROLL. YOU'VE JUST GOT TO LOVE IT AND WANT TO PLAY IT."
>
> *Lee Brilleaux, Dr Feelgood*

Right
Dr. Feelgood's original line up included the menacing vocals of Lee Brilleaux and the Mick Green-styled guitar prowess of Wilko Johnson.

LEADING EXPONENTS

Eggs Over Easy
Brinsley Schwarz
Bees Make Honey
Ace
Chilli Willi & the Red
 Hot Peppers
Ducks Deluxe
Dr Feelgood
Ian Dury
Eddie & the Hot Rods
The 101'ers
Elvis Costello
Nick Lowe
Graham Parker

THE beginning of pub rock is largely credited to a little-known American band, Eggs over Easy, gigging at the Tally-Ho pub in London with a mixture of original songs and cover material which inspired other bands and, just as importantly, encouraged other pubs to book live bands on what was soon to become a vibrant gig circuit.

Opening Time

Brinsley Schwarz's mixture of folk, prog rock and hippie affectations on their self-titled debut album in 1970 sounds even worse on record than on paper, and along with a disastrous showcase gig in the US it effectively ended all interest there. Returning to the UK, Schwarz honed their sound culminating with *Nervous on the Road* (1972), a pub rock masterpiece that helped pave the way for fellow pub rockers Bees Make Honey, Ace, Chilli Willi and the Red Hot Peppers and Ducks Deluxe. Emerging towards the end of the pub rock era, Dr. Feelgood's lively and aggressive R&B sound made them an exciting live band, who managed to capture that energy on their debut album *Down By The Jetty* (1975). Eddie & the Hot Rods were similarly energetic and had a hit single with 'Do Anything You Wanna Do' in 1977.

Last Orders At The Tally-Ho

The music press and many listeners turned their attention to punk in the latter half of the 1970s and the pub rock bands were unable to compete. Most faded into obscurity or disbanded, the notable exception being Dr. Feelgood. Band members left and were replaced until the only remaining original member was singer Lee Brilleaux. Brilleaux died from cancer in 1994 but the band has carried on.

Pub rock had a significant influence on punk rock. The Clash's frontman, the late Joe Strummer, began his musical career with pub rockers the 101'ers. Ex-Brinsley Schwarz songwriter Nick Lowe became the in-house producer with the Stiff record label, one of the foremost punk labels working with the Damned, the Pretenders and Elvis Costello, before going on to enjoy a successful solo career.

Singer/songwriters Elvis Costello and the late Ian Dury straddle the divide between pub rock and punk rock, albeit a more restrained and literate side of punk rock, and their pub rock roots can be heard on their respective debut albums *My Aim Is True* (1977) and *New Boots And Panties!!* (1977). These artists were strongly influenced by Van Morrison and the Rolling Stones, influences rendered very unfashionable by punk rock. Fellow singer/songwriter Graham Parker's debut album *Howlin' Wind* gained critical acclaim but unlike Costello and Dury he was sidelined by punk rock.

PUB ROCK

In pub rock the snare drum plays a pattern normally associated with the hi-hat or ride cymbals, accompanied by a punchy bassline.

THE ROCK INTRO ➡74 ROCK PEOPLE A-Z ➡116 INSTRUMENTS A-Z ➡436 ROCK: BRITISH PUNK ➡88 FOLK: FOLK ROCK ➡235

Proto-Punk

PROTO-PUNK BANDS, LIKE ALL "PROTO" GENRES, ARE BY DEFINITION ONLY IDENTIFIED RETROSPECTIVELY AND GENERALLY SHARE SUBVERSIVE AND ANTI-ESTABLISHMENT ATTITUDES. ALTHOUGH PUNK ROCK WAS PRIMARILY A BRITISH PHENOMENON, THERE WERE SEVERAL NOTABLE AMERICAN PUNK BANDS AND ITS MUSICAL ROOTS LIE MORE WITH THESE AMERICAN BANDS THAN WITH BRITISH BANDS.

THE energy of pub rockers like Dr. Feelgood and Eddie & the Hot Rods may be heard in the punk bands but they lacked the anger, nihilism, and artistic and political overtones.

Although the Velvet Underground's debut album *The Velvet Underground & Nico* (1967) didn't sell huge amounts on its release, its impact on non-mainstream forms of rock music was significant, with its disregard for conventional song structures and lyrics that dealt head-on with sex and drugs. The roots of punk rock, goth rock and glam rock can all be traced back to this album.

Anti-Establishment

The MC5 gathered a loyal following on the strength of their exciting and anarchic live performances, so much so that they elected to record a live show for their debut album, *Kick out the Jams* (1969). Beginning with singer Rob Tyners rabble rousing cry of "Kick out the jams, motherfuckers", the early use of the "mf" word – nearly 30 years before it became commonplace on rap records – led to some shops refusing to stock the record. Elektra Records had to release an alternative version with "brothers and sisters" replacing "motherfuckers". With their radical anti-establishment politics, the MC5 became the figurehead for the White Panther Party whose manifesto included "an assault on the culture by any means necessary, including dope and fucking in the streets."

Self-Destruction

You won't find an anti-establishment manifesto with Iggy and the Stooges, but they certainly helped themselves to the sex and drugs. A band with one finger permanently on the self-destruct button, singer Iggy Pop would cut himself onstage or smear himself with peanut butter or raw meat – then launch himself into the audience. *Raw Power* (1973) reveals a wild, wired and weird band, with raw and spontaneous music and lyrics, thanks to the band's habit of improvising in the studio.

And speaking of self-destruction, the New York Dolls' second album *Too Much Too Soon* (1974) became a self-fulfilling prophesy and the band split shortly afterwards, despite hapless manager Malcolm McLaren's attempts to promote the band to a wider audience. McLaren would put his experience to use afterwards as the infamous manager of the Sex Pistols.

Having established herself as a poet, Patti Smith released her debut album *Horses* (1975) to critical acclaim, and revealed a poet's sensibilities with her imaginative use of language in loosely constructed song forms.

Smith described her music as, "three chord rock merged with the power of the word". Her debut single 'Piss Factory' (1974) describes the boredom of working in a factory, something the punks could relate to.

Britain was not without its proto-punk bands. The Troggs had a hit single in the UK in 1966 with 'Wild Thing', based on a three chord riff and the archetypical example of their "caveman rock". The Kinks also had a knack for primitive, aggressive guitar riff based songs such as 'You Really Got Me' and 'All Day And All of the Night', the latter being covered by punk band the Stranglers.

Above

Distinctive artwork adorns Velvet Underground's album, emphasizing Pop Art roots and Andy Warhol connections.

> ## "WE'RE MUSICAL PRIMITIVES."
> *John Cale, Velvet Underground*

Below

Iggy Pop's legendary onstage performances were always controversial and caused one UK television show, So It Goes, to be withdrawn permanently after a bout of particularly colourful language.

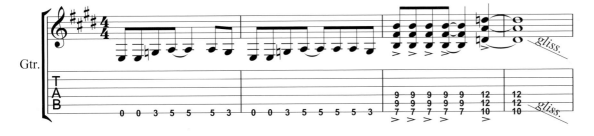

Gtr.

PROTO-PUNK

Proto-punk tunes feature heavily distorted guitar riffs and crash chords, frenetic drums and screaming vocals.

LEADING EXPONENTS

The Velvet Underground
The MC5
Iggy & the Stooges
New York Dolls
Patti Smith
The Troggs

THE ROCK INTRO ➡ 74   ROCK PEOPLE A-Z ➡ 116   INSTRUMENTS A-Z ➡ 436   ROCK: AMERICAN PUNK ➡ 90

British Punk

PUNK EXPLODED ON TO THE STAGNANT BRITISH MUSIC SCENE IN THE MID-1970S WITH SHORT, FAST SONGS, PLAYED WITH MAXIMUM ENERGY AND OFTEN FUELLED BY ANGRY LYRICS. A MUSICAL AND SOCIAL PHENOMENON, PUNK WAS A REACTION TO THE INDULGENCE OF GLAM ROCK BANDS, AND THE PERCEIVED ELITISM OF THE OFTEN HIGHLY MUSICALLY PROFICIENT MUSICIANS WHO PLAYED IN THE PROG ROCK BANDS.

IT was also a reaction to the perceived artificialness of the "corporate rock" manufactured supergroups such as Boston, Kansas and Foreigner, and the perceived slickness of the equally artificial disco scene. Socially, punk appealed to the disenfranchised British youth who felt at best bored and at worst alienated by what British society had to offer them – unemployment or dead end jobs.

Looking back from the perspective of a more permissive and (slightly!) more tolerant society, it is difficult to believe the profoundly shocking effect punk had on the nation's morals. Arguably the last musical movement to have such a huge social impact, British TV shows would earnestly debate the "evils" of punk rock. Goaded into swearing on live daytime television, Sex Pistols guitarist Steve Jones recalled this turning point: "It was hilarious, it was one of the best feelings, the next day, when you saw the paper. You thought, 'Fucking hell, this is great!' From that day on, it was different. Before then, it was the music: the next day, it was the media."

"THIS IS A CHORD. THIS IS ANOTHER. THIS IS A THIRD. NOW FORM A BAND."

Sideburns fanzine

Above

Johnny Rotten got the gig as vocalist for the Sex Pistols after he was spotted with green hair, wearing an "I Hate Pink Floyd" T-shirt.

No Future

At the height of their fame – or infamy – the Sex Pistols with Johnny Rotten (aka John Lydon) as their lead singer, had a number one single 'God Save the Queen' during the Queen's Silver Jubilee, which was banned by the BBC on the grounds of its allegedly offensive lyrics. The opening of 'God Save the Queen' bears the hallmarks of classic rock'n'roll, albeit with a louder, faster and more aggressive character. Its anti-establishment lyrics and "no future" outro sum up the Sex Pistols' outlook perfectly: bleak and nihilistic. Fittingly, the Sex Pistols imploded shortly after releasing their debut album, *Never Mind The Bollocks, Here's The Sex Pistols* (1977).

The Clash, fronted by the late Joe Strummer, were equally exciting but offered a more positive agenda, particularly with

LEADING EXPONENTS

The Sex Pistols
The Clash
The Jam
The Stranglers
The Damned
The Buzzcocks
Elvis Costello
The Adverts
X-Ray Spex

BRITISH PUNK

The raw aggression of punk is created by physically striking the guitar hard, to produce crashing chords. Most tunes are restricted to three chords and basic melodies.

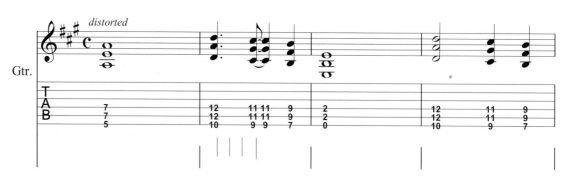

THE ROCK INTRO ➡ 74   ROCK PEOPLE A–Z ➡ 116   INSTRUMENTS A–Z ➡ 436   POP: SKIFFLE ➡ 22   POP: MOD ➡ 36   POP: NEW WAVE ➡ 48

their anti-racism messages. The Clash were able to develop their sound from the impressive frenetic self-titled debut in 1977, culminating in *London Calling* (1979), which reveals influences as diverse as rockabilly, reggae, ska and hard rock.

Several other bands offered significant variations on the stereotypical manic punk three chord thrash. The Jam had an altogether smarter image than the punks, and *In The City* (1977) reveals 1960s mod leanings. After the Jam split up, singer Paul Weller went on to enjoy a successful solo career, although his solo offerings do not reflect his punk and mod roots with the Jam and he remains unwilling to play songs from that era. The Stranglers, significantly older than the other punk bands, offered a psychedelic tinge, as can be heard on the groovy organ solo on the title track of *No More Heroes* (1977). Other notable punk debuts included the Damned's *Damned, Damned, Damned* (1977) and the Buzzcocks' *Spiral Scratch* (1977). The Damned had a distinctly less political agenda than, for example, the Clash, and came across as drunken pranksters out for a laugh, although 'New Rose' and 'Neat Neat Neat' from their debut are classics of the punk genre – short, energetic and highly memorable. Inspired by the Sex Pistols, the Buzzcocks mixed punk and pop, with occasionally humorous lyrics.

Elvis Costello started his career on the pub rock circuit, then successfully jumped ship to get lumped in with the punk generation, although lyrically and musically he was considerably more sophisticated, as demonstrated on *My Aim Is True* (1977). Consequently the media labelled him "new wave", a loosely-defined genre for artists less hard-edged than the punk rockers.

DIY

Punk's lasting musical legacy was its DIY (do-it-yourself) ethic, encouraging youngsters

from all walks of life to form bands. In this respect, punk mirrored the skiffle craze that had swept the UK twenty years earlier, offering aspiring musicians a road to stardom regardless of their musical ability and standard of equipment. Punk also encouraged people to set up their own independent or indie record labels, so-called because they didn't rely on what punk rockers regarded as the BOFs ("boring old farts") and accountants in the traditional record companies.

The Sex Pistols effectively destroyed their credibility by reforming for a tour in the 1990s, a shameless venture which they readily admitted was driven by financial reasons, the justification being that they didn't make any money the first time around. The Clash's mainman Joe Strummer died in 2003 before the Clash could reform for a proposed Rock'n'Roll Hall Of Fame gig.

American Punk

LIKE THE MAJORITY OF THEIR BRITISH COUNTERPARTS, THE ORIGINAL AMERICAN PUNKS HAD BEEN MAKING MUSIC FOR YEARS BEFORE THEY BEGAN TO RECEIVE ACKNOWLEDGEMENT IN LATE-1975. IN COMMON WITH THE BRITS ONCE AGAIN, THE BIGGEST PROBLEM WAS THAT NOBODY HAD A CLUE WHAT TO CALL IT.

Above

Punks at New York's CBGB's club in 1978.

DRAWING their wild, high-energy style from such Detroit-based rock acts of the late-1960s and early 1970s as MC5 and the Stooges, and boasting an androgynous, long-haired look that made the Rolling Stones look like choirboys, glammed-up east coast quintet the New York Dolls were America's first real punk rock band. Debauched and dangerous, loud and lewd, the Dolls had formed as far back as 1971, but it didn't take long for them to fulfill the cliché of living fast and dying young. Original drummer Billy Murcia succumbed to a mixture of alcohol and drugs during a British tour in late-1972, and was succeeded by Jerry Nolan.

In 1973 and 1974, a pair of albums for Mercury Records – the Todd Rundgren-produced *New York Dolls* and *Too Much Too Soon* – barely dented the US chart despite receptive reviews, and the band were dropped, meeting future Sex Pistols manager Malcolm McLaren shortly afterwards. Still perfecting his manipulative skills, McLaren attempted to revive their career by dressing the Dolls in red leather and demanding they pose in front of the USSR flag. Accusations of communism followed,

"PUNK WAS ABOUT CREATING NEW, IMPORTANT, ENERGETIC MUSIC THAT WOULD HOPEFULLY THREATEN THE STUPIDITY OF THE 1970S. YOU CAN ARGUE ABOUT WHETHER OFFSPRING SOLD OUT BY SIGNING TO SONY UNTIL YOU'RE BLUE IN THE FACE, IT WON'T FEED THE HOMELESS PERSON OUTSIDE YOUR FRONT DOOR."

Jello Biafra, Dead Kennedys

and one by one the members began to depart. By 1977, with McLaren riding high as the Pistols manager, it was all over. Jerry Nolan and guitarist Johnny Thunders teamed up with Richard Hell to form the Heartbreakers, though former Television bassist Hell – who had turned down McLaren's offer to front the Sex Pistols – departed soon afterwards to form the Voidoids. After many notoriously drug addicted years, Thunders himself was found dead in 1991, with Nolan succumbing to a heart attack soon afterwards.

An Undercurrent Of Subterfuge

In early 1976, a new magazine called *Punk* gave the movement focus. The personnel and inner circles of the post-Dolls bands included more than their fair share of arty bohemian types – painters, filmmakers, writers, poets and artists; like the waitresses and house-decorators, all refreshingly free of the baggage of "serious" musicians. Television, Suicide and Patti Smith were among the acts to play New York dives like Max's Kansas City

LEADING EXPONENTS

New York Dolls

Richard Hell

Black Flag

The Dead Kennedys

Ramones

Blondie

Talking Heads

Television

X

Germs

The Dead Boys

Green Day

The Offspring

AMERICAN PUNK

In comparison to British punk American punk is more sophisticated, with rests between the sparse chords and a less physically aggressive playing style.

Gtr.

THE ROCK INTRO ➡ 74   ROCK PEOPLE A-Z ➡ 116   INSTRUMENTS A-Z ➡ 436   POP: NEW WAVE ➡ 48   ROCK: PROTO-PUNK ➡ 87

and the Country, Bluegrass & Blues Club (CBGB's for short). The sounds of these bands, and others like the Ramones, Talking Heads and Blondie, were radically different, yet united by an exciting undercurrent of subterfuge. In the words of Smith, "I was wondering what I could do as a writer or poet to inspire people to reclaim rock'n'roll as a revolutionary, grass-roots base for the people."

A New Wave Of Punk

The first of the new wave acts to be signed were the Ramones, a band that relied more upon goofy, dark humour than anarchy. Given their near-legendary musical minimalism, it was highly remarkable that the Ramones made music for some twenty years after *Ramones*, their May 1976 debut.

Cleveland chipped in with the Dead Boys, and over on the west coast, Black Flag, X, the Germs and the Dead Kennedys were spearheading a more aggressive, politically aggrieved strike at the nation's underbelly. Of the four, Black Flag were more inclined to incorporate humour into their edgy blend of rage and sarcasm – an asset that frontman Henry Rollins retained when the band fragmented in 1986. The Dead Kennedys, meanwhile, were deadly serious … and then some. 'California Über Alles', their debut single, lambasted San Francisco's then governor, Jerry Brown. In 1979, frontman Jello Biafra contested the city's mayorship, finishing fourth. Despite being banned, the group's 'Too Drunk To Fuck' single broached the British chart, but worse followed when a poster for 1985's *Frankenchrist* album resulted in an obscenity prosecution. The Kennedys fragmented after a two-year court battle with Biafra left hopping mad at the group's reformation without him, the re-issue of their catalogue and the pressing of the live album, *Mutiny On The Bay*.

If the DKs are guilty of undermining the original principles of punk rock, they're far from alone. The Offspring's reported $10 million (£6.7 m) switch to Sony Records subsidiary Columbia from Epitaph – a credible indie label owned by Bad Religion's Brett Gurewitz – created a backlash, though the Californians underlined both underground credentials and popularity by permitting an MP3 of their song 'Pretty Fly (For A White Guy)' to be downloaded an incredible 22 million times in just ten weeks.

Consequently, survivors like Sick Of It All have had their noses rubbed in the success of airwave-friendly, younger acts like Sum 41, Blink 182 and Finch, not to mention Green Day who, though more pop today, started out with a punk attitude. As SOIA singer Lou Koller observes, punk is now freely "available at the mall".

Left

The New York Dolls were the missing link between glam rock and punk. Their gigs mixed cross-dressing with swearing and hard rock music.

Below

The Ramones specialized in a very basic sound; their songs, incorporating simple chords and lyrics and no solos, rarely lasted more than two and a half minutes, but this did not detract from their fans' enjoyment of their gigs.

THE RISE OF ARENA ROCK BEGAN IN NORTH AMERICA DURING THE MID-1970S WITH A SURGE IN THE POPULARITY OF BANDS LIKE JOURNEY, FOREIGNER, BOSTON AND STYX. EMBRACED BY A NETWORK OF FM RADIO STATIONS, THESE BANDS AND OTHERS LIKE THEM BECAME SO PROFITABLE TO THEIR RECORD COMPANIES THAT THEY ALMOST REPRESENTED A LICENCE TO PRINT MONEY.

Arena Rock

Above

The anthems on Journey's Escape *brought Steve Perry's powerful, sweeping vocals to the album and singles charts.*

THE formula was deliciously simple: slick, commercial material, underpinned by memorable hard rock riffs and a glossy production. Radio-friendly ballads also encouraged a wider audience, although these were used in moderation.

A Stylistic Journey

The arena rock sound resembled an aural marshmallow; encased in an apparently tough outer casing, but sticky and sweet on the inside. In fact, many of its original bands had gravitated towards the genre from other styles of music. Formed in 1973 by the ex-Santana guitarist Neal Schon, and joined later that year by keyboard player Gregg Rolie, Journey had made three poor-selling jazz rock albums before the simplified strains of *Infinity* enabled them to top a million sales in 1978.

Two years earlier, in 1976, a New York-based English guitarist/songwriter called Mick Jones had almost turned his back on the music business after the dissolution of the Leslie West Band, but fuelled by the success of the singles 'Cold As Ice' and 'Feels Like The First Time', Jones achieved out-of-the-box success with Foreigner's, five-million-selling, self-titled debut.

The rags to riches story of Boston was more unlikely still. Essentially a vehicle for guitarist/songwriter/producer Tom

> ## "YOU HAVE TO BE ABLE TO SURVIVE CHANGE AND KEEP YOUR INTEGRITY. "
>
> *Tommy Shaw, Styx*

Above

Foreigner's original line-up was a mixture of Londoners and New Yorkers, which was the basis of the band's name.

Scholz, the band's 1976 *Boston* album – a glorified collection of basement demos – shot to the top of the US chart and became the best-selling pop debut effort in history until dislodged by Whitney Houston in 1986. By 1995, *Boston* had sold over 15 million copies in America alone, though the perfectionist streak of the reclusive Scholz has created just four more albums in the ensuing quarter of a century.

MTV And Mass Appeal

In the 1980s, Aerosmith, Heart and Whitesnake – all acts with uniquely different roots – moved in to stake their claims in the arena rock market. With their leaner, more blues-based heritage, Aerosmith had already tasted considerable success during the 1970s and brought their sound into a new decade with the help of songwriters Desmond Child and Holly Knight and producer Bruce Fairbairn. Heart, too, already had a proven track record for folk-based acoustic melancholy, but the *Heart* album gave them their most popular release in 1985. Likewise, former blues-rockers Whitesnake, lead by former Deep Purple vocalist David Coverdale, cunningly engineered a re-birth to capitalize upon the MTV boom in 1987.

Rush, too, began to court mass appeal. Their prog roots were homogenized via such synth-friendly albums as *Power Windows* (1985) and *Hold Your Fire* (1987), although the Canadian trio were to become increasingly reclusive.

The grunge-rock revolution would render arena rock deeply unfashionable during the next decade. However, many of its big hitters live on, and continue to play live. Bands like Journey, Styx and REO Speedwagon continue to undertake major tours.

LEADING EXPONENTS

Aerosmith
Styx
Journey
Foreigner
Heart
Kansas
REO Speedwagon
Rush
Boston
Whitesnake

ARENA ROCK

Arena rock often uses simple drum patterns and fills, together with guitar crash chords to create a dramatic sound capable of filling a stadium.

THE ROCK INTRO ➡ 74   ROCK PEOPLE A-Z ➡ 116   INSTRUMENTS A-Z ➡ 436   ROCK: HARD ROCK ➡ 78

Melodic Rock

DURING THE 1970S, TUNEFUL HARD ROCK LOOMED OVER THE US CHARTS LIKE A FLUFFY, PINK COLOSSUS. THE ARRIVAL OF BABY-FACED GUITARIST TOMMY SHAW LED CHICAGO ROCKERS STYX TO BECOME THE FIRST AMERICAN GROUP TO ACHIEVE FOUR CONSECUTIVE TRIPLE-PLATINUM ALBUMS, AND WHEN JOURNEY APPOINTED SINGER STEVE PERRY, IT MADE THEM ONE OF THE BIGGEST BANDS IN THE WORLD.

FOREIGNER have now sold an incredible 60 million albums – 35 million of those in the US alone – as a consequence of such airwave standards as the 1980s hits 'Waiting For A Girl Like You', 'I Want To Know What Love Is' and 'Hot Blooded'.

In the 1980s, British band Def Leppard utilized state-of-the-art technology, clever marketing and widespread touring to tap into the pop market with their *Pyromania* and *Hysteria* albums, a blueprint later used more ruthlessly still by Bon Jovi. The latter pair of bands were among the few to survive the grunge rock revolution, though Leppard surprised many by daring to flirt with the style themselves on their 1996 album *Slang*. Having overhauled themselves for a new generation of MTV viewers, ex-Deep Purple frontman David Coverdale and his former blues band Whitesnake also received long-overdue US attention as the 1980s drew to a close.

Ebbing Enthusiasm

Post-grunge, the only real metamorphosis that melodic rock has undergone is a downsizing of its audience. All save a tiny minority of acts have long since abandoned the pretence of

creatively advancing their music. Like no other genre, except perhaps progressive rock, fans of AOR (album-oriented rock) demand rehashes of the same old ideas. At grass-roots level, Vaughan, Von Groove, Ten, Harem Scarem, Mecca and Westworld all represent a glut of highly entertaining though inward-looking artists. Even new albums

from top-tier bands often elicit scant enthusiasm, and Journey and Van Halen both ended long-term deals with Sony and Warner Brothers in 2002.

However, a decent living can be made on the lucrative summer touring circuit, and perhaps for that reason alone many of melodic rock's main players continue to exist. Although Journey sold just 200,000 copies of *Arrival*, their debut with ex-Tall Stories singer Steve Augeri replacing Steve Perry, they and others like them seem determined to continue.

Invaluable exposure on TV's *South Park*, *Austin Powers: Goldmember* and the Adam Sandler movie *Big Daddy* has rewarded Styx – these days without keyboard player Dennis De Young, the voice of 'Come Sail Away', 'The Best Of Times' and 'The Grand Illusion' – with an unlikely renewed credibility that peaked when Brian Wilson of the Beach Boys, Tenacious D and Billy Bob Thornton all made guest appearances on the group's fourteenth album, *Cyclorama*.

Guitarist Mick Jones and vocalist Lou Gramm, the latter recovered from a life-threatening brain tumor, have celebrated Foreigner's 25th anniversary with 50 US dates and embarked upon their first album together since *Mr Moonlight* in 1994. Boston came back with a new album, *Corporate America*, in 2002. Unfortunately, it's now unlikely that Van Halen will work again with either of their ex-singers, David Lee Roth or Sammy Hagar, although Hagar and bassist Michael Anthony are both in Planet US, a project including Journey's Neal Schon and Deen Castronovo.

Above

Although never a great hit with critics or "serious" rock fans, Styx enjoyed great popularity during their heyday, packing clubs throughout America and releasing three triple-platinum albums.

"HOW DID I FEEL DURING THE GRUNGE YEARS? UNEMPLOYED."

Kip Winger, Winger

Left

After landing a recording contract in 1983, New Jersey band Bon Jovi's extensive touring, phenomenal record sales and good-looking frontman quickly transformed them into one of the world's top rock acts.

LEADING EXPONENTS

Bon Jovi
Journey
Styx
Van Halen
Foreigner
Def Leppard
Whitesnake
Boston
Toto
Chicago

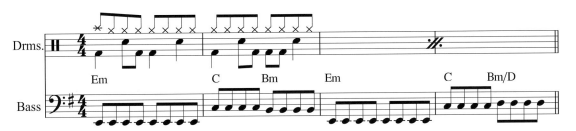

MELODIC ROCK

Melodic rock features pulsing bass eighth notes and a heavy off-beat snare behind finely crafted guitar and vocal lines.

THE ROCK INTRO ➡ 74   ROCK PEOPLE A-Z ➡ 116   INSTRUMENTS A-Z ➡ 436   ROCK: ARENA ROCK ➡ 92

MUCH DERIDED BY MUSIC (AND FASHION) JOURNALISTS, GOTH ROCK IS SLOW, INTROSPECTIVE, GLOOMY AND DOOM-RIDDEN, WITH ELEMENTS FROM HARD ROCK AND PSYCHEDELIA, OFTEN WITH SWATHES OF COLD KEYBOARDS AND ANGULAR GUITAR PARTS.

Goth Rock

Above

Bela Lugosi of Bauhaus's landmark single 'Bela Lugosi's Dead' played Dracula during the 1930s. The song covered two of goth's top subjects – horror and death – in the title.

The dress code was rigid: black clothes, big black hair and face made up to look deathly white. Critics often found the music pretentious and overblown and the goth fashion cartoonish and reminiscent of the Addams Family, but that didn't stop hordes of angst-ridden adolescents finding something they could relate to.

The roots of goth rock can be heard in Joy Division who provide the missing link between punk and goth rock. Formed in true punk style after an inspiring gig by the Sex Pistols by guitarist Bernard Sumner and bassist Peter Hook – but before they had had any musical experience – Joy Division replaced the energy of punk with melancholy, atmosphere and introspection, as heard on *Unknown Pleasures* (1979) and *Closer* (1980). On the verge of their first American tour, the troubled singer Ian Curtis hanged himself. The remaining members regrouped and formed New Order, taking the music in a more dance-oriented direction.

"WE WERE ANTI-ROCK'N'ROLL AND THAT MIGHT BE PRETENTIOUS BUT THERE'S PRETENCE IN EVERY ASPECT OF ART. IT'S ALL AN ACT."

Peter Murphy

Right

The dark, gloomy music of Joy Division, along with the untimely death of singer Ian Curtis, made the band a perfect role model for fledgling goths.

Horror And Death

The goth rock flag was handed over to Bauhaus, whose epic single 'Bela Lugosi's Dead' marked the beginning of full-on goth. Their debut album, *In The Flat Field* (1980), similarly provided a template for Goth – self-obsessed and despairing lyrics over moody and atmospheric music.

Starting as a post-punk band, by the time of their fifth album, *Pornography* (1982), the Cure had miserablism down to a fine art, firmly establishing their goth credentials and achieving a UK Top 10 album despite its rather relentless monotony. Of all the prominent goth bands, the Cure went on to enjoy the longest and most commercially successful career, with Robert Smith managing to combine their goth roots with a more varied, accessible and poppy sound – but without ditching the black clothes and the big black hair.

As goth established itself as a commercial proposition, Bauhaus had a hit single with a cover of David Bowie's 'Ziggy Stardust' in 1982 and their most successful album to date, *The Sky's Gone Out* (1982), reaching number four in the charts.

Zeppelin-Esque

The Sisters Of Mercy's *Floodland* (1987) benefited from Meat Loaf producer Jim Steinman's widescreen production, which helped give the music the scale and depth it required to have full effect. In 1988, The Mission (a Sisters of mercy splinter

group) released *Little Children* which benefited from the production and playing of ex-Led Zeppelin bassist John Paul Jones, who not surprisingly gave the album a Zeppelin-esque tinge.

By the end of the 1980s goth had largely run its course, although its musical influence can be heard in doom metal and industrial metal, and its visual influence can be seen in artists like Marilyn Manson.

LEADING EXPONENTS

Joy Division
Bauhaus
The Cure
Sisters Of Mercy
The Mission
Christian Death
Fields Of the Nephilim
Flesh For Lulu
Gene Loves Jezebel
Siouxsie & the
 Banshees

GOTH ROCK

The gothic sound is epitomized by layered guitars and echo effects to which a heavy bass is added, producing an atmospheric, sinister feel.

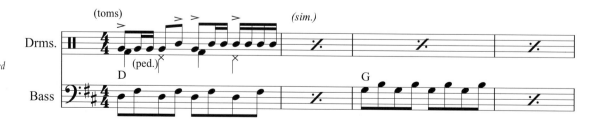

THE ROCK INTRO ➡ 74   ROCK PEOPLE A-Z ➡ 116   INSTRUMENTS A-Z ➡ 436   ROCK: HARD ROCK ➡ 78

Doom Metal

INSPIRED LARGELY BY HEAVY METAL FOUNDERS BLACK SABBATH, THE DOOM METAL BANDS BASED THEIR SOUND ON THE SLOWER AND MORE "SLUDGY" ELEMENTS OF SABBATH'S SOUND, AS CAN BE HEARD ON 'PLANET CARAVAN' FROM PARANOID (1970) AND 'SWEET LEAF' FROM MASTER OF REALITY (1971), RATHER THAN THE FASTER AND MORE BRUTAL ELEMENTS OF THEIR MUSIC.

AS the name suggests, doom metal is sad, melancholic and brooding, and like heavy metal the prominent instrument is distorted guitar, but unlike speed metal, doom metal is not particularly aggressive. Vocally, bands may use straightforward "clean" and traditional vocals or the more extreme "grunting".

The movement began to take shape in the mid-1980s with bands such as St Vitus, Trouble and Candlemass from Sweden. Doom metal contrasts strongly with, and was partly a reaction to, the speed metal bands of the early 1980s, such as Metallica and Slayer who played as fast as possible – many of the doom metal bands make a virtue out of playing slowly.

"The Heaviest Band In The World"

Once described as "the heaviest band in the world", Candlemass' *Epicus Doomicus Metallicus* (1986) is a classic of the genre, and is thought to have christened the genre, although others believe the name comes from the Black Sabbath song 'Hand

of Doom' from *Paranoid*. Cathedral's *In Memorium* (1992) also sets the standard and illustrates neatly the musicians' motivation. Singer Lee Dorrian had previously been with the highly influential Napalm Death, whose style had been characterized by speed and brutality. With Cathedral though, he slowed the music right down, with detuned guitars for extra heaviness and his own unique "singing" style

In the 1990s, My Dying Bride, Paradise Lost and Anathema, three British bands on the Peaceville record label, mixed their Black Sabbath-derived doom metal influences with elements of goth rock. Paradise Lost's *Gothic* (1991) acknowledges the goth influence in their music and, as befits the band's name, My Dying Bride create a mood of doomed romanticism as can be heard on *Turn Loose The Swans* (1993).

Stoner Metal, Drone Doom And Sludge Metal

Just as heavy metal inspired doom metal, doom metal in turn inspired the 1970s-obsessed stoner metal, and also overlaps with this 1990s style. As the name suggests, stoner rock has an added preoccupation with recreational drug use. In a seemingly limitless spiral of possibilities, another offshoot from doom metal is the so-called "drone doom" as practised by Earth. Retaining the heaviness, slowness and brooding of doom, Earth exploit drones in their music, that is, notes or riffs ringing on or being repeated against change in other instruments. On the other side of the Atlantic, yet another branch of doom metal crawled from New Orleans – the so-called "sludge metal" bands like Crowbar and Eyehategod who also drew inspiration from the Seattle grunge bands such as Soundgarden.

Above

Black Sabbath-inspired Cathedral, with Lee Dorrian's grunting, gargling vocals perfectly punctuated by Gaz Jennings' power guitar riffs, created a new "doom-groove" sound.

> "TO ME, DOOM METAL IS A HOME FOR THE TROUBLED SOUL."
>
> *Hammy, Peaceville Records*

Left

To the chagrin of many of their original fans, Paradise Lost have continued to grow creatively throughout their career, moving from their metal roots to electronic and pop music.

DOOM METAL

The characteristic melancholy sound of doom metal is produced by playing minor chords which are then distorted through the amps.

LEADING EXPONENTS

St Vitus

Trouble

Candlemass

Cathedral

My Dying Bride

Paradise Lost

Anathema

THE ROCK INTRO ➡ 74   ROCK PEOPLE A-Z ➡ 116   INSTRUMENTS A-Z ➡ 436   ROCK: SPEED & THRASH METAL ➡ 97

Heavy Metal

THE TERM "HEAVY METAL" CAME FROM THE CONTROVERSIAL US BEAT MOVEMENT NOVEL, NAKED LUNCH, IN WHICH THE AUTHOR, WILLIAM BURROUGHS, TALKED ABOUT "HEAVY METAL THUNDER". THIS PHRASE WAS USED IN STEPPENWOLF'S 1968 SINGLE 'BORN TO BE WILD', AND HELPED CHRISTEN AN EMERGING SUB-GENRE OF HARD ROCK.

Above

Eddie, Iron Maiden's album cover character and mascot, has saved the band members from being constantly recognized on the streets, even at the height of their popularity.

"IT WASN'T SUPPOSED TO BE A PRETTY THING."

Robert Plant, Led Zeppelin

Right

Before an MTV docu-soap relaunched his career, Ozzy Osbourne of Black Sabbath was known for many years as "the bloke who bit the head off a bat".

LEADING EXPONENTS

Led Zeppelin
Black Sabbath
Judas Priest
Motorhead
Ozzy Osbourne
Iron Maiden
Def Leppard
Metallica
AC/DC
Anthrax
Deep Purple
Megadeth
Slayer
Whitesnake
Tool
Godsmack

THE origins of heavy metal are heard in the hard rock bands of the late-1960s and early 1970s such as the Jimi Hendrix Experience, Led Zeppelin and Cream, and in the strident guitar playing of Dave Davies in the Kinks and Pete Townshend in the Who in the mid-1960s. The difference between hard rock and heavy metal is rather subtle – and for many listeners the terms are interchangeable. However, heavy metal is generally more brutal, louder and without the blues influence heard in hard rock, and often the lyrics have satanic, black magic or fantasy overtones. It's a male dominated style of music, and popular with angst-ridden adolescents. There's also a strict dress code – denim, leather, and perhaps most important of all, long hair. Needless to say, music critics hate heavy metal.

The defining albums are Led Zeppelin's *Led Zeppelin II* (1969), particularly the bombastic 'Whole Lotta Love', and Black Sabbath's *Paranoid* (1971). While Zeppelin moved onto new musical pastures, Sabbath continued to plough the same furrow. Guitarist Tony Iommi came up with some of the style's most memorable guitar riffs such as 'Paranoid' and 'Iron Man', while singer Ozzy Osbourne added his trademark nasal whine. Other prominent exponents include Judas Priest with singer Rob Halford's trademark semi-operatic vocals as heard on *British Steel* (1980), and Motorhead (*Ace of Spades* (1980) is a prime example of their fare) who claimed to be so heavy that if they moved in next door to you then your lawn would die!

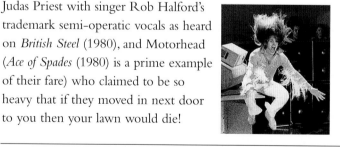

NWOBHM

Dead lawns notwithstanding, a younger generation of British musicians was inspired by the hard rock and heavy metal bands of the 1970s, spawning the New Wave Of British Heavy Metal, or NWOBHM for short. The NWOBHM included Iron Maiden, Def Leppard, Saxon, Samson, Venom, Diamond Head and many others.

Of all the NWOBHM bands, the most successful were Iron Maiden and Def Leppard. Maiden's trademark galloping rhythm and lyrics about fantasy or the Devil has changed little over the years. *The Number Of The Beast* (1982) marked a commercial breakthrough with little compromise in their sound. Def Leppard consistently strove to develop their sound and produced the best-selling *Hysteria* (1987), an expertly produced and painstakingly composed piece of pop metal.

The NWOBHM had a profound impact on drummer Lars Ulrich, who later formed Metallica, the most successful of the big four so-called thrash metal bands, the others being Slayer, Megadeth and Anthrax. As Metallica's sound developed they smoothed off their brutal edges and became a heavy metal band, with *Metallica* (1991) becoming one of the best-selling metal albums.

Happy Families

Meanwhile, Ozzy Osbourne left and rejoined Black Sabbath, along the way releasing *Blizzard of Ozz* (1980) under his own name, featuring the formidable guitar talents of the late Randy Rhoads. Bizarrely, instead of being revered as the Godfather of Heavy Metal, Osbourne is now better known as the hapless head of his dysfunctional, but loving, family thanks to the MTV real-life hit documentary TV series *The Osbournes*.

HEAVY METAL

Heavy drums, pulsing bass and 'pushes' are typical of heavy metal music.

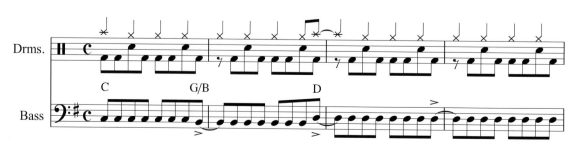

THE ROCK INTRO ➡ 74   ROCK PEOPLE A-Z ➡ 116   INSTRUMENTS A-Z ➡ 436   ROCK: HARD ROCK ➡ 78

Speed & Thrash Metal

SPEED AND THRASH METAL SPRANG TO PROMINENCE IN AMERICA DURING THE EARLY 1980S, WITH FANS AROUND THE GLOBE FORMING THEIR OWN GROUPS. EQUALLY INDEBTED TO THE DO-IT-YOURSELF ETHOS OF THE NEW WAVE OF BRITISH HEAVY METAL AND THE UNDERGROUND SPIRIT OF HARDCORE PUNK, THE STYLE'S ORIGINAL PROGENITORS WERE FRIGHTENINGLY YOUNG, BUT HAD SPENT YEARS SHARPENING THEIR MUSICIANSHIP.

SPEED metal's culture of mindless exuberance was perhaps best summed up by Metallica's 'Whiplash', a galloping exercise in precision riffing that appeared on their 1983 debut album, *Kill 'Em All*. If other self-penned numbers like 'Jump In The Fire' suggested that Metallica had been influenced by the UK's Diamond Head, the covering of the Stourbridge quartet's 'Am I Evil?' on an early B-side was definitive proof.

More than any of their rivals, Metallica exhibited a willingness to grow, and although initially sworn against the music industry's corporate gamesmanship, the San Franciscans had signed to a major label by their fourth album, 1988's *…And Justice For All*. Sooner or later, the rest of the movement's so-called "big four" – Anthrax, Megadeth and Slayer – had done likewise. For other pacesetters like Exodus and Testament, approval from the mainstream came too late, sometimes even resulting in boardroom interference.

Regardless of the labels that released them, some of the best speed/thrash albums attained only cult status, among them *Bonded By Blood* by Exodus (1985), Testament's *The Legacy* (1987), *Darkness Descends* by Dark Angel (1986), *Terrible Certainty* by Kreator (1988) and Death Angel's *Act III* (1990). Swiss band Celtic Frost added their own fascinating idiosyncracies when creating *Into The Pandemonium* in 1987.

Extreme Metal

To many, Slayer made the definitive thrash metal album in the form of 1986's controversial, Rick Rubin-produced *Reign In Blood*. Less than half an hour in duration, the savagery of 'Necrophobic', 'Raining Blood' and 'Angel Of Death' – the latter written by guitarist Jeff Hanneman about war criminal Joseph Mengele – elevated speed metal to death metal and a new plateau of extremity.

By the early 1990s, Metallica's fabled *Metallica* (also known as *The Black Album*) had effectively put them out of reach of the chasing pack, topping the US chart and selling seven million copies. The combination of the ballads 'The Unforgiven' and 'Nothing Else Matters' and the crunching stadium rock of 'Enter Sandman' made Metallica more accessible than any had believed possible, and they had also moved the goalposts for hard rock bands in general. Three years afterwards, Pantera's *Far Beyond Driven* entered the Billboard chart at number one, and later that decade, Megadeth – formed by Dave Mustaine, the sacked Metallica guitarist – released a string of platinum and multi-platinum albums before disbanding in 2002.

With Metallica and Megadeth long since moving on, Anthrax and especially Slayer profited through remaining faithful to speed metal's roots. More recently, Swedish quartet the Haunted added a brutal, contemporary twist, with colourful Floridians Iced Earth demonstrating what a little extra ingenuity can achieve.

Above
Metallica *combined the band's rough sounds and hard riffs with the more commercial flavour brought by mainstream producer Bob Rock.*

> "LARS [ULRICH, DRUMMER] WAS ALWAYS NERVOUS ONSTAGE, SO HE'D PLAY FASTER AND FASTER. WE JUST FIGURED, 'HELL, WE'LL PLAY FASTER, TOO.'"
> *James Hetfield, Metallica*

Left
Man O War entered the Guiness Book Of Records during their "Spectacle Of Might" tour as the world's loudest rock'n'roll band.

LEADING EXPONENTS
Metallica
Slayer
Anthrax
Megadeth
Exodus
Pantera
Man O War
Hüsker Dü
Iced Earth
The Haunted
Celtic Frost

Gtr.

SPEED & THRASH METAL
Played slowly, thrash metal shares many musical characteristics with doom and goth rock. Played fast, it becomes an archetypal speed/thrash metal riff.

Death Metal & Grindcore

DEATH METAL AND GRINDCORE BOTH HAD ROOTS IN THE DECAYING THRASH METAL SCENE OF THE MID-1980S. AS THAT DECADE CONCLUDED, MUSICIANS ON BOTH SIDES OF THE ATLANTIC WERE LOOKING FOR NEW AND HORRIFIC WAYS TO SHOCK. THE STYLES ENDED UP GRAVITATING TOWARDS ONE ANOTHER, BUT BEGAN LIFE AS VERY DIFFERENT ENTITIES.

Above
Napalm Death's sound was so extreme that at first some critics though it was a joke.

DEATH metal bands like Morbid Angel and Death set their violence, suffering and pain-obsessed lyrics to a more intricate framework than the more punk rock-influenced early grindcore acts. As well as the sharing of guitarist Bill Steer, the debut albums from Napalm Death and Carcass (1987's legendary *Scum* and the following year's *Reek Of Putrefaction*) had much in common. Both were showcases for breathtakingly fast and often jarringly short material as well as biting social comment. However, both quickly realized the limited possibilities of what they were doing and began more rounded careers. Carcass eventually found themselves stranded in no man's land with the more mainstream *Swansong* album in 1996, fragmenting soon afterwards. Fiercely defensive of their underground status,

Napalm Death have rarely sounded more ferocious or incisive than on their last two albums, *Enemy Of The Music Business* and *Order Of The Leech*.

"WE'RE OUT TO WIND UP AS MANY PEOPLE AS POSSIBLE"
Jeff Walker, Carcass

A Gruesome Glut

Just as Napalm and Carcass lit the touchpaper in the UK, Chuck Schuldiner's band Death were doing likewise with their own 1987 debut, *Scream Bloody Gore*. Fellow Floridians Morbid Angel weren't lagging far behind guitarist/singer Schuldiner, and by the early 1990s the North American death metal scene included thousands of bands. Each seemed personified by a gruesome name and indecipherable logo. Among the first to make an impression were Slayer, Cannibal Corpse, Obituary, Deicide, Immolation, Autopsy, Malevolent Creation, Gwar and Suffocation. Brazil also had Sepultura,

with Scandinavia throwing forth Dismember, Entombed, At The Gates, Carnage and Hypocrisy.

As quickly as death metal became big business, its quality control mechanism flew out of the window. Major labels began signing such generic second-wavers as Cancer, and before too long records were being judged upon who had produced them, and where.

Melodic Death Metal

After a period of stagnation, In Flames, Dark Tranquillity, Soilwork and Sentenced have all revitalized death metal. The juxtaposition of tuneful segments and traditional intensity has resulted in a melodic death metal that is known as the Gothenburg sound. Meanwhile, former Carnage/Carcass guitarist Mike Amott and his fellow Scandinavians Arch Enemy have dared to appoint an unknown female, Germany's Angela Gossow, as their lead vocalist and are reaping the increased rewards of their best release to date, 2001's *Wages Of Sin*. South Carolina's Nile have also given death metal a cinematic, symphonic twist with their highly recommended 2002 album, *In Their Darkened Shrines*.

LEADING EXPONENTS

Morbid Angel
Dissection
Death
Napalm Death
Carcass
Sepultura
Deicide
Nile
Cannibal Corpse
In Flames
Arch Enemy
Gwar

DEATH METAL
Musically death metal and grindcore have much in common with thrash metal and black metal, but with a biting satirical element to the lyrics that adds intensity.

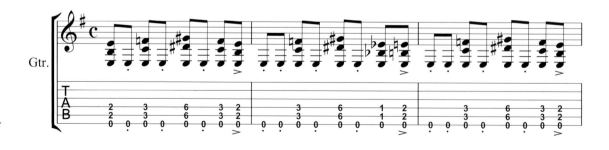

Madchester

OCCASIONALLY, A TOWN OR CITY IS SO INTEGRAL TO A STYLE OF MUSIC THAT THE MUSIC TAKES ITS NAME FROM THE PLACE. IN THE EARLY 1960S, LIVERPOOL GAVE RISE TO THE MERSEY SOUND AND MERSEYBEAT; IN THE LATE-1980S AND EARLY 1990S, ENGLAND'S MANCHESTER SPAWNED SO-CALLED MADCHESTER.

AS much a clubbing scene and youth sub-culture as a style of music, Madchester was also known as "Baggy" due to the baggy clothes worn by the kids. The foremost band of the Madchester scene was the Happy Mondays with their drugged-out, almost psychedelic take on dance music. Embracing funky rhythms and hip hop beats topped off with stream of consciousness lyrics, often with a menacing undercurrent, the Mondays' *Bummed* (1988) shows their unique style beginning to gel.

Manchester had already produced arguably the most important British guitar band of the 1980s, the Smiths, and then went on to produce another significant British guitar band – the Stone Roses. Both bands were heavily influenced by 1960s guitar pop, and although the Stone Roses self-titled debut album from 1989 has little in the way of dance influence, a more dance-orientated remix of 'Fool's Gold' helped establish the Stone Roses as the main Madchester band alongside the Happy Mondays.

The Happy Mondays came into their own with their second album, *Pills, Thrills and Bellyaches* (1990). An intoxicating and heady mix of trippy beats and surreal lyrics sung in a thugish and occasionally threatening tone by vocalist Shaun Ryder, the album represents the pinnacle of the Madchester scene. It also revealed the Mondays' shameless appropriation – 'Step On' is basically John Kongos' 'He's Gonna Step On You Again' and the melody of 'Kinky Afro' is "borrowed" from LaBelle's 'Lady Marmalade'.

The Stone Roses and the Happy Mondays were by no means the only players in the Madchester scene. Eclectic leftfielders James crossed paths with the Madchester, and their *Gold Mother* (1990) album produced the hit single 'Sit Down', a mini-anthem for the Madchester generation, although their sound was too diverse to make them a pure Madchester band, with their distinctly folky influences and even stadium-rock leanings.

Above
The Stone Roses found widespread success with their psychedelia-influenced jangly guitar pop, but legal battles with their record companies led to an early retirement from the limelight.

> "MANCHESTER'S GOT EVERYTHING EXCEPT A BEACH."
>
> *Ian Brown, singer, Stone Roses*

Left
The Hacienda was opened in 1982 by a group of people – including Manchester band New Order – who felt that the city did not offer a night-club suited to their needs. The innovative, space-age venue soon gained legendary status.

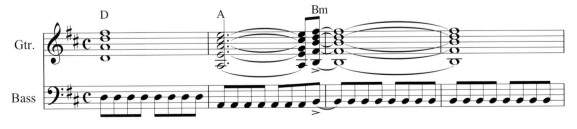

Gtr.

Bass

MADCHESTER

The madchester sound is characterized by 1960s-style melodies, and a jangly, metallic guitar sound.

LEADING EXPONENTS

The Happy Mondays
The Stone Roses
James
The Charlatans
Inspiral Carpets
The Farm

THE ROCK INTRO ➡ 74   ROCK PEOPLE A–Z ➡ 116   INSTRUMENTS A–Z ➡ 436   POP: BRIT POP ➡ 62   ROCK: ALTERNATIVE/INDIE ROCK ➡ 101

Mighty Throbbing Organ

The Hammond organ played a big part in the sound of both the Inspiral Carpets and the Charlatans. Clint Boon's organ work makes an integral contribution to Inspiral Carpets' *Life* (1990), although the band's inconsistency meant their biggest claim to fame in music history was that Oasis songwriter and creative force Noel Gallagher started his musical career as a roadie for the Inspiral Carpets, learning the ropes of the music business. The Charlatans' *Some Friendly* (1991) reveals them to be a more traditional rock band than the Stone Roses and the Happy Mondays with their Rolling Stones-ish swagger and "wakka wakka" organ, as blueprinted by Deep Purple on their 'Hush' single way back in 1968.

On the fringes of the Madchester scene, the Farm's struggled for an identity before aligning themselves with a Madchester-inspired sound. Perceived as rather goofy and a bit of a novelty act, their album *Spartacus* (1991) nevertheless produced two hit singles, 'Groovy Train' and 'All Together Now', the latter of which lifted the melody from classical composer Johann Pachelbel's 'Canon'.

Just as psychedelic rock was heavily influenced and associated with LSD, the Madchester scene was heavily influenced by and associated with the drug

Ecstasy. "Es", as they are known, induce a feeling of blissed-out "loviness" and an understanding of one's fellow clubber. In fact, clubbing played a big part in the Madchester scene, and Madchester often utilized the acid-house dance rhythms heard by the musicians while out clubbing. As with many labels, the precise origins of the "Madchester" term are open to speculation, although it is thought that the Happy Mondays *Rave On Manchester EP* (1989) gave the scene its name. However, it also ties in the Manchester expression "mad fer it" meaning "up for it", and the "mad" part is appropriate since the the drug taking associated with the scene gave rise to some, well, pretty mad behaviour.

The Stone Roses became embroiled in a long-running court case with their former record company, then a bout of laziness resulted in a five-year delay before the release of their modestly-titled second album, *The Second Coming* (1994). The loss of momentum led to the end of the band, with singer Ian Brown pursuing a solo career and guitarist John Squire leading the ill-fated trad rock band the Seahorses. The Happy Mondays disintegrated, largely due to Ryder's drug abuse, although he got himself sufficently together to form Black Grape who continued where the Happy Mondays had left off.

Below

The Happy Mondays perhaps best summed up the spirit of Madchester, combining vocalist Shaun Ryder's deadpan drawl, Bez's frenzied onstage antics and a dancey, "urban folk" sound.

Alternative/ Indie Rock

RATHER A "CATCH-ALL" CATEGORY THAT INCLUDES MANY MUSICALLY DIVERSE BANDS FROM THE 1980S AND 1990S. "ALTERNATIVE" IS GENERALLY AN AMERICAN TERM REFERRING TO ANY REMOTELY LEFTFIELD AND NON-MAINSTREAM BAND. WHEREAS "INDIE ROCK" ORIGINALLY REFERS GENERALLY TO THE UK BANDS RECORDING FOR SMALLER, INDEPENDENT LABELS, AGAIN USUALLY MEANING NON-MAINSTREAM BANDS.

ALTERNATIVE encompasses many sub-styles. To complicate matters, many bands can be said to have started their career as "alternative", simply because they are little known and therefore non-mainstream, but as they become more successful and consequently incorporated into the mainstream, they are no longer "alternative" even though they may have changed their music little. Mainstream bands such as Radiohead, U2 and INXS have all at some point in their careers been described as "alternative". Confused? You should be! Just don't take this "alternative" category too rigidly!

Stateside, the first two alternative bands of lasting significance were REM and Hüsker Dü, both of whom emerged in the mid-1980s. REM started off as a guitar pop band, inspiring many bands in their wake, and went on to become one of the biggest and most successful bands on the planet; Hüsker Dü's speed pop was similarly influential although they never broke into the mainstream.

In the 1990s, the most influential alternative band was Nirvana, who emerged from the so-called Seattle-based grunge scene, with *Nevermind* (1991), breaking down the barrier between hard rock and alternative. Influenced by the Pixies' use of dynamics (that is, quiet passages followed by loud passages as heard on 'Smells Like Teen Spirit') as on *'Surfer Rosa'* (1988), Nirvana were described as "the Guns 'n' Roses it's OK to like" – melodic hard rock

smashing pumpkins • siamese dream

Above

The Smashing Pumpkins' Siamese Dream *is an emotional roller coaster of rock music.*

"WE PROVED THAT ALTERNATIVE MUSIC IS A VIABLE COMMODITY."

Krist Novoselic, Nirvana

Left

Morrissey was the spokesman for a disillusioned generation with his bleak sound and thought-provoking lyrics.

LEADING EXPONENTS
REM
Hüsker Dü
Nirvana
The Pixies
The Butthole Surfers
Sonic Youth
Jane's Addiction
Smashing Pumpkins
Nine Inch Nails
My Bloody Valentine
The Happy Mondays
Blur
Oasis
The Sisters Of Mercy
The Fall
The Smiths
Radiohead
U2
INXS

Drms.

ALTERNATIVE/INDIE ROCK
Although alternative rock features distorted guitar riffs, it relies on solid, traditional rock rhythms to dictate the pace.

THE ROCK INTRO ➡ 74   ROCK PEOPLE A-Z ➡ 116   INSTRUMENTS A-Z ➡ 436   POP: BRIT POP ➡ 62   ROCK: MADCHESTER ➡ 99

Above

Above

Thom Yorke from England's Radiohead. Receiving critical acclaim for albums such as The Bends *(1995) and* OK Computer *(1997), Radiohead's musical style continues to evolve with each record they release.*

without the macho and misogynistic trappings that traditionally accompany many hard rock bands.

The alternative scene is so broad that it encompasses experimental bands such as the Butthole Surfers from Austin, Texas, and Sonic Youth, who emerged from the New York Noise scene. At the other end of the spectrum, it includes bands with traditional rock influences such as Jane's Addiction with their Led Zeppelin (heard on *Nothing's Shocking* (1988)) and the Smashing Pumpkins, led by alternative guitar hero Billy Corgan, who "widdles" with the best of them on 1993's *Siamese Dream*. Nine Inch Nails took traditionally conservative heavy metal into new areas with drum machines in industrial metal and Danzig took metal into new musical territories with *Danzig III: How The Gods Kill* (1992).

Lollapalooza Festival

Perry Farrell, the Jane's Addiction singer, packaged the alternative scene into the Lollapalooza tour in the 1990s, a travelling musical circus showcasing many of the alternative bands but also celebrating alternative counter-culture 1990s-style with tattooing and piercing stands. Controversy was caused in 1996 when the festival was headlined by Metallica, again illustrating the broadness of the "alternative" category. Metallica certainly started out as a broadly alternative band, albeit of the speed metal variety, but many alternative purists felt they were really unreconstructed heavy metal dinosaurs.

Indie In The UK

The indie rock scene in the UK has many parallels with the alternative scene in the US. Inspired by the DIY ethic of the punk rockers, many independent small labels sprung up offering a refreshing alternative to the big, lumbering corporate labels who were perceived as boring and run by men in suits. Ironically, many of these labels became absorbed by the major record labels.

Although indie rock is more pop-based than the alternative scene in the US, it similarly encompasses several other styles such as the shoegazers, My Bloody Valentine being the leaders of this movement, Madchester, as celebrated by the Happy Mondays, Brit pop, as exemplified by Blur and Oasis, and goth rock, represented by the Sisters Of Mercy.

The longest-lasting and most prolific indie rock band is probably the Fall, led by Mark E. Smith. Despite an ever-changing line-up, the Fall's unique sound – courtesy of Smith's half-sung, half-spoken vocals, backed by spiky and sometimes almost cacophonic guitar and keyboards (as on 1980's *Grotesque (After The Gramme)*) – has changed little over the years.

The Smiths self-titled debut album in 1984 heralded the most influential British guitar rock of the 1980s and, like REM across the pond, the Smiths were influenced by 1960s guitar pop like the Byrds but with singer Morrissey's uniquely English slant on life.

Shoegazing

ORIGINALLY COINED AS A CRITICISM OF THE BANDS' STATIC STAGE PERFORMANCES – BAND MEMBERS WERE SAID TO STAND STOCK STILL STARING AT THEIR SHOES – THE SO-CALLED SHOEGAZERS PLAYED SLOW- OR MEDIUM-PACED ROCK, GENERALLY WITH HEAVILY DISTORTED OR HEAVILY REVERBED GUITARS TOPPED BY DREAMY, MELODIC AND ETHEREAL VOCALS.

INFLUENCED by the use of distorted guitars by the Jesus & Mary Chain and the otherworldliness of the Cocteau Twins, the shoegazers were primarily a British movement, the most prominent exponent being My Bloody Valentine.

My Bloody Valentine took a long and tortuous path from their debut recording *This Is Your Bloody Valentine*, released in 1985, to their masterpiece album *Loveless* in 1991. Starting as a goth band, their distinctive sound began to emerge with the addition of singer Bilinda Butcher and the development of bandleader Kevin Shields' guitar sound.

Retreating to the recording studio for two years to further refine their sound, spending around £200,000 ($310,000) in studio time and nearly bankrupting their label, Creation, the band's painstaking attention to sound detail is confirmed by the "engineered and assisted by" credit that runs to 18 different names (including two band members). Centring around Shields' awesome guitar sounds and the sensual interplay between Shields and Butcher's airy vocals, *Loveless* defines the shoegazing sound.

Bandwagon

Such was My Bloody Valentine's hold on the shoegazer style that some bands inspired by Loveless were accused of jumping on the shoegazer bandwagon – Curve in particular suffered from such bad press, although *Doppelganger* (1992) sees them finding their own take on the *Loveless* sonic landscape. The Verve emerged from darkest Wigan with a psychedelic take on the shoegazer sound, as heard on *A Storm In Heaven* (1993).

Insular

A rather inward-looking and insular movement, some of the shoegazer bands such as Ride, Chapterhouse, Curve, Slowdive and Lush struggled to develop their sound. Others managed to evolve and reach a wider audience. The shoegazer influence can be heard on Blur's *Leisure* (1991), but by the time of *Parklife* (1994) they had established themselves as forerunners of Brit pop. The Verve broke into the mainstream with their massive hit single 'Bitter Sweet Symphony' from *Urban Hymns* (1997). Similarly, the Boo Radleys' *Everything's Alright Forever* (1992) reveals a debt to the shoegazer sound, but by *Wake Up!* they were more of a straightforward pop band.

The shoegazer bands' notoriously static live performances didn't endear them as live acts and few were able to move in new directions. Even Kevin Shields found it hard to follow up *Loveless* and My Bloody Valentine still hadn't recorded a full-length follow-up album when Shields joined Primal Scream as a guitarist on a semi-permanent basis in the late-1990s. The shoegazer's influence can be heard in trip hop.

Above
My Bloody Valentine pioneered the ethereal sound that came to define shoegazing.

> "WE TRY TO MAKE THE MUSIC THE PERSONALITY AND KEEP OURSELVES QUITE ANONYMOUS."
>
> *Andy Bell, Ride*

Left
Toni Halliday, whose languid vocals cut through Curve's multi-layered, dreamy sound. Halliday went on to contribute guest vocals to Leftfield's 'Original' on their 1995 album Leftism.

SHOEGAZING

Several guitars are used to create the layered sound of shoegazing, with an additional rhythm guitar to create a swamped sound and ethereal vocals over the top.

LEADING EXPONENTS
My Bloody Valentine
Curve
The Verve
Ride
Chapterhouse
Slowdive
Lush
Blur

US Underground & Garage Rock

TAKING THEIR NAME FROM THE MEAGRE REHEARSAL FACILITIES OF ITS EARLY PRACTITIONERS, GARAGE ROCK BEGAN IN THE US DURING THE MID-1960S. THE LOUD, FUZZ-TONED GUITARS OFTEN FAILED TO DISGUISE LINKS TO UK POP MENTORS LIKE THE BEATLES, ROLLING STONES AND THE WHO. LATER ACID ROCK BANDS SUCH AS THE ELECTRIC PRUNES INCORPORATED PROGRESSIVE AND PSYCHEDELIC INFLUENCES.

Above
The White Stripes' 2001 album White Blood Cells *showcased the band's raw, garrage rock sound.*

MOSTLY, however, the first wave of garage rock bands were destined for short-lived cult appeal, then obscurity. Garage rock became rawer and more raucous, evolving into something more politicized during the early 1970s. Among the first indications that something was afoot, future Patti Smith guitarist Lenny Kaye assembled *Nuggets, Vol 1: The Hits*, a legendary double compilation that cherrypicked the likes of the Chocolate Watch Band, the Electric Prunes, Blue Cheer, Seeds and Todd Rundgren's Nazz, even coining the term "punk rock" for the first time in his sleeve notes.

"WHEN WE STARTED WE WERE PART OF THE BURGEONING USA UNDERGROUND BAND SCENE, BUT WE WERE DERIDED BY PUNK ROCK PURISTS AS AN 'ART' BAND. NOW BEING 'ART' HAS A HIP CACHET AND PUNK IS FOR POSERS – GO FIGURE."

Thurston Moore, Sonic Youth

Prose And Punk Rock

By 1975, Kaye was providing musical backing for Patti Smith's poetry readings. Produced by ex-Velvet Underground man John Cale, Smith's watershed album *Horses* had successfully married her adventurous prose to a proto-garage rock sound, making it one of the most influential albums in the growth of punk rock.

An early single sleeve of John F. Kennedy being shot had rendered the Misfits so notorious that labels were genuinely afraid to release their product. Eventually, such albums as 1982's *Walk Among Us* – or, perhaps more accurately, the patronage of thrash metal giants Metallica, who covered 'Last Caress' during the 1980s – belatedly secured the place of the

LEADING EXPONENTS

The 13th Floor Elevators
Patti Smith Group,
Dinosaur Jr.
Hüsker Dü
Sonic Youth
Melvins
Misfits
Jon Spencer Blues
    Explosion
The Hives
The White Stripes
The Strokes

US UNDERGROUND & GARAGE ROCK

A strong bass figure, featuring tight rhythms and often in a minor key, is reflected by the drums to characterize the underground rock style.

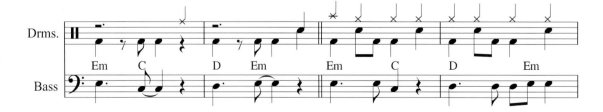

THE ROCK INTRO ➡ 74   ROCK PEOPLE A–Z ➡ 116   INSTRUMENTS A–Z ➡ 436   ROCK: PSYCHEDELIC ROCK ➡ 80   ROCK: PROTO-PUNK ➡ 87

New Jersey punks in the annals of underground rock.

America's alternative rock scene was thriving. West coast punk act Black Flag had played their part, though by 1986 guitarist Greg Ginn had disbanded the group, his SST label introducing the world to the free-thinking idealism of Meat Puppets, Sonic Youth, Hüsker Dü, Soundgarden, Screaming Trees, the Minutemen and Firehose, becoming one of the most important independent imprints of its day. SST also distinguished itself by issuing *I Against I*, the pièce de résistance of Washington D.C.-based metal-punk-hardcore-reggae fusionists the Bad Brains, and the Black Sabbath-flavoured sludge rock of St Vitus.

Twisted Eclectism

The Butthole Surfers and Big Black crystalized the twisted eclecticism of the US underground, which mutated hard and punk rock with alternating strains of psychedelia, art rock, folk and even country. Both were formed in 1982 and lead by gifted, uncompromising mavericks in the shape of Gibby Haynes and Steve Albini, making music that was powerful, cynical, crazed and often wryly amusing. The unhinged Haynes, in particular, based his career upon shockingly bad behaviour, though he remained forgiveable while creating records as brilliantly frazzled as 1987's *Locust Abortion Technician*. Splitting up at their peak, Big Black lasted for just five short years, Albini becoming a producer (or to use the term he prefers "recording engineer") of distinction through his work with Nirvana, the Pixies and even his heroes Cheap Trick.

Unlike their rivals REM, Minneapolis bands Hüsker Dü and the Replacements never quite became household names. However, the songwriting skills of guitarist Bob Mould and drummer Grant Hart remain among the most celebrated of the US underground and beyond. Like Sonic Youth, Hüsker Dü moved onto a major label as the 1980s drew to a close, although the band split up in January of 1988 when the long-running rivalry between Mould and Hart became unworkable. The Replacements, meanwhile, formed in 1979, playing some of the noisiest and most chaotic gigs of the following decade, although sometimes they were unable to complete shows due

to drunkenness – or worse. A reluctance to make accessible videos also speeded up the Replacements' demise, though singer/songwriter Paul Westerberg has a cult solo career and former bassist Tommy Stinson toured with Guns 'n' Roses.

At least Sonic Youth were sussed enough to have ensured that their contract gave them total creative control when they signed with the Geffen Records offshoot DGC, offering genuine hope that independent artistry could work hand-in-hand with corporate distribution and marketing. However, since then, the twin driving forces of guitarist Thurston Moore and bassist Kim Gordon have regained indie credibility through the formation of their own label SYR Records.

In common with many garage rock acts, Pussy Galore were also plagued by substance problems. The bass guitar-less Washington DC quartet, who took their name from the female James Bond character, created a scuzzy, nihilistic wall of sound that was jointly inspired by the New York Dolls and the Velvet Underground. When the band split in 1990, frontman Jon Spencer adopted the tongue-in-cheek name of the Blues

Above

Sonic Youth emerged from New York's "no-wave" scene with a ferocious sound, blending infectious melodies and intense instrumentation, which the band refined over time.

Left

Jon Spencer, the charismatic frontman of the Jon Spencer Blues Explosion (or JSBX). Although influenced by the blues, the band play a manic mixture of musical styles which combines punk rock with blues-flavoured grooves.

ROCK: BRITISH PUNK ➡ 88   ROCK: AMERICAN PUNK ➡ 90   ROCK: ALTERNATIVE/INDIE ROCK ➡ 101

Post-Pussy Galore, Spencer had in fact played with wife Cristina Martinez in Boss Hog, famously accepting a last-minute cancellation at CBGB in New York as their debut gig – a show that Martinez is said to have performed naked. The Jon Spencer Blues Explosion's energetic blend of punk, funk, rockabilly and soul was equally hard to ignore, and the support of Steve Albini further validated the band's credentials. Now onto their eighth album, last year's acclaimed *Plastic Fang*, the Explosion's future success is assured.

Albini has also worked with Californian art rockers Neurosis, another band that have helped to erode the very boundaries of underground rock with their highly charged industrial metal and progressive-influenced arrangements. The multi-platinum success of both *Tool* and *A Perfect Circle* have certainly helped to break down barriers in that respect, though nothing, it seems, is sacred anymore.

A Garage Rock Revival

In recent years garage rock has undergone a revival, a new wave of often besuited upstarts from around the planet re-invigorating the style. Between them, Sweden's the Hives, New York five-piece the Strokes and the Detroit-based duo White Stripes have somehow injected urgency and fashionability into a form of music that was in danger of becoming redundant. However, *Rolling Stone* magazine had no hesitation in putting Jack and Meg White of the White Stripes on their prestigious front cover, touting the minimalist pair as the "next big thing".

Above

Underground queen Patti Smith, who has described her unique sound as "three chord rock merged with the power of the word". Smith's 1975 debut Horses was the first underground rock album to enter the Billboard *Top 50.*

Explosion (aka JSBX) for his new project, while guitarist Neil Haggerty formed the similarly confrontational Royal Trux with vocalist Jennifer Herrema. The latter were once described as sounding like: 'two hopeless junkies in a cheap studio making up a horrid squall of off-key guitars, out-of-time drums, and tuneless moaning in lieu of vocals as they go along', so it's no surprise that of the two acts, JSBX have fared better.

Among the acts snapping at the heels of this elite bunch are the Vines, the Australians whose debut album *Highly Evolved* debuted in August 2002 at number 11 on the *Billboard 200*, plus fellow Detroit combo the Von Bondies, New Zealand's the Datsuns and D4, the BellRays from Britain and Finland's the Flaming Sideburns.

Progressive Metal

CANADIAN TRIO RUSH HAD LITTLE IDEA OF THE MAGNITUDE OF THEIR ACTIONS WHEN THEY RELEASED CARESS OF STEEL IN SEPTEMBER OF 1975. JUST SEVEN MONTHS AFTER THE GROUP'S SECOND ALBUM, FLY BY NIGHT, IT SAW THEM BOARD A CREATIVE WAVE THAT FOR MANY FANS WOULD PEAK WITH THEIR NEXT STUDIO RELEASE, 1976'S CONCEPTUAL ALBUM 2112.

THOUGH still recognizeable as a Led Zeppelin/Cream-inspired bar act, the increasingly progressive *Caress...* introduced 'The Necromancer' and 'The Fountain Of Lamneth' – 12-and-a-half minutes and 20-minutes-long, respectively – epic numbers which were infused with an adventurous new spirit and embellished by drummer Neal Peart's sci-fi lyrics.

Then as now, critics dismissed the trio's endeavours as overblown and pretentious, but the fans did not care. Rush would release better focused albums than *Caress Of Steel* over the course of a still unfolding 30-year career, though it undoubtedly served as a launch pad for their own endeavors, as well as a sub-genre now known as progressive metal.

Heirs To Rush's Throne

In the 1980s, with Rush busy exploring synthesizers, bands like Watchtower and Fate's Warning took up the baton, mostly missing the point with their combination of unnecessarily shrill vocals and super-technical instrumentation. However, Queensrÿche and King's X eventually emerged as fitting heirs to the throne, with Savatage lurking not too far behind.

In 1988, Queensrÿche unveiled *Operation: Mindcrime*. Offering power in the Iron Maiden mould and soaring melodies, the Seattle quintet found themselves billed as the thinking man's hard rock band. The album tipped its hat at Rush's own *2112* for its concept of futuristic censorship, and also to Michael Kamen for its lavish orchestral arrangements, yet Queensrÿche's masterwork is rightly regarded as a power metal watershed moment in its own right. *Operation: Mindcrime* stayed on the American charts for a year, selling over a million copies, though even those figures were eclipsed in the 1990 *Empire* album, with its haunting hit 'Silent Lucidity'.

Above
Lengthy drum solos, in the style of Led Zeppelin's John Bonham, have found a home in the progressive metal genre.

The departure of guitarist Chris DeGarmo accelerated Queensrÿche's gradual process of unravelling. Things reached a nadir with the dreary *Q2K* in 1999, by which time the band had a serious rival. Originally known as Majesty, Dream Theater's earliest recording line-up had shown potential on 1989's debut *When Dream And Day* Unite. Replacing frontman Charlie Dominici with beefy Canadian James LaBrie helped the quintet to gain invaluable MTV exposure for their excellent 1992 follow-up, *Images And Words*, after which Dream Theater never looked back. The group's insistence upon performing lengthy drum, keyboard, guitar and bass solos infuriated reviewers, only cementing the enthusiasm of their following. In creative terms, Dream Theater peaked in 1999 with *Metropolis Pt 2: Scenes From A Memory*, an ambitious conceptual piece that the band had modeled upon *Dark Side Of The Moon* and *The Wall* by Pink Floyd, Genesis' *The Lamb Lies Down On Broadway* and even *OK Computer* by Radiohead.

> "EVERY DAY'S A TEST OF FRIENDSHIP FOR THIS BAND..."
> *Mike Portnoy, Dream Theater*

Most of the best progressive metal now emanates from Scandinavia, such groundbreaking acts as Opeth, Meshuggah and Therion proving that a little serious thought is all it takes to carve new and unique ideas from what's gone before.

Left
Rush are Canada's biggest rock act and have retained a large fan base throughout their lengthy career, despite frequent panning by critics – as well as sometimes by the fans themselves.

PROGRESSIVE METAL
Multilayered syncopation over a steady rhythm (usually provided by one percussion instrument) provide the distinguishing characteristics of progressive metal.

LEADING EXPONENTS
Rush
Queensrÿche
Dream Theater
Opeth
King's X
Fates Warning
Savatage
Symphony X
Katatonia
Spock's Beard

THE ROCK INTRO ➡ 74   ROCK PEOPLE A–Z ➡ 116   INSTRUMENTS A–Z ➡ 436   ROCK: PROG ROCK ➡ 82   THE BLUES INTRO ➡ 160

BY THE END OF THE 1980S, THRASH METAL WAS ON ITS LAST LEGS. METALLICA AND SLAYER WERE ON THE PATH TOWARDS ACCEPTANCE BY THE MAINSTREAM AND IT SEEMED AS THOUGH HEAVY METAL WAS IN DANGER OF LOSING NOT ONLY THE EXTREMITY UPON WHICH IT HAD BEEN FOUNDED, BUT ALSO ITS SHOCK VALUE. HOW ILL-FOUNDED THOSE ASSUMPTIONS TURNED OUT TO BE.

Black Metal

Above

Burzum's Count Grishnackh, who ended up behind bars after killing fellow black metal star Euronymous, from the band Mayhem.

IN America, death metal had already raised the stakes, but an even more violent new breed of metal musician was lurking in Norway. Jointly inspired by the Satanic writings of Aleister Crowley and the groundbreaking evil noise of UK trio Venom, whose 1982 watershed release *Black Metal* effectively gave the new style its name, groups like Mayhem, Burzum and Emperor were soon to achieve worldwide notoriety.

Satanic Crimes

The bleak, icy extremity of black metal was quickly rendered infamous through a succession of twisted, criminal acts. The features of its protagonists were disguised by "corpse paint", a ghostly white type of facial make-up, their identities further cloaked by such grim pseudonyms as Count Grishnackh, Euronymous and Dead. Such anonymity allowed them to pursue a variety of alleged causes, including satanism, paganism and nationalism, not forgetting self-promotion.

Although rivalry between the early front-runners was fierce, a ten-man "inner circle" eventually established itself. Together they swore to rid Norway of Christianity and would torch wooden Christian churches by night and afterwards openly boast of their satanic influence. Ultimately, many of their number would eventually die – some at the hands of fellow conspirators – while others ended up imprisoned for murder, arson or grave desecration.

> ## "HE DIED FROM ONE STAB TO THE HEAD, THROUGH THE SKULL. I ACTUALLY HAD TO KNOCK THE KNIFE OUT."
>
> *Count Grishnackh of Burzum after he had murdered Mayhem's Euronymous*

Above right

Venom's penchant for using extreme pyrotechnic effects during their stage act significantly reduced their choice of venues.

Murder And Mayhem

Chillingly, none of those apprehended went on to express remorse for their deeds. Indeed, Mayhem frontman Euronymous – stabbed to death in his underwear in 1993 by former friend Count Grishnackh of Burzum – once stated: "I don't want to see people respecting me, I want them to hate and fear." Grishnackh (real name Varg Vikernes) is likely to be freed in October of 2006, though he has added to the Burzum catalogue since his incarceration.

Of all the black metal bands, Emperor became the most popular and influential. Having dropped the corpse paint and refined their sound with *Anthems To The Welkin At Dusk* in 1997, the quartet had seemed on the verge of big things before announcing a decision to retire from touring. This was followed by a full-blown split in 2001.

Black metal has gradually divided into numerous offshots, newcomers like Dimmu Borgir choosing to add keyboards and proceed down more orchestrally embellished routes. But while many of the music's original goals have thankfully been laid to rest, its popularity continues to thrive. In late 2002, Norwegian duo Satyricon and Capitol Records offered the genre's first major label release, *Volcano*, and in the UK the Sony corporation have also entered the market via the signing of Cradle Of Filth. With their forthcoming *Damnation And A Day* album, the self-styled vampiric rockers from Suffolk are optimistic of reaching sales of a cool half-million copies.

LEADING EXPONENTS

Emperor

Burzum

Venom

Bathory

Cradle Of Filth

Mayhem

Satyricon

Dimmu Borgir

Darkthrone

Immortal

BLACK METAL

Another doom-laden genre, black metal frequently uses the tritone, or augmented fourth – also called the "diabolus in musica" since medieval times, when it was thought to represent the Devil and so was banned from church music.

THE ROCK INTRO ➡ 74   ROCK PEOPLE A-Z ➡ 116   INSTRUMENTS A-Z ➡ 436   ROCK: DEATH METAL & GRINDCORE ➡ 98

Southern Rock

TAKING ITS LEAD FROM THE LOUD BLUES ROCK OF LATE-1960S BANDS SUCH AS CREAM AND THE GRATEFUL DEAD, SOUTHERN ROCK MATERIALIZED WITH THE RELEASE OF THE ALLMAN BROTHERS BAND'S EPONYMOUS 1969 DEBUT ALBUM, WHICH EMBELLISHED A FUSION OF ROCK'N'ROLL, BLUES, COUNTRY AND JAZZ WITH A DISTINCT GOOD OL' BOY EDGE FROM DIRECTLY BELOW THE MASON-DIXON LINE.

NATIVES of Macon, Georgia, the Allmans always resisted the southern rock label. The band underwent many personnel changes over the years, the first of these being due to the motorcyle death of guitarist Duane Allman in October 1971, and that of bass player Berry Oakley just over a year later. Before Duane's fatal accident, through the *Idlewild South* and *Live at the Fillmore East* albums, he and fellow lead guitarist Dickey Betts traded solos with keyboardist/vocalist Gregg Allman in a balanced line-up that enhanced its blues rock performances with sophisticated jazz structures and classical techniques. Following Duane's death midway through the recording of the *Eat A Peach* album, Betts assumed all of the lead guitar duties and, while also emerging as a singer and songwriter, he led the band in a more laid-back, country-oriented direction, evident on 1973's, *Brothers And Sisters*.

Hereafter, a combination of internal disputes and drink-and-drug-related problems would contribute to the Allman Brothers' diminishing accomplishments throughout the remainder of the decade. Nevertheless, the band had changed the musical map of America, and in so doing it had also paved the way for numerous other southern rock acts to enjoy mainstream success. Ironically however, the band who brought the southern rock sound closest to the mainstream were a Californian outfit, Creedence Clearwater Revival. Their stomping, bayou-influenced rock is encapsulated in hits such as 'Proud Mary' and the ubiquitous 'Bad Moon Rising', which has since become a standard in every amatuer band's repertoire.

The Success Of Skynyrd

The definitive southern rock outfit, Jacksonville, Florida natives Lynyrd Skynyrd boasted a heavy blues rock sound, the songwriting talents of lead singer Ronnie Van Zant, and the three-pronged guitar formation of Allen Collins, Gary Rossington and Ed King that featured prominently on the band's first hit song, 'Freebird', a tribute to the late, lamented Duane Allman. In 1974, following a support slot on the Who's *Quadrophenia* tour, Skynyrd achieved a multi-platinum breakthrough with its sophomore album, *Second Helping*, which spawned the hit single 'Sweet Home Alabama' and helped to cement the group's credentials both in the studio and on the road. Van Zant was flowering as a composer and lyricist, yet tragedy struck in October 1977 when, just three days after the release of the band's *Street Survivors* album, he was killed in a plane crash en route to Baton Rouge, Louisiana. The accident also claimed backing vocalist Cassie Gaines and her brother Steve, who had joined Skynyrd as a guitarist following Ed King's departure.

Like the Allman Brothers Band, Lynyrd Skynyrd broke up and subsequently reformed with a revamped line-up. Despite the emergence of outfits such as the Georgia Satellites, the Black Crowes, Widespread Panic and the Dave Matthews Band during the 1980s and 1990s, the halcyon days of southern rock were over having, never recovered from the decimation of its two leading lights.

Above and Below Left
Two of the defining bands of the southern rock sound, Lynyrd Skynyrd and the Allman Brothers.

> "ROCK'N'ROLL WAS BORN IN THE SOUTH, SO SOUTHERN ROCK IS LIKE SAYING ROCK ROCK."
> *Gregg Allman*

LEADING EXPONENTS

The Allman Brothers Band
The Marshall Tucker Band
Creedence Clearwater Revival
Blackfoot
The Charlie Daniels Band
The Dixie Dregs
The Molly Hatchet Band
Lynyrd Skynyrd
The Outlaws
Sea Level
.38 Special
Wet Willie
The Georgia Satellites
The Black Crowes
Widespread Panic
The Dave Matthews Band

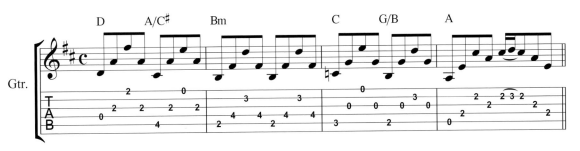

SOUTHERN ROCK
Southern rock took blues-based riffs and added southern-fried honky tonk flavours, resulting in a lazy, swinging sound.

THE ROCK INTRO ➡ 74   ROCK PEOPLE A-Z ➡ 116   INSTRUMENTS A-Z ➡ 436   BLUES: BLUES ROCK ➡ 175   COUNTRY: COUNTRY ROCK ➡ 209

WHEN THE GRATEFUL DEAD STARTED ATTRACTING A LARGE FAN FOLLOWING ON THE BAY AREA CONCERT SCENE DURING THE LATE-1960S, COURTESY OF FREE-FORM JAMS THAT SHOWCASED THE BAND'S FUSION OF FOLK, ROCK, COUNTRY AND BLUES, IT SIGNALLED THAT ROCK'N'ROLL WAS LATCHING ONTO A TRADITION OF IMPROVIZATION THAT HAD LONG BEEN PREVALENT IN OTHER FORMS OF WESTERN MUSIC.

Jam Bands

Above and Right
Jamming was introduced to the rock scene by acts such as Frank Zappa and then adopted and expanded by bands like Blues Traveler.

THIS had been a key feature of the classical music of the Baroque era in Europe, where even composers such as Mozart were renowned improvizors on the keyboard. However, by the early-nineteenth century, at the height of the Romantic movement, the complex musical language of the composers was set down, providing little room for the musicians to improvize. At the start of the twentieth century, this was still the norm in Europe, whereas in America an air of greater collaboration prevailed among the pioneering jazz musicians who virtually created music as they performed it. And it was this approach, passed down the generations by greats like Louis Armstrong, Duke Ellington, Charlie Parker, Ornette Coleman, Miles Davis and John Coltrane, which was subsequently adopted by, among others, the Grateful Dead, Frank Zappa & the Mothers of Invention and the Allman Brothers Band, who also echoed the jazz musicians' penchant for fusing diverse musical styles onstage and on albums such as the Dead's *Anthem of the Sun* and *American Beauty*; and the Allmans' *Idlewild South* and *Eat A Peach*.

> "IT'S LIKE YOU'RE SURFING: THE WAVE IS STRONGER THAN YOU. IF YOU RELAX AND HAVE NO FEAR, AND YOU'RE WITH THE FLOW OF THE WAVE, YOU CAN RIDE IT. BUT IF YOU TRY TO FIGHT IT, YOU'LL WIPE OUT."
>
> *Trey Anastasio, Phish*

Musical Eclecticism

During the 1990s, a new generation of jam bands emerged. Taking their lead from the Dead and the Allmans, while fusing anything from rock, soul and jazz to bluegrass and worldbeat,

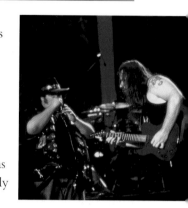

groups such as the Spin Doctors, Blues Traveler, Widespread Panic and Phish began carving out their own niche. Building their following by way of constant touring, what they and their predecessors have usually shared is a solid bond with their audience – even encouraging them to tape concerts – as well as an understandable ability to fully transfer their live appeal to record. Nevertheless, this isn't to say that some of them haven't enjoyed chart triumphs.

New York's Spin Doctors saw sales of their 1991 album *Pocket Full of Kryptonite* rocket after radio and MTV helped turn 'Little Miss Can't Be Wrong' into a hit on the singles charts, and much the same was experienced by another band out of the Big Apple, Blues Traveler. When *Four*, Traveler's aptly-titled fourth album, was released in September 1994, it eventually achieved quintuple-platinum sales in the wake of the single 'Run Around' becoming one of 1995's biggest hits.

Conversely, the outfit that has led the way on the jam band scene while coming closest to assuming the Grateful Dead's mantle, is one from Vermont that has never been able to translate its concert following into record sales via studio albums such as *Junta* and *A Picture of Nectar*. Melding folk, bluegrass, country, jazz and rock'n'roll Phish has set new standards of originality in terms of free-form rock improvization, while becoming an institution on the American college circuit. And therein lies the appeal of the jam scene, which has far more to do with live performance than with recorded encapsulations.

LEADING EXPONENTS

The Allman Brothers Band
The Black Crowes
Big Head Todd & the Monsters
Blues Traveler
The Disco Biscuits
The Grateful Dead
Leftover Salmon
The Dave Matthews Band
Medeski, Martin & Wood
Moe
Phish
The Spin Doctors
Widespread Panic

JAM BANDS

The nature of the songs and duration of the concerts gives jam bands plenty of scope to display their versatility, with changes in tempo and melody that move from country to funk in one song.

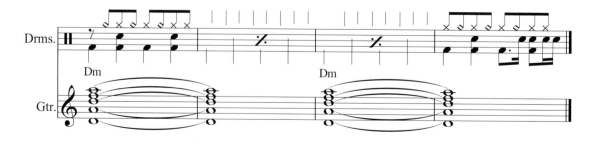

THE ROCK INTRO ➡ 74   ROCK PEOPLE A-Z ➡ 116   INSTRUMENTS A-Z ➡ 436   ROCK: PSYCHEDELIC ROCK ➡ 80   FOLK: FOLK ROCK ➡ 235

Grunge

WITH LYRICS WRITTEN MINUTES BEFORE THEY WERE RECORDED AND THE MOST RAMSHACKLE PRODUCTION IMAGINEABLE, NIRVANA'S 1989 DEBUT ALBUM BLEACH DIDN'T SOUND LIKE THE WORK OF A GROUP CAPABLE OF TOPPLING MTV'S FIXATION WITH HAIRSPRAY ROCK; NOR DID ITS INITIAL SALES OF AROUND 15,000 COPIES. BUT THAT'S EXACTLY WHAT THE TRIO FROM ABERDEEN, WASHINGTON, WENT ON TO ACHIEVE.

ARMED with just the simplicity of guitarist/vocalist Kurt Cobain's songs and a refreshingly fundamentalist view of what making music should really be about, Nirvana went on to revolutionize rock music as it was known in the 1990s and beyond.

Such was the impact of the band's addictive breakthrough single 'Smells Like Teen Spirit', it mattered little that the track's riff was borrowed from 'More Than A Feeling' by melodic rock staples Boston. With hindsight, Nirvana were doing little that the Pixies hadn't already attempted over a cult four-album career, though the group's talismanic 1991 album *Nevermind* was greeted by media overkill. Indeed, the grunge phenomenon eventually found itself suffering from many of the ailments that it had seemed like curing.

Seattle Stars

Third-rate imitators were soon crawling out of the woodwork, though the credentials of fellow Seattle originals like Soundgarden, Pearl Jam, Alice In Chains and Mudhoney were never in doubt. The same couldn't be said for Stone Temple Pilots, who despite achieving major stardom with their three-million-selling *Core* debut in 1992, were cast as plagiarists. Strange then that along with Pearl Jam, STP were among the few grunge acts with any real staying power. The fickle nature of fortune also ensured that one of the longest lasting and most talented of the Seattle bands, the Screaming Trees, also fell by the wayside (though vocalist Mark Lanegan is now a member of Queens Of The Stone Age).

The pressure of stardom was too much for the waif-like, increasingly self-destructive Cobain. The singer attempted suicide many times, and had several heroin overdoses; in 1993 after another overdose, he failed to complete a rehabilitation programme and went missing. Many conspiracy theories suggest otherwise, but it's certain that Kurt shot himself on 5 April 1994, leaving behind a wife, Courtney Love of Hole, and daughter Frances Bean. Her marriage and subsequent tragedy obscured Courtney Love's own musical achievement with Hole, whose breakthrough 1993 album *Live Through This* was widely acclaimed.

A New Stripped-Down Style

Pearl Jam's popularity is only marginally diminished. Meanwhile, drugs terminated the life of singer Layne Staley and the career of his band Alice In Chains. Staley died of a heroin overdose eight years to the day after Cobain's suicide.

Elsewhere, the Soundgarden frontman Chris Cornell is now a member of Audioslave, who are completed by the three instrumentalists from Rage Against The Machine. A self-titled album has received rave reviews.

The glory days of what we traditionally recognize as grunge rock are long gone, but Nirvana drummer Dave Grohl has found success with the Foo Fighters and Creed, Live, Silverchair, Bush, Everclear and 3 Doors Down have all borrowed liberally from grunge's stripped-down formula, reaping their own multi-platinum rewards.

Above

Pearl Jam, dismissed as "corporate" by Kurt Cobain, have remained true to their ideals by playing less-established venues – in a bid to enrage the all-pervasive Ticketmaster – and by voicing their opinions, however controversial (notably against the war in Iraq in 2003).

> "A LOT OF KIDS WERE LOOKING FOR SOMETHING THAT FELT MORE REAL AND HAD MORE PASSION..."
>
> *Butch Vig, Nevermind producer*

Left

Krist Novoselic (bass) and Dave Grohl (drums) of Nirvana, the band which both created and epitomized the grunge movement. Their album Nevermind became an anthem for the so-called "Generation X".

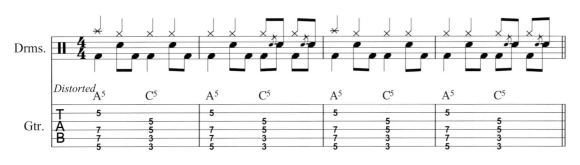

GRUNGE

Innocuous guitar riffs made up of simple melodies and structured rhythms are turned into the riffs characteristic of grunge by distorting the guitar sound through the amps.

LEADING EXPONENTS

Nirvana
Pearl Jam
Soundgarden
Alice In Chains
Hole
Stone Temple Pilots
Screaming Trees
Bush,
The Pixies
Mudhoney

THE ROCK INTRO ➡ 74   ROCK PEOPLE A-Z ➡ 116   INSTRUMENTS A-Z ➡ 436   ROCK: HARD ROCK ➡ 78   ROCK: ALTERNATIVE/INDIE ROCK ➡ 101

FUNK STARS OF THE 1970S LIKE THE OHIO PLAYERS, SLY & THE FAMILY STONE AND FUNKADELIC DIDN'T REALIZE FOR A DECADE THAT HARD ROCK EARS HAD BEEN PAYING ATTENTION. THAT SAME DECADE, AEROSMITH'S COMBINATION OF WHITE-BOY ELECTRIC BLUES AND PROPULSIVE ARENA HARD ROCK HAD BEEN DEEMED AS UNIQUE, WITH JUST GRAND FUNK RAILROAD WORKING ALONG THE SIMILAR LINES.

Funk Metal

Above

Faith No More have long struggled with their conflicting opinions of the rock mainstream, of which they have unwittingly become a part.

"LIVING IN PORTLAND WAS A GREAT MIXTURE OF THE EAST AND WEST COASTS. AT THE SAME TIME AS WE GOT AC/DC, WE ALSO GOT SLY & THE FAMILY STONE. WE GOT CAMEO, WE GOT PARLIAMENT, HUMBLE PIE, FREE AND BAD COMPANY."

Dan Reed

Right

The irrepressible Red Hot Chili Peppers.

LEADING EXPONENTS

Red Hot Chili Peppers

Faith No More

The Beastie Boys

Dan Reed Network

Primus

Fishbone

No Doubt

Sugar Ray

Living Colour

Rage Against The
Machine

IT would be more than ten years before a revamped version of Aerosmith's 'Walk This Way', recorded with Run-DMC, took the mixture of styles to its logical conclusion, and when the collaboration charted all over the globe it opened the floodgates for an avalanche of other like-minded acts. In 1986, the Beastie Boys, whose rock-fuelled *Licensed To Ill* was the first hip hop album to top the American chart.

Aerosmith frontman Steven Tyler himself had described the Red Hot Chili Peppers as "fuckin' great", and the Chilis' breakthrough arrived with their 1991 album, the Rick Rubin-produced *Blood Sugar Sex Magik*. By this time broader-based material like 'Under The Bridge', 'Give It Away' and 'Breaking The Girl' had rewarded them with a popularity that only drug addiction had seemed likely to destroy.

Faith No More paired a simmering internal tension with a pooled record collection that included punk, heavy metal and Tibetan Buddhism. In 1989, it all came to the boil for an album called *The Real Thing*, but the stardom that such hits as 'Epic' and 'Midlife Crisis' brought the San Francisco five-piece affected them in so many different ways that they simply could not last.

In 1988, the Prince-meets-Van Halen groove of the Dan Reed Network's self-titled debut had thrilled and puzzled in equal measures. However, frontman Reed's humanitarian streak meant he was not cut out for the music business, and the DRN went their separate ways in 1993. Formed the following year, New York's Mick Jagger-approved Living Colour burned brightly at first but fragmented after four albums. However, the group has since reformed.

Ska Meets Funk Metal

Sugar Ray and the ska-flavoured No Doubt have brought the funk metal sound into the new millennium, though when *Californication* (1999) and *By The Way* (2002) came around, the Chilis' had long since moved onto more mellow, stadium-friendly strains of rock. Newcomers like the Bloodhound Gang have since taken Anthony Kiedis and company's harmless innuendo to its vulgar limits. "You and me baby ain't nuthin' but mammals/So let's do it like they do on the

Discovery Channel", sing the vacant Philadelphia crew on 2000's *Hooray For Boobies*, setting both funk-rock and the male species back several generations in one fell swoop. Fortunately, old-timers Fishbone remain determined to uphold traditional values, even if it means proceeding down the independent label route.

FUNK METAL

Funk metal combines heavy metal drums with a funky bass line, in which the emphasis is put on the half-beat, creating the characteristic pause in rhythm.

THE ROCK INTRO ➡ 74   ROCK PEOPLE A–Z ➡ 116   INSTRUMENTS A–Z ➡ 436   ROCK: PROTO-PUNK ➡ 87   SOUL AND R&B: FUNK ➡ 376

Riot Grrrl

A POTENT THOUGH SHORT-LIVED FORCE IN THE EARLY 1990S. LYRICALLY, RIOT GRRRL HAD A STRONG FEMINIST AGENDA. WHILST MUSICALLY IT WAS STRONGLY INFLUENCED BY PUNK ROCK. THE SPIRITUAL ROOTS OF RIOT GRRRL CAN BE TRACED BACK TO THE ALL-FEMALE BRITISH PUNK BAND THE SLITS FROM THE 1970S.

WITH its origins in America, and an agenda of "cutting the tripwires of alienation that separate girls from boys", riot grrrl was pioneered by Bikini Kill in the US, and by their spiritual cousins Huggy Bear in the UK. The movement sought to by-pass the traditional male-dominated structures of the music business by generally recording for small, independent labels and using fanzines to reach their followers while refusing to play the media game of giving interviews to the traditional mainstream music press.

In keeping with their political agenda, Bikini Kill even recorded for the Olympia, Washington-based Kill Rock Stars label. *The CD Version Of The First Two Records* (1992) draws together the band's first two albums – angry, aggressive and confrontational, but also intelligent. Bikini Kill teamed up with Huggy Bear for *Yeah! Yeah! Yeah!* (1992), each band taking one side of the 12-inch release. Bikini Kill's *Pussy Whipped* (1994) is more experimental, varied and accessible, but the band's preference for enthusiastic performances over polished production values doesn't help broaden their listening appeal. Ex-Runaways singer and solo artist Joan Jett helped address this by producing Bikini Kill's 'New Radio' single, included on *The Singles* (1998).

Female-Friendly Gigs

At live shows, audiences were asked to allow women to the front. At a Huggy Bear gig in England in 1993, a male member of the audience objected to the "girls only at the front" policy, the resulting melée meaning the gig ended in chaos. Bikini Kill would invite female members of the audience to take the microphone and discuss matters of sexual misconduct and sexual abuse.

Above
The UK's Brighton-based Huggy Bear comprised two male and three female members and scored hits with songs such as 'Her Jazz'.

Negative Publicity

The British and American media were keen to run stories on riot grrrl, but a lack of co-operation from the bands meant media publicity was outside the bands' influence. Huggy Bear attracted controversy when they disrupted UK youth culture programme *The Word* because they objected to an item on "bimbos". In the States, Bikini Kill's singer Kathleen Hanna gained similar non-musical publicity when she was punched in the face by Hole's Courtney Love – not much sisterhood there, then!

Ironically, despite having a valid feminist agenda, particularly regarding sexism in the music industry, refusing to give interviews to the music press limited the movement's impact, and musically neither Bikini Kill nor Huggy Bear were able to move forward or capture a wider audience. Some of the spirit and influence of riot grrrl can be heard in British band Bis and in American bands L7, Babes In Toyland and Hole. The movement largely faded away with Kathleen Hanna going to graduate school in 1998, although Sleater-Kinney formed from the remnants of two first generation riot grrrl bands and kept the flag flying with *Call The Doctor* (1996).

> "BECAUSE WE DON'T WANNA ASSIMILATE TO SOMEONE ELSE'S (BOY) STANDARDS OF WHAT IS OR ISN'T."
> *From Kathleen Hanna's Riot Grrrl Manifesto.*

Above Left
As pioneers of the riot grrrl movement, Bikini Kill offered a similar brand of aggressive musical frustration and promises of female liberty to 1990s women as the Slits had done to female punks in the 1970s.

RIOT GRRRL

Heavily politicized lyrics, an elementary on-beat snare drum and aggressive guitar riffs sum up the riot grrrl genre.

LEADING EXPONENTS
Bikini Kill
Huggy Bear
Sleater-Kinney
Babes In Toyland
Tribe 8

THE ROCK INTRO ➡ 74   ROCK PEOPLE A–Z ➡ 116   INSTRUMENTS A–Z ➡ 436   ROCK: BRITISH PUNK ➡ 88   ROCK: GRUNGE ➡ 111

AS THE GENRE'S NAME SO BOLDLY IMPLIES, TIMING AND IMAGE WERE BOTH OF CRITICAL IMPORTANCE TO THE REALM OF NU METAL. IN PURE MUSICAL TERMS THERE WAS LITTLE TO UNITE THE SCENE'S LEADING EXPONENTS, SAVE FOR THE RADICAL DETUNING OF THEIR INSTRUMENTS AND A DESIRE TO DISTANCE THEMSELVES FROM SUCH OLD-SCHOOL HARD ROCK FAVOURITES AS IRON MAIDEN AND METALLICA.

Nu Metal

FROM the rap-flavoured pop rock of Limp Bizkit to the hate-driven, theatrical metal of Slipknot, the nu metal crowd was indeed a disparate gathering. Marilyn Manson and Nine Inch Nails, for example, were both established names before the critics began lumping them in with an ever-widening array of musical misfits.

Although Faith No More will forever be irked by the suggestion, the San Franciscan quintet's provocative, chaotically eccentric brand of funk metal helped to define the roots of nu metal during the mid-1980s. Later that decade, the grunge of Nirvana also helped to tear down lyrical, philosophical and visual barriers, paving the way for a far darker, nihilistic and stripped-down approach.

Above

Korn brought about the 1990s renaissance of metal music, with their raw, hip hop-tinged sound and honest songs that spoke to misunderstood teenagers everywhere.

The Setting Of Nu Metal Standards

Among the first act to crystallize the nu metal sound were Korn, a five-piece from Bakersfield in California. Railing against the suffocation of smalltown USA, Korn were lead by vocalist and former undertaker Jonathan Davis. The group's compellingly miserable self-titled debut album surfaced in 1994, overseen by Ross Robinson, the producer whose name quickly became a watermark of approval from within the nu metal circle. Davis'

"THERE IS GOOD AND EVIL WITHIN ALL OF US, AND I ENJOY SEARCHING TO BRING THAT OUT THROUGH MY MUSIC. I LIKE IT THAT THERE ARE QUESTIONS BROUGHT OUT BY MY MUSIC."
Marilyn Manson

violent lyrics addressed such previously taboo subjects as childhood bullying and even sexual abuse, connecting with many confused souls in the process.

Korn was a slowburner, though it eventually sold two million copies, and two years later the band confirmed their star quality with *Life Is Peachy*. Three more studio albums and seven years later, Korn have set standards of consistency and longevity that other nu metal acts can only dream of. However, their chief rivals are Slipknot and Limp Bizkit.

LEADING EXPONENTS

Limp Bizkit
Slipknot
Korn
System Of A Down
Marilyn Manson
Linkin Park
Deftones
Papa Roach
Nine Inch Nails
Staind

NU METAL

Unsettling melodic intervals, such as the minor second, and the augmented fourth in this riff are used as a repeating pattern in nu metal to create a disturbing and hypnotic sound

Electric Guitar

Electric Guitar

THE ROCK INTRO ➡ 74   ROCK PEOPLE A-Z ➡ 116   INSTRUMENTS A-Z ➡ 436   ROCK: GOTH ROCK ➡ 94   ROCK: GRUNGE ➡ 111

Hailing from Des Moines, Iowa, the nine members of Slipknot also used the repressions of their own collective youth as highly effective subject matter for songs like 'Wait And Bleed', 'Spit It Out' and 'People = Shit'. Fusing jagged, grinding riffs with barbaric percussion, plus samples and keyboards, Slipknot became overnight heroes after signing to Roadrunner Records in 1999 for their platinum-selling second album, *Slipknot* (their first album, 1997's *Mate. Feed. Kill. Repeat*, was self-financed). The group's refusal to be photographed without their trademark scary masks and boiler suits polarized opinions on levels of musicianship and validity, though to most it only heightened their mystique.

Proof of Slipknot's mushrooming popularity arrived in 2001 when their third album, *Iowa*, entered the Billboard chart at number three. However, with the group currently busying themselves in a variety of side-projects like the Murderdolls, Stone Sour and DJ Starscream – and even stating: "We've [got] one more album in us, then we'll call it a day" – question marks must be raised against their long-term future.

The very public face of nu metal, Limp Bizkit's Fred Durst is as famous for his red baseball cap and cheeky grin as for a series of childish feuds and disposable one-liners. Once a frustrated tattooist-cum-rap-rock frontman, the ubiquitous Durst astutely plotted the route to his current, enviable position of influence. It was Durst who appointed turntable wizard DJ Lethal to play on Limp Bizkits's first album, 1997's *Three Dollar Bill, Y'All$*, and who discovered future US chart-toppers Staind. He also recognized the importance of internet file-trading, controversially aligning the group to a tour sponsored by the music industry's avowed bête noire, Napster.

Nevertheless, it remains to be seen how Limp Bizkit will fare minus Wes Borland, the enigmatic guitarist that departed under mysterious circumstances following 2000's American chart-topping third album, *Chocolate Starfish And The Hotdog Flavored Water*. Borland is also due to return to action with his own project, *Eat The Day*.

Unpredictable Antics

If one single factor unites nu metal, it's the genre's sheer unpredictability. From the chameleon-like, shock rock-inspired antics of Marilyn Manson to the electrifying unconformity of Armenian-American four-piece System Of A Down and the commercially infused Linkin Park, bands once again seem happy to take chances. The power of the electric guitar – sometimes offered in seven-string format – remains central to the appeal of acts like Papa Roach, Staind, Amen and Taproot, but integration of electronica, hip hop, gothic and dance music is steadily growing.

Just a decade ago, it would have been hard to accept the notion of a hard rock group brave enough to absorb the Cure's influence, in the case of Sacramento's Deftones, or Duran Duran and Depeche Mode in that of Linkin Park. However, the mounting Grammy nominations and sales figures suggest that, for the moment at least, the listening public cannot get enough of such avid cross-pollination.

Left

The constantly masked band Slipknot consists of nine members, including three percussionists, two guitarists, a bassist, a DJ, a sampler and a lead singer. This line-up shows a marked departure from the traditional rock band and gives some idea of how rock music is evolving.

Below

Limp Bizkit guitarist Wes Borland, whose departure from the band in 2000 left a gaping hole. Borland was an important part of LB's stage act and his outrageous outfits and eccentric behaviour were popular with the fans.

Artists: Rock

Entries appear in the following order: name, music style, year(s) of popularity, type of artist, country of origin

.38 Special, Southern Rock, 1970s-, Artist, American
? & the Mysterians, US Underground & Garage Rock, 1960s; 1990s-, Artist, American
10,000 Maniacs, Alternative/Indie Rock, 1980s-1990s, Artist, American
101'ers, The, Pub Rock, 1970s, Artist, British
10cc, Prog Rock, 1970s-1990s, Artist, British
13th Floor Elevators, Psychedelic Rock, 1960s-1980s, Artist, American
7 Year Bitch, Riot Grrrl; Alternative/Indie Rock; Hard Rock, 1990s, Artist, American
999, British Punk, 1970s-1990s, Artist, British
A-Bones, The, US Underground & Garage Rock, 1980s-1990s, Artist, American
AC, Death Metal & Grindcore, 1990s-, Artist, American
AC/DC, Heavy Metal, 1970s-, Artist, Australian
Accept, Heavy Metal, 1970s-1990s, Artist, German
Ace, Pub Rock, 1970s, Artist, British
Addicts, The, Hard Rock; British Punk, 1970s-, Artist, British
Adolescents, The, US Underground & Garage Rock, 1970s-1980s, Artist, American
Adrenalin OD, US Underground & Garage Rock; Thrash & Speed Metal, 1980s-1990s, Artist, American
Adverts, The, British Punk, 1970s, Artist, British
Aerosmith, Hard Rock; Arena Rock; Heavy Metal, 1970s-, Artist, American
Afghan Whigs, Alternative/Indie Rock, 1980s-, Artist, American
Agent Orange, US Underground & Garage Rock, 1980s-1990s, Artist, American
Agitation Free, Alternative/Indie Rock, 1970s, Artist, German
Agnostic Front, US Underground & Garage Rock, 1980s-, Artist, American
Air Miami, Alternative/Indie Rock, 1990s, Artist, American
Alan Parsons Project, The, Prog Rock, 1970s-1890s, Artist, British
Alastis, Death Metal & Grindcore, 1990s, Artist, Swiss
Alexander, Willie "Loco", American Punk, 1970s-1990s, Artist, American
Alice Cooper, Heavy Metal; Hard Rock, 1960s-, Artist, American
Alice In Chains, Grunge; Alternative/Indie Rock, 1990s-, Artist, American
Alien Sex Fiend, Goth Rock, 1980s-, Artist, British
Allman Brothers Band, The, Southern Rock; Jam Rock, 1960s-, Artist, American
Allman, Duane, Southern Rock, 1960s-1970s, Artist, American
Allman, Gregg, Southern Rock, 1970s-1990s, Artist, American
Alternative TV, British Punk; Alternative/Indie Rock, 1970s-1990s, Artist, British
Ambitious Lovers, US Underground & Garage Rock; Alternative/Indie Rock, 1980s-1990s, Artist, American
Ambrosia, Prog Rock; Melodic Rock, 1970s-1990s, Artist, American
America, Melodic Rock, 1970s-1990s, Artist, British
American Music Club, Alternative/Indie Rock, 1980s-1990s, Artist, American
Anacrusis, Thrash & Speed Metal, 1980s-1990s, Artist, American
Anathema, Doom Metal; Death Metal & Grindcore, 1990s-, Artist, British
Angelic Upstarts, British Punk; Hard Rock, 1970s-, Artist, British
Angry Samoans, US Underground & Garage Rock, 1970s-1990s, Artist, American
Annihilator, Thrash & Speed Metal, 1980s-, Artist, Canadian
Anthrax, Thrash & Speed Metal, 1980s-, Artist, American
Aphrodite's Child, Prog Rock, 1960s-1970s, Artist, Greek
Arch Enemy, Death Metal & Grindcore, 1990s-, Artist, British
Archers Of Loaf, Alternative/Indie Rock, 1990s-, Artist, American
Area, Prog Rock, 1970s, Artist, Italian
Argent, Prog Rock, 1960s-1970s, Artist, British
Art Bears, The, Prog Rock, 1970s-1980s, Artist, British
Ash Ra Tempel, Prog Rock, 1970s-, Artist, German
Asia, Prog Rock; Arena Rock, 1980s-, Artist, British
At The Gates, Death Metal & Grindcore, 1990s-, Artist, Swedish
Atheist, Death Metal & Grindcore, 1980s-1990s, Artist, American
Atlanta Rhythm Section, The, Southern Rock, 1970s-1980s, Artist, American
Au Pairs, The, British Punk, 1980s, Artist, British
Avail, Alternative/Indie Rock, 1990s-, Artist, American
Avengers, The, American Punk, 1970s-1980s, Artist, American
Average White Band, The, Funk Metal, 1970s-1980s, Artist, British
Ayers, Kevin, Prog Rock, 1960s-1990s, Artist, British
Babes In Toyland, Riot Grrrl; Alternative/Indie Rock; Grunge, 1980s-1990s, Artist, American
Babys, The, Arena Rock; Hard Rock, 1970s-1980s, Artist, British
Bachman-Turner Overdrive, Arena Rock; Hard Rock, 1960s-1980s, Artist, British
Bad Brains, US Underground & Garage Rock; Alternative/Indie Rock, 1980s-1990s, Artist, American
Bad Company, Hard Rock; Arena Rock, 1970s-1990s, Artist, British
Bad Religion, US Underground & Garage Rock; Alternative/Indie Rock, 1980s-, Artist, American
Bantam Rooster, US Underground & Garage Rock; Alternative/Indie Rock, 1990s-, Artist, American
Barbarians, The, Pub Rock, 1960s-1970s, Artist, British
Barenaked Ladies, Alternative/Indie Rock, 1990s-, Artist, Canadian
Barracudas, The, US Underground & Garage Rock, 1980s; 2000s, Artist, Anglo-American
Barrett, Syd, Psychedelic Rock, 1960s-1970s, Artist, British
Barry & the Remains, US Underground & Garage Rock, 1960s, Artist, American
Bathory, Death Metal & Grindcore, 1980s-, Artist, Swedish
Bauhaus, Goth Rock; Alternative/Indie Rock, 1970s-1990s, Artist, British
Beastie Boys, The Alternative/Indie Rock; Funk Metal, 1980s-, Artist, American
Beasts Of Bourbon, Alternative/Indie Rock; Pub Rock, 1980s-1990s, Artist, Australian
Beat Happening, Alternative/Indie Rock, 1980s-1990s, Artist, American
Beatles, The, Psychedelic Rock, 1960s-1970s, Artist, British
Beck, Alternative/Indie Rock, 1990s-, Artist; Songwriter, American
Beck, Jeff, Hard Rock, 1960s-, Artist, British
Bees Make Honey, Pub Rock, 1970s, Artist, British
Belew, Adrian, Prog Rock; Alternative/Indie Rock, 1980s-, Artist, American
Believer, Thrash & Speed Metal, 1980s-1990s, Artist, American
Benatar, Pat, Arena Rock; Hard Rock, 1970s-, Artist, American
Bettii Serveert, Alternative/Indie Rock, 1990s-, Artist, Dutch
Betts, Dickey, Funk Metal, 1970s-, Artist, American
Bevis Frond, The, Alternative/Indie Rock, 1980s-, Artist, British
Big Black, US Underground & Garage Rock; Alternative/Indie Rock, 1980s, Artist, American
Big Boys, The, US Underground & Garage Rock; Alternative/Indie Rock, 1980s-1990s, Artist, American
Big Head Todd & the Monsters, Jam Rock, 1980s–, Artist, American
Big Star, Proto-Punk, 1970s, Artist, American
Bikini Kill, Riot Grrrl; Alternative/Indie Rock, 1990s, Artist, American
Birthday Party, The, Alternative/Indie Rock, 1970s-1980s, Artist, Australian
Bitch Magnet, Alternative/Indie Rock, 1980s-1990s, Artist, American
Björk, Alternative/Indie Rock, 1990s-, Artist, Icelandic
Black Crowes, The, Southern Rock; Jam Rock, 1990s-, Artist, American
Black Flag, US Underground & Garage Rock; American Punk, 1970s-1980s, Artist, American
Black Sabbath, Heavy Metal, 1960s-, Artist, British
Blackfoot, Southern Rock, 1970s-1990s, Artist, American
Blind Guardian, Heavy Metal, 1980s-, Artist, German
Blonde Redhead, Alternative/Indie Rock, 1990s-, Artist, American
Blondie, American Punk, 1970s-1990s, Artist, American
Blossom Toes, Psychedelic Rock, 1960s, Artist, British
Blue Cheer, Psychedelic Rock; Hard Rock1960s-1990s, Artist, American
Blue Oyster Cult, Arena Rock; Hard Rock, 1970s-, Artist, American
Blues Magoos, The, US Underground & Garage Rock; Psychedelic Rock, 1960s-1970s, Artist, American
Blues Traveler, Jam Rock, 1990s–, Artist, American
BMX Bandits, Alternative/Indie Rock, 1980s-1990s, Artist, British
Bolan, Marc, Glam Rock & Glitter; Psychedelic Rock, 1960s-1970s, Artist; Songwriter, British
Bolt Thrower, Death Metal & Grindcore, 1980s-, Artist, British
Bon Jovi, Arena Rock; Melodic Rock, 1980s-, Artist, American
Bongwater, US Underground & Garage Rock; Alternative/Indie Rock, 1980s-1990s, Artist, American
Boo Radleys, The, Shoegazing; Alternative/Indie Rock, 1990s, Artist, British
Boomtown Rats, The, British Punk, 1970s-1980s, Artist, British
Boredoms, Alternative/Indie Rock, 1980s-, Artist, Japanese
Borknager, Death Metal & Grindcore, 1990s-, Artist, Norwegian
Boss Hog, Alternative/Indie Rock, 1980s-, Artist, American
Boston, Arena Rock; Hard Rock, 1970s-1990s, Artist, American
Bowie, David, Hard Rock; Proto-Punk; Prog Rock; Glam Rock & Glitter, 1960s-, Artist, British
Brainiac, Alternative/Indie Rock, 1990s, Artist, American
Bratmobile, Riot Grrrl; Alternative/Indie Rock, 1990s-, Artist, American
Breeders, The, Alternative/Indie Rock, 1990s-, Artist, American
Brinsley Schwarz, Pub Rock, 1970s, Artist, British
Brown Arthur, Psychedelic Rock, 1960s-1990s, Artist, British
Brutal Truth, Death Metal & Grindcore, 1990s-, Artist, American
Budgie, Heavy Metal; Hard Rock, 1970s-1980s, Artist, British
Built To Spill, Alternative/Indie Rock, 1990s-, Artist, American
Burzum, Black Metal, 1990s-, Artist, Norwegian
Bush, Grunge; Alternative/Indie Rock, 1990s-, Artist, British
Butchies, The, Riot Grrrl; Alternative/Indie Rock, 1990s-, Artist, American
Butterglory, Alternative/Indie Rock, 1990s, Artist, American
Butthole Surfers, The, US Underground & Garage Rock; Alternative/Indie Rock, 1980s-1990s, Artist, American
Buzzcocks, British Punk, 1970s-, Artist, British
Byrds, The, Psychedelic Rock, 1960s-1970s, Artist, American
Byrne, David, Alternative/Indie Rock, 1980s-, Producer; Artist, British
Cabaret Voltaire, Alternative/Indie Rock, 1970s-1990s, Artist, British
Cale, John, Proto-Punk; Prog Rock, 1960s-, Artist, British
Camel, Prog Rock, 1970s-1990s, Artist, British
Camper Van Beethoven, US Underground & Garage Rock; Alternative/Indie Rock, 1980s, Artist, American
Can, Prog Rock, 1960s-1990s, Artist, German
Cancer, Death Metal & Grindcore, 1980s-1990s, Artist, American
Candlebox, Grunge; Alternative/Indie Rock, 1990s, Artist, American
Candlemass, Doom Metal, 1980s-1990s, Artist, Swedish
Cannibal Corpse, Death Metal & Grindcore, 1980s-, Artist, American
Captain Beefheart, Psychedelic Rock; Proto-Punk; Prog-Rock, 1960s-1980s, Artist, American
Caravan, Prog Rock, 1960s-1990s, Artist, British
Carcass, Death Metal & Grindcore, 1980s-1990s, Artist, British
Carroll, Jim, Proto-Punk; American Punk, 1970s-1990s, Artist, American
Cathedral, Doom Metal; Heavy Metal, 1990s-, Artist, British
Catherine Wheel, Shoegazing; Alternative/Indie Rock, 1990s-, Artist, British
Caustic Resin, Alternative/Indie Rock, 1990s-, Artist, American
Cavaliere, Felix, Prog Rock, 1970s; 1990s, Artist, American
Cave, Nick, Alternative/Indie Rock, 1980s-, Artist; Songwriter, Australian
Celibate Rifles, Alternative/Indie Rock, 1980s-1990s, Artist, Australian
Celtic Frost, Thrash & Speed Metal, 1980s-1990s, Artist, Swiss
Cemetary, Doom Metal; Death Metal & Grindcore, 1990s, Artist, Swedish
Chapterhouse, Alternative/Indie Rock; Shoegazing, 1980s-1990s, Artist, British
Charlatans, The, Madchester; Alternative/Indie Rock, 1980s-, Artist, British
Charlie & the Wide Boys, Pub Rock, 1970s, Artist, British
Charlie Daniels Band, The, Southern Rock, 1970s-1990s, Artist, American
Chavez, Alternative/Indie Rock, 1990s, Artist, American
Cheap Trick, Hard Rock; Arena Rock, 1970s-, Artist, American
Cherubs, Alternative/Indie Rock, 1990s, Artist, American
Chesterfield Kings, US Underground & Garage Rock, 1980s-1990s, Artist, American
Chicago, Melodic Rock, 1960s-, Artist, American
Childish, Billy, Alternative/Indie Rock, 1970s-, Artist, British
Chilli Willi & the Red Hot Peppers, Pub Rock, 1970s, Artist, British
Chocolate Watchband, The, US Underground & Garage Rock; Psychedelic Rock, 1960s; 1990s, Artist, American
Chokebore, Alternative/Indie Rock, 1990s, Artist, American
Church, The, Alternative/Indie Rock, 1980s-, Artist, Australian
Cinderella, Heavy Metal; Hard Rock, 1980s-1990s, Artist, American
Circle Jerks, The, American Punk, 1980s-1990s, Artist, American
Clan Of Xymox, Goth Rock, 1980s-, Artist, Dutch
Clapton, Eric, Hard Rock, 1960s-, Artist; Songwriter, British
Clash, The, Hard Rock; British Punk, 1970s-1980s, Artist, British
Cockney Rebel, Glam Rock & Glitter, 1970s-1990s, Artist, British
Cockney Rejects, British Punk, 1980s-1990s, Artist, British
Coctails, The, Alternative/Indie Rock, 1990s, Artist, American
Colosseum II, Prog Rock; Hard Rock, 1970s, Artist, British
Come, Alternative/Indie Rock, 1990s, Artist, American
Conflict, British Punk, 1980s-, Artist, British
Connors, Loren MazzaCane, Alternative/Indie Rock, 1980s-, Artist, American
Coroner, Thrash & Speed Metal, 1980s-1990s, Artist, Swiss
Corrosion Of Conformity, Thrash & Speed Metal, 1980s-, Artist, American
Costello, Elvis, British Punk; Pub Rock, 1970s-, Artist; Songwriter, British
Count Five, US Underground & Garage Rock; Psychedelic Rock, 1960s, Artist, American
Counting Crows, Alternative/Indie Rock, 1990s-, Artist, American
Country Joe & Fish, Psychedelic Rock, 1960s-1970s, Artist, American
Cowboy Junkies, Alternative/Indie Rock, 1980s-, Artist, Canadian
Cows, The, US Underground & Garage Rock; Alternative/Indie Rock, 1980s-1990s, Artist, American
Cradle Of Filth, Black Metal, 1990s-, Artist, British
Cramps, The, US Underground & Garage Rock, 1980s-1990s, Artist, American
Crass, British Punk, 1970s-1980s, Artist, British
Cream, Hard Rock; Psychedelic Rock, 1960s, Artist, British
Creation, The, Psychedelic Rock, 1960s, Artist, British
Creatures, The, Goth Rock, 1980s-1990s, Artist, British
Creedence Clearwater Revival, Southern Rock, 1960s-1970s, Artist, American
Crimson Glory, Heavy Metal, 1980s-1990s, Artist, American
Cro-Mags, US Underground & Garage Rock; Thrash & Speed Metal, 1980s-, Artist, American
Crow, Sheryl, Alternative/Indie Rock, 1990s-, Artist, American
Crowded House, Alternative/Indie Rock, 1980s-1990s, Artist, New Zealander
Cub, Alternative/Indie Rock, 1990s, Artist, American
Cul de Sac, Alternative/Indie Rock, 1990s-, Artist, American
Cult, The, Goth Rock; Hard Rock, 1980s-, Artist, British
Cure, The, Goth Rock; Alternative/Indie Rock, 1970s-1990s, Artist, British
Curved Air, Prog Rock, 1970s; 1990s, Artist, British
Cynic, Death Metal & Grindcore, 1990s, Artist, American
Cynics, US Underground & Garage Rock; Alternative/Indie Rock, 1980s-1990s, Artist, American
Czukay, Holger, Prog Rock, 1960s-, Artist, German
Dag Nasty, US Underground & Garage Rock, 1980s-, Artist, American
Damned, The, British Punk; Goth Rock, 1970s-1990s, Artist, British
Dan Reed Netwrok, Funk Metal, 1980s–, Artist, American
Dantalion's Chariot, Psychedelic Rock, 1960s, Artist, British
Danzig, Heavy Metal, 1980s-, Artist, American
Dark Tranquillity, Death Metal & Grindcore, 1990s-, Artist, Swedish
Darkthrone, Black Metal, 1990s-, Artist, Norwegian
Das Damen, US Underground & Garage Rock; Alternative/Indie Rock, 1980s-1990s, Artist, American
Dave Matthews Band, Southern Rock; Jam Rock, 1990s-, Artist, American
De Burgh, Chris, Melodic Rock; Prog Rock, 1970s-, Artist, British
Dead Boys, American Punk, 1970s-1980s, Artist, American
Dead Can Dance, Shoegazing, 1980s-, Artist, Australian
Dead Kennedys, US Underground & Garage Rock; American Punk, 1970s-1980s, Artist, American

Death Angel, Thrash & Speed Metal, 1980s-1990s, Artist, American
Death, Death Metal & Grindcore, 1980s-, Artist, American
Death, Christian, Goth Rock; Thrash & Speed Metal, 1980s-1990s, Artist, American
Deep Purple, Hard Rock, 1960s-, Artist, British
Def Leppard, Hard Rock; Heavy Metal, 1980s-, Artist, British
Defectors, The, Alternative/Indie Rock, 1990s-, Artist, Danish
Deftones, Nu Metal, 1990s-, Artist, American
Deicide, Death Metal & Grindcore, 1990s-, Artist, American
Demons & Wizards, Heavy Metal, 2000s-, Artist, American
Depeche Mode, Alternative/Indie Rock, 1980s-, Artist, British
Derek & the Dominoes, Hard Rock, 1970s, Artist, British
Descendents, US Underground & Garage Rock, 1980s-1990s, Artist, American
Destroy All Monsters, Proto-Punk; Hard Rock, 1970s-1990s, Artist, American
DeVille, Mink, American Punk, 1970s-1990s, Artist, American
Devo, US Underground & Garage Rock; American Punk, 1970s-1990s, Artist, American
Dickies, The, American Punk, 1970s-, Artist, American
Dicks, US Underground & Garage Rock, 1980s, Artist, American
Dictators, The, American Punk; Proto-Punk, 1970s-1980s, Artist, American
Die Kreuzen, US Underground & Garage Rock, 1980s-1990s, Artist, American
Died Pretty, Alternative/Indie Rock, 1980s-, Artist, Australian
Dils, American Punk, 1970s-1980s, Artist, American
Dimmu Borgir, Black Metal, 1990s-, Artist, Norwegian
Dinosaur Jr., US Underground & Garage Rock; Alternative/Indie Rock, 1980s-1990s, Artist, American
Dio, Heavy Metal; Hard Rock, 1970s-, Artist, American
Dire Straits, Melodic Rock, 1970s-1990s, Artist, British
Disco Biscuits, The, Jam Rock, 1990s–, Artist, American
Dissection, Death Metal & Grindcore, 1990s-, Artist, Swedish
Dixie Dregs, The, Southern Rock, 1970s-1980s, Artist, American
DMZ, US Underground & Garage Rock, 1970s-1980s, Artist, American
Donnas, The, Alternative/Indie Rock; Hard Rock, 1990s-, Artist, American
Donovan, Psychedelic Rock, 1960s-, Artist, British
Doors, The, Psychedelic Rock; Proto-Punk, 1960s-1970s, Artist, American
Dr. Feelgood, Pub Rock, 1970s-, Artist, British
Dream Syndicate, US Underground & Garage Rock; Alternative/Indie Rock, 1980s, Artist, American
Dream Theater, Heavy Metal; Hard Rock, 1980s-, Artist, American
DRI, US Underground & Garage Rock; Thrash & Speed Metal, 1980s-, Artist, American
Drive Like Jehu, Alternative/Indie Rock, 1990s, Artist, American
Ducks Deluxe, Pub Rock, 1970s-1980s, Artist, British
Dukes Of Stratosphear, The, Psychedelic Rock; Alternative/Indie Rock, 1980s, Artist, British
Dury, Ian, British Punk; Pub Rock, 1970s-1990s, Artist, British
Eagles, The, Melodic Rock, 1970s-1990s, Artist, American
Echo & the Bunnymen, Alternative/Indie Rock, 1970s-, Artist, British
Eddie & the Hot Rods, British Punk; Pub Rock, 1970s-1990s, Artist, British
Edge Of Sanity, Death Metal & Grindcore, 1990s, Artist, Swedish
Edmunds, Dave, Pub Rock, 1970s-, Artist, British
Eels, Alternative/Indie Rock, 1990s-, Artist, American
Eggs Over Easy, Pub Rock, 1970s, Artist, American
Eggs, Alternative/Indie Rock, 1990s, Artist, American
Eight-Eyed Spy, US Underground & Garage Rock, 1980s, Artist, American
Electric Eels, Proto-Punk, 1970s, Artist, American
Electric Light Orchestra, Prog Rock, 1970s-, Artist, British
Electric Prunes, The, Psychedelic Rock; US Underground & Garage Rock, 1960s, Artist, American
Eleventh Dream Day, Alternative/Indie Rock, 1980s-, Artist, American
Eloy, Prog Rock, 1970s-1990s, Artist, German
Embarrassment, The, US Underground & Garage Rock; Alternative/Indie Rock, 1970s-1990s, Artist, American
Emerson, Lake & Palmer, Prog Rock, 1970s-1990s, Artist, British
Emperor, Black Metal, 1990s-, Artist, Norwegian
Eno, Brian, Prog Rock; Proto-Punk, 1970s-, Artist, British
Entombed, Death Metal & Grindcore, 1980s-, Artist, Swedish
Enuff Znuff, Hard Rock, 1980s-, Artist, American
Eric's Trip, Alternative/Indie Rock, 1990s, Artist, Canadian
E-Types, The, US Underground & Garage Rock, 1960s; 1990s, Artist, American
Everclear, Grunge; Hard Rock; Alternative/Indie Rock, 1990s-, Artist, American
Ex, The, Alternative/Indie Rock, 1980s-, Artist, Dutch
Exodus, Thrash & Speed Metal, 1980s-1990s, Artist, American
Exploited, The, British Punk, 1980s-, Artist, British
Extreme Noise Terror, Death Metal & Grindcore, 1980s-, Artist, British
Extreme, Heavy Metal; Hard Rock, 1980s-1990s, Artist, American
Faces, Hard Rock; Proto-Punk, 1970s, Artist, British
Fair, Jad, US Underground & Garage Rock; Alternative/Indie Rock, 1980s-, Artist, American
Faith Healers, Th', Shoegazing; Alternative/Indie Rock, 1990s, Artist, British
Faith No More, Funk Metal, 1980s-1990s, Artist, American
Falco, Tav, Alternative/Indie Rock, 1980s-, Artist, American
Fall, The, Alternative/Indie Rock, 1970s-, Artist, British
Family, Prog Rock, 1960s-1970s, Artist, British
Fankhauser, Merrell, Prog Rock, 1960s-, Artist, American
Farm, The, Madchester, 1980s-1990s, Artist, British
Fastbacks, Alternative/Indie Rock, 1980s-1990s, Artist, American
Faster Pussycat, Heavy Metal; Hard Rock, 1980s-1990s, Artist, American
Fate's Warning, Heavy Metal, 1980s-, Artist, American
Faust, Prog Rock, 1970s-, Artist, German
Fear Factory, Heavy Metal, 1990s-, Artist, American
Fear, US Underground & Garage Rock, 1970s-, Artist, American
Feelies, The, US Underground & Garage Rock; Alternative/Indie Rock, 1970s-1990s, Artist, American
Felt, British Punk, 1970s-1980s, Artist, British
Ferry, Bryan, Prog Rock; Glam Rock & Glitter, 1970s-, Artist, British
Fields Of The Nephilim, Goth Rock, 1980s-1990s, Artist, British
Firehouse, Heavy Metal, 1980s-, Artist, American
Fishbone, Funk Metal, 1980s-, Artist, American
Flamin' Groovies, The, Proto-Punk, 1960s-1990s, Artist, American
Flaming Lips, The, US Underground & Garage Rock; Alternative/Indie Rock, 1980s-, Artist, American
Flash, Prog Rock, 1970s, Artist, British
Fleetwood Mac, Prog Rock, 1960s-, Artist, British
Flesh Eaters, US Underground & Garage Rock; Hard Rock, 1970s-1990s, Artist, American
Flesh For Lulu, Goth Rock, 1980s-1990s, Artist, British
Fleshcrawl, Death Metal & Grindcore, 1980s-, Artist, American
Fleshtones, The, US Underground & Garage Rock; Alternative/Indie Rock, 1970s-, Artist, American
Fleur de Lys, Les, Psychedelic Rock, 1960s, Artist, British
Flipper, US Underground & Garage Rock; Alternative/Indie Rock, 1980s-1990s, Artist, American
Flotsam & Jetsam, Thrash & Speed Metal, 1980s-, Artist, American
Flowered Up, Madchester, 1990s, Artist, British
Flying Saucer Attack, Alternative/Indie Rock, 1990s-, Artist, British
FM, Prog Rock, 1970s-, Artist, Canadian
Focus, Prog Rock, 1970s-1980s, Artist, Dutch
Folk Implosion, Alternative/Alternative/Indie Rock, 1990s-, Artist, American
Foo Fighters, Grunge; Alternative/Indie Rock, 1990s-, Artist, American
Foreigner, Hard Rock; Arena Rock, 1970s-, Artist, American
Frampton, Peter, Arena Rock, 1970s-, Artist, British
Free, Hard Rock, 1960s-1970s, Artist, British
Frumpies, Riot Grrrl; Alternative/Indie Rock, 1990s, Artist, American
Fuck, Alternative/Indie Rock, 1990s-, Artist, American
Fugazi, US Underground & Garage Rock; Alternative/Indie Rock, 1980s-, Artist, American
Fushitsusha, Alternative/Indie Rock, 1980s-1990s, Artist, Japanese
Fuzztones, The, US Underground & Garage Rock; Alternative/Indie Rock, 1980s-1990s, Artist, American
Gabriel, Peter, Prog Rock, 1970s-, Artist, British
Galactic Cowboys, The, Heavy Metal; Hard Rock, 1990s-, Artist, American
Galaxie 500, Alternative/Indie Rock; Shoegazing, 1980s-1990s, Artist, American
Gamma Ray, Heavy Metal, 1990s-, Artist, American
Gang Of Four, Alternative/Indie Rock, 1970s-1990s, Artist, British
Gastr del Sol, Alternative/Indie Rock, 1990s, Artist, American
Gathering, The, Death Metal & Grindcore, 1990s-, Artist, Dutch
Gaza Strippers, US Underground & Garage Rock; Alternative/Indie Rock, 1990s-, Artist, American
Gene Loves Jezebel, Goth Rock, 1980s-, Artist, British
Generation X, British Punk, 1970s-1980s, Artist, British
Genesis, Prog Rock, 1960s-1990s, Artist, British
Gentle Giant, Prog Rock, 1970s-1980s, Artist,
Georgia Satellites, The, Southern Rock, 1980s-1990s, Artist, American
Germs, The, US Underground & Garage Rock; American Punk, 1970s-1980s, Artist, American
Ginn, Greg, US Underground & Garage Rock; Alternative/Indie Rock, 1990s, Artist, American
Girls Against Boys, Alternative/Indie Rock, 1990s-, Artist, American
Glitter Band, Glam Rock & Glitter, 1970s-1990s, Artist, British
Glitter, Gary, Glam Rock & Glitter, 1960s-1990s, Artist, British
Goblin, Prog Rock; Hard Rock, 1970s-1980s, Artist, Italian
Godflesh, Death Metal & Grindcore, 1980s-, Artist, British
Godspeed You Black Emperor, Alternative/Indie Rock, 1990s-, Artist, Canadian
Gomm, Ian, Pub Rock, 1970s-, Artist, British
Gone, US Underground & Garage Rock; Alternative/Indie Rock, 1980s-, Artist, American
Gong, Prog Rock, 1070s-, Artist, Australian
Goo Goo Dolls, Alternative/Indie Rock; Hard Rock, 1980s-, Artist, American
Gorefest, Death Metal & Grindcore, 1980s-1990s, Artist, Dutch
Government Issue, US Underground & Garage Rock, 1980s-1990s, Artist, American
Graham, Ernie, Pub Rock, 1970s, Artist, British
Grand Funk Railroad, Hard Rock; Arena Rock, 1960s-1990s, Artist, American
Grateful Dead, The, Psychedelic Rock; Jam Rock, 1960s-1990s, Artist, American
Great White, Heavy Metal; Hard Rock, 1980s-, Artist, American
Green River, Grunge; Alternative/Indie Rock, 1980s, Artist, American
Grifters, Alternative/Indie Rock, 1990s, Artist, American
Grindcrusher, Death Metal & Grindcore, 1990s, Artist, British
Grodes, The, US Underground & Garage Rock, 1960s, Artist, American
Groundhogs, The, Heavy Metal; Psychedelic Rock, 1960s-1990s, Artist, British
Grubbs, David, Alternative/Indie Rock, 1990s-, Artist, American
Guess Who, The, Hard Rock, 1960s-1970s; 1990s, Artist, Canadian
Guided By Voices, Alternative/Indie Rock, 1980s-, Artist, American
Gumball, Grunge; Alternative/Indie Rock, 1990s, Artist, American
Gun Club, US Underground & Garage Rock; Hard Rock; Alternative/Indie Rock, 1980s-1990s, Artist, American
Guns 'n' Roses, Hard Rock, 1980s-, Artist, American
Hackett, Steve, Prog Rock, 1970s-, Artist, British
Haino, Keiji, Alternative/Indie Rock, 1970s-, Artist, Japanese
Half Japanese, US Underground & Garage Rock; Alternative/Indie Rock, 1970s-, Artist, American
Half Man Half Biscuit, Alternative/Indie Rock, 1980s-, Artist, British
Hammerfall, Heavy Metal, 1990s-, Artist, Swedish
Hangman's Beautiful Daughters, US Underground & Garage Rock, 1980s, Artist, American
Happy Mondays, Madchester; Alternative/Indie Rock, 1980s-1990s, Artist, British
Harvey, P. J., Alternative/Indie Rock, 1990s-, Artist, British
Haunted, The, Death Metal & Grindcore, 1990s-, Artist, Swedish
Hawkwind, Prog Rock; Hard Rock, 1970s-, Artist, British
Head Of David, Death Metal & Grindcore, 1980s-1990s, Artist, British
Heart, Hard Rock; Arena Rock, 1970s-, Artist, American
Heartbreakers, The, American Punk; Hard Rock; Proto-Punk, 1970s-1980s, Artist, American
Heat, Reverend Horton, Alternative Rock, 1990s-, Artist, American
Heavens To Betsy, Riot Grrrl, 1990s, Artist, American
Helium, Alternative/Indie Rock, 1990s, Artist, American
Hell, Richard, Proto-Punk, 1970s-, Artist, American
Helloween, Thrash & Speed Metal, 1980s-, Artist, German
Help Yourself, Pub Rock, 1970s, Artist, British
Hendrix, Jimi, Hard Rock; Psychedelic Rock, 1960s-1970s, Artist; Songwriter, American
Hentchmen, US Underground & Garage Rock; Alternative/Indie Rock, 1990s-, Artist, American
Herd, The, Psychedelic Rock, 1960s-1970s, Artist, British
Hillage, Steve, Prog Rock, 1970s-1980s, Artist, British
His Name Is Alive, Alternative/Indie Rock, 1990s-, Artist, American
Hitchcock, Robyn, Alternative/Indie Rock, 1980s-, Artist, British
Hole, Grunge; Alternative/Indie Rock, 1990s-, Artist, American
Hoodoo Gurus, Alternative/Indie Rock, 1980s-1990s, Artist, Australian
Hootie & the Blowfish, Alternative/Indie Rock, 1990s-, Artist, American
Hornsby, Bruce, Alternative/Indie Rock, 1980s-, Artist, American
Huggy Bear, Riot Grrrl; Alternative/Indie Rock, 1990s, Artist, British
Human Beinz, The, US Underground & Garage Rock; Psychedelic Rock, 1960s, Artist, American
Humble Pie, Hard Rock, 1960s-1980s, Artist, British
Hüsker Dü, US Underground & Garage Rock; American Punk, 1980s, Artist, American
Hypocrisy, Death Metal & Grindcore, 1990s-, Artist, Swedish
Iced Earth, Heavy Metal, 1980s-, Artist, American
Idle Race, The, Prog Rock; Psychedelic Rock, 1960s-1970s, Artist, British
Immortal, Black Metal, 1990s, Artist, Norwegian
Impala, US Underground & Garage Rock, 1990s, Artist, American
In Flames, Death Metal & Grindcore, 1990s-, Artist, Swedish
Incredible String Band, The, Psychedelic Rock, 1960s-, Artist, British
Inspiral Carpets, Madchester, 1980s-1990s, Artist, British
Intruders, The, US Underground & Garage Rock, 1960s, Artist, American
Iron Butterfly, Psychedelic Rock; Hard Rock, 1960s-1970s, Artist, American
Iron Maiden, Heavy Metal, 1970s-, Artist, British
Ishtar, Death Metal & Grindcore, 1990s-, Artist, Danish
It Bites, Prog Rock; Hard Rock, 1980s-1990s, Artist, British
J. Geils Band, Hard Rock, 1970s-1980s, Artist, American
Jaguars, The, US Underground & Garage Rock; Psychedelic Rock, 1960s, Artist, American
Jale, Alternative/Indie Rock, 1990s, Artist, Canadian
Jam, The, British Punk, 1970s-1980s, Artist, British
James Gang, Arena Rock; Hard Rock, 1960s-1970s, Artist, American
James, Madchester; Alternative/Indie Rock, 1980s-2000s, Artist, British
Jane's Addiction, Alternative/Indie Rock, 1980s-1990s, Artist, American
Japan, Prog Rock, 1970s-1980s, Artist, British
Jawbox, Alternative/Indie Rock, 1990s-, Artist, American
Jawbreaker, Grunge; Alternative/Indie Rock, 1980s-1990s, Artist, American
Jefferson Airplane, Psychedelic Rock; Hard Rock, 1960s-1980s, Artist, American
Jefferson Starship, Arena Rock; Hard Rock, 1970s-, Artist, American
Jesus & Mary Chain, The, Alternative/Indie Rock, 1980s-1990s, Artist, British
Jesus Lizard, The, US Underground & Garage Rock; Alternative/Indie Rock, 1980s-1990s, Artist, American
Jethro Tull, Prog Rock; Arena Rock; Hard Rock, 1960s-, Artist, British
Jett, Joan, Hard Rock; Arena Rock, 1980s-, Artist, American
Jobriath, Glam Rock & Glitter, 1970s, Artist, American
Johansen, David, American Punk; Hard Rock, 1970s-, Artist, American
Jon & Vangelis, Prog Rock, 1970s-1990s, Artist, Greek
Jon Spencer Blues Explosion, Alternative/Indie Rock, 1990s, Artist, American
Journey, Arena Rock; Melodic Rock; Hard Rock, 1970s-, Artist, American
Joy Division, Alternative/Indie Rock, 1970s-1980s, Artist, British
Judas Jump, Prog Rock, 1970s, Artist, British
Judas Priest, Heavy Metal; Hard Rock, 1970s-1990s, Artist, British
Kaiser, Henry, Prog Rock; Alternative/Indie Rock, 1970s-, Artist, American
Kansas, Prog Rock; Arena Rock, 1970s-1990s, Artist, American
Kenny, Glitter, 1970s, Artist, British
Kid Rock, Heavy Metal; Hard Rock, 1990s-, Artist, American
Kilburn & the High Roads, Pub Rock, 1970s, Artist, British
Killdozer, US Underground & Garage Rock; Alternative/Indie Rock, 1980s-1990s, Artist, American
King Crimson, Prog Rock, 1960s-, Artist, British

King Diamond, Thrash & Speed Metal, 1980s-, Artist, American
King's X, Prog Rock; Hard Rock, 1980s-, Artist, American
Kingsmen, The, US Underground & Garage Rock, 1960s, Artist, American
Kinks, The, Hard Rock, 1960s-, Artist, British
Kiss, Hard Rock; Arena Rock, 1970s-, Artist, American
Korn, Nu Metal, 1990s-, Artist, American
Kravitz, Lenny, Psychedelic Rock, 1980s-, Artist, American
Kreator, Thrash & Speed Metal, 1980s-, Artist, German
Kuepper, Ed, Alternative/Indie Rock, 1980s-1990s, Artist, German
Kursaal Flyers, Pub Rock, 1970s-1980s, Artist, British
Kyuss, Heavy Metal; Hard Rock, 1990s, Artist, American
L7, Riot Grrrl; Grunge; Alternative/Indie Rock, 1990s, Artist, American
La De Das, The, Alternative/Indie Rock, 1960s-1970s, Artist, New Zealander
LA Guns, Heavy Metal; Hard Rock, 1980s-, Artist, American
La's, The, Alternative/Indie Rock, 1980s-, Artist, British
Lake Of Tears, Doom Metal; Heavy Metal, 1990s-, Artist, Sweden
Lambchop, Alternative/Indie Rock, 1990s-, Artist, American
Leaves, The, US Underground & Garage Rock, 1960s, Artist, American
Leaving Trains, US Underground & Garage Rock; Alternative/Indie Rock, 1980s-1990s, Artist, American
Led Zeppelin, Hard Rock, 1960s-1980s, Artist, British
Leftover Salmon, Jam Rock, 1990s-, Artist, American
Lemonheads, The, Alternative/Indie Rock; US Underground & Garage Rock, 1980s-1990s, Artist, American
Lewis, Huey, Arena Rock, 1980s-, Artist, American
Lilys, Shoegazing; Alternative/Indie Rock, 1990s-, Artist, American
Lime Spiders, Alternative/Indie Rock, 1980s-1990s, Artist, Australian
Limp Bizkit, Nu Metal, 1990s–, Artist, American
Linkin Park, Nu Metal, 1990s–, Artist, American
Litter, The, US Underground & Garage Rock; Psychedelic Rock, 1960s-1970s, Artist, American
Little Feat, Hard Rock, 1970s-, Artist, American
Live Skull, US Underground & Garage Rock, 1980s-1990s, Artist, American
Living Colour, Funk Metal, 1980s-1990s, Artist, Anglo-American
Loop, Alternative/Indie Rock; Shoegazing, 1980s-1990s, Artist, British
Los Lobos, Alternative/Indie Rock, 1970s-, Artist, American
Los Mockers, Alternative/Indie Rock, 1960s, Artist, Uruguayan
Love & Rockets, Goth Rock, 1980s-1990s, Artist, British
Love Battery, Grunge; Alternative/Indie Rock, 1990s, Artist, American
Love, Psychedelic Rock; US Underground & Garage Rock, 1960s-1970s, Artist, American
Loverboy, Arena Rock; Hard Rock, 1970s-1990s, Artist, Canadian
Lowe, Nick, Pub Rock, 1970s-, Producer; Songwriter; Artist, British
Lunch, Lydia, US Underground & Garage Rock, 1970s-, Artist, American
Lush, Shoegazing; Alternative/Indie Rock, 1980s-1990s, Artist, British
Luv'd Ones, US Underground & Garage Rock, 1960s, Artist, American
Lynyrd Skynyrd, Southern Rock; Arena Rock, 1970s-, Artist, American
Lyres, The, US Underground & Garage Rock; Alternative/Indie Rock; American Punk, 1970s-1990s, Artist, American
MacColl, Kirsty, Alternative/Indie Rock, 1980s-, Artist, British
Machine Head, Heavy Metal, 1990s-, Artist, American
Mad Season, Grunge; Alternative/Indie Rock, 1990s, Artist, American
Magazine, Alternative/Indie Rock, 1970s-1980s, Artist, British
Magnetic Fields, Alternative/Indie Rock, 1990s, Artist, American
Make-Up, The, Alternative/Indie Rock, 1990s-, Artist, American
Malevolent Creation, Death Metal & Grindcore, 1990s-, Artist, American
Malmsteen, Yngwie, Heavy Metal; Hard Rock, 1980s-, Artist, Swedish
Man, Prog Rock; Hard Rock; 1960s-1990s, Artist, British
Manic Street Preachers, Alternative/Indie Rock, 1990s-, Artist, British
Manzanera, Phil, Prog Rock, 1970s-, Producer; Artist, British
Margana Lefay, Heavy Metal, 1990s, Artist, Swedish
Marillion, Prog Rock, 1970s-, Artist, British
Marilyn Manson, Nu Metal, Goth Rock, 1990s-, Artist, American
Marshall Tucker Band, The, Southern Rock, 1970s-, Artist, American
Massive Attack, Alternative/Indie Rock, 1990s-, Artist, British
Material, Prog Rock; Alternative/Indie Rock, 1980s-1990s, Artist, American
Mayhem, Black Metal, 1980s-, Artist, Norwegian
MC5, Hard Rock; Proto-Punk, 1960s-1970s, Artist, American
McCarthy, Alternative/Indie Rock, 1980s-1990s, Artist, British
Meat Loaf, Arena Rock; Hard Rock, 1970s-, Artist, American
Meat Puppets, US Underground & Garage Rock; American Punk; Alternative/Indie Rock, 1980s-, Artist, American
Meatmen, US Underground & Garage Rock; American Punk, 1980s-1990s, Artist, American
Medaski, Martin & Wood, Jam Rock, 1990s–, Artist, American
Medicine, Alternative/Indie Rock, 1990s, Artist, American
Megadeth, Thrash & Speed Metal, 1980s-, Artist, American
Mekong Delta, Thrash & Speed Metal, 1980s-, Artist, American
Mekons, The, Alternative/Indie Rock, 1970s-, Artist, British
Mellencamp, John Cougar, Hard Rock, 1970s-, Artist, American
Melvins, Grunge; Alternative/Indie Rock, 1980s-, Artist, American
Memento Mori, Doom Metal, 1990s, Artist, American
Mercury Rev, Alternative/Indie Rock, 1990s-, Artist, American
Mercyful Fate, Thrash & Speed Metal, 1980s-1990s, Artist, Danish
Meshuggah, Death Metal & Grindcore, 1990s-, Artist, Swedish
Metal Church, Thrash & Speed Metal, 1980s-1990s, Artist, American
Metallica, Thrash & Speed Metal, 1980s-, Artist, American
Midnight Oil, Alternative/Indie Rock, 1970s-, Artist, Australian
Mighty Lemon Drops, The, Alternative/Indie Rock, 1980s-1990s, Artist, British
Milkshakes, The, Alternative/Indie Rock, 1980s-1990s, Artist, British
Miller, Frankie, Pub Rock, 1970s-1990s, Artist, British
Miller, Steve, Arena Rock, 1960s-1990s, Artist; Songwriter, American
Ministry, Alternative/Indie Rock, 1980s-, Artist, American
Minor Threat, US Underground & Garage Rock; American Punk, 1980s, Artist, American
Minutemen, US Underground & Garage Rock, 1980s, Artist, American
Miracle Workers, The, US Underground & Garage Rock; Hard Rock, 1980s-1990s, Artist American
Miranda Sex Garden, Goth Rock, 1990s-, Artist, British
Misfits, The, US Underground & Garage Rock, 1970s-1990s, Artist, American
Mission Of Burma, American Punk, 1980s-1990s, Artist, American
Mission, The, Goth Rock, 1980s-, Artist, British
Misunderstood, The, US Underground & Garage Rock , 1960s, Artist, American
Moby Grape, Psychedelic Rock, 1960s-1980s, Artist, American
Modern Lovers, The, American Punk; Proto-Punk, 1970s, Artist, American
Modest Mouse, Alternative/Indie Rock, 1990s-, Artist, American
Moe, Jam Rock, 1990s-, Artist, American
Mojo Men, The, US Underground & Garage Rock; Psychedelic Rock, 1960s, Artist, American
Molly Hatchet Band, The, Southern Rock, 1970s–, Artist, American
Monks Of Doom, US Underground & Garage Rock; Alternative/Indie Rock, 1980s-1990s, Artist, American
Monks, The, US Underground & Garage Rock, 1960s, Artist, American
Mono Men, US Underground & Garage Rock; Alternative/Indie Rock, 1980s-1990s, Artist, American
Monster Magnet, Heavy Metal; Hard Rock, 1990s-, Artist, American
Montrose, Hard Rock; Arena Rock, 1970s, Artist, American
Moody Blues, The, Prog Rock, 1960s-, Artist, British
Moore, Thurston, US Underground & Garage Rock; Alternative/Indie Rock, 1980s-, Artist, American
Moose, Shoegazing; Alternative/Indie Rock, 1990s-, Artist, British
Morbid Angel, Death Metal & Grindcore, 1980s-, Artist, American
Morrissey, Alternative/Indie Rock, 1980s-, Artist, British
Mother Love Bone, Grunge; Hard Rock, 1980s-1990s, Artist, American
Mötley Crüe, Heavy Metal; Hard Rock, 1980s-, Artist, American
Motörhead, Heavy Metal, 1970s-, Artist, British
Mott the Hoople, Hard Rock; Proto-Punk; Glam Rock & Glitter, 1960s-1970s, Artist, British
Mould, Bob, Alternative/Indie Rock, 1980s-, Artist, American
Mount McKinleys, US Underground & Garage Rock; Alternative/Indie Rock, 1990s, Artist, American
Mouse & the Traps, US Underground & Garage Rock; Psychedelic Rock, 1960s, Artist, American
Move, The, Prog Rock, 1960s-1970s, Artist, British
Moving Targets, US Underground & Garage Rock; Alternative/Indie Rock, 1980s-1990s, Artist, American
Mr. Big, Heavy Metal; Hard Rock, 1980s-, Artist, American
Mud, Glam Rock & Glitter, 1960s-1980s, Artist, British
Mudhoney, US Underground & Garage Rock; Grunge, 1980s-, Artist, American
Mummies, The, US Underground & Garage Rock; Alternative/Indie Rock, 1990s, Artist, American
Mumps, The, American Punk, 1970s, Artist, American
Murphy, Peter, Goth Rock, 1980s-, Artist, British
My Bloody Valentine, Shoegazing; Alternative/Indie Rock, 1980s-1990s, Artist, Irish
My Dad Is Dead, US Underground & Garage Rock; Alternative/Indie Rock, 1980s-, Artist, American
My Dying Bride, Doom Metal; Death Metal & Grindcore, 1990s-, Artist, American
Mystic Eyes, US Underground & Garage Rock; Alternative/Indie Rock, 1990s-, Artist, American
Naked Raygun, US Underground & Garage Rock, 1980s-1990s, Artist, American
Napalm Death, Death Metal & Grindcore, 1980s-, Artist, British
Nation Of Ulysses, US Underground & Garage Rock; Alternative/Indie Rock, 1990s, Artist, American
National Health, Prog Rock, 1970s-1980s, Artist, British
Necros, The, US Underground & Garage Rock; Thrash & Speed Metal, 1980s, Artist, American
Ned's Atomic Dustbin, Alternative/Indie Rock, 1980s-1990s, Artist, British
Negative Approach, US Underground & Garage Rock, 1980s, Artist, American
Nevermore, Heavy Metal, 1990s-, Artist, American
New Bomb Turks, US Underground & Garage Rock; Alternative/Indie Rock, 1990s-, Artist, American
New Colony Six, US Underground & Garage Rock, 1960s, Artist, American
New Order, Alternative/Indie Rock, 1980s-, Artist, British
New York Dolls, The, Proto-Punk, 1970s, Artist, American
Nice, The, Prog Rock, 1960s-1970s, Artist, British
Nichtcrawlers, The, US Underground & Garage Rock, 1960s, Artist, American
Nine Inch Nails, Alternative/Indie Rock; Nu Metal, 1980s-, Artist, American
Nirvana, Grunge; Alternative/Indie Rock, 1980s-1990s, Artist, American
No Doubt, Funk Metal, 1980s-, Artist, American
Nomads, The, Alternative/Indie Rock, 1980s-, Artist, Swedish
NoMeansNo, US Undeground & Garage Rock; Alternative/Indie Rock, 1970s-, Artist, Canadian
Nuclear Assault, Thrash & Speed Metal, 1980s-1990s, Artist, American
Nugent, Ted, Arena Rock; Hard Rock, 1960s-, Artist, American
O'Rourke, Jim, Alternative/Indie Rock, 1980s-, Artist, American
Oasis, Hard Rock; Alternative/Indie Rock, 1990s-, Artist, British
Obituary, Death Metal & Grindcore, 1980s-1990s, Artist, American
Oblivians, US Underground & Garage Rock; Alternative/Indie Rock, 1990s, Artist, American
Oldfield, Mike, Prog Rock, 1970s-, Artist, British
Opeth, Death Metal & Grindcore, 1990s-, Artist, Swedish
Optic Nerve, The, US Underground & Garage Rock, 1980s, Artist, American
Osborne, Joan, Alternative/Indie Rock, 1990s-, Artist, American
Osbourne, Ozzy, Hard Rock; Heavy Metal, 1980s-, Artist, British
Outcasts, The, US Underground & Garage Rock, 1960s, Artist, American
Outlaws, The, Southern Rock, 1970s-1980s, Artist, American
Outsiders, The, Psychedelic Rock, 1960s, Artist, Dutch
Overkill, Thrash & Speed Metal, 1980s-, Artist, American
Palace, Alternative/Indie Rock, 1990s, Artist, American
Pale Saints, Shoegazing; Alternative/Indie Rock, 1980s-1990s, Artist, British
Palmer, Robert, Arena Rock, 1970s-, Artist, British
Pantera, Thrash & Speed Metal; 1980s-, Artist, American
Panzer, Jag, Heavy metal; Hard Rock, 1980s-, Artist, American
Pavement, Alternative/Indie Rock, 1990s-, Artist, American
Papa Roach, Nu Metal, 1990s-, Artist, American
Parker, Graham, Pub Rock, 1970s-, Artist; Songwriter, British
Pastels, The, Alternative/Indie Rock, 1980s-, Artist, British
Pavement, Alternative/Indie Rock, 1990s-, Artist, American
Paw, Grunge; Alternative/Indie Rock, 1990s-, Artist, American
Pearl Jam, Grunge; Hard Rock; Alternative/Indie Rock, 1990s-, Artist, American
Pearls Before Swine, Psychedelic Rock, 1960s-1970s, Artist, American
Pentagram, Doom Metal; Heavy Metal, 1970s-, Artist, British
Pere Ubu, US Underground & Garage Rock; American Punk, 1970s-, Artist, American
Petty, Tom, Hard Rock, 1970s-, Artist, American
Phair, Liz, Alternative/Indie Rock, 1990s-, Artist, American
Phillips, Sam, Alternative/Indie Rock, 1980s-, Artist, American
Phish, Jam Rock, 1980s-, Artist, American
Pink Floyd, Psychedelic Rock; Prog Rock, 1960s-, Artist, British
Pixies, Alternative/Indie Rock, 1980s-1990s, Artist, American
Plasticland, US Underground & Garage Rock, 1980s-, Artist, American
Pleasure Seekers, US Underground & Garage Rock, 1960s, Artist, American
Poco, Prog Rock, 1960s-1990s, Artist, American
Pogues, The, Alternative/Indie Rock, 1980s-1990s, Artist, British
Poison, Heavy Metal, 1980s-, Artist, American
Pop Group, The, Alternative/Indie Rock, 1970s-1980s, Artist, British
Pop, Iggy, Proto-Punk; Hard Rock, 1970s-, Artist, American
Portishead, Alternative/Indie Rock, 1990s, Artist, British
Possessed, Thrash & Speed Metal, 1980s, Artist, American
Presidents Of The United States Of America, Grunge; Alternative/Indie Rock, 1990s-, Artist, American
Pretenders, The, Hard Rock, 1970s-1990s, Artist, British
Pretty Things, The, Psychedelic Rock; Prog Rock; Hard Rock, 1960s-, Artist, British
Primal Scream, Alternative/Indie Rock, 1980s-, Artist, British
Primus, Funk Metal, 1990s, Artist, American
Prisoners, The, Alternative/Indie Rock, 1980s-1990s, Artist, British
Procol Harum, Psychedelic Rock; Prog Rock, 1960s-1990s, Artist, British
Psychedelic Furs, Alternative/Indie Rock, 1980s-, Artist, British
Psyclone Rangers, The, US Underground & Garage Rock; Alternative/Indie Rock, 1990s, Artist, American
Public Image Limited, British Punk; Alternative/Indie Rock, 1970s-1990s, Artist, British
Pulp, Alternative/Indie Rock, 1980s-, Artist, British
Pussy Galore, US Underground & Garage Rock; Alternative/Indie Rock, 1980s-, Artist, American
Quasi, Alternative/Indie Rock, 1990s-, Artist, American
Quatro, Suzi, Glam Rock & Glitter, 1970s-1990s, Artist, American
Queen, Arena Rock; Glam Rock & Glitter; Prog Rock; Hard Rock, 1970s-1990s, Artist, British
Queensrÿche, Melodic Rock, 1980s-, Artist, American
Quicksilver Messenger Service, Psychedelic Rock, 1960s-1990s, Artist, American
Quickspace, Alternative/Indie Rock, 1990s-, Artist, British
Rachel's, Alternative/Indie Rock, 1990s , Artist, American
Radio Birdman, Hard Rock, 1970s-1980s, Artist, Australian
Radiohead, Alternative/Indie Rock, 1990s-, Artist, British
Rage Against The Machine, Funk Metal, 1990s–, Artist, American
Ramones, The, American Punk, 1970s-1990s, Artist, American
Ranaldo, Lee, US Underground & Garage Rock; Alternative/Indie Rock, 1980s-1990s, Artist, American
Rancid, Alternative/Indie Rock, 1990s-, Artist, American
Rapeman, US Underground & Garage Rock, 1980s, Artist, American
Rationals, The, US Underground & Garage Rock, 1960s-1970s, Artist, American
Ratt, Heavy Metal; Hard Rock, 1980s-1990s, Artist, American
Reagan Youth, American Punk; US Underground & Garage Rock, 1980s, Artist, American
Real Kids, The, American Punk, 1970s-1980s, Artist, American
Red Hot Chili Peppers, Funk Metal, 1980s-, Artist, American
Red Krayola, The, Psychedelic Rock; Prog Rock, 1960s-, Artist, American
Redd Kross, US Underground & Garage Rock, 1980s-1990s, Artist, American
Reed, Lou, Proto-Punk; Hard Rock, 1970s-, Artist; Songwriter, American
Reef, Alternative/Indie Rock, 1990s Artist, British,
REM, US Underground & Garage Rock; Alternative/Indie Rock, 1980s-, Artist, American
Renaissance, Prog Rock, 1960s-, Artist, British
REO Speedwagon, Arena Rock, 1970s-, Artist, American
Replacements, The, Hard Rock; Alternative/Indie Rock, 1980s-1990s, Artist, American
Revere, Paul, & the Raiders, US Underground & Garage Rock, 1960s-1990s, Artist, American
Rezillos, The, British Punk, 1970s, Artist, British
Richman, Jonathan, Proto-Punk; US Underground & Garage Rock, 1970s-, Artist, American
Ride, Shoegazing; Alternative/Indie Rock, 1980s-, Artist, British
Rising Storm, The, US Underground & Garage Rock, 1960s; 1980s, Artist, American
Rivieras, The, US Underground & Garage Rock, 1960s, Artist, American
Robinson, Tom, British Punk; Hard Rock, 1970s-, Artist, British
Rocket From The Crypt, Alternative/Indie Rock, 1990s-, Artist, American

Rocket From The Tombs, Proto-Punk, 1970s, Artist, American
Rockpile, Pub Rock, 1970s-1980s, Artist, British
Rodan, Alternative/Indie Rock, 1990s, Artist, American
Rolling Stones, The, Hard Rock; Psychedelic Rock, 1960s-, Artist, British
Rollins, Henry, Alternative/Indie Rock; US Underground & Garage Rock, 1980s-, Artist, American
Roogalator, Pub Rock, 1970s, Artist, American
Rotary Connection, Psychedelic Rock, 1960s-1970s, Artist, American
Rotting Christ, Death Metal & Grindcore, 1990s-, Artist, Greek
Roxy Music, Prog Rock; Glam Rock & Glitter, 1970s-1980s, Artist, British
Royal Trux, Alternative/Indie Rock, 1980s-, Artist, American
Rundgren, Todd, Prog Rock; Proto-Punk; Hard Rock, 1970s-, Artist, American
Rush, Prog Rock; Arena Rock; Hard Rock, 1970s-, Artist, Canadian
Saccharine Trust, US Underground & Garage Rock, 1980s, Artist, American
Saint Vitus, Doom Metal; Alternative/Indie Rock, 1980s-1990s, Artist, American
Saints, The, Alternative/Indie Rock, 1970s-1990s, Artist, Australian
Samael, Death Metal & Grindcore, 1990s, Artist, Swiss
Samson, Prog Rock, 1960s-1970s, Artist, British
Santana, Hard Rock; Psychedelic Rock, 1960s-, Artist, American
Sarge, Alternative/Indie Rock, 1990s, Artist, American
Satyricon, Black Metal, 1990s-, Artist, Norwegian
Savatage, Heavy Metal, 1980s-, Artist, American
Scared Reich, Thrash & Speed Metal, 1980s-1990s, Artist, American
Scientists, Alternative/Indie Rock, 1970s-1990s, Artist, Australian
Scorpions, Heavy Metal; Hard Rock, 1970s-, Artist, German
Scratch Acid, US Underground & Garage Rock; Alternative/Indie Rock, 1980s , Artist, American
Scrawl, Alternative/Indie Rock, 1980s-1990s, Artist, American
Screaming Trees, US Underground & Garage Rock; Grunge, 1980s-1990s, Artist, American
Screeching Weasel, Alternative/Indie Rock, 1980s-, Artist, American
Sea Level, Southern Rock, 1970s, Artist, American
Seahorses, Alternative/Indie Rock, 1990s, Artist, British
Sebadoh, Alternative/Indie Rock, 1980s-1990s, Artist, American
Seeds, The, Psychedelic Rock, 1960s-1970s, Artist, American
Seger, Bob, Hard Rock, 1960s-1990s, Artist; Songwriter, American
Sepultura, Thrash & Speed Metal; Death Metal & Grindcore, 1980s-, Artist, Brazilian
Sex Gang Children, Goth Rock, 1980s-, Artist, British
Sex Pistols, The, British Punk, 1970s; 1990s, Artist, British
Shadows Of Knight, US Underground & Garage Rock, 1960s, Artist, American
Sham 69, British Punk, 1970s-, Artist, British
Showaddywaddy, Glam Rock & Glitter, 1970s-1980s, Artist, British
Silkworm, Alternative/Indie Rock, 198s0-, Artist, American
Silver Apples, Proto-Punk, 1960s; 1990s, Artist, American
Silver Jews, The, Alternative/Indie Rock, 1990s-, Artist, American
Silverchair, Grunge; Alternative/Indie Rock, 1990s-, Artist, Australian
Siouxsie & the Banshees, British Punk; Goth Rock, 1970s-1990s, Artist, British
Sisters Of Mercy, The, Goth Rock, 1980s-1990s, Artist, British
Skid Row, Heavy Metal, 1980s-, Artist, American
Skyclad, Thrash & Speed Metal, 1990s-, Artist, British
Slade, Glam Rock & Glitter, 1960s-1990s, Artist, British
Slaughter, Heavy Metal; Hard Rock, 1980s-1990s, Artist, American
Slayer, Thrash & Speed Metal, 1980s-, Artist, American
Sleater-Kinney, Riot Grrrl; Alternative/Indie Rock, 1990s-, Artist, American
Slint, US Underground & Garage Rock; Alternative/Indie Rock, 1980s-1990s, Artist, American
Slipknot, Nu Metal, 1990s-, Artist, American
Slits, The, British Punk, 1970s-1980s, Artist, British
Slowdive, Shoegazing; Alternative/Indie Rock, 1980s-1990s, Artist, British
Small Faces, Psychedelic Rock, 1960s, Artist, British
Small Factory, Alternative/Indie Rock, 1990s, Artist, American
Smashing Pumpkins, The, Alternative/Indie Rock, 1990s-, Artist, American
Smith, Patti, Proto-Punk; Hard Rock, 1980s-, Artist, American
Smiths, The, Alternative/Indie Rock, 1980s-1990s, Artist, British
Smog, Alternative/Indie Rock, 1980s-, Artist, British
Smoke, The, Psychedelic Rock, 1960s, Artist, British
Soft Boys, The, British Punk, 1970s-1980s, Artist, British
Soft Machine, The, Psychedelic Rock; Prog Rock, 1960s-1990s, Artist, British
Solitude Aeternus, Doom Metal, 1990s, Artist, American
Some Velvet Sidewalk, US Underground & Garage Rock; Alternative/Indie Rock, 1990s, Artist, American
Sonic Boom, Alternative/Indie Rock, 1980s-1990s, Artist, British
Sonic Youth, Alternative/Indie Rock; US Underground & Garage Rock, 1980s-, Artist, American
Sonics, The, US Underground & Garage Rock, 1960s, Artist, American
Soul Asylum, US Underground & Garage Rock; Hard Rock, 1980s-1990s, Artist, American
Soulfly, Heavy Metal, 1990s-, Artist, Brazilian
Soundgarden, Grunge; Alternative/Indie Rock, 1980s-1990s, Artist, American
Soup Dragons, The, Alternative/Indie Rock, 1980s-1990s, Artist, British
Southern Culture On The Skids, Alternative/Indie Rock, 1980s-, Artist, American
Southern Death Cult, Goth Rock; Hard Rock, 1980s, Artist, British
Spacemen 3, Alternative/Indie Rock, 1980s-1990s, Artist, British
Spence, Skip, Psychedelic Rock, 1960s, Artist; Songwriter, American
Spin Doctors, The, Jam Rock, 1990s, Artist, American
Spinanes, The, Alternative/Indie Rock, 1990s, Artist, American
Spirit, Psychedelic Rock; Prog Rock, 1960s-1990s, Artist, American
Spiritualized, Alternative/Indie Rock, 1990s-, Artist, British
Spooky Tooth, Prog Rock; Hard Rock, 1960s-1970s, Artist, British
Spoozys, Alternative/Indie Rock, 1990s-, Artist, Japanese
Springsteen, Bruce, Arena Rock, 1970s-, Artist; Songwriter, American
Squirrel Bait, US Underground & Garage Rock; Alternative/Indie Rock, 1980s, Artist, American
Staind, Nu Metal, 1990s–, Artist, American
Standells, The, US Underground & Garage Rock, 1960s, Artist, American
Sta-Prest, Riot Grrrl; Alternative/Indie Rock, 1990s, Artist, American
Steppenwolf, Hard Rock; Psychedelic Rock, 1960s-1990s, Artist, American
Stereolab, Alternative/Indie Rock, 1990s-, Artist, British
Stewart, Rod, Hard Rock; Arena Rock, 1960s-, Artist; Songwriter, British
Stiff Little Fingers, British Punk, 1970s-1990s, Artist, British
Stillroven, The, US Underground & Garage Rock; Prog Rock, 1960s, Artist, American
Sting, Alternative/Indie Rock, 1970s-, Artist, British
Stone Roses, The, Madchester; Alternative/Indie Rock, 1980s-1990s, Artist, British
Stone Temple Pilots, Grunge; Hard Rock; Alternative/Indie Rock, 1990s-, Artist, American
Stooges, The, Hard Rock; Proto-Punk, 1960s-1970s, Artist, American
Stormtroopers Of Death, Thrash & Speed Metal, 1980s-, Artist, American
Stranglers, The, British Punk, 1970s-1990s, Artist, British
Strapping Fieldhands, Alternative/Indie Rock, 1990s-, Artist, American
Stratovarius, Heavy Metal, 1980s-, Artist, Finnish
Strawbs, The, Prog Rock, 1960s-1980s, Artist, British
Styx, Prog Rock; Arena Rock; Hard Rock, 1970s-, Artist, American
Sugar Ray, Funk Metal, 1990s-, Artist, American
Sugar Shack, US Underground & Garage Rock, 1990s-, Artist, American
Sugarcubes, Alternative/Indie Rock, 1980s-1990s, Artist, Icelandic
Suicidal Tendencies, US Underground & Garage Rock; Thrash & Speed Metal, 1980s-, Artist, American
Suicide, American Punk, 1970s-1990s, Artist, American
Sunny Day Real Estate, Alternative/Indie Rock, 1990s-, Artist, American
Superchunk, Alternative/Indie Rock, 1980s-, Artist, American
Supertramp, Prog Rock; Arena Rock, 1970s-, Artist, British
Swamp Rats, US Underground & Garage Rock, 1980s, Artist, American
Swans, US Underground & Garage Rock, 1980s-1990s, Artist, American
Sweet, Glam Rock & Glitter, 1970s-1990s, Artist, British
Swell Maps, British Punk, 1970s-1980s, Artist, British
Swervedriver, Shoegazing; Alternative/Indie Rock, 1990s, Artist, British
Swirlies, The, Shoegazing; Alternative/Indie Rock, 1990s-, Artist, American
Sylvian, David, Prog Rock, 1980s-, Artist, British
Symphony X, Heavy Metal, 1990s-, Artist, American
Syndicate Of Sound, US Underground & Garage Rock, 1960s, Artist, American
System Of A Down, Nu Metal, 1990s–, Artist, American
T Rex, Glam Rock & Glitter, 1960s-1970s, Artist, British
Tad, Grunge; Alternative/Indie Rock, 1980s-1990s, Artist, American
Tad Morose, Heavy Metal, 1990s-, Artist, Swedish
Talking Heads, US Underground & Garage Rock, 1970s-1980s, Artist, American
Tangerine Dream, Prog Rock, 1960s-, Artist, German
Team Dresch, Riot Grrrl; Alternative/Indie Rock, 1990s, Artist, American
Teardrop Explodes, The, British Punk, 1970s-1990s, Artist, British
Television, American Punk; Proto-Punk, 1970s; 1990s, Artist, American
Tell-Tale Hearts, US Underground & Garage Rock, 1980s, Artist, American
Temple Of The Dog, Grunge; Alternative/Indie Rock; Hard Rock, 1990s, Artist, American
Terrorizer, Death Metal & Grindcore, 1990s, Artist, American
Tesla, Heavy Metal; Hard Rock, 1980s-, Artist, American
Testament, Thrash & Speed Metal, 1980s-, Artist, American
Thee Midniters, US Underground & Garage Rock, 1960s, Artist, American
Therion, Death Metal & Grindcore, 1990s-, Artist, Swedish
They Might Be Giants, Alternative/Indie Rock, 1980s-, Artist, American
Thin Lizzy, Heavy Metal; Hard Rock, 1970s-1990s, Artist, Irish
Thin White Rope, US Underground & Garage Rock; Alternative/Indie Rock, 1980s-1990s, Artist, American
Three Fourgiven, US Underground & Garage Rock; Alternative/Indie Rock, 1980s-1990s, Artist, American
Three Headcoats, Alternative/Indie Rock, 1980s-, Artist, British
Three O'Clock, The, US Underground & Garage Rock; Alternative/Indie Rock, 1980s, Artist, American
Throbbing Gristle, Alternative/Indie Rock, 19760d-1980s, Artist, British
Throwing Muses, Alternative/Indie Rock, 1980s-1990s, Artist, American
Thrush Hermit, Alternative/Indie Rock, 1990s, Artist, American
Thunders, Johnny, Hard Rock; American Punk, 1970s-1990s, Artist, American
Tiamat, Death Metal & Grindcore, 1980s-1990s, Artist, Swedish
Tiger Trap, Alternative/Indie Rock, 1990s, Artist, American
Time, The, Funk Metal, 1980s-1990s, Artist, American
Tintern Abbey, Psychedelic Rock, 1960s, Artist, British
Toad the Wet Sprocket, Alternative/Indie Rock, 1980s-1990s, Artist, American
Tomorrow, Psychedelic Rock, 1960s, Artist, British
Tones on Tail, Goth Rock, 1980s, Artist, British
Tool, Heavy Metal, 1990s-, Artist, American
Tortoise, Alternative/Indie Rock, 1990s-, Artist, American
Toto, Melodic Rock, 1970s-1990s, Artist, American
Townshend, Pete, Hard Rock; Prog Rock, 1960s-, Artist; Songwriter, British
Traffic, Psychedelic Rock; Prog Rock, 1960s-1970s; 1990s, Artist, British
Transambient Communication, Alternative/Indie Rock, 1990s-, Artist, British
Trapeze, Prog Rock; Hard Rock, 1970s-1990s, Artist, British
Treepeople, Grunge; Alternative/Indie Rock, 1980s-1990s, Artist, American
Tricky, Alternative/Indie Rock, 1990s-, Artist, British
Trouble, Doom Metal, 1980s-1990s, Artist, American
Tsunami, Alternative/Indie Rock, 1990s, Artist, American
Tubes, The, Arena Rock; Hard Rock, 1970s-, Artist, American
Type O Negative, Heavy Metal, 1990s-, Artist, American
U2, Alternative/Indie Rock, 1970s-, Artist, Irish
UFO, Arena Rock; Hard Rock, 1970s-, Artist, British
UK, Prog Rock, 1970s, Artist, British
UK Subs, British Punk, 1970s-, Artist, British
United States Of American, The, Psychedelic Rock, 1960s, Artist, American
Unrelated Segments, US Underground & Garage Rock, 1960s, Artist, American
Unrest, Alternative/Indie Rock; US Underground & Garage Rock, 1980s-1990s, Artist, American
Unsane, US Underground & Garage Rock; Alternative/Indie Rock, 1980s-1990s, Artist, American
Unwound, Alternative/Indie Rock, 1990s-, Artist, American
Urge Overkill, Hard Rock; Alternative/Indie Rock, 1980s-1990s, Artist, American
Uriah Heep, Prog Rock; Heavy Metal, 1970s-1990s, Artist, British
Utopia, Prog Rock; Arena Rock, 1970s-1990s, Artist, American
Vai, Steve, Heavy Metal; Hard Rock, 1980s-, Artist, American
Van Der Graf Generator, Prog Rock, 1960s-1970s, Artist, British
Van Halen, Hard Rock; Arena Rock; Heavy Metal, 1970s-1990s, Artist, American
Velocity Girl, Alternative/Indie Rock, 1990s, Artist, American
Velvet Underground, The, Proto-Punk, 1960s-1970s; 1990s, Artist, American
Venom, Black Metal, 1980s, Artist, British
Veronica, Riot Grrrl; Alternative/Indie Rock, 1990s, Artist, American
Versus, Alternative/Indie Rock, 1990s-, Artist, American
Veruca Salt, Grunge; Alternative/Indie Rock, 1990s-, Artist, American
Verve, The, Shoegazing; Alternative/Indie Rock, 1990s, Artist, British
Vibrators, The, British Punk, 1970s-, Artist, British
Violent Femmes, Alternative/Indie Rock, 1980s-, Artist, American
Vipers, The, US Underground & Garage Rock Revival, 1980s-1990s, Artist, American
Vixen, Heavy Metal; Hard Rock, 1980s-1990s, Artist, American
Voivod, Thrash & Speed Metal, 1980s-, Artist, Canadian
Waits, Tom, Alternative/Indie Rock, 1970s-, Artist, American
Walker, Scott, Alternative/Indie Rock, 1960s-1990s, Artist, American
Wallflowers, The, Alternative/Indie Rock, 1990s-, Artist, American
Warped, Alternative/Indie Rock, 1990s, Artist, American
Warrant, Heavy Metal; Hard Rock, 1980s–, Artist, American
Watchtower, Thrash & Speed Metal, 1980s, Artist, American
We The People, US Underground & Garage Rock; Psychedelic Rock, 1960s-1970s, Artist, American
Wedding Present, The, Alternative/Indie Rock, 1980s-1990s, Artist, British
Ween, Alternative/Indie Rock, 1990s-, Artist, American
Weirdos, The, American Punk, 1970s-1980s, Artist, American
Weller, Paul, Alternative/Indie Rock, 1990s-, Artist; Songwriter, British
Wet Willie, Southern Rock, 1960s-, Artist; American
White Lion, Hard Rock; Glam Rock & Glitter, 1980s-1990s, Artist, American
White Winged Moth, Alternative/Indie Rock, 1990s, Artist, American
Whitesnake, Heavy Metal; Hard Rock, 1970s-1990s, Artist, British
Who, The, Hard Rock; Psychedelic Rock, 1960s-, Artist, British
Widespread Panic, Southern Rock; Jam Rock, 1990s, Artist, American
Wimple Winch, Psychedelic Rock, 1960s, Artist, British
Windy & Carl, Alternative/Indie Rock, 1990s-, Artist, American
Winger, Heavy Metal; Hard Rock, 1980s-1990s, Artist, American
Wipers, US Underground & Garage Rock; Alternative/Indie Rock, 1970s-, Artist, American
Wire, British Punk; Alternative/Indie Rock, 1970s-1990s, Artist, British
Wishbone Ash, Prog Rock; Hard Rock, 1970s-, Artist, British
Wolfhounds, The, Alternative/Indie Rock, 1980s-1990s, Artist, British
Wood, Roy, Glam Rock & Glitter; Hard Rock; Prog Rock, 1960s-, Artist; Songwriter, British
Wright, Gary, Prog Rock, 1970s-1990s, Artist, American
Wurm, US Underground & Garage Rock, 1980s, Artist, American
X, US Underground & Garage Rock; American Punk, 1980s-, Artist, American
X-Ray Spex, British Punk, 1970s-1990s, Artist, British
XTC, Alternative/Indie Rock, 1970s-, Artist, British
Yardbirds, The, Psychedelic Rock, 1960s, Artist, British
Yes, Prog Rock, 1960s-, Artist, British
Yo La Tengo, Alternative/Indie Rock, 1980s-, Artist, American
You Am I, Grunge; Alternative/Indie Rock, 1980s-1990s, Artist, Australian
Young, Neil, Hard Rock, 1960s-, Artist; Songwriter, Canadian
Youth Of Today, US Underground & Garage Rock, 1980s-1990s, Artist, American
Zappa, Frank, Prog Rock; Proto-Punk; Hard Rock, 1960s-1990s, Artist, American
Zeni Geva, Alternative/Indie Rock, 1980s-, Artist, Japanese
ZZ Top, Hard Rock; Arena Rock, 1970s-1990s, Artist, American

BRITISH PUNK ➡ 88 AMERICAN PUNK ➡ 90 ARENA ROCK ➡ 92 MELODIC ROCK ➡ 93 GOTH ROCK ➡ 94 DOOM METAL ➡ 95
SHOEGAZING ➡ 103 US UNDERGROUND & GARAGE ROCK ➡ 104 PROGRESSIVE METAL ➡ 107 BLACK METAL ➡ 108 SOUTHERN ROCK ➡ 109
JAM BANDS ➡ 110 GRUNGE ➡ 111 FUNK METAL ➡ 112 RIOT GRRRL ➡ 113 NU METAL ➡ 114

Jazz

Above

On Blues & Roots, Charles Mingus concentrated on the blues and gospel elements of his musical heritage.

LIKE a great river that runs endlessly, forming numerous tributary streams as it flows, jazz continues to evolve over time. And no matter how far the River Jazz may flow from its source – whether through stylistic evolution or technological innovation – the essential spirit of the music remains intact.

Granted, the more academic and esoteric extrapolations of avant-gardists such as Anthony Braxton and Cecil Taylor may, on the surface of it, appear to be light years away from the early innovations and earthy expressions of Louis Armstrong and Sidney Bechet. In essence, however, both widely divergent approaches are imbued with that spirit of spontaneous creativity, risk-taking and discovery that is at the core of all jazz. Regardless of what instruments are being used; whether the general tone is harshly electric or purely acoustic; and whether the form is defined by straight 4/4 time, or more intricate rhythmic variations, or no time at all; jazz is, in all of its manifestations, fundamentally about improvising and the art of playing without premeditation – or, in the parlance of Louis Armstrong, "taking a scale and making it wail".

Cool jazz or fusion, swing-era big bands or bebop quintets, Dixieland or the avant-garde: the music thrives on a collective spirit of interplay and the daring chances taken by the participants individually or as a group, and strictly in the moment. Jazz is, as the noted critic Whitney Balliett once called it, "the sound of surprise". The phrase could be applied as accurately to Armstrong's 1928 duets with Earl Hines as it could to Charlie Parker's pyrotechnic excursions in 1945 with kindred spirit Dizzy Gillespie; or to Eric Dolphy's 1960 opus *Out There*, the Art Ensemble of Chicago's 1973 classic *Fanfare For The Warriors*, alto-saxophonist Steve Coleman's radical M-Base experiments of the mid-1980s, or trumpeter Dave Douglas's compelling, Middle Eastern-flavored offering from 2001, *Witness*.

Jazz has been called the quintessential American music, the ultimate in rugged individualism and the creative process incarnate. In its infancy, it was dismissed by one pointed newspaper editorial as "a manifestation of a low streak in man's taste that has not yet come out in civilization's wash". In more modern times, it has been hailed as one of the noblest forms of human expression, with a deep and direct connection to the soul. It is about individuals filling space with invention while negotiating their agendas within a group; an improvisational art that thrives on freedom of expression yet demands selfless collaboration.

New Orleans was the nexus for its genesis. A cultural melting pot where people of all nationalities lived side by side, New Orleans was one of the richest, most cosmopolitan cities in America during the early 1800s. It was in this integrated society that strains of melodies from the West Indies began to mingle with traces of African polyrhythms, carried over by slaves and European classical music played by Creoles (the free and prosperous light-skinned descendants of French and Spanish colonists and their African wives and mistresses). Many of these Creole musicians, who identified with their

> "JAZZ HAS GOT TO HAVE THAT THING. YOU HAVE TO BE BORN WITH IT. YOU CAN'T LEARN IT, YOU CAN'T BUY IT AND NO CRITIC CAN PUT IT INTO ANY WORDS. IT SPEAKS IN THE MUSIC. IT SPEAKS FOR ITSELF."
>
> *Miles Davis*

STYLES

Ragtime
New Orleans
Chicago
Swing
Bebop
Dixieland Revival
Cool Jazz
Hard Bop
Free Jazz
Soul Jazz
Fusion & Jazz Rock
Acid Jazz
Smooth Jazz
Latin Jazz
Brazilian Jazz

JAZZ STYLE

Born in 1873, W.C. Handy provided the link between Joplin and the early jazz ragtime pianists as seen in this excerpt from 'Beale St. Rag'.

Louis Armstrong

Above

It was in New Orleans that Creole and African musical influences combined to create the musical style we know as jazz. This scene shows Canal Street in 1924, when New Orleans jazz was well under way.

led to the formation of various repertoire bands in the United States, chief among them the Lincoln Center Jazz Orchestra in New York (for which the trumpeter Wynton Marsalis serves as artistic director). Since its formation in 1988, the LCJO has taken on the task of presenting the works of jazz masters such as Duke Ellington, Sidney Bechet, Jelly Roll Morton, Thelonious Monk and others to largely subscription audiences at the prestigious Alice Tully Hall in the Lincoln Center complex.

European and not their African ancestors, were classically trained. Added to the mix were minstrel tunes and plantation songs, work songs and spirituals, along with the constant sound of brass bands parading around the Crescent City at weddings, funerals and picnics, as well as during the six- to eight-week Carnival season leading up to Mardi Gras. This incredible hodgepodge of sound would eventually lead to ragtime at the outset of the 1890s.

In 1896, a landmark decision by the US Supreme Court would change the face of New Orleans music forever. This "separate but equal" ruling institutionalized segregation between the races, effectively forcing classically trained Creole musicians into the black community, where they merged their technical fluency on various instruments with the blues-inflected music of black bands. Together, they would create a new music that began to emerge at the dawn of the new twentieth century. Something beyond ragtime or blues, it was initially called "hot music", to convey its fiery nature, and later dubbed "jass" (a name that came from the jasmine perfume favoured by prostitutes in Storyville). By 1907, around the time that the pianist-composer Jelly Roll Morton began to blend ragtime with minstrel songs, the blues and habanera dance rhythms from the Caribbean (which he described as the all-important "Spanish tinge"), the term had eventually morphed into "jazz" and it has remained there to this day.

While the facts of where jazz came from and how it evolved over time are indisputable, the question of where jazz is going – or, indeed, should be headed – is a topic of heated debate. On the one hand, staunch traditionalists believe jazz to be a precious, homemade American art music that ought to be preserved and disseminated intact. This "curator" notion has

Others maintain that the jazz tradition is one of innovation itself, and that the music must adapt to new times in order to survive. Indeed, many movements that came along throughout the course of jazz history were direct reactions to some previous, prevailing movement: as bebop was to swing, as hard bop was to the cool school, as the avant-garde movement was to mainstream jazz, and so on. Rather than supplanting a previous style, each new movement is an extension, that builds on the past while retaining some inherent qualities of previous styles. So, in Dizzy Gillespie's pyrotechnic trumpet work at the height of the bebop era in

Right

Sidney Bechet played the clarinet and soprano saxophone with a clear, penetrating tone that soared above the other instruments in the band. As a young man Bechet played in Bunk Johnson's Eagle Band.

the late 1940s we can still hear something of Louis Armstrong; in Cecil Taylor's turbulent piano work we can still hear traces of his heroes Duke Ellington, Bud Powell and Fats Waller; in revolutionary, alto saxophonists such as Ornette Coleman and Eric Dolphy we can hear a direct connection to Charlie Parker.

Through the miracle of technology, we are now hearing something of the past masters (quite literally) in new hybrid forms such as hip hop jazz and smooth jazz. Countless beats from early 1960s Blue Note and Prestige soul-jazz recordings have been digitally sampled and looped to create the foundation for rhythm tracks on modern-day, cutting-edge recordings. The smooth jazz saxophone star Kenny G went one step further by brazenly "dueting" with Louis Armstrong (via sampling) on 'What A Wonderful World', from his 1999 CD, *Classics In The Key Of G.*

Whether jazz remains an exclusive or inclusive art form, there is no denying the impact of other cultures on this quintessentially American music as it reaches ever outward. From its earliest manifestations at the turn of the twentieth century in the cultural gumbo of New Orleans, to the Afro-Cuban jazz collaborations of Dizzy Gillespie and Machito in the 1940s, to the groundbreaking cross-pollination efforts of Stan Getz in the early 1960s with *Jazz Samba* and *Getz/Gilberto*, to the incorporation of Eastern rhythms and scales during the 1970s by fusion groups such as the Mahavishnu Orchestra and Weather Report, jazz has a history of embracing other cultural expressions.

Above

After experimenting with the "jungle sound", involving the heavily muted trumpet of Bubber Miley, Duke Ellington Orchestra found nationwide fame by accepting the position of house band at Chicago's Cotton Club.

Today, numerous jazz artists (such as trumpeter Roy Hargrove, alto saxophonist Steve Coleman and soprano saxophonist Jane Bunnett, among others) have travelled to Havana to soak up and document the authentic Afro-Cuban vibe in their music. Others, such as Panamanian pianist Danilo Pérez, Argentine pianist-composer-arranger Guillermo Klein, Czech bassist George Mraz, Cameroonian bassist Richard Bona,

Cuban trumpeter Arturo Sandoval, Norwegian alto saxophonist Jan Garbarek, Armenian percussionist Arto Tuncboyaçyin, Lithuanian pianist Vyacheslav Ganelin, Cuban piano sensation Gonzalo Rubalcaba, Tunisian oud player Anouar Brahem, Chinese pianist/composer Jon Jang, Indian alto saxophonist Rudresh Mahanthappa, Pakistani guitarist Fareed Haque, Chinese baritone saxophonist Fred Ho, Vietnamese guitarist Nguyên Lê, Swedish keyboard player Esbjörn Svensson, Cuban saxophonist/clarinetist Paquito D'Rivera, Swiss-Dutch vocalist Susanne Abbuehl, Japanese pianist/composer/arranger and big band leader Toshiko Akiyoshi, Indian percussionist Zakir Hussain, Japanese pianist Satoko Fujii, Norwegian keyboard player Bugge Wesseltoft, Puerto Rican saxophonist David Sanchez, Brazilian percussionist Airto Moreira, Australian bassist Nicki Parrott, Irish guitarist David O'Rourke and Indian percussionist Trilok Gurtu (the list goes on and on) have mined the richness of their own cultural heritages to come up with other new and exciting hybrid forms of jazz. In the process, all have advanced the cause of jazz, taking the essence of the music to a new place through their bold experimentation and honest expression.

This living drama continues to unfold. Every trumpeter today, 100 years after the birth of jazz, still carries a little piece of Buddy Bolden, or King Oliver, or Louis Armstrong with him; every alto sax player a bit of Bird, every pianist something of Jelly Roll, every drummer a touch of Baby Dodds and so it goes on. Like Olympians carrying the eternal flame across the ages, they represent the past while charging full steam ahead into the future. In his own time and in his own way, each has made a unique contribution. This is the nature of jazz – continually flowing and changing, like the never-ending river.

Left

Two of the greatest innovators in jazz, Charlie Parker (centre) and Miles Davis (right), together with bass player Tommy Potter. Parker and Davis were instrumental in bringing jazz forward to a new era.

JAZZ: COOL ➡ 134   THE BLUES INTRO ➡ 154

Ragtime

A FORERUNNER OF JAZZ, RAGTIME WAS DERIVED FROM BRASS-BAND MUSIC AND
EUROPEAN FOLK MELODIES, AFRICAN-AMERICAN BANJO MUSIC AND SPIRITUALS,
MINSTREL SONGS, MILITARY MARCHES AND EUROPEAN LIGHT CLASSICS.

Above
*Eubie Blake and Noble Sissle
began writing songs together
in 1915 and went on to have
a successful writing and
performing partnership, calling
themselves "The Dixie
Duo". They made their last
recording together in 1968.*

THE "raggy" style, or ragged-time feeling, of this jaunty,
propulsive, toe-tapping piano music refers to its inherent
syncopation, where loud right-hand accents fall between the
strong beats of the left-hand rather than on top of them. One
noted practitioner, the pianist Eubie Blake (composer of the
1920s hit song 'I'm Just Wild About Harry'), summed it up
simply: "Ragtime is syncopation and improvising and accents".

While this highly syncopated style involved only limited
improvisation and lacked a jazz-swing feel, it directly informed
the work of the early jazz giant Jelly Roll Morton and served
as a precursor to the Harlem stride piano movement of the
1920s, pioneered by James P. Johnson, Willie "The Lion" Smith
and Fats Waller. Ragtime could be heard as early as the 1880s
in camps of workers building the great railroads across the
American continent, as
well as in travelling minstrel
shows and vaudeville shows.
By 1892, the composer
Charles Ives had come
across it in his hometown
of Danbury, Connecticut.
At the Chicago World's Fair
that same year, many people
heard ragtime for the first
time. By 1896, the first
pieces labelled "ragtime"
were published. The
following year, some 20
rags were published.
By 1899, 120 rags were
issued in New Orleans.

"SCORNED BY
THE ESTABLISHMENT
AS EPHEMERAL AT BEST,
TRASHY AT WORST,
RAGTIME WAS THE
FOUNTAINHEAD OF
EVERY RHYTHMIC AND
STYLISTIC UPHEAVAL
THAT HAS FOLLOWED
IN A CENTURY OF EVER-
EVOLVING AMERICAN
POPULAR MUSIC."

Max Morath

LEADING EXPONENTS

Tom Turpin
James Scott
Scott Joplin
Eubie Blake
Joseph Lamb
Max Morath
Joshua Rifkin
Reginald R. Robinson
David Thomas Roberts
Marcus Roberts

RAGTIME STYLE

*Ragtime is a composed piano
style which consists of pieces
of simple, cheerful-sounding
melodies with simple
syncopation in which the
right hand is rhythmically
supported by the left.*

    THE JAZZ INTRO ➡ 118   JAZZ PEOPLE A-Z ➡ 152   INSTRUMENTS A-Z ➡ 436   JAZZ: DIXIELAND REVIVAL ➡ 132

As piano rolls and sheet music appeared at the turn of the century, a ragtime fad swept the nation. Hordes of young people shocked their parents by kicking up their heels to this infectious new music, which was described alternately by critics and newspaper columnists as "syncopation gone mad" and "the product of our decadent art culture".

The Ragtime King

Although Scott Joplin became the figurehead for this burgeoning new American music movement, there were several ragtime piano players who preceded him, including Walter Gould (known as One Leg Shadow), Tom Turpin, James Scott and One-Leg Willie Joseph, along with other ivory-tinkling "professors" who plied their trade in brothels, gambling joints, saloons and private clubs. Following the phenomenal success of Joplin's 'Maple Leaf Rag', which sold 75,000 copies of sheet music in 1899 for the publisher John Stark and 500,000 copies within 10 years, he was dubbed "King of Ragtime Writers" and presided over ragtime's reign as the main popular musical style of the US for nearly 20 years.

The son of a former slave, born in Texarkana, a town in the northeast corner of Texas, on 24 November 1868, Joplin was a piano prodigy with a musical education financed by his mother's work as a domestic servant. With aspirations to become a classical concert pianist, he played at the Chicago World's Fair in 1892 and later enrolled at the George R. Smith College for Negroes in Sedalia, Missouri (where he would write 'Maple Leaf Rag'). In 1901, Joplin moved to St. Louis to begin working with Stark, where he began to expand his writing from ragtime tunes to full-length pieces such as ballets and operas. The first of these, *A Guest Of Honor*, emerged in 1903.

Rather than being improvised, Joplin's music was as formally composed and carefully worked out as any of Frédéric Chopin's études. And while he easily enchanted the masses with catchy numbers such as 'Maple Leaf Rag' and 'The Entertainer' (an infectious quality that Irving Berlin strived to emulate in 1911 with his 'Alexander's Ragtime Band'), Joplin longed to be taken seriously as a composer. He saw himself as a black American counterpart to Chopin or Strauss, a composer of new music for a new century. Joplin's death in 1917, just before the end of the First World War, effectively marked the beginning of the end of ragtime's supremacy in America. And although Zez Confrey had some success in the early 1920s with tunes such as 'Kitten On The Keys' and 'Dizzy Fingers', by the second decade of the twentieth century, attention had shifted dramatically to the new phenomenon of "hot music" or "jazz". By 1930, ragtime was largely extinct. The legacy of the early ragtime pioneers lived on only through sheet music and piano rolls of their compositions: there were no recordings of any of the music. In fact, the year Joplin died was the same year in which the Original Dixieland Jazz Band made the first jazz recording.

Ragtime Revival

More than half a century after Joplin's death, this rollicking, syncopated music enjoyed a revival in the early 1970s, sparked by three significant events. In 1971, the musicologist and pianist Joshua Rifkin recorded an album of Joplin's pieces for Nonesuch, which caught on with critics and the public alike. The following year, Joplin's 1915 ragtime opera, *Treemonisha*, was resurrected and staged at Atlanta's Memorial Arts Center. Then, in 1973, the pianist-composer Marvin Hamlisch used Joplin's 'The Entertainer' as the main theme for the Hollywood blockbuster *The Sting*, starring Paul Newman and Robert Redford. That Academy Award-winning film made Joplin a household name, helping to trigger renewed interest in his jaunty and sophisticated music.

Treemonisha was again staged by the Houston Grand Opera in May 1975 and brought to Broadway that October, contributing to Joplin being posthumously awarded a special Pulitzer Prize in 1976 for his contribution to American music. Joplin's legacy has been kept alive through the 1980s and 1990s by ragtime piano interpreters such as Terry Waldo, Butch Thompson, Dick Hyman and Marcus Roberts, as well as by prominent jazz instrumentalists such as Anthony Braxton, Archie Shepp, Ran Blake, Ron Miles, Bill Frisell and Wynton and Branford Marsalis. Original composers in the ragtime style, such as Mississippi's David Thomas Roberts and Chicago's Reginald Robinson, have helped to keep this nearly extinct music alive on the concert and recording scene over the past 10 years.

Far left

Thomas "Fats" Waller, along with his one-time piano tutor James P. Johnson, pioneered the stride piano style that grew out of ragtime. Stride (originally called "shout") shared the basic structure of ragtime but was rhythmically looser.

Below

Scott Joplin wisely secured a royalty contract on 'Maple Leaf Rag', one of his most successful compositions. He received one cent for each copy sold, which, although hardly a princely sum, provided him with a steady income.

New Orleans

CONDITIONS WERE RIPE FOR JAZZ TO EVOLVE IN NEW ORLEANS AT THE TURN OF THE TWENTIETH CENTURY. A THRIVING PORT OF IMMIGRATION, WHERE AFRICANS AND CREOLES LIVED SIDE BY SIDE WITH ITALIANS, GERMANS, IRISH, FRENCH, MEXICANS AND CUBANS, NEW ORLEANS' UNPRECEDENTED ETHNIC DIVERSITY ALLOWED FOR A FREE AND EASY MINGLING OF MUSICAL IDEAS BETWEEN CULTURES.

Above

The Red Hot Peppers sessions, led by pianist, composer and band-leader Jelly Roll Morton represent some of the finest recordings in the New Orleans style.

OTHER factors contributed to the coalescing of jazz as a cultural expression unique to New Orleans. The call-and-response tradition of West African music was retained in many Baptist churches of the South, particularly in New Orleans, while concepts of polyrhythm and improvisation within group participation (qualities inherent in African drumming ensembles) were kept alive in the Crescent City at Congo Square, an authorized venue where slaves would gather to recreate their drumming and dancing traditions. These African drumming concepts, and indeed the very notion of percussiveness as musical expression, would seep into the cultural consciousness of New Orleans.

the West Indies and the Caribbean, and factor in the slightly decadent and pervasive "party time" atmosphere of the City That Care Forgot (typified by the pageantry of Mardi Gras, as well as the city's unofficial motto, "Laissez les bons temps rouler" or "Let the good times roll"), and you have a potent recipe for jazz.

"ARGUABLY THE HAPPIEST OF ALL MUSIC IS NEW ORLEANS JAZZ. THE SOUND OF SEVERAL HORNS ALL IMPROVISING TOGETHER ON FAIRLY SIMPLE CHORD CHANGES WITH DEFINITE ROLES FOR EACH INSTRUMENT BUT A LARGE AMOUNT OF FREEDOM CANNOT HELP BUT SOUND CONSISTENTLY JOYFUL."

Scott Yanow

Let The Good Times Roll

The foundation for a new hybrid music was set by a combination of the African notion of rhythm that swings, or has a propulsive motion, with the European classical influences brought into the mix by ragtime and sophisticated Creole musicians. Add a thriving brass band tradition, which developed in the late-nineteenth century from the plentiful supply of cheap brass band instruments left behind after the Civil War, blend in rhythmic and melodic elements from Cuba,

LEADING EXPONENTS

Buddy Bolden
Freddie Keppard
King Oliver
Jelly Roll Morton
Louis Armstrong
Kid Ory
Sidney Bechet
Johnny Dodds
Jimmie Noone
Original Dixieland Jazz Band

NEW ORLEANS STYLE

New Orleans is an ensemble style in which each instrument has a specific role. The piano and banjo provide rhythm and harmony, the trumpet plays the main melody and the clarinet is used for melodic embellishment.

 THE JAZZ INTRO ➡ 118   JAZZ PEOPLE A-Z ➡ 152   INSTRUMENTS A-Z ➡ 436   JAZZ: RAGTIME ➡ 122   THE BLUES INTRO ➡ 154

Out of this rich cultural gumbo came Charles "Buddy" Bolden, the first bona fide jazz star of the twentieth century. A cornetist of unparalleled power, Bolden's innovative approach took the essence of ragtime and put a looser, hotter, bluesier spin on it, grabbing dancers in the process. By 1895, Bolden was leading his own group in residence at New Orleans' Globe Theater, where he held court as "King" Bolden. By 1901, his popularity spread from playing dance halls scattered throughout the city and in outlying communities, including Preservation Hall, the Tin Roof Café and Funky Butt Hall. In 1903, he began to fade from the scene, plagued by spells of dementia and drunkenness, until he was committed to the East Louisiana State Mental Hospital on 5 June 1907: the first jazz casualty.

Succeeding Bolden as the cornet king of New Orleans was Freddie Keppard, who, in 1906, led the Olympia Orchestra. Legend has it that Keppard, leery of having other cornet players "steal his stuff", turned down an offer from the Victor Talking Machine Company to become the first New Orleans musician to record. Another prominent cornetist was Joe Oliver, who began playing in local dance bands and with the Onward Brass Band in 1907. By 1917, he became the star cornetist in a popular band led by the trombonist Edward "Kid" Ory, who billed him as "King" Oliver. An early master of mutes, Oliver pioneered the "wah-wah" and other vocal effects on his horn, which would later become a signature of the Ellington trumpeter Bubber Miley. When Oliver went north to Chicago in February 1919, Ory hired the 18-year-old Louis Armstrong as his replacement on cornet.

The Jazz Age

Oliver's contemporary on the New Orleans scene was the Creole clarinettist Sidney Bechet. A child prodigy, Bechet held his own with Freddie Keppard's band at the age of 10. He left school at 16 and began working with various bands, thrilling audiences and players alike with his forceful attack, soaring passion and unusually fast vibrato. Bechet relocated to Chicago in 1918 and, a year later, became one of the first Americans to spread jazz to Europe as a member of the travelling Southern Syncopated Orchestra. It was while he was in London that he ran across the instrument with which he would eventually make jazz history: the soprano saxophone.

A key figure in New Orleans jazz was the pianist, composer, entertainer and raconteur Jelly Roll Morton. A natural extrovert who bragged that he had invented jazz, Morton began embellishing on ragtime, blues and light classics while performing at the "sporting houses" of the Storyville red-light district as early as 1902.

By 1907, he began touring in vaudeville shows throughout the Gulf Coast and the Midwest. He settled in Chicago in 1914, then relocated to the West Coast from 1917 to 1922. He had composed numerous works by that time, including his classic 'King Porter Stomp' and 'Winin' Boy Blues', but remained unrecorded until 1923.

A plethora of jazz musicians were active in New Orleans during the first decade of the twentieth century, but the first jazz recording was not made until 1917. That honour went not to pioneers such as Keppard, Ory, Oliver, Bechet or Morton (all of whom went unrecorded until after they had left New Orleans), but to a group of five young, white New Orleans musicians calling themselves the Original Dixieland Jazz Band. Led by Sicilian-American cornetist Nick LaRocca, the ODJB assembled in the Victor studio in New York City on 26 February 1917 to record 'Livery Stable Blues'. A lively novelty number that featured passages where the instruments imitated barnyard animals, it immediately caught on with the public. Following the extraordinary success of their recording debut (it would eventually sell 1.5 million copies), the ODJB toured British variety theatres, where they audaciously billed themselves as "The Creators of Jazz". The ODJB later introduced such Dixieland standards as 'Margie', 'Indiana' and 'Tiger Rag', spawning a number of copy bands and sparking a craze that quickly swept America, as well as setting the stage for what the writer F. Scott Fitzgerald characterized as "The Jazz Age" of the 1920s.

Far left
Kid Ory's "tailgate" playing style – in which the trombone plays a rhythmic line beneath the band's trumpets and cornets – may have been influenced by his earlier experiences as a banjo player.

Below
King Oliver's Creole Jazz Band made some of the most important jazz recordings of the 1920s. The band, including such greats as Louis Armstrong, Johnny Dodds and King Oliver himself, took group improvization to new heights.

JAZZ WAS THE BY-PRODUCT OF CULTURES COMING TOGETHER IN NEW ORLEANS AT THE TURN OF THE TWENTIETH CENTURY. THE MUSIC, ALONG WITH SOME OF ITS GREATEST PRACTITIONERS, MOVED NORTH BY 1917. THAT YEAR STORYVILLE, THE RED-LIGHT DISTRICT, WAS FORCED TO CLOSE AND JAZZ MUSICIANS HEADED NORTH TO CHICAGO, WHERE JAZZ MATURED INTO A FINE ART FORM.

Chicago

Above
Bix Beiderbecke and Frankie Trumbauer had a unique musical and recording partnership with Bix on cornet and Frankie on saxophone.

CHICAGO held the promise of a new life for the Southern black population, which migrated from the fields of the cotton industry to the blast furnaces and factories of big Northern cities. A centrally located, active transportation hub that provided easy access to Los Angeles and New York, Chicago was an attractive destination for working jazz musicians, many of whom worked in the gangster-owned speakeasies created by the Volstead Act of 1919 (outlawing the manufacture and sale of alcohol in the United States).

Blow The Way You Feel

While the North Side of Chicago had its famous clubs – the Green Mill, College Inn, Blackhawk, Kelly's Stables and Friar's Inn – the hottest jazz bands of the early 1920s could, primarily, be found on a nine-block stretch of State Street on the city's predominantly black South Side, known as "The Stroll". There, jazz lovers could choose between the Pekin Inn, Dreamland Café, Plantation Café, Elite Café and Sunset Café. Among the patrons who frequented The Stroll was a group of jazz-hungry, white teenage students who attended Chicago's Austin High School – cornetist Jimmy McPartland, tenor saxophonist Bud Freeman, drummer Dave Tough and reedman Frank

Teschemacher. Along with developing young players, such as guitarist Eddie Condon, pianist Joe Sullivan, cornetists Muggsy Spanier and Leon "Bix" Beiderbecke, clarinetist Benny Goodman and drummer Gene Krupa, this next generation of jazz musicians originated the "Chicago style", building on the rhythmic innovations of the New Orleans pioneers while injecting a frenetic intensity and reckless spirit that reflected the city itself.

> "ARMSTRONG PLAYS WITH SUCH BRAVURA AND RHYTHMIC INTENSITY THAT WHEN YOU LISTEN TO IT YOU HEAR THE FUTURE. AT THAT MOMENT YOU KNOW THAT SOMETHING IS IN THE WORKS AND IT'S NEVER GOING TO BE CONTAINED."
>
> *Gary Giddins, critic, 2000*

LEADING EXPONENTS

New Orleans
  Rhythm Kings
Joe "King" Oliver
Louis Armstrong
Jimmy McPartland
Frank Teschemacher
Joe Sullivan
Bix Beiderbecke
Max Kaminsky
Cutty Cutshall
Bud Freeman
Jess Stacy
Miff Mole

CHICAGO STYLE

Several instrumentalists playing together, with a tight, rhythmically polished co-ordination, create the dense textures of Chicago jazz, which are then richly interspersed with solos.

Hypnosis At First Hearing

The Austin Gang and other architects of the extrovert Chicago style were fans of the Original Dixieland Jazz Band, but they quickly fell under the spell of another white group from New Orleans, playing in Chicago in 1920 under the name of the New Orleans Rhythm Kings. They made their recording debut in 1922, and a year later teamed up in the studio with Jelly Roll Morton for one of the first-ever integrated sessions. Another focal point for the Austin Gang's adulation, and a great source of inspiration for aspiring cornetists McPartland and Beiderbecke, was the dazzling cornet virtuoso Louis Armstrong, who came to town in 1922 to join his mentor King Oliver in the ranks of the Creole Jazz Band. (The band also included the great New Orleans clarinettist Johnny Dodds and his younger brother Warren "Baby" Dodds on drums, along with Honoré Dutrey on trombone, Bill Johnson on bass and banjo, and Lil Hardin on piano.) With its two-cornet frontline, underscored by an intuitive call-and-response chemistry between its leader and 22-year-old star, the impact of King Oliver's Creole Jazz Band on young audiences was devastating. As guitarist Eddie Condon recalled in his memoirs, *We Called It Music: A Generation of Jazz* (Henry Holt): "It was hypnosis at first hearing. Armstrong seemed able to hear what Oliver was improvising and reproduce it himself at the same time. Then the two wove around each other like suspicious women talking about the same man".

In the early part of 1923, Oliver's pace-setting group went into a rickety studio in Richmond, Indiana, and cut its first historic recording ('Chimes Blues') for the small but influential Gennett label.

Armstrong left Chicago in 1924 to join Fletcher Henderson's band in New York. The following year, he returned to Chicago to lead a band organized by his new wife, Lil (Hardin) Armstrong, at the Dreamland Café. Soon afterward, he began doubling with Erskine Tate's Vendome Theater Orchestra, where he was the featured hot soloist. Then, on 12 November 1925, he went into the Okeh studios in Chicago to make the first of a series of five dozen tracks recorded between 1925 and 1928, which have come to be known as the Hot Fives and Hot Sevens sessions. With these revolutionary recordings, Armstrong single-handedly shifted the focus from jazz as an ensemble music to a soloist's art form. As noted critic Gary Giddins put it, "It's the moment when jazz becomes an art form. With these pivotal recordings, he virtually codifies what jazz is going to be for the next half century".

By 1929, Armstrong shifted his home base from Chicago to New York, where jazz was poised for its next evolution.

Above

Featuring ex-members of King Oliver's band, Louis Armstrong's Hot Five recordings may represent the greatest jazz of all time. Pictured from left to right are Armstrong, Johnny St. Cyr, Johnny Dodds, Kid Ory and Lil Hardin-Armstrong.

Far left

Eddie Condon never took solos, preferring to work as a steady rhythm player. He played an important part in the desegregation of jazz, as well as in moving jazz performances from under-ground clubs to concert halls.

THE POPULARITY OF JAZZ HIT A PEAK AFTER THE DEPRESSION YEARS OF 1929-1933. BY THE END OF 1934, HUGE NUMBERS WERE TUNING IN TO THE NBC RADIO SERIES LET'S DANCE, WHICH BROADCAST PERFORMANCES BY THE XAVIER CUGAT, KEL MURRAY AND BENNY GOODMAN ORCHESTRAS. GOODMAN'S ORCHESTRA IN PARTICULAR CAUGHT ON WITH THE PUBLIC AND CREATED A DEMAND FOR LIVE PERFORMANCES.

Swing

WHEN Goodman went on tour in the US, scoring his first big success before a packed house of ecstatic teenagers at the Palomar Ballroom in Los Angeles on 21 August 1935, it signalled the beginning of a new national youth craze to rival the turn-of-the-century ragtime fad. Symbolically, it was the birth of the swing era, the predominance of big bands in jazz.

Reaching Fever Pitch

Following Goodman's triumph at the Palomar Ballroom, the floodgates opened wide and several bands followed in his wake. By 1937, Kansas City pianist and bandleader William "Count" Basie had recorded his first swinging sides, including the anthemic 'Jumpin' at the Woodside' and 'One O'Clock Jump', both featuring the tenor saxophonist Lester Young and the all-American rhythm section of bassist Walter Page, drummer Papa Jo Jones and guitarist Freddie Green. That same year, Jimmy Dorsey scored hits with 'Marie' and 'Song of India', featuring classic trumpet solos by Bunny Berigan. Shortly after, Berigan formed his own big band and had a hit

in August 1937 with 'I Can't Get Started', still part of the standard jazz repertoire to this day. Swing-era momentum reached fever pitch with Benny Goodman's historic Carnegie Hall concert in New York in January 1938, which was recorded for posterity and included the classic instrumental version of Louis Prima's 'Sing, Sing Sing', the frantic number that made drummer Gene Krupa such a star that he left the BG Orchestra to form his own big band.

"THERE WAS A TIME, FROM 1935–1946, WHEN TEENAGERS AND YOUNG ADULTS DANCED TO JAZZ-ORIENTED BANDS, WHEN JAZZ ORCHESTRAS DOMINATED POP CHARTS AND WHEN INFLUENTIAL CLARINETTISTS WERE HOUSEHOLD NAMES. THIS WAS THE SWING ERA."

Scott Yanow

LEADING EXPONENTS

Fletcher Henderson
Count Basie
Duke Ellington
Chick Webb
Cab Calloway
Benny Goodman
Artie Shaw
Glenn Miller
Tommy Dorsey
Jimmy Dorsey
Woody Herman
Harry James
Gene Krupa
Bunny Berigan
Charlie Barnet

SWING STYLE

One feature of swing is the drumming. As drum kits developed drummers moved away from four-in-a-bar bass drum to more subtle patterns.

The year 1939 saw a flurry of activity in swing: Harry James, an outstanding trumpeter in the Goodman organization, formed his own orchestra. The clarinettist Woody Herman scored his first big band hit with 'At the Woodchopper's Ball'. The saxophonist Charlie Barnet became a household name that same year on the strength of his big- band hit 'Cherokee'. Singer Ella Fitzgerald took over the Chick Webb Orchestra following the drummer-bandleader's death that summer. Glenn Miller's Orchestra rose to prominence by blending pop elements with the highly polished big band formula, scoring several Top Ten hits in 1939 and 1940 with popular recordings such as 'Little Brown Jug', 'In The Mood' and 'Pennsylvania 6-5000'. In that same year, trumpeter Dizzy Gillespie joined the Cab Calloway Orchestra; tenor-sax great Coleman Hawkins recorded his immortal 'Body And Soul'; and bassist Jimmy Blanton and tenor saxophonist Ben Webster joined the great orchestra led by Duke Ellington. Ellington's orchestra had been a monumental force in jazz since the early 1920s and he remained a major name during the swing era on the strength of anthemic hits such as 'It Don't Mean A Thing If It Ain't Got That Swing', 'Rockin' in Rhythm' and 'Drop Me Off In Harlem'.

Swing Is The Thing

As the 1930s came to a close, one thing was eminently clear: swing had become as commercially viable and lucrative as rap music is today. While the swing-era dance bands enjoyed unprecedented popularity, there was never any attempt at playing to the lowest common denominator. The general level of musicianship had risen incrementally in the early 1930s due to the towering influence of Louis Armstrong, whose pyrotechnic playing on the Hot Five sessions of 1925 and collaboration with Earl Hines in 1928 (particularly on anthemic showpieces like 'Weather Bird' and 'West End Blues') had raised the bar for instrumental virtuosity in jazz. The combination of Armstrong-influenced hot soloing, well-honed ensemble playing and an infectious 4/4 beat proved irresistible for listeners and dancers through the 1930s and into the early 1940s.

With the size of the ensembles ranging from 10 to 20 pieces or more, big band music flowed smoothly on a steady 4/4 pulse, propelled by a foundation of string bass "walking" in synch with the drums, which kept time on the high-hat cymbal and bass drum while providing syncopated accents on snare and tom-toms. The distinctive big band quality came from the use of separate trumpet, trombone and saxophone (alto, tenor, baritone) sections to provide chordal or contrapuntal blocks of sound or add rhythmic punch to an arrangement. Over the top of these intricately voiced, highly polished arrangements was room designated for individual soloists to tell their story. That juxtaposition of discipline and freedom is a hallmark of big band music.

From A Flurry To A Fall

By 1942, the first full year of American participation in the Second World War, the swing era had suffered some setbacks. Key players and bandleaders like Glenn Miller and Artie Shaw had enlisted in the Armed Services and a recording strike by the Musicians Union from 1942–1944 effectively halted the documenting of this new music's development. By the end of the Second World War in 1945, the swing era was feeling competition from the Dixieland revival and the advent of bebop, creating a kind of Civil War that split the jazz audience into three factions. By 1946, many of the big bands had broken up. Combos were the wave of the future. Name-orchestras like Duke Ellington's, Count Basie's and Woody Herman's persisted in the face of changing times but the swing era as a cultural force was clearly over.

Far left

Django Reinhardt was a key player in European jazz during the swing era. After losing two fingers on his fretting hand in a caravan fire, Reinhardt developed his own unique style of playing which became hugely influential.

Centre

Virtuoso clarinettist Benny Goodman messes around with Gene Krupa, a drummer so innovative that he was able to upstage Goodman, leading to a falling out between the pair in the late 1930s.

Left

Count Basie was taught piano in the Harlem stride tradition by Fats Waller. He worked in the vaudeville circuit for a number of years before going on to become one of the world's greatest big band leaders.

Bebop

THOUGH IT WAS OFTEN REFERRED TO AS A MUSICAL REVOLUTION, BEBOP WAS ACTUALLY A NATURAL EVOLUTION OF JAZZ, INVOLVING INNOVATIVE APPROACHES TO HARMONY AND RHYTHM THAT ADVANCED THE MUSIC FORWARD TO A MODERN ERA.

Above

The bebop movement established the saxophone as the future sound of modern jazz.

TRACES of bebop began to emerge during the early 1940s, in orchestras led by Earl Hines and Billy Eckstine. Those adventurous impulses were further developed in Harlem nightspots such as Minton's Playhouse and Clark Monroe's Uptown House, where the architects of an iconoclastic new movement conducted experiments with time, tempo and extended techniques.

An Iconoclastic New Movement

It was there that drummer Kenny Clarke began to employ new methods on the kit – implying time, accenting in unpredictable ways and generally colouring and embellishing the music spontaneously from measure to measure, rather than keeping strict metronomic time in the manner of swing-era drummers. It was there that pianist Thelonious Monk began to map out sophisticated harmonic modulations and new melodic contours around familiar songs. In the same spirit of discovery, the trumpeter Dizzy Gillespie and alto saxophonist Charlie Parker began to effectively eliminate bar lines by soaring over the chord changes with impunity, injecting their lines with a stream-of-consciousness creativity that cascaded effortlessly through their horns. These young modernists were, largely, reacting to clichés that had begun to saddle big bands towards the end of the swing era. Their ambitious efforts at developing a new lexicon of expression coalesced into a new kind of music that was publicly unveiled on "Swing Street", the vibrant strip of nightclubs that lined 52nd Street between Fifth and Seventh Avenues in Midtown Manhattan.

> "'BEBOP' WAS A LABEL THAT CERTAIN JOURNALISTS LATER GAVE IT, BUT WE NEVER LABELED THE MUSIC. IT WAS JUST MODERN MUSIC, WE WOULD CALL IT. WE WOULDN'T CALL IT ANYTHING, REALLY, JUST MUSIC."
>
> *bebop drummer Kenny Clarke*

LEADING EXPONENTS

Charlie Parker
Dizzy Gillespie
Thelonious Monk
Kenny Clarke
Max Roach
Bud Powell
Roy Haynes
Miles Davis
Fats Navarro
Dexter Gordon
Oscar Pettiford

BEBOP STYLE

This example characterises the bebop rhythm section. Swing drums combine with walking bass and offbeat piano stabs. Melodies and solos typically used counter rhythms.

THE JAZZ INTRO ➡ 118   JAZZ PEOPLE A–Z ➡ 152   INSTRUMENTS A–Z ➡ 436   JAZZ: NEW ORLEANS ➡ 124   JAZZ: SWING ➡ 128

A Divisive Movement

With the emergence of bebop around 1945, the jazz world was suddenly divided into opposing (and at times hostile) camps: those who thrived on the new music and those threatened by its incursion. Some old-guard icons, such as trumpeter Louis Armstrong and bandleader Cab Calloway, readily dismissed bebop, branding its frantic tempos, eccentric rhythms, advanced harmonies and discordant melodies as undanceable and indecipherable. But others, such as tenor saxophonists Coleman Hawkins and Don Byas, successfully made the transition from the old into the new.

John Birks "Dizzy" Gillespie, with his outrageous stage persona, became a figurehead of the rebellious new movement. Aside from his peerless virtuosity as a trumpeter, Dizzy was also a beloved showman throughout his long and illustrious career. Gillespie, along with his kindred spirit and musical partner Charlie "Yardbird" Parker, whose blinding speed and dazzling facility placed him a cut above every other improviser of his day, unleashed a torrent of new ideas (some of which were based on pre-existing chord patterns from swing-era standards) that set a new standard for instrumental virtuosity and changed the course of jazz.

Born in South Carolina in 1917, Gillespie began playing trombone at the age of 14, before switching to trumpet the following year. He played with Philadelphia's Frank Fairfax Band, before he joined Teddy Hill's Orchestra in 1937, filling a spot formerly held by his trumpet-playing idol, Roy Eldridge. In 1939, Gillespie found himself in fast company on a Lionel Hampton all-star date for Victor. He distinguished himself with some singular, muted trumpet work on 'Hot Mallets', which showed a distinct departure from Eldridge's influence and pointed to a new path for jazz trumpet. Following a two-year stint in Cab Calloway's band, Gillespie worked in a succession of bands led by musicians including Ella Fitzgerald, Benny Carter, Duke Ellington and, in 1943, Earl Hines. In January 1944, he put together the Hepsations, the first bebop-oriented jazz group to play on 52nd Street. In June 1944, he joined Billy Eckstine's all-star big band, and by spring 1945 he had teamed up with Parker at The 3 Deuces on Swing Street. Together, they dominated the bop era from 1945 to 1949.

A Jazz Messiah

With remarkable technical proficiency, coupled with the sheer force of his charismatic personality, Charlie Parker became a jazz messiah in the mid-1940s. His solos were sermons to a faithful flock, hungering for a hipper alternative to Benny Goodman and Glenn Miller. Parker's virtuosic flights on alto sax, marked by an uncanny fluidity, an inherent bluesy quality and an intuitive harmonic logic that was complex yet crystal clear, earned him a lofty status among critics, fans and contemporaries alike. An early apprenticeship with the Jay McShann Orchestra in 1937 helped him hone his technique, and by the time he first visited New York City in 1939 as an eager 19-year-old, he was prepared to deal with the advanced playing of Art Tatum and take the next step in his musical journey. Parker met and began exchanging ideas with Gillespie as early as 1940. The two later met in Earl Hines' band in 1943 and, for a few months, in Billy Eckstine's Orchestra in 1944. But it was not until late 1944 that they worked together on 52nd Street, startling the world with bop anthems such as 'Groovin' High', 'Hot House' and 'Shaw 'Nuff'.

In the wake of landmark small group recordings by Bird & Diz, documented in May 1945 on the Guild label, other modernists would add to the bebop canon, including pyrotechnic virtuosos such as pianist Bud Powell, trumpeters Howard McGhee and Fats Navarro, saxophonists Dexter Gordon and Edward "Sonny" Stitt, trombonist J. J. Johnson, and pianists Tadd Dameron and Al Haig, all of whom placed a premium on speed of thought and execution in their music. By 1950, bebop had run its course as a burgeoning new movement. Some of its early practitioners and disciples had evolved, and were already experimenting with two new jazz tributaries – hard bop and cool jazz.

Left

Earl Hines, a jazz pianist who had played on Louis Armstrong's Hot Five sessions, led a big band throughout the 1930s and 1940s that served as a launch pad for the up-and-coming bebop movement.

Below

Dizzy Gillespie's incredibly varied and unpredictable playing style created a feeling of excited suspense. Charlie Parker may have developed bebop beyond all expectations, but without Diz it would never have begun.

Dixieland Revival

BY THE END OF THE 1930S, THE SWING ERA WAS IN FULL FORCE, USHERED IN BY BIG BANDS LED BY BENNY GOODMAN, CHICK WEBB, THE DORSEY BROTHERS (JIMMY AND TOMMY) AND GLENN MILLER. NEW ORLEANS JAZZ AND ITS STYLISTIC OFF-SHOOT, DIXIELAND, HAD BOTH LARGELY FADED FROM POPULARITY.

Above

Ken Colyer helped to keep traditional New Orleans-style jazz alive in Britain.

NEW ORLEANS pioneers King Oliver and Jelly Roll Morton drifted into obscurity. Original Dixieland Jazz Band leader Nick LaRocca left music altogether and became a building contractor, while New Orleans trombonist-bandleader Edward "Kid" Ory (once a mentor to the teenage Louis Armstrong in New Orleans and later appearing on Armstrong's revolutionary Hot Five and Hot Seven sessions from 1925–28) had gone into chicken farming.

Goodtime Music From The Past

By 1939, Dixieland was making a solid comeback. A generation of players, including clarinettists Pee Wee Russell and Joe Marsala, saxophonist Bud Freeman, trumpeters Bobby Hackett, Muggsy Spanier, Max Kaminsky and Wild Bill Davison, guitarist Eddie Condon and others, began reinvestigating the extroverted collective improvisational style of early New Orleans music and Chicago-style jazz of the 1920s. Part of the impetus for the revival of Dixieland came in 1938, when New York record store owner Milt Gabler launched his Commodore Records label to document these prominent Dixieland revivalists. Responding to the renewed interest in old-style New Orleans

music, Jelly Roll Morton (who had made only one appearance on record between 1931–37 on a little-known Wingy Manone date) led sessions in 1939 with such notable New Orleans sidemen as Sidney Bechet, Red Allen and Albert Nicholas. Ironically, Morton's music became popular again after his death in July 1941, just as the Dixieland revival really started to take off.

Another figure who spearheaded the Dixieland revival was Bob Crosby. A former singer in the Dorsey Brothers' band from 1934–1935, Crosby led a band through the late 1930s and early 1940s that revived such New Orleans evergreens as 'South Rampart Street Parade', 'Sugarfoot Strut' and 'Muskrat Ramble' while also interpreting popular hits of the day in a Dixieland two-beat style. Following the example of Tommy Dorsey (who in 1935 formed his Dixieland-flavoured Clambake Seven as a featured smaller group within his big band), Crosby formed the Bobcats from the ranks of his own big band. This smaller Dixieland ensemble featured several New Orleans-born musicians performing faithful renditions of classic fare by Louis Armstrong, King Oliver and the Original Dixieland Jazz Band.

> "BY THE MID-1930S THE WORD 'DIXIELAND' WAS BEING APPLIED FREELY TO CERTAIN CIRCLES OF WHITE MUSICIANS, FIRST BY THE TRADE PRESS, THEN BY THE PUBLIC. BY THE END OF THE DECADE IT HAD ALL BUT LOST ANY DIRECT 'SOUTHERN' ASSOCIATION."

Richard Sudhalter

LEADING EXPONENTS

Bunk Johnson
Kid Ory
George Lewis
Eddie Condon
Muggsy Spanier
Bob Crosby
Bob Scobey
Lu Watters Yerba Buena
  Jazz Band
Louis Armstrong
Yank Lawson
Wingy Manone
Bob Haggart
Doc Cheatham
Bud Freeman
Pee Wee Russell

DIXIELAND STYLE

Dixieland rejected the more melodically, harmonically and rhythmically complex forms of jazz in favour of simple rhythmic and harmonic structures.

Spirited Ensemble Music

By the early to mid-1940s, New Orleans jazz pioneers like Kid Ory, Bunk Johnson and George Lewis were being persuaded to return to recording studios and concert halls, which touched off renewed interest in the original New Orleans-style jazz and placed more emphasis on interactive ensemble playing and less on extroverted soloing, as was the style of the Dixielanders. Their pure, spirited playing directly inspired the British cornetist and trumpeter Ken Colyer, who would spearhead a wave of traditional New Orleans jazz throughout England in the 1950s.

A primary force for a west coast Dixieland revival was Lu Watters' Yerba Buena Jazz Band, which issued its first records in 1942. This revivalist octet emulated the two-cornet approach of King Oliver's Creole Jazz Band with trumpeters Watters and Bob Scobey on the frontline alongside trombonist Turk Murphy and clarinettist Ellis Horne. By the mid to late 1940s, with the advent of the modernist bebop movement, traditional New Orleans jazz and Dixieland players were being dismissed by progressives as "moldy figs". Yet the music was carried on in the late 1940s and through the 1950s by its figurehead, Louis Armstrong, who broke up his big band in 1947 and spent the rest of his career leading an all-star sextet which specialized in playing old New Orleans jazz and Dixieland standards like 'Basin Street Blues', 'Royal Garden Blues', 'Sleepy Time Down South', 'Tiger Rag', 'Indiana' and 'Struttin' With Some Barbecue'.

Guitarist Eddie Condon, a major propagandist for the Dixieland cause, recorded prolifically throughout the 1940s and 1950s with notable Dixieland players such as trumpeters Wild Bill Davison and Max Kaminsky, trombonists Jack Teagarden and Cutty Cutshall, and clarinettists Pee Wee Russell and Peanuts Hucko. Other Dixieland revivalists during the 1950s included trumpeter Adolphus "Doc" Cheatham, New Orleans clarinettist George Lewis, trombonist Wilbur de Paris (whose band featured the great New Orleans-born clarinettist Omer Simeon), San Francisco trumpeters Bob Scobey and Turk Murphy and former Bobcats bandmates trumpeter Yank Lawson and bassist Bob Haggart (who would team up in the late 1960s to form their Dixieland-inspired World's Greatest Jazz Band).

In 1961, Preservation Hall opened in New Orleans to keep the tradition alive and provide steady work for old-time New Orleans jazzmen, such as the trumpeters Kid Thomas Valentine and Punch Miller, clarinetist Willie Humphrey and, on trumpet, his older brother Percy. Trumpeter Al Hirt and clarinettist Pete Fountain also brought greater visibility to Dixieland with their popular recordings and frequent television appearances throughout the 1950s and 1960s.

This spirited ensemble music is still being championed today by New Orleans clarinettists Dr. Michael White and Pete Fountain, New Orleans-based singer-bandleader Banu Gibson, soprano saxophonist Bob Wilber (whose Bechet Legacy group was active in the early 1980s), cornetists Jim Cullum Jr. and Warren Vaché, New Orleans trumpeter Wynton Marsalis and the current edition of the Preservation Hall Jazz Band.

Above

New Orleans jazzman Bunk Johnson ceased playing in 1931 after a fellow trumpeter was stabbed to death on stage. He was rediscovered in the early 1940s by two jazz biographers, who encouraged him to make his first recordings.

Left

Humphrey Lyttleton, a self-taught trumpeter, is one of Britain's leading revivalists. His engaging style earned praise from Satchmo himself, who proclaimed Lyttleton "the top trumpet man in England".

IN THE WAKE OF THE PYROTECHNIC MANIFESTO THAT CHARLIE "BIRD" PARKER AND DIZZY GILLESPIE JOINTLY ISSUED ON THEIR FIRST RECORDING TOGETHER IN 1945, MOST MUSICIANS ON THE NEW YORK JAZZ SCENE BEGAN FANNING THE FLAMES OF BEBOP. TEMPOS PICKED UP SPEED, INTENSITY INCREASED ON THE BANDSTAND AND BLAZING VIRTUOSITY BECAME A MEANS TO AN END, IN A FIERY PURSUIT OF BIRD AND DIZ.

Cool Jazz

AND yet, the task of topping the two trendsetters who originated and mastered the art of bebop seemed insurmountable to many of their disciples, who, at best, might be considered great imitators but never originators. This frustrating fact caused several forward-thinking musicians to break from the extroverted bebop mould and forge a new, more reflective and deliberate musical path. Like pouring water on the flames of the bebop movement, these thoughtful young player-composers came to epitomize a "cool school" in jazz.

> "IT WAS AN ETHEREAL, DRIFTING CLOUD MUSIC THAT USED FRENCH HORNS AS WELL AS REGULAR JAZZ INSTRUMENTS, HIGHLY WROUGHT ARRANGEMENTS AND RICH TONE COLORS, THROUGH WHICH THE SOLOISTS PLAYED IN A MEASURED, WALKING-ON-EGGSHELLS MANNER."
>
> *John Fordham*

Velvety, Sensuous And Swinging

The roots of this antidote to the hyperactivity of bebop can be heard in the work of Claude Thornhill & His Orchestra, a dreamy-sounding ensemble from the early 1940s that utilized such unusual instrumentation as French horns and tuba as melodic voices. Some of the finest charts in the band's book, circa 1946–47, were contributed by the composer-arranger Gil Evans, who brought his own boppish inclinations to the ensemble's softer, inherently sweet quality. By the end of 1947, Evans had become acquainted with Miles Davis, a promising 22-year-old trumpeter from East St. Louis who had apprenticed alongside Parker at the height of the bebop craze.

While Davis did not possess the dazzling, high-note virtuosity of his idol Dizzy Gillespie, he began developing a sparser, middle-register approach to trumpet soloing, contrasting with the explosive bravura of the beboppers. This quieter, cooler style finally came to fruition on Davis' *Birth Of The Cool*, the 1949 recording that helped usher in a new musical movement in jazz.

Davis' landmark nonet sessions of 1949–50 were characterized by a relaxed yet disciplined integration of elements, featuring cool-toned soloists such as alto saxophonist Lee Konitz, trombonists J. J. Johnson and Kai Winding, and baritone saxophonist Gerry Mulligan. Working with the larger canvas of a nonet, the arrangers Evans ('Boplicity', 'Moon Dreams'), Mulligan ('Venus De Milo', 'Darn That Dream'),

LEADING EXPONENTS

Claude Thornhill
Miles Davis
Gerry Mulligan
Lee Konitz
Gil Evans
John Lewis/Modern Jazz
  Quartet
Lennie Tristano
Shorty Rogers
Howard Rumsey
Bud Shank
Jimmy Giuffre
Chet Baker
Paul Desmond
Dave Brubeck
Chico Hamilton

COOL JAZZ STYLE

The laid back sound of cool jazz is created by using instruments that are traditionally part of the rhythm section, such as the double bass, to provide melody instead.

THE JAZZ INTRO ➡ 118   JAZZ PEOPLE A-Z ➡ 152   INSTRUMENTS A-Z ➡ 436   JAZZ: BEBOP ➡ 130

Johnny Carisi ('Israel'), John Lewis ('Move') and Davis ('Deception') incorporated the lush tones of French horns, trombone and tuba in creating a velvety, sensuous yet swinging body of work, that has stood the test of time.

Offshoots Of The Cool School

Key participants in the seminal *Birth Of The Cool* sessions went on to incorporate various musical precepts of the Davis nonet experience in their own work: Gerry Mulligan with his celebrated, pianoless quartet, featuring trumpeter and kindred spirit Chet Baker; John Lewis with the chamber like Modern Jazz Quartet; Lee Konitz in his mid-1950s work with tenor saxophonist Warne Marsh. So pervasive was the influence of *Birth Of The Cool* among musicians that it spawned a separate movement, known as "West Coast Jazz". Some of the leaders of this West Coast branch of the cool school included bassist Howard Rumsey and his Lighthouse All-Stars, trumpeter-arranger Milton "Shorty" Rogers and his Giants, alto saxophonist Bud Shank with his tenor saxophonist partner Bill Perkins, valve trombonist Bob Brookmeyer, trumpeter Conte Candoli, multi-reedman Jimmy Giuffre, vibist Teddy Charles, tenor saxophonist-oboeist Bob Cooper, trombonist Frank Rosolino and drummer-composer Chico Hamilton, who introduced a group in 1955 that featured the unusual instrumentation of cello (Fred Katz), guitar (Jim Hall), flute (Buddy Collette) and bass (Carson Smith).

Another leading light of west coast Jazz was the alto saxophonist Paul Desmond, whose tone was once described as "sounding like a dry martini". In 1951 Desmond teamed up with the pianist Dave Brubeck, a protégé of the contemporary classical composer Darius Milhaud, who had led an experimental third-stream octet during the late 1940s. Together Desmond

and Brubeck found phenomenal success on college campuses, reaching new audiences and turning a younger generation on to jazz. In the wake of 1954's *Jazz Goes To College*, the Dave Brubeck Quartet was so popular that its leader appeared on the cover of *Time* magazine. From the quartet's million-selling 1959 album, *Time Out*, Desmond's anthemic 'Take Five' remains an oft-covered jazz classic.

While the rich tonal colours, highly wrought arrangements and relaxed, measured solos of west coast or cool jazz emerged in reaction to the urgency and all-out burn of bebop, it in turn triggered another movement that followed in the mid-1950s and prospered through to the mid-1960s: hard bop.

By 1959 Miles Davis, who had helped usher in the cool jazz movement a decade earlier with *Birth Of The Cool*, was already on to other groundbreaking work. His landmark album of that year, the influential and bestselling *Kind Of Blue*, would popularize modal jazz – a system of improvising based on modes or scales rather than running chord progressions – and pave the way for the free jazz movement of the 1960s.

Above

The Dave Brubeck Quartet experimented with unusual time signatures on tracks such as the now-classic 'Take Five'. They were advised that such records would not sell, as they were too difficult to dance to.

Far left

Chet Baker's ethereal, melodic playing style, combined with his androgynous vocals, introduced a fragile element to cool jazz.

Centre

Percy Heath (bass) and Milt Jackson (vibes) of the Modern Jazz Quartet, a band led by John Lewis, employed classical musical forms, such as the fugue.

HARD BOP EVOLVED OUT OF BEBOP DURING THE EARLY 1950S BUT ITS RHYTHMS WERE MORE DRIVING AND SYNCOPATED. HARD BOP ALSO TENDED TO HAVE A MORE FULL-BODIED SOUND, A BLUESY FEEL WITH DARKER TEXTURES AND SHORTER IMPROVISED LINES, AND ITS CHORD PROGRESSIONS WERE USUALLY COMPOSED RATHER THAN BORROWED FROM POPULAR TUNES.

Hard Bop

The Fathers Of Hard Bop

Many listeners underestimate the impact Horace Silver had on contemporary mainstream jazz: the hard bop style he and Art Blakey developed in the 1950s is still one of the dominant forms of the genre. Silver studied piano at school in Connecticut, where he formed a trio for local gigs. They impressed tenor saxophonist Stan Getz, who immediately hired them and brought them over to New York in 1950. Silver worked with Getz for a year there and also began to play with other top jazzers, including the saxophonists Coleman Hawkins and Lester Young. In 1953 he joined forces with Art Blakey to form a band under their joint leadership. Their first album, *Horace Silver And The Jazz Messengers* (1955), proved to be a milestone in the development of hard bop, with some of the tunes Silver penned for the recording later becoming jazz standards. Silver left the band in 1956 to record a series of albums that showcased his original, funky piano style. His recordings throughout the ensuing five decades have featured many jazz notables, including the trumpeters Donald Byrd, Art Farmer and Randy Brecker, as well as the saxophonists Hank Mobley and Michael Brecker.

Art Blakey began as a pianist before he switched to the drums in the 1940s. He drummed with Mary Lou Williams, Fletcher Henderson's Swing Band and Billy Eckstine's band before forming the original Jazz Messengers in 1955. The band varied in size, and there were countless personnel changes over the next 40 years (a list of the band's alumni is basically a who's who of mainstream jazz from the 1950s onwards), but they always delivered top-notch jazz, powered by Blakey's driving drums. His accompaniment style was relentless, and even the best players in his bands had to be on

"IF ART BLAKEY'S OLD-FASHIONED, I'M WHITE."
Miles Davis

ALTHOUGH Miles Davis made an early foray into hard bop with *Walkin'* (1953), the style did not become established until drummer Art Blakey and pianist Horace Silver joined forces later that year. They played with the trademark hard-driving grooves and gospel-inspired phrasings that would later be associated with the genre.

LEADING EXPONENTS:
Art Blakey
Sonny Rollins
Horace Silver
John Coltrane
Miles Davis
Wes Montgomery
Max Roach
Art Farmer
Freddie Hubbard
Cannonball Adderley

HARD BOP STYLE
The 4th bar of this example shows a typical snare "bomb". Tempos became ever more frenetic and solos and chords ever more adventurous.

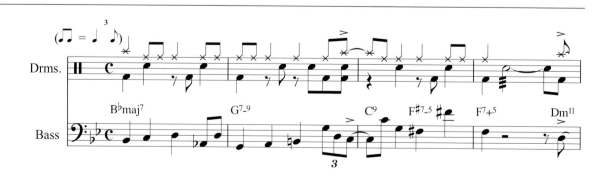

THE JAZZ INTRO ➡ 118   JAZZ PEOPLE A–Z ➡ 152   INSTRUMENTS A–Z ➡ 436   JAZZ: BEBOP ➡ 130

their toes to keep up with him. He was never really the jazz world's most subtle or versatile drummer, but what he played, he played exceedingly well and with spirit, until his death in 1990.

Other Hard Bop Players

Max Roach was another hugely influential bebop and hard bop drummer. He and Kenny Clarke were the first drummers to spell out the pulse of a groove with the ride cymbal to get a lighter texture. This gave them more freedom to explore their drum kits, and to drop random snare "bombs" while

allowing the frontline virtuosos to play with greater freedom at faster speeds. Roach possessed a broader range than Blakey; he was capable of creating a furious drive, but also drum solos with storylines. He was also very creative with his use of silence, using cymbals as gongs and handling the brushes as deftly as the sticks.

Sonny Rollins, one of jazz's most influential and most-loved saxophonists, also played a key role in the development of hard bop. Rollins started out on the piano before he permanently switched to the tenor sax in the mid-1940s. After a recording debut with Babs Gonzales in 1949, he worked with Miles Davis from 1951, Thelonious Monk from 1953 and the

classic Max Roach-Clifford Brown quintet from 1955. He became a band leader in 1956 and produced a series of brilliant recordings for Blue Note, Prestige, Contemporary and Riverside, including *Saxophone Colossus* (1956), *Tour De Force* (1957), *A Night At The Village Vanguard* (1957) and *Our Man In Jazz* (1962). Rollins was such a good soloist that Miles Davis once called him "the greatest tenor ever", and a sax player cannot get a better compliment than that! Other notable hard bop saxophonists who helped to expand the style included Julian "Cannonball" Adderley, John Coltrane and, more recently, Michael Brecker.

The trumpet was also a prominent instrument in hard bop, and some of the trumpeters who played it were exceptional musicians. Freddie Hubbard, one of the all-time great trumpeters, made a number of acclaimed recordings with Sonny Rollins, Philly Joe Jones (drummer) and Slide Hampton (trombonist), while Art Farmer's trumpet gave a lyrical feel to recordings by the Horace Silver Quintet and the Gerry Mulligan Quartet during the mid-to-late 1950s. The electric guitar was not originally a prominent instrument in hard bop, but Wes Montgomery's great soloing on *The Incredible Jazz Guitar Of Wes Montgomery* (1960) and *Smokin' At The Half Note* (1965) influenced a later generation of jazz guitar giants, including Pat Metheny and Mike Stern.

Far left

Sonny Rollins (left) and Max Roach (standing, centre) played some incredible music together that was not always popular with the critics, but was admired by peers such as Miles Davis.

Left

Art Blakey's style of drumming set a new precedent for jazz percussionists. During the other musicians' solos, Blakey would spur them on with a drum roll when they seemed to be running out of inspiration.

Below

Wes Montgomery's mellow tone was a result of his picking technique; whereas other guitarists tended to use a plectrum, Wes used his thumb, which one recording engineer described as "the fastest thing I've ever seen".

FREE JAZZ IS SEEN BY MANY AS AN AVANT-GARDE ART FORM RATHER THAN A TYPE OF JAZZ, WITH ITS UNPREDICTABLE RHYTHM AND CHORD PROGRESSIONS. EVOLVING OUT OF BEBOP IN THE 1940S AND 1950S THE EXPONENTS OF FREE JAZZ ABANDONED TRADITIONAL FORMS TO EXPAND THE MUSIC'S CREATIVE POSSIBILITIES, CHALLENGING MAINSTREAM LISTENERS AND PLAYERS ALIKE.

Free Jazz

Above

Rumour has it that when gigging with Pee Wee Crayton's band in 1953, Ornette Coleman was paid to forfeit his solos, as audiences would stop dancing when he began to play.

THE first documented free jazz recordings were made by the pianist Lennie Tristano and his band for Capitol Records in 1949. He asked the other players to ignore keys, chord structures, time signatures and melodies for the sessions, and just focus on "reading into each others' minds". Capitol were not exactly happy about this, but they released the sessions as *Crosscurrents* (1949). Tristano was a pioneer; his unique contrapuntal and improvisational ideas inspired other bebop musicians to try expanding the boundaries of jazz.

Coleman And Taylor

Although Tristano and his fellow musicians had been indulging in free jazz improvisation in the 1940s, the term free jazz was not used in earnest until the saxophonist Ornette Coleman released his first album in 1958. Coleman started out by playing Charlie Parker-style alto sax in Fort Worth, Texas, during the 1940s, before he moved to Los Angeles in 1950. He worked there as a lift operator, studied music theory and developed some radical ideas about jazz composition. Although these ideas were initially rejected by most of LA's jazz elite, Coleman eventually found enough allies to form a band: Don Cherry (trumpet), Don Payne (bass), Walter Norris (piano)

> "I HAVE ALWAYS WANTED MUSICIANS TO PLAY ON A MULTIPLE LEVEL WITH ME. I DON'T WANT THEM TO FOLLOW ME. I WANT THEM TO FOLLOW THEMSELVES, BUT TO BE WITH ME AT THE SAME TIME."
>
> *Ornette Coleman*

and Billy Higgins (drums). They recorded *Something Else!!!!* (1958), an original collection of atonal jazz compositions, for Contemporary Records, and it took the jazz world by storm. Coleman's next record, *The Shape Of Jazz To Come* (1959), featured himself, Cherry and Higgins with bassist Charlie Haden. This trimmed-down band line-up showed more focus and a better realization of Coleman's vision. The next offering,

Free Jazz (1960), was the album that gave the style its name, although Coleman denied later that he had any intention of naming the new type of music he had been developing.

LEADING EXPONENTS

Ornette Coleman
Cecil Taylor
John Coltrane
Lennie Tristano
Anthony Braxton
Eric Dolphy
Albert Ayler
Sun Ra
Derek Bailey
Keith Tippett
Elton Dean
Peter Bratzman
Misha Mengleberg

FREE JAZZ STYLE

Free jazz disposes of the inhibitions of diatonic harmony and regular rhythm, relying instead on musicians' interaction. Less standard playing techniques are often used.

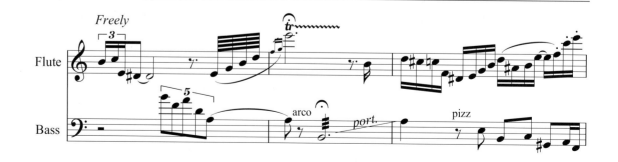

THE JAZZ INTRO ➡ 118   JAZZ PEOPLE A-Z ➡ 152   INSTRUMENTS A-Z ➡ 436

Coleman's music was nothing short of revolutionary. He used traditional instrumentation and his music swung in a relatively conventional way, but the manner in which he dealt with tonality was extremely unusual. His tunes were based around quirky bebop motifs, and he would use the overall tonality of these to create space for unusually free and expressive solos. Traditional jazz critics initially dismissed this music as "anti-jazz" because it did not fit in with their conceptions of what jazz should sound like. Nowadays, though, Coleman is seen as a true jazz pioneer, on a par with the likes of Charlie Parker, Louis Armstrong and Miles Davis.

A seminal figure in the free jazz movement was Cecil Taylor who was inspired by Fats Waller's single-note melodies and Dave Brubeck's chord clusters, and went on to develop what many critics consider to be one of the most extraordinary jazz piano techniques ever heard; recordings such as *Jazz Advance* (1956), *Looking Ahead!* (1958) and *The World Of Cecil Taylor* (1960) featured highly original versions of standards and atonal tunes, the likes of which had never been heard before. Taylor's approach was very different to Coleman's, as Whitney Balliett once observed in *The New Yorker*: "Coleman's music is accessible, but he is loath to share it; Taylor's music is difficult, and he is delighted to share it". "The American aesthetic landscape is littered with idiosyncratic marvels – Walt Whitman, Charles Ives, D. W. Griffith, Duke Ellington, Jackson Pollock – and Taylor belongs with them," Balliett continued.

From Coltrane To Braxton

Possibly the most influential free jazz player to emerge during the late 1950s was John Coltrane. Unlike Coleman, 'Trane was already a well-known figure in the mainstream jazz scene; he had played on seminal recordings by Dizzy Gillespie and Miles Davis. While Coleman was defining his art by reducing jazz's tonal base to its bare essence, Coltrane increased the complexity of jazz harmony many times over with his *Giant Steps* (1959) recording. He also began to explore modal jazz concepts, and recorded a series of more progressively "free" jazz albums up until his premature death at the age of 40 in 1967. Other notable free jazz musicians from this period include multiple reed player Eric Dolphy, saxophonist Albert Ayler and the eccentric keyboard playing band leader, Sun Ra, who claimed to have arrived here on Earth from Saturn on a date that cannot be revealed because of its mystical astrological significance!

Free jazz developed throughout the early 1960s and 1970s as a growing number of new players such as the Art Ensemble of Chicago and David Murray in the US; Keith Tippett, Steve Beresford, Elton Dean, Trevor Watts, Ian Coxhill and Maggie Nichols amongst others in the UK; Peter Brotzman and Peter Kowald in Germany; and in the Netherlands' Willem Breuker,

Misha Mengleberg and Han Bennick decided to follow in the footsteps of Coleman, Coltrane and Taylor, throwing original ideas into the ever-filling free-jazz pot. Derek Bailey, an eccentric guitarist from the UK, pioneered the use of unusual guitar effects and developed a highly idiosyncratic style, completely avoiding conventional melodies, chords or rhythms while Anthony Braxton and Steve Lacy coaxed extraordinary textures out of saxophones and clarinets, on solo and ensemble recordings. These and other free jazz exponents are continuing to produce original and challenging music.

Above

John Coltrane's eagerness to experiment with chords and musical structure led to his being labelled "eccentric" and even "unmusical".

Left

Cecil Taylor was a leading figure in free jazz until his success was eclipsed by the advent of Ornette Coleman in 1959.

SOUL JAZZ STOOD OUT FROM OTHER PREVIOUS JAZZ FORMS. ITS MELODIES WERE SIMPLER AND MORE RHYTHMIC COMPARED TO HARD BOP, AND INFLUENCES FROM GOSPEL AND R&B WERE EVIDENT. IN MORE TRADITIONAL JAZZ FORMS, SOLOISTS WOULD FOLLOW WALKING BASSLINES OR METRIC CYMBAL RHYTHMS. IN SOUL JAZZ, THEY FOLLOWED A WHOLE GROOVE, WHICH ENCOURAGED A DIFFERENT STYLE OF PHRASING.

Soul Jazz

SOUL jazz, also known as jazz-funk, can be traced back as far as the early 1950s, when Horace Silver was writing groovy jazz numbers for his now famous trio. One of their recordings, *Horace Silver Trio & Art Blakey* (1952), featured one of the earliest recorded jazz-funk tunes, 'Opus de Funk', which even helped to name the emerging style. The much celebrated hard-bop classic, *Horace Silver And The Jazz Messengers* (1954), also boasts a couple of funky little numbers, including 'The Preacher', one of Silver's most well-known tunes.

The music developed during the 1960s and 1970s within both the jazz and soul music fraternities, although the more modern sounds of fusion and smooth jazz were to overshadow it by the 1980s.

"FUNKY MEANS EARTHY AND BLUES-BASED. IT MIGHT NOT BE BLUES ITSELF, BUT IT DOES HAVE THAT 'DOWN-HOME' FEEL TO IT. SOUL IS BASICALLY THE SAME, BUT THERE'S AN ADDED DIMENSION OF FEELING AND SPIRIT."

Horace Silver

Above
Cannonball Adderley's impassioned, open-hearted playing style ensured that he quickly shook off the inevitable, early comparisons to Charlie Parker and established his own role in the jazz scene.

King Of The Organ

One of the first musicians to be associated with soul jazz was the legendary organist Jimmy Smith. Both of Jimmy's parents played the piano, so it was not long before he did too; he worked with his father in clubs during the 1940s and formed his own trio in 1955. His brand of "late night" soul jazz met with almost instant success, and albums such as *Home Cookin'* (1958), *Back At The Chicken Shack* (1960) and *Bashin'* (1962)

inspired countless other Hammond B3 maestros, including "Brother" Jack McDuff, Jimmy McGriff, Richard "Groove" Holmes and Big John Patten. Smith's influence also extended to many major figures in rock and pop, including Steve Winwood, John Mayall, Georgie Fame, Brian Auges and Jon Lord of Deep Purple. After a string of hits in the 1960s, he went off the boil and recorded a series of unremarkable albums in the 1970s and 1980s. By then, though, his reputation as an influential pioneer of soul-jazz organ was assured.

LEADING EXPONENTS

Horace Silver

Jimmy Smith

Cannonball Adderley

Ronnie Foster

Ramsey Lewis

Lou Donaldson

Jack McDuff

Grover Washington Jr.

Big John Patton

SOUL JAZZ STYLE

Soul Jazz heralded a return to simple blues-influenced melodies and is characterized by melodic and rhythmic repetition.

THE JAZZ INTRO ➡ 118   JAZZ PEOPLE A-Z ➡ 152   INSTRUMENTS A-Z ➡ 436   JAZZ: FUSION ➡ 142   JAZZ: SMOOTH JAZZ ➡ 146

Another soul jazz pioneer was the saxophonist Julian "Cannonball" Adderley. Nicknamed "Cannibal" at school because of his capacious liking for food, Julian changed this to "Cannonball" during his early jazz years. He directed a local high school band during the early 1950s, formed his own jazz combo in 1956, and signed to Riverside Records in 1958. They produced a series of albums, often live, that contributed greatly to the soul jazz style. The first of these, *Somethin' Else* (1958), featured the legendary trumpeter Miles Davis as a sideman. In turn, Cannonball played alto sax on Miles's universally acclaimed *Kind Of Blue* (1959). The most influential Adderley soul jazz recordings were made a few years later, with keyboardist Joe Zawinul in the band; *Jazz Workshop Revisited* (1963) spawned a soul jazz classic in 'Mercy, Mercy, Mercy', penned by Zawinul. The keyboard player's electric piano sound became another recognizable texture in jazz-funk and fusion (he later formed Weather Report with the saxophonist Wayne Shorter).

The guitar also began to appear in soul jazz music during the 1960s, and the velvet-toned Wes Montgomery, an exceptional soloist, often appeared with Jimmy Smith. Wes picked out melodies with his right thumb and fingers, a soft style which originally developed out of trying not to upset his neighbours! His albums were among the first jazz recordings to appeal to a non-jazz public, but in 1968, at the peak of his popularity and aged only 43, he died suddenly of a heart attack. Kenny Burrell was another cool-toned player who graced countless soul jazz recordings during the 1960s and 1970s. His successful career, spanning six decades, has also encompassed hard bop and jazz funk, and his most popular album, *Midnight Blue* (1963), was cited as the main influence for Van Morrison's jazz-pop classic, *Moondance* (1970).

The Next Generations

Many new soul jazz and jazz funk artists began to appear during the 1970s. As the decade progressed, the music became more dance oriented. The guitarist/singer George Benson

effortlessly switched between soulful and smooth jazz styles, and the organist Ronnie Foster emerged as a talented mainstream funk keyboardist, whose Blue Note records later became cult items among a younger generation of listeners raised on acid jazz.

A number of soul jazz hits appeared during the 1970s, one of the most famous of which is The Crusaders' 1979 classic 'Street Life'. The guest vocalist on the song was Randy Crawford, who also sang on Cannonball Adderley's *Big Man* (1975), released after the great saxophonist's death. Artists such as the pianist Ramsey Lewis and saxophonist Grover Washington Jr. also produced a lot of lighter instrumental soul jazz during the 1970s and 1980s. Although jazz purists dismissed most of this as borderline muzak, it introduced soul jazz – and, indeed, jazz itself – to a wider audience.

Left

Jimmy Smith has remained faithful to the Hammond organ sound despite advances in keyboard technology. His pioneering, bluesy style was influenced more by saxophonists than fellow keyboard players.

Below

Horace Silver's relationship with the innovative Blue Note label lasted for 28 years. Blue Note is the most famous and influential jazz label and has remained open-minded about emerging jazz styles since it began in 1939.

"FUSION" CAN BE APPLIED TO ANY MUSIC THAT BLENDS TWO OR MORE DIFFERENT STYLES, THOUGH IT IS NORMALLY USED TO DESCRIBE THE ELECTRONIC JAZZ ROCK MOVEMENT THAT EMERGED IN THE LATE 1960S. SOME OF THE MUSICIANS EXPANDED THE BOUNDARIES OF BOTH JAZZ AND ROCK, WHILE OTHERS FOCUSED ON PRODUCING SOPHISTICATED, BUT SHALLOW, "BACKGROUND" MUSIC.

Fusion & Jazz Rock

ALTHOUGH fusion records have never sold in huge quantities, the style has remained popular within the musical community during the past 30 years. The term "musician's musician" is often used to describe the top exponents.

It is widely accepted that Miles Davis's *Bitches Brew* (1969) album was the first influential jazz rock recording. It combined modal jazz with rock guitar and drum sounds, and introduced jazz to a wider rock audience. The album featured an extraordinary selection of musicians, including Joe Zawinul and Chick Corea (keyboards), Wayne Shorter (saxophone), John McLaughlin (electric guitar) and Lenny White (drums). These players went on to form three of the most celebrated and influential fusion bands in the early 1970s: Weather Report (Zawinul and Shorter), Return To Forever (Corea and White) and the Mahavishnu Orchestra (McLaughlin).

Weather Report And Mahavishnu

Weather Report was one of the most successful fusion bands, with albums reaching the Top 50 charts on both sides of the Atlantic. Their earliest recordings were patchy, but *Black Market* (1976) featured strong compositions and introduced the legendary Jaco Pastorius on bass guitar. The combination of strikingly original tunes, Shorter's searing sax lines, Zawinul's colourful synth passages (played on Arp and Oberheim instruments) and Pastorius's jaw-dropping bass work

(ranging from "singing" melodic passages to unusual harmonics and ultra-fast riffs) proved to be an even bigger success with their next album, *Heavy Weather* (1977). Further recordings, such as *Mr. Gone* (1978), *Night Passage* (1980) and *Weather Report* (1982), confirmed the band's status as a top-flight jazz act, although Pastorius left in 1982 and the band eventually split in 1986. Sadly, Pastorius died in 1987 after he was beaten up outside a nightclub in Fort Lauderdale, Florida.

The Mahavishnu Orchestra was more rock-oriented than Weather Report. Formed by John McLaughlin during the early 1970s and influenced by Eastern mysticism, the original band featured McLaughlin on electric guitar, along

> "BITCHES BREW HAS A KIND OF SEARCHING QUALITY BECAUSE MILES WAS ONTO THE PROCESS OF DISCOVERING THIS NEW MUSIC AND DEVELOPING IT."
>
> *Dave Holland (bass player on Bitches Brew)*

LEADING EXPONENTS:

Weather Report
Mahavishnu Orchestra
Return To Forever
Tony Williams' Lifetime
Al Di Meola
Pat Metheny
Frank Zappa
Jean-Luc Ponty
Allan Holdsworth
John Scofield

JAZZ ROCK STYLE

Jazz rock utilizes traditional jazz melodies and rhythms and uses rock instrumentation and electrification to create a typical "fusion" sound.

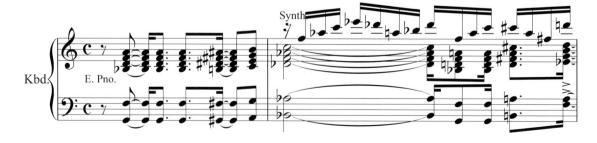

THE JAZZ INTRO ➡ 118   JAZZ PEOPLE A-Z ➡ 152   INSTRUMENTS A-Z ➡ 436   THE ROCK INTRO ➡ 74   THE WORLD INTRO ➡ 276

with Jan Hammer (keyboards), Jerry Goodman (violin), Rick Laird (bass) and Billy Cobham (drums). Their explosive creativity broke new boundaries in jazz, both in terms of virtuosity and complexity, and their albums *The Inner Mounting Flame* (1971) and *Birds of Fire* (1972) are widely regarded as fusion classics. Hammer, Goodman and Cobham left to work on their own projects a year later, and McLaughlin reformed the band with various other line-ups for the next two decades. He also formed Shakti, an exploratory "Eastern" acoustic fusion band, with renowned Indian classical musicians such as L. Shankar (violin) and Zakir Hussain (tablas) during the mid-1970s, as well as a much-celebrated acoustic guitar trio with flamenco virtuoso Paco de Lucía and fusion ace Al Di Meola. The trio's live recording, *Friday Night In San Francisco* (1980), features some breathtakingly fleet guitar work that has to be heard to be believed.

Other Influential Bands

The other primary 1970s fusion band to directly emerge out of the *Bitches Brew* scene was Chick Corea's Return To Forever. Their first line-up was a Latin-style band led by Chick on keyboards, but by 1975 the group had developed into an all-out fusion outfit featuring Al Di Meola (guitar), Stanley Clarke (bass) and Lenny White (drums). Their *Romantic Warrior* (1976) recording was a landmark jazz-rock album, featuring six complex, intricately crafted instrumentals that were to inspire rock and jazz musicians for years to come.

It also acted as a launching pad for Di Meola's solo career; he went on to record *Land Of The Midnight Sun* (1976), *Elegant Gypsy* (1976), *Casino* (1977) and *Splendido Hotel* (1979), which resulted in *Guitar Player* magazine readers voting him Best Jazz Player for five consecutive years.

There were a number of other seminal fusion recordings made during the 1970s: *Believe It* (1975) by Tony Williams introduced Allan Holdsworth's unique but influential legato lead-guitar style; Frank Zappa's *Roxy & Elsewhere* (1974) fused jazz and rock with a warped, but much-loved sense of humour; and the Pat Metheny Group with its self-titled album (1978) forged a new, earthy jazz style that eventually earned the group huge audiences, critical acclaim and Grammy awards. Across the Atlantic, Brand X's *Unorthodox Behaviour* (1976) and Soft Machine's *Third* (1970) proved that British bands were also capable of producing world-class fusion, while the French and Belgians also showed their fusion mettle with violinist Jean-Luc Ponty's *Enigmatic Ocean* (1977) and Marc Moulin's *Placebo* (1973).

By contrast, the 1980s were relatively quiet for fusion, although Corea, Holdsworth and the American guitarist John Scofield made some significant recordings during this period. In more recent years, Tribal Tech, led by guitarist Scott Henderson and bass virtuoso Gary Willis, has kept the fusion flag flying. Their recent recordings, *Thick* (1999) and *Rocket Science* (2000), show that jazz rock is still alive and kicking. The latest platform for "jazz rock" has evolved into the "jam band scene".

Above
An incredibly talented and versatile pianist, Chick Corea made forays into fusion jazz that were only a part, albeit an important one, of his musical output. He also peformed Latin and free jazz and music from the classical repertoire.

Left
The groundbreaking Bitches Brew *marked an irrevocable change in the development of jazz. The dark but fiery combination of Miles Davis' horn and Wayne Shorter's saxophone on the album blew away all who heard it.*

Far left
The Fender Jazz Bass has a warm but punchy sound and sounds not unlike an upright string bass. Jaco Pastorius of Weather Report *used a fretless version on the track 'Night Passage'.*

ACID JAZZ IS A LIVELY, GROOVE-ORIENTED MUSIC STYLE THAT COMBINES ELEMENTS FROM JAZZ, FUNK AND HIP HOP, WITH AN EMPHASIS ON JAZZ DANCE. THE TERM "ACID JAZZ" WAS FIRST USED DURING THE LATE 1980S, BOTH AS THE NAME OF AN AMERICAN RECORD LABEL AND THE TITLE OF A BRITISH JAZZ FUNK, "RARE GROOVE" COMPILATION SERIES.

Acid Jazz

INTEREST had originally been sparked by a thriving London club scene, where hip DJs were playing rare 1970s jazz funk records. This encouraged British and American underground musicians such as The Brand New Heavies, Jamiroquai, Stereo MC's, Galliano and Groove Collective, who began to popularize the style by the 1990s.

One of the first DJs to be identified with acid jazz was the London-based Gilles Peterson, who began broadcasting jazz funk sets from his garden shed at home and DJing at London clubs in the late 1980s.

He teamed up with Eddie Piller, who had previously released a debut album by a young, contemporary Hammond organ virtuoso, James Taylor, to form Acid Jazz Records. The label's first releases were a series of compilations titled *Totally Wired*, which alternated jazz funk obscurities from the 1970s with updated tracks from the new acid jazz movement. Peterson later formed his own acid jazz label, Talkin' Loud Records.

"ACID JAZZ WAS THE MOST SIGNIFICANT JAZZ FORM TO EMERGE OUT OF THE BRITISH MUSIC SCENE."
Q magazine, UK.

Above

N'Dea Davenport, as a member of the Brand New Heavies, was an important figure in the development of acid jazz. After leaving the band in 1994, she embarked on a solo career, releasing her debut album four years later.

Mainstream Acid Jazz

Acid jazz entered into the mainstream in 1990, after The Brand New Heavies released their self-titled debut album on the Acid Jazz label. Formed in 1985 by drummer Jan Kincaid, guitarist Simon Bartholomew and bassist/keyboardist Andrew

LEADING EXPONENTS

The Brand New Heavies
Jamiroquai
Galliano
Groove Collective
James Taylor Quartet
Courtney Pine
United Future
  Organisation
Stereo MC's

ACID JAZZ STYLE

Acid jazz artists have effectively cross-fertilized jazz harmonies and melodies with funk basslines and dance orientated drum patterns.

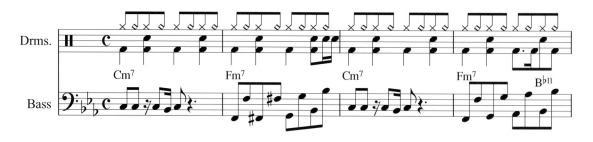

THE JAZZ INTRO ➡ 118   JAZZ PEOPLE A-Z ➡ 152   INSTRUMENTS A-Z ➡ 436   THE WORLD INTRO ➡ 276   THE DANCE INTRO ➡ 310

Levy – old school friends from London – they were originally an instrumental band inspired by James Brown and The Meters, whose records were getting extensive play around the rare groove scene. The band began recording their own material, added a singer and a brass section, and gained exposure via the club circuit. Their first album was a success and it was followed by a string of hit singles in 1991 in the UK and US. Then came *Heavy Rhyme Experience, Vol. 1* (1992), featuring guest appearances by the rappers Main Source, Gang Starr, Grand Puba and The Pharcyde. The following album, *Brother Sister* (1994), went platinum in Britain, and the band's success has since continued on both sides of the Atlantic with *Original Flava* (1994) and *Delicious* (1997).

After the emergence of the Heavies, Galliano and a few smaller UK acid jazz bands, a spate of compilations were launched en masse by record labels, leaving many consumers confused over exactly what the style was or who played it. The confusion increased when even more independent acid jazz communities began to spring up all over the US during the early 1990s. By then, the term could refer to anything from Jamiroquai's commercial soul funk to the James Taylor Quartet's rendering of the 'Starsky And Hutch Theme', or from the ethnic eclecticism of the Japanese producers United Future Organisation to the hip hop poetry of New York's Groove Collective.

The creation of the UK singer/songwriter Jason Kay, Jamiroquai has perhaps popularized acid jazz more than any other band. Although some listeners today dismiss them as mere Stevie Wonder imitators, the band has experienced chart success all over the world with an irresistible blend of house rhythms and 1970s-era soul/funk. As he did not originally have a band to back up his songs, Jay came up with his own project and coined its moniker by adding the name of an American Indian tribe, Iroquois, to the music term "jam". He assembled a group of musicians and produced some demos, which impressed the Acid Jazz label enough to issue the debut single 'When You Gonna Learn?' in late 1992. A hit, it led to a long-term and lucrative recording contract with Sony, who released *Emergency On Planet Earth* (1992) and *The Return Of The Space Cowboy* (1994), both major hit albums in the UK. This success spread to America with Jamiroquai's third effort, *Travelling Without Moving* (1996), which contained the worldwide hit 'Virtual Insanity'. The band is still going strong, although they now appear to be past their prime.

Cutting-Edge Jazz

A number of more "serious" jazz artists, including the UK's Courtney Pine, the American veteran Pharaoh Sanders (saxophonists) and the American Pat Metheny (guitarist),

were also associated with acid jazz forms during the 1990s. Pine and Sanders both contributed to a British compilation series titled *Rebirth Of The Cool* (named after the classic Miles Davis album *Birth Of The Cool*), while The Pat Metheny Group used hip hop-style grooves to great effect on their *We Live Here* (1995) album.

Nu Jazz

Since the 1990s, acid jazz has moved more left-field, evolving into the nu jazz (nu-fusion or future-jazz) movement via the house music-led club dance floor. The cutting edge, springing from the underground, has been exploited commercially by France's St. Germain and even the 'establishment's' Herbie Hancock (*Future2Future,* 2002). A serious jazz vibe is being combined with percussion-led, acousto-electric keyboards and programmed beats transfused with the hip hop/drum 'n' bass repetitions of house music, Afro-Brazilian beats and live jazz. Leading the nu jazz field are labels such as Germany's Compost (Jazzanova, Beanfield, Les Gammas, Kyoto Jazz Massive and Minus 8) and UK's 'West London collective' working with producer-DJ IG Culture and artists such as Kaidi Tatham, Modaji and Seiji. In nu jazz, vocalists are coming into their own again, high in both profile and mix – Vikter Duplaix, Robert Owens, Peven Everett and Ursula Rucker in the US, Victor Davies, Joseph Malik, Kate Phillips (Bembé Segué) and Marcus Begg in the UK and Europe.

Producers collaborating with live musicians are mixing (today's technological equivalent of scoring/arranging), remixing and sampling to brilliant effect, and new technology is opening up even more possibilities for jazz. Indeed, as Sun Ra predicted as long ago as 1972, "Space Is The Place", especially for the MP3 generation.

Smooth Jazz

SLICK, "RADIO-FRIENDLY" SMOOTH JAZZ EMERGED IN THE 1970S, AND IT HAS CONTINUED TO EVOLVE EVER SINCE. THE MOST ARTFUL EXAMPLES CAN MAKE FOR REWARDING LISTENING, WHILE BLANDER COMPOSITIONS CAN BE RECOGNIZED BY ANY COMBINATION OF MUSICAL CLICHÉS: LIGHT FUNK GROOVES, COOL JAZZ CHORDS, SLAPPED BASS LINES, CORNY HORN ACCOMPANIMENTS AND PREDICTABLE SOLOS.

Above

There are many who would dispute the music of Kenny G deserving the name jazz; to his credit he prefers to describe his music as "instrumental pop". His records are popular as relaxing background music.

THE style has drawn fierce criticism from jazz purists, but its unobtrusiveness has often made it popular with restaurants, wine bars and other public places where sophisticated-sounding background music is required to give clients or customers a chill-out vibe. Many would use the term "fusion" to describe smooth jazz, even though the same word is more commonly used to describe the more exploratory jazz rock scene that emerged out of Miles Davis's *Bitches Brew* period. This seems rather contradictory, as smooth jazz is normally cool background music while jazz rock is often complex and demanding. But it probably explains why jazz rock fans tend to pour scorn over even the most distinguished smooth jazz acts whenever they are mentioned.

Cool Sounds In The 1970s

The earliest smooth jazz artists were musicians who wanted to make more commercial, accessible music without losing their jazz roots. Born in Pittsburgh, Pennsylvania on 22 March, 1943, George Benson is perhaps the best example of this. His stepfather was a musician who taught him to play the ukulele and guitar, and after being enticed by the jazz sounds of saxophonist Charlie Parker and guitarist Grant Green, he decided

"KENNY G HAS LONG BEEN THE MUSICIAN MANY JAZZ LISTENERS LOVE TO HATE."
All Music Guide

to become a jazz guitarist. He emerged as a popular soloist in the style of Wes Montgomery, and played alongside top artists such as Herbie Hancock, Jack McDuff and Ron Carter during the 1960s. In the 1970s, he switched over to a more commercial, jazz funk style, and was rewarded with serious album sales. *Breezin'* (1976) sold more than two million units and was the first of several Grammy-winning recordings with Warner Brothers, while *In Flight* (1976) was a polished album that featured Benson – an accomplished vocalist – "scat" singing in unison with his trademark cool solos. He switched to a more overtly pop vocal sound during the 1980s, to the disgust of

LEADING EXPONENTS

George Benson
Yellowjackets
Steely Dan
Kenny G
Larry Carlton
Spyro Gyra
The Rippingtons

SMOOTH JAZZ STYLE

Smooth Jazz rejects ensemble pieces in favour of unchallenging melodies played by one or two principle instruments.

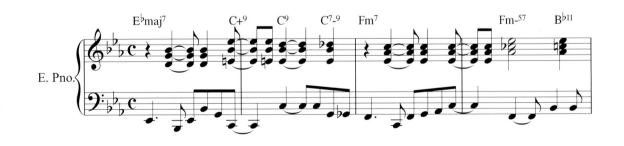

THE JAZZ INTRO ➡ 118   JAZZ PEOPLE A-Z ➡ 152   INSTRUMENTS A-Z ➡ 436

some jazz purists, but he later compensated by recording with Count Basie's old band in 1990.

Benson's popularity inspired other jazz guitarists to go "smooth" during the 1970s. Earl Klugh appeared with acoustic guitar albums, including the acclaimed *Earl Klugh* (1976) and *Finger Painting* (1977), while Lee Ritenour produced Latin-influenced recordings such as *Guitar Player* (1976) and *Captain Fingers* (1977), and Larry Carlton delighted listeners with his excellent soloing on *Larry Carlton* (1977). Keyboard players were at it too, with Herbie Hancock using electronically synthesized vocals on *Sunlight* (1977), Ramsey Lewis producing slick recordings such as *Tequila Mockingbird* (1978) and George Duke recording many albums, including his critically acclaimed *Solo Keyboard Album* (1976). On the band side, Spyro Gyra delivered the infectious *Morning Dance* (1979) and even jazz rock heroes Steely Dan fully developed their own unique and sophisticated brand of jazz pop on the albums *Aja* (1977) and *Gaucho* (1980).

Further Refinements

Some of the most polished, artistic and commercial examples of smooth jazz emerged during the 1980s and 1990s. Perhaps the most respected band in this period was the Yellowjackets. They formed in 1977, when the guitarist Robben Ford assembled a group of veteran session musicians to work on one of his albums. Ford and the trio of musicians – keyboardist Russell Ferrante, bassist Jimmy Haslip and drummer Ricky Lawson – enjoyed working together, hence the Yellowjackets. Ford and Lawson left after two well-received albums, but the band continued to refine its sound: by the late 1980s, recordings such as *Politics* (1988) and *The Spin* (1989) demonstrated that they were already a cut above most other smooth jazz bands in terms of artistry. By the mid-1990s, they had developed a definitive smooth jazz sound on the albums *Greenhouse* (1991), *Like A River* (1992) and *Blue Hats* (1997). They are still going

strong, and their lively 2002 *Mint Jam* album (Heads Up label) featured among the 2003 Grammy nominations.

At the more commercial end of the musical spectrum, Kenny Gorelick (Kenny G) has been introducing larger pop audiences to smooth jazz. He began playing professionally with Barry White in 1976, and, after graduating from the University of Washington, worked with the keyboardist Jeff Lorber before signing to Arista as a solo artist in 1982. His first three albums were moderately successful, but his fourth, *Duotones* (1986), hit the big time with a hugely popular instrumental hit, 'Songbird'. Since then, he has released a succession of popular smooth jazz albums, which have sold more than 30 million copies and annoyed jazz purists who consider them innocuous and one-dimensional. Various other smooth jazz bands, such as the Rippingtons, Fattburger and Acoustic Alchemy, as well as solo artists such as Joyce Cooling, Dave Koz and Boney James, have helped to maintain the popularity of this style.

Above

Donald Fagan, whose distinctive vocals added yet another unusual dimension to the logic-defying band Steely Dan. Their music is an obscure but strangely accessible combination of jazz, rock and pop, with a hint of country.

Left

The musically open-minded guitarist George Benson infuriated jazz fans with his covers of pop records, but he refuses to be constricted by what is expected of him, explaining that his first duty is as an entertainer.

LATIN JAZZ IS COMMONLY DEFINED AS THE FUSION OF AMERICAN JAZZ MELODIES, IMPROVISATION AND CHORDS WITH LATIN AMERICAN RHYTHMS, PREDOMINANTLY THOSE OF AFRO-CUBAN ORIGIN. HOW THIS MARRIAGE OF STYLES OCCURRED IS ALSO ONE OF THE MOST SIGNIFICANT CULTURAL, MUSICAL EXCHANGES IN HISTORY.

Latin Jazz

Above

Harlem-born Puerto Rican Tito Puente's arrangements of the mambo and cha-cha earned him admiration across a wide cultural sphere. He recorded over a hundred albums and has a star on the Hollywood Walk of Fame.

MENTION the birth of Latin jazz to any aficionado of the art form and they will invariably reply with two names: Machito and Mario Bauzá. The former was born Francisco Raul Gutiérrez Grillo on 16 February 1912, in Cuba. The young vocalist/maraca man hit New York City in 1937, where he played stints with Xavier Cugat and Noro Morales before forming his own band, Machito's Afro-Cubans. By 1940, Machito asked his brother-in-law, Mario Bauzá (who was married to his sister Estella), a trumpeter, pianist, arranger and composer who had already worked with the likes of Dizzy Gillespie and Chick Webb, to be his band's musical arranger. It was this orchestra that two American musicians – one in Los Angeles, one in New York City – would hear, and the musical world would never be the same again.

The Night That Changed Dizzy's Life

On 31 May 1943, the already legendary Gillespie went to the Park Place Ballroom in New York. There, he heard Machito and his orchestra perform 'Tanga' (meaning marijuana), a dazzling new Afro-Cuban composition written by Bauzá during a rehearsal. The piece is widely recognized to be a breakthrough in the creation of a new style of music, which has been called Afro-Cuban jazz,

Cubop and Latin jazz, a term Bauzá reportedly hated. Still, Gillespie would often recall that night as one that changed his life. The trumpet virtuoso was so taken with the conga, bongos, and "clave" rhythms that he immediately incorporated them into his own group.

In January 1946, the influential American pianist/bandleader Stan Kenton was awestruck when he heard the same 'Tanga' at a club in Los Angeles. Soon, he too added Latin elements to virtually all of his music. Gillespie made

Latin music history himself with his 30 December 1947 recording of 'Manteca' on RCA Victor, which he co-wrote with a musician introduced to him by Bauzá. It was the master conguero Chano Pozo, another seminal figure in the birth of Latin jazz and the key figure in Gillespie's continued "latinization" of jazz. 'Manteca' would subsequently become Gillespie's signature tune and one of the most covered standards in the history of the genre.

> "WE PLAY JAZZ WITH THE LATIN TOUCH, THAT'S ALL, YOU KNOW."
>
> *Tito Puente*

LEADING EXPONENTS

Machito
Mario Bauzá
Chano Pozo
Dizzy Gillespie
Israel "Cachao" López
Arturo Sandoval
Paquito D'Rivera
Eddie Palmiéré
Danilo Pérez
David Sánchez
Tito Puente
Patato Valdés

LATIN JAZZ STYLE

A growing Hispanic population in the US brought with them latin percussion rhythms, such as uptempo sambas, which blended with traditional jazz melodies to produce Latin jazz.

THE JAZZ INTRO ➡ 118   JAZZ PEOPLE A–Z ➡ 152   INSTRUMENTS A–Z ➡ 436   WORLD: LATIN ➡ 300

Following closely behind Machito, Pozo, Gillespie and Kenton is master timbalero, bandleader and composer Tito Puente, also known as El Rey del Timbal and The Mambo King. Born in New York to Puerto Rican parents, Puente was instrumental in taking jazz to a broader audience thanks to his big band orchestrations and his on stage flourish. And, of course, he wrote and recorded 'Oye Cómo Va', later popularized by Carlos Santana, which incorporated a coro section and used other eminently Latin elements, such as a charanga-style flute and, of course, the characteristic syncopated piano cha-cha riff.

Another pioneer who took Latin jazz to the mainstream was master conguero Ramón "Mongo" Santamaría, best known for his hit rendition of Herbie Hancock's 'Watermelon Man' and for authoring jazz standard 'Afro Blue'. It was with Santamaria's band, that a then-young Chick Corea first received major exposure, while present-day conguero Poncho Sánchez cites Santamaría as his mentor and major influence.

A New Generation

Other direct descendants of Latin jazz's founding fathers include brothers Charlie and Eddie Palmieri, born in New York to Puerto Rican parents. Both of them pianists, composers, bandleaders and arrangers, they created their separate bands and helped shape the New York salsa sound. While Eddie is best known for his work with his band La Perfecta, which incorporated trombones and trumpets, Charlie revived the concept of the *descarga* (Latin jam session) originally popularized by veteran Cuban bassist Israel López "Cachao". Largely forgotten in the 1980s, Cachao lived a brilliant revival in the mid-1990s when he was rediscovered by Cuban-born Hollywood film star Andy García, who directed a documentary on Cachao's life, *Cachao: como su ritmo no hay dos*. Later on, García would also be involved in a film project based on the life of another Cuban musician, trumpeter Arturo Sandoval. Those two projects, coupled with the 2000 film *Calle 54*, which features a series of Latin jazz performances by the likes of Jerry González and the Fort Apache Band, Cuban

percussionist Patato Valdés and fellow countryman and pianist Chucho Valdés, has renewed interest in the genre. Currently, pianist Valdés is the elder statesman of a new generation of highly virtuosic Latin jazz pianists, including Gonzalo Rubalcaba, who freely blend American standards with Cuban rhythms and are also highly experimental in their own compositions.

Other current leaders of the movement include Sandoval and countryman Paquito D'Rivera, who, like Valdés, were once members of experimental Cuban jazz ensemble Irakere, and are currently living in the US. D'Rivera in particular, expanded beyond his brand of Afro-Cuban jazz to delve extensively in to other styles of Latin jazz, incorporating rhythms from Venezuela, Peru and Puerto Rico into his music.

The openness to rhythms outside of Cuba is congruent with the rise of several Latin jazz musicians from other countries, including pianists Danilo Pérez (Panama) and Michel Camilo (Dominican Republic).

Above

Machito (right) inspired players such as Dizzy Gillespie and Stan Kenton to experiment with Latin sounds. Kenton described him as the "greatest exponent of Afro-Cuban jazz" and even named a track after him.

Centre

Mario Bauzá started out as a professional clarinet and oboe player in the Havana Philharmonic before moving to New York in 1930. It was there, while playing with Noble Sissle, that he took up the trumpet.

Brazilian Jazz

IN THE MID-1950S, A CULTURAL CROSSFERTILIZATION OF BRAZILIAN SAMBA RHYTHMS, AMERICAN COOL JAZZ AND SOPHISTICATED HARMONIES LED TO THE DEVELOPMENT OF BOSSA NOVA. IN THE EARLY 1960S THE BOSSA NOVA MOVEMENT SWEPT THROUGH THE UNITED STATES AND EUROPE PRODUCING A STRAIN OF BRAZILIAN-INFLUENCED JAZZ THAT REMAINS A VITAL PART OF THE JAZZ SCENE.

Above

Black Orpheus was an updating of the Orpheus & Eurydice myth, set against the background of a Brazilian Carnival. The intense vitality of the music in the film fascinated viewers and the soundtrack sold in the millions.

BY the early 1950s, a few pioneering Brazilian composers began listening seriously to American jazz, particularly the limpid-toned west coast variety practised by Chet Baker, Gerry Mulligan and Shorty Rogers. In absorbing that cool influence, composers such as Antonio Carlos Jobim, João Gilberto, Baden Powell and Luiz Bonfá stripped the complex polyrhythms of Afro-Brazilian samba down to their undulating essence and offered a more intimate approach, in which melodies were caressed rather than belted out in the raucous Carnival fashion.

Blame It On The Bossa Nova

Around the same time, American jazz saxophonist Bud Shank (from the west coast branch of cool jazz) had joined forces with Brazilian guitarist Laurindo Almeida in a quartet that blended Brazilian rhythms and folk melodies with cool jazz improvising. Recorded five years before the term "bossa nova" was even coined, their 1953 collaboration on the World Pacific label, *Brazilliance*, would have a significant impact on the ultimate architects of the bossa nova movement.

In 1956, the Bahian guitarist/composer João Gilberto relocated from Salvador to Rio de Janeiro, where the colourful cultural mix was inspiring another brilliant guitarist/composer, Antonio Carlos Jobim. The two began to collaborate, and in July 1958, Gilberto recorded Jobim and Vinícius de Moraes's 'Chega de Saudade' ('No More Blues'), which became the

> ## "I JUST THOUGHT IT WAS PRETTY MUSIC. I NEVER THOUGHT IT WOULD BE A HIT."
>
> *Stan Getz on his first involvement with Brazilian music, the album Jazz Samba*

Right

Versed in rural blues as a boy, Charlie Byrd turned to jazz in 1945 after meeting Django Reinhardt in Paris.

hit single (backed by his own 'Bim Bom') widely considered to be responsible for launching the bossa nova movement in Brazil. Their follow-up single, Jobim's 'Desafinado' ('Off-Key') was a fully formed masterpiece that floated on Gilberto's distinctive, syncopated guitar rhythm, which would become the basis for this new, hybrid form. Momentum for the movement picked up the following year with the popularity of the Oscar-winning film *Black Orpheus*, a romance set in Rio de Janeiro during Carnival, featuring a beguiling score by Jobim and fellow Brazilian guitarist/composer Luiz Bonfá,

LEADING EXPONENTS

Laurindo Almeida

Bud Shank

João Gilberto

Antonio Carlos Jobim

Luiz Bonfá

Charlie Byrd

Stan Getz

Astrud Gilberto

Hermeto Pascoal

Baden Powell

BRAZILIAN JAZZ STYLE

This example shows the standard Bossa Nova drum pattern, which features an off-beat counter rhythm played by the sidestick over two bars.

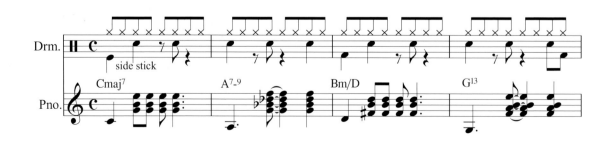

THE JAZZ INTRO ➡ 118   JAZZ PEOPLE A–Z ➡ 152   INSTRUMENTS A–Z ➡ 436   WORLD: LATIN & SOUTH AMERICA ➡ 300

and introducing such enduring bossa nova anthems as 'Manhã de Carnaval' and 'Samba de Orfeo'. Then, in 1960, Gilberto and Jobim recorded 12 original bossa nova pieces on the largely overlooked Capitol release, *Samba de Uma Note So*.

Meanwhile, this "quiet revolution" continued to unfold. In 1961, the US State Department sponsored a good-will jazz tour of Latin America that included American guitarist Charlie Byrd. A swing through Brazil on that tour was a revelation to Byrd, igniting the guitarist's love affair with bossa nova. Back in the States, Byrd played some bossa nova tapes to his friend, the soft-toned tenor saxophonist Stan Getz, who then convinced Creed Taylor at Verve to record an album of the alluring Brazilian music with himself and Byrd. Their historic 1962 collaboration, *Jazz Samba*, introduced the bossa nova sound to mass North American audiences. *Jazz Samba* enjoyed immense popularity on the strength of the hit single, Jobim's "Desafinado" ("Off-Key"), prompting a rush by American jazz record labels to repeat its success, which produced a flood of copycat releases between 1962 and 1963, including Gene Ammons' *Bad! Bossa Nova*, Dave Brubeck's *Bossa Nova USA*, Herbie Mann's *Do The Bossa Nova With Herbie Mann* and Eddie Harris' *Bossa Nova*.

A Universally Appealing Message

In 1963, Jobim and Gilberto came to New York to collaborate with Stan Getz on another bossa nova classic, *Getz/Gilberto*. The album made Gilberto an international superstar and also introduced his then-wife, the singer Astrud Gilberto, whose seductive vocals graced the mega-hit single, 'The Girl From Ipanema', written by Jobim and Vinícius de Moraes. At this time, de Moraes was also working with the influential guitarist Baden Powell, composing a number of important Afro-sambas, paying tribute to the African tradition in Brazilian music.

Getz's recorded output for Verve during the bossa nova craze also included a collaboration with bandleader/arranger Gary McFarland (1962's *Big Band Bossa Nova*), guitarist/composer Luiz Bonfá (1963's *Jazz Samba Encore!*) and guitarist/bossa nova pioneer Laurindo Almeida (1963's *Stan Getz With Guest Artist Laurindo Almeida*). All of Getz's important recordings in this genre have been compiled on a five-CD set by Verve, entitled *The Bossa Nova Years (Girl From Ipanema)*.

While Getz passed away in 1991, Gilberto continues to perform and record. Today, the veteran architect of Brazil's bossa nova movement is known in his native country as simply O Mito (The Legend). His 2000 recording, *João Voz E Violão*, is stripped down to the bare essentials – João's magnificent voice and his silky-sounding guitar accompaniment.

The alluring sound of bossa nova has continued to thrive over the past four decades. Its universally appealing message

has been and is continuing to be spread by prominent Brazilian artists such as singer-composers Milton Nascimento and Ivan Lins; pianist/composer/orchestrator Hermeto Pascoal; pianist/vocalist Eliane Elias; vocalists Joyce and Flora Purim; guitarists Toninho Horta, Carlos Barbosa-Lima, Oscar Castro-Neves and Baden Powell; percussionist Airto Moreira; and the group Trio da Paz (comprised of guitarist Romero Lubambo, bassist Nilson Matta and drummer Duduka da Fonseca), as well as by scores of jazz artists all over the world.

Below

Jobim's prolific songwriting and adaptability to concert hall performances led to comparisons with George Gershwin. His studio albums showcase his gentle strumming technique and haunting vocals.

Artists: Jazz

Entries appear in the following order: name, music style, year(s) of popularity, type of artist, country of origin.

3 Mustaphas 3, Fusion and Jazz Rock, 1980s-, Artist, Balkan
Abercrombie, John, Bebop, 1970s-, Artist, American
Abou-Khalil, Rabih, World Fusion, 1980s-, Artist; Composer, Lebanese
Abrams, Muhal Richard, Free Jazz, 1960s-, Artist, American
Adams, Pepper, Hard Bop, 1950s-1980s, Artist, American
Adderley, Cannonball, Hard Bop, 1950s-1970s, Artist, American
Adderley, Nat, Hard Bop, 1950s-1990s, Artist, American
Air, Free Jazz, 1970s-1980s, Artist, American
Albion Jazz Band, Dixieland Revival, 1990s, Artist, Canadian
Albright, Gerald, Smooth Jazz, 1980s-, Artist, American
Alegre All Stars, Latin Jazz, 1960s, Artist, American
Ali, Rashied, Free Jazz, 1960s, Artist, American
Allen, Byron, Free Jazz, 1960s, Artist, American
Allen, Henry 'Red', New Orleans Jazz; Swing; Chicago Jazz, 1920s-1960s, Artist, American
Allen, Marshall, Free Jazz, 1950s-, Artist, American
Allison, Mose, Hard Bop, 1950s-, Artist, American
Almeida, Laurindo, Brazilian Jazz; Latin Jazz, 1950s-1990s, Artist, Brazilian
Ammons, Albert, Swing, 1930s-1940s, Artist, American
Ammons, Gene, Bebop; Hard Bop, 1940s-1970s, Artist, American
Amram, David, Fusion and Jazz Rock; Latin Jazz; Bebop, 1950s-1990s, Artist; Composer, American
Anderson, Ernestine, Cool Jazz, 1940s-, Artist, American
Anderson, Fred, Free Jazz, 1960s-, Artist, American
Anthony, Ray, Swing, 1940s-, Artist, American
Armstrong, Louis, New Orleans Jazz; Swing; Chicago Jazz, 1920s-1970s, Artist, American
Art Ensemble of Chicago, Free Jazz, 1960s-, Artist, American
Ashby, Harold, New Orleans Jazz, 1950s-1990s, Artist, American
Assad, Badi, Brazilian Jazz, 1990s, Artist, Brazilian
Auger, Brian, Jazz Rock; Fusion, 1960s-, Artist, British
Ayers, Roy, Soul Jazz; Fusion, 1960s-, Artist, American
Ayler, Albert, Free Jazz, 1960s-1970s, Artist, American
Azymuth, Brazilian Jazz; Fusion, 1970s-1990s, Artist, Brazilian
Babarin, Paul, New Orleans Jazz, 1940s-1960s, Artist, American
Back Bay Ramblers, Dixieland Revival, 1980s-, Artist, American
Bailey, Buster, Swing, 1920s-1960s, Artist, American
Bailey, Derek, Free Jazz, 1960s-, Artist, British
Bailey, Mildred, Swing, 1920s-1950s, Artist, American
Baker, Chet, Cool Jazz, 1950s-1980s, Artist, American
Baker, Ginger, Jazz Rock; Fusion, 1970s-, Artist, British
Ball, Kenny, New Orleans Jazz; Chicago Jazz, 1950s-1990s, Artist, British
Barber, Chris, New Orleans Jazz; Chicago Jazz, 1940s-1990s, Artist, British
Barbieri, Gato, Latin Jazz, 1960s-1990s, Artist, Argentinean
Barker, Danny, New Orleans Jazz; Swing, 1930s-1990s, Artist, American
Barnet, Charlie, Swing, 1930s-1960s, Artist, American
Barretto, Ray, Latin Jazz, 1950s-, Artist, American
Barron, Kenny, Hard Bop, 1950s-, Artist, American
Barroso, Ary, Brazilian Jazz; Latin Jazz, 1930s-1970s, Composer, Brazilian
Basie, Count, Swing, 1920s-1980s, Artist, American
Batish, Ashwin, Fusion and Jazz Rock; Fusion, 1980s-1990s, Artist, Indian
Batuque, Grupo, Brazilian Jazz, 1990s, Artist, Brazilian
Bauer, Billy, Cool Jazz, 1940s-1950s, Artist, American
Bauza, Mario, Latin Jazz, 1930s-1990s, Artist, Cuban
Bechet, Sidney, Chicago Jazz; New Orleans Jazz, 1920s-1950s, Artist, American
Beck, Joe, Fusion, 1950s-, Artist, American
Beiderbecke, Bix, New Orleans Jazz, 1920s-1930s, Artist, American
Bellson, Louie, Swing; Bebop, 1940s-1990s, Artist, American
Bennink, Han, Free Jazz, 1960s-, Artist, Dutch
Benoit, David, Fusion; Jazz Rock, 1970s-, Producer; Artist, American
Benson, George, Smooth Jazz; Hard Bop, 1960s-, Artist, American
Berigan, Bunny, Swing, 1930s-1940s, Artist, American
Berne, Tim, Free Jazz, 1970s-, Artist, American
Berry, Chu, Swing, 1930s-1940s, Artist, American
Bhatt, Vishwa Mohan, Fusion and Jazz Rock, 1980s-1990s, Artist, Indian

Bigard, Barney, New Orleans Jazz; Swing, 1920s-1970s, Artist, American
Bilk, Acker, New Orleans Jazz, 1950s-1990s, Artist, British
Bishop, Walter Jr, Bebop; Hard Bop, 1960s-1990s, Artist, American
Blackwell, Ed, Free Jazz, 1950s-1990s, Artist, American
Blades, Rubén, Latin Jazz, 1970s-, Artist, Panamanian
Blake, Eubie, Ragtime, 1910s-1980s, Composer; Artist, American
Blakey, Art, Hard Bop, 1940s-1990s, Artist, American
Blanchard, Terence, Hard Bop, 1980s-, Artist, American
Bley, Paul, Free Jazz, 1950s-, Artist, Canadian
Bobo, Willie, Latin Jazz, 1950s-1980s, Artist, Spanish
Bonano, Sharkey, Chicago Jazz, 1920s-1960s, Artist, American
Bonfá, Luiz, Brazilian Jazz, 1950s-1990s, Artist; Composer, Brazilian
Boswell Sisters, The, Swing, 1920s-1930s, Artist, American
Boti, Chris, Smooth Jazz, 1990s-, Artist, American
Bowie, Lester, Free Jazz, 1960s-1990s, Artist, American
Braff, Ruby, Dixieland Revival; New Orleans Jazz; Swing, 1940s-, Artist, American
Brand New Heavies, Acid Jazz, 1990s-, Artist, British
Braxton, Anthony, Free Jazz, 1960s-, Artist, American
Brecker Brothers, Fusion, 1960s-1990s, Artist, American
Brecker, Michael, Fusion, 1960s-, Artist, American
Brecker, Randy, Fusion; Hard Bop, 1960s-, Artist, American
Bregman, Buddy, Swing, 1950s-1960s, Producer, American
Brookmeyer, Bob, Cool Jazz, 1950s-, Artist, American
Brooks, Tina, Hard Bop, 1950s-1960s, Artist, American
Brötzmann, Peter, Free Jazz, 1960s-, Artist, German
Brown, Carlinhos, Brazilian Jazz, 1990s-, Artist, Brazilian
Brown, Clifford, Hard Bop; Bebop, 1950s, Artist, American
Brown, Marion, Free Jazz, 1960s-1990s, Artist, American
Brown, Ray, Bebop, 1940s-, Artist, American
Brubeck, Dave, Cool Jazz, 1950s-, Artist, American
Bryant, Ray, Soul Jazz; Swing; Bebop, 1950s-, Artist, American
Bryant, Rusty, Soul Jazz; Hard Bop, 1950s-1980s, Artist, American
Buckley, Tim, Jazz Rock, 1960s-1970s, Artist; Songwriter, American
Buckner, Teddy, Chicago Jazz, 1930s-1980s, Artist, American
Budwig, Monty, Cool Jazz; Bebop, 1950s-1990s, Artist, American
Buena Vista Social Club, Latin Jazz, 1990s-, Artist, Cuban
Bull, Sandy, Fusion and Jazz Rock, 1960s-1980s, Artist, American
Burrell, Dave, Free Jazz, 1960s-, Artist, American
Burrell, Kenny, Bebop; Hard Bop; Cool Jazz, 1950s-, Artist, American
Butterfield, Billy, Chicago Jazz; Swing, 1930s-1980s, Artist, American
Byard, Jaki, Free Jazz, 1940s-1990s, Artist, American
Byas, Don, Swing; Bebop, 1930s-1970s, Artist, American
Byrd, Charlie, Brazilian Jazz; Latin Jazz, 1950s-1990s, Artist, American
Byrd, Donald, Hard Bop; Fusion, 1950s-, Artist, American
Cachao, Latin Jazz, 1940s-, Artist, Cuban
California Ramblers, New Orleans Jazz, 1920s-1930s, Artist, American
Callender, Red, Cool Jazz; Swing; Bebop, 1940s-1980s, Artist, American
Calloway, Cab, Swing, 1920s-1980s, Artist, American
Candido, Latin Jazz, 1950s-, Artist, Cuban
Candoli, Conte, Cool Jazz; Bebop, 1940s-1990s, Artist, American
Carle, Frankie, New Orleans Jazz, 1940s-1960s, Artist, British
Carlton, Larry, Fusion; Smooth Jazz, 1960s-, Artist, American
Carmichael, Hoagy, New Orleans Jazz, 1920s-1960s, Composer; Artist, American
Carson, Ernie, Dixieland Revival, 1950s-1990s, Artist, American
Carter, Benny, Swing, 1920s-1990s, Artist, American
Carter, Betty, Bebop, 1950s-1990s, Artist, American
Carter, James, Hard Bop, 1990s-, Artist, American
Carter, Ron, Hard Bop, 1960s-, Artist, American
Centipede, Jazz Rock, 1970s, Artist, British
Chambers, Paul, Hard Bop, 1950s-1960s, Artist, American
Charles, Teddy, Cool Jazz, 1950s-1990s, Artist, American
Cheatham, Doc, Swing; Chicago Jazz, 1920s-1990s, Artist, American
Cherry, Don, Free Jazz; Fusion and Jazz Rock, 1950s-1990s, Artist, American
Christian, Charlie, Swing; Bebop, 1930s-1940s, Artist, American
Christie Brothers Stompers, New Orleans Jazz; Chicago Jazz, 1950s, Artist, British
Christy, June, Cool Jazz, 1940s-1980s, Artist, American
Clark, Sonny, Bebop; Hard Bop, 1950s-1960s, Artist, American
Clarke, Kenny, Bebop, 1940s-1980s, Artist, American
Clarke, Stanley, Fusion, 1960s-1990s, Artist, American
Clayton, Buck, Swing, 1930s-1990s, Artist; Composer, American
Cobb, Arnett, Soul Jazz, 1930s-1980s, Artist, American
Cobb, Jimmy, Hard Bop, 1950s-, Artist, American
Cobham, Billy, Fusion, 1970s-, Artist, American
Codona, Fusion and Jazz Rock; Free Jazz, 1970s-1980s, Artist, American
Cohn, Al, Bebop; Cool Jazz, 1940s-1980s, Artist, American
Cole, Cozy, Swing, 1930s-1970s, Artist, American
Cole, Nat King, Swing, 1930s-1960s, Artist, American
Cole, Richie, Bebop, 1970s-1990s, Artist, American
Coleman, George, Hard Bop, 1950s-, Artist, American
Coleman, Ornette, Free Jazz, 1950s-1990s, Artist; Composer, American
Coles, Johnny, Hard Bop, 1950s-1990s, Artist, American
Collette, Buddy, Cool Jazz, 1950s-, Artist, American
Collie, Max, New Orleans Jazz, 1950s-, Artist, Australian
Colon, Willie, Latin Jazz, 1960s-, Artist, American
Coltrane, Alice, Free Jazz, 1960s-1980s, Artist, American
Coltrane, John, Modal Jazz; Free Jazz; Hard Bop, 1950s-1960s, Artist, American
Colyer, Ken, New Orleans Jazz, 1940s-1980s, Artist, British
Concord Allstars, Swing; Bebop, 1970s-1990s, Artist, American
Condon, Eddie, Chicago Jazz; Swing, 1920s-1970s, Artist, American
Connolly, Dolly, Ragtime, 1900s-1920s, Artist, American
Connor, Chris, Cool Jazz, 1950s-, Artist, American
Connors, Norman, Fusion, 1970s-, Artist, American
Coolbone Brass Band, Acid Jazz, 1990s-, Artist, American
Cooper, Bob, Cool Jazz; Hard Bop, 1940s-1990s, Artist, American
Corduroy, Acid Jazz, 1990s-, Artist, British
Corea, Chick, Fusion; Free Jazz, 1960s-, Artist; Composer, American
Coryell, Larry, Fusion, 1960s-, Artist, American
Costa, Paulinho Da, Brazilian Jazz; Latin Jazz; Fusion and Jazz Rock, 1970s-1990s, Artist, Brazilian
Counce, Curtis, Hard Bop, 1940s-1960s, Artist, American
Count Basic, Acid Jazz, 1990s-, Artist, American
Cranshaw, Bob, Hard Bop, 1960s-1990s, Artist, American
Crawford, Hank, Soul Jazz; Hard Bop, 1950s-1990s, Artist, American
Criss, Sonny, Hard Bop, 1940s-1970s, Artist, American
Crosby, Israel, Cool Jazz; Swing, 1930s-1960s, Artist, American
Crusaders, The, Hard Bop; Soul Jazz; Fusion, 1960s-, Artist, American
Cruz, Celia, Latin Jazz, 1950s-, Artist, Cuban
Cuba, Joe, Latin Jazz, 1950s-1970s, Artist, American
Cugat, Xavier, Latin Jazz, 1930s-1960s, Artist, Spanish
Cullum, Jim Jr, Dixieland Revival, 1960s-1990s, Artist, American
Cutler, Chris, Jazz Rock; Fusion, 1970s-, Artist, American
Cyrille, Andrew, Free Jazz, 1960s-, Artist, American
D'Note, Acid Jazz, 1990s-, Artist, British
D'Influence, Acid Jazz, 1990s-, Artist, British
D'Rivera, Paquito, Latin Jazz, 1970s-, Artist, Cuban
Dameron, Tadd, Bebop, 1940s-1960s, Composer; Songwriter; Artist, American
Dapogny, James, Dixieland Revival; Swing, 1960s-1990s, Artist, American
Davern, Kevin, Dixieland Revival; Swing, 1950s-, Artist, American
Davis, Eddie 'Lockjaw', Bebop; Hard Bop, 1940s-1980s, Artist, American
Davis, Miles, Bebop; Hard Bop; Cool Jazz; Jazz Rock; Fusion, 1940s-1990s, Artist; Composer, American
Davis, Richard, Hard Bop, 1950s-, Artist, American
Davis, Walter Jr, Bebop; Hard Bop, 1950s; 1970s-1980s, Artist, American
Davison, Wild Bill, Dixieland Revival, 1920s-1980s, Artist, American
DeFrancesco, Joey, Soul Jazz; Hard Bop, 1980s-, Artist, American
DeFranco, Buddy, Bebop, 1940s-1990s, Artist, American
DeJohnette, Jack, Fusion, 1960s-, Artist, American
DeParis, Sidney, Chicago Jazz, 1920s-1960s, Artist, American
Desmond, Paul, Cool Jazz, 1940s-1970s, Artist, American
Dibango, Manu, Fusion and Jazz Rock, 1970s-, Artist, African
Dickenson, Vic, Swing, 1930s-1980s, Artist, American
DiMeola, Al, Fusion; Jazz Rock; Fusion and Jazz Rock, 1970s-, Artist, American

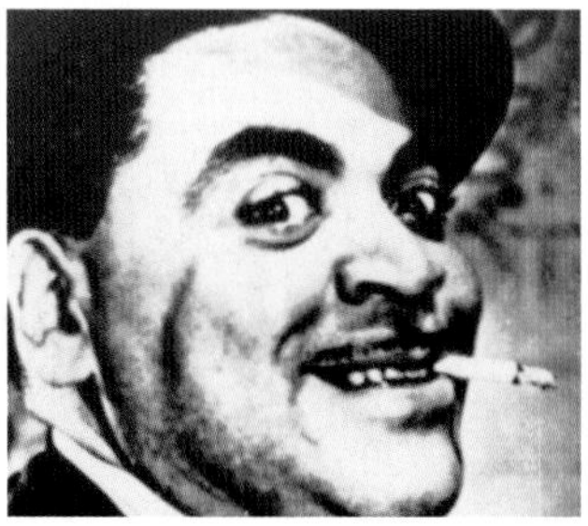

Din, Hamza el, Fusion and Jazz Rock, 1960s-1990s, Artist, African
Dissidenten, Fusion and Jazz Rock, 1970s-1990s, Artist, German
Dixon, Bill, Free Jazz, 1960s-, Artist, American
DJ Greyboy, Acid Jazz, 1990s, Artist, American
DKV Trio, Free Jazz, 1990s-, Artist, American
Dodds, Baby, New Orleans Jazz, 1920s-1950s, Artist, American
Dodds, Johnny, New Orleans Jazz, 1920s-1940s, Artist, American
Doky Brothers, Hard Bop, 1990s, Artist, American
Dollar Brand, Fusion and Jazz Rock, 1970s-1980s, Artist, South African
Dolphy, Eric, Free Jazz, 1950s-1960s, Artist, American
Donaldson, Lou, Bebop; Hard Bop, 1950s-, Artist, American
Donato, João, Brazilian Jazz, 1960s-1970s, Artist, Brazilian
Dorham, Kenny, Hard Bop, 1940s-1970s, Artist, American
Dorough, Bob, Cool Jazz; Bebop; Swing, 1940s-, Artist, American
Dorsey, Jimmy, Swing, 1920s-1950s, Artist, American
Dorsey, Tommy, Swing, 1920s-1950s, Artist, American
Dread Flimstone, Acid Jazz, 1990s, Artist, American
Drew, Kenny, Hard Bop, 1950s-1990s, Artist, American
Duke, George, Fusion, 1960s-, Producer; Artist, American
Dukes of Dixieland, Dixieland Revival, 1950s-, Artist, American
Duvivier, George, Swing; Bebop, 1950s-1990s, Artist, American
Eardley, Jon, Cool Jazz; Bebop, 1950s-1970s, Artist, American
Earland, Charles, Soul Jazz; Hard Bop, 1960s-1990s, Artist, American
Eça, Luíz, Brazilian Jazz, 1970s-1990s, Artist, Brazilian
Eckstine, Billy, Bebop, 1940s-1980s, Artist, American
Edison, Harry "Sweets", Swing, 1940s-1990s, Artist, American
Edwards, Teddy, Bebop; Hard Bop, 1940s-, Artist, American
Eldridge, Roy, Swing, 1930s-1980s, Artist, American
Elias, Eliane, Brazilian Jazz; Latin Jazz, 1970s-, Artist, Brazilian
Ellington, Duke, Swing, 1920s-1970s, Artist; Composer, American
Ellington, Mercer, Swing, 1940s-1990s, Artist, American
Elliott, Don, Cool Jazz; Swing; Fusion, 1950s-1970s, Artist, American
Ellis, Herb, Swing; Bebop, 1940s-1990s, Artist, American
Ervin, Booker, Hard Bop, 1950s-1960s, Artist, American
Erwin, Pee Wee, Swing, 1950s-1980s, Artist, American
Escovado, Pete, Latin Jazz; Fusion, 1960s-, Artist, American
Etting, Ruth, New Orleans Jazz, 1920s-1950s, Artist, American
Evans, Bill, Cool Jazz; Modal Jazz, 1940s-1980s, Artist, American
Evans, Gil, Cool Jazz; Fusion, 1940s-1980s, Artist, Canadian
Faddis, John, Bebop, 1970s-1990s, Artist, American
Fagerquist, Don, Cool Jazz; Bebop, 1950s, Artist, American
Farlow, Tal, Bebop; Cool Jazz, 1950s-1990s, Artist, American
Farmer, Art, Bebop; Hard Bop; Cool Jazz, 1950s-1990s, Artist, American
Farrell, Joe, Hard Bop, 1960s-1980s, Artist, American
Fasteau, Zusaan Kali, Fusion and Jazz Rock; Free Jazz, 1970s-, Artist, American
Favors, Malachi, Free Jazz, 1960s-1990s, Artist, American
Feldman, Victor, Cool Jazz, 1950s-1980s, Artist, British
Ferguson, Maynard, Hard Bop, 1950s-1990s, Artist, Canadian
Fest, Manfredo, Brazilian Jazz; Latin Jazz, 1960s-1990s, Artist; Composer, Brazilian
Firehouse Fire Plus Two, Dixieland Revival, 1940s-1960s, Artist, American
Fitzgerald, Ella, Swing; Bebop, 1930s-1990s, Artist, American
Flanagan, Tommy, Bebop; Hard Bop, 1940s-1990s, Artist, American
Fontana, Carl, Cool Jazz; Bebop, 1950s-1990s, Artist, American
Foseter, Ronnie, Soul Jazz, 1970s-1990s, Artist, American
Foster, Frank, Hard Bop; Swing, 1950s-1990s, Artist, American
Foster, Pops, New Orleans Jazz, 1910s-1940s, Artist, American
Fountain, Pete, Dixieland Revival, 1940s-1990s, Artist, American
Fourplay, Smooth Jazz, 1990s-, Artist, American
Freeman, Bud, Swing, 1920s-1980s, Artist, American
Freeman, Russ, Cool Jazz; Bebop, 1940s-1980s, Artist, American
Freeman, Stan, Cool Jazz; Swing; Bebop, 1950s-1960s, Artist, American
Frisell, Bill, Fusion, 1970s-, Artist, American
Fuller, Curtis, Hard Bop, 1950s-1990s, Artist, American
G., Kenny, Smooth Jazz, 1980s-, Artist, American
Gaillard, Slim, Swing, 1930s-1950s, Artist, American
Galliano, Acid Jazz, 1990s, Artist, British
Garber, Jan, Swing, 1920s-1970s, Artist, American
Garland, Red, Hard Bop, 1950s-1980s, Artist, American
Garner, Erroll, Bebop; Swing, 1940s-1970s, Artist, American
Garrison, Jimmy, Free Jazz, 1960s-1980s, Artist, American
Gershwin, George, Ragtime, 1900s-1930s, Artist; Composer, American
Getz, Stan, Cool Jazz; Hard Bop, 1940s-1990s, Artist, American
Gibbs, Terry, Bebop, 1950s-1990s, Artist, American
Gibson, Banu, Dixieland Revival, 1970s-1990s, Artist, American
Gilberto, João, Brazilian Jazz, 1950s-, Artist, Brazilian
Gillespie, Dizzy, Bebop, 1930s-1990s, Artist, American
Gilmore, John, Free Jazz; Bebop, 1950s-1990s, Artist, American
Giordano, Vince, Dixieland Revival, 1980s-1990s, Artist, American
Girard, George, Chicago Jazz, 1950s, Artist, American
Gismonti, Egberto, Brazilian Jazz; Fusion and Jazz Rock, 1960s-1990s, Artist, Brazilian
Giuffre, Jimmy, Bebop; Cool Jazz, 1940s-, Artist, American
Golson, Benny, Hard Bop, 1950s-, Artist; Composer, American
Gonsalves, Paul, Swing; Bebop, 1950s-1970s, Artist, American
Gonzales, Ruben, Latin Jazz, 1980s-, Artist, Cuban
Goodman, Benny, Swing, 1920s-1970s, Artist, American
Gordon, Dexter, Bebop; Hard Bop, 1940s-1980s, Artist, American
Gottschalk, Louis Moreau, Ragtime, 1890s, Artist; Composer, American
Granz, Norman, Bebop, 1940s-1990s, Artist, American
Grappelli, Stephane, Swing, 1930s-1990s, Artist, American
Grassy Knoll, The, Acid Jazz, 1990s, Artist, American
Graves, Milford, Free Jazz, 1960s-, Artist, American
Gray, Wardell, Bebop; Swing, 1940s-1950s, Artist, American
Green, Benny, Swing; Bebop, 1950s-1960s, Artist, American
Green, Bunky, Hard Bop, 1940s-1980s, Artist, American
Green, Charlie, New Orleans Jazz, 1920s-1930s, Artist, American
Green, Freddie, Swing, 1940s-1980s, Artist, American
Green, Grant, Hard Bop, 1950s-1970s, Artist, American
Greer, Sonny, Swing, 1920s-1940s, Artist, American
Grey, Al, Bebop; Swing, 1940s-1990s, Artist, American
Greyboy Allstars, Acid Jazz, 1990s, Artist, American
Griffin, Johnny, Bebop; Hard Bop, 1940s-, Artist, American
Grimes, Tiny, Bebop, 1940s-1970s, Artist, American
Groove Collective, Acid Jazz, 1990s-, Artist, American
Grosz, Marty, Dixieland Revival, 1950s-1990s, Artist, American
Grusin, Dave, Fusion, 1960s-, Producer; Composer; Artist, American
Gryce, Gigi, Hard Bop, 1950s-1970s, Artist, American
Guaraldi, Vince, Cool Jazz, 1950s-1970s, Artist, American
Guarnieri, Johnny, Swing, 1930s-1980s, Artist, American
Gullin, Lars, Cool Jazz; Bebop, 1950s-1970s, Swedish
Gurtu, Trilok, Fusion and Jazz Rock; Fusion, 1970s-, Artist, Indian
Guyer, Bobby, Swing; Chicago Jazz, 1930s-1980s, Artist, American
Hackett, Bobby, Chicago Jazz; Swing, 1930s-1970s, Artist, American
Haden, Charlie, Free Jazz; Hard Bop, 1950s-, Artist, American
Haig, Al, Bebop, 1940s-1980s, Artist, American
Hall, Edmond, New Orleans Jazz; Swing, 1930s-1960s, Artist, American
Hall, Jim, Cool Jazz, 1950s-, Artist, American
Hamilton, Chico, Cool Jazz; Hard Bop, 1950s-, Artist, American
Hamilton, Jimmy, Bebop; Swing, 1950s-1980s, Artist, American
Hammer, Jan, Fusion, 1960s-, Artist, Czech
Hampton, Lionel, Swing, 1920s-1990s, Artist, American
Hampton, Slide, Bebop; Hard Bop, 1950s-, Artist; Composer, American
Hancock, Herbie, Modal Jazz; Hard Bop; Fusion, 1960s-, Artist, American
Hanrahan, Kip, Fusion and Jazz Rock; Fusion, 1980s-1990s, Producer; Artist, American
Hanshaw, Annette, New Orleans Jazz, 1920s-1930s, Artist, American
Harewood, Al, Bebop, 1940s-1960s, Artist, American
Harney, Ben, Ragtime, 1890s-1900s, Artist; Composer, Austrian
Harris, Barry, Bebop, 1950s-, Artist, American
Harris, Benny, Bebop, 1950s-, Artist, American
Harris, Eddie, Soul Jazz; Hard Bop, 1960s-1990s, Artist, American
Harris, Gene, Soul Jazz; Hard Bop; Fusion, 1950s-1990s, Artist, American
Harrison, Lou, Fusion and Jazz Rock, 1940s-1990s, Artist, American
Hawes, Hampton, Bebop; Hard Bop, 1950s-1970s, Artist, American
Hawkins, Coleman, Swing; Bebop, 1920s-1960s, Artist, American
Hawkins, Erskine, Swing, 1930s-1970s, Artist, American
Hayes, Clifford, New Orleans Jazz, 1920s-1930s, Artist, American

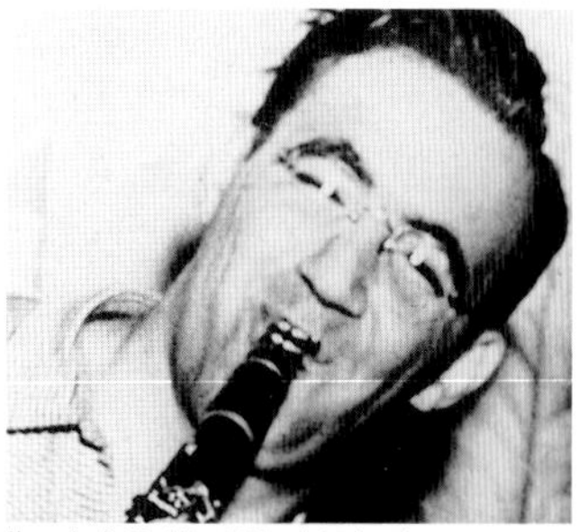

Hayes, Louis, Hard Bop, 1950s-, Artist, American
Haynes, Roy, Bebop; Hard Bop, 1940s-, Artist, American
Heard, J. C., Swing; Bebop, 1940s-1980s, Artist, American
Heath, Albert 'Tootie', Hard Bop, 1940s-1990s, Artist, American
Heath, Jimmy, Hard Bop, 1940s-1990s, Artist, American
Heath, Percy, Bebop; Hard Bop; Cool Jazz, 1940s-1990s, Artist, American
Heath, Ted, Swing, 1940s-1960s, Artist, British
Hefti, Neal, Swing, 1940s-1990s, Artist; Composer, American
Helm, Bob, Dixieland Revival, 1940s-1990s, Artist, American
Hemphill, Julius, Free Jazz, 1960s-1990s, Artist; Composer, American
Henderson, Fletcher, Swing, 1920s-1950s, Artist, American
Henderson, Joe, Hard Bop, 1960s-1990s, Artist, American
Hendricks, Jon, Bebop, 1940s-, Artist, American
Henry Cow, Jazz Rock, 1960s-1970s, Artist, British
Herman, Woody, Swing; Cool Jazz, 1930s-1980s, Artist, American
Heywood, Eddie, Swing, 1920s-1980s, Artist, American
Hidalgo, Giovanni, Latin Jazz; Fusion and Jazz Rock, 1980s-1990s, Artist, Puerto Rican
Higgins, Billy, Hard Bop; Free Jazz, 1950s-1990s, Artist, American
Hill, Andrew, Modal Jazz, 1950s-, Artist, American
Hines, Earl, Swing, 1920s-1980s, Artist; Composer, American
Hinton, Milt, Swing, 1930s-1990s, Artist, American
Hiroshima, Fusion and Jazz Rock, 1970s-1990s, Artist, American
Hirt, Al, Dixieland Revival, 1950s-1990s, Artist, American
Ho, Fred, Fusion and Jazz Rock, 1980s-, Artist, American
Hodes, Art, Chicago Jazz, 1930s-1990s, Artist, American
Hodges, Johnny, Swing, 1920s-1960s, Artist, American
Hogan, Ernest, Ragtime, 1890s-1900s, Composer, American
Holdsworth, Allan, Jazz Rock; Fusion, 1970s-, Artist, British
Holiday, Billie, Swing, 1930s-1950s, Artist, American
Holland, Dave, Free Jazz, 1970s-, Artist, British
Holloway, Red, Soul Jazz; Swing; Bebop, 1950s-, Artist, American
Holmes, Richard 'Groove', Soul Jazz; Hard Bop, 1950s-1990s, Artist, American
Hope, Elmo, Hard Bop; Bebop, 1940s-1960s, Artist; Composer, American
Hope, Stan, Hard Bop, 1940s-1990s, Artist, American
Horn, Paul, Fusion and Jazz Rock; Hard Bop, 1950s-, Artist, American
Horn, Shirley, New Orleans Jazz, 1950s-, Artist, American
Howard, George, Smooth Jazz, 1970s-1990s, Artist, American
Hubbard, Freddie, Hard Bop; Fusion, 1960s-, Artist, American
Hucko, Peanuts, Chicago Jazz; Swing, 1940s-1990s, Artist, American
Humphrey, Bobbi, Soul Jazz; Fusion, 1970s-1990s, Artist, American
Hussain, Zakir, Fusion and Jazz Rock, 1960s-, Artist, Indian
Hutcherson, Bobby, Hard Bop, 1960s-, Artist, American
Hyman, Dick, Swing, 1940s-, Artist, American
Incognito, Acid Jazz, 1980s-, Artist, British
Ingham, Keith, Dixieland Revival; Swing, 1980s-, Artist, American
Irakere, Latin Jazz, 1970s-, Artist, Cuban
Jackson, Milt, Bebop; Hard Bop, 1940s-1990s, Artist, American
Jackson, Preston, New Orleans Jazz, 1920s-1930s, Artist, American
Jackson, Ronald Shannon, Fusion; Free Jazz; Hard Bop, 1970s-, Artist, American
Jackson, Willis 'Gator', Soul Jazz; Hard Bop, 1940s-1980s, Artist, American
Jacquet, Illinois, Swing; Bebop, 1940s-1990s, Artist, American
Jamal, Ahmad, Cool Jazz, 1950s-, Artist, American
James, Bob, Fusion, 1960s-, Artist, American
James, Boney, Smooth Jazz, 1990s-, Artist, American
James, Harry, Swing, 1930s-1970s, Artist, American
Jamiroquai, Acid Jazz, 1990s-, Artist, British
Jarman, Joseph, Free Jazz, 1960s-1990s, Artist, American
Jarrett, Keith, Fusion, 1960s-, Artist, American
Jarvis, Clifford, Free Jazz, 1960s-1990s, Artist, American
Jazz at the Philharmonic, Swing; Bebop, 1940s-1980s, Artist, American
Jazz Crusaders, The, Soul Jazz; Acid Jazz, 1960s, Artist, American
Jazz Warriors, The, Acid Jazz, 1980s-, Artist, British
Jefferson, Eddie, Bebop, 1950s-1970s, Artist; Songwriter, American
Jenkins, Gordon, Swing; Cool Jazz, 1930s-1990s, Composer, American
Jenkins, Leroy, Free Jazz, 1970s-1990s, Artist, American
Jhelisa, Acid Jazz, 1990s, Artist, British
Jobim, Antonio Carlos, Brazilian Jazz; Fusion and Jazz Rock; Latin Jazz, 1950s-1990s, Artist, Brazilian
Johnson, Budd, Swing; Bebop, 1930s-1980s, Artist, American
Johnson, Bunk, New Orleans Jazz, 1910s-1940s, Artist, American
Johnson, Dink, New Orleans Jazz, 1940s-1950s, Artist, American
Johnson, J. J., Bebop; Hard Bop, 1940s-1990s, Artist, American
Johnson, James P., Ragtime, 1910s-1950s, Composer; Artist, American
Johnson, Lonnie, New Orleans Jazz, 1920s-1960s, Artist, American
Jolly, Pete, Cool Jazz; Bebop, 1950s-1990s, Artist, American
Jolson, Al, Ragtime, 1910-1940s, Producer; Artist, American
Jones, Elvin, Hard Bop, 1960s-, Artist, American

RAGTIME ➡ 122 NEW ORLEANS ➡ 124 CHICAGO ➡ 126 SWING ➡ 128 BEBOP ➡ 130 DIXIELAND REVIVAL ➡ 132 COOL JAZZ ➡ 134

Jones, Hank, Swing; Bebop, 1950s-1990s, Artist, American
Jones, Isham, New Orleans Jazz, 1920s-1940s, Artist, American
Jones, Jo, Swing, 1930s-1970s, Artist, American
Jones, Joe 'Boogaloo', Soul Jazz, 1960s-1970s, Artist, American
Jones, Philly Joe, Hard Bop, 1950s-, Artist, American
Jones, Quincy, Swing; Bebop, 1950s-, Producer; Artist; Composer, American
Jones, Sam, Hard Bop, 1950s-1980s, Artist, American
Jones, Thad, Bebop; Hard Bop, 1950s-1980s, Artist; Composer; Producer, American
Joplin, Scott, Ragtime, 1900s-1910s, Composer; Artist, American
Jordan, Clifford, Hard Bop, 1950s-1990s, Artist, American
Jordan, Duke, Bebop; Hard Bop, 1940s-1990s, Artist, American
Jordan, Louis, Swing, 1930s-1970s, Artist, American
Jordan, Ronny, Acid Jazz, 1990s-, Artist, British
Kamuca, Richie, Cool Jazz, 1950s-1970s, Artist, American
Kay, Connie, Cool Jazz, 1940s-1990s, Artist, American
Kelly, Wynton, Hard Bop, 1950s-1970s, Artist, American
Kenton, Stan, Swing, 1930s-1970s, Artist; Composer, American
Keppard, Freddie, New Orleans Jazz, 1920s-1930s, Artist, American
Kessel, Barney, Bebop; Cool Jazz, 1940s-, Artist, American
Kid Thomas, New Orleans Jazz, 1920s-1970s, Artist, American
King Oliver, New Orleans Jazz, 1920s-1930s, Artist, American
Kirk, Andy, Swing, 1920s-1950s, Artist, American
Klugh, Earl, Fusion, 1970s-, Artist, American
Konitz, Lee, Cool Jazz, 1940s-, Artist, American
Krall, Diana, Swing, 1990s-, Artist, Canadian
Krupa, Gene, Swing, 1920s-1970s, Artist, American
Lacy, Steve, Free Jazz, 1950s-, Artist, American
Ladnier, Tommy, New Orleans Jazz, 1920s-1930s, Artist, American
Lake, Oliver, Free Jazz, 1970s-, Artist, American
Lamb, Joseph, Ragtime, 1950s, Artist, American
Lambert, Hendricks and Ross, Bebop, 1950s-1960s, Artist, American
Lambert, Michael, Bebop, 1980s-1990s, Artist, American
Land, Harold, Hard Bop, 1950s-, Artist, American
Lang, Eddie, Swing, 1920s-1930s, Artist, American
Last Exit, Free Jazz, 1980s-1990s, Artist, American
Lateef, Yusef, Hard Bop, 1950s-, Artist, American
Laws, Hubert, Hard Bop, 1950s-1990s, Artist, American
Lawson, Yank, Chicago Jazz; Swing, 1930s-1980s, Artist, American
Levey, Stan, Cool Jazz; Bebop, 1950s, Artist, American
Levy, Lou, Cool Jazz; Bebop, 1940s-1990s, Artist, American
Lewis, George, New Orleans Jazz, 1920s-1960s, Artist, American
Lewis, John, Bebop; Cool Jazz, 1940s-, Artist, American
Lewis, Mel, Bebop, 1940s-1980s, Artist, American
Lewis, Ramsey, Soul Jazz, 1950s-1990s, Artist, American
Lewis, Ted, New Orleans Jazz, 1910s-1960s, Artist, American
Lighthouse All-Stars, The, Cool Jazz; Bebop, 1950s, Artist, American
Little, Booker, Hard Bop, 1950s-1960s, Artist, American
Lobo, Edu, Latin Jazz, 1960s-1990s, Artist, Brazilian
Loeb, Chuck, Fusion; Hard Bop, 1970s-, Artist, American
Lorber, Jeff, Smooth Jazz, 1970s-, Artist; Composer, American
Lovano, Joe, Hard Bop, 1970s-, Artist, American
Lowe, Frank, Free Jazz, 1970s-1990s, Artist, American
Lowe, Mundell, Cool Jazz; Swing, 1950s-, Artist, American
Lunceford, Jimmie, Swing, 1920s-1940s, Artist, American
Lyons, Jimmy, Free Jazz, 1960s-1980s, Artist, American
Lyttleton, Humphrey, New Orleans Jazz; Chicago Jazz, 1940s-1960s; 1980s-1990s, Artist, British
Machito, Latin Jazz, 1940s-1980s, Artist, Cuban
Mahavishnu Orchestra, Jazz Rock; Fusion, 1970s-1980s, Artist, American
Man Called Adam, A, Acid Jazz, 1980s-1990s, Artist, British
Mance, Junior, Soul Jazz; Bebop, 1950s-, Artist, American
Maneri, Joe, Free Jazz, 1960s-, Artist, American
Mangione, Chuck, Fusion, 1960s-, Artist, American
Manhattan Transfer, Smooth Jazz, 1970s-, Artist, American
Mann, Herbie, Soul Jazz, 1950s-, Artist, American
Manne, Shelley, Bebop; Cool Jazz, 1940s-1980s, Artist, American
Manone, Wingy, Chicago Jazz, 1920s-1960s, Artist, American
Mariano, Charlie, Bebop, 1950s-, Artist, American
Marmarosa, Dodo, Bebop, 1940s-1960s, Artist, American
Marsala, Joe, Chicago Jazz; Swing, 1930s-1940s, Artist, American
Marsalis, Branford, New Orleans Jazz; Hard Bop, 1980s-, Artist, American
Marsalis, Wynton, New Orleans Jazz; Swing, 1980s-, Artist, American
Marsh, Warne, Cool Jazz, 1940s-1980s, Artist, American
Martinez, Sabú, Latin Jazz, 1940s-1970s, Artist, Cuban
Masekela, Hugh, Fusion and Jazz Rock; Soul Jazz, 1960s-, Artist, South African
May, Billy, Swing, 1940s-1970s, Composer; Artist, American
McCall, Steve, Free Jazz, 1960s-1980s, Artist, American
McCann, Les, Soul Jazz; Hard Bop, 1960s-, Artist, American
McDuff, Jack, Soul Jazz; Hard Bop, 1950s-1990s, Artist, American
McFarland, Gary, Hard Bop, 1950s-1990s, Artist; Composer, American
McGhee, Howard, Bebop; Hard Bop, 1940s-1980s, Artist, American
McGriff, Jimmy, Soul Jazz; Hard Bop, 1960s-, Artist, American
McIntyre, Kalaparusha Maurice, Free Jazz, 1960s, Artist, American

McKenna, Dave, Swing, 1950s-, Artist, American
McKibbon, Al, Bebop; Hard Bop, 1940s-1990s, Artist, American
McKinley, Ray, Swing, 1930s-1960s, Artist, American
McKinney's Cotton Pickers, Swing, 1920s-1930s, Artist, American
McKusick, Hal, Cool Jazz, 1950s-1990s, Artist, American
McLaughlin, John, Fusion; Fusion and Jazz Rock, 1960s-, Artist, British
McLean, Jackie, Hard Bop, 1950s-, Artist, American
McPartland, Jimmy, Chicago Jazz, 1930s-1970s, Artist, American
McPhee, Joe, Free Jazz, 1960s-, Artist, American
McPherson, Charles, Bebop; Hard Bop, 1950s-1990s, Artist, American
McShann, Jay, Swing, 1930s-, Artist, American
Meirelles, Pascoal, Brazilian Jazz, 1980s-1990s, Artist, Brazilian
Melle, Gil, Hard Bop; Bebop; Cool Jazz, 1950s-1990s, Artist; Composer, American
Metheny, Pat, Fusion, 1970s-, Artist; Composer, American

Miley, Bubber, Swing, 1920s, Artist, American
Miller, Glenn, Swing, 1920s-1940s, Artist, American
Mills Brothers, The, Swing; New Orleans Jazz, 1930s-1970s, Artist, American
Mills, Irving, New Orleans Jazz, 1920s-1930s, Artist, American
Mingus Big Band, Swing, 1990s-, Artist, American
Mingus, Charles, Bebop; Hard Bop, 1940s-1970s, Artist; Composer, American
Miranda, Carmen, Brazilian Jazz; Latin Jazz, 1930s-1950s, Artist, Brazilian
Mitchell, Blue, Hard Bop, 1950s-1970s, Artist, American
Mitchell, Red, Cool Jazz; Hard Bop, 1950s-1990s, Artist, American
Mitchell, Roscoe, Free Jazz, 1960s-, Artist, American
Mobley, Hank, Hard Bop, 1950s-1970s, Artist, American
Modern Jazz Quartet, The, Cool Jazz, 1950s-, Artist, American
Mole, Miff, Chicago Jazz, 1920s-1950s, Artist, American
Mondo Grosso, Acid Jazz, 1990s-, Artist, Japanese
Monk, Thelonious, Bebop; Modal Jazz; Hard Bop, 1940s-1970s, Artist, American
Monterose, J. R., Hard Bop, 1950s-1980s, Artist, American
Montgomery Brothers, The, Soul Jazz, 1950s-1960s, Artist, American
Montgomery, Wes, Hard Bop, 1940s-1960s, Artist, American
Montrose, Jack, Cool Jazz, 1950s-1990s, Artist, American
Moody, James, Bebop; Hard Bop, 1940s-, Artist, American
Mooney, John, Ragtime, 1970s-, Artist, American
Moraes, Vinícius de, Latin Jazz, 1940s-1980s, Artist, Brazilian
Morath, Max, Ragtime, 1970s-1990s, Artist, American
Moreira, Airto, Brazilian Jazz; Latin Jazz, 1970s-, Artist, Brazilian
Morello, Joe, Cool Jazz; Hard Bop, 1950s-1990s, Artist, American
Morgan, Frank, Hard Bop; Bebop, 1950s-1990s, Artist, American
Morgan, Lee, Hard Bop, 1950s-1970s, Artist, American
Morrison, Van, Jazz Rock, 1960s-, Artist; Songwriter, British
Morton, Jelly Roll, New Orleans Jazz, 1920s-1940s, Artist; Composer, American
Mosca, Sal, Cool Jazz, 1950s-1990s, Artist, American
Moten, Bennie, Swing, 1920s-1930s, Artist, American
Muhammad, Idris, Soul Jazz, 1970s-1990s, Artist, American
Mulligan, Gerry, Cool Jazz, 1940s-1990s, Artist; Composer, American
Murphy, Turk, Chicago Jazz, 1930s-1980s, Artist, American
Murray, David, Free Jazz, 1970s-, Artist, American
Murray, Sunny, Free Jazz, 1950s-1990s, Artist, American
Navarro, Fats, Bebop, 1940s-1950s, Artist, American
Neidlinger, Buell, Free Jazz, 1950s-1990s, Artist, American
Nelson, Oliver, Hard Bop, 1950s-1970s, Artist; Composer, American
New Orleans Rhythm Kings, Chicago Jazz, 1920s-1960s, Artist, American
Newborn, Phineas, Hard Bop, 1950s-1980s, Artist, American
Newman, David 'Fathead', Soul Jazz; Hard Bop, 1950s-, Artist, American
Newman, Joe, Swing, 1940s-1990s, Artist, American
Newsom, Tommy, Cool Jazz; Bebop, 1950s-, Artist, American
Nichols, Herbie, Dixieland Revival; Swing; Bebop, 1950s, Artist; Composer, American
Nichols, Red, Chicago Jazz, 1920s-1960s, Artist, American
Niehaus, Lennie, Cool Jazz; Bebop, 1950s-1990s, Artist, American
Noone, Jimmie, New Orleans Jazz, 1920s-1930s, Artist, American
Norvo, Red, Swing; Cool Jazz, 1930s-1980s, Artist, American
O'Bryant, Jimmy, New Orleans Jazz, 1920s, Artist, American
O'Day, Anita, Swing; Bebop, 1940s-1990s, Artist, American
O'Farrill, Chico, Latin Jazz; Bebop, 1940s-1970s, Artist, Cuban
Olympia Brass Band, New Orleans Jazz, 1960s-1990s, Artist, American
Oquendo, Manny, Latin Jazz, 1970s-, Artist, American
Oregon, Fusion; Fusion and Jazz Rock, 1970s-1990s, Artist, American
Original Dixieland Jazz Band, New Orleans Jazz, 1910s-1950s, Artist, American
Original Salty Dogs, The, Dixieland Revival, 1960s, Artist, American
Ory, Kid, New Orleans Jazz; Chicago Jazz, 1920s-1960s, Artist, American
Outback, Fusion and Jazz Rock, 1990s, Artist, British
Page, Hot Lips, Swing, 1930s-1950s, Artist, American
Paich, Marty, Bebop; Cool Jazz, 1950s-1990s, Artist, American
Palm Skin Productions, Acid Jazz, 1990s-, Producer, British
Palmieri, Charlie, Latin Jazz, 1950s-1980s, Artist, American
Palmieri, Eddie, Latin Jazz, 1960s-, Artist, American
Papete, Brazilian Jazz, 1970s-1980s, Artist, Brazilian
Parenti, Tony, New Orleans Jazz, 1910s-1970s, Artist, American
Parker, Charlie, Bebop; Swing, 1930s-1950s, Artist, American
Parker, Evan, Free Jazz, 1960s-, Artist, British
Parker, Maceo, Soul Jazz, 1970s-, Artist, American
Parker, William, Free Jazz, 1970s-, Artist, American
Parlan, Horace, Hard Bop, 1960s-, Artist, American
Partch, Harry, Fusion and Jazz Rock, 1920s-1970s, Artist, American
Pascoal, Hermeto, Latin Jazz; Brazilian Jazz, 1960s-1990s, Artist, Brazilian
Pass, Joe, Bebop; Hard Bop, 1950s-1990s, Artist, American
Passport, Fusion, 1970s-, Artist, American
Pastorius, Jaco, Fusion, 1970s-1980s, Artist, American
Patitucci, John, Fusion, 1980s-, Artist, American
Patrick, Pat, Free Jazz, 1950s-1990s, Artist, American
Patterson, Don, Soul Jazz; Hard Bop, 1960s-1970s, Artist, American
Patton, Big John, Soul Jazz; Hard Bop, 1960s-1990s, Artist, American
Payne, Cecil, Bebop; Hard Bop, 1950s-, Artist, American
Peacock, Gary, Free Jazz, 1960s-1990s, Artist, American
Pearson, Duke, Hard Bop, 1950s-1970s, Producer; Artist, American
Pedersen, Niels-Henning Orsted, Bebop; Hard Bop, 1960s-1990s, Artist, Danish
Pena, Ralph, Cool Jazz; Bebop, 1960s, Artist, American
Pepper, Art, Bebop; Hard Bop; Cool Jazz, 1940s-1980s, Artist, American
Perkins, Bill, Cool Jazz; Hard Bop, 1950s-, Artist, American
Person, Houston, Soul Jazz; Hard Bop; Swing, 1960s-, Artist, American
Peterson, Giles, Acid Jazz, 1990s-, Artist, British
Peterson, Oscar, Swing; Bebop, 1940s-, Artist, Canadian
Pettiford, Oscar, Bebop, 1940s-1950s, Artist, American
Phillips, Sonny, Soul Jazz, 1960s-1970s, Artist, American
Piazzolla, Astor, Latin Jazz, 1940s-1990s, Artist, Argentinean
Ponder, Jimmy, Soul Jazz; Hard Bop, 1960s-, Artist, American
Ponty, Jean-Luc, Fusion, 1960s-, Artist, American
Potter, Tommy, Bebop, 1940s-1950s, Artist, American
Powell, Baden, Latin Jazz, 1960s-, Artist, Brazilian
Powell, Bud, Bebop, 1940s-1960s, Artist; Composer, American
Powell, Mel, Swing, 1940s-1960s, Artist; Composer, American
Pozo, Chano, Latin Jazz, 1940s, Artist, Cuban
Preservation Hall Jazz Band, Dixieland Revival, 1950s-, Artist, American

Previn, André, Cool Jazz; Bebop, 1940s-, Artist, French
Pucho and His Latin Soul Brothers, Latin Jazz, 1960s-1970s, Artist, American
Puente, Tito, Latin Jazz, 1940s-1990s, Artist, American
Pullen, Don, Free Jazz, 1960s-1990s, Artist, American
Purdie, Bernard "Pretty" Soul Jazz, 1960s-1990s, Artist, American
Purim, Flora, Brazilian Jazz; Latin Jazz; Fusion, 1970s-, Artist, Brazilian
Quebec, Ike, Hard Bop; Soul Jazz; Swing, 1940s-1960s, Artist, American
Raeburn, Boyd, Bebop, 1940s-1950s, Artist, American
Ramzy, Hossam, Fusion and Jazz Rock, 1970s-, Artist, Egyptian
Raney, Jimmy, Cool Jazz, 1950s-1990s, Artist, American
Red Rodney, Bebop; Hard Bop, 1940s-1990s, Artist, American
Red Snapper, Acid Jazz, 1990s-, Artist, British
Red, Sonny, Hard Bop, 1950s-1970s, Artist, American
Redd, Freddie, Hard Bop, 1950s-1990s, Composer; Artist, American
Redman, Dewey, Free Jazz, 1960s-1990s, Artist, American
Redman, Don, Swing, 1920s-1950s, Artist; Composer, American
Reed, Wayman, Hard Bop, 1960s-1980s, Artist, American
Reid, Steve, Free Jazz, 1970s-, Artist, American
Reinhardt, Django, Swing, 1920s-1950s, Artist, Belgian
Return to Forever, Fusion, 1970s, Artist, American
Rich, Buddy, Swing; Bebop; Swing, 1940s-1980s, Artist, American
Richards, Johnny, Latin Jazz, 1940s-1960s, Composer, Brazilian
Richardson, Jerome, Cool Jazz; Hard Bop, 1950s-1990s, Artist, American
Rippingtons, The, Smooth Jazz, 1980s-, Artist, American
Ritenour, Lee, Fusion, 1970s-1990s, Artist, American
Rivers, Sam, Free Jazz, 1960s-, Artist, American
Roach, Freddie, Soul Jazz, 1960s-1970s, Artist, American
Roach, Max, Bebop; Hard Bop, 1940s-1990s, Artist, American
Roca, Pete la, Latin Jazz; Hard Bop, 1950s-1990s, Artist, American
Rogers, Shorty, Cool Jazz, 1950s-1990s, Artist, American
Rollins, Sonny, Bebop; Hard Bop, 1940s-, Artist; Composer, American
Romao, Dom Um, Latin Jazz; Brazilian Jazz; Fusion and Jazz Rock, 1970s-, Artist, Brazilian
Rouse, Charlie, Hard Bop, 1940s-1980s, Artist, American
Rowles, Jimmy, Bebop; Swing, 1950s-1990s, Artist, American
Royal, Ernie, Bebop; Swing, 1940s-1980s, Artist, American
Rubalcaba, Gonzalo, Latin Jazz, 1980s-, Artist, Cuban
Rudd, Roswell, Free Jazz, 1950s-, Artist, American
Ruff, Willie, Hard Bop; Bebop, 1950s-1990s, Artist, American
Rugolo, Pete, Swing, 1950s-1990s, Artist, American
Ruiz, Hilton, Latin Jazz, Bebop, 1970s-1990s, Artist, Cuban
Rumsey, Howard, Cool Jazz; Bebop, 1950s-1960s, Artist, American
Rushing, Jimmy, Swing, 1920s-1970s, Artist, American
Russell, Curly, Bebop, 1940s-1950s, Artist, American
Russell, Luis, Swing, 1920s-1940s, Artist, American
Russell, Pee Wee, Swing; Chicago Jazz, 1920s-1960s, Artist, American
Rypdal, Terje, Fusion, 1970s-1990s, Artist, Norwegian
Salvador, Sal, Cool Jazz; Bebop, 1950s-1990s, Artist, American
Sample, Joe, Hard Bop; Fusion; Soul Jazz, 1960s-, Artist, American
Sanborn, David, Smooth Jazz, 1970s-, Artist, American
Sanchez, Poncho, Latin Jazz, 1970s-, Artist, American
Sandals, Acid Jazz, 1990s, Artist, British
Sanders, Pharaoh, Free Jazz; Hard Bop, 1960s-, Artist, American
Sandoval, Arturo, Latin Jazz, 1970s-, Artist, Cuban
Santamaria, Mongo, Latin Jazz, 1950s-1990s, Artist, Cuba
Schifrin, Lalo, Bebop, 1950s-, Composer; Artist, Argentinean
Schulz, Bob, Dixieland Revival, 1980s-, Artist, American
Scobey, Bob, Chicago Jazz, 1950s-1960s, Artist, American
Scofield, John, Fusion, 1970s-, Artist, American
Scott, Hazel, Cool Jazz, 1940s-1950s, Artist, American
Scott, Shirley, Soul Jazz; Hard Bop, 1950s-1990s, Artist, American
Scott, Tony, Cool Jazz, 1950s-1990s, Artist, American
Shakti, Fusion and Jazz Rock; Fusion, 1970s, Artist, American
Shank, Bud, Cool Jazz; Hard Bop, 1950s-, Artist, American
Shankar, Lakshminarayana, Fusion and Jazz Rock; Fusion, 1970s-1990s, Artist, Indian
Sharrock, Sonny, Free Jazz, 1960s-1990s, Artist, American
Shavers, Charlie, Swing, 1930s-1970s, Artist, American
Shaw, Artie, Swing, 1930s-1950s, Artist, American
Shaw, Woody, Hard Bop, 1960s-1980s, Artist, American
Shearing, George, Cool Jazz; Bebop, 1930s-1990s, Artist, British
Sheldon, Jack, Bebop, 1950s-, Artist, American
Shepp, Archie, Free Jazz; Hard Bop, 1960s-, Artist, American
Shihab, Sahib, Bebop; Hard Bop, 1950s-1990s, Artist, American
Shirley, Don, Cool Jazz, 1950s-1970s, Artist, Jamaican
Sidran, Ben, Smooth Jazz; Cool Jazz, 1970s-, Artist, American
Silva, Alan, Free Jazz, 1960s-, Artist, American
Silva, Robertinho, Brazilian Jazz, 1990s, Artist, Brazil
Silveira, Ricardo, Brazilian Jazz; Fusion, 1980s-1990s, Artist, Brazilian
Silver, Horace, Hard Bop; Fusion, 1950s-, Artist, American
Simeon, Omer, New Orleans Jazz; Swing, 1920s-1950s, Artist, American
Simmons, Sonny, Free Jazz, 1960s-, Artist, American
Simone, Nina, Smooth Jazz, 1950s-, Artist, American
Sims, Zoot, Bebop; Cool Jazz, 1940s-1980s, Artist, American
Sinatra, Frank, Swing, 1930s-1990s, Artist, American
Slide Five, Acid Jazz, 1990s, Artist, American
Smith, Bessie, New Orleans Jazz, 1920s-1930s, Artist, American
Smith, Jabbo, Bebop, 1920s-1970s, Artist, American
Smith, Jimmy, Hard Bop, 1950s-, Artist, American
Smith, Johnny, Cool Jazz, 1950s-1970s; 1990s, Artist, American
Smith, Keely, Swing, 1950s-, Artist, American
Smith, Lonnie Liston, Fusion, 1970s-1990s, Artist, American
Smith, Lonnie, Soul Jazz; Hard Bop, 1960s-, Artist, American
Smith, Louis, Hard Bop, 1950s-, Artist, American
Smith, Stuff, Swing, 1920s-1960s, Artist, American
Smith, Tab, Swing, 1940s-1950s, Artist, American
Smith, Wadado Leo, Free Jazz, 1970s-, Artist, American
Smith, Willie "The Lion", New Orleans Jazz, 1920s-1970s, Artist, American
Snowden, Elmer, New Orleans Jazz, 1920s-1960s, Artist, American
Soft Machine, The, Jazz Rock, 1960s-1990s, Artist, British
South Frisco Jazz Band, Dixieland Revival, 1950s-1990s, Artist, American
South, Eddie, Swing, 1920s-1950s, Artist, American
Southern, Jeri, Cool Jazz, 1950s-1960s, Artist, American
Spanier, Muggsy, Chicago Jazz, 1920s-1960s, Artist, American
Spyro Gyra, Smooth Jazz; Fusion, 1970s-, Artist, American
St Cyr, Johnny, New Orleans Jazz, 1920s-1930s, Artist, American
State Street Ramblers, New Orleans Jazz, 1920s-1930s, Artist, American
Steely Dan, Jazz Rock, 1970s-, Artist, American
Stereo MCs, Acid Jazz, 1980s-, Artist, British
Stewart, Rex, Chicago Jazz; Swing, 1920s-1960s, Artist, American
Stewart, Slam, Swing, 1940s-1980s, Artist, American
Stitt, Sonny, Bebop, 1940s-1980s, Artist, American
Strayhorn, Billy, Chicago Jazz, 1930s-1960s, Composer; Artist, American
Sullivan, Joe, Chicago Jazz; Swing, 1930s-1960s, Artist, American
Sun Ra, Free Jazz, 1940s-1990s, Artist, American
Sunshine, Monty, New Orleans Jazz; Chicago Jazz, 1960s-, Artist, British
Tate, Buddy, Swing, 1930s-1990s, Artist, American
Tate, Grady, Hard Bop, 1950s-1990s, Artist, American
Tatum, Art, Swing, 1920s-1950s, Artist, American
Taylor, Art, Bebop; Hard Bop, 1950s-1990s, Artist, American
Taylor, Billy, Bebop; Hard Bop; Swing, 1940s-, Artist, American
Taylor, Cecil, Free Jazz, 1950s-, Artist, American
Taylor, James, Acid Jazz; Soul Jazz, 1980s-, Artist, British
Tchicai, John, Free Jazz, 1960s-, Artist, Danish
Teagarden, Jack, Swing; Chicago Jazz, 1920s-1960s, Artist, American
Terry, Clark, Bebop; Swing, 1950s-, Artist, American
Teschemacher, Frank, New Orleans Jazz, 1920s-1930s, Artist, American
Thielemans, Toots, Brazilian Jazz; Latin Jazz; Swing; Bebop, 1950s-, Artist, Belgian
Thigpen, Ed, Bebop; Hard Bop, 1950s-1990s, Artist, American
Thompson, Barbara, Free Jazz; Fusion, 1970s-1990s, Artist, British
Thompson, Lucky, Bebop; Hard Bop, 1940s-1970s, Artist, American
Thornhill, Claude, Cool Jazz, 1930s-1950s, Artist, American
Three Sounds, The, Soul Jazz; Hard Bop, 1950s-1960s, Artist, American
Tibbetts, Steve, Fusion, 1970s-, Artist, American
Timmons, Bobby, Soul Jazz; Hard Bop, 1950s-1960s, Composer; Artist, American
Tippett, Keith and Julie, Free Jazz; Fusion, 1960s-1990s, Artist, British
Tiso, Wagner, Brazilian Jazz; Latin Jazz, 1970s-1990s, Artist, Brazilian

Tizol, Juan, Swing, 1930s-1960s, Artist, Puerto Rican
Tjader, Cal, Cool Jazz; Latin Jazz, 1950s-1980s, Artist, American
Tolliver, Charles, Hard Bop, 1960s-1980s, Artist, American
Tormé, Mel, Swing; Bebop, 1940s-1990s, Artist, American
Tristano, Lennie, Cool Jazz; Bebop, 1940s-1960s, Artist, American
Tucker, Sophie, Ragtime, 1920s-1960s, Artist, American
Turner, Big Joe, Swing, 1930s-1980s, Artist, American
Turpin, Tom, Ragtime, 1890s, Composer, American
Turre, Steve, Latin Jazz; Hard Bop; Bebop, 1970s-, Artist, American
Turrentine, Stanley, Hard Bop; Fusion, 1960s-1990s, Artist, American
Tyner, McCoy, Hard Bop, 1960s-, Artist, American
Ulmer, James Blood, Free Jazz, 1970s-, Artist, American
United Future Organization, Acid Jazz, 1990s-, Artist, Japanese
Urbaniak, Michal, Fusion, 1970s-, Artist, Polish
Vache, Warren, Swing; Chicago Jazz, 1970s-, Artist, American
Valdes, Carlos 'Patato', Latin Jazz, 1950s-, Artist, Cuban
Valdes, Chucho, Latin Jazz, 1970s-, Artist, Cuban
Vandermark, Ken, Free Jazz, 1980s-, Artist, American
Vaughan, Sarah, Bebop; Cool Jazz, 1940s-1980s, Artist, American
Venuti, Joe, Swing, 1920s-1970s, Artist, American
Vick, Harold, Soul Jazz; Hard Bop, 1960s-1980s, Artist, American
Vinnegar, Leroy, Cool Jazz, 1950s-1990s, Artist, American
Vinson, Eddie 'Cleanhead', Bebop, 1940s-1980s, Artist, American
Walcott, Colin, Fusion and Jazz Rock, 1970s-1980s, Artist, American
Waldo, Terry, 1970s-1980s, Artist, American,
Waldron, Mal, Hard Bop, 1950s-, Artist, American
Waller, Fats, Swing, 1920s-1940s, Artist, American
Wallington, George, Bebop, 1940s-1960s, Artist, American
Walton, Cedar, Hard Bop, 1950s-, Artist; Composer, American
Washington, Grover Jr, Soul Jazz, 1960s-1990s, Artist, American
Wasserman, Rob, Fusion, 1970s-, Artist, American
Waters, Benny, Swing, 1940s-1990s, Artist, American
Waters, Ethel, Swing, 1920s-1960s, Artist, American
Watrous, Bill, Bebop, 1960s-, Artist, American
Watters, Lu, Chicago Jazz, 1930s-1960s, Artist, American
Weather Report, Fusion, 1970s-1980s, Artist, American
Webb, Chick, Swing, 1920s-1930s, Artist, American
Webster, Ben, Swing, 1930s-1970s, Artist, American
Wellstood, Dick, New Orleans Jazz; Ragtime, 1950s-1980s, Artist, American
Wess, Frank, Swing; Cool Jazz; Bebop, 1940s-, Artist, American
West Coast All Stars, New Orleans Jazz, 1990s, Artist, American
West Jemond Rhythm Kings, Dixieland Revival, 1980s-1990s, Artist, American
Weston, Randy, Hard Bop, 1950s-1990s, Artist, American
Wettling, George, Chicago Jazz, 1920s-1950s, Artist, American
Whalum, Kirk, Smooth Jazz, 1980s-, Artist, American
White, Michael, Dixieland Revival; New Orleans Jazz, 1980s-, Artist, American
Wiggins, Gerald, Swing; Bebop, 1950s-1990s, Artist, American
Wilber, Bob, New Orleans Jazz, 1940s-, Artist, American
Wilkins, Ernie, Bebop; Swing, 1950s-1990s, Artist, American
Willette, Baby Face, Soul Jazz; Hard Bop, 1960s, Artist, American
Williams, Buster, Hard Bop, 1960s-, Artist, American
Williams, Clarence, Swing, 1920s-1940s, Artist; Composer, American
Williams, Cootie, Swing, 1930s-1970s, Artist, American
Williams, Joe, Swing, 1930s-1990s, Artist, American
Williams, John, Swing, 1940s-1960s, Artist, American
Williams, Mary Lou, Swing; Bebop, 1920s-1970s, Artist; Composer, American
Williams, Tony, Fusion; Hard Bop, 1960s-1990s, Artist, American
Williamson, Claude, Cool Jazz; Bebop, 1950s-1990s, Artist, American
Willis, Larry, Fusion, 1960s-, Artist, American
Wilson, Cassandra, Fusion and Jazz Rock, 1980s-, Artist, American
Wilson, Gerald, Swing; Bebop, 1940s-1990s, Artist; Composer, American
Wilson, Reuben, Soul Jazz; Hard Bop; Fusion, 1960s-1990s, Artist, American
Wilson, Teddy, Swing, 1930s-1980s, Artist, American
Winding, Kai, Bebop, 1940s-1970s, Artist, American
Winter, Paul, Fusion and Jazz Rock, 1960s-, Artist; Producer, American
Woods, Phil, Bebop; Hard Bop, 1950s-, Artist, American
World Saxophone Quartet, Free Jazz, 1970s-, Artist, American
World's Greatest Jazz Band, Dixieland Revival, 1960s-1970s, Artist, American
Wright, Eugene, Cool Jazz; Swing, 1950s-1970s, Artist, American
Yellowjackets, The, Smooth Jazz; Fusion, 1980s-1990s, Artist, American
Young, Larry, Soul Jazz; Hard Bop; Fusion, 1960s-1970s, Artist, American
Young, Lester, Swing; Cool Jazz, 1930s-1950s, Artist, American
Young, Snooky, Swing, 1950s-1990s, Artist, American
Young, Trummy, Swing, 1930s-1960s, Artist, American
Young, Webster, Cool Jazz, 1950s-1960s, Artist, American
Zappa, Frank, Jazz Rock; Fusion, 1960s-1990s, Artist, American
Zawinul, Joe, Fusion; Fusion and Jazz Rock; Soul Jazz; Hard Bop, 1950s-1990s, Artist, Austrian

HARD BOP ➡ 136 FREE JAZZ ➡ 138 SOUL JAZZ ➡ 140 FUSION & JAZZ ROCK ➡ 142 ACID JAZZ ➡ 144 SMOOTH JAZZ ➡ 146
LATIN JAZZ ➡ 148 BRAZILIAN JAZZ ➡ 150

Blues

FEW would deny that the blues has played a more important role in the history of popular culture than any other musical genre. As well as being a complete art form in itself, it is a direct ancestor to the different types of current popular music we know and love today. Without the blues there would have been no Beatles or Jimi Hendrix, no Led Zeppelin or Nirvana, Louis Armstrong or Miles Davis, James Brown or Stevie Wonder, Pink Floyd or Frank Zappa, Oasis or Blur … the list is endless.

The blues emerged out of the hardships endured by generations of African American slaves during the late nineteenth and early twentieth centuries. By 1900, the genre had developed to a

> "THE BLUES IS A LOW-DOWN, ACHING CHILL; IF YOU AIN'T NEVER HAD 'EM, I HOPE YOU NEVER WILL."
>
> *Robert Johnson*

1910, the word "blues" was commonly used in southern states to describe this musical tradition. Capitalizing on its popularity, the music industry published 'Memphis Blues' by the black composer W. C. Handy in 1912.

By the 1920s, rural African-Americans had migrated to the big cities in search of work, bringing their music with them. Mamie Smith, a New York vaudeville singer, made the

three-line stanza, with a vocal style derived from southern work songs. "Call and response" songs were a fundamental part of African slave labour, with the gang leader singing a line and the other workers following in response. This style was developed further by early blues guitar players, who would sing a line and then answer it on the guitar. They would often sing when they were feeling depressed, or "blue", and by

first known blues recording, 'Crazy Blues', with Okeh Records in 1920. Its success convinced singers such as Bessie Smith and Ma Rainey to follow suit. Louis Armstrong accompanied them on their recordings, absorbing some of their blues vibes into his jazz singing and trumpeting styles. Street musicians such as Blind Lemon Jefferson also started to make recordings, which inspired a whole generation of blues guitar players.

STYLES

Work Songs

Delta/Country Blues

Louisiana Blues

Texas Blues

Boogie-Woogie

Chicago Blues

Piedmont Blues (East Coast Blues)

Jump Blues

British Blues

Rhythm & Blues

Blues Rock

Modern Electric Blues

THE BLUES STYLE

This extract shows a typical blues style, with lowered ("blue") notes in the vocal, a loose guitar accompaniment and simple yet haunting lyrics.

I went to the cross - roads Fell down on my knees

BLUES PEOPLE A-Z ➡ 180   INSTRUMENTS A-Z ➡ 436

Previous Overleaf
Bessie Smith's powerful, roaring voice brought intense misery and despair to numbers such as 'Nobody Knows You When You're Down And Out'.

The 1930s were a crucial period in the development of the blues, for it was then that early Mississippi Delta blues performers Charley Patton, Son House and Robert Johnson travelled throughout the southern states, singing about their woes, freedom, love and sex to community after community. Johnson, who allegedly made a pact with the Devil in order to become a better guitar player, was the first true blues performance artist. On the east coast, musicians such as Blind Boy Fuller, Sonny Terry and the Rev. Gary Davis developed a more folky, "Piedmont" blues style. In Kansas City, Count Basie was absorbing the blues and reinjecting it into the big band jazz style of the swing era. And in New York, Billie Holiday, one of the most famous blues/jazz singers of all time, began captivating audiences with her haunting, sensuous voice.

As urban blues grew and developed in cities all over the country, the 1940s witnessed the birth of a wide range of new musical styles. In Los Angeles, bandleaders Louis Jordan and Tiny Bradshaw pioneered jump blues, an energetic style based around singers and saxophone players. They still used the traditional call-and-response blues approach, but this time it was the singers ("shouters") and saxophonists ("honkers") who were exchanging phrases and passages. By the end of the decade, jump blues developed into rhythm and blues (R&B), in which more emphasis was placed on the singers than the instrumentalists. In Chicago, electric blues began to develop, as local bluesmen took Mississippi Delta ideas, amplified them and put them into a small-band context. The harmonica also became a more prominent instrument, thanks to players such as Little Walter and Otis Rush.

By the 1950s, electric blues was in full swing, with B. B. King, Muddy Waters, John Lee Hooker, T-Bone Walker and Howlin' Wolf playing to packed houses in major cities. King pioneered across-the-string vibrato and note-bending techniques on his beloved guitar, "Lucille"; these are now used today by all blues lead-guitar players. Hooker developed a different style, where he stomped continuously with his right foot while singing and playing. Wolf injected more power and frustration into the blues and Walker jazzed things up, but it was perhaps Muddy Waters, with his passionate singing and biting guitar tones, who popularized the style more than anyone else from this period. Some bluesmen,

including Big Bill Broonzy, visited England, where their performances inspired local musicians to adopt the style. Chris Barber, a jazz bandleader, assembled his own blues outfit with guitarist Alexis Korner and harmonica player Cyril Davies; they went on to become Blues Incorporated.

The 1960s witnessed a musical and cultural revolution, as British guitar players such as Eric Clapton and Peter Green began to mimic American bluesmen, using solid body guitars and more powerful amps to get a harder, more driving sound than their American mentors. The Rolling Stones (named after a Muddy Waters song) developed a blues-influenced style, injecting rawness and attitude into mainstream chart music. These Brits had enormous worldwide success with their anglicized blues, much to the surprise of the American traditionals. But what went around came around, and the success of British bluesmen encouraged more listeners to check out some of the earlier, more authentic blues artists, whose audience numbers began to swell. "They stole my music," Muddy Waters said of the Rolling Stones, "but they gave me my name." Another musical phenomenon of the 1960s was Jimi Hendrix, an avant-garde bluester who expanded the boundaries of the electric

lead-guitar style. His and Clapton's guitar tones prompted the birth of a number of other styles, including blues rock, hard rock and heavy metal.

From the 1970s onwards, fewer and fewer dedicated blues musicians have appeared, as more singers and players have adopted the spin-off styles that emerged out of it. However, Stevie Ray Vaughan and Gary Moore still managed to inject energy into it, Robben Ford expanded the blues-jazz chops repertoire and Robert Cray introduced the genre to a larger, more mainstream audience throughout the 1980s and 1990s. Other artists, including Bernard Allison, Walter Trout, Dave Hole and Susan Tedeschi, continue to play the blues to enthusiastic audiences around the world.

It might seem paradoxical that a music born out of loneliness, misery, poverty and depression should give so many listeners so much joy, but in reality the first blues songs were sung to raise the spirits of impoverished African-American slaves. The earliest blues singers empathized with their audiences because they had been through the same experiences. It seems fitting that such a sincere and worthy art form has endured to this day, spawning numerous musical children of its own.

Above
The Rolling Stones were inspired by the likes of Muddy Waters, Howlin' Wolf and Jimmy Reed. They started out playing covers of blues songs, which were largely unknown to British audiences at the time.

Left
The harmonica is one of the most expressive blues instruments. The Marine Band was used by such greats as Sonny Terry, Little Walter, Sonny Boy Williamson II and Paul Butterfield.

Far Left
Muddy Waters was first recorded by Alan Lomax on a Mississippi plantation before heading to Chicago in the 1940s and hitting the big time with songs like Willie Dixon's 'Hoochie Coochie Man'.

JAZZ, BLUES, SPIRITUALS AND GOSPEL MUSIC, WERE ROOTED IN THE WORK SONGS OF BLACK LABOURERS OF THE SOUTH. AS CHET WILLIAMSON WROTE "THESE WERE SONGS AND CHANTS THAT KEPT A PEOPLE MOVING AND ADVANCING THROUGH DREADFUL OPPRESSION. THESE ARE THE VOICES OF THOSE WHO HARVESTED THE FIELDS, DROVE THE MULES, LAUNCHED THE BOATS, AND HAMMERED THE RAILS."

Work Songs

Above

Alan Lomax made these recordings in 1959, when the African-American music of the century's early years was still alive in the South. The collection includes field hollers, Delta blues, spirituals and prison recordings.

BASED on the compelling rhythms, sliding-pitch intonation and overlapping call-and-response traditions of West African music, which persevered in North America during the time of slavery, these work songs resounded in the South during the Reconstruction years following the Civil War, which ended in 1865. Whether sung by slaves and, later, sharecroppers picking cotton or husking corn, workers laying track on the railroad line, prisoners on the chain gang breaking rocks and draining swamps or coal miners with pickaxes, work songs were structured in a very similar way to West African percussion ensembles.

A Fount Of Creativity And Personal Expression

In a typical drum ensemble of Ghana, the leader/drummer would give signals or motifs to the rest of the group, which would then respond in overlapping call-and-response fashion. The leader, in effect, poses a question and the group offers an answer (the overlap occurring where the call is still in the air when the response begins, or the call begins again before the response is done).

"THESE LONG, MOURNFUL, ANTIPHONAL SONGS ACCOMPANIED THE WORK ON COTTON PLANTATIONS, UNDER THE DRIVER'S LASH."

Tony Palmer, All You Need Is Love: The Story Of Popular Music

Above Right

Work songs, often secular and usually relating to the slaves' predicament, helped the slaves in the cotton fields to pick in rhythm and also served to lift their spirits, relieving the pain and boredom of their labour.

Responsorial singing follows this same procedure, with the leader often improvising above a rhythmic pulse by varying the timing, pitch, attack or decay of words at the beginning or end of a phrase. The leader might also toy with the phrasing by employing rhythmic displacement or a slight altering of phrases in relation to the underlying beat.

In most work songs, the rhythm was tied into the pattern of the work itself – the swinging back and down and the blow of a sledgehammer or pickaxe, the hoisting of ropes on a block and tackle – while the lead chanter acted as a coach, directing the teamwork until the job was done. Each new line was often punctuated by a grunt as the axe or hammer found its mark:

"Dis ole hammer – hunh!
Ring like silver – hunh!
Shine like gold, baby – hunh!
Shine like gold – hunh!"

Field hollers, work songs and the cries of street vendors advertising their wares all incorporated imaginative vocal sounds and various pitch-altering decorations of a note, including the use of "blue notes". A good example of this can be heard on an Alan Lomax recording from 1959 of 'Louisiana', sung by prisoner Henry Ratcliff, who was serving time at the Mississippi State Penitentiary at Parchman Farm. Other examples from Lomax's recording include 'Stewball', sung by Ed Lewis leading a group of prisoners at the Lambert State Penitentiary in Mississippi, and 'Berta Berta', sung by Leroy Miller leading a hoeing group at Parchman Farm. Another well-known field holler is 'Mama Lucy', sung by Leroy Gary and recorded by Lomax in 1959, also at Parchman Farm.

The work song was fluid and organic and never repeated exactly the same way twice. This idea of an endless fount of creativity and personal expression within a simple, finite structure, through the use of vocal slurs, falsetto leaps and patches of melisma, is an inherently African device also readily apparent in the blues idiom.

LEADING EXPONENTS

Sid Hemphill
Ervin Webb
Ed Young
Ed Lewis
Miles Pratcher
Fred McDowell

WORK SONGS

Work songs retain a strong African influence, with irregular rhythms that often follow speech patterns, "bent" pitches and emotionally inflected vocal sounds.

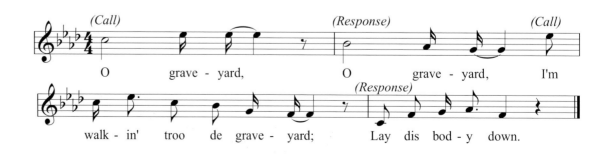

THE BLUES INTRO ➡ 154   BLUES PEOPLE A-Z ➡ 180   INSTRUMENTS A-Z ➡ 436   THE JAZZ INTRO ➡ 118   THE GOSPEL INTRO ➡ 384

Delta/Country Blues

IT WAS IN THE RICH COTTON-PRODUCING DELTA STRETCHING FROM MISSISSIPPI TO TENNESSEE THAT BLACK LABOURERS WORKING THE PLANTATIONS GAVE FERMENT TO AN EARTHY STYLE OF MUSIC BORN OUT OF AFRICAN SONGS, CHANTS, SPIRITUALS AND GOSPEL TUNES THAT HAD BEEN HANDED DOWN FOR GENERATIONS. THEY CALLED IT THE BLUES.

THE man usually recognized as the first star of Delta country blues is Charley Patton. An acoustic guitarist of impressive facility with a hoarse, impassioned singing style, Patton was a house-rocking entertainer who played plantation dances and juke joints throughout the Mississippi Delta during the early 1920s. Combined with a high-energy performance style, the strong rhythmic pulse of his music was so galvanizing that he held emotional sway over audiences everywhere he played. Legend has it that workers would often leave crops unattended to listen to him play guitar.

Patton's Prototype

When he finally documented his entertaining tunes in the studio (beginning with 'Pony Blues', for the Paramount label, in 1929), his records could be heard on phonographs throughout the South. And while he did not invent the form (nor was he the first Delta bluesman to record), Patton was the genre's most popular attraction: a genuine celebrity whose appetite for food, liquor and women were legendary, and who travelled from one engagement to the next with a flashy, expensive-looking guitar fitted with a custom-made strap and case. In essence, he was the prototypical rock star. When Patton died in 1934, he left behind a total of only 60 recorded tracks but his legacy was a colorful one, thoroughly addressed in 2001's Grammy-winning seven-CD box set, *Screamin' And Hollerin' The Blues: The Worlds Of Charley Patton,* on the Revenant label.

By the late 1920s, at the time of Patton's first recordings, other Mississippi bluesmen were also making their mark on records, including Patton contemporaries such as Tommy Johnson and Son House. While Johnson emulated Patton's powerful, rough-hewn vocal delivery and showboating style – playing the guitar behind his neck and the like – he lacked the ambition that drove Patton to the pinnacle of stardom in the late 1920s. Instead, Johnson spent most of the 1920s drinking, gambling and womanizing, until his slow descent into alcoholism started to take its toll. Canned Heat,

Above

Mississippi John Hurt's delicate picking style in fact had more in common with the east coast ragtime guitarists than the Delta guitar sound.

> "BLUES ACTUALLY IS AROUND YOU EVERY DAY. DOWNHEARTEDNESS AND HARDSHIP. YOU EXPRESS IT THROUGH YOUR SONG."
>
> *Arthur Lee Williams*

LEADING EXPONENTS

Charley Patton
Tommy Johnson
Son House
Robert Johnson
Bukka White
Skip James
Mississippi John Hurt
Mississippi Fred
  McDowell
Johnny Shines
Robert Lockwood Jr.
Junior Kimbrough
R. L. Burnside
Big Jack Johnson
Roosevelt "Booba"
  Barnes
Paul "Wine" Jones

I went to the cross-roads
Fell down on my knees

Gtr.

DELTA/COUNTRY BLUES

Early blues artists were unconstrained by European musical sensibilities, adding or subtracting beats at will.

THE BLUES INTRO ➡ 154   BLUES PEOPLE A-Z ➡ 180   INSTRUMENTS A-Z ➡ 436   WORLD: AFRICA ➡ 290   THE GOSPEL INTRO ➡ 384

the popular, California-based boogie-blues band of the 1960s, took its name from the title of a Johnson song about drinking Sterno-denatured alcohol used for artificial heat.

The Major Innovators

Another major innovator of the Delta blues style, Eddie James "Son" House brought an extraordinary degree of emotional power to his singing and slide guitar playing on his first recordings in the early 1930s for the Paramount label. A main source of inspiration for both Robert Johnson and Muddy Waters, Son (unlike his contemporary Charley Patton) lived long enough to experience his own rediscovery during the folk blues revival of the mid-1960s. A one-time Baptist

preacher, House imbued his blues with an almost demonic intensity on recordings such as 'My Black Mama', 'Preachin' The Blues' and 'Walkin' Blues'. His 1965 recording of 'Death Letter' (cut while in his 60s for the Columbia label) is one of the most anguished and emotionally stunning laments in the Delta blues oeuvre and has been covered in dramatic fashion by a diverse list of artists such as David Johansen, Cassandra Wilson, Diamanda Galas, James Blood Ulmer, Derek Trucks

and the White Stripes. In 1965, he played Carnegie Hall in New York and subsequently became an attraction on the folk blues coffee house network, where he was rightly hailed as the greatest living Delta singer still actively performing.

Perhaps the most celebrated and mythic figure in Delta blues was Robert Johnson, a guitarist of dazzling technique who could simultaneously juggle independent rhythms and pianistic-type lines by employing the unique finger-style approach he developed. Legend has it that one night Johnson met the Devil at the crossroads and exchanged his everlasting soul for the gift of unparalleled virtuosity on the guitar. Whether that is folklore or not, Johnson's incredible skills as both a player and a profoundly blue singer soon became apparent to all around the Delta, including elders and inspirations such as Son House, who marvelled at his talent. An itinerant performer, Johnson had a wandering nature that took him well beyond the Delta to places like St. Louis, Chicago, Detroit and New York. His only recordings were made between 1936 and 1937.

Though Johnson died on 16 August 1938 at the age of 27, his approach to playing guitar and singing had a profound effect on a generation of blues musicians, including Jimmy Reed, Elmore James, Hound Dog Taylor and hundreds of others. His most famous songs, such as 'Sweet Home Chicago', 'Crossroads' and 'Love In Vain', have become blues standards, covered endlessly by the likes of the Rolling Stones, Led Zeppelin, Cream, Eric Clapton, Steve Miller and Cassandra Wilson. Other key, early country blues players include the idiosyncratic Skip James, Bukka White, Mississippi John Hurt, Mississippi Fred McDowell and Robert Johnson partners and disciples Robert Lockwood Jr. (Johnson's step-son and taught by the master himself) and Johnny Shines.

In recent years, renewed interest in Delta or country blues has been triggered by the spirited work of guitarists/singer-songwriters like Corey Harris, Keb' Mo', Guy Davis, Eric Bibb and Alvin Youngblood Hart, who have blended in touches of Delta-style acoustic blues along with their more contemporary pop-oriented offerings on record and in concert appearances all over the world. Present-day exponents of an edgier, electrified version of the raw, uncut Delta blues sound include Mississippi-based guitarists-singers R. L. Burnside, Big Jack Johnson, Paul "Wine" Jones, Roosevelt "Booba" Barnes and James "Super Chikan" Johnson.

Louisiana Blues

NEW ORLEANS IS WIDELY ACKNOWLEDGED AS THE BIRTHPLACE OF JAZZ, BUT IT ALSO PRODUCED ITS OWN INDIGENOUS BRAND OF BLUES, WHICH BORROWED FROM TEXAS AND KANSAS CITY WHILE ALSO MAKING USE OF CAJUN AND AFRO-CARIBBEAN RHYTHM PATTERNS.

A MIX of croaking and yodeling, floating over the top of the music in an independent time scheme, Professor Longhair's singular vocals added to his idiosyncratic charm. Influenced by New Orleans barrelhouse pianists Tuts Washington, Kid Stormy Weather and Sullivan Rock, Longhair developed his unique conception and made his recording debut in 1949 with the anthemic 'Mardi Gras In New Orleans', for the Dallas-based Star Talent label. In typically enigmatic fashion, he named his band the Shuffling

Hungarians and scored a hit in 1950 for the Mercury label with 'Bald Head', which combined his rolling piano with some good-time bounce and hilarious lyrics.

Rolling Piano And Good-Time Bounce

In 1953, Longhair recorded another New Orleans anthem, 'Tipitina', for the Atlantic label, and in 1959 he revived his 'Mardi Gras In New Orleans' (retitled 'Go To The Mardi Gras') for the regional Ron imprint. After fading from the scene in the 1960s, his performance at the first New Orleans Jazz & Heritage Festival in 1971 ignited a comeback, leading to a slew of recordings and international festival appearances. His last recording, the triumphant *Crawfish Fiesta* (Alligator Records), was released after his death on 30 January 1980. Longhair's irrepressible piano style was carried on by such Crescent City disciples as James Booker, Allen Toussaint, Fats Domino, Dr. John (Mac Rebennack) and Henry Butler.

An accompanist to Longhair during his comeback years, Snooks Eaglin distinguished himself as a guitarist who could cover any style of music convincingly. Blind since birth, he developed a dazzling finger-style approach, which allowed him to shift easily from Delta-style blues to flamenco, to gospel, R&B, rock, surf guitar or jazz. His earliest recordings, for the Folkways label in 1958, present him in an acoustic folk blues

> "BLACK OR WHITE, LOCAL OR OUT-OF-TOWN, THEY ALL HAD LONGHAIR'S MUSIC IN COMMON, JUST THAT MAMBO-RHUMBA BOOGIE THING."
>
> *Allen Toussaint*

Snooks Eaglin
COUNTRY BOY IN NEW ORLEANS
With Lucious Bridges And Percy Randolph

Above
Blind finger-picker Snooks Eaglin was Longhair's favourite guitarist and can be heard on many 'Fess tracks, as well as on Sugar Boy Crawford's rocking Mardi Gras anthem 'Jock-A-Mo'.

LEADING EXPONENTS
Champion Jack Dupree
Tuts Washington
Professor Longhair
James Booker
Dr. John
Guitar Slim
Snooks Eaglin
Earl King
Slim Harpo
Lightnin' Slim
Lazy Lester
Raful Neal
Kenny Neal

LOUISIANA BLUES
Louisiana blues is imbued with latin influences – usually mambo or rhumba – incorporated into the rhythms of the left-hand.

THE BLUES INTRO ➡ 160   BLUES PEOPLE ➡ 204   INSTRUMENTS A-Z ➡ 436   WORLD: CAJUN & ZYDECO ➡ 302

setting, accompanied only by harmonica and washboard. His early 1960s sides for the Imperial label show him excelling at New Orleans R&B, while his output for the Black Top label from the late 1980s onward highlight his blistering, rock-tinged guitar work in funky, New Orleans-style settings. He remains a top attraction in the Crescent City, at both the Jazz & Heritage Festival and showcase venues such as Tipitina's.

Swamp And Gospel

Another significant figure on the New Orleans blues scene was Eddie Jones (a.k.a Guitar Slim). Hailing from the Delta, he turned up in New Orleans at the age of 24, heavily influenced by Texas guitarist Clarence "Gatemouth" Brown.

His 1951 debut on the Imperial label featured the eerily distorted, nasty-toned guitar work and gospel-drenched vocals that would become his trademark. In 1954, his swampy, gospel-tinged track 'The Things I Used To Do', cut in New Orleans for the Specialty label, topped the R&B charts for 14 weeks and influenced a generation of young players, including the guitarist-songwriter Earl King. After recording throughout the 1950s for the Savoy, Specialty and Ace labels,

King scored his biggest hits in the 1960s with Imperial, including 1960's rock-flavored 'Come On' (later covered by Jimi Hendrix), 1961's funky 'Trick Bag' and 1962's 'Always A First Time'.

King also wrote for Fats Domino, Professor Longhair and Lee Dorsey during the 1960s. Following a lull in the 1970s, his career was revived in the 1980s through a series of first-rate releases for the Black Top label. He remains a top attraction in the Big Easy, thrilling fans with his scintillating showmanship, as well as his irresistible blend of high-energy jump blues and second-line rhythms.

A swampy side of the blues can be heard in the music of Baton Rouge artists such as harmonica aces Slim Harpo and Lazy Lester, as well as guitarists Silas Hogan and Lightnin' Slim, the latter scoring a national hit in 1959 with 'Rooster Blues'. The Baton Rouge style was characterized by reverb-laden production, laid-back beats, relaxed vocals, snakey guitar riffs and raw, wailing harmonica. That tradition was continued by the harmonica player Raful Neal in the 1970s, and is being continued today by his son, the talented harmonica player/guitarist/ songwriter Kenny Neal.

Accordion player Clifton Chenier melded traditional French Cajun dance music with R&B, rock'n'roll and the blues, originating the southwestern Louisiana hybrid known as zydeco. He made his first recordings in 1955, for the Los Angeles-based Specialty label. By the mid-1970s, Chenier's Red Hot Louisiana Band was an international touring act. He recorded regularly throughout the 1980s for the blues/folk revival label Arhoolie, winning a Grammy in 1982 for the album *I'm Here!* and maintained a relentless touring schedule on the international festival circuit until his death in 1987. Chenier's zydeco heirs include such blues-drenched accordionists and bandleaders as his son C. J. Chenier, Boozoo Chavis, Buckwheat Zydeco and Rockin' Dopsie.

Texas Blues

ALTHOUGH TEXAS HAS A RICH LEGACY OF ACOUSTIC COUNTRY BLUES ARTISTS, ITS PRIMARY CONTRIBUTION TO THE BLUES WAS ELECTRIC. AN INORDINATE NUMBER OF DAZZLING ELECTRIC GUITARISTS HAILED FROM THE LONE STAR STATE, INCLUDING T-BONE WALKER, CLARENCE "GATEMOUTH" BROWN, ALBERT COLLINS, FREDDIE KING AND SCORES OF HOTSHOT SIX-STRINGERS STILL ON THE SCENE.

OFTEN accompanied by flamboyant showmanship, the Texas electric-guitar style has always been overtly aggressive and rhythmically driving. As Billy Gibbons, of the Texas blues rock band ZZ Top, put it: "The Texas sound could be described as heavier than light and bluesier than anything else… And the flamboyancy of most Texans, which is now an established fact throughout the world, has created the flashiness that goes right along with the technical skills of most musicians".

Aggressive Showmanship

That flamboyance was perhaps best exemplified by the archetypal blues guitarist/vocalist/showman Aaron Thibeaux (T-Bone) Walker. Although Walker made his mark in Los Angeles in the late 1930s, before spearheading the west coast blues movement following his 1947 signature tune 'Stormy Monday', his roots were in Texas. Born on 28 May, 1910 in Linden, Texas, the young T-Bone learned all the stringed

"IN EAST TEXAS ... GUITAR ACCOMPANIED BLUES TENDED TO BE RHYTH-MICALLY DIFFUSE, WITH GUITARISTS LIKE BLIND LEMON JEFFERSON PLAYING ELABORATE, MELODIC FLOURISHES TO ANSWER THEIR VOCAL LINES."

Robert Palmer

instruments – including mandolin, violin, ukulele, upright bass and banjo – but gravitated toward guitar. As a teenager, he often served as "lead boy" for the Texas acoustic blues master Blind Lemon Jefferson, while the older, sightless man walked the Dallas streets playing for tips.

Above
T-Bone Walker's electric lead guitar play and singing set a precedent for future musicians.

Left
Sam "Lightnin'" Hopkins took up his name after pairing up with pianist Wilson "Thunder" Smith.

LEADING EXPONENTS

Blind Lemon Jefferson
Blind Willie Johnson
Johnny Winter
Lightnin' Hopkins
T-Bone Walker
Clarence "Gatemouth" Brown
Albert Collins
Johnny "Guitar" Watson
Freddie King

Gtr.

TEXAS BLUES

Blues guitarists intersperse their rhythmic accompaniment with more expressive solo passages, adding flavour to the music and demonstrating their technical skills.

THE BLUES INTRO ➡ 160   BLUES PEOPLE A-Z ➡ 204   INSTRUMENTS A-Z ➡ 436   BLUES: JUMP BLUES ➡ 170

Below

*Clarence "Gatemouth"
Brown is an extremely
versatile musician; he plays a
wide variety of instruments
and his compositions embrace
a range of musical styles.*

Walker later worked in touring carnivals and medicine shows with the blues singers Ida Cox and Bessie Smith, sharing the bill with stars such as Bill "Bojangles" Robinson and Cab Calloway, who had a major impact on T-Bone's concept of showmanship. He formed his own group in 1928 and recorded his first single for Columbia a year later, billed as Oak Cliff T-Bone (named after the Dallas neighbourhood where he grew up). When he relocated to Los Angeles in

1934, Walker vacated a position in the 16-piece, Dallas-based Lawson Brooks Band, which was promptly filled by his younger friend and jamming partner, the guitarist Charlie Christian. At the height of his popularity in the late-1940s, Walker exuded star quality. His audacious stage act – doing splits while playing his newly amplified Gibson electric guitar behind his head, with his teeth or under his leg – made him the Jimi Hendrix of his day.

Clarence "Gatemouth" Brown's big break came in the mid-1940s, when he filled in for an ailing T-Bone at the Bronze Peacock Lounge in Houston's Fifth Ward and thrilled the audience with his crowd-pleasing boogie-woogie and blistering finger-picked riffs. He was leading his own 25-piece band by 1947, and in 1949, scored a hit with 'My Time Is Expensive' on the Peacock label. His next hit, the influential 'Okie Dokie Stomp', came in 1951. In the mid-1960s, Brown served as musical director for the house band on *The!!!Beat*, a groundbreaking syndicated blues and R&B television show (a black alternative to *American Bandstand*), broadcast out of Dallas and hosted by the influential WLAC radio DJ Bill "Hoss" Allen. Today, at 79, the eternally youthful Gatemouth continues to pay tribute to his two biggest influences, jump blues master Louis Jordan and fellow Texan T-Bone Walker, while also blending in bits of country, Cajun and swinging, Count Basie-styled small band arrangements.

Stinging Intensity

Albert Collins emulated both T-Bone's patented licks and his flamboyant stage presence. While his stinging intensity earned him the nickname "Master of the Telecaster", Collins also engaged the audience by jumping off the stage and strolling through the house with a 46 m (150ft) guitar cord. His first hit came in 1962 with the million-selling 'Frosty'. He cut his classic sides for the Imperial label from 1968 to 1970. Collins had signed to the Chicago-based Alligator label by 1977, while the late 1980s saw him releasing a string of well-received recordings, including the Grammy-winning *Showdown!*, a 1987 collaboration with the guitarists Robert Cray and his fellow Texan Johnny Copeland.

Two other Texas guitar slingers of note are Houston's Johnny "Guitar" Watson and Gilmer's Freddie King. A flamboyant showman and nasty-toned picker in the T-Bone Walker tradition, Watson recorded throughout the 1950s before hitting it big in 1961 with his 'Gangster Of Love'. He reinvented himself as a raunchy disco-funkster in the 1970s, scoring hits with popular numbers such as 'A Real Mother For Ya', 'Ain't That A Bitch' and 'Superman Lover'. Freddie King, nicknamed "The Texas Cannonball" for his dynamic stage presence and intense attack on his Gibson guitar, made a great impact on a generation of players with his electrified output from the 1960s and early 1970s. His signature tune, the 1961 instrumental hit 'Hideaway', remains a staple in the modern blues repertoire.

Boogie-Woogie

A ROLLICKING, FAST PIANO STYLE CHARACTERIZED BY REPETITIVE EIGHTH-NOTE BASS FIGURES IN THE LEFT HAND, MESHED WITH SHARP, BLUESY SINGLE-NOTE RUNS IN THE RIGHT HAND, BOOGIE-WOOGIE WAS AN INFECTIOUS FORM THAT HAD AN IMMEDIATE APPEAL TO DANCERS.

WHILE the left hand remained tied to the task of covering driving basslines in a kind of "automatic pilot" approach through chord changes (repeating continuous eighth-note bass figures in each different harmony), the right hand was liberated to explore, express and create with bluesy impunity.

Although the boogie-woogie fad swept the nation in the late 1930s, its roots go back much further. Jelly Roll Morton and W. C. Handy recalled hearing boogie-woogie-style piano in the American South during the first decade of the twentieth century. By the 1920s, boogie-woogie pianists were making their mark in saloons, juke joints, honky-tonks and at rent parties throughout both the South and North, where their powerfully rhythmic attack could cut through the din of a good time.

A Powerfully Rhythmic Attack

One of the pioneers of this raucous, rapid-fire, eight-to-the-bar piano style was Jimmy Yancey. Born in 1894 in Chicago, he worked in vaudeville as a singer and tap dancer – starting at the age of six – before taking up the piano in 1915. Although he did not make a recording until 1939, his most famous student, Meade "Lux" Lewis, would become one of the first to document the boogie-woogie piano style on record with his 1927 'Honky Tonk Train Blues', a masterpiece of intricate cross-rhythms that highlights Lewis's remarkable independence between hands. That same year, Pine Top Smith garnered widespread attention with his catchy 'Pine Top's Boogie-Woogie', in which the pianist shouts instructions to dancers over the top of his rolling keyboard work. The hit tune, covered by several artists – including Bing Crosby with the Lionel Hampton Orchestra – also featured the rhythmic "breaks" that were an essential part of early ragtime.

From Spirituals To Swing

In 1938, a single event helped bring boogie-woogie to wider public exposure. Jazz impresario John Hammond, a producer and talent scout who had a keen interest in boogie-woogie piano (and particularly in Meade Lux Lewis), arranged to have Lewis and fellow boogie-woogie pianists Albert Ammons and Pete Johnson appear on the bill of his "From Spirituals To Swing" concert, held at Carnegie Hall on 23 December 1938. The gala event (which also featured Count Basie's Orchestra, gospel singer-guitarist Sister Rosetta Tharpe, blues shouters Jimmy Rushing and Big Joe Turner, blues harmonica ace Sonny Terry, soprano sax genius Sidney Bechet and his New Orleans Feet Warmers and the Kansas City Six featuring tenor saxophonist Lester Young on the bill) not only helped launch the boogie-woogie boom but also led directly to the formation of Blue Note Records by the German immigrant Alfred Lion.

As Michael Cuscuna wrote in *The Blue Note Years* (Rizzoli): "Lion attended the legendary 'From Spirituals To Swing' concert at Carnegie Hall. He was so moved by the

Above

Albert Ammons (left) was a flexible enough player to record with his son Gene Ammons, the founder of the 1940s Chicago saxophone sound. Pete Johnson (right) found success playing piano for the great Joe Turner.

"THEY PLAYED A ROLLING RHYTHM IN THE LEFT HAND SO THAT THEY COULD REACH FOR A DRINK OR A SANDWICH WITH THE RIGHT HAND."

Donald Clark, The Rise and Fall of Popular Music

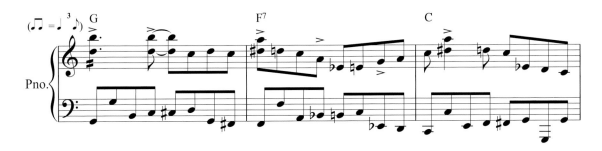

BOOGIE-WOOGIE

Boogie piano is characterized by its rolling rhythmic left hand. The right hand melodies and solos often feature syncopation and cross-rhythms, as in this example.

LEADING EXPONENTS

Pine Top Smith

Albert Ammons

Meade "Lux" Lewis

Pete Johnson

Jimmy Yancey

Amos Milburn

Floyd Dixon

THE BLUES INTRO ➡ 160   BLUES PEOPLE A-Z ➡ 204   INSTRUMENTS A-Z ➡ 436   JAZZ: RAGTIME ➡ 122   THE DANCE INTRO ➡ 310

Above

John Hammond kick-started the careers of the key boogie-woogie players as well as discovering Bessie Smith, Billie Holiday, Bob Dylan, and Robert Johnson.

Below

Amos Milburn (piano) & his Chicken Shackers, as the group called themselves after the runaway success of their hit 'Chicken Shack Boogie'.

pulsating, dazzling boogie-woogie artistry of pianists Albert Ammons, Meade Lux Lewis and Pete Johnson that he scraped up enough money for one day's rental on a studio. Exactly two weeks later on January 6, 1939, he recorded Ammons and Lewis. By that evening, Alfred Lion found himself in the record business – Blue Note Records was born".

Lion pressed 50 copies each of two 78rpm singles, one by Ammons, the other by Lewis. There followed other sessions with the two boogie-woogie pianists, including an innovative 1941 session with Lewis on celeste, Charlie Christian on guitar, Edmond Hall on clarinet and Israel Crosby on bass. Ammons recorded in the 1940s with the blues singer Sippie Wallace and in 1949 he cut a session with his son, the great tenor saxophonist Gene Ammons, before passing away later that year. Lewis continued playing after the boogie-woogie craze died down, relocating to Los Angeles and recording until 1962. Pete Johnson, the third member of the Big Three of boogie-woogie (the others being Albert Ammons and Meade Lux Lewis), forged a musical rapport with his Kansas City compatriot, blues shouter Big Joe Turner, releasing popular recordings such as 'Roll 'Em Pete'

and 'Cafe Society Rag'. He spent 1947–49 in Los Angeles before moving to Buffalo in 1950 and, subsequently, drifting into obscurity.

Down-Home Double Entendre And Humour

Born the year Meade Lux Lewis cut his first tracks, Amos Milburn was a jovial boogie-woogie disciple who picked up the torch and ran with it. The Houston-born pianist pounded out some of the most explosive boogie grooves of the post-war era, beginning in 1946 on the Los Angeles-based Aladdin label. His first hits included the driving, countrified boogie of 'Down The Road Apiece' (covered in 1960 by Chuck Berry and in 1965 by the Rolling Stones). Milburn excelled at good-natured, upbeat romps about booze and partying, imbued with a vibrant sense of humour and double entendre, as well as vivid, down-home imagery in his lyrics. He scored successive Top 10 R&B hits with 1948's 'Chicken Shack Boogie', 1949's 'Roomin' House Boogie', 1950's 'Bad, Bad Whiskey' and 1953's 'One Scotch, One Bourbon, One Beer'.

Milburn's frantic piano-pumping style would have a profound effect on seminal rock'n'rollers such as Floyd Dixon, Fats Domino, Little Richard and Jerry Lee Lewis in the early 1950s. That boogie-woogie piano lineage continues today with explosive players such as Marcia Ball, Billy C. Wirtz and Mitch Woods.

Chicago Blues

CHICAGO BLUES IS A RAW, ROUGH-AND-TUMBLE MUSIC, DEFINED BY SLASHING, DELTA-ROOTED ELECTRIC SLIDE GUITARS, RAUNCHY-TONED HARMONICAS OVERBLOWN INTO HANDHELD MICROPHONES TO THE POINT OF DISTORTION, UPTEMPO SHUFFLE DRUMMERS, INSISTENTLY WALKING BASS PLAYERS AND DECLAMATORY, SOULFUL VOCALISTS WHO IMBUED THE TUNES WITH SOUTHERN GOSPEL FERVOUR.

IT became a universally recognized sound by the 1960s, fuelling the British blues movement in the early part of the decade (spearheaded by Alex Korner, Cyril Davies, John Mayall and the Rolling Stones) and the American blues boom of the late 1960s (spearheaded by blues rock pioneers such as Paul Butterfield, Michael Bloomfield, Elvin Bishop and Johnny Winter, and bands such as the Blues Project and Canned Heat).

Urban And Amplified

Just as a generation of New Orleans jazz musicians had migrated from the source of the music to Chicago in the 1920s, a generation of Mississippi bluesmen migrated from the fertile Mississippi Delta region to Chicago in the 1940s. Mississippians such as Sunnyland Slim, Bukka White, Robert Nighthawk, Arthur "Big Boy" Crudup, Muddy Waters, Otis Spann, Otis Rush, Homesick James, Johnny Young, Eddie Taylor, Jimmy Reed and Hound Dog Taylor were among the Delta blues musicians who came north to the Windy City, where they helped forge an urban, amplified take on the Delta sound. A second wave, including Howlin' Wolf, Hubert Sumlin, Elmore James, Sonny Boy Williamson II, Buddy Guy, Pinetop Perkins, Big Walter "Shakey" Horton, James Cotton, Magic Sam, Magic Slim, David Honeyboy Edwards and Carey Bell, followed that same path north in the early 1950s, contributing to the post–war Chicago blues explosion.

By the 1960s, Chicago's south side was a bustling hub of blues activity. Bands led by Muddy

Above
Elmore James took the Delta blues and brought it closer to rock'n'roll.

"MUDDY WATERS, HOWLIN' WOLF AND ELMORE JAMES WERE ALREADY SEEMING "OLD", BUT THEIR DYNAMISM, THEIR FIERCE SHOUTING … EXPRESSED THE SWELLING ANGER OF THE YOUNGER BLACKS."
Paul Oliver

LEADING EXPONENTS

Muddy Waters
Howlin' Wolf
Big Walter Horton
Little Walter Jacobs
Elmore James
Willie Dixon
James Cotton
Jimmy Reed
Buddy Guy
Junior Wells
Hound Dog Taylor
Hubert Sumlin
Magic Sam
Otis Rush

CHICAGO BLUES

In Chicago Blues the emphasis is on lead and rhythm playing, rather than finger-style playing. Electric guitars expand on the traditional blues sound , with scales enhanced by a wide variety of string bends and vibrato.

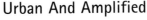

THE BLUES INTRO ➡ 160   BLUES PEOPLE A–Z ➡ 204   INSTRUMENTS A–Z ➡ 436   BLUES: DELTA BLUES ➡ 159   THE GOSPEL INTRO ➡ 384

Waters, James Cotton, Otis Rush, Homesick James, J. B. Hutto, Otis Spann, Junior Wells and Howlin' Wolf performed regularly at South Side nightclubs such as Peppers Lounge, Turner's Blue Lounge, Theresa's, the J&C Lounge and Curley's. A significant recording from 1965 documented this vital scene and helped spread the word about lesser-known Chicago blues artists to a much wider audience. Produced by Samuel Charters for the Vanguard label, the three-volume *Chicago/The Blues/Today!* became the Rosetta Stone for many young blues initiates. As Eric Clapton recalled: "It was a very important slice of history which helped me to understand the nature of modern blues music."

The acknowledged father of the Chicago blues scene was McKinley Morganfield (aka Muddy Waters). A product of the fertile Mississippi Delta, he grew up in Clarksdale on Stovall's plantation, where he emulated the passionate slide-guitar

stylings of Delta patriarch Son House. In 1941, the musicologist Alan Lomax made important field recordings of Waters at Stovall's under the auspices of the Library of Congress, documenting for all time the intensity and unfettered expression of the Mississippi Delta bluesman. Two years later, Waters moved to Chicago, where he sharpened his slide-guitar skills. He took up with the pianist Sunnyland Slim, who played a large role in launching Muddy's career by inviting him to provide guitar accompaniment for his 1947 Aristocrat session. That same day in the studio, Waters cut his own first recordings for Aristocrat. A year later, he had his first national hit with the 78 'I Can't Be Satisfied' backed with 'I Feel Like Going Home'.

Waters enjoyed a string of chart-toppers throughout the 1950s, backed by a tight band of superior musicians that included harmonica ace Little Walter, guitarist Jimmy Rogers and pianist Otis Spann. His supremacy continued through the first half of the 1960s, until the emerging psychedelic rock movement rendered his old-school Chicago sound passé. After a relatively low profile in the 1970s, Muddy's recording career was resuscitated in the later part of the decade by his disciple Johnny Winter, who produced a triumphant triumvirate of hard-hitting Chicago blues albums announcing the great man's comeback.

A Thriving Blues Centre

Other important players on the Chicago blues scene include Elmore James, the most influential slide guitarist of the post-war period; Little Walter (Marion Walter Jacobs), the king of amplified blues harp and a key man in Muddy Waters' powerful band of the late-1940s and 1950s; harmonica ace Junior Wells, who replaced Little Walter in Waters' band and later formed a potent partnership with the guitarist Buddy Guy; and Howlin' Wolf (aka Chester Arthur Burnett), who migrated to Chicago from Mississippi in 1953 and would be challenging Muddy Waters' blues supremacy in the Windy City by 1958.

No summary of Chicago blues can be written without mentioning the ubiquitous session bassist-producer and Chess Records songwriter Willie Dixon, who penned numerous hits for Muddy Waters, Howlin' Wolf, Little Walter, Bo Diddley and Koko Taylor among others. His most famous tunes, including 'Hoochie Coochie Man', 'Evil', 'My Babe', 'Wang Dang Doodle' and 'Spoonful', are staples of the blues repertoire, having been covered countless times by rock and blues bands.

Chicago remains a thriving blues centre, boasting several vibrant nightclubs on the city's south and west sides, as well as two important blues labels in Alligator Records and Delmark. The city also hosts an annual, free summer blues festival in Grant Park, which draws fans from around the world.

Piedmont Blues (East Coast Blues)

WHILE THE MISSISSIPPI DELTA GAVE BIRTH TO GUITAR-BASED ACOUSTIC BLUES, IN THE AREA KNOWN AS THE PIEDMONT REGION – WHICH STRETCHES ALONG THE ATLANTIC SEABOARD FROM VIRGINIA TO FLORIDA – A WIDE RANGE OF BLUES STYLES FLOURISHED. FROM THE BACKWOODS SOUND OF THE APPALACHIAN FOOTHILLS OF VIRGINIA TO THE MORE URBANE SOUND OF BIG CITIES SUCH AS ATLANTA.

THE characteristic that these varying Piedmont styles have in common, distinguishing them from the Delta blues style, is an emphasis on a sophisticated, syncopated kind of rhythm playing, with a complex fingerstyle technique that closely emulated a pianistic or ragtime approach on the guitar. Some of the earliest and most famous practitioners of the Piedmont style include three virtuosic sightless players: Blind Blake

(whose signature ragtime guitar piece 'Diddie Wah Diddie' was covered nearly 50 years later by Leon Redbone), Blind Boy Fuller (famed for 'Step It Up And Go' and 'Rag Mama Rag') and the formidable 12-string dazzler Blind Willie McTell (whose 'Broke Down Engine' was covered in the 1960s by blues guitar star Johnny Winter and whose 'Statesboro Blues' is still being performed as a blues-rock anthem to this day by the Allman Brothers Band). Other Piedmont pioneers included Curley Weaver and Robert "Barbecue Bob" Hicks, both of whom recorded in the late 1920s.

In the late-1950s, a folk revival swept college campuses from coast to coast, helping to revive the careers of many Piedmont bluesmen. Pink Anderson, John Jackson, Etta Baker and the duo of harmonica ace Sonny Terry and guitarist Brownie McGhee were rediscovered and soon performing on college campuses and in coffee houses. Budding folk artists such as Bob Dylan, Taj Mahal, Joan Baez and Bonnie Raitt championed the cause of Rev. Gary Davis, while Ry Cooder, David Bromberg and Jorma Kaukonen studied with him.

A Uniquely American Artist

Also a blind artist and strictly self-taught on guitar, Davis developed remarkably quickly and, by his twenties, had an advanced technique that was unmatched in the blues field. Davis recorded for the first time in the early 1930s and became an ordained minister in 1937. An appearance at the 1958 Newport Folk Festival helped bring greater attention to Davis, leading to his becoming one of the most popular figures of the folk and blues revival scenes. Some of his signature tunes include 'Cocaine Blues', 'Samson and Delilah', 'Twelve Gates to the City' and 'Lovin' Spoonful'.

One of the most outstanding exponents of the Piedmont style today is the Washington DC based duo of guitarist John Cephas and harmonica player Phil Wiggins.

> "...EMPHASIS ON GOOD EXECUTION, RHYTHM ICALLY FREE-FLOWING, LIGHTER IN TEXTURE... IT HAD A DISTINCT FLAVOUR WHICH MINGLED WITH THAT OF THE HILLBILLY AND MOUNTAIN SINGERS OF THE WHITE RURAL TRADITION."
>
> *Paul Oliver*

Above

Brownie McGhee's smooth sound contrasted perfectly with the rough harmonica style of Sonny Terry.

Left

Joan Baez's admiration of Rev. Gary Davis was presumably mutual, judging by the poster on his wall. Davis's musical experimentations showed him to be musically ahead of his time.

Drms.

Bass

E⁷ A⁷ E⁷ E⁷

PIEDMONT BLUES

In this extract the bass plays a one bar riff. The rhythm is closely followed by the drums, giving a solid base for the soloist.

LEADING EXPONENTS

Blind Blake

Blind Boy Fuller

Blind Willie McTell

Rev. Gary Davis

Sonny Terry

Brownie McGhee

Jump Blues

INFECTIOUSLY SWINGING, FULL OF GOOD HUMOUR AND HUGELY POPULAR FOR ITS TIME, THE JUMP BLUES MOVEMENT OF THE PRE- AND-POST-SECOND WORLD WAR YEARS WAS A PRECURSOR TO THE BIRTH OF BOTH R&B AND ROCK'N'ROLL.

Above

A Clarksdale juke joint in 1939. Blacks went to juke joints to drink and dance and it was in these venues that jump blues gained popularity, due to its raucous, danceable, feel-good sound.

KANSAS City was an incubator for jump blues in the late 1930s, via the infectious, rolling rhythms of Walter Page's Blue Devils and the Bennie Moten and Count Basie bands. But in the years following America's involvement in the Second World War, Los Angeles became a major breeding ground for a west coast branch of this new sound, characterized by shuffling uptempo rhythms, raucously upbeat spirits, honking tenor saxophones and swaggering vocalists who shouted about partying, drinking and good times. It was there, in the clubs that lined Central Avenue in Los Angeles, that a bevy of saxophonists dubbed "honkers" for their piercing, squealy tones and frantic showmanship helped to define the scene. Among them were Big Jay McNeely, Chuck Higgins and Joe Houston, all players influenced by Illinois Jacquet's rambunctious tenor soloing on Lionel Hampton's huge 1942 hit, 'Flying Home'.

Setting The Pattern

The undisputed heavyweight champion of the jump blues movement was Louis Jordan, who with his Tympany Five came to personify the spirit of the times with his theme song 'Let The Good Times Roll'. From 1941 to 1952, Jordan reigned as the "King of Jukeboxes", with a string of catchy, uptempo boogie-woogie influenced hits like 'Caldonia', 'Choo Choo Ch'Boogie', 'Ain't Nobody Here But Us Chickens', 'Five Guys Named Mo' and 'Saturday Night Fish Fry'. Jordan's infectious rhythms, aggressive alto sax playing and dynamic stage presence set the pattern for jump blues.

> "LOUIS JORDAN WAS A GREAT MUSICIAN AND, IN MY OPINION, HE WAS WAY AHEAD OF HIS TIME."
>
> *B. B. King*

Many of the most popular west coast performers who followed in the wake of Jordan's success based themselves in Los Angeles during the 1940s but originally hailed from Texas. Chief among them were pianist-singer Charles Brown, whose ultra-mellow style made a big impact in 1945 with 'Driftin' Blues' and again in 1947 with the Yuletide classic 'Merry Christmas Baby' (both cut with Johnny Moore's Three Blazers) and the pioneering electric guitarist T-Bone Walker, whose inherent soulfulness and jazzy dexterity on the instrument would influence generations of bluesmen from B. B. King, Lowell Fulson and Pee Wee Crayton to proto-rocker Chuck Berry and blues rock pioneers like Duane Allman, Johnny Winter and Eric Clapton.

Pioneer Spirit

Walker arrived in Los Angeles in 1934 and by 1939 was singing in Les Hite's popular Cotton Club Orchestra. After striking out on his own in 1941, he signed with Capitol Records and cut 'Mean Old World' backed with 'I Got A Break Baby' for the fledgling label. The momentum of his

LEADING EXPONENTS

Louis Jordan

T-Bone Walker

Roy Milton

Jimmy Liggins

Joe Liggins

Pee Wee Crayton

Johnny Otis

Wynonie Harris

Big Joe Turner

Roy Brown

Charles Brown

JUMP BLUES

In jump blues the piano is used to reinforce the rhythm. The left hand plays a broken chord while the right plays off beat stab chords.

THE BLUES INTRO ➡ 154   BLUES PEOPLE A-Z ➡ 180   INSTRUMENTS A-Z ➡ 436   THE DANCE INTRO ➡ 310

recording career was halted by the American Federation of Musicians' recording band which lasted from 1942 to 1944. After spending two years in Chicago, Walker returned to Los Angeles in 1946 and signed with Black & White Records. His third session for the label, the anthemic 'Call It Stormy Monday', became an immediate and huge hit in 1947, leading to a string of other successful recordings like 'T-Bone Shuffle' and 'West Side Baby'. Walker's success directly inspired guitarist Pee Wee Crayton, another transplanted Texan who relocated to Los Angeles, signed with the Bihari brothers in 1948 and hit big with 'Blues After Hours'.

Another successful bandleader on the west coast blues scene was drummer/singer Roy Milton, who followed both Jordan's and Walker's example with his Solid Senders, a lively jump blues small combo. Milton's steady backbeat and infectious, Jo Jones-styled ebullience behind the kit provided the kinetic pulse behind such mid-1940s hits as 'R. M. Blues', 'Milton's Boogie' and 'Hop, Skip, Jump'. By late 1947, at the peak of the west coast blues boom, Roy Milton & his Solid Senders became the number two jump blues band in the land, second only to Louis Jordan & his Tympany Five. Camille Howard, an outstanding boogie-woogie pianist, was the group's secret weapon and was heavily featured in the band throughout the Specialty label years, which ended in 1954.

The Liggins Brothers

Two other key figures on the west coast blues scene were brothers Joe and Jimmy Liggins. In 1945, pianist-bandleader Joe Liggins had a two-million-seller hit with 'The Honeydripper'. After joining Specialty in 1950, he hit big again with 'Pink Champagne', which became his signature song and was promptly covered by both Tommy Dorsey and Lionel Hampton. Jimmy's younger and more frantic brother Joe (who was originally the bus driver for the Honeydrippers), jumped into the recording business himself after signing with Specialty in 1947, and scored a hit the following year with 'Cadillac Boogie'. After leaving Specialty in 1953, he cut some sessions for Aladdin that anticipated the coming rock'n'roll movement, including the rousing novelty number 'I Ain't Drunk' (later covered by Texas blues guitarist Albert Collins). Joe's wild stage presence and manic delivery also had a direct and lasting impact on rock'n'rollers like Little Richard, Chuck Berry, Bill Haley and Elvis Presley.

Another key figure on the west coast blues scene was bandleader, producer and talent scout Johnny Otis. By 1947, with the decline of the big bands, Otis downsized his larger ensemble to a septet, patterning his new band after the wildly successful examples of Louis Jordan & his Tympany Five and Roy Milton & his Solid Senders. In 1958 he scored a hit with 'Willie and the Hand Jive' and in 1972 formed the Blues Spectrum label to document many of the living jump blues legends of the day like Big Joe Turner, Roy Milton, Roy Brown and Pee Wee Crayton.

Above

This image of Big Jay McNeely really sums up the spirit of jump blues – the raw, dirty sound of the sax, the performer putting every-thing into the swinging soul of the music and, above all, the audience going wild.

Left

The jump king Louis Jordan (centre) with his band. Jordan helped bring about the musical transition from big band swing and early R&B to the rock'n'roll sound of artists like Little Richard.

British Blues

BRITISH BLUES WAS BORN WHEN BRITISH MUSICIANS ATTEMPTED TO EMULATE MISSISSIPPI AND CHICAGO BLUESMEN DURING THE 1960S. LED BY ERIC CLAPTON AND THE ROLLING STONES, THESE MUSICIANS COPIED THE STYLES OF BIG BILL BROONZY, MUDDY WATERS, HOWLIN' WOLF AND B. B. KING. AND, AIDED BY POWERFUL AMPLIFIERS, DEVELOPED A SOUND OF THEIR OWN.

Above

On this album the inclusion of Eric Clapton, fresh from the Yardbirds, helped British blues to reach a wider audience. Clapton's incredible guitar work on the record inspired "Clapton Is God" graffiti across London.

IN the early 1950s, the first American blues musician to appear in England was Big Bill Broonzy. Although he was a popular, Chicago-style bluesman, his UK performances consisted of acoustic folk blues and protest songs. It was Muddy Waters' visit to the country in 1958 that really sparked off the beginning of the British blues movement. Muddy played with an electric, solid-body Fender guitar, backed by Chris Barber's English blues group featuring guitarist Alexis Korner and blues harpist Cyril Davies. They played at a volume that shocked folk purists, but delighted a growing younger audience.

Inspiration For A New Generation

After Muddy's tour, Korner and Davies pursued their musical ambitions even more passionately and formed Blues Incorporated, the first of the British blues bands. By 1962, the group had a regular slot at London's Marquee Club and a recording contract with Decca. Blues Incorporated inspired a younger generation of musicians, who then formed the three most influential British blues bands: John Mayall's Bluesbreakers featuring Eric Clapton, the Rolling Stones and the original Fleetwood Mac, with Peter Green. Clapton was a phenomenon with the Bluesbreakers – he turned his amp up to gig volume for recordings and obtained a more modern electric sound

> "I SPENT MOST OF MY TEENS AND EARLY TWENTIES STUDYING THE BLUES – THE GEOGRAPHY OF IT AND THE CHRONOLOGY OF IT, AS WELL AS HOW TO PLAY IT."
>
> *Eric Clapton*

Right

Alexis Korner was the main man behind the 1960s British blues scene.

that influenced the likes of Jimi Hendrix and also Jimmy Page, who went on to form Led Zeppelin.

Sex, Drugs And Rock'n'Roll

The Rolling Stones were perceived to be the definitive British blues band. They made a stream of hit records during the mid-1960s, including a chart-topping version of Willie Dixon's 'Little Red Rooster' (1964). They also covered songs by Muddy Waters and Howlin' Wolf, even insisting that Howlin' was a featured guest at a special US appearance. Their legendary "sex, drugs and rock'n'roll" lifestyle contrasted sharply with the Beatles' squeaky-clean image during the 1960s.

By 1966, British blues was in full flight: the legendary *John Mayall's Bluesbreakers With Eric Clapton* album was released that year; bands such as Fleetwood Mac, the Yardbirds (with Jeff Beck) and Ten Years After (with Alvin Lee) were forming, and the Animals started to develop their inimitable brand of blues pop. By the end of the decade, the British blues movement was carried back across to the United States, where it was reabsorbed by larger audiences than the original Chicago and Mississippi bluesmen had enjoyed. The success of the British blues bands also encouraged early American blues rock bands such as the Allman Brothers and ZZ Top, who had already developed their own unique styles.

Although British blues is now seen by many as an early step in the conversion of blues into rock and heavy metal, it was a distinct style in its own right. Even today, musicians such as John Mayall, Eric Clapton and Aynsley Lister are waving the British blues flag.

LEADING EXPONENTS

John Mayall's
  Bluesbreakers
The Rolling Stones
Blues Incorporated
Eric Clapton
Cyril Davies
Peter Green
Alexis Korner
Ten Years After
The Yardbirds

BRITISH BLUES

In British blues the rhythm guitar provides the structure and melody, keeping the beat solid and sound continuous, with electric virtuosos over the top.

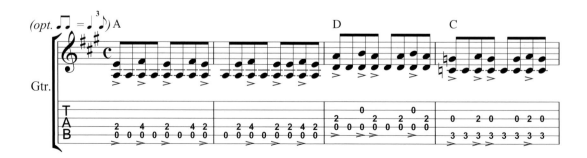

THE BLUES INTRO ➡ 154   BLUES PEOPLE A–Z ➡ 180   INSTRUMENTS A–Z ➡ 436   BLUES: DELTA BLUES ➡ 159   BLUES: CHICAGO BLUES ➡ 404

Rhythm & Blues

RHYTHM & BLUES (R&B) MUSIC EVOLVED OUT OF JUMP BLUES RHYTHMS DURING THE LATE-1940S, BUT IT ALSO HAD RIFFS AND LYRICS THAT WERE BEGINNING TO POINT MORE TOWARDS THE EMERGENCE OF ROCK'N'ROLL. USING SPARSER INSTRUMENTATION THAN JUMP BLUES, R&B WAS BASED UPON TRADITIONAL BLUES CHORD CHANGES PLAYED OVER A STEADY BACKBEAT.

R&B placed more emphasis on the singer and the song than on the band's instrumentalists. Although it branched out into rock'n'roll during the 1950s, and soul during the 1960s, it always retained its own following, and R&B artists continue to draw large audiences all over the world.

Legendary R&B Singers

As rock'n'roll continued to emerge, R&B branched out into further distinct styles, including doo wop, electric blues and New Orleans. Each of these exerted its influence on other R&B forms, as well as popular music in general.

During the late 1940s and early 1950s, a number of great singers began to emerge from the R&B scene. Ruth Brown was perhaps the first of these. Initially inspired by jazz singers such as Sarah Vaughan, Billie Holiday and Dinah Washington, Ruth developed her own expressive tone and

was recommended to the bosses of a fledgling Atlantic Records in 1948. After she was promptly signed up, they produced a string of R&B classics, including 'So Long' (1949), 'Teardrops From My Eyes' (1950), 'I'll Wait For You' (1951), '(Mama) He Treats Your Daughter Mean' (1953) and 'Mambo Baby' (1954). She became well known as "Miss Rhythm", appeared on the TV program *Showtime At The Apollo* with Miles Davis and Thelonious Monk, and proved to be a big influence on subsequent female R&B singers.

Ray Charles was another hugely influential figure in the 1950s R&B movement, and one of the forefathers of soul music. Born Ray Charles

> ## "I WAS BORN WITH MUSIC INSIDE ME. THAT'S THE ONLY EXPLANATION I KNOW OF."
>
> *Ray Charles*

Robinson in Albany, Georgia, on 23 September 1930, and blind since the age of seven, he studied composition and learned to play a number of musical instruments at the St. Augustine School for the Deaf and the Blind in Florida. He drew from gospel and Southern blues music to develop a unique singing and songwriting style, which encouraged Atlantic Records to sign him up in 1953.

Above
Clyde McPhatter's compelling vocals combined blues and gospel influences, giving a stunning, emotionally charged tenor voice that served as a forerunner to the 1960s and 1970s soul sounds.

Left
Owing to the seemingly endless string of hits enjoyed by Ruth Brown on Atlantic Records, the then fledgling label came to be known as "The House That Ruth Built".

Pno.

RHYTHM & BLUES
Gospel vocals combined with blues piano riffs, and the frequent inclusion of elements of country produce the archetypal rhythm & blues sound.

LEADING EXPONENTS
Ray Charles
Ruth Brown
Clyde McPhatter
Johnny "Guitar" Watson
Bo Diddley

THE BLUES INTRO ➡ 154   BLUES PEOPLE A–Z ➡ 180   INSTRUMENTS A–Z ➡ 436   THE ROCK INTRO ➡ 74   BLUES: JUMP BLUES ➡ 170

Lebanon Singers in New York, Clyde switched over to R&B when he joined the Dominoes in 1950. They signed to Syd Nathan's King label and recorded 'Sixty Minute Man' (1951), the biggest R&B hit of the year and, according to some, the earliest identifiable example of a rock'n'roll song. He quit the Dominoes in early 1953 and formed his own band, the Drifters, the same year. They recorded 'Money Honey' (1954) and several other big R&B hits for Atlantic Records during the mid-1950s and McPhatter's extremely versatile tenor voice proved capable of handling both sensitive ballads and raucous rock'n'roll. He left the band for a solo career and released several other hits during the late-1950s, but he had less success in the following decade and, undeservedly, faded into obscurity. Other notable R&B singers from the 1950s included Jackie Wilson and James Brown, who both became soul superstars during the 1960s.

R&B Guitar Icons

Other R&B artists, such as Bo Diddley and Johnny "Guitar" Watson, were associated with their instruments as much as their singing. Diddley developed an unorthodox, "hambone" rhythm guitar style, which he played on a trademark rectangular guitar. Perhaps his most famous hit was the two-sided 'Bo Diddley'/'I'm A Man' (1955), which he recorded for Chess records. Watson grew up listening to bluesmen T-Bone Walker and Clarence "Gatemouth" Brown and developed a biting, high-treble guitar tone, which he used to strong effect on albums such as *Gangster Of Love* (1958) and *Johnny Guitar Watson* (1963). An eccentric performer, he was reputed to have played the guitar standing upside-down, using a 46m (150 ft) cord so he could get on top of the auditorium with his instrument. "Those things Jimi Hendrix was doing; I started that shit!" he said to a music journalist.

Above

Although undoubtedly a key influence in R&B, Ray Charles has successfully turned his hand to a number of musical styles, including blues, gospel, pop, country, jazz, and early rock'n'roll.

Above right

A plectrum, as used by Bo Diddley to create his distinctive, percussive guitar sound.

Charles and Atlantic hit the jackpot: 'I Got A Woman' was a number two R&B hit in 1955, and Charles followed it with a string of other chart-toppers, combining his unmistakably soulful vocal delivery with R&B rhythms. Ray influenced countless R&B singers and became one of the first soul superstars in the 1960s. He later worked with many popular artists, including Aretha Franklin and Michael Jackson.

Another important name in early R&B music is Clyde McPhatter. Originally a gospel singer with the Mount

Although R&B branched off into a number of different music styles between the 1950s and 1970s, countless blues and soul stars have released R&B hits over the past 40 years. Recent R&B revival artists, such as Big Boy Bloater & his Southside Stompers, continue to ensure that the genre is very much alive.

Blues Rock

BLUES ROCK GREW OUT OF THE BRITISH BLUES MOVEMENT THAT STARTED DURING THE LATE-1950S, WHICH WAS IN TURN DEVELOPED IN THE 1960S. THE BRITS USED MORE POWERFUL AMPLIFICATION THAN THEIR AMERICAN COUNTERPARTS, RESULTING IN A HARDER, MORE IMPOSING SOUND. JIMI HENDRIX, LED ZEPPELIN AND OTHER ARTISTS DEVELOPED THIS INTO A RIFF-ORIENTED ROCK STYLE.

AMONG the earliest blues rock bands were Cream, the Paul Butterfield Blues Band and Canned Heat. Cream were formed when Ginger Baker, drummer with the Graham Bond Organisation, decided to start his own band with guitarist Eric Clapton and bassist Jack Bruce. "Things were going badly with Graham", Baker told music journalist Chris Welch, "so I decided to get my own thing together. I was unaware that Eric had such a huge following. I just dug his playing, so I went to a Bluesbreakers gig in Oxford. In the interval Eric asked if I'd play a number with them, and it really took off! So I told him I was getting a band together and was wondering if he'd be interested. He said that he was and recommended Jack as the bass player."

As all three band members were well known around the British blues circuit when they formed, each with a reputation for being a virtuoso on his respective instrument,

Cream was, effectively, the first "supergroup". They were louder and more riff-oriented than previous blues-influenced bands, and their style incorporated extended solos – a regular feature for subsequent blues rockers. Despite only lasting for three years, Cream's first three albums, *Fresh Cream* (1966), *Disraeli Gears* (1967) and *Wheels Of Fire* (1967), are widely accepted as both blues rock classics and milestones in the birth of rock music. Influential American bands had also developed blues rock styles by the late 1960s: the Paul Butterfield Blues Band, with Mike Bloomfield and Elvin Bishop on guitars, and Canned Heat, a white blues band formed by singer Bob "The Bear" Hite and harmonica player Alan "Blind Owl" Wilson, were the most notable of these.

Above
Jeff Beck's Guitar Shop, *released in 1989, is a showcase for Beck's incredible guitar skills.*

A Dazzling Showman

Another key figure in the transition from blues to rock was the legendary Jimi Hendrix. Born Johnny Allen Hendrix in Seattle on 27 November 1942, he later changed his name to James (Jimi) Marshall Hendrix. Influenced by legendary bluesmen such as Robert Johnson and B. B. King as a schoolboy, he taught himself to play guitar before working with musicians such as Little Richard in the early 1960s. His break came when Chas Chandler, the bassist with the Animals, heard him play in

"I HAD A LES PAUL BEFORE ERIC BUT I DIDN'T HAVE A MARSHALL. AND WHEN ERIC GOT ALL OF THAT TOGETHER HE WAS A DELIGHT TO LISTEN TO. HE REALLY UNDERSTOOD THE BLUES."
Jimmy Page

Left
The brilliant Cream fused blues and rock.

LEADING EXPONENTS
Cream
The Paul Butterfield
  Blues Band
Canned Heat
Jimi Hendrix
The Rolling Stones
Led Zeppelin
The Allman Brothers
  Band
Free
Carlos Santana
Rory Gallagher

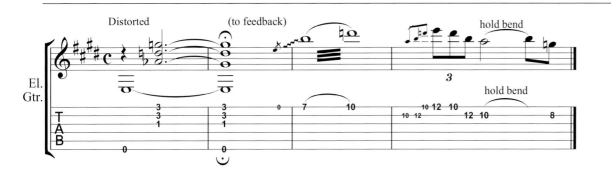

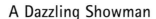

BLUES ROCK
Sliding the fingers from one note to another, instead of lifting the fingers off the strings, creates the blues sound, characteristic of blues rock. A freeform rhythm and performances embellished by long improvizations add to the sound.

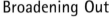

New York's Greenwich Village. Chas persuaded him to move over to London, where the Jimi Hendrix Experience was formed, with Jimi on guitar, Noel Redding on bass and Mitch Mitchell on drums.

Jimi was a dazzling showman, playing the guitar behind his head and with his teeth, but it was his extraordinary soloing and mastery of controlled feedback that set a new standard in electric blues lead guitar playing. His best albums, *Are You Experienced?* (1967), *Axis: Bold As Love* (1968) and *Electric Ladyland* (1968), demonstrate that something seriously interesting was happening to the blues by the late-1960s. Although he tragically died in 1970, Jimi was to influence countless blues and rock players for many years to come.

Broadening Out

By the end of the 1960s, blues rock began to diversify into heavy metal in the UK and southern blues rock in the US. Led Zeppelin was, perhaps, the first band to be described as heavy metal, but the group's blues roots are apparent in all of its recordings, including the hugely popular *Led Zeppelin II* (1969) and *Led Zeppelin IV* (1971) albums. The band's guitarist, Jimmy Page, grew up listening to blues and rock'n'roll recordings, but one of his biggest influences was hearing Eric Clapton's Gibson Les Paul guitar through a cranked-up Marshall amp at a Bluesbreakers gig. "I had a Les Paul before Eric but I didn't have a Marshall," Page recalled. "And when Eric got all of that together he was a delight to listen to. He really understood the blues."

Meanwhile, in the States, the Allman Brothers Band was fusing electric blues with country and folk elements, to form what is now known as "southern rock". Albums such as *The Allman Brothers Band* (1969), *Idlewild South* (1970) and *Live At The Fillmore East* (1971) paved the way for a whole family of southern rock bands, including Lynyrd Skynyrd and Black Oak Arkansas. ZZ Top, a trio from Texas, also emerged out of the blues rock

scene. Led by the bearded Billy Gibbons (guitar, vocals) and Dusty Hill (bass, vocals), the trio developed their own style of boogie-style blues rock, which became hugely popular in the 1970s and 1980s.

Meanwhile, over in the UK, the group Free inspired generations of British blues rockers with major hits like 'All Right Now' (1970) and 'Wishing Well' (1973). Many other notable blues rock artists have since appeared on both sides of the Atlantic, including Bernard Allison, Bonnie Raitt, Walter Trout, Dave Hole and Ronnie Earl.

Modern Electric Blues

ALTHOUGH THE FIRST GENERATIONS OF ELECTRIC BLUESMEN PLAYED LOUDER AND MORE FLAMBOYANTLY THAN THEIR ACOUSTIC FOREFATHERS, THEIR MUSIC WAS STILL TRADITIONAL IN ITS DELIVERY AND STRUCTURE. THE BRITISH BLUES PLAYERS WHO EMULATED THEM DURING THE 1960S WERE ALSO FAIRLY TRADITIONAL IN THEIR APPROACH TO THE GENRE.

JIMI Hendrix opened things up a bit more when he first appeared on the scene in 1967, but the musicians he in turn influenced tended to lean towards the rock side of the musical spectrum.

Another group of electric bluesmen also began to emerge during the late-1960s and early 1970s – guitar players such as Roy Buchanan and Johnny Winter, who had taken on board the new sounds of rock but were steeped in the traditions of the blues.

"STEVIE RAY VAUGHAN IS THE BEST FRIEND I'VE EVER HAD, THE BEST GUITARIST I EVER HEARD AND THE BEST PERSON ANYONE WILL EVER WANT TO KNOW."

Buddy Guy

Above

Robert Cray was largely responsible for the 1980s blues guitar revival and his versatile playing style ensured a wide crossover success. He even had videos played on MTV, which was unheard of for a blues artist.

Blues Got Them Early

The son of a Pentecostal preacher, Roy Buchanan grew up in California and, as a teenager, joined Dale Hawkins' band in 1958. After a stint as a session player in the 1960s, he decided to try his luck as a solo artist with *Roy Buchanan* (1972), an accomplished album highlighting his distinctive, treble-sounding Fender Telecaster tone. He was asked to join the Rolling Stones after Brian Jones died but, surprisingly, he turned the offer down. His career, like that of many other blues musicians, was plagued by booze and drug problems, and, after a number of unsuccessful suicide attempts, he hung himself in a police cell in 1988.

LEADING EXPONENTS	MODERN ELECTRIC BLUES
Stevie Ray Vaughan	*Refinements in guitar*
Robben Ford	*and amplification technology*
Roy Buchanan	*have helped the development*
Johnny Winter	*of blues playing by enabling*
Robert Cray	*a 'wailing' guitar sound, in*
Jimmie Vaughan	*which the very highest notes can be sustained.*

THE BLUES INTRO ➡ 154   BLUES PEOPLE A-Z ➡ 180   INSTRUMENTS A-Z ➡ 436   BLUES: DELTA BLUES ➡ 159   BLUES: CHICAGO BLUES ➡ 167

Johnny Winter, an albino bluesman who grew up in Texas, also began playing and singing the blues early in life; he cut his first record at the age of 15, and produced a demonstration disc known as *The Progressive Blues Experiment* in 1968. An excellent review in *Rolling Stone* magazine led to lucrative management and recording deals. His first proper album, *Johnny Winter* (1969), established his standing as an outstanding performer with an exceptionally dexterous guitar style and paved the way for more than 20 further, critically acclaimed Winter blues albums.

Blues Fusions

Robben Ford is another great blues artist who emerged during the early 1970s. He also showed a mastery of jazz, unlike most blues guitar players, and his music developed into a compelling blend of the two styles. Inspired by Eric Clapton and Mike Bloomfield, Robben learned blues guitar during the 1960s and performed with Charlie Musselwhite in 1970. He also toured and recorded with George Harrison and Joni Mitchell in the mid-1970s and with Miles Davis in the 1980s. His *Talk To Your Daughter* album (1988) was nominated for a Grammy, while later, *Robben Ford And The Blue Line* (1992) won considerable acclaim for its original, earthy approach to the blues. Robben's soloing is more sophisticated than that of most other blues players and his chord progressions are often laced with rich jazz harmonies.

Another musician who effortlessly fused jazz with the blues is the Connecticut-born John Scofield. Although John spent many of his early years studying the work of jazz and fusion players such as Jim Hall and John McLaughlin, his *Still Warm* (1986) and *Blue Matter* (1987) albums are full of original, angular blues-style licks.

The two blues giants of the 1980s were undoubtedly Robert Cray, from Georgia, and Stevie Ray Vaughan, from Texas. Cray formed his first band in 1974, but did not really hit the big time until his *Bad Influence* album was released to critical and commercial acclaim in 1983. A mainstream fusion of blues, soul and rock, his style was particularly popular throughout the 1980s, introducing a wider pop audience to the blues. He was invited to play with Eric Clapton during the ex-Bluesbreaker's famous series of concerts at London's Albert Hall in 1989.

A Recent Legend

Stevie Ray Vaughan was heavily influenced by his older brother, Jimmie Vaughan (of the Fabulous Thunderbirds), as well as by Albert King and Hendrix. He played in various local bands in Austin, Texas before forming Double Trouble (named after an Otis Rush song), with bassist Tommy Shannon and drummer Chris "Whipper" Layton. In 1982 the ensemble played at the Montreux Jazz Festival, where Vaughan's stunning, high-energy blues style was noted by David Bowie, who poached him for his *Let's Dance* album (1983). The same year, Double Trouble also recorded *Texas Flood* with the legendary blues producer John Hammond, to critical and commercial acclaim. The second Double Trouble album, the Hendrix-influenced *Couldn't Stand The Weather* (1984), was an even bigger success – it went platinum.

Vaughan battled with alcohol and drug problems during the mid-1980s, and was admitted to a rehabilitation centre in Georgia, but he straightened out to make the Grammy-winning *In Step* (1989). Tragically, he died in a helicopter accident in 1990, after playing at an Eric Clapton concert in Milwaukee. As with Hendrix, Vaughan's reputation has grown since his death, with recent guitar magazine reader polls indicating that he is one of the most popular blues artists of all time.

Thanks to players such as Vaughan and Ford, modern electric blues evolved during the 1980s and 1990s and, like every current musical style, continues to do so. Players including Walter Trout, Susan Tedeschi, Dave Hole, Tinsley Ellis and Bernard Allison continue to delight audiences.

Left

Robben Ford started out as a saxophonist and it was his love for this instrument – and its masters, such as John Coltrane and Wayne Shorter – that helped to shape his unique jazz-tinged blues guitar sound.

Below

Stevie Ray Vaughan's amazing guitar technique and understanding of the blues won him two W. C. Handy National Blues Awards in 1984: Entertainer of the Year and Blues Instrumentalist of the Year. He was the first white person to win either award.

Artists: Blues

Entries appear in the following order: name, music style, year(s) of popularity, type of artist, country of origin

AB Skhy, Blues Rock, 1960s-1970s, Artist, American
Abrahams, Mick, Blues Rock; Rhythm & Blues, 1970s-1990s, Artist, British
Abshire, Nathan, Chicago Blues, 1940s-1980s, Artist, American
Ace, Johnny, Rhythm & Blues, 1950s, Artist, American
Adams, Arthur, Modern Electric Blues, 1970s-1990s, Artist, American
Adams, Faye, Piedmont Blues; Jump Blues; Rhythm & Blues, 1950s-1960s, Artist, American
Adams, Johnny, Rhythm & Blues, 1950s-1990s, Artist, American
Agee, Ray, Jump Blues, 1950s-1970s, Artist, American
Akers, Garfield, Delta/Country Blues, 1920s-1930s, Artist, American
Alabama Sheikhs, Delta/Country Blues, 1930s, Artist, American
Alexander, Arthur, Rhythm & Blues, 1960s-1970s, Artist, American
Allison, Luther, Chicago Blues; Modern Electric Blues, 1960s-1990s, Artist, American
Allison, Mose, Delta/Country Blues, 1950s-, Artist, American
Allman Brothers Band, The, Blues Rock, 1960s-, Artist, American
Allman, Duane, Blues Rock, 1960s-1970s, Artist, American
Allman, Greg, Blues Rock, 1970s-1990s, Artist, American
Ammons, Albert, Boogie-Woogie, 1920s-1940s, Artist, American
Anderson, Little Willie, Modern Electric Blues; Chicago Blues, 1970s-1980s, Artist, American
Anderson, Miller, Blues Rock, 1960s-1990s, Artist, British
Anderson, Pink, Delta/Country Blues, 1930s-1960s, Artist, American
Andrews, Ernie, Jump Blues, 1950s; 1980s-, Artist, American
Animals, The, British Blues; Blues Rock, 1960s-1980s, Artist, British
Arc Angels, The, Blues Rock, 1990s, Artist, American
Arnold, Billy Boy, Chicago Blues, 1950s-, Artist, American
Arnold, Kokomo, Chicago Blues, 1930s-1940s, Artist, American
Ashton, Gardner & Dyke, Blues Rock, 1960s-1970s, Artist, British
Austin, Sil, Piedmont Blues; Jump Blues, 1950s-1970s, Artist, American
Bacon Fat, Jump Blues, 1970s, Artist, American
Bad Company, Blues Rock, 1970s-1990s, Artist, British
Bailey, Mildred, Delta/Country Blues, 1920s-1950s, Artist, American
Baker, Edythe, Boogie-Woogie, 1920s, Artist, American
Baker, Etta, Delta/Country Blues, 1950s; 1980s-1990s, Artist, American
Baker Gurvitz Army, Blues Rock, 1970s, Artist, British
Baker, Ginger, Blues Rock, 1970s-, Artist, British
Baker, Lavern, Rhythm & Blues; Jump Blues, 1950s-1960s; 1980s-1990s, Artist, American
Baker, Mickey, Rhythm & Blues; Piedmont Blues, 1950s-1970s, Artist, American
Baldry, Long John, British Blues; Blues Rock, 1950s-, Artist, British
Ball, Marcia, Modern Electric Blues, 1970s-, Artist, American
Ballard, Hank, Rhythm & Blues, 1950s-1990s, Artist; Songwriter, American
Barbee, John Henry, Delta/Country Blues, 1930s, Artist, American
Barbeque Bob, Delta/Country Blues, 1920s-1930s, Artist, American
Barker, Blue Lu, Piedmont Blues, 1930s-1980s, Artist, American
Barnes, Roosevelt 'Booba', Modern Electric Blues, 1970s-1990s, Artist, American
Bartholomew, Dave, Rhythm & Blues, 1940s-1990s, Artist; Songwriter, American
Barton, Lou Ann, Texas Blues; Blues Rock, 1980s-, Artist, American
Basie, Count, Boogie-Woogie, 1920s-1980s, Artist, American
Bass, Ralph, Texas Blues, 1940s-1970s, Producer, American
Beale Street Sheikhs, The, Delta/Country Blues, 1920s, Artist, American
Beck, Jeff, British Blues; Blues Rock, 1960s-, Artist, British
Bedard, George, Blues Rock, 1990s, Artist, American
Bell, Carey, Modern Electric Blues; Chicago Blues, 1960s-1990s, Artist, American

Bell, Lurrie, Modern Electric Blues; Chicago Blues, 1980s-1990s, Artist, American
Bell, Maggie, Blues Rock, 1970s-1980s, Artist, British
Bell, T. D. , Texas Blues; Modern Electric Blues, 1990s, Artist, American
Bennett, Duster, British Blues; Blues Rock, 1960s-1970s, Artist, British
Benoit, Tab, Modern Electric Blues, 1990s-, Artist, American
Benton, Brook, Rhythm & Blues, 1950s-1970s, Artist, American
Benton, Buster, Modern Electric Blues; Chicago Blues, 1960s-1990s, Artist, American
Berry, Richard, Rhythm & Blues, 1950s-1960s, Artist, American
Big Brother & the Holding Company, Blues Rock, 1960s-1990s, Artist, American
Big Dave & the Ultrasonics, Blues Rock; Modern Electric Blues, 1990s, Artist, American
Big Maybelle, Piedmont Blues; Jump Blues; Rhythm & Blues, 1940s-1960s, Artist, American
Big Three Trio, The, Chicago Blues, 1940s-1950s, Artist, American

Big Time Sarah, Modern Electric Blues, 1970s-, Artist, American
Binder, Roy Book, Delta/Country Blues, 1970s-1990s, Artist, American
Bishop, Elvin, Modern Electric Blues, 1960s-, Artist, American
Bizor, Billy, Texas Blues, 1960s, Artist, American
Black Ace, Delta/Country Blues; Texas Blues, 1920s-1940s, Artist, American
Blackwell, Otis, Piedmont Blues, 1950s-1970s, Songwriter; Artist, American
Blackwell, Scrapper, Chicago Blues, 1920s-1930s; 1950s-1960s, Artist, American
Bland, Bobby Blue, Texas Blues; Rhythm & Blues, 1950s-, Artist, American
Blind Blake, Delta/Country Blues, 1920s-1930s, Artist, American
Blind Faith, Blues Rock; British Blues, 1960s, Artist, British
Blodwyn Pig, Blues Rock, 1960s-1990s, Artist, British
Bloomfield, Michael, Modern Electric Blues; Chicago Blues, 1960s-1980s, Artist, American
Blue, Little Joe, Jump Blues; Modern Electric Blues, 1950s-1980s, Artist, American
Bluebirds, The, Blues Rock, 1990s-, Artist, American
Blues Brothers, The, Rhythm & Blues, 1970s-, Artist, American
Blues Incorporated, British Blues, 1960s, Artist, British
Blues Project, The, Blues Rock, 1960s-1970s, Artist, American
Blues Traveler, Blues Rock, 1990s-, Artist, American
Bluesbusters, The, Blues Rock, 1980s, Artist, American
Bo, Eddie, Rhythm & Blues, 1950s-, Artist, American
Bogan, Lucille, Delta/Country Blues, 1920s-1930s, Artist, American
Bollin, Zuzu, Texas Blues, 1980s, Artist, American
Bond, Graham, British Blues; Blues Rock, 1960s-1970s, Artist, British
Bonds, Son, Delta/Country Blues, 1920s-1940s, Artist, American
Bonner, Juke Boy, Jump Blues; Texas Blues, 1950s-1970s, Artist, American
Boogie-Woogie Red, Boogie-Woogie, 1940s-1970s, Artist, American
Booker, James, Boogie-Woogie; Louisiana Blues, 1950s-1980s, Artist, American
Bostic, Earl, Rhythm & Blues, 1930s-1960s, Artist, American
Bourelli, Jean-Paul, Blues Rock , 1980s-, Artist, American
Box Of Frogs, Blues Rock, 1980s, Artist, British
Boyd, Eddie, Chicago Blues, 1940s-1980s, Artist; Songwriter, American
Bracey, Ishman, Delta/Country Blues, 1920s-1930s, Artist, American
Bradshaw, Tiny, Jump Blues; Rhythm & Blues, 1930s-1950s, Artist, American
Bramhall, Doyle, Texas Blues; Modern Electric Blues, 1980s-1990s, Artist, American
Bramlett, Bonnie, Blues Rock, 1970s-, Artist, American
Bramlett, Delaney, Blues Rock, 1970s, Artist, American
Brenston, Jackie, Jump Blues, Rhythm & Blues, 1940s-1960s, Artist, American
Brim, John, Chicago Blues, 1950s-1960s; 1990s, Artist, American
Brooks, Elkie, Blues Rock, 1970s-, Artist, British
Brooks, Hadda, Boogie-Woogie, 1940s-1960s, Artist, American
Brooks, Lonnie, Modern Electric Blues, 1950s-1990s, Artist, American
Broonzy, Big Bill, Delta/Country Blues; Chicago Blues, 1920s-1950s, Artist, American
Brown, Charles, Jump Blues, 1940s-1990s, Artist, American
Brown, Clarence 'Gatemouth', Texas Blues; Delta/Country Blues, 1940s-, Artist, American
Brown, James, Rhythm & Blues, 1950s-, Artist; Songwriter, American
Brown, Lee, Piedmont Blues; Boogie-Woogie, 1930s-1940s, Artist, American
Brown, Maxine, Rhythm & Blues, 1960s-1970s, Artist, American
Brown, Nappy, Jump Blues; Rhythm & Blues, 1950s-1960s; 1980s-1990s, Artist, American
Brown, Roy, Jump Blues, 1940s-1970s, Artist; Songwriter, American
Brown, Ruth, Jump Blues; Rhythm & Blues, 1940s-1960s; 1980s-1990s, Artist, American
Brown, Willie, Delta/Country Blues, 1920s-1930s, Artist, American
Brozman, Bob, Delta/Country Blues, 1980s-, Artist, American
Bruce, Jack, British Blues, 1960s-, Artist, Scottish
Buchanan, Roy, Blues Rock; Modern Electric Blues, 1970s-1980s, Artist, American
Bull City Red, Delta/Country Blues; Piedmont Blues, 1930s, Artist, American
Bumble Bee Slim, Delta/Country Blues; Jump Blues, 1930s-1950s, Artist, American
Burnside, R. L., Delta/Country Blues; Modern Electric Blues, 1960s-, Artist, American
Butler, Jerry, Rhythm & Blues, 1950s-1990s, Artist, American
Butterbeans & Susie, Delta/Country Blues, 1920s-1930s, Artist, American
Butterfield, Paul, Chicago Blues; Blues Rock, 1960s-1980s, Artist, American
Cadets, The, Rhythm & Blues, 1950s-1960s, Artist, American
Cale, J. J. , Blues Rock, 1970s-1990s, Artist; Songwriter, American
Campbell, Gene, Delta/Country Blues, 1920s-1930s, Artist, American
Canned Heat, Blues Rock; Modern Electric Blues, 1960s-, Artist, American
Cannon, Gus, Delta/Country Blues, 1920s-1960s, Artist, American
Cannon's Jug Stompers, Delta/Country Blues, 1920s-1930s, Artist, American
Captain Beefheart, Blues Rock, 1960s-1980s, Artist, American
Carr, Leroy, Boogie-Woogie, 1920s-1930s, Artist; Songwriter, American
Carr, Sister Wynona, Jump Blues; Rhythm & Blues, 1950s, Artist, American
Carter, Benny, Piedmont Blues; Jump Blues, 1920s-1990s, Artist; Composer, American
Carter, Bo, Delta/Country Blues, 1920s-1940s, Artist, American
Cephas & Wiggins, Piedmont Blues, 1980s-, Artist, American
Charles, Ray, Rhythm & Blues, 1940s-, Artist, American
Chatmon, Sam, Delta/Country Blues, 1930s-1980s, Artist, American
Chicken Shack, British Blues; Blues Rock, 1960s-1980s, Artist, British
Clapton, Eric, British Blues; Blues Rock, 1960s-, Artist; Songwriter, British
Clark, Dee, Rhythm & Blues, 1950s-1980s, Artist, American
Clark, W. C., Texas Blues; Modern Electric Blues, 1980s-1990s, Artist, American
Clarke, Mick, British Blues; Blues Rock, 1970s-, Artist, British
Clarke, William, Modern Electric Blues, 1970s-1990s, Artist, American

Clayborn, Reverend Edward, Delta/Country Blues, 1920s, Artist, American
Clearwater, Eddy, Modern Electric Blues; Rhythm & Blues; Chicago Blues, 1950s-, Artist, American
Climax Blues Band, Blues Rock, 1960s-1990s, Artist, British
Clovers, The, Rhythm & Blues, 1940s-1950s, Artist, American
Coasters, The, Rhythm & Blues, 1950s-1970s, Artist, American
Cobb, Arnett, Jump Blues, 1930s-1980s, Artist, American
Cocker, Joe, Blues Rock, 1960s-, Artist, British
Coleman, Deborah, Modern Electric Blues, 1990s-, Artist, American
Coleman, Jaybird, Delta/Country Blues, 1920s-1930s, Artist, American
Collette, Buddy, Jump Blues, 1950s-, Artist, American
Collins, Albert, Texas Blues; Modern Electric Blues, 1950s-1990s, Artist; Songwriter, American
Collins, Sam, Delta/Country Blues, 1920s-1940s, Artist, American
Cooder, Ry, Blues Rock, 1970s-1990s, Artist, American
Cooke, Sam, Rhythm & Blues, 1950s-1960s, Artist, American
Cookie & the Cupcakes, Rhythm & Blues, 1950s-1960s, Artist, American
Copeland, Johnny, Modern Electric Blues; Texas Blues, 1960s-1990s, Artist, American
Copeland, Shemekia, Modern Electric Blues, 1990s-, Artist, American
Cotton, Elizabeth, Rhythm & Blues, 1950s-1980s, Artist; Composer, American
Cotton, James, Modern Electric Blues; Chicago Blues, 1950s, Artist, American
Cox, Ida, Delta/Country Blues, 1920s-1960s, Artist, American
Cray, Robert, Modern Electric Blues, 1970s-, Artist, American
Crayton, Pee Wee, Jump Blues; Texas Blues, 1940s-1980s, Artist, American
Cream, British Blues; Blues Rock, 1960s, Artist, British
Crudup, Arthur "Big Boy", Delta/Country Blues; Rhythm & Blues, 1940s-1970s, Artist, American
Dale, Larry, Piedmont Blues; Rhythm & Blues, 1950s-1960s, Artist, American
Darby, Blind Teddy, Delta/Country Blues, 1920s-1930s, Artist, American
Davenport, Charles "Cow Cow", Boogie-Woogie, 1920s-1950s, Artist, American
Davies, Cyril, British Blues, 1960s, Artist, British
Davis, Blind John, Boogie-Woogie, 1930s-1950s, Artist, American
Davis, James, Modern Electric Blues, 1930s-1980s, Artist, American
Davis, Larry, Texas Blues, 1950s-1990s, Artist, American
Davies, Rev. Gary, Piedmont Blues, 1930s-1970s, Artist, American
Dawkins, Jimmy, Modern Electric Blues; Chicago Blues, 1960s-1990s, Artist, American
Delaney & Bonnie, Blues Rock, 1960s-1970s, Artist, American
Derek & the Dominoes, British Blues; Blues Rock, 1970s, Artist; Songwriter, American
Diddley, Bo, Rhythm & Blues; Chicago Blues, 1950s-, Artist, American
Dixon, Floyd, Jump Blues, Rhythm & Blues, 1940s-1970s; 1990s, Artist, American
Dixon, Willie Dee, Chicago Blues; Modern Electric Blues, 1990s, Artist, American
Dixon, Willie, Jump Blues; Chicago Blues, 1940s-1990s, Artist; Songwriter; Producer, American
Doctor Ross, Delta/Country Blues, 1950s-1990s, Artist, American
Domino, Fats, Louisiana Blues, 1940s-1980s, Artist, American
Dominoes, The, Rhythm & Blues, 1950s-1960s, Artist, American
Don & Dewey, Rhythm & Blues, 1950s-1960s, Artist, American
Donegan, Dorothy, Boogie-Woogie, 1940s-1990s, Artist, American
Dorsey, Georgia Tom, Delta/Country Blues, 1920s-1930s, Songwriter; Artist, American
Dorsey, Lee, Rhythm & Blues, 1960s-1980s, Artist, American
Douglas, K. C., Delta/Country Blues, 1950s-1970s, Artist, American
Dr. John, Louisiana Blues, 1960s-, Artist, American
Dranes, Arizona, Delta/Country Blues, 1920s, Artist, American
Drifters, The, Rhythm & Blues, 1950s-1990s, Artist, American
Du Droppers, The, Rhythm & Blues, 1950s, Artist, American
Duarte, Chris, Blues Rock, 1990s-, Artist, American
Dunn, Johnny, Delta/Country Blues, 1920s, Artist, American
Dupree, Champion Jack, Louisiana Blues; Rhythm & Blues, 1940s-1990s, Artist, American
Duskin, Big Joe, Boogie-Woogie, 1940s-1980s, Artist, American
Eaglin, Snooks, Louisiana Blues, 1950s-, Artist, American
Ealey, Robert, Texas Blues, 1980s-1990s, Artist, American
Earl, Ronnie, Blues Rock; Modern Electric Blues, 1970s-, Artist, American
Edwards, Archie, Modern Electric Blues, 1980s, Artist, American
Edwards, Honeyboy, Modern Electric Blues, 1940s-, Artist, American
Edwards, Susie, Delta/Country Blues, 1920s-1960s, Artist, American
Egan, Willie, Boogie-Woogie, 1950s, Artist, American
Electric Flag, Blues Rock, 1960s-1970s, Artist, American
Ellis, Tinsley, Modern Electric Blues, 1980s-, Artist, American
Erickson, Craig, Modern Electric Blues, 1990s-, Artist, American
Estes, Sleepy John, Delta/Country Blues, 1930s; 1960s-1970s, Artist, American
Fabulous Thunderbirds, The, Blues Rock, 1970s-, Artist, American
Fats Domino, Rhythm & Blues, 1940s-1990s, Artist, American
Five Keys, The, Piedmont Blues; Piedmont Blues, 1950s-1960s, Artist, American
Five Royales, The, Rhythm & Blues, 1950s-1960s, Artist, American
Fleetwood Mac, British Blues; Blues Rock, 1960s-, Artist, British
Ford, Frankie, Louisiana Blues, 1950s-, Artist, American
Forest City Joe, Chicago Blues, 1940s-1950s, Artist, American
Free, Blues Rock, 1960s-1970s, Artist, British
Frost, Frank, Modern Electric Blues, 1950s-1990s, Artist, American
Fuller, Blind Boy, Piedmont Blues, 1930s-1940s, Artist, American
Fuller, Jesse, Delta/Country Blues; Jump Blues, 1950s-1960s, Artist, American
Fulson, Lowell, Jump Blues; Texas Blues, 1940s-1990s, Artist, American
Funderburgh, Anson, Modern Electric Blues, 1980s-, Artist, American
Gaines, Roy, Modern Electric Blues, 1970s-, Artist, American
Gallagher, Rory, British Blues; Blues Rock, 1970s-1980s, Artist, Irish
Gant, Cecil, Jump Blues; Rhythm & Blues, 1940s-1950s, Artist, American
Gibson, Clifford, Delta/Country Blues, 1920s-1930s, Artist, American
Gillespie, Dana, Blues Rock, 1960s-2000s, Artist, British
Gillum, Bill, Delta/Country Blues, 1930s-1940s, Artist, American
Glenn, Lloyd, Jump Blues, 1940s-1950s, Producer; Artist, American
Grant, Coot, Delta/Country Blues, 1920s-1940s, Artist, American
Graves, Blind Roosevelt, Delta/Country Blues, 1920s-1930s, Artist, American
Green, Clarence, Texas Blues, 1950s-1990s, Artist, American

Green, Leothus Lee, Delta/Country Blues, 1920s-1930s, Artist, American
Green, Peter, British Blues; Blues Rock, 1970s-, Artist, British
Greer, Big John, Piedmont Blues, 1940s-1950s, Artist, American
Grey Ghost, Texas Blues, 1960s; 1980s, Artist, American
Grimes, Tony, Jump Blues, 1940s-1970s, Artist, American
Groundhogs, The, Blues Rock, 1960s-1990s, Artist, British
Guitar Junior, Chicago Blues, 1960s, Artist, American
Guitar Shorty, Modern Electric Blues, 1950s-, Artist, American
Guitar Slim, Louisiana Blues, 1950s, Artist, American
Guy, Buddy, Modern Electric Blues; Chicago Blues, 1960s-, Artist, American
Hammond, John Jr., Blues Rock; Rhythm & Blues, 1960s-, Artist, American
Hampton, Lionel, Jump Blues, 1920s-1990s, Artist, American
Handy, W. C., Delta/Country Blues, 1900s-1920s, Songwriter; Artist, American
Hare, Pat, Modern Electric Blues, 1950s-1960s, Artist, American
Harlem Hamfats, Piedmont Blues, 1930s, Artist, American
Harmonica Slim, Jump Blues, 1950s-1960s, Artist, American
Harper, Toni, Boogie-Woogie; Rhythm & Blues, 1950s-1960s, Artist, American
Harpo, Slim, Louisiana Blues, 1950s-1960s, Artist, American
Harris, Corey, Delta/Country Blues; Modern Electric Blues, 1990s-, Artist, American
Harris, Peppermint, Jump Blues, 1940s-1970s, Artist, American
Harris, Wynonie, Jump Blues; Rhythm & Blues, 1940s-1960s, Artist, American
Harrison, Wilbert, Rhythm & Blues, 1950s-1970s, Artist, American
Hawkins, Erskine, Jump Blues, 1930s-1970s, Artist, American
Hawkins, Roy, Jump Blues; Rhythm & Blues, 1940s-1950s, Artist, American
Hawkins, Ted, Rhythm & Blues, 1980s-1990s, Artist, American
Henderson, Duke, Jump Blues, 1940s-1950s, Artist, American
Hendrix, Jimi, Blues Rock, 1960s-1970s, Artist; Songwriter, American
Henry, Clarence "Frogman", Louisiana Blues, 1950s-1960s, Artist; Songwriter, American
Hibbler, Al, Jump Blues, 1940s-1990s, Artist, American
Hicks, Edna, Delta/Country Blues, 1920s, Artist, American
Hill, Jessie, Louisiana Blues, 1960s-1970s, Artist, American
Hill, Z. Z., Modern Electric Blues, 1960s-1980s, Artist, American
Hoax, The, British Blues; Blues Rock, 1990s-, Artist, British
Holiday, Billie, Piedmont Blues; Rhythm & Blues, 1930s-1950s, Artist, American
Holland, Jools, Boogie-Woogie, 1980s-, Artist, British
Holmes Brothers, Modern Electric Blues, 1980s-, Artist, American
Hooker, Earl, Delta/Country Blues; Chicago Blues, 1950s-1970s, Artist, American
Hooker, John Lee, Chicago Blues; 1940s-1990s, Artist; Songwriter, American
Hopkins, Lightnin', Texas Blues, 1950s-1970s, Artist, American
Hopkins, Linda, Piedmont Blues; Jump Blues, 1950s-1980s, Artist, American
Hornbuckle, Linda, Modern Electric Blues, 1990s-, Artist, American
Horton, Big Walter "Shakey", Chicago Blues, 1940s-1980s, Artist, American
House, Son, Delta/Country Blues, 1930s-1960s, Artist; Songwriter, American
Houston, Bee, Texas Blues, 1950s-1980s, Artist, American
Hovington, Fred, Delta/Country Blues, 1970s, Artist, American
Howard, Rosetta, Piedmont Blues, 1930s-1940s, Artist, American
Howell, Peg Leg, Delta/Country Blues , 1920s-1930s, Artist, American
Howlin' Wolf, Chicago Blues, 1930s-1970s, Artist, American
Hughes, Joe "Guitar", Texas Blues; Modern Electric Blues, 1950s-, Artist, American
Humble Pie, Blues Rock; British Blues, 1960s-1980s, Artist, British
Humes, Helen, Delta/Country Blues; Jump Blues, 1920s-1970s, Artist, American
Hunter, Alberta, Rhythm & Blues, 1920s-1980s, Artist, American
Hunter, Ivory Joe, Jump Blues; Rhythm & Blues, 1930s-1970s, Artist; Songwriter, American
Hunter, Long John, Modern Electric Blues; Texas Blues, 1960s-1990s, Artist, American
Hurt, Mississippi John, Delta/Country Blues; Work Songs, 1920s-1940s; 1960s, Artist; Songwriter, American
Hutto, J. B., Chicago Blues, 1960s-1980s, Artist, American
Isley Brothers, The, Rhythm & Blues, 1950s-, Artist, American
J. Geils Band, Blues Rock, 1970s-1980s, Artist, American
Jacks, The, Rhythm & Blues, 1950s-1960s, Artist, American
Jackson, Bull Moose, Jump Blues; Rhythm & Blues, 1940s-1950s, Artist, American
Jackson, Chuck, Rhythm & Blues, 1970s-1980s, Artist, American
Jackson, Jim, Delta/Country Blues, 1910s-1930s, Artist, American
Jackson, John, Delta/Country Blues, 1960s-1990s, Artist, American
Jackson, Melvin "Lil' Son", Texas Blues, 1940s-1960s, Artist, American
Jackson, Papa Charlie, Delta/Country Blues, 1920s-1930s, Artist, American

WORK SONGS ➡ 158 DELTA/COUNTRY BLUES ➡ 159 LOUISIANA BLUES ➡ 161 TEXAS BLUES ➡ 163 BOOGIE-WOOGIE ➡ 165

James, Elmore, Chicago Blues, 1950s-1960s, Artist; Songwriter, American
James, Etta, Rhythm & Blues, 1950s-, Artist, American
James, Skip, Delta/Country Blues; 1930s; 1960s, Artist; Songwriter, American
Jaxon, Frankie "Half-Pint", Piedmont Blues, 1920s-1940s, Artist, American
Jefferson, Blind Lemon, Delta/Country Blues; Texas Blues, 1920s, Artist, American
Jelly Roll Kings, The, Modern Electric Blues, 1970s-1990s, Artist, American
Johnson, Blind Willie, Texas Blues, 1920s-1940s, Artist, American
Johnson, Buddy, Jump Blues; Rhythm & Blues, 1930s-1060s, Artist; Songwriter, American
Johnson, Ella, Piedmont Blues; Jump Blues; Rhythm & Blues, 1940s-1950s, Artist, American
Johnson, Johnnie, Boogie-Woogie; Rhythm & Blues, 1950s-1990s, Artist, American
Johnson, Larry, Modern Electric Blues, 1960s-1970s, Artist, American
Johnson, Lonnie, Delta/Country Blues, 1920s-1960s, Artist, American
Johnson, Luther, Modern Electric Blues, 1990s, Artist, American
Johnson, Marv, Rhythm & Blues, 1950s-1960s, Artist, American
Johnson, Pete, Boogie-Woogie, 1920s-1960s, Artist, American
Johnson, Robert, Delta/Country Blues; 1930s, Artist; Songwriter, American
Johnson, Tommy, Delta/Country Blues; 1920s-1930s, Artist, American
Jones, Eddie "One String", Delta/Country Blues, 1960s, Artist, American
Jones, Etta, Swing, 1940s-, Artist, American
Jones, Floyd, Chicago Blues, 1960s, Artist; Songwriter, American
Jones, Little Johnny, Chicago Blues; Boogie-Woogie, 1940s-1960s, Artist, American
Jones, Tuta, Modern Electric Blues, 1990s-, Artist, American
Joplin, Janis, Blues Rock, 1960s-1970s, Artist, American

Jordan, Charley, Delta/Country Blues, 1920s-1940s, Artist, American
Jordan, Louis, Jump Blues, 1930s-1970s, Artist, American
Julian, Don, Rhythm & Blues, 1950s-1970s, Artist, American
K-Doe, Ernie, Rhythm & Blues, 1960s-1990s, Artist; Songwriter, American
Keb' Mo', Blues Rock, 1990s-, Artist, American
Kelly, Jo Ann, British Blues, 1960s-1990s, Artist, British
Kennedy, Tiny, Piedmont Blues; Jump Blues, 1950s, Artist, American
Kimbrough, Junior, Modern Electric Blues; Delta/Country Blues; 1960s-1990s, Artist, American
King Curtis, Rhythm & Blues; Piedmont Blues, 1950s-1970s, Artist, American
King, Albert, Modern Electric Blues; Rhythm & Blues, 1960s-1980s, Artist, American
King, B. B., Modern Electric Blues; Rhythm & Blues, 1940s-, Artist, American
King, Earl, Louisiana Blues, 1950s-2000s, Artist, American
King, Freddie, Texas Blues; Rhythm & Blues; Modern Electric Blues, 1950s-1970s, Artist, American
King, Shirley, Modern Electric Blues, 1990s, Artist, American
Kirkland, Eddie, Modern Electric Blues, 1960s-1990s, Artist, American
Korner, Alexis, British Blues; Blues Rock, 1960s-1980s, Artist, Greek
Kubek, Smokin' Joe, Modern Electric Blues, 1990s-, Artist, American
Lazy Lester, Modern Electric Blues, 1950s-, Artist, American
Leake, Lafayette, Boogie-Woogie, 1960s, Artist, American
Led Zeppelin, British Blues; Blues Rock, 1960s-1980s, Artist, British
Ledbetter, Huddie "Leadbelly", Delta/Country Blues, 1920s-1940s, Artist, American
Lennox, Alan, Work Songs, 1930s-1990s, Artist, American
Lenoir, J. B., Chicago Blues, 1950s-1960s, Artist, American
Levy, Ron, Modern Electric Blues, 1970s-, Artist, American
Lewis, Furry, Delta/Country Blues, 1920s; 1960s-1970s, Artist, American
Lewis, Meade "Lux", Boogie-Woogie, 1930s-1960s, Artist, American
Lewis, Noah, Delta/Country Blues, 1920s-1960s, Artist, American
Lewis, Smiley, Louisiana Blues, 1940s-1960s, Artist, American
Liggins, Jimmy, Jump Blues; Rhythm & Blues, 1940s-1950s, Artist, American
Liggins, Joe, Jump Blues; Rhythm & Blues, 1940s-1950s, Artist, American
Lightnin' Slim, Louisiana Blues, 1950s-1970s, Artist, American
Lil' Ed & the Blues Imperials, Modern Electric Blues, 1980s-, Artist, American
Lincoln, Charley, Delta/Country Blues, 1920s-1930s, Artist, American
Linden, Colin, Modern Elecrtci Blues, 1970s-, Artist, Canadian
Lipscomb, Mance, Delta/Country Blues, 1950s-1970s, Artist, American
Little Charlie & the Nightcats, Modern Electric Blues, 1980s-1990s, Artist, American
Little Feat, Blues Rock, 1970s-, Artist, American
Little Milton, Modern Electric Blues; Rhythm & Blues, 1950s-, Artist, American
Little Richard, Rhythm & Blues, 1950s-1990s, Artist, American
Little Walter, Chicago Blues, 1940s-1960s, Artist; Songwriter, American
Little Willie John, Rhythm & Blues, 1950s-1960s, Artist, American
Littlefield, Little Willie, Jump Blues; Boogie-Woogie; Rhythm & Blues, 1940s-1990s, Artist, American
Littlejohn, John, Chicago Blues; Modern Electric Blues, 1960s-1990s, Artist, American
Lockwood, Robert Jr., Delta/Country Blues; Chicago Blues, 1930s-, Artist, American
Lomax, Alan, Work Songs, 1930s-1990s, Producer, American
Lonesome Sundown, Chicago Blues, 1950s-1970s, Artist, American
Long, Joey, Texas Blues, 1970s-1990s, Artist, American
Louis, Big Joe, & his Blues Kin, British Blues, 1990s, Artist, British
Louis, Joe Hill, Delta/Country Blues, 1940s-1950s, Artist, American
Love Sculpture, Blues Rock, 1960s-1970s, Artist, British
Love, Billy, Delta/Country Blues, 1950s, Artist, American
Lutcher, Joe, Rhythm & Blues, 1940s-1950s, Artist, American
Lynn, Barbara, Rhythm & Blues; Modern Electric Blues, 1960s-1990s, Artist, American
Mabon, Willie, Chicago Blues; Rhythm & Blues, 1950s-1980s, Artist, American
Mack, Lonnie, Modern Electric Blues; Rhythm & Blues, 1960s-, Artist, American
Madcat & Kane, Rhythm & Blues, 1990s, Artist, American
Magic Dick, Blues Rock; Modern Electric Blues, 1990s, Artist, American
Magic Sam, Modern Electric Blues; Chicago Blues, 1950s-1960s, Artist, American
Magic Slim, Modern Electric Blues, 1970s-, Artist, American
Magpie, Work Songs, 1970s-, Artist, American
Manfreds, The, Blues Rock; Rhythm & Blues, 1990s-, Artist, British
Margolin, Bob, Modern Electric Blues, 1960s-, Artist, American
Martin, Carl, Piedmont Blues, 1930s-1970s, Artist, American
Martin, Sara, Delta/Country Blues, 1920s-1930s, Artist, American
Mayall, John, British Blues; Blues Rock, 1960s-, Artist, British
Mayfield, Percy, Jump Blues; Rhythm & Blues, 1940s-1970s, Artist, American
McCain, Jerry "Boogie", Modern Electric Blues, 1950s-1960s; 1980s-, Artist; Songwriter, American
McClennan, Tommy, Delta/Country Blues, 1930s-1940s, Artist, American
McClinton, Delbert, Blues Rock; Modern Electric Blues, 1960s-, Artist, American
McCoy, Joe, Delta/Country Blues, 1920s-1930s, Artist, American
McCoy, Viola, Delta/Country Blues, 1920s-1930s, Artist, American
McCracklin, Jimmy, Jump Blues; Rhythm & Blues, 1950s-1990s, Artist, American
McDowell, Mississippi Fred, Delta/Country Blues, 1950s-1970s, Artist, American
McGhee, Brownie, Piedmont Blues; Delta/Country Blues, 1940s-1990s, Artist, American
McNeely, Big Jay, Jump Blues, Rhythm & Blues, 1940s-1990s, Artist, American
McPhatter, Clyde, Rhythm & Blues, 1950s-1960s, Artist, American
McShann, Jay, Jump Blues, 1930s-, Artist, American
McTell, Blind Willie, Piedmont Blues; Delta/Country Blues, 1920s-1950ss, Artist, American
Medicine Head, British Blues, 1960s-1970s; 1990s, Artist, British
Memphis Jug Band, Delta/Country Blues, 1920s-1930s, Artist, American
Memphis Minnie, Delta/Country Blues; Chicago Blues, 1920s-1950s, Artist, American
Memphis Sheikhs, Delta/Country Blues, 1990s, Artist, American
Memphis Slim, Boogie-Woogie, 1930s-1980s, Artist, American
Merriweather, Big Maceo, Chicago Blues, 1930s-1950s, Artist, American
Meters, The, Rhythm & Blues, 1960s-1990s, Artist, American
Mickey & Sylvia, Rhythm & Blues, 1950s-1960s, Artist, American
Milburn, Amos, Jump Blues; Rhythm & Blues, 1940s-1960s, Artist, American
Miles, Lizzie, Delta/Country Blues, 1920s-1930s, Artist, American
Millinder, Lucky, Jump Blues, 1930s-1950s, Artist, American
Milton, Roy, Jump Blues; Rhythm & Blues, 1940s-1980s, Artist, American
Mississippi Sheikhs, Delta/Country Blues, 1920s-1930s, Artist, American
Montgomery, Little Brother, Boogie-Woogie, 1930s-1970s, Artist, American
Mooney, John, Delta/Country Blues, 1970s-, Artist, American
Moonglows, The, Rhythm & Blues, 1950s, Artist, American
Moore, Merrill, Boogie-Woogie; Rhythm & Blues, 1950s-1970s, Artist, American
Morgan, Mike, Modern Electric Blues; Texas Blues, 1990s-, Artist, American
Morris, Thomas, Delta/Country Blues, 1920s, Artist, American
Moss, Buddy, Piedmont Blues; Delta/Country Blues, 1930s-1940s, Artist, American
Muddy Waters, Delta/Country Blues; Chicago Blues, 1940s-1980s, Artist, American
Musselwhite, Charlie, Modern Electric Blues, 1960s-, Artist, American
Neal, Raful, Louisiana Blues, 1950s-1960s, Artist, American
Nelson, Jimmy, Jump Blues; Rhythm & Blues, 1950s-1960s, Artist, American
Neville Brothers, The, Rhythm & Blues, 1960s-, Artist, American
Neville, Aaron, Rhythm & Blues, 1960s-, Artist, American
Newbern, Hambone Willie, Delta/Country Blues, 1920s, Artist, American
Newman, Jack, Delta/Country Blues, 1930s, Artist, American
Nighthawk, Robert, Chicago Blues, 1930s-1960s, Artist, American
Nix, Willie, Chicago Blues, 1940s-1970s, Artist, American
Numbers Band, The, Blues Rock, 1960s-1990s, Artist, American
Odetta, Delta/Country Blues, 1950s-, Artist, American
Olympics, The, Rhythm & Blues, 1950s-1960s, Artist, American
Omar & the Howlers, Modern Electric Blues; Blues Rock, 1980s-, Artist, American
Orioles, The, Rhythm & Blues, 1940s-1960s, Artist, American
Otis, Johnny, Jump Blues; Rhythm & Blues, 1940s-1990s, Artist, American
Owens, Jack, Delta/Country Blues, 1960s-1970s, Artist, American
Page, Jimmy, British Blues, 1980s-, Artist; Composer; Producer, British
Palmer, Earl, Rhythm & Blues, 1950s-, Artist, American
Parker, Junior, Rhythm & Blues, 1950s-1970s, Artist, American
Parrish, Michael, Delta/Country Blues, 1990s, Artist, American
Patton, Charley, Delta/Country Blues, 1920s-1930s, Artist, American
Peg Leg Sam, Delta/Country Blues, 1930s-1970s, Artist, American
Pena, Paul, Rhythm & Blues, 1970s; 1990s, Artist, American
Perkins, Pinetop, Boogie-Woogie; Chicago Blues, 1940s-, Artist, American
Phillips, Esther, Rhythm & Blues, 1950s-1970s, Artist, American
Phillips, Flip, Piedmont Blues; Jump Blues, 1940s-1990s, Artist, American
Phillips, Gene, Jump Blues, 1940s-1950s, Artist, American
Piano Red, Boogie-Woogie, 1950s-1960s, Artist, American
Piazza, Rod, Jump Blues; Modern Electric Blues, 1960s-, Artist, American
Pickett, Charlie, Delta/Country Blues, 1980s-1990s, Artist, American
Pickett, Dan, Delta/Country Blues, 1940s-1950s, Artist, American
Poets, The, British Blues, 1960s-1970s, Artist, British
Price, Lloyd, Rhythm & Blues, 1950s-1960s; 1980s, Artist, American
Price, Sammy, Boogie-Woogie; Jump Blues, 1920s-1980s, Artist, American
Prima, Louis, Jump Blues, Rhythm & Blues, 1930s-1970s, Artist, American
Primer, John, Modern Electric Blues, 1970s-, Artist, American
Professor Longhair, Louisiana Blues, 1940s-1980s, Artist; Songwriter, American
Pryor, Snooky, Chicago Blues, 1940s-1990s, Artist, American
Prystock, Red, Jump Blues; Rhythm & Blues, 1950s-1960s, Artist, American
Qualls, Henry, Texas Blues; Modern Electric Blues, 1990s, Artist, American
Rachell, Yank, Delta/Country Blues, 1930s-1980, Artist, American
Rainey, Ma, Delta/Country Blues, 1920s-1930s, Artist, American
Raitt, Bonnie, Blues Rock, 1970s-, Artist; Songwriter, American
Ravens, The, Rhythm & Blues, 1940s-1950s, Artist, American
Reed, Jimmy, Chicago Blues; Rhythm & Blues, 1950s-1970s, Artist, American

Robins, The, Rhythm & Blues, 1940s-1950s, Artist, American
Robinson, Fenton, Texas Blues, 1960s-1980s, Artist, American
Rogers, Jimmy, Chicago Blues, 1950s-1990s, Artist, American
Rogers, Roy, Blues Rock, 1970s-, Artist; Producer, American
Roland, Walter, Boogie-Woogie; Delta/Country Blues, 1930s, Artist, American
Rolling Stones, The, Blues Rock, 1960s-, Artist, British
Roomful Of Blues, Jump Blues; Modern Electric Blues, 1970s-, Artist, American
Rush, Otis, Chicago Blues, 1950s-1990s, Artist, American
Rushing, Jimmy, Piedmont Blues; Jump Blues, 1920s-1970s, Artist, American
Sahm, Doug, Delta/Country Rock; Blues Rock, 1950s-1990s, Artist; Songwriter, American
Sane, Dan, Delta/Country Blues, 1920s-1930s, Artist, American
Santana, Blues Rock, 1960s-, Artist, American
Savoy Brown, Blues Rock; British Blues, 1960s-, Artist, British
Scott-Adams, Peggy, Modern Electric Blues, 1960s-1970s, Artist, American
Seals, Son, Modern Electric Blues, 1970s-, Artist, American
Shade, Will, Delta/Country Blues, 1920s-1960s, Artist, American
Shariff, Omar, Texas Blues, 1960s-, Artist, American
Sharpe, B. J., Blues Rock, 1990s, Artist, American
Sharpe, Ray, Texas Blues, 1950s, Artist, American
Shaw, Robert, Boogie-Woogie, 1930s; 1960s-1980s, Artist, American
Shepard, Ollie, Delta/Country Blues, 1930s-1940s, Artist, American
Shines, Johnny, Delta/Country Blues; Chicago Blues, 1960s-1990s, Artist, American
Shirley & Lee, Rhythm & Blues, 1950s-1960s, Artist, American
Short, J. D., Delta/Country Blues, 1930s-1960s, Artist, American
Showmen, The, Rhythm & Blues, 1960s, Artist, American
Siegel-Schwall Band, Modern Electric Blues, 1960s-1980s, Artist, American
Sims, Frankie Lee, Delta/Country Blues, 1940s-1960s, Artist, American
Slack, Freddie, Boogie-Woogie, 1940s-1950s, Artist, American
Slim, Sunnyland, Delta/Country Blues, 1940s-1980s, Artist, American
Slim, Tarheel, Rhythm & Blues, 1950s-1970s, Artist, American
Slim, T. V., Delta/Country Blues; Rhythm & Blues, 1950s-1960s, Artist, American
Smith, Bessie, Delta/Country Blues, 1920s-1930s, Artist, American
Smith, Clarence "Pine Top", Boogie-Woogie, 1920s, Artist, American
Smith, Funny Paper, Texas Blues, 1930s, Artist, American
Smith, George "Harmonica", Modern Electric Blues, 1940s-1980s, Artist, American
Smith, Huey "Piano", Louisiana Blues, 1950s-1960s, Artist, American

Smith, Ivy, Delta/Country Blues, 1920s-1930s, Artist, American
Smith, Laura, Delta/Country Blues, 1920s, Artist, American
Smith, Mamie, Delta/Country Blues, 1920s, Artist, American
Smith, Willie "Big Eyes", Modern Electric Blues, 1990s-, Artist, American
Smokey Babe, Jump Blues, 1960s, Artist, American
Spaniels, The, Rhythm & Blues, 1950s-1970s, Artist, American
Spann, Otis, Chicago Blues, 18950s-1960s, Artist, American
Speckled Red, Boogie-Woogie, 1920s-1930s, Artist, American
Spellman, Benny, Rhythm & Blues, 1960s, Artist, American
Spencer, Jeremy, British Blues; Blues Rock, 1970s, Artist, British
Spiders, The, Rhythm & Blues, 1950s, Artist, American
Spivey, Victoria, Delta/Country Blues, 1920s-1930s, Artist, American
Steampacket, British Blues, 1960s, Artist, British
Stokes, Frank, Delta/Country Blues, 1910s-1920s, Artist, American
Strong, Nolan, Rhythm & Blues, 1950s-1960s, Artist, American
Sugar Blue, Modern Electric Blues, 1970s-1990s, Artist, American
Sumlin, Hubert, Chicago Blues; Modern Electric Blues, 1950s-, Artist, American
Sykes, Roosevelt, Chicago Blues, 1920s-1980s, Artist, American
Taggart, Blind Joe, Delta/Country Blues, 1920s-1930s, Artist, American
Taj Mahal, Blues Rock, 1960s-, Artist, American
Talley, James, Delta/Country Blues; Modern Electric Blues, 1970s-, Artist; Songwriter, American
Tampa Red, Chicago Blues, 1920s-1960s, Artist, American
Taylor, Eddie, Modern Electric Blues; Rhythm & Blues, 1950s-1980s, Artist, American
Taylor, Hound Dog, Chicago Blues, 1960s-1970s, Artist, American
Taylor, Koko, Modern Electric Blues; Chicago Blues; Rhythm & Blues, 1960s-, Artist, American
Taylor, Melvin, & the Slack Band, Modern Electric Blues, 1990s, Artist, American
Taylor, Sam, Jump Blues, 1990s, Artist; Songwriter, American
Temple, Johnnie "Geechie", Delta/Country Blues; Chicago Blues, 1930s-1950s, Artist, American
Temple, Johnny, Piedmont Blues, 1980s-, Artist, American
Ten Years After, British Blues; Blues Rock, 1960s-1990s, Artist, British
Terry, Sonny, Piedmont Blues, 1930s-1980s, Artist, American
Tharpe, Sister Rosetta, Jump Blues, 1930s-1960s, Artist, American
Them, British Blues; Blues Rock, 1960s, Artist, British
Thomas, Henry, Delta/Country Blues, 1920s-1930s, Artist; Songwriter, American
Thomas, Irma, Rhythm & Blues, 1960s-, Artist, American
Thomas, James "Son", Delta/Country Blues, 1960s-1980s, Artist, American
Thomas, Jesse, Texas Blues, 1930s-1990s, Artist, American
Thomas, Ramblin', Delta/Country Blues, 1920s-1930s, Artist, American
Thomas, Rockin' Tabby, Chicago Blues, 1950s-1990s, Artist, American
Thompson, Ron, Modern Electric Blues, 1970s-1980s, Artist, American
Thorogood, George, Blues Rock, 1970s-1990s, Artist, American
Thornton, Big Mama, Rhythm & Blues, 1940s-1970s, Artist, American
Toussaint, Allen, Louisiana Blues, 1950s-1990s, Artist, American
Townsend, Henry, Delta/Country Blues, 1920s-1980s, Artist, American
Tramp, British Blues, 1960s-1970s, Artist, British
Treniers, The, Jump Blues, Rhythm & Blues, 1940s-1980s, Artist, American
Tucker, Bessie, Delta/Country Blues, 1920s, Artist, American
Turner, "Big" Joe, Jump Blues; Rhythm & Blues, 1930s-1980s, Artist, American
Turner, Ike, Rhythm & Blues, 1950s-, Producer; Songwriter; Artist, American
Turner, Titus, Piedmont Blues; Jump Blues; Rhythm & Blues, 1950s-1970s, Artist, American
Turner, Zeb, Boogie-Woogie, 1940s-1950s, Artist, American
Twice As Much, British Blues, 1960s, Artist, British
Tyson, Willie, Delta/Country Blues, 1970s, Artist, American
Vaughan, Jimmie, Modern Electric Blues; Blues Rock, 1980s-, Artist, American
Vaughan, Stevie Ray, Texas Blues; Modern Electric Blues; Blues Rock, 1980s-1990s, Artist, American
Vinson, Eddie "Cleanhead", Jump Blues; Rhythm & Blues, 1940s-1980s, Artist, American
Vinson, Walter, Delta/Country Blues, 1920s-1940s; 1960s-1970s, Artist, American
Walker, Joe Louis, Modern Electric Blues, 1980s-, Artist, American
Walker, Philip, Modern Electric Blues, 1970s-1990s, Artist, American
Walker, T-Bone, Texas Blues, 1920s-1970s, Artist; Songwriter, American
Wallace, Sippie, Delta/Country Blues, 1920s-1940s, Artist, American
Walton, Mercy Dee, Jump Blues, 1940s-1960s, Artist, American
Ward, Billy, Rhythm & Blues, 1950s, Artist, American
Washington, Leroy, Chicago Blues, 1960s, Artist, American
Washington, Tuts, Louisiana Blues, 1980s, Artist, American
Waters, Ethel, Delta/Country Blues, 1920s-1960s, Artist, American
Watson, Johnny "Guitar", Modern Electric Blues; Texas Blues; Rhythm & Blues, 1950s-1990s, Artist, American
Watson, Junior, Jump Blues, 1990s, Artist, American
Watts, Noble, Piedmont Blues; Jump Blues, 1950s-1990s, Artist, American
Weathersby, Carl, Modern Electric Blues, 1990s-, Artist, American
Weaver, Curly, Country Blues, 1920s-1930s; 1950s, Artist, American
Weaver, Sylvester, Country Blues, 1920s, Artist, American
Webb, Boogie Bill, Rhythm & Blues; Country Blues, 1950s-1980s, Artist, American
Webster, Katie, Rhythm & Blues, 1960s; 1980s-1990s, Artist, American
Weldon, Casey Bill, Country Blues, 1920s-1940s, Artist, American
Wellington, Valerie, Modern Electric Blues, 1980s-1990s, Artist, American
Wells, Junior, Chicago Blues; Modern Electric Blues, 1950s-1990s, Artist, American
Wheatstraw, Peetie, Country Blues, 1930s-1940s, Artist, American
Whispering Smith, Rhythm & Blues, 1970s, Artist, American
White, Bukka, , 1930s-1940s; 1960s-1970s, Artist, American
White, Charles, Jump Blues, 1990s-, Artist, American
White, Josh Jr, Country Blues, 1970s-1980s, Artist; Songwriter, American
Wilkins, Robert, Country Blues, 1920s-1930s, Artist, American
Williams, André, Rhythm & Blues, 1950s-1970s; 1990s-, Artist, American
Williams, Big Joe, Delta/Country Blues, 1930s-1980s, Artist; Songwriter, American
Williams, Cootie, Jump Blues, 1930s-1970s, Artist, American
Williams, Larry, Rhythm & Blues, 1950s-1970s, Artist, American
Williams, Lester, Rhythm & Blues, 1940s-1950s, Artist, American
Williams, Robert Pete, Country Blues, 1950s-1970s, Artist, American
Williamson, Homesick James, Chicago Blues, 1930s-1990s, Artist, American
Williamson, Sonny Boy (I), Delta/Country Blues, 1930s-1940s, Artist, American
Williamson, Sonny Boy (II), Chicago Blues, 1930s-1960s, Artist; Songwriter, American
Willis, Chuck, Rhythm & Blues, 1950s, Artist, American
Willis, Ralph, Country Blues, 1940s-1950s, Artist, American
Wilson, Hop, Texas Blues, 1950s-1970s, Artist, American
Wilson, Jackie, Rhythm & Blues, 1950s-1970s, Artist, American
Winston, Edna, Country Blues, 1920s, Artist, American
Winter, Johnny, Blues Rock; Modern Electric Blues, 1960s-, Artist, American
Witherspoon, Jimmy, Jump Blues, 1940s-1990s, Artist, American
Woods, Mitch, Boogie Woogie; Jump Blues, 1980s-, Artist, American
Yancey, Jimmy, Boogie Woogie, 1930s-1950s, Artist, American
Yardbirds, The, British Blues; Blues Rock, 1960s, Artist, British
Young, Mighty Joe, Chicago Blues, 1960s-1990s, Artist, American
Zwingenberger, Axel, Boogie Woogie, 1970s-1980s, Artist, German
ZZ Top, Blues Rock, 1970s-1990s, Artist, American

CHICAGO BLUES ➡167 PIEDMONT BLUES (EAST COAST BLUES) ➡169 JUMP BLUES ➡170 BRITISH BLUES ➡172 RHYTHM & BLUES ➡173
BLUES ROCK ➡175 MODERN ELECTRIC BLUES ➡178

Country

COUNTRY music has been euphemistically called "white man's blues" or "the poetry of the common man". While both descriptions have elements of truth, neither is quite accurate. It is, in fact, a broad, nebulous, over-reaching category with no exact boundaries or parameters.

Over the decades country music has grown to encompass a greatly varied assortment of music styles and sub-styles. These include everything from the keening old-time hillbilly music of Roy Acuff and bluegrass king Bill Monroe (both long-time favourites on the *Grand Ole Opry*, broadcast from Nashville since 1925), and the electrified gut-bucket honky-tonk of Texans Ernest Tubb and Hank Thompson, to the ethnic strains of south Louisiana Cajun and south Texas-style conjunto/Tex Mex music, and the high-gloss country-pop of contemporary stars like Shania Twain and Faith Hill.

Also included under country's catch-all umbrella are the great Texas and Oklahoma western swing bands of the 1930s and 1940s, the influential southern California country rock bands of the 1960s and 1970s and the progressive bluegrass artists of 1970s, 1980s and 1990s. All told, country music is a sprawling, ill-defined yet glorious 80-year-long amalgamation of many different styles, eras, phases and attitudes.

Country music – at least mainstream country music, which generally means the music that is played on commercial country radio stations, turns up in *Billboard*'s country charts and is mass media-friendly – is to some degree a popular American art form. Yet during the last half-century it has also

become a numbers- and profit-driven commercial art form, as well – much like prime time television, for that matter. This owes much to the fact that music's rise since the 1920s has

> ## "COUNTRY MUSIC IS THREE CHORDS AND THE TRUTH."
> *Harlan Howard*

STYLES

Early & Old-Time
  Country
Cowboy Music
Western Swing
Bluegrass
Honky Tonk
The Nashville Sound
Mainstream Country
The Outlaw Movement
Country Rock
Urban Cowboys
Neo-Traditionalists
Alternative Country
Young Country

THE COUNTRY STYLE

This classic country music guitar figure would be played on an acoustic instrument, providing a simple but steady melodic and rhythmic structure.

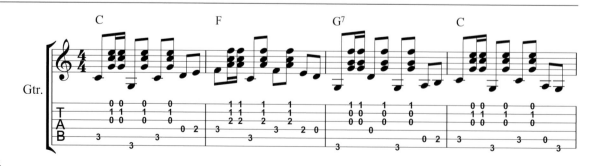

Hank Williams

been made possible by the for-profit radio and recording industries and, more recently, television, the printed media and mass media in general.

Because of this for-profit argument, there has been, through the decades, an enduring tension between the polarities of popular grassroots/creative innovation and the commercial realities of catering, and occasionally pandering, to changing public tastes in order to sell more records and increase market share. As a result, the country music industry has, when prevailing public tastes warranted it, chosen to celebrate and revive its rustic rural roots. At other times it has seemed embarrassed and commercially confined by these roots, so there have been resulting attempts to marginalize and minimize their presence in the music by adding sheens and layers of uptown pop or crossover embellishments.

Geography has, of course, played a major part in country music's development and sense of identity, although it's safe to say that today there are probably more country radio listeners living in large cities and their suburbs than on farms and in small towns. While Nashville, Tennessee – with its powerful record industry and the presence of the *Grand Ole Opry*, the most popular and enduring of the nation's many live country music radio shows – has become synonymous with country music, other southern and southwestern states like Texas, Oklahoma, Kentucky, Virginia and South Carolina have also produced an amazing number of the music's most talented artists and have offered fresh alternatives to the styles produced and marketed by Nashville's Music Row.

Other leading artists have come from midwestern states such as Ohio (1970s outlaw Bobby Bare) and Illinois (celebrated bluegrass singer/bandleader Alison Krauss). Southern California has similarly produced its share of leading lights, such as Merle Haggard, Buck Owens and neo-traditionalist divas like Iris DeMent and Gillian Welch. Some have even hailed from unlikely places such as New Jersey (Eddie Rabbitt) and New England (progressive bluegrass banjo masters Bill Keith and Dan Tyminski). Canada has also produced its share of artists: long-time *Grand Ole Opry* favourite Hank Snow, easy listening country-pop diva Anne Murray and alternative country queen k.d. lang.

Although Charley Pride is the only African-American to achieve enduring stardom in mainstream country, other eminently gifted African-American singers like DeFord Bailey (whose firing from the *Grand Ole Opry* in 1941 is still a subject of controversy), O. B. McClinton, Big Al Downing, Dobie Gray and Cleve Francis have also made significant contributions before ultimately bumping their heads on country's "glass ceiling". Certainly the rise of the nascent radio and recording industries in the 1920s and 1930s played an essential role in elevating country music from a relatively isolated melting pot of regional styles to a commercial force with national implications.

Yet long before that, and even long before sheet music was the sole medium for disseminating music nationwide, modern country music's earliest roots were already being nourished by an array of regional, ethnic and popular musical styles – everything from transplanted British folk balladry, protestant hymns, rural black blues and string band music to the Tin Pan Alley proto-pop tunes heard on the stages of the travelling minstrel, vaudeville and medicine shows that were popular throughout the south in the late nineteenth and early twentieth centuries.

In the past century, country music has gone through countless permutations, evolving with a changing culture and sprouting new stylistic branches. Some of these stylistic changes, like the rise of honky-tonk and western swing in the 1930s and 1940s and the advent of country rock in the 1960s and 1970s, have been grassroots innovations which in some way reflected periods of dramatic social upheaval – for example, the Great Depression of the 1930s, the post-Second World War rural-to-urban and suburban migration and the rise of youth culture in the closing decades of the twentieth century.

Other stylistic developments, like the 1930s and 1940s cowboy (western) music boom, the Nashville sound era of the late-1950s and 1960s, and the young country phenomenon of the 1990s, were driven more by industry considerations and borrowed heavily from prevailing pop music styles. To understand the cumulative change that these grassroots and commercial forces have wrought over the decades, one need only play a rustic and old-timey 1920s Vernon Dalhart hit back-to-back with a sample of the aggressively surreal pschobilly of a 1990s alt. country band like the Bad Livers.

The result is a contemporary country landscape whose diversity is dazzling to the point of perplexity. Today, the catch-all rubric of "country" has expanded and branched out to include everything from the delightfully archaic-sounding sounds of old-time country revivalists like Norman Blake and the celebratory Cajun (French-Acadian) strains of a south Louisiana band like Beausoleil, to mainstream young country stars like Shania Twain – whose slick, youth-oriented sound is virtually indistinguishable from mainstream pop.

Shania Twain

Left

Ernest Tubb's admiration of Jimmie Rodgers was such that he befriended Rodgers' widow, who arranged for him to have a recording session and lent him one of Jimmie's guitars for the occasion.

Early & Old-Time Country

THERE IS NO DISTINCT BOUNDARY LINE BETWEEN THE EARLY AND OLD-TIME COUNTRY ERA, WHEN THE MUSIC WAS STILL RELATIVELY UNSHAPED BY THE AMERICAN MAINSTREAM, AND THE MODERN AGE, WHEN COUNTRY MUSIC'S POPULARITY AND UBIQUITY HAVE MADE IT VERY MUCH A PART OF THE MASS CULTURE.

Above

The Ryman Auditorium, home to the Grand Ole Opry from 1943–74 and the place where many country stars rose to fame.

BUT it was in the 1920s, due to the emerging radio and recording industries, that the US's varied regional and ethnic rural, grassroots musical forms began to find popularity beyond the isolated regions that spawned them. By the 1940s and early 1950s, as the commercial country radio and record industries gathered force, the music's connections to its grassroots origins became a bit more tenuous, and the old-time era was beginning to come to an end.

Blue Yodellers And Family Values

Though many successful and noteworthy artists preceded him, Meridian, Mississippi-born Jimmie Rodgers is most often hailed as the "father of modern country music" and one of its earliest national stars. Though Rodgers died of tuberculosis in 1933 aged 35, his ubiquitous influence was unrivaled until the emergence of Hank Williams in the late 1940s. Even 70 years after his death, his impact can still be heard in the music of latter-day stars such as Merle Haggard, Lefty Frizzell, George Jones, Gene Autry, Hank Snow and Ernest Tubb. With his warm, laconic, seemingly effortless vocal style (which included a thrilling falsetto and yodel), Rodgers brought to the country table a strong feel for black blues. Some of his classic recordings sold hundreds of thousands of copies – huge numbers for the time – and their sales were bolstered by his many live appearances on radio and in the vaudeville and tent shows that were popular throughout the southern US in the 1920s and early 1930s.

> "THE SONGS WERE DIFFERENT THAN THE NORM. THEY HAD MORE OF AN INDIVIDUAL NATURE AND AN ELEVATED CONSCIENCE ... I WAS DRAWN TO THEIR POWER."
>
> *Bob Dylan on Jimmie Rodgers*

The Singing Brakeman.

LEADING EXPONENTS

J. E. Mainer's
  Mountaineers
Jimmie Rodgers
The Carter Family
Uncle Dave Macon
Gid Tanner & his Skillet
  Lickers
Roy Acuff
Molly O'Day
Kitty Wells
Hank Snow
Carl Smith
Marty Robbins

OLD TIME COUNTRY

Old time country was a direct descendant of ballad, hymnal and folk styles, with a strong vocal storytelling tradition, and simple melodies with harmonization.

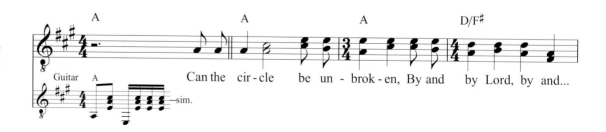

Can the cir-cle be un-brok-en, By and by Lord, by and...

THE COUNTRY INTRO ➡ 182   COUNTRY PEOPLE A-Z ➡ 220   INSTRUMENTS A-Z ➡ 436   THE BLUES INTRO ➡ 154   FOLK: TRADITIONAL FOLK ➡ 228

The Carter Family, often hailed as the "first family of country music", came from Virginia. Like Rodgers before them, they were first captured on disk by pioneering record executive Ralph Peer in Bristol, Tennessee in 1927. While Jimmie Rodgers' music was edgy and adventurous for its time, the Carter Family made music that was soothing, acoustic and heavily steeped in mountain traditions. Timeless recordings like 'Keep On The Sunny Side', 'Wildwood Flower' and 'Will The Circle Be Unbroken' (a Tin Pan Alley tune that they rustically reinterpreted) often spoke of the comfort of home, hearth and the old ways. With these songs and others the Carter Family explored a wide variety of genres, including blues, gospel, traditional ballads and nineteenth-century parlour songs.

This emphasis on the family tradition continued from the 1930s to the 1950s, when there was a rise of various influential sibling harmony ensembles like the Delmore Brothers, the Blue Sky Boys and Charlie & Bill Monroe. Familial vocal harmonies were further popularized by the Bailes Brothers from west Virginia, the Allen Brothers, the Dixon Brothers and Johnnie (Edwards) & Jack (Anglin – Johnnie's brother-in-law).

Showtime At The Grand Ole Opry

From the time it first went on the air, the *Grand Ole Opry* on Radio WSM in Nashville was a springboard for dozens of country music's most important artists – Roy Acuff, Hank Williams and Loretta Lynn not least among them. One of the earliest figures to find fame via the *Opry* was Tennessee-born Uncle Dave Macon. Macon started out as a banjoist and comedian on the vaudeville circuit before appearing on the *Opry*'s first formal broadcast in 1925. He was an accomplished banjo player and an effervescent showman and raconteur, with a vast repertoire of songs, including many of the rural ballads he'd learned as a child. Yet Macon was also amazingly adept at tailoring down-home adaptations of the pop hits he'd learned on the vaudeville stage as well as spinning out vivid originals like 'Farm Relief' and 'From Earth To Heaven'.

Music From The Mountains

J. E. Mainer's Mountaineers, from North Carolina, were foremost among the numerous guitar-fiddle-banjo Appalachian string bands that were popular in the 1930s. J. E.'s brother Wade left the Mountaineers in 1936 and formed his own band, the Sons of the Mountaineers. Wade Mainer's band, driven by its leader's innovative two-finger banjo style, foresaw the bluegrass music style, which would rise out of the string band tradition in the mid- and late-1940s.

Another archetypal and influential string band was Gid Tanner and his Skillet Lickers, often referred to as country music's first "supergroup". Tanner (real name James Gideon) was a chicken farmer from Dracula, Georgia and a gifted singer, showman and old-time fiddler. In 1924, he began

187

recording for Columbia and performing – most notably on Atlanta's Radio WSB – as a duo with blind singer-guitarist Riley Puckett. A couple of years later they were joined by two other popular musicians featured on WSB: fiddler Clayton McMichen and five-string banjo player Fate Norris. Fueled by Tanner's and McMichen's spirited fiddling and Puckett's adept, driving guitar rhythms, the Skillet Lickers brought an extroverted, often comic bent to a repertoire that included everything from old-time mountain ballads and humorous skits to popular Tin Pan Alley tunes of the day.

Below

Uncle Dave Macon was almost 60 when he found fame on the Grand Ole Opry. *He was a popular figure who had a vaudeville-inspired act that involved dancing around his banjo.*

It was during the 1930s that Roy Acuff, the roughhewn, diminutive son of an east Tennessee preacher/lawyer, made his sensational debut on the *Grand Ole Opry*. Acuff sang in a bold, emotional, high-keening style. Many of his signature hits from the 1940s – 'Great Speckled Bird', 'Night Train To Memphis' and 'Fire Ball Mail' – intimated his direct links to the east Tennessee mountain ballad singers and string bands that he listened to as a youngster. Acuff would remain a dominant figure in country music well into the 1950s and "the grand old man of the *Opry*" until shortly before his death in 1992.

One of the first women to enter country's front ranks, if only briefly, was Kentuckian Molly O'Day. O'Day was in many ways rooted in the same Appalachian mountain styles as Roy Acuff. She possessed a clear, booming voice that imbued with earnestness and earthy conviction everything she sang, whether maudlin tearjerkers like 'The Drunken Driver', gospel standards like 'Tramp On The Street' or her early covers of Hank Williams originals like 'Six More Miles'.

The Ghost Of Country Past

The 1940s was in some ways the end of the era of old-time country and the beginning of the modern age. Popular sounds of the 1920s and 1930s by the Carter Family and others would gradually give way to more modern styles. As early as the 1940s, *Grand Ole Opry* stars like Eddie Arnold and Red Foley were bringing their smoother, more sentimental musical temperaments to country's mainstream, thus foreshadowing the Nashville sound crossover style that would come into fruition by the early 1960s. It was during the mid-1940s that the first recording sessions took place in Nashville, and the city soon began to solidify its position as the de facto world capital of the country music industry. At the same time, *Billboard* began publishing the first record charts devoted exclusively to country music and, by 1944, more than 600 radio stations nationwide were playing country music either full or part-time.

Amidst this market expansion, a few traditional-flavoured singers like Rose Maddox, Kitty Wells and Wilma Lee and Stoney Cooper continued to gain airplay, and enjoyed considerable popularity into the 1950s. Others, like Kentucky guitar master Merle Travis, would artfully combine the old with the new. Travis scored hit versions of his original tradition-spirited coal mining songs like 'Sixteen Tons' (later a pop hit for Tennessee Ernie Ford) and 'Nine Pound Hammer', energetically updating them with his intricate thumb-and-finger-picking lead guitar style.

Chet Atkins, as an asthma-ridden teenager in east Tennessee, was heavily influenced by Merle Travis when he heard him on the radio. Atkins soon perfected his own unique

THE COUNTRY INTRO ➡ 182   COUNTRY PEOPLE A–Z ➡ 220   INSTRUMENTS A–Z ➡ 436   THE BLUES INTRO ➡ 154   FOLK: TRADITIONAL FOLK ➡ 228

thumb-and-two-finger-picking style, and by the early 1950s he was in Nashville as a *Grand Ole Opry* member and an "A Team" studio session guitarist. As a musician, Atkins would go on to influence countless country guitarists as well as celebrated rock'n'rollers like George Harrison, Duane Eddy and Mark Knopfler. He would also become one of Nashville's most influential record producers and was largely responsible for the celebrated Nashville sound.

Old-Time Habits Die Hard

Hank Snow, who would be overshadowed only by Roy Acuff in terms of his longevity and enduring popularity on the *Grand Ole Opry*, made his inauspicious debut on that live radio show in 1950. Heavily steeped in American cowboy music and the legacy of Jimmie Rodgers, Snow brought a droll, growling hard country sensibility to everything he sang. Throughout his career, which extended into the 1970s, he often experimented with blues-style and even Latin rhythms.

In 1951 Carl Smith, a pivotal figure, also emerged on the scene. Smith's early recordings contained elements of Ernest Tubb-style hardcore honky tonk, along with traces of more subtle vocal refinements that would become a defining element of the Nashville sound in the late 1950s and early 1960s. The year 1951 also marked the recording debut of Arizona-born Marty Robbins, a versatile singer who, throughout his long career, was as adept with cowboy saga songs like 'El Paso' as he was with soft-shoe 1950s teen ballads like 'Singin' The Blues' and 'A White Sport Coat And A Pink Carnation'.

Below
Country music king and master fiddler Roy Acuff impresses the other members of his band with a balancing trick.

Cowboy Music

THE MYTHS, LEGENDS AND LORE OF THE WILD WEST, FOR BETTER OR WORSE, HAVE DONE MUCH TO SHAPE THE AMERICAN CHARACTER. THEY HAVE GIVEN RISE TO THE NATION'S LINGERING INFATUATION WITH GUNS, OUTLAWS, THE RUGGED ETHOS OF SELF-RELIANCE, INDIVIDUALISM AND A WORLD WITH SIMPLISTIC DEFINITIONS.

Above

Tex Ritter featured in many cowboy films and had a big hit with the title track to the 1952 Gary Cooper film High Noon.

Right

William Cody, or "Buffalo Bill", created his travelling show in order to bring the rugged excitement of the Wild West to those who were at a geographical disadvantage.

"VICTORIAN AMERICANS WENT CRAZY FOR COWBOYS ... IT WAS ONLY A MATTER OF TIME BEFORE SOMEONE BROUGHT TOGETHER THESE THREE FACETS – ENTERTAINER, SINGER, AND COWBOY."

Douglas B. Green

THESE themes, usually portrayed in an earnest and nostalgic manner, lie at the heart of cowboy, or western, music. The style is marked by dreamy harmonies and subdued arrangements that suggest yearning and nostalgia for the long-gone ethos of the American West, or at least a romanticized version of it.

The Wild West Meets Tin Pan Alley

Some of the songs that have become western music standards, such as 'Home On The Range', 'The Streets of Laredo', 'The Yellow Rose Of Texas', 'Bury Me Not On The Lone Prairie', evolved directly out of a folk tradition and were once passed from one itinerant ranch hand or range rider to the next. These home-spun tunes were often set to the familiar melodies of Old World folk ballads, brought to the US by earlier waves of settlers. As early as 1895, Buffalo Bill's Wild West Show featured cowboy singers among its attractions.

In fact, many of the songs most closely associated with cowboy music today, like 'I'm An Old Cowhand', 'Don't Fence Me In' and 'Tumbling Tumbleweeds', were actually penned by Tin Pan Alley and Hollywood pop composers in the 1930s and 1940s, when western music reached its peak. Even pop singers of the day such as Bing Crosby included the occasional western song in their recorded repertoires. But the form's popularity was largely due to two "singing cowboy"

LEADING EXPONENTS

Gene Autry

Roy Rogers

Tex Ritter

Rex Allen, Sr.

Marty Robbins

Michael Martin
   Murphey

Riders In The Sky

COWBOY MUSIC

The harmonies in cowboy music consist of the tonic, dominant and sub-dominant chords, within a flowing, simple chord progression that produces a classic hymnal sound.

THE COUNTRY INTRO ➡ 182   COUNTRY PEOPLE A-Z ➡ 220   INSTRUMENTS A-Z ➡ 436

movie stars who have influenced countless country artists since and whose names have become more or less synonymous with the genre: Gene Autry and Roy Rogers.

Range Rovers

Autry, the archetypal singing cowboy, was the son of a Texas rancher. He began his career as a singer, actor and comedian in a medicine show, but by the late 1920s had immersed himself deeply in the musical style of Jimmie Rodgers and embarked on a solo career. By the early 1930s, he had shifted his style to the western song, and his singing conveyed the warm, expansive sincerity that is inherent to the "aw-shucks" cinematic cowboy image.

In 1931, Autry joined the *National Barndance*, a popular live radio show in Chicago, billing himself as "Oklahoma's Singing Cowboy". In 1934 he appeared with Ken Maynard, the most popular cowboy star of the day, in his first film, *In Old Santa Fe*. A year later he landed his first starring role, in *Tumbling Tumbleweeds*, and by 1937 was voted America's most popular western star. In the following years Autry continued to top both film box-office lists and the record charts with hits like 'South Of The Border' and 'Tumbling Tumbleweeds'.

In terms of musical sophistication, the benchmark practitioners of western music were the Sons of the Pioneers, headed by Roy Rogers. The group's illustrious line-up, which included greats like Bob Nolan and Tim Spencer, was first assembled in 1933 by young Ohio-born Roy Rogers (real name: Leonard Slye) in a Hollywood boarding house, where they spent hours perfecting their rich, seamless vocal harmonies. These were often delivered in a "block style" in which three voices essentially become one.

The Pioneers' soaring, ethereal, yet forceful harmonies, buttressed by the country-flavoured instrumentation of fiddle-guitar brother duo Hugh and Karl Farr, have never been surpassed. Canadian-born Bob Nolan is still considered one of the most gifted songwriters of the movement, having penned western standards like 'Tumbling Tumbleweeds' and 'Cool Water'. Such songs stand in sharp contrast to the earthier and more rough-hewn western songs of early singing cowboy stars like the handsome Carl T. Sprague (one of the first cowboys to achieve a level of popularity in the mid-1920s that approached stardom).

By 1943, Rogers had left the Pioneers and embarked on a successful film career, rivaling Gene Autry as America's most popular singing cowboy – a status he maintained into the early 1950s, when he made a transition to television and became one of its early stars. It's a sign of his enduring popularity and influence that Rogers, who died in 1998, is the only man twice elected to the Country Music Hall of Fame – first as an original member of the Sons of the Pioneers and later as a solo musician.

The Cowboys Ride On

By the early 1950s, the popularity of western music had nearly run its course, but in the decades since it has been gloriously revived now and again by artists like Marty Robbins ('Big Iron', 'El Paso'), Johnny Cash ('Don't Take Your Guns To Town') and, more recently, former pop star Michael Martin Murphey. The leading contemporary purveyor of cowboy music is a lively vocal group called Riders In The Sky, headed by singer/music historian Douglas B. Green. The Riders have carved out a contemporary niche by blending the Sons of the Pioneers' vocal harmony tradition with strains of thoroughly modern humour and satire.

Western Swing

WESTERN SWING IS AN INNOVATIVE, FREE-WHEELING YET COMPLEX INSTRUMENTAL AMALGAM DRAWN FROM BLUES, JAZZ AND DIXIELAND SYNCOPATIONS AND HARMONIES. CENTRAL TO THE STYLE IS AN EMPHASIS ON INSTRUMENTAL SOLOS, OFTEN INVOLVING THE TRANSPOSITION OF JAZZ-STYLE HORN PARTS TO FIDDLE, GUITAR AND STEEL GUITAR.

IT is indicative of western swing's sophistication that Bob Wills' Texas Playboys, the definitive western swing band, included at various times a Dixieland drummer (Smokey Dacus), a jazz piano player (Al Stricklin) and a jazz-flavoured guitarist (Eldon Shamblin). Wills' innovations with his long-time band the Texas Playboys were crucial to the emergence of this hybrid music that merged horns and the free-wheeling, improvisatory spirit of jazz big bands with country fiddle music and elements of honky tonk instrumentation like the electric guitar, steel guitar and twin fiddles.

Rivaling Wills' influence in establishing and propagating early western swing was his fellow Texan and one-time band mate, Milton Brown – the two played together briefly in the early 1930s as part of a trio called the Aladdin Laddies, and

later the Light Crust Doughboys. Brown and his band the Musical Brownies were, until Brown's untimely death in a car accident in 1936, pioneers of a number of the genre's essential ingredients, including New Orleans jazz rhythms, twin fiddles

playing in harmony, slap-bass fiddle playing and some of the earliest uses of electrified instruments in country music. Brown, just as importantly, brought a smooth and rhythmic vocal style to western swing that drew more heavily from jazz masters like Jack Teagarden and Cab Calloway than from country sources. He also recorded and popularized songs like 'Right Or Wrong' and 'Corrine Corrina' that still endure as western swing standards. Unfortunately, without Brown, the Brownies' innovations ceased and the band's popularity quickly waned.

Doughboys And Playboys

Bob Wills' career began modestly in 1929 when a trio he'd formed landed a spot on a Fort Worth, Texas radio station. In the early 1930s, as he moved on to larger radio stations and his budget increased, Wills added additional players (including Milton Brown) to his band, which was called at various times the Aladdin Laddies and the Light Crust Doughboys (depending on what company was sponsoring his show at the time). In Tulsa, Oklahoma in 1934 the name Texas Playboys finally stuck for good. By then Wills had further expanded his instrumental line-up to include two fiddles, two guitars

Left

Not only is Hank Thompson a great musician, songwriter and all-round entertainer, he is also an electronics wizard and develops his own lighting and sound arrangements for his shows.

"WHEN DANCERS SPOTTED THE TEXAS PLAYBOYS AT ONE END OF CAIN'S DANCEHALL OUTSIDE TULSA, WHAT THEY SAW WAS A TRADITIONAL COUNTRY STRING BAND. WHAT THEY HEARD, HOWEVER, WAS A NEW KIND OF JAZZ BAND."

Charles Townsend

LEADING EXPONENTS

Bob Wills & the Texas Playboys

Milton Brown & his Musical Brownies

Leon McAuliffe

Cliff Bruner's Texas Wanderers

Tommy Duncan & the Western All-Stars

Hank Thompson

Johnny Gimble

Ray Benson & Asleep At The Wheel

Merle Haggard

George Strait

WESTERN SWING

Western swing adopted and adapted the rhythms of swing jazz including the characteristic "walking bass", usually in a fairly simple form.

THE BLUES INTRO ➡ 154   COUNTRY: COWBOY MUSIC ➡ 190

Above & Below Right

Bob Wills (repeated below right) shows jazz and blues influences in his music, which he absorbed from working and playing with the cotton-field slaves. He once travelled 50 miles on horseback to see Bessie Smith perform.

and a bass, piano and banjo. Four years later, he had boosted the band to 14 members, including a third fiddle, two saxophones and a trumpet player.

By 1935, after more personnel shuffles, Wills assembled what some consider to be the most talented line-up of Playboys. Players included vocalist Tommy Duncan, banjo player Johnnie Lee Wills, bass player Son Lansford, trumpeter Everett Stover, saxophonist Zeb McNally, guitarist Herman Arnspiger, trombonist Art Haines, fiddler Jesse Ashlock, steel guitarist Leon McAuliffe, guitarist Sleepy Johnson, drummer Smokey Dacus, piano player Al Stricklin and Wills himself, also on fiddle. In the next few years, Wills enlarged his already substantial band still more, adding an entire six-man horn section and innovative guitarist Eldon Shamblin. He soon was recording some of the songs that have endured as western swing's universal standards, including 'Time Changes Everything', 'San Antonio Rose', 'Take Me Back To Tulsa' and 'Cherokee Maiden'.

Western Swing's The Thing

Wills' popularity continued unabated throughout most of the 1940s and the personnel shifts continued. In the late 1940s, he added the brilliant Texas fiddler Johnny Gimble to the Playboys' line-up and employed his younger brother Billy Jack Wills as his vocalist after Tommy Duncan — western swing's most celebrated singer, who sang lead on many of Wills' landmark recordings — left in 1948 to form his own band, the Western All-Stars. Wills also gradually reduced his once-expansive horn section to a single trumpet. During these years he added yet another enduring hit, 'Faded Love,' to his celebrated repertoire.

As Wills' popularity had begun to spread in the 1930s, the Texas Playboys became the inspiration for a number of other talented western swing bands. Many of these were led by former Texas Playboys like Leon McAuliffe, Jesse Ashlock and Wills' brothers Lee and Billy Jack. The western swing sound even spread as far afield as Kentucky, where a band called the

Prairie Ramblers picked up on it. Adding Patsy Montana, a talented Arkansas singer, to their line-up, they became popular members of Chicago's *National Barndance* radio show during the 1930s and 1940s.

However, practically all these bands, as well as notables like Cliff Bruner's Texas Wanderers and Jimmie Revard & his Oklahoma Playboys, borrowed heavily from Wills' arrangements and repertoire and never quite escaped his long shadow. By the mid-1950s, Wills' star was on the wane, as was his health, and the golden age of western swing had largely run its course. The western swing king was sidelined forever in 1969 by a debilitating stroke and died in 1975 following a series of strokes.

Bob Wills Is Still The King

Even decades after its 1930s and 1940s heyday, western swing in general and Wills' repertoire and Texas-style big-band sound in particular, have been revisited time and again by contemporary country stars like Merle Haggard and George Strait, as well as celebrated honky tonkers like Ray Price, Red Steagall and, most notably, Texan Hank Thompson. A real

milestone in western swing revivalism came in 1970 when Merle Haggard, a lifelong admirer of Wills, reassembled many of the original Texas Playboys and recorded a magnificent album-length salute to Wills called *A Tribute To The Best Damn Fiddle Player In The World*. Numerous artists, including George Strait and Ray Benson, have cited the album as a seminal influence on their musical coming of age.

Oddly enough, western swing also got a fresh hearing in the 1970s and 1980s through the music of several eclectic, youthful hippy-era bands like Commander Cody & his Lost Planet Airmen, Dan Hicks & his Hot Licks and Asleep At The Wheel, who became enthralled with the Bob Wills musical tradition. The most enduring of these neo-western swingers is Asleep At The Wheel, a band headed by Texas singer Ray Benson. Benson originally formed Asleep At The Wheel in west Virginia and the band cut its teeth playing clubs in the nearby Washington, DC area in the late 1960s. Through thick and thin, countless personnel changes and several Grammy Awards, Benson and the Wheel are still going strong as the most vital contemporary purveyors of this intricate yet robust and eminently danceable music.

Above

Asleep At The Wheel play a highly original fusion of country, jazz and swing, but their inherent love of the Bob Wills sound was commemorated on their 1999 album Ride With Bob.

UNLIKE PRACTICALLY ANY OTHER STRAIN OF INDIGENOUS AMERICAN MUSIC, BLUEGRASS CAN BE TRACED BACK TO A PARTICULAR TIME AND A PARTICULAR GROUP OF MEN: KENTUCKY-BORN MANDOLIN PLAYER/ BANDLEADER BILL MONROE AND A SELECT HANDFUL OF MUSICIANS HE GATHERED IN HIS BAND, THE BLUEGRASS BOYS.

Bluegrass

MONROE and the celebrated 1940s vintage line-up of the Bluegrass Boys first transformed traditional acoustic guitar-fiddle-bass-fiddle country stringband music into something fresh, exciting and revolutionary in its innovation. They did this by kicking it into a higher gear and giving it a driving, syncopated beat along with close, high-pitched, "high lonesome" lead and harmony vocals on favourites like 'Uncle Pen', 'Muleskinner Blues' and 'Blue Moon Of Kentucky'. Monroe also elevated the mandolin from a rhythmic to a fully fledged lead instrument. Earl Scruggs essentially did the same with the five-string banjo.

"I THINK BILL MONROE'S IMPORTANCE TO AMERICAN MUSIC IS AS IMPORTANT AS SOMEONE LIKE ROBERT JOHNSON WAS TO BLUES, OR LOUIS ARMSTRONG. HE WAS SO INFLUENTIAL; I THINK HE'S PROBABLY THE ONLY MUSICIAN THAT HAD A WHOLE STYLE OF MUSIC NAMED AFTER HIS BAND."

Ricky Scaggs

The Grass Is Always Bluer

The music that Monroe and a handful of his talented contemporaries forged more than half a century ago has not only endured, but has also enjoyed renewed popularity in recent decades. In fact, one of the most acclaimed and best-selling country albums of the new millennium, despite getting practically no airplay on country stations, is the soundtrack from the 2000 feature film *O Brother, Where Art Thou?* A quirky, dark comedy directed by the Coen Brothers, *O Brother* transferred a Homeric epic to a rural 1930s setting. Its rich

soundtrack featured vintage bluegrass by veterans such as Ralph Stanley, as well as old-time country and gospel music by an imaginative line-up of popular and obscure musicians, and contemporary newgrass and alt. country figures like Alison Krauss and Gillian Welch. The soundtrack sold several million copies, won five Grammy Awards and sparked yet another revival in rural musical Americana.

It was the stellar 1945–48 line-up of Bill Monroe's Bluegrass Boys – Earl Scruggs on five-string banjo and vocals, Lester Flatt on guitar and vocals, Chubby Wise on fiddle, Cedric Rainwater and Monroe himself on mandolin – that deserves the lion's share of credit for forging this intricate, high-energy musical hybrid from its more traditional antecedents. To this day the seminal late- and mid-1940s Bluegrass Boys recordings serve as the template, and the Holy Grail, of the traditional bluegrass sound.

Tennessee-born Flatt and North Carolina-born Scruggs, a pair of former textile mill workers, left the Bluegrass Boys in 1948 and formed their own band, the Foggy Mountain Boys. This new ensemble would play nearly as central a role as Monroe and the Bluegrass Boys in further defining the bluegrass spirit and style. With his intricate three-finger banjo style, Scruggs elevated the banjo from a traditional rhythmic role to a lead instrument as crucial to bluegrass's soul as Monroe's

LEADING EXPONENTS

Bill Monroe & the
  Bluegrass Boys
Lester Flatt & Earl
  Scruggs
Carter & Ralph Stanley
Don Reno & Red Smiley
Jim & Jesse McReynolds
The Country Gentlemen
The Seldom Scene
J. D. Crowe & the New
  South
New Grass Revival
Del McCoury

BLUEGRASS

The violin, mandolin, guitar and banjo are the predominant instruments of Bluegrass. The violin's double stopping with open strings reinforces the underlying harmony.

THE COUNTRY INTRO ➡ 182   COUNTRY PEOPLE A–Z ➡ 220   INSTRUMENTS A–Z ➡ 436   THE BLUES INTRO ➡ 154   FOLK: FOLK SONGS ➡ 226

kinetic mandolin style. The Foggy Mountain Boys also imbued their bluegrass sound with smoother lead vocals while adding a second guitar and speeding the rhythm up even more, with an emphasis on Scruggs's intricate breakneck speed banjo playing. In 1955 Flatt & Scruggs added the dobro (resonator guitar) of Josh Graves to the Foggy Mountain Boys. It was Graves' expertise that has since established the dobro's mournful presence as a central ingredient in bluegrass. Until they went their separate ways in 1966, Flatt & Scruggs did much to popularize bluegrass with non-country audiences with favourites like 'Foggy Mountain Breakdown', 'Roll In My Sweet Baby's Arms' and 'Old Salty Dog Blues'.

O Brother …

Monroe's innovations on the *Grand Ole Opry*, both with Flatt & Scruggs and after their departure from the Bluegrass Boys, did not go unnoticed in the heartlands where the *Grand Ole Opry's* powerful 50,000-watt AM signal boomed far and wide on Saturday nights. It had a particularly important impact on a pair of young Virginia musicians, Ralph and Carter Stanley. The Stanley Brothers, who were steeped in the harmony-driven old-time music traditions of their native state, began covering songs by Monroe and the Bluegrass Boys and incorporating the new bluegrass sound into their own distinct mountain style on classic recordings like 'Molly And Tenbrooks'.

The Stanley Brothers soon became one of bluegrass's most popular bands and they remained in the front ranks until Carter Stanley's death in 1966. After that, Ralph, who until then had pretty much worked in older brother Carter's shadow, assumed the role of lead singer and bandleader of the Clinch Mountain Boys and has since enjoyed great musical longevity.

Virginians Jim and Jesse McReynolds rose to bluegrass's front ranks in the 1960s on the strength of Jim's brilliant tenor and Jesse's imaginative transposition of the syncopated "cross-picking" banjo technique to the mandolin. Jim & Jesse, much like the Stanley Brothers, were anchored in the traditional mountain stringband sound early in their career, but by 1964, when they became members of the *Grand Ole Opry*, they were expanding bluegrass's parameters by masterfully weaving mainstream country elements into their repertoire and sometimes even using electrified instruments.

In the 1960s, the Osborne Brothers from Hyden, Kentucky, also found success on country radio (which by and large had shied away from playing bluegrass, which it deemed too strident and old-timey for its listeners). The Osbornes adventurously augmented their individualized bluegrass sound with typically non-bluegrass instrumentation like steel guitars, drums and pianos. Mac Wiseman, a lead vocalist and rhythm guitarist with Monroe's Bluegrass Boys, also achieved popularity with country audiences by occasionally refashioning pop songs

Above

The unprecedented success of the O Brother, Where Art Thou *soundtrack inspired concerts by the contributors at the Ryman Auditorium and Carnegie Hall, a documentary film of the Ryman concert and a further soundtrack album of the documentary.*

Left

Bill Monroe, creator and undisputed king of the bluegrass sound. Monroe's plaintive, wailing vocals, combined with the dense textures and frenetic playing of his band, took country music in a new and exciting direction

Far Left

The banjo was brought to the bluegrass foreground by Earl Scruggs, with his incredibly fast, three-finger-picking style. Scruggs set a trend for wearing the banjo over one shoulder, later explaining this was so that he could take his banjo on and off without having to remove his hat.

Above

Earl Scruggs and Lester Flatt perform at the Grand Ole Opry *with the other Foggy Mountain Boys. Flatt & Scruggs' popularity was furthered by the popular 1960s TV show* The Beverly Hillbillies, *which featured music by the duo, as well as cameo appearances.*

of the day like 'Love Letters In The Sand' into bluegrass odes. Other ensembles, like the great, innovative banjo-guitar-vocal duet team Don Reno and Red Smiley and fiddler Kenny Baker, would enrich and expand upon bluegrass's traditional roots throughout the 1960s and 1970s.

Bluegrass To Newgrass

Young, progressive bluegrass artists like the Dillards, Clarence and Roland White and Byron Berline were part of a 1960s and 1970s renaissance that came to be called newgrass. Other pioneering newgrass bands like the New Grass Revival, Ricky Skaggs's short-lived but influential Boone Creek and J. D. Crowe & the New South broke ranks by infusing traditional bluegrass with youthful energy, electrified instruments and wide-ranging eclecticism.Beginning in the late 1950s, the greater Washington, DC area began to emerge as a hotbed

of fine bluegrass innovation, due in large part to the presence in the region of many Kentucky and Virginia musicians who had moved there in search of work. Top-notch bands like the Seldom Scene and the Country Gentlemen reinvigorated bluegrass in their own fashion by adding smooth, urbane harmonies, increased emphasis on flashy instrumental leads and broad song repertoires that included distinctly non-bluegrass folk and rock tunes from distinctly non-bluegrass songwriters like Bob Dylan, Gordon Lightfoot and even Eric Clapton.

Since the 1970s, bluegrass has enjoyed a golden age of renewal, vitality and popularity through artists and ensembles like Alison Krauss, Nickel Creek, Larry Sparks, Del McCoury, the Seldom Scene, IIIrd Tyme Out, the Lonesome River Band, Blue Highway, Claire Lynch and Rhonda Vincent.

Honky Tonk

AT LEAST UNTIL THE 1930S AND 1940S THE DOMINANT THEMES IN COUNTRY MUSIC WERE A CELEBRATION OF BEDROCK RURAL VALUES LIKE FAMILY, FAITH, FIDELITY AND THE REDEEMING POWERS OF TRUE LOVE AND HONEST LABOUR. THE MUSIC SERVED AS MUCH AS ANYTHING TO OFFER LISTENERS COMFORT, REASSURANCE AND A SOOTHING SENSE OF PLACE AND IDENTITY.

BUT as America's national zeitgeist began to reflect dramatic social shifts like the industrial-age migration from country to city, country music, especially in the unsettled, temporary, Second World War-era oil field, factory and shipyard settlements of Texas and the great American Southwest, underwent a similar transformation. The rise of honky tonk music was a manifestation of that social upheaval. It is strident, electrified and utterly worldly music that drew its very name from the rough-hewn saloons and dancehalls, known as "honky tonks", in grungy working-class cities like Houston, Beaumont and Port Arthur, Texas. Honky tonk really became a force in country music during the 1940s and particularly during the era of the Second World War.

Honky tonk's emphasis on electrification and heavier percussion was also a departure from largely acoustic-based traditional country music. It was both a reflection of a faster-paced life as well as a practical means of being heard over the late-night din in an oil-field or factory-town barroom.

The Kings Of Honky Tonk

The first major star to arise in the genre was Texas-born Ernest Tubb, whose illustrious recording career stretched from 1936 until 1982. A gruff-voiced yet plaintive singer, Tubb started out in the 1930s as an earnest disciple of Jimmie Rodgers, but he found his own laconic voice with earthy honky tonk anthems like 'Walking The Floor Over You', 'Wasting My Life Away' and 'Warm Red Wine'. Tubb further widened honky tonk's audience in the early 1940s when he became a member of Nashville's *Grand Ole Opry*.

But few if any artists would transfigure country music, write and sing the standards and define honky tonk for decades to come in the way that Alabama-born former shipyard worker and itinerant musician Hank Williams did, beginning in the late 1940s. Williams' timeless originals ('Cold, Cold Heart', 'I'm So Lonesome I Could Cry', 'Jambalaya', 'Your Cheatin' Heart', etc.) and his stark, lonesome and evocative singing style both personified and transcended honky tonk's earthbound parameters.

Despite Williams' early and untimely death at age 29 in 1953, his immense musical legacy and ill-starred legend loom even larger with each passing year. His original compositions, in the half-century since his death, have been recorded hundreds of times by everyone from George Jones and Patsy Cline to Tony Bennett and Cassandra Wilson.

> "WE GOTTA PLAY MUSIC THAT'LL MAKE THEM GODDAMN BEER BOTTLES BOUNCE ON THE TABLE."
> *Moon Mullican*

Above
The legendary Hank Williams, who has strongly influenced countless musicians, country or otherwise, with his poignant songs.

Left
An original performer, Lefty Frizzell also had his own sharp way of dressing and was the first country star to wear rhinestones onstage.

LEADING EXPONENTS
Al Dexter
Ernest Tubb
Hank Williams
Lefty Frizzell
Hank Thompson
Kitty Wells
Ray Price
George Jones
Jerry Lee Lewis
Merle Haggard

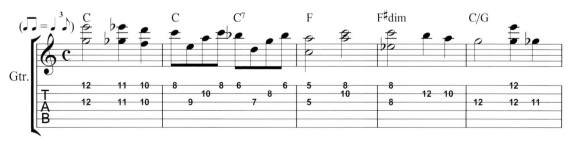

HONKY TONK
This excerpt shows descending sixths played by electric guitar (or pedal steel). The diminished chord was an addition to the traditional tonic, dominant and sub-dominant.

Another major player who has enjoyed great longevity in the field is Texan Hank Thompson, who had parallel importance as a proponent of western swing and scored hits with 'Humpty Dumpty Heart' (1948) and 'The Wild Side Of Life' (1952). Kitty Wells, the demure, retiring wife of singer Johnny Wright (of Johnny & Jack) unwittingly became one of the first and only honky tonk queens when 'It Wasn't God Who Made Honky Tonk Angels', her answer song to Hank Thompson's 'Wild Side Of Life', became a surprise number one radio and jukebox hit in 1952.

Though best known for lighter 1960s and 1970s Nashville sound crossover-style hits like 'Danny Boy' and 'For The Good Times', Texan Ray Price began his recording career in the 1950s with pivotal hits like 'Crazy Arms' and 'City Lights'. The intense rhythmic brand of honky tonk that Price introduced with these recordings has been so widely emulated that it has since become known as the 'Ray Price Beat'.

The Legacy Of The Honky Tonk Blues

The man whose music has became as synonymous with 1960s–1990s honky tonk as Frizzell's and Williams' names were to the 1950s is east Texas native George Jones. An early devotee of Frizzell, Williams and *Grand Ole Opry* star Roy Acuff, Jones, by the late 1950s, had subsumed these worthy vocal influences into his own uncannily powerful and subtle octave-swooping baritone that plumbs the depths of emotional profundity and clenched-teeth sorrow like almost no one before. Also like Williams and Frizzell before him, Jones, throughout his half-century recording career, has emerged as a tortured, ambivalent soul whose despair and confusion often echo hauntingly in his music. As such, his hit, beer-stained lamentations like 'He Stopped Loving Her Today' and 'Bartender's Blues' and his unabashed celebrations of the wild side like 'Tennessee Whiskey' and 'White Lightning' have come to embody honky tonk for many country fans.

The honky tonk influence has persisted over the decades, even through the more mellow eras of the Nashville sound and the urban cowboys. Today it's clearly heard in the music of contemporary stars like Alan Jackson (chart-topping hits like 1991's 'Don't Rock The Jukebox' and 1992's 'She's Got The Rhythm (And I've Got The Blues)') and Dwight Yoakam (his brilliant 1986 cover of Johnny Horton's 'Honky Tonk Man' and his 1988 hit duet with Buck Owens, 'Streets of Bakersfield') whose vocal styles have been profoundly inspired by an earlier generation of practitioners like Hank Williams, Merle Haggard, Lefty Frizzell and George Jones.

Humpty-Dumpty And Honky Tonk Angels

Nearly as influential as Williams as a honky tonk vocalist was Corsicana, Texas-born Lefty Frizzell. Like Tubb before him, Frizzell was heavily steeped in the Jimmie Rodgers legacy. Yet by the early 1950s, when he had an almost unprecedented flurry of hits like 'If You've Got The Money I've Got The Time' and 'Mom And Dad's Waltz', Frizzell had developed his own vividly original and emotional clenched-teeth, slip-note, vowel-bending vocal style. His vocal influence lingers vividly today in the voices of more recent honky tonk and country stars like George Jones, George Strait, Randy Travis and Merle Haggard. Although Haggard's vocal mannerisms are heavily rooted in the Lefty Frizzell style and as an artist he has been a major proponent of honky tonk since the late 1960s, his amazing versatility and stylistic range transcend any one particular strain of country music.

The Nashville Sound

THE NASHVILLE SOUND HAS BEEN BOTH PRAISED AND MALIGNED. OCCASIONALLY CALLED "CROSSOVER COUNTRY", "EASY LISTENING COUNTRY" OR "COUNTRYPOLITAN", IT WAS A TREND MORE THAN AN INNOVATION. AS SUCH, IT AROSE AS MUCH FROM COMMERCIAL CONSIDERATIONS AS IT DID FROM PERSONAL ARTISTRY.

ALL through the decades there have been periodic cross-pollinations between the country world and the wider pop audience. From the 1930s well into the 1950s *Grand Ole Opry* star Red Foley charmed both country folk and urbanites alike with his smooth voice and mellow musical sensibilities. In the 1950s and early 1960s Patti Page, an Oklahoman who started out singing western swing music, had a few best-selling pop hits with covers of country tunes. Her 1950 recording of Pee Wee King's 'Tennessee Waltz' sold nearly five million copies. Crooner Bing Crosby even got in on the act with a cover of Ernest Tubb's 'Walkin' The Floor Over You'.

An Antidote To Rock'n'Roll

Oddly enough, it was the advent of rock'n'roll that really spurred the late-1950s and early 1960s Nashville crossover era. The emergence of Elvis Presley, Jerry Lee Lewis and other

rock'n'rollers with early hits like 'Hound Dog', 'Jailhouse Rock', 'Whole Lotta Shakin' ' and 'Great Balls Of Fire' unleashed a national craze that for a while seriously impacted country record sales. The negative impact on the country record market was such that even hardcore country artists like George Jones responded by trying their hands at rockabilly and rock'n'roll. Others, like Sonny James, Marty Robbins and Don Gibson, broke through the late-1950s crossover market with mellow teen ballads like 'Young Love' and 'A White Sport Coat (And A Pink Carnation)'. The success of such records was not lost upon Nashville producers Chet Atkins and Owen Bradley, the widely acknowledged pioneers of the Nashville sound. They, along with any number of other Music Row producers, had been trying to figure out for a long time how to make country records that could jump the fence into the far more lucrative pop crossover market.

Their appetites were further whetted by the success of Nashville-based artists like the Everly Brothers, Roy Orbison and Brenda Lee, who managed to achieve longevity in the 1950s and 1960s as teen pop idols with hits that were written by Nashville-based songwriters and recorded and produced in Nashville studios.

> "NOW WE'VE CUT OUT THE FIDDLE AND STEEL GUITAR AND ADDED CHORUSES TO COUNTRY MUSIC. BUT IT CAN'T STOP THERE. IT ALWAYS HAS TO KEEP DEVELOPING TO KEEP FRESH."
>
> *Producer Owen Bradley*

Left
Nashville, Tennessee, the "Music City", in 1933. Home to the Grand Ole Opry and country music's top producers, Nashville was the destination of many a hopeful hillbilly dreaming of a recording contract.

NASHVILLE SOUND

The harshness of the fiddle and steel string guitar are softened in Nashville sound by the use of additional vocal back-up, and string sections or a full orchestra.

LEADING EXPONENTS

Eddy Arnold
Patsy Cline
Jim Reeves
George Morgan
Faron Young
David Houston
Charlie Rich
Tammy Wynette

THE COUNTRY INTRO ➡ 182   COUNTRY PEOPLE A–Z ➡ 220   INSTRUMENTS A–Z ➡ 436   POP: FIFTIES POP ➡ 12

From Nashville To "Cashville"

What distinguished the Nashville sound was the way it aggressively dressed up mainstream country music for pop airplay. Producers like Atkins and Bradley found tasteful ways of toning down the clatter and clang of country music's raw edges and nudging it in a more uptown direction. They eased up on – or eliminated altogether – the vocal twang and replaced raucous fiddles and steel guitars with lush vocal arrangements, bright, sparkling slip-note piano embellishments and laid-back string and horn arrangements.

The term "Nashville sound" also refers to the increasingly regimented, almost factory-like approach to hit-making that producers like Atkins and Bradley utilized during the heyday of the Nashville sound. By the early 1960s, the Music Row studio system had become dominated by a relatively small,

tight-knit group of "A Team" studio musicians who played on hundreds of recording sessions, conducted with the precision and efficiency of a factory time clock.

Many fans of traditional and honky tonk-style country music – particularly those of older generations – took such Nashville sound refinements as an affront to the music's integrity and even a harbinger of the impending death of country music as they knew and loved it. They found it even more irritating when a few premier honky tonk singers such as Ray Price blithely segued into a mellow, easy listening pop cushiness with hits like 'Danny Boy' and 'For The Good Times' that seemed the very antithesis of hard country.

Some artists most closely associated with the Nashville sound, like crooner Eddy Arnold ('What's He Doing In My World'), *Grand Ole Opry* star George Morgan and Virginia-born songstress Patsy Cline (who before her untimely death in a 1963 plane crash cracked the pop Top 10 with 'Crazy') flourished and found their natural voices in the Nashville sound setting. So did others like Marty Robbins (who topped the pop charts with the western ballad 'El Paso' in 1959), Ferlin Husky ('Gone', 'Wings Of A Dove') and former honky tonkers Don Gibson ('Oh Lonesome Me') and Faron Young, who reached the pop Top 20 in 1961 with Willie Nelson's 'Hello Walls'. Ironically, practically all of these singers had begun their careers in a much more traditional spirit.

Crossing over from a slightly different angle were artists like Bobby Bare ('500 Miles Away From Home'), George Hamilton IV ('Abilene') and Johnny Cash ('Ring Of Fire'), who enjoyed some success in the country charts and at least some in the pop charts, with a subgenre often referred to as folk country. Roger Miller managed to cross over in his own quirky way and won 11 Grammy Awards with hip, scat-sung novelty tunes like 'King Of The Road' and 'Dang Me'.

The Sherrillization Of Nashville

The producer who inherited the Nashville sound mantle in the 1970s was Billy Sherrill, a talented and somewhat enigmatic former Alabama rhythm & blues saxophone player. Sherrill would earn both kudos and scorn for upping the Nashville sound ante even further by adapting the "wall of sound" approach pioneered by legendary rock producer Phil Spector on pop hits by artists like the Righteous Brothers. Sherrill applied his own heavily layered wall of sound to hits he produced for stars of the day like Tammy Wynette (who, despite the overblown arrangements on hits like 'Stand By Your Man,' usually avoided the Nashville sound tag simply because her voice was so countrified), David Houston ('Almost Persuaded') and Charlie Rich.

Rich, a gifted former white R&B and supper-club jazz singer who made it big with slick crossover chart-toppers in the 1970s like 'Behind Closed Doors' and 'The Most Beautiful Girl In The World', became a particular embodiment of what has been both praised and damned as the "Sherrillization" of country music. Love it or hate it, many of the Billy Sherrill-produced records by Rich and Wynette, like 'Stand By Your Man' and 'Behind Closed Doors', were runaway best-sellers.

Permutations of the Nashville sound have, to one extent or another and in one form or another, persisted right up into the present era. But by the early 1970s, its refinements had begun to lapse into predictability and stagnation. The trend reached its embarrassing nadir in 1975 when the Country Music Association saw fit to bestow its highest honour, the "Entertainer of the Year" award, on pop star John Denver, to the chagrin of innumerable country music performers and enthusiasts. Although the Nashville sound remains a factor in mainstream country to this day, it fell upon a handful of strong-willed mavericks, popularly known as country's outlaws, to rise from the late-1960s and 1970s Nashville sound morass and revitalize country's mainstream by swinging it back toward its rustic, unadorned roots.

Above

Chet Atkins, session guitarist and producer, has worked with all the greats, including the Carter Family, Hank Williams, Ray Charles, Roy Orbison and Elvis Presley. Atkins, together with Merle Travis and Doc Watson, is considered one of the "holy trinity" of country guitarists.

Mainstream Country

THE NAMES OF THIS ARRAY OF LANDMARK ARTISTS WHOSE MUSIC EITHER STRADDLED OR TRANSCENDED SPECIFIC GENRES, – JOHNNY CASH, DOLLY PARTON, TAMMY WYNETTE, LORETTA LYNN, GEORGE JONES, CONWAY TWITTY, CHARLEY PRIDE AND BUCK OWENS AMONG OTHERS – HAVE BECOME SYNONYMOUS WITH COUNTRY MUSIC.

Above

Tammy Wynette, whose unmistakable country twang graced the charts as a solo artist, in duets with her one-time husband George Jones and as a trio with Dolly Parton and Loretta Lynn.

DURING the 1950s, 1960s and 1970s, country's popularity penetrated deeper into the American psyche and even won an international following. In 1953 there was only one full-time country music station in the US; by the late-1950s there was still only a handful, but by 1969 the scope of the "country explosion" was such that the number of full-time country stations had risen to 606. Country music also found a handy vehicle in popular network musical variety TV shows like *Hee Haw* and *The Johnny Cash Show*.

The Top Dogs Of Country

Foremost among this era's artists was Johnny Cash. Cash first emerged from the Memphis/Sun Records 1950s rockabilly stable with songs like 'I Walk The Line', but by the early 1960s he had embarked on an amazing four-decade country career, releasing such classics as 'Ring Of Fire' and 'Folsom Prison Blues'. With his unmistakably gruff, sonorous voice and his incredible breadth as a writer and interpreter of songs, Cash delved masterfully into everything from historic Americana ballads to gut-bucket prison songs and politically charged, folk-style ballads.

Nearly as formidable a figure was Merle Haggard. He first emerged from the Bakersfield, California music scene as a Buck Owens protégé, but by the early 1970s, Haggard manifested nearly unparalleled creative and stylistic ambition. With his vivid songwriting, rich, fluid Lefty Frizzell-style baritone, accomplished lead guitar work and finesse as a country-jazz bandleader, Haggard became a dominant figure throughout the 1970s and 1980s. As a revivalist, he had a profound influence on the next generation of artists, with his masterful reprises of music by greats like Jimmie Rodgers, Lefty Frizzell and western swing king Bob Wills, as well as original material such as 'The Fugitive', 'Okie From Muskogee' and 'I Think I'll Just Stay Here And Drink'.

"BACK WHEN YOU'RE TRYING TO MAKE A LIVING, YOU'VE GOT TO DO EVERYTHING YOU CAN TO GET A RECORD PLAYED TO MAKE ENOUGH MONEY, TO BE ACCEPTED ON THE CHARTS. I JOKE THAT I HAD TO GET RICH IN ORDER TO SING LIKE I'M POOR AGAIN."

Dolly Parton

LEADING EXPONENTS

Johnny Cash
Loretta Lynn
Buck Owens
Tammy Wynette
Merle Haggard
Dolly Parton
Charley Pride
Conway Twitty
The Statler Brothers
Tom T. Hall

MAINSTREAM COUNTRY

At the very heart of mainstream country music is the strummed or picked acoustic guitar. This example plays bass notes alternating with rhythmic strummed chords.

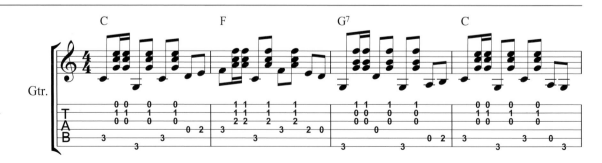

THE COUNTRY INTRO ➡182   COUNTRY PEOPLE A-Z ➡220   INSTRUMENTS A-Z ➡436   THE POP INTRO ➡8

Willie Nelson had a similarly pervasive impact. By the mid-1970s the vastly talented and musically adventurous singer-songwriter-guitarist transcended his spearhead role of the early 1970s outlaw movement to forge a remarkable career that has covered a panoply of styles – from hardcore honky tonk and country rock to pop balladry and even inspired excursions into soft jazz and 1930s and 1940s show tunes.

Straddling these two extremes was Conway Twitty ('Hello Darlin'', 'You've Never Been This Far Before', 'I'd Love To Lay You Down'). Though his instincts were more unerringly commercial than Cash's or Haggard's, Twitty (another Sun Records alumnus) would consistently top the charts from the late 1960s into the 1990s with everything from hardcore honky tonk ballads to syrupy countrified remakes of pop and rock ballads. Other country stars, such as Ferlin Husky, Mac Davis, Ronnie Milsap, Glen Campbell, Kenny Rogers and Barbara Mandrell, would thrive with more low-key and refined styles connected to the 1960s Nashville sound – which remained alive and well in one form or another even during the 1970s and 1980s.

The Rise Of The Cowgirls

The 1960s through to the 1980s also saw the rise of women as a dominant force in country. Central to the countrified "women's movement" was Kentucky-born coal-miner's daughter Loretta Lynn. With a singing style and songwriter's sensibility that was resolutely twangy, rustic and sassy, Lynn, like Johnny Cash, would ultimately achieve the stature of folk hero. Like Cash, her authentic musical roots were firmly anchored in the backwoods temperament of her humble, rural upbringing. Nearly as emblematic for millions of "unliberated" American women was Mississippi-born former hairdresser Tammy Wynette, best remembered for anthems like 'Stand By Your Man' and 'D-I-V-O-R-C-E'. Though she would later segue into a more pop-oriented sound, Dolly Parton first gained prominence in the early and mid-1970s with unadorned yet eloquent original songs that celebrated her east Tennessee Smoky Mountain heritage.

Other Country Chart Sounds

The 1950s and 1960s also saw the rise of prototypical singer-songwriters like Don Gibson, Roger Miller, Tom T. Hall and Kris Kristofferson, who enriched the music with eloquent and often idiosyncratic compositional styles. A few, like Don Williams, a former member of folk group the Pozo Seco Singers, brought a laconic, introspective folk influence to the country field. Others, like the Statler Brothers, drew upon a gospel vocal quartet flavour to popularize sentimental story-songs like 'Countin' Flowers On The Wall'. Still others,

Above
The "Man In Black", Johnny Cash. Cash has a huge fan base from a wide range of musical spheres and has found receptive audiences in prisons and at mainstream pop festivals, as well as on the country circuit.

like Vern Gosdin, Stonewall Jackson, Johnny Paycheck and Cal Smith, found passing chart success by revitalizing the honky tonk sound.

Brother harmony groups like the Louvin Brothers, the Wilburn Brothers, the Osbornes and Johnny & Jack also had occasional hits. Their sibling vocal sounds in turn inspired the Everly Brothers, who had a string of early Nashville-produced rock-pop classics like 'Wake Up, Little Susie' in the 1960s. The Kendalls, a talented father-and-daughter vocal duo, also hit big around 1980 with the song 'Heaven's Just A Sin Away'. This "family tradition" would be gloriously revived in the mid-1980s by the Judds, a mother-daughter vocal team that achieved huge popularity.

It is artists like these who forged the template for most of the country music recorded over the years since. And perhaps more than any other generation of musicians, they have had an indelible influence on the younger artists who followed them.

Left
Dolly Parton, for many people the epitome of country music, performs onstage with country-pop crooner Kenny Rogers. The duo had a smash hit in 1983 with the Bee Gees-penned 'Islands In The Stream'.

The Outlaw Movement

BY THE LATE-1960S, THE NASHVILLE MUSIC INDUSTRY HAD GROWN SLICK, COMPLACENT AND PREDICTABLE, EVEN AS THE GREATER NATIONAL CULTURE, IN THE SHADOW OF THE VIETNAM WAR, WAS ENTERING AN ERA OF TUMULT AND REBELLION. LARGELY AS A RESULT OF THIS, THE OUTLAW MOVEMENT AROSE.

IT began as a rudimentary grassroots uprising, instigated by a handful of talented artists whose rough edges and quirky individualism simply didn't fit the prescribed Nashville mold. But, as it gained momentum and the Nashville music industry sensed its commercial viability, the outlaw movement soon became part of the mainstream. As a result, it reinvigorated country music with its vital, restless anti-heroic spirit.

Outlaw music was a musical throwback that drew from the raw spirit of 1950s and 1960s Texas-style honky tonk while infusing it with the aggressive spirit of rock'n'roll urgency and rebellion. While the image of the typical Nashville sound practitioner was that of the clean-cut singer in a well-pressed western suit and an ingratiating "aw-shucks" smile, the outlaw image was about shaggy hair, dirty blue jeans and a wary, world-weary, hungover scowl.

Instrumentally, the outlaws favoured a raw, bedrock guitar-steel guitar-drum-fiddle sound that flew in the face of Nashville sound refinements.

Wanted! The Outlaws

The outlaw movement was in large part launched by two artists: fellow Texans Waylon Jennings (from Texas's northern Panhandle region) and Willie Nelson (who was born in central Texas, not too far south of Dallas). Nelson and Jennings both spent the better part of the 1960s in Nashville as outsiders in an industry that didn't seem to know quite what to make of them. Both men experienced years of frustration while struggling to rise through Nashville's highly regimented, producer-dominated studio system.

Shotgun Willie

Willie Nelson enjoyed considerable success as a Nashville songwriter in the 1960s. The steady string of hits he penned for artists like Patsy Cline ('Crazy') earned him a six-figure income. Though he spent years trying to break through as a recording artist, only two of the many singles he released between 1962 and 1975 even reached the country Top 10. His unconventional baritone possesses roughhewn but powerful gravity, but Nelson has always favoured jazz-like vocal inflections and a propensity for singing slightly ahead of or behind the beat, which confounded Nashville producers.

"THE REASON EVERYBODY CAN RELATE TO OUR MUSIC, I GUESS, IS BECAUSE IT'S SO BASIC. [THE OUTLAW'S] MUSIC IS HONEST AND SIMPLE. WE SYMBOLIZE TO MANY PEOPLE HONESTY AND FIGHTING FOR WHAT YOU BELIEVE IN. AND HONESTY IS SOMETHING YOU CAN'T WEAR OUT."

Waylon Jennings

LEADING EXPONENTS

Willie Nelson

Waylon Jennings

Bobby Bare

Billy Joe Shaver

Kris Kristofferson

David Allan Coe

Johnny Paycheck

Guy Clark

Townes Van Zandt

Jerry Jeff Walker

OUTLAW MOVEMENT

Outlaw country owes its sound to blues lyrics and tempos, combined with rock rhythms and bass lines.

Nelson's commercial and artistic breakthrough began in the early 1970s with a pair of raw, back-to-basics and somewhat autobiographical albums (*Shotgun Willie* and *Phases and Stages*) that he recorded for Atlantic Records at the encouragement of noted rock producer/executive Jerry Wexler. But Nelson really defined his sound and persona with *Red Headed Stranger*, released in 1975 by Columbia Records, a musically austere, thematically complex song-cycle set in the mythical Old West. Nelson recorded the album on a shoestring budget of $20,000 in a small Texas studio, having written most of the songs and produced it himself. With its minimalist arrangements and stark semi-mystical themes of betrayal, murder and redemption, *Red Headed Stranger* was the antithesis of the average, over-produced Music Row album. It eventually sold over a million copies. A single from the album, 'Blue Eyes Crying In The Rain', an old-timey ballad written in 1945 by Fred Rose (Hank Williams' publisher and occasional co-writer), became Nelson's first number one hit and earned him his first Grammy Award.

The Ramblin' Man

Waylon Jennings, at least chart-wise, fared better in the 1960s; he even won a Grammy Award in 1969 for his melancholy country rendition of the syrupy pop hit 'MacArthur Park'. But he really began finding his own voice in the early 1970s when he demanded and attained artistic control over his own music. His initial upward momentum came with a series of landmark albums, including *Ladies Love Outlaws*, *Lonesome On'ry And Mean* and *Honky Tonk Heroes*, on which he called the musical shots and sometimes produced himself.

It was Nelson who, after moving from Nashville back to Texas in the late 1960s, first sensed the winds of change and discovered a new, youthful audience of hippies and long-haired cowboys in the dancehalls of south and central Texas. Most of these were rock'n'rollers with a closet appetite for hard-edged country and honky tonk that was not being satisfied by the more tame styles of country played on the radio. Nelson convinced his friend Jennings that this open-minded young audience might just prove to be the elusive fan base they'd

Above

Willie Nelson and Waylon Jennings, the "most wanted" stars of the outlaw movement. One of Jennings' best outlaw statements was the song 'Are You Sure Hank Done It This Way', a satire on the commercialism of Nashville.

Far Left

Bobby Bare has avoided mainstream success by recording material that he likes personally, regardless of whether it is controversial, darkly humorous or strange.

Left

The Fender Precision Bass. There is a photograph of Waylon Jennings playing one of these on Buddy Holly's fateful 1959 tour.

at RCA, Jennings' long-time label, the outlaws' breakthrough came in 1976. Its cornerstone was *Wanted! The Outlaws*, an uneven compilation album that was cleverly packaged by Bradley. 'Good Hearted Woman', a rowdy Jennings-Nelson duet that was released as a single from the album, topped the country charts in 1975 and won the Country Music Association's "Single of the Year" Award. It became the first country album to achieve million-selling platinum status. And, though largely comprised of previously released material by Nelson and Jennings, along with tracks by their outlaw compatriot, producer/publisher/singer Tompall Glaser and Jennings' wife, singer Jessi Colter, *Wanted! The Outlaws* quickly transformed the outlaw movement from a regional musical uprising to a national commercial force.

The Other Highwaymen

Riding on Jennings' and Nelson's coat-tails came a host of kindred artists, such as Texan Jerry Jeff Walker (who had already achieved considerable notoriety as a folksy country rocker in the 1960s and 1970s with self-penned hits like 'Mr. Bojangles'), Guy Clark and Townes Van Zandt. There were also rough-and-rowdy Nashville-based fellow travellers, including the flamboyant David Allan Coe ('You Never Even Called Me By My Name', 'Longhaired Redneck', 'Waylon & Willie & Me') and 1960s honky tonker Johnny Paycheck ('Take This Job and Shove It'). But one of the movement's central figures and unsung heroes was Ohio-born Bobby Bare, a laconic yet thematically adventurous singer whose influence was also felt behind the scenes. As one of the first Nashville artists to achieve sufficient autonomy to produce his own records and choose his own material, Bare served as a role model for contemporaries like Jennings and Nelson. With his uncanny ear, Bare was also one of the first to discover songwriters like Kris Kristofferson and Billy Joe Shaver, whose compositions would become unofficial anthems of the iconoclastic outlaw movement.

been searching for. As he and Jennings began playing dancehalls around central and south Texas, young "Lone Star State" listeners quickly embraced the raw vitality of outlaw music and the rowdy, long-haired image of its practitioners.

By this time at least a few Nashville music executives began to sense the commercial potential of the youthful rock'n'roll audience Nelson and Jennings had successfully cultivated in the Lone Star State. And thanks to Jerry Bradley, an executive

The very nature of the outlaws' ascendance in some ways presaged the movement's demise. By the late 1970s, perennial outsiders Jennings and Nelson had become industry darlings and quintessential insiders. The gypsy-ish, iconoclastic spirit of their vital, definitive 1960s and early 1970s recordings eventually mellowed into the sort of quieter introspection and soulfulness that great material success and middle age tend to engender. And, once again, complacency became the name of the game along Nashville's Music Row.

Country Rock

IN TERMS OF INFLUENCES AND ORIGINS, COUNTRY AND ROCK'N'ROLL DRAW SO CLOSELY FROM THE SAME ANTECEDENTS THAT THEY ARE PRACTICALLY MUSICAL FIRST COUSINS: BRANCHES FROM THE SAME TREE THAT SHARE THE SAME BASIC INSTRUMENTATION OF GUITAR, BASS AND DRUMS.

TWO of country music's greatest practitioners, Johnny Cash and Jerry Lee Lewis, launched their careers in the mid-1950s as part of the rock'n'roll/rockabilly explosion that took place at Sam Phillips' Sun Studios in Memphis. Even Elvis Presley, the star of the Sun Studio stable, was billed as a country singer and was a regular performer on *Louisiana Hayride*, a live country music radio extravaganza, broadcast from Shreveport.

Dylan Hits Nashville

An early harbinger of the modern country rock movement was Bob Dylan, who journeyed to Nashville in the mid- and late-1960s to record a trio of albums – *Blonde On Blonde*, *John Wesley Harding* and *Nashville Skyline*. For these projects, Dylan utilized "A Team" Music Row session musicians to underpin his dense and surreal lyrics with austere guitar- and steel guitar-driven country arrangements. Dylan's country rock explorations gave added impetus to a vital country rock movement that, by the late-1960s, was underway in southern California, spearheaded by pioneering bands like the Byrds, the Flying Burrito Brothers and Poco. These bands and a handful of others like them imaginatively re-conjoined the two musical styles, which had drifted far apart since the mid-1950s.

The California Country Rock Explosion

These southern California bands grew out of a generation of young musicians who had been raised on rock'n'roll, but were just as influenced and enthralled by the bedrock country sounds of honky tonkers like Hank Williams, Merle Haggard and Buck Owens and the vintage bluegrass and western swing of artists like Bill Monroe and Bob Wills. In various ways, these California bands, like almost none before, melded the

1960s spirit of counter-cultural rebelliousness and the youthful hubris of rock'n'roll with the more down-home attitudes, arrangements and repertoires of country music.

Gram Parsons, The Grievous Angel

A central figure in the California country rock scene was Gram Parsons, a Florida-born, Harvard University dropout and former teenage rock'n'roller. By the time Parsons joined the Byrds in late 1967, he was already resolutely pursuing a musical vision that sought a seamless fusion of acoustic rock- and blues-tinged country honky tonk into an elusive sound that he described as "cosmic American music". What Parsons strived for with the Byrds, then with the Flying Burrito Brothers, and later still as a solo artist, was, in the words of Byrds bandmate Roger McGuinn, "to blend the Beatles and country; to really do something revolutionary".

Parsons found a country music-loving kindred spirit in California-born singer and multi-instrumentalist Chris Hillman, who was the Byrds' bass player at the time. Under Parsons' and Hillman's influence, the band, best remembered today for rock hits like 'Turn Turn Turn', immersed itself in a country idiom. Journeying to Nashville, the Byrds worked

"SO WE TRIED THE COMBINATION OF PUTTING COUNTRY MUSIC, WHICH WAS OUR ROOTS, AND ROCK'N'ROLL TOGETHER TO TRY TO FORM SOMETHING NEW."
Jim Messina

Above
Bob Dylan's 1969 album Nashville Skyline *saw the sometime-protest singer in a more mellow mood. Dylan's singing voice on the album is softer than his usual rasping tone and the songs are short and sweet, with simple lyrics.*

LEADING EXPONENTS
Bob Dylan
Gram Parsons
Chris Hillman
The Byrds
The Flying Burrito
   Brothers
Commander Cody & his
   Lost Planet Airmen
Poco
The Eagles
Charlie Daniels
Hank Williams Jr.

COUNTRY ROCK
The example is a typical country rock rhythm. A strummed acoustic guitar would complete the rhythmic "bed" for electric guitars and vocals.

THE COUNTRY INTRO ➡ 182   COUNTRY PEOPLE A–Z ➡ 220   INSTRUMENTS A–Z ➡ 436   THE ROCK INTRO ➡ 74   FOLK: FOLK ROCK ➡ 235

with Music Row session pickers on tracks that culminated in their 1968 album *Sweetheart Of The Rodeo*, a country rock landmark. Country music critic and historian Geoffrey Himes, praising the album's subtle and masterful blend of steel guitar and lovely country-style three-part vocal harmonies with rock drumming and vocal irony, hailed *Sweetheart Of The Rodeo* as "perhaps the most influential alternative country album ever made... no matter how closely the Byrds tried to imitate traditional country music, their rock'n'roll sensibility gave everything a subtle spin that made this something new." Shortly after its release, Parsons and Hillman left the Byrds and formed the Flying Burrito Brothers, yet another cornerstone country rock ensemble. The Burrito Brothers' 1969 *Gilded Palace Of Sin*, like *Sweetheart Of The Rodeo*, masterfully blended country roots with rock'n'roll brio, and is still considered a country rock classic.

The ever-restless Gram Parsons next struck out on his own and, in the early 1970s, recorded a pair of highly influential solo albums, *GP* and *Grievous Angel*, which featured his then-musical protégé Emmylou Harris. Chris Hillman, for his part, would resurface on the country scene in the late-1980s in the Desert Rose Band, whose membership included several other celebrated west coast bluegrass/country rock practitioners like Herb Pedersen. Though the Desert Rose Band's records were heavily steeped in a traditional and bluegrass-flavoured harmony sound, intimations of the glorious 1970s southern California country rock era seemed to echo in every groove.

Poco, another influential California country rock ensemble included at various times both future members of the Eagles and former members of Buffalo Springfield. Poco, in its earliest late-1960s–early 1970s incarnation, forged its own rousing country rock blending, in which Clapton- and Hendrix-style electric lead guitar runs were often thrillingly transposed on Rusty Young's electrified pedal steel guitar. It was the Eagles, including Poco alumni Randy Meisner and Timothy Schmit, with their smooth, soft rock/country-pop sound – captured on early hits like 'Tequila Sunrise' and 'Desperado' – whose influence on modern country has been most widely felt and persistent. During the 1980s and 1990s there seemed to be at least a half-dozen different Nashville-based male harmony bands that were masterfully emulating the early Eagles' soft country rock groove, with its clean, subdued drum and guitar sound and pop-smooth tenor vocals.

In 1972, California-based country rock group the Nitty Gritty Dirt Band also played an important part in closing the cultural gap between country and rock audiences, when they came to Nashville and recorded the landmark LP *Will The Circle Be Unbroken*. This ambitious three-record set featured the Dirt Band in various traditional settings with country and bluegrass masters like Roy Acuff, Mother Maybelle Carter (of the Carter Family) and bluegrass banjo king Earl Scruggs.

The Evolution Of Country Rock

The 1970s saw the rise of a handful of Nashville-based country rockers like former Music Row session man Charlie Daniels. Hank Williams Jr., on the strength of landmark country boogie albums like *Hank Williams Jr. and Friends* and *Family Tradition*, won a huge national following of rowdy, youthful rock fans

that were already tuned in to the music of formative southern rock bands like the Allman Brothers and Lynyrd Skynyrd. Williams, the son of honky tonk legend Hank Williams Sr., was actually more stylistically aligned with these formative 1970s southern rock ensembles than he was with his country contemporaries. While his records always contained elements of country, his live concerts, more often than not, were pure, eardrum-splitting hard rock.

In the 1980s, Texas singer-songwriters like Joe Ely and Steve Earle earned cult followings with muscular styles that incorporated the intensity of rock'n'roll with the twang and grittiness of Texas-style honky tonk. Also in the early 1980s a handful of Nashville bands like Jason & the Scorchers – once described as "non-compromising rock'n'rollers with hillbilly hearts" – pioneered a frenzied strain of punk country rock that foreshadowed the alt. country movement of the 1990s.

Above

The Nitty Gritty Dirt Band started out jamming together in the 1960s, influenced by folk and rock'n'roll. As they delved more deeply into their musical heritage, they discovered bluegrass music, which began to appear in their own repertoire.

Urban Cowboys

ONE OF COUNTRY MUSIC'S RARE DEPARTURES FROM ITS DOWN-HOME VALUES, THE URBAN COWBOY PHENOMENON OF THE EARLY 1980S WAS MUCH MORE A FLEETING TREND, DRIVEN BY COMMERCIAL GREED, THAN A GENUINE GRASSROOTS MOVEMENT.

Above

John Travolta smoulders in the leading role of Hollywood smash Urban Cowboy, *as a city boy who moves to Texas and is drawn into the local lifestyle, including the thrill of riding the rodeo.*

THE term "urban cowboy" gained currency with the 1980 release *Urban Cowboy*, a hit Hollywood feature film of middling quality, starring John Travolta and Debra Winger. *Urban Cowboy*'s country-themed soap opera story line was set in Gilley's, a hangar-sized country dance club in Houston. The movie's fleeting box-office popularity, and its million-plus-selling double-LP soundtrack, succeeded in unleashing a fad.

Hollywood Conquers Nashville

The *Urban Cowboy* soundtrack was, like the film, aimed at the mass pop market and featured country-flavoured tracks by pop and soft rock stars of the day like the Eagles and Linda Ronstadt, along with offerings from quite a few second-string country artists like Johnny Lee and Mickey Gilley (an owner of Gilley's club in Pasadena, Texas, which was famous for its electronic bucking bull that simulated an actual rodeo ride).

But for a brief while, the country music-inspired lifestyle depicted in *Urban Cowboy* captured the fleeting attention of young urban hipsters everywhere. Country dance clubs (many with their own mechanical bulls) began popping up in New York City and other unlikely places. Stetson hats and Durango boots suddenly became de rigueur attire for former disco dancers. As a result, many adult contemporary (pop and light rock) radio stations begrudgingly began to add uptown strains of country music to their play lists.

> "WE'RE ALL SUBURBAN. WE ALL HAVE TVS AND RADIOS, AND WE'RE ALL EXPOSED TO A LOT OF DIFFERENT SOUNDS."

Linda Ronstadt

Right

Linda Ronstadt, one of the stars of the Urban Cowboy *soundtrack, shows that she is a country girl at heart.*

The Nashville music industry, anxious to capitalize on this new post-Nashville sound audience, once again shifted its focus to more subdued, pop- and rock-tinged strains of country that lightened up on the twang and went easy on the fiddles and steel guitar (if not eliminating them all together). The early 1980s crossover-style artists who spearheaded the urban cowboy craze were in many ways stylistic successors to the 1960s Nashville practitioners.

Sweet Home Alabama

Alabama, a tame, occasionally formulaic foursome from Fort Payne, was one of the first groups to arise during this time frame to have lasting impact. Since this quartet first hit the charts in 1980 with the single 'Tennessee River', it has sold more than 57 million albums. Alabama has since sustained enormous success with a calculated yet intriguing blend of country balladeering and soft country rock that strikes an agreeable balance between the predictability of urban cowboy and the spontaneity of more bedrock styles.

Other urban cowboy-era artists like Janie Fricke, Razzy Bailey and particularly Earl Thomas Conley did reveal occasional flashes of inspiration and vitality. But, by and large, urban cowboy music did not represent innovation so much as a mere watering-down of prevalent grassroots styles such as honky tonk and the Nashville sound.

LEADING EXPONENTS

Janie Fricke
Razzy Bailey
Lee Greenwood
T.G. Sheppard
Earl Thomas Conley
Mickey Gilley
Johnny Lee
Silvia
Alabama
Kenny Rogers

URBAN COWBOYS

The use of electric guitars and pianos in country-influenced ballads gives country music a more modern, urban feel.

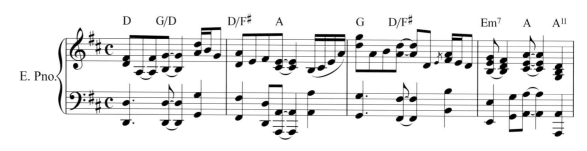

212

Neo-Traditionalists

FROM THE URBAN COWBOYS CAME THE NEO-TRADITIONALISTS, WHO OFFERED A STARK AND WELCOME ALTERNATIVE. THEIR MUSIC, WITH ITS RESOLUTE DEVOTION TO EARLIER STYLES LIKE HONKY TONK, BLUEGRASS AND OLD-TIME COUNTRY, BRISTLED WITH THE VITALITY AND SPIRIT OF INNOVATION THAT URBAN COWBOY LACKED.

EMMYLOU Harris, a lovely, ethereal singer, came of age in the country and bluegrass clubs of the greater Washington, DC area and was briefly a protégée of pioneering California country rocker Gram Parsons. Harris was almost reverentially steeped in the 1950s and 1960s hard country traditions – her first Top 10 country hit was 'If I Could Only Win Your Love',

an inspired reprise of an old Louvin Brothers ballad. With her warm, sweet singing style she was able to revive rustic honky tonk and old-time country gems by Buck Owens and the Carter Family in a way that was vital and meaningful to a new generation of youthful urban- and suburban-dwelling music fans. In recent years, Harris has remained faithful to her love of tradition, while also embarking on adventurous projects like *Red Dirt Girl*, a highly autobiographical 2000 album, and 1995's atmospheric *Wrecking Ball*. The latter album was produced by Daniel Lanois, best known for his work with U2 and Bob Dylan.

Revival Of The Old Masters

Another key new traditionalist is Ricky Skaggs, a Kentucky-born former bluegrass child prodigy who did stints in the bands of both bluegrass king Ralph Stanley and Emmylou Harris before pursuing a solo career in Nashville. With number one hits like 'Uncle Pen' (Skaggs' revival of an old Bill Monroe bluegrass chestnut), 'Heartbroke' and 'Don't Cheat In Our Hometown', he tastefully retro-fitted and subtly electrified the traditional bluegrass sound.

George Strait, a shy south Texan heavily steeped in the musical traditions of western swing king Bob Wills and the consummate honky tonk/country jazz sound of

> "THE REASON FOR ME BEING SO TRADITIONAL – OR RICKY SKAGGS OR GEORGE STRAIT BEING SO TRADITIONAL – IS JUST THAT IT'S A PART OF WHAT HAS BEEN HANDED DOWN TO US AND IT'S WHAT'S COMING OUT."
>
> *John Anderson*

Above
Emmylou Harris's Roses In The Snow *is an album of traditional country and bluegrass sounds.*

Left
George Strait, who constantly sets new records in album and ticket sales.

LEADING EXPONENTS

Emmylou Harris
Ricky Skaggs
John Anderson
John Conlee
George Strait
Reba McEntire
Randy Travis
Dwight Yoakam
Patty Loveless
Steve Earle

NEO-TRADITIONAL COUNTRY

Although opinions may differ as to what traditional country music actually is, neo-traditionalists generally abandon the influences of pop, jazz and blues.

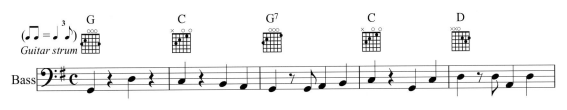

THE COUNTRY INTRO ➡ 182   COUNTRY PEOPLE A–Z ➡ 220   INSTRUMENTS A–Z ➡ 436   COUNTRY: EARLY & OLD-TIME COUNTRY ➡ 186

Other figures like John Anderson, a Florida-born former hard rocker turned twangy honky tonk balladeer ('Wild And Blue', 'Swingin'), also held the hard country line during the urban cowboy explosion and, in so doing, paved the way for a neo-traditional renaissance that unfolded in the mid-1980s. Kentucky-born former mortician and DJ John Conlee also helped to keep the traditional spirit alive with hearty, countrified late-1970s and early 1980s chart-topping ballads like 'Rose Colored Glasses', 'Backside Of Thirty', 'Lady Lay Down' and his Top 10 cover of Ray Charles' 'Busted'.

Country's Renaissance Artists

Spearheading the mid-1980s renaissance was a diverse new generation of artists who collectively managed to swing the mainstream temporarily back towards its roots with a fresh infusion of honky tonk, rockabilly and even contemporary folk and big-band influences. Dwight Yoakam, a Kentucky native who eschewed Nashville and instead rose through the southern California roots rock scene, stormed the country charts and even secured a little rock airplay with his hard-edged, freewheeling musical approach. His sound combined the best of 1950s and 1960s honky tonk with the swagger of rock'n'roll and the raw Appalachian soulfulness of his native Kentucky, in songs like 'Guitars, Cadillacs' and 'I Sang Dixie'. On the Nashville front, eminently talented neo-honky tonk singers like North Carolina-born Randy Travis (a marvellous stylistic throwback to the great Lefty Frizzell, with hits such as 'Diggin' Up Bones' and 'On The Other Hand') and Kentucky-born Patty Loveless (a distant cousin of Loretta Lynn) also rose to prominence with resolutely tradition-flavoured sounds.

Oklahoma's Reba McEntire, a former rodeo rider from a family of rodeo champions, had modest success in the late-1970s and early 1980s. By 1984, with the encouragement of MCA Records producer Jimmy Bowen, she began co-producing her own albums and almost immediately set about revisiting her back-to-basics roots with albums like 1984's *My Kind Of Country* and the follow-up *Have I Got A Deal For You*, which paved the way for her future stardom.

Even as country music moves uneasily into a new century and Nashville's relentless music machine behind it seems more attuned than ever to the allure of the crossover pop market, many fans still look back at the mid-1980s neo-traditionalist renaissance as a golden age of innovation, diversity and open-mindedness on Music Row.

Above

Unlike many country artists, Randy Travis writes songs celebrating the good things in life and the positive aspects of human nature. His music defines his own take on the traditions of Merle Haggard and Lefty Frizzell.

Merle Haggard and his band, the Strangers, quietly slid into Nashville and went politely against the grain with his superlative Texas neo-honky tonk-style sound. Strait has since emerged as one of country's all-time most popular stars, with 50 number one records at last count. His best-known songs include 'Unwound' and 'Does Fort Worth Ever Cross Your Mind?'.

COUNTRY: BLUEGRASS ➡ 196   COUNTRY: HONKY TONK ➡ 199

Alternative Country

THERE HAVE ALWAYS BEEN AVANT-GARDE ARTISTS AND BANDS THAT TAKE ELEMENTS OF COUNTRY AND FUSE THEM WITH OTHER MUSICAL IDIOMS TO MAKE THEIR OWN HIGHLY ORIGINAL, OFTEN IDIOSYNCRATIC STYLES. MANY OF THESE ARTISTS ALSO ADDRESS CONTROVERSIAL ISSUES THAT ARE TABOO IN THE POLITICALLY CORRECT COUNTRY MAINSTREAM.

IT was the late-1960s and early 1970s, when America's anti-war "alternative" sub-culture was in full swing, that such artists were first referred to as alternative country musicians. Most managed to earn a following without the benefit of airplay on mainstream country radio. Their music has often had special appeal to younger, more urbane listeners who tend to be put off by the bland, predictable commercial constraints of the mainstream and hunger for a grassroots alternative.

John Prine

A Patchwork Of Alternative Country Styles

Alternative country – and its 1990s iteration, called "alt. country" or "alt country" – has since devolved into a one-size-fits-all category for an array of artists so numerous and stylistically diverse as to defy any precise categorization. Their only common thread is that they offer intriguing alternative sounds and styles that are often in sharp contrast to what is heard in country's rather predictable and trend-savvy mainstream.

Over the years, quite a few of these artists have found limited niches within Nashville's music industry. Some, like John Prine, John Hiatt, Guy Clark, Rodney Crowell, Jim Lauderdale, Lucinda Williams, Buddy & Julie Miller, Kieran Kane and Kevin Welch have prospered by writing songs for best-selling mainstream artists while doing their own recording for small, independent "boutique" labels and performing in non-country venues like listening rooms and coffeehouses.

"THEY [BILL MONROE AND FLATT & SCRUGGS] TOOK THE EXISTING FORMS OF MUSIC OF THE DAY, AND RADICALLY INNOVATED A NEW MUSIC FORM. SO THE SPIRIT OF THAT IS HAPPENING TODAY. IT'S TAKING THE ROOTS AND TURNING IT INTO A NEW THING THAT'S UNIQUELY YOUR OWN."
Ron Block

Left

The late, great Townes Van Zandt, whose powerful songs are better known to many as covers by artists such as Emmylou Harris, Doc Watson and Don Williams.

ALTERNATIVE COUNTRY

Alt. country absorbs a wide range of musical influences from rock to punk, but uses such influences to return to a less-produced, country sound, such as in this example of a picked pattern with descending bass.

LEADING EXPONENTS

Guy Clark
John Prine
Alison Krauss
Gillian Welch
Steve Earle
Nickel Creek
Lucinda Williams
Rodney Crowell
Buddie & Julie Miller

Gtr.

E   D   A/C#   Am/C   D

Austin, Texas, with its vibrant live music scene, has long served as a viable springboard for a wide assortment of cutting-edge alternative artists and ensembles. These include Junior Brown, who combines droll, gut-bucket country vocals with dazzling lead work on a double-necked instrument of his own design called the "git-steel" – half electric lead guitar and half electrified steel guitar. Others run the gambit from the Bad Livers (whose raunchy and often bizarre sound can aptly be called psycho-billy), to gentle old-time yodelling country/cowboy music revivalists like Don Walser and satirical hipsters like Kinky Friedman & his Texas Jewboys.

Below

Gillian Welch's conversion to bluegrass came about one Sunday morning as she was cleaning out the bathtub, when one of her housemates put on a live Stanley Brothers record.

Country Fusion

Many of these earliest alternative country artists, who have become role models for several younger musicians, emerged during the open-minded eras of the 1970s outlaw movement and the 1980s neo-traditionalist movement. These include Texas singer-songwriters Guy Clark, Nanci Griffith, Steve Earle, the late Townes Van Zandt and Illinois-born John Prine. Meanwhile, the west coast has given rise to influential roots-oriented singer-songwriters like Iris DeMent and Gillian Welch, as well as neo-western swing bands like Big Sandy & the Fly-Rite Boys.

The music of south Louisiana's Cajun (French Acadian) community has contributed yet another strand to alternative country's vast DNA. Familiar names from this genre include historic figures like Hackberry Ramblers, Iry LeJeune, Harry Choates and D. L. Menard, as well as contemporary ensembles like The Balfa Brothers and Beausoleil. Most present-day Cajun musicians earn their livings on the club and festival circuit. Yet a few, like *Grand Ole Opry* member Jimmy C. Newman ('Alligator Man', 'Bayou Talk'), Doug Kershaw ('Louisiana Man', 'Diggy Diggy Lo') and Jo-El Sonnier ('Tear Stained Letter'), have found some success in the mainstream country charts over the years.

The wildly – often *willfully* – diverse and eclectic styles encompassed by the alt. country free-for-all draw from a slurry of styles – western swing, bluegrass, honky tonk, cowboy, folk-blues, rockabilly and even punk rock, thrash rock, Brit rock and art rock. The movement is often traced back to a pair of definitive groups. One of these is Canada's Cowboy Junkies, whose 1988 album *Trinity Sessions* paid tribute to the traditions of Patsy Cline and Hank Williams while casting them in a melancholy, post-modern blues- and jazz-tinged folk vein.

In 1990, Uncle Tupelo, another definitive alt. country band based in Illinois, released their debut album *No Depression* on the independent Rockville label. Uncle Tupelo, though relatively short-lived (the band disbanded in 1994 and its members went on to form other influential offshoot bands like Son Volt and Wilco), released four albums between 1990 and 1993. These captured the imaginations of post-punk rockers and other young eclectic music fans and earned kudos from music critics. Uncle Tupelo's *No Depression* even inspired an alt. country Internet forum of the same name, which in 1995 was expanded into a bi-monthly magazine that continues to chronicle the thriving alt. country movement.

Uncle Tupelo's music was often built around an unlikely but passionate and emotionally direct fusion of punk rock's fuzz-tone aggression with traditional country's twangy soul in a mix that was often tinged with contemporary malaise

Above

Nickel Creek's innovative sound has been described as "polystylistic" by critics. Their music reflects their diverse influences, which include Bill Monroe, Bach, Radiohead and Pat Metheny.

and acute social consciousness. These elements offered a marked alternative to mainstream country's largely apolitical laments and unquestioning celebrations of the status quo. Alt. country music is also, more often than not, imbued with rock'n'roll angst, sexual candor and political consciousness.

The Return To Roots

The dominant sound in alternative country took another shift around the turn of the millennium, this time in the direction of bluegrass and newgrass (progressive bluegrass). The catalyst was, somewhat ironically, *O Brother, Where Art Thou?*, a 2000 Hollywood film, and its best-selling soundtrack.

One of the most prominent figures featured on the soundtrack to *O Brother, Where Art Thou?* was Illinois-born Alison Krauss, an extraordinarily gifted singer, fiddler and bandleader (her long-time band Union Station is considered to be one of the best ensembles in contemporary bluegrass). Krauss, who is equally at home with a soft country ballad as she is with a bluegrass breakdown, has earned large followings in both bluegrass and country circles. Also prominent on the

soundtrack was Gillian Welch, another highly influential alt. country practitioner. Not since Emmylou Harris's emergence in the mid-1970s has a woman artist showed such intensity and artistry in recreating the spirit of traditional country. Though Welch's songs often resonate with old-timey mountain soul, she was born in southern California and attended Boston's Berklee College of Music before embarking on a singing and songwriting career in the early 1990s.

Although not featured on the *O Brother* soundtrack, Nickel Creek, a California-based youthgrass (or alt. grass) trio, have risen to prominence in recent years with a musical fusion of introspective and urbane pop and folk melodies, moods and atmospherics and top-notch bluegrass instrumentation. The result is a sound that's both something more and something less than authentic bluegrass, yet utterly appealing and contemporary. Recently hailed by *Time* magazine as the "musical innovators of the millennium", Nickel Creek have won a following that effortlessly cuts across the urban/rural pop/country divide.

Young Country

THE YOUNG COUNTRY MOVEMENT WAS AN INDUSTRY-DRIVEN TREND AIMED AT THE MASS MARKET OF TEENS AND TWENTY-SOMETHING MUSIC FANS. LIKE THE URBAN COWBOYS, YOUNG COUNTRY ARTISTS OFTEN CONTEMPORIZED OR DILUTED PREVAILING STYLES LIKE HONKY TONK AND POP COUNTRY FOR MASS CONSUMPTION.

Above
The Dixie Chicks, a combination of confidence, energy and outspoken opinions, have brought country music to a wider audience, appealing to teenagers and families as well as country fans.

THE early 1990s saw a continuation of the mid- and late-1980s neo-traditionalist movement and produced a glut of gifted young male singers like Mark Chesnutt, Clay Walker, Rick Trevino, Travis Tritt and Marty Stuart, for the most part grounded in honky tonk and hard country.

Of these, Alan Jackson, a handsome, unassuming singer from Georgia, would rise to the fore. Jackson's 1990 debut album, *Here In The Real World*, features unabashedly twangy vocals and robust fiddle-guitar-steel guitar arrangements, while also showcasing Jackson as a tradition-flavoured songwriter of artistry and insight. Other men, like Steve Wariner, Mike Reid, Collin Raye, Bryan White, Kevin Sharp and Vince Gill (an Oklahoma-born tenor singer who has also emerged as one of country's most popular figures in the past decade) thrived in the late-1980s and the 1990s with softer, more refined ballad-oriented styles, equally accessible to pop and country fans.

"SOME OF THE MUSICAL CHANGES HAVE BEEN HIGHLY CREATIVE, OTHERS STRICTLY COMMERCIAL. NO ONE KNOWS WHERE THE WHOLE THING WILL LEAD, CHIEFLY BECAUSE … THE MUSIC IS HEADING IN A BUNCH OF WEIRD DIRECTIONS ALL AT ONE TIME."

Frye Gaillard

Invasion Of The Youngsters

Though his dramatic rise preceded the young country movement by a few years, Oklahoman Garth Brooks' phenomenal success in conquering the youthful crossover audience (he sold 60 million albums between 1989 and 1996 alone) did much to shift the country record

LEADING EXPONENTS

Vince Gill
Garth Brooks
Trisha Yearwood
Alan Jackson
Lee Ann Womack
Faith Hill
Tim McGraw
The Dixie Chicks
LeAnne Rimes

YOUNG COUNTRY

Musicians like Alan Jackson have incorporated rock-based rhythm sections while maintaining a strong country feel through harmony, instrumentation and singing style.

THE COUNTRY INTRO ➡ 182   COUNTRY PEOPLE A-Z ➡ 220   INSTRUMENTS A-Z ➡ 436   COUNTRY: MAINSTREAM COUNTRY ➡ 204

industry's focus to an increasingly younger crossover crowd. Brooks' success lay in his uncanny ability to combine the drawl and whine of a neo-honky tonker with effective pop country balladeering, an animated performance style, an introspective new age persona and a shrewd marketing acumen.

Nearly parallel with Brooks' rise was the ascendance of Georgia-born Trisha Yearwood, who debuted in 1991 with the number one single 'She's In Love With The Boy'. Yearwood's confident, Linda Ronstadt-like soprano, which often effortlessly bridges the rocky gap between country and pop, won instant appeal. She has since followed up with a string of chart-topping hits, from the soulful 'The Song Remembers When' to the sprightly 'XXX's And OOO's'.

Mississippi-born LeAnne Rimes, another harbinger of young country, first topped the national charts aged 13 in 1996, with the number one crossover single 'Blue'. 'Blue' was originally written for Patsy Cline, who died before she could record it. Rimes herself has a powerful Patsy Cline-like pop country voice, but audiences found a novelty appeal in her ability to sound like she was 13 going on 39. Like Brooks, Rimes racked up incredible sales figures. Her debut album, *Blue*, sold three million, and she sold twelve and a half million albums in 1997 alone.

A dozen or more under-20 artists were soon rolling down the pathway that Rimes paved for them. By the late-1990s there was hardly a Nashville record label that hadn't signed at least one teenage sensation with a sweet voice, a revealing halter-neck top and tight knickers. These youngsters' shared affinity for bare midriffs earned them the dubious tag of "the belly-button brigade".

Country Chicks

Mississippi-born Faith Hill was well into her twenties when she first hit the charts in 1993 with her debut single, 'Wild One', then went on to become one of the most popular women in country music. Yet much of her appeal also stems from the beauty and glamour of her youthful image. Hill (who married fellow young country star Tim McGraw in 1995) is also emblematic of her times in that she is a powerful singer largely unburdened by any resolute stylistic vision. Her records have taken on a progressively shinier pop sheen over time. This progression culminated in her best-selling 2002 album, *Cry*, a full-blown excursion into pop music, on which she (at least temporarily) left country behind.

The Dixie Chicks, a trio from Texas, also rose to stardom in the late 1990s with an appealing and somewhat predictable formula of musical brio and appealing looks. But, unlike Hill, they have displayed a wider breadth of imagination with each record release and a stronger grounding in retro-country styles. The Chicks' first two albums, *Wide Open Spaces* (1998) and *Fly* (1999), have sold more than 14 million copies. Their third album, *Home*, released in 2002, earned widespread critical praise for its roots-oriented power.

Texan Lee Ann Womack emerged in the late-1990s with tradition-leaning hits like 'The Fool' and 'A Little Past Little Rock' that earned her warm comparisons to the likes of Dolly Parton and Tammy Wynette. With 2002's *Something Worth Leaving Behind*, her fourth album and her follow-up to 2001's three million-selling *I Hope You Dance*, Womack took a sharp turn toward adult-contemporary pop sophistication.

Soviet Swing

What does the new millennium hold for country music? The only thing for certain is that the surprises won't cease. To wit, one of 2003's most talked-about country artists is a critically acclaimed band called Bering Strait. Though one would hardly know it on first listen, Bering Strait hail from the former Soviet Socialist Republic. Ironically these young Russian upstarts actually sound a lot more "country" than many of the all-American artists now topping *Billboard*'s "hot country" charts.

Above
The phenomenal success of stars such as Garth Brooks and the lavish production costs that finance their recordings and tours show how far country music has come from its simple roots in the rural backwaters of the southern states.

Left
Alan Jackson's guitar bears a traditional country message. Jackson, despite being a commercially successful artist, has remained true to his roots and still plays benefit shows in his hometown of Newnan, Georgia.

Artists: Country

Entries appear in the following order: name, music style, year(s) of popularity, type of artist, country of origin.

Ace In The Hole Band, Alternative Country, 1970s-1990s, Artist, American
Acuff, Roy, Honky Tonk, 1930s-1960s, Artist, American
Adams, Ryan, Alternative Country; Country Rock, 1990s-, Artist; Songwriter, American
Adcock, Eddie, Bluegrass, 1970s-1990s, Artist, American
Adkins, Trace, Young Country, 1990s-, Artist, American
Alabama, Urban Cowboys; Country Rock, 1970s-, Artist, American
Alan, Buddy, Country Rock, 1960s-1970s, Artist, American
Alger, Pat, Young Country, 1980s-1990s, Artist, American
Allan, Gary, Young Country; Neo-Traditionalists, 1990s-, Artist, American
Allanson, Susie, Urban Cowboys, 1970s-1980s, Artist, American
Allen Brothers, The, Early & Old-Time Country, 1920s-1930s, Artist, American
Allen, Deborah, Urban Cowboys, 1980s-1990s, Artist, American
Allen, Harley, Young Country, 1990s-, Artist, American
Allen, Jules Verne, Cowboy Music, 1910s-1930s, Artist, American
Allen, Red, Bluegrass, 1950s-1990s, Artist, American
Allen, Rex, Cowboy Music, 1940s-1970s, Artist, American
Allen, Rosalie, Cowboy Music, 1940s-1960s, Artist, American
Allen, Terry, Alternative Country; Country Rock, 1970s-1990s, Artist, American
Allsup, Tommy, Western Swing, 1960s, Artist, American
Alverson, Tommy, Young Country, 1990s-, Artist, American
Alvin, Dave, Alternative Country, 1980s-, Artist; Songwriter, American
Amazing Rhythm Aces, Country Rock, 1970s-, Artist, American
Ambel, Eric, Alternative Country; Country Rock, 1980s-, Artist, American
American Flyer, Country Rock, 1970s, Artist, American
Anderson, Bill, The Nashville Sound, 1960s-, Artist; Songwriter, American
Anderson, John, The Outlaw Movement; Honky Tonk, 1970s-, Artist, American
Anderson, Lynn, The Nashville Sound, 1960s-, Artist, American
Anderson, Pete, Alternative Country, 1980s-1990s, Producer; Artist, American
Anderson, Sharon, Young Country, 1990s, Artist, American
Archer Park, Young Country, 1990s, Artist, American
Armstrong, Billy, Western Swing, 1970s, Artist, American
Arnold, Eddy, The Nashville Sound; Cowboy Music; Honky Tonk, 1940s-1990s, Artist, American
Asleep At The Wheel, Neo-Traditionalists, 1970s-1990s, Artist, American
Atcher, Bob, Cowboy Music; Early & Old-Time Country, 1940s-1960s, Artist, American
Atkins, Chet, The Nashville Sound, 1940s-1990s, Artist, American
Atkins, Rhett, Neo-Traditionalists, 1990s-, Artist, American
Atlanta, Urban Cowboys, 1980s, Artist, American
Austin, Bryan, Young Country, 1990s, Artist, American
Austin, Sherrie, Young Country, 1990s-, Artist, Australian
Autry, Gene, Old-Time County; Cowboy Music, 1920s-1960s, Artist; Songwriter, American
Avalon, Young Country, 1990s-, Artist, American
Axton, Hoyton, Early & Old-Time Country, 1960s-1990s, Artist; Songwriter, American
Azar, Steve, Young Country, 1990s-, Artist, American
Backsliders, The, Alternative Country; Country Rock, 1990s, Artist, American
Bailey Brothers, The, Bluegrass; Early & Old-Time Country, 1940s-1950s; 1970s-1980s, Artist, American
Bailey, Linda, Young Country, 1990s, Artist, American
Baillie & the Boys, Young Country, 1980s-, Artist, American
Baker & Myers, Young Country, 1990s, Artist, American
Baker, Butch, Young Country, 1980s-1990s, Artist, American
Baldknobbers, Young Country, 1990s, Artist, American
Ball, David, Young Country, 1980s-, Artist, American
Ball, Tom, Young Country; Bluegrass, 1980s, Artist, American
Ballard, Roger, Young Country, 1990s, Artist, American
Banach, Karen, Young Country, 1990s, Artist, American
Band, The, Country Rock, 1960s-1970s; 1990s, Artist, Canadian
Bandy, Moe, Honky Tonk; Early & Old-Time Country, 1970s-1990s, Artist, American
Bare, Bobby, The Outlaw Movement; The Nashville Sound, 1950s-1980s, Artist, American
Barker, Aaron, Urban Cowboys, 1970s, Artist, American
Barlow, Randy, Neo-Traditionalists, 1970s-1980s, Artist, American
Barmby, Shane, Young Country, 1980s-1990s, Artist, American
Barnes, Max D., Young Country; Neo-Traditionalists, 1980s-, Artist, American
Barnett, Mandy, Young Country; Neo-Traditionalists, 1990s, Artist, American
Bashful Brother Oswald, Early & Old-Time Country, 1930s-1990s, Artist, American
Beau Brummels, The, Country Rock, 1960s-1970s, Artist, American
Beaudry, David, Young Country, 1990s, Artist, American
Bellamy Brothers, The, Country Rock, 1970s-, Artist, American
Bentley, Stephanie, Young Country, 1990s, Artist, American
Berg, Matraca, Young Country, 1990s, Artist, American
Berline, Byron, Bluegrass, 1960s-1990s, Artist, American
Bernard, Crystal, Young Country, 1990s, Artist, American
Berry, John, Young Country, 1990s-, Artist, American
Berryman, Pete and Lou, Early & Old-Time Country, 1980s-1990s, Artist, American
Big House, Young Country, 1990s-, Artist, American
Big Sandy & his Fly-Rite Boys, Country Rock; Bluegrass; Western Swing, 1990s-, Artist, American
Black, Clint, Neo-Traditionalists; Young Country, 1980s-1990s, Artist, American
Blackhawk, Young Country, 1990s-, Artist, American
Blake, Norman, Bluegrass, 1970s-, Artist, American
Blood Oranges, The, Alternative Country; Country Rock, 1990s, Artist, American
Blue Mountain, Alternative Country, 1990-, Artist, American
Blue Rags, Alternative Country, 1990s, Artist, American
Blue Rodeo, Alternative Country, 1980s-, Artist, American
Blue Sky Boys, The, Bluegrass; Early & Old-Time Country, 1930s-1970s, Artist, American
Bluegrass Album Band, The, Bluegrass, 1970s-1980s, Artist, American
Bluegrass Cardinals, The, Bluegrass, 1970s-1980s, Artist, American
Blundell, James, Young Country, 1980s, Artist, American
Boggs, Doc, Early & Old-Time Country, 1920s; 1960s, Artist, American
Boggs, Noel, Western Swing, 1950s-1960s, Artist, American
Bogguss, Suzy, Neo-Traditionalists, 1980s-1990s, Artist, American
Bonamy, James, Young Country, 1990s, Artist, American
Bond, Johnny, Country Rock, 1940s-1970s, Artist, American
Bonnie Lou, Cowboy Music, 1950s, Artist, American
Boone, Larry, Young Country; Neo-Traditionalists, 1980s-1990s, Artist, American
Boosinger, Laura, Early & Old-Time Country, 1990s, Artist, American
Booth, Tony, Country Rock, 1970s, Artist, American
Bosworth, Libbi, Alternative Country, 1990s-, Artist; Songwriter, American
Bottle Rockets, The, Alternative Country, 1990s-, Artist, American
Bowers, Bryan, Early & Old-Time Country, 1970s-, Artist, American
Boy Howdy, Young Country; Country Rock, 1990s, Artist, American
Boyd, Bill, Western Swing, 1930s-1950s, Artist, American
BR5-49, Neo-Traditionalists; Alternative Country, 1990s-, Artist, American
Bradley, Harold, Western Swing, 1960s, Artist, American
Bradley, Owen, The Nashville Sound, 1950s-1970s, Producer; Artist, American
Brandt, Paul, Young Country, 1990s, Artist, Canadian
Brannon, Kippi, Young Country, 1990s, Artist, American
Branson Brothers, Young Country, 1990s, Artist, American
Brinsley Schwarz, Country Rock, 1970s, Artist, British
Brody, Lane, Urban Cowboys, 1980s, Artist, American
Brokop, Lisa, Young Country, 1990s, Artist, American
Brooks & Dunn, Neo-Traditionalists; Young Country, 1990s-, Artist, American
Brooks, Garth, Neo-Traditionalists, 1980s-, Artist, American
Brooks, Karen, Young Country, 1980s-1990s, Artist, American
Brooks, Kix, Young Country, 1990s, Artist, American
Brother Phelps, Young Country, 1990s, Artist, American
Brower, Cecil, Western Swing, 1960s, Artist, American
Brown, Alison, Bluegrass, 1990s-, Artist, American
Brown, Jim Ed, The Nashville Sound; Honky Tonk, 1950s-1990s, Artist, American
Brown, Junior, Neo-Traditionalists; Alternative Country, 1990s-, Artist, American
Brown, Marty, Young Country, 1990s, Artist, American
Brown, Milton, Western Swing, 1930s, Artist, American
Brown, Roger, Young Country, 1990s-, Artist, American
Brown, T. Graham, Urban Cowboys; Country Rock, 1980s-, Artist, American
Browne, Jann, Young Country, 1990s-, Artist; Songwriter, American
Browns, The, The Nashville Sound, 1950s-1960s; 1990s, Artist, American
Bruce, Ed, The Outlaw Movement, 1960s-1980s, Artist; Songwriter, American
Bruner, Cliff, Honky Tonk; Western Swing, 1930s-1940s, Artist, American
Bryant, Boudleaux, The Nashville Sound, 1960s, Songwriter, American
Bryant, Cody, Bluegrass; Western Swing, 1990s, Artist, American
Bryant, Felice, The Nashville Sound, 1940s-1950s, Songwriter; Composer, American
Buckner, Richard, Alternative Country, 1990s-, Artist, American
Buffalo Club, Young Country, 1990s, Artist, American
Buffalo Springfield, Country Rock, 1960s, Artist, American
Buffet, Jimmy, Country Rock, 1970s-, Artist, American
Burch Sisters, Young Country, 1980s, Artist, American
Burnette, Billy, Country Rock, 1970s-, Artist, American
Burnette, Smiley, Cowboy Music, 1950s-1960s, Artist, American
Burnin' Daylight, Young Country, 1990s, Artist, American
Burton, James, Country Rock, 1960s-1970s, Artist, American
Bush, Johnny, Honky Tonk; Western Swing, 1960s-, Artist, American
Byrd, Tracy, Young Country, 1990s-, Artist, American
Byrds, The, Country Rock, 1960s-1970s, Artist, American
Cactus Brothers, The, Alternative Country, 1990s, Artist, American
Callahan Brothers, The, Cowboy Music, 1930s-1940s, Artist, American
Camp Creek Boys, The, Early & Old-Time Country; Bluegrass, 1960s, Artist, American
Campbell, Glen, Mainstream Country; The Nashville Sound, 1960s-, Artist, American
Campbell, Stacy Dean, Young Country, 1990s, Artist, American
Carlin, Bob, Early & Old-Time Country, 1990s, Artist, American
Carlisle, Bill, Cowboy Music, 1930s-1990s, Artist, American
Carlisle, Cliff, Cowboy Music, 1930s-1940s, Artist, American
Carlson, Paulette, Young Country, 1990s, Artist, American
Carpenter, Mary Chapin, Young Country, 1980s-, Artist; Songwriter, American
Carpetbaggers, The, Alternative Country, 1990s, Artist, American
Carson, Fiddlin' John, Early & Old-Time Country, 1920s-1930s, Artist, American
Carson, Jeff, Young Country, 1990s-, Artist, American
Carson, Mindy, Young Country, 1990s-, Artist, American
Carter Family, The, Early & Old-Time Country, 1920s-1960s, Artist, American
Carter, Anita, Early & Old-Time Country, 1960s, Artist, American
Carter, Carlene, Neo-Traditionalists, 1970s-1990s, Artist, American
Carter, Deana, Young Country; Neo-Traditionalists, 1990s-, Artist, American
Carter, Mother Maybelle, Early & Old-Time Country, 1950s-1960s, Artist, American
Carter, Wilf, Cowboy Music, 1930s-1980s, Artist, Canadian
Cartwright, Lionel, Young Country, 1980s-1990s, Artist, American
Case, Neko, Alternative Country, 1990s-, Artist, American
Cash, Johnny, Mainstream Country; Country Rock, 1950s-, Artist, American
Cash, Rosanne, Neo-Traditionalists, 1970s-1990s, Artist; Songwriter, American
Cason, Buzz, Western Swing, 1970s, Artist, American
Cassell, Pete, Early & Old-Time Country, 1930s-1940s, Artist, American
Chance, Dean, Young Country, 1990s, Artist, American
Chance, Jeff, Young Country, 1990s, Artist, American
Chapman, Beth Nielson, Young Country, 1980s-, Artist, American
Chapman, Ce Ce, Young Country, 1980s-1990s, Artist, American
Chase, Charlie, Young Country, 1990s, Artist, American
Chesney, Kenny, Neo-Traditionalists, 1990s-, Artist, American
Chesnutt, Mark, Young Country, 1990s-, Artist, American
Chesterman, Charlie, Alternative Country, 1990s, Artist, American
Chicken Chokers, The, Alternative Country, 1980s, Artist, American
Childers, Bob, Young Country, 1980s-1990s, Artist, American
Childre, Lou, Early & Old-Time Country, 1930s-1950s, Artist, American
Choates, Harry, Western Swing, 1930s-1950s, Artist, American
Clark, Gene, Country Rock, 1960s-1990s, Artist; Songwriter, American
Clark, Guy, Alternative Country; The Outlaw Movement, 1970s-1990s, Artist; Songwriter, American
Clark, Roy, The Nashville Sound, 1950s-, Artist, American
Clark, Terri, Young Country; Neo-Traditionalists, 1990s-, Artist, Canadian
Clark, Yodelling Slim, Cowboy Music, 1950s-1970s, Artist, American
Claypool, Philip, Young Country, 1990s, Artist, American
Clayton, Lee, The Outlaw Movement, 1970s-1990s, Artist; Songwriter, American
Clement, Jack, The Outlaw Movement, 1970s, Producer, American
Clements, Vassar, Bluegrass, 1970s-, Artist, American
Clifton, Bill, Bluegrass, 1950s-1970s, Artist, American
Cline, Patsy, The Nashville Sound, 1950s-1960s, Artist, American
Clover, Country Rock, 1970s, Artist, American
Cochran, Anita, Young Country; Neo-Traditionalists, 1990s-, Artist, American
Cochran, Hank, Honky Tonk, 1960s-1990s, Artist, American
Coe, David Allen, The Outlaw Movement, 1960s-, Artist; Songwriter, American
Collie, Mark, Neo-Traditionalists, 1980s-1990s, Artist, American
Collins, Tommy, Honky Tonk, 1950s-1970s, Artist; Songwriter, American
Colter, Jessi, The Outlaw Movement, 1970s-1980s, Artist, American
Comeaux, Amie, Young Country, 1990s, Artist, American
Commander Cody, Country Rock, 1970s-, Artist, American
Confederate Railroad, Young Country; Neo-Traditionalists, 1990s-, Artist, American
Conlee, John, Neo-Traditionalists, 1970s-1990s, Artist, American
Conley, Earl Thomas, Urban Cowboys; Neo-Traditionalists, 1980s-1990s, Artist, American
Cooley, Spade, Western Swing, 1940s-1950s, Artist, American
Coon Creek Girls, The, Early & Old-Time Country; Bluegrass, 1930s-1950s, Artist, American
Cooper, Roger, Early & Old-Time Country, 1990s, Artist, American
Cooper, Stoney, Early & Old-Time Country; Bluegrass, 1940s-1970s, Artist, American
Cooper, Wilma Lee, Early & Old-Time Country; Bluegrass, 1930s-1990s, Artist, American
Copas, Cowboy, Honky Tonk, 1940s-1960s, Artist, American
Copley, Jeff, Young Country, 1990s, Artist, American
Country Gazette, The, Bluegrass, 1970s-1990s, Artist, American
Country Gentlemen, The, Bluegrass, 1950s-1990s, Artist, American
Cowboy Jazz, Cowboy Music, 1980s, Artist, American
Cowboy Junkies, Alternative Country, 1980s-, Artist, Canadian
Cox, Ronnie, Young Country, 1990s-, Artist, American
Craig, Cathryn, Young Country, 1990s, Artist, American
Cramer, Floyd, The Nashville Sound, 1950s-1990s, Artist, American
Crowe, J. D., Bluegrass, 1960s-1990s, Artist, American
Crowell, Rodney, Neo-Traditionalists; Country Rock, 1970s-, Artist; Songwriter, American
Crutchfield, Captain Sam, Neo-Traditionalists, 1990s, Artist, American
Cryner, Bobby, Young Country, 1990s, Artist, American
Curless, Dick, Early & Old-Time Country, 1950s-1990s, Artist, American
Curtis, Ken, Cowboy Music, 1960s, Artist, American
Cyrus, Billy Ray, Young Country, 1990s-, Artist, American
Dale, Ernie, Young Country, 1990s, Artist, American
Dalhart, Vernon, Cowboy Music; Early & Old-Time Country, 1920s-1940s, Artist, American
Dallas County Line, Young Country, 1990s, Artist, American
Dalton, Dan, Cowboy Music, 1960s-1970s, Artist, American
Dalton, Lacy J., Neo-Traditionalists, 1970s-, Artist, American
Daniel, Dale, Young Country, 1990s, Artist, American
Daniel, Davis, Young Country, 1990s, Artist; Songwriter, American
Daniels, Charlie, Urban Cowboys; Country Rock, 1970s-, Artist, American
Darby and Tarlton, Early & Old-Time Country, 1920s-1930s, Artist, American
Darling, Denver, Cowboy Music, 1930s-1950s, Artist, American
Dash Rip Rock, Alternative Country, 1980s-, Artist, American
Dave and Deke Combo, The, Alternative Country, 1990s, Artist, American
Davis, Danny, The Nashville Sound, 1960s-1970s, Artist, American
Davis, Jimmie, The Nashville Sound, 1920s-1980s, Artist; Songwriter, American
Davis, Linda, Young Country, 1990s, Artist, American
Davis, Link, Western Swing, 1930s-1960s, Artist, American
Davis, Mac, The Nashville Sound; Country Rock, 1970s-1990s, Artist, American
Davis, Skeeter, The Nashville Sound; Country Rock, 1960s-1990s, Artist, American
Dawson, Julian, Alternative Country, 1980s-1990s, Artist, American
Day, Curtis, Young Country, 1990s-, Artist, American
Day, Jimmy, Honky Tonk; Western Swing, 1960s; 1990s, Artist, American
Dayton, Jesse, Alternative Country, 1990s-, Artist, American
Dean, Billy, Neo-Traditionalists, 1990s, Artist, American
Dean, Eddie, Cowboy Music, 1930s-1970s, Artist, American
Dean, Jimmy, The Nashville Sound, 1950s-1970s, Artist, American
Dean, Larry, Cowboy Music, 1980s-1990s, Artist, American
Delmore Brothers, The, Honky Tonk; Early & Old-Time Country, 1930s-1950s, Artist, American
Delray, Martin, Neo-Traditionalists, 1990s, Artist, American
Dement, Iris, Neo-Traditionalists; Alternative Country, 1990s, Artist; Songwriter, American
Dennis, Wesley, Young Country, 1990s, Artist, American
Denver Darling, Cowboy Music, 1930s-1950s, Artist, American
Derailers, Alternative Country; Honky Tonk; Country Rock, 1990s-, Artist, American
Desert Rose Band, Country Rock, 1980s-1990s, Artist, American
Dexter, Al, The Nashville Sound; Honky Tonk; Cowboy Music, 1950s-1960s, Artist; Songwriter, American
Diamond Rio, Neo-Traditionalists, 1970s; 1990s-, Artist, American
Diamond, Davis, Young Country, 1990s, Artist, American
Dickens, Hazel, Early & Old-Time Country, 1960s-1990s, Artist, American
Dickens, Little Jimmy, The Nashville Sound, 1940s-1960s, Artist, American
Diesel Smoke, Honky Tonk, 1960s, Artist, American
Diffie, Joe, Young Country, 1990s–, Artist, American
Dillard and Clark, Country Rock; Bluegrass, 1960s-1970s; 1990s, Artist, American
Dillards, The, Country Rock; Bluegrass, 1960s-1990s, Artist, American
Dillon, Dean, Neo-Traditionalists, 1970s-1990s, Artist, American
Disturbingly Lo, Young Country, 1990s, Artist, American
Dixiana, Young Country, 1990s, Artist, American
Dixie Chicks, Young Country, 1990s-, Artist, American
Dixie Gentlemen, Bluegrass, 1960s, Artist, American
Dodd, Deryl, Neo-Traditionalists; Honky Tonk, 1990s-, Artist, American
Doucet, Camey, Young Country, 1990s-, Artist, American
Douglas, Jerry, Bluegrass, 1970s-, Artist, American
Douglas, Steve, Young Country, 1960s, Artist, American
Dowd, Johnny, Alternative Country, 1990s-, Artist, American
Dr Hook, Country Rock, 1960s-1970s, Artist, American
Driftwood, Jamie, Early & Old-Time Country, 1950s-1960s; 1990s, Artist, American
Drusky, Roy, The Nashville Sound, 1960s-1990s, Artist, American
Ducas, George, Young Country, 1990s, Artist, American
Dudley, Dave, Honky Tonk, 1960s-, Artist, American
Duncan, Steve, Alternative Country, 1990s, Artist, American
Duncan, Tommy, Western Swing, 1930s-1960s, Artist, American
Dunn, Holly, Young Country, 1980s-1990s, Artist, American
Durham, Bobby, Honky Tonk, 1970s-1980s, Artist, American
Dylan, Bob, Country Rock, 1960s-, Artist; Songwriter, American
Eagles, The, Country Rock, 1970s-1990s, Artist, American
Eaglesmith, Fred, Alternative Country, 1980s-, Artist; Songwriter, Canadian
Earle, Steve, Alternative Country; Neo-Traditionalists, 1980s-, Artist; Songwriter, American
Edwards, Daniel, Young Country, 1990s, Artist, American
Edwards, Don, Cowboy Music, 1980s-, Artist, American
Ellington, Harvey, Early & Old-Time Country, 1950s, Artist, American
Ellis, Darryl & Don, Young Country, 1990s, Artist, American
Ely, Joe, The Outlaw Movement; Country Rock, 1970s-, Artist, American
Emilio, Young Country, 1990s, Artist, American
England, Ty, Young Country, 1990s, Artist, American
Escovedo, Alejandro, Alternative Country, 1990s-, Artist; Songwriter, American
Evans, Dale, Cowboy Music, 1940s-1960s, Artist, American
Evans, Sara, Young Country; Neo-Traditionalists, 1990s-, Artist, American
Everette, Leon, Urban Cowboys, 1970s-1980s, Artist, American
Everly Brothers, The, Country Rock, 1950s-1990s, Artist, American
Ewing, Skip, Neo-Traditionalists, 1980s-1990s, Artist; Songwriter, American
Exile, Urban Cowboys, 1970s-1990s, Artist, American
Fargo, Donna, The Nashville Sound, 1970s-1980s, Artist, American
Farr, Hugh & Karl, Western Swing; Cowboy Music, 1930s-1950s, Artist, American
Firefall, Country Rock, 1970s-1980s, Artist, American
Fjellgard, Gary, Young Country, 1970s-1990s, Producer, Canadian
Flatlanders, The, The Outlaw Movement; Alternative Country, 1970s; 1990s-, Artist, American
Flatt & Scruggs, Bluegrass, 1940s-1970s, Artist, American
Flying Burrito Brothers, The, Country Rock, 1960s-1990s, Artist, American
Foley, Red, Honky Tonk; Bluegrass, 1940s-1960s, Artist, American
Ford, Brownie, Cowboy Music, 1980s, Artist, American
Ford, Jim, Country Rock, 1960s, Artist; Songwriter, American
Ford, Tennessee Ernie, The Nashville Sound, 1940s-1980s, Artist, American
Forester Sisters, The, Neo-Traditionalists, 1980s-1990s, Artist, American
Foster & Lloyd, Neo-Traditionalists; Young Country, 1980s-1990s, Artist, American
Foster, Radney, Neo-Traditionalists, 1990s-, Artist, American
Fox, George, Young Country, 1980s-1990s, Artist, Canadian
Foxworthy, Jeff, Young Country, 1980s-, Artist, American
Francis, Cleve, Young Country, 1990s, Artist, American
Frazier River, Young Country; Country Rock, 1990s, Artist, American
Frazier, Dallas, The Nashville Sound; Honky Tonk, 1950s-1970s, Artist; Composer; Songwriter, American
Freakwater, Alternative Country, 1980s-1990s, Artist, American
Freight Hoppers, The, Early & Old-Time Country; Neo-Traditionalists, 1990s, Artist, American
Friedman, Kinky, The Outlaw Movement, 1970s-1990s, Artist; Songwriter, American
Frizzell, Lefty, Honky Tonk, 1950s-1970s, Artist; Songwriter, American
Fulks, Robbie, Alternative Country; Neo-Traditionalists, 1990s-, Artist; Songwriter, American
Fuller & Kaz, Country Rock, 1970s, Artist, American
Gatlin Brothers, Urban Cowboys; Neo-Traditionalists, 1970s-, Artist, American
Gatlin, Larry, Urban Cowboys; Neo-Traditionalists, 1970s-1990s, Artist, American
Gatton, Danny, Neo-Traditionalists; Country Rock, 1970s, Artist, American
Gayle, Crystal, Urban Cowboys, 1970s-, Artist, American
Gemrino, Mark, Country Rock, 1990s, Artist; Songwriter, American
Gibbs, Terri, Urban Cowboys, 1980s-1990s, Artist, American
Gibson, Don, The Nashville Sound, 1940s-1990s, Artist; Songwriter, American
Gill, Vince, Neo-Traditionalists; Bluegrass; Young Country, 1980s-, Artist, American
Gillette, Steve, Young Country, 1960s-, Artist, American
Gilley, Mickey, Urban Cowboys; Honky Tonk, 1960s-1990s, Artist, American
Gillman, Jane, Young Country, 1970s-1980s, Artist; Songwriter, American
Gilmore, Jimmie Dale, Alternative Country, 1980s-, Artist; Songwriter, American
Gilmour, Amanda, Young Country, 1990s, Artist, American
Gimble, Johnny, Western Swing; Bluegrass, 1970s-1980s, Artist, American
Girls Next Door, Young Country, 1980s-1990s, Artist, American
Glaser, Jim, Mainstream Country, 1950s-1980s, Artist; Songwriter, American
Glaser, Tompall, The Outlaw Movement, 1960s-1990s, Artist, American
Glenn, Darrell, Western Swing, 1950s, Producer, American
Glory Fountain, Alternative Country, 1990s-, Artist, American
Golbey, Brian, Early & Old-Time Country, 1960s, Artist, British
Golden Smog, Alternative Country, 1990s, Artist, American
Goldens, The, Young Country, 1980s-1990s, Artist, American
Gordon, Noah, Young Country; Bluegrass, 1990s, Artist, American
Gorman, Skip, Cowboy Music, 1970s-1990s, Artist, American
Gosdin Brothers, Neo-Traditionalists; Bluegrass, 1960s-1990s, Artist, American
Gosdin, Vern, Bluegrass, 1970s-1990s, Artist, American
Grateful Dead, The, Country Rock, 1960s-1990s, Artist, American
Graves, Josh, Bluegrass, 1940s-, Artist, American
Gray, Billy, Western Swing, 1950s-1960s, Artist, American
Grayson & Witter, Early & Old-Time Country, 1920s-1930s, Artist, American
Great Divide, The, Neo-Traditionalists; Honky Tonk, 1990s-, Artist, American
Great Plains, The, Young Country; Country Rock, 1990s, Artist, American
Greenwood, Lee, Urban Cowboys, 1980s-, Artist, American
Gregory, Clinton, Young Country, 1990s-, Artist, American
Griffith, Nanci, Young Country, 1970s-, Artist; Songwriter, American
Grisman, David, Bluegrass, 1970s-, Artist, American
Grissom, Rich, Young Country, 1980s-1990s, Artist, American
Haggard, Marty, Neo-Traditionalists, 1990s, Artist, American
Haggard, Merle, Western Swing; Honky Tonk; Mainstream Country, 1960s-, Artist; Songwriter, American
Haley, Bill, Western Swing, 1950s-1970s, Artist, American
Hall, Connie, The Nashville Sound, 1960s, Artist, American
Hall, Dickson, Cowboy Music, 1950s-1960s, Artist, American
Hall, Tom T., Mainstream Country, 1960s-1990s, Artist; Songwriter, American
Hamilton, George IV, The Nashville Sound, 1950s-1980s, Artist, American
Hammond, Lorraine Lee, Alternative Country, 1970s-1990s, Artist, American
Hancock, Butch, Alternative Country, 1970s-, Artist, American
Hancock, Wayne, Neo-Traditionalists; Alternative Country, 1990s-, Artist, American
Harbour Voices, Young Country, 1990s, Artist, American
Hardwick, Billy Jr., Neo-Traditionalists, 1990s, Artist, American
Hargrove, Linda, Urban Cowboys; Country Rock, 1970s-1980s, Artist; Songwriter, American
Harlow, Camp, Young Country, 1990s, Artist, American
Harms, Joni, Young Country, 1990s-, Artist, American
Harris, Emmylou, Alternative Country; Country Rock; Young Country, 1960s-, Artist, American
Hartford, John, Early & Old-Time Country, 1960s-, Artist, American
Harvey, Alexander, Urban Cowboys, 1970s-1980s, Artist, American
Hawkins, Hawkshaw, Honky Tonk, 1950s-1960s, Artist, American
Hayes, Wade, Honky Tonk; Neo-Traditionalists, 1990s-, Artist, American
Hazlewood, Lee, Country Rock, 1950s-1970s; 1990s-, Producer; Artist; Songwriter, American
Health And Happiness Show, Alternative Country; Country Rock, 1990s, Artist, American
Heap, Jimmy, Honky Tonk; Western Swing, 1950s-1970s, Artist, American
Hearts And Flowers, Country Rock, 1960s; 1990s, Artist, American
Hellecasters, The, Alternative Country, 1990s-, Artist, American
Helms, Don, Cowboy Music; Honky Tonk, 1960s, Artist, American
Henderson, Michael, Young Country, 1990s, Artist, American
Hennen, Joe Pat, Neo-Traditionalists, 1990s, Artist, American
Henry, Don, Young Country, 1990s-, Artist; Songwriter, American
Henry, Joe, Alternative Country, 1980s-, Artist, American
Herndon, Ty, Young Country, 1990s-, Artist, American
Hiatt, John, Country Rock, 1970s-, Artist, American
Hickman, Sara, Alternative Country, 1980s-, Artist; Songwriter, American
High Country, Young Country, 1980s-1990s, Artist, American
Highway 101, Young Country, 1980s-, Artist, American
Hill, Faith, Young Country, 1990s-, Artist, American
Hofner, Adolph, Western Swing, 1950s, Artist, American
Holladay, Dave, Urban Cowboys, 1980s-, Artist, American
Holt, David, Early & Old-Time Country, 1980s-, Artist, American
Hood, Bobby, Young Country, 1990s, Artist, American
Hood, Ray, Young Country, 1990s-, Artist, American
Hoosier Hotshots, Early & Old-Time Country, 1930s-1960s, Artist, American
Horton, Johnny, The Nashville Sound; Honky Tonk, 1950s-1960s, Artist, American
Hot Rize, Bluegrass, 1970s-1990s, Artist, American
Howard, Harlan, Honky Tonk, 1950s-1980s, Artist; Composer, American
Hummer, Buzz, Young Country, 1990s, Artist, American
Hummon, Marcus, Alternative Country, 1990s, Artist; Songwriter, American
Hunter, Jesse, Young Country, 1990s, Artist, American
Husky, Ferlin, The Nashville Sound; Honky Tonk, 1950s-1990s, Artist, American
Hutchinson, Frank, Early & Old-Time Country, 1920s, Artist, American
Hyatt, Walter, Alternative Country, 1990s, Artist; Songwriter, American
Ingram, Jack, Neo-Traditionalists, 1990s-, Artist, American
Insley, Mark, Young Country, 1990s-, Artist, American
International Submarine Band, Country Rock, 1960s, Artist, American
Intveld, James, Neo-Traditionalists; Country Rock, 1990s-, Artist, American
Jackson, Alan, Neo-Traditionalists; Young Country, 1990s-, Artist, American
Jackson, Aunt Molly, Early & Old-Time Country, 1930s-1950s, Artist, American
Jackson, Stonewall, The Nashville Sound; Honky Tonk, 1950s-1980s, Artist, American
Jackson, Tommy, Western Swing, 1950s-1970s, Artist, American
James, Brett, Neo-Traditionalists, 1990s, Artist, American
James, Sonny, The Nashville Sound, 1950s-1980s, Artist, American
Jason, Alternative Country, 1990s, Artist, American
Jayhawks, The, Alternative Country, 1980s-, Artist, American
Jefferson, Paul, Young Country, 1990s, Artist; Songwriter, American
Jennings, Waylon, The Outlaw Movement, 1950-, Artist, American
Jim & Jesse, Bluegrass, 1930s-1990s, Artist, American
Johnson Mountain Boys, The, Bluegrass, 1970s-1990s, Artist, American
Johnston, Freedy, Alternative Country, 1990s-, Artist; Songwriter, American
Jones, Davis Lynn, Young Country, 1970s-1990s, Artist, American
Jones, George, The Nashville Sound; Honky Tonk, 1950s-, Artist, American
Jones, Grandpa, Early & Old-Time Country, 1930s-1970s, Artist, American
Jones, Larry Lee, Young Country, 1990s, Artist, American
Jones, Stan, Cowboy Music, 1960s, Artist, American
Jordanaires, The, The Nashville Sound, 1940s-, Artist, American
Joss, Scott, Neo-Traditionalists, 1980s-, Artist, American
Judd, Wynonna, Neo-Traditionalists; Young Country, 1990s-, Artist, American
Judds, The, Young Country, 1980s-1990s, Artist, American
Kane, Kieran, Young Country, 1990s, Artist, American

EARLY & OLD-TIME COUNTRY ➡ 186 COWBOY MUSIC ➡ 190 WESTERN SWING ➡ 193 BLUEGRASS ➡ 196 HONKY TONK ➡ 199

Keen, Robert Earl Jr., Alternative Country, 1980s-, Artist; Songwriter, American
Keith, Toby, Young Country, 1990s-, Artist, American
Kennedy Rose, Country Rock, 1980s-1990s, Artist, American
Kentucky Colonels, The, Bluegrass, 1960s-1990s, Artist, American
Kentucky Headhunters, Young Country, 1980s-, Artist, American
Kerr, Anita, The Nashville Sound, 1950s-1990s, Producer; Artist, American
Kersh, David, Young Country; Neo-Traditionalists, 1990s, Artist, American
Kershaw, Sammy, Young Country; Neo-Traditionalists, 1980s-, Artist, American
Ketchum, Hal, Neo-Traditionalists, 1980s-,Artist, American
Kilgore, Merle, Cowboy Music; Country Rock; Honky Tonk, 1960s-1970s, Artist, American
Killbilly, Alternative Country, 1990s, Artist, American
Kimes, Royal Wade, Neo-Traditionalists, 1990s, Artist, American
Kincaid, Bradley, Early & Old-Time Country, 1930s-1970s, Artist, American
King, Bob, Cowboy Music, 1950s-1960s, Artist, Canadian
King, Don, Urban Cowboys, 1970s-1980s, Artist; Songwriter, American
King, Pee Wee, Western Swing; Cowboy Music; Early & Old-Time Country, 1930s-1970s, Artist, American
King, Sid, Western Swing, 1960s-1980s, Artist, American
Kirchen, Bill, Alternative Country; Country Rock, 1990s-, Artist, American
Kitten, Young Country, 1990s, Artist, American
Knight, Jeff, Young Country, 1990s, Artist; Songwriter, American
Knitters, The, Alternative Country, 1980s, Artist, American
Koller, Fred, Young Country, 1980s-, Artist; Songwriter, American
Krauss, Alison, Bluegrass; Neo-Traditionalists, 1980s-, Artist, American
Kristofferson, Kris, The Outlaw Movement, 1970s-1990s, Artist; Songwriter, American
LaFave, Jimmy, Alternative Country, 1980s-, Artist; Songwriter, American
Lambchop, Alternative Country, 1990s-, Artist, American
Land, Gene, Young Country, 1990s-, Artist, American
Lang, k. d., Neo-Traditionalists; Alternative Country, 1980s-, Artist, Canadian
Lansdowne, Jerry, Young Country, 1990s, Artist, American
Larson, Nicolette, Urban Cowboys; Country Rock, 1970s-1990s, Artist, American
Last Round, Alternative Country; Neo-Traditionalists, 1990s, Artist, American
Lauderdale, Jim, Young Country, 1990s-, Artist, American
Laughton, Charles, Western Swing, 1960s, Artist, American
Lawrence, Tracy, Young Country, 1990s-, Artist, American
Lawson, Doyle, Bluegrass, 1970s-, Artist, American
LeBlanc, Will, Young Country, 1980s-1990s, Artist; Songwriter, American
Ledford String Band, Early & Old-Time Country, 1930s-1940s, Artist, American
LeDoux, Chris, Urban Cowboys; Neo-Traditionalists; Cowboy Music;Young Country, 1970s-, Artist, American
Lee, Albert, Neo-Traditionalists; Country Rock, 1960s-, Artist, British
Lee, Brenda, The Nashville Sound, 1950s-1990s, Artist, American
Lee, Johnny, Urban Cowboys, 1970s-1990s, Artist, American
Lee, Robin, Urban Cowboys, 1980s-1990s, Artist, American
Lee, Rory, Young Country, 1990s, Artist, American
Lee, Wilma, and Stoney Cooper, Early & Old-Time Country; Bluegrass, 1940s-1970s, Artist, American
Lee, Woody, Young Country, 1990s, Artist, American
Levin, Danny, Western Swing, 1990s, Artist, American
Lewis, Jerry Lee, Honky Tonk, 1950s-, Artist, American
Light Crust Doughboys, The, Western Swing, 1930s-, Artist, American
Lilly Brothers, The, Bluegrass, 1960s-1970s, Artist, American
Little Texas, Young Country, 1990s, Artist, American
Locklin, Hank, The Nashville Sound, Honky Tonk, 1940s-1970s, Artist, American
Logan, Josh, Young Country, 1980s, Artist, American
London, Eddie, Young Country, 1990s, Artist, American
Lonesome Strangers, Alternative Country; Country Rock, 1980s-1990s, Artist, American
Lonestar, Neo-Traditionalists, 1990s-, Artist, American
Louisiana Boys, Alternative Country, 1990s, Artist, American
Louvin Brothers, The, Bluegrass, 1940s-1960s, Artist, American
Loveless, Patty, Neo-Traditionalists, 1980s-, Artist, American
Lovett, Lyle, Alternative Country, 1980s-, Artist; Songwriter, American
Lowe, Nick, Country Rock, 1970s-, Producer; Songwriter; Artist, British
Lunsford, Bascon Lamar, Early & Old-Time Country, 1900s-1970s, Artist, American
Lynn, Loretta, Mainstream Country; Honky Tonk, 1960s-, Artist, American
Lynne, Shelby, Alternative Country, 1980s-, Artist; Songwriter, American
Macon, Uncle Dave, Early & Old-Time Country, 1920s-1950s, Artist, American
Maddox Brothers & Rose, The, Western Swing, 1930s-1960s, Artist, American
Mainer, J. E., Early & Old-Time Country, 1930s-1960s, Artist, American
Major, Charlie, Young Country, 1980s-, Artist; Songwriter, Canadian
Malchak, Tim, Urban Cowboys, 1980s-1990s, Artist, American
Manders, Mark David, Young Country, 1990s-, Artist, American
Mandrell, Barbara, Mainstream Country, 1960s-1990s, Artist, American
Mandrell, Louise, Urban Cowboys, 1970s-1980s, Artist, American
Maphis, Joe, Honky Tonk, 1940s-1980s, Artist, American
Marcy Brothers, Young Country, 1990s, Artist, American
Martin, Asa, Early & Old-Time Country, 1920s-1930s, Artist, American
Martin, Jimmy, Bluegrass, 1940s-1990s, Artist, American
Martin, Roger, Young Country, 1990s, Artist, American
Marvin, Alternative Country, 1990s, Artist; Songwriter, American
Mason, Mila, Young Country, 1990s, Artist, American
Matt, Jim, Young Country, 1990s, Artist; Songwriter, Canadian
Mattea, Kathy, Young Country, 1980s-, Artist, American
Matthews, Wright & King, Country Rock, 1990s, Artist, American
Maule, Brad, Young Country, 1990s, Artist, American
Mavericks, The, Neo-Traditionalists, 1990s, Artist, American
McAuliffe, Leon, Western Swing, 1950s-1970s, Artist, American
McBride & the Ride, Young Country, 1990s-, Artist, American
McBride, Martina, Young Country, 1990s, Artist, American
McCall, C. W., Urban Cowboys, 1970s-1990s, Artist, American
McCarter, Jennifer, Young Country, 1990s, Artist, American
McCarty, Fred, Young Country, 1990s, Artist, American
McClain, Charly, Urban Cowboys, 1970s-1980s, Artist, American
McClinton, Delbert, Country Rock, 1960s-, Artist, American
McCoury, Del, Bluegrass, 1960s-, Artist, American
McCoy, Neal, Young Country; Neo-Traditionalists, 1990s-, Artist, American
McCready, Mindy, Young Country, 1990s-, Artist, American
McDaniel, Mel, Urban Cowboys, 1970s-1980s, Artist, American
McDowell, Ronnie, Urban Cowboys, 1970s-, Artist, American
McEntire, Reba, Neo-Traditionalists;Young Country, 1970s-, Artist, American
McGee, Sam, Early & Old-Time Country, 1930s-1970s, Artist, American
McGraw, Tim, Young Country; Neo-Traditionalists, 1990s-, Artist, American
Meade, Donna, Honky Tonk, 1920s, Artist, American
Meesina, Jo Dee, Neo-Traditionalists, 1990s-, Artist, American
Mellons, Ken, Young Country, 1990s, Artist, American
Memphis Exchange, Alternative Country, 1990s, Artist, American
Mercury Dime, Young Country, 1990s, Artist, American
Miller, Buddy, Alternative Country; Neo-Traditionalists, 1990s-, Artist, American
Miller, Dean, Young Country, 1990s, Artist, American
Miller, Emmett, Early & Old-Time Country, 1920s-1950s, Artist, American
Miller, Joe, Cowboy Music, 1990s, Artist, American
Miller, Lisa, Alternative Country, 1990s-, Artist, American
Miller, Roger, The Nashville Sound; Honky Tonk, 1950s-1980s, Artist; Songwriter, American
Milsap, Ronnie, Mainstream Country, 1960s-, Artist, American
Mitchell, Waddie, Cowboy Music, 1990s-, Artist, American
Mize, Bill, Western Swing, 1980s-, Artist, American
Moffatt, Katy, Alternative Country, 1970sl; 1990s-, Artist, American
Molsky, Bruce, Early & Old-Time Country, 1990s-, Artist, American
Monroe, Bill, Bluegrass, 1930s-1990s, Artist, American
Montana, Patsy, Cowboy Music, 1930s-1990s, Artist, American
Montgomery, John Michael, Young Country, 1990s-, Artist, American
Mooney, Ralph, Honky Tonk, 1960s, Artist, American
Moonshine Willie, Alternative Country, 1990s, Artist, American
Moore, Tiny, Western Swing; Bluegrass, 1970s, Artist, American
Morgan, George, The Nashville Sound, 1940s-1970s, Artist, American
Morgan, Lorrie, Neo-Traditionalists, 1980s-, Artist, American
Morris, Joni, Neo-Traditionalists, 1990s, Artist, American
Mullican, Moon, Honky Tonk; Western Swing, 1940s-1960s, Artist, American
Murphey, Michael Martin, Neo-Traditionalists; Country Rock; Cowboy Music, 1970s-, Artist; Songwriter, American
Murphy, David Lee, Nweo-Traditional Country, 1990s, Artist, American
Murray, Anne, Country Rock, 1960s-, Artist, Canadian
Nashville Bluegrass Band, The, Bluegrass, 1980s-1990s, Artist, American
Nashville West, The Outlaw Movement, 1960s-1970s, Artist, American
Nelson, Ricky, Country Rock, 1950s-1980s, Artist, American
Nelson, Willie, The Outlaw Movement; Mainstream Country, 1950s-, Artist; Songwriter, American
Nesmith, Michael, Country Rock, 1960s-, Artist; Songwriter, American
New Coon Creek Girls, Bluegrass, 1980s-, Artist, American
New Grass Revival, Bluegrass, 1970s-1990s, Artist, American
New Riders Of The Purple Sage, The, Country Rock, 1960s-1990s, Artist, American
Newbury, Mickey, The Outlaw Movement, 1960s-1990s, Artist; Songwriter, American
Newton, Juice, Urban Cowboys, 1970s-, Artist, American
Nichols, Joe, Neo-Traditionalists, 1990s-, Artist, American
Nichols, Roy, Honky Tonk, 1990s, Artist, American
Nitty Gritty Dirt Band, Country Rock; Bluegrass, 1960s-, Artist, American
Norwood, Daron, Young Country, 1990s, Artist, American
O'Connell, Chris, Western Swing, 1990s, Artist, American
O'Day, Molly, Honky Tonk, 1950s-1970s, Artist, American
O'Hara, Jamie, Neo-Traditionalists, 1990s-, Artist; Songwriter, American
O'Kanes, The, Neo-Traditionalists; Country Rock; Bluegrass, 1980s-1990s, Artist, American
Old 97's, Alternative Country, 1990s-, Artist, American
Old And In The Way, Bluegrass, 1970s, Artist, American
Olson, Carla, Country Rock, 1970s-, Artist, American
Olson, Kim, Young Country, 1990s, Artist, American
Original River Road Boys, Neo-Traditionalists, 1990s, Artist, American
Orozco, Rick, Young Country, 1990s, Artist, Mexican
Orrall & Wright, Young Country, 1990s, Artist, American
Osborne Brothers, Bluegrass, 1940s-1990s, Artist, American
Oslin, K. T., Young Country, 1980s-, Artist, American
Overstreet, Paul, Young Country, 1980s-, Artist, American
Owens, Bonnie, Honky Tonk, 1960s-1970s, Artist, American
Owens, Buck, Mainstream Country; Honky Tonk, 1950s-1980s, Artist, American
Owens, Tex, Cowboy Music, 1930s-1950s, Artist; Songwriter, American
Palace, Alternative Country, 1990s, Artist, American
Palomino Road, Young Country, 1990s, Artist, American
Parker, Caryl Mack, Young Country, 1990s, Producer, American
Parker, Chubby, Early & Old-Time Country, 1920s-1940s, Artist, American
Parker, Fess, Cowboy Music, 1950s-1960s, Artist, American
Parker, Knocky, Western Swing, 1940s-1970s, Artist, American
Parks, John Andrew, Young Country, 1990s, Artist, American
Parnell, Lee Roy, Western Swing, 1990s-, Artist, American
Parsons, Gram, Country Rock, 1960s-1970s, Artist, American
Parton, Dolly, Mainstream Country; Honky Tonk; Young Country, 1960s-, Artist; Songwriter, American
Patton, Wayland, Young Country, 1990s, Artist, American
Pawtuckets, Alternative Country, 1990s-, Artist, American
Paycheck, Johnny, The Outlaw Movement; Honky Tonk, 1960s-, Artist, American
Pearl River, Young Country, 1990s, Artist, American
Penn, Dan, Alternative Country, 1990s, Artist; Songwriter, American
Pennington, J. P., Young Country, 1990s, Artist, American
Penny, Hank, Western Swing, 1940s-1960s, Artist, American
Perfect Stranger, Neo-Traditionalists, 1990s-, Artist, American
Peters, Gretchen, Young Country, 1990s-, Artist; Songwriter, American
Peterson, Michael, Neo-Traditionalists; Honky Tonk, 1990s-, Artist, American
Pierce, Jo Carol, Alternative Country, 1980s-1990s, Artist; Songwriter, American
Pierce, Webb, Honky Tonk, 1950s-1980s, Artist, American
Poco, Country Rock, 1960s-1990s, Artist, American
Poole, Charley, Early & Old-Time Country, 1920s-1930s, Artist, American
Posey, Sandy, The Nashville Sound, 1960s-1980s, Artist, American
Potterm Curtis, Western Swing, 1950s-1990s, Artist, American
Prairie Oyster, Young Country, 1990s, Artist, American
Price, Ray, The Nashville Sound; Honky Tonk, 1950s-, Artist, American
Pride, Charley, The Nashville Sound; Mainstream Country, 1960s-, Artist, American
Puckett, Riley, Early & Old-Time Country, 1920s-1940s, Artist, American
Pure Prairie League, Country Rock, 1970s-1980s, Artist, American
Rabbitt, Eddie, Urban Cowboys, 1970s-1990s, Artist, American
Ranch Romance, Alternative Country; Western Swing, 1990s, Artist, American
Randolph, Boots, The Nashville Sound, 1960s-1990s, Artist, American
Rattlesnake Annie, The Outlaw Movement, 1980s-1990s, Artist, American
Rausch, Leon, Western Swing, 1950s-1980s, Artist, American
Raven, Eddy, Mainstream Country, 1960s-, Artist, American
Ray, Wade, Western Swing, 1950s-1970s, Artist, American
Raye, Collin, Young Country; Neo-Traditionalists, 1990s-, Artist, American
Raye, Susan, Country Rock, 1970s, Artist, American
Red Clay Ramblers, The, Early & Old-Time Country, 1960s-, Artist, American
Red Meat, Alternative Country; Neo-Traditionalists, 1990s-, Artist, American
Red Rivers, Neo-Traditionalists, 1990s, Artist, American
Reed, Blind Alfred, Early & Old-Time Country, 1920s, Artist, American
Reed, Ola Belle, Early & Old-Time Country; Bluegrass, 1970s, Artist, American
Reeves, Jim, The Nashville Sound, 1950s-1960s, Artist, American
Reeves, Ronna, Young Country, 1990s, Artist, American
Reid, Mike, Young Country, 1980s-1990s, Artist; Songwriter, American
Remington, Herbie, Western Swing, 1950s-, Artist, American
Remingtons, The, Young Country, 1990s, Artist, American
Reno & Smiley, Bluegrass, 1950s-1990s, Artist, American
Restless Heart, Young Country, 1980s-1990s, Artist, American
Revard, Jimmy, Western Swing, 1930s, Artist, American
Rhodes, Kimmie, Alternative Country, 1980s-, Artist; Songwriter, American
Rice, Tony, Bluegrass, 1970s-, Artist, American
Rich, Charlie, The Nashville Sound, 1950s-1990s, Artist, American
Richey, Kim, Young Country, 1990s-, Artist, American
Ricochet, Young Country, 1990s-, Artist, American
Riddle, Bo, Young Country, 1990s, Artist, American
Riders In The Sky, Western Swing; Cowboy Music, 1970s-, Artist, American
Rigas, Ellen, Young Country, 1990s, Artist, American
Rigby, Amy, Alternative Country, 1990s-, Artist; Songwriter, American
Right, Robin, Young Country, 1990s, Artist, American
Riley, Thomas Michael, Young Country, 1990s, Artist, American
Rimes, LeAnn, Young Country, 1990s-, Artist, American
Riptones, Alternative Country, 1990s-, Artist, American
Ritter, Tex, Cowboy Music, 1930s-1970s, Artist, American
Rivers, Jerry, Cowboy Music, 1960s, Artist, American
Rivers, Jimmie, Western Swing, 1960s, Artist, American
Rizzetta, Sam, Bluegrass, 1970s-, Artist, American
Road Music, Honky Tonk, 1990s, Artist, American
Robbins, Dennis, Young Country, 1980s-1990s, Artist; Songwriter, American
Robbins, Hargus 'Pig', Western Swing; The Nashville Sound; Country Rock, 1960s-1990s, Artist, American
Robbins, Marty, The Nashville Sound; Cowboy Music, 1950s-1990s, Artist, American
Roberts, Kenny, Cowboy Music, 1940s-1980s, Artist, American
Robertson, Kathy, Western Swing, 1990s, Artist, American
Robinson, Bruce, Young Country, 1990s, Artist, American
Robinson, Charlie, Young Country, 1990s-, Artist, American
Robison, Bruce, Alternative Country, 1990s-, Artist; Songwriter, American
Robison, Carson, Cowboy Music; Early & Old-Time Country, 1920s-1950s, Artist; Songwriter, American
Robison, Charlie, Alternative Country, 1990s-, Artist; Songwriter, American
Roddy, Ted, Alternative Country, 1990s-, Artist; Songwriter, American
Rodgers, Jimmie, Early & Old-Time Country, 1920s-1930s, Artist; Songwriter, American
Rodman, Judy, Young Country, 1980s, Artist, American
Rodriguez, Johnny, The Outlaw Movement, 1970s-1990s, Artist, American
Rogers, Kenny, Mainstream Country, 1960s-, Artist, American
Rogers, Ron, Young Country, 1990s, Artist; Songwriter, American
Rogers, Roy, Cowboy Music; Early & Old-Time Country, 1930s-1960s; 1980s-1990s, Artist, American
Rogers, Tammy, Young Country, 1990s, Artist, American
Ronstadt, Linda, Country Rock, 1960s-, Artist, American
Rowan, Peter, Bluegrass, 1970s-1990s, Artist, American
Rowans, The, Bluegrass, 1970s-1980s, Artist, American
Runaway Express, Young Country, 1990s-, Artist, American
Russell, Tom, Young Country, 1980s-R, Artist; Songwriter, American
Sahm, Doug, Country Rock, 1950s-1990s, Artist, American
Satherly, Art, Cowboy Music, 1930s-1950s, Producer, British
Sawyer Brown, Young Country, 1980s-, Artist, American
Schlitz, Don, Urban Cowboys, 1980s, Artist; Songwriter, American
Schneider, John, Urban Cowboys, 1980s, Artist, American
Schramms, Alternative Country, 1990s-, Artist, American
Schwaggert, Young Country, 1990s, Artist, American
Scud Mountain Boys, Alternative Country, 1990s, Artist, American
Sears, Dawn, Alternative Country; Young Country, 1990s, Artist, American
Seeger, Mike, Early & Old-Time Country, 1960s-1990s, Artist, American
Seldom Scene, The, Bluegrass, 1970s-, Artist, American
Sharp, Kevin, Young Country, 1990s, Artist, American
Shaver, Billy Joe, The Outlaw Movement; Honky Tonk, 1970s-, Artist; Songwriter, American
Shaw, Victoria, Young Country, 1990s, Artist, American
Shea, Rick, Honky Tonk, 1980s-, Artist, American
Shelton, Ricky van, Young Country, 1980s-, Artist, American
Shenandoah, Young Country, 1980s-, Artist, American
Shepard, Jean, Honky Tonk, 1950s-1990s, Artist, American
Sheppard, T. G., Urban Cowboys, 1970s-1990s, Artist, American
Sherrill, Billy, The Nashville Sound, 1960s, Producer; Songwriter, American
Shivers, Alternative Country, 1990s, Artist, American
Sholes, Steve, The Nashville Sound, 1940s-1960s, Producer, American
Six Shooter, Young Country, 1990s, Artist, American
Six String Drag, Alternative Country, 1990s, Artist, American
Skaggs, Ricky, Bluegrass; Young Country, 1970s-, Artist, American
Skillet Lickers II, The, Early & Old-Time Country, 1980s-1990s, Artist, American
Skinner, Tom, Alternative Country, 1990s, Artist, American
Smith Brothers, The, Cowboy Music, 1950s-1960s, Artist, American
Smith, Carl, Western Swing; Honky Tonk, 1950s-1980s, Artist, American
Smith, Darden, Young Country, 1980s-, Artist, American
Smith, Sammi, The Outlaw Movement, 1970s-1990s, Artist, American
Smokin' Armadillos, Alternative Country, 1990s, Artist, American
Snider, Todd, Alternative Country, 1990s-, Artist; Songwriter, American
Snow, Hank, Honky Tonk; Cowboy Music, 1930s-1980s, Artist, Canadian
Sometime Band, Young Country, 1990s, Artist, American
Son Volt, Alternative Country, 1990s, Artist, American
Sonnier, Jo-El, Alternative Country, 1970s-, Artist, American
Sons Of The Pioneers, The, Cowboy Music, 1930s-1970s, Artist, American
Sons Of The San Joaquin, Cowboy Music, 1990s-, Artist, American
Sons Of The West, The, Western Swing, 1930s-1940s, Artist, American
South Mountain, Young Country, 1990s, Artist, American
Souther, J. D. , Urban Cowboys; Country Rock, 1970s-1990s, Artist; Songwriter, American
Sovine, Red, Honky Tonk; Early & Old-Time Country, 1950s-1970s, Artist, American
Sparks, Larry, Bluegrass, 1970s-, Artist, American
Spencer, Sid, Young Country, 1990s, Artist, American
Sprague, Carl T., Cowboy Music, 1920s-1930s;19780s, Artist, American
Stanley Brothers, The, Bluegrass, 1940s-1960s, Artist, American
Stanley, Ralph, Bluegrass, 1950s-, Artist, American
Statler Brothers, The, Mainnstream Country, 1960s-, Artist, American
Steagal, Red, The Nashville Sound; Honky Tonk; Cowboy Music, 1970s-1990s, Artist, American
Steele, Jeffrey, Alternative Country, 1990s-, Artist, American
Stegall, Keith, Urban Cowboys, 1980s-1990s, Artist; Songwriter, American
Steven, Jeff, Young Country, 1980s-1990s, Artist, American
Stevens, Doug, Young Country, 1990s-, Artist, American
Stewart, Larry, Young Country, 1990s, Artist, American
Stewart, Wynn, Early & Old-Time Country, 1950s-1970s, Artist, American
Stone, Doug, Young Country; Neo-Traditionalists, 1980s-1990s, Artist, American
Stoneman Family, The, The Nashville Sound; Early & Old-Time Country, 1950s-1980s, Artist, American
Strait, George, Western Swing; Neo-Traditionalists, 1970s-, Artist, American
Streeter, Shelley, Young Country, 1990s, Artist, American
Strickland, Gayle, Young Country, 1990s, Artist, American
Stringbean, Bluegrass; Early & Old-Time Country, 1930s-1970s, Artist, American
Stuart, Marty, Neo-Traditionalists; Bluegrass; Country Rock, 1980s-, Artist, American
Sunshine Boys, Western Swing, 1960s, Artist, American
Sutton, Shane, Young Country, 1990s, Artist, American
Sweethearts Of The Rodeo, Young Country, 1980s-1990s, Artist, American
Sylvia, Urban Cowboys, 1980s, Artist, American
Tanner, Gid, Early & Old-Time Country, 1920s-1930s, Artist, American
Tarnation, Alternative Country, 1990s, Artist, American
Taylor, Les, Young Country, 1990s, Artist, American
Taylor, Tut, Early & Old-Time Country; Bluegrass, 1960s-1970s, Artist, American
Texas Kellys, Young Country, 1990s, Artist, American
Texas Tornados, The, Alternative Country, 1990s, Artist, American
Thomas, B. J., Country Rock, 1960s-1990s, Artist, American
Thompson Brothers, Young Country, 1990s, Artist, American
Thompson, Hank, Honky Tonk; Western Swing, 1940s-1990s, Artist, American
Thompson, Verlon, Young Country, 1990s, Artist, American
Thornton, Marsha, Young Country, 1990s, Artist, American
Threadgill Troubadors, Alternative Country, 1990s, Artist, American
Tillis, Mel, Early & Old-Time Country, 1960s-1990s, Artist, American
Tillis, Pam, Young Country; Urban Cowboys, 1980s-, Artist, American
Tillman, Floyd, Honky Tonk, 1940s-1970s, Artist, American
Tin Star, Alternative Country, 1980s, Artist, American
Tippin, Aaron, Young Country, 1990s-, Artist, American
Tobin, Karen, Alternative Country, 1990s, Artist, American
Toliver, Tony, Young Country, 1990s, Artist, American
Tractors, The, Neo-Traditionalists, 1990s-, Artist, American
Trailer Bride, Alternative Country, 1990s-, Artist, American
Trailer Park Rangers, Alternative Country, 1990s, Artist, American
Travis, Merle, Early & Old-Time Country, 1940s-1970s, Artist, American
Travis, Randy, Neo-Traditionalists, 1980s-, Artist, American
Trevino, Geronimo, Alternative Country, 1990s, Artist, American
Trevino, Rick, Young Country, 1990s-, Artist, American
Trickett, Kate, Young Country, 1990s, Artist, American
Trischka, Tony, Bluegrass, 1970s-1990s, Artist, American
Tritt, Travis, Neo-Traditionalists, 1990s-, Artist, American
Tubb, Ernest, Honky Tonk, 1930s-1980s, Artist, American
Tucker, Tanya, Young Country, 1970s-1990s, Artist, American
Tupelo, Uncle, Alternative Country, 1980s-1990s, Artist, American
Twain, Shania, Young Country, 1990s-, Artist, American
Twister Alley, Young Country, 1990s, Artist, American
Twitty, Conway, The Nashville Sound, 1950s-1990s, Artist, American
Two Dollar Pistols, Alternative Country, 1990s-, Artist, American
Tyree & Company, Young Country, 1990s, Artist, American
Tyson, Ian, Cowboy Music, 1970s-1990s, Artist, Canadian
Ulisse, Donna, Young Country, 1990s, Artist, American
Van Shelton, Ricky, Young Country, 1980s-, Artist, American
Van Zandt, Townes, Alternative Country, 1960s-1990s, Artist; Songwriter, American
Vezner, Jon, Young Country, 1990s, Artist, American
Vidalias, The, Alternative Country, 1990s, Artist, American
Vincent, Rick, Alternative Country, 1990s, Artist, American
Volebeats, The, Alternative Country, 1980s-, Artist, American
Waco Brothers, The, Alternative Country, 1990s-, Artist, American
Wade, Stephen, Early & Old-Time Country, 1990s, Artist, American
Wagoner, Porter, The Nashville Sound, 1950s-1980s; 2000s-, Artist; Songwriter, American
Wagoners, The, Alternative Country, 1980s, Artist, American
Wakefield, Frank, Bluegrass, 1950s-1990s, Artist, American
Wakely, Jimmy, Cowboy Music, 1940s-1970s, Artist, American
Wakeman, Dusty, Alternative Country, 1980s-1990s, Artist, American
Walkabouts, The , Alternative Country, 1980s-, Artist, American
Walker, Billy, Western Swing; Honky Tonk, 1940s-1990s, Artist, American
Walker, Cindy, Young Country, 1960s, Artist, American
Walker, Clay, Young Country, 1990s-, Artist, American
Walker, Jerry Jeff, The Outlaw Movement, 1960s-, Artist; Songwriter, American
Wall, Chris, Alternative Country, 1990s, Artist; Songwriter, American
Waller, Juliana, Young Country, 1990s, Artist, American
Walser, Don, Alternative Country; Western Swing, 1990s, Artist, American
Ward, Chris, Young Country, 1990s, Artist, American
Ward, Fields, Early & Old-Time Country, 1930s-1940s; 1960s, Artist, American
Warden, Monte, Alternative Country, 1990s, Artist, American
Wariner, Steve, Neo-Traditional, 1980s-, Artist, American
Warren, Jamie, Young Country, 1980s-1990s, Artist; Producer, American
Watson Family, The, Bluegrass, 1960s, Artist, American
Watson, Dale, Alternative Country, 1990s-, Artist, American
Watson, Doc, Early & Old-Time Country, 1960s-, Artist, American
Weissman, Shari, Young Country, 1990s, Artist, American
Welch, Gillian, Alternative Country, 1990s-, Artist; Songwriter, American
Welch, Kevin, Alternative Country, 1990s-, Artist; Songwriter, American
Wells, Kitty, The Nashville Sound; Honky Tonk, 1940s-1980s, Artist, American
West, Dottie, The Nashville Sound, 1950s-1980s, Artist, American
West, Shelly, Urban Cowboys, 1980s, Artist, American
Western, Johnny, Cowboy Music, 1950s-1980s, Artist, American
Whiskeytown, Alternative Country, 1990s, Artist, American
White, Bryan, Young Country, 1990s-, Artist, American
White, Clarence, Bluegrass, 1960s-1970s, Artist, American
Whitley, Chris, Alternative Country, 1990s-, Artist; Songwriter, American
Whitley, Dwight, Alternative Country, 1990s, Artist, American
Whitley, Keith, Neo-Traditionalists; Bluegrass, 1980s-1990s, Artist, American
Whitley, Ray, Cowboy Music, 1930s-1950s, Artist, American
Whitman, Slim, Cowboy Music, 1940s-1980s, Artist, American
Wilco, Alternative Country, 1990s-, Artist, American
Wild Rose, Neo-Traditionalists, 1990s, Artist, American
Wilds, Honey, Early & Old-Time Country, 1930s-1950s, Artist, American
Wilkin, Marijohn, Outlaw County; Honky Tonk, 1950s-1970s, Artist; Songwriter, American
Williams, Don, Country Rock, 1960s-, Artist, American
Williams, Hank Jr., Country Rock, 1960s-, Artist, American
Williams, Hank, Honky Tonk, 1940s-1950s, Artist, American
Williams, Jett, Alternative Country; Hony Tonk; Neo-Traditionalists, 1990s, Artist, American
Williams, Lucinda, Alternative Country, 1970s-, Artist, American
Williams, Tex, Western Swing, 1940s-1980s, Artist, American
Williams, Victoria, Alternative Country, 1980s-, Artist; Songwriter, American
Willing, Foy, Cowboy Music, 1940s-1960s, Artist, American
Willis Brothers, The, Western Swing, 1960s-1970s, Artist, American
Willis, Kelly, Young Country, 1990s-, Artist, American
Wills, Billy Jack, Western Swing, 1950s, Artist, American
Wills, Bob, Western Swing, 1930s-1970s, Artist; Songwriter, American
Wills, Johnnie Lee, Western Swing, 1940s-1970s, Artist, American
Wills, Mark, Young Country, 1990s-, Artist, American
Wilson, Slim, Young Country, 1990s, Artist, American
Wise, Chubby, Western Swing, 1940s-1990s, Artist, American
Wiseman, Mac, Bluegrass, 1950s-, Artist, American
Womack, LeeAnn, Young Country, 1990s-, Artist, American
Wood, Jeff, Young Country, 1990s, Artist, American
Woods, Bill, Honky Tonk, 1960s, Artist, American
Wooley, Sheb, Cowboy Music, 1940s-1970s, Artist, American
Wopat, Tom, Young Country, 1980s-, Artist, American
Wright, Curtis, Young Country, 1990s, Artist, American
Wright, Michelle, Young Country, 1980s-1990s, Artist, Canadian
Wyble, Jimmy, Western Swing, 1950s, Artist, American
Wylie & the Wild West Show, Alternative Country; Western Swing, 1990s-, Artist, American
Wynette, Tammy, The Nashville Sound; Mainstream Country, 1960s-1990s, Artist, American
Yearwood, Trisha, Young Country, 1990s-, Artist, American
Yoakam, Dwight, Neo-Traditionalists; Alternative Country; Country Rock, 1980s-, Artist, American
Young, Faron, The Nashville Sound, Honky Tonk, 1950s-1990s, Artist, American
Young, Harvey Thomas, Young Country, 1990s, Artist, American
Young, Neil, Country Rock, 1960s-, Artist; Songwriter, Canadian
Young, Steve, The Outlaw Movement, 1960s-, Artist, American

THE NASHVILLE SOUND ➡ 201 MAINSTREAM COUNTRY ➡ 204 THE OUTLAW MOVEMENT ➡ 206 COUNTRY ROCK ➡ 209 URBAN COWBOYS ➡ 212
NEO-TRADITIONALIST ➡ 213 ALTERNATIVE COUNTRY ➡ 215 YOUNG COUNTRY ➡ 218

Folk

IT was Louis Armstrong (or Leadbelly, depending on whom you believe) who came up with the famous final word on the definition of folk music: "It's ALL folk music … I ain't never heard no horse sing…."

The quote has been repeated ad nauseam throughout the years, but it has not prevented strenuous debate about the meaning of folk music in every country in which it is performed. Which is every country in the world. "Music of the people, by the people, for the people" was the neat description favoured by early British folklorists, giving it a social and political context free of the stylistic parameters that tend to tag it in modern days.

It means different things in different countries. In its purest form, folk is the natural expression of a people and, therefore, arguably the most natural and organic musical genre of all, whether it comes in the form of African tribal chants, the ceremonial songs of Native Americans, or old England fertility rituals. In many cases, the cultural history of a country is reflected in its indigenous music, which evolves to meet the changing nature of the times and people, blurring the boundaries of genre definition. Cowboy songs, sea shanties, romantic ballads, prison work songs, gypsy music… all might legitimately be recognized as folk music. A century ago, African-American spirituals and, later on, the blues and even hillbilly country music might have justifiably been considered the true folk music of America. Logically, you could make a strong argument for rap being modern folk music. Common

> ## "IT'S ALL FOLK MUSIC … I AIN'T NEVER HEARD NO HORSE SING…."
> *Leadbelly (or Louis Armstrong)*

Right
A prolific songwriter and performer, Woody Guthrie sang songs of economic, political and social woe with a grace and effectiveness that led him to be called the greatest folk singer ever.

perception today, however, tends to associate folk music with acoustic guitars and storytelling lyrics.

The very nature of the music's history means that its repertoire encompasses many shapes and styles. It has metamorphosed dramatically through vagaries of fashion and shifting opinions of its relevance. It is one of the sadder and most mystifying characteristics of modern culture that the indigenous folk music of the people is rarely accorded the respect of its own people in its own land – whatever land that may be. In many cases, it has been left to enthusiasts to march against the tide, collecting and protecting traditional songs and tunes, and providing the raw material that has fuelled folk revivals at different times. It is often said that one country with an unbroken folk tradition is Ireland, but in pre-war times even Irish music was confined to remote rural areas. It survived courtesy of émigrés in America, playing to provide a few home thoughts from abroad.

By the end of the nineteenth century, British folk music had long been in decline, singers having been discouraged from performing their old songs of simple emotions and heartfelt expressions of working-class life. The songs had often been handed down to them through several generations, but many had been conditioned to be ashamed of their legacy and refused to sing them. There was a concerted campaign at the beginning of the twentieth century, directed by the middle classes, to annotate and market the old "peasants' music" as a way of recapturing the soul of the country in the face of European cultural incursions. Most famously, Cecil Sharp, Ralph Vaughan Williams, George Butterworth and George Gardiner collated and published many songs, tunes and dances that have sustained the folk repertoire to this day.

STYLES

Folk Songs
Traditional Folk
Political Folk & Protest
    Songs
The Folk Revival
Folk Rock
Folk Pop
UK Folk
Irish Folk
Alternative Folk
Contemporary Folk
Neo-Traditional Folk

THE FOLK STYLE

The essence of folk music lies in its simplicity. Here the fiddle, a traditional folk instrument in many cultures, plays an up-tempo tune suitable for dancing to, accompanied by the loose drone of a second fiddle.

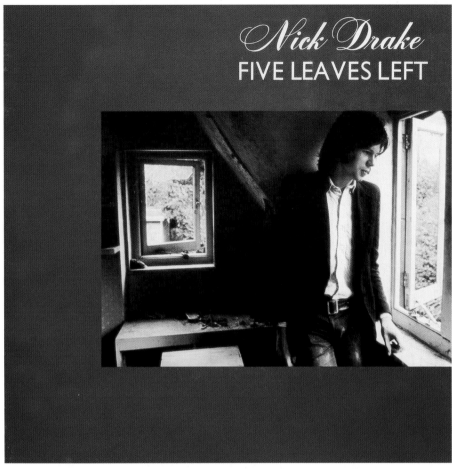

Above
Nick Drake's Five Leaves
Left *remains for many his
masterwork and a testament
to the mental and emotional
anguish he wrestled with
until his tragic death at the
age of 26.*

The work of the Lincolnshire traditional singer Joseph Taylor still survives on early cylinder recordings, and his song 'Brigg Fair' was used by the composer Frederick Delius as the basis of an influential orchestral work in 1907. Other fine traditional singers and musicians were discovered, but they had mostly been ignored and forgotten by the time of the Second World War. Yet the short-lived skiffle fad that hit Britain in the mid-1950s had profound significance for folk music. The flagship star of skiffle was Lonnie Donegan, whose roots were in jazz, but the key appeal of skiffle was the primitive skill required to play it. The music such artists were generally drawn to play was the American folk blues that had recently become popular in the States on the back of spectacular chart successes by the Weavers and later the Kingston Trio.

Major folk revivals subsequently emerged in the US and the UK, though they went in different directions. Woody Guthrie, Leadbelly, and Sonny Terry & Brownie McGhee became the heartbeat of the American revival – giving crucial reference and impetus to the arrival of Bob Dylan in Greenwich Village and igniting

Right
*From 1957 to 1963, the
Kingston Trio transformed
folk music into a popular
genre while becoming the
most well-known group in
the world during their time.*

a new movement of protest song that had massive reverberations around the rest of the world. In the UK, interest in the folk blues of the skiffle bands metamorphosed into a real hunger to uncover the British equivalent. A network of folk clubs emerged and the maligned repertoires of the old traditional singers were gleefully rediscovered, analyzed and reinvented by a new generation with long hair and idealist attitudes. "This machine kills fascists", the sticker on Woody Guthrie's guitar proudly proclaimed. In America, certainly, folk music had a major influence on shifts in public opinion, particularly relating to the Vietnam War.

When Dylan dumped his acoustic guitar, acquired a band and plugged in an electric guitar, the purists were unforgiving. Pete Seeger tried to pull the plug at the Newport Folk Festival and hardcore fans howled "Judas", but the fuse had been lit and nothing was ever quite the same again. Musical boundaries shattered as the folk revival splintered. Electric folk bands emerged from all corners, leftfield fusion artists mixed'n'matched the music with other forms, and some artists hit the mainstream. A new sub-genre emerged with a forceful upsurge of Celtic musicians in the 1970s. The climax was Bill Whelan's *Riverdance* stage show, which has seduced many parts of the world into giving Irish dancing its highest ever profile and promoted Irish music to previously unimagined heights.

Many people's impressions of folk music remain riddled with clichés, from hippy images of long beards and new-age characters, to songs associated with an irrelevant rural idyll. But as many listeners seek refuge from modern pop music,

the heart and soul associated with much folk music wins it new respect. The greater availability and accessibility of local music from different parts of the world has helped open ears to new sounds, arrangements and instrumentation, offering varied ideas and fresh perspectives. It gets called different things now ("world music", "roots" and the like, arguably as a marketing ploy), but folk music has defied the sceptics, surviving into the twenty-first century with its credibility and sense of purpose intact. While a string of rock acts have turned to the "unplugged" album as a means of displaying their true colours, others have been drawn from different fields by the inherent drama of the old ballads and the integrity of the music. A certain idealism binds them all, though conventional success seldom results, for folk music is a genre that has largely remained outside the reach of the mass music industry; and that may just be why it remains so strong.

Folk Songs

TO THIS DAY, MANY STILL CONTEND THAT A WRITTEN SONG IS NOT A FOLK SONG. PURISTS CLAIM THAT ONLY A TRADITIONAL SONG, SHAPED AND HONED BY THE ENVIRONMENTAL CONTEXT THAT PRODUCED IT AND HANDED DOWN BY WORD OF MOUTH THROUGH THE GENERATIONS, CAN JUSTLY CLAIM TO BE TRUE FOLK MUSIC.

Above

A major figure in the English folk revival is Martin Carthy, whose talents in songwriting and knowledge of a vast range of instruments influenced such greats as Bob Dylan and Steeleye Span.

INDEED, the great Scots folklorist, writer and performer Hamish Henderson – so admired that he was offered (but refused) an MBE (Member of the Order of the British Empire) – insisted that songs should be learned only by the aural tradition. He refused to write songs or tunes down, or allow potential performers of them to record him on tape, but he was quite happy to spend hours singing or humming a piece of music to his students until they had learned it. Another great Scots folk legend, Ewan MacColl, once famously decreed that singers and musicians should only perform songs and music of their own national culture. He refused to allow them to appear in his own folk club unless they agreed.

Yet both MacColl and Henderson wrote some classic material that, heavily structured in a traditional style, could not be considered anything but folk song. Some of Henderson's best work was based on his experiences in the Second World War, and it provided genuine insights into the minds of those sent to serve.

Himself a fine performer of traditional ballads, MacColl swiftly developed into the finest songwriter of his generation with a whole catalogue of songs, still widely performed, that many assume to be traditional. Among these are 'Dirty Old Town', written about his experiences in Salford, where he grew up; 'Freeborn Man', about the plight of gypsies; and 'Manchester Rambler', about freedom of the countryside.

> "MY FUNCTION IS NOT TO REASSURE PEOPLE. I WANT TO MAKE THEM UNCOMFORTABLE, TO SEND THEM OUT OF THE PLACE ARGUING AND TALKING."
>
> *Ewan MacColl*

LEADING EXPONENTS

Hamish Henderson
Ewan MacColl
Peggy Seeger
Pete Seeger
Martin Carthy
Woody Guthrie
Billy Bragg
Bob Dylan
Christy Moore
Dick Gaughan
Martin Carthy
Paul Simon
Leadbelly
Nic Jones

FOLK SONG

A style which very much uses simple melody and structure, with usually guitar accompaniment and simple key structure and chord sequence. As with many forms of folk, the words of the song are the primary focus.

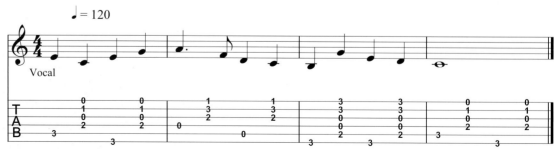

THE FOLK INTRO ➡ 222   FOLK PEOPLE A–Z ➡ 248   INSTRUMENTS A–Z ➡ 436   THE BLUES INTRO ➡ 154   WORLD: CELTIC ➡ 282

MacColl's visionary Radio Ballads series, written in the late-1950s and early 1960s with his wife, Peggy Seeger, portrayed the reality of working-class lives in a folk music context. But they were not merely brilliant snapshots of Britain's social history; they also established a strong catalogue of new MacColl songs that have sustained the folk movement ever since. And yet, MacColl wrote many tender, personal songs too – most famously 'The First Time Ever I Saw Your Face'. Should these qualify as folk songs?

The outspoken singer/songwriter Billy Bragg, made his own telling analysis of the topic, arguing that once songwriters moved from a journalistic stance, painting descriptive pictures of events to expressing more oblique personal emotions about their own lives, they ceased to be folk singers. In this context, it is easy to see why many fine songwriters are overlooked simply because their work is assumed to be traditional. Indeed, for some of those writers it has become the ultimate compliment that their music has passed into such common parlance that it is regarded as traditional. The edges become even more blurred as modern writers and performers amend and adapt existing traditional songs, or simply write their own lyrics. The great English singer Nic Jones took delight in adapting existing folk songs – to such an extent that he was effectively creating original material – but always gleefully passed it off as part of the tradition. This has occasionally led to dispute, notably when Martin Carthy taught the young Paul Simon his own highly individual arrangement of the ballad 'Scarborough Fair' and was not very pleased when the arrangement later turned up on a Simon & Garfunkel album with Simon credited as the song-writer. One of Britain's prime interpreters of traditional songs over four decades, Martin Carthy – like those other great folk singers, Christy Moore and Dick Gaughan – has occasionally written modern songs in a traditional style.

Hey, Hey Woody Guthrie

The father of modern folk songwriting, Woody Guthrie rewrote old hillbilly and blues songs as a matter of course. Far from demeaning his incredible body of work, however, this allies him even more closely with the tradition, both musically and politically. His ballads portraying the human misery of the dust-bowl storms – later imbued with a sharp political edge – remain a significant landmark in the modern folk song revival.

From a simple, poor background in Oklahoma, Guthrie had many acolytes. He was enduring a long and painful death when the folk singer/songwriter scene exploded in Greenwich Village in the early to mid-1960s, inspired by his legacy. None more so than the young Bob Dylan, who, at one time, based his whole persona on Guthrie's rambling lifestyle

and fundamental values. His first original song of real note was, indeed, a straightforward homage to his hero, 'Song To Woody' ("Hey, hey Woody Guthrie"), though Dylan and others of his generation made an intensive study of the great eccentric Harry Smith's *Anthology Of American Folk Music*. Smith devoted much of his life to travelling the US, collecting old records of ballads, blues and folk songs from a colourful assortment of local performers in all corners. Reissued in a six-CD box set by Smithsonian Folkways in 1997, that extraordinary collection sounds as powerful as ever.

An Act Of Betrayal?

There was intense debate about the meaning of folk music during that pivotal time in the 1960s. Much vitriol was directed at Dylan – not least by other musicians, notably the one American singer/songwriter who matched him for lyricism, Phil Ochs – for what they saw as an act of betrayal when he turned from folk music to pursue his own path. The boundaries of music are less clear-cut these days, and the idea of what does and what does not constitute a folk song is a less animated debate. There are many modern writers, of many musical styles and backgrounds, who use the influence of folk songs liberally when it suits them. Few would associate the rock star Sting with writing folk songs, but his beautiful 'Fields Of Gold' has been embraced so enthusiastically by the folk fraternity that it has acquired all the characteristics of a traditional song.

Traditional Folk

TRADITIONAL IS THE TERM GIVEN TO FOLK MUSIC SO OLD ITS ORIGINS HAVE BEEN LONG FORGOTTEN. DIFFERENT SONGS ARE OFTEN PERFORMED TO THE SAME TUNES AND SOMETIMES THE SAME BALLAD IS PLAYED WITH VARIOUS TUNES. SONGS WITH THE SAME STORY POP UP ON BOTH SIDES OF THE ATLANTIC WITH DIFFERENT TREATMENTS, AFTER BEING TRANSPORTED BY EMIGRANTS AND ADAPTED THROUGH THE YEARS.

> "SOMETIMES YOU HAVE TO LOOK TO THE PAST TO MOVE INTO THE FUTURE AND WE'RE LUCKY THERE ARE SO MANY FANTASTIC SONGS AND TUNES. IT'S IMPORTANT IT SURVIVES."
>
> *Eliza Carthy*

LEADING EXPONENTS

Shirley Collins
John & Alan Lomax
Harry Smith
Joseph Taylor
Harry Cox
Phil Tanner
Willie Scott
Pop Maynard
Charlie Wills
Fred Jordan
Walter Pardon
Jeannie Robertson
Margaret Barry
Paddy Tunney
Phoebe Smith
Sam Larner

IN some ways, it's a miracle that British traditional music has survived at all. That it has, and in such rich quantities, is due in no small part to the zealous collectors who travelled Britain annotating the old songs. What we do not know is how much they left out or censored. The early song and dance collectors were largely motivated by a sense of nationalism, and if an old singer performed something overly bawdy or offensive to the collector, it was likely to have been ignored or amended. It is impossible, therefore, to know how much of the tradition has been lost, or tampered with, through time.

One of the major forces of traditional song is *The English And Scottish Popular Ballads*, a five-volume collection by the American Francis Child, published in 1882 and including the texts of more than 300 songs. Child's ballads provided the backbone of material in the 1960s folk revival, reinforced by the work of other collectors such as Lucy Broadwood, George Butterworth, Ralph Vaughan Williams

and – most famously in England – Cecil Sharp. Inspired by seeing the Headington Quarry morris dancers in Oxfordshire, Sharp set off with missionary zeal and, famously, collected his first song, 'The Seeds Of Love', from the Somerset gardener John England in a vicarage in 1903. Subsequently, he travelled across Britain and America, collecting folk songs with Maud Karpeles. Unlike Child, Sharp annotated the tunes as well as the words, and recognized that many of the songs he found in America were variants of those he had collected in Britain and that he was merely following the songs' original journey.

Field Recordings

And yet, despite the importance of the collectors, the most crucial element of folk song is the oral tradition. Modern folklorists contend that the spirit and feeling of the tradition is more important than slavish recreations gleaned from book collections, which may have been sanitized in the first place. Cylinder discs made it possible to preserve the feeling of the traditional singers, as well as the words and music (Percy Grainger's 1908 cylinder recordings of Joseph Taylor are the oldest in existence), while the advent of tape recorders transformed the credibility of the collectors' work.

The field recordings of John Lomax and his son Alan provide a massive catalogue of traditional music of many different facets. John published his first collection, *Cowboy Songs And Other Frontier Ballads*, in 1910, but his immortality is ensured by the field recordings that he and Alan, who was then a teenager, began making for the Library of Congress in the 1930s. Their important discoveries ranged from the Appalachian mountain music of the Ritchie family to the penitentiary blues of Leadbelly, Jelly Roll Morton and Muddy

TRADITIONAL FOLK

The flavour of traditional folk comes from its use of traditional musical instruments; violin, wooden flute etc. Here, the second fiddle provides the "drone" for the upper melody, rather like the drone pipes on a set of bagpipes giving an extremely simple harmonic structure, over which vocals are added.

Waters. Alan's subsequent field trips across America, Britain, Europe and other parts of the world – some of them with the English singer Shirley Collins – remain a vital ingredient of the folk process. His 10-disc collection on the Caedmon label in the UK in the 1950s proved to be a vital inspiration for the folk revival that was beginning to stir. Equally, the extra-ordinary collection of obscure commercial recordings made by the eccentric American Harry Smith – originally released as the *Anthology Of American Folk Music* on Folkways in 1952 and later acquired by the Smithsonian Institution – was pivotal to the American revival.

A Living English Tradition

Mostly, though, credit for the survival of traditional music and song must go to the performers themselves. These rural folk sang and played music in their own families as a matter of course, but had no idea that it was called folk music and, in many cases, were too shy, ashamed or fearful of ridicule to perform in public. And yet the work of post-Second World War folklorists such as Peter Kennedy, Hamish Henderson, Seamus Ennis, Tony Engle, Reg Hall, Bill Leader and Mike Yates ensured that great traditional artists such as Harry Cox, Phil Tanner, Willie Scott, Pop Maynard, Charlie Wills, Fred Jordan, Walter Pardon, Jeannie Robertson, the Stewarts of Blairgowrie, Margaret Barry, Paddy Tunney, Phoebe Smith and Sam Larner attained their rightful place in British folk music legend.

The work of Topic Records in preserving the tradition should not be underestimated, either; its amazing, 20-CD collection, *The Voice Of The People*, is particularly worthy of note. While most genuine traditional singers and musicians have long since died, a living English tradition still survives in the form of morris dance sides, annual folk customs – notably the "Obby Oss" parade at Padstow in Cornwall – and the most celebrated singing family of all,

the Coppers of Rottingdean in Sussex. Having passed through generations of the family, their songs and unaccompanied harmony singing still light up concerts, festivals and informal pub gatherings, providing links with the past and roots for the future.

Far Left

Along with his father, John, Alan Lomax is one of the most influential and important contributors to the preservation and documentation of American folk and blues. His vast field recordings have salvaged what could have been lost forever.

Left

The Copper Family of Sussex, England had amassed a large collection of folk songs prior to being visited by folklorist Katie Lee, who exposed their talents to the world in the early twenty-first century.

Political Folk & Protest Songs

THE RELATIONSHIP BETWEEN POLITICS AND FOLK MUSIC HAS ALWAYS BEEN FUEL FOR LIVELY DEBATE. SOME ARGUE THAT THE TWO SHOULD NOT MIX, AND THAT ALIGNING TRADITIONAL SONG WITH POLITICS DEMEANS IT. FRONT-LINE SINGERS SUCH AS DICK GAUGHAN AND ROY BAILEY, HOWEVER, ARGUE THAT FOLK SONGS ARE INEXTRICABLY LINKED WITH POLITICS, AND PERFORM PLENTY OF STRIDENT MATERIAL TO PROVE IT.

Above

An ex-convict plucked from prison under the influence of John and Alan Lomax, Leadbelly was the first black singer of blues and soul to captivate a white audience.

IN fact, Bailey's occasional shows with the veteran left-wing former MP (Member of Parliament) Tony Benn have entertainingly detailed the history of social dissent in stories and music, and been a popular staple diet of the British scene for many years.

The modern folk revival, in fact, is indelibly linked with songs of dissent. While the folk music that Shirley Collins talks about is merely an expression of people's daily lives – whether it involves ploughing fields, falling in love or getting drunk – protest song is inextricably tied to modern folk song. Protest music of the 1960s took its cue from Woody Guthrie and his acolytes, who founded the Almanac Singers and People's Songs musical co-operative in the 1940s and devoted themselves to union benefits and workers' groups. Most of Guthrie's best work had a political edge, from his early songs about the plight of the migrants heading west after their lives had been wrecked by dust storms, to championing causes and fighting the corner of

> "NEVER UNDERESTIMATE THE POWER OF SONGS. MARTIN LUTHER KING WASN'T MUCH OF A SINGER BUT HE STILL MADE 'WE SHALL OVERCOME' SOUND BEAUTIFUL."
>
> *Pete Seeger*

Right

Woody Guthrie's refusal to profit from any of his music during his lifetime did not prevent him from reaching legendary status after his death.

the oppressed wherever he found them – as in 'Deportees', a song about a group of nameless refugees killed in a plane crash. Even his most famous song, 'This Land Is Your Land', was conceived as a workers' antidote to Irving Berlin's sentimental patriotic anthem, 'God Bless America'. The folk movement was outraged when Guthrie's edgiest verse was removed from this work, and the song was used as an anthem in Ronald Reagan's

presidential election campaign. Bruce Springsteen's later version, though, reclaimed it for the people.

Guthrie adapted many of his songs from existing country blues, itself a fiery conduit of protest, and became close friends with the great blues star Leadbelly. Leadbelly himself wrote a catalogue of protest songs that have long passed into folk legend, such as 'Midnight Special', 'Scottsboro Boys' and 'Bourgeois Blues', all confronting the realities of racism,

---

LEADING EXPONENTS

Woody Guthrie

Pete Seeger

Phil Ochs

Chumbawamba

Billy Bragg

Leon Rosselson

Dick Gaughan

Victor Jara

Buffy Sainte-Marie

POLITICAL FOLK & PROTEST SONGS

The political folk style combines a sparse guitar accompaniment with a simple yet catchy melody and words encouraging social change.

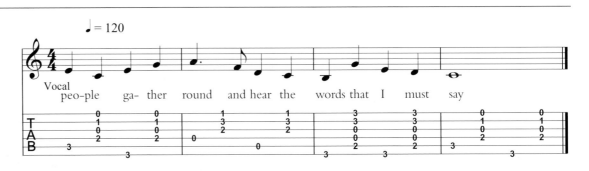

burn their draft cards; Peter, Paul & Mary audiences chanted "Make love not war"; and half the nation bopped along to Country Joe & Fish's brilliantly sardonic singalong anthem 'Fixing To Die Rag'. Folk music, then, played a big role in shaping the anti-war movement that helped force an end to the Vietnam conflict.

Pete Seeger, with songs such as 'If I Had A Hammer' and 'Where Have All The Flowers Gone?', continued to play a key role in protest song and the civil rights movement. His adaptation of the old gospel/work song 'We Shall Overcome' became the anthem of protest marches and human rights

Left

Pete Seeger performed some of the best-known and most enduring of the 1960s folk protest songs. His adaptation of the work song 'We Shall Overcome' became an unofficial anthem for civil rights and is still sung by protesters all over the world.

poverty and workers' rights. The politicization of folk music created various causes célèbres. Swedish railwayman and songwriter Joe Hill became a martyr of the American union movement in 1915 when he was convicted for murder on flimsy evidence and executed in Utah. Hill, whose most famous song was 'Casey Jones (The Union Scab)', written in aid of striking railwaymen, wrote his last song, 'My Will', the night before he died. On the 10th anniversary of his death, Alfred Hayes wrote a tribute, 'I Dreamed I Saw Joe Hill', set to music by Carl Robinson. Hill's name was prominent when protest music rose again, with artists ranging from Paul Robeson to Joan Baez covering 'I Dreamed I Saw Joe Hill'.

campaigns all over the world. At the height of such movements in the US, Seeger sang it while marching shoulder to shoulder with Martin Luther King. In the UK, too, plenty of artists were adapting existing gospel, blues or folk songs to fit their own pet causes, and many fine songwriters emerged to put their spin on protest music. The Scotsman Ian Campbell wrote one of the best of them in 'The Sun Is Burning', a

chilling account of a nuclear explosion that was regularly sung on the annual Aldermaston marches for nuclear disarmament. And Ewan MacColl, an influential giant of the British folk revival who was originally noted as a traditional singer, had a long career as a compelling political songwriter, from his telling insights into the lives of working people in the Radio Ballads, to a suite of songs reacting to apartheid and the Sharpeville Massacre in South Africa. Age didn't wither the conviction of MacColl, who, with his wife, Peggy Seeger, continued to write barbed songs of social

A Blaze Of Blistering Social And Political Tirades

In the 1950s, Pete Seeger, one of Guthrie's main cohorts in New York, found himself on the front line of the struggle when, as a communist, he was targeted by Senator Joseph McCarthy's witch-hunt, and even briefly imprisoned after he refused to testify before the House Un-American Activities Committee. Seeger was blacklisted – effectively killing the career of his group the Weavers, who had taken the songs of Guthrie and Leadbelly to the top of the US charts – and it was 17 years before he appeared on network TV again. This was the background from which Bob Dylan, Phil Ochs and others launched their careers in a blaze of blistering social and political tirades. Dylan's 'The Times They Are A-Changin' ' was the call to arms for a rebellious new generation, and songs such as his 'Masters Of War', Ochs's 'I Ain't Marching Anymore' and Buffy Sainte-Marie's 'Universal Soldier' became a powerful soundtrack to the anti-Vietnam War campaign. Joan Baez invited audiences at her concerts to form orderly lines to

Below

By including introspective lyrics, politics and poetry in his songs, Bob Dylan became one of the greatest singer/ songwriters of all time.

consciousness all his life. Indeed, he spent many of his final years writing vitriolic material pillorying the evils of the Margaret Thatcher administration, which held sway over Britain during the 1980s. Peggy Seeger also wrote one of the defining songs about women's rights, 'I'm Gonna Be An Engineer'.

The stormy history of Ireland, too, has provided inspiration for plenty of stirring political material. Rebel songs have been a staple diet of Irish Republicanism for more than a century, and heroic figures of the Irish struggle such as James Connolly, Robert Emmett and Kevin Barry have long been lionized in popular folk song. Christy Moore, one of the greatest modern figures in Irish music, raised a few eyebrows when he started performing material by Bobby Sands, the IRA prisoner who starved himself to death in 1981. The songs themselves were not overtly political, but Moore has never shirked from tackling sensitive issues in his songs. Many songs have been written about "The Troubles", but the most memorable of them have probably been the pleas for peace – notably Paul Brady's 'The Island', Phil & June Colclough's 'Song For Ireland' and Tommy Sands's 'There Were Roses', a harrowing account of two innocent friends, one a Catholic, the other a Protestant, who become victims of the war. Those campaigning for peace in Northern Ireland in the 1990s adopted the song.

Below
After establishing her very own record label at the age of 20, Ani DiFranco enjoyed complete grassroots success as word of mouth touted her talents as a contemporary female folk singer.

Taking On The System

Songs of social consciousness had fallen out of fashion by the 1980s, but they enjoyed a renaissance with the emergence of Eric Bogle (whose anti-war epics 'And The Band Played Waltzing Matilda' and 'No Man's Land' were covered widely all over the world) and Billy Bragg. Articulate Londoner Bragg had a Top 10 hit with his personal socialist anthem, 'Between The Wars', inspiring a new generation of singer/songwriters. 'Between The Wars' has since become a standard on a British folk scene rediscovering its social conscience. The right-wing Thatcher administration – and the 1984 miners' strike – focused a lot of minds and re-ignited the art of radical songwriting, with Ewan MacColl, Dick Gaughan and the Oyster Band all penning stirring material.

The most consistently radical of the English singer/songwriters, though, has perhaps been Leon Rosselson, who boasts a long history of writing scathing, topical songs, effectively denouncing the establishment and fearlessly tackling unspoken taboos such as religion, the royal family, business corporations, marriage and ecology. His greatest song of all is 'The World Turned Upside Down', a dramatic and ultimately disturbing account of the Diggers uprising of workers in 1649, which was so brutally put down. It set a benchmark for radical songwriting that few have been able to match, and as the record industry has become more corporate, it has not been conducive to songs of dissent.

One who has taken on the system and won, however, is Ani DiFranco, a singer/songwriter from Buffalo, New York, who, with her daring lyrics, acerbic songs, razor-sharp wit, charismatic personality and outrageous sense of humour, has established a huge live following. DiFranco has gained much respect for her opposition to the commercial record industry, refusing offers from all the major companies to manage herself and release material on her own label, Righteous Babe.

Historically, music has always played a big role in voicing dissent, and the roots of some national anthems can even be traced back to radical folk songs. Originally named 'Chant De Guerre', 'La Marseillaise' was written by the soldier Joseph De Lisle as a revolutionary song before it was adopted as the French national anthem in 1795. The song 'L'Internationale' also came out of revolution; Eugène Pottier, one of the Communards who wrested power in Paris in 1871, but who had to flee to England when the Commune was overthrown, wrote it.

Inspiring songs of struggle have played a central role in the lives of working people ever since. The great folk singer Victor Jara was targeted and murdered in the military coup in which General Pinochet overthrew the Marxist government of Salvador Allende in Chile in 1973. It was a chilling reminder of the enduring perceived power of folk song: for where there is oppression or injustice, folk music will usually have something to say about it.

The Folk Revival

MENTION OF THE FOLK REVIVAL IS GENERALLY APPLIED TO THE LATE-1950S AND EARLY 1960S, WHEN A NEW GENERATION OF ENTHUSIASTS EARNESTLY SET ABOUT EXPLORING THE HISTORY OF FOLK MUSIC AND RECREATING ITS PASSIONATE, SOCIAL IDEALS.

THERE had been other folk revivals throughout history, but they tended to stem from the middle classes in search of a purer identity, resulting in the tendency to patronize real folk music. The folk revival of the 1950s and 1960s, however, was a naturally organic affair generated by the musicians themselves, rather than the academic view of social culture that had been at the heart of previous revivals.

Its American roots began with groups such as the Kingston Trio, the Weavers and the New Christy Minstrels bringing folk, blues and country songs to the masses. Their arrangements may have been trite and sanitized, but the Weavers had massive hits with Woody Guthrie's 'So Long (It's Been Good To Know You)' and Leadbelly's 'Goodnight Irene'. They also opened the commercial door to a roots music that had previously been confined to its rural locality, be it the Appalachian mountains, Mississippi cotton fields or Texas bars. It was enough to inflame the curiosity of a new, young generation of guitarists and singers researching those roots, who were further spurred on by the political implications of the McCarthy witch-hunt and the refusal of Pete Seeger and others to bow to establishment values. Their guru was Oklahoma-born Woody Guthrie, whose own songs vehemently addressed issues close to him, including the human agony caused by the dust storms, or were created at singalongs for his own children. Though Woody himself was incapacitated through the wasting disease Huntington's chorea long before his death in 1967, his legacy was a new generation of acolytes who were inspired by his simple tunes and abrasive lyrics and sought to embody his maverick lifestyle. Most famously, Bob Dylan visited Woody at his bedside and wrote his first song as a tribute to his hero, but a closer embodiment of the Guthrie spirit was represented by his friend Ramblin' Jack Elliot, who travelled extensively with Woody, aped his

Above

The 1971 release of Joni Mitchell's Blue *album marked the singer's ascent into stardom.*

"WITHOUT WOODY GUTHRIE THERE'D BE NO RAMBLIN' JACK ELLIOT AND WITHOUT RAMBLIN' JACK ELLIOT THERE'D BE NO BOB DYLAN."
Arlo Guthrie

Left

With shifts in her folk music to country and pop, Joan Baez remains one of the most influential artists on the folk scene. This image shows a performance in a typical Greenwich Village folk venue in the 1960s; note the artist in the audience, busy sketching Baez.

LEADING EXPONENTS

Bob Dylan
The Weavers
Woody Guthrie
Ramblin' Jack Elliot
Ewan MacColl
Shirley Collins
Lonnie Donegan
Joan Baez
Martin Carthy
A. L. Lloyd

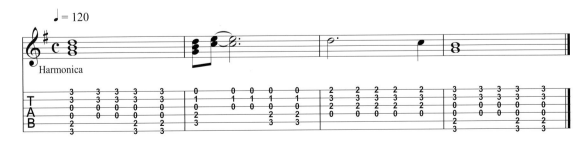

FOLK REVIVAL

An extract much in the style of Bob Dylan, with strummed acoustic guitar and harmonica accompaniment.

Above

Known as Britain's first musical superstar, Lonnie Donegan's mix of folk, jazz, gospel and blues continues to influence British folk music today.

voice and attitude and performed many of his songs. Yet Guthrie's legend was best perpetuated by his own son Arlo Guthrie, who went on to achieve a commercial breakthrough that obliterated anything his father had done, with the long, autobiographical singing blues tome 'Alice's Restaurant', which captured the anti-Vietnam War mood of the times so acutely it was made into a film.

Woody Guthrie's legacy flowered in Greenwich Village, where a new breed of singer/song-writer with attitude, wordy songs and idealistic values descended to energize a new scene. With his sharp lyrics and revolutionary message, Bob Dylan was the most visible and successful of the new breed of folk star. But there were many others, too, including Dylan's then-partner, Joan Baez. She was a highly rated singer of ballads, stridently political and often to be found on the front line of various anti-war demonstrations and marches. An explosion of singer/songwriters with acoustic guitars followed, with Paul Simon, Joni Mitchell, James Taylor, Phil Ochs, Tom Paxton, Tim Hardin, Gordon Lightfoot, Dave Van Ronk, Judy Collins and Buffy Sainte-Marie among them. Despite their mix of styles and backgrounds, they were all associated with the folk revival.

The growing popularity of the scene also refocused attention on the lesser-known artists providing inspiration – and often material – for the main attraction. The likes of Doc Watson, the Carter Family, Sonny Terry & Brownie McGhee, Muddy Waters and Mississippi John Hurt thus came to prominence, the focus on the latter accelerated by the emergence of British bands such as the Rolling Stones and the Yardbirds, with a rock take on the blues tradition. Odetta, a black folk-blues singer from Alabama who worked early on with Harry Belafonte and Pete Seeger, also achieved an important international breakthrough. A network of clubs, coffeehouses and informal "hootenannies" emerged, along with famous festivals, such as the Newport Folk Festival in Rhode Island, to give the music a high profile. The revival achieved widespread commercial success for a while, too, with Peter, Paul & Mary playing huge concerts all over the world.

An Abiding Interest In Folk Blues

The UK folk revival had similar roots, and it occurred at about the same time. But it emerged in a very different form. Those Kingston Trio and Weavers hits caught the imagination of young British fans and musicians, too, but interest in the roots of this music manifested itself in an unexpected way. Lonnie Donegan was playing rhythm guitar with Ken Colyer's jazz band and, as a leftfield concert-filler, started playing primitive American folk blues. After a 1930s term coined to describe bands that played household implements because they could not afford instruments, he gave it the name "skiffle". Donegan broke through with 'Rock Island Line' in 1956 and the following year went to number one with 'Cumberland Gap'. This gave licence to young hopefuls to form groups whether or not they had talent, instruments or places to play, and in 1958 skiffle was everywhere. Although it did not last, its legacy was an abiding interest in the folk blues songs that had driven it. Many of those who had started in skiffle bands shifted gear, reshaped their musical policy and became folk groups.

While several of them, such as the Ian Campbell Folk Group, homed in on the songs of Dylan and the rest coming across the Atlantic, a network of clubs with different values was also emerging. Ewan MacColl opened one of the first dedicated folk music venues – the Ballad & Blues Club – in London and caused great debate when he declared that musicians would only be permitted to perform music of their own culture at his club. It may have seemed bizarre, but MacColl's aim was to force young British musicians to research their own tradition for material rather than slavishly copy songs off Kingston Trio albums. It was controversial, but it worked, as artists such as the Watersons, Martin Carthy, Shirley Collins, Young Tradition, Anne Briggs and Louis Killen quickly developed into popular performers, playing a rapidly growing network of folk clubs throughout the country.

It was an exciting time as the revival artists competed to find undiscovered traditional songs in the library at Cecil Sharp House, the headquarters of the English Folk Dance & Song Society, or, better still, directly from a source singer. A. L. Lloyd, too, was a guru of the folk revival. A fine, slightly eccentric singer in his own right, he wrote articles and books, lectured, travelled the world finding material and was generally an inspirational figure in the British revival.

The momentum of those early days of the revival lasted into the 1970s, when other musical forces came into play and folk music splintered into different sub-genres. Folk clubs are not as plentiful now, but the music is still there and it generally wields the same values. That is its own tribute to the work of the folk revival pioneers.

Folk Rock

FOR MANY PEOPLE IN THE 1960S, FOLK WAS EQUATED WITH ACOUSTIC MUSIC OR EVEN UNACCOMPANIED MUSIC – AND ELECTRIC GUITARS WERE THE GREAT TABOO. THE SENSE OF PROPRIETY AMONG THE REVIVALISTS OF THE TIME MADE THEM FIERCELY PROTECTIVE OF THE MUSIC, DETERMINED TO PRESERVE ITS PURITY IN THE FACE OF ATTACK FROM THE EVIL FORCES OF POP. MANY SAW THE ELECTRIC GUITAR AS THE ENEMY.

THAT is why Pete Seeger is said to have tried to pull the plug on Bob Dylan during his infamous performance at the 1965 Newport Folk Festival with members of the electric Paul Butterfield Blues Band. In England, the cry of "Judas" was heard when he repeated the formula. In essence, though, the first rumblings of a new fusion of folk and rock came not from the hardcore folk fraternity, but from rock bands seeking a fresh ideology. There had long been a course of great blues artists interpreted by young white guys, and with spectacular results from the likes of Elvis, the Rolling Stones and the Yardbirds, among others. As rock music diversified in the late-1960s, it was not unnatural for young musicians to seek to develop what they saw as a rigid format for playing folk music.

Dylan's move towards rock opened the doors. Subsequently, when the Byrds began to have hits with Dylan songs, and bands such as Jefferson Airplane emerged in San Francisco with a strong folk blues flavour, it was obvious that the times were indeed a-changin'. In England, Fairport Convention modelled themselves on Jefferson Airplane with little thought of the implications, but it led them to the realization that there was a rich treasury of indigenous music in their own backyard, untouched by bass, drums or electric guitar. It was the bass player Ashley Hutchings who really led Fairport Convention's drive into traditional music, with the landmark album *Liege & Lief*. Recorded in the aftermath of a tragic band road crash, which resulted in the death of the drummer, Martin Lamble, *Liege & Lief* was hailed as the first

" ... TO ME IT SEEMED A VERY NATURAL AND EXCITING EXPERIMENT FOR A ROCK BAND TO EXPLORE ITS OWN CULTURE OF FOLK MUSIC."
Ashley Hutchings

Above
One of the most successful and enduring British folk rock groups in the 1970s was Steeleye Span, whose lead singer Maddy Prior's impressive vocals helped promote the group's success.

Left
Fairport Convention, who have had a phenomenal number of changes in their line-up over the years, performed revved up versions of traditional folk songs from the British Isles to great critical acclaim.

FOLK ROCK
The folk rock genre includes many of the chord progressions and folk "riffs" employed in other folk styles, but transposed to classic rock ensemble instrumentation, here with a tab for lead guitar.

LEADING EXPONENTS
The Byrds
Fairport Convention
Jethro Tull
Steeleye Span
Albion Country Band
Mr Fox
Five Hand Reel
Pentangle
Home Service

THE FOLK INTRO ➡ 222   FOLK PEOPLE A-Z ➡ 248   INSTRUMENTS A-Z ➡ 436   THE ROCK INTRO ➡ 74

way (neither Hutchings nor Carthy were to stay long), Steeleye became an enduringly successful outfit. They not only achieved the seemingly impossible feat of making folk music hot again, but sold out tours all over the world and even enjoyed some unlikely hit singles, notably with a song in Latin, 'Gaudete', and a feelgood version of the traditional standard 'All Around My Hat'. The singer Maddy Prior, like Martin Carthy, was later awarded the MBE.

While Steeleye was achieving pop success, Ashley Hutchings was experimenting ever more deeply with traditional song and dance through numerous incarnations of the Albion Band. He achieved his most spectacular results with his then-wife, Shirley Collins, singing on the classic *No Roses* album, which featured most of the leading British folk musicians of the day. Hutchings also masterminded *Morris On* and (with John Kirkpatrick) *The Compleat Dancing Master*, early 1970s albums stimulating a rebirth of dance tunes. At one point, the Albion Band even toured with a morris-dancing side in tow.

A Lasting Legacy

The early success of folk rock had a profound effect on folk music. For one, it triggered the emergence of a host of Steeleye/Fairport/Albion imitators. Few of them brought anything new to the party, however, apart from Bob and Carole Pegg's Mr Fox (playing contemporary songs written in a traditional style), Five Hand Reel (with Dick Gaughan on lead vocal and electric guitar) and the Albion offshoot Home Service, gloriously fronted by two of the scene's most colourful characters and best songwriters, John Tams and Bill Caddick. By the 1980s, the record industry and the media had lost interest, and hard economics prevented many folk rock outfits from surfacing. The one group to buck the trend has been the Oyster Band (later Oysterband), which emerged from the folk dance circuit to achieve credibility and success as folk rockers well versed in traditional music, but using it as a launch pad for their own highly charged, often political material.

But more than that, folk rock had a lasting legacy with a new generation familiar with the music. The long-term result is that its influence has spread far and wide, and continues to do so. In 1970, rock band Traffic played an elaborate arrangement of the trad song 'John Barleycorn', while other iconic artists – such as Robert Plant and Jimmy Page of Led Zeppelin, Mike Oldfield and Jethro Tull – have drawn on elements of the tradition. More recently, the Northumbrian piper Kathryn Tickell has found herself playing on records by Sting, and nobody bats an eyelid when they hear bass, drums and electric guitar on a folk record. Or, more significantly, a traditional song or folk arrangement creeping into a rock record.

British folk rock album, attracting a new audience to both the band and the traditional music they were experimenting with. More than 30 years after its 1969 release, it was still voted Britain's favorite folk album in a national poll – although it did lead to dissension in the ranks. The two obvious front members of the band, Sandy Denny and Richard Thompson, were both keen to develop their own songwriting rather than pursue the traditional path. Ultimately, this rift resulted in the departure of Denny and Thompson, as well as Ashley Hutchings.

A Bold Blend Of Ancient And Modern

Hutchings went on to become the seminal figure in English folk rock, forming Steeleye Span with two young stalwarts of the folk club scene, Maddy Prior and Tim Hart. When Martin Carthy, the most admired young revival singer on the scene, joined too, a lot of hardcore purists had to revise their attitudes towards the folk rock fusion. Steeleye, named after a character in the traditional song 'Horkstow Grange', released a second album, *Please To See The King*, a bold, seminal blend of ancient and modern that genuinely captured the spirit of traditional songs in a modern format. It caught the imagination of the public, too, and despite changes of personnel along the

Folk Pop

FOLK POP IS OFTEN LOOKED DOWN ON BY CONNOISSEURS OF THE MUSIC WHO BELIEVE THAT IN ITS PUREST FORM IT SHOULD HAVE NOTHING IN COMMON WITH THE CHARTS AND THE COMMERCIAL WORLD. YET FOLK HAS PUNCTURED THE MAINSTREAM MORE OFTEN THAN MOST WOULD IMAGINE, AND IN MANY WAYS ITS POPULARITY HAS BEEN RELIANT ON THOSE WHO'VE BROADENED THE MARKET BY TAKING IT INTO THE POP ERA.

PART of the cachet of folk music is its alternative status. It has drifted in and out of fashion through the years, but the purity of the music and its ideals means that it could never co-exist naturally in a commercial environment. Yet every genre needs a visible face to fire the imagination as well as attract new audiences and musicians, and folk is no different. The early folk boom was built on the back of hits by the Weavers, the Kingston Trio and Harry Belafonte, and the vision of Bob Dylan inspired a whole generation of singer/songwriters.

Succeeding generations have accessed traditional music as an important source, but the fusion of folk music with other musical genres has increasingly provided interest for a less specialized audience. The advent of folk rock certainly rejuvenated the fading folk revival, led by bands such as the Byrds and Flying Burrito Brothers in America and, in the UK, Fairport Convention and Steeleye Span. The Byrds enjoyed several hits – most spectacularly with Bob Dylan's 'Mr Tambourine Man' and 'All I Really Want To Do' and Pete Seeger's adaptation of the biblical passage 'Turn Turn Turn' – and there have been sporadic UK folk hits, too. One of the earliest came from the Irish folk pioneers the Dubliners, who, championed by the pirate station Radio Caroline, took the risqué traditional song 'Seven Drunken Nights' into the Top 10 in 1967, following it up with 'Black Velvet Band'. It was 20 years before they made the charts again, in a collaboration with one of the bands they helped inspire, the Pogues, on a raucous treatment of the popular pub song 'Irish Rover'. The Pogues themselves scored one of the most memorable folk-inspired hits of all with their classic, bittersweet Christmas song 'Fairytale Of New York', which reached number two in the UK in 1987.

Above
Melding elements of the British Invasion with psychedelic pop and folk, American group the Byrds became a powerful force in music, influencing artists such as the Beatles and the Rolling Stones.

"IT WAS AMAZING WHEN WE GOT OUR FIRST HIT SINGLE ... EVERYONE CAME OUT TO APPLAUD US. THEN WE WENT INTO OUR DAD'S PUB AND HE MADE US WORK BEHIND THE BAR. FOLK MUSIC KEEPS YOU GROUNDED."
Máire Brennan, Clannad

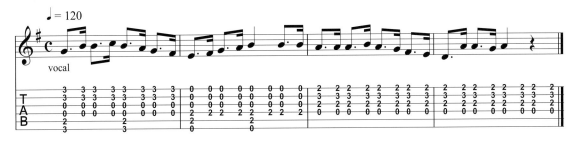

FOLK POP

This style utilizes standard rock band instrumentation, with chords strummed rather than plucked with the fingers, and a standard 4/4 drum beat. The tab here should be strummed alternately with down- and up-strokes.

LEADING EXPONENTS

The Kingston Trio
The Weavers
Harry Belafonte
Enya
Sinéad O'Connor
The Byrds
The Corrs
Ladysmith Black Mambazo

The Irish have a good track record of giving folk music populist appeal. In 1973, Thin Lizzy enjoyed its first Top 10 hit with a rocking cover of another old pub classic, 'Whiskey In The Jar'. In 1982, Donegal's Clannad had a massive hit with 'Harry's Game', the atmospheric, haunting theme of a TV drama. Clannad went on to enjoy several more hits in the same style, and inspired a new genre of highly produced, richly layered Celtic music of tranquil overtones. In fact, Enya, a member of the same Donegal family as Clannad, has enjoyed the greatest crossover success of all in this sphere; her 'Orinoco Flow' went to number one in 1988 and her various albums have sold in the millions. The lead singer of Clannad, Máire Brennan, even enjoyed a pop hit dueting with Bono of U2. In the 1990s, the family group the Corrs gave their pop sensibility an enticing dose of their traditional Irish background, scoring a series of major hits. Even more oddly, the Scots band Capercaillie had a hit with the ancient walking song 'Coisich A Ruin', the first Gaelic-language record ever to make the charts.

Fairport Convention had a novelty hit in 1969 with a bizarre version of Bob Dylan's 'If You've Gotta Go, Go Now', which the band translated into French and performed as 'Si Tu Dois Partir'. And yet they did not have as much pop success as their folk rock cousins Steeleye Span, who first hit the charts with the Latin hymn 'Gaudete' in 1973, and scored an even bigger hit two years later with an upbeat version of the traditional song 'All Around My Hat'. But even Steeleye could not match Fiddler's Dram, who later metamorphosed into Oysterband and had a Top Three smash with the singalong anthem 'Day Trip To Bangor' in 1979.

One of the most influential names in British folk music, Ewan MacColl scored a huge, unexpected hit when one of his self-written songs 'The First Time Ever I Saw Your Face', was covered by Roberta Flack. Written in a matter of hours, this song has had more cover versions than most, and MacColl was highly amused when he heard Elvis Presley's version.

Folk Pop Of A Certain Type

Paul Simon has had a variety of pop folk hits through the years, but his most significant crossover contribution was the *Graceland* album. Although it was, controversially, recorded in South Africa at the time of a cultural boycott, it effectively sparked interest in African music throughout the world. Launched to fame on the back of it, Ladysmith Black Mambazo subsequently enjoyed a series of crossover hits. Not that this was the first time music of African origin had hit the charts. Miriam Makeba's Xhosa music brought her international acclaim as far back as the 1950s, while Harry Belafonte's various calypso hits, including 'Banana Boat Song' and 'Island In The Sun', might be considered folk pop of a certain type.

As musical boundaries fall, folk music is increasingly integrated into other musical forms. Sinéad O'Connor won acclaim for her traditional Irish album *Sean-Nòs Nua* in 2002, and it could be argued that the Seattle grunge band Nirvana touched on folk roots with its *MTV Unplugged* show, which included a powerful acoustic version of Leadbelly's 'Black Girl'. The techno dance world, too, has occasionally used folk samples, proving that, no matter how ancient it is, folk music can still make its impact felt on contemporary music.

UK Folk

FOLK MUSIC IN BRITAIN HAS AN ERRATIC HISTORY, SUSCEPTIBLE TO THE FICKLE FATES OF FASHION AND IMAGE AND ALMOST ERADICATED COMPLETELY BY THE APATHY OF THE PEOPLE WHOSE CULTURE IT REPRESENTS. YET A HUGELY COLOURFUL TREASURE CHEST OF MUSIC AND TRADITIONS SURVIVES IN THE NETWORK OF FOLK CLUBS THAT STILL EXIST UP AND DOWN THE COUNTRY.

BRITISH folk clubs have little in common with the rest of the entertainment industry. Elsewhere, it is extremely rare for new, untried artists to be allowed to get up and play "floor spots" as support for the main attraction. While this sometimes results in painful performances, as would-be stars learn in public, it has also allowed some exceptional talents to flourish. Some clubs have applied hard attitudes to support purist ideals, but essentially, the grassroots folk scene operates an open-house policy that fosters creativity and imagination. Blues, country, jazz, comedy and even pop musicians have been embraced by the folk fraternity, which makes it an alternative forum well beyond the radar of the mainstream music scene.

A flood of richly inventive young acoustic guitarists gravitated to the folk clubs in the early boom days of the 1960s and 1970s, effectively re-inventing the way the guitar was played. In particular, Davy Graham had a profound influence on young guitarists everywhere. Constantly experimenting with techniques and rhythmic patterns, he embraced musical styles from different parts of the world long before it was fashionable, and perfected the DAGDAD tuning that became standard for folk playing. His fearless, trailblazing *Folk, Blues & Beyond* and visionary *Folk Roots, New Routes* fusion album with Shirley Collins, both released in 1964, set a landmark for folk music.

Above
Eliza Carthy's modern and youthful approach to traditional English folk vocals and fiddle playing has garnered much critical acclaim and praise.

> "ALL THE KIDS AT SCHOOL WOULD BE WEARING THEIR HEADPHONES LISTENING TO ROCK OR HEAVY METAL BAND AND I'D BE LISTENING TO SOME FIDDLE MUSIC."
> *Kate Rusby*

Left
Considered to be one of the most important figures in contemporary British folk, Bert Jansch's acoustic guitar prowess so impressive that he has influenced such electric guitar devotees as Jimmy Page and Neil Young.

LEADING EXPONENTS

Kate Rusby
Waterson Carthy
Cara Dillon
Davy Graham
Shirley Collins
Bert Jansch
Nic Jones
Oysterband
Billy Bragg
Capercaillie

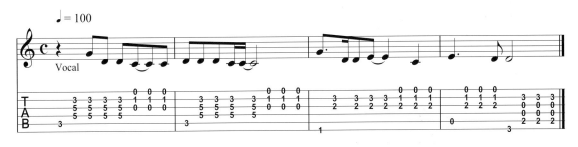

UK FOLK

UK folk is performed in a similar style to other modern folk categories, but often using chords with suspended 2nds and 4ths, and a rhythmically complex vocal line.

There was consistent brilliance, too, from Bert Jansch and John Renbourn, who built on Graham's breakthrough to develop the styles they were to employ so successfully in the band Pentangle, fronted by singer Jacqui McShee. Other brilliant musicians who emerged from the thriving Soho folk scene in London included Roy Harper, Al Stewart and Ralph McTell, and at different times extraordinary standards were also set for the folk guitar by Wizz Jones, John James and Martin Simpson. They were heady times, as American artists such as Bob Dylan, Paul Simon and Jackson C. Frank could be found playing at various clubs, among them Les Cousins and The Troubadour, at the dead of night.

Rampant With Subversive Talent

Scotland, meanwhile, had its own hive of creativity with the Incredible String Band emerging from Glasgow with a mad charm that captivated the hippy era. Elsewhere stars such as Julie Felix and Nadia Cattouse were virtually household names, regularly featured on national television. The Spinners, the Ian Campbell Folk Group, the Corries and the Yetties were the big groups of the period, dominating radio and TV with populist songs and presentation, but the underground scene was rampant with more subversive talents. Fashions came and went, and singer/songwriters, Celtic bands, dance musicians and folk comedians all predominated at different times. The folk scene, in fact, produced a series of funny men who went on to become household names, led by Billy Connolly (who first came to

attention with the group Humblebums, alongside Gerry Rafferty), Jasper Carrott, Mike Harding and Tony Capstick.

Various bands emerged from the grassroots scene. Tim Hart & Maddy Prior had been a successful club scene duo before they joined another of the scene's major figures, Martin Carthy, in the electric folk band Steeleye Span. Carthy had worked for several years in a duo with the great fiddle player Dave Swarbrick, who had been playing with the Ian Campbell Folk Group and later joined Fairport Convention, with whom he remained for many years. Economics have always made it difficult for bands to survive on the grassroots scene, but others who emerged to go on to greater glories have included Pentangle, Albion Band, Home Service, the Boys Of The Lough, Oysterband, Capercaillie, Five Hand Reel, Battlefield Band, Silly Wizard, Hedgehog Pie and Tannahill Weavers.

An Exciting New Generation

Yet even through the hard times the grassroots folk club scene has been sustained by a strong nucleus of outstanding artists. The Watersons and Young Tradition set the standards for harmony singing, and the legacy of their passionate, unaccompanied vocals can still be heard in the likes of Waterson:Carthy and the male trio Coope, Boyes & Simpson, who occasionally team up under the guise Blue Murder. Many other great artists have graced the scene, including Nic Jones (who has not performed in public since a terrible car crash in 1982), Tony Rose (who died of cancer in 2002), Vin Garbutt, June Tabor, Dick Gaughan, Archie Fisher, Roy Bailey and Ashley Hutchings' various incarnations of the Albion Band.

Yet the Waterson:Carthy dynasty has been the UK scene's heartbeat for three decades. Martin Carthy and his wife Norma Waterson were both awarded MBEs for their services to folk music, and have continued to excel in different guises, not least with their family group Waterson:Carthy. Their daughter Eliza Carthy has also emerged as a formidable performer, championing English music and proving herself to be an accomplished singer and fiddle player. She also welcms other influences, experimenting with techno, fronting an ambitiously varied band, and making one album of her own contemporary songs, *Angels & Cigarettes*. Nominated for a Mercury Music Prize for her 1998 album, *Red Rice*, Eliza is at the vanguard of an exciting new generation of young British folk musicians. Kate Rusby has also won wide acclaim (including a Mercury Music Prize nomination for *Sleepless*) for her tender traditional interpretations, while other young artists have emerged to suggest that the British folk tradition is in good hands.

Right

The Incredible String band's 1967 release, 5000 Spirits Or The Layers Of The Onion, *saw the band reduce in size to only two members, with Robin Williamson and Mike Heron producing the well-known song, 'First Girl I Loved'.*

Irish Folk

IF THERE IS A STRAND OF FOLK MUSIC THAT SEEMS UNIVERSALLY POPULAR, IT'S IRISH. THIS IS NOT SURPRISING CONSIDERING IRELAND'S SAD HISTORY OF EMIGRATION AND THE TRANSPORTATION OF THEIR MUSIC TO ALL CORNERS OF THE GLOBE. THROUGH THOSE CLAIMING ANCESTRY OR SIMPLY CONNECTING WITH A MUSIC THAT CONVEYS EXTREMES OF EMOTION, IT HAS THE PROVEN ABILITY TO CONNECT WITH MANY DIFFERENT CULTURES.

MOVING into the twenty-first century, arguably the most forceful – and most popular – type of folk music has been Celtic. Whether everything marketed under the umbrella of

"Celtic music" does justice to great artists such as the Bothy Band and Alan Stivell, who first coined the term for their exciting music in the 1970s, is another matter. But still, massive worldwide hits for the likes of Clannad, Enya and Loreena McKennit turned Celtic into a powerful marketing tool. The incredible international success of the stage show *Riverdance* – based around a breathtaking display of Irish dancing, originally put together by Bill Whelan with Planxty as a seven-minute interlude in the Eurovision Song Contest – cemented the massive commercial possibilities of Irish folk culture. When the *Riverdance* star Michael Flatley broke away to produce his own show along the same lines, *Lord Of The Dance*, it seemed that no corner of the world was untouched by Irish music. Numerous smash-hit movies – from *Barry Lyndon* to *Titanic* – have liberally used Irish music to popular effect in their soundtracks.

If the lush, arranged manner in which much of the atmospheric, new-age approach to the music is played does not always meet with the approval of the hardcore fans, it is fitting that the music itself enjoys such popularity. Ireland is rare in being able to claim an unbroken traditional music history at the forefront of its culture. The rural west, in particular, harbours a myriad of different styles of playing and dancing that have all survived to some degree today.

"IT ALL HAPPENED BY ACCIDENT. THE GROUP, THE SONGS, THE ARAN SWEATERS, WE WERE JUST HAVING A LAUGH. ALL OF A SUDDEN WE WERE BEING TAKEN SERIOUSLY BY THE FOLK AROUND . . . IT WAS MAD!"
Liam Clanaf

Left
Fans brandish the Irish flag at a Pogues gig. The people of Ireland's pride in their heritage is reflected in the integrity of their folk music, which has remained to a certain extent untarnished by external musical influences.

♩ = 100
Flute

Bodhran

IRISH FOLK
This extract shows the characteristic "feel" of Irish folk in a more contemporary form, with keyboards as a "drone" and a jig-style flute; simple repetitive percussion and vocals would also be included.

LEADING EXPONENTS
The Clancy Brothers
The Dubliners
Christy Moore
The Bothy Band
Planxty
Moving Hearts
Altan
Clannad
The Chieftains
De Dannan

THE FOLK INTRO ➡ 222 FOLK PEOPLE A-Z ➡ 248 INSTRUMENTS A-Z ➡ 436 FOLK: POLITICAL FOLK & PROTEST SONGS ➡ 230 WORLD: CELTIC ➡ 282

Right

*By maintaining a raw "pub"
sound and their scruffy,
unkempt appearances, the
Dubliners managed to carve
their own niche in the Irish
folk scene.*

The Salvation Of Irish Music

Not that it has always thrived, however. Despite various
attempts at revival, the music was on its knees in the early part
of the twentieth century; it was falling out of fashion and the
old techniques of instrument-making (notably of uillean pipes)
were being lost. The tradition was saved, essentially, by the
country's ongoing curse of emigration. The thousands of Irish
forced to leave their homeland in search of work sought
comfort in any semblance of home life, and found it in the
traditional music being played – and establishing a vibrant
scene – in certain Irish strongholds of America, such as New
York, Boston, Chicago and Philadelphia. The records of the
leading lights on the American Irish scene, particularly by
the Flanagan Brothers and the Sligo fiddle players Michael
Coleman, Paddy Killoran and James Morrison, found their way
back to Ireland and inspired an upsurge of musicians at home.

America, then, has always played a big role in the
salvation of Irish music. Indeed, in the early 1900s, the
Chicago police chief Francis O'Neill, who was originally
from Cork, collected and published extensive collections
of traditional tunes that had already played a big role in
rejuvenating interest in the music.

Another crucial figure in modern Irish music was
O'Neill's fellow Cork man Sean O'Riada, a classical
composer who, in the 1960s, created the band Ceoltoiri
Chualann to play traditional tunes in an orchestral setting,
most strikingly the gorgeous tunes of the blind seventeenth-
and eighteenth-century harpist Turlough O'Carolan. O'Riada
himself played harpsichord and the bodhran – the distinctive
drum made of goat skin – and he crucially recruited the
young uillean piper Paddy Moloney. When O'Riada
disbanded the orchestra, Moloney and several like-minded
musicians involved in the project formed the Chieftains, who

Right

*Debuting to the mainstream
in 1961 on* The Ed
Sullivan Show, *the Clancy
Brothers' theatrical and close-
harmony approach to their
mix of Irish and American
folk and protest songs became
an influential sound that
enthralled the masses.*

have subsequently taken the music to all corners of the
world. They transformed the emphasis of Irish music from
the barnstorming ballad singing of the Clancy Brothers &
Tommy Makem, who took America by storm in the 1960s,
and the Dubliners, who enjoyed big UK hit singles with
'Seven Drunken Nights' and 'Black Velvet Band'.

During the 1970s, a new wave of bands such as
Planxty, the Bothy Band, De Dannan, Clannad, Horslips
and Moving Hearts came along to reinvigorate Irish
music with their contemporary image, virtuoso playing
and explosive rhythms, eliciting the "Celtic" references in
tribute to their thrilling wildness.

A Major Selling Point

Since then, Irish music – and dancing – has thrived. The
annual fleadh cheoil festivals are a testament to the talent on
display, and the music is a major selling point in the thriving
tourist industry that has transformed the country. The
Chieftains are still going, despite the death of their popular
harpist Derek Bell; Christy Moore continues to perform to
packed audiences; and Sinéad O'Connor has turned to
traditional Irish music. Younger bands like Altan, Dervish,
Danu, Lunasa, Kila and Providence continue to thrive, and
more young people than ever are attending the summer
schools and competing in fleadh cheoils to guarantee the
survival of the music and maintain its standards. It is hard to
imagine that, less than a century ago, complicated techniques
of both playing and making the uillean – elbow – pipes were
fast being lost, seriously threatening the existence of Ireland's
unique instrument. Now, the pipes, bodhran, fiddle, melodeon
and tin whistle are regular ingredients of the informal sessions
that take place all over Ireland virtually every night of the
week, and the legend of "the craic" now dominates the
image of Ireland as one of Europe's most thriving countries.

Alternative Folk

ALTERNATIVE MUSIC IS OFTEN SEEN AS A CONTROVERSIAL IDIOM, REFLECTING THOSE WHO HAVE SOUGHT TO CHANGE THE EXISTING STYLES BY FUSING IT WITH OTHERS, OR APPROACHING IT FROM A DIFFERENT ANGLE. IT IS CRITICIZED BY PURISTS WHO BELIEVE IN THE FOLK IDEAL, BUT SUPPORTED BY THOSE WHO ARGUE THAT STAGNANT MUSIC IS A DEAD MUSIC AND THAT IT MUST BE CHANGED FOR IT TO SURVIVE.

FOR all those who say there is nothing new under the sun, where there is an established musical style, there will always be somebody trying to turn it on its head and create something new. Purists invariably get angry, the media is reprimanding, and, more often than not, the experiment turns out to be a never-to-be-repeated disaster. And yet occasionally, often more by luck than judgement, a genuinely exciting, significant break-through emerges from the most unlikely of fusions.

Folk music has long been a target for young artists with new ideas, determined to shake off the cobwebs and make it relevant and vibrant for contemporary audiences. This has happened almost since the folk revival began, when Davy Graham and Shirley Collins sought to blend English traditional song with jazz, blues and Indian music on the *Folk Roots, New Routes* album in 1964. The early stabs at folk rock were radical

for their time, but it would not be too long before these fusions had graduated to the mainstream. Critics were soon bemoaning the lack of initiative and imagination in the bass-and-drums format, which was the rhythmic norm for these bands. The injection of brass into the equation, primarily via the Albion Band and Home Service, opened up another alternative, as did 1980s punk folk bands such as the Pogues, the Men They Couldn't Hang and the more country-influenced Boothill Foot-Tappers.

Above

The Chieftains' music centres around member Paddy Moloney's pipes, and they have collaborated with artists such as Van Morrison and Sinéad O'Connor.

The growth of importance in technology in recording studios opened another hornet's nest for an organic music that prides itself on instrumental virtuosity and live performance. Technology is still the enemy for many folk artists and commentators, and yet folk has a natural affinity with dance music. On occasion, traditional tunes have worked spectacularly well in the hands of a judicious producer or mixer, adding beats and samples for a new audience of clubbers. Afro Celt Sound System has, perhaps, been the most successful, employing the extremes of both the oral tradition and the new dance culture in a bold amalgamation of African and Celtic styles. Eyebrows were raised when the great Irish *sean-nos* singer Iarla O'Lionaird became involved with the London producer Simon Emmerson's attempt to find common links in Irish and African

"WE HAVE SAMPLED A LOT OF FOLK MUSIC ON OUR RECORDS BECAUSE IT'S REAL AND IT'S RELEVANT AND IT PROVIDES A GOOD BASIS FOR SONGWRITING."
Boff, Chumbawamba

Left

Performing a blend of punk and hippy/Celtic-inspired folk, the Levellers became a popular act in the UK and were regulars on the festival circuit playing songs like 'One Way'.

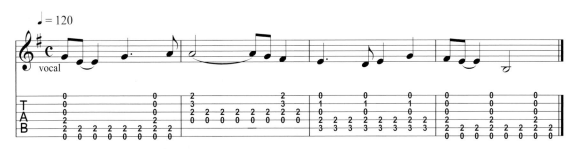

♩ = 120

vocal

ALTERNATIVE FOLK

The alternative folk style shows influences from a number of musical genres that have been assimilated into the more traditional folk sound. This sample shows syncopated jazz-influenced rhythms and a rock-style guitar accompaniment.

LEADING EXPONENTS

Afro Celt Sound System
Mouth Music
The Levellers
Ani DiFranco
Chumbawamba
The Boggs
Asian Dub Foundation
Martyn Bennett
Sharon Shannon

THE FOLK INTRO ➡ 222 FOLK PEOPLE A–Z ➡ 248 INSTRUMENTS A–Z ➡ 436 FOLK: POLITICAL FOLK & PROTEST SONGS ➡ 230 THE WORLD INTRO ➡ 276

Right

Rebellious and anarchic group Chumbawamba performed in relative obscurity until the mid-1990s when their anti-big-business message was delivered to millions with their Top 10 hit 'Tubthumping'.

music, but it was important to Emmerson that both the Irish and African ingredients were authentic. As a result, the Afro Celts have become a hugely successful international band.

But they have not been the only ones to experiment with technology. While regularly busking in Edinburgh, the Newfoundland-born fiddle and bagpipe player Martyn Bennett one day found himself playing jigs and reels to a techno backing track. The crowd liked it and so did Bennett, who went on to make a couple of breakthrough techno folk records, notably *Bothy Culture*. The Scots have been at the forefront of this alternative approach, with Shooglenifty, Seelyhoo, Mouth Music and Mac Umba pushing back the barriers. Paul Mounsey, too, converted a decade of living in Brazil into a unique fusion of Celtic, Latin and Caribbean music.

Landmark Collaborations

Some such fusions have come from unlikely sources. Built around the traditional heritage of Karen Mattheson and the songwriting of Donald Shaw, Capercaillie was long established as a well-respected band when, unexpectedly, the group experimented with techno. The band acknowledged that its efforts were not entirely successful, but it did produce at least one landmark collaboration, with Hijas Del Sol from Equatorial Guinea. The brilliant Irish accordion star Sharon Shannon has also never been shy about diving into other musical genres, perhaps most memorably when she recorded her *Out The Gap* album with the Jamaican reggae producer Denis Bovell in 1994. Other famed Shannon collaborations include work with the Galician piper Carlos Nuñez.

Fiddle players have also become involved in modern dance culture at various times, with Natalie McMaster, Eileen Ivers and Eliza Carthy all emerging from the experience with their reputations unscathed. They have never gone as far as experimenting with techno, but the kings of leftfield collaboration are the Chieftains. Not content with being the first Western band to play in China, they jammed onstage with Chinese musicians, setting a blueprint for similarly

unlikely liaisons in different corners of the world. In some circles, their occasional work with Van Morrison, and one notable track with the Rolling Stones (playing 'Rocky Road To Dublin'), would qualify them as the most alternative of all.

Roots Are Where You Find Them

Other diverse artists who have been labelled as alternative folk include Billy Bragg, Ani DiFranco, the Handsome Family, the Levellers and De Dannan, the Irish band whose regular leftfield excursions have ranged from Celtic interpretations of Handel to gospel, the Beatles and Queen. With such a natural propensity for dance, folk tunes and singers do occasionally get sampled by bona-fide dance collectives, dating right back to 1988 when the legendary Israeli singer Ofra Haza's 'Im Nin'alu' became a pan-European hit after being sampled by Coldcut/Eric B Rakim.

Even more intriguingly, the anarchist Yorkshire band Chumbawamba – which had a massive international hit in the late-1990s with the single 'Tubthumping' – made an inventive pop rock album, *Readymades*, that sampled heavily from some of folk music's most admired singers, including Coope, Boyes & Simpson, Kate Rusby and the great Norfolk traditional singer Harry Cox. Asian Dub Foundation's full-blooded, politically slanted merger of Asian and British dance cultures could be interpreted as a vignette of modern folk music, too. The ex-Led Zeppelin singer Robert Plant's interest in blues and world music has developed to such an extent in recent years – he even headlined at the Cambridge Folk Festival – that he might now merit recognition as a fully fledged alt-folk figure. America, too, has no shortage of crusading, maverick figures providing a radical, alternative take on traditional culture. Nirvana flirted with the roots, while the ex-New York Dolls singer, David Johansen, explored it more deeply with his band the Harry Smiths. Even the White Stripes dip into it at regular intervals, and the Boggs do it almost as a matter of course. Roots music is alive and well, but sometimes it is found where you least expect it.

Contemporary Folk

IT MAY NOT FIT INTO THE PURISTS' IDEAL, BUT CONTEMPORARY SONG HAS LONG BEEN AN ESSENTIAL ELEMENT OF FOLK MUSIC. THE ART OF THE SINGER/SONGWRITER, FROM WOODY GUTHRIE THROUGH TO BOB DYLAN, AND A WHOLE HOST OF ARTISTS WHO EMERGED IN THEIR WAKE, FUELLED MUCH OF THE EARLY FOLK REVIVAL.

TODAY'S singer/songwriters borrow heavily from many disparate influences and styles, yet the image of the solo performer with an acoustic guitar writing songs about social issues remains a vivid and precious image of folk music.

The days of the contemporary folk artist ruling the music world are long gone, but people have not stopped writing modern folk songs. Many are applying their own music to folk values so neatly that, sometimes, it can be difficult to see the join. The great English revival singer Nic Jones – who sadly hasn't performed since a major car crash in 1982 – used to write original music so closely in the style of traditional songs that most people assumed they were traditional – and he took great delight in not correcting them. In 2002, Ashley

Hutchings put together an interesting album called *Street Cries*, which updated old folk songs and rewrote them in modern contexts. There is such emotional drama in traditional music that it is not surprising when modern writers employ the form. The young Barnsley singer Kate Rusby has written several songs that could easily pass as traditional, one of which – 'Who Will Sing Me Lullabies?' – even won an award.

On songs such as 'Nobody's Wedding' and 'New St. George', Richard Thompson was one of the first to use the mechanics of traditional music in his own writing. He continued to employ the technique with later material such as 'Beeswing' and 'Galway To Graceland', a magnificent modern opera about an Irishwoman who thinks she is married to Elvis Presley. In many cases, it is the form in which they are presented, rather than the songs themselves, that is used to identify their pedigree and terms of reference. Most people assume that the great chorus ballad 'Will Ye Go, Lassie, Go?' is a traditional song, but the McPeakes, a Belfast family who were prominent in the early days of the UK folk revival in the 1950s and 1960s, insist it was written by their ancestor Francis McPeake. They claim that when a folk song collector visited, the song was confused with a selection of traditional songs McPeake performed for the tape recorder.

Above
John Martyn's 1973 release Solid Air *incorporated an innovational guitar effect known as the echoplex, which creates an otherworldly sound when attached to an electrified acoustic guitar.*

"THERE ARE JUST SO MANY GREAT TRADITIONAL SONGS AROUND AND IT'S VERY CHALLENGING AND DAUNTING FOR ANY SONGWRITER TO TRY AND COME UP WITH SOMETHING TO MATCH."
Pete Morton

Above Left
With his anti-folk electrified sound and deep lyrics, Billy Bragg's reputation earned him the privilege to record archived Woody Guthrie songs.

LEADING EXPONENTS
Bob Dylan
Paul Simon
Richard Thompson
Lal Waterson
Paul Brady
Joni Mitchell
Ani DiFranco
Loudon Wainwright III
Tom Paxton
John Prine

CONTEMPORARY FOLK
This is a more contemporary musical style, reflected in the use of minor 7th chords played on acoustic guitar. The vocal line remains uncluttered and the accompaniment can include piano and other instruments. The tab here can be picked.

Story Songs Of Working-Class People

Contemporary folk, though, has also been fuelled from an unlikely source. In the early days of the folk revival, performers and audiences alike were often split into the two camps of traditional and contemporary music. There were

Right

Shane MacGowan's slurred vocals and drug- and alcohol-laden behaviour may have caused the Pogues to fire him as lead singer, but his actions only enhance the aesthetic nature of his lyrics.

distinct borders, but they became blurred when the great traditional singer Ewan MacColl started writing his own songs. In more recent times, fine performers of traditional song such as Christy Moore, Dick Gaughan and Martin Carthy have written contemporary songs. "I will only write a song," Gaughan once commented, "if there is a subject I want to sing about and there isn't an existing song to sing about it." Some of the best modern songs were written by the late Lal Waterson, whose evocative works were showcased alongside those of her brother Mike on the landmark 1970 album *Bright Phoebus*.

The UK contemporary tradition was forged by the likes of Roy Harper, Al Stewart, Ralph McTell, John Martyn and Bert Jansch, and Jansch took it further with John Renbourn and the hugely successful concert attraction, *Pentanple*. Billy Bragg took it to a new level with his acerbic, lyrical songs, backed by an electric-guitar style weaned on the Clash and punk rock. Bragg never minded being called a folk singer but he swore he would never play acoustic guitar in public. Many years after saying it, though, he reneged on the promise. The Irish singer Paul Brady recorded an epic solo album of traditional song called *Welcome Here Kind Stranger*, and then announced that he would pursue a career as a singer/song-writer. He did it, too, with a vast catalogue of songs that have been covered widely by singers ranging from Bonnie Raitt to Tina Turner. John Tams has also contributed some magnificent

songs, while Bill Caddick, Pete Morton and Kieran Halpin have maintained the genre with excellent material. Bands such as the Men They Couldn't Hang and the Levellers might also stake a claim to being contemporary folk acts, given that their story songs of working-class people adhere to the values of traditional song.

Modern Parables

Fuelled by Dylan and his contemporaries, the American singer/songwriter legacy is more entrenched, with the likes of Tom Paxton, Loudon Wainwright, John Prine and James Taylor largely maintaining a style that never deviated unduly from the original concepts of contemporary folk. Wainwright's Canadian ex-wife, Kate McGarrigle, also played a leading role in this process, writing many outstanding songs in a folk context. So has her sister Anna, and between them, they have successfully recorded and performed together for three decades. New additions along the way have included, notably, Ani DiFranco, leading an extraordinary upsurge of female singer/songwriters from the States. Michelle Shocked and Suzanne Vega were early incarnations of a modern folk approach, but there have been many since whose songs flirt with the form, from Tori Amos to Jewel – even if both would probably run screaming from any association with folk music. A closer bond with the form may come from artists generally associated with a country background, such as Emmylou Harris, Steve Earle and the late Townes Van Zandt, whose colorful story songs often seemed like modern parables.

Perhaps the most important contemporary folk writer of modern times, however, is Shane MacGowan. Raised on punk, MacGowan formed the Pogues as a loud, brash, hard-drinking, devil-may-care stage act, taking the templates of the Clancy Brothers and the Dubliners, and increasing the volume, speed and energy to excessive extremes. They drew a raucous, dedicated following, but what nobody was quite prepared for was the rare quality of the new material being written by MacGowan. Songs such as 'A Pair Of Brown Eyes', 'Fairytale Of New York' and 'Sally MacLennane' will eventually submerge into the folk tradition in time-honoured fashion. Much of the success of 'Fairytale Of New York' was due to the vocal contribution of Kirsty MacColl, daughter of Ewan, whose death in 2000 robbed the world of a fine singer and also one of its most original songwriters, with the rare talent of being able to blend comedy and pathos credibly.

With established younger artists like Kate Rusby, Eliza Carthy, James Fagan and Cara Dillon contributing new material alongside the British tradition and artists like the Be Good Tanyas, Gillian Welch, Alison Krauss and Nanci Griffith doing the same across the Atlantic, the signs are still strong.

Neo-Traditional Folk

IN 1996, THE CALIFORNIAN SINGER GILLIAN WELCH RELEASED HER DEBUT ALBUM, REVIVAL. HER UNASSUMING, FOLKSY SONGS AND PLAINTIVE, OLD-TIME SINGING COULD HAVE COME STRAIGHT OUT OF THE APPALACHIANS AT ANY TIME IN THE LAST HUNDRED YEARS. WITH GUITARIST DAVID RAWLINGS, WELCH CAME TO PINPOINT AND DEFINE A NEW STYLE OF FOLK MUSIC: THE NEO-TRADITIONAL PERFORMER.

WELCH personified a modern embodiment of the old-fashioned values of mountain folk, rural country and bluegrass music. This reached fruition in a startling manner with the massive sales of the T-Bone Burnett-produced *O Brother, Where Are Thou?* movie soundtrack in 2000, featuring the music of Welch and Rawlings alongside kindred spirits Norman Black, Emmylou Harris, Alison Krauss, Dan Tyminski and bluegrass legend and banjo hero Ralph Stanley.

Others soon followed the neo-traditional path. A whole new genre – marketed as Americana – has subsequently emerged to encompass those who attempt to reflect the roots of American music. Those who might be assimilated under the umbrella are not necessarily new, young artists such as Welch,

Krauss and Tyminski, either. Nanci Griffith might be called something of a veteran, though she has always drawn on the finest American traditions of gospel, blues and country as well as folk music. Emmylou Harris emerged from the influential late-1960s country rock. However, her later outputs put her firmly in the neo fold. Her Daniel Lanois-produced album,

Wrecking Ball, set new standards, and she followed it in 2000 with *Red Dirt Girl*, revealing a natural instinct for the soul of traditional music.

The Neo-Traditional Folk Star Arrives

Plenty of others might fit reasonably into the neo-traditional mould. New Lost City Ramblers successfully revived the old-time string-band music of the 1920s and 1930s associated with Gid Tanner & his Skillet Lickers, Fruit Jar Drinkers and the Kessinger Brothers. Later, the Holy Modal Rounders reinvented old-timey music with an eccentric modern edge that appealed to young audiences. For many years, Townes Van Zandt lived a relatively humble existence in the mountains, experiencing the simple lifestyle and experiences that shaped the music of his forefathers. And it showed, too, in the late singer/songwriter's own earthy, rootsy style. His great friend Steve Earle has similar values. There are plenty of others, too, who sporadically flit into the neo-folk realms: Lucinda Williams, Shawn Colvin, Dwight Yoakam, Kathy Mattea and – one of the earliest – the late Kate Wolf.

Neo-folk continues to gather ground, as proven by the unexpected success of the Vancouver girl band, the Be Good Tanyas. The Tanyas – who named themselves after an Obo Martin song – sang together for their own entertainment when they made their first album, *Blue Horse*. They pressed up 500 copies and never anticipated success; instead, it launched them on a successful international career.

Above

Performing a kind of updated honky tonk, Dwight Yoakam has flouted many of country music's rules by weaving folk and roots-rock elements through his performances.

> "I FEEL DRAWN TO A LOT OF OLD MUSIC, I LOVE THE PURITY AND SIMPLICITY."
> *Gillian Welch*

Left

With a sound reminiscent of rural Appalachia in the early twentieth century, Gillian Welch has been featured on the soundtrack to O Brother, Where Art Thou? and on acclaimed alternative country artist Ryan Adams' debut album, Heartbreaker.

♩ = 80

NEO-TRADITIONAL FOLK

This music, with a modern feel, often arranged for standard 4-piece band, incorporates simple vocal melody echoing the more traditional roots of folk. This extract could also include an electric guitar plucking the strings of each chord.

LEADING EXPONENTS

Gillian Welch
Emmylou Harris
Be Good Tanyas
The Holy Modal
　Rounders
New Lost City Ramblers
Nanci Griffith
Steve Earle
Alison Krauss
Townes Van Zandt

Artists: Folk

Entries appear in the following order: name, music style, year(s) of popularity, type of artist, country of origin

4 Bitchin' Babes, Contemporary Folk, 1990s–, Artist, American
Acoustic Junction, Contemporary Folk, 1990s–, Artist, American
Acousticats, The, Contemporary Folk, 1990s, Artist, American
Addison's Walk, Folk Rock, 1990s, Artist, American
Agnelli & Rave, Folk Rock; Folk Pop, 1990s, Artist, American
Aguilar, Freddie, Folk Rock, 1970s–1990s, Artist, Filipino
Albion Band, The, UK Folk; Folk Rock, 1970s–, Artist, British
Allen, Jamie, Traditional Folk, 1990s, Artist, American
Almanac Singers, Traditional Folk; Political Folk & Protest Songs, 1940s, Artist, American
Alsop, Peter, Folk Pop, 1970s–1990s, Artist, American
ALT, Folk Rock, 1990s, Artist, Irish
Aman Folk Orchestra, Contemporary Folk, 1990s, Artist, American
Amy & Leslie, Contemporary Folk, 1980s–1990s, Artist; Songwriter, American
Anam, Irish Folk, 1990s–, Artist, Irish
Anderson, Eric, Contemporary Folk; Folk Rock, 1960s–, Artist, American
Anderson, Jamie, Folk Pop, 1980s–, Artist; Songwriter, American
Anderson, Marian, Traditional Folk, 1920s–1960s, Artist, American
Armstrong, Frankie, UK Folk, 1960s–1980s, Artist, British
Arnold, Linda, Contemporary Folk, 1980s–1990s, Artist, American
Arranmore, Folk Pop, 1990s–, Artist, American
Art Institute, The, Folk Pop, 1990s, Artist, American
Arundel, Jeff, Contemporary Folk, 1990s–, Artist, American
Ashes, The, Folk Rock, 1960s, Artist, American
Asylum Street Spankers, Neo-Traditional Folk, 1990s–, Artist, American
Au Go-Go Singers, The Folk Revival; Traditional Folk, 1960s, Artist, American
Aztec Two-Step, Folk Rock, 1970s–1990s, Artist; Songwriter, American
Bad Livers, Neo-Traditional Folk, 1990s–, Artist, American
Badlees, The, Contemporary Folk, 1990s–, Artist, American
Baez, Joan, Traditional Folk; Folk Rock; Political Folk & Protest Songs; The Folk Revival, 1950s–, Artist, American
Bailey, Roy, UK Folk, 1970s–1980s, Artist; Songwriter, British
Baker, Duck, Folk Rock, 1970s–1990s, Artist; Songwriter, American
Balancing Act, The, Folk Rock, 1980s, Artist, American
Ball, Patrick, Irish Folk, 1980s–, Artist, Irish
Band, The, Folk Rock, 1960s–1970s, Artist, Canadian
Banjo Express Ensemble, Traditional Folk, 1990s, Artist, American
Barclay James Harvest, Folk Rock, 1970s–, Artist, British
Bare, Bobby, Alternative Folk, 1950s–1980s, Artist, American
Barry, Margaret, Folk Songs, 1950s, Artist, Irish
Bartley, Geoff, Contemporary Folk, 1980s–, Artist, American
Barton, Cathy, Traditional Folk, 1970s, Artist, American
Battlefield Band, The, The Folk Revival, 1970s–, Artist, British
Beatles, The, Folk Rock, 1960s–1970s, Artist, British
Beau Brummels, The, Folk Rock, 1960s–1970s, Artist, American
Beers Family, Traditional Folk, 1960s–1970s, Artist, British
Bellamy, Peter, UK Folk; The Folk Revival, 1960s–1990s, Artist, British
Belle & Sebastian, Folk Rock, 1990s–, Artist, British
Bennett, Martyn, Traditional Folk, 1990s, Artist, British
Bently Boys, Folk Songs; Traditional Folk, 1920s, Artist, American
Berry, Heidi, Folk Rock, 1980s–1990s, Artist, American
Berryhill, Cindy Lee, Folk Rock, 1980s–1990s, Artist; Songwriter, American
Berryman, Peter & Lou, Contemporary Folk, 1980s–1990s, Artist, American
Bibb, Leon, Traditional Folk, 1960s, Artist, American
Big Fish Ensemble, Folk Rock, 1990s–, Artist, American

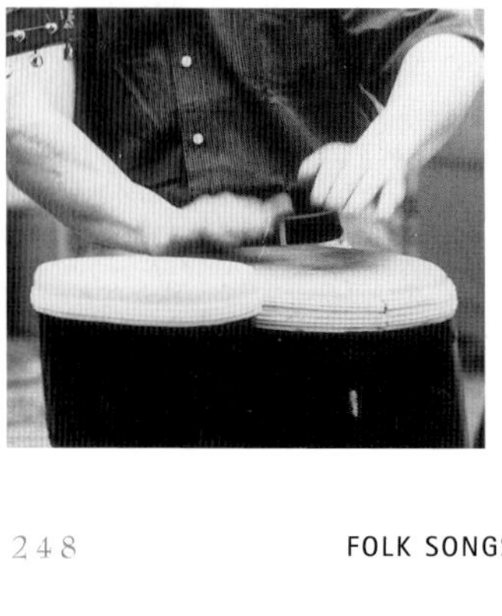

Big Three, The, Folk Pop; The Folk Revival, 1960s, Artist, American
Bikel, Thoedore, Traditional Folk, 1950s–1990s, Artist, Austrian
Bin, Aly, UK Folk, 1980s–, Artist, British
Binder, Milo, Folk Pop; Contemporary Folk, 1990s, Artist; Composer, American
Bird, Tony, Traditional Folk, 1970s, Artist, American
Black, Mary, Contemporary Folk; Irish Folk, 1980s–, Artist, Irish
Blackgirls, Folk Rock; Folk Pop, 1980s–1990s, Artist; Songwriter, American
Blake, Norman, Neo-Traditional Folk; Traditional Folk, 1970s–, Artist, American
Bloom, Ken, Traditional Folk, 1970s–, Artist, American
Bloom, Luka, Alternative Folk; Contemporary Folk, 1980s–, Artist; Songwriter, Irish
Blue Rodeo, Folk Rock, 1980s–, Artist, American
Blue Things, The, Folk Rock, 1960s, Artist, American
Blue, David, Folk Rock, 1960s–1970s, Artist; Songwriter, American
Blues Project, The, Folk Rock, 1960s–1970s, Artist, American
Blumenfeld, Hugh, Contemporary Folk, 1980s–1990s, Artist; Songwriter, American
Boggs, Dock, Traditional Folk; The Folk Revival, 1920s; 1950s, Artist, American
Bolan, Marc, Folk Rock, 1960s–1970s, Artist, British
Bonti, Michael, Folk Pop, 1990s, Artist, American
Bothy Band, The, Irish Folk, 1970s, Artist, Irish
Bragg, Billy, UK Folk; Alternative Folk, 1980s–, Artist, British
Brandywine Singers, The, Folk Pop; The Folk Revival, 1960s, Artist, American
Brennan, Máire, 1970s–1990s, UK Folk; Folk Pop, Artist, Irish
Brewer & Shipley, 1960s–1970s, Folk Rock, Artist, American
Brickell, Edie, Folk Rock, 1980s–1990s, Artist, American
Briggs, Anne, UK Folk, 1950s–1970s, Artist, British
Brislin, Kate, Contemporary Folk; Neo-Traditional Folk, 1990s, Artist, American
Brodsky, Chuck, Contemporary Folk, 1980s–, Artist; Contemporary, American
Bromberg, David, Contemporary Folk, 1960s–1980s, Artist; Songwriter, American
Brooke, Jonathan, Contemporary Folk, 1990s–, Artist; Songwriter, American
Brothers Figaro, Folk Rock; Folk Pop, 1980s, Artist, American
Brothers Four, The, The Folk Revival; Traditional Folk, 1950s–1990s, Artist, American
Broudy, Saul, Contemporary Folk, 1970s, Artist, American
Brown, Greg, Contemporary Folk, 1980s–, Artist; Songwriter, American
Brown, Herschel, Traditional Folk, 1920s, Artist, American
Broza, David, Contemporary Folk, 1980s–, Artist; Songwriter, Israeli
Bucklew, Wendy, Folk Rock, 1990s, Artist; Songwriter, American
Buckley, Jeff, Folk Rock, 1990s, Artist, American
Buckley, Tim, Folk Rock, 1960s–1970s, Artist, American
Buckner, Richard, Alternative Folk; Contemporary Folk, 1990s–, Artist, American
Bud & Travis, Traditional Folk, 1950s–1960s, Artist, American
Buffalo Springfield, Folk Rock, 1960s, Artist, American
Bull, Sandy, Folk Rock; Contemporary Rock, 1960s–1980s, Artist, American
Burke, Kevin, Irish Folk, 1970s–, Artist, British
Burnett, Richard, Folk Songs; Traditional Folk, 1920s, Artist, American
Burnett, T-Bone, Folk Rock, 1970s–1990s, Artist, American
Burns Sisters, The, Contemporary Folk; Folk Rock, 1980s–, Artist, American
Buskin, David, Traditional Folk, 1970s, Artist; Songwriter, American
Byaela, Jane, Contemporary Folk, 1990s, Artist; Songwriter, American
Byrds, The, Folk Rock, 1960s–1970s, Artist, American
Cabrel, Francis, Contemporary Folk, 1970s–, Artist; Songwriter, French
Caedmon's Call, Folk Rock, 1990s–, Artist, American
Calhoun, Andrew, Alternative Folk; Contemporary Folk, 1980s–1990s, Artist; Songwriter, American
Cameron, Isla, The Folk Revival; Folk Songs, 1950s–1960s, Artist, British
Camp, Bob, The Folk Revival, 1960s, Artist, American
Camp, Hamilton, The Folk Revival; Traditional Folk, 1960s, Artist; Songwriter, American
Capercaillie, Contemporary Folk, 1980s–, Artist, Scotland
Carawan, Guy, Folk Songs; Traditional Folk, 1950s–1990s, Artist; Composer, American
Carolina Tar-Heels, The, Traditional Folk, 1920s–1930s, Artist, American
Carpenter, Mary Chapin, Contemporary Folk, 1980s–, Artist; Songwriter, American
Carter, Deana, Contemporary Folk, 1990s–, Artist; Songwriter, American
Carthy, Eliza, UK Folk; Contemporary Folk, 1990s–, Artist, British
Carthy, Martin, UK Folk; The Folk Revival, 1960s–, Artist, British
Case, Peter, Contemporary Folk, 1980s–, Artist, American
Ceolbeg, Irish Folk, 1990s–, Artist, Irish
Cervenka, Exene, Folk Rock, 1980s–1990s, Artist, American
Chandler, Len, Traditional Folk, 1960s, Artist, American
Chapman, Beth Nielsen, Contemporary Folk, 1980s–, Artist, American
Chapman, Marshall, Folk Rock, 1970s–1990s, Artist, American
Chapman, Tracy, Alternative Folk; Contemporary Folk, 1980s–, Artist, American
Charlatans, The, Folk Rock, 1960s, Artist, American
Chesapeake, Contemporary Folk; Neo-Traditional Folk, 1990s, Artist; Songwriter, American
Chesnutt, Vic, Contemporary Folk, 1990s–, Artist; Songwriter, American
Chieftains, The, Irish Folk; UK Folk, 1960s–, Artist, Irish
Chimera, Folk Rock, 1990s, Artist, British
Christian, Frank, Traditional Folk; Contemporary Folk, 1980s–1990s, Artist, American
Christian, Meg, Folk Pop, 1970s–1980s, Artist, American
Christmas Jug Band, Traditional Folk, 1980s–1990s, Artist, American
Chrysalis, Folk Rock, 1960s, Artist, American
Cincinnati Jug Band, Folk Songs; Traditional Folk, 1920s, Artist, American
Clancy Brothers, The, The Folk Revival; Traditional Folk, 1950s–, Artist, Irish
Clannad, UK Folk; Irish Folk, 1970s–, Artist, Irish
Clark, Gene, Folk Rock, 1960s–1990s, Artist; Songwriter, American
Clark, Guy, Contemporary Folk, 1970s–1990s, Artist; Songwriter, American
Clark, Sheila, Folk Songs; Neo-Traditional Folk; Contemporary Folk, 1980s, Artist, British
Claypool, Philip, Contemporary Folk, 1990s, Artist, American
Clayton, Paul, Traditional Folk, 1950s–1960s, Artist, American
Cockburn, Bruce, Contemporary Folk, 1960s–1990s, Artist; Songwriter, Canadian
Cohen, Leonard, Folk Rock, 1960s–, Artist; Songwriter, Canadian
Collins, Judy, The Folk Revival; Folk Rock, 1950s–, Artist, American
Collins, Shirley, UK Folk; The Folk Revival, 1950s–1970s, Artist, British
Collister, Christine, UK Folk; Contemporary Folk, 1980s–, Artist; Songwriter, British

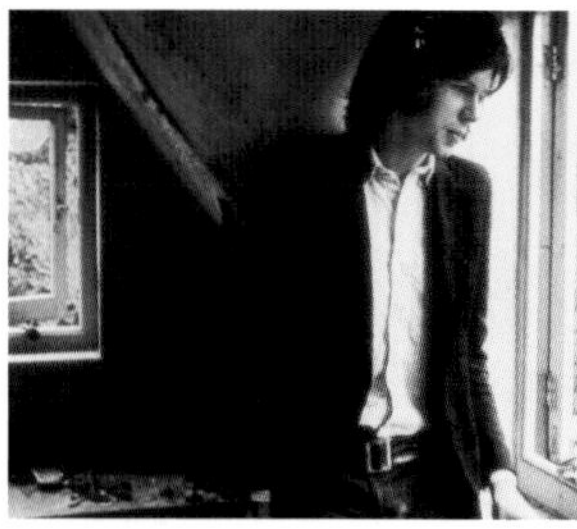

Colvin, Shawn, Contemporary Folk, 1980s–, Artist; Songwriter, American
Continental Divide, Traditional Folk, 1990s–, Artist, American
Copper Family, The, UK Folk, 1980s, Artist, British
Cordelia's Dad, Folk Rock; Neo-Traditional Folk, 1990s–, Artist, American
Cormier, Joseph, Traditional Folk, 1990s–, Artist, Canadian
Cotten, Elizabeth, Traditional Folk; The Folk Revival, 1950s–1980s, Artist, American
Cox Family, The, Neo-Traditional Folk, 1990s, Artist, American
Crazy Bugs, The, Folk Rock, 1980s, Artist, Italian
Creach, Papa John, Folk Rock, 1970s–1990s, Artist, American
Critic's Group, The, UK Folk, 1960s–1970s, Artist, British
Critters, The, Folk Rock, 1960s, Artist, American
Crosby, David, Folk Rock, 1970s–1990s, Artist; Songwriter, American
Crosby, Rob, Contemporary Folk, 1990s, Artist; Songwriter, American
Crosby, Stills & Nash, Folk Rock, 1960s–1990s, Artist; Songwriter, American
Cross, Mike, Contemporary Folk, 1970s–1990s, Artist; Songwriter, American
Cunningham, Phil, Traditional Folk, 1970s–1990s, Artist, British
Curtis, Catie, Contemporary Folk, 1980s–, Artist; Composer, American
Daily Flash, The, Folk Rock, 1960s, Artist, American
Damien Youth, Folk Rock, 1980s–1990s, Artist, British
Danann, De, Irish Folk, 1970s–1990s, Artist, Irish
Darin, Bobby, Folk Rock, 1950s–1970s, Artist, American
Darling, Eric, The Folk Revival, 1960s–, Artist, American
Davies, Gail, Contemporary Folk, 1980s–, Artist; Songwriter, American
Days Like These, Folk Pop, 1990s, Artist, American
Del Amitri, Folk Rock, 1980s–1990s, Artist, British
Dement, Iris, Contemporary Folk; Neo-Traditional Folk, 1990s, Artist; Songwriter, American
Denny, Sandy, Folk Rock; UK Folk, 1960s–1970s, Artist, British
Denver, John, Folk Rock, 1960s–1990s, Artist; Songwriter, American
DeShannon, Jackie, Folk Rock, 1960s–1980s, Artist; Songwriter, American
Dhomhnaill, Triona Ni, Irish Folk, 1970s–1990s, Artist, Irish
Dickens, Hazel, Neo-Traditional Folk; Political Folk & Protest Songs, 1960s–1990s, Artist, American
DiFranco, Ani, Alternative Folk, 1980s–, Artist; Songwriter, American
Dobkin, Alix, Political Folk & Protest Songs, 1970s–1990s, Artist, American
Donegan, Lonnie, UK Folk, 1950s–1990s, Artist, British
Donovan, Folk Rock; UK Folk, 1960s–, Artist; Songwriter, British
Dr Strangely Strange, Irish Folk; Folk Rock, 1960s–1970s, Artist, Irish
Drake, Nick, Folk Rock; UK Folk, 1960s–1970s, Artist; Songwriter, British
Driscoll, Julie, Folk Rock, 1960s–1970s, Artist, British
Drovers, The, Folk Rock, 1990s, Artist, American
Dry Branch Fire Squad, Neo-Traditional Folk, 1960s–, Artist, American
Dubliners, The, Irish Folk, 1960s–, Artist, Irish
Dunaway, Judy, Contemporary Folk, 1990s, Artist, American
Dunford, Uncle Eck, Folk Songs, 1920s, Artist, American
Dyer-Bennett, Richard, Traditional Folk, 1950s–1980s, Artist, British
Dylan, Bob, Political Folk & Protest Songs; Folk Rock, 1960s–, Artist; Songwriter, American
Eaglesmith, Fred, Contemporary Folk, 1980s–, Artist; Songwriter, American
Eatman, Heather, Folk Rock, 1990s–, Artist; Songwriter, American
Eberhardt, Cliff, Contemporary Folk, 1980s–1990s, Artist; Songwriter, American
Eddie From Ohio, Contemporary Folk, 1990s–, Artist, American
Eden Burning, Folk Rock, 1980s–1990s, Artist, British
Edgerton, Clyde, Traditional Folk, 1990s, Artist, American
Edwards, Jonathan, Folk Rock, 1970s–1990s, Artist; Songwriter, American
Egan, Seamus, Irish Folk, 1970s–1990s, Artist, Irish
Eikhard, Shirley, Contemporary Folk, 1980s–, Artist, American
Elders, Betty, Contemporary Folk, 1980s–1990s, Artist; Songwriter, American
Electric Bonsai Band, Contemporary Folk, 1980s–1990s, Artist, American
Elliot, Ramblin' Jack, Traditional Folk; The Folk Revival, 1950s, Artist, American
Elman, Tony, Traditional Folk, 1980s–1990s, Artist, American
Emmet Swimming, Folk Rock, 1990s, Artist, American
Ennis, Seamus, Irish Folk, 1930s–1980s, Artist, Irish
Enya, Irish Folk; Contemporary Folk, 1980s–, Artist, Irish
Everly Brothers, The, Folk Rock, 1950s–1990s, Artist, American
Everly, Don, Folk Rock, 1970s, Artist, American
Everly, Phil, Folk Rock, 1970s–1980s, Artist, American
Fahey, John, Neo-Traditional Folk; Traditional Folk, 1950s–1990s, Artist, American
Faier, Billy, Traditional Folk, 1950s, Artist, American
Fairport Convention, Folk Rock; UK Folk, 1960s–1990s, Artist, British
Fapardokly, Folk Rock, 1960s, Artist, American
Farina, Mimi, Traditional Folk; The Folk Revival, 1960s–1990s, Artist, American
Farina, Richard, The Folk Revival; Folk Rock, 1960s, Artist; Songwriter, American
Farr, Natalie, Contemporary Folk, 1990s, Artist, American
Feliciano, José, Folk Rock, 1960s–, Artist, Puerto Rican
Ferron, Contemporary Folk, 1970s–1990s, Artist; Songwriter, Canadian
Fielding, Rick, Contemporary Folk, 1990s, Artist; Songwriter, Canadian
Fingerett, Sally, Contemporary Folk, 1970s–1990s, Artist; Songwriter, American
Finister, Howard, Traditional Folk; Neo-Traditional Folk, 1990s, Artist, American
Fink, Cathy, Contemporary Folk, 1980s–1990s, Artist; Songwriter, American
Flophouse, Contemporary Folk, 1990s, Artist, American
Forbert, Steve, Contemporary Folk, 1970s–, Artist; Songwriter, American
Foster, Stephen, Folk Songs, 1840s–1860s, Artist; Composer, American
Fotheringay, UK Folk, 1970s, Artist, British
Four Men & A Dog, Contemporary Folk, 1990s, Artist, British
Fox, Ted, Folk Pop, 1990s, Artist, American
Freakwater, Neo-Traditional Folk, 1980s–1990s, Artist, American
Free Hot Lunch, Contemporary Folk, 1980s–1990s, Artist, American

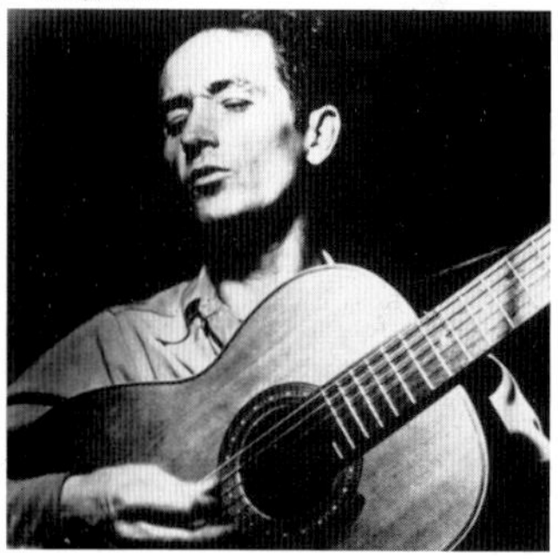

Fruvous, Moxy, Contemporary Folk; Folk Rock, 1990s–, Artist, Canadian
Fugs, The, Folk Rock, 1960s–1990s, Artist, American
Fuller & Kaz, Folk Rock, 1970s, Artist, American
Fureys, The, Irish Folk, 1970s–1990s, Artist, Irish
Gallup, Annie, Contemporary Folk, 1990s–, Artist; Songwriter, American
Gants, The, Folk Rock, 1960s, Artist, American
Garcia, Jerry, Folk Rock, 1970s–1990s, Artist, American
Gaspard, Blind Uncle, Folk Songs; Traditional Folk, 1920s, Artist, American
Gateway Singers, The Folk Revival; Traditional Folk, 1950s–1960s, Artist, American
Gaughan, Dick, Political Folk & Protest Songs; UK Folk; Contemporary Folk; Irish Folk, 1970s–, Artist, British
Gibson, Bob, Folk Songs; Traditional Folk, 1950s–1990s, Artist, American
Gilmore, Jimmie Dale, Alternative Folk; Contemporary Folk, 1980s–, Artist; Songwriter, American
Giteck, Janice, Contemporary Folk, 1960s–1990s, Songwriter, American
Golbey, Brian, Traditional Folk, 1960s, Artist, British
Gooding, Cynthia, Traditional Folk, 1950s, Artist, American
Goodman, Steve, Contemporary Folk, 1970s–1980s, Artist; Songwriter, American
Gorka, John, Contemporary Folk, 1980s–, Artist; Songwriter, American
Gorman, Skip, Contemporary Folk; Traditional Folk, 1970s–1990s, Artist, American
Grace Pool, Folk Rock, 1980s–1990s, Artist, American
Graham, Davy, UK Folk, 1960s–1980s, Artist, British
Grammer, Reg, Folk Rock, 1970s–1990s, Artist, American
Grateful Dead, The, Folk Rock, 1960s–1990s, Artist, American
Grayson, G. B., Folk Songs; Traditional Folk, 1920s–1930s, Artist, American

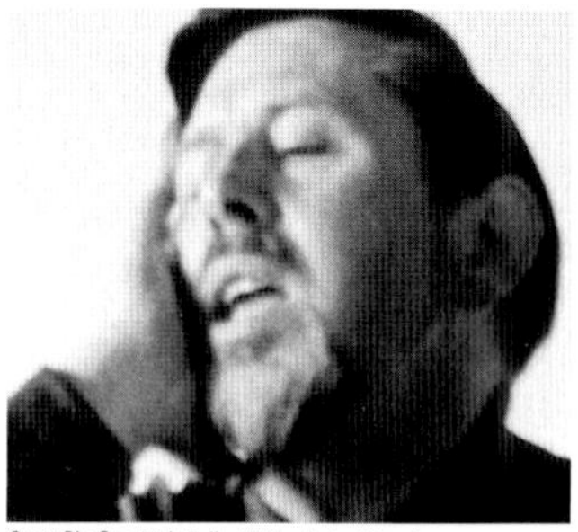

Great Big Sea, Irish Folk, 1990s–, Artist, Canadian
Great Speckled Bird, Folk Rock; Contemporary Folk, 1970s, Artist, Canadian
Greenbriar Boys, The, Traditional Folk, 1950s–1960s, Artist, American
Greenstein, Robin, Contemporary Folk, 1980s–1990s, Artist, American
Greenway, Greg, Contemporary Folk, 1970s–1990s, Artist; Songwriter, American
Gregson, Clive, Contemporary Folk; Folk Rock, 1970s–1990s, Artist; Songwriter, British
Grievous Angels, Contemporary Folk, 1990s, Artist, American
Griffin, Patty, Contemporary Folk; Folk Pop, 1990s–, Artist; Songwriter, American
Griffith, Nanci, Contemporary Folk, 1970s–, Artist; Songwriter, American
Guthrie, Arlo, Political Folk & Protest Songs; Contemporary Folk; Folk Rock, 1960s–1990s, Artist, American
Guthrie, Woody, Traditional Folk; Political Folk & Protest Songs, 1930s–1960s, Artist, American
Hall, Chuck, Contemporary Folk, 1990s, Songwriter, American
Hall, Tom T., Neo-Traditional Folk, 1960s–1990s, Artist; Songwriter, American
Hamilton IV, George, Traditional Folk, 1950s–1980s, Artist, American
Hamilton Pool, Folk Rock, 1990s, Artist, American
Hamilton, Dirk, Folk Rock, 1970s–, Artist; Songwriter, American
Hammond, John Jr, The Folk Revival, 1960s–, Artist, American
Hancock, Butch, Contemporary Folk, 1970s–, Artist, American
Handsome Family, The, Neo-Traditional Folk, 1990s–, Artist, American
Hardin, Tim, Folk Rock, 1960s–1970s, Artist; Songwriter, American
Harding, John Wesley, Alternative Folk; Contemporary Folk, 1980s–, Artist, British
Harper, Ben, Folk Rock, 1990s–, Artist, American
Harper, Roy, Folk Rock; UK Folk, 1960s–, Artist, British
Harris, Emmylou, Folk Rock, 1960s–, Artist, American
Hartford, John, Neo-Traditional Folk, 1960s–, Artist, American
Havens, Richie, Folk Rock, 1960s–, Artist; Songwriter, American
Hayes, Martin, Irish Folk, 1990s, Artist, Irish
Heart of Gold Band, Folk Rock, 1980s, Artist, American
Heartbeats Rhythm Quartet, The, Irish Folk, 1990s, Artist, Irish
Hearts & Flowers, Folk Rock, 1960s, Artist, American
Helm, Levon, Folk Rock, 1960s–, Artist, American
Henske, Judy, The Folk Revival; Folk Rock, 1960s–1970s, Artist, American
Hester, Carolyn, Traditional Folk; The Folk Revival; Folk Rock, 1960s–1970s; 1990s, Artist, American
Hewerdine, Boo, Contemporary Folk, 1980s–1990s, Artist; Songwriter, British
Hickman, Sara, Folk Pop, 1980s–, Artist, American
Highwaymen, The, The Folk Revival; Folk Pop, 1960s, Artist, American
Hill, Kim, Folk Rock, 1980s–1990s, Artist, American
Hills, Ann, Contemporary Folk, 1970s–1990s, Artist; Songwriter, American
Hinojosa, Tish, Contemporary Folk, 1980s–, Artist, American
Hinton, Sam, The Folk Revival; Traditional Folk, 1940s–1960s, Artist; Songwriter, American
Hitchcock, Robyn, Folk Rock, 1980s–, Artist, British
Holcomb, Robin, Contemporary Folk, 1980s–, Artist; Songwriter, American
Holt, David, Traditional Folk, 1980s–, Artist, American
Holy Modal Rounders, The, Folk Rock, 1960s–1990s, Artist, American
Hopkin, Mary, Folk Rock, 1960s–1970s, Artist, British
Horseflies, The, Traditional Folk; Contemporary Folk, 1970s–1990s, Artist, American
Horslips, Folk Rock, 1970s–1980s, Artist, Irish
Hot Tuna, Folk Rock, 1970s–, Artist, American
House Band, The, Irish Folk, 1980s–1990s, Artist, British
Houston, Cisco, Traditional Folk, 1940s–1960s, Artist; Songwriter, American
Hoyle, Linda, Folk Rock, 1970s, Artist, American
Hull, Alan, UK Folk, 1970s–1990s, Artist; Songwriter, British
Hunter, Robert, Folk Rock, 1970s–1990s, Artist; Songwriter, American
Hutchings, Ashley, UK Folk; Traditional Folk, 1960s–, Artist, British
Ian & Sylvia, The Folk Revival; Folk Rock; Folk Pop, 1960s–1970s, Artist, Canadian
Ian, Janis, Folk Rock; Contemporary Folk, 1960s–, Artist, American
Idha, Folk Rock, 1990s, Artist, Swedish
Incredible String Band, The, Folk Rock; UK Folk, 1960s–, Artist, British
Indians, The, Folk Rock, 1990s, Artist, American
Indigo Girls, Folk Rock, 1980s–, Artist, American

FOLK SONGS ➡ 226 TRADITIONAL FOLK ➡ 228 POLITICAL FOLK & PROTEST SONGS ➡ 230 THE FOLK REVIVAL ➡ 233 FOLK ROCK ➡ 235

Innocence Mission, Folk Rock, 1980s–, Artist, American
Insect Trust, Folk Rock, 1960s–1970s, Artist, American
Irvine, Andy, Irish Folk, 1960s–, Artist, British
It's A Beautiful Day, Folk Rock, 1960s–1970s, Artist, American
Ives, Burl, Traditional Folk; Folk Pop, 1940s–1960s, Artist, American
Jackopierce, Folk Rock, 1990s, Artist; Songwriter, American
Jan Dukes de Grey, UK Folk; Folk Rock, 1970s, Artist, British
Jansch, Bert, Folk Rock; UK Folk, 1960s–, Artist, British
Jara, Victor, Contemporary Folk, 1960s–1970s, Artist, Chilean
Jefferson Airplane, Folk Rock, 1960s–1980s, Artist, American
Jerling, Michael, Contemporary Folk, 1980s–1990s, Artist; Songwriter, American
Jethro Tull, Folk Rock, 1960s–, Artist, British
Jim & Jean, The Folk Revival; Folk Rock, 1960s, Artist, American
JK & Co., Folk Rock, 1960s, Artist, American
Joffen, Josh, Contemporary Folk, 1980s–1990s, Artist, American

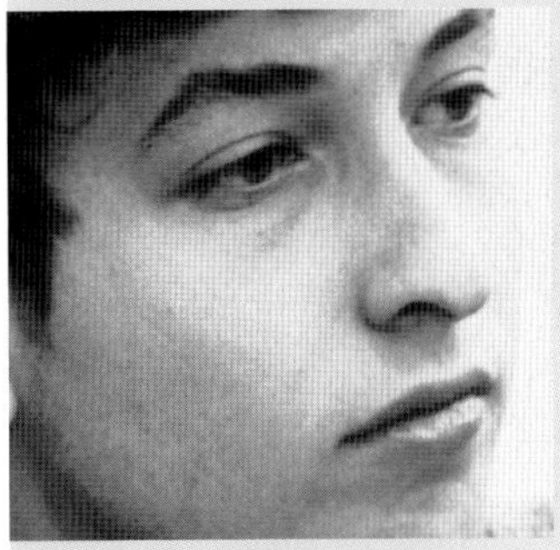

John & Mary, Contemporary Folk, 1990s, Artist, American
Johnson, Prudence, Contemporary Folk, 1980s–1990s, Artist, American
Johnston, Freedy, Folk Rock, 1990s–, Artist, American
Johnstone, Jimmy, Irish Folk, 1990s, Artist, Irish
Jones, Nic, UK Folk; Contemporary Folk, 1960s–1980s, Artist; Songwriter, British
Jones, Rickie Lee, Folk Rock, 1970s–, Artist; Songwriter, American
Jones, Wizz, UK Folk, 1970s–1990s, Artist, British
Journeymen, The Folk Revival; Contemporary Folk; Folk Pop, 1960s, Artist, American
Juggling Suns, Folk Rock, 1990s, Artist, American
Jump In The Water, Folk Rock, 1990s, Artist, American
Kahn, Brenda, Contemporary Folk; Folk Rock, 1990s, Artist; Songwriter, American
Kaldor, Connie, Contemporary Folk, 1980s–1990s, Artist; Songwriter, Canadian
Kaleidoscope, Folk Rock, 1960s–1990s, Artist, American
Kane, Kieran, Traditional Folk, 1990s–, Artist, American
Kantner, Paul, Folk Rock, 1970s–1990s, Artist, American
Kaplan, Paul, Contemporary Folk, 1980s, Artist, American
Kaplansky, Lucy, Contemporary Folk; Alternative Folk, 1990s–, Artist, American
Kaukonen, Jorma, Folk Rock, 1970s–, Artist, American
Kazee, Buell, Traditional Folk, 1920s–1970s, Artist, American
Keane, Dolores, Irish Folk, 1970s–, Artist, Irish
Keen, Robert Earl Jr, Contemporary Folk, 1980s–, Artist, American
Kell, Tom, Contemporary Folk, 1990s, Artist, American
Kelly, Jeff, Folk Rock, 1980s–, Artist, American
Kelly, Matt, Folk Rock, 1990s, Artist, American
Kelly, Paul, Folk Rock, 1980s–, Artist, Australian
Kennedy, Bap, Irish Folk, 1990s–, Artist, Irish
Key, Steve, Contemporary Folk, 1970s–1990s, Artist; Songwriter, American
Khan, Brenda, Folk Rock, 1990s, Artist, American
Khan, Si, Contemporary Folk; Political Folk & Protest Songs, 1970s–, Artist, American
Kincaid, Bradley, Traditional Folk, 1930s–1970s, Artist, American
King Fish, Folk Rock, 1970s–, Artist, American
King, Bob, Alternative Folk, 1950s–1960s, Artist, Canadian
King, Grant, Folk Pop, 1990s, Artist, American
Kingston Trio, The, Traditional Folk; The Folk Revival; Folk Pop, 1950s–1990s, Artist, American
Kinney, Kevin, Folk Rock, 1990s–, Artist, American
Kirkpatrick, John, UK Folk, 1960s–, Artist, British
Koerner, John "Spider John", The Folk Revival, 1960s–1990s, Artist, American
Koller, Fred, Contemporary Folk, 1980s–, Artist; Songwriter, American
Kossoy Sisters, The Folk Revival; Traditional Folk, 1950s, Artist, American
Kottke, Leo, Contemporary Folk, 1960s–1990s, Artist, American
Krikorian, Rob, Folk Pop, 1990s, Artist, American
Kweskin, Jim, Traditional Folk; The Folk Revival, 1960s–1970s, Artist, American
LaFarge, Peter, Traditional Folk, 1960s, Artist, American
Laing, Shona, Folk Rock, 1980s–1990s, Artist, New Zealander
Larkin, Patty, Contemporary Folk, 1980s–, Artist; Songwriter, American
Larner, Sam, UK Folk; Traditional Folk, 1900s–1960s, Artist, British
Last Fair Deal, Folk Pop, 1980s, Artist, American
Lavin, Christine, Contemporary Folk, 1980s–, Artist; Songwriter, American
Leadbelly, Folk Songs; The Folk Revival, 1920s–1940s, Artist; Composer, American
Leaves, The, Folk Rock, 1960s, Artist, American
Leftover Salmon, Folk Rock, 1990s–, Artist, American
Leslie Spit Treeo, Folk Pop, 1990s, Artist, Canadian
Lester, Julius, Traditional Folk, 1960s, Artist, American
Lewis & Clarke Expedition, Folk Rock, 1960s, Artist, American
Lewis, Laurie, Neo-Traditional Folk, 1980s–1990s, Artist, American
Lightfoot, Gordon, Folk Rock, 1960s–, Artist; Songwriter, Canadian
Lilac Time, Folk Rock, 1980s–, Artist, British
Limeliters, The, Traditional Folk; The Folk Revival; Folk Pop, 1960s–1990s, Artist, American
Lind, Bob, Folk Rock, 1960s, Artist; Songwriter, American
Lindisfarne, UK Folk; Folk Rock, 1960s–, Artist, British
Loggins & Messina, Folk Rock, 1970s, Artist, American
Lomax, Alan, Traditional Folk, 1930s–1990s, Artist, American
London Madrigal Singers, UK Folk, 1960s, Artist, British
Lonesome Val, Alternative Folk, 1990s, Artist; Songwriter, American
Love, Folk Rock, 1960s–1970s, Artist, American
Lovin' Spoonful, The, Folk Rock, 1960s–1970s; 1990s, Artist, American
Lowe, Jez, Irish Folk; UK Folk; Political Folk & Protest Songs, 1970s–, Artist, British
Lunsford, Bascom Lamar, Traditional Folk, 1910s–1970s, Artist, American
MacColl, Ewan, Folk Songs; The Folk Revival; UK Folk, 1950s–1990s, Artist, British
MacColl, Kirsty, Folk Rock, 1980s–1990s, Artist, British
MacDonald, Rod, Contemporary Folk, 1980s–1990s, Artist; Songwriter, American
MacLean, Brian, Folk Rock, 1970s–1990s, Artist; Songwriter, American
MacLean, Dougie, Traditional Folk; Contemporary Folk, 1970s–, Artist; Songwriter, British
MacMaster, Natalie, Irish Folk, 1980s–, Artist, Irish
MacNeill, Finlay, Traditional Folk, 2000s, Artist, British
Magpie, Political Folk & Protest Songs; Traditional Folk, 1970s–, Artist, American
Makem, Tommy, Irish Folk, 1960s–1990s, Artist, Irish
Mamas & the Papas, The, Folk Rock, 1960s, Artist, American
Mangsen, Cindy, Traditional Folk; UK Folk, 1980s–1990s, Artist; Songwriter, American
Manning, Roger, Contemporary Folk; Folk Rock, 1980s–, Artist; Songwriter, American
Martin, Paul, Folk Rock, 1990s, Artist, American
Martyn, John, Folk Rock; UK Folk, 1960s–, Artist; Songwriter, British
Masen, Sarah, Folk Pop, 1990s–, Artist, American
Mason Proffit, Folk Rock, 1960s–1970s, Artist, American
Massengill, David, Contemporary Folk, 1980s–1990s, Artist; Songwriter, American
Mattea, Kathy, Contemporary Folk, 1980s–, Artist, American
Matthews, Ian, Folk Rock; UK Folk, 1960s–1990s, Artist; Songwriter, British
Maze, Folk Rock, 1960s, Artist, American
McAnally, Mac, Folk Pop, 1970s–1990s, Artist; Songwriter, American
McCalla, Deidre, Contemporary Folk, 1990s, Artist; Songwriter, American
McCaslin, Mary, Contemporary Folk, 1960s–1990s, Artist; Songwriter, American
McCurdy, Ed, Traditional Folk; The Folk Revival, 1950s–1960s, Artist, American
McCutcheon, John, Traditional Folk, 1970s–, Artist, American
McDonald, Country Joe, Folk Rock; Political Folk & Protest Songs, 1960s–1990s, Artist; Songwriter, American
McDonough, Megon, Traditional Folk, 1970s, Artist; Songwriter, American
McGarrigle, Kate & Anna, Contemporary Folk, 1970s–1990s, Artist; Songwriter, Canadian
McGee, Kieran, Folk Rock, 1990s, Artist, American
McGuinn, Clark & Hillman, Folk Rock, 1970s–1980s, Artist, American
McGuire, Barry, Folk Rock, 1960s–1980s, Artist; Songwriter, American
McKenna, Joe & Antoinette, Irish Folk, 1970s, Artist, Irish
McKenzie, Scott, Folk Rock, 1960s–1970s, Artist, American
McLachlan, Sarah, Folk Pop, 1980s–, Artist, Canadian
McLauchlan, Murray, Folk Rock, 1970s, Artist, British
McLennan, Grant, Folk Rock, 1990s, Artist, Australian
McMeen, El, Traditional Folk, 1970s, Artist, American
McTell, Ralph, UK Folk, 1960s–, Artist; Songwriter, British
Meat Purveyors, The, Neo-Traditional Folk, 1990s–, Artist, American
Melanie, Folk Pop, 1960s–, Artist, American
Messina, Jim, Folk Rock, 1960s–1990s, Artist, American
Miller, Bill, Contemporary Folk, 1970s–, Artist; Songwriter, American
Miller, Jody, Alternative Folk, 1960s–1970s, Artist, American
Miller, Julie, Folk Pop, 1990s, Artist; Songwriter, American
Ming, Hoyt "Floyd", Traditional Folk; Folk Songs, 1920s; 1970s, Artist, American
Minogue, Aine, Irish Folk, 1990s, Artist, Irish
Mitchell, Chad, Traditional Folk; The Folk Revival; Folk Pop, 1950s–1990s, Artist, American
Mitchell, Joni, Folk Rock, 1960s–, Artist; Songwriter, Canadian
Moby Grape, Folk Rock, 1960s–1980s, Artist, American
Modern Folk Quartet, The Folk Revival, 1960s, Artist, American
Moffatt, Hugh, Alternative Folk, 1980s–1990s, Artist; Songwriter, American
Moffatt, Katy, Alternative Folk, 1970s; 1990s–, Artist, American
Mollys, The, Irish Folk, 1990s–, Artist, Irish
Mondlock, Buddy, Traditional Folk, 1980s–1990s, Artist; Songwriter, American
Moore, Hamish, Irish Folk; UK Folk, 1990s–, Artist, British
Morris On, UK Folk, 1970s, Artist, British
Morris, Gary, Alternative Folk, 1980s–1990s, Artist, American
Morrisey, Bill, Contemporary Folk, 1980s–, Artist; Songwriter, American
Morrison, Van, Folk Rock, 1960s–, Artist; Songwriter, British
Moving Cloud, Irish Folk, 1980s–1990s, Artist, Irish
Mugwumps, Folk Rock, 1960s, Artist, American
Murphy, Elliott, Folk Rock, 1970s–, Artist, American
Mustard's Retreat, Traditional Folk, 1980s–1990s, Artist, American
Nash, Graham, Folk Rock, 1970s–1980s, Artist; Songwriter, British
Near, Holly, Political Folk & Protest Songs; Folk Rock; Folk Pop, 1970s–, Artist; Songwriter, American
Neil, Fred, Folk Rock, 1960s–1970s, Artist; Songwriter, American
Nesmith, Michael, Folk Rock, 1960s–, Artist; Songwriter, American
Nestor, J. P., Traditional Folk; Folk Songs, 1920s, Artist, American
New Christy Minstrels, The, The Folk Revival; Folk Pop, 1960s–1970s, Artist, American
New Coon Creek Girls, Traditional Folk, 1980s–, Artist, American
New Lost City Ramblers, The, Traditional Folk; The Folk Revival, 1950s–1990s, Artist, American
Newcomer, Carrie, Contemporary Folk; Folk Rock, 1990s–, Artist, American
Nightcrawlers, The, Folk Rock, 1960s, Artist, American
Niles, John Jacob, Traditional Folk, 1920s–1970s, Artist, American
O'Brien, Connolly & Len, Traditional Folk, 1990s, Artist, Irish
O'Hara, Mary, Irish Folk, 1970s–1990s, Artist, Irish
Ochs, Phil, Political Folk & Protest Songs; Folk Rock, 1960s–1970s, Artist; Songwriter, American
October Project, The, Folk Rock, 1990s, Artist, American
Odetta, Folk Songs; The Folk Revival, 1950s–, Artist, American
Old Time Radio Gang, Traditional Folk, 1980s–1990s, Artist, American
Olney, David, Traditional Folk, 1970s–, Artist, American
Orton, Beth, Alternative Folk, 1990s–, Artist; Songwriter, British
Ostroushko, Peter, Traditional Folk, 1970s–, Artist, Ukrainian
Oysterband, UK Folk; Contemporary Folk, 1980s–, Artist, British
Paleface, Folk Rock, 1990s, Artist, American
Palmer, Joe, Irish Folk, 1990s, Producer, Irish
Parker, Chubby, Traditional Folk; Folk Songs, 1920s–1940s, Artist, American
Parsons, Gene, Folk Rock, 1970s–1990s, Artist, American

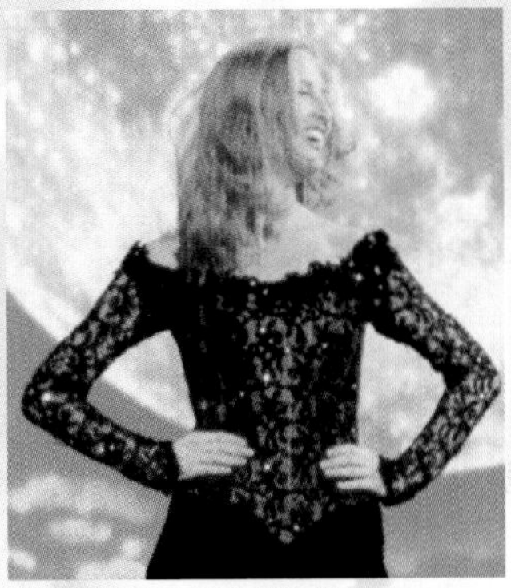

Paul, Ellis, Contemporary Folk, 1980s–, Artist; Songwriter, American
Paxton, Tom, The Folk Revival, 1960s–, Artist; Songwriter, American
Pearls Before Swine, Folk Rock, 1960s–1970s, Artist, American
Pentangle, Folk Rock; UK Folk, 1960s–1990s, Artist, British
Peter, Paul & Mary, Traditional Folk; The Folk Revival; Folk Pop, 1960s–1990s, Artist, American
Peterson, Colleen, Folk Rock, 1970s–1990s, Artist; Songwriter, Canadian
Petric, Faith, Traditional Folk, 1980s–, Artist, American
Petteway, Al, Traditional Folk, 1990s–, Artist, American
Pettis, Pierce, Contemporary Folk, 1980s–, Artist; Songwriter, American
Phillips, Utah, Traditional Folk; Political Folk & Protest Songs, 1960s–1990s, Artist, American
Phranc, Folk Rock; Alternative Folk, 1980s–1990s, Artist, American
Pierce, Jo Carol, Alternative Folk, 1980s–1990s, Artist; Songwriter, American
Plainsong, Folk Rock, 1970s; 1990s, Artist, British
Pogues, The, UK Folk, 1980s–1990s, Artist, British
Pozo-Seco Singers, The, Folk Pop, 1960s–1970s, Artist, American
Prine, John, Contemporary Folk, 1970s–, Artist; Songwriter, American
Prior, Maddy, UK Folk; Contemporary Folk, 1970s–, Artist, British
Prophet, Chuck, Folk Rock, 1990s–, Artist, American
Rankin Family, The, Contemporary Folk, 1990s, Artist, American
Rare Air, Irish Folk, 1980s–1990s, Artist, Canadian
Rave-Ups, The, Folk Rock, 1980s–1990s, Artist, American
Ray, Dave Snaker, The Folk Revival, 1960s–1990s, Artist, American
Red Clay Ramblers, The, Neo-Traditional Folk, 1960s–, Artist, American
Reed, Blind Alfred, Traditional Folk, 1920s, Artist, American
Reeves, Goebel, Traditional Folk, 1920s–1930s, Artist, American
Renbourn, John, UK Folk, 1960s–, Artist, British
Reser, Harry, Alternative Folk, 1920s–1950s, Artist, American
Rising Sun, Folk Rock, 1960s, Artist, American
Robinson, Earl, Traditional Folk, 1950s–1980s, Artist, American
Roche, Suzzy, Contemporary Folk, 1990s–, Artist; Songwriter, American
Roches, The, Contemporary Folk, 1970s–1990s, Artist; Songwriter, American
Rodgers, Jimmy F., Folk Pop, 1950s–1970s, Artist, American
Ronstadt, Linda, Folk Rock, 1960s–, Artist, American
Rooftop Singers, Traditional Folk; Folk Pop; The Folk Revival, 1950s–1960s, Artist, American
Rose, Tim, Folk Rock; Contemporary Folk, 1960s–1990s, Artist; Songwriter, British
Rosmini, Dick, The Folk Revival, 1950s–1960s, Artist, American
Rosselon, Leon, UK Folk, 1960s–, Artist, British
Rowan, Peter, Contemporary Folk; Neo-Traditional Folk, 1970s–1990s, Artist, American
Runrig, Contemporary Folk; Folk Rock, 1970s–, Artist, British
Rush, Tom, Traditional Folk, 1960s–, Artist; Songwriter, American
Russell, Tom, Contemporary Folk, 1980s–, Artist; Songwriter, American
Saint John, Bridget, Folk Rock, 1960s–1970s, Artist, British
Sainte-Marie, Buffy, Folk Rock; Contemporary Folk; Folk Pop, 1960s–, Artist; Songwriter, Canadian
Salem 66, Folk Rock, 1980s–1990s, Artist, American
Sallyangie, The, UK Folk; Folk Rock, 1960s, Artist, British
Samples, The, Folk Rock, 1980s–, Artist, American
Sandpipers, The, The Folk Revival; Folk Pop, 1960s–1970s, Artist, American
Sands, Tommy, Political Folk & Protest Songs; Irish Folk, 1960s–, Artist, Irish
Sarstedt, Peter, UK Folk, 1960s–, Artist; Songwriter, British
Schlamme, Martha, Traditional Folk, 1950s, Artist, German
Schneider, Mimi, Folk Pop, 1990s, Artist; Songwriter, American
Schuyler, Knobloch & Bickhardt, Contemporary Folk, 1980s, Artist, American
Searchers, The, Folk Rock, 1960s–, Artist, British
Sebastian, John, Contemporary Folk; Folk Rock, 1970s–, Artist; Songwriter, American
Seeger, Mike, Traditional Folk; Neo-Traditional Folk, 1960s–1990s, Artist, American
Seeger, Peggy, Folk Songs; The Folk Revival; Traditional Folk, 1950s–, Artist, American
Seeger, Pete, Traditional Folk; Folk Songs; Political Folk & Protest Songs; The Folk Revival, 1940s–, Artist, American
Seekers, The, Folk Rock, 1960s–1970s, Artist, Australian
Serendipity Singers, Folk Pop; The Folk Revival, 1960s, Artist, American
Setters, Jilson, Folk Songs; Traditional Folk, 1880s–1940s, Artist, American
Sexton, Martin, Alternative Folk; Contemporary Folk, 1990s–, Artist; Songwriter, American
Shakers, The, UK Folk; Folk Rock, 1970s–1980s, Artist, British
Shocked, Michelle, Alternative Folk, 1980s–1990s, Artist, American
Siebel, Paul, Contemporary Folk; Folk Rock, 1970s–1990s, Artist; Songwriter, American
Silly Sisters, UK Folk, 1970s–1980s, Artist, British
Silos, The, Folk Rock, 1980s–, Artist, American
Silverstein, Shel, Folk Songs; The Folk Revival, 1950s–1980s, Artist, American
Simon & Garfunkel, Folk Rock, 1960s–1980s, Artist, American
Simon Sisters, The, The Folk Revival, 1960s, Artist, American
Simon, Paul, Folk Rock, 1960s–, Artist; Songwriter, American
Simpson, Martin, Contemporary Folk; UK Folk, 1970s–, Artist; Songwriter, British
Sky, Patrick, Irish Folk, 1960s–1990s, Artist, American
Sloan, P. F., Folk Rock, 1960s–1990s, Artist; Songwriter, American
Snow, Kilby, Folk Songs; Traditional Folk, 1960s, Artist, American
Snow, Phoebe, Contemporary Folk, 1970s–1990s, Artist; Songwriter, American
Song Project, The, Contemporary Folk, 1980s, Artist, American
Sonny & Cher, Folk Rock, 1960s–1970s, Artist, American
Sordid Humor, Folk Rock, 1990s, Artist, American
Sorrels, Rosalie, Traditional Folk; Contemporary Folk, 1970s–, Artist, American
Spence, Skip, Folk Rock, 1960s, Artist, Canadian
Spheeris, Chris, Folk Pop, 1980s–, Artist; Composer, Greek
Spillane, Davy, Irish Folk; Contemporary Folk, 1970s–, Artist, Irish
Springfields, The Folk Revival; Folk Pop; Traditional Folk, 1960s, Artist, British
Stackabones, Folk Rock, 1990s, Artist, American
Staines, Bill, Contemporary Folk; Traditional Folk, 1960s–, Artist; Songwriter, American
Stealers Wheel, Folk Rock, 1970s, Artist, British
Steeleye Span, UK Folk; Folk Rock, 1970s–, Artist, British
Stephens, Uncle Bunt, Folk Songs; Traditional Folk, 1920s–1930s, Artist, American
Stewart, Al, Folk Rock; UK Folk, 1960s–, Artist; Songwriter, British
Stewart, John, Folk Rock; Contemporary Folk, 1960s–, Artist; Songwriter, American
Stewart, Rod, Folk Rock, 1960s–, Artist; Songwriter, British
Stills, Stephen, Folk Rock, 1960s–1990s, Artist, American
Stone Poneys, Folk Rock, 1960s–1970s, Artist, American
Strawbs, The, Folk Rock; UK Folk, 1960s–1980s, Artist, British
Street, Patrick, Irish Folk, 1980s–1990s, Artist, Irish
Swarbrick, Dave, UK Folk, 1960s–1990s, Artist, British
Sweet Thursday, Folk Rock, 1960s, Artist, American
Tabor, June, Folk Rock; Contemporary Folk; UK Folk, 1970s–, Artist, British
Talley, James, Alternative Folk, 1970s–, Artist, American
Tamarack, Contemporary Folk, 1980s–, Artist, Canadian
Tannahill Weavers, The, Traditional Folk, 1970s–, Artist, British
Tarriers, The, The Folk Revival, 2000s–, Artist; Songwriter, American
Tashian, Barry & Holly, Contemporary Folk, 1980s–1990s, Artist, American
Taylor, Alex, Folk Rock, 1970s–1980s, Artist; Songwriter, American
Taylor, Kate, Traditional Folk; Folk Rock, 1970s, Artist; Songwriter, American
Tester, Scan, UK Folk , 1950s–1960s, Artist, British
Tetes Noires, Folk Rock, 1980s, Artist, American
Thompson, Linda, UK Folk; Folk Rock, 1960s–, Artist; Songwriter, British
Thompson, Richard, Folk Rock; UK Folk, 1960s–1990s, Artist; Songwriter, British
Tickell, Kathryn, UK Folk; Irish Folk, 1980s–, Artist, British
Tiny Lights, Folk Rock, 1980s–1990s, Artist, American
Tom & Jerry, Folk Rock, 1960s, Artist, American
Touchstone, Irish Folk, 1970s–1980s, Artist, Irish
Trader Horne, Folk Rock, 1970s, Artist, British
Traum, Artie, Traditional Folk, 1970s–, Artist; Songwriter, American
Traum, Happy, Traditional Folk, 1960s–1980s, Artist, American

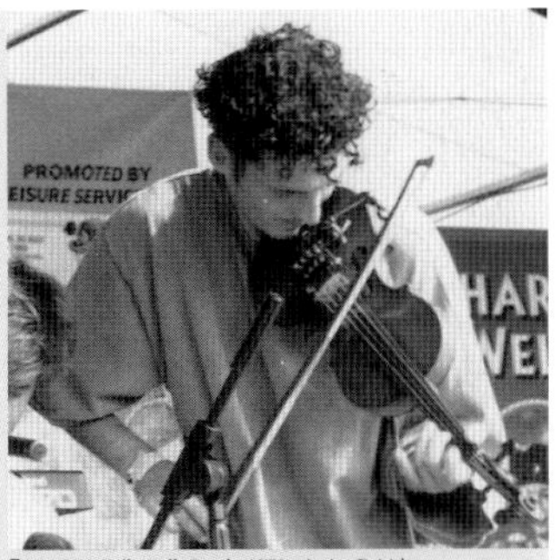

Trees, UK Folk; Folk Rock, 1970s, Artist, British
Turtles, The, Folk Rock, 1960s, Artist, American
Tyminski, Dan, Neo-Traditional Folk, 1980s–, Artist, American
Tyson, Ian, Contemporary Folk, 1970s–1990s, Artist, Canadian
Ugly Americans, The, Folk Rock, 1990s, Artist, American
Ungar, Jay, Traditional Folk; Contemporary Folk, 1970s–, Artist, American
Val, Joe, Traditional Folk, 1990s, Artist, American
Van Ronk, Dave, Traditional Folk, 1950s–1990s, Artist, American
Van Zandt, Townes, Contemporary Folk, 1960s–1990s, Artist; Songwriter, American
Varttina, Folk Pop, 1980s–, Artist, Finnish
Vega, Suzanne, Alternative Folk; Contemporary Folk, 1980s–, Artist, American
Vejtables, The, Folk Rock, 1960s, Artist, American
Venice, Folk Rock, 1990s, Artist, American
Vigilantes Of Love, Folk Rock, 1990s–, Artist, American
Vogl, Nancy, Folk Rock, 1980s–1990s, Artist; Songwriter, American
Voice Squad, The, Irish Folk, 1990s, Artist, Irish
Wade, Stephen, Traditional Folk, 1990s, Artist, American
Wainwright, Loudon III, Contemporary Folk, 1970s–, Artist; Songwriter, American
Wallin, Doug, Folk Songs, 1990s, Artist, American
Warriner, Steve, Contemporary Folk, 1980s–, Artist, American
Watchman, The, Contemporary Folk, 1980s–1990s, Artist; Songwriter, Dutch
Waterboys, The, Folk Rock, 1980s–1990s, Artist, British
Waterson, Norma, UK Folk, 1960s–, Artist, British
Watersons, The, UK Folk, 1960s–1970s, Artist, British
Watson Family, The, Traditional Folk, 1960s, Artist, American
Watson, Doc, Traditional Folk, 1960s–, Artist, American
Wayfarers Trio, The Folk Revival; Folk Pop, 1960s, Artist, American
We Five, Folk Rock, 1960s, Artist, American
Weavers, The, Traditional Folk; Political Folk & Protest Songs; The Folk Revival, 1940s–1960s, Artist, American
West, Harry & Jeanie, Traditional Folk, 1950s–1980s, Artist, American
West, Hedy, The Folk Revival, 1990s, Artist; Songwriter, American
Wheeler, Cheryl, Contemporary Folk, 1980s–1990s, Artist; Songwriter, American
Whelan, John, Irish Folk, 1980s–, Artist, Irish
While, Chris, Traditional Folk, 1990s, Artist, British
White, Andy, Folk Rock, 1990s–, Artist; Songwriter, American
White, Josh, Political Folk & Protest Songs, 1920s–1960s, Artist, American
Whitman, Slim, Folk Pop, 1940s–1980s, Artist, American
Why Store, The, Folk Rock, 1990s, Artist, American
Wilcox, David, Contemporary Folk, 1980s–, Artist; Songwriter, American
William St James, Folk Rock, 1970s, Artist, American
Williams Brothers, The, Folk Rock, 1970s–, Artist, American
Williams, Dar, Alternative Folk, 1990s–, Artist; Songwriter, American
Williams, Lucinda, Alternative Folk, 1970s–, Artist; Songwrite r, American
Williams, Victoria, Alternative Folk; Contemporary Folk, 1980s–, Artist, American
Williamson, Robin, UK Folk; Folk Rock, 1960s–, Artist, British
Willson-Piper, Marty, Folk Rock, 1980s–, Artist; Songwriter, Australian
Winchester, Jesse, Contemporary Folk; Folk Rock, 1970s–, Artist; Songwriter, American
Winter Hours, Folk Rock, 1980s–1990s, Artist, American
Wolf, Kate, Contemporary Folk, 1970s–1990s, Artist; Songwriter, American
Yarbrough, Glenn, Traditional Folk; The Folk Revival; Folk Pop, 1950s–1990s, Artist, American
Young, Neil, Folk Rock, 1960s–, Artist; Songwriter, Canadian
Youngbloods, The, Folk Rock, 1960s–1970s, Artist, American

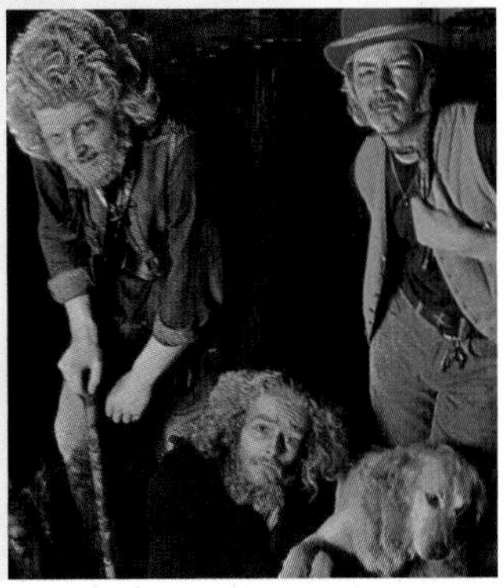

Classical

THE story of classical music is not bound up simply with the traditions of any one country: it is tied up with the cultural development of Europe as a whole. This section attempts to pick out the composers from each successive age who, looked at from one point of view, exerted the greatest influence on their contemporaries and subsequent generations, as well as both within their own countries and internationally.

Even then, the full picture can only be appreciated by taking into account music by the many recognized masters who do not feature here: among them Dufay, Tallis, Byrd, Palestrina, Domenico Scarlatti, Gluck and a whole pantheon of Romantic and twentieth-century figures. Women are also absent from the story because, for reasons too complex to be merely regrettable, they have had little impact on the development of classical music. Despite this, there are talented women composers whose music *does* survive: Hildegard von Bingen from the eleventh century, or Barbara Strozzi from the seventeenth, Clara Schumann in the nineteenth and Lili Boulanger in the twentieth.

The 1,000-year period has been sliced up into generally agreed periods that are, of course, not set in stone. You do not have to look far to find evidence to contradict them: for instance, a tradition of unaccompanied vocal music, following the Late Renaissance model of Palestrina, flourished well into the Early Baroque; and Richard Strauss's Late Romantic

masterpieces were composed at the dawn of the Contemporary era, long after Late Romanticism had supposedly run its course. History often contradicts "definitive" readings, and the stories of both twentieth-century and contemporary music could be written in many different ways.

Still, the language of music, its principal genres and its circumstances of performance have changed considerably over 10 centuries. Status and social roles also changed, as musicians gained increasing independence – at first from the Church, then from aristocratic patrons – before attaining a kind of "aristocracy of the spirit" in the eyes of an admiring nineteenth-century public. During the last millennium, and especially in recent centuries, European society has seen its dynamism reflected in the progressive drive of its music.

The idea of progress has played a key role in the development of music since the Early Baroque era. In particular, composers in the nineteenth century became increasingly preoccupied with advancing the common musical

Above

The manuscript of George Frideric Handel's Messiah. *With its joyous 'Hallelujah Chorus', it is one of the most famous oratorios ever written, and certainly the most recognizable.*

> "THE HISTORY OF MUSIC, UNTIL OUR DAY, MAY BE SEEN AS A GRADUAL BREAKDOWN OF ALL THE VARIOUS ISOLATING FORCES OF THE ART."
>
> *Charles Rosen*

Above Right

The original production of Stravinsky's Rite of Spring *featured deliberately un-graceful choreography by Njinsky. Pictured here third from left is Serge Diaghilev, the mastermind behind the legendary Ballets Russes.*

STYLES

Medieval
Renaissance
Early Baroque
Late Baroque
Classical
Early Romantic
Late Romantic
Twentieth Century
Contemporary

THE CLASSICAL STYLE

Classical music relies on melody, harmony and interplay between instruments. The string quartet has a perfect sound balance; the first violin's melody and the cello's bassline are combined with the texture and harmonies of the second violin and viola.

  CLASSICAL PEOPLE A-Z ➡ 274   INSTRUMENTS A-Z ➡ 436

Above

*The great virtuoso violinist
Yehudi Menuhin teaching a
future virtuoso, Nigel
Kennedy. With their dazzling
techniques and artistic
brilliance, virtuoso performers
have always added a touch of
glamour to the solo concerto,
a form developed in the
Baroque era which is still part
of today's standard repertoire.*

Previous Overleaf

*The great conductor, Yan
Pascal Tortelier. The conductor
is responsible for controlling
the performance, and for
shaping individual phrases.
The conductor's central role
dates back to the early
nineteenth century with the
development of expressive,
Romantic elements in music.*

shaped by the music of their time, and possibly that of the preceding generation. Since then, the widely agreed canon of finest works has grown hand in hand with the development of the major vocal and instrumental genres – principally opera, oratorio, symphony, concerto, string quartet – and the orchestras and opera houses that perform them.

The most popular works, however, have not always been the most historically significant. Audience favourites, such as Rossini's 'William Tell' Overture, Grieg's Piano Concerto or Barber's Adagio, exerted far less influence on their contemporaries than other more challenging works. Any survey of the high points from the last 1,000 years will inevitably omit tranches of memorable music in its attempt to answer the fundamental question of why classical music developed in the way it did.

A short answer would surely acknowledge the central importance of notation, from the early monastic records of plainsong (made towards the end of the first millennium) to more recent, visually arresting scores by the likes of Karlheinz Stockhausen and George Crumb. The use of scores has given us priceless access to the minds of musicians who lived before the first universities were founded. The complexity of classical music carries with it the need for notation and, therefore, the means of creating a permanent archive. We take for granted the abundance of music that does survive – until we realize that, say, in the case of Monteverdi, the great majority of his opera scores have been lost. The three extant works are so fine that the loss of so many others must rank as a cultural tragedy.

language to the point where, like the society around it, the language exhausted its own potential. In contrast to previous ages, originality became de rigueur, as nineteenth-century musicians became increasingly aware of their historical context. With greater knowledge comes greater self-consciousness and pressure to act as an individual; as a result, twentieth-century composers often struggled to forge a personal musical style.

Instead of finding a single solution to the collapse of the common language, in recent years composers have had a plethora of options from which to construct a personal idiom. The norms from which musicians in previous ages could hammer out striking innovations that their audiences would instantly recognize, and be shocked or delighted by, have almost disappeared. In the same way, society norms in general have weakened over the past 100 years. When composers adopt the old models today, they do so more self-consciously.

Still, you could argue that our age is the most historically self-conscious there has been. Indeed, the idea that music could have a significant history dates back no further than the late-eighteenth century (a great age of historical writing), when the first comprehensive music histories were written. Before then, the musical tastes of the public tended to be

Just as notation arose because of the liturgical importance of plainsong in the monasteries of pre-medieval Europe, so the sacred genres were the keenest test of any composer's skill throughout the medieval period and a good chunk of the Renaissance. Though it ceased to be a predominantly sacred style as much as five centuries ago, classical music, like Western society, has never managed to wholly divorce itself from the influence of the Western church. Secular composers such as Igor Stravinsky and György Ligeti have reserved some of their greatest utterances for religious forms such as the requiem mass, a genre that stretches back to the Middle Ages. The original task of finding a suitable musical language for the business of praising God set a standard of musical rhetoric that contributed to the high concept of much secular music.

You could argue that this elevated rhetoric has, in part, led to the popular image of the classical composer as someone aloof from the world. At various times throughout its history, and for long periods in the twentieth century, the musical avant-garde has lost touch with a large part of its potential audience. Perhaps the biggest task facing today's composers is to reach an audience that may have little knowledge of, or time for, the established classics. Still, in attempting to reconnect with society at large in an increasingly globalized culture, classical music of the last 40 years or so has absorbed influences from the music of other cultures, as well as from various styles of pop music.

Certainly, the trick of being both popular and serious, of finding a balance between a high concept of music and the need to communicate directly with the ordinary music lover, is one that the greatest composers have nearly always achieved. It may well be the highest art form of all.

Left

Standing at the crossroads of the Classical and Romantic eras, Ludwig van Beethoven is one of the greatest composers in history, excelling in virtually every genre of his day.

Below

A nineteenth-century state visit to the Royal Opera House in London's Covent Garden shows the popularity of the opera as a social event – as much as a musical one – among the upper classes.

THE MIDDLE AGES IS THE FIRST PERIOD IN THE HISTORY OF CLASSICAL MUSIC WHOSE COMPOSERS CAN BE IDENTIFIED BY NAME. FOR CENTURIES, FOLLOWING THE ROMAN EMPIRE'S COLLAPSE, THE MAIN CENTRES OF LEARNING IN WESTERN EUROPE HAD BEEN THE MONASTERIES.

Medieval

THE monks' vast repertory of Gregorian chant, or plainsong – highly ornate, unaccompanied melodies set to sacred Latin texts – emerged from the Dark Ages as the single resource upon which much of the most important music of the medieval period would be based.

The Notre Dame School

At the same time, the Middle Ages were a time of social upheaval, set against the backdrop of a divided Church. For instance, the Pope lived in exile from Rome, at Avignon in southern France, for much of the fourteenth century, and there were numerous rival contenders to the papal throne. In this atmosphere, composers – particularly French composers, whose music shows the greatest technical and artistic development during the medieval period – were at liberty to write serious secular music. Equally, their sacred works often mixed in secular elements, even extending to being accompanied by instruments, which the Church had previously forbidden. It regarded the human voice as the only instrument pure enough to praise God.

Perhaps the most significant musical advance of this period was the development of a style of writing known as polyphony. This technique entails the simultaneous coordination of two or more distinct parts, or voices, in a harmonically unified composition. First elaborated in a style known as *organum*, it has been a cornerstone of classical music ever since. By the end of the twelfth century, composers affiliated with the newly built cathedral of Notre Dame in Paris had developed a sophisticated style of polyphonic composition. Three, sometimes even four voices would be combined in extended works that would have sumptuously exploited the building's generous acoustics.

Composed by a man we know only as Pérotin, *Viderunt Omnes* offers a mesmerizing example of the Notre Dame style. Like many works of the period, its upper voices are composed around a given plainsong melody in the tenor part. The tenor melody itself has been slowed so that it functions as a shifting drone, around which the other parts play out faster, dancing patterns. The effect is like an impression of eternity, whose jarring harmonies sound surprisingly modern.

Machaut's Secular Music

If Pérotin and his contemporaries had a different concept of what later musicians would come to define as dissonance, composers of the fourteenth century expanded the idea of what constituted a serious composition beyond the practice of the previous generation. Defined as the *Ars Nova*, in contrast to the so-called *Ars Antiqua* of the Notre Dame School, the music of the fourteenth century added a wide variety of new forms to the inventory of notated, or written-down, music. Many of them, such as the *rondeau*, the *virelai* and the *ballade*, were types of secular song that were well-established in the oral tradition; composers of the Ars Nova developed their

> ## "MACHAUT HIMSELF DECLARED THAT TRUE SONG AND POETRY COULD COME ONLY FROM THE HEART."
> *Donald Grout and Claude V. Palisca*

LEADING EXPONENTS

Hildegard von Bingen
Léonin
Pérotin
Philippe de Vitry
Guillaume de Machaut
Francesco Landini
Johannes Ciconia
John Dunstable
Guillaume Dufay
Gilles Binchois

MEDIEVAL

Unaccompanied chanted recitations of the liturgy in Latin, with one syllable extended across two or more notes, are characteristic of medieval church music.

THE CLASSICAL INTRO ➡ 250   CLASSICAL PEOPLE A-Z ➡ 274   INSTRUMENTS A-Z ➡ 436

essential characteristics in sometimes highly elaborate polyphonic settings. Principal among these forms was the motet, a complex polyphonic work for at least three voices.

The motets of Guillaume de Machaut (*c*. 1300–77) are highly serious works, often featuring texts on secular subjects that he had written. He was the most celebrated composer of his day and one of its principal poets, and much of his poetry reflects his sexual experiences. The musical settings of these texts are as intricate as those of his religious works, and Machaut frequently added further layers of complexity by setting two or three texts simultaneously, one part per voice. This practice was typical of the *Ars Nova*, though no one exercised complexity of this kind to the same emotional effect as Machaut. The haunting *Dame, je sui cilz/Fins cuers doulz* is a good example, setting two separate texts written to, perhaps, the same woman.

Machaut's La Messe De Nostre Dame

We can witness the blurring of boundaries between the Church and the outside world in the emblematic figure of Machaut. Most importantly, perhaps, the sound of Machaut's secular music is no different from that of his sacred compositions. In the volatile religious climate of the

fourteenth century, composers such as Machaut had more freedom than before to express the range of their musical personalities. His secular music represents the greater part of his output. It is, perhaps, paradoxical that his most significant composition, the scope and magnificence of which parallels the architectural achievements of the great Gothic cathedrals, was a religious work.

The first complete setting of the Ordinary of the Mass, *La Messe de Nostre Dame* was composed for performance in the cathedral of Reims in northern France in the 1360s. As a work for four voices, it equals in polyphonic complexity anything he ever wrote. A 30-minute span of music planned as a whole, its six movements share a hypnotic unity of mood and style that exceed in ambition and grandeur any work of the period. Indeed, it would not be matched until the Masses of Guillaume Dufay (1400–74), some 75 years later. Its scale laid down a template for large-scale classical compositions for the next six centuries, making it by far the most significant work of the Middle Ages.

AS A PERIOD IN ART HISTORY, THE RENAISSANCE DATES FROM THE BEGINNING OF THE FIFTEENTH CENTURY TO THE FIRST PART OF THE SIXTEENTH. UNDER THE INFLUENCE OF PERSPECTIVE AND THE REDISCOVERY OF ANCIENT GREEK STATUARY, PAINTING AND SCULPTURE IN WESTERN EUROPE, AND PARTICULARLY ITALY, WERE TRANSFORMED BY A WORLDVIEW WE NOW KNOW AS "HUMANISM".

Renaissance

THIS phenomenon led to a new interest among the arts and sciences in human beings and their passions. In music, fundamental changes tend to take longer to emerge than in other arts, and are less conspicuous when they do. During the fifteenth century, composers continued to develop the techniques handed down to them by Machaut and his contemporaries.

New Centres Of Excellence

The main European centre of compositional excellence moved from northern France to Burgundy, an area that today would comprise Holland, Belgium, Luxembourg, Lorraine and north-eastern France. Though other traditions continued to flourish – in particular the English school of the sixteenth century, whose greatest exponents were Thomas Tallis (1505–85) and William Byrd (1543–1623) – from the late-fifteenth century onwards, the music of Burgundian composers starts to dominate the general practice of this period. Throughout the sixteenth century the Burgundians found lucrative employment and artistic freedom in the service of the various courts associated with the powerful Italian city states. There, they developed new forms that gave more attention to expressing the meaning of the text, marking perhaps the most significant difference between Renaissance and medieval music.

> "HE IS THE MASTER OF THE NOTES. THEY MUST DO AS HE WILLS; AS FOR THE OTHER COMPOSERS, THEY HAVE TO DO AS THE NOTES WILL."
>
> *Martin Luther on Josquin des Prez*

Above

English composer Thomas Tallis's career spanned the reigns of Henry VIII and his three children, and reflected the associated religious upheavals. His first compositions were Latin motets and Masses, and he became one of the greatest Anglican composers of his time.

LEADING EXPONENTS

Johannes Ockeghem
Jacob Obrecht
Josquin des Prez
Heinrich Isaac
Adrian Willaert
Carlo Gesualdo
Orlando di Lasso
Thomas Tallis
William Byrd
Giovanni da Palestrina
Giovanni Gabrieli

Ockeghem's Masses

During the fifteenth century, the musical form that offered the greatest scope to an ambitious composer was the Mass. The Burgundian musician Johannes Ockeghem (*c.*1420–97) composed 13 Masses, the technical ingenuity and expressiveness of which represent a high-water mark in the genre.

Perhaps the most obvious difference between Ockeghem's music and that of Machaut is its sweeter sound. This was the result of the increasing harmonic importance of intervals of 3rds and 6ths. The staple harmonic unit of all modal and tonal music up to the end of the nineteenth century, 3rds and 6ths (as opposed to the 4ths and 5ths regarded as "perfect" by earlier musicians) were first used extensively by English composers such as John Dunstable (1390–1453), before the Burgundian generation that included Dufay brought them into mainstream European practice. Ockeghem's harmonic sense is therefore fully contemporary. His melodic writing, on the other hand, denotes a return to the melismatic style of Gregorian chant, in which a long melodic phrase might be sung over a single syllable. Ockeghem's music still retains many features of the earlier style in this sense, though in other ways – particularly its elaborate use of canon, a technique whereby voices enter in sequence in strict imitation of each other – his music offers resources that were taken up and used more freely by composers of the sixteenth century. His *Missa Mi-Mi* is a fine example of how these new resources enabled him to compose sacred music of sustained power and beauty. His death was duly mourned across the whole of Europe.

RENAISSANCE

In the Renaissance style, motet writing supports four unaccompanied voices, which at times imitate one another in pairs.

La   la - la   la - la-la   la - la la   la   la   la

THE CLASSICAL INTRO ➡ 250   CLASSICAL PEOPLE A-Z ➡ 274   INSTRUMENTS A-Z ➡ 436

Ave Maria By Josquin Des Prez

Josquin des Prez (1440–1521) raised the art of setting words to music to new heights. His output includes 18 Masses and several dozen *chansons*, but his 100 motets provide the best evidence of his genius.

In the superb four-part motet *Ave Maria*, for example, the aural complexity of the fourteenth-century motet gives way to a greater variety of textures, even in such a short piece, reflecting a musical treatment that strives to dramatize the meaning of the text – in this case, a paean to the Virgin Mary. Pairs of voices imitating each other follow the canonic passages that open the work, where the four voices enter sequentially in strict imitation. Imitation was a mainstay of Josquin's technique, as well as his main legacy to later composers. Further on in the work, the prevailing duple meter, or march time, is briefly replaced by a delicate triple time to depict the verse beginning "Hail true virginity, immaculate chastity". The most sublime moment is reserved for the climax of this motet, where the words "O Mother of God, remember me" are set homophonically, all four voices singing together. In this setting, the composer seems to appeal personally to the Virgin through his art. This sense of the human drama of music was entirely new, and it anticipates the larger dramatic forms – principally, opera and oratorio – of the Baroque era.

The Sixteenth-Century Madrigal

During the late-fifteenth and sixteenth centuries, the secular song forms of the Middle Ages were gradually replaced by genres – principally the chanson, the *Lied* and the madrigal – incorporating the contemporary techniques of imitative counter-point and word-painting. Each was associated with a particular region: the chanson with Burgundy, the Lied with Germany and the madrigal with Italy. As the most skilful European composers found work in the Italian courts, it follows that the madrigal saw the greatest range of development.

One of the most prolific madrigal composers, and one of the best, was Orlande de Lassus, or Orlando di Lasso (1532–94). His name can be correctly spelt in more than one language, as he was a Burgundian who later

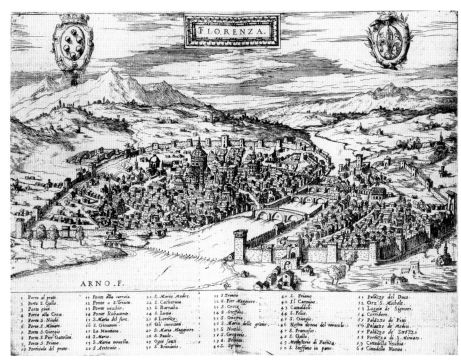

found employment in Italy and southern Germany. A cosmopolitan figure and the most celebrated composer of the Late Renaissance, he shows equal mastery of chanson, Lied and madrigal. *Cantai hor piango*, a madrigal setting of a sonnet by the fourteenth-century Italian poet Petrarch, achieves a sustained lyrical intensity through dramatic word-painting, a greater degree of chromaticism – harmony remote from the home key – and the controlled use of dissonance, which increasingly featured in Renaissance harmonic practice.

Above

The Renaissance is believed to have begun in the city state of Florence in the fourteenth century. The movement diffused through the whole of Europe, influencing philosophy, art, architecture, literature and music.

Left

The Renaissance saw the flowering of many new types of secular music, accompanied by a range of instruments, some of the most popular of which are pictured here: the lute, flute and harp.

Early Baroque

SPANNING NEARLY THE ENTIRE SEVENTEENTH CENTURY, THE EARLY BAROQUE ERA WAS A TIME OF GREAT CHANGE IN MUSIC. IN THE ITALIAN CITIES THAT LED MUSICAL TASTE AT THE END OF THE RENAISSANCE, A FLOWERING OF NEW GENRES OF VOCAL MUSIC ACCOMPANIED BY INSTRUMENTS SUPPLANTED THE UNACCOMPANIED MASS AND MOTET. AMONG THESE, THE OPERA AND ORATORIO STILL EXIST IN MODERN TIMES.

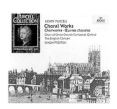

Above

Henry Purcell was a distinguished English composer, equally at home writing for the court, the theatre or the Church. His word-painting skills were second to none, evident particularly in his opera Dido and Aeneas, *and choral music, such as the odes he wrote to celebrate the Feast of St Cecilia.*

Monteverdi And Early Opera

THE way in which music was composed shifted from the modal melodic method of the previous half-millennium towards the tonal harmonic system that would underpin music of the Classical and Romantic eras. Gradually formalized during the Baroque period, this way of conceiving music placed harmonic organization above other considerations, allowing a greater range of both musical associations and emotions. In terms of the way the music sounded, there was a new emphasis on the bass part, and on the melody in the upper voice, at the expense of the inner parts. This allowed swift modulations (changes of key), and a greater responsiveness to the emotional nuances of a text. The development of the extended genres, and opera in particular, would have been inconceivable without the globally organizing principle of tonality.

The genre of music theatre most typical of Western classical music emerged during the first decade of the seventeenth century, initially as an entertainment for the Florentine aristocracy. It then spread to Mantua, Rome and other Italian cities, before its arrival at the Teatro San Cassiano in Venice, the first operatic venue dependent on a fee-paying general public.

Opera was a way of writing an extended dramatic work that embraced both narrative action and lyrical beauty. It was the first time in Western music history that identifiable characters had been portrayed on stage, and a new musical technique, known as "recitative", was devised to make their utterances

sound lifelike. Based on contemporary ideas of how the poems of Ancient Greece were performed, the recitative style preserved the natural speech rhythms of the words and set them melodically over a simple chordal accompaniment,

> "HAVE FAITH THAT THE MODERN COMPOSER BUILDS ON FOUNDATIONS OF TRUTH."
>
> *Claudio Monteverdi*

LEADING EXPONENTS

Giulio Caccini
Jan Sweelinck
Claudio Monteverdi
Girolamo Frescobaldi
Heinrich Schütz
Samuel Scheidt
Giacomo Carissimi
Louis Couperin
Jean-Baptiste Lully
Henry Purcell

EARLY BAROQUE

Baroque music is characterized by the addition of a definite bass line (carried here by the cello) underlying a melodic treble line, often taken by the violin.

Piano

usually played on either harpsichord or organ, and known as the "continuo" part. In the hands of a musician as skilled as Claudio Monteverdi (1567–1643), an experienced composer of the Late Renaissance madrigal – which showed an increasing tendency towards dramatic declamation – recitative became an expressive vehicle for conveying emotion as well as the semblance of speech.

In *L'Orfeo* (1607), he employed an orchestra of about 40 instruments, far greater than in other works of the period, which he used in various ensembles in the *ritornelli*, or refrains, that intersperse the various vocal solos, duets and choruses. Lasting almost two hours in performance, *L'Orfeo* was the first opera of any significance, and a work that drastically expanded both the scale and dramatic scope of what music could say about the human condition.

Seventeenth–Century Sacred Music

Although the composition of unaccompanied vocal Masses declined almost to nothing, sacred music in various guises continued to interest composers in the Baroque era. In Germany, Heinrich Schütz (1585–1672) adapted the Venetian manner of his teacher Giovanni Gabrieli (1554–1612), with its majestic use of spatially separated instrumental groups. His *Psalmen Davids* (1619), for instance, is scored for multiple choruses, soloists and concertato instruments; that is, instruments playing a role equal to that of the singers.

The same Venetian influence can be heard in another Monteverdi piece: his *Vespers* (1610), a magnificent work as ingenious in its varying of vocal and instrumental resources as was *L'Orfeo*. Three decades later, his *Selva morale e spirituale* (1641) is a diverse collection of unaccompanied psalms, motets and songs, in Latin and Italian, and both as harmonically daring and texturally varied as any of his secular works.

The sacred genre from this period that has matched the longevity of opera is the oratorio, an extended work written for large forces on a biblical subject. Combining narrative and meditative elements, oratorios of this period were generally performed in church. Perhaps the most remarkable example from the seventeenth century is *Jephte* (1650), by the Roman Giacomo Carissimi (1605–74). The lament and chorale finale of this work provide moving evidence that, despite the restricted circumstances of performance, the oratorio could rival opera for sheer musical drama.

Henry Purcell

As has often been the case in music and the other arts, England was a special case in the seventeenth century. Somewhat removed from the influence that Italian music exerted on the rest of Europe, English composers developed their own musical forms, and an indigenous harmonic sense that still owed something to Renaissance practice. This distinctive plangency is discernible in many vocal works of the late-seventeenth century, particularly those of Henry Purcell (1659–95) – such as his glorious, eight-part anthem *Hear my prayer, O Lord*.

English composers also continued developing their own genres, so that while much of Europe in the later seventeenth century was drawn by the spell of either French opera, whose chief exponent was the Italian-born Jean-Baptiste Lully (1632–87), or Italian opera, led by Alessandro Scarlatti (1660–1725), Purcell composed only one true opera, albeit the finest English opera written prior to the twentieth century, *Dido and Aeneas* (1689). Purcell thrived in home-grown genres such as the anthem or the English-language ode. Perhaps his most magnificent achievement was *Hail! Bright Cecilia* (1692), the fourth and final ode he composed for the Musical Society in London and first performed on the patron saint of music's name day. A secular oratorio in spirit, if not in subject matter, its vivid word-setting and general variety of moods offered a challenge to later composers of oratorios in English, most notably George Frideric Handel.

Far Left

Claudio Monteverdi had one aim in his music: to express the text as convincingly as he could, and as a result his works display a supremely seamless union of music and words.

Below

In 1973, conductor Christopher Hogwood revived the Academy of Ancient Music, which originally began in the eighteenth century. The internationally renowned orchestra play on period instruments, and perform works from the Baroque, Classical and Early Romantic eras.

Late Baroque

THE SEVENTEENTH AND EARLY EIGHTEENTH CENTURIES WERE INFUSED WITH A SPIRIT OF SCIENTIFIC AND PHILOSOPHICAL ENQUIRY. IN 1722'S TRAITÉ DE L'HARMONIE ('TREATISE ON HARMONY'), JEAN-PHILIPPE RAMEAU (1683-64), WHO DOMINATED FRENCH OPERA IN THE 1730S – CASTOR ET POLLUX (1737) – SET OUT THE RULES OF THE TONAL METHOD THAT COMPOSERS HAD LONG BEEN DEVELOPING IN PRACTICE.

Above

Today, Antonio Vivaldi's The Four Seasons is one of classical music's best-known and loved works, featuring on countless CDs, TV commercials and call-waiting systems. However, for many years the work was lost, only re-surfacing in the early 1950s.

At the same time, the tuning system known as equal temperament, still in use today, enabled diverse instruments with previously different tuning systems to be harmoniously united in large ensembles.

The Late Baroque Concerto

During the later seventeenth century, instrumental music had emerged as a medium in its own right. The increasing vogue for public recitals and orchestral concerts was the result of a number of factors, such as the rise in amateur music-making and a new middle-class appetite for courtly dancing. With the rise in status of the violin and the technical improvements in this and other instrumental families, came genres associated with specific solo instruments or ensembles: for the organ, the toccata and fugue and the chorale prelude; for the harpsichord or clavichord, the suite and the sonata; for the chamber ensemble of two violins and continuo, the trio sonata; for the orchestra of strings, continuo and occasional other instruments, the orchestral concerto, concerto grosso and solo concerto.

The composer most readily associated with the development of instrumental music at the turn of the eighteenth century is the Roman Arcangelo Corelli (1653–1713). An accomplished violinist, with works such as the *12 Concerti Grossi*, Opus 6, first published in 1714, Corelli raised the violin family to the prominent position it occupies today.

> ## "WHETHER I WAS IN MY BODY OR OUT OF MY BODY AS I WROTE IT I KNOW NOT. GOD KNOWS."
> *Handel on the 'Hallelujah Chorus' in his Messiah*

Right

Although he was not court composer, Handel wrote many works for George I. Here we see a performance of Handel's music attended by the king at St George's Church in Hanover Square, London.

LEADING EXPONENTS

Dietrich Buxtehude
Arcangelo Corelli
Alessandro Scarlatti
François Couperin
Georg Philipp Telemann
Jean-Philippe Rameau
Antonio Vivaldi
George Frideric Handel
Johann Sebastian Bach
Domenico Scarlatti

LATE BAROQUE

Composers of the Late Baroque period explored the new concept of "key"; this example uses notes from the D minor key.

Piano

 THE CLASSICAL INTRO ➡250   CLASSICAL PEOPLE A-Z ➡274   INSTRUMENTS A-Z ➡436

The concerto grosso pits a small, or concertino, group of solo instruments – in this case, two violins and a violoncello – against a larger string group. A typical Corelli concerto comprises five or six short movements, with tempi alternating between fast and slow. Their customary contrapuntal texture, frequent instances of weak-to-strong-beat dissonance (known as suspensions), repeated use of harmonic sequences and clear tonal structures lend these pieces an elegance and poise that was widely admired in the early eighteenth century.

Of the next generation, two-thirds of the concertos of Antonio Vivaldi (1678–1741) are for solo instruments, with a string orchestra that sometimes included wind instruments or horns. Vivaldi brought a new rhetoric to orchestral music. Works such as *Le Quattro Stagioni* ('The Four Seasons'), from his set of *12 Concerti*, Opus 8 (1725), which were as popular in the composer's lifetime as they are now, depend less on intricate counterpoint than on a compelling sense of the abstract drama of music, realized in stark contrasts of mood and orchestral texture. They were highly influential in the development of the solo concerto of the Classical period.

Handel's Vocal Music

In the early eighteenth century, England saw a great flourishing of musical activity – especially in London, where the music-loving public developed an appetite for Italian opera. During the 1720s, the German composer George Frideric Handel (1685–1759), who had settled in London in 1714, scored one success after another with works on classical or mythological subjects. *Giulio Cesare* ('Julius Caesar') (1724)

shows how far the genre had developed in 100 years. Recitative is now a much more responsive tool, the rapid interplay of voices in some passages suggesting the naturalistic dialogue of a stage play. Perhaps his greatest operatic legacy, however, are the arias, or solo vocal numbers, which became an increasingly important aspect of the genre in the previous 30 years. In *Giulio Cesare*, the noble simplicity of arias such as Cornelia's '*Priva son d'ogni conforto*' show why these works remain a staple of the modern opera repertoire.

With the declining taste for Italian opera in London in the 1730s, Handel turned his attention to the oratorio in English, a secular genre intended for concert performance. Adopting biblical subjects that were more familiar to the new middle-class audience, Handel brought his own cosmopolitan influences to bear on the genre, the most striking of which is the dramatic contrapuntal choral writing that has made works such as his *Messiah* (1742) perennial favourites with British choral societies.

J. S. Bach

In his own lifetime, the works of Johann Sebastian Bach (1685–1750) were regarded as somewhat old-fashioned. Bach persisted with a contrapuntal style that gradually fell out of favour during the eighteenth century, raising every genre he worked in to a pitch of perfection that has never been surpassed. He wrote works of every kind – for solo instruments, especially the keyboard, for orchestra and for voices and orchestra – which have become cornerstones of the modern repertoire for those genres.

If Bach's music is built on a thorough mastery of counterpoint – in particular, the strictest contrapuntal form, known as fugue – a profound grasp of tonal harmony and, above all, an exquisite balance of these two elements, its overriding impulse was a religious one. One of the greatest musical dramatists, he never wrote an opera, regarding himself primarily as a servant of God. His mature years were spent as cantor of a church school in Leipzig, Germany, for which he wrote a staggering 250 church cantatas and two complete Passions, among numerous other works, in less than a decade. Bach carried the oratorio Passion tradition of the Lutheran Church, previously developed by Schütz and his contemporaries, to its loftiest peak. The *St. Matthew Passion* BWV 244 (1727) unites diverse musical elements – chorale, recitative, aria and passages for concertato instruments – in a work whose sublime grandeur is unmatched anywhere in Western music history.

Above

As the violin acquired musical respectability, the upper-middle classes became interested in amateur music-making and a market grew for tutors, or instruction books (the earliest-known of which dates from 1693).

Left

J. S. Bach wrote some of the world's most powerful vocal music, demonstrated best in his Passion settings. He used the range and colour of the human voice to great effect, generally using the bass for Christ's words, the tenor for the storyteller, alto for the Holy Spirit and the soprano for the voice of the soul.

ONE REASON WHY MUSIC OF THE CLASSICAL PERIOD LENDS ITS NAME TO WESTERN ART MUSIC IN GENERAL IS BECAUSE IT BEST EMBODIES THE VALUES ON WHICH THE MODERN WORLD WAS BUILT. THE IDEAS OF THE ENLIGHTENMENT MOVEMENT EMPHASIZED THE RIGHTS OF THE INDIVIDUAL, AND WOULD LEAD TO THE AMERICAN WAR OF INDEPENDENCE AND THE FRENCH REVOLUTION.

Classical

Above

Until Haydn's day, the string quartet had not been firmly established. Haydn was a master of the form, and raised the string quartet's formerly humble profile to new heights with exquisite ensemble writing and a wide range of musical expression.

ONE of the Enlightenment's principal thinkers, Jean-Jacques Rousseau was concerned with making music accessible a wider audience, and defined it as "the art of inventing tunes and accompanying them with suitable harmonies".

Haydn's Symphonies And String Quartets

Abandoning the contrapuntal complexities of the Baroque, this new style was fundamentally harmonic. With its complex but logical sets of key relationships to the main (tonic) key tonality allowed subtle or dramatic contrasts of mood through changes of key that could be carefully planned, often over long periods. The principal formal model was the Sonata-Allegro movement – the fast movement that opens most symphonies, sonatas, concertos and string quartets of the Classical era. The inherent tension and excitement in so many Sonata-Allegro movements derives from the relationship between the tonic key and the secondary, or dominant, key.

"MELODY IS THE ESSENCE OF MUSIC. I COMPARE A GOOD MELODIST TO A FINE RACER, AND COUNTERPOINTS TO HACK POST-HORSES."

Wolfgang Amadeus Mozart

Most sonata movements describe a journey away from the tonic to the dominant key and beyond, before returning again to the tonic key.

The new style brought with it new genres of instrumental music: one chamber, the other orchestral. Both the symphony and the string quartet owe their development at the end of the eighteenth century to Joseph Haydn (1732–1809), the first in a line of great Viennese

composers who would dominate Western music until the end of the nineteenth century. Haydn established the four movements that remained the standard pattern for the symphony and string quartet until well into the twentieth century.

In successive series of symphonies and quartets, Haydn extended the logic of key relationships within and between movements. In the symphonies, he defined new roles for wind instruments within the orchestra and transformed the genre

LEADING EXPONENTS

C. P. E. Bach

J. C. Bach

Christoph Willibald Gluck

Joseph Haydn

Antonio Salieri

Wolfgang Amadeus Mozart

Muzio Clementi

Jan Ladislav Dussek

Ludwig van Beethoven

Johann Nepomuk Hummel

CLASSICAL

Classical compositions are charcterized by a prominent melody and harmonic accompaniment, and would often have been played out by a string quartet. (This example shows a simplified melody for the piano.)

from the light, crowd-pleasing form he had inherited into what, in the nineteenth century, became the medium of choice for a composer's serious musical thoughts. His last 12 symphonies, written in the early 1790s for subscription concerts in London and collectively known as the *London Symphonies*, are his finest achievements in this genre. On the other hand, his string quartets are the medium in which Haydn's personality is perhaps most apparent. The regular phrasing and recognizable musical sentences of the archetypal Classical work are disrupted in these pieces by a charming wit – one that is never gratuitous, but the result of the music's inner logic. In an age that placed great store in the art of conversation, Haydn also increased a sense of equality among the four instruments. In the best of these works, such as Quartets nos. 75-80 Opus 76, a new application of the art of counterpoint enables a dialogue of musical ideas to pass back and forth between the four players.

Mozart's Operas And Piano Concertos

Although his achievements in the realms of symphony and string quartet bear comparison with the works of any composer, Wolfgang Amadeus Mozart (1756–91) was primarily a vocal composer, and a melodist of seemingly inexhaustible facility. Famous across Europe as a child prodigy, he was already an experienced stage composer by the mid-1780s, when he wrote his greatest operas. In works such as *Le nozze di Figaro* ('The Marriage of Figaro') K.492 (1786) and *Don Giovanni* K.527 (1787), Mozart imparted to Italian *opera buffa*, or comic opera, a depth and sensitivity of musical characterization that applied to all social classes. For this reason, aside from the intrinsic quality of the music, many regard him as the finest of opera composers.

Mozart's sense of individuality was, no doubt, a by-product of his genius and the spirit of the age, and it prompted him to favour the life of a freelance musician. In Vienna during the early 1780s, he was in great demand as a composer and performer for the middle-class public, which had become the main arbiter of taste. The pianoforte was a new keyboard instrument, louder and more percussive than either the harpsichord or clavichord it had quickly replaced. Mozart wrote his mature piano concertos during his first years in Vienna, more or less inventing the genre. Combining

the *ritornello* practice of the Baroque concerto with the dynamism inherent in the new sonata principle, these three-movement works, in which soloist and orchestra play equal roles, are conceived on the scale of a symphony. For the grandeur of its opening movement and the daring variation-form finale, his Piano Concerto No. 24 in C minor K.491 (1786), is among his finest achievements.

Beethoven The Revolutionary

In a creative life spanning only three decades, Ludwig van Beethoven (1770–1827) transformed almost every genre he worked in – symphony, string quartet, piano concerto, solo piano sonata – beyond the recognition of his contemporaries. Beethoven was an admirer of Napoleon Bonaparte, the original dedicatee of his magnificent Symphony No. 3 in E flat Opus 55, known as the 'Eroica', and a conscious musical revolutionary whose most radical innovations were not properly understood even 100 years after his death.

He turned the essentially light-hearted solo piano sonata (as developed by Haydn and Mozart) into a genre of often ferocious seriousness. Beethoven's last five sonatas belong to his "late period", when the experiments with form which had shocked his audiences hitherto ventured into territory which still has the power to disturb. His Sonata in B flat Opus 106, the 'Hammerklavier', is in four movements as opposed to the conventional three, and it ends with a three-part fugue that was considered unplayable when it was written. One of the shorter items in conventional sonatas, the slow movement lasts almost 25 minutes in performance, almost half the entire length of the piece, achieving an intense stillness that is both beautiful and terrifying. The sonata assumes the monumental proportions of a symphony, making unprecedented demands on the performer and taking the listener on an exhausting "journey of the soul" – repeated in Beethoven's late works.

BEETHOVEN'S SHADOW LOOMS LARGE OVER THE EARLY ROMANTIC PERIOD. MANY OF THE AGE'S MOST REMARKABLE COMPOSERS – SCHUBERT, BERLIOZ, WAGNER, BRAHMS – REVERED HIM ABOVE ALL. HE HAD STRETCHED THE LOGIC OF TONAL HARMONY, WEAKENING ITS TONIC-DOMINANT FOUNDATIONS. IN THE PROCESS, THE DRAMATURGY OF THE CLASSICAL SONATA HAD BEEN ALTERED.

Early Romantic

Above

As well as writing some of the world's supreme melodies, Schubert is equally revered for his mastery of large-scale structures and his innovative approach to harmony.

Schubert's Lieder

THE Romantic imagination was more confessional than any previous artistic mindset. The extended tonality and proliferation of new forms suited the exploration of new states of feeling. One of the paradoxes of the age was the public celebrity now afforded to composers whose minds were often withdrawn into private imaginative worlds. Some of the most characteristic public statements of the Early Romantic period were in the realms of tragic opera and the increasingly virtuosic solo concerto, both highly individualistic styles.

Above all, the Romantic period was a literary age. Its most distinctive genre in the field of chamber music was the song with piano accompaniment. In different forms, the German Lied had existed since the Renaissance, but as an intimate medium for solo voice and piano it dated back to the mid-eighteenth century. The great Viennese composers of the Classical period had all contributed to the genre, but it was another Viennese, Franz Schubert (1797–1828), who, with Robert Schumann (1810–56) in the 1840s, raised the Lied's profile so that it ranked alongside the established chamber forms of sonata and string quartet.

Schubert was the first of the Early Romantic composers, though his music still bears certain hallmarks of the late Classical period in which he lived.

In his short life, which ended only a year after Beethoven's, Schubert wrote an astonishing amount of music, including

more than 600 Lieder. He set texts by a wide range of German Romantic poets, including Goethe and Heine, but his two great song cycles, *Die Schöne Müllerin* (1823) and *Winterreise* (1827), use poems by the lesser-known Wilhelm Müller. Schubert's gift for melody and constantly surprising harmonic sense pervade all his music, but perhaps his greatest legacy to the Lied was to make the piano accompaniment an active part of the song, further dramatizing the poetry through the allusive use of musical imagery. In these two cycles, there are many examples of this practice, a technique that became crucial to much of the music composed in the Early Romantic period.

> "MUSIC…PRESENTS AT ONE AND THE SAME TIME THE INTENSITY AND EXPRESSION OF FEELING; IT IS THE EMBODIED AND INTELLIGIBLE ESSENCE OF FEELING."
>
> *Franz Liszt*

LEADING EXPONENTS

Franz Schubert
Robert Schumann
Frédéric Chopin
Felix Mendelssohn
Hector Berlioz
Franz Liszt
Richard Wagner
Giuseppe Verdi
Anton Bruckner
Johannes Brahms
Pyotr Ilyich Tchaikovsky
Antonin Dvořák
Modest Mussorgsky

EARLY ROMANTIC

Early Romantic music mesmerizes the listener with unbroken rhythmic patterns, as in this inner figure from a piano sonata.

(Left hand piano)

Chopin's Piano Music

If the piano virtuoso is the stereotypical Romantic musician, the most characteristic genre of piano music is the piano miniature or character piece. Along with the Lied, these pieces, also known as intermezzo, ballade, nocturne, prélude, étude – saw the greatest range of innovation in nineteenth-century chamber music. The standard of piano manufacture improved a great deal during the Early Romantic era, affording the pianist a wider range of dynamics and subtleties of tone, and the composer more possibilities for poetic expression. Frédéric Chopin (1810–49), himself a celebrated virtuoso, stands out among nineteenth-century composers in having written almost exclusively for the piano. He was also unusual for the period in that he wrote works with no apparent poetic programme. His many works in this genre include two books of études, Opus 10 and Opus 25. Originally, the étude was a study written to test an aspect of a player's technique. In these two cycles – which are among the most idiomatic works written for the instrument – Chopin explores every conceivable facet of the piano technique of his day in compositions of exquisite beauty and stunning virtuosity, judged for musical effect.

Berlioz's Orchestral Music

The technical improvements enjoyed by the piano applied to almost every instrument, leading to a greater standard of orchestral playing as well as a wider palette of sounds and available sound combinations. Symphonies were written in great numbers: in Germany by Schumann and Felix Mendelssohn (1809–47); in Vienna by Anton Bruckner (1824–96) and Johannes Brahms (1833–97); in Russia by Pyotr Ilyich Tchaikovsky (1840–1893); and in Czechoslovakia by Antonín Dvořák (1841–1904). Perhaps the most characteristic symphonic form of this period, however, was the symphonic poem, a term invented by Franz Liszt (1811–86) to denote a loosely structured orchestral work based on subjects from literature, history or mythology. Even some so-called symphonies could only casually wear the name.

Among these, the works of Hector Berlioz (1803–69) made extraordinary use of all the instruments of the orchestra, in works such as the *Symphonie fantastique* Opus 14 (1830), which follows a poetic and imaginatively autobiographical programme, and the "dramatic symphony" *Roméo et Juliette* Opus 17 (1839), which lasts nearly an hour and a half in performance. Structured in seven "tableaux", it features three soloists, a chorus and a very large orchestra that includes Berlioz's characteristically expanded brass section. The famous 'Queen Mab' scherzo from this movement is founded on a ghostly orchestral texture in the string section, anticipating twentieth-century orchestral techniques.

Verdi's Operas And Richard Wagner's Music Dramas

Opera achieved a dramatic apotheosis in the second half of the nineteenth century: in France with the works of Berlioz; in Russia with operas by members of "the mighty handful" group of composers, particularly those by Modest Mussorgsky (1839–81); and in Italy with those of Giuseppe Verdi (1813–1901).

Verdi's music is rooted in the long tradition of Italian opera that had begun with Monteverdi, and in the early nineteenth century included the works of Gioacchino Rossini (1792–1868), Gaetano Donizetti (1797–1848) and Vincenzo Bellini (1801–35). Italian opera in the Early Romantic era was a popular art form, and innovations in Verdi's music were introduced only gradually over the course of his 60-year career. Any new developments deepened the portrayal of human dramas that was central to Verdi's view of his art: *Falstaff* (1892), his last opera, shows a more subtle depiction of his characters than *Rigoletto* (1851), an opera from the middle of his career, for example.

The radical transformation of opera, and the entire language of Western music, was left to the German composer Richard Wagner (1813–83). Wagner wrote his own libretti and coined the term *Gesamtkunstwerk* ("the total artwork unifying all the elements comprised in music theatre"). In this vein, he referred to his own mature operas as "music dramas". Works such as the epic *Der Ring des Nibelungen* ('The Ring Cycle') (1853–74), a cycle of four long music dramas composed over a 20-year period, forged a new relationship between singers and orchestra.

Wagner was more interested in his characters' states of mind than in providing his singers with memorable tunes, and he gradually dispensed with the operatic convention of separating the parts of an act into distinct musical numbers in which the orchestra serves as accompaniment to the singer's aria, a pattern typical of nineteenth-century Italian opera from Rossini right through to Verdi's later works. In its place Wagner adopted long skeins of semi-declamatory melody endlessly reshaping itself to the characters' shifting emotions. Wagner's music dramas also use the orchestra symphonically, ceaselessly recombining, or reharmonizing, the web of melodic fragments, or leitmotifs, associated with particular characters or elements in the drama.

Wagner's greatest legacy, however, was in what he undid. The radical chromatic harmony of *Tristan und Isolde* (1859) superbly reflects the volatility of the characters' inner lives. At the same time, it weakened the bonds of tonality to the point where, referring to this work, later generations of composers would regard the harmonic system that underpinned Western music for hundreds of years as moribund.

Above

Richard Wagner's Der Ring des Nibelungen *('The Ring') is a great parable of human existence, spread over four evenings, and involves a vast orchestra, taxing vocal parts and incredible special effects, including rivers, a dragon and horses.*

Far Left

'Swan Lake' by Tchaikovsky has proved to be his most popular and enduring work, however it was not well received at its first performance in 1877. The choreography was inept, costumes and sets were a mish-mash, and the orchestra played badly.

Late Romantic

COMPOSERS AT THE END OF THE NINETEENTH CENTURY WERE AWESTRUCK BY THE MUSIC DRAMAS OF RICHARD WAGNER. HIS COLOSSAL ACHIEVEMENTS COULD NOT BE FOLLOWED, AND YET THE CHALLENGE HIS MUSIC LAID DOWN, PARTICULARLY IN THE REALMS OF HARMONY, HAD TO BE RECKONED WITH – EITHER DEVELOPED OR REJECTED – BY ANY EUROPEAN COMPOSER OF THE NEXT GENERATION.

Above

It was to be at least 50 years after his death that Mahler's symphonies were to be fully appreciated. They were orchestrated on a grand scale with richness and refinement, and were perfectly realized in the hands of conductors such as Herbert von Karajan.

MUSIC was more international than ever. By the end of the nineteenth century, Russia developed a distinctive tradition and, across the continent, smaller, emerging nations such as Norway, Denmark, Finland and Czechoslovakia, together with a resurgent Great Britain, added composers of some stature to the French, Italian and German/Viennese traditions.

The Great Conductors

To the great virtuoso in the Late Romantic period we can add a new kind of musical star. Many of the world's great orchestras were founded in the late-nineteenth and early twentieth centuries, and along with them came the great conductors – the "maestros", who could draw crowds more easily than the composers whose music they performed. Above all, the Late Romantic period was an age of orchestral music in which, as a matter of course, composers wrote scores requiring more than 100 players, and often hundreds of choral singers. The common musical language ripened, to the point where the key of a work was either in flux or barely recognizable.

This inflation of musical forces was played out against the political backdrop of imperial land grabbing in Africa, as well as the tense stand off between the political powers that led to the First World War. But even when the war had ended,

> "THE SYMPHONY MUST BE LIKE THE WORLD. IT MUST EMBRACE EVERYTHING."
>
> *Gustav Mahler*

and the radical innovations of twentieth-century music made the post-Wagnerian idiom seem irrelevant, many composers, like old soldiers still proudly wearing their medals, persisted with a Late Romantic style. In many ways, it had become the swan song for an era of European civilization.

Richard Strauss

Internationally fêted as both a conductor and composer from the late-1880s onwards, Richard Strauss (1864–1949) was the central figure in German music after Wagner. His musical language is founded on Wagner's chromaticism, but his sense of structure drew more on traditional models. In a series of symphonic poems written before 1900, he developed an orchestral virtuosity and a deliberately emotional musical rhetoric, illustrating the diverse programmes that lay behind these pieces. The most mercurial of these works was *Till Eulenspiegels lustige Streiche* (1895), an exuberant, orchestral showpiece that remains a favourite with concert audiences.

After 1900, Strauss increasingly turned to opera. In first *Salome* (1905), then *Elektra* (1909), he treated melodramatic subjects with a histrionic musical language that verged on the atonal. These works of musical expressionism are contemporaneous with the radical, atonal experiments of Arnold Schoenberg (1874–1951), but in his next opera, *Der Rosenkavalier* (1911), and in his music of the following 37 years, Strauss retreated from the precipice into an intentionally old-fashioned, nostalgic-sounding musical idiom. And yet, almost certainly as a result of this, *Der Rosenkavalier*, which sets its quasi-Mozartian story in the Hapsburg Vienna of the 1740s, contains some of the most rapturous music ever written.

LEADING EXPONENTS

Nikolai Rimsky-
   Korsakov

Gabriel Fauré

Antonín Dvořák

Edward Elgar

Giacomo Puccini

Gustav Mahler

Hugo Wolf

Richard Strauss

Jean Sibelius

Carl Nielsen

Leos Janáček

Alexander Skryabin

Sergei Rachmaninov

LATE ROMANTIC

Late Romantic compositions are defined by dramatic dynamics and extreme harmonies that sound as though they conflict, represented here as alternating chords.

As Mahler's personal aesthetic was world-embracing, his symphonies, many of which are long enough to occupy an entire concert programme, make melancholic references to funeral marches, folk dances and the environmental sounds of his childhood. Mahler wrote almost nothing but masterpieces, but perhaps his most profound statement is the Symphony No. 9 in D Major (1910). The composer Alban Berg (1885–1935), another Viennese composer of the next, radical generation, whose music is strongly foreshadowed in Mahler's late work, described this symphony's funereal first movement as "permeated by premonitions of death". This morbid foreboding in the midst of the most outwardly joyous, life-affirming music is a central contradiction in Mahler's symphonies. Like Beethoven's, his works are deeply personal statements, charting his spiritual journey. The tendency towards harmonic chaos, in this and other late works, hints at a threefold mortality: Mahler's own, that of the common musical language of Europe, and, because of war, the common European culture of which the Viennese musical tradition had been a pillar.

If Mahler's approach to the symphony was compendious, his Finnish contemporary, Jean Sibelius (1865–1957), tended towards terse concentration and a classical balance. He achieved this by means of a smaller orchestra, a simpler harmonic language, and the clear formal models against which he worked. Sibelius admired Beethoven for his structural ingenuity, and his own symphonies, despite being quite harmonically conservative for the period, are so formally surprising that they continue to exert a strong influence on contemporary composers.

His approach to each work was unique, but he seems to have come closest to his own ideal in the Symphony No. 7 in C, Opus 105 (1924) – his last, because he wrote nothing of any significance after 1926. They are cast in a single movement, but it is possible to make out the usual four, held together in a work of compelling grandeur and characteristic simplicity of manner.

The Late Romantic Symphony

Beethoven's achievements continued to haunt composers throughout the Romantic era. Johannes Brahms (1833–96) did not compose his first symphony until he was in his forties, and completed only four. Following the example of Brahms and, in particular, Bruckner, Gustav Mahler (1860–1911) became the last great exponent of the Viennese symphonic tradition that stretched back as far as Haydn, and his awareness of this is central to his music.

Like Strauss, Mahler was a renowned orchestral conductor; so it is, perhaps, no surprise that his musical output is dominated by nine completed symphonies and five orchestral song cycles, a genre he played a large part in creating. These works employ a typically large Late Romantic orchestra, though the instrumentation is magnificently varied – from massive statements for full orchestra to delicate chamber ensembles.

Far Left

Until the early nineteenth century, the oboe had only two keys. In the 1830s the modern oboe was developed by French instrument-maker Guillaume Tribert. Its sound was more refined than its predecessor, and its keys worked differently.

Left

Catherine Malfitano plays Salome in a 1997 production of Strauss's violent, erotic masterpiece at London's Royal Opera House.

Below

Brahms's music was strongly influenced by the Classical style; he revived and enlarged the principles laid down by Mozart, Beethoven and Haydn. It was seen by many as a reaction to the "new music" of the Romantic era.

Twentieth Century

BY THE TURN OF THE TWENTIETH CENTURY, WESTERN CLASSICAL MUSIC SEEMED TO HAVE REACHED A CRISIS IN LANGUAGE. TONALITY HAD BECOME ENFEEBLED BY ITS OWN PROGRESSIVE TENDENCY, VIA INCREASING CHROMATICISM, TOWARD SUBTLER AND MORE COMPLEX FORMS OF EXPRESSION. EUROPEAN SOCIETY HAD BECOME SIMILARLY ENERVATED BY THE FAMILIAR COMFORTS OF A BOURGEOIS EXISTENCE.

Above

Arturo Toscanini conducted the New York Philharmonic in the 1920s and 1930s, and his artistic devotion, respect for the composer's intentions and the electricity of his performances made him one of the early twentieth century's great musical personalities.

IN many quarters across the Continent, before war was imminent, there was a sense that a cataclysm was needed in order for things to change.

The Loss Of A Common Language

In 1900, Sigmund Freud published *The Interpretation Of Dreams*, the book that ushered in his revolutionary psychiatric method of psychoanalysis. The subsequent awareness of the unconscious mind contradicted notions of the supremacy of the will that underpinned so much nineteenth-century thought – in particular, the philosophy of Friedrich Nietzsche – and made itself felt in much late-nineteenth-century music. The exhaustion of the tonal system, for example, forced composers to confront the loss of a common language. In the various solutions they found, we can now see that what had been lost was not just language, but whole realms of experience that several centuries of increasing civilization had either obscured or annulled.

> "BEAUTY IN MUSIC IS TOO OFTEN CONFUSED WITH SOMETHING THAT LETS THE EARS LIE BACK IN AN EASY CHAIR."
>
> *Charles Ives*

LEADING EXPONENTS

Claude Debussy

Charles Ives

Maurice Ravel

Béla Bartók

Igor Stravinsky

Arnold Schoenberg

Anton Webern

Alban Berg

Edgard Varèse

Aaron Copland

George Gershwin

Dmitri Shostakovich

Ralph Vaughan Williams

Michael Tippett

Benjamin Britten

Sound For Sounds' Sake

If the giddy expansion of tonality at the end of the nineteenth century held composers in a kind of spell, the first to break it was a Frenchman. Beginning with *Prélude à l'après-midi d'un faune* ('Prelude to an afternoon of the faun'), a brief orchestral work whose 1894 premiere caused a scandal, Claude Debussy (1862–1918) adopted a radical new approach to harmony. He freed chords from their place within a functional, tonal

hierarchy of keys, valuing them instead for their own intrinsic beauty or interest. In *La Cathédrale engloutie* ('The Sunken Cathedral'), a piece from the first book of *Préludes* (1910) for solo piano, a series of rising chords made up of fourths and fifths depicts a medieval cathedral rising from the waves in a passage appropriately suggestive of medieval *organum*. The chord sequence is twice repeated over a series of descending bass notes, but it leads nowhere, giving way to a passage of entirely new material in a completely unrelated key.

After the French Impressionist painters, Debussy's intention is to depict the phenomena or sensations of the physical world, using resources that have no meaning within the tonal system. To this end, he frequently employs modes such as the pentatonic scale, or even the tonally neutral whole-tone scale. In *Voiles* ('Veils'), for instance, from the same book of *Préludes*, a fragmentary, whole-tone melody is subtly suggestive of the sensual movements of an exotic dancer. Like so much of Debussy's music, the piece seems aimless because it has no aim: it exists for and in the moment.

TWENTIETH CENTURY

This melody, characterized by the pentatonic scale, is indicative of the simple and effective modes that are utilized to create vivid impressions of a subject.

Left hand piano

The Vitality Of Folk Music

In the late-nineteenth century, composers from countries on the musical periphery of Europe increasingly turned to their own native folk music, adjusted to fit the tonal system, to help them forge an idiom distinct from the prevailing styles of the musical superpowers. In the early twentieth century, composers such as Ralph Vaughan Williams (1872–1958), in England, and Leos Janácek (1854–1928), in a province of the latter-day Czech Republic, assiduously notated their own countries' folk songs in the field and incorporated them into their music.

Béla Bartók (1881–1945) went further, recording onto wax cylinders the songs of his native Hungary, as well as songs from regions such as Turkey and North Africa, before notating their rhythmic and melodic subtleties. Deeply immersed in folk idioms, Bartók found latent structural possibilities within these rhythmically irregular melodies, together with ways of combining them contrapuntally in classical forms.

His six String Quartets – the most substantial contribution to the genre since Beethoven's, and a huge influence on string quartet writing since the 1940s – chart the development of this remarkable composer. The first, completed in 1909, is a Late Romantic work; the third and fourth, from 1927 and 1928 respectively, depend on a dense, astringent harmony that veers toward atonality; the fifth (1934) and sixth (1939) are written in a more relaxed style. Many of these works feature a sonata-form first movement, adapted to Bartók's modal idiom. They are a vigorous demonstration of his attempts to unite the vitality of folk music with the enduring forms of Western art music.

Far Left

Claude Debussy was fascinated by the musical evocation of nature: the effects of light on water; a still, dark forest. This, as well as the evocative names he gave his music, caused him to be dubbed "Impressionist".

Below

Last Night of the Proms. This very British tradition began in 1895 with the first series of Promenade Concerts at the Queen's Hall, London. Now held at the Royal Albert Hall, the Proms continue to be an annual musical celebration.

The Second Viennese School

Few could have felt the crisis in musical language more keenly than Arnold Schoenberg (1874–1951). A Viennese who began composing with a ripe Late Romantic language, he was the first to give up the ghost of tonality in a series of atonal works – that is, music without a fixed harmonic system – written from 1909–13. The essential formlessness of atonality was well suited to portraying disturbed states of mind. Schoenberg's monodrama *Erwartung* ('Expectation') Opus 17 (1909), for soprano and orchestra, is a fine example, focused on a woman walking in the woods at night and looking for her lover. The text is written in an ungrammatical stream of consciousness, and the orchestra is consistently moulded to the woman's nightmarish declamatory monologue, in music that is still unsettling to listen to.

Paralyzed by the continuing crisis in musical language, Schoenberg wrote almost nothing between 1913 and 1921. He re-emerged with what he called the dodecaphonic, or 12-note, method. In the absence of any governing key, Schoenberg's method applies the 12 notes of the chromatic scale equally in note rows, or series, which function something like plain-chant does in medieval music. His most compelling application of this new principle, which would wield a huge influence over Western music after 1945, is perhaps his impressive, unfinished opera, *Moses und Aaron* (1932).

Schoenberg's pupils, Alban Berg (1885–1935) and Anton Webern (1883–1945), wrote music as enduring as their master's. The three of them comprise what has come to be known as the Second Viennese School. Probably one of the finest pieces of expressionist music theatre, Berg's atonal opera, *Wozzeck* (1922), is intriguingly

structured, using old-fashioned formal models stripped of their tonal implications. His elegiac Violin Concerto (1935), one of the most lyrical ever written, was composed using a 12-note row, allowing him to seamlessly incorporate a Bach chorale into the final movement. Berg's temperament was essentially Romantic, and his works frequently inhabit a hinterland between the new keyless music and the lost tonal world of his native Vienna.

Webern was the most reticent composer of the three. His output amounts to only around 30 short works, mostly Lieder or chamber pieces, none of which lasts more than 15 minutes in performance. In works such as the eerily sublime Symphony Opus 21 (1928), Webern organizes his 12-note material in two short movements. The first operates along sonata principles and features myriad use of canon, a contrapuntal technique he learned from studying Renaissance polyphonic music; the second is also in a traditional form, the theme and variations, as used by tonal composers such as Bach and Beethoven. Webern's rigorous application of the 12-note

method and his complete lack of Romantic rhetoric, which in the symphony manifests itself in a pointillistic approach to melody and orchestration, exerted a profound influence on Western composers after the Second World War.

Stravinsky And The Search For Ritual

Igor Stravinsky (1882–1971) is, perhaps, the name most synonymous with twentieth-century music. His ballet score *Le Sacre du printemps* ('The Rite Of Spring') caused a scandal at its premiere in 1913, and is the work in which he revolutionized rhythm. Fifty years later, in connection with another work, he wrote that "in the absence of harmonic modulation it [rhythm] must play a considerable part in the delineation of form". Stravinsky liberated rhythm from the strict measurement imposed on it by the bar line. In *Le Sacre*, the constant syncopations and changes of time signature disrupt the metrical pattern of the music, creating a new kind of musical tension. Nearly a century after it was first performed, it is still a work of astonishing primitive power, utterly suited to the depiction of an ancient pagan ritual. Scored for a huge Late Romantic orchestra, it appears, on the surface, to have little in common with the composer's later music.

After 1920, Stravinsky turned to the works of the tonal masters for inspiration, adopting forms such as sonata and symphony, though radically recasting them with his rhythmic invention in a skewed tonal language that altered with every piece. Scored for chorus and orchestra, the 'Psalms' Symphony (1930) is not so much a symphony in the conventional sense as a sacred oratorio of transcendent grandeur, almost unimaginable in the twentieth century. Following the death of Schoenberg, Stravinsky adopted the 12-note method in a series of mainly religious works. His last major composition, the *Requiem Canticles* (1966), which the composer referred to as a "pocket requiem", is structured in nine short movements of an austere beauty that is strangely reminiscent of medieval music. What links his later music with *Le Sacre du printemps*, regardless of the changes in musical language, is the composer's compelling, continual rediscovery of a fundamental human need for sacred ritual.

Charles Ives And The Lost World Of Childhood

Fifty years ago, the music of Charles Ives (1874–1954) was hardly known to all but the composer's intimate circle. Indeed, Ives died without hearing some of his major works performed, though he is regarded as the first great American classical composer. Ives studied music in the 1890s at Yale University but had no time for the straight music world, preferring to earn his living as a businessman and compose in his spare time. Born in Connecticut, he grew up in the shadow of the

Transcendentalist philosophers, the American Civil War and the outdoor music making of revivalist religious gatherings.

Ives' biggest influence, however, was a father unschooled in the European tradition and unashamed of musical experimentation without reference to the past. These forces come to bear upon his greatest works, among them the extraordinary Symphony No. 4, completed in 1916 but first performed 50 years later. In particular, the second and last movements layer popular songs, hymns and Civil War marching tunes one on top of the other, regardless of their differing tonalities; the cumulative effect is a world-affirming cacophony of remembered life. Sandwiched between them is a conventional fugue, which might sound bland in another context but is bizarrely appropriate here.

Ives' eclecticism and experimental techniques have been among the major influences on contemporary composers, but his purpose in writing such original music seems, at least in part, to have been a straightforward act of remembrance.

Above

Charles Ives' earliest and greatest musical influence was his father, George. A bandsman in the American Civil War, he encouraged young Ives to experiment with music, such as by playing a tune in one key and accompanying it in another.

THE CONTEMPORARY ERA CAN BE DATED BACK TO ANTON WEBERN'S DEATH IN
SEPTEMBER 1945. WEBERN'S INFLUENCE ON THE GENERATION OF POST-SECOND WORLD
WAR COMPOSERS MEANS THAT MUCH OF THE MUSIC FROM THE 1950S SOUNDS MORE
MODERN THAN MUSIC FROM THE LAST 20 YEARS.

Contemporary

Above
*Steve Reich's music is
characterized by phasing: a
number of instruments play
identical music starting one
after the other, creating an
echo effect, best evident in
Clapping from 1970.*

COMPOSERS such as Karlheinz Stockhausen
(b. 1928) and Pierre Boulez (b. 1925) extended the
12-note, or serial, principles of Webern to all the
elements of music: not only pitch, but duration (the
basic component of rhythm), timbre (instrumental
colour) and dynamics (loudness). The results of this
method, in works such as Stockhausen's *Gruppen*
(1957), scored for three spatially separated orchestras with their
own conductors, could be explosive, if seldom easy on the ear.

Postmodernism And Messiaen

The widespread influence of this method was short-lived, so
that by the mid-1960s a wide range of possible styles lay open
to composers. This eclecticism, the increasing influence of
non-Western music in particular, is the essential quality of
an artistic philosophy that has come to be known as post-
modernism. This phenomenon has led some commentators
to pronounce the Western tradition well and truly dead, while
in the minds of others, it is the path of renewal.

Olivier Messiaen
(1908–92) towers above the
contemporary era. In his
analysis classes at the Paris
Conservatoire in the late-
1940s, he introduced many
of the movers and shakers
of the next generation, among them Boulez and Stockhausen,
to the music of Stravinsky and the Second Viennese School.
His influence on music of the post-war period would be
profound had it stopped there. But by that time, Messiaen, a
devout Catholic, had evolved a unique compositional idiom to

communicate a powerful, personal vision of God. This was
sometimes apocalyptic, as in the *Quatuor pour la fin du temps*
('Quartet For The End Of Time') (1940), composed and first
performed in a Nazi prison camp, and sometimes erotic, as in
the joyous, 10-movement *Turangalîla-symphonie* (1948).

Conceived on a vast scale, many of his works take up an
entire concert programme. His musical language is founded on
a highly individual modal approach to harmony; a conception
of rhythm that owes more to the principles of Indian classical
music than to the West, and a melodic voice that owes almost
everything to his love of ornithology and a painstaking ear.
Over many decades, Messiaen accurately notated thousands of
bird songs, and reproduced these extremely complex melodies
verbatim in pieces from the 1950s onwards, often densely
layered on top of each other. In works such as the lustrous

> "THERE ARE A
> THOUSAND WAYS OF
> PROBING THE FUTURE."
> *Olivier Messiaen*

LEADING EXPONENTS
John Cage
Elliott Carter
Witold Lutoslawski
Karlheinz Stockhausen
Pierre Boulez
György Ligeti
Luciano Berio
Per Nørgård
Alfred Schnittke
Harrison Birtwistle
Peter Maxwell Davies
George Crumb
Steve Reich
Arvo Pärt
Olivier Messiaen

CONTEMPORARY
*Contemporary classical music
often incorporates naturalistic
sounds within the melodies,
which are accompanied by
word-painting. This example
includes birdsong, in which
three whistles are heard before
the bird flies off in the final bar.*

(Top B flat and E)

Flute

f

orchestral piece *Des canyons aux étoiles* ('From The Canyons To The Stars') (1974), the most striking element is Messiaen's sense of time, which owes more to a pervasive idea of eternity than the strictly measured periods of the Western world.

The Influence Of Asia

Messiaen's absorption of aspects of Indian music is just one instance of how Asian philosophy and music has changed Western musical practice since the 1960s. During the 1950s, alongside his concert music, Karlheinz Stockhausen began composing in the recording studio, directly onto tape or for live electronics with acoustic instruments. These experiences opened up a new world of sound, which, coupled with his tendency towards an Eastern-influenced mysticism not uncommon in the late-1960s, led him to write music that explored the essence of sounds. The extraordinary *Stimmung* ('Tuning') (1968) is "scored" for six amplified vocalists, each given one note to sing of a chord based on the B-flat overtone series. This intimate, meditative, often funny piece lasts for more than an hour and, in a good performance, has an expressive range that equals most conventional music, but in a more relaxed style.

Arnold Schoenberg regarded John Cage (1912–92) more "an inventor of genius" than a composer. His Sonatas and Interludes (1948) are written for prepared piano (a conventional piano whose strings have been threaded with small objects to alter the pitch and timbre of those notes). This exquisite music is as delicate as anything in the piano repertoire, but the sound is more like a Balinese gamelan orchestra than a Western instrument.

The influence of the East on Cage's music went further still. His conversion to Zen Buddhism led him to eventually abandon the Western idea of the composer as controller of every aspect of a composition. The groundbreaking *4'33"* (1952) instructs the player to sit or stand with their instrument for four and a half minutes without playing a note. The piece has achieved a certain infamy, but the point is a serious one for a Western audience that seldom has the time to notice the music all around them.

The Influence Of Africa

Via the blues and other black American styles, African music is the rhythmic ancestor of more or less all genres of contemporary pop music. Western classical composers have also absorbed the rhythmic vitality of, in particular, West African music. In the case of Steve Reich (b. 1936), the experience of Ghanaian drumming techniques led him to a style based on complex, repeated rhythmic patterns. The magnificent *Drumming* (1971), scored for various percussion instruments with male and female voices, creates a hypnotic momentum over the course

of almost an hour. It is a seminal work in the style that came to be known as minimalism, a term that embraces the music of other composers including Terry Riley (b. 1935) and Philip Glass (b. 1937), whose musical language is based on repetitive melodic or rhythmic elements. The discovery of African music led Hungarian composer György Ligeti (b. 1923), formerly Bartókian in manner, to take his work in new directions. *Désordre* ('Disorder') (1985), from his first book of études for solo piano, achieves a fascinating rhythmic complexity, based on West African polyrhythm.

The Dawn Of A New Millennium

For the generation born since the end of the Second World War, the challenge of building on a tradition that nowadays has so many roots will be a central part of any story that is told of classical music a thousand years from now. The vast array of voices on which to draw has resulted in there being an enormous range of styles among contemporary composers. In the UK the music of Harrison Birtwistle (b. 1934) unites lyrical beauty with a stark rhythmic energy, and Peter Maxwell Davies (b. 1934) has, throughout his career, made frequent, sometimes highly ironic, reference to music of the past. In the USA, Elliott Carter (b. 1908) is an unapologetic modernist still composing music of bracing vigour in his nineties, while the eclectic scores of George Crumb (b. 1929) seem to have absorbed the music of a vast number of cultures, uniting them in music of exquisite poetry that is possibly unmatched in recent times.

There are also composers from Europe, from China and Japan, from Australasia and elsewhere who have made a name for themselves in an increasingly international tradition. For the generation born since the end of the Second World War, the challenge of building on a tradition that nowadays has so many roots will be a central part of any story that is told of Classical music a thousand years from now.

Artists: Classical

Entries appear in the following order: name, music style, year(s) of popularity, type of artist, country of origin

Abel, Carl Friedrich, Classical, 1740s–1780s, Composer, German
Adam, Adolphe, Early Romantic, 1820s–1850s, Composer, French
Adams, John, Contemporary, 1970s–, Composer, American
Ades, Thomas, Contemporary, 1990s–, Composer, British
Agricola, Alexander, Renaissance, 1460s–1500s, Composer, Franco-Flemish
Alain, Jehan Arista, 20th Century, 1920s–1930s, Composer, French
Albéniz, Isaac, Late Romantic, 1880s-1900s, Artist; Composer, Spanish
Albinoni, Tomaso, Late Baroque, 1690s–1750s, Composer; Artist, Italian
Alfonso X, Medieval, 1240s–1280s, Composer, Spanish
Alfvén, Hugo, 20th Century, 1900s–1960s, Composer; Artist, Swedish
Alkan, Charles Henri Valentin, Late Romantic, 1830s–1880s, Artist; Composer, French
Allen, Thomas, Contemporary, 1960s–, Artist, British
Alwyn, William, 20th Century, 1920s–1980s, Composer, British
Anderson, Leroy, 20th Century, 1930s–1970s, Composer, American
Andriessen, Louis, Contemporary, 1950s–, Composer, Dutch
Animuccia, Giovanni, Renaissance, 1520s–1570s, Composer, Italian
Antheil, George, 20th Century, 1920s–1950s, Composer; Artist, American
Arcadelt, Jacques, Renaissance, 1530s–1560s, Composer, French
Arensky, Anton Stepanovich, Late Romantic, 1880s–1900s, Composer; Artist, Russian
Argento, Dominick, Contemporary, 1950s–, Composer, American
Arne, Thomas Augustine, Classical, 1730s–1770s, Composer, British
Arnold, Malcolm, 20th Century, 1950s–present, Composer, British
Arrau, Claudio, 20th Century, 1920s–1970s, Artist, Chilean
Arriaga y Balzola, Juan Crisostomo, Classical, 1820s, Composer, Spanish
Ashkenazy, Vladimir, Contemporary, 1950s–, Artist, Russian
Auber, Daniel-François-Esprit, Early Romantic, 1800s–1870s, Composer, French
Auric, Georges, 20th Century, 1920s–1980s, Composer, French
Avison, Charles, Late Baroque, 1720s–1770s, Composer, British
Babbitt, Milton, 20th Century, 1930s–1970s, Composer, American
Bacewicz, Graznya, 20th Century, 1930s–1960s, Composer, Polish
Bach, Carl Philipp Emanuel, Classical, 1730s–1780s, Composer, German
Bach, Johann Christian, Classical, 1760s–1780s, Composer, German
Bach, Johann Christoph Friedrich, Classical, 1950s–1790s, Composer, German
Bach, Johann Sebastian, Late Baroque, 1700s–1750s, Composer; Artist, German
Bach, Wilhelm Friedemann, Classical, 1730s–1780s, Composer, German
Baker, Janet, Contemporary, 1950s–, Artist, British
Balakirev, Mily Alexeyevich, Late Romantic, 1850s–1910s, Composer, Russian
Balfe, Michael, Early Romantic, 1820s–1870s, Composer, Irish
Banchieri, Adriano, Renaissance, 1580s–1630s, Composer, Italian
Barber, Samuel, 20th Century, 1930s–1980s, Composer, American
Barbirolli, John, 20th Century, 1920s–1960s, Artist, British
Barraqué, Jean, 20th Century, 1950s–1970s, Composer, French
Bartók, Béla, 20th Century, 1900s–1940s, Composer; Artist, Hungarian
Bartoli, Cecilia, Contemporary, 1980s, Artist, Italian
Bashmet, Yuri, Contemporary, 1970s–, Artist, Russian
Bax, Arnold, 20th Century, 1900s–1950s, Composer, British
Beach, Amy, Late Romantic, 1880s–1940s, Composer, American
Beethoven, Ludwig van, Classical, 1780s–1820s, Composer; Artist, Austrian
Bellini, Vincenzo, Early Romantic, 1820s–1830s, Composer, Italian
Benda, Franz, Classical, 1730s–1780s, Composer, Czech
Benda, Georg, Classical, 1740s–1790s, Composer, Bohemian
Benjamin, George, Contemporary, 1980s–, Composer, British
Bennett, William Sterndale, Late Romantic, 1830s–1870s, Composer, British
Berg, Alban, 20th Century, 1900s–1930s, Composer, Austrian
Berganza, Teresa, Contemporary, 1950s, Artist, Spanish
Bergonzi, Carlo, 20th Century, 1940s–1980s, Artist, Italian
Berio, Lucio, 20th Century, 1950s–1990s, Composer, Italian
Berkeley, Lennox, 20th Century, 1920s–1980s, Composer, British
Berlin, Irving, 20th Century, 1910s–1980s, Composer, American
Berlioz, Louis-Hector, Early Romantic, 1820s–1860s, Composer, French
Bernstein, Leonard, 20th Century, 1940s–1990s, Composer, American
Berwald, Franz, Early Romantic, 1810s–1860s, Composer, Swedish
Biber, Heinrich von, Early Baroque, 1660s–1700s, Composer; Artist, German
Biggs, E. Power, 20th Century, 1930s–1970s, Artist, American
Binchois, Gilles, Medieval, 1420s–1460s, Composer, Franco-Flemish
Bingen, Hildegard von, Medieval, 1110s–1170s, Composer, German
Birtwistle, Harrison, Contemporary, 1960s–, Composer, British
Bizet, Georges, Late Romantic, 1850s–1870s, Composer, French
Björling, Jussi, 20th Century, 1930s–1960s, Artist, Swedish
Blades, James, 20th Century, 1940s–1980s, Artist, British
Bliss, Arthur Drummond, 20th Century, 1910s–1970s, Composer, British
Blitzstein, Marc, 20th Century, 1930s–1960s, Composer, American
Bloch, Ernest, 20th Century, 1900–1950s, Composer, Swiss-American
Blow, John, Early Baroque, 1670s–1700s, Composer, British
Boccherini, Luigi, Classical, 1760s–1800s, Composer, Italian
Böhm, Georg, Early Baroque, 1680s–1730s, Composer, German
Boieldieu, François-Adrien, Early Romantic, 1790s–1830s, Composer, French
Boito, Arrigo, Late Romantic, 1860s–1920s, Composer, Italian
Bolcom, William, Contemporary, 1960s–, Composer, American
Bologna, Jacopo da, Medieval, 1360s–1380s, Composer, Italian
Bononcini, Giovanni, Late Baroque, 1690s–1740s, Composer; Artist, Italian
Borodin, Alexander, Late Romantic, 1860s–1880s, Composer, Russian
Boulanger, Lili, 20th Century, 1910s, Composer, French
Boulez, Pierre, 20th Century, 1950s–1990s, Composer, French
Bordoni, Faustina, Early Baroque, 1720s–1780s, Artist, Italian
Bowman, James, Contemporary, 1960s–, Artist, British
Boyce, William, Classical, 1740s–1770s, Composer, British
Brahms, Johannes, Late Romantic, 1850s–1890s, Composer, German
Brain, Dennis, 20th Century, 1940s–1950s, Artist, British
Bream, Julian, Contemporary, 1950s–, Artist, British
Brendel, Alfred, Contemporary, 1950s–, Artist, Austrian
Brian, Havergal, 20th Century, 1900s–1970s, Composer, British
Bridge, Frank, 20th Century, 1900s–1940s, Composer, British
Britten, Benjamin, 20th Century, 1930s–1970s, Composer, British
Brouwer, Leo, Contemporary, 1960s–, Composer; Artist, Cuban
Brown, Earle, 20th Century, 1950s–2000s, Composer; Artist, American
Bruch, Max, Late Romantic, 1860s–1920s, Composer, German
Bruckner, Anton, Late Romantic, 1840s–1890s, Composer, Austrian
Bruhns, Nicolaus, Early Baroque, 1680s–1690s, Composer, German
Bull, John, Renaissance, 1580s–1620s, Composer; Artist, British
Bull, Ole, Early Romantic, 1830s–1880s, Artist; Composer, Norwegian
Bülow, Hans von, Late Romantic, 1850s–1890s, Composer, German
Busnoys, Antoine, Medieval, 1450s–1490s, Composer, French
Busoni, Ferrucio, 20th Century, 1900s–1920s, Composer, Italian-German
Butterworth, George, 20th Century, 1900s–1910s, Composer, British
Buxtehude, Dietrich, Early Baroque, 1650s–1700s, Composer, German
Byrd, William, Renaissance, 1570s–1620s, Composer, British
Caballé, Montserrat, Contemporary, 1950s–, Artist, Spanish
Cabanilles, Juan Bautista, Early Baroque, 1660s–1710s, Composer, Spanish
Cabezón, Antonio de, Renaissance, 1530s–1560s, Artist; Composer, Spanish
Caccini, Giulio, Early Baroque, 1560s–1610s, Composer; Artist, Italian
Cage, John, 20th Century, 1930s–1990s, Composer, American
Caldara, Antonio, Late Baroque, 1690s–1730s, Composer, Italian
Callas, Maria, 20th Century, 1940s–1970s, Artist, American
Cambini, Giuseppe Maria, Classical, 1760s–1820s, Composer, Italian
Campion, Thomas, Renaissance, 1590s–1620s, Composer, British
Campra, André, Late Baroque, 1680s–1740s, Composer, French
Carissimi, Giacomo, Early Baroque, 1620s–1670s, Composer, Italian
Carpenter, John Alden, 20th Century, 1900s–1950s, Composer, American
Carreras, José, Contemporary, 1970s–, Artist, Spanish
Carter, Elliot, 20th Century, 1930s–1980s, Composer, American
Carulli, Ferdinando, Classical, 1790s–1840s, Composer, Italian
Caruso, Enrico, 20th Century, 1900s–1920s, Artist, Italian
Carver, Robert, Renaissance, 1510s–1540s, Composer, Scottish
Casals, Pablo, 20th Century, 1900s–1950s, Artist, Spanish
Casella, Alfredo, 20th Century, 1900s–1940s, Composer; Artist, Italian
Castelnuovo-Tedesco, Mario, 20th Century, 1910s–1960s, Composer; Artist, American-Italian
Casulana, Maddalena, Renaissance, 1560s–1590s, Artist; Composer, Italian
Catalani, Alfredo, Late Romantic, 1870s–1890s, Composer, Italian
Cavalieri, Emilio de', Early Baroque, 1570s–1600s, Composer, Italian
Cavalli, Francesco, Early Baroque, 1620s–1670s, Composer; Artist, Italian
Certon, Pierre, Renaissance, 1520s–1570s, Composer, French
Cesti, Antonio, Early Baroque, 1640s–1660s, Composer, Italian
Chabrier, Emmanuel, Late Romantic, 1860s–1890s, Composer, French
Chadwick, George, Late Romantic, 1870s–1930s, Composer, American
Chambonnières, Jacques Champion, Early Baroque, 1620s–1670s, Composer, French
Chaminade, Cécile, Late Romantic, 1870s–1940s, Composer, French
Charpentier, Gustav, 20th Century, 1890s–1950s, Composer, French
Charpentier, Marc-Antoine, Early Baroque, 1660s–1700s, Composer, French
Chausson, Ernest, Late Romantic, 1880s–1890s, Composer, French
Chávez, Carlos, 20th Century, 1930s–1970s, Composer, Mexican
Cherubini, Luigi, Early Romantic, 1780s–1840s, Composer, Italian
Chopin, Frédéric, Early Romantic, 1830s–1840s, Composer; Artist, Polish
Christof, Boris, 20th Century, 1940s–1980s, Artist, Bulgarian
Ciconia, Johannes, Medieval, 1390s–1410s, Composer, Franco-Flemish
Cilèa, Francesco, 20th Century, 1890s–1950s, Composer, Italian
Cimarosa, Domenico, Classical, 1770s–1800s, Composer, Italian
Clarke, Jeremiah, Late Baroque, 1690s–1700s, Composer, British
Clemens non Papa, Renaissance, 1530s–1550s, Composer, Franco-Flemish
Clementi, Muzio, Classical, 1770s–1830s, Artist; Composer, Italian
Clérambault, Louis-Nicolas, Late Baroque, 1690s–1740s, Composer, French
Codax, Martin, Medieval, 1230s, Composer, Portuguese
Coin, Christophe, Contemporary, 1970s–, Artist, French
Copland, Aaron, 20th Century, 1920s–1990s, Composer, American
Coprario, Giovanni, Early Baroque, 1590s–1620s, Composer, British
Corelli, Arcangelo, Early Baroque, 1670s–1710s, Composer; Artist, Italian
Corigliano, John, Contemporary, 1960s–, Composer, American
Cornelius, Peter, Late Romantic, 1850s–1870s, Composer, German
Cornysh, William, Renaissance, 1490s–1520s, Composer, British
Cortot, Alfred, 20th Century, 1900s–1950s, Artist, French
Couperin, François, Late Baroque, 1680s–1730s, Composer, French
Couperin, Louis, Early Baroque, 1650s–1660s, Composer, French
Cowell, Henry, 20th Century, 1930s–1960s, Composer, American
Crawford Seeger, Ruth, 20th Century, 1920s–1950s, Composer, American
Crecquillon, Thomas, Renaissance, 1500s–1550s, Composer, French
Creston, Paul, 20th Century, 1920s–1980s, Composer, American
Crumb, George, 20th Century, 1950s–1990s, Composer, American
Cui, César, Late Romantic, 1850s–1910s, Composer, Russian
Curzon, Clifford, 20th Century, 1930s–1970s, Artist, British
Czerny, Carl, Early Romantic, 1810s–1850s, Composer; Artist, Austrian
D'Albert, Eugene, Late Romantic, 1880s–1930s, Artist; Composer, German
D'Indy, Vincent, Late Romantic, 1870s–1930s, Composer, French
Da Ponte, Lorenzo, Classical, 1770s–1830s, Librettist, Italian
Dallapiccola, Luigi, 20th Century, 1930s–1970s, Composer, Italian
Danzi, Franz, Early Romantic, 1780s–1820s, Composer, German
Dargomïzhsky, Alexander, Late Romantic, 1830s–1860s, Composer, Russian
Davidovsky, Mario, Contemporary, 1950s–, Composer, Argentinean
Davies, Peter Maxwell, Contemporary, 1960s–, Composer, British
Debussy, Claude, 20th Century, 1880s–1910s, Composer, French
Delibes, Léo, Late Romantic, 1860s–1890s, Composer, French
Delius, Frederick, 20th Century, 1890s–1930s, Composer, British
Deller, Alfred, 20th Century, 1930s–1960s, Artist, British
Denisov, Edison, 20th Century, 1940s–1990s, Composer, Russian
Diamond, Dave, 20th Century, 1930s–1980s, Composer, American
Dibdin, Charles, Classical, 1770s–1810s, Composer, British
Distler, Hugo, 20th Century, 1920s–1940s, Composer; Songwriter, German
Dittersdorf, Carl Ditters von, Classical, 1750s–1790s, Composer, Austrian
Dohnányi, Ernö, 20th Century, 1900s–1960s, Composer, Hungarian
Domingo, Plácido, Contemporary, 1960s–, Artist, Spanish
Donizetti, Gaetano, Early Romantic, 1810s–1840s, Composer, Italian
Dowland, John, Renaissance, 1580s–1620s, Composer; Artist, British
Druckman, Jacob, 20th Century, 1940s–1990s, Composer, American
Dufay, Guillaume, Medieval, 1410s–1470s, Composer, French
Du Pré, Jacqueline, 20th Century, 1960s–1980s, Artist, British
Dukas, Paul, 20th Century, 1890s–1910s, Composer, French
Dun, Tan, Contemporary, 1980s–, Composer; Producer, Chinese
Dunstaple, John, Medieval, 1410s–1450s, Composer, British
Duparc, Henri, Late Romantic, 1860s–1880s, Composer, French
Dupré, Marcel, 20th Century, 1930s–1970s, Artist, French
Duruflé, Maurice, 20th Century, 1920s–1980s, Composer; Artist, French
Dussek, Jan Ladislav, Early Romantic, 1780s–1810s, Artist; Composer, Bohemian
Dutilleux, Henri, 20th Century, 1940s–1980s, Composer, French
Dvorák, Antonín, Late Romantic, 1860s–1900s, Composer, Czech
Eisler, Hans, 20th Century, 1920s–1960s, Composer, German
Elgar, Edward, Late Romantic, 1890s–1930s, Composer, British
Enescu, George, 20th Century, 1900s–1950s, Composer, Romanian
Erkel, Ferenc, Late Romantic, 1830s–1890s, Composer, Hungarian
Escobar, Pedro de, Renaissance, 1490s–1530s, Composer, Portuguese
Evans, Geraint, 20th Century, 1940s–1980s, Artist, British
Falla, Manuel de, 20th Century, 1900s–1940s, Composer, Spanish
Farnaby, Giles, Early Baroque, 1590s–1640s, Composer, British
Fauré, Gabriel, Late Romantic, 1860s–1920s, Composer, French
Fayrfax, Robert, Renaissance, 1480s–1520s, Composer, British
Feldman, Morton, 20th Century, 1950s–1980s, Composer, American
Ferneyhough, Brian, Contemporary, 1970s–, Composer, British
Ferrier, Kathleen, 20th Century, 1940s–1950s, Artist, British
Feuermann, Emmanuel, 20th Century, 1910s–1940s, Artist, Austrian
Fibich, Zdenek, Late Romantic, 1870s–1900s, Composer, Czech
Field, John, Early Romantic, 1800s–1830s, Composer; Artist, Irish
Finzi, Gerald, 20th Century, 1920s–1950s, Composer, British
Fischer, Edwin, 20th Century, 1900s–1950s, Artist, Swiss
Fischer, Johann, Early Baroque, 1670s–1740s, Composer, German
Fischer-Dieskau, Dietrich, 20th Century, 1940s–1990s, Artist, German
Flagstad, Kirsten, 20th Century, 1930s–1960s, Artist, Norwegian
Flotow, Friedrich, Early Romantic, 1830s–1880s, Composer, German
Floyd, Carlisle, 20th Century, 1940s–1990s, Composer, American
Foote, Arthur, Late Romantic, 1870s–1930s, Composer, American
Forquerey, Antoine, Late Baroque, 1690s–1740s, Composer, French
Foss, Lukas, 20th Century, 1940s–1980s, Composer, American
Fournier, Pierre, 20th Century, 1920s–1970s, Artist, French
Fox, Virgil, 20th Century, 1920s–1960s, Artist, American
Françaix, Jean, 20th Century, 1930s–1990s, Composer, French
Franck, César, Late Romantic, 1840s–1890s, Composer, Belgian
Frescobaldi, Girolamo, Early Baroque, 1600s–1640s, Composer, Italian
Froberger, Johann Jacob, Early Baroque, 1630s–1660s, Composer, German
Fux, Johann Joseph, Late Baroque, 1680s–1740s, Composer; Artist, German
Gabriel, Virginia, Late Romantic, 1850s–1870s, Songwriter, Italian
Gabrieli, Andrea, Renaissance, 1530s–1580s, Composer, Italian
Gabrieli, Giovanni, Renaissance, 1580s–1610s, Composer, Italian
Gade, Niels, Late Romantic, 1840s–1890s, Composer, Danish
Galieli, Vincenzo, Renaissance, 1540s–1590s, Artist, Italian
Galuppi, Baldassare, Classical, 1720s–1780s, Composer, Italian
Galway, James, Contemporary, 1960s–, Artist, British
Gardiner, John Eliot, Contemporary, 1960s–, Artist, British
Gastoldi, Giovanni, Renaissance, 1570s–1620s, Composer, Italian
Gaultier, Denis, Early Baroque, 1620s–1670s, Composer, French
Geminiani, Francesco, Late Baroque, 1700s–1760s, Composer; Artist, Italian
Gerhard, Roberto, 20th Century, 1930s–1970s, Composer, Catalan
Gershwin, George, 20th Century, 1920s–1930s, Composer; Artist, American
Gesualdo, Carlo, Renaissance, 1580s–1610s, Composer, Italian
Ghiaurov, Nicolai, 20th Century, 1950s–1990s, Artist, Bulgarian
Gibbons, Orlando, Renaissance, 1590s–1620s, Composer, British
Gieseking, Walter, 20th Century, 1920s–1950s, Artist, German
Gigli, Beniamino, 20th Century, 1910s–1950s, Artist, Italian
Gilels, Emil, 20th Century, 1930s–1970s, Artist, Russian
Ginastera, Alberto, 20th Century, 1930s–1980s, Composer, Argentinean
Giordano, Umberto, 20th Century, 1890s–1940s, Composer, Italian
Giuliani, Mauro, Classical, 1800s–1820s, Composer, Italian
Glass, Philip, Contemporary, 1960s–, Composer, American
Glazunov, Alexander, Late Romantic, 1880s–1930s, Composer, Russian
Glière, Reinhold Moritsovich, Late Romantic, 1920s–1950s, Composer, Russian
Glinka, Mikhail, Early Romantic, 1820s–1850s, Composer, Russian
Gluck, Christoph Willibald von, Classical, 1730s–1780s, Composer, Bohemian
Gobbi, Tito, 20th Century, 1930s–1970s, Artist, Italian
Goehr, Alexander, Contemporary, 1960s–, Composer, British
Goldmark, Karl, Late Romantic, 1850s–1910s, Composer, Hungarian
Gombert, Nicolas, Renaissance, 1510s–1560s, Composer, Flemish
Gomes, Carlos, Late Romantic, 1860s–1890s, Composer, Brazilian
Goossens, Leon, 20th Century, 1910s–1960s, Artist, British
Górecki, Henryk, Contemporary, 1960s–, Composer, Polish
Gossec, François-Joseph, Classical, 1750s–1820s, Composer, Belgian
Gottschalk, Louis Moreau, Late Romantic, 1840s–1860s, Composer, American
Goudimel, Claude, Renaissance, 1530s–1570s, Composer, French
Gould, Glenn, 20th Century, 1950s–1980s, Artist, Canadian
Gounod, Charles-François, Late Romantic, 1830s–1890s, Composer, French
Grainger, Percy, 20th Century, 1910s–1960s, Composer, Australian
Granados, Enrique, Late Romantic, 1890s–1910s, Composer, Spanish
Graun, Carl Heinrich, Classical, 1720s–1750s, Composer, German
Grétry, André-Ernest-Modest, Classical, 1760s–1810s, Composer, Belgian
Grieg, Edvard, Late Romantic, 1860s–1900s, Composer, Norwegian
Griffes, Charles Tomlinson, 20th Century, 1900s–1920s, Composer, American
Grofé, Ferde, 20th Century, 1910s–1970s, Composer, American
Gruber, Karl-Heinz, Contemporary, 1970s–, Composer, Austrian
Grumiaux, Arthur, 20th Century, 1940s–1980s, Artist, Belgian

Gubaydulina, Sofiya, Contemporary, 1960s–, Composer, Russian
Hába, Alois, 20th Century, 1920s–1970s, Composer, Czech
Hahn, Reynaldo, 20th Century, 1890s–1940s, Composer, French
Halévy, Jacques-François-Fromental, Early Romantic, 1810s–1860s, Composer, French
Halle, Adam de la Medieval, 1270s–1290s, Artist, French
Handel, George Frideric, Late Baroque, 1700s–1750s, Composer; Artist, German
Hanson, Howard, 20th Century, 1920s–1980s, Composer, American
Harbison, John Harris, Contemporary, 1960s–, Composer, American
Harnoncourt, Nicolaus, Contemporary, Artist, German
Harris, Roy, 20th Century, 1920s–1970s, Composer, American
Harrison, Lou, 20th Century, 1930s–1990s, Composer, American
Hasse, Johann Adolf, Classical, 1720s–1780s, Composer; Artist, German
Hassler, Hans Leo, Renaissance, 1580s–1610s, Composer, German
Haydn, Joseph, Classical, 1760s–1800s, Composer, Austrian
Haydn, Michael, Classical, 1760s–1800s, Composer, Austrian
Heifetz, Jascha, 20th Century, 1910s–1960s, Artist, American
Heinichen, Johann David, Late Baroque, 1700s–1720s, Composer, German
Heinrich, Anthony Philip, Early Romantic, 1810s–1860s, Composer, American
Hensel, Fanny, Early Romantic, 1840s, Composer, German
Henze, Hans Werner, 20th Century, 1950s–1980s, Composer, German
Herbert, Victor, Late Romantic, 1880s–1920s, Composer; Songwriter, American
Herrmann, Bernard, 20th Century, 1930s–1970s, Composer, American
Hess, Myra, 20th Century, 1900s–1950s, Artist, British
Hiller, Johann Adam, Classical, 1740s–1800s, Composer, German
Hindemith, Paul, 20th Century, 1920s–1960s, Composer; Artist, German
Hoffmann, E. T. A., Early Romantic, 1790s–1820s, Composer, German
Hogwood, Christopher, Contemporary, 1970s, Artist, British
Holborne, Antony, Renaissance, 1580s–1600s, Composer, British
Hollinger, Heinz, Contemporary, 1960s–, Composer; Artist, Swiss
Holst, Gustav, 20th Century, 1910s–1930s, Composer, British
Honegger, Arthur, 20th Century, 1920s–1950s, Composer, Swiss
Hook, James, Classical, 1770s–1820s, Composer; Artist, British
Horne, Marilyn, Contemporary, 1960s–, Artist, American
Horowitz, Vladimir, 20th Century, 1920s–1980s, Artist, American
Hotter, Hans, 20th Century, 1940s–1970s, Artist, Austrian
Hovhaness, Alan, 20th Century, 1930s–1990s, Composer; Songwriter, American
Howells, Herbert, 20th Century, 1920s–1980s, Composer, British
Humfrey, Pelham, Early Baroque, 1660s–1670s, Composer, British
Hummel, Johann, Early Romantic, 1790s–1830s, Composer; Artist, Austrian
Humperdinck, Engelbert, Late Romantic, 1880s–1920s, Composer, German
Husa, Karel, 20th Century, 1940s–1990s, Composer, Czech
Ibert, Jacques, 20th Century, 1920s–1960s, Composer, French
India, Sigismondo d', Early Baroque, 1600s–1620s, Composer, Italian
Ippolitov-Ivanov, Mikhail, Late Romantic, 1880s–1930s, Composer, Russian
Ireland, John, 20th Century, 1900s–1960s, Composer, British
Isaac, Heinrich, Renaissance, 1470s–1510s, Composer, Flemish
Ives, Charles, 20th Century, 1900s–1950s, Composer, American
Jacobs-Bond, Carrie, Late Romantic, 1880s–1940s, Songwriter, American
Jacquet de la Guerre, Elisabeth-Claude, Late Baroque, 1680s–1720s, Composer; Artist, French
Janácek, Leos, 20th Century, 1880s–1920s, Composer, Czech
Janequin, Clément, Renaissance, 1500s–1550s, Composer, French
Jehannot de Lescaurel, Medieval, 1400s–1430s, Composer, French
Joachim, Joseph, Late Romantic, 1840s–1900s, Artist, German
Joio, Norman Dello, 20th Century, 1930s–1980s, Composer, American
Jolivet, André, 20th Century, 1920s–1970s, Composer, French
Jommelli, Nicolo, Classical, 1730s–1774, Composer, Italian
Josquin des Prez, Renaissance, 1460s–1520s, Composer, Franco-Flemish
Kabalevsky, Dmitri, 20th Century, 1940s–1980s, Composer; Artist, Russian
Kagel, Maurizio, 20th Century, 1950s–1980s, Composer, Argentinean
Kalinnikov, Vasily, Late Romantic, 1980s–1900s, Composer, Russian
Kancheli, Giya, Contemporary, 1950s–, Composer, Russian
Karajan, Herbert von, 20th Century, 1920s–1980s, Artist, Austrian
Keiser, Reinhard, Late Baroque, 1690s–1730s, Composer, German
Kellog, Clara Louise, Late Romantic, 1860s–1880s, Artist, American
Kempff, Wilhelm, 20th Century, 1910s–1980s, Artist, German
Kern, Jerome, 20th Century, 1910s–1940s, Composer; Artist, American
Kernis, Aaron Jay, Contemporary, 1980s–, Composer, American
Khachaturian, Aram, 20th Century, 1920s–1970, Composer, Armenian

MEDIEVAL ➡ 254 RENAISSANCE ➡ 256 EARLY BAROQUE ➡ 258 LATE BAROQUE ➡ 260 CLASSICAL ➡ 262 EARLY ROMANTIC ➡ 264

Kincaid, William, 20th Century, 1920s–1950s, Artist, American
Kirchner, Leon, 20th Century, 1940s–1990s, Composer, American
Kirkby, Emma, Contemporary, 1970s–, Artist, British
Klemperer, Otto, 20th Century, 1910s–1960s, Artist; Composer, German
Knussen, Oliver, Contemporary, 1980s–, Composer, British
Kodály, Zoltán, 20th Century, 1920s–1960s, Composer, Hungarian
Koechlin, Charles, 20th Century, 1890s–1950s, Composer, French
Koopman, Ton, Contemporary, 1970s–Artist, Dutch
Korngold, Erich Wolfgang, 20th Century, 1920s–1950s, Composer, American
Krebs, Johann Ludwig, Classical, 1730s–1780s, Composer, German
Kreisler, Fritz, 20th Century, 1890s–1950s, Artist, American
Krenek, Ernst, 20th Century, 1920s–1990s, Composer, Austrian
Kuhlau, Friedrich, Early Romantic, 1810s–1830s, Composer; Artist, Danish
Kuhnau, Johann, Late Baroque, 1680s–1720s, Composer, German
Kurtág, György, 20th Century, 1950s–1980s, Composer, Hungarian
La Rue, Pierre de, Renaissance, 1480s–1510s, Composer, Flemish
Lalande, Michel-Richard de, Late Baroque, 1670s–1720s, Composer, French
Lalo, Édouard, Late Romantic, 1840s–1890s, Composer, French
Landi, Stefano, Early Baroque, 1600s–1630s, Composer, Italian
Landini, Farncesco, Medieval, 1340s–1390s, Composer; Artist, Italian
Landowska, Wanda, 20th Century, 1900s–1950s, Artist, Polish
Lansky, Paul, Contemporary, 1970s–, Composer, American
Larsson, Lars-Erik, 20th Century, 1930s–1980s, Composer; Artist, Swedish
Lassus, Orlande de, Renaissance, 1550s–1590s, Composer, Franco-Flemish
Lawes, Henry, Early Baroque, 1630s–1660s, Composer, British
Lawes, William, Early Baroque, 1620s–1640s, Composer, British
Le Jeune, Claude, Renaissance, 1550s–1600s, Composer, French
Leclair, Jean-Marie, Late Baroque, 1710s–1760s, Composer; Artist, French
Lehár, Franz, 20th Century, 1890s–1940s, Composer, Austrian
Leoncavallo, Ruggero, Late Romantic, 1880s–1910s, Composer, Italian
Leonhardt, Gustav, 20th Century, 1950s–1990s, Artist, Dutch
Léonin, Medieval, 1150s–1200s, Composer, French
Le Rochois, Marthe, Early Baroque, 1670s–1720s, Artist, French
Ligeti, György , 20th Century, 1950s–1980s, Composer, Hungarian
Lind, Jenny, Early Romantic, 1840s–1880s, Artist, Swedish
Lipatti, Dinu, 20th Century, 1940s, Artist, Romanian
Liszt, Franz, Early Romantic, 1840s–1880s, Composer; Artist, Hungarian
Lloyd Webber, Andrew, Contemporary, 1970s–, Composer, British
Lloyd, George, 20th Century, 1930s–1990s, Composer, British
Locatelli, Pietro Antonio, Late Baroque, 1710s–1760s, Composer; Artist, Italian
Locke, Matthew, Early Baroque, 1640s–1670s, Composer, British
Loewe, Carl, Early Romantic, 1820s–1860s, Composer; Artist, German
Lortzing, Albert, Early Romantic, 1920s–1850s, Composer, German
Ludwig, Christa, 20th Century, 1940s–1980s, Artist, German
Lully, Jean-Baptiste, Early Baroque, 1650s–1680s, Composer, French
Lutoslawski, Witold, 20th Century, 1930s–1980s, Composer, Polish
MacDowell, Edward, Late Romantic, 1880s–1900s, Composer, American
Machaut, Guillaume de, Medieval, 1320s–1370s, Composer, French
Maderna, Bruno, 20th Century, 1940s–1970s, Composer, Italian
Mahler, Gustav, Late Romantic, 1880s–1910s, Composer, Austrian
Malibran, Maria, Early Romantic, 1820s–1830s, Artist, Italian
Malipiero, Gian Francesco, 20th Century, 1900s–1970s, Composer, Italian
Marais, Marin, Late Baroque, 1670s–1720s, Composer; Artist, French
Marcello, Alessandro, Late Baroque, 1690s–1740s, Composer, Italian
Marcello, Benedetto, Late Baroque, 1700s–1730s, Composer, Italian
Marenzio, Luca, Renaissance, 1570s–1590s, Composer, Italian
Marriner, Neville, Contemporary, 1940s–, Artist, British
Marschner, Heinrich, Early Romantic, 1820s–1860s, Composer, German
Martin, Frank, 20th Century, 1920s–1970s, Composer, Swiss
Martín y Soler, Vicente, Classical, 1770s–1800s, Composer, Spanish
Martini, Giovanni Battista, Classical, 1720s–1780s, Composer, Italian
Martino, Donald, 20th Century, 1950s–1990s, Composer, American
Martinu, Bohuslav, 20th Century, 1910s–1950s, Composer, Czech
Mascagni, Pietro, Late Romantic, 1890s–1940s, Composer, Italian
Mason, Lowell, Early Romantic, 1820s–1870s, Composer, American
Massenet, Jules, Late Romantic, 1870s–1910s, Composer, French
Mattheson, Johann, Late Baroque, 1700s–1760s, Composer, German
Maw, Nicholas, Contemporary, 1950s–, Composer, British
Mayr, Johannes Simon, Early Romantic, 1780s–1840s, Composer, German
McCormack, John, 20th Century, 1910s–1940s, Artist, Irish
McPhee, Colin, 20th Century, 1920s–1960s, Composer, Canadian
Medtner, Nikolay, 20th Century, 1900s–1950s, Composer, Russian
Méhul, Etienne-Nicolas, Early Romantic, 1780s–1810s, Composer, French
Melchior, Lauritz, 20th Century, 1920s–1960s, Artist, American
Mendelssohn, Felix, Early Romantic, 1820s–1840s, Composer, German
Mennin, Peter, 20th Century, 1940s–1980s, Composer, American
Menotti, Gian Carlo, 20th Century, 1930s–1990s, Composer, Italian-American
Menuhin, Yehudi, 20th Century, 1920s–1990s, Artist, American-British
Mercadente, Saverio, Early Romantic, 1810s–1870s, Composer, Italian
Merula, Tarquino, Early Baroque, 1610s–1660s, Composer, Italian
Merulo, Claudio, Renaissance, 1550s–1600s, Composer, Italian
Messiaen, Olivier, 20th Century, 1930s–1990s, Composer, French
Metastasio, Pietro, Classical, 1720s–1780s, Librettist, Italian
Meyerbeer, Giacomo, Early Romantic, 1820s–1860s, Composer, German
Milán, Luis de, Renaissance, 1530s–1560s, Composer, Spanish
Milhaud, Darius, 20th Century, 1920s–1970s, Composer, French
Mompou, Federico, 20th Century, 1920s–1980s, Composer, Spanish
Moniuszko, Stanislaw, Early Romantic, 1830s–1870s, Composer, Polish
Monk, Meredith, Contemporary, 1970s–, Composer, American
Monn, Matthias Georg, Classical, 1730s–1750s, Composer, Austrian
Monte, Philippe de, Renaissance, 1540s–1600s, Composer, Flemish
Monteverdi, Claudio, Early Baroque, 1580s–1640s, Composer; Artist, Italian
Moore, Douglas S., 20th Century, 1910s–1960s, Composer, American
Morales, Cristóbal de, Renaissance, 1520s–1550s, Composer, Spanish
Moreno Torroba, Federico, 20th Century, 1920s–1980s, Composer, Spanish
Morley, Thomas, Renaissance, 1570s–1600s, Composer, British
Moszkowski, Moritz, Late Romantic, 1880s–1920s, Composer, German
Mouton, Jean, Renaissance, 1470s–1520s, Composer, French
Moyse, Marcel, 20th Century, 1910s–1970s, Artist, French
Mozart, Leopold, Classical, 1740s–1790s, Artist; Composer, Austrian
Mozart, Wolfgang Amadeus, Classical, 1760s–1790s, Composer; Artist, Austrian
Muffat, Georg, Early Baroque, 1670s–1700s, Composer, German
Musgrave, Thea, 20th Century, 1940s–1990s, Composer, British
Mussorgsky, Modest, Late Romantic, 1850s–1880s, Composer, Russian
Mutter, Anne,-Sophie Contemporary, 1970s–, Artist, German
Myaskovsky, Nikolay, 20th Century, 1900s–1950s, Composer, Russian
Nancarrow, Conlon, 20th Century, 1930s–1990s, Composer, Mexican
Neveu, Ginette, 20th Century, 1930s–1940s, Artist, French
Nicolai, Otto, Early Romantic, 1830s–1840s, Composer, German
Nielsen, Carl, 20th Century, 1890s–1930s, Composer, Danish
Nilsson, Birgit, 20th Century, 1940s–1980s, Artist, Swedish
Nono, Luigi, 20th Century, 1950s–1980s, Composer, Italian
Norgard, Per, Contemporary, 1950s–, Composer, Danish
Norman, Jessye, Contemporary, 1960s–, Artist, American
Norrington, Roger, Contemporary, 1960s–, Artist, British
Nyman, Michael, Contemporary, 1970s–, Composer, British
Obrecht, Jacob, Renaissance, 1470s–1500s, Composer, Franco-Flemish
Ockeghem, Johannes, Medieval, 1450s–1490s, Composer; Artist, Franco-Flemish
Offenbach, Jacques, Late Romantic, 1850s–1880s, Composer, French
Oistrakh, David, 20th Century, 1920s–1960s, Artist, Russian
Orff, Carl, 20th Century, 1920s–1980s, Composer, German
Pachelbel, Johann, Early Baroque, 1670s–1700s, Composer, German
Paderewski, Ignacy, Late Romantic, 1880s–1940s, Artist; Composer, Polish
Paer, Ferdinando, Early Romantic, 1800s–1830s, Composer, Italian
Paganini, Niccolò, Early Romantic, 1800s–1840s, Artist; Composer, Italian
Paine, John Knowles, Late Romantic, 1860s–1900s, Composer, American
Paisello, Giovanni, Classical, 1760s–1810s, Composer, Italian
Palestrina, Giovanni Pierluigi da, Renaissance, 1540s–1590s, Composer, Italian
Parker, Horatio, Late Romantic, 1890s–1910s, Composer, American
Parry, Charles Hubert, Late Romantic, 1870s–1910s, Composer, British
Pärt, Arvo, Contemporary, 1960s–, Composer, Estonian
Partch, Harry, 20th Century, 1920s–1970s, Composer, American
Pasquini, Bernando, Early Baroque, 1650s–1710s, Composer; Artist, Italian
Pasta, Giuditta, Early Romantic, 1820s–1860s, Artist, Italian
Patti, Adelina, Late Romantic, 1870s–1910s, Artist, Italian
Pavarotti, Luciano, Contemporary, 1960s–, Artist, Italian
Pears, Peter, 20th Century, 1930s–1970s, Artist, British
Peeters, Flor, 20th Century, 1920s–1980s, Composer, Belgian
Penderecki, Krzysztof, Contemporary, 1960s–, Composer, Polish
Perahia, Murray, Contemporary, 1970s–, Artist, American
Pergolesi, Giovanni Battista, Late Baroque, 1730s, Composer, Italian
Peri, Jacopo, Early Baroque, 1580s–1630s, Composer, Italian
Perlman, Itzhak, Contemporary, 1960s–, Artist, Israeli
Perotin, Medieval, 1200s, Composer, French
Persichetti, Vincent, 20th Century, 1930s–1980s, Composer, American
Pettersson, Gustaf Allan, 20th Century, 1930s–1980s, Composer, Swedish
Pfitzner, Hans, 20th Century, 1900s–1940s, Composer, German
Philidor, François-André-Danican, Classical, 1740s–1790s, Composer, French
Piatigorsky, Gregor, 20th Century, 1920s–1960s, Artist, American
Piazzolla, Astor, 20th Century, 1940s–1990s, Composer, Argentinean
Piccinni, Niccolò, Classical, 1750s–1800s, Composer, Italian
Pinnock, Trevor, Contemporary, 1970s–, Artist, British
Piston, Walter, 20th Century, 1920s–1970s, Composer, American
Pizzetti, Ildebrando, 20th Century, 1900s–1960s, Composer, Italian
Pleyel, Ignace Joseph, Classical, 1770s–1830s, Composer, Austrian
Pollini, Maurizio, Contemporary, 1960s–, Artist, Italian
Ponce, Manuel, 20th Century, 1900s–1940s, Composer, Mexican
Ponchielli, Amilcare, Late Romantic, 1850s–1880s, Composer, Italian
Ponselle, Rosa, 20th Century, 1910s–1950s, Artist, American
Poulenc, Francis, 20th Century, 1920s–1960s, Composer, French
Pousseur, Henri, 20th Century, 1950s–1980s, Composer, Belgian
Power, Leonel, Medieval, 1400s, Composer, British
Praetorius, Michael, Renaissance, 1590s–1620s, Composer, German
Primrose, William, 20th Century, 1920s–1970s, Artist, Scottish
Prokofiev, Sergei, 20th Century, 1910s–1950s, Composer, Russian
Puccini, Giacomo, Late Romantic, 1880s–1920s, Composer, Italian
Purcell, Henry, Early Baroque, 1680s–1690s, Composer; Artist, British
Quantz, Johann Joachim, Late Baroque, 1710s–1770s, Composer; Artist, German
Quilter, Roger, 20th Century, 1900s–1950s, Composer, British
Rachmaninov, Sergei, Late Romantic, 1890s–1940s, Composer, Russian
Raff, Joachim, Late Romantic, 1840s–1880s, Composer, Swiss
Rameau, Jean-Philippe, Late Baroque, 1700s–1760s, Composer, French
Rampal, Jean-Pierre, 20th Century, 1940s–1980s, Artist, French
Rattle, Simon, Contemporary, 1970s–, Artist, British
Rautavaara, Einojuhani, 20th Century, 1950s–1990s, Composer, Finnish
Ravel, Maurice, 20th Century, 1900s–1930s, Composer, French
Rebel, Jean-Féry, Late Baroque, 1680s–1740s, Composer, French
Reger, Max, Late Romantic, 1890s–1910s, Composer, German
Reich, Steve, Contemporary, 1960s–, Composer, American
Reicha, Antonin, Early Romantic, 1790s–1830s, Composer, Czech-French
Reincken, Johann Adam, Late Baroque, 1640s–1720s, Composer, Dutch-German
Reinecke, Carl, Late Romantic, 1850s–1910s, Composer, German
Respighi, Ottorino, 20th Century, 1900s–1930s, Composer, Italian
Revueltas, Silvestre, 20th Century, 1920s–1940s, Composer, Mexican
Rhodes, Helen, Late Romantic, 1870s–1930s, Songwriter, French
Richter, Sviatoslav, 20th Century, 1930s–1980s, Artist, Russian
Riegger, Wallingford, 20th Century, 1910s–1960s, Composer, American
Rihm, Wolfgang, Contemporary, 1970s–, Composer, German
Riley, Terry, Contemporary, 1960s–, Composer, American
Rimsky-Korsakov, Nicolai, Late Romantic, 1860s–1900s, Composer, Russian
Rochberg, George, 20th Century, 1940s–1990s, Composer, American
Rodrigo, Joaquin, 20th Century, 1920s–1990s, Composer, Spanish
Roman, Johan Helmich, Late Baroque, 1720s–1750s, Composer, Swedish
Ropartz, Joseph, 20th Century, 1890s–1950s, Composer, French
Rore, Cipriano de, Renaissance, 1530s–1560s, Composer, Franco-Flemish
Rorem, Ned, 20th Century, 1950s–1990s, Composer, American
Rossi, Luigi, Early Baroque, 1610s–1650s, Composer, Italian
Rossi, Salamone, Early Baroque, 1590s–1630s, Composer; Artist, Italian
Rossini, Gioacchino, Early Romantic, 1810s–1860s, Composer, Italian
Rostropovich, Mstislav, Contemporary, 1950s–, Artist, Russian
Rouse, Christopher, Contemporary, 1970s–, Composer, American
Roussel, Albert, 20th Century, 1890s–1930s, Composer, French
Rubbra, Edmund, 20th Century, 1920s–1980s, Composer, British
Rubinstein, Anton, Late Romantic, 1850s–1890s, Artist; Composer, Russian
Rubinstein, Arthur, 20th Century, 1900s–1980s, Artist, American
Rue, Pierre de la, Renaissance, 1480s–1510s, Composer, Dutch
Ruffo, Tito, 20th Century, 1900s–1940s, Artist, Italian
Ruggles, Carl, 20th Century, 1920s–1970s, Composer, American
Rutter, John, Contemporary, 1960s–, Composer, British
Rzewski, Frederic, Contemporary, 1950s–, Composer; Artist, American
Saint-Saëns, Camille, Late Romantic, 1840s–1920s, Composer, French
Salieri, Antonio, Classical, 1770s–1820s, Composer, Italian
Sallinen, Aulis, Contemporary, 1960s–, Composer, Finnish
Salzedo, Carlos, 20th Century, 1910s–1960s, Composer, American
Sammartini, Giovanni Battista, Classical, 1720s–1770s, Composer, Italian
Sarasate, Pablo de, Late Romantic, 1860s–1900s, Composer, Spanish
Satie, Erik, 20th Century, 1890s–1920s, Composer, French
Sauguet, Henri, 20th Century, 1920s–1980s, Composer, French
Scarlatti, Alessandro, Late Baroque, 1680s–1720s, Composer, Italian
Scarlatti, Domenico, Late Baroque, 1700s–1750s, Composer; Artist, Italian
Scelsi, Giacinto, 20th Century, 1920s–1980s, Composer, Italian
Scheidt, Samuel, Early Baroque, 1600s–1650s, Composer, German
Schein, Johann Hermann, Early Baroque, 1600s–1630s, Composer, German
Schmidt, Franz, 20th Century, 1900s–1930s, Composer, Austrian
Schmitt, Florent, 20th Century, 1890s–1950s, Composer, French
Schnabel, Artur, 20th Century, 1900–1950s, Artist, American
Schnittke, Alfred, 20th Century, 1950s–1990s, Composer, Russian
Schobert, Johann, Classical, 1750s–1760s, Composer, German
Schoeck, Othmar, 20th Century, 1900s–1950s, Composer, Swiss
Schoenberg, Arnold, 20th Century, 1890s–1940s, Composer, Austrian
Scholl, Andreas, Contemporary, 1990s–, Artist, German
Schorr, Friedrich, 20th Century, 1900s–1940s, Artist, American
Schreier, Peter, Contemporary, 1960s–, Artist, German
Schreker, Franz, 20th Century, 1900s–1930s, Composer, Austrian
Schubert, Franz, Early Romantic, 1810s–1820s, Composer, Austrian
Schuller, Gunther, 20th Century, 1940s–1990s, Composer, American
Schuman, William, 20th Century, 1930s–1990s, Composer, American
Schumann, Clara, Early Romantic, 1830s–1890s, Artist, German
Schumann, Robert, Early Romantic, 1830s–1850s, Composer, German
Schütz, Heinrich, Early Baroque, 1600s–1670s, Composer, German
Schwanter, Joseph, Contemporary, 1960s–, Composer, American
Schwarzkopf, Elisabeth, 20th Century, 1930s–1970s, Artist, German
Schweitzer, Albert, 20th Century, 1900s–1950s, Artist, German-French
Scriabin, Alexander, 20th Century, 1900s–1910s, Composer; Artist, Russian
Sculthorpe, Peter, 20th Century, 1950s–1990s, Composer, Australian
Segovia, Andrés, 20th Century, 1900s–1960s, Artist, Spanish
Senfl, Ludwig, Renaissance, 1500s–1540s, Composer, Swiss
Serkin, Rudolf, 20th Century, 1910s–1970s, Artist, American
Sermisy, Claudin de, Renaissance, 1510s–1560s, Composer, French
Sessions, Roger, 20th Century, 1920s–1980s, Composer, American
Shchedrin, Rodion, Contemporary, 1950s–, Composer, Russian
Shostakovich, Dmitri, 20th Century, 1920s–1970s, Composer, Russian
Sibelius, Jean, Late Romantic, 1890s–1950s, Composer, Finnish
Simpson, Robert, 20th Century, 1940s–1990s, Composer, British
Smetana, Bedrich, Late Romantic, 1840–1880s, Composer, Czech
Smyth, Ethel, Late Romantic, 1890s–1940s, Composer, British
Solange, Medieval, 1340s–1370s, Composer, French
Soler, Antonio, Classical, 1750s–1780s, Composer, Spanish
Solti, Georg, 20th Century, 1930s–1990s, Artist, Hungarian
Sor, Fernando, Classical, 1790s–1830s, Composer, Spanish
Sorabji, Kaikhosru, 20th Century, 1910s–1980s, Composer, British
Sousa, John, Philip 20th Century, 1880s–1930s, Composer, American
Sowerby, Leo, 20th Century, 1910s–1960s, Composer, American
Spohr, Louis, Early Romantic, 1800s–1850s, Composer; Artist, German
Spontini, Gaspare, Early Romantic, 1800s–1850s, Composer, Italian
Stamitz, Johann Wenzel Anton, Classical, 1730s–1750s, Composer, Bohemian
Stanford, Charles Villiers, Late Romantic, 1870s–1920s, Composer, British
Stenhammar, Wilhelm, 20th Century, 1900s–1920s, Composer, Swedish
Stern, Isaac, Contemporary, 1940s–, Artist, American
Still, William Grant, 20th Century, 1920s–1970s, Composer, American
Stockhausen, Karlheinz, Contemporary, 1950s–, Composer, German
Storace, Stephen, Classical, 1780s–1790s, Composer, British
Stradella, Alessandro, Early Baroque, 1660s–1680s, Composer, Italian
Strauss, Johann I, Early Romantic, 1820s–1940s, Composer, Austrian
Strauss, Johann II, Late Romantic, 1840s–1890s, Composer, Austrian
Strauss, Richard, Late Romantic, 1890s–1940s, Composer, German
Stravinsky, Igor, 20th Century, 1910s–1960s, Composer, Russian
Strozzi, Barbara, Early Baroque, 1630s–1660s, Composer; Artist, Italian
Suk, Josef, Late Romantic, 1890s–1930s, Artist; Composer, Czech
Sullivan, Arthur, Late Romantic, 1860s–1900s, Composer, British
Suppé, Franz von, Late Romantic, 1840s–1890s, Composer, Austrian
Sutherland, Joan, Contemporary, 1950s–, Artist, Australian
Svendsen, Johann Sverin, Late Romantic, 1870s–1910s, Composer, Norwegian
Sweelinck, Jan Pieterszoon, Early Baroque, 1580s–1620s, Composer, Dutch
Szigeti, Joseph, 20th Century, 1900s–1960s, Artist, American
Szymanowski, Karol, 20th Century, 1910s–1930s, Composer, Polish
Tailleferre, Germaine, 20th Century, 1910s–1980s, Composer, French
Takemitsu, Toru, 20th Century, 1960s–1990s, Composer, Japanese
Tallis, Thomas, Renaissance, 1530s–1580s, Composer, British
Taneyev, Sergei Ivanovich, Late Romantic, 1880s–1910s, Composer, Russian
Tárrega, Francisco, Late Romantic, 1870s–1900s, Composer, Spanish
Tartini, Giuseppe, Late Baroque, 1710s–1770s, Composer, Italian
Tauber, Richard, 20th Century, 1910s–1940s, Artist, Austrian
Tavener, John, Contemporary, 1970s–, Composer, British
Taverner, John, Renaissance, 1510s–1540s, Composer, British
Tchaikovsky, Pyotr Ilyich, Late Romantic, 1860s–1890s, Composer, Russian
Tcherepnin, Alexander, 20th Century, 1920s–1970s, Composer, Russian
Tebaldi, Renata, 20th Century, 1940s–1970s, Artist, Italian
Telemann, Georg Philipp, Late Baroque, 1700s–1760s, Composer, German
Terfel, Bryn, Contemporary, 1980s–, Artist, Welsh
Tertis, Lionel, 20th Century, 1900s–1960s, Artist, British
Teyte, Maggie, 20th Century, 1900s–1960s, Artist, British
Thibaud, Jacques, 20th Century, 1900s–1950s, Artist, French
Thomas, Ambroise, Late Romantic, 1830s–1880s, Composer, French
Thompson, Randall, 20th Century, 1920s–1980s, Composer, American
Thomson, Virgil, 20th Century, 1920s–1980s, Composer, American
Tippett, Michael, 20th Century, 1930s–1990s, Composer, British
Toch, Ernst, 20th Century, 1900s–1960s, Composer, Austrian
Katharine Tofts, Late Baroque, 1700s–1750s, Artist, British
Tomkins, Thomas, Early Baroque, 1590s–1650s, Composer, British
Torelli, Giuseppe, Early Baroque, 1670s–1700s, Composer, Italian
Torke, Michael, Contemporary, 1980s–, Composer, American
Toscanini, Arturo, Late Romantic, 1880s–1950s, Artist, Italian
Tower, Joan, Contemporary, 1950s–, Composer, American
Traetta, Tommaso, Classical, 1750s–1770s, Composer, Italian
Tredici, David del, Contemporary, 1960s–, Composer, American
Turina, Joaquin, 20th Century, 1910s–1940s, Composer, Spanish
Turner, Eva, 20th Century, 1910s–1960s, Artist, British
Ullman, Viktor, 20th Century, 1920s–1940s, Composer, Czech
Varèse, Edgard, 20th Century, 1920s–1960s, Composer, French-American
Vaughan Williams, Ralph, 20th Century, 1900s–1950s, Composer, British
Vengerov, Maxim, Contemporary, 1990s, Artist, Russian
Ventadorn, Bernart de, Medieval, 1150s–1190s, Artist, French
Verdelot, Philippe, Renaissance, 1500s–1530s, Composer, French
Verdi, Giuseppe, Late Romantic, 1830s–1890s, Composer, Italian
Viardot-Garcia, Pauline, Early Romantic, 1840s–1910s, Artist, Italian
Vickers, Jon, 20th Century, 1950s–1990s, Artist, Canadian
Victoria, Tomás Luis de, Renaissance, 1560s–1610s, Composer, Spanish
Vierne, Louis, 20th Century, 1890s–1930s, Composer, French
Vieuxtemps, Henri, Late Romantic, 1840s–1880s, Composer, Belgian
Villa-Lobos, Heitor, 20th Century, 1900s–1950s, Composer, Brazilian
Viotti, Giovanni Battista, Early Romantic, 1770s–1820s, Artist; Composer, Italian
Vitry, Philippe de, Medieval, 1310s–1360s, Composer, French
Vivaldi, Antonio, Late Baroque, 1690s–1740s, Composer; Artist, Italian
Wagenseil, Georg Christoph, Classical, 1730s–1770s, Composer, Austrian
Wagner, Richard, Late Romantic, 1830s–1880s, Composer, German
Wallace, Vincent, Early Romantic, 1830s–1860s, Composer, Irish
Walther von der Vogelweide, Medieval, 1200s, Artist, German
Walton, William, 20th Century, 1920s–1980s, Composer, British
Warlock, Peter, 20th Century, 1920s–1930s, Composer, British
Weber, Carl Maria von, Early Romantic, 1800s–1820s, Composer, German
Webern, Anton, 20th Century, 1910s–1940s, Composer, Austrian
Weelkes, Thomas, Renaissance, 1590s–1620s, Composer, British
Weill, Kurt, 20th Century, 1920s–1950s, Composer, German-American
Weiss, Sylvius Leopold, Late Baroque, 1700s–1750s, Composer, Germany
Widor, Charles-Marie, Late Romantic, 1860s–1930s, Composer, French
Wieniawski, Henri, Late Romantic, 1860s–1880s, Composer, Polish
Wilby, John, Renaissance, 1590s–1630s, Composer, British
Willaert, Adrian, Renaissance, 1510s–1560s, Composer, Flemish
Williams, John, Contemporary, 1960s–, Composer, American
Wolf, Hugo, Late Romantic, 1880s–1900s, Composer, German
Wolff, Christian, Contemporary, 1950s–, Composer, American
Wolf-Ferrari, Ermanno, 20th Century, 1890s–1940s, Composer, Italian
Wolpe, Stefan, 20th Century, 1920s–1960s, Composer, American
Woodforde-Finden, Amy, Late Romantic, 1880s–1910s, Composer, British
Wuorinen, Charles, Contemporary, 1960s–, Composer, American
Xenakis, Iannis, 20th Century, 1950s–1980s, Composer, French-Greek
Zarlino, Gioseffo, Renaissance, 1530s–1590s, Composer, Italian
Zelenka, Jan Dismas, Late Baroque, 1690s–1740s, Composer, Czechoslovakian
Zemlinsky, Alexander, 20th Century, 1910s–1940s, Composer, Austrian
Zimmerman, Bernd Alois, 20th Century, 1940s–1970s, Composer, German
Zwilich, Ellen Taafe, Contemporary, 1960s–, Composer, American

World

Above

The World of Music, Arts and Dance Festival brings together artists from across the globe.

Right

The Manipuri pung cholom is a ritualistic dance. The music is characterized by sharp contrasts of tempo and volume and an intricate network of accompanying rhythms.

AS the worldwide success of artists such as Shakira, Björk and Baha Men proves, world music is not antithetical to pop music, or to dance music, or to any other music form. For artists like India's Ravi Shankar, the music of their world is classical music; for many Latin musicians, it is jazz; for others, such as Nusrat Fateh Ali Khan, it is the equivalent of gospel.

So, if world music does not stand in oppostition to pop, what exactly does it stand for? What criteria make Paul Simon's *Graceland* world music, but exclude 'Bridge Over Troubled Water'? The crucial thing is the existence of cultural roots within the music, an understanding of where the components began life. By asking South African musicians to play in the manner to which they were accustomed, Simon acknowledged their culture. The Beatles may be everybody's idea of a Liverpool band, but nothing in their music contains "essence of Liverpool", so we can file them under pop.

However, the parameters of world music are as rigid as a line drawn in sand. If Senegal's Youssou N'Dour recorded Beatles songs accompanied by musicians playing West African instruments, it would be world music; if he was accompanied by Western musicians and sang in a Liverpudlian accent, it would be a pop album. Fortunately, musicians don't think too hard about parameters, lines or labels, nor is world music designed by focus groups.

> ## "IN CHINA, TRADITIONAL MUSIC IS ALIVE AND THAT INFLUENCES US. WHAT WE ARE DOING IS SOMETHING COMPLETELY DIFFERENT."
>
> *Xiao Suo, Beijing punk musician*

So nobody makes world music, but many people listen to it. The term was coined by a group of concerned parties only because they wanted a neat marketing term, something that record shops could file records under. "They call my music 'world music'," argues Jocelyne Beroard of Kassav', "but what they mean is 'Third World music', it's just a racist term."

Beroard has a point but, in defence of the indefensible, world music is no longer the sole provenance of oppressed black people in Africa, the Caribbean and South America. World music thrives in Europe, where multicultural centres such as Paris, Barcelona and London are producing fast-mutating fusions of every global music imaginable. In cities that an Anglocentric perspective would view as the homes of world music – Rio de Janeiro, Mexico City, Senegal, Tokyo and so on – young musicians are creating styles that owe as much to their own roots as they do to the all-pervasive hip hop and rock heard on the radio. While major record companies are forever chasing "the new Michael Jackson", musicians are wondering what would have happened if Jackson had been from Peru.

With rock, jazz and blues, there are consensus starting points, both in time and geography; this is not possible in world music unless you are prepared to include the first Neanderthal dance. This is not a flippant point, because rock, jazz and blues

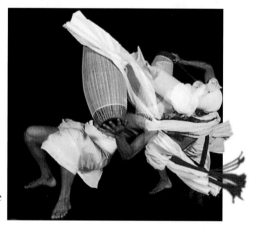

STYLES

East Asia
Celtic
India
Southeast Asia
Caribbean
Africa
Australia & Oceania
Middle East
Native America
Latin & South America
Cajun & Zydeco
Europe
Russia & Central Asia

THE WORLD STYLE

World music comprises a great many different styles and so there is no "typical" sound. However, African music, such as the example shown here, has influenced musical styles across the globe, including the jazz and blues of the West.

PAUL·SIMON
GRACELAND

Above

An album often described as one of the best of the 1980s, Paul Simon's Graceland *is an exploratory and deeply moving blend of folk music diffused with South African tribal rhythms.*

Previous Overleaf

Hailing from Senegal, Youssou N'Dour has put a modern spin on African pop that has brought him worldwide fame.

Right

Yothu Yindi, from the Aboriginal northeastern region of Australia's Northern Territory, celebrate their spiritual connections with the land through song, dance and ceremony.

have all reached a point where, it can be argued, the full range of their possibilities has been explored. With world, there is no start, no centre and no limits. World music is the most exciting music on the planet in the twenty-first century; it is the oldest music, but the one with the greatest possible future.

In the early years of the twentieth century, the classical composer Bela Bartók travelled around Eastern Europe recording folk music, which he then incorporated into his own works. The father-and-son team of John and Alan Lomax were collecting the music of the Americas; Hugh Tracey, an Englishman living in southern Africa, produced 210 LPs of field recordings. Others went to Asia, the Middle East, the Caribbean – wherever music was being created.

Although some genres can claim thousands of years of history, it was almost all passed between generations orally. Death could wipe out an entire style of music without leaving any trace except, perhaps, a cave painting or sculpture. Slavery and genocide decimated cultures in the "civilized" centuries; nobody knows the extent of what could have been lost before then.

So the history of world music is, with a few exceptions and some odd precursors, the history of the twentieth century. There were no recordings before the start of it, and by the end of it the entire globe had been explored. The creeping onslaught of progress and urbanization brought with it the portable microphones of ethnomusicologists, who taped what they could for libraries, universities and museums, often thinking it was the product of "inferior" civilizations. The idea that the world's population might find some sort of enjoyment in the music was still a pipe dream.

The twentieth century also saw mass migration, which was not new, and broadcasting, which was. Suddenly, Caribbean émigrés in New York could hear Cuban music being played live and people in the Sierra Madre could hear the same musicians on the radio. Moisés Simóns' 'The Peanut

Vendor' was a smash hit in North America; Rita Hayworth and Carmen Miranda were Hollywood stars; mambomania took over New York. Music was being listened to by people who were not its target audience. World music existed.

However, the idea that world music is African, Asian or South American music exported to the rest of the world is wide of the mark. In many cases, the musicians in these places were trying to play what they heard via the colonial powers. "When we sang to Americans in Havana, we had to sing in English," remembers Omara Portuondo of 1950s Cuba. "But when we went to America we had to sing in Spanish to be accepted."

In Africa, guitarists were influenced by country music artists playing pedal-steel guitar, an instrument developed by musicians in Hawaii; horn players and the rhythm sections preferred Cuban orchestras; others heard James Brown and Elvis Presley and decided that funk or rock were the true paths. But the availability of instruments and like-minded souls – both to play with or to provide an audience – would guide them in a different direction. And then there is the possibility that they might just get it totally wrong and come up with something brilliantly different in the process.

World music: nobody agrees on what it is and nobody will admit to playing it, but 80 per cent of the globe is listening to it.

THE RECENT HISTORY OF EAST ASIA IS ONE OF CONFLICT: HOSTILITIES HAVE BROKEN OUT OVER WHETHER A KOREAN TUNE SOUNDS JAPANESE OR NOT. WHILE MUSICIANS IN OTHER COUNTRIES TALK ABOUT CROSSING BORDERS, MUSIC HERE HAS STRATEGIC USES.

East Asia

Above

Used by farmers and peasants during festivals, Taiwanese gongs and drums are instruments of celebration and are often played very quickly with fast rhythms, producing a hypnotic sound.

THE communist North Korea is dominated by patriotic work songs; South Korea celebrates history; mainland Japanese musicians absorb Western influences and reinvent them, but different rules apply on Okinawa. And China? How do you sum up the musical tastes of more than a billion people?

Korea

Although religious music still has an important place in Korean society, other traditional music survives only through government support. Traditional instruments are still common, however, with chimes, bells, gongs, zithers, flutes and double-headed drums used in folk music. The country's most famous group, Samul Nori, plays a variety of folk known as nongak, which involves barrel drums, hourglass drums, gongs and a spectacular whirling dance. The group are so famous that, thanks to exposure during the 2002 World Cup and the Seoul Olympics, an entire genre has sprung up bearing its name.

> "EVERYWHERE YOU GO HERE, THERE'S A REAL PRIDE IN THE CULTURE. THE MINUTE YOU GET OFF THE PLANE, OKINAWAN MUSIC IS ALL AROUND YOU."
>
> *Keith Gordon, Ryukyu Underground*

Partly as a result of overseas influence, popular music on the peninsula has been dominant since the second half of the twentieth century. The Japanese occupation saw the arrival of ppongtchak, a deliberate attempt to spread the imperialists' culture into its satellites. From 1950, American influence was strongest in the south, and Ch'oe Hi-jun became a star because he sounded like America's greatest asset in the early years of the Cold War, Nat King Cole.

LEADING EXPONENTS

Korea

Ch'oe Hi-jun

Samul Nori

Seoul Ensemble Of
 Traditional Music

Japan

Miyako Harumi

Hibari Misora

Nenes

Takashi Hirayasu

Ryuichi Sakamoto

China

Guo Brothers

Chow Hsuan

EAST ASIA

This type of song is often used in geisha parlours to entertain the guests. The vocalist accompanies her own melody with a shamisen, singing: a typical pentatonic-style scale.

voice, shamisen

The following decades saw pop developing in ways similar to the West: the 1970s introduced tong guitar, corresponding to American protest folk; pap, a variation on hippy singer/songwriters; and eventually indigenous rock, dance and rap, each using Korean idioms to retain a unique flavour.

North Korea, in contrast, has been locked in a communist time warp since 1953. Music is rigorously controlled there, with military bands, factory choirs and faux pop all singing the praises of the party, the state and the joys of work rather than celebrating imperialist fripperies such as love.

Japan

It is the world's second-biggest market for music, but to outsiders Japan is a stronghold of bubblegum pop, with teen singers queuing up for their 15 seconds of fame. The view from inside is very different. Classical music – orchestral, theatrical and Buddhist – all retain strong followings, and the three paradigm instruments are the shakuhachi flute, koto zither and the shamisen lute, all of which have centuries of history and feature in contemporary music.

Folk music (minyo) differs from the Western form, in that it is regulated by guilds and requires extensive apprenticeships – you cannot just stand up, stick your finger in your ear and sing. As a result, professional performers, such as Asano Sanae, are all of an extremely high standard.

Until 1868, Japan had been isolated from outside influences, thus protecting its indigenous musics. When the walls came down, the Japanese absorbed what they heard with unrivalled enthusiasm. Just as today's bands play Japanese variations on punk, heavy metal or rap, their predecessors used jazz, Latin and blues to create new strains. However, the result (kayokyoku) was unmistakably Japanese, as the recordings of the celebrated pop singer Hibari Misora prove.

The composer Ryuichi Sakamoto rose to international fame thanks to his soundtrack for *Merry Christmas, Mr Lawrence*, but it was one of his former colleagues in the Yellow Magic Orchestra, Haruomi Hosono, who introduced the music of Okinawa (or Ryukyu) to both the rest of Japan and the outside world. The southern archipelago, under American control until 1972, clung to its traditions while watching the rest of Japan modernize. Hence, when the rootsy harmonies of Nenes and steel-guitar-like sanshin of Takashi Hirayasu were exported, it was almost as if the previous 600 years of progress had never happened.

China

While Hong Kong and Taiwan specialize in bubblegum pop, and Beijing youth develop their own varieties of punk and metal, the recent history of Chinese music is dominated by the events of the Cultural Revolution, in which Mao's Red Guards tried to obliterate every trace of the country's feudal heritage. Fortunately, they failed.

Western influence in Chinese music stretches back no further than 1911, and even then, it hardly extended beyond the cities. But the graceful pop that came from Shanghai and Canton in this period, featuring singers like Bai Kwong and Chow Hsuan, was exquisite. After 1949 and the communist takeover, however, the music and film industries fled to Hong Kong.

With no pop music, then, the media was dominated by the so-called national music, played on fiddles, lutes, flutes and zithers, and military marches, all of which were supposed to reflect pan-Chinese heterogeneity. However, they did so in just the same way as New York or London could be said to represent the USA or Britain. Outside the urban areas, folk music still plays a crucial part in keeping cultures alive, with drums, gongs, mouth organs (sheng) and flutes continuing to score rituals, festivals and daily life.

BY 200BC, THE CELTS OCCUPIED EUROPE FROM THE BALKANS TO FRANCE, WITH OUTPOSTS IN TURKEY, SPAIN AND THE BRITISH ISLES. HOWEVER, THE RISE OF ROME, FOLLOWED BY A GERMANIC DRIFT SOUTH, PUSHED THE CELTS TO THE EDGE OF THE CONTINENT: IRELAND, SCOTLAND, WALES, BRITTANY AND THE BASQUE COUNTRY.

Celtic

Above

Alan Stivell, who brought Breton Celtic music to the attention of the musical world. He has transgressed the confines of folk music to play with pop and rock acts.

ONE theory suggests that the Celts also had a Mediterranean heritage, and arrived in the west carrying traces of black African culture. By the time they had put roots down in Ireland, the West African kora had been slowly changed into the harp and the tama (talking drum) had become the bodhran. Neither theory necessarily contradicts the other, but if you take the African instruments and add those of the European route – a fiddle, the Greek bouzouki and a set of pipes (found in Greece, Eastern Europe, Scotland and Ireland) – you have the perfect Celtic group, an ensemble with a 2,500-year pedigree.

However, the length of this heritage has not always deemed it worth preserving. In Spain, during Franco's dictatorship, there were attempts to enforce homogeneity upon the country; in Britain, Celts were exported to populate the colonies and their culture held up to ridicule. The tradition has remained unbowed only in Ireland, inspiring others to do the same. Fortunately, they succeeded: in the twenty-first century, Celtic music is the healthiest European roots music.

Keeping Culture And Language Alive

Northwestern Spain is home to a thriving Celtic music scene, strengthened by years of resistance to attempts to subordinate the Basques. Rather than submit, the musicians of Euskadi (the Basque country) dug deep. Today, music and poetry are vital to keeping culture and language alive. Kepa Junkera is among the best-known exponents of trikitrixa, Spanish bagpipe

music that has been adapted for the accordion. In Galicia, it is the piper Carlos Núñez who leads the roots revival. His affinity with other Celts is clear: his piping style came about through studying Scottish pipers, while he served his apprenticeship with the Irish icons the Chieftains. After learning that many Galicians emigrated to the Caribbean, he travelled to Havana and established a Celtic-Cuban connection.

In France, the Celts inhabit Brittany, where pipe-and-drum ensembles are known as bagad. The most important development in the revival of Celtic music was the success of Alan Stivell, a harpist and piper who mixed folk and rock in the late-1960s, partly as a response to British folk rock groups such as the Incredible String Band.

England is not often thought of as a Celtic nation, but the music of the Northumbrian piper Kathryn Tickell reflects the proximity of north-east England to Celtic Scotland. Further south, the Afro Celt Sound System could only have come about in London: an Irish-Senegalese collaboration that searches for the musical links between West Africa and Europe's western coasts, and then adds cutting-edge dance beats.

Wales is home to the outstanding feature of the rebirth of Celtic culture: where once the language was thought doomed, it is now a growth industry outside its northern and western heartlands. The pipes have a lesser status in Welsh music, however; the most emblematic instrument of Celtic identity is the harp, particularly during summer's eisteddfod season.

Scotland's New Celtic Pride

It was not until the early 1970s that traditional musicians started to replace cartoon tartanalia as the public face of Scotland's Celtic heritage. Much of this was due to the folk

> ## "THE CHAIN OF TRADITION WAS BROKEN, BUT WHAT WE ARE SEEING NOW IS THE REBIRTH OF IT ALL."
> *Carlos Núñez*

LEADING EXPONENTS

Carlos Núñez
Kepa Junkera
Alan Stivell
Afro Celt Sound System
Aly Bain
The Waterboys
Iarla O'Lionaird
Clannad
The Chieftains
Ashley MacIsaac
Natalie MacMaster
Jerry Holland
Mary Black
Karan Casey

CELTIC

Many Scottish melodies are pentatonic. The characteristic 6/8 time signature is also used in Welsh and Irish traditional music.

THE WORLD INTRO ➡ 276   WORLD PEOPLE A-Z ➡ 308   INSTRUMENTS A-Z ➡ 436   FOLK: FOLK SONGS ➡ 226

revival of the 1960s, but tribute must also be paid to growing knowledge of separate Scottish and Irish identities. While the bagpipes are the national instrument, they are the sound of Highland and military music (pibroch) rather than folk (or country) and have less of a place in contemporary Celtic groups than Ireland's uillean pipes. In the late-1970s, Scotland's new Celtic pride was cemented by the rise of rock bands playing musical fusions: Runrig were the first, but the high-water mark was the Waterboys' *Fisherman's Blues*, an unashamedly Irish album from the Edinburgh-born Mike Scott and his band.

Although Irish folk and Celtic music are at times interchangeable, it is through sean nos (old-style) singing that the links are most strong. Donegal's Iarla O'Lionaird, one of the finest sean nos singers, is now a member of the Afro Celt Sound System, a group that has also used Sinéad O'Connor, piper Ronan Browne and Robert Plant to further its journey into the heart of bardic culture. Mixing Celtic airs with contemporary music is not a new fad for Irish musicians, however, as Clannad, Planxty, Altan and Van Morrison prove.

In the eighteenth century, the clearances that decimated rural Scotland and Ireland resulted in a great number of musicians moving to Canada, where Celtic communities thrived. While those who remained in Britain adapted to laws intended to neuter their culture, the emigrant fiddlers could retain a truer hold on their roots. As a result, when Ashley MacIsaac emerged from Cape Breton in the 1990s, a punk flash in a kilt who played fast, hard and loud, he was immediately denounced for everything he was ... just like every other Celt.

Above

In creatively blending traditional Irish music with West African rhythms and hip dance beats, the Afro Celt Sound System, now known simply as AfroCelts, have created an innovative sound.

Left

The Waterboys, based in Ireland but fronted by a Scotsman, perform a mixture of folk and traditional Irish music to create their own signature sound, which further evolves with their ever-changing line-up.

FOLK: POLITICAL FOLK & PROTEST SONGS ➡ 230   FOLK: IRISH FOLK ➡ 241

THE PHRASE "INDIAN MUSIC" IS MOST OFTEN EQUATED TO AN IMAGE OF RAVI SHANKAR AND THE SITAR, BUT THERE IS MUCH MORE TO IT THAN THAT. THE SOUTH IS THE HEARTLAND OF KARNATIC CLASSICAL MUSIC, WHOSE HISTORY STRETCHES BACK FOR 6,000 YEARS.

India

Above

Indian wind-blown instruments are collectively known as "sushir".

SHANKAR may be emblematic of Hindustani classical music, but that is a much younger style, a blend of Karnatic music and influences from the Middle East and northern Asia. Both styles share basic rules: those of the raga, a scale that will be played throughout any composition; and the tala, the rhythmic cycle.

Further north, the qawwali singers of Pakistan have the power to transport even Western atheists to another spiritual plane. Thanks to the efforts of the band Cornershop, Bollywood film soundtracks have never been so popular outside the subcontinent, and you hardly need to be au fait with Satyajit Ray to be brimful of Asha Bhosle. With so many people involved in music at an expert level, it is not surprising that there is a burgeoning contemporary scene – albeit one that relies on musicians such as London's Talvin Singh, with experience of cultures outside India. Midival Punditz from New Delhi combine classical Indian ragas and electronic music with great success. They are the first Indian electronica band to sign to an international label and feature on the soundtrack to *Monsoon Wedding* (2002) and Talvin Singh's second Anokha collection.

> ## "IT IS THE GREATEST THRILL FOR THE MUSICIAN AND THE LISTENER WHEN YOU GET INTO THE WORLD OF THE RAGA AND YOU CAN ROAM FREELY."
>
> *Ravi Shankar*

Ravi Shankar

Arguably the first hero of world music, Shankar was born into a musical family in 1920, just as the globe was opening up to the "exotic". His timing was perfect. By the end of the 1930s, he had toured France and America with his brother's dance

LEADING EXPONENTS

Hindustani Classical Music
Ravi Shankar
Ali Akbar Khan
Alla Rakha

Karnatic Classical Music
U. Srinivas
L. Subramaniam

Bollywood
Asha Bhosle
Mohammed Rafi

Pakistan
Nusrat Fateh Ali Khan
Rizwan-Muazzam Qawwali
Sabri Brothers

Contemporary
Talvin Singh
Midival Punditz

INDIA

The gat (melody) of 'Rag Kafi' begins on the 7th beat of a 16-beat cycle. The Sam (first beat) coincides with the most prominent note of the raga.

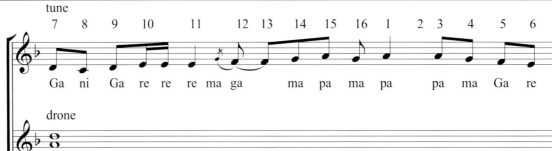

tune

| 7 | 8 | 9 | 10 | 11 | 12 | 13 | 14 | 15 | 16 | 1 | 2 | 3 | 4 | 5 | 6 |

Ga ni Ga re re re ma ga ma pa ma pa pa ma Ga re

drone

troupe. "When I started playing the sitar I would practice for 12 to 14 hours daily, sometimes 16. We had to do it like this because of the hand techniques, the music itself and because of our oral tradition."

By the 1950s, Shankar was able to play Carnegie Hall in New York, to great acclaim from both the jazz community (John Coltrane named his son Ravi) and Western classical musicians (he released a series of astounding duets with the violinist Yehudi Menuhin). But in 1966, George Harrison (then of the Beatles) became his student and Indian music briefly entered the pop mainstream. Subsequently, Shankar played both the Monterey and Woodstock festivals accompanied by his long-term collaborator, the tabla (twin drums) maestro Alla Rakha. "In India, I was accused of jazzifying my music. It bothered some people that I had two identities, as a classicist and as a creator of new music. They thought I was a goner."

Karnatic Classical Music

Although the sitar and tabla are often thought of as the main instruments of Indian music, in the south it is the vina (like a pedal steel with a gourd at both ends) that supplies the string sound, and the mridangam (double-headed drum) and ghatam (clay pot) that add percussion. Although it is the older of the two styles, karnatic music is also open to outside influence. Since the Raj, instruments such as the violin, clarinet and saxophone are common and the former child prodigy U. Srinivas has made the five-stringed mandolin his own.

Bollywood

Filmi is India's pop music, and the fact that it comes from the world's two largest movie centres (Mumbai and Madras) is not incidental to its appeal: think of it as an MTV that people pay to watch en masse. The most popular films are all-singing, all-dancing Technicolor musical spectaculars, but their popularity depends as much on the music as the action. Behind the scenes, playback singers such as Asha Bhosle, her sister Lata Mangeshkar, or Mohammed Rafi would provide hit after hit. The scores, which borrow from every conceivable style, from Indian classical to American funk, are provided by peerless composers, including S. D. Burman and the current hero, A. R. Rahman, who has expanded his horizons to include *Bombay Dreams*, a stage musical collaboration with Andrew Lloyd Webber.

Qawwali

Although the death of Nusrat Fateh Ali Khan saw the end of the career of Pakistan's most famous musician, it was perhaps fitting that his passing was announced on the twentieth anniversary of the death of Elvis Presley. He was "the brightest

of stars", a qawwali singer who brought the sufi message of spirituality to the Western masses. His extraordinary voice, a frenzied yet perfectly controlled tenor, spilled out torrents of words, and made him a favourite with stars like Jeff Buckley and Trent Reznor. Thus he made the transition from the intensity of devotional sufi music to almost-pop star.

Like the guitar-bass-drums rock line-up, qawwali ensembles have a tradition: a lead singer, harmonium players who take solo vocals and a chorus that also contains percussionists. The lyrics use metaphors and poetry to praise God, raising both performers and listeners to a state of trance-like euphoria. Nusrat Fateh Ali Khan explained it thus: "The sign of a good qawwal, or any other musician, is his ability to absorb his listeners into the reality of his message. A good qawwal does not himself exist when he is performing." Hence the phrase that best describes a qawwal in full flight, "dead man walking".

Above
The making of drums in India is often viewed as more than just a craft process; many see it as a spiritual journey, which involves respect for the materials involved and a strong connection to the object created.

Left
After becoming the director of All India Radio in 1949, composer and instrumentalist Ravi Shankar resolved to introduce an international audience to the wonders of Indian music, which he has certainly achieved.

SOUTHEAST ASIAN MUSIC OWES MUCH TO ITS NEIGHBOURS. TRAVELLERS, MOVING SOUTH FROM CHINA, MIXED WITH TRADERS FROM INDIA AND ARABIA. LATER ARRIVALS ADDED TO THE MIX; THE PHILIPPINES ARE SPANISH-AMERICAN, VIETNAM IS FRENCH-CHINESE, AND MALAYSIA IS ARABIC-CHINESE-INDIAN-PORTUGUESE-BRITISH. ADD THE LATEST ECONOMIC INVASION AND IT'S A WONDER THAT ANY UNADULTERATED MUSIC SURVIVES. BUT IT DOES.

Southeast Asia

Above

Hollow woodblock instruments have been used in Vietnamese pagoda ceremonies for centuries. These unique instruments are called danmos.

IN Indonesia, Javanese gamelan ensembles still play court music that dates back to the eighteenth century; the tribes of Borneo are trying to preserve their folk traditions and the Buddhist orchestras of Myanmar, Thailand, Laos and Cambodia celebrate the heroes of the Hindu Ramayana, introduced to Indochina from Indonesia in the ninth century.

pinpeat orchestras (gongs laid out in large horseshoes, xylophones, drums and woodwind) are still to the fore at festivals. However, enthusiasm is limited among the local population, and performances by orchestras or the classical ballet companies are rare.

In Thailand, which has never been colonized by a European power, the orchestra tradition (known as piphat, but influenced by Khmer and Laotian music) is stronger, and a number of ensembles are able to support themselves. The most famous is Bangkok's Duriyapraneet, which formed in 1898, while Fong Naam are highly regarded for their fusing of classical music with jazz.

In Vietnam – isolated by its politics for much of the late-twentieth century – the classical traditions resemble the Chinese folk operas (hat cheo) and historical tales (hat boi) from which they developed. Both are in danger of losing the

"MUSIC OF A VERY STRANGE KIND, YET THE SOUND WAS PLEASANT AND DELIGHTFUL."

Sir Francis Drake, Java, 1580

LEADING EXPONENTS

Indonesia

Banyumas Bamboo
  Gamelan

Jugala Orchestra

Nasida Ria

Philippines

Sindao Banisil

Freddie Aguilar

Thailand

Duriyapraneet

Fong Naam

Suraphon Sombatjalern

Nasida Ria

Vietnam

Huong Thanh

Classical

In a region where traditions have been casually discarded, it is noticeable that those who have been isolated have the strongest links with their classical roots. Laos and Cambodia were backwaters when the French ruled Indochina, and the

SOUTHEAST ASIA

Musicians number the notes according to an eight-note scale. Lines above and below the numbers indicate the octave. (See table)

Larger metallophones play at half- and quarter-speeds according to size and pitch.

3	5	6̄		3	2	3	2
3		6	5	3		3	2
3̲				3̲			

tune

1 2 3 5 6   3 5 6 5 3 2 3 2

THE WORLD INTRO ➡ 276   WORLD PEOPLE A–Z ➡ 308   INSTRUMENTS A–Z ➡ 436

support of the indigenous population, although the Nhac Cung Dinh group is trying to keep alive the court music of Hué, the capital prior to the abdication of the last emperor in 1945.

Folk

Although Western pop seems to be all-conquering in the cities, the prevalence of isolated tribes has ensured the survival of many unique forms of folk music. To hear it, though, often requires a trip into the wilderness, as it may not even travel as far as the nearest city. The gamelan (orchestras that feature metal or bamboo xylophones, gongs and drums) is still synonymous with Indonesia, especially Java, Lombok and Bali. The latter island is also home to kecak, the monkey chant, in which men imitate the animals' cries while sitting as if in a trance.

In the Philippines, there is a tradition of music in the islands of Mindanao, although much of the traditional knowledge has been lost. Only a few singers and musicians, such as Sindao Banisil, are still flying the flag. In eastern Malaysia, gong ensembles can be found throughout Sabah and Sarawak, and the sape (a cricket-bat-shaped guitar) is making a comeback of sorts. In peninsular Malaysia, the ronggeng, a Portuguese-Arabic fusion from Malacca, has ascended to the position of unofficial national folk music.

For the Thais, the music of the country, pleng luk thung, rose to prominence in the 1960s, under the stewardship of the great singer Suraphon Sombatjalern. However, in the north-east, the dominant culture is Laotian and the khaen (bamboo pipes) is the most emblematic instrument of a style known as mor lam. In Vietnam, the Hanoi Conservatoire has done its best to take the people's music and modernize and "improve" it, to the chagrin of the hill tribes and music lovers.

Pop

If you can hear it on the radio in America or Europe, there is a local version in Southeast Asia. It can even be sold back to the originators, as the Filipino Freddie Aguilar discovered when his song 'Anak' sold millions in Europe in the 1970s. Although Indonesia dominates, the label the "Manila sound" bestows musical credibility on any band.

Indonesian pop has a pedigree that stretches back centuries, to the kroncong ukulele bands, and often swamps its neighbours. In the 1970s, Latin music arrived (dangdut), turning Rhoma Irama into a regional star. Later, the Jugala Orchestra, from western Java, updated folk music, turning it into pop (jaipongan). Middle Eastern Arabic music became popular when played by local groups (gambus, also popular in Malaysia through such singers as Fadzil Ahmad); Nasida Ria, an all-female group who developed Islamic rock (qasidah modern), also updated it.

While other countries lag behind Indonesia in developing long-lasting stars, there are some significant exceptions. Thailand has its own indie scene, in which Modern Dog excel, and the eastern half of the country resonates to kantrum, a frantic, Thai-Khmer hybrid led by Darkie. In Cambodia, the biggest name is Sin Sisamouth, a crooner who dominates airplay, despite having been killed by the Khmer Rouge sometime in the 1970s.

FROM PORT OF SPAIN ON TRINIDAD TO NASSAU IN THE BAHAMAS. FROM MIAMI THROUGH TO PORT-AU-PRINCE: YOU ARE NEVER FAR FROM A GREAT RHYTHM IN THE CARIBBEAN. WHILE JAMAICAN REGGAE AND CUBA'S SON, MAMBO AND SALSA HAVE BEEN EXPORTED TO THE WORLD, THERE IS A WEALTH OF GREAT MUSIC ON THE OTHER ISLANDS, FROM CALYPSO AND ZOUK TO PLENA AND CHUTNEY.

Caribbean

Above

The music of Antilles band Kassav' was so popular at "zouk" parties that it created a new genre known as zouk music. Their style drew from traditional carnival music, which was updated with more modern beats and instruments.

FROM the moment Christopher Columbus set foot on Cuba in 1492, the Caribbean has seen settlers arrive, usually to the detriment of the indigenous population. Slaves from Africa, colonists from Britain, America, Spain, France and beyond: all have brought their own music, making Havana, Kingston, Fort-de-France and San Juan among the most fertile cities for musicians, particularly if you are around during the Easter carnival season.

Antilles

Primarily influenced by the French and Africans, the islands of Martinique and Guadeloupe are strongholds of zouk, a mix of Haitian compas, brought by musicians fleeing that island's poverty and repression; and the beguine, a dance dating back to the 1920s, when visitors to Martinique even introduced it to Europe. The undoubted stars are Kassav', led by Jocelyne Beroard, a forceful presence both musically and culturally.

> "WE WRITE FOR OUR HOME AUDIENCE, WE PLAY MUSIC THAT APPEALS TO THOSE AT HOME, A MUSIC THAT FEELS NATURAL AND INTUITIVE."
>
> *Juan Luis Guerra*

Bahamas

On the surface, the islands are a mix of Africans (proximity to America making them a favoured bolthole for runaway slaves) and strict English Protestantism (although obeah, African witchcraft, is also strong). The current music scene on the islands is less inspiring, but Joseph Spence (1910-84), a self-taught guitarist who always sounded precisely out of tune to other ears, remains a towering presence. Often compared to Thelonious

LEADING EXPONENTS

Kassav'

Joseph Spence

Johnny Ventura

Juan Luis Guerra

Tabou Combo

Boukman Eksperyans

Canario

Rafael Cortijo

Lord Executor

Machel Montano

Mighty Sparrow

CARIBBEAN

Syncopated chords on guitar or keyboards is a strong feature in the rhythmic accompaniment to calypso, the first music of the Caribbean, which draws from West African influences.

bass

hi hat

cowbell

Monk, Spence was a notable influence on Ry Cooder, the Grateful Dead, Taj Mahal and other modern slide players.

Dominican Republic

The further north you get, the more Latin the sound. The eastern half of the island of Hispaniola (which it shares with Haiti) has always been overshadowed by Cuba, but merengue has been around for hundreds of years and always comes back stronger whenever it feels that salsa has been stealing the limelight. When disco was beamed in by US radio stations, an entrepreneur-musician such as Johnny Ventura would co-opt the instruments and arrangements. In the 1980s, Juan Luis Guerra added sweet, Motown-style harmonies; thus the music kept moving.

This was originally the music of the plantations, where workers would sit and play drums, accordions and box bass. Today, however, the modern band has adopted the horn section from Cuba and pushed the African percussion and indigenous guira to the front. The latest unlikely development is merenhouse, particularly among the immigrant population in New York.

Haiti

Despite being the poorest country in the western hemisphere, Haiti was once the region's only rival to Havana for the richness of its nightlife. Unsurprisingly, there is a close relationship with the Dominican Republic's music: in the Spanish neighbour, they have merengue, in Haiti, meringue, with guitars rather than accordions. Other outside influences include Cuban son and Congolese rumba. When America occupied Haiti (1915-34), jazz and swing were introduced. The result of this blend was compas, which rose to international attention in the 1970s with Tabou Combo, the most famous Haitian musicians prior to Wyclef Jean. As outcasts in the Caribbean, Haitian musicians, like Cubans, have returned to their roots – voodoo. But in a land where dictators and military governments have ruled through fear, the main stars of the movement, such as Boukman Eksperyans or Boukan Ginen, have often found themselves threatened for playing in a style that gives their followers something positive and uncontrollable in which to believe.

Puerto Rico

East of the Dominican Republic, dwarfed by Cuba, Puerto Ricans – as demonstrated in *West Side Story* – were the prime movers when it came to turning New York into Nu Yorica. The island may have its own national rhythm (plena), but its expat musicians (Tito Puente among them) can take the credit for turning Cuban son into global salsa. Back home, plena was country music that escaped to the cities in the 1930s through musicians such as Canario, who augmented acoustic guitar and drum ensembles with brass and keyboards, and stayed popular into the 1960s with Rafael Cortijo.

Trinidad And Tobago

Growing out of work songs, calypso spread throughout the Windward and Leeward Islands, where carnival meant calypso and steel bands. By the 1930s, calypso was the sound of Trinidad, with stars such as Lord Executor, Mighty Sparrow and Roaring Lion fêted internationally; the biggest international star, though, was the Jamaican Harry Belafonte. While the tunes were simple, the lyrics were potent: scabrous, obscene and politically charged. In the 1970s, Trinidadian musicians fused their music with the people of Tobago, and soca was born – a mixture of Indian and calypso rhythms (not, as is often suggested, soul and calypso). The most notable difference was the switch in emphasis from lyrics to rhythm. Detractors point to this as the moment the music ceased to be interesting, but stars such as Machel Montano, who also uses reggae and hip hop, may prove them wrong. Another style that has grown out of the area's Indian heritage blends sounds of the subcontinent with calypso, soca and ragga. The name for this music? Chutney.

Centre

Johnny Ventura, shown performing at the 1997 New Orleans Jazz & Heritage Festival. The following year, Ventura became mayor of Santo Domingo but still performs as often as his political duties will allow.

Left

The Mighty Sparrow (Slinger Francisco), the calypso king, has won countless awards over his 50-year career, but in July 2001 he was given the ultimate accolade in the form of a statue at St Ann's roundabout in Port of Spain.

AFRICAN MUSIC DOMINATES THE WORLD IN THE EXPORTED FORMS OF BLUES, JAZZ, FUNK AND THEIR CHILDREN, BUT THE MUSIC WITHIN THE CONTINENT IS OFTEN OVERLOOKED. AFRICA STILL EXPORTS BUT IT IS ALSO AN IMPORTER, ADAPTING SALSA, RAP AND COUNTRY TO ITS OWN CIRCUMSTANCES.

Africa

Above

The marimba, an African xylophone, is a versatile instrument. Its tone and pitch range varies depending on the type and thickness of the wood used. In some regions, marimbas are used to communicate news across villages.

AFRICA is a metaphorical and geographical crossroads, making the continent the home of world music. People moved from north to south, from east to west within Africa; Europeans came, Islam and Christianity came, each reshaping what they found; people left for the New World across the ocean, some forced, others by choice; expatriate communities reached out to those who remained. There is no musical form on Earth that could have remained impervious to those cultural exchanges. Try to think what music might sound like if there had never been slavery.

A Vast Catalogue Of Styles

African geography, demographics and communications have created a catalogue of styles that is too vast to fit in one section of one book. Some became conspicuous influences on pop and rock, for example, turning hymns into gospel, then soul, then funk, then rap; some – rai, soukous, mbalax – achieved worldwide popularity; others would exasperate anyone raised on white musical traditions. What follows is a guide to the styles that took the most from the outside and went on to have the greatest appeal and influence within and outside Africa. True world music.

> "MUSIC IS LIKE A TREE. ROCK AND JAZZ ARE THE BRANCHES, BUT IN MALI WE HAVE THE TRUNK AND THE ROOTS."
>
> *Salif Keita*

Algeria

What Liverpool was to British pop, Oran is to rai: a port where musicians knew all about sex, drugs and rock'n'rebellion. It was not until the mid-1970s that the recording industry exploded, with young ("cheb") punks making pop-rai mainstream. Led by Cheb Khalèd, these flouted the rules of classical Arabic music. In the 1980s, fearing persecution from religious extremists, the scene moved to France, where record companies provided

LEADING EXPONENTS

Khalèd
Cesaria Evora
OK Jazz
Mahmoud Ahmed
Tarika
Salif Keita
Fela Kuti
Youssou N'Dour
Ladysmith Black
  Mambazo
Thomas Mapfumo
Gigi
Habib Koité

AFRICA

Two mbiras (thumb piano with gourd resonator) playing distinct simultaneous patterns produce a melody from their combined parts.

budgets to turn Khalèd and Cheb Mami into global pop stars, and to support such maverick rockers as Rachid Taha and the Maghreb magpies, Orchestra National De Barbes.

Congo–Zaire

In the mid-twentieth century, Africa went crazy for Cuban music – African in origin, but twisted by influences from elsewhere. In Kinshasa, guitarists hijacked the piano and horn lines, creating Congolese rumba (soukous). The kingpins were dance bands such as African Jazz and OK Jazz, who produced generations of virtuoso musicians and singers, among them Joseph Kabasele, Franco Luambo Makiadi, Manu Dibango, Sam Mangwana and Mose Fan Fan. When the economy collapsed, the soukous scene quit for Paris, where Kanda Bongo Man and Papa Wemba were already established, having emigrated to achieve recognition away from the competition.

Ethiopia

The funkiest rhythms and horn sections to come out of Africa could be found in Addis Ababa from the late-1960s until the mid-1970s, when dictatorship brought an end to the city's nightlife. More importantly, it also brought war, famine and the flight of most of the country's greatest artists. Not the exodus that Bob Marley was dreaming of. Fortunately, the Éthiopiques series of albums (released on the French Buda Musique label) captures the flavour of the period when Mahmoud Ahmed ruled the music scene, with a band that could have graced Stax.

Ghana

In the 1970s, Osibisa had three Top 10 hits in Britain – no other Africans have enjoyed this level of UK success. The musical relationship between Ghana and Britain was forged in 1928, when Kwame Asare made the first highlife recordings in London. This was the sound of *la dolce vita* on the Gold Coast, music for polite ballroom dances, but the Africans had their own, street-level version: guitar music influenced by swing. Independence came in 1957, leading to the rise of E. T. Mensah's Cuban-influenced Tempos. However, the cost of running big bands was prohibitive. By the 1970s, the highlife was in decline.

Madagascar

The island of Madagascar is African, but only just. The people look more Asian, the instruments are unique (the most famous is the valiha, a zither featuring strings around the outside of a bamboo tube) and the music is at once incomparable and reminiscent of everything. On their album *Son Egal*, Tarika, the island's most famous export, reconciled their culture with that of the Senegalese transported there by France; on *Soul Makassar*, they investigated their links with Indonesia. Such split personalities are common: Njava sound like the Rolling Stones circa 1969.

Left
In many African cultures, music plays an important part in all aspects of life; whether the situation is a religious or cultural ceremony, a social occasion or a particular musical event, there is always an excuse to sing and dance.

Left
King Sunny Ade, "The Minister of Enjoyment", tours with his band, the African Beats. Their music, known as juju, involves many different sounds and they use a mixture of traditional African and modern Western instruments.

Mali

The country's pedigree stretches back to the thirteenth century, the Mande empire and the singers who praised the warrior Sunjata Keita. The occupation of musician was hereditary, and your family name determined your caste. Salif Keita (an aristocratic name) was disowned for wanting to be a musician; Toumani Diabate (a virtuoso on the kora, a 21-string harp) had little choice. Ali Farka Touré, on the other hand, was a farmer who claimed to have been possessed by spirits. In return, they made him into a blues guitarist, often compared to John Lee Hooker (Touré argues that Hooker is playing African music). In the capital, Bamako, the Super Rail Band has groomed fine musicians for more than 30 years, among them Djelimady Tounkara and Mory Kanté. In the south, female singers are the stars, whether praise singers, such as Kandia Kouyate, or the proto-feminist Oumou Sangaré. One of the most significant changes of the 1990s was the growth of a new strain of modern singer/songwriters, not all of them from the musical caste, and the names of Rokia Traore and Habib Koité are already well known beyond the country's borders.

Nigeria

As in Ghana, Nigeria swung to highlife, although black drinking dens had their own juju music. The early stars included Tunde Nightingale, I. K. Dairo's Morning Star Orchestra and King Sunny Ade, whose speedy percussive take on the music would see him proclaimed as "the new Bob Marley" in the 1980s. In 1969, the leader of Lagos group Koola Lobitos moved to America, where he discovered black consciousness and James Brown. When he returned to Nigeria, Fela Kuti was a man possessed by pan-African politics and funk (retitled Afrobeat). For the next 20 years, he was also public enemy number one for the government. In the 1990s, juju and Afrobeat were toppled from their pre-eminence by fuji and bandleaders such as Barrister, whose groups featured only furiously fast percussionists and the occasional Hawaiian guitar.

Senegal

Senegal shares the praise-singer tradition with Mali, but Cuban sailors brought in outside influences and the countries' paths diverged. The newly independent Senegal's leaders preferred the Star Band or Orchestre Baobab, who played rough facsimiles of the music of Havana's orquestas. Although this love of Cuba has continued with Africando, who export salsa to New York, by the 1980s the youth wanted something more African. It arrived with Youssou N'Dour, Étoile De Dakar and the style of music they called mbalax, which kept the Latin swing but introduced complex polyrhythms and ditched the horn section. In the north of the country, Baaba Maal was listening to mbalax and learning traditional music from his family's griot. He exploded onto the world stage with *Firin' In Fouta*, an album that also used Western dance beats.

South Africa

South Africa's nightclubs blossomed under curfew – you could either go home or stay in a club listening to jazz all night. In the mid-1950s, there was a boom in pennywhistle jive (kwela, with similarities to Jamaican ska). This made stars of Spokes Moshiyane (an early collaborator with Miriam Makeba) and West Nkosi, who went on to greater things as a saxophonist when kwela was superseded by township jive (mbaqanga) and as a producer when South African vocal groups such as Mahlathini and the Mahotella Queens and Ladysmith Black Mambazo (Zulu a cappella) adapted traditional harmonies to become the country's biggest musical exports. The post-apartheid freeing up of black musicians resulted in kwaito, a brand of hip hop using local samples that has made stars of the Prophets Of Da City.

Zimbabwe

In the mid-1980s, a Zimbabwean guitar band called the Bhundu Boys arrived in Scotland, cold and having difficulty adapting to local conditions (they did not own their own instruments). What they did have, however, was a desire to play gigs whenever and wherever, and to record and be heard. Their contribution to the growth of world music may never be truly understood. Back home, there are two permanent kings on the music scene; Thomas Mapfumo's mbira (thumb piano) orchestras have been playing chimurenga protest songs since the days of the Rhodesian white-minority government and continued into the 1990s, turning their wrath on President Robert Mugabe. The current ruler in Harare, though, is Oliver Mtukudzi, a charismatic guitarist and singer who mixes mbira music with US soul, Congolese rumba and South African jive.

Left

Biggie Tembo, lead singer of Zimbabwe's Bhundu Boys, named his band after his experiences in his country's struggle for liberation, in which he had been a runner – or "bundhu boy" – for the rebels.

Australia & Oceania

OCEANIA COVERS A VAST PORTION OF THE WORLD'S SURFACE, AND EACH ISLAND OR ARCHIPELAGO IS SEPARATED BY THOUSANDS OF MILES OF PACIFIC, YET THESE DISTINCT CULTURES SHARE ONE SOURCE: THE SOUTHWARD MIGRATION OF SEAFARERS FROM SOUTHEAST ASIA, WHO ARRIVED ON THE SINGLE LANDMASS THAT WAS NEW GUINEA, AUSTRALIA AND TASMANIA APPROXIMATELY 50,000 YEARS AGO.

Above
New Zealand group Wai aim to keep the Maori culture alive through their music. Band founder Mina Ripia once joined the Fugees on stage in Auckland, rapping in Maori to the delight of the audience.

IT would take more than 45,000 years before they would set foot on the islands of Melanesia, travelling east to Fiji, Tonga and Samoa by 1300 BC, and then on to Hawaii, French Polynesia and, eventually, New Zealand about 1,250 years ago.

These time spans, the distances covered and the rising seas that saw New Guinea, Australia and Tasmania become three islands, brought significant variations to the separated cultures. The effect of colonization has been no less important, with the Indonesian, British, Dutch, Portuguese, German, French and American peoples being among those laying claim to the islands, and Christian missionaries laying claim to the souls of their inhabitants. Nevertheless, indigenous cultures have survived, often against the odds.

An Indigenous Folk Music

Australian history once began in the eighteenth century with Captain Cook, at a time when the Aborigine population stood at three times the 250,000 it was at the end of the twentieth century. Attempts to "keep Australia white" have included separating Aborigine children from their parents and deliberate extermination. Language, culture and land rights have been ignored and people have been resettled. In the late-twentieth century, immigration from the north meant that Australia had to face up to its status as a de facto Asian country.

> **"I'M USING WHITE MAN'S SKILLS, YOLNGU [ABORIGINE] SKILLS AND PUTTING THEM TOGETHER FOR A NEW BEGINNING."**
> *Mandawuy Yunupingu*

But just as the American folk revival of the 1960s is irrevocably tied to civil rights, so the Aborigines' fight for recognition fostered an indigenous folk music and an appreciation of Aboriginal art – from painting to dance to the didgeridoo – that has spread to every continent and rock festival. The singers Kev Carmody, Archie Roach and Ruby Hunter have become standard bearers for this movement, bringing an awareness of the oppression their people had to bear to the wider audience, at home and abroad. As their names suggest, all three were raised by white people.

Festivals of Aboriginal culture gather indigenous people from all over Australia, the Torres Strait islands and Papua New Guinea, and are now visited by tens of thousands of Australians whose claim to the title goes back less than two centuries. But, given that Aborigines constitute only one-and-a-half per cent of the population, it is unsurprising

LEADING EXPONENTS

Yothu Yindi
Kev Carmody
Archie Roach
Ruby Hunter
George Telek
The Tahitian Choir
Te Vaka
Wai

AUSTRALIA & OCEANIA

This traditional hymn is typical of the acapella Fijian Methodist singing. The use of four part harmony (SATB) is common and is frequently "ad-libbed" by the singers.

SA

Kei - ma - mi va - ka - ma - du - o   vei   Ji - su

TB

THE WORLD INTRO ➡ 276   WORLD PEOPLE A–Z ➡ 308   INSTRUMENTS A–Z ➡ 436   FOLK: POLITICAL FOLK & PROTEST SONGS ➡ 230

that Yothu Yindi, the first band to break into the mainstream, were a multiracial rock band that could play a set in which a pop hit such as 'Treaty' could be followed by a tune that was 10,000 years older.

Very Little Cultural Interaction

Melanesia stretches from New Guinea (the island is divided into Indonesian Irian Jaya and Papua New Guinea) to Fiji. Although George Telek, from Papua New Guinea, is the only singer to have a profile outside the archipelago, there is much music to be found, particularly at a village singsing or at Christian festivals. Ukuleles and guitars dominate, but the 12 ft garamut slit drum is a spectacular sight. To the east, the Solomon Islands are home to panpipe orchestras and bamboo bands, who bang various lengths of tube with their sandals.

Culturally, Fiji shares more with Polynesia than its neighbours to the west, and is home to a form of apartheid. The population is evenly split between indigenous Fijians and transplanted Indians, but very little cultural interaction takes place.

The Polynesia of Gauguin no longer exists, and perhaps it never did. Instead, string bands playing relaxed Polynesian calypsos on ukuleles and guitars are the one thing visitors are guaranteed to find. Missionaries introduced Christianity and deplored native belief systems: the result was a tradition of polyphonic choral music that was developed in varying ways by the different churches in their isolated strongholds, with particularly beautiful versions to be heard on Tahiti and the Cook Islands. What separates the islands, though, is their sensuality. In western Polynesia, particularly Tonga and Samoa, the hip-shaking hula dances found on Tahiti are considered vulgar; far more acceptable are seated dances in which storytellers use their arms and faces to illustrate "action songs".

Contemporary Pop Sounds

Although not the capital of New Zealand, Auckland, which is by far the largest city in the Pacific's post-Australia diaspora, has become the centre of its recording industry. Maori culture survives primarily in the haka (a group chant of welcome or, most famously when performed by the national rugby union team, war) and the poi dance, but it is Polynesian immigrants to the North Island who have raised the international profile of their music, using contemporary pop sounds where necessary.

The multi-cultural Te Vaka (led by Opetaia Foa'i, a man with roots in Samoa, Tuvalu and Tokelau) are the best-known, having toured beyond the Pacific several times. They use Western rock and traditional Polynesian music, and promote both traditional instruments – such as log drums (pate) and goatskin bass drum (pau'u malu) – and dances. Having started out as the first band playing "original contemporary Pacific music", Te Vaka have been followed by Oceania, a Maori group that performs haka singing, and Wai, whose *Wai 100%* album staked a claim to containing the first Maori techno recordings, along with traditional musicians, action sounds, samples and hip hop rhythms.

THE STORY OF MIDDLE EASTERN MUSIC IN THE TWENTIETH CENTURY IS THE STORY OF UMM KALTHUM. UNTIL THE EARLY PART OF THE CENTURY, THE AREA HAD BEEN DIVIDED, CONQUERED AND RULED BY INVADERS FOR TWO MILLENNIA. KALTHUM PLAYED NO TANGIBLE PART IN THE STRUGGLE FOR INDEPENDENCE, BUT HER VOICE UNITED ARABS WHEREVER ARABIC IS SPOKEN.

Middle East

Above

Transglobal Underground's Psychic Karaoke *is a cocktail of musical styles from all over the world – including the Middle East, India, Africa, Jamaica – mixed together with dance, rap and pop influences from closer to home.*

BEYOND geographical boundaries, the Middle East is dominated by the music of Egypt, which imports musicians from and exports music to the Arab countries, and Turkey, which has the eastern Mediterranean world sewn up. But others such as Iran and Syria have strong musical traditions, particularly in classical music, while the influence of African Arabs such as the Sudanese oud maestro Hamza el Din should not be underestimated. Then there are the songs of struggle and survival, of reconciliation and peace, from both sides in the Israeli-Palestinian conflict. And then, from the north, from Armenia, comes the most melancholy music in the world, a sound shaped by a massacre.

A Strongly Patriotic Repertoire

Umm Kalthum was born in 1904, the daughter of an impoverished village imam who taught her religious songs. By the time she was 19, the family had decided she should become a professional singer and moved to Cairo. The next two decades saw her rise as a singer and film star, improvizing emotional love songs that stretched past the 60-minute mark, but it was the 1952 coup that was the catalyst for turning her into an icon. Befriending Gamal Abdul Nasser, the head of the new republic, she developed a strongly patriotic repertoire that won the hearts of the people. She never forgot her roots, however, or the hard work she put in before she became famous. Once asked if she had ever been nervous in front of

"IN THE 1950S, TWO LEADERS EMERGED IN THE MIDDLE EAST: GAMAL ABDUL NASSER AND UMM KALTHUM."

Egyptian saying

LEADING EXPONENTS

Djivan Gasparyan

Chava Alberstein

Ofra Haza

Umm Kalthum

Hamza el Din

Musicians Of The Nile

The Kamkars

Whirling Dervishes

Burhan Ocal

The Istanbul Oriental

Ensemble

MIDDLE EAST

Two notable characteristics of Middle Eastern music are the augmented 2nd between the sixth and seventh degrees of the scale, and the steady upbeat rhythm of the accompaniment.

crowds when she was an unknown, her answer said much about her character: "No. They were scared of me."

Three-Minute Fixes And Deep Melancholy

As Egypt opened up to outside influences in the 1970s, American rock and pop started to appeal to the youth. However, they already had their own equivalents: the rough-and-ready shaabi, which had grown up on the streets from the late-1960s, and al-jil, an Arabic techno-dance pop. Polite society was initially shocked by these working-class louts with their potent, three-minute fixes and *Pop Idol*-style aesthetics. But in countries where Umm Kalthum's legacy mattered less, al-jil sounded like the next best thing, the London-based Transglobal Underground being by far the most famous exploiters of the sound of young Cairo.

It's not all light-hearted frolics, however. In 1915, hundreds of thousands of Armenians were massacred by their Turkish neighbours. The survivors immediately fled their land, which is now part of Turkey, and the new rulers embarked on an elaborate operation to erase this episode from history. Twenty years later, Djivan Gasparyan would sit in his local cinema watching silent films and listening to the musicians accompanying them. The Armenian recorder, the duduk, is made of apricot wood and has a deep, melancholic tone, although a virtuoso can imbue it with warmth and joy. But the pain of Armenian history weighs heavily in Gasparyan's music, and one listen to his masterpiece, the album *I Will Not Be Sad In This World*, expresses his feelings better than words.

The Daily Struggle Of Getting Their Music Heard

The creation of Israel in 1948 brought an influx of new settlers to the Middle East, and a further degree of instability to the region. As new arrivals (Noa and Ofra Haza, for example, had roots in Yemen, while Chava Alberstein is Polish) with a desire to fit in, a large proportion of the musicians sing for peace in the region. Although the Palestinians who lived on the same disputed land did use music for entertainment, it was not until the uprising of the late-1980s that it began to have a real sense of purpose. However, the musician who has done most to take Palestinian music into world spheres is Adel Salameh, an oud player who left his country to live in Britain.

For the Kurds, even disputed land would be a blessing: in 1923, Kurdistan was carved up by Iran, Iraq, Soviet Armenia, Syria and Turkey. Since then, the Kurds and their culture have been systematically oppressed and excluded from mainstream life. For singers such as Sivan (based in Germany) and bands such as the Kamkars, the daily struggle is based around getting their music heard.

With the creation of modern, secular Turkey, Kemal Ataturk came down hard on music that was, in his view, tainted by Arabic influences. It was not until the 1980s that the renowned Mevlevi whirling dervishes, who practised Turkish sufism, were once again allowed to perform their rituals for believers rather than tourists. Non-religious music – folk, based around the sound of the saz, a long-necked lute; the classical music of the cities; and gypsy fasil and belly dancing – prospered in the interim, as did arabesk, an unpretentious, specifically Turkish pop music that has grown since Arabic was banned in the 1940s and follows a parallel path to rock in the West.

Above
Combining traditional Yemenite songs with a dance beat, Ofra Haza left Israel for success in the golden West. At first she was considered unpatriotic, but she went on to become an unofficial "musical ambassador" for her country.

Centre
Armenian music legend Djivan Gasparyan plays a duduk, a type of recorder capable of producing an intensely emotional sound, adding great depth to Gasparyan's music.

Native America

THE MUSIC OF THE INDIGENOUS PEOPLES OF NORTH AMERICA IS TIGHTLY BOUND TO THEIR STRUGGLE FOR SELF-DETERMINATION, HUMAN RIGHTS AND LAND, AS WELL AS THE TRADITIONAL CEREMONIES THAT WERE CREATED TO DEVELOP SPIRITUAL TIES WITH NATURE, TO PROVIDE STRENGTH FOR BATTLE AND TO RELATE GREAT VICTORIES. THE ARRIVAL OF EUROPEANS ALTERED THE DETAILS, BUT NOT THE ESSENCE.

Above

Native American music plays a big part in powwows and social dances. Here, a Mohawk performs the smoke dance, a former war dance that often features in powwow competitions.

HOWEVER, such is the precarious nature of a culture founded on oral history, even the most emblematic of ceremonies raise some controversy. The origins of the powwows that today bring together representatives of tribes from all corners of the continent, and which climax in elaborate celebrations featuring dances, drumming, vocable chanting (singing sounds that have no meaning outside the chants) and the throat-singing shared with Mongolian and Siberian nomads, may date from hundreds of years ago, but sceptics argue that they were the creation of white settlers and are about as authentic as a Wild West show or John Wayne movie.

Hollywood Cliché

In its early years, the all-pervasive influence of the Hollywood western reduced many of the Native Americans' sacred beliefs to cliché. The true significance of rain dances, war dances (particularly the Sioux Ghost Dance that eventually led to their final defeat in 1890), medicine men and the sacred use of smoking have become hard to comprehend or even take seriously for outsiders. However, as European and Native American cultures started to trade influences on an equal footing (and Hollywood started revising its image of the "Injun"), new musical forms started to emerge.

> "THE CHANTS ARE A TOY IN A LOT OF PEOPLE'S HANDS, BUT THIS IS MY HERITAGE. I HAVE ALL THESE SOUNDS THAT I'VE BEEN CARRYING AROUND FOR YEARS, ALL MY LIFE."
>
> *Robbie Robertson*

Among the first Europeans to venture onto the reservations were missionaries, and gospel music has a strong tradition among Native Americans. However, just as in other continents where Christianity has been introduced to a population with its own beliefs, hybrid strains have grown up, fusing animism, shamanism and hallucinogenic cacti. Chester Mahooty, Robert Tree Cody and the Sioux/Navajo duo Verdell Primeaux & Johnny Mike have become the foremost practitioners of peyote-inspired sacred music, singing prayers over drums and ambient electronics.

Singing For Civil Rights

In the 1960s, at the height of the civil rights struggle in the United States, a new breed of Native American singers started making themselves heard with music that was both contemporary and held hard-hitting messages. Born on a Saskatchewan reservation, the Cree singer Buffy Saint-Marie was the first politicized Native American to make real headway. Her 1964 breakthrough album, *It's My Way*, tackled topics such as war, incest, the destruction of the indigenous way of life and the perils of drug addiction. Although her singing career foundered in the 1970s, she later married the Phil Spector and Rolling Stones collaborator Jack Nitzsche and shared an Oscar with him for the theme to the film *An Officer And A Gentleman*.

Robbie Robertson was another with roots in the Canadian reservations. In the 1960s, he was Bob Dylan's guitarist on the folk singer's early electric tours; he then became one of the pioneers of Americana as songwriter for the Band. Although his songs for the Band described a lost America that had little to do with its indigenous people, in

LEADING EXPONENTS

Robbie Robertson
Buffy Sainte-Marie
Walela
Primeaux & Mike
Robert Mirabal
Without Rezervation
Redbone
Southern Scratch

NATIVE AMERICA

A major feature of music from the Andes is the use of pan pipes playing the melodies. Accompaniment is provided by pipes, guitars and charangos (guitars made from armadillo shells) and percussion.

pan pipes

THE WORLD INTRO ➡ 276   WORLD PEOPLE A–Z ➡ 308   INSTRUMENTS A–Z ➡ 436   FOLK: TRADITIONAL FOLK ➡ 228

1994 he composed the music for a TV series, *The Native Americans*, on which he collaborated with the likes of Rita Coolidge and her family vocal trio Walela, the Silvercloud Singers and the flautist Douglas Spotted Eagle. His 1998 album *Contact From The Underworld Of Redboy* took the themes he had grown up with a step further, mixing anger at the contemporary treatment of his people with cutting-edge dance beats, peyote chants and stomp dances. Among the contributors were Primeaux & Mike, and Inuit throat singers Tudjaat and Coolidge.

Led by Tom Bee, the New Mexican group XIT were unlikely members of the Motown family in the early 1970s, when they released two albums on the Rare Earth imprint, the folky *Plight Of The Redman* and the straight-ahead rock album *Silent Warrior*. The most successful band to

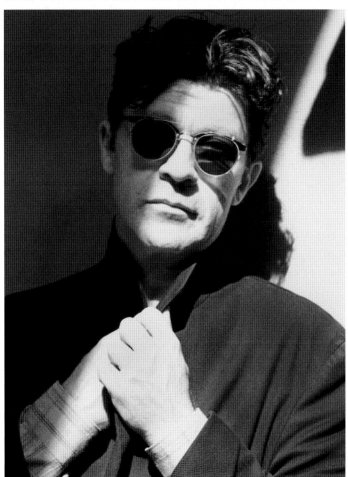

mix rock and funk with traditional music was arguably Redbone, led by Pat and Lolly Vegas, whose chart hits included 'Witch Queen Of New Orleans'.

A style of Native American music that seems determined to stay resolutely outside the mainstream, however, is chicken scratch, which rarely ventures far from its home on the Arizona/Mexico border. The proximity with Spanish influences flavours its unique brand of polkas, waltzes and mazurkas, played on acoustic guitars, fiddles and, in more contemporary bands such as Southern Scratch, accordions.

The Flute Revival

After *Changes*, the 1983 debut album by R. Carlos Nakai, there was renewed interest in the flute, which had traditionally been the favoured instrument of courting rituals. Nakai's recordings have sold almost three million copies, but the flute revival was soon co-opted by the new age movement. Without doubting the sincerity of the musicians, the jury is still out on whether every non-Native new age flautist understands the depths of the spirituality they are invoking. A flautist with perhaps more imagination, however, is Robert Mirabal, who conjured up the sound of a buffalo stampede on his 1995 album *Land*.

The future, unsurprisingly, will belong to hip hop and bands such as Without Rezervation, who mix the sound of urban America with ancient chants and beliefs, resulting in the same anger and directness that brought Sainte-Marie to the fore. You can take the people out of their land, but you can't take the land out of the people.

Left

Native American singer/ songwriter Buffy Sainte-Marie's lyrics proved too honest for the White House, which allegedly included her in its list of outspoken musicians that "deserved to be suppressed".

Left

Ex-Band member Robbie Robertson's collaborative work with Native American musicians often underlines the similarities between indigenous tribal culture and the current dance music scene.

Latin & South America

LATIN AMERICA IS PARTICULARLY RICH AND VARIED IN ITS MUSICAL TRADITIONS, WITH EACH COUNTRY BOASTING A BROAD AND VERY DISTINCT COLLECTION OF GENRES WHOSE DEVELOPMENT HAS BEEN SHAPED BY INDIGENOUS RHYTHMS, MIGRATION PATTERNS FROM EUROPE AND THE INFLUX OF SLAVERY.

Above

Ry Cooder's creation was an effort to resurrect the sensual melodies, patriotic hymns and lovelorn ballads of pre-Castro Cuba, played by semi-retired musicians to appeal to a diverse, worldwide audience.

AT the uppermost tip of Latin America is Mexico, a country whose musical sub-genres are too many to name, but may be best known for its mariachi music. Played by a large ensemble that includes violins, guitars, trumpets and vihuelas (five-string guitars), and which dresses in traditional, silver-studded charro attire, the mariachi may well be Mexico's most-recognized cultural expression, even though it does not include indigenous instruments such as flute or percussion. The origins of the word "mariachi", and indeed of the music itself, remain murky, but the mariachi is a staple in both Mexican pop and folk music. Although any song can be adapted to the format, there is a standard mariachi repertoire that includes classics such as 'Cielito Lindo', with its recognizable "Ay, ay, ay, ay" chorus and sweeping violin lines. Thanks to emissaries such as the band Mariachi Vargas de Tecalitlán, and ranchero icons such as Vicente Fernández (known for his rendition of 'El Rey'), mariachi music has also become part of the culture of other countries, including Colombia.

> "I'VE ALWAYS LIKED TO SING CORRIDOS, SINCE I WAS A KID. PEOPLE LOOKED FOR US ON THE RANCH TO SING THEM STORIES".
>
> *Jorge Hernández, Los Tigres del Norte*

LEADING EXPONENTS

Mariachi Vargas de
  Tecalitlán
Pedro Infante
Vicente Fernández
Carlos Gardel
Astor Piazzolla
Toto la Momposina
Rafael Escalona
Diómedes Díaz
João Gilberto
Luiz Bonfá
Ary Barroso
Los Tigres del Norte
Ry Cooder
Rubén González
Compay Segundo
Tom Jobim
Ibrahim Ferrer

Another Mexican musical form that stemmed from folk traditions was the corrido, which became popular during the Mexican revolution – much later than mariachi, thought to have made its appearance in the 1860s. The root of the corrido is its narrative quality (imagine a Mexican version of the troubadours!), as it often dealt with the tales and stories of revolutionary heroes. Through the years, corridos evolved to incorporate anti-heroes, ranging from bandits to Robin Hood types, and gained notoriety in the 1970s with the so-called narco-corridos of Los Tigres del Norte. Based in California, the group was one of the first to talk about drug smuggling and drug dealers in their songs. Los Tigres have become icons in the corrido genre and in 2002 their 1971 hit 'Contrabando y Traicion', a tale of treason and murder, was adapted into a best-selling novel, *La Reina del Sur*, by the Spanish author Arturo Pérez-Reverte.

LATIN & SOUTH AMERICA

Melodies are flamboyant with colourful syncopations, as in this example where the rhythmic stresses across the main beats produce a jovial and lilting effect.

The Cumbian Beat Goes On

The traditional music of Colombia – the cumbia – has been adopted in Mexico and, in turn, mariachi has become part of the culture of Colombia. The original cumbia, as with other Caribbean rhythms, has an African rhythm base and dates as far back as the seventeenth century, where it developed on Colombia's northern coasts. The music, which also takes elements from Spain and Colombia's indigenous population, uses drums and flutes (called gaitas) and is meant to be danced to, with emphasis placed on hip movement. Over the years, cumbia has evolved and adapted urban characteristics; today, a cumbia orchestra will include horns and keyboard, and play at a faster clip. But the cumbia beat remains unchanged, and the standard repertoire, notably 'La Pollera Colorá' and 'La Piragua', is still played and updated by numerous pop bands.

Colombia's other renowned musical export is vallenato, the music of the coastal state of Valledupar, characterized by the accordion and by songs with an emphasis on storytelling. Carlos Vives has contemporized the genre and its representative icons include Rafael Escalona and Diómedes Díaz.

Aggressively Sensual And Hugely Popular

Just as cumbia and mariachi have become universal, so has the Argentine-born tango, a dance and song form which grew in the brothels of Buenos Aires and was initially aggressive and often violent, like its milieu. The early tango used flute, violin and guitar, later expanding to accommodate the bandoneón (a German accordion), now the instrument most associated with the music. As it developed from being aggressive to aggressively sensual, tango became hugely popular in the US and Europe, thanks in part to the singer Carlos Gardel, who went so far as to make films in the US in the 1930s, before he died in a plane crash in 1935. Among Gardel's numerous signature tunes is the lovely 'El Día Que Me Quieras', also the title of a movie. In the latter part of the 1900s, there was a tango revival thanks to the "new tango" of Astor Piazzolla, who studied with Nadia Boulanger in Paris and brought new harmonies and orchestration to the genre, concentrating on the instrumental rather than the vocal parts. Tango has continued to evolve and be immortalized in multiple art forms, including the film *Last Tango In Paris* and, more recently, a series of travelling shows, such as *Tango Argentino* and *Forever Tango*.

Perhaps the most recent and phenomenal revival of traditional Latin music is that of Cuban Son, the nineteenth-century fusion of African and Spanish elements that evolved into Son Montuno and contemporary salsa. But the more traditional Cuban Son, exemplified by the song 'Son de la Loma', was brought to the international spotlight with Ry Cooder's recordings of Buena Vista Social Club, featuring veteran icons of Cuban music such as Rubén González and Compay Segundo. The standard Son instrumentation includes guitar, tres (a six- or nine-string guitar), clave (the two sticks that are struck together, playing the signature rhythm), bongos and bass. Later, trumpet, piano and conga were added. The lead vocals, of course, went to the sonero, who improvises.

Brazilian Bossa Nova

In Brazil, local rhythms captured the international spotlight in the form of the bossa nova of the 1960s, popularized by the likes of Tom Jobim and João Gilberto. But the country's premier rhythm is probably samba, a blend of Afro-Brazilian,

European and Cuban influences that converged in the street and was often sung by dancers, backed by throbbing percussion. Brazil and samba became known worldwide through the Ary Barroso composition 'Aquarela do Brasil', also known simply as 'Brazil'. The main ambassador of the music was the singing star Carmen Miranda, who sported her trademark fruit headgear in Hollywood films and recorded the hit 'Mama Eu Quero', a carnival samba of the likes developed yearly for the Rio de Janeiro carnival and others around Brazil.

Centre
Astor Piazzolla began to play the bandoneón while standing with one leg up on a chair, a trait that distinguished him on the music scene, as most bandoneonists play while seated.

Above
The romantic softness of bossa nova was founded and brought to the jazz mainstream by Brazil's João Gilberto, whose tremendous impact on the genre will always remain due to the archetypal hit, 'The Girl From Ipanema'.

Cajun & Zydeco

CAJUN EMERGED FROM A EUROPEAN TRADITION OF CONTREDANSES, TWO-STEPS AND WALTZES; ZYDECO, THE BLACK EQUIVALENT, GREW OUT OF THE WORK SONGS OF THE BLACK FARMERS WHO HAD SETTLED IN LOUISIANA. LIFE IN THE POOREST STATE IS STILL HARD, AND COTTON AND CRAWFISH STILL RULE: AT LEAST THERE ARE SOME THINGS THE SETTLERS OF THE EIGHTEENTH CENTURY WOULD RECOGNIZE AS THEIRS.

Above

The conga drum often provides the rhythms in Cajun and zydeco music

> ### "MUSIC IS THE GLUE THAT HOLDS THE WHOLE CULTURE AND SOCIETY TOGETHER."
>
> *Marc Savoy*

LEADING EXPONENTS

Cajun

Doug Kershaw

Joseph & Cleoma
    Falcon

The Balfa Brothers/Balfa
    Toujours

Michael
    Doucet/BeauSoleil

Iry LeJeune

Dewey, Will, Rodney &
    Harry Balfa

Zydeco

Clifton Chenier

Boozoo Chavis

Rockin' Dopsie

Buckwheat Zydeco

Queen Ida

C. J. Chenier

Nathan & the Zydeco
    Cha-Chas

Terrance Simien

Rosie Ledet

FRENCH expansion into the Americas began in Acadia (later renamed Nova Scotia by the British) and ran through the Great Lakes, from Ontario on the St Lawrence River to Fort St Joseph at the southern end of Lake Michigan, then south towards the Gulf of Mexico and New Orleans, that city being founded in 1718. Conflict between the French and the British, both planning global domination, erupted in 1754, and the British evicted French settlers from Acadia, resulting in many of them relocating to Louisiana.

By 1763, France's North American territories had been claimed by Britain, and subsequent years saw Spain stake out possession of Florida and Louisiana, although the large number of French Acadians (renamed Cajuns) made them the largest culture around the prairies of Baton Rouge and Lafayette, cities that still bear French names.

Although the Cajun dialect was banned by ruling outsiders as the Union expanded and the autonomy of French and Spanish settlements disappeared, the music of the Cajuns has always held on to its French roots. However, the modern Cajun style started only in the 1920s, when the traditional fiddlers were supplemented by guitarists and accordion players. Although the accordion was able to stay in tune in the humid conditions of a dancehall in the tropics, it was unable to play the same tunes as the fiddle. So the tunes changed.

In 1928, the recording industry sought out the good-time dance music and a 78rpm disc, 'Allons à Lafayette', by Joseph and Cleoma Falcon, was released. Cleoma Falcon's brother Amédé Breaux then released a recording of 'Jolie Blonde' ('Pretty Blonde Girl'), which would become as important to Cajun music as the phrase "Woke up this morning" would be to the blues. Another duo, Amédé Ardoin and Dennis McGee, caused a stir with their accordion and fiddle recordings, Ardoin also being a remarkable singer. What was truly striking, though, was that Ardoin was black and McGee white.

A Brief Interlude From The Hardships Of Life

In the 1930s, Cajun music changed again, as American migration from the dust-bowls along with the growth of radio, meant that people in the south were hearing country & western tunes. Drums, bass and steel guitars began to make an impact. But the tide swung back in the post-war years, thanks to two

CAJUN & ZYDECO

Cajun music originating from French Acadia (Canada) employs accordion techniques along with jazz/blues elements. The grace notes in bars 2 and 4 emulate "note-bending" on guitar.

THE WORLD INTRO ➡ 276   WORLD PEOPLE A–Z ➡ 308   INSTRUMENTS A–Z ➡ 436   BLUES: LOUISIANA BLUES ➡ 161   THE COUNTRY INTRO ➡ 182

accordionists: the near-blind Iry LeJeune, who was influenced by Amédé Ardoin, and Nathan Abshire, who was a fan of the blues.

For Louisiana's black population, known as Creoles, their music, la-la, was a brief interlude from the hardships of life. La-la (from the French for a house party) was noticeably more African in origin, with greater emphasis on rhythm and less on melody, though the main instruments were still accordion and fiddle. Of the earliest players, the duo of Canray Fontenot (fiddle) and the accordionist Bois Sec (a cousin of Amédé Ardoin) is the most celebrated today.

As rock'n'roll and blues took hold among the black population throughout America, la-la underwent rapid changes in order to keep its audience. Thus was born zydeco, a turbo-charged R&B that took black Louisiana's music in an alternative direction from that of the whites, a gap that remains to this day. The man at the forefront of this revolution was the accordionist Clifton Chenier, who was signed to the same label, Specialty, as rockers Little Richard and Lloyd Price.

Despite Chenier's death in 1987, zydeco had established itself as a bona fide rock style, with such eye-catching performers as Queen Ida, Boozoo Chavis, Rockin' Dopsie (who contributed to Paul Simon's *Graceland*) and Rockin' Sidney, who took zydeco in to the international pop charts with the breakout hit 'My Toot Toot'.

A Newly Recognized American Roots Music

For Cajun music, it was the folk revival rather than rock'n'roll that was the catalyst for acceptance on its own terms. A 1950s recording of the brothers Dewey, Will, Rodney and Harry Balfa was part of the folk revival curriculum, but the music was seen as a relic of a bygone age until Dewey performed a rapturously received set at the 1964 Newport Folk Festival. At last, Cajun music had an audience outside French Louisiana. A new generation of musicians, such as Doug "The Ragin' Cajun" Kershaw, had started adapting rock rhythms for their own purpose and singing in English to widen their appeal (Kershaw's 'Louisiana Man' was the first tune played in outer space – how much wider can you get?). The acclaim for this newly recognized American roots music meant that groups such as Balfa Toujours and BeauSoleil, and the accordionist Eddie LeJeune (son of Iry), were suddenly finding popularity throughout the country.

Where once young Cajuns tried to assimilate into the greater scheme of things and their language was proscribed, French has become part of Louisiana's education curriculum and annual festivals take place to promote both Cajun and zydeco music. As a result of the growing interest in all things Cajun – from the music to the food – a once-threatened subculture has found new strength and looks set to thrive.

Centre

Clifton Chenier was the first to combine blues with the accordian, and helped to popularize the zydeco sound. An intense performer, Chenier would put everything he had into each song, and he rarely needed to record more than one take.

Left

Doug Kershaw is a talented multi-instrumentalist, whose manic fiddle playing often leaves him barely visible in a cloud of rosin dust, and can result in his getting through three or four bows in one gig.

PERVERSE AS IT MAY SEEM, EUROPE IS AN IMPORTANT CENTRE FOR WORLD MUSIC.
ALL THE PREREQUISITES EXIST: LARGE POPULATIONS IN A SMALL AREA, TRANSPORT,
PROXIMITY TO OTHER CONTINENTS, AFFLUENT CONSUMERS, COMMUNICATIONS …

Europe

Above
Edith Piaf, whose raw, impassioned delivery and touching songs brought her global fame. She remained intrinsically linked to her native country and, for many people, Piaf came to symbolize France itself.

AS rural migrants moved to urban areas and immigrants arrived, Europeans were leaving for the New World (making New York the best place to hear klezmer, the music of Eastern Europe's Jews). As a result, various forms of folk music achieved popularity far from their home crowd: in the 1980s, Le Mystère des Voix Bulgares, the Bulgarian women's national radio choir, became a hit on the indie rock scene. Paris is now at the heart of North Africa: Rachid Taha is a Franco-Algerian rock star who mixes heavy metal guitars with dance beats and rai. Flamenco, the sound of Spain, is a hybrid of Moorish and gypsy influences, and its greatest exponents, such as the singer El Camarón de la Isla, or the most popular, the Gipsy Kings (from southern France), come from cultures that are still outcasts in society.

In Britain, the first time the general population was exposed to world music came when calypso musicians arrived from the West Indies in the 1950s, although there had been earlier flourishes of polite Latin music. The 1960s brought sitars, *Brian Jones Presents The Pipes Of Jajouka* and the Incredible String Band. By the 1970s, reggae, Indian classical and bhangra, a Punjabi folk music, were well established, creating a situation in which the Nigerian King Sunny Ade was launched as the successor to Bob Marley as a Third World superstar. In 1982, Peter Gabriel launched WOMAD (World of Music, Arts and Dance) to promote world music through album releases, tours

and festivals. After a short period of success, however, the mainstream audience proved resistant to music in foreign tongues, record sales rarely matched expectations and eventually the accountants pulled the plug. Despite the demise of WOMAD, the seeds of acceptance had been sown.

> "ONE HALF OF MY BAND – THE OUD AND PERCUSSION – IS WORLD; THE OTHER HALF – THE GUITARS AND DRUMS – THEY ARE ROCK'N'ROLL, BABY."
>
> *Rachid Taha*

LEADING EXPONENTS

Talvin Singh
Serge Gainsbourg
Les Négresses Vertes
Le Mystère des Voix Bulgares
El Camarón de la Isla
Muzsikás
Márta Sebestyén
Amália Rodrigues
Vera Bila
Taraf de Haidouks

EUROPE

This Croatian dance is typical of folk music from Eastern Europe, using a pentatonic scale accompanied by simple dance rhythms.

tune: vocal, guitar, flute etc

accompaniment: accordion, guitar, bass etc

THE WORLD INTRO ➡ 276 WORLD PEOPLE A–Z ➡ 308 INSTRUMENTS A–Z ➡ 436

Music Aimed At The Streets

It was not until the early 1990s that Britain produced its first lasting indigenous world music, bringing something from outside to the sounds of London's clubs. The standard-bearers were Transglobal Underground, the former Public Image Limited bassist Jah Wobble (with the Invaders Of The Heart) and Natacha Atlas. This was music aimed at the streets rather than the coffee tables, and it opened many ears and minds to far wider possibilities.

The next stage was the so-called Asian Underground, which collected musicians, primarily from India and Pakistan, and offered them the chance to voice their thoughts on being Asian and British. It was a fashion that soon faded in the mainstream media's eyes, but the likes of Talvin Singh, Nitin Sawhney and Asian Dub Foundation had already transcended categorization and become international stars.

In Paris, the archetypal café accordion music was a folk sound that had, like flamenco in Spain, become part of the national identity. Lacking an (anglophonic) rock culture, French music was dominated by chanson, the ballads of Edith Piaf and the Armenian Charles Aznavour, updated in the 1960s by the Belgian Jacques Brel and the one-man scandal factory that was Serge Gainsbourg (whose parents were Russian Jews). This was world music in waiting.

It came together in the early 1980s, when reggae, chanson, punk, rai and accordions melded in riotous assemblies such as Les Négresses Vertes and Mano Negra. At the same time, the government started offering grants to African musicians, and the likes of Salif Keita and Manu Dibango arrived. France not had its own new music and Paris became a centre of sub-Saharan music.

Cultures For The Dispossessed

Although no other cities offer such startling examples of pan-world music cultures (a theory Barcelona, home to Manu Chao, might dispute), there are dozens of regional centres where you can find musicians whose influence on London and Paris is immense.

In Portugal, fado reigns supreme: it's a passionate music, influenced by immigrants from Brazil, which highlights life's tough breaks. The death of the leading singer of the modern era, Amália Rodrigues, merited a state funeral and cast a long shadow. New stars, such as the Angola-born Mariza, carry the flame knowing they will forever be compared to Rodrigues.

Rembetika, an urban blues not unlike fado, occupies a similar position in Greece, although its roots lie in Constantinople. The music of the dispossessed and disenfranchised, it was often attacked by repressive governments throughout the twentieth century, and would not achieve respectability until

the 1970s, when a revival brought the singer Eleftheria Arvantaki to the international stage.

From Greece to Paris, however, there has always been a culture for the dispossessed: the gypsies, whose roots stretch back to northern India. The most popular European styles are flamenco, the Parisian jazz of Django Reinhardt, the Bessie Smith-style blues of Vera Bila and the Romanian frenzy of Taraf de Haidouks, examples of musicians adapting themselves to local needs in order to make a living rather than serve as exponents of living traditions. The Nazi Holocaust and Soviet Persecution brought many such traditions to an end, and the support of gypsy human rights is a modern development hastened by the success of folk musicians such as Hungary's Márta Sebestyén and Muzsikás, who have done their bit to learn and preserve centuries-old songs.

Above

Mariza's powerful yet sensual voice is perfectly suited to fado, which translates as "fate". She started out singing in her parents' restaurant in the Lisbon suburb of Mouraria, considered to be the birthplace of fado.

Centre

Asian Dub Foundation grew out of a community music workshop and released their first album in 1995. The band experiment with new sound combinations and voice strong political beliefs in their music.

Russia & Central Asia

THE TURBULENT HISTORY AND IMMENSE SIZE OF RUSSIA AND THE SOVIET UNION MAKE IT A DIFFICULT PLACE TO SUM UP IN MUSICAL TERMS – NOT BECAUSE THERE ARE INCALCULABLE VARIETIES, AND GENERALIZING WOULD NECESSARILY FAVOUR ONE STYLE OR REGION OVER ANOTHER, BUT BECAUSE WHAT IS AUTHENTIC IS BOUND UP IN POLITICS.

Above

Tuvan band Yat-Kha's music successfully fuses their country's traditions with the modern recording world, while managing to remain untainted by popular Western influences.

THE Tzars wanted to hear professional musicians demonstrating the national culture and real peasants could not be introduced to the court, so at least one layer of authenticity would be stripped away before the music was heard in the cities.

Under Soviet control, folk music had to be controlled and approved by the state. But the further from Moscow one travelled, the looser this control became. While the Red Army Choir could captivate sympathetic audiences with their artistry, this was not the true sound of their comrades in the rural soviets.

It was not until the 1960s that musicians felt confident enough to replicate the real music of the country without preparing them for outside consumption. Dmitri Pokrovsky and Vyacheslav Shchurov would send singers out to the country to record and transcribe amateur folk singers, thus preserving the true music of the people, under threat in the rest of the world from urbanization and homogeneity.

> "FUSION HAS BEEN GOING ON FOR THOUSANDS OF YEARS IN DIFFERENT SPHERES OF HUMAN CULTURE. IT MOVES THE WORLD FORWARD."
>
> *Albert Kuvezin, Yat-Kha*

Strings That Are Too Spiky

However, the Soviet attitude to music that was not Russian was less encouraging. In Mongolia and Tuva, the move to create a pan-USSR music meant that local styles were subordinated to types of music made by people who lived 4,000 miles to the west. The nomadic lifestyles of the

LEADING EXPONENTS

Yat-Kha
Huun-Huur-Tu
Sainkho Namtchylak
Egschiglen
The Red Army Choir
Terem Quartet
Ashkhabad
Alim Qasimov

RUSSIA & CENTRAL ASIA

Russian folk melodies, especially those in the minor key, are a mix of modal and oriental scales with strong accidental changes at cadence points.

melody - accordion, balalaika

indigenous people were also controlled, their shamans stripped of their status and their Buddhist monks forced from their monasteries.

Like many other teens in the 1970s and 1980s, Albert Kuvezin had no interest in traditional music, but taught himself music via bootleg tapes of the Beatles and Iron Butterfly. He remembers being forbidden from playing concerts by panels charged with making sure his music was suitable for Soviet youth: he failed on 14 counts, including having strings that were "too spiky".

It was not until the fall of communism that the traditional music of these two states made their mark outside, but the effect was spectacular. Throat (or overtone) singing involves collapsing the lungs to produce two or three vocal lines. One singer can simultaneously sing a baritone drone and add other noises on top. It is a skill shared with Native Americans, and comes in a variety of styles, notably kargyraa (wheezing), ezengileer (horse trotting), borbannadyr (rolling), sygyt (whistle) and khoomei (similar to sygyt but more nasal).

In 1992, Huun-Huur-Tu were formed by Tuvans Sacha and Sayan Bapa, Kaiga-ool Khovalyg and Albert Kuvezin, who had all been members of a state-run troupe. The same year, Shu-De were invited to Wales to take part in the eisteddfod. With their shaman performing mystical rituals, and their traditional costumes and instruments (horse-head, four-ear and spike fiddles), they quickly came to the attention of the WOMAD organization and recorded an album of folk songs.

Huun-Huur-Tu and Mongolia's Egschiglen were the next ensembles to appear in the West, but Kuvezin soon split from the former band to found Yat-Kha, in an attempt to make the music more progressive and appealing to young Tuvans. By 2000, they were combining throat singing with hard rock to great international acclaim.

Although throat singing by women is often frowned upon (it is believed to cause infertility), Sainkho Namtchylak became Tuva's leading export after moving to western Europe in the 1980s. Considerably more arty than the other artists mentioned, she has taken her vocal skills to jazz, avant-garde and dance spheres.

The Barriers Are Down

The musics of the former Soviet republics of Central Asia share Islam, Russian discrimination, and roots in Turkey and western China. But the contemporary artists who have had success in the wider world display the distinctiveness that comes from centuries of conflict mixed with isolation.

Like Europe's nomad people, the gypsies, the music of Central Asia reflects South Asian and Middle Eastern traits; it is also commonly used to provide entertainment at family gatherings and celebrations. Yulduz Usmanova has made a name for herself internationally by updating the traditional music of Uzbekistan. At home, however, she is best known as the country's most popular wedding singer. Similarly, the Turkmenistan ensemble Ashkhabad arrived in Britain to tour and record wedding music, playing clarinet, violin, accordion and frame drum. In Azerbaijan, Alim Qasimov, a former shepherd, has become known as the greatest singer of the country's most famous song style, the mugam, a devotional love poem resembling the singing of the sufis of Pakistan. In 1999, he was awarded a prize by UNESCO for his contribution to the art.

Back in Russia, the barriers are down, and pop, punk and heavy metal have moved in. All is not lost, however: the folk revival continues, and lost musics (not least that of the Russian Orthodox church) have been rediscovered. For a good night out, though, the Terem Quartet play the classics and throw in some folk tunes for good measure – all with a coating of comedy. The Party would not be pleased.

Left

Sainkho Namtchylak blends the throat singing style of the Republic of Tuva with Siberian shamanic culture and folklore, as well as Bhuddist traditions. Her exotic sound and looks have established her as a rising star in the Western world.

Below

Alim Qasimov's amazing vocal abilities and haunting delivery rank him among the world's top singers. His first instrument was a frame drum made from the skin of a goat slaughtered by his father.

Artists: World

Entries appear in the following order: name, music style, year(s) of popularity, type of artist, country of origin

Abana Ba Nasery, Africa, 1960s-1990s, Artist, Kenyan
Abaquondidi Brothers, Africa, 1990s, Artist, South African
Abdelli, Africa, 1990s, Artist, Algerian
Abdo, George, India, 1990s, Artist, Indian
Abdy, Africa, 2000s-, Artist, Moroccan
Abe, Keiko, East Asian, 1980s-1990s, Artist, Japanese
Abraham, Paul, Europe, 1920s-1960s, Composer, Hungarian
Abreu, Vania, Latin & South America, 1990s, Artist, Brazilian
Abshire, Nathan, Cajun & Zydeco, 1940s-1980s, Artist, American
Absolut Folk, Europe, 1990s, Artist, Swedish
Abyssinia Band, Africa, 1990s, Artist, Ethiopian
Adamo, Europe, 1960s-, Artist, Italian
Adawia, Ahmed, Middle East, 1970s-, Artist, Egyptian
Addy, Mustapha Tettey, Africa, 1970s-1990s, Artist, Ghanaian
Addy, Obo, Africa, 1970s-, Artist, Ghanaian
Ade, King Sunny, Africa, 1970s-, Artist, Nigerian
Adewale, Segun, Africa, 1980s, Artist, Nigerian
African Brothers Band, Africa, 1960s-1980s, Artist Ghanaian
African Fiesta, Africa, 1960s, Artist, Zaire
Agyeman, Eric, Africa, 1970s, Artist, Ghanaian
Ahlam, Middle East, 1990s, Artist, Moroccan
Ahmed, Mahmoud, Africa, 1970s-1990s, Artist Ethiopian
Ahmed, Sherhabeel, Africa, 1980s, Artist, Sudanese
Aichi, Houria, Africa, 1990s, Artist, Algerian
Aisha Kandisha's Jarring Effects, Middle East, 1990s-, Artist, Moroccan
Aj-Jelad, Agd, Africa, 1980s-1990s, Artist, Sudanese
Akanni Animashaun, Africa, 1980s, Artist, Nigerian
Akendengue, Pierre, Africa, 1970s-, Artist, Gabonese
Al Said, Mokhtar, Middle East, 1990s, Artist, Lebanese
Alakotila, Timo, Europe, 1990s, Artist, Finnish
Alame, Ragheb, Middle East, 1990s-, Artist, Lebanese
Al-Amin, Mohamad, Africa, 1960s-1980s, Artist, Sudanese
Alangolla, Europe, 1990s, Artist, Finnish
Al-Bakheit, Abu Araky, Africa, 1980s, Artist, Sudanese
Alberto Y Roberto, Latin & South America, 2000s-, Artist, Mexican
Alexiou, Haris, Europe, 1990s, Artist, Greek
Algarner, Loy, Australia & Oceania, 1990s, Artist, Hawaiian
Ali, Meher, Russia & Central Asia, 1990s, Artist, Pakistani
Ali, Muzaffar, Russia & Central Asia, 2000s-, Artist, Pakistani
Alisha, India, 1980s-1990s, Artist, Indian
Allen, Tony, Africa, 1960s-, Artist, Nigerian
Al-Matah, Talal, Middle East, 1990s, Artist, Saudi Arabian
Al-Saher, Kazem, Middle East, 2000s-, Artist, Iraqi
Altan, Celtic, 1980s-, Artist, British
Amadinda Percussion Group, Europe, 1980s-, Artist, Hungarian
Amaduduzo, Africa, 1980s-1990s,, Artist, South Africa
Aman, Ehsan, Middle East, 1980s, Artist, Afghan
Amayenge, Africa, 2000s-, Artist, Zambian
Ambolley, Gyedu-Blay, Africa, 2000s-, Artist, Ghanaian
Amdursky, Asaf Middle East 2000s- Artist Israeli
Amigo, Vicente Latin & South America 1980s- Artist Mexican
Amira Saqati, Middle East, 1990s, Artist, Moroccan
Amrouche, Marguerite Taos, Africa, 1960s, Artist, Algerian
Anam, Celtic, 1990s-, Artist, Irish
Anand, Vijaya, India, 1990s, Artist, Indian
Anastacia, Latin & South America, 1990s-, Artist, Brazilian
Angelin Tytot, Europe, 1990s, Artist, Swedish
Animashaun, Akanni, Africa, 1980s, Artist, Nigerian
Anjelit, Europe, 1980s-1990s, Artist, Finnish
An-Nil, Hanan, Africa, 2000s-, Artist, Sudanese
Anouar, Africa, 1990s-, Artist, Algerian
Antunez, Rafael Ramos, Europe, 1920s-1930s, Artist, Spanish
Apaka, Alfred, Australia & Oceania, 1940s-1950s, Artist, Hawaiian
Arafeh, Souheil, Middle East, 1990s, Artist, Syrian
Argan, Middle East, 1990s, Artist, Moroccan
Armstrong, Frankie, Celtic, 1960s-1980s, Artist, British
Arrow, Caribbean, 1980s-, Artist, Trinidadian
Arun, Ila, India, 1990s, Artist, Indian
Asebido, Rachel, Australia & Oceania, 1990s, Artist, Hawaiian
Ashland Singers, The, Native America, 2000s-, Artist, American
Ashmahan, Middle East, 1930s-1940s, Artist, Egyptian
Astatke, Mulatu, Africa, 1960s-1970s, Artist, Ethiopian
Athenians, The, Europe, 1980s- , Artist, Greek
Au Kwan-Cheng, East Asia, 2000s-, Artist, Chinese
Awali, Leila, Middle East, 1990s, Artist, Saudi Arabian
Awapuhi, Hale, Australia & Oceania, 1990s, Artist, Hawaiian
Aweke, Aster, Africa, 1980s-1990s, Artist, Ethiopian
Ay Lazzat, Russia & Central Asia, 1990s, Artist, Russian
Azim, Erica Kundidzora, Africa, 1990s-, Artist, Zimbabwe
Azizi, Sear, Middle East, 2000s-, Artist, Afghan
Azrie, Abed, Middle East, 1990s-, Artist, Syrian
Azuma, East Asia, 1980s, Producer, Japanese
Baah, Rebop Kwaku, Africa, 1970s-1980s, Artist, Nigerian
Baden Powell, Latin & South America, 1960s-, Artist, Brazilian
Badjie, Saikouba, Africa, 1990s, Artist, Senegalese
Baha Men, Caribbean, 1990s-, Artist, Bahamian
Balai, Alberto, Europe, 1970s, Artist, Italian
Balalaika-Ensemble Wolga, Russia & Central Asia, 1990s, Artist, Russian
Balfa, Dewey, Cajun & Zydeco, 1970s-1980s, Artist, American
Ball, Patrick, Celtic, 1980s-, Artist, American
Bally, Caribbean, 1980s-, Artist, Trinidadian
Balogh, Istvan, Europe, 2000s-, Artist, Hungarian
Balogh, Kalman, Europe, 1990s, Artist, Hungarian
Balogh, Kalman, Europe, 1990s, Artist, Hungarian
Baluchi Ensemble Of Karachi, The, India, 1990s, Artist, Middle Eastern
Bamba, Amadu, Africa, 1990s, Artist, Senegalese
Banda Karembe, Latin & South America, 2000s-, Artist, Mexican
Banda Zagal, Latin & South America, 2000s-, Artist, Mexican
Banerjee, Nikhil, India, 1960s-1980s, Artist, Indian
Bano, Iqbal, India, 1990s, Artist, Indian
Bar, Shlomo, Middle East, 1970s-, Artist, Moroccan
Baron, Caribbean, 1980s-, Artist, Trinidadian
Barong, Southeast Asia, 2000s-, Artist, Javanese
Barzaz, Europe, 1980s-1990s, Artist, French
Basho-Junghans, Steffan, Europe, 1990s-, Artist, German
Bask, Europe, 1990s, Artist, Swedish
Batish, Ashwin, India, 1980s-1990s, Artist, Indian
Bawa, Gurmeet, India, 1980s, Artist, Indian
Bear, Keith, Native, America, 2000s, Artist, American
Beausoleil, Cajun & Zydeco, 1950s-, Artist, American
Beaver Chief, Native America, 1990s, Artis,t American
Begley, Brendan, Celtic, 1980s-1990s, Artist, Irish
Begley, Seamus, Celtic, 1990s, Artist, Irish
Begum, Shamshad, India, 1930s-1940s, Artist, Indian
Belafonte, Harry, Caribbean, 1940s-1990s, Artist, American
Bellamy, Peter, Celtic, 1960s-1990s, Artist, British
Bellemou, Messaoud, Africa, 1960s-, Artist, Algerian
Belloni, Alessandro, Europe, 1980s-, Artist, Italian
Bembeya Jazz National, Africa, 1960s-1990s, Artist, Guinean
Ben, Jorge, Latin & South America, 1960s-, Artist, Brazilian
Ben, Zehava, Middle East, 1990s-, Artist, Israeli
Benani, Hamdi, Africa, 1990s, Artist, Algerian
Bengal Tigers, The, India, 1990s, Artist, Indian
Benkadi International, Africa, 1990s, Artist, African
Benson, Bobby, Africa, 1950s-1970s, Artist, Nigerian
Beroard, Jocelyne, Caribbean, 1980s-1990s, Artist, West Indian
Bey, Tamuril Cemil, Middle East, 1910s, Artist, Turkish
Bhattacharya, Tarun, India, 1980s-, Artist, Indian
Bhengu, John, Africa, 1950s-1960s, Artist, Zulu
Bhosle, Asha, India, 1970s-1990s, Artist, Indian
Bhundu Boys, The, Africa, 1980s-1990s, Artist, Zimbabwe
Bichevskaya, Jeanne, Russia & Central Asia, 1990s, Artist, Russian
Billie, Chief Jim, Native America 1980s-, Artist, American
Bix, Europe, 1970s, Artist, Lithuanian
Black Eagle, Native America, 1990s-, Artist, American
Black Lodge Singers, Native America, 1990s-, Artist, American
Black Umfolosi, Africa, 1990s, Artist, Zimbabwe
Black, Frances, Celtic, 1990s, Artist, Irish
Black, Mary, Celtic, 1980s-, Artist, Irish
Blades, Ruben, Latin & South America, 1970s-, Artist, Panamanian
Blanasi, David, Australia & Oceania, 1990s-, Artist, Australian
Blanca de la Rosa, Latin & South America, 1990s-, Artist, Mexican
Blue Notes, The, African, 1960s-1980s, Artist, African
Boden, Ulrika, Europe, 1990s-, Artist, Swedish
Boka Marimba, Africa, 2000s-, Artist, Zimbabwe
Bolat, Latif, Middle East, 1990s, Artist, Turkish
Boot, Europe, 1990s, Artist, Swedish
Boross, Lajos, Europe, 1990s, Artist, Hungarian
Bose, Sipra, India, 1980s-, Artist, Indian
Bothy Band, The, Celtic, 1970s, Artist, Irish
Boutouk, Ian, Europe, 2000s-, Artist, Hungarian
Bowane, Henri, Africa, 1950s-1970s, Artist, Zaire
Bowhouse Quintet, Celtic, 1990s, Artist, Irish
Boys Of The Lough, The, Celtic, 1960s-1990s, Artist, Irish
Branco, Waltel, Latin & South America, 1970s, Artist, Brazilian
Braten-Berg, Kirsten, Africa, 1990s-, Artist, Senegalese
Brathanki, Europe, 2000s-, Artist, Polish
Brett, Seamus, Celtic, 1990s, Artist, Irish
Briggs, Anne, Celtic, 1950s-1970s, Artist, British
Bright, Teresa, Australia & Oceania, 1980s-, Artist, Hawaiian
Brotherhood Of Breath, African, 1970s, Artist, African
Brothers Kanilau, Australia & Oceania, 1990s, Artist, Hawaiian
Bruce, Vin, Cajun & Zydeco, 1960s-, Artist, American
Brulé, Native America, 1970s-1990s, Artist, American
Buckwheat Zydeco, Cajun & Zydeco, 1970s-, Artist, American
Budvarka, Russia & Central Asia, 1990s, Artist, Sri Lankan
Buen, Knut, Europe, 1970s-, Artist, Norwegian
Bukkene Bruse, Europe, 1990s-, Artist, Norwegian
Bulgarian National Folk Ensemble, Europe, 1990s, Artist, Bulgarian
Bulkin, Anatholi, African, 1980s-, Artist, African
Bulu-Bulu, Hana, Africa, 1980s, Artist, Sudanese
Burke, Kevin, Celtic, 1970s-, Artist, Irish
Burman, R. D. India, 1960s-1990s, Artist, Indian
Burning Sky, Native America, 1990s, Artist, American
Buti, Carlo, Europe, 2000s-, Artist, Italian
Cabang, Mel, Australia & Oceania, 1990s, Artist, Hawaiian
Calf Robe Singers, Native America, 2000s-, Artist, American
Calypso Rose, Caribbean, 1980s-1990s, Artist, Trinidadian
Can, Libel, Middle East, 2000s-, Artist, Turkish
Canoe Club, Australia & Oceania, 1990s, Artist, Hawaiian
Cardoso, Wanderley, Latin & South America, 1950s-, Artist, Brazilian
Carrier, Chubby, Cajun & Zydeco, 1990s, Artist, American
Carter, John, Native America, 1960s-1990s, Artist, American
Carthy, Martin, Celtic, 1960s-, Artist, British
Casimero, Roland, Australia & Oceania, 1970s, Artist, Hawaiian
Cathedral Lake Singers, The, Native America, 1990s, Artist, American
Cerny, Jozka, Europe, 1980s, Artist, Moravian
Cespedes, Bobi, Latin & South America, 1980s-, Artist, West African
Chandra, Sheila, India, 1980s-, Artist, Indian
Chateau Neuf, Europe, 1990s, Artist, Swedish
Chatterjee, Anindo, India, 1990s, Artist, Indian
Chaudhuri, Shri Swapan, India, 1990s, Artist, Indian
Chaurasia, Hariprasad, India, 1950s-, Artist, Indian
Chavis, Boozoo, Cajun & Zydeco, 1950s-, Artist, American
Chen, Louis, East Asia, 1990s, Artist, Chinese
Chenier, C. J. Cajun & Zydeco 1970s- Artist, American
Chenier, Clifton, Cajun & Zydeco, 1950s-1980s, Artist, American
Cherokee Rose, Native America, 2000s-, Artist, American
Chieftains, The, Celtic, 1960s-, Artist, Irish
Chinese Instrumental Ensemble, East Asia, 1990s, Artist, Chinese
Ching, Wong, East Asia, 1990s, Artist, Chinese
Chisala, P. K. Africa, 1980s, Artist, Zambian
Chiweshe, Stella, Africa, 1970s-1990s, Artist, Zimbabwe
Choates, Harry, Cajun & Zydeco, 1930s-1950s, Artist, American
Cigliano, Fausto, Europe, 2000s, Artist, Italian
Cigliano, Fausto, Europe, 1980s-, Artist, Italian
Cissoko, Kaouding, Africa, 1990s, Artist, Senegalese
Ciurlionis, Mikolajus Konstitantinus, Europe, 1900s, Composer, Lithuanian
Clancy Brothers, The, Celtic, 1950s-, Artist, Irish
Clannad, Celtic, 1970s-, Artist, Irish
Clark, Ned Tsosie, Native America, 2000s-, Artist, American
Clegg, Johnny, Africa, 1980s-1990s, Artist, Anglo-African
Clipman, Nakai Eaton, Native America, 1990s, Artist, American
Cobra, Latin & South America, 1990s, Artist, Mexican
Cody, Radmilla, Native America, 2000s-, Artist, American
Colon, Willie, Latin & South America, 1960s-, Artist, American
Colonial Cousins, India, 1990s, Artist, Indian
Cook, Jesse, Latin & South America, 1990s-, Artist, Spanish
Cordova, Jimmy, Native America, 2000s-, Artist, American
Coulter, Phil, Celtic, 1980s-, Artist, British
Cracow Klezmer Band, The, Europe, 1990s-, Artist, Polish
Crazy, Caribbean, 1980s-1990s, Artist, Trinidadian
Crentsil, A. B. Africa, 1980s-, Artist, Ghanaian
Crow, Joseph Fire, Native America, 2000s-, Artist, American
Cruz, Celia, Latin & South America, 1950s-, Artist, Cuban
Cunningham, Phil, Celtic, 1970s-1990s, Artist, British
Czerwone Gitary, Europe, 1960s, Artist, Polish
Czokolom, Europe, 1990s-, Artist, Hungarian
D'Gary, Africa, 1990s-, Artist, Madagascan
Dakar, Etoile de, Africa, 1970s-1980s, Artist, Senegalese
Daktaris, The, Africa, 1990s, Artist, American
Dale, Heather, Europe, 1990s-, Artist, British

Dale, Lennie, Latin & South America, 1960s, Artist, Brazilian
Dalgas, Andonis, Europe, 1930s-, Artist, Greek
Daniels, Luke, Celtic, 1990s, Artist, Irish
Danish Folk Orchestra, Europe, 1990s, Artist, Danish
Darko, George, Africa, 1980s, Artist, Ghanaian
Das Baul, Paban India 1990s Artist Indian
D'Auri, Gino, Latin & South America, 1980s-1990s, Artist, Italian
De Dannan, Celtic, 1970s-1990s, Artist, Irish
De Lucia, Paco, Europe, 1960s-, Artist, Spanish
De Palo, Jarabe, Europe, 1990s-, Artist, Spanish
De Ricardo, Nino, Europe, 1990s, Artist, Spanish
Debebe, Neway, Africa, 1970s-1990s, Artist, Ethiopian
Decimus, Georges, Caribbean, 1980s-1990s, Artist, West Indian
Del Gastor, Paco, Europe, 1990s, Artist, Spanish
Demessae, Seleshe, Africa, 1980s-1990s, Artist, Ethiopian
Derrane, Joe, Celtic, 1940s-1950s, Artist, American
Dervish, Celtic, 1980s-, Artist, Irish
Designer, Caribbean, 1980s-1990s, Artist, Trinidadian
DeSouza, Ignace, Africa, 1990s, Artist, Ghanaian
Desvariuex, Jacob, Caribbean, 1980s, Artist, West Indian
Dhomhnaill, Triona Ni, Celtic, 1970s-1990s, Artist, Irish
Dia, Anka, Africa, 2000s-, Artist, West African
Diabate, Sona, Africa, 1980s-1990s, Artist, West African
Diabate, Toumani, Africa, 1970s-1990s, Artist, Malian
Diamond, Leo, Australia & Oceania, 1950s-1960s, Artist, Polynesian
Diatta, Pascal, Africa, 2000s-, Artist, Senegalese
Dibala, Diblo, Africa, 1960s-, Artist, Zaire
Dibango, Mahu, African, 1970s-, Artist, African
Dieng, Fallou, Africa, 1990s, Artist, Senegalese
Diop, Mapathe, Africa, 1990s, Artist, Senegalese
Diop, Vieux, Africa, 1970s-, Artist, West African
Diop, Wassis, Africa, 1980s-1990s, Artist, Senegalese
Distel, Sacha, Europe, 1960s-1970s; 1990s, Artist, French
Djembe, Tahirou, Africa, 1990s-, Artist, West African
Doctor Nico, Africa, 1960s, Artist, Zaire
Doran, Johnny, Celtic, 1920s-1950s, Artist, Irish
Doucet, Michael, Cajun & Zydeco, 1980s-1990s, Artist, American
Dozzler, Christian, Europe; Zydeco, 1990s, Artist, Hungarian
Draghici, Damian, Europe, 1990s, Artist, Romanian
Drew, Ronnie, Celtic, 1960s-1990s, Artist, Irish
Drummers Of Burundi, Africa, 1980s-1990s, Artist, Burundian
Dubliners, Celtic, 1960s-, Artist, Irish
Dumitrescu, Iancu, Europe, 1970s-1990s, Composer, Romanian
Dyani, Johnny, African, 1960s-1980s, Artist, African
Egan, Seamus, Celtic, 1970s-1990s, Artist, Irish
Egeland, Anon, Europe, 1990s, Artist, Norwegian
Eggen, Mari, Europe, 1990s-, Artist, Norwegian
Eksperyans, Boukman, Caribbean, 1990s-, Artist, Haitian
El Amin, Muhamed, Africa, 1990s, Artist, Sudanese
El Din, Hamza, Africa, 1960s-1990s, Artist, Sudanese
El Hindi, Africa, 1990s-, Artist, Algerian
El-Mosili, Yousif, Africa, 1980s-, Artist, Sudanese
Emma, Australia & Oceania, 1990s-, Artist, Tahitian
Engelbrecht, Jens, Europe, 1990s, Artist, Danish
Ennis, Seamus, Celtic, 1930s-1980s, Artist, Irish
Ensemble Sadiyana, East Asia, 1990s-, Artist, Chinese
Enya, Celtic, 1980s-, Artist, Irish
Erguner, Kudsi, Middle East, 1960s-, Artist, Turkish
Erkose Ensemble, The, Middle East, 1990s-, Artist, Turkish
Eshete, Alemayehu, Africa, 1960s-1990s, Artist, Ethiopian
Eskenazi, Roza, Europe, 1920s-1970s, Artist, Greek
Esperados de la Sierra, Latin & South America, 2000s-, Artist, Mexican
Estopa, Latin & South America, 1990s-, Artist, Spanish
Ethio Stars, Africa, 1980s-1990s, Artist, Ethiopian
Evora, Cesaria, Africa, 1990s-, Artist, African
Fadela, Chaba, Africa, 1990s, Artist, Algerian
Fadl, Mahmoud, Middle East, 1990s-, Artist, Egyptian
Faikava, Australia & Oceania, 1980s-1990s, Artist, Tongan
Faiz, Faiz Ahmad, Russia & Central Asia, 1940s-1960s, Artist, Pakistani
Faraco, Marcio, Latin & South America, 1990s, Artist, Brazilian
Farid el Atache, Middle East, 1930s-1970s, Artist, Egyptian
Farkas, Andras Jr., Europe, 1990s-, Artist, Hungarian
Farmen, Oivind, Europe, 2000s-, Artist, Norwegian
Fashek, Majek, Africa, 1980s-1990s, Artist, Nigerian
Fataar, Steve, African, 1960s-1970s, Artist, British
Fernandez, Gerardo, Latin & South America, 2000s-, Artist, Mexican
Fetia, Australia & Oceania, 2000s-, Artist, Tahitian
Fevers, The, Latin & South America, 1970s, Artist, Brazilian
Feza, Mongezi, African, 1960s-1970s, Artist, African
Floro, Gilles, Caribbean, 1980s-1990s, Artist, West Indian
Former, Frie, Europe, 2000s-, Artist, Norwegian
Four Brothers, The, Africa, 1980s-, Artist, Zimbabwe
Four Mountain Nation Singers, The, Native America, 1990s, Artist, American
Franco, Africa, 1950s-1980s, Artist, Zaire
Frifot, Europe, 1990s, Artist, Swedish
Fu Chan Chang, East Asia, 2000s-, Artist, Chinese
Funkadesi, Caribbean, 2000s-, Artist, Jamaican
Gabilou, John, Australia & Oceania, 1960s-1970s, Artist, Tahitian
Gambuh Ensemble Of Batuan, Southeast Asia, 1990s, Artist, Indonesian
Gamelan Jegog Werdi Senatana, Southeast Asia, 1990s, Artist, Indonesian
Gamelan Joged Bumbung, Southeast Asia, 1990s, Artist, Indonesian
Gamelan Sangburni, Southeast Asia, 1990s, Artist, Indonesian
Garbarek, Anja, Europe, 1990s-, Artist, Norwegian
Garmana, Europe, 1990s-, Artist, Swedish
Garner, Loyal, Australia & Oceania, 1990s, Artist, Hawaiian
Gasparyan, Djivan, Europe, 1940s-, Artist, Armenian
Gaughan, Dick, Celtic, 1970s-, Artist; Songwriter, British
Gazzola, Ana, Latin & South America, 1990s, Artist, Brazilian
German, Anna, Russia & Central Asia, 1960s-1970s, Artist, Russian
Gigi, Africa, 2000s-, Artist, Ethiopian
Gil, Gilberto, Latin & South America, 1960s-, Artist, Brazilian
Gilliom, Amy Hanaiali'I, Australia & Oceania, 2000s-, Artist, Hawaiian
Gipsy Kings, Europe, 1980s-, Artist, Spanish
Gjallarhorn, Europe, 1990s-, Artist, Finnish
Gnawa Diffusion, Africa, 1990s, Artist, Algerian
Goddard, Pelham, Caribbean, 1960s-1990s, Artist, Trinidadian
Golana, Native America, 1990s-, Artist, American
Goodall, Medwyn, Celtic, 1980s-, Artist, British
Goode, Daniel, Southeast Asia, 1970s-1990s, Artist, American
Gopalnath, Kadri, India, 1970s-, Artist, Indian
Gora, John, Europe, 1980s-1990s, Artist, Polish
Gorby, Sarah, Europe, 1980s-1990s, Artist, Polish
Gorn, Steve, India, 1980s-1990s, Artist, American
Gorniak, Edyta, Europe, 1990s, Artist, Polish
Gralak, Don, Europe, 2000s-, Artist, Polish
Great Big Sea, Celtic, 1990s-, Artist, Canadian
Great Lakes Indians, Native America, 2000s-, Artist, American
Groupa, Europe, 1980s-, Artist, Swedish
Grupo Tequila, Latin & South America, 2000s-, Artist, Mexican
Grupo Um, Latin & South America, 1980s, Artist, Brazilian
Guccini, Francesco, Europe, 1980s-, Artist, Italian
Gudmundson, Per, Europe, 1980s-, Artist, Swedish
Gulda, Friedrich, Europe, 1950s-1980s, Artist; Composer Austria
Gumuz Tribe, Africa, 1980s, Artist, Sudanese
Guo Brothers & Shung Tian, East Asia, 1980s-, Artist, Chinese
Gupta, Buddhadev Das, India, 1980s-, Artist, Indian
Gwangwa, Jonas, African, 1950s-, Artist African
Hackberry Ramblers, Cajun & Zydeco, 1960s, Artist, American
Hadi, Africa, 2000s-, Artist, Sudanese
Hadidjah, Idjah, Southeast Asia, 1970s-1980s, Artist, Indonesian
Haidouks, Taraf de, Europe, 1990s-, Artist, Romanian
Hamar, Daniel, Europe, 1970s-1990s, Artist, Hungarian
Hammer, Jan Europe 1960s- Artist Czech
Handy, W. C. Native America, 1900s-1920s, Artist, American
Hart-Rouge, Europe, 1990s, Artist, French-Canadian
Harv, Europe, 1990s-, Artist, Swedish
Har-You Percussion Group, Africa, 1990s, Artist, American
Hayes, Martin, Celtic, 1990s, Artist, Irish
Hedningarna, Europe, 1980s-, Artist, Swedish
Heredia, Ray, Europe, 1990s-, Artist, Spanish
Heroes del Silencio, Latin & South America, 1980s-1990s, Artist, Spanish
Hevia Europe 1990s- Artist Spanish
Hime, Olivia, Latin & South America, 1980s, Artist, Brazilian
Hirayasu, Takashi, East Asia, 1970s-, Artist, Japanese
Horvath, Europe, 1980s, Artist, Hungarian
Houdini, Wilmouth, Caribbean, 1920s-1940s, Artist, Trinidadian
House Band, The, Celtic, 1980s-1990s, Artist, British
Hoven Droven, Europe, 1980s-, Artist, Swedish
Hrant, Udi, Middle East, 1990s, Artist, Turkish
Huayucaltia, Latin & South America, 1980s-1990s, Artist, Mexican
Huello, Paul, Europe, 1990s, Artist, French
Hui 'Ohana, Australia & Oceania, 1970s-, Artist, Tahitian
Humphrey, Annie, Native America, 1980s-, Artist, American
Hungarian Gypsy Orchestra, Europe, 1990s, Artist, Hungarian
Hungarian State Folk Ensemble, Europe, 1990s, Artist, Hungarian
Hurley, Red, Celtic, 1990s, Artist, Irish
Hussain, Zakir, India, 1960s-, Artist, Indian
Ibarra, Jesus Beltran, Latin & South America, 1990s-, Songwriter, Mexican
Ibrahim, Abdullah, Africa, 1960s-, Artist, South African
Indian Nation, Native America, 1990s, Artist, American
Inkuyo, Latin & South America, 1980s-, Artist, American
Inti-Illimani, Latin & South America, 1960s-1990s, Artist, American
Irvine, Andy, Europe, 1960s-, Artist, British
Ishola, Haruna, Africa, 1940s-1970s, Artist, Nigerian
Iza, Europe, 1990s, Artist, Polish
Jagoda, Flory, Europe, 1990s, Artist, Yugoslav
Jahasinga, A. Russia & Central Asia, 1990s, Artist, Sri Lankan
Jara, Victor, Latin & South America, 1960s-1970s, Artist, Chilean
Jarvela, Arto, Europe, 1980s-, Artist, Finnish
Jarvela, Mauno, Europe, 1960s-, Artist, Finnish
Jasraj, Pandit, India, 1980s-, Artist, Indian
Jehan, Noor, Russia & Central Asia, 1930s-, Artist, Pakistani
Jobarteh, Amadu Bansang, Africa, 1940s-, Artist, West African
Jobim, Antonio Carlos, Latin & South America, 1950s-1990s, Artist; Composer, Brazilian
Jocque, Beau, Cajun & Zydeco, 1990s-, Artist, American
Jodlerclub, Europe, 1990s, Artist, Swiss
Jog, Pandit V. G. India, 1980s-1990s, Artist, Indian
Johansson, Olov, Europe, 1990s, Artist, Scandinavian
Jongo Trio, Latin & South America, 1960s, Artist, Brazilian
Jordanova, Victoria, Europe, 1990s, Artist, Bosnian
JPP, Europe, 1990s, Artist, Finnish
Jugala Group, Southeast Asia, 1990s-, Artist, Indonesian
Juluka, Africa, 1970s-1980s, Artist, African
Junkera, Kepa, Europe, 1980s-1990s, Artist, Spanish
Jurad, Simon, Caribbean, 1980s-1990s, Artist, West Indian
Jylha, Konsta, Europe, 1940s-1980s, Artist, Finnish
Kabasele, Joseph, Africa, 1950s-1990s, Artist, Zaire
Kabra, Brij Bhushan, India, 1960s-1980s, Artist, Indian
Kader, Cheb, Africa, 2000s-, Artist, Algerian
Kahauanu Lake Trio, Australia & Oceania, 1990s, Artist, Hawaiian
Kaiwa, Bill, Australia & Oceania, 1990s, Artist, Hawaiian
Kalaniemi, Maria, Europe, 1980s-, Artist, Finnish
Kalapana, Harry, Australia & Oceania, 1990s, Artist, Hawaiian
Kalle, Pepe, Africa, 1960s-1990s, Artist, Zaire
Kalyi Jag Group, Europe, 1990s, Artist, Hungarian
Kamae, Eddie, Australia & Oceania, 2000s-, Artist, Hawaiian
Kamuku, Duke, Australia & Oceania, 2000s-, Artist, Hawaiian
Kanahele, Kekuhi, Australia & Oceania, 1990s-, Artist, Hawaiian
Kanda Bongo Man, Africa, 1970s-, Artist, Zaire
Kanté, Mory, Africa, 1970s-, Artist, West African
Karas, Antojn, Europe, 1940s-1960s, Artist; Composer, Austria
Karolinka, Europe, 2000s-, Artist, Polish
Kassav', Caribbean, 1970s-1990s, Artist, French
Kaszowski Brothers, Europe, 1990s, Artist, Polish
Kayirebwa, Cecile, Africa, 1960s-, Artist, Rwandan
Kaziu, Stary, Europe, 2000s, Artist, Polish
Kealoha, William, Australia & Oceania, 2000s-, Artist, Hawaiian
Keane, Dolores, Celtic, 1970s-, Artist, Irish
Keita, Salif, Africa, 1960s-, Artist, Malian
Kelly Family, The, Celtic, 1980s-1990s, Artist, German-Irish
Kester, Emeneya, Africa, 1970s-1980s, Artist, Zaire
Khaled, Cheb, Africa, 1970s-, Artist, Algerian
Khan, Ali Akbar, India, 1960s-1990s, Artist, Indian
Khan, Mohammed Sharif, Russia & Central Asia, 2000s-, Artist, Pakistani
Khan, Nusrat Fateh Ali, Russia & Central Asia, 1970s-1990s, Artist, Pakistani
Khan, Shafqat Ali, Russia & Central Asia, 1970s-, Artist, Pakistani
Khan, Ustad Imrat, East Asia, 1980s-1990s, Artist, Pakistani
Khan, Ustad Vilayat, India, 1980s-, Artist, Indian
Khanyile, Jabu, Africa, 1980s-1990s, Artist, South African
Khaznadji, Mohamed, Africa, 1990s, Artist, Algerian
Kheira, Africa, 1990s-, Artist, Algerian
Khmer Dance Troup, Southeast Asia, 2000s-, Artist, Cambodia
Khoza, Valanga, Africa, 1990s, Artist, South Africa
Kidjo, Angélique, Africa, 1980s-, Artist, Benin
Kincaid, David, Celtic, 1990s, Artist, Irish
King Bruce, Africa, 1950s-1960s, Artist, Ghanaian
King, Gershon, Latin & South America, 1970s, Artist, Brazilian
Klegetoh Swingers, Native America, 1970s-, Artist, American
Knight, Chester, Native America, 2000s-, Artist, American
Kodo, East Asia, 1980s-, Artist, Japanese
Kolinda, Europe, 1970s-1990s, Artist, Hungarian
Kolo Dancing Ensemble, Europe, 1980s-1990s, Artist, Serbian
Komariah, Euis, Southeast Asia, 1990s, Artist, Indonesian
Konadu, Alex, Africa, 1990s, Artist, Ghanaian
Kong Nay, Southeast Asia, 2000s-, Artist, Cambodia
Konte, Dembo, Africa, 1980s-, Artist, Senegalese
Konte, Lamine, Africa, 1980s-1990s, Artist, Senegalese
Koray, Erkin, Middle East, 1960s-1990s, Artist, Turkish

Kormoran, Europe, 1980s, Artist, Hungarian
Kornog, Europe, 1970s-1990s, Artist, French
Kotoja, Africa, 1980s-, Artist, West African
Kounkou, Theo Blaise, Africa, 2000s-, Artist, Zaire
Kouyate, Djimo, Africa, 1980s, Artist, Senegalese
Kouyate, Kandia, Africa, 1970s-, Artist, West African
Kraton, Jogja, Southeast Asia, 1990s, Artist, Indonesian
Krisiun, Latin & South America, 2000s-, Artist, Brazilian
Kubik, Europe, 2000s-, Artist, French
Kulthum, Umm, Middle East, 1920s-1970s, Artist, Egyptian
Kuomboka, Distro, Africa, 2000s-, Artist, Zambian
Kurki-Suoni, Sanna, Europe, 1990s, Artist, Finnish
Kurnia, Detty, Southeast Asia, 1960s-, Artist, Indonesian
Kurtis, Milo, Europe, 1990s-, Artist, Polish
Kuti, Fela, Africa, 1960s-1990s, Artist, Nigerian
Kuti, Femi, Africa, 1980s-, Artist, Nigerian
Laazaz, Abderahman, Africa, 1990s-, Artist, Algerian
Ladysmith Black Mambazo, Africa, 1980s-, Artist, South African
Laezar Ensemble, The, Middle East, 2000s-, Artist, Turkish
Lakatos, Sandor Deki, Europe, 1990s-, Artist, Hungarian
Lakota Thunder, Native America, 2000s-, Artist, American
Lam, Kine, Africa, 1970s-, Artist, Senegalese
Lane, Julia, Celtic, 1990s, Artist, Irish
Larafyette Afro Rock Band, Africa, 1970s, Artist, American
Larasati, Niken, Southeast Asia, 1990s-, Artist, Indonesian
Laughing, Lawrence, Native America, 2000s-, Artist, American
Lawson, Rex, Africa, 1960s-1970s, Artist, Nigerian
Lazard, Sasha, Russia & Central Asia, 2000s-, Artist, American
Le Forestier, Maxime, Europe, 1970s-1990s, Artist, French
Leahy, Celtic, 1990s-, Artist, Canadian
Lee, CoCo, East Asia, 1990s-, Artist, Japanese
Lefel, Edith, Caribbean, 1980s-, Artist, West Indian
Lemeut, Jean, Celtic, 1990s, Artist, Irish
Lenine, Latin & South America, 1990s-, Artist, Brazilian
Lewis, Kevin, Native America, 1980s-1990s, Artist, American
Li He, East Asia, 1990s-, Artist, Chinese
Li Xiang-Ting, East Asia, 2000s-, Artist, Chinese
Lien, Annbjorg, Europe, 1980s-, Artist, Norwegian
Lindsay, Tony, Australia & Oceania, 2000s-, Artist, Hawaiian
Little, Archie, Native America, 2000s-, Artist, American
Liu Ming-Yuan, East Asia, 1990s-, Artist, Chinese
Liu Ying, East Asia, 2000s-, Artist, Chinese
Lo, Cheikh, Africa, 1980s-, Artist, Senegalese
Lo, Ismaël, Africa, 1990s-, Artist, Senegalese
Lobi, Kakraba, Africa, 1990s-, Artist, Ghanaian
Lobitos, Koola, Africa, 1950s-1960s, Artist, Nigerian
Loituma, Europe, 1990s, Artist, Finnish
Loketo, Africa, 1980s-1990s, Artist, Zaire
Lomax, Alan, Europe, 1930s-1990s, Artist; Producer, American
Longo, N'Yoka, Africa, 1970s-, Artist, Zaire
Longomba, Vicky, Africa, 1950s-1970s, Artist, Zaire
Lord Burgess, Caribbean, 1950s-1960s, Artist, Trinidadian
Lord Invader, Caribbean, 1940s-1960s, Artist, Trinidadian
Lord Kitchener, Caribbean, 1940s-1990s, Artist, Trinidadian
Lord Melody, Caribbean, 1940s-1980s, Artist, Trinidadian
Los Madrugadores, Latin & South America, 1930s-1960s, Artist Mexican
Los Maynas, Latin & South America, 2000s-, Artist, Mexican
Los Titanes del Norte, Latin & South America, 2000s-, Artist, Mexican
Love, M'Pongo, Africa, 1970s-1980s, Artist, Zaire
Lucky Ali, India, 1990s-, Artist, Indian
Luna Band, Russia & Central Asia, 1980s-, Artist, American
Lunar Drive, Native America, 1990s, Artist, American
Ly, Mabadou, Africa, 1980s-1990s Artist, Senegalese
Maal, Baaba, Africa, 1980s-, Artist, Senegalese
Maanam, Europe, 1990s, Artist, Polish
Mabulu, Africa, 2000s-, Artist, African
Mac Umba, Celtic, 1990s, Artist, British
MacDonald, Catriona, Celtic, 1990s-, Artist, British
MacInnes, Mairi, Celtic, 1990s-, Artist, Irish
MacLean, Dougie, Celtic, 1970s-, Artist, British
MacLeod, Kate, Celtic 1990s-, Artist, American
MacMaster, Natalie, Celtic, 1980s-, Artist, Irish
Maes, Christian, Celtic, 1990s, Artist, Irish
Mahone, Keith, Native America, 1990s, Artist, American
Majaivana, Lovemore, Africa, 1970s-1990s, Artist, Zimbabwe
Makeba, Miriam, Africa, 1950s-, Artist, South African
Makem, Tommy, Celtic, 1960s-1990s, Artist, Irish
Makiadi, Franco Luambo, Africa, 1950s-1980s, Artist, Zaire
Malavoi, Caribbean, 1980s-, Artist, West Indian
Malcolm, Jim, Celtic, 1990s, Artist, Irish
Malvicino, Latin & South America, 1960s, Artist, Brazilian
Mamelang, Africa, 1990s-, Artist, Zulu
Mami, Cheb, Africa, 1980s-, Artist, Algerian
Mangeshkar, Lata, India, 1950s-1990s, Artist, Indian
Mangwana, Sam, Africa, 1960s-, Artist, Zaire
Mann, C. K., Africa, 1960s-1980s, Artist, Ghanaian
Manu, Charley, Australia & Oceania, 2000s-, Artist, Polynesian
Manuiti, Australia & Oceania, 1990s, Artist, Tahitian
Mapfumo, Thomas, Africa, 1980s-, Artist, Zimbabwe
Marabu Combo, Latin & South America, 2000s-, Artist, Mexican
Maraire, Dumisani, Africa, 1970s-1990s, Artist, Zimbabwe
Marais & Miranda, Africa, 1940s-1960s, Artist, American
Marchand, Erik, Europe, 1990s-, Artist, French
Mariam, Middle East, 1990s-, Artist, Afghan
Marquee, Andrea, Latin & South America, 2000s-, Artist, Brazilian
Marssaoui, Nouredine, Africa, 1990s-, Artist, Algerian
Martenitsa Choir, The, Europe, 1990s, Artist, Bulgarian
Martinez, Narciso, Latin & South America, 1920s-1990s, Artist, Mexican
Masekela, Hugh, African, 1960s-, Artist, African
Massa, Bumba, Africa, 1970s, Artist, Zambian
Masuka, Dorothy, Africa,, 1960s; 1990s-, Artist, Zimbabwe
Matsumoto, Chihiro, East Asia, 1980s-1990s, Artist, Japanese
Mauro, Jose, Latin & South America, 1970s, Artist, Brazilian
Mazowsze, Europe, 1960s-1970s; 1990s-, Artist, Polish
Mazzotti, Ana, Latin & South America, 1980s, Artist, Brazilian
Mbarga, Prince Nico, Africa, 1970s-1990s, Artist, Nigerian
Mbaye, Dial, Africa, 1990s-, Artist, Senegalese
Mbaye, Jimi, Africa, 1970s-, Artist, Senegalese
McCormack, John, Celtic, 1910s-1940s, Artist, Irish
McGovern, Betsy, Celtic, 1990s, Artist, Irish
McGraw, Hugh, Native America, 1990s, Artist, American
McGregor, Chris, African, 1960s-1990s, Artist, African
Mchunu, Sipho, Africa, 1970s-, Artist, Zulu
McKee, Larry, Celtic, 1990s, Artist, Irish
McKennitt, Loreena, Celtic, 1980s-1990s, Artist, Canadian
McKeown, Susan, Celtic, 1990s-, Artist, Irish
McMahon, Katie, Celtic, 1990s-, Artist, Irish
McManus, Tony, Celtic, 1990s-, Artist, British
McMathuna, Padraic, Celtic, 1990s, Artist, Irish
McNaughton, Adam, Celtic, 1970s; 1990s, Artist, Irish
McPhee, Colin, Southeast Asia, 1930s-1950s, Artist, Canadian
Means, Russell, Native America, 1990s, Artist, American
Medicine Dream, Native America, 2000s-, Artist, American
Megama, Middle East, 1980s, Artist, Israeli
Meisfjord, Sondre, Europe, 2000s-, Artist, Norwegian
Mensah, E. T., Africa, 1930s-1990s, Artist, Ghanaian
Mensah, Kwaku A., Africa, 1950s-1970s, Artist, Ghanaian
Mhlanga, Louis, Africa, 1980s-, Artist, Zimbabwe
Mhlongo, Busi, Africa, 1990s, Artist, Zulu
Mian, Aziz, Russia & Central Asia, 2000s-, Artist, Pakistani
Mighty Sparrow, Caribbean, 1950s-, Artist, Trinidadian
Mighty Terror, Caribbean, 1950s-, Artist, Trinidadian
Mighty Zandolie, Caribbean, 1990s, Artist, Trinidadian
Mila & Loma, Australia & Oceania, 2000s-, Artist, Tahitian
Minogue, Aine, Celtic, 1990s, Artist, Irish
Min'yo, East Asia, 1990s, Artist, Japanese
Misiani, Daniel Owino, Africa, 1960s-1980s, Artist, Kenyan
Mitchell, Davis, Native America, 1990s, Artist, American
Miucha, Latin & South America, 1970s-1990s, Artist, Brazilian
Mkwamba, Patrick, Africa, 1980s, Artist; Songwriter, Zimbabwe
Moholo, Louis, African, 1960s-1990s, Artist, African
Moller, Ale, Europe, 1970s-, Artist, Swedish
Mollys, The, Celtic, 1990s-, Artist, Irish-American
Monsoon, Indian, 1980s-1990s, Artist, Indian
Montano, Machel, Caribbean, 1980s-, Artist, Trinidadian
Montero, Doris, Latin & South America, 1970s, Artist, Brazilian
Montero, Germaine, Europe, 1990s-, Artist, Spanish
Moore, Christy, Celtic, 1960s-, Artist, Irish
Moraito, Europe, 1990s-, Artist, Spanish
Morgane, Celtic, 1990s, Artist, Scottish
Moriarty, Brendan, Celtic, 1990s, Artist, Irish
Morris, Ned, Native America, 2000s-, Artist, American
Mounir, Mohamed, Middle East, 1960s-, Artist, Egyptian
Moustaki, Georges, Europe, 1980s-, Artist; Composer, French
Mtukudzi, Oliver "Tuku", Africa, 1970s-, Artist, Zimbabwe,
Muana, Tshala, Africa, 1980s-, Artist, Zaire
Muchena, Amai, Africa, 2000s-, Artist, Zimbabwe
Mujuru, Ephat, Africa, 1960s-, Artist, Zimbabwe
Mukeshwa, Virginia, Africa, 2000s-, Artist, Zimbabwe
Mukhtar, Hafiz A., Africa, 1990s, Artist, Sudanese
Mulcahy, Mick, Celtic, 1990s, Artist, Irish
Murolo, Roberto, Europe, 1990s-, Artist, Italian
Murphy, John, Celtic, 1980s-1990s, Artist, Irish
Mursal, Maryam, Africa, 1960s-, Artist, Somalian
Musafir, India, 1990s, Artist, Indian
Mustafov, King Ferus, Europe, 1990s, Artist, Macedonian
Mutukudzi, Oliver, Africa, 1980s-1990s, Artist, Zimbabwe
Muzsikas, Europe, 1970s-, Artist, Hungarian
Mweda, Jean Bosco, Africa, 1950s-1960s; 1980s, Artist, Zaire
Mynta, India, 1970s-, Artist, Indian
Najma, Indian, 1980s-1990s, Artist, Indian
Naranjo, Monica, Europe, 1990s-, Artist, Spanish
Narayan, Udit, Indian, 1970s, Artist, Indian
Nassima, Africa, 1980s-, Artist, Algerian
Nataraj XT, India, 2000s-, Artist, Indian
Natay, Ed Lee, Native America, 1940s-1960s, Artist, American
Navajo Nation Swingers, Native America, 1990s, Artist, American
N'Dour, Youssou, Africa, 1970s-, Artist, Senegalese
Nevaquayah, Doc Tate, Native America, 1970,s Artist, American
Ngonda, Wally, Africa, 1990s, Artist, Zaire
Ni Uallachain, Padraigin, Celtic, 1990s-, Artist, Irish
Niang, Magay, Africa, 1960s-, Artist, Senegalese
Nightingale, Tunde, Africa, 1950s-1960s, Artist, Nigerian
Nikolic, Jovica, Europe, 1990s, Artist, Yugoslav
Niles, John Jacob, Native America, 1920s-1970s, Artist, American
Nimo, Koo, Africa, 1950s-, Artist, Ghanaian
No Smoking, Europe, 1990s-, Artist, Serbian
Norudde, Anders, Europe, 1990s-, Artist, Swedish
Notomi, Judo, Australia & Oceania, 1980s, Artist, Japanese
Nouria, Cheb, Africa, 2000s-, Artist, Algerian
Nova Menco, Europe, 1990s-, Artist, Spanish
Novalia, Europe, 1960s-, Artist, Italian
Núnez, Carlos, Celtic, 1990s-, Artist, Spanish
Nyame, E. K., Africa, 1990s-, Artist, Ghanaian
Nyami Nyami Sounds, Africa, 1980s, Artist, Zimbabwe
Nyhus, Sven, Europe, 2000s-, Artist, Norwegian
Obeng, Kwaku Kwaakye, Africa, 1990s, Artist, Ghanaian
Obey, Ebenezer, Africa, 1970s-1990s, Artist, Nigerian
O'Brien, Paddy, Celtic, 1980s, Artist, Irish
Ocal, Burhan, Middle East, 1970s-, Artist, Turkish
Occasionals, Celtic, 1990s-, Artist, Irish
Odadaa, Africa, 1980s-, Artist, Ghanaian
O'Domhnaill, Michael, Celtic, 1990s, Producer; Artist, Irish
Ogada, Ayub, Africa, 1990s, Artist, Kenyan
Ogur, Erkan, Middle East, 1970s-, Artist, Turkish
O'Keefe, Marie, Celtic, 1990s, Artist, Irish
Okosun, Sonny, Africa, 1980s-, Artist, Nigerian
Okros Ensemble, Europe, 1980s-, Artist, Hungarian
Olatunji, Babatunde, Africa, 1960s-1990s, Artist, Nigerian
Oldarra, Europe, 1930s-, Artist, Spanish
Olsson, Hjort Anders, Europe, 1990s, Artist, Swedish
Ongala, Remmy, Africa, 1970s-, Artist, Zaire
Opetum, Ndombe, Africa, 1990s, Artist, Zaire
Opium Jukebox, India, 2000s-, Artist, Indian
Orchestre Baobab, Africa, 1970s-1980s, Artist, Senegalese
Orchestre Makassy, Africa, 1970s-1980s, Artist, Zaire
Orchestre Marrabenta Star de Mocambique, Africa, 1990s-, Artist, African
Orchestre Super Matamilla, Africa, 1980s-, Artist, Zaire
Ordorika, Ruper, Europe, 1980s-, Artist, Spanish
Original Evening Birds, Africa, 1940s-1950s, Artist, South African
Ortolan, Celtic, 1990s, Artist, Irish
Osadebe, Chief Stephen Osita, Africa, 1960s-1990s, Artist, Nigerian
Osman Alamu, Africa, 1960s, Artist, Sudanese
Our Boys Steel Orchestra, Caribbean, 1980s-1990s, Artist, Trinidadian
Ozgen, Mesut, Middle East, 1980s-, Artist, Turkish
Ozkan, Talip, Middle East, 1980s-1990s, Artist, Turkish
Paco de Lucia, Europe, 1960s-, Artist, Spanish
Pahunini, Gabby, Australia & Oceania, 1940s-1980s, Artist, Hawaiian
Palermo Boogie Gang, Europe, 1990s, Artist, Hungarian
Palomo, Latin & South America, 2000s-, Artist, Mexican
Panjab, Russia & Central Asia, 1990s, Artist, Pakistani
Pantoja, Flavio, Latin & South America, 1980s, Artist, Brazilian
Papadakis, Yannis, Europe, 1990s, Artist, Greek

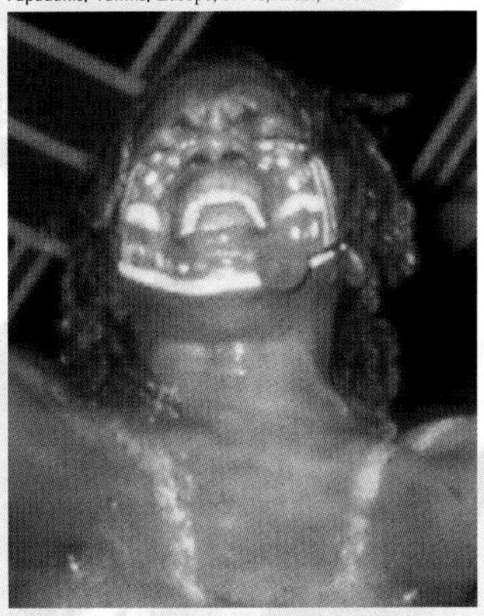

Papagika, Marika, Europe, 1900s-1920s,, Artist, Greek
Paralamas, Australia & Oceania, 1980s-, Artist, Tahitian
Paseando, Europe, 1990s-, Artist, Spanish
Passos, Rosa, Latin & South America, 1990s-, Artist, Brazilian
Pasteles, Latin & South America, 2000s-, Artist, Mexican
Paterson, Rod, Celtic, 1980s-1990s, Artist, Scottish
Pena, Paco, Europe; Latin & South America, 1970s-, Artist, Spanish
Pene, Omar, Africa, 1970s-1990s, Artist, Senegalese
Perez, Avi, Middle East, 1990s, Artist, Israeli
Perrone, Luciano, Latin & South America, 1990s, Artist, Brazilian
Peters, Sir Shina, Africa, 1980s-1990s, Artist, Nigerian
Philemon Zulu, Africa, 1990s, Artist, Zulu
Piazzolla, Astor, Latin & South America, 1940s-1990s, Artist, Argentinean
Pima Express, Native America, 1990s-, Artist, American
Ponce, Daniel, Latin & South America, 1980s-1990s, Artist, Cuban
Popovic, Anna, Europe, 1990s-, Artist, Yugoslav
Poroi, Australia & Oceania, 2000s-, Artist, Tahitian
Prado, Perez, Latin & South America, 1940s-1970s, Artist; Composer, Mexican
Pukwana, Dudu, African, 1950s-1980s, Artist, African
Queen Ida, Cajun & Zydeco, 1970s-1990s, Artist, American
Quinn's Tahitian Hut, Australia & Oceania, 1950s-1970s, Artist, Tahitian
Radev, Petko, Europe, 2000s-, Artist, Bulgarian
Radio Tarifa, Europe; Africa, 1990s-, Artist, Spanish
Raffi, Caribbean, 1970s-1990s, Artist, Canadian
Rafi, Mohammad, Indian, 1940s-1970s, Artist, Indian
Rahman, A. R., Indian, 1990s-, Producer, Indian
Rakha, Alla, India, 1940s-1990s, Artist, Indian
Ramzy, Hossam, Middle East, 1970s-, Artist, Egyptian
Ranarim, Europe, 1990s-, Artist, Swedish
Rankin Family, The, Celtic, 1990s, Artist, Canadian
Rasha, Africa, 1990s-, Artist, Sudanese
Rayo, Latin & South America, 2000s-, Artist, Mexican
Rebroff, Ivan, Russia & Central Asia, 2000s-, Artist, Russian
Red Tail Chasing Hawks, Native America, 1990s, Artist, American
Redhouse Family, The, Native America, 1990s, Artist, American
Remitti, Cheikha, Africa, 1930s-1950s, Artist, Algerian
Reyes, Jessita, Native America, 1990s, Artist, American
Reyes, Jose, Europe, 1970s-1980s, Artist, Spanish
Richard, Zachary, Cajun & Zydeco, 1970s-1990s, Artist, American
Rimestad, Hege, Europe, 1990s, Producer, Scandinavian
Rinken Band, East Asia, 2000s-, Artist, Japanese
Risk, Laura, Celtic, 1990s-, Artist, Irish
Roaring Lion, Caribbean, 1930s-1980s, Artist, Trinidadian
Rochereau, Tabu Ley, Africa, 1950s-, Artist, Zaire
Roches, Yves, Australia & Oceania, 1990s, Artist, Tahitian
Rock Point Singers, Native America, 2000s-, Artist, American
Rockin' Dopsie, Cajun & Zydeco, 1970s-1990s, Artist, American
Rockin' Sidney, Cajun & Zydeco, 1970s-1990s, Artist, American
Rodowicz, Maryla, Europe, 2000s-, Artist, Polish
Rodriguez, Roman, Latin & South America, 2000s, Artist, Mexican
Rogie, Sooliman E., Africa, 1970s-1990s, Artist, African
Roine, Erik, Europe, 1990s, Artist, Norwegian
Rondalla de las Flores, Latin & South America, 2000s-, Artist, Mexican
Rosenberg 7, Europe, 1990s-, Artist, Swedish
Rosier, Pierre, Caribbean, 1980s-1990s, Artist, West Indian
Roswall, Niklas, Europe, 1990s-, Artist, Swedish
Rubin, Joel, Europe, 1980s-1990s, Artist; Songwriter, German
Rubinel, Ronald, Caribbean, 1980s, Artist, West Indian
Rudder, Davis, Caribbean, 1980s-, Artist, Trinidadian
Sacred Spirit, Native America, 1990s-, Artist, American
Safam, Middle East, 1980s, Artist, American
Sage Point Singers, Native America, 2000s-, Artist, American
Sahotas, Indian, 1980s-, Artist, Indian
Salim, Abdel Gadir, Africa, 1980s-1990s, Artist, Sudanese
Sam-Ang Sam, Southeast Asia, 1990s-, Artist, Cambodian
Samba Brasil, Latin & South America, 2000s-, Artist, Brazilian
Sam's Trio, Africa, 1920s-1930s, Artist, Ghanaian
San Juan Singers, Native America, 2000s-, Artist, American
Sanden, Sofia, Europe, 1990s-, Artist, Swedish
Sands, Tommy, Celtic, 1960s-, Artist, Irish
Sangare, Oumou, Africa, 1980s-1990s, Artist, Malian
Santa, Ferenc Jr., Europe, 1990s, Artist, Hungarian
Santor, Irene, Europe, 2000s-, Artist, Polish
Santos, Sonia, Latin & South America, 2000s-, Artist, Brazilian
Sanu, Kumar, Indian, 1990s, Artist, Indian
Sardou, Michel, Europe, 1960s-, Artist, French
Savuka, Africa, 1980s-1990s, Artist, Zulu
Sayyah, Emad, Middle East, 1990s-, Artist, Lebanese
Schneider, Mary, Europe, 1990s, Artist, Swiss
Schola Hunarica, Europe, 1990s, Artist, Hungarian
Seanachie, Celtic, 1980s-1990s, Artist, British
Sebo Ensemble, Europe, 1970s-1980s, Artist, Hungarian
Seck, Mansour, Africa, 1990s, Artist, Senegalese
Seck, Theone, Africa, 1980s-, Artist, Senegalese
Sedrenn, Celtic, 1990s, Artist, Irish
Seelyhoo, Celtic, 1990s, Artist, Irish
Seghal, Baba, Indian, 1990s, Artist, Indian
Selsar, Selim, Middle East, 1990s, Artist, Turkish
Senghour, Sonar, Africa, 1990s, Artist, Senegalese
Serrano, Jose, Europe, 1990s, Artist, Spanish
Setona, Africa, 1990s, Artist, Sudanese
Shanachie, Celtic, 1990s, Artist, German
Shankar, Lakshmi, India, 1960s-, Artist, Indian
Shankar, Ravi, India, 1950s-, Artist, Indian
Sharma, Rahul, Caribbean, 2000s-, Artist, Jamaican
Sharma, Shivkumar, India, 1970s-, Artist, Indian
Sidahmed, Mustafa, Africa, 2000s-, Artist, Sudanese
Silly Sisters, Celtic, 1970s-1980s, Artist, British
Silverbird, J. Reuben, Native America, 1990s, Producer, American
Simien, Terence, Cajun & Zydeco, 1980s-, Artist, American
Sin Samadekcho, Southeast Asia, 1990s, Artist, Cambodia
Singh, Jagjit, India, 1990s, Artist, Indian
Singh, Malkit, India, 1990s-, Artist, Indian
Sir Lancelot, Caribbean, 1940s-1970s, Artist, Trinidadian
Skeduz, Celtic, 1990s, Artist, Irish
Skjerve, Heidi, Europe, 2000s-, Artist, Norwegian
Skomsvoll, Erlend, Europe, 2000s-, Artist, Norwegian
Skrzynecka, Katarzyna, Europe, 1990s, Artist, Polish
Sky, Patrick, Celtic, 1960s-1990s, Artist, American
Society Of Ubud, Southeast Asia, 1990s, Artist, Indonesian
Sok Torng, Southeast Asia, 1990s, Artist, Cambodia
Soler, Pedro, Europe, 1990s-, Artist, Spanish
Sorten Muld, Europe, 1990s-, Artist, Swedish
Soul Ethiopia Afro Beat Band, Africa, 1970s, Artist, Ethiopian
Southern Scratch, Native America, 1990s, Artis,t American
Spillane, Davy, Celtic, 1970s-, Artist, Irish
Spotted Eagle, Douglas, Native America, 1990s, Artist, American
Srivinas, U., India, 1980s-, Artist, Indian
St Val, Tanya, Caribbean, 1980s-, Artist, West Indian
Stanislawski Brothers, Europe, 1980s-1990s, Artist, Polish
Star Band de Dakar, Africa, 1960s, Artist, Senegalese
Stare Dobre Malzenstwo, Europe, 1990s, Artist, Polish
Steel Band, Caribbean, 1990s, Artist, Trinidadian
Steel Orchestra Of Trinidad, Caribbean, 1990s, Artist, Trinidadian
Stivell, Alan, Europe, 1970s-, Artist, French
Stonecoat, Native America, 1990s, Artist, American
Street, Patrick, Celtic, 1980s-, Artist, Irish
Stringer, Dave, India, 2000s-, Artist, American
Stroutsos, Gary, Native America, 1990s-, Artist, American
Sudha, Sur, India, 1990s, Artist, Indian
Sugar Aloes, Caribbean, 1990s, Artist, Trinidadian
Sunni, Mustafa Al, Africa, 1990s, Artist, Sudanese
Suso, Foday Musa, Africa, 1960s-1990s, Artist, Gambian
Swallow, Caribbean, 1980s-1990s, Artist, Trinidadian
Swap, Europe, 1990s, Artist, Swedish
Sweet Talks, The, Africa, 1970s-1980s, Artist, Ghanaian
Tabor, June, Celtic, 1970s-, Artist, British
Taha, Rachid, Africa, 1990s-, Artist, Algerian
Takapuna City Silver Band, Australia & Oceania, 2000s-, Artist, Tahitian
Takfarinas, Middle East, 2000s-, Artist, Turkish
Tallari, Europe, 1990s, Artist, Finnish
Talsam, Hadia, Africa, 2000s-, Artist, Sudanese
Tambu, Caribbean, 1980s-1990s, Artist, Trinidadian
Tamburitza Ensemble, Europe, 1990s-, Artist, Yugoslav
Tansey, Seamus, Celtic, 1990s, Artist, Irish
Tartan Omoebas, Celtic, 1990s, Artist, Irish
Tatiana, Latin & South America, 1980s-, Artist, American
Ta'u Tahiti, Australia & Oceania, 2000s-, Artist, Tahitian
Taubman, Craig, Middle East, 1970s-1990s, Artist, American
Taw Band, Africa, 2000s-, Artist, Rwandan
Tayfa, Laco, Middle East, 2000s-, Artist, Turkish
Tazi, Ustad Massano, Africa; Middle East, 1980s, Artist, Moroccan
Te Vaka, Australia & Oceania, 1990s-, Artist, New Zealand
Tekameli, Europe, 2000s-, Artist, Hungarian
Tekbilek, Omar Faruk, Middle East, 1990s-, Artist, Turkish
Telek, Australia & Oceania, 2000s-, Artist, Papua New Guinean
Tempos, The, Caribbean, 1950s, Artist, Trinidadian
Terem Quartet, Russia & Central Asia, 1990s-, Artist, Russian
Tha Tribe, Native America, 1990s-, Artist, American
Thamar, Ralph, Caribbean, 1980s-1990s, Artist, West Indian
Thomas, Pat, Africa, 1970s-1990s, Artist, Ghanaian
Thulbion, Celtic, 1990s, Artist, Irish
Thu-Zaina, Africa, 1990s, Artist, Zaire
Tiare, Don, Australia & Oceania, 2000s-, Artist, Hawaiian
Tickell, Kathryn, Celtic, 1980s-, Artist, British
Tiger, Caribbean, 1970s-1990s, Artist, Trinidadian
Tonnere, Michael, Celtic, 1990s, Artist, Irish
Toure, Ali Farka, Africa, 1970s-1990s, Artist, Malian
Trejo, Judy, Native America, 1990s, Artist, American
Tres Reinas, Latin & South America, 2000s-, Artist, Mexican
Triakel, Europe, 1990s-, Artist, Swedish
Tridruga, Russia & Central Asia, 2000s-, Artist, Russian
Trinidad Tripoli Steel Band, Caribbean, 1950s-1990s, Artist, Trinidadian
Trio da Paz, Latin & South America, 1990s-, Artist, Brazilian
Trisakti, Seheke Joged, Southeast Asia, 1990s, Artist, Indonesian
Troka, Europe, 1990s, Artist, Finnish
True, Chris, Russia & Central Asia, 1970s-, Artist, American
Trueno Norteno, Latin & South America, 2000s-, Artist, Mexican
Tsitsanis, Vassilis, Europe, 1930s-1970s, Artist, Greek
Turtle Mountain Singers, Native America, 2000s-, Artist, American
Tweed, Karen, Europe, 1990s-, Artist, British
Ukranians, The, Russia & Central Asia, 1990s-, Artist, British
Ulali, Native America, 1980s-1990s, Artist, American
Uttara-Kuru, East Asia, 1990s, Artist, Japanese
Vamvakaris, Markos, Europe, 1940s-1960s, Artist, Greek
Varis, Tapani, Europe, 1990s, Producer, Scandinavian
Varius Manx, Europe, 1990s, Artist, Polish
Värttinä, Europe, 1980s-, Artist, Finnish
Väsen, Europe, 1990s-, Artist, Swedish
Vaughan, Palani, Australia & Oceania, 2000s-, Artist, Hawaiian
Vei, Yiotta, Europe, 1990s, Artist, Greek
Veloso, Caetano, Latin & South America, 1960s, Artist, Brazilian
Vicente, Don, Europe, 2000s-, Artist, Spanish
Vincent, Francky, Caribbean, 1980s-1990s, Artist; Composer, West Indian
Vintermane, Europe, 2000s-, Artist, Norwegian
Viseur, Gus, Europe, 1930s-1940s, Artist, French
Volga Choir, The, Russia & Central Asia, 1990s, Artist, Russian
Vujicsics, Europe, 1970s-, Artist, Hungarian
Walela, Native America, 1990s, Artist, American
Walker, Lawrence, Cajun & Zydeco, 1950s, Artist, American
Wang Yi-Dong, East Asia, 2000s-, Artist, Chinese
Wanyika, Simba, Africa, 1970s-1990s, Artist, Kenyan
Wardi, Mohammed, Africa, 1980s-1990s, Artist, Sudanese
Warren, Guy, Africa, 1950s-1960s, Artist, Ghanaian
Weisbarth, Agnes Malabey, Australia & Oceania, 2000s-, Artist, Hawaiian
Wemba, Papa, Africa, 1970s-, Artist, Zaire
Wertheimer, Benjy, Indian, 2000s-, Artist, American
West African Instrumental Quintet, Africa, 1920s-1930s, Artist, West African
Westberg, Tron Steffen, Europe, 2000s-, Artist, Norwegian
Whelan, Bill, Celtic, 1980s-1990s, Artist, Irish
Whelan, John, Celtic, 1980s-, Artist, Irish
White, Andrew, Celtic, 1980s-1990s, Artist, Irish
Whitewind, Native America, 2000s-, Artist, American
Williams, Arliene Nofchissey, Native America, 2000s-, Artist, American
Wimme, Europe, 1990s-, Artist, Finnish
Winkler, Henriette, Australia & Oceania, 2000s-, Artist, Tahitian
Wolfsong, Leah, Native America, 2000s-, Artist, American
Xalam, Africa, 1970s-1980s, Artist, Senegalese
Ximba, Vusi, Africa, 2000s-, Artist, Zulu
Xit, Native America, 1970s-1980s, Artist, American
Yama Sari Ensemble, Southeast Asia, 1990s, Artist, Indonesian
Yamil, Latin & South America, 2000s-, Artist, Mexican
Yamparika Singers, Native America, 2000s-, Artist, American
Youcef, Cheb, Africa, 2000s-, Artist, Algerian
Young Dubliners, The, Celtic, 1990s-, Artist, Irish
Youngblood, Mary, Native America, 1990s-, Artist, American
Zahir, Ahmad, Middle East, 1960s-1970s, Artist, Afghan
Zahouanian, Chaba, Africa, 1990s, Artist, Algerian
Zaiko Langa Langa, Africa, 1970s-1990s, Artist, Zaire
Zamfir, Europe, 1970s-1990s, Artist, Romanian
Zawose, Hukwe Ubi, Africa, 1990s-, Artist, Tanzanian
Zhang Wei-Liang, East Asia, 1990s-, Artist, Chinese
Zhou Yu, East Asia, 1980s-, Artist, Chinese
Zvuci, Kalesiski, Europe, 1990s-, Artist, Bosnian

MIDDLE EAST ➡296 NATIVE AMERICA ➡298 LATIN & SOUTH AMERICA ➡300 CAJUN & ZYDECO ➡302 EUROPE ➡304 RUSSIA & CENTRAL ASIA ➡306

Dance

Above

Above

Jimmy Saville – BBC DJ and the first person to use two turntables simultaneously, thus reducing the gap between the records played.

> "IF I CAN'T DANCE, IT'S NOT MY REVOLUTION."

Emma Goldman, American feminist writer

STYLES

Disco
House
Acid
Tribal/Progressive
Hardcore
Happy Hardcore
Trance
Jungle
Drum'n'Bass
Techno
Gabba
Breakbeat
Big Beat
UK Garage
US Garage
Tech-House

DANCING is as old as time, and its one constant is music that you can do it to. And while not all music is designed for dancing, some revolutionary dance music has been produced since records began. Some of it is intentionally disposable, but it is surprising just how much of the dance music made in the last 50 years stands the test of time.

A catch-all term, "dance music" has come to refer to any derivation of electronic music designed for dancing. The metronomic 120 beats per minute boom-boom-boom of house music – resembling the speed of the human heartbeat – is the standard, and this has been accelerated or morphed according to taste at different times. Most electronic music is designed for club consumption, so this section is concentrating strictly on the dance-floor side.

In the twentieth century, developments in the way people listened to music ran in tandem with the role that music events played in their social lives. At dancehalls, live bands would play the traditional jazz or swing hits of the day. By the latter half of the century, however, it became acceptable to have pre-recorded music as a form of entertainment at a nightspot. This is thanks to an innovator who, in retrospect, might seem a little unlikely – Mr Fix-It himself, Jimmy Saville.

In the early 1940s, this ex-miner hired a room above a working men's club in Otley, West Yorkshire, to play his 78s on a hastily constructed mobile system. Little did he know that in so doing, he would, effectively, be a godfather to club culture. Soon after, Saville put two turntables together for a gig and toured his DJ nights around the north of England. He went on to become a rather odd TV presenter as well as a charity marathon runner, but in 1946 he faced objections from the Musicians Union in the UK, which lobbied so that venues could only receive licences if "records aren't used in substitution of a band or orchestra".

Being interactive, 1950s jukeboxes helped pre-recorded music to become acceptable as a form of entertainment in venues. Jukeboxes also established the need for a "selector", responsible for choosing the music that a certain set of people wanted to hear. Once going out had become the accepted means by which young people were exposed to new trends and sounds, nightclubs took on a new cultural importance – as did the significance of the DJ.

Some may argue that DJs should be only a footnote to a history of music, and that live music is infinitely preferable. But, discounting the fact that most DJs become producers when they can afford the equipment necessary, the cultural significance of DJs in the last 100 years has been considerable – initially on radio and then in clubs, dance music's global popularity having grown in tandem with the rise of DJ culture.

What is a DJ? In one sense, a latter-day club DJ such as Judge Jules is scarcely different to Jimmy Saville – who also pioneered the more dubious innovation of talking live between records. According to context, a DJ might play future hits, whatever is in the charts or a seamless flow of minimalist

THE DANCE STYLE

As it is made for dancing to, dance music is characterized by a strong, steady drum beat. It is performed mainly on electronic instruments, such as the synth bass shown here.

♩ = 200

Syn Bass

Above
DJs are now rated on a level with rock stars. Decks are the musical instruments of dance music and top DJs combine technical and musical know-how with a perfect sense of rhythm to link and mix records together.

Right
The music of Richard James, a.k.a Aphex Twin, is always innovative and defiant of categorization. His work ranges from slow, ambient tones to high-speed hardcore. He even released pop tunes so as to appear on Top Of The Pops – a long-held ambition.

of a space needs lifting up or taking down, and whether the music needs to be harsher or more soulful at any particular time.

Dancing is participatory: rather than passively consuming music, you join in with it. People dance for all sorts of reasons, and after the onset of rock'n'roll, the practice seemed to be liberated from the conventions of boy-girl couplings. Some night-time groovers have been inclined to use illegal drugs to alter their physical and mental states, narcotics having long been a part of youth culture – whether it is jazz dudes with their blunts, mods with speed or ravers with ecstasy.

While you could argue that the British and Americans have an inflated sense of their cultural and political importance, most of the innovations in dance music actually have come from these two places. As technologies developed, producers took to fusing different sounds so that, to an extent, genres are perpetually morphing, with as many overlapping variants (theoretically) as the human mind can perceive. For the most part, however, some sort of consensus has formed around certain genres, usually involving an innovation or set of tracks, employing similar techniques or sounds.

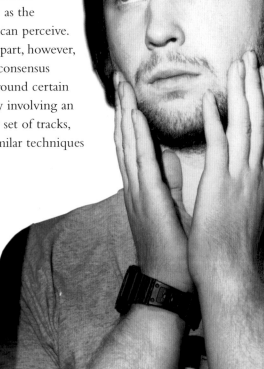

tech-house sounds. It depends where and when they are playing. Essentially, a DJ is simply the medium between the music and the crowd, operating as both a point of focus and a disseminator.

While a DJ is, ostensibly, just somebody who plays other people's records, the practice has become a hugely popular one, despite being frequently maligned and misunderstood. As DJ culture evolved through northern soul, funk and reggae and towards disco, the art of DJing came to be about communicating with a roomful of people through music. With a box of records to play, a DJ would endeavour to turn the practice into an improvizational art form by playing their music in a certain order. Weaving a tapestry of sound, DJs in the sixties and seventies started to knit together records on two turntables so you could not tell where one track ended and the next began.

In a sense, a DJ is a sort of postmodern artist: part obsessive record collector, part mad scientist and part intuitive psychologist of the party groove. Equally, they could be seen as presenters of new music, filtering what is fresh and groovy – though an increasing number of records are made especially with the DJ in mind these days. At times, both a performer and promoter, the DJ has also been referred to as a harmonic navigator, entrusted with the responsibility of the group mood or mind. A good DJ should be able to sense when the mood

Many artists dislike being pigeonholed, but others will wave a flag for their chosen genre. And while some genres seem to exist solely for the convenience of categorization in record shops, the quantity of electronic dance-floor music has necessitated splits into varying sounds and tribes.

Evolving out of what were principally black/gay clubs in America, dance music has become a worldwide phenomenon. It has been related to outrage over drug usage and constitutional criminality, but also moved from being largely ignored to being co-opted by the mainstream in the mid-1990s. You can now find it soundtracking sports TV programmes and even gardening shows.

Meanwhile, some DJs have been elevated to superstar status – more kids now buy decks than guitars, as DJs have become the new pop stars – and dance music has been the most important new musical trend for a generation. For some, it is easy to dismiss this type of music as disposable, computer-generated noise that all sounds the same. Delve a little deeper, though, and there is a whole world of innovation to be found and enjoyed.

Disco

THE AFRO WIG. THE MIRROR BALL. PLATFORM HEELS. A PAIR OF LURID FLARES. THE ENDURING ICONOGRAPHY OF THE MASS-MARKET DISCO ERA MIGHT SEEM LAUGHABLE NOW, BUT TO REDUCE SUCH A REVOLUTIONARY SOCIAL FORCE, AND CREATIVE MUSICAL EXPLOSION TO A FEW ITEMS OF FASHION TAT WOULD BE VERY SHORT-SIGHTED INDEED.

Above

The soundtrack to the 1977 film Saturday Night Fever proved to be the biggest-selling soundtrack album in history, selling over 25 million copies.

AS has happened with many other musical forms, the black (and, in this case, also gay) origins of disco have tended to be somewhat brushed over. Indeed, for many, disco is summed up by the movie *Saturday Night Fever* or disco latecomers like the Bee Gees. It may be true that the all-dancing John Travolta film took disco overground, and the previously washed-up Gibb brothers made disco more widely known in the late-1970s, but the first discotheque dates back to the 1940s.

Discotheque literally means "record library", derived from the French word *bibliotheque*. During their Second World War occupation of France, the Nazis banned dancing to, or playing, American-sounding music. The French Resistance took to playing the jazz records of black America furtively in the dark, makeshift cellar bars, and the term *discotheque* gained a more widespread parlance. When English speakers picked up on the concept of discotheques, their very Frenchness leant these early establishments a degree of sophistication.

As New York DJs like Francis Grasso began mixing records together in late-night joints – keeping the beat going so that the music constantly flowed – revellers could begin to party harder and longer. Boundaries and prejudices were being broken down on the dance floors, and the cultural climate was heading towards a kind of post-civil rights inclusivity. Other DJs, such as David Mancuso, at his New York loft parties, would emphasize the

> "THE DISCO SCENE IS A CLASSIC CASE OF SPILLED RELIGION, OF SEEKING TO OBTAIN THE SPIRITUAL EXALTATION OF THE SACRED WORLD BY INTENSIFYING THE PLEASURES OF THE SECULAR."

Albert Goldman, 'Disco'

Right

Donna Summer combined sultry vocals with songwriting talent to become the undoubted Queen of Disco.

spiritual journey a musical evening could take, while Nicky Siano – opening The Gallery – realised that Mancuso's vibe could still work on a more commercial club level. By the mid-1970s, there were more than 100 nightclubs in NYC. The disco sound had genuinely begun to germinate.

Soul, Sex And Dancing

In general, disco had a soulful feel about it, boosted by a quality, post-Spector production that incorporated uplifting,

LEADING EXPONENTS
The Bee Gees
Francis Grasso
David Mancuso
MFSB
Gloria Gaynor
Sister Sledge
Chic
Donna Summer

DISCO
The traditional disco style, with prominent bass line, sweeping strings and the characteristic "Pea-Soup" rhythm, created by open hi-hat and snare/bass.

THE DANCE INTRO ➡310 DANCE PEOPLE A-Z ➡332 INSTRUMENTS A-Z ➡436 POP: EUROPOP ➡42 DANCE: HOUSE ➡316 THE SOUL AND R&B INTRO ➡368

orchestral strings or brass. In addition, Giorgio Moroder's productions introduced a hi-NRG European influence, on classic cuts such as 'Love To Love You Baby' and 'I Feel Love', by Donna Summer. The definition of disco remained quite open: essentially, it referred to what would work on the dance floor. Even non-disco songs would become disco tunes, such as the Sugar Hill Gang's hip-hop prototype 'Rapper's Delight', or Blondie's 'Heart Of Glass'. Some artists even seemed to become disco for one week only, and not simply to revive a flagging career – the list of opportunists included Kiss, Cher, Bryan Adams, Queen, Bay City Rollers, Burt Bacharach and Diana Ross.

Some key musical innovations went hand in hand with the rise of disco. DJs fuelled the demand for remixes or re-edits of records, many of which were, initially, done by Tom Moulton. By 1974, labels were releasing DJ-only vinyl pressings of remixes, and 12 percent of vinyl was cut to allow for more space between the grooves. The results included such bona fide sex-and-dancing classics as 'Love Is The Message', 'Never Can Say Goodbye', 'Ring My Bell', 'Disco Inferno' and 'Funky Town', the big name artists including Gloria Gaynor, MFSB, Lipps Inc., Sister Sledge, Ottawan, Gamble & Huff, The O'Jays and The Temptations. With indie labels such as Salsoul and Prelude rising to challenge the majors, there was no shortage of tuneage with which DJs could provide the soundtrack for a night of hedonism.

How The Bubble Burst

By 1977 a New York celebrity haunt called Studio 54 was stealing the headlines. With its velvet-rope exclusivity, 54 was the sort of place where you could see Bianca Jagger riding in on a white horse – and indeed, the attending glitterati were probably more important than the music. It was the sort of joint that Nile Rodgers and Bernard Edwards of Chic loved, but their exclusion one night prompted them to return to their studio and, enraged, pen one of disco's most enduring anthems, originally called 'Fuck Off', its title was soon changed to 'Le Freak'.

By 1978, the USA boasted 20,000 nightclubs. Disco dominated a third of the singles chart and radio airwaves, and the industry's worth rose into the billions. The majors tried to make a fast buck, of course, but the bubble finally burst.

Disco soon fell out of favour, becoming unfashionable, kitsch and naff. The backlash was aided in part by US rock DJ Steve Dahl who called on disco-haters to demolish disco records at a Detroit Tigers baseball game

in Comiskey Park. The fans rioted, causing the game to be cancelled and chanted repeatedly "Disco sucks!". Punk rock by now was the new rock'n'roll, and disco for some was just fluff pop, becoming increasingly a watered-down version of black funk music stripped of its funk and blackness. Zipping up its boots, disco went back to its gay roots, already having laid the foundations for many more dance music genres to come.

Below

The co-founder of the disco band, Chic, Nile Rodgers is known for his distinctive style of bass guitar. Since Chic he has written and produced songs for David Bowie, Diana Ross and Eric Clapton.

DISCO HAD SUCCESSFULLY BEEN PORTRAYED IN THE BACKLASH AS UN-AMERICAN, OF QUESTIONABLE SEXUALITY, LACKING THE SUBSTANCE AND RESONANCE OF ROCK. IN UNDERGROUND CLUBS, HOWEVER, HOUSE MUSIC CONSTITUTED A MUTATION OF THE SOUND, CONCENTRATING ITS ENERGIES ON THE SYNTHETIC NOISES AND ELEMENTS OF REPETITION THAT WERE COMMON IN MANY DISCO CUTS.

House

Above

One of the leading Chicago house DJs, Farley "Jackmaster" Funk, was also influential in bringing house to the UK. His single 'Love Can't Turn Around' entered the UK Top 10, confirming the new style's popularity.

HOUSE music derived its name from the Warehouse gay club in Chicago, where Frankie Knuckles would spin records to an adoring crowd. Taking just the instrumental break of a disco record, Knuckles would splice and loop it onto reel-to-reel tape, or boost the bottom-end rhythm section of dance records with a drum machine. This 4/4 kick-drum house music is still maintained today.

The first house record, however, is widely thought to be 'On & On' by Jesse Saunders and Vince Lawrence, released in 1983 on their own Jes Say label before Larry Sherman's Trax stamp picked it up. Along with the DJ International imprint, Jes Say helped to spread these new "tracks" (rather than songs) to other US cities and beyond. Farley "Jackmaster" Funk and Jesse Saunders' 'Love Can't Turn Around' (a cover of the Isaac Hayes song) is credited as being the first worldwide house hit.

At any rate, house was a new approach, which made old music relevant again with cut-and-paste montages and the judicious use of sampling techniques, borrowed from early hip hop. It was, like disco before it, a DJ-led form, but in a creative explosion facilitated by new technology in the mid-1980s, with tracks by US producers such as Marshall Jefferson and Steve "Silk" Hurley spreading out of the house clubs and into the pop charts.

> "HOUSE MUSIC AIN'T NOTHING BUT A HARDER KICK-DRUM THAN DISCO, THAT'S IT."
>
> *Farley "Jackmaster" Funk*

Right

Frankie Knuckles has had a long and prestigious music career. He spent 15 years DJing in Chicago before recording his own work. He has since mixed and produced records for many top pop stars, including Michael Jackson.

Divisions In The House Sound

While disco popularized remixes of bands, house dispensed with the band altogether, leaving just a producer and his machines. Studio producers recruited gospel-trained vocalists, such as Robert Owens and Daryl Pandy and disco divas such as Jocelyn Brown and Loleatta Holloway. House split into two camps. The soulful side – featuring humanist sentiments and skilled musicianship – with direct linkage to disco, emphasized elements of R&B. A deep-house track such as Joe Smooth's 'Promised Land' evoked the civil rights movement by echoing Martin Luther King's equality speeches.

Meanwhile, on tracks such as Steve "Silk" Hurley's 'Jack Your Body', the freaky sounds of impersonal machine music were emphasized, their repetition attempting to offer a kind of spiritual enlightenment by encouraging trance dancing. Jacking in clubs – a kind of object-humping, jerky dance, performed as if you were plugged into the national grid – developed to these stripped-down acid tracks. The acid house sound would soon provide the impetus for the revolutionary new dance scene in the UK.

As it matured, house music dominated dance floors. As the 1990s progressed, house consolidated its position as the dominant worldwide dance-floor sound, increasingly being produced at faster than the 120bpm heartbeat speed – such as in the "handbag" offshoot of the mid-1990s. In addition, the late-1990s saw Subliminal introducing filtered disco sounds and loops, while others reverted to minimalist, quirky sounds or punky noises – such as in the click, boompty and punk house subgenres.

LEADING EXPONENTS

Frankie Knuckles

Farley "Jackmaster"
   Funk

Jesse Saunders

Steve "Silk" Hurley

Marshall Jefferson

HOUSE

A lighter rhythm than most dance music, usually with vocal and piano or keyboard predominating

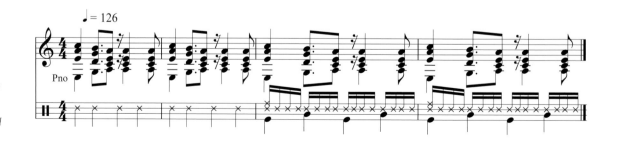

♩ = 126

THE DANCE INTRO ➡ 310   DANCE PEOPLE A-Z ➡ 332   INSTRUMENTS A-Z ➡ 436   DANCE: DISCO ➡ 314   DANCE: ACID ➡ 314

Acid

IN THE MID-1980S, THE CHICAGO DJ PIERRE WAS FIDDLING AROUND WITH A NEW PIECE OF TECHNOLOGY, THE ROLAND TB 303 MACHINE. TAMPERING WITH ITS BASS SOUND PRODUCED ALL SORTS OF SQUIGGLY, COMPLEX PATTERNS. PIERRE AND THE DJ/PRODUCER MARSHALL JEFFERSON GAVE A 12-MINUTE TAPE OF THESE DOODLINGS TO A LOCAL DJ, RON HARDY, WHO PLAYED IT AT THE MUSIC BOX CLUB.

IT became known as Ron Hardy's Acid Trax, a reference to the rumour about LSD being put in the water supply at the club, and spawned many copycat tunes, such as Bam Bam's 'Where's Your Child' and Fast Eddie's 'Acid Thunder'. DJ Pierre, however, soon moved away from the acid sound after a while, claiming it was "soulless".

The Summer Of Love

The acid sound in dance music has become virtually synonymous with the sounds produced out of a 303. Early producers of acid tracks often insisted that the genre had nothing to do with hallucinogenics, although considering the amount of drugs consumed in Chicago at this time, the claim was probably a reflex defence. It was the drug ecstasy, however, that helped kick off the acid house scene in the UK and Europe, as it grew from a few people wielding a 303 in Chicago to the most important youth movement in the UK since punk.

DJs such as Mike Pickering (who later formed M People), at Manchester's Hacienda, began to play the new house sounds from Chicago and New York, and in 1987, four London DJs were turned onto house by the Balearic DJ Alfredo, at Amnesia in Ibiza. Returning home, Danny Rampling, Paul Oakenfold, Nicky Holloway and Johnny Walker kick-started the acid house explosion in the UK. The term "acid house" came to apply to the whole house explosion in the UK in 1987, which also became known as the first Summer of Love, with a knowing nod towards San Fran twenty years previously.

Rave On

It was a somewhat exclusive secret for a while, but acid house and the drug that fuelled it – ecstasy – soon swept the UK. Finding clubs too restrictive, some punters took to putting on acid house parties in disused warehouses, as tracks such as D-Mob's 'We Call It Acieed', Jolly Roger's 'Acid Man' and Humanoid's 'Stakker Humanoid' smashed into the charts. However, the notoriously moralistic British tabloids soon took note of the scene, and "Acid House Horror" stories began to creep into the headlines. As police raided these illegal acid parties, some promoters became more daring and started to throw big outdoor parties in fields – events that became known as raves.

Tracks in a 303 style may have given way to the pianos and breakbeats of hardcore at these turn-of-the-decade raves, but the acid sound was destined to make a reappearance every so often in ensuing years. 'Higher State Of Consciousness' by Philadelphia's Josh Wink would be one of the biggest and most memorable dance tracks of the 1990s, a cut reliant on its manic 303 scribbling.

As Fatboy Slim, Norman Cook extolled the virtues of the Roland machine in 'Everybody Needs A 303', while in the illegal warehouse parties of London and beyond, the punishing-yet-cerebral acid techno of labels such as Stay Up Forever, Smitten and Cluster became the soundtrack of choice at squat party raves.

Left

A clean-living vegan, Josh Wink rejected the hedonistic lifestyle so closely associated with dance music culture by adopting an anti-drug stance. He reached the peak of his success in the mid-1990s.

> "DJ PIERRE WAS OVER AND HE WAS JUST MESSING WITH THIS THING, AND HE CAME UP WITH THAT PATTERN, MAN."
>
> *Marshall Jefferson, DJ/Producer*

Above

A youth-culture movement, acid house provided an escape from the oppressions of 1980s society. Raves allowed clubbers to absorb themselves completely in the music and escape everyday life.

♩ = 140

Synth

ACID

Differs from many of the dance styles by including "off-beats" in the rhythm, rather than a straight 4-in-the-bar kick-drum. Always accompanied by repeated sequences or "loops" on synthesizer.

LEADING EXPONENTS

DJ Pierre
Marshall Jefferson
Danny Rampling
DJ Ron Hardy
Paul Oakenfold
Nicky Holloway
Johnny Walker
D-Mob
Humanoid

THE DANCE INTRO ➡ 310   DANCE PEOPLE A-Z ➡ 332   INSTRUMENTS A-Z ➡ 436   ROCK: PSYCHEDELIC ROCK ➡ 80   THE ELECTRONIC INTRO ➡ 392

Tribal/ Progressive

DRUMS ARE THE BASIS OF TRIBAL HOUSE. WHILE THE PERCUSSION MAY BE SIMPLE AND REPETITIVE, ITS APPEAL LIES IN A CERTAIN PRIMAL, DRIVING ENERGY, STEMMING FROM THE RHYTHMICAL DRUMMING ANTICS OF TRIBESPEOPLE IN PRE-INDUSTRIALIZED SOCIETIES.

Above

Leftism includes vocals from Curve singer Toni Halliday, ex-Sex Pistol John Lydon and reggae vocalist Earl Sixteen.

"WHAT'S THE DIFFERENCE BETWEEN TRIBAL AND PROGRESSIVE? ME! HA HA HA!"

Danny Tenaglia

Right

Underworld consists of vocalist Karl Hyde, guitarist Rick Smith and DJ Darren Emerson. The group gained huge commercial success with the track 'Born Slippy', which appeared on the soundtrack to the film Trainspotting *and prompted chanting of the lyric 'shouting lager, lager lager'.*

LEADING EXPONENTS

Danny Rampling
Leftfield
William Orbit
Underworld
Fluke
The Aloof
Deep Dish
Sasha
John Digweed
Dave Seaman
Danny Howells

FROM Middle Eastern prayer call to Brazilian batucada rhythms, many musical styles are culture-specific. However, the West often lumps together this rich variety of cultural nuances, rather insultingly, under the tag of "ethnic". Nevertheless, some of these sounds have made their way onto buttons on keyboards and drum machines. A true tribal track respectfully utilizes such sounds, which are derived either from the authentic tribal rhythms of indigenous cultures or sampled from the field.

After house's US inception, American producers like Murk, the Latin-tinged Masters At Work or labels such as Strictly Rhythm were early exponents of tribal house. The first wave of early 1990s progressive house in the UK, meanwhile, was largely centred around acts like Spooky and the Drum Club or others on William Orbit's Guerilla label or Leftfield's Hard Hands imprint. The exquisite use of field sample sounds on Leftfield's *Leftism* album remain a principal reason as to why it's so often dubbed the best dance album ever.

With its slightly trippy, dub inflections and multi-level percussion, "progressive" was intended to signify a thoughtful development for house music. It was more refined than hardcore rave or marauding jungle, and it began to dominate London's West End clubs.

Millennial House

Progressive's first incarnation produced live dance bands such as Underworld, Leftfield, Fluke and the Aloof. By the mid-1990s, genres such as hard house had eclipsed it but as the 1990s progressed, however, a transatlantic synthesis of underground producers from the States, such as Deep Dish and Danny Tenaglia, along with UK DJ superstars like Sasha and John Digweed, was developing.

With his reputation as the DJ's DJ, Italian-American New York DJ Danny Tenaglia was a linchpin in this late-1990s musical synthesis. Even as late as 1999, DJs like Sasha, Dave Seaman and Danny Howells were allowing themselves to be categorized as deep trance. But the explosion of big-riff commercial trance into the pop charts led to a necessary distancing by these serious jocks from what they saw as undesirable cheesy pap and a move towards Tenaglia's dark house strain. Progressive house Mk II, taking tribal inflections and overlaying them with various modern sounds and effects, crystallized around the millennium into the international dance scene.

In 2001 progressive supplanted the Hoovers and horns of hard house as the UK dance industry's favourite genre. Some argued, however, that its subtle, stripped-down sound was not suited to the big venues prog DJs found themselves playing in. Others complained that a prog set from the likes of John Digweed – with its extended breakdowns and seemingly identical, dinosaur-lumbering loops – was pompous prog rock for post-ecstasy accountants. Still, the ability of its versatile DJs and producers to move between genres, and the vision of labels such as Kismet, Bedrock, Renaissance and SAW, meant that there was plenty of invention and fun to be had from the genre.

TRIBAL/PROGRESSIVE

A more complex rhythm than many of the dance styles, with a slightly more "earthy" feel. Usually features long sustained chords over the top, and can include vocal line.

THE DANCE INTRO ➡ 310   DANCE PEOPLE A-Z ➡ 332   THE WORLD INTRO ➡ 276   WORLD: MIDDLE EAST ➡ 296   WORLD: LATIN & SOUTH AMERICA ➡ 300

Hardcore

AS THE 1990S BEGAN, DANCE MUSIC WAS REALLY ONLY SUBDIVIDED INTO HOUSE OR TECHNO. HOWEVER, ANOTHER GENRE WAS FORMING ALONGSIDE THE EXPLOSION OF BIG OUTDOOR RAVES – HARDCORE, WHERE EXTREME HEDONISM MET A KIND OF UNDERCLASS DESPERATION.

HARDCORE has meant different things at different times. In the early 1990s, different parts of Europe had different words for hardcore dance music, such as the Belgian *skizzo* (schizophrenic) and the German *bretter*. UK hardcore was less acceptable to the media than electronic sounds such as house, because it was the preferred choice of the sweaty, drug-gobbling working class. Hardcore ravers seemed to be pushing the boundaries of sensation, and producers and DJs made a virtue out of doing the same with the music-making or -playing equipment.

Hardcore was what sounded good at big raves, on one level, but within the new sound several distinct strains developed. At varying times in the early 1990s, hardcore could mean the bleep'n'bass of Sheffield-based Warp Records acts such as LFO and Nightmares On Wax; the hip-house/ragga techno sounds on the north London Shut Up & Dance label; the pop-rave of N-Joi and K-Klass; Belgian (and German) brutalist outfits such as T99, with their Hoover noises and 'Mentasm' stabs; and, by 1993, the proto-jungle sound of breakbeat hardcore.

In the more segregated USA, the hip hop and house scenes were poles apart. In the UK, however, they were more or less part of the same continuum – street beats derived from America. Both the black and white youth got involved in mutating techno out of all recognition. The Detroit pioneers were horrified at Europe's unruly bastardization of techno.

Raving In Toytown

Using the new technology – a great leveller in terms of access and affordability – British youth particularly began experimenting with sounds such as increased sub-bass frequencies. Some, like the Prodigy, Shut Up & Dance and Liquid on 'Sweet Harmony' began looping breakbeats to add a scuttling oomph to the metronomic 4/4 house sound, and started seeking out and grabbing cheeky samples from the most unlikely sources. Police sirens, public information film snippets, classical string sweeps, and the theme tunes to half-forgotten kids' TV programmes were all fair game.

One act, Altern8, had an image that inverted the hardcore raver's pseudo-military get-up. Their chemical protection jump-suits and gas masks, not to mention standing-for-Parliament stunts, won them brief acclaim. But when Shut Up & Dance based 'Raving I'm Raving' on the old 'Walking In Memphis' standard, the might of the record industry came down upon them and, effectively, shut them down. Sample royalties was still a grey area, and the fresh naivety of the sampler as instrument led to a rash of "obvious" sampled hits. 'Sesame's Treet' by Smart Es, 'Trip To Trumpton', 'Charly' and 'Roobarb & Custard' all used references from children's television. These were humorous, quite innovative tracks taken on their own, but as a simultaneous glut, hardcore was starting to seem increasingly toytown.

Eventualy hardcore developed into new genres, and in 2001 was briefly revived by a rash of compilation CDs of old skool.

> ## "WE'RE NOT A RAVE GROUP, WE'RE A FAST HIP HOP GROUP."
> *Shut Up & Dance, hardcore pioneers*

Above

'Sesame's Treet' reached number 5 in the UK chart in 1992. Smart E's took the theme tune to the children's TV series Sesame Street *and added hip hop break-beats. Hardcore had hit the Top 10!*

Left

Although together only three years, Altern8's exploits gained a good deal of media coverage. It was rumoured that they provided the audience with ecstasy spiked pastries and were themsleves addicted to Vicks Vapo-Rub.

♩ = 140

Synth

HARDCORE

Fast and loud 4-in-a-bar kick-drum and hi-hat, often with high-register vocal and dominant bass-line, give hardcore its instantly recognizable sound.

LEADING EXPONENTS

K-Klass
N-Joi
Nightmares On Wax
Altern8
Shut Up & Dance
The Prodigy
Smart E's
T99

THE DANCE INTRO ➡ 310   DANCE PEOPLE A–Z ➡ 332   ROCK: PSYCHEDELIC ROCK ➡ 80   DANCE: ACID ➡ 317   DANCE: HAPPY HARDCORE ➡ 320

Happy Hardcore

IN THE UK, HARDCORE SPLIT INTO TWO CAMPS IN THE EARLY 1990S. ONE HALF WOULD LEAD TO JUNGLE, BUT WITHIN BREAKBEAT HARDCORE, A FACTION OF DJS AND RAVERS FELT THAT THE MUSIC WAS GETTING TOO GLOOMY. PRODUCERS AND DJS SUCH AS SLIPMATT, SEDUCTION, VIBES, BRISK AND DOUGAL EFFECTIVELY LED AN EXODUS OF WHITE RAVERS AWAY FROM WHAT THEY SAW AS A TOO-MOODY JUNGLE SCENE.

Above

One of the many happy hardcore compilations. The eighth in the series of Wow – What A Rush compilations, it features many joint efforts by happy hardcore stars such as Slipmatt & Frisky.

THE sound largely stemmed from the antics of Slipmatt, a.k.a Matt Nelson. As one half of SL2, DJ Lime being the other half, Slipmatt took Jimi Polo's old house anthem, 'Better Days', and created the happy blueprint using techniques evident in the 'On A Ragga Tip' hardcore hit. Selling 10,000 copies on the underground scene, 'SMD#1' led to Slipmatt forming his own Universal label to release productions by other DJs/artists such as Hixxy, Sy and Force & Styles.

Essentially running at about 170bpm with sped-up breakbeats alongside the 4/4 stomp, happy hardcore made a virtue of the elements of hardcore that had been derided as too "cheesy" – the piano chords borrowed from Italo-house, searing synth stabs, wailing divas, quick and easy samples, and absurdly catchy choruses. The juvenile, toytown vibe that had, for some, signalled the death of rave seemed to be maximized in happy hardcore. Witness the success of 'Toy Town' by Sharkey and Hixxy, a track that celebrated the playtime antics of children's cartoons.

> ## "IT WAS MOSTLY DJS WHO WERE INTO DARK. ALL I HEARD FROM THE CROWD WAS MOANS."
> *DJ Slipmatt*

Right

Happy hardcore was all about having fun. The music had a very positive vibe, and the appearance of some of the clubbers reflected this euphoric mood.

The peace-and-love vibes prevalent in happy hardcore were undoubtedly boosted by the continuing presence of ecstasy. Many clubbers at jungle raves preferred marijuana and alcohol to ecstasy, but happy hardcore was always very much an ecstasy scene. At clubs such as Kinetic in Stoke-on-Trent, or the Labyrinth in Dalston, clubbers wore white gloves, waved glo-sticks and sported comedy clubwear. For them, raving was still about fun and being happy – hence the emphasis, in case anyone had any doubt, on the genre's prevailing mood.

Crappy Hardcore?

Apart from Slipmatt's show on the London radio station KISS FM, the sound was largely ignored by the mainstream, although it did find an unlikely ally in the UK's maverick Radio 1 DJ John Peel, a long-time champion of misfit embryonic musical styles. "People often say to me, 'Why are you playing happy hardcore? It's crap'," Peel said. "That just makes me want to play more of it."

In the mid-1990s, Sharkey and his colleague Hixxy released the 'Bonkers' triple-mix CD on compilation specialist label React. Amazingly, it sold a quarter of a million copies, propelling the sound into the homes of dance-music types who would otherwise not have known about the underground sound. As well as 'Toy Town', other happy tracks, such as 'Rainbow In The Sky' by Paul Elstak (on loan from happy-gabba), 'Wonderland' by Force & Styles, and 'Is This Love?' by Fade & Melody, would follow. But producers such as Billy Bunter, Ramos and Sharkey himself soon moved away from the happy sound.

"Not everyone goes to a rave and wants to be happy and not everyone goes and wants to be dark," Sharkey exclaimed. "It's about giving people the choice." Sharkey's outlook on twenty-first-century hardcore underlines the pick'n'mix element evident in the latter-day scene. Mixing hard trance, gabba, acid techno and hardcore old and new, the juvenile rush of hardcore is still evident in outposts in Germany, France, Holland and Scotland, as well as territories outside Europe such as Australia.

LEADING EXPONENTS

Matt Nelson (DJ Slipmatt)

DJ Lime

Seduction Vibe

Brisk & Dougal

Sharkey

Hixxy

Force & Styles

Fade & Melody

HAPPY HARDCORE

A more "happy" and tuneful sound than straight hardcore, with a more melodic vocal style, usually with chord accompaniment on keyboards.

THE DANCE INTRO ➡ 160   DANCE PEOPLE A-Z ➡ 332   INSTRUMENTS A-Z ➡ 436   ROCK: PSYCHEDELIC ROCK ➡ 80   DANCE: HARDCORE ➡ 319

Trance

EFFECTIVELY A HYBRID OF TANGERINE DREAM-STYLE COSMIC SYNTH-ROCK AND GIORGIO MORODER EURO-DISCO, TRANCE BEGAN TO CRYSTALLIZE OUT OF TURN-OF-THE-DECADE TRIPPY TECHNO AT THE END OF THE 1980S (ALTHOUGH DISCO RECORDS SUCH AS GRACE'S 'NOT OVER YET' OR DONNA SUMMER'S 'I FEEL LOVE', PRODUCED BY MORODER AND PETE BELLOTTE, COULD LAY CLAIM TO BEING EARLIER TRANCE CUTS).

IT was Hardfloor's 'Acperience' on Harthouse that set the blueprint for the haunting textures of trance. Layering 303 acid sounds across each other like intertwining snakes the track sold shed-loads, paving the way for the rise of German, Dutch and British labels like MFS, Platipus, Eye Q, Noom and Rising High and the eventual conquest of many dance floors in the US.

Going To Goa

In the early 1990s, nights at The Omen in Frankfurt, Trance Buddha in Amsterdam and Megatripolis in London swiftly became techno-trance meccas. The coalescing sound began to become popular at outdoor techno parties in Goa on the west coast of India, a stop-off haven on the hippy trail. Hosted by the likes of Goa Gil and Mark Allen, Goa trance emphasized the spiritual and ethnic elements of the sound. Key components of Goa began to filter back to Europe, with Brit DJs such as Danny Rampling and Paul Oakenfold briefly adopting the sound after visits to the region and German producer Sven Vath sampling sounds from the jungle on the Indian subcontinent for his *An Accident In Paradise* album.

In addition, many Israelis would visit the region when travelling after national service. Returning home, revellers would try to recreate the spirit of those memorable outdoor Goa trance parties in clubs in their own home countries.

Cheese With Your Cerebral Ethnodelia?

In London, Raja Ram's TIP label, Youth's Dragonfly, and acts such as Eatstatic, Juno Reactor, Hallucinogen, Total Eclipse, Man With No Name and Shpongle fed 150bpm cerebral ethnodelia into fluoro-tastic club nights Return to the Source, Escape From Samsara and Pendragon. From Denmark, Koxbox introduced a more psychedelic component to the sound, and outdoor full-moon parties kicked off at exotic locations around the globe. Some would sneer that the scene was full of trustafarians (trust-fund hippies) seeking both enlightenment and druggy hedonism, but for many, the psychedelic-trance scene and lifestyle was life-changing.

In Europe in the late-1990s, a watered-down strain was starting to creep into the German charts. Promotions such as the UK's Gatecrasher and GodsKitchen took the sound into the superclubs. Trance was beginning to dominate dance floors everywhere. As the sound became more commercialized, some DJs jumped ship ("I've had enough," said Sven Vath in 1998), and tracks by Euro-trance acts like Alice Deejay, Lange and ATB – who produced trance's first UK number one with '9PM (Till I Come)' – hit paydirt.

Inevitably, there was a backlash, in which trance became increasingly derided as too cheesy and lacking any sort of authentic funk. However, 2002 saw a resurgence in its popularity, with credible underground Dutch trance DJs such as Tiësto, Armin Van Buuren and Ferry Corsten reviving the scene.

Above
Judge Jules works hard to maintain his position as the UKs most popular DJ. He has two weekend shows and plays around five gigs a week.

> "WE WENT TO GOA, HEARD THE TECHNO BEING PLAYED THERE, CAME BACK AND SET UP OUR OWN PARTIES."
>
> *Raja Ram, psychedelic trance producer*

Left
A pioneer of dance music, Danny Rampling set up the influential club Shoom in 1987. Rampling has always been a passionate music fan and hardcore clubber; so much so that in 1997 he suffered a breakdown caused by exhaustion.

$\quad = 140$

Synth

TRANCE

A repetitive and monotonous style (hence the name), usually with repeated sequenced keyboard loops, 4-in-a-bar kick-drum, and 16ths on hi-hat.

LEADING EXPONENTS

Raja Ram
Paul Van Dyck
Man With No Name
Pigs In Space
Tiësto
Armin Van Buuren
Jam and Spoon
Ferry Corsten

THE DANCE INTRO ➡ 160   DANCE PEOPLE A-Z ➡ 332   INSTRUMENTS A-Z ➡ 436   ROCK: PSYCHEDELIC ROCK ➡ 80   DANCE: ACID ➡ 317

JUNGLE WAS A REACTION AGAINST HAPPY RAVE'S CROSSOVER COMMERCIALISM. THE MUSIC DID NOT SO MUCH DIE AS GO BACK UNDERGROUND, BECOMING DARKER AND MORE SINISTER IN ORDER TO REFLECT THE PREVAILING, EARLY 1990S MOOD.

Jungle

Above

An experimental DJ, Fabio is associated with the more mellow, jazzy strands of jungle. He began his career on the pirate radio Phase 1 and then joined forces with Grooverider, whom he worked with for more than 10 years.

BY this time in dance music, there had been plenty of media scare stories about ecstasy fatalities. As drug use spiralled for some clubbers, tracks such as 4Hero's 'Mr Kirk's Nightmare' (Reinforced), Ed Rush's 'Bloodclot Artattack' (No U-Turn) and Origin Unknown's 'Valley Of The Shadows' (Ram), reflected the mood of a scene riven with drug casualties and near-death experiences.

DJs such as Fabio and Grooverider would increase the tempo on breakbeat house tracks by pitching up the speed on the record decks. In a mutually beneficial synergy of DJ/producer development, producers began creating more of a mutated, Jamaican ragamuffin/dancehall techno sound, which DJs aimed to emulate with their cutting-up turntable tricks. With dancehall samples and other sound system traditions, such as the use of exclusive solitary vinyl dubplate pressings by DJs and the exuberance of motormouth MCs, a black element became more evident in the music, although jungle was avowedly multiracial from its inception.

The actual origins of the term "jungle" are disputable. One story claims that it sprang from a sample used by the producer Rebel MC citing "alla the junglists". One of DJ Hype's crew, Pascal, recording as Johnny Jungle, was the first producer to use the term on vinyl. Another tale has it that the urban-jungle metaphor, used in black music history by everyone from Sly Stone and Grandmaster Flash to the Wailers, simply seemed to fit the music perfectly.

"YOU HAVE TO KNOW THIS MUSIC TO BE ABLE TO GET INSIDE IT. AND YOU CAN'T MAKE THIS MUSIC UNLESS YOU ARE INSIDE IT."

Goldie

Right

Having originally been part of Double Trouble, Rebel MC pursued a solo career as a pop rapper. His 1991 album, however, took a different direction. Black Meaning Good is considered a precursor to jungle music.

It's A Jungle Out There

Cascading like tangled vines, the polyrhythmic breakbeats almost gave the dance floor the feel of a sonic jungle. As producers experimented with new techniques such as time-stretching, an identifiable sound emerged. The rhythm is the melody in jungle, and its deadly, half-speed bassline gives it two levels at which you can dance – skanking at 70 beats per minute as if dancing to ska, then flailing to the skittering drums where desired. Some saw this new sound as devoid of a feminine element, and the combative dancing as too masculine. But the number of ragga gals who would wind their bodies to the music put an end to that notion.

Turned onto the music by future DJs Kemistry and Storm at Rage, a young graffiti artist named Goldie began to make exhilarating, disturbing, futuristic opuses such as 'Terminator'. Despite its uniqueness, the sound was pointedly ignored by the media, even the newly formed dance-music press.

The number of black faces on the scene seemed to scare some people too, and jungle nights were largely restricted to the outskirts of a city. When the media did decide to look into the scene, scare stories involving crack and guns at raves tarnished its image, leading some, mistakenly, to believe that jungle was dominated by gun-toting, crack-smoking bad boys.

LEADING EXPONENTS

Goldie
Fabio
Grooverider
Kemistry & Storm
Doc Scott
Pascal
DJ Hype
Ed Rush
4Hero

JUNGLE

A style very dependent on the rhythm, no melody or chord structure, usually long bass notes to accompany the increasingly complex jungle rhythm through the song.

Drum'n'Bass

DRUM'N'BASS WAS A KIND OF RE-BRANDING THAT CAME FROM THE SCENE ITSELF – THE PRODUCER SIDE THAT WANTED TO ALLOW FILMIC SOUNDS TO SPEAK FOR THEM RATHER THAN SOME PATOIS MC. BY DOWNPLAYING THE RAGGA, PRODUCERS AND DJS WERE EFFECTIVELY SAYING THAT THEY WISHED TO COMMUNICATE A MESSAGE OR MOOD SONICALLY RATHER THAN VERBALLY.

SOME have argued that drum'n'bass is the UK's equivalent to hip hop, and as such, this distinction mirrors the hip hop/ trip hop raison d'être.

Still immersed in breakbeat manipulation, some producers began experimenting with sound textures or female vocals, speeding up the breaks so much that they ceased to be visceral triggers for dancing limbs and actually became soothing. One DJ, LTJ Bukem, had pre-empted the split from the ragga sound with his mellowcore 'Logical Progression', 'Demon's Theme' and 'Music' releases. For his part, Goldie delivered 'Angel' and his masterpiece, 'Inner City Life', which he described as "ghetto blues for the 1990s". Others such as Omni Trio, Foul Play, A Guy Called Gerald and hardcore stalwarts 4Hero began moving away from what they increasingly saw as juvenile or druggy sounds and into the realms of artcore.

The scene effectively became split between the roughneck and the elegantly suave. At new central London club-night Speed, DJs Fabio and Bukem aired the jazzy, oceanic side of the sound, and suddenly, drum'n'bass was the buzzword on the lips of fashionistas everywhere. The major labels duly came begging.

Hearing Is Believing

As a parallel to jazzy jungle, others began to develop a science out of painstakingly building percussive breakbeats. Producers such as Lemon D and Dillinja produced tearaway monsters such as 'The Acid Track' and 'Tudor Rose'; avant-gardists such as Aphex Twin, Squarepusher and U-Ziq took breakbeat manipulation to absurd extremes with their non-dancefloor "drill'n'bass" oddities; the Jump-Up style popularized by DJ Hype and the Ganja Kru flourished; Roni Size and his Reprazent crew from Bristol won the prestigious Mercury Music Prize; and when DJ Trace tore up the sax-tastic 'Mutant Jazz' by T-Power vs Mk Ultra to make 'The Mutant', a new d&b style crystallized. Tech-step allowed producers to explore their sci-fi or martial arts obsessions, and was a reaction to the perceived coffee-table acceptability of the sound. Pockets of drum'n'bass DJ/producers began springing up in countries such as Norway, France and the USA.

This premillennial darkness proved too much for some, and they heartily welcomed the positive, sunshiny Latino element brought into the music by Brazilian junglists Marky, Patife and XRS, and hits such as 'Shake Ur Body'. Drum'n'bass is now a global genre, and the term is used more frequently (but still more or less interchangeably) with jungle.

> "I COULD KNOCK OUT 17 MILLION JUNGLE TRACKS A WEEK JUST BY GETTING ALL MY OLD REGGAE SEVEN INCHES AND STICKING THEM OVER AN AMEN BREAK. I THINK PEOPLE ARE MORE INTELLIGENT THAN THAT."
>
> *LTJ Bukem*

Above
London-born DJ/producer Danny Williamson, a.k.a LTJ Bukem, has remained true to his drum'n'bass roots.

Left
In the guise of A Guy Called Gerald, Gerald Simpson has contributed to virtually all the leading dance music genres.

♩ = 120

DRUM'N'BASS

Predominantly, as the name suggests, dependent on the drum'n'bass guitar parts, usually a simple 4/4 drum line.

LEADING EXPONENTS

LTJ Bukem
Roni Size
A Guy Called Gerald
Goldie
4Hero
DJ Hype & the
   Ganja Kru
Fabio
Aphex Twin
Squarepusher

IN THE EARLY 1980S, DERRICK MAY WAS ONE OF A TRIUMVIRATE OF TECHNO PIONEERS IN DETROIT WHO BEGAN PROVIDING A SOUNDTRACK FOR THE FUTURE. MAY WAS FRIENDS WITH KEVIN SAUNDERSON AND JUAN ATKINS AT JUNIOR HIGH SCHOOL IN BELLEVILLE. ATKINS TURNED THEM ON TO MUSIC BY THE LIKES OF GIORGIO MORODER, KRAFTWERK AND THE SPRAWLING CLINTON/PARLIAMENT/FUNKADELIC FUNK BEAST.

Techno

Above

The Technics 1210 turntable is an international version of the 1200 Mark2. The original 1200 was released by Technics in the early 1970s and then developed further in the late-1970s.

THE home of Motown, Detroit certainly was a funk city but its car industry also lent itself well to the *motorik* rhythms of Kraftwerk. The Detroit Belleville three were as inspired by Kraftwerk as Afrika Bambaataa was to make electro blueprint 'Planet Rock' in New York. They would sit around and dream up sci-fi phenomena and future possibilities, in music and in life. Atkins had already started making paranoid, synthetic socio-funk, first as Cybotron (together with Rick Davis) and then as Model 500. Once they began DJing on the social club circuit around Detroit as Deep Space Soundworks, they wanted to release their own compositions on vinyl.

The Detroit pioneers – who were soon joined by a fourth musketeer, Eddie "Flashin'" Fowlkes – embraced the techno-logical developments of the twentieth century as a means of empowerment and resistance against corporations that mass-produce new machines. Atkins actually described himself as "a warrior for the technological revolution", and he was projecting so far into the future that he began developing a techno-speak dictionary known as *The Grid*.

> "IT'S LIKE GEORGE CLINTON AND KRAFTWERK ARE STUCK IN AN ELEVATOR WITH ONLY A SEQUENCER TO KEEP THEM COMPANY."
>
> *Derrick May, techno pioneer*

Right

Joey Beltram started DJing at an early age. At 18 he was working with Transmat, the influential Detroit techno label. He began playing Chicago house, but is best known for his Belgian-style acid and techno.

The Detroit pioneers set up their own record labels (May: Transmat; Saunderson: KMS; Atkins: Metropole), and if Atkins' music was eerily futuristic, Derrick May's was splendidly symphonic. Recording under the name Rhythim Is Rhythim, he sampled recorded moments of the Detroit Symphony Orchestra for his epic 'Strings Of Life' track. Meanwhile,

LEADING EXPONENTS

Derrick May
Kevin Saunderson
Juan Atkins
Eddie "Flashin'" Fowlkes
Jeff Mills
Orbital
Laurent Garnier
Dave Angel

TECHNO

A fast and heavy 4/4 beat, with the bar of silence followed by rapid and accelerating sequenced snare, characteristic of this style.

THE DANCE INTRO ➡ 310   DANCE PEOPLE A–Z ➡ 332   INSTRUMENTS A–Z ➡ 436   DANCE: DISCO ➡ 314   SOUL AND R&B: FUNK ➡ 376

under the name Inner City, Kevin Saunderson – with roots in Chicago, the most disco-minded of the Belleville boys – produced the uplifting ditties 'Big Fun' and 'Good Life' with vocalist Paris Grey, both of which went on to become international chart hits.

Burning Down The House

DJs started to play techno tracks in the US alongside early house records, but the compilation album that helped spread the sound far and wide was *Techno! The New Dance Sound Of Detroit* on Virgin. "We're tired of hearing about being in love or falling out, so a new progressive sound has emerged," said Atkins at the time. "We call it techno."

"House still has its heart in 1970s disco," May observed. "We don't have any of that respect for the past, it's strictly future music." He would play techno on the radio in Detroit sometimes, but it was the fast cuts of The Wizard – aka Jeff Mills – on Detroit's WJLB station that captured people's imaginations. Meeting up with Mike Banks and Robert Hood, Mills formed the militantly minded Underground Resistance (UR), a project/label so covert it generated as much mystique as the semi-mythical, world-domination secret society the Bilderberg group.

Producing first the hypnotic 'Energy Flash' and then the synth-stabbing 'Mentasm', a New Yorker, Joey Beltram, changed the course of techno twice before his 21st birthday. The Belgians were the first to pick up on this embryonic, brutalist hardcore sound, replacing energy with noise – much to the despair of the original Detroitists. In the UK, techno became the sound of free festivals, taking up the space once occupied by space rock or dub.

Five years after the first so-called Summer of Love in 1987, a huge, illegal techno gathering of 20,000 travellers and ravers took place on Castlemorton Common in Worcestershire. After outrage in the tabloids, police arrested who they believed to be the organizers of this spontaneous gathering – the "terra-technic" collective Spiral Tribe. Alarmed at such a huge word-of-mouth gathering of undesirables playing and listening to alien machine music, the Conservative government introduced the Criminal Justice Act, which outlawed unlicensed gatherings at which the amplified music played is "characterised by the emission of a succession of repetitive beats". Despite initial establishment outrage caused by

jazz, rock'n'roll and punk, this was the first time that a genre of music had been specifically legislated against in UK law.

Throughout the 1990s, producers and DJs emerged who would take techno to new levels. The Londoner Carl Cox went from being a DJ hawking his own sound system around the south coast of the UK for illegal parties, to the current worldwide ambassador for the sound. Taking their name from the parties around the London M25 ring-road, Orbital – Hartnoll brothers Phil and Paul – took their increasingly Heath Robinson-esque take on the sound live and to *Top Of The Pops* with momentous tracks like 'Chime' and 'Belfast'. Laurent Garnier, Luke Slater, Richie Hawtin, Carl Craig, Dave Angel, Dave Clarke, Ken Ishii, Stacey Pullen, Umek, Jim Masters, Brenda Russell (not to be confused with the American R&B singer of the same name), Marco Carola, C1, Adam Beyer and Slam have all become important players on the dance scene. In the main, the future funk sound has remained true to its roots, concentrating on the vocal-free, machine-generated rhythms that hark back to nothing except the future.

Above

The techno guru Carl Cox while playing at Tribal Gathering in 1996; the third of the annual dance festival to be held in the UK.

Below

Derrick May was one of the first American techno artists to tour England following the UK success of his single 'Strings of Life' in 1987–1988.

GROWING OUT OF BELGIAN "HOOVER" TRACKS (SEEMINGLY FEATURING THE SOUNDS OF INSANELY TRUMPETING HARMONIC VACUUM CLEANERS) BY THE LIKES OF T99, AND OLD HARDCORE TUNES SUCH AS BELTRAM'S 'ENERGY FLASH', A DUTCH STRAIN OF RAVE ADDED AN ABSURDLY FAST ROLAND 909 DRUM MACHINE TO THE MUSIC.

Gabba

Above
Michael Wells and his wife, Lee Newman, gained chart success as the duo Technohead.

THIS shuddering, rapid kick-drum sound took off in Rotterdam, which was attempting to distinguish itself from the tasteful house music scene in Amsterdam, and echo football and other rivalries.

Gabba literally meant "hooligan" or "ruffneck", but youth in Rotterdam reclaimed the derogatory word as a distinguishing badge of pride. Appropriately enough, Euromasters (a.k.a Paul Elstak) 'Where The Fuck Is Amsterdam?' was the first gabba anthem to hit big. Another early gabba Euro-wide hit was 'Poing', by Rotterdam Termination Source. Sounding like a demented ping-pong ball let loose in a wind tunnel, 'Poing' was an early example of pushing music-making equipment to the extreme. Moby also experimented in his song 'Thousand' by pushing the tempo up to 1,000bpm, although most gabba tracks found their feet at about 200bpm.

Gabba is more than just the living embodiment of the generation gap. Not only would your parents detest its pneumatic drill syncopation, your brothers and sisters probably would, too. As would many of your friends. With samples from heavy metal guitars, apocalyptic preachers or other doomcore sounds, the gabba scene echoes the death metal strain of rock with the knobs turned up to destroy.

"THE APOCALYPTIC, SCI-FI AND HORROR MOVIE IMAGERY IN GABBA IS... VERY SIMILAR TO THE WAY HEAVY METAL USES THE IMAGERY OF DEATH, DESTRUCTION AND ANTI-RELIGION."

Michael Wells, Technohead

Right
Gabba, a radical strain of techno, was popular in Scotland and Amsterdam, but a divide developed as certain gabbers took the scene to extremes.

Gabba's nihilism and blood-and-guts imagery is evident from the names of some of the record labels feeding the scene. Bloody Fist, War, Killout and Napalm all sprang up as the 1990s progressed. One gabba act, Ultraviolence, trailed their *Psycho Drama* LP with the promise of "10,000 Nagasakis in your head". This sound is not for the faint-hearted or squeamish.

Gabba Gabba Hey Hey

Gabba began to get a bad reputation as the 1990s progressed. Its pseudo-skinhead regalia, combined with tracks such as Sperminator's 'No Women Allowed', seemed to echo bellicose Nazi machismo. Most Dutch gabba labels were aware of this possible perception, however, and took care to wear their antiracist credentials on their (record) sleeves.

One DJ/producer, Paul Elstak, deserted the dark, noisecore faithful to record chart hits in a happy-gabba style. His 'Life Is Like A Dance' track cracked the Dutch Top 10, and the follow-up, 'Luv U More', reached number two. Other happy-gabba tracks, such as Technohead's 'I Want To Be A Hippy', dented the pop charts. These were largely dismissed by the Nasenbluten-loving hardcore faithful, who would claim that "Happy is for homos" – preferring, perhaps, the nosebleed thrash-gabba of DJ Smurf.

LEADING EXPONENTS

Rotterdam Termination Source
Paul Elstak
Technohead
T99
Ultraviolence
DJ Smurf
Agent Orange
Sperminator

GABBA

An extremely fast version of hardcore/techno, with a frantic drum line and sequenced synth bass.

♩ = 200

Syn Bass

THE DANCE INTRO ➡ 310 DANCE PEOPLE A-Z ➡ 332 INSTRUMENTS A-Z ➡ 436 ROCK: DOOM METAL ➡ 95 DANCE: HOUSE ➡ 316 THE DANCE INTRO ➡ 310

Breakbeat

THE BREAKBEAT IS, LITERALLY, THE PERCUSSION-ONLY SEGMENT OF A FUNK OR DISCO TRACK, WHERE THE DANCERS WOULD CUT LOOSE. FINDING THAT THIS WAS OFTEN THE SEGMENT THEY MOST WANTED TO PLAY, DISCO DJS WOULD CUT BETWEEN TWO COPIES OF THE SAME RECORD TO CREATE A FUNKY DRUMMER MÉLANGE.

IN the mid-1970s, too, Kool Herc invented the hip-hop technique of looping breaks into a continuous groove by using two turntables. The basis for future rappers' street-poetry polemics had been laid.

Seething Percussive Polyrhythms

Hip-hop producers began using new sampling and sequencing technology to loop beats, some of which were collected on "beats & breaks" compilation albums, primarily for use as a DJ tool. By the early 1990s, house and techno producers were also using breakbeats on tracks, and producers with a hip hop background, such as the Prodigy's Liam Howlett or future junglist DJ Hype, created seething, percussive polyrhythms of sound.

From house maestro Todd Terry's late 1980s experiments in hip-house, to breakbeat hardcore and jungle/drum'n'bass, breakbeat has often been a key component of 1990s electronic dance music. But by the late 1990s, some DJs were starting to see it as the main component of a new style. The emergence of the nu-skool breaks sound came out of the Friction club night, started by Rennie Pilgrem at London's Bar Rumba. A former hardcore DJ and producer, alongside cohort Ellis Dee, Pilgrem began pioneering a new breakbeat-driven sound on his label TCR.

Friction was populated by proto-breakbeat DJs and producers who had come together out of other London scenes. FreQ Nasty, Blim and T-Power came from drum'n'bass, Mob Records boss Tayo came from house, and DJs Adam Freeland and Ali B were former press officers with a company called Slice PR before they became headline makers themselves. In part, they were also taking their cue from the breaks sound and big beat emerging from the US west coast but without the glaringly obvious hip hop samples thrown into the mix.

Something For Anyone

When Jason Nevins remixed the 1980s Run-DMC hip hop classic 'It's Like That', it shot to the top of the UK charts and brought the street craze of breakdancing back into vogue. Acts such as the Freestylers and the Plump DJs emerged out of breaks nights such as Passenger in Kings Cross, the former establishing themselves as one of dance music's most popular live acts and the latter going on to act as ambassadors for the breaks sound worldwide. In the US, the crossover of breakbeats into rock was aided by acts like Crystal Method and even nu metallists such as Limp Bizkit.

Within breakbeat's accepted step, you probably can find something for virtually everyone, and with such diverse contributors the future for breaks is looking very healthy indeed.

"WHEN HARDCORE GOT TO 150BPM, IT GOT A BIT CHEESY. THAT'S NOT A VERY GOOD DANCING SPEED EITHER, SO WE'VE DOWNED THE TEMPO TO 130, WHICH IS LIKE HOUSE SPEED. IT'S FUNKIER THAT WAY."
TCR label boss, Rennie Pilgrem

Above
DJ Tayo, one of the instigators of the breakbeat sound, performing at Bugged Out in Brighton.

Left
Aston Harvey and Matt Cantor combined their talents as producers, breakdancers, MCs and vocalists to produce infectious breakbeat tunes as the Freestylers.

♩ = 100

Pno

Elec Gtr

BREAKBEAT
As the name suggests, this music has a prominent beat which is occasionally "broken", giving a bar of silence in the rhythm part, filled with a solo instrument.

LEADING EXPONENTS
Rennie Pilgrem
The Prodigy
Todd Terry
Ellis Dee
Adam Freeland
Ali B
The Freestylers
Plump DJs

DANCE PEOPLE A-Z ➡ 332 INSTRUMENTS A-Z ➡ 436 DANCE: DISCO ➡ 314 DANCE: HOUSE ➡ 316 SOUL AND R&B: FUNK ➡ 376

Big Beat

THE 1990S ELECTRONICA THAT CAME TO BE KNOWN AS BIG BEAT IS RECOGNISED BY ITS RHYTHMIC CLOUT AND PROPULSIVE FORCE. WITH THEIR FREAKY FX AND MENTAL 303 ACID LINES SET TO BLOCK ROCKIN' BEATS, THE CHEMICAL BROTHERS WERE THE ARCHITECTS OF THIS FUSION OF HIP HOP AND TECHNO; NORMAN COOK, A.K.A FATBOY SLIM, WOULD LATER EMULATE THEIR SOUND.

Above
Considered by some as the definitive big beat album, You've Come a Long Way, Baby was the second of Norman Cook's albums to be released under the name of Fatboy Slim. It lived up to all expectations.

FIRST at Naked Under Leather in Manchester, and then at the Heavenly Social in London, Tom Rowlands and Ed Simons (The Chemical Brothers) DJ'd across the board, Balearic-style. There was already a rich history of dance music to plunder by the early 1990s, from old-skool hip hop to breakbeat house, through indie dance or Northern soul, but Tom and Ed wanted to make their own mark. Their 'Chemical Beats' track is considered to be the first 1990s big-beat record, the "chemical generation" already being a much-used term for post-acid house, ecstasy-using clubbers. The Chemical Brothers would draw on old hardcore sounds, breaks and, crucially, guitars for their own tracks. Recorded in 1996 with Oasis guitarist Noel Gallagher, 'Setting Sun' topped the UK charts, and the album it came from, *Dig Your Own Hole*, sold a million and helped convert a swathe of alt-rock fans to electronica.

A former bassist in the Housemartins, Norman Cook had been dabbling in dance music since the mid-1980s, first fronting the dub-a-delic band Beats International, then putting out house records under names such as Mighty Dub Katz and Pizzaman. Legend has it that Norman Cook (Fatboy Slim) took fellow Brighton pal Damian Harris to the amyl nitrate-fuelled Heavenly Social in London to give the Midfield General (Harris) a vision for his new label, Skint. They soon started a night in their seaside hometown, with Norman as resident – the Big Beat Boutique.

> "I LIKE TO MAKE THE MUSIC MORE ACCESSIBLE TO PEOPLE, RATHER THAN BEING COOLER-THAN-THOU AND MOODY OR WHATEVER."
>
> *Norman Cook, a.k.a Fatboy Slim*

Right
Jacques Lu Cont is the man behind Les Rhythmes Digitales. Despite both the French names, he is English. A colourful character, he is known for his excellent live shows.

While some dance music innovations inevitably became clichés, the big beat DJs kept ahead of the pack with their interest in technological developments. Crescendos, explosions, time-stretching, sirens, huge hip hop samples – no quick-fix trick was too much for the emerging sound, which would often come out as kitsch in-synch. This was blasphemy for some, a dumbing-down of refined electronic tweakery that turned dance music into pub rock, but its importance in converting rock doubters to dance music is inestimable.

Party Time

Big beat also re-introduced a sense of fun to a dance scene that had become quite po-faced and studied. Trainspotting trip hop or chin-stroking, obscure European electronica was all very well, but hardly the heady "abandon and party" spirit of original acid house. Big beat's "Fuck art, let's party" ethos would soon lead to a number of other artists, DJs and labels banding together under this umbrella – although virtually everybody soon professed disdain for the terminology.

Aside from Skint, Wall Of Sound with Wiseguys, Propellerheads, Les Rhythmes Digitales and Monkey Mafia were the other chief label exponents of big beat. Acts such as Eboman, the Lo-Fi Allstars, Bentley Rhythm Ace, Dub Pistols, FC Kahuna, the Crystal Method, Lunatic Calm and Deejay Punk-Roc all became associated with the sound, but when the inevitable backlash came, most of them successfully side-swerved into other genres, such as house, breakbeat or electro.

LEADING EXPONENTS

Norman Cook
  (a.k.a Fatboy Slim)
The Chemical Brothers
Bentley Rhythm Ace
Propellerheads
Lo-Fi Allstars
Damian Harris
  (a.k.a Midfield General)
Dub Pistols
Les Rhythmes Digitales

BIG BEAT
Much the same as breakbeat, but without the rhythmic "breaks", and usually has a full and heavy rhythm with bass or keyboard sequences.

THE DANCE INTRO ➡310 DANCE PEOPLE A–Z ➡332 INSTRUMENTS A–Z ➡436 DANCE: HOUSE ➡316 DANCE: TECHNO ➡324 HIP HOP: HIP HOP ➡336

UK Garage

THE UK GARAGE SCENE BEGAN IN LONDON IN THE 1990'S WHEN ENTERPRISING DJ'S SUCH AS NORRIS "DA BASS" WINDROSS AND KARL "TUFF ENUFF" BROWN SET UP AFTER-HOURS PARTIES IN THE CAPITAL'S PUBS FOR CLUBBERS RELUCTANT TO END THE REVELRY AFTER SPENDING THE EVENING AT ONE OF LONDON'S NEW SUPERCLUBS, SUCH AS THE MINISTRY OF SOUND.

"WE used to pitch it up a bit, give it a bit more energy cos people used to come from Ministry vibed up and we didn't want to chill them out," remembers Matt "Jam" Lamont, another of the London DJs. The records these DJs played were by Americans such as Todd Edwards, MK and Victor Simonelli. But London's poly-cultural creative musical heritage would, inevitably, lead DJs and producers such as Grant Nelson and RIP to put their own twist on the sound.

It was another American, though, Armand Van Helden, who threw away the rule book, putting big basslines and junglist nuances into garage remixes of the Sneaker Pimps and Tori Amos, and thereby creating the space for disaffected drum'n'bass heads with drum programming experience, to enter the scene. Records such as 'Closer Than Close', by Rosie Gaines, Double 99's 'RIP Groove' and 'Gunman', by 187 Lockdown, would break on illegal pirate radio stations before crossing over into the UK pop charts. The media dubbed the sound "speed garage", but the bubble burst after the initial 1997 hype, as the scene to back up the hyperbole had not developed sufficiently.

So Solid Headline Snatchers

It was another American, Kelly G, with a remix of Tina Moore's 'Never Gonna Let You Go', who blueprinted the non-4/4 off-beat two-step sound of UKG. In 1999, songs such as Shanks & Bigfoot's 'Sweet Like Chocolate' and Craig David and Artful Dodger's 'Rewind' zoomed to the top of the UK charts. The national UK radio station, Radio 1, soon had its own UK garage show, hosted by the Dreem Teem.

Although varying musical styles would develop – from MJ Cole's smooth, soulful dubs to the breakbeat garage of Dee Kline or DJ Zinc, and from bassline-heavy bits by Wookie or DJ Narrows, to the gangsta-rap stylings of So Solid Crew – it was the latter that inevitably stole the headlines. UK garage raves became peppered with gun-toting idiots, but with DJs such as EZ reintroducing the 4/4 sound, and MCs such as the Mercury Prize-winning Ms Dynamite speaking out against violence, the music looks set to prosper once more.

> "LONDON IS A MULTICULTURAL CITY... IT'S LIKE A MELTING POT OF YOUNG PEOPLE, AND THAT'S REFLECTED IN THE MUSIC OF UK GARAGE."
>
> *MJ Cole, UK Garage DJ/producer*

Above

Only 19 when he had his first UK number one in 2000, Craig David enjoyed a phenomenal rise to success.

Left

Niomi McLean-Daley (a.k.a Ms Dynamite) was a former member of So Solid Crew, but with her solo career came a move towards British ragga and R&B. In 2002 she became the first female black solo artist to win the Mercury Music Prize.

♩ = 140

Pno

UK GARAGE

Similar to house, but a more mellow "poppy" sound, often with predominant keyboard chords and vocal line.

LEADING EXPONENTS

MJ Cole
Roger Sanchez
David Morales
Armand Van Helden
Shanks & Bigfoot
Craig David
Artful Dodger
So Solid Crew
Ms Dynamite

US Garage

DISCO MAY HAVE DIED AFTER IT WENT OVERGROUND IN THE LATE-1970S. BUT ONE NEW YORK DJ CONTINUED SPINNING HIS FAVOURITE TUNES AT THE SAME CLUB FROM 1977 TO 1987 – LARRY LEVAN. THOUGH LEVAN'S DJING STYLE WAS WILDLY ECLECTIC. THE SMOOTH. SOULFUL FLAVOURS HE FAVOURED WOULD BECOME KNOWN AS "GARAGE" – NAMED AFTER THE CLUB LEVAN RULED FOR 10 YEARS. THE PARADISE GARAGE.

Above

An important figure in the development of garage music, Tony Humphries has played at over 300 venues worldwide and completed over 200 studio remixes.

THE Garage was predominantly black and gay, like the Warehouse in Chicago, and to those who heard him, Levan was an inspirational DJ. It was widely felt that he was communicating messages of hope, love, freedom and brotherhood directly to the dance floor – via vinyl. His dialogue with the dancers was the songs he played, but the style of house music that developed around him in early 1980s New York was different from Chicago tracky cuts. Full of organic textures, with perhaps Latin percussion, and a jazzy or even gospel feel, what would become garage took its cue from Philadelphia (Philly) soul, disco and R&B. The only historical glitch in the naming of this genre is that Levan was as likely to drop a punky-reggae Clash record as a soulful Loleatta Holloway song at the Paradise Garage.

Literally worshipped every Saturday night for a decade, Levan was an early example of the DJ as shaman, and one of the first DJ/producers. He also co-founded the Peech Boys, who, along with acts such as D-Train and Sharon Redd, and producers such as Arthur Baker and Jellybean Benitez, were part of the nascent NYC electro-funk sound that rose out of the ashes of disco.

Meanwhile, just outside New York in New Jersey, Tony Humphries played the soulful stuff at the Zanzibar. Effectively pairing R&B with house, Humphries pioneered what became known as the Jersey sound. But it was not until after the Paradise Garage closed in 1987, and house had spread internationally, that soulful house came to be called garage, in memory of Levan's legendary club. Humphries held a huge showcase of all his Zanzibar protégés at the 1988–89 New Music Seminar, and suddenly everyone was talking about the Jersey garage sound.

The Spirit Of Paradise

Larry Levan developed AIDS and died in 1992, of heart problems brought on by his addictions to heroin and cocaine. "People should remember the positive things, though," cautions Mel Cheren, a contemporary of Levan and the owner of West End Records. "Of course he had a drug problem, like many people do. But he was a genius and people should remember that first and foremost."

Acts such as Blaze, Todd Edwards and Masters At Work developed the soulful house sound as the 1990s progressed. Slippery, slidy beats prospered on labels such as Strictly Rhythm, Nu Groove and Slip N Slide, and wherever soul was preferred over power.

In Europe, US garage has now largely slipped out of favour, with deep house being the preferred notation for "authentic", garage-sounding records. But at club nights such as the long-running Shelter, and the now-defunct Body & Soul in New York and Soul Heaven in London, the spirit of the Paradise Garage lives on.

> "A LOT OF IT WAS REALLY PHILLY ELEMENTS. IT WAS LIKE PHILLY LIVING ON FOREVER AND THAT WAS OUR FLAVOR."
>
> *Tony Humphries, US garage DJ*

Right

Masters At Work consist of "Little" Louie Vega and Kenny "Dope" Gonzales. The duo have been involved in many other projects, including Nuyorican Soul and the Bucketheads, all released on the Masters At Work record label.

LEADING EXPONENTS

Tony Humphries
Larry Levan
The Peech Boys
D-Train
Sharon Redd
Arthur Baker
Masters At Work
Blaze
Todd Edwards

US GARAGE

A style similar to UK garage, though without the "pop" overtones, tending to owe more to the hip hop genre, although a more mellow sound.

♩ = 80

Bass

THE DANCE INTRO ➡ 310   DANCE PEOPLE A-Z ➡ 332   INSTRUMENTS A-Z ➡ 436   DANCE: DISCO ➡ 314   SOUL AND R&B: FUNK ➡ 376

Tech-House

THE TERM TECH-HOUSE CAME FROM ONE OF THE MUSIC'S MAIN PROPONENTS AND CHAMPIONS. MR C. THE FORMER SHAMEN RAPPER, COINED IT TO DESCRIBE THE FUSION OF TOUGH, US GARAGE "DUBS" – INSTRUMENTAL VERSIONS OF VOCAL TRACKS – AND DEEP, DETROIT TECHNO THAT LONDON DJS SUCH AS EDDIE RICHARDS, COLIN DALE, TERRY FRANCIS AND C HIMSELF WERE PLAYING FROM THE EARLY TO MID-1990S.

IT would, however, be incorrect to categorize tech-house as one easily definable style. Mr C – one of the scene's most influential producers – famously called it "a genre without a genre". Tech-house is dance-floor-friendly, but it takes its cues from reggae, dub, breaks, electro and even two-step sources, as well as using funky techno and US house as its dance-floor basis.

Long before tech-house was a recognized sound, Detroit producers such as Octave One (with their 430 West label), Blake Baxter and Kevin Saunderson were experimenting with techno and house fusions. Octave One's Burden brothers' dense rhythm funk, Baxter's Chicago-influenced sounds and Saunderson's earliest productions – even mainstream cuts such as 'Good Life' and 'Big Fun' – were explorations of futuristic techno depth and utopian house rhythms.

By the early to mid-1990s, the style had spread beyond its London roots and the Scottish label Soma and the imprint 20/20 Vision (based in the north of England) adopted this open-minded aesthetic. Subsequently, releases by Random Factor, Maas and Slam preempted London's affiliation with tech-house. However, it was the UK capital's club and under-ground party scene that eventually forced dance music's media to realize that there were lasting and significant changes taking place in the middle ground between house and techno.

Future Possibilities

Mr C and Layo's End nightclub, Terry Francis' Wiggle parties, and word-of-mouth events such as Heart & Soul and Whoop Whoop brought a new wave of UK-based producers to the fore, including Tribalation, Mark Ambrose, Pure Science, Get Fucked, Matthew B, Asad Rizvi, Haris and Alien Funk Movement. Characterized by dense and dubby rhythms,

futuristic and trippy sounds and deeply musical elements, this new wave of producers have been supported by mainstream names of late, with big-name DJs such as John Digweed and Pete Tong professing their support for tech-house.

While this is viewed as a positive development by most tech-house producers, there are fears that the music is being hijacked by progressive DJs and producers desperately seeking fresh, post-backlash sounds. However, in spite of this development and a lack of obviously spottable "songs", tech-house has never been in a healthier state.

Producers such as Mazi, EBE, Patrick Turner and Jay Tripwire have given tech house a distinct North American identity. Meanwhile, Brazilian producers such as Renato Lopez and Anderson Noise have given it a fresh Latino slant. The Visitor label and Haris' releases have helped build support for tech-house in Belgium and Croatia, while the minimal approach favoured by German producers such as Steve Bug, MRI and Ricardo Villalobos has opened up possibilities for the music on other fronts.

"IT'S BECOME A GENRE OUT OF A NAME, IT CAME FROM TRYING TO MAKE OURSELVES MORE ACCEPTED AS A GROUP OF INDIVIDUALS."

Mr C, tech-house DJ and former Shamen rapper

Above

When in the mid-1990s the success of the Shamen was dwindling, Mr C returned to DJing and was soon releasing mix albums that were to be the beginings of tech-house.

Left

Colin Dale used his radio show Abstrakt Dance *on London's KISS FM to promote his progressive techno. In 2000 he launched* Groovetech UK, *an Internet radio show.*

♩ = 115

Bass

TECH-HOUSE

A mixture of the techno-style sequences, but with the lighter rhythm of house.

LEADING EXPONENTS

The Shamen
Eddie Richards
Colin Dale
Terry Francis
Octave One
Blake Baxter
Jay Tripwire

THE DANCE INTRO ➡ 310   DANCE PEOPLE A-Z ➡ 332   INSTRUMENTS A-Z ➡ 436   DANCE: DISCO ➡ 314   DANCE: HOUSE ➡ 316   DANCE: TECHNO ➡ 324

Artists: Dance

Entries appear in the following order: name, music style, year(s) of popularity, type of artist, country of origin

2 Bad Mice, Jungle; Drum'n'Bass, 1990s, Artist, British
2 Unlimited, House, 1990s–, Artist, Dutch
4Hero, Breakbeat, 1990s–, Artist, British
808 State, House; Acid, 1980s–, Artist, British
Aalon, Disco, 1970s, Artist, American
Abrams, Colonel, US Garage; House, 1980s-1990s, Artist, American
Acid Farm, Trance; Techno, 1990s, Artist, American
Acid Rob, Techno, 1990s–, Artist, German
Acid Scout, Trance; Techno, 1990s, Artist, American
Adeva, Disco; US Garage; House, 1980s-1990s, Artist, American

Adonis, House; Acid, 1980s–, Producer, American
Advent, The, Techno, 1990s–, Artist, British
Afronaut, Breakbeat, 1990s–, Artist, British
Agent K, Breakbeat, 2000s–, Artist, British
Air Liquide, Techno, 1990s–, Artist, German
Allspice, Disco, 1970s, Artist, American
Ali B, Breakbeat, 1990s–, Artist; Producer, British
Alice Deejay, Trance, 1990s–, Artist, Dutch
Aloof, The, Techno, 1990s–, Artist, British
Alter Ego, Techno, 1980s-1990s, Artist, German
Altern 8, Hardcore, 1990s, Artist, British
Ambient Temple Of Imagination, Trance, 1990s, Artist, American
Angel, Dave, Techno, 1990s–, Artist; Producer, British
Anglo-Saxon Brown, Disco, 1970s, Artist, American
Aphex Twin, Acid; Techno; Trance, 1990s–, Producer, British
Aphrodite, Jungle; Drum'n'Bass, 1990s–, Artist; Producer, British
Aquarian Dream, Disco, 1970s-1980s, Artist, American
Aquasky, Jungle; Drum'n'Bass, 1990s–, Artist, British
Arc, Trance; Techno, 1990s, Artist, American
Arcon 2, Jungle; Drum'n'Bass, 1990s–, Producer, British
Armando, House; Acid, 1980s-1990s, Artist; Producer, American
Arpeggio, Disco, 1970s, Artist, American
Art Of Trance, Trance, 1990s–, Artist, American
Artful Dodger, The, UK Garage, 1990s–, Artist, British
As One, Techno; House; Breakbeat, 1990s–, Producer; Artist, British
Ashford & Simpson, Disco, 1970s-1980s, Artist, American
Astral Pilot, Trance; Techno, 1990s, Artist, German
Astral Projection, Trance, 1990s–, Artist, Israeli
Astralasia, Trance, 1990s–, Artist, British
Atari Teenage Riot, Gabba; Techno, 1990s–, Artist, German
Atkins, Juan, Techno, 1980s–, Artist; Producer, American
Atlantic Starr, Disco, 1970s-1990s, Artist, American
Atom Heart, Trance; Techno, 1990s–, Producer, German
Attius, Alex, Breakbeat, 2000s–, Artist, Swiss
Attius, Stephane, Breakbeat, 2000s–, Artist, Swiss
Aurra, Disco, 1980s, Artist, American
Aviance, Kevin, House, 1990s–, Artist, American
B., Rich, Trance; Techno, 1990s, Artist, British
B12, Techno, 1990s–, Artist, British
Baccara, Disco, 1970s, Artist, Spanish
Baker, Arthur, US Garage, 1980s–, Artist; Producer, American
Ballistic Brothers, Progressive, 1990s–, Artist, British
Bandulu, Techno, 1990s–, Artist, British
Barry, Claudja, Disco, 1970s-1980s, Artist, Canadian
Bartz, Richard, Trance; Techno, 1990s, Producer, German
Basement Jaxx, House; UK Garage, 1990s–, Artist, British
Baxter, Blake, Techno; Tech-House, 1990s, Artist; Producer, American
BBE, Trance, 1990s–, Artist; Producer, French
Beats International, Big Beat, 1990s, Artist, British
Beck, Robin, Disco, 1980s, Artist, American
Bedrock, Progressive; Trance; House, 1990s–, Artist, British
Bee Gees, The, Disco, 1960s–, Artist, British
Bee, Celi, Disco, 1990s, Artist, Puerto Rican
Beedle, Ashley, House, 1990s–, Artist; Producer, British
Begg, Si, Jungle; Drum'n'Bass; Techno, 1990s–, Producer, British
Bell, Archie, Disco, 1960s-1970s, Artist; Songwriter, American
Beltram, Joey, Techno, 1980s–, Artist; Producer, American
Beltran, John, Techno, 1990s–, Producer, American
Bentley Rhythm Ace, Big Beat, 1990s–, Artist, British
Beyer, Adam, Techno, 1990s–, Artist; Producer, Swedish
Bicknell, Steve, Trance; Techno, 1990s–, Artist, British
Biggun, Ivor, Disco, 1970s-1980s, Artist, British
Bizarre Inc, Acid; House, 1990s–, Artist, British
Black Box, House, 1990s–, Artist, Italian
Black Britain, Disco, 1980s, Artist, British
Black Dog, The, Techno, 1980s–, Artist, British
Black Jazz Chronicles, Progressive, 1990s, Producer, British
Black Science Orchestra, Progressive; House, 1990s–, Artist, British
Blame, Jungle; Drum'n'Bass, 1990s–, Artist; Producer, British
Blank & Jones, Trance; Techno; Progressive, 1990s–, Artist, German
Blaze, House; US Garage, 1980s–, Artist, American
Blue Mercedes, Disco, 1980s, Artist, British
Bohannon, Disco, 1970s-1980s, Artist, American
Bolland, C. J., Techno; Trance, 1990s–, Artist; Producer, British
Bombers, Disco, 1970s, Artist, Australian
Bones, Frankie, Tribal; Techno; House, 1990s–, Artist; Producer, American
Boney M, Disco, 1970s–, Artist, German
Boom Boom Satellites, Big Beat, 1990s–, Artist, Japanese
Boom, Taka, Disco, 1970s-1980s, Artist, American
Boriqua Brothers, The, Tribal; House, 1990s, Artist, American
Boxcar, Trance, 1990s, Artist, Australian
Boymerang, Jungle; Drum'n'Bass, 1990s–, Producer, British
Brass Construction, Disco, 1960s-1980s, Artist, American
Breakbeat Era, Jungle; Drum'n'Bass, 1990s–, Artist, British
Breaks, Danny, Jungle; Drum'n'Bass; Techno, 1990s–, Producer, British
Brick, Disco, 1970s-1980s, Artist, American
Bridges, Alicia, Disco, 1970s-1980s, Artist, American
Brook, Michael, Tribal; Techno, 1980s-1990s, Composer; Artist, Canadian
Broom, Mark, Techno, 1990s–, Producer, British
Brown, Jocelyn, Disco; House, 1980s–, Artist, American
Brown, Peter, Disco, 1970s-1990s, Artist, American
Brown, Terry Lee Jr, House, 1990s–, Producer, German
BT, House; Trance, 1990s–, Producer, American
BT Express, Disco, 1970s-1980s, Artist, American
Bugz In The Attic, Breakbeat, 1990s–, Artist, British

Bukem, L. T. J, Jungle; Drum'n'Bass; Breakbeat, 1990s–, Artist, British
Bump & Flex, UK Garage, 1990s, Artist, British
Burton, Jenny, Disco, 1980s, Artist, American
Butch Quick, Disco; House, 1990s, Artist, American
C+C Music Factory, House, 1990s, Artist, American
Cajmere, House; Acid, 1990s–, Artist; Producer, American
Camouflage, Disco, 1980s–, Artist, German
Candelario, Benji, US Garage, 1990s–, Artist, American
Cappella, House, 1980s–, Artist, Italian
Carola, Marco, Techno, 1990s–, Producer, Italian
Carter, Derrick, House, 1980s–, Artist; Producer, American
Case, Ed, UK Garage, 1990s–, Artist; Producer, British
Cerrone, Disco; House, 1970s–, Producer, French
Chandler, Kerri, House; US Garage, 1990s–, Artist; Producer, American
Chanson, Disco, 1970s, Artist, American
Charism, Disco, 1970s, Artist, American
Charles, Tina, Disco, 1970s-1980s, Artist, American
Chateau Flight, Breakbeat, 1990s–, Artist, French
Chemical Brothers, The, Big Beat, 1990s–, Artist, British
Chic, Disco, 1970s-1990s, Artist, American
Chicane, Progressive; Trance; House, 1990s–, Producer, British
Child, Desmond, Disco, 1970s, Artist, American
Choice Four, The, Disco, 1970s, Artist, American
CJ & Co, Disco, 1970s, Artist, American
Clarke, Dave, Acid; Techno, 1990s–, Artist; Producer, American
Claussell, Joe, House; US Garage, 1990s–, Artist, American
Club 69, House, 1990s–, Artist, American
Club Nouveau, Disco, 1980s-1990s, Artist, American
Coffee, Disco, 1980s, Artist, American
Coldcut, House; Acid, 1980s–, Artist, British
Cole, M. J., UK Garage; House, 1990s–, Artist; Producer, British
Collins, Bootsy, Disco, 1970s–, Artist, American
Collins, Kimball, Progressive; Trance, 1990s–, Artist, American
Collins, Sandra, Progressive; Trance, 1990s–, Artist; Producer, American
Commander Tom, Trance; Techno, 1990s–, Artist, German
Cook, Norman (a.k.a Fatboy Slim), Big Beat, 1990s–, Artist; Producer, British
Corsten, Ferry, Trance, 1990s–, Artist; Producer, Dutch
Cosmic Baby, Trance; Techno, 1990s–, Producer, German
Cox, Carl, House; Techno; Acid, 1990s–, Artist; Producer, British
Craig, Carl, Techno, 1980s–, Producer, American
Cristina, Disco, 1980s, Artist, American
Croisette, Disco, 1990s, Artist, American
Crown Heights Affair, Disco, 1970s-1980s, Artist, American
Crystal Method, The, Big Beat, 1990s–, Artist, American
Curtin, Dan, Techno, 1990s–, Producer, American
Cybotron, Techno, 1980s–, Artist, American
D-Mob, Acid, 1980s–90s, Artist, British
D Train, US Garage; House, 1980s-1990s, Artist, American
D:Fuse, Progressive; House; Trance, 1990s–, Artist, American
Daft Punk, House, 1990s–, Artist, French
Dale, Colin, Tech-House, 1990s, Artist; Producer, British
Damier, Chez, House; US Garage, 1980s-1990s, Producer, American
Dance, Acid; House, 1980s, Artist, American
Daniel, Jeffrey, Disco, 1980s, Artist, American
David, Craig, UK Garage, 1990s–, Artist, British
Davis, Roy Jr. House; US Garage, 1980s–, Artist; Producer, American
De Paul, Lynsey, Disco, 1990s, Artist, American
De Vit, Tony, Trance; House, 1990s, Artist; Producer, British
Dead Or Alive, Disco, 1980s–, Artist, British
Dean, Hazell, Disco, 1980s-1990s, Artist; Songwriter, American
Dearborn, Mike, Techno; House, 1990s–, Producer, American
Death In Vegas, Big Beat, 1990s–, Artist, British
Decoder, Jungle; Drum'n'Bass, 1990s–, Artist, British
Dee, Ellis, Breakbeat, 1990s–, Artist; Producer, British
Deee-Lite, House, 1980s-1990s, Artist, American
Deep Dish, House, 1990s–, Artist, American
Deejay Punk-Roc, Big Beat, 1990s–, Producer, American
Delegation, Disco; House, 1970s-1980s, Artist, British
Dem 2, UK Garage, 1990s–, Artist, British
Denham, Jay, Techno, 1990s–, Producer, American
Deodato, Disco, 1960s-1980s, Artist, Brazilian
Depth Charge, Techno; Acid; House, 1980s–, Producer, British
Detroit Escalator Company, Techno, 1990s–, Producer, American
Digweed, John, Tribal/Progressive, 1990s–, Artist; Producer, British
Dimitri From Paris, House, 1980s–, Artist; Producer, French
Disco Circus, Disco, 1990s, Artist, American
Disco Tex & the Sex-O-Lettes, Disco, 1970s, Artist, American
Diversions, Disco, 1970s, Artist, American
DJ Brisk, Happy Hardcore; Gabba, 1990s–, Artist, British
DJ Choci, Happy Hardcore; Techno, 1990s–, Artist, British
DJ Crystl, Jungle; Drum'n'Bass; Techno, 1990s, Artist; Producer, British
DJ Dara, Jungle; Drum'n'Bass, 1990s–, Artist; Producer, Irish

DJ Dee Kline, UK Garage, 1990s–, Artist, British
DJ Dougal, Happy Hardcore; Techno, 1990s–, Artist, American
DJ Eruption, Happy Hardcore, 1990s, Artist, British
DJ Hell, Techno, 1990s–, Artist; Producer, German
DJ Hype, Jungle; Drum'n'Bass, 1990s–, Artist; Producer, British
DJ Hyperactive, Trance; Techno, 1990s–, Producer, American
DJ Isaac, Gabba; Techno, 1990s, Artist, British
DJ Keoki, Trance; Techno; House, 1990s–, Artist; Producer, American
DJ Lime, Happy Hardcore, 1990s–, Artist; Producer, British
DJ Marky, Drum'n'Bass; Jungle, 1990s–, Artist; Producer, Brazilian
DJ Misjah, Trance; Techno; House, 1990s–, Producer, Dutch
DJ Pierre, House; Acid, 1980s–, Artist; Producer, American
DJ Rap, Jungle; Drum'n'Bass, 1990s–, Artist; Producer, British
DJ Rolando, Techno, 1990s–, Artist, American
DJ Slipmatt, Happy Hardcore; Techno, 1990s–, Artist, British
DJ Smurf, Gabba, 1990s, Artist; Producer, British
DJ Sneak, House, 1990s–, Artist; Producer, American
DJ SS, Jungle; Drum'n'Bass, 1990s–, Artist; Producer, British
DJ Sy, Happy Hardcore; Techno, 1990s, Artist, British
DJ T-1000, Techno, 1990s–, Artist, American
DJ Trace, Jungle; Drum'n'Bass, 1990s–, Artist; Producer, British
DJ Zinc, Drum'n'Bass, Jungle, UK Garage, 1990s–, Artist; Producer, British
Dlugosch, Boris, House; UK Garage, 1990s–, Artist, German
Dom & Roland, Jungle; Drum'n'Bass, 1990s–, Artist, British
Domu, Breakbeat, 1990s, Artist, British
Donatello, Joe, Disco; House, 1990s, Producer, American
Doolally, UK Garage, 1990s–, Artist, British
Double 99, UK Garage; Techno; House, 1990s, Artist, British
Double Exposure, Disco, 1970s, Artist, American
Douglas, Carl, Disco, 1970s, Artist, Jamaican
Douglas, Carol, Disco, 1970s, Artist, American
Dr Buzzard's Original Savannah Band, Disco, 1970s-1980s, Artist, American
Dreadzone, Trance; Techno, 1990s–, Artist, British
Dreem Teem, The, UK Garage; House, 1990s–, Artist, British
Drum Club, The, House; Progressive, 1990s, Artist, British
Dub Federation, Techno; Disco, 1990s, Artist, British
Dub Pistols, Big Beat, 1990s–, Artist, British
Dubtribe, Tribal, 1990s, Artist, American
Dury, Ian, Disco, 1970s-1990s, Artist; Songwriter, British
Earth, Wind & Fire, Disco, 1970s–, Artist, American
Eat Static, Trance, 1990s–, Artist, British
E-Dancer, Techno, 1980s-1990s, Producer, American
Edwards, Todd, UK Garage; House, 1990s–, Artist, British
El Coco, Disco, 1970s, Artist, American
Elliman, Yvonne, Disco, 1970s, Artist, American
Ellis, Jimmy, Disco, 1970s, Artist, American
Elstak, Paul, Gabba; Techno, 1990s–, Artist, Dutch
Emerson, Darren, Trance; Techno, 1990s–, Artist, British
Empire State, Trance, 1990s–, Artist, American
Endemic Void, Jungle; Drum'n'Bass, 1990s, Producer, British
English, Kim, Trance; House, 1990s–, Artist, American
Eruption, Disco, 1970s-1980s, Artist, British
Euphoria, Trance; Techno, 1960s-1970s, Artist, American
Evolution, Trance; House, 1980s–, Artist, British
E-Z Rollers, Jungle; Drum'n'Bass, 1990s–, Artist, British
EZ, UK Garage, 1990s, Artist, British
F., Adam, Jungle; Drum'n'Bass, 1990s–, Producer, British
Fabio, Jungle; Drum'n'Bass, 1980s-1990s, Artist; Producer, British
Facts Of Life, Disco, 1970s, Artist, American
Faithless, House; Progressive; Trance, 1990s–, Artist, British
Farley & Heller, House; Progressive; Trance, 1990s–, Artist, British
Farley Jackmaster Funk, House; Acid, 1980s–, Artist; Producer, American
Fatboy Slim, Big Beat, 1990s–, Artist; Producer, British
Fauna Flash, Jungle; Drum'n'Bass, 1990s–, Artist, German
Faver, Colin, Trance; Techno, 1990s, Artist, British
FC Kahuna, Big Beat, 1990s–, Artist; Producer, British
Felix Da Housecat, House; Acid, 1980s–, Artist; Producer, American
Fingers Inc., Acid; House, 1980s–, Artist, American
Fiocco, Trance; Techno, 1990s, Artist, Belgian
Fisher, Cevin, House; US Garage, 1990s–, Producer, American
Fleming, John "00", Progressive; House; Trance, 1990s–, Artist, British
Fluke, House; Techno, 1990s–, Artist, British
Force & Styles, Happy Hardcore, 1990s–, Artist, British
Foul Play, Jungle; Drum'n'Bass, 1990s, Artist, British
Fowlkes, Eddie "Flashin", Techno, 1980s–, Artist; Producer, American
Francis, Terry, House; Tech-House, 1990s, Artist; Producer, British
François K, House, 1970s–, Artist; Producer, French
Freaky Chakra, Techno, 1990s, Producer, American
Freeland, Adam, Breakbeat, 1990s–, Artist; Producer, British
Freestylers, Big Beat, 1990s–, Artist, British
Fretless AZM, Techno, 1990s, Artist, British
Funky Green Dogs, House; Progressive, 1990s–, Artist, American
Future Sound Of London, The, Techno, 1990s–, Artist, British
Gaines, Rosie, US Garage, 1990s–, Artist, American
Gamble & Huff, 1960s–80s, Disco, Artist, American
Garnier, Laurent, House; Acid; Techno, 1980s–, Artist; Producer, French
Gaynor, Gloria, Disco, 1970s–, Artist, American
Geist, Morgan, Techno, 1990s–, Producer, American
Gemini, House; Acid, 1990s–, Producer, American
Genaside II, Jungle; Drum'n'Bass; Techno; Acid; House, 1990s–, Artist, British
Gibbons, Walter, House; Disco, 1970s-1980s, Artist; Producer, American
Global Communication, House, 1990s, Artist, British
Goldie, Jungle; Drum'n'Bass, 1990s–, Artist; Producer, British
Graham, Max, Progressive; Trance, 1990s–, Producer, Canadian
Grasso, Francis, Disco, 1960s–80s, Artist, American
Gray, Chris, House, 1990s, Producer, American
Green Velvet, House; Progressive; Acid, 1990s–, Artist; Producer, American
Grid, The, Techno; Acid, 1990s, Artist, British
Grooverider, Jungle; Drum'n'Bass, 1980s-1990s, Artist; Producer, British
Ground Zero, Techno, 1990s, Artist, Japanese
Guillaume, Jephté, House, 1990s–, Artist; Producer, American
Gusto, Tribal; House, 1990s, Artist, American
Guy Called Gerald, A, House; Acid, 1980s–, Artist; Producer, British
Hallucinogen, Trance, 1990s–, Artist, British
Halpern, Steve, Tribal, 1970s–, Artist, American
Hand, K., Techno; House, 1990s–, Artist; Producer, American
Hardfloor, Acid; Trance, 1990s–, Artist, German
Hardkiss, Trance; Techno, 1990s, Artist, American
Hardway, James, Jungle; Drum'n'Bass, 1990s–, Producer, British
Hardy, Ron, House; Acid, 1970s-1980s, Artist; Producer, American
Harris, Damian (a.k.a Midfield General), Big Beat, 1990s–, Artist; Producer, British
Hartnoll, Phil & Paul, Techno, 1980s–, Artist, British
Hassell, Jon, Tribal; Techno, 1970s–, Artist; Composer, American

Hawtin, Richie, Techno, 1990s–, Artist, British/Canadian
Headrillaz, Big Beat, 1990s, Artist, British
Heard, Larry, House; Acid, 1980s–, Producer; Artist, American
Hixxy, Happy Hardcore; Techno, 1990s, Artist, British
Holloway, Loleatta, Disco; House; US Garage, 1990s–, Artist, American
Holloway, Nicky, Acid, 1980s–, Artist, British
Holmes, David, Techno, 1990s–, Artist; Producer, British
Hood, Robert, Techno, 1990s–, Artist; Producer, American
Hosono, Haruomi, Trance; Techno, 1970s–, Producer; Artist, Japanese
House Of 909, House, 1990s, Artist, British
Houston, Thelma, Disco, 1970s-1990s, Artist, American
Howells, Danny, Tribal/Progressive, 1990s– Artist; Producer, British
Humanoid, Acid, 1980s, Artist, British
Humphries, Tony, House; US Garage, 1980s–, Artist; Producer, American
Hurley, Steve "Silk", House, 1980s-1990s, Artist; Producer, American
Hybrid, Progressive; Trance, 1990s–, Artist, British
Infected Mushroom, Trance, 1990s–, Artist, Israeli
Infiniti, Techno, 1990s, Producer, American
Inner City, House, 1980s-1990s, Artist, American
Ishii, Ken, Techno, 1990s–, Artist; Producer, Japanese

Ishino, Takkyu, Trance; Techno, 1990s–, Producer, Japanese
Jam & Spoon, Techno; Trance, 1990s–, Artist, German
Jefferson, Marshall, House; Acid, 1980s-1990s, Artist; Producer, American
Jellybean, House; US Garage, 1980s-1990s, Artist; Producer, American
Johnson, Paul, Trance; Techno, 1980s–, Artist, British
Jolly Roger, Acid, 1980s, Artist, British
Jon The Dentist, Trance; Progressive, 1990s–, Artist, American
Jones, Grace, Disco, 1970s–, Artist, American
Junkie XL, Big Beat; Techno, 1990s, Artist, Dutch
Juno Reactor, Trance; Techno, 1990s–, Artist, British
Justice, Jungle; Drum'n'Bass, 1990s–, Producer, British
K Hand, Techno; House, 1990s–, Artist; Producer, American
K., François, House; Techno, 1970s–, Artist; Producer, French
Karet, Djam, Tribal; Techno, 1980s–, Producer; Artist, American
KC & the Sunshine Band, Disco, 1970s-1990s, Artist, American
Keith, Ray, Jungle; Drum'n'Bass, 1990s, Artist; Producer, British
Kemistry & Storm, Drum'n'Bass; Jungle, 1990s, Artist; Producer, British
Ken, Kenny, Jungle; Drum'n'Bass, 1990s, Artist, British
Kevorkian, François, House; Disco, 1990s, Artist; Producer, French
Kid Batchelor, House; Acid, 1980s, Artist; Producer, British
King, Evelyn "Champagne", Disco; House, 1970s-1990s, Artist, American
K-Klass, Progressive; House, 1990s–, Artist, British
KLF, The, House; Acid, 1980s-1990s, Artist, British
Knuckles, Frankie, House; Acid, 1980s–, Artist; Producer, American
Koxbox, Trance; Progressive, 1990s, Artist, Danish
Krivit, Danny, US Garage, 1970s–, Artist, American
Krust, Jungle; Drum'n'Bass, 1990s–, Artist; Producer, British
L., Jonny, Jungle; Drum'n'Bass, 1990s–, Producer, British
LaBelle, Disco, 1960s-1970s, Artist, American
Lamb, Jungle; Drum'n'Bass, 1990s–, Artist, British
Landstrumm, Neil, Techno, 1990s–, Artist; Producer, British
Lange, Trance, 1990s–, Artist, British
Larkin, Kenny, Techno, 1990s, Producer, American
Lawrence, Christopher, Progressive; Trance, 1990s–, Artist, American
Lawrence, Vince, House, 1990s, Artist, American
Leftfield, House; Progressive, 1990s–, Artist, British
Leiner, Robert, Trance; Acid; House; Techno, 1990s, Producer, Swedish
Les Rhythmes Digitales, Big Beat, 1990s–, Artist, French
Levan Larry, Disco; House; US Garage, 1970s-1990s, Producer; Artist, American
LFO, House; Techno; Acid, 1980s-1990s, Artist, British
Liberator, Chris, Trance; Techno, 1990s–, Artist, British
Lieb, Oliver, Trance, 1980s–, Producer, German
Lil' Louis, House; Acid, 1980s-1990s, Artist; Producer, American
Lionrock, Big Beat; House, 1990s, Artist, British
Lipps Inc., Disco, 1970s-1980s, Artist, American
Lo Fidelity Allstars, Big Beat, 1990s–, Artist, British
LSG, Trance, 1990s–, Artist, German
M People, House, 1990s–, Artist, British
m-Ziq, Techno, 1990s–, Producer, British
Maas, Tech-House, 1990s, Artist, British
M/A/R/R/S, Acid, 1980s, Artist, British
Majik, J. , Jungle; Drum'n'Bass, 1990s–, Artist; Producer, British
Malice, Tribal; House, 1990s, Artist, American
Man Called Adam, A, House; Acid, 1980s-1990s, Artist, British
Man With No Name, Trance, 1990s–, Artist, British
Mancuso, David, Disco, 1970s–, Artist, American
Mantronik, Kurtis, Big Beat, 1980s–, Producer, Jamaican
Masters At Work, House; US Garage, 1990s–, Artist, American
Masters, Jim, Techno, 1990s, Artist; Producer, British
Masterstepz, UK Garage, 1990s–, Artist, British
Mateo & Matos, House, 1990s–, Artist, American
Matrix, Jungle; Drum'n'Bass, 1990s–, Producer, British
May, Derrick, Techno, 1980s-1990s, Artist; Producer, American
McCoy, Van, Disco, 1960s-1970s, Producer; Songwriter; Artist, American
McCrae, George, Disco, 1970s, Artist, American
McCrae, Gwen, Disco, 1970s-1990s, Artist, American
Mekron, Big Beat, 1990s–, Producer, American
Metamatics, Techno, 1990s–, Artist, British
MFSB, Disco, 1970s–80s, Artist, American
Midney, Boris, Progressive; Trance; Disco, 1990s, Producer, Russian
Miles, Robert, Progressive; Trance; House, 1990s–, Artist; Producer, Italian
Mills, Jeff, Techno, 1980s–, Artist, American
MJ Cole, UK Garage, 1990s–, Artist; Producer, British
MK, US Garage; House, , 1990s, Producer
Moby, House; Trance; Techno, 1980s–, Artist; Producer, American
Model 500, Techno; House, 1980s–, Producer, American
Monkey Mafia, Big Beat; House, 1990s–, Artist, British
Montauk P, Trance, 1990s–, Artist, American
Mood II Swing, House, 1990s, Artist; Producer, American
Morales, David, House, 1990s, Artist; Producer, American
Morel, George, House, 1990s–, Producer, American
Moroder, Giorgio, Disco, 1960s–, Producer; Composer; Artist, Italian
Mr C, Techno; Tech-House, 1990s–, Artist; Producer, British
Ms Dynamite, UK Garage, 1990s–, Artist, British
Murk, House; Progressive, 1990s, Artist, American
Negro, Joey, UK Garage, 1990s–, Artist; Producer, British
Neon Phusion, Breakbeat, 1990s, Artist, British
Nevins, Jason, Breakbeat, 1990s–, Artist; Producer, American
New Sector Movements, Breakbeat, 1990s, Artist, British
N-Joi, Hardcore, 1990s, Artist, British
Nu Birth, UK Garage, 1990s, Artist, British
Nu Era, Breakbeat; Techno, 1990s–, Artist, British
Nubian Mindz, Breakbeat; Techno, 1990s–, Artist, British
Numbers, Breakbeat, 1990s–, Artist, British
O'Brien, Ian, Breakbeat; Techno, 1990s, Producer, British
Oakenfold, Paul, House; Trance; Progressive; Acid, 1990s–, Producer; Artist, British
Octave One, Techno, 1990s, Artist, American
O'Jays, Disco, 1960s–, Artist, American
Omni Trio, Jungle; Drum'n'Bass, 1990s, Producer, British
Operator & Baffled, UK Garage, 1990s, Artist, British
Optical, Jungle; Drum'n'Bass, 1990s, Producer, British
Orbit, William, Tribal/Progressive, 1980s–, Artist; Artist, British
Orbital, Techno, 1980s–, Artist, British
Origin Unknown, Drum'n'Bass; Jungle, 1990s, Artist, British
Ottowan, Disco, Artist, 1970s–80s, French
Panacea, Jungle; Drum'n'Bass, 1990s–, Producer, German
Paperclip People, House; Techno, 1990s, Producer, American
Pappa, Anthony, Progressive; Trance; House, 1990s–, Artist; Producer, Australian
Parker, Terrence, House; Techno, 1990s, Artist; Producer, American
Pascal, Drum'n'Bass; Jungle, 1990s–, Artist; Producer, British
Patife, Drum'n'Bass; Jungle, 1990s– Artist; Producer, Brazilian
Peech Boys, The, House; US Garage, 1980s–, Producer, American
Peshay, Jungle; Drum'n'Bass, 1990s–, Artist; Producer, British
Pet Shop Boys, House, 1980s–, Artist, British
Photek, Jungle; Drum'n'Bass, 1990s–, Producer, British
Phuture, House; Acid, 1980s-1990s, Artist, American
Pickering, Mike, House, 1990s–, Producer, British
Pilgrem, Ronnie, Breakbeat, 1990s–, Artist; Producer, British
Planet BEN, Trance; techno, 1990s, Artist, British
Plastikman, Techno; Acid, 1990s–, Artist; Producer, British
Playford, Rob, Jungle; Drum'n'Bass, 1990s, Artist; Producer, British
Plug, Jungle; Drum'n'Bass, 1990s, Producer, British
Plump DJs, Breakbeat, 1990s–, Artist, British
Posford, Simon, Trance, 1990s–, Artist; Producer, British
Principle, Jamie, House; Acid, 1980s-1990s, Artist; Producer, American
Prodigy, The, Big Beat; Techno, 1990s–, Artist, British
Propellerheads, Big Beat, 1990s, Artist, British
Pullen, Stacey, Techno, 1990s–, Artist; Producer, American

Ralph, Dave, Progressive; House; Trance, 1990s–, Artist, British
Ram, Raja, Trance, 1990s–, Artist; Producer, 1990s–, British
Rampling, Danny, House; Acid; Trance, 1990s–, Artist, British
Random Factor, Tech-House, 1990s, Artist; Producer, British
Real McCoy, The, House, 1990s, Artist, German
Rebel MC, Drum'n'Bass; Jungle, 1980s–90s, Artist; Producer, British
Recloose, Breakbeat; Techno, 1990s–, Producer, American
Redd, Sharon, US Garage, 1970s–, Artist, American
Reece, Alex, Jungle; Drum'n'Bass, 1990s, Artist; Producer, American
Reel 2 Real, House, 1990s, Artist, American
Resistance D, Trance; Techno, 1990s–, Artist, German
Return To The Source, Trance, 1990s, Artist, British
Reyes, Jorge, Tribal; Techno, 1980s-1990s, Artist, Mexican
Rich, Robert, Tribal; Techno, 1980s–, Producer; Composer; Artist, American
Richards, Eddie, House; Tech-House, 1980s–, Artist; Producer, British
Roach, Steve, Tribal; Techno, 1970s–, Artist; Producer, American
Robinson, Vicky Sue, Disco, 1970s-1990s, Artist, American
Rodgers, Nile, Disco, 1970s-1980s, Producer; Songwriter; Artist, American
Romanthony, House; Acid, 1990s, Artist, American
Rosario, Ralphi, House; Acid, 1980s–, Artist; Producer, American
Ross, Diana, Disco, 1960s–, Artist, American
Roth, Gabrielle, Tribal; Techno, 1980s–, Artist, American
Rotterdam Termination Source, Gabba, 1990s, Artist, Dutch
Royce, Rose, Disco, 1970s-1980s, Artist, American
RuPaul, House, 1990s, Artist, American
Rush, Ed, Jungle; Drum'n'Bass, 1990s, Artist; Producer, British
Sabres Of Paradise, The, Techno, 1990s, Artist, British
Salsoul Orchestra, The, Disco, 1970s-1980s, Artist, American
Sanchez, Roger, House, 1990s–, Artist; Producer, American
Sasha & John Digweed, House; Progressive; Trance, 1990s–, Artist, British
Sasha, Progressive; House; Trance, 1990s–, Artist; Producer, British
Saunders, Jesse, House, 1980s–, Artist, American
Saunderson, Kevin, House; Techno, 1980s–, Artist; Producer, American
Scanner, Techno, 1990s–, Producer, British
Scott, Doc, Jungle; Drum'n'Bass, 1990s–, Artist; Producer, British
Seaman, Dave, Tribal/Progressive, 1990s–, Artist; Producer, British
Seiji, Breakbeat, 1990s–, Artist, British
Shake, Techno, 1990s–, Producer, American
Shakir, Anthony "Shake", Techno, 1990s, Producer, American
Shamen, The, Acid; Techno, 1980s-1990s, Artist, British
Shanks & Bigfoot, UK Garage, 1990s–, Artist; Producer, British
Sharkey, Happy Hardcore, 1990s, Artist; Producer, German
Shut Up And Dance, Acid; House, 1980s-1990s, Artist, British
Shpongle, Trance, 1990s–, Artist, British
Shy FX, Jungle; Drum'n'Bass, 1990s, Artist; Producer, British
Sister Sledge, Disco, 1970s–, Artist, American
Size, Roni, Jungle; Drum'n'Bass, 1990s–, Producer, British
SL2, Happy Hardcore, 1990s, Artist, British
Slam, House; Techno, 1990s–, Artist, British
Slater, Luke, Techno, 1990s–, Artist; Producer, British
Slave, Disco, 1970s-1990s, Artist, American
Smart E's, Hardcore, 1990s, Artist, British
Smooth, Joe, House, 1980s–90s, Producer, American
Smith & Mighty, Jungle; Drum'n'Bass, 1990s–, Artist, British
So Solid Crew, UK Garage, 2000s–, Artist, British
Solitaire, Tribal; Trance; Techno, 1990s, Artist, German
Soul II Soul, House; Acid, 1980s-1990s, Artist, British
Source Direct, Jungle; Drum'n'Bass, 1990s, Artist, British
Speedy J, Techno; Trance, 1990s–, Artist; Producer, Dutch
Spicelab, Trance; Techno, 1990s, Artist, German
Spooky, House; Progressive; Techno, 1990s, Artist, British
Spring Heel Jack, Jungle; Drum'n'Bass, 1990s–, Artist, British
Squarepusher, Jungle; Drum'n'Bass, 1990s–, Artist; Producer, British
Stereo MCs, House, 1980s–, Artist, British
Sticks & Stones, Tribal; House, 1990s–, Artist, American
Sticky Fingers, Tribal; House, 1970s, Artist, American
Stingily, Byron, House; Acid, 1990s–, Artist, American
Stoll, Steve, Techno, 1990s, Producer, American
Summer, Donna, Disco, 1970s–, Artist, American
Sun Electric, Techno, 1990s, Artist, German
Sunkings, Trance, 1990s, Artist, British
Surgeon, Techno; Trance, 1990s–, Artist; Producer, British
Sylvester, Disco, 1970s-1980s, Artist, American
Sylvia, Disco, 1960s-1980s, Producer; Songwriter; Artist, American
T99, Hardcore, 1990s, Artist, Belgian
T Power, Jungle; Drum'n'Bass; Techno, 1990s, Producer, British
Tavares, Disco, 1960s–, Artist, American
Technical Itch, Jungle; Drum'n'Bass, 1990s, Artist, British
Technohead, Gabba; Techno, 1990s, Artist, Dutch
Technotronic, House; Acid, 1980s-1990s, Artist, Belgian
Tee Bone, UK Garage, 1990s, Artist, British
Temptations, Disco, 1960s–90s, American, Artist
Ten City, House, 1980s-1990s, Artist, American
Tenaglia, Danny, House; US Garage, 1980s–, Artist, American
Terry, Todd, House; US Garage, 1980s-1990s, Artist; Producer, American
Tieghem, David van, Tribal; Techno, 1980s-1990s, Artist, American
Tiësto, Trance, 1900s–, Artist, Dutch
Tobin, Amon, Jungle; Drum'n'Bass, 1990s–, Artist; Producer, Brazilian
Tong, Pete, House; Trance; Progressive, 1980s–, Artist; Producer, British
Total Eclipse, Trance, 1990s, Artist, French
Tracid, Kai, Progressive; Trance, 1990s–, Artist, German
Trammps, The, Disco, 1960s-1970s, Artist, American
TransGlobal Underground, Tribal, 1990s–, Artist, British
Trent, Ron, House; Techno, 1990s–, Artist; Producer, American
True, Andrea, Disco, 1970s, Artist, American
Tucker, Keith, Techno, 1990s–, Artist; Producer, American
Tuff Jam, UK Garage; House, 1990s, Artist, British
Twisted Science, Jungle; Drum'n'Bass; Techno, 1990s–, Producer, British
Two Lone Swordsmen, Techno, 1990s–, Artist, British
Ultra Naté, Tribal; House; US Garage, 1980s–, Artist, American
Ultraviolence, Gabba; Techno, 1990s–, Producer, British
Underground Resistance, Techno, 1990s–, Artist, American
Underground, Glenn, House, 1990s–, Artist; Producer, American
Underworld, House; Progressive; Techno, 1980s–, Artist, British
Umek, Techno, 1990s–, Artist; Producer, Slovenian
Van Buuren, Armin, Trance, 2000s–, Producer, Dutch
Van Dyk, Paul, Trance, 1990s–, Artist; Producer, German
Van Helden, Armand, House, 1990s–, Artist; Producer, Dutch
Vasquez, Junior, House; US Garage, 1980s–, Artist, American
Vath, Sven, Techno; Trance, 1990s–, Artist; Producer, German
Village People, Disco, 1970s-1990s, Artist, American
Vinylgroover, Happy Hardcore; Techno, 1990s–, Artist, British
Vit, Tony de, House; Trance, 1990s, Artist; Producer, British
Vogel, Cristian, Techno, 1990s–, Artist; Producer, Chilean
W., Christine, House, 1990s–, Artist, American
Walker, Johnny, Acid, 1980s–, Artist, British
Wamdue Kids, House; Techno; Progressive, 1990s, Artist, American
Ward, Anita, Disco, 1970s; 1990s–, Artist, American
Wax, Tom, Trance; Techno, 1990s–, Artist, German
WestBam, Acid; Techno, 1980s–, Artist, German
White, Barry, Disco, 1970s–, Artist; Songwriter, American
Wink, Josh, House, 1990s, Artist, American
Wiseguys, The, Big Beat, 1990s–, Artist, British
Wookie, UK Garage, 1990s–, Artist, British
XRS, Drum'n'Bass; Jungle, 1990s–, Artist; Producer; Brazilian
Yost, Kevin, House, 1990s–, Producer, American
Young, Claude, Techno, 1990s, Artist; Producer, American
Zed Bias, UK Garage, 1990s–, Artist, British

Hip Hop

Above

Hip hop culture emerged from rap and consisted of four main facets of self-expression: break-dancing, DJing (cutting and scratching), rapping and graffiti art.

> "HIP HOP WAS AN ATTITUDE. IT WAS A VIBE THAT BEGAN IN THE GHETTO AND SPREAD ACROSS THE WHOLE CITY, IT BEGAN WITH THE MUSIC AND EMBRACED CLOTHES, ART, FILM, DANCE ... EVERYTHING."

LL Cool J

LIKE so many of black America's most enduring musical genres, hip hop was born out of invention. When, as the 1970s came to a close, a combination of disco and big record company involvement had diluted funk and soul to the extent that it had become boring to go out to a club on a Saturday night, something rumbled out of New York's South Bronx that would change the music business for ever – hip hop.

Always more than simply a type of music, hip hop was a whole youth culture, with rap as one of its component pieces. Musically, hip hop took exactly what it wanted from what already existed – beats, breaks, hooks – and recut them into something exciting, edgy and tailor-made for a new generation of teenage party people. That it could be done more or less anytime, anywhere, gave it a rebel status that flew in the face of disco's orderly 4/4 beats and exclusive venues.

Simply by wiring two turntables into a streetlamp, a DJ was ready to start wrecking records and turn a playground or basketball court into a dance floor. To put rap on top of it further exercised an inner city ownership as it continued black America's oral tradition and allowed a healthy dose of the "dozens" to be stirred in (the dozens is a ghetto game where kids insult each other with escalating vigour; the loser is the one who gives in first). This was always going to make for a very different accent and

jargon from the much smoother world of soul singing, and the very idea of it infuriated the mainstream for years. Rap was the most obvious musical expression, and late-1970s/early 1980s records like the Sugarhill Gang's 'Rapper's Delight' and Kurtis Blow's 'Christmas Rapping' introduced the style to a wider audience, where it remains essentially unchanged right up to today's Jay-Z and 50 Cent.

Graffiti art was a natural visual counterpart to the music. It began life as kids scrawling their customized signatures everywhere, thus rudely announcing their presence in environments beyond their own. Their art had the same DIY feel as what the DJs were doing with the turntables; just as they could make something rather marvellous out of the blandest of records, so graffiti blossomed into mural painting that turned some of New York's worst eyesores into art gallery-style beauty. Break-dancing, too – the physical expression of the music – was something that anybody who owned a couple of square yards of cardboard could do. It also brought a unique style of self-expression that remained part of the hip hop community for a long time because first, break-dancing was difficult to master, and second, new moves were developed and unleashed continuously, so that it was always shifting beyond any notions of corporateness.

In the same way that jazz and blues were conjured up out of imagination, innovation and sheer raw talent, so hip hop was another example of the spirit of a people being expressed in musical terms. Indeed, during its 20-or-so-year existence, hip hop has continued to shift its own goalposts in an effort to stay outside the more conventional music scene and service its own community first. Every time hip hop appears to have allowed itself to become co-opted into the mainstream

---

STYLES

Hip Hop

British

Old School

Golden Age

Political

Gangsta

Alternative

THE HIP HOP STYLE

Most hip hop styles have a fairly simple melodic backing, with a more intricate bass-and-drum rhythm section. The focal point of the style is the vocals, which add another rhythmical dimension to the overall sound.

HIP HOP PEOPLE A-Z ➡ 347   INSTRUMENTS A-Z ➡ 436   THE BLUES INTRO ➡ 154   WORLD: AFRICA ➡ 290   DANCE: DISCO ➡ 314

Above

*Regarded as one of the best
live performance groups in
hip hop, LA outfit Cypress
Hill was the first band to
successfully straddle the fence
between hardcore gangsta rap
and grunge rock.*

industry, another offshoot pops up with a style guaranteed to get up suburbia's nose. For that reason, hip hop has remained as much a metaphor for rebellion as it was back in its early graffiti-tagging and quick-mixing days.

Even as it has progressed to become one of the most successful pop genres on the planet, hip hop still stands for social and musical mutiny all over the world. While in Britain it plays a large part in UK garage culture, and in Jamaica its influences are felt throughout the reggae world, in other places hip hop has developed on its own terms. France has long had a healthy hip hop scene, best known for MC Solaar (part of Guru's Jazzmatazz project), the more hardcore Stomy Bugsy and Passi (the pure old school vibe of the Saïan Supa Crew) and more recently, the innovative Cuban rap crew Orishas

which has set up home in Paris. Canadian hip hop has been a force ever since the Dream Warriors broke onto the international scene at the end of the 1980s and currently, like its French and UK counterparts, it seems to draw from a wider circle of inspiration to produce some unique sounds: witness rappers Madchild, Prevail and DJ A-Trak, who can hold their own with any Americans.

In essence, hip hop remains stylistically the same across time and space. In spite of the advances made in studio technology over the last two decades, hip hop records are still being created to sound like someone with two turntables cutting up and relaying beats, while somebody else raps on top. Maybe that's because that is what the people want, and hip hop remains very much a people's music.

AS THE 1970S PLAYED OUT AND DISCO TOOK OVER, A NEW GENERATION REACTED AGAINST THE COMMERCIAL HOMOGENIZATION OF BLACK MUSIC BY CREATING A COMPLETELY NEW SOUND. THIS SOUND CAME FROM THE STREETS AND WAS ACCOMPANIED BY ITS OWN DRESS CODE, LANGUAGE, DANCE STYLES AND ATTITUDE: HIP HOP WAS A WAY OF LIFE.

Hip Hop

Above

A teenage rapper in Harlem plays hip hop beats on a "ghetto blaster".

Whereas disco was symbolized by the swank Manhattan nightclubs, these new sounds swaggered out of the street corners and house parties of the Bronx, where the most plentiful resource was ingenuity. During the second half of the 1970s, young black America was literally cutting disco up as DJs made their sets more challenging by working two turntables with the same record on each, mixing between them to prolong the interesting bits at the expense of the banalities. The DJ credited with starting this is Jamaican ex-pat DJ Kool Herc, who noticed, when operating his sound system, that it was the instrumental breaks in the extended 12-inch mixes that particularly moved the crowds, and began to mix two such sections together to create one seamless segment. It is from these extended instrumental breaks that the terms "break beats", "break-dancers", and "b-boys" (an abbreviation of "break boys") originated.

"I WANTED TO BE THE FIRST BLACK ELECTRONIC GROUP. SOME FUNKY MECHANICAL CRAZY SHIT WITH NO BAND, JUST ELECTRONIC INSTRUMENTS."

Afrika Bambaata

Taking It Further

However, these impromptu remixes soon took on lives of their own and entirely different tunes were created out of parts of others as sections of vocals or melody were cut up and repeated to assume completely altered vibes. An extra rhythmic thrust was provided by scratching, as a turntable's stylus was manipulated in a record's groove by moving the record itself backwards and forwards for beat-sized snatches. The burgeoning technology worked in tandem with this creativity as samplers and drum machines

Right

Break-dancing first emerged onto the New York street scene in the 1970s and competing gangs would regularly square up and seek to outdo each other with increasingly outrageous (and dangerous) moves.

began to be used with increasingly sophisticated mixers and turntables allowing far more imaginative effects to be put into hip hop tunes. By the beginning of the 1980s, producers and mixers such as Arthur Baker, Grandmaster Flash and Afrika Bambaataa began to put this sound on record.

LEADING EXPONENTS

Afrika Bambaataa

Fab Five Freddie

Futura

Arthur Baker

Soul Sonic Force

Double Trouble

DJ Kool Herc

HIP HOP

A fairly mellow sound, with light rhythm and bass under sustained chords, usually with a melodic or rap vocal, or a combination of the two.

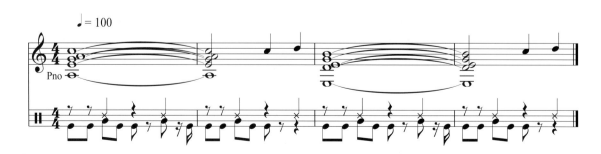

THE HIP HOP INTRO ➡ 334   HIP HOP PEOPLE A-Z ➡ 347   INSTRUMENTS A-Z ➡ 436   THE BLUES INTRO ➡ 154   WORLD: AFRICA ➡ 290

It also made stars of the slick-talking streetwise likes of the Furious Five, Spoonie Gee, the Cold Crush Brothers, the Sequence and Soul Sonic Force. Bringing a further, impromptu, anyone-can-join-in vibe to proceedings, DJs and MCs began rapping. Although such carryings-on are not unheard of in black American music – think of jazz's scat singing or jive-talking radio DJs – this was the first time it had been a sustained and featured part of proceedings instead of an optional extra. Essentially publicizing themselves, the club or the sound system, commenting on what was going on around them and just whooping with exuberance, the rappers were the glue that held the early hip hop scene together as they vibed it up and, more importantly, kept it exclusive.

Creative Spin-Offs

Break-dancing and graffiti were the physical manifestations of hip hop, each, like the music, representing a street expression that relied on little more than inventiveness and practised expertise. In the same way as the music, they also made use of their own environments to create something unique, energized and extraordinary out of not very much. For these reasons dancing was at the very heart of hip hop; it gave anybody who could scare up a square of cardboard or linoleum the chance – with a bit of hard work – to show off for the neighbourhood and excel at something. As dancers threw down increasingly audacious moves – body-popping, moon-walking, head spins, windmills – break-dancing competitions in clubs and parties echoed the dance floor cutting contests of the big band era. It was this healthy spirit of competition that former New York street-gang leader Afrika Bambaataa recognized as a far more viable and far less life-threatening alternative to fighting. Using his influence, gained from his notorious Black Spades gang, he set up dance competitions and created the Zulu Nation, named after the heroic African warriors in the film *Zulu*, as a kind of umbrella organization for the city's growing number of hip hop crews.

It is entirely understandable that graffiti art should grow up alongside rap and break-dancing as part of hip hop. Again, it is a spontaneous street expression and one that had the added bonus of being genuinely outlawed as it outgrew "tagging" (kids scrawling their customized initials, or tags, on any visible surface) to become "bombing" (painting detailed murals on subway trains in the stockyards). No early hip hop show was complete without a graffiti-style mural as a backdrop. Graffiti became quite a political statement, inasmuch as its mere appearance represented a degree of anarchy or loss of order, yet it blossomed into one of the most vibrant art forms of the late-twentieth century. Naturally, it ended up in smart uptown galleries. Fab Five Freddie, Futura and Phase II were hip hop's most influential graffiti artists, and were a vital part of its flourishing as a culture. Freddie went on to become a filmmaker of note, while the modern art world considers Futura a vital late twentieth-century talent.

Once hip hop went wide, marketing men became the decision makers rather than the kids themselves, which is why so much later hip hop does not have a sense of a "nation" in the way the old school used to. While hip hop has gained a great deal of logic, hip hop has also lost an equal amount of the raw, unpredictable spirit that originally served to unify it.

Below
Respectfully known as the "Godfather" and "Grandfather" of hip hop culture, Afrika Bambaataa was initially a gang warlord who went on to spread rap and hip hop culture around the world through his Zulu Nation.

British Hip Hop

IT IS A COMMON ENOUGH OPINION THAT THE WORDS "BRITISH" AND "RAP" ARE CONTRADICTIONS IN TERMS. UNFORTUNATELY, THIS IS INDEED THE CASE AND IT IS SOLELY BECAUSE OF THE LANGUAGE BARRIER: RAP DELIVERED IN ANY FORM OF ENGLISH OTHER THAN AMERICAN DOES NOT SOUND AUTHENTIC.

Above
Neneh Cherry, the daughter of jazz legend Don Cherry and older sister to Eagle Eye, boasts genetic credentials that first bore fruit with the massive success of her 1989 debut solo album, Raw Like Sushi.

TO attempt rap in the Queen's English became known as the "Derek B Syndrome", after the enthusiastic British rapper who, at the end of the 1980s, became the most successful of a slew of British rappers – the Cookie Crew, Wee Papa Girl Rappers, Overlord X and She-Rockers included – who failed to equate sales figures with hip-hop credibility. Although, perhaps in Overlord X's case sales and credibility did run in tandem. Derek B, the self-styled Bad Young Brother, had all the attitude, but his mish-mash cockney/New York accent sounded so out of place in rap's very stylized vocabulary that it was never going to be anything other than novelty.

Made In Britain

British rappers always seemed confused as to whether they should be "keeping it real" with local speech patterns or going as close to Yankee as they could manage. Either way, this tended to open them up to ridicule from the UK's hardcore hip hop community. It is no coincidence that British rappers Monie Love and Neneh Cherry (the most successful, in terms of credibility) both spent so much time with family in New York that they had more or less authentic American accents on 'Down to Earth' and 'Buffalo Stance',

> "THE BRITISH MUSIC PRESS WILL NEVER TIRE OF BEMOANING THE STATE OF ITS HOME-GROWN HIP HOP."
>
> *Peter Shapiro*

respectively. This situation has not changed much today, as the slick-talking Phi-Life Crew are taken more seriously than their counterparts by sounding far more New York than New Malden.

This is not to say that what went on behind the rappers was not worth tuning into. British hip hop producers and turntable wizards soaked up the influences of reggae, rock and numerous other styles, unlike US rappers working within the rigidly structured US music system. As a result, mixmasters like DJ Vadim, the Creators and the Scratch Perverts can hold their own anywhere in the world. This hip hop-based creativity seeped back into the pop sphere too, as outfits like Bomb The Bass, S'Express, Beatmasters, Coldcut and Beats International, an earlier incarnation of Norman "Fatboy Slim" Cook, appeared on the UK charts in the late-1980s.

Finding Its Way

In the early 1990s British hip hop found a new potency, acknowledging the ways it differed from US rap and building on its own unique foundations. Jamaican patois – the basis of much UK urban street slang – began driving the lyrical style, encouraging those from solid hip hop traditions to experiment wildly. Rappers Roots Manuva, Black Twang and the more pop-oriented Ms Dynamite are all riding high, and all deliver their lyrics in clear Jamaican timbres. Meanwhile drum'n'bass, jungle and UK garage are all the result of fusing rap with reggae and other dance styles, with a sense of adventure that goes back to SoulIISoul in the 1980s. UK garage collective So Solid Crew and solo artist the Streets are perfect examples of how hip hop can bind a multitude of other musical genres to produce a powerful and eclectic street style.

LEADING EXPONENTS
Monie Love
Neneh Cherry
Fatboy Slim
Roots Manuva
SoulIISoul
So Solid Crew
Ms Dynamite
The Streets

BRITISH HIP HOP
A gentle rhythm, often with piano or keyboard accompaniment, over which a vocalist could rap.

Old School

IT USED TO BE EASY TO TALK ABOUT RAP OR HIP HOP, BECAUSE ESSENTIALLY EVERYBODY KNEW WHERE THEY STOOD: THE ARTISTS MADE 12-INCH SINGLES THAT DIDN'T GET PLAYED ON THE RADIO; THEY DRESSED IN ACRES OF BRIGHTLY COLOURED LEATHER, WITH PEOPLE BREAK-DANCING AND BODY-POPPING AROUND THEM; AND NOBODY CAME FROM FARTHER WEST THAN NEW JERSEY.

BACK in the day, the Sugarhill Gang was the group everybody had heard of, as their 'Rappers' Delight' single stormed pop charts all over the world in late-1979, followed up almost immediately by Kurtis Blow's 'Christmas Rapping'. While the mainstream pop industry was quick to pass these records off as mere novelty, they were the tip of a hip hop iceberg that until then had been an underground, almost strictly live scenario, with sound-system-duplicated tapes being the only recordings available. The records were also splitting the hip hop community – was this recording success a sell-out, or was it the way forward? Thankfully, the latter camp won out and hip hop committed itself to wax with gusto.

Advancing The Cause

Understandably, with a start like that, the New Jersey-based Sugarhill Records led the way, and their early 1980s catalogue was a Who's Who of hip hop: alongside the Sugarhill Gang were the Sequence, Lady B, the Treacherous Three, the Funky Four and Grandmaster Flash & the Furious Five. These were all acts who had made their names at New York clubs such as the Roxy and Danceteria, and put an emphasis on performance (hence the leatherwear they tended to favour). It was the last

group that did the most to advance hip hop's cause. While the rappers rapped pretty much exclusively about their money, their sexual prowess or themselves, which quickly got tedious on record, Flash breathed life into the scene with the single 'Adventures On The Wheels Of Steel', a virtuoso display of turntable manipulation that introduced the world at large to scratching and quick-mixing. It changed the face of hip hop recordings, as artists now felt much freer to represent club culture instead of trying to sound as conventional as possible.

Meanwhile, in Sugarhill's slipstream were acts like the Cold Crush Brothers, Double Trouble, the Fearless Four and the Force MDs, and New York record labels Enjoy, Tommy Boy and West End, all of whom expanded hip hop's visions. It was in 1982 that Zulu Nation leader Afrika Bambaataa teamed up with producer Arthur Baker and rap crew Soul Sonic Force to create 'Planet Rock', one of the year's biggest club hits and the vanguard of the electro style that was to take hip hop in a new, more accessible direction.

Evidence of these times and a mark of how, within a few years, hip hop had seeped into a far broader marketplace, can be found in the slew of rapping/break-dancing films that were released in the early 1980s; *Wild Style, Breakdance* and *Beat Street* being the most successful. By 1984, Def Jam Records had been launched by Russell Simmons and Rick Rubin, whose initial acts included LL Cool J and Public Enemy. These acts are the last surviving links between the old school and hip hop today.

Above

Kurtis Blow was the first rapper to sign with a major record label and was instrumental in bringing rap to the masses.

> "FRIENDS OF MINE USED TO SAY, 'LET'S GO TO THE PARK, HANG OUT WITH GIRLS,' I'M LIKE, 'NAW MAN, I'M WORKING ON SOMETHING.'"
> *Grandmaster Flash*

Above Left

With a string of hits, the Furious Five and their frontman, Grandmaster Flash, became one of the most well-known rap acts in the early 1980s, before parting ways in 1984.

♩ = 80

Elec Gtr

OLD SCHOOL

The old school sound, referring to hip hop styles of the 1970s and 1980s, has a fairly simple rhythmical structure. Simple raps fit squarely to the beats, unlike the more complex rhythms often used in more modern rap styles.

LEADING EXPONENTS

Grandmaster Flash &
  the Furious Five
The Sugarhill Gang
Spoonie Gee
Kurtis Blow
The Cold Crush Brothers
The Sequence
Afrika Bambaataa

THE HIP HOP INTRO ➡ 334   HIP HOP PEOPLE A–Z ➡ 347   INSTRUMENTS A–Z ➡ 436   SOUL AND R&B: FUNK ➡ 376

WHEN THE SUGARHILL GANG AND KURTIS BLOW MADE AN IMPACT ON THE MAINSTREAM POP CHARTS IN 1979, RAP WAS IMMEDIATELY PALMED OFF AS A NOVELTY. HOWEVER, THE STYLE NOT ONLY SURVIVED, BUT HAS PROVED TO BE SO INFLUENTIAL THAT, IN VARYING DEGREES, POP, ROCK, HEAVY METAL AND REGGAE HAVE ALL BORROWED FROM HIP HOP AT SOME POINT. ALSO, ASTONISHINGLY, HIP HOP'S GOLDEN AGE HAS LASTED MORE THAN TWENTY YEARS.

Golden Age

Above
Run-DMC – Joseph Simmons (Run), Darryl McDaniels (DMC) and Jason Mizell (Jam Master Jay) – were childhood friends who grew up together in Queens, NY, before becoming a rap phenomenon.

HIP HOP has survived because it has continued to reinvent itself to a staggering degree, absorbing a turnover of influences matched only by its appropriation of musical technology. Whether it was the old school Sugarhill era, Def Jam's rap'n'rock extravaganza or the west coast's gangsta, like the beat itself hip hop's golden era just won't stop.

In The Beginning ...

It is those three high profile areas that serve best to define hip hop's success story, representing, respectively, the introduction, the consolidation and the pre-eminence. When Sugarhill Records became the first company to concentrate on recording and marketing rap, it was all relatively unsophisticated, inasmuch as technology didn't extend past two turntables and a cross-fader, while rapping was confined to street-corner braggadocio in the simplest rhyming couplets. However, as an alternative to disco, rap found a wider following and quickly convinced its fans of a dazzling potential when 'Rapper's Delight' gave way to 'The Message', 'White Lines' and 'Adventures On The Wheels Of Steel'.

The whole hip hop experience spread across the media-friendly Manhattan nightclub scene as break-dancing, graffiti art and street style became as trendy as the electro and scratch-mixed soundtrack. B-boys and -girls, as the hip hop crowd was known, assumed iconic status, as pop videos all seemed to feature body-popping and the world's sharper style magazines rushed to investigate these South Bronx goings-on. It was during this period, in the early 1980s that the moonwalk first went public and the baseball cap got turned back to front.

However, in spite of the obvious popularity and hipness quota of characters such as Grandmaster Flash, Whodini, Afrika Bambaataa, Kool Moe Dee and Soul Sonic Force, hip hop was still being ignored by the increasingly powerful MTV and so much

> ## "NO ONE EVER GOT SHOT AT ONE OF MY PARTIES. BACK THEN PEOPLE HAD TOO MUCH RESPECT, FOR ME AND FOR THE MUSIC."
> *DJ Kool Herc*

Right
Co-founders of Def Jam Records Rick Rubin (left) and Russell Simmons (right) began their partnership in 1984. They split acrimoniously a few years later, but not before making hip hop history with acts like Run-DMC, LL Cool J, the Beastie Boys and Public Enemy.

LEADING EXPONENTS
Run-DMC
LL Cool J
The Beastie Boys
Salt-N-Pepa
Warren G
Will Smith

GOLDEN AGE
Similar to old school, though with slightly more of a hip hop flavour. The vocal line tends to alternate between pure melody and rap, underpinned by sustained keyboard chords.

THE HIP HOP INTRO ➡ 334   HIP HOP PEOPLE A-Z ➡ 347   INSTRUMENTS A-Z ➡ 436   THE POP INTRO ➡ 8   THE ROCK INTRO ➡ 74

mainstream radio. In the early 1980s, Russell Simmons and Rick Rubin came on the scene – a street-smart black artist manager and a heavy metal-loving white college boy, respectively – who together founded Def Jam Records. They took hip hop to a level way beyond its cottage industry status in 1984, with their very first release – LL Cool J's 100,000-selling song 'I Need A Beat'.

Where Simmons and Rubin immediately made their mark on music was by combining their own personal preferences – hip hop and heavy metal – on Def Jam productions to create a whole new, ultra-obnoxious hip hop sound: denser, more in-your-face and technologically superior. It instantly took rap to a mainstream market by airing Run-DMC's 'Walk This Way', a single and video featuring hard rock favourites Aerosmith, on MTV. Ironically, although it was not a Def Jam record, and despite the fact that Simmons managed Run-DMC (his brother Joseph is Run) and had a hand in the production, he had signed the group to Polygram before he teamed up with Rubin. However, Def Jam's Public Enemy, LL Cool J and the Beastie Boys made up for this by dominating rap throughout the mid-1980s with a string of mainstream album successes with, respectively, *Fear Of A Black Planet*, *Bigger & Deffer* and *Licence To Ill*. Def Jam has remained a force, as the company shifted with the times to have hits throughout the 1990s and into the new millennium with Warren G, Montell Jordan, Method Man, Jay-Z and Ja Rule.

A New Direction

Def Jam continued into hip hop's third era, when the focus shifted to California and became gangsta, as opposed to the New York scene stylistically as it was geographically. Heralded by NWA's *Straight Outta Compton*, it marked a new nihilistic era in which lyrical concerns were the supposed reality tales drawn from the street-gang playgrounds of South Central Los Angeles. Artists such as Snoop Dogg, Tupac Shakur, Ice-T, Ice Cube and Dr. Dre took hip hop to new levels of expertise and invention, soon to be matched beat for beat by east coast gangstas Notorious BIG, MOP and Capone-N-Noriega. Thanks to TV exposure and shrewder business plans, it is this age of rap that has survived to the degree that gangsta artists like Snoop, Dr. Dre, Jay-Z and Mobb Deep are now, more or less, a legitimate part of the mainstream music scene, where, incidentally, hip hop sells more to whites than it does to its assumed black audience.

But while these are easily defined areas, for the last twenty-odd years, rap's golden age has maintained itself with an almost perpetual chart presence – Salt-N-Pepa, the Fat Boys, the Fresh Prince (aka Will Smith), Doug E. Fresh, MC Hammer, Kid 'N Play, Coolio and Mantronix have all scored mainstream hits before hip hop technique became an intrinsic part of the pop process. And they did so without necessarily having underground success first, implying that hip hop has come of age and is more than capable of taking on the rest of the music world on its own terms.

Below

James Todd Smith, aka Ladies Love Cool James. His ability to marry rap and pop has resulted in a long career that saw him release his tenth album in 2002.

IT HAS BEEN ARGUED THAT ALL RAP IS POLITICAL: A GENUINE BLACK STREET STATEMENT, GIVING VOICE TO THOSE OUTSIDE THE MUSICAL OR SOCIAL ESTABLISHMENTS IN A WAY THAT CONNECTS WITH A SIMILARLY DISPOSSESSED AUDIENCE, AND SO ITS VERY EXISTENCE IS A POLITICAL ACT. WHILE MANY WILL BE JUSTIFIED IN THINKING THIS IS PATENTLY NONSENSE, IT IS, ACTUALLY, HALF RIGHT.

Political

Above

With their debut album 3 Years, Five Months and 2 Days in the Life of... in 1992, Arrested Development became an "alternative" rap group with a spiritual sound in an era when gangsta acts dominated the scene.

THE essence of Afrika Bambaataa's hip hop culture was that of rebelliousness: youngsters rebelling against disco's homogenizing of street funk's spikiness; the kicking against a typecast that viewed them as inherently violent; and a DIY methodology that gave the music biz the finger. It was a rebel assertion in the same vein as the first UK punks of half a decade earlier. But in his determination to organize the New York street gangs into a force for good (he was once a leader of the fearsome Black Spades) and his close ties with the Nation of Islam, Bambaataa was always far more politicized than could be gleaned from his musical output.

Spreading The Word

Although rap is a distillation of a long-standing black oral tradition, the formalizing of any narrative technique lies in the revolutionary street poetry of Gil Scott-Heron and the Last Poets. Here, removed from the mainstream's considerations, was the perfect opportunity to take up the baton from soul's politically aware icons such as James Brown and Curtis Mayfield. In fact, through early 1980s singles like Grandmaster Flash's 'The Message', Melle Mel's anti-drug hymn 'White Lines', The Rake's 'Street Justice' and Brother D's 'How We Gonna Make The Black Nation Rise?', rap always had an overtly political edge to it. And it didn't take long for a large

> "WE WAS LOOKING TO MAKE SOME CHANGES. OUR ATTITUDE WAS 'IF WE DON'T MAKE IT HAPPEN THEN IT AIN'T GONNA HAPPEN' AND WE WOULD INTELLECTUALIZE DEEP INTO THE NIGHT."
>
> *Chuck D*

proportion of rappers to start thinking deeper than merely rhyming "hands in the air" with "just don't care".

Since the late-1980s Public Enemy have remained the market leaders in rap consciousness, as the verbal and visual dynamics of Chuck D and Flavour Flav's relationship – the former a thundering sermonizer, the latter a counterpointing

LEADING EXPONENTS

Public Enemy
KRS-One
Grandmaster Flash
Queen Latifah
Nas
Digital Underground
Ms Dynamite

POLITICAL HIP HOP

Political hip hop bears the rhythmic and melodic hall-marks of standard hip hop, but uses the lyrics to promote black consciousness and many black community issues.

THE HIP HOP INTRO ➡ 334   HIP HOP PEOPLE A-Z ➡ 347   INSTRUMENTS A-Z ➡ 436   THE BLUES INTRO ➡ 154

class clown – backed up with Professor Griff (the Minister Of Information) researching their subject matter and Terminator X's explosive beats – put them out front. Albums like *It Takes A Nation Of Millions To Hold Us Back* and *Fear Of A Black Planet* may have delivered a brutal political message as a blast of barely contained rage, but the sonic mayhem that backed it was powerful enough to floor (probably literally) the most demanding rap fan.

Beyond this broad-brush black nationalism, though, is a host of tireless soldiers for the cause with more tightly focussed agendas. KRS-One raged as righteously as Public Enemy, coming down hard on black-on-black violence; likewise the softer X-Clan, who laced their lyrics with the kind of co-Egyptology the band Earth, Wind & Fire would have been proud of. Queen Latifah, Salt-N-Pepa, Roxanne Shanté and Monie Love flew the feminist flag while Poor Righteous Teachers and Brand Nubian expounded the Five Percent belief that men are innately superior to women. Then Wu Tang and Digital Underground served up their politics with a generous helping of entertainment and sheer silliness. In this, they owed a big debt to George Clinton's P-Funk, a group which combined political focus with stage shows involving outrageous costumes and an enormous mothership. The need to be saying something was definitely seeping into rap's consciousness.

On The Other Hand

On the west coast in the 1990s, it was never all nihilism, as gangsta maintained its own robust approach to politics with tales of ghetto life as a valid statement in themselves. Indeed, NWA's *Straight Outta Compton*, Ice-T's 'The Gun Tower', Kam's 'Neva Again' and Coolio's 'Gangsta Paradise' are undeniably modern protest songs, as they call attention to the plights of urban youth. But as gangsta seemed to take over the hip hop nation, it provoked a reaction in the deliberately anti-gangsta stance of "Afrocentricity". As practiced by the Jungle Brothers, Arrested Development, A Tribe Called Quest, De La Soul and Digable Planets, it was a gentle, more cerebral, entirely saleable form of rap consciousness, by collections of hip hoppers who wanted to let the world know there was more to contemporary black music and culture than gang-banging in Los Angeles. They'd dress almost hippy-style, smile a great deal, wear leather and wooden Africa-emblem jewellery and threatened to bring back the afro. In many ways, they represented a continuation of the more traditional threads in black music: consciousness, righteousness, playfulness and sex that was not necessarily devoid of love. It was following along the same lines as Afrika Bambaataa and his Zulu Nation, a concept that had got rather lost in that west coast heat haze.

These days, with the exception of Nas, this part-time embracing of politics amid the more commercially viable party music, gangsta fantasies and sex talk best represents the current crop of rappers' attitudes. Types like Ja Rule and Jay-Z know they can sell records in quantities their predecessors never dreamed of, yet they remain very aware that they have to stay rooted in some kind of black consciousness in order to retain a hold on credibility.

Far Left

One of the most controversial and influential rap groups, Public Enemy's mixture of Chuck D's political rhetoric and Flavour Flav's wacky humour set the agenda for rap and hip hop music as a channel for social force.

Left

The Wu Tang Clan is a collective of MCs from Staten Island, NY, known under several names and pseudonyms including Rza (formerly Prince Rakeem), Ol' Dirty Bastard, Method Man, Raekwon The Chef, Ghostface Killah, U-God, Inspecta Deck (aka Rebel INS) and Masta Killa.

FOLK: POLITICAL FOLK & PROTEST SONGS ➡ 230   SOUL AND R&B: FUNK ➡ 376   HIP HOP: GANGSTA ➡ 344

RUMBLING OUT OF LOS ANGELES WITH DIFFERENT BEATS, A DIFFERENT LOOK AND A VERY DIFFERENT ATTITUDE, GANGSTA RAP WAS HIP HOP'S BELLIGERENT STREET CHILD. THIS NEW SOUND GREW UP AT BLACK DISCOS AND PARTIES AWAY FROM MAINSTREAM INTERFERENCE, AND SO, MUCH AS THE ORIGINAL HIP HOP HAD, IT QUITE LITERALLY PLEASED ITSELF AND HARKED BACK TO STREET FUNK FOR MUSICAL INSPIRATION.

Gangsta

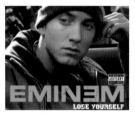

Above

Detroit rapper Eminem has raised the credibility of white rap through his phenomenal worldwide success. His song 'Lose Yourself', from the semi-autobiographical film 8 Mile, won the singer an Academy Award.

It was the first time rap had achieved any identity other than on the East Coast, but now, as hip hop moved closer to heavy metal and mainstream rock, upping its tempo and musical intensity, it appeared to be edging away from its home crowd. There had been signs that a change was due, when Eric B & Rakim's minimalist *Paid In Full* was the biggest rap album of 1987, and the following year EPMD's acclaimed *Strictly Business* proved how hip hop could still be funky. In the wake of these underground successes, it was not too much of a surprise when, at the end of the 1980s, west coast rap built itself almost exclusively on P-Funk samples – George Clinton's ParliamentFunkadelic always had huge support in California – for a bouncing, open-top car, hot-fun-in-the-California-sun type of vibe, laid-back in all but the lyrics.

"WE CALLED THE LABEL DEATH ROW 'CAUSE A MAJORITY OF OUR PEOPLE WAS PAROLEES OR INCARCERATED – IT'S NO JOKE. WE GOT PEOPLE REALLY WAS ON DEATH ROW."

Suge Knight

Right

Biggie Smalls, aka Notorious BIG, and Tupac Shakur epitomized the east coast/west coast rivalry. Both were gunned down within six months of each other.

Street Level

When NWA (Niggaz With Attitude, as they were known back then) unleashed their *Straight Outta Compton* album on an unsuspecting world in 1988, it epitomized the state of their particular nation; both geographically and situationally. The album's narrative told of the neglected world that was south central Los Angeles, which some 20 years after the Watts riots had slipped into decay and was ruled by the violent carryings-on of the Bloods and Crips street gangs. Songs from that LP like 'Fuck Tha Police', 'Straight Outta Compton' and the track that gave the genre its name, 'Gangsta Gangsta' summed up a situation in a way that came to represent black rage's new tone of voice – foul-mouthed, hate-filled, vitriolic and nihilistic.

In the city that, a few years later, would be notorious for the Rodney King beating, such an anti-authority attitude was understandable. The worrying factor was that in many ways this new attitude demonstrated a deep-rooted self-hatred, never more noticeable than in gangsta's apparent relationship with women. At the time, the notions that women were nothing more than "bitches" and "hos", whose main role in life was to be scantily clad in videos, attracted more media flack than the preoccupations with violence. The fact that female rappers such as Foxy Brown and Lil' Kim endorsed that state of affairs – instead of using their success to prove the world otherwise – didn't help matters.

LEADING EXPONENTS

Ice-T

NWA

Snoop Dogg

Suge Knight

Notorious BIG

Lil' Kim

Tupac Shakur

Jay-Z

Eminem

GANGSTA

A rap style characterized by the lyric themes, usually street life, crime, poverty etc.

THE HIP HOP INTRO ➡ 334   HIP HOP PEOPLE A-Z ➡ 347   INSTRUMENTS A-Z ➡ 436   HIP HOP: POLITICAL ➡ 342   THE SOUL AND R&B INTRO ➡ 368

As Cool As Ice

But in spite of – or perhaps *because of* – initial mainstream disapproval, gangsta rap flourished, as NWA became the alma mater for the genre's two most significant figures, lyricist/ rapper Ice Cube and producer Dr. Dre. Also out of Los Angeles was Ice-T, who may ultimately have fallen from grace, but earned respect as one of the genre's most powerful writers and performers for his *OG* album alone. Then there was the infamous Death Row Records, the label formed in 1991 by Suge Knight, a terrifying, physically huge figure who was rumoured to have connections with the Mafia. For him, gangsta was not just a musical style but a genuine way of life. However questionable Knight's methods were, Death Row attracted the cream of west coast talent, and before he was incarcerated in 1997, his company had released three of the genre's most memorable albums: Snoop Dogg's *Doggy Dogg Style*, Dr. Dre's *The Chronic* and Tupac Shakur's *All Eyez On Me*.

Naturally, New York was not going to be left out of the picture for too long. By the early 1990s, the Big Apple had its own thriving gangsta rap scene, but didn't achieve much wider acclaim until Notorious BIG released his *Ready To Die* album in 1994. It proved him to be one of the best from any hip hop era, with a sense of humour that drove his audacious rhyming skills and delivery to match the very best beats. In his slipstream were the Junior MAFIA posse, MOP, Capone-N-Noriega (who met in jail), Mobb Deep and Jay-Z, all of whom were a match for most of what came out of LA, shifting the power base eastwards. Too often, though, the rivalry between the two coasts, which occasionally escalated from merely a war of words, became the industry's and the media's focus and the quality of some of the music got overshadowed.

But whereas gangsta rap may originally have been an expression of black rage or frustration, it was quickly co-opted (by MTV and the fact that rap was now mainstream) as a kind of ghetto-style entertainment for thrill-seeking, socially rebelling whites. The audience changed and the artists began to play up to what was required of them. By the end of the 1990s, two of gangsta's biggest stars – Notorious BIG and Tupac – had been shot dead and the form had become a caricature of itself, providing an almost cartoon world of black violence and unpleasantness, increasingly irrelevant to many of its original audience. Ironically, the narrative power and vocabulary of the medium was taken up in spectacular fashion by Eminem (who also used Dr. Dre as a producer) to create a situation where the world's greatest rapper is white. But then the world's greatest golfer is black, so anything's possible.

Above
NWA was formed in 1986 by former drug-dealer Eazy-E (Eric Wright). Its line-up included luminaries Ice Cube (O'Shea Jackson) and Dr. Dre (Andre Young), who both went on to successful solo careers. Eazy-E died of AIDS in 1995.

ONCE HIP HOP HAD EXPANDED BEYOND APPARENTLY USING THE HOOK LINES FROM CHIC'S 'GOOD TIMES' AS THE BASIS FOR JUST ABOUT EVERYTHING, IT QUICKLY BECAME AS DIVERSE AS ANY OTHER BLACK MUSIC GENRE. ITS EVOLUTION IN RECORDING STUDIOS TOOK IT WAY BEYOND THE SCOPE OF CONVENTIONAL INSTRUMENTS. CAN'T PLAY PIANO LIKE HERBIE HANCOCK OR BASS LIKE BOOTSY? SO WHAT? SAMPLE IT.

Alternative

Above

Gang Starr is the Brooklyn-based duo of Keith Elam, aka Guru (left), and DJ Premier (right), whose innovative and captivating fusion of jazz and rap continue to earn popularity and critical acclaim.

THE downside to this is that almost anybody can duplicate what just about anybody else does. Successful sounds and riffs get copied to trend-setting proportions, meaning that on the populist level, hip hop can sound unimaginative and uniform. But below this surface, in terms of influences and achievements, nothing could be further from the truth. This was the case practically from day one.

A Stylistic Melting Pot

Founding father Afrika Bambaataa was as partial to a bit of Teutonic rock as he was solid funk, and his synth-heavy early collaborations with Arthur Baker and John Robie owed a great deal to Kraftwerk, his favourite group. Rock, rather than soul, played a big part in Run-DMC's introducing rap to MTV: their marrying of heavy metal with hip hop was highlighted in 'Walk This Way', a collaboration with Aerosmith. This style went on to become the basis of Def Jam's sound – hip hop's most successful record label in the 1980s.

Jazz was always a popular alternative foundation, as used to particular effect by Gang Starr, Digable Planets, the Pharcyde, the Roots and A Tribe Called Quest, the latter creating a mellow, contemplative, sophisticated experience. Chilling out was the rap lifestyle explored famously by De La Soul, which produced a popular alternative to the more high-profile macho posturings. They were followed down this flowered-up, rural-type road by the laid-back

> "THE WHOLE MEANING OF DIGABLE PLANETS IS THEY OPERATE ON THEIR OWN TERMS, WHICH IS THE ESSENCE OF HIP HOP. NOT FOR SELFISH REASONS, BUT AS AN EXAMPLE OF UNITY."
>
> *Mecca, Digable Planets*

Above Right

De La Soul became an instant sensation with their 1989 debut album, Three Feet High and Rising. Tracks such as 'Me, Myself and I' offered intricate rhythms that changed the face of hip hop.

likes of Black Eyed Peas and Arrested Development. Mantronix cleverly evolved from straight-ahead rap – albeit with a very musical bent – into an unique hip hop-flavoured dance style. The albums *Three Feet High And Rising* (De La Soul), *Bizarre Ride II* (the Pharcyde) and *Reachin'* (Digable Planets) all worked hard to redefine rap as the 1980s eased into the 1990s.

Taking It Further

Rap's Irish contingent was represented by House Of Pain ('Jump Around'), while the Beastie Boys introduced an *Animal House*, frat-boy wildness to hip hop and took it to a whole new pop audience. Hispanic hip hop has been well established by Kid Frost, who aimed squarely at LA's barrios with his low-riding ways, while Cypress Hill, which may have been mostly about getting stoned, remains overtly Latino. Most interesting in this area of late are Orishas, Paris-based Cuban exiles, who combine hip-hop techniques and rapping (in Spanish) spectacularly with traditional Cuban music (scratched-mixed) and singing.

Today, although gangsta seems to dominate, there are still plenty of alternatives. Rap and rock are common bedfellows: bands such as Fun Lovin' Criminals, Limp Bizkit and Linkin Park have all adopted a hip hop way of doing things, and Ice-T's thrash metal band Body Count is built on Onyx's punk rock/rap leanings. Digital Underground's cartoon antics paved the way for Ludacris, and Wu Tang Clan's whole presentation owes a great deal to the P-Funk concepts of twenty years previously. Then there's Eminem …

LEADING EXPONENTS

Gang Starr
Mantronix
De La Soul
Cypress Hill
Orishas
Arrested Development
The Goats

ALTERNATIVE

Repetitive bass lines and keyboard/synthesizer loops, together with a slightly more complex sequenced drum pattern, make up this style. The overall effect is a full and heavy sound, with the drum track very much in the foreground.

Synth Bass

Seq Drums

THE HIP HOP INTRO ➡ 334   HIP HOP PEOPLE A-Z ➡ 347   INSTRUMENTS A-Z ➡ 436   FOLK: POLITICAL FOLK & PROTEST SONGS ➡ 230

Artists: Hip Hop

Entries appear in the following order: name, music style, year(s) of popularity, type of artist, country of origin

2 Live Crew, Hip Hop, 1980s–, Artist, American
3rd Bass, Golden Age; Alternative, 1980s–1990s, Artist, American
Aceyalone, Hip Hop; Alternative, 1990s–, Artist, American
America's Most Wanted, Gangsta, 1990s, Artist, American
Ancient Beatbox, Old School, 1990s, Artist, American
Ant Banks, Gangsta, 1990s–, Artist, American
Arrested Development, Political; Alternative; Hip Hop 1990s, Artist, American
Artifacts, British, 1990s–, Artist, British
Assorted Phlavors, Gangsta, 1990s, Artist, American
AZ, Hip Hop; Gangsta, 1990s–, Artist, American
Badu, Erykah, Alternative; Hip Hop, 1990s, Artist, American
Ball, Kimberley, Old School, 1990s, Artist, American
Bambaataa, Afrika, Hip Hop; Old School, 1980s–, Artist; Producer, American
Base, Rob, Hip Hop, 1980s–, Artist, American
Basehead, Alternative; Political, 1990s, Artist, American
Beastie Boys, The, Old School; Golden Age; Alternative; Hip Hop, 1980s–, Artist, American
Beatnuts, The, Hip Hop, 1990s–, Artist, American
Big Daddy Kane, Hip Hop; Golden Age; Gangsta, 1980s–1990s, Artist, American
Big Punisher, Gangsta; 1990s, Artist, American
Biz Markie, Golden Age, 1980s–1990s, Artist, American
Blac Monks, Gangsta, 1990s, Artist, American
Black Grape, British, 1990s, Artist, British
Black Mophia Clan, Gangsta, 1990s, Artist, American
Black Sheep, Alternative; Golden Age; Hip Hop, 1990s, Artist, American
Black-Eyed Peas, Alternative, 1990s–, Artist, American
Blackstreet, Hip Hop, 1990s, Artist, American
B-Legit, Gangsta, 1990s–, Artist, American
Blige, Mary J., Hip Hop, 1990s–, Artist, American
Blood & Cripps, Gangsta, 1990s, Artist, American
Blow, Kurtis, Old School; Hip Hop 1970s–1980s, Artist, American
Bog Noyd, Gangsta, 1990s, Artist, American
Bone Thugs N Harmony, Gangsta; Hip Hop 1990s–, Artist, American
Boo, Gangsta, 1990s, Artist, American
Booby Jimmy & The Critters, Old School, 1980s–1990s, Artist, American
Boogie Boys, Old School, 1980s, Artist, American
Boogie Down Productions, Golden Age; Political; Gangsta, Hip Hop 1980s–1990s, Artist, American
Brand Nubian, Golden Age; Alternative, 1980s–1990s, Artist, American
Brotha Lynch Hung, Gangsta, 1990s–, Artist, American
Brown, Foxy, Hip Hop; Gangsta, 1990s–, Artist, American
Brown, Shawn, Old School, 1990s–, Artist, American
Bums, The, Gangsta, 1990s, Artist, American
Busta Rhymes, Gangsta; Alternative; Hip Hop, 1990s–, Artist, American
Busy Bee, Old School, 1990s, Artist, American
Canibus, Gangsta, 1990s–, Artist, Jamaican
Capone-N-Noriega, Gangsta, 1990s–, Artist, American
Captain Rapp, Old School, 1990s, Producer, American
Casper, Old School, 1980s, Artist, American
C-Bo, Gangsta, 1990s–, Artist, American
Celly Cell, Gangsta, 1990s–, Artist, American
Channel Live, Gangsta, 1990s–, Artist, American
Chino XL, Gangsta, 1990s, Artist, American
Chuck D., Hip Hop; Gangsta, 1980s–1990s, Artist, American
CIN, Gangsta, 1990s, Artist, American
Cold Crush Brothers, The Old School, 1990s, Artist, American
Common, Alternative; Political, 1990s–, Artist, American
Company Flow, Political, 1990s–, Artist, American
Compton's Most Wanted, Gangsta, 1990s–, Artist, American
Conscious Daughters, Gangsta, 1990s, Artist, American
Cool Nutz, Gangsta, 1990s–, Artist, American
Coolio, Hip Hop, 1990s, Artist, American
Cowboy, Old School, 1970s, Artist, American
Credit To The Nation, British, 1990s, Artist, British
Crime Boss, Gangsta, 1990s–, Artist, American
Cru, Gangsta, 1990s, Artist, American
Cypress Hill, Gangsta; Alternative, 1990s–, Artist, American
D Of Trinity Garden Cartel, Gangsta, 1990s, Artist, American
Da Bush Babees, Gangsta, 1990s, Artist, West Indian
Da Lench Mob, Gangsta, 1990s, Artist, American
Dan The Automator, Hip Hop; Alternative, 1990s–, Artist; Producer, American
Dane, Dana, Old School, 1980s–1990s, Artist, American
Darkroom Familia, Gangsta, 1990s–, Artist, American
Darkstar, Old School, 1980s–1990s, Artist, American
Das EFX, Golden Age; Hip Hop, 1990s, Artist, American
Dat Nigga Daz, Gangsta, 1990s, Artist, American
Davy DMX, Old School, 1990s, Artist, American
Daze, Gangsta, 1990s, Artist, Danish
De La Soul, Alternative; Golden Age, 1980s–, Artist, American
Dead Ringas, Gangsta, 1990s, Artist, American
Def Squad, Gangsta, 1980s–, Artist, American
Del Tha Funkee Homosapien, Alternative; Hip Hop, 1990s–, Artist, American
Delinquent Habits, Gangsta, 1990s–, Artist, American
Detroit's Most Wanted, Gangsta, 1990s–, Artist, American
Digable Planets, Alternative, 1990s, Artist, American
Digital Underground, Alternative; Hip Hop, 1980s–1990s, Artist, American
Disco Daddy, Old School, 1980s–, Artist, American
Disposable Heroes Of Hiphoprisy, The, Political; Alternative, 1990s, Artist, American
DJ Clue, Hip Hop, 1990s, Producer, American
DJ Flash, Old School, 1990s, Artist, American
DJ Hollywood, Old School, 1990s, Artist, American
DJ Jazzy Jeff & The Fresh Prince, Hip Hop, 1980s–1990s, Artist, American
DJ Kool Herc, Old School, 1970s–1990s, Artist, American
DJ Kool, Hip Hop; Old School, 1990s–, Artist; Producer, American
DJ Matrix, Old School, 1990s, Artist, American
DJ MT, Gangsta, 1990s–, Producer, American
DJ Muggs, Gangsta; Alternative, 1990s–, Artist; Producer, American
DJ Pooh, Gangsta, 1980s–, Producer, American
DJ Quik, Gangsta, 1990s–, Artist, American
DJ Red Alert, Old School; Hip Hop, 1980s–, Artist, American
DJ Shadow, Hip Hop, 1990s–, Artist; Producer, American
DMX, Gangsta, 1990s–, Artist, American
Do Or Die, Gangsta, 1990s–, Artist, American
DOC, The Gangsta, 1980s–1990s, Artist, American
Dog House Posse, Gangsta, 1990s, Artist, American
Doomsday Productions, Gangsta, 1990s–, Artist, American
Dr. Dre, Gangsta, 1980s–, Producer; Artist, American
Dr. Octagon, Hip Hop, 1990s–, Artist, American
Dream Warriors, Political, 1990s, Artist, Canadian
Dru Hill, Hip Hop, 1990s, Artist, American
D-Shot, Gangsta, 1990s, Artist, American
Dubee, Gangsta, 1990s–, Artist, American
Dupri, Jermaine, Hip Hop, 1990s–, Producer, American
Dust Brothers, The, Hip Hop, 1980s–, Artist, American
E-40, Gangsta, 1990s–, Artist, American
Eazy-E, Gangsta, 1980s–1990s, Artist, American
Ed OG & Da Bulldogs, Gangsta, 1990s, Artist, American
Egyptian Lover, The, Old School, 1980s–1990s, Artist, American
Elliot, Missy, Alternative; Hip Hop, 1990s–, Artist, American
Eminem, Gangsta; Hip Hop, 1990s–, Artist, American
EPMD, Golden Age; Gangsta, 1980s–1990s, Artist, American
Eric B & Rakim, Golden Age; Hip Hop, 1980s–1990s, Artist, American
ESG, Old School, 1980s–, Artist, American
Esham, Gangsta, 1990s–, Artist; Producer, American
Everlast, Alternative; Gangsta, 1980s–, Artist, American
Excalibur, Old School, 1990s, Artist, American
Facemob, Gangsta, 1990s–, Artist, American
Fat Boys, Old School; Hip Hop 1980s–1990s, Artist, American
Fat Joe, Gangsta, 1990s–, Artist, American
Fiend, Gangsta, 1990s, Artist, American
Fifth Ward Boyz, Gangsta, 1990s–, Artist, American
Filthy Rich, Gangsta, 1990s, Artist, American
Fo' Clips Eclipse, Gangsta, 1990s, Artist, American
Foe, Gangsta, 1990s, Artist, American
Freestyle Fellowship, Hip Hop; Political, 1990s–, Artist, American
Fresh Gordon, Old School, 1990s, Producer, American
Fresh, Doug E., Old School; Golden Age; Hip Hop 1980s–1990s, Artist, American
Fugees, The, Alternative; Hip Hop, 1990s, Artist, American
Full Force, Old School, 1980s–, Artist, American
Fun-Da-Mental, British, 1990s–, Artist, English
Funkmaster Flex, Hip Hop; Old School, 1990s–, Artist, American
Funky Four Plus One, Old School, 2000s–, Artist, American
Gang Starr, Golden Age; Political; Hip Hop, 1980s–1990s, Artist, American
Geto Boys, Gangsta, 1980s–1990s, Artist, American
Grand Puba, Golden Age, 1990s–, Artist, American
Grandmaster Flash, Old School; Hip Hop, 1980s–, Artist, West Indian
Gravediggaz, Gangsta, 1990s–, Artist, American
Heavy D & The Boyz, Hip Hop, 1980s–1990s, Artist, American
Hill, Lauryn, Alternative; Hip Hop, 1990s–, Artist, American
House Of Pain, Hip Hop; Gangsta, 1990s–, Artist, Irish
Ice Cube, Golden Age; Gangsta, 1980s–, Artist, American
Ice-T, Golden Age; Gangsta, 1980s–, Artist, American
Intelligent Hoodlum, Political, 1990s, Artist, American
Jayo Felony, Gangsta, 1990s–, Artist, American
Jay-Z, Hip Hop; Gangsta, 1990s–, Artist; Producer, American
Jean, Wyclif, Hip Hop; Alternative, 1990s–, Producer; Artist, American
Jeru The Damaja, Gangsta; Hip Hop 1990s, Producer; Songwriter; Artist, American
Jungle Brothers, Golden Age; Political; Alternative; Hip Hop, 1980s–, Artist, American
Junior MAFIA, Gangsta, 1990s, Artist, American
Jurassic 5, Alternative; Hip Hop, 1990s–, Artist, American
Kid Frost, Old School, 1990s, Artist, American
King, Dee Dee, Old School, 1980s, Artist, American
Knights Of The Turntables, Old School, 1990s, Artist, American
Kool G. Rap & DJ Polo, Golden Age; Gangsta, 1980s–1990s, Artist, American
Kool Keith, Hip Hop, 1990s–, Artist; Producer, American
Kool Moe Dee, Golden Age; Old School, 1980s–1990s, Artist, American
KRS-One, Political; Gangsta; Hip Hop, 1990s–, Artist, American
Kurupt, Gangsta, 1990s–, Artist; Producer, American
LA Dream Team, Old School, 1980s, Artist, American
Lightnin' Rod, Old School, 1970s, Artist, American
Lil' Blunt, Gangsta, 1990s–, Artist, American
Lil' Kim, Gangsta; Hip Hop, 1990s–, Artist, American
LL Cool J, Golden Age; Hip Hop, 1980s–, Artist; Songwriter, American
Lords Of The Underground, Hardcore; Golden Age; Gangsta, 1990s, Artist, American
Mack 10, Gangsta, 1990s–, Artist, American
Mack, Craig, Hip Hop, 1990s–, Artist, American
Madrok, Old School, 1990s, Artist, American
Main Source, Golden Age; Alternative; Hip Hop, 1980s–1990s, Artist, American
Mantronix, Golden Age; Old School; Hip Hop, 1980s–1990s, Artist, American
Marley Marl, Golden Age; Old School; Hip Hop, 1980s–, Artist, American
Masta Ace Incorporated, Gangsta, 1990s, Artist, American
Master P, Gangsta; Hip Hop, 1990s–, Artist; Producer, American
MC Breed, Gangsta, 1990s–, Artist, American
MC Hammer, Hip Hop, 1980s–, Artist, American
MC Ren, Gangsta, 1990s–, Artist, American
MC Shan, Golden Age; Old School, 1980s–1990s, Artist, American
Melle Mel, Old School, 1980s–1990s, Artist, American
Method Man, Gangsta; Hip Hop, 1990s–, Artist, American
Mia X, Gangsta, 1990s, Artist, American
Mix Master Mike, HipHop; Alternative, 1990s–, Artist, American
Mobb Deep, Gangsta; Hip Hop, 1990s–, Artist, American
Monch, Pharaoh, Hip Hop; Alternative, 1990s–, Artist, American
Monie Love, British, 1980s–, Artist, British
Mos Def, Political; Hip Hop, 1990s–, Artist, American
Mr Quikk, Gangsta, 1990s–, Artist, American
Naughty By Nature, Golden Age; Gangsta, 1990s–, Artist, American
Newcleus, Old School, 1980s, Artist, American
Nice & Smooth, Hip Hop; Golden Age, 1980s–1990s, Artist, American
Noriega, Gangsta, 1990s–, Artist, American
Notorious BIG, Gangsta; Hip Hop, 1990s, Artist, American
NWA, Golden Age; Gangsta, 1980s–1990s, Artist, American
Onyx, Gangsta, 1990s–, Artist, American
OutKast, Alternative; Hip Hop, 1990s–, Artist, American
P. Diddy/Puff Daddy, Hip Hop, 1990s–, Artist, American
Padilla, Rocky, Old School, 1990s, Producer, American
Paris, Political; Gangsta, 1980s–1990s, Artist, American
Pharcyde, The, Political; Alternative; Hip Hop, 1990s–, Artist, American
PM Dawn, Alternative, 1990s, Artist, British
Poor Righteous Teachers, Golden Age; Political, 1980s–, Artist, American
Positive Force, Old School, 1990s, Artist, American
Prime Minister Pete Nice & Daddy Rich, Alternative, 1990s, Artist, American
Prince Paul, Alternative; Hip Hop, 1990s, Producer, American
Public Enemy, Golden Age; Political; Hip Hop, 1980s–, Artist, American
Puff Daddy/P. Diddy, Hip Hop, 1990s–, Artist, American
Q-Tip, Alternative, 1980s–, Artist, American
Queen Latifah, Golden Age; Alternative, Hip Hop, 1980s–1990s, Artist, American
Rakim, Hip Hop; Gangsta, 1990s, Artist, American
Rappin' 4-Tay, Gangsta, 1990s, Artist, American
Redman, Hip Hop; Gangsta, 1990s–, Artist; Producer, American
Rock, Pete, & CL Smooth, Golden Age; Hip Hop, 1990s, Artist, American
Rodney O.. Old School, 1980s–1990s, Artist, American
Roots, The, Alternative; Hip Hop, 1990s–, Artist, American
Run-DMC, Golden Age; Hip Hop, 1980s–, Artist, American
RZA, Gangsta, Alternative, 1990s–, Artist, American
Salt-N-Pepa, Golden Age; Hip Hop, 1980s–1990s, Artist, American
Scarface, Gangsta, 1990s–, Artist, American
Schoolly D, Golden Age; Gangsta, 1980s–, Artist, American
Sequence, The, Old School, 1980s–1990s, Artist, American
Shakur, Tupac, Gangsta, 1990s, Artist, American
Shanté, Roxanne, Golden Age; Old School, 1980s–1990s, Artist, American
Silkk The Shocker, Gangsta, 1990s–, Artist, American
Sister Souljah, Political; Gangsta, 1990s, Artist, American
Skinny Boys, The, Old School, 1970s–1980s, Artist, American
Skinyele, Gangsta, 1990s–, Artist, American
Slick Rick, Golden Age; Gangsta; Hip Hop, 1980s–1990s, Artist, British
Smith, Will, Hip Hop, 1990s–, Artist, American
Snoop Dogg, Gangsta, 1990s–, Artist, American
Soul Assassins, Gangsta, 1990s, Artist, American
Spearhead, Political; Alternative, 1990s–, Artist, American
Spice 1, Gangsta, 1980s, Artist, American
Spoonie Gee, Old School; Hip Hop, 1970s–1980s, Artist, British
Spyder-D, Old School, 2000s–, Producer, American
Stetsasonic, Hip Hop; Golden Age, 1980s–1990s, Artist, American
Sugarhill Gang, The, Old School, 1970s–1990s, Artist, American
Tee, Howie, Old School, 1980s, Producer, American
Tee, Toddy, Old School, 1990s, Producer, American
Timbaland, Hip Hop, 1990s–, Producer, American
Timex Social Club, Old School, 1980s, Artist, American
TLC, Hip Hop, 1990s–, Artist, American
Too Short, Golden Age; Gangsta, 1980s–, Artist, American
Treacherous Three, Old School, 1980s–, Artist, American
Tribe Called Quest, A, Alternative; Hip Hop, 1980s–1990s, Artist, American
Trouble Funk, Old School, 1970s–1990s, Artist, American
Two-Bigg MCs, Old School, 1990s, Artist, American
Ultramagnetic MCs, Golden Age; Hip Hop, 1980s–1990s, Artist, American
Uncle Jam's Army, Old School, 1980s, Artist, American
Unknown DJ, The, Old School, 1980s–1990s, Artist; Producer, American
UTFO, Old School, 1980s–1990s, Artist, American
Westside Connection, Gangsta, 1990s, Artist, American
Whodini, Golden Age; Old School;Hip Hop 1980s–1990s, Artist, American
Wildbunch, The, British, 1990s–, Artist, British
World Class Wreckin' Crew, Old School Rap, 1980s, Artist, American
Wu-Tang Clan, Hip Hop; Gangsta, 1990s–, Artist, American
X-Clan, Political; Golden Age, 1980s–1990s, Artist, American
X-Ecutioners, The,Hip Hop, 1990s–, Artist, American
Young MC, British, 1980s–, Artist, British

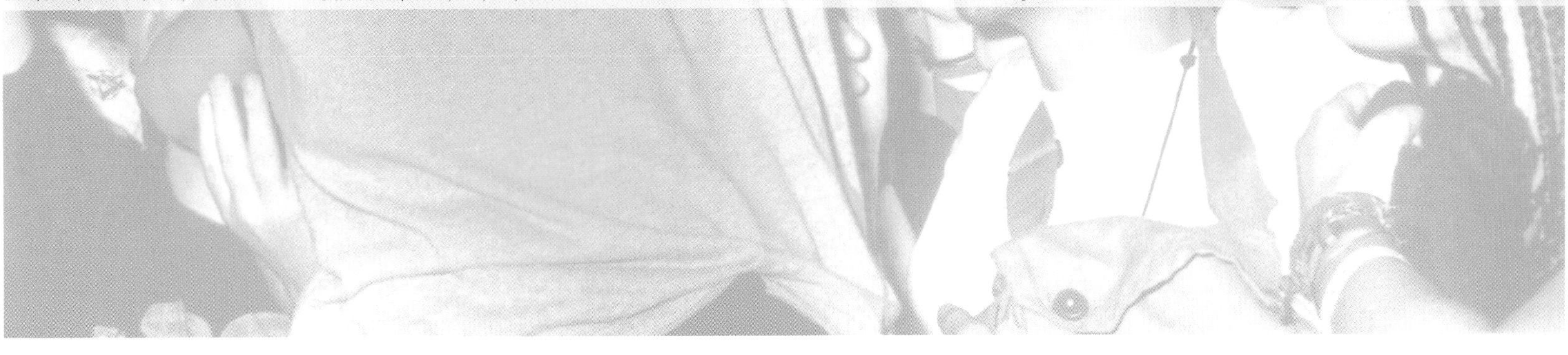

Reggae

REGGAE is unique. No other style has made so much out of its original musical resources to present itself in so many different guises with only a couple of structural changes in over 40 years. No other style has so accurately reflected the people that create and consume it. Jamaican music's relationship with its people is such that it is not unusual for music to influence political and social change as much as it does the other way around. No other community has had such a large and successful musical output. The music is also extremely influential: without dub the reggae remix culture would not exist, and reggae's deejay style is directly responsible for one of the biggest international genres of recent times – rap. But then no other music serves its audience first and its industry second. To understand this and, indeed, reggae and its various subsections, it is necessary to appreciate the importance of the sound system.

The sound system has existed longer than Jamaican music itself. In the late 1950s, an enterprising generation of dance promoters found it made much more sense to play records instead of hiring bands. This opened dances up to a much wider section of the population and the sound system lawns, huge open-air spaces where the latest American R&B records boomed out, became the entertainment staple of downtown Kingston's poor. The sound system lawn was the place to be, something uniquely ghetto which was looked down on by the middle classes: all local life could be found there, presided over by sound men who would be local

heroes. To keep themselves ahead of the rest, the sound men continually searched for new and exclusive records to play, and it was not too long before they started making their own. Jamaica's first record producers, Prince Buster, Duke Reid and Coxsone Dodd, were all sound men recording tunes to play at their dances, with no intention of offering anything up for sale.

And nothing has really changed, other than the fact that they soon found it was possible to sell the records that got the best reactions, so every sound man worth his system started his own record label. The sound system soon became a valuable testing ground, and the recording side of their businesses would stay in touch with market forces by seeing which versions of which tunes were most eagerly received. The reaction of the sound system crowds were responsible for the sound men taking reggae down new avenues: Dodd and Buster switched from playing R&B records to something more indigenous and came up with ska and records like 'Easy Snappin'' and 'Oh Carolina'. Duke Reid saw the potential in having instrumental versions of tunes and a deejay "toasting" records (where the deejay talks in rhyme in time to the beat), and released singles such as U-Roy's 'Wear You To The Ball' and 'Wake The Town'. King Tubby's live sound system mixes convinced him there was a market for dub records, and Big Youth tuned into the demand for roots and culture by deejaying on a sound system. King Jammy's 'Sleng Teng' experiment in 1985, which changed the face of reggae forever, would have gone no further if the crowd at its sound system had not gone wild for the first tune with no bass line…

It is this mutual participation and shared sense of ownership of reggae that has kept it as a genuine folk music, and as one of the world's most exciting, vibrant pop cultures.

"WE DIDN'T SET OUT TO DELIBERATELY CORRUPT AMERICAN R&B, WE JUST WANTED TO DO IT WITH OUR JAMAICAN FEELING."

Ernest Ranglin

Above
Some 100,000 records have been released in Jamaica over the last 45 years, which is not bad considering the current population stands at just over two and a half million.

STYLES

Ska

Rock Steady

Roots

Dub

UK Reggae

Reggae Pop

Ragga

Dancehall

Bobo Dread Deejays

US Reggae

Deejays

REGGAE STYLE

Reggae music is characterized by the emphasis on the off-beat, which pulls the tempo back and gives the music a laid-back feel. A strong bass line makes the music easier to dance to.

Bob Marley

SKA REPRESENTS THE BIRTH OF MODERN POPULAR JAMAICAN MUSIC, AND IT DOES SO WITH THE ACCENT ON "JAMAICAN". WHILE THIS RAUCOUS, UPTEMPO, GOOD-TIMES MUSIC MAY HAVE HAD ITS ROOTS IN AMERICAN BIG-BAND JAZZ AND R&B, IT WAS CONCEIVED AS A CELEBRATION OF JAMAICAN INDEPENDENCE.

Ska

SKA is the link between the virtuoso playing of Kingston's sophisticated nightclub musicians and the vibrancy of the downtown sound systems. It revolutionized Jamaican life and the island's place in the world at the time.

As an alternative to the very English radio programming in pre-independence Jamaica (light classics, light jazz and light chat), citizens were tuning into the powerful radio stations broadcasting from New Orleans and Miami, which presented a steady diet of R&B, blues and jump jazz. As a result, American music was informing Jamaican popular taste, and while it might have been a great deal of fun, such cultural colonialism in the 1950s, after the island's independence process had been set in motion, no longer fitted the mood. By then, Jamaican-ness was what counted, and so a home-grown soundtrack was obligatory. Ska was that music, and it was taken straight to people's hearts because it was born downtown among those same people at their sound system dances.

> ## "SKA WAS OUR TYPE OF MUSIC THAT COULD LIFT THE YOUTH AND MAKE JAMAICA KNOWN AROUND THE WORLD."
> *Lloyd Brevett*

Above

Officially formed in 1964 in Jamaica, the Skatalites were central to the ska age. A prodigious group of musicians, they backed most of the top singing stars of the day.

Identifiably Jamaican

At its essence, ska is an R&B structure and a jazz attitude, mixed together with enough Jamaican flavouring to give it its own identity. And, like practically every subsequent musical development on the island, it was precipitated by sound men. Coxsone Dodd and Prince Buster, two of Jamaica's biggest sound men, read the mood and wanted to change the beat. By the start of the 1960s, they were running out of new R&B

LEADING EXPONENTS

Prince Buster
The Skatalites
Desmond Dekker
Don Drummond
Jimmy Cliff
Rico Rodriguez
Theophilus Beckford
The Maytals
The Wailers
Derrick Morgan

SKA

Ska features a very simple bass on the beat with the keyboards and guitar bouncing off the beat. The um-ska sound given, which gave ska its name, is the basis for virtually all reggae styles that followed.

THE REGGAE INTRO ➡ 348   REGGAE PEOPLE A–Z ➡ 367   INSTRUMENTS A–Z ➡ 436   POP: 2-TONE ➡ 52   THE JAZZ INTRO ➡ 118

records to play at their dances. They needed a change of music to keep them out in front of their rivals, and they and their crowds were getting swept along by independence fever. As a result, and independently of each other, Buster and Dodd both devised variations on the standard R&B boogie rhythm to create something new that was also identifiably Jamaican.

Buster and Dodd both retained the shuffle beat from R&B to power ska along as a dance style, and this can be heard when they cut, respectively, tracks like 'Oh Carolina' by the Folkes Brothers or 'They Got To Go' by Buster himself, and 'Easy Snappin'' by Theophilus Beckford or 'Time to Play' by the Mello Larks. As can also be heard on these (almost) prototype records, they both switched the arrangement's emphasis around from the first and third beats of the bar to the second and fourth, creating the off-beat focus that remained at the centre of Jamaican music for years to come. Whereas Dodd, a jazz fan, then looked to add instrumental passages, Buster opted for more intrinsically Jamaican additions such as Rasta drumming and mento (Jamaican calypso) references. This was the basis of the ska sound and it expanded into music that was galloping, virtuosic and largely instrumental, thanks to a pool of superb players on the island. Many of these players had been classically trained and studied the likes of Dizzy Gillespie, Charlie Parker and Thelonius Monk, and made their livings playing dance music to demanding American hotel crowds. These musicians at last had their own medium – ska – through which they could express themselves as they pleased among their own people (many lived in the ghettos and went uptown only to work). Players as talented as the Skatalites, Don Drummond and Prince Buster's All Stars produced tracks like 'Guns Of Navarone', 'Phoenix City', 'Man In The Street', 'Madness', 'The Reburial', 'Al Capone' and 'Confucius'.

Establishing The Sound

For much of its lifetime, ska was played more in the dancehalls than in the recording studios, and the classic ska orchestra, rhythm-driven and horn-heavy, involved between 10 and 20 players. In true jazz style the soloists worked as hard to impress each other as much as they did the paying customers, and cutting contests were commonplace, in which musicians strove to outdo each other by alternating increasingly tricky lines, fired by sheer musical audacity as much as by conventional skill. Central to ska were the Skatalites, from the rhythm section of Lloyd Knibbs (drums) and Lloyd Brevett (bass) through guitarists Jah Jerry and Ernest Ranglin and pianist Jackie Mittoo, and the brass players: trombonist Don Drummond, saxmen Tommy McCook, Lester Sterling and Roland Alphonso and trumpeter Dizzy Moore. They were the

epitome of a ska band and one of the best Jamaican groups ever. The ska era also benefited greatly from a generation of brass players that all came from the Alpha Boys School, an establishment run by nuns for wayward or abandoned boys that mixed strict discipline with the best music department and marching bands in Jamaica. Horn players Don Drummond, Tommy McCook, Rico Rodriguez, Lester Sterling, Dizzy Moore and Eddie Thornton are all Alpha alumni.

Of course, ska wasn't all about playing, and singers such as Jimmy Cliff ('King Of Kings'), the Wailers ('Simmer Down'), Ken Boothe, Desmond Dekker, Lee Perry, Delroy Wilson, the Maytals ('Never Grow Old'), Millie Small and Derrick Morgan ('Forward March') were all ska stars. It was as much them as the musicians and producers, including Prince Buster, Leslie Kong, Duke Reid, Coxsone Dodd and Vincent Chin, that were responsible for ska's laying the foundations of the Jamaican recording industry and taking its music all over the world.

Left

Prince Buster, who dubbed himself "the Voice of the People", was responsible for giving a voice to the people with 'Oh Carolina', which expressed black Jamaican-ness through a commercially viable medium.

Below

Clement "Coxsone" Dodd, the sound system man and prolific producer, opened a recording studio and launched his Studio One label in 1963, working with top names of the day, including the Wailers and the Skatalites.

Rock Steady

SELDOM HAS A STYLE OF MUSIC BEEN NAMED WITH GREATER ACCURACY THAN ROCK STEADY. LIKE SO MANY OTHER JAMAICAN GENRES, IT TOOK ITS NAME FROM A DANCE, IN WHICH PARTICIPANTS PLANTED THEIR FEET AND "ROCKED STEADY". WHEN ROCK STEADY BEGAN TO DOMINATE THE DANCEHALLS IN THE MID-1960S, IT WAS THE ANTITHESIS TO SKA'S ROLLICKING, BIG-BAND, JAZZ-BASED, HORN-HEAVY FRENZY.

Above

The material issued from Arthur "Duke" Reid's Treasure Island studios during the rock steady era exemplifies the cool and elegant feel of the music.

WHILE it presented a silkier, smoother aspect of the music, it also pushed singing and singers to the fore in a way that hadn't been fashionable in Jamaican music for the previous few years. Rock steady owed a great deal to the soul groups who were doing so well in the US at that time – the Impressions, the Drifters, the Dells. But the undisputed king of rock steady was Duke Reid, sound system owner, record producer and fearsome former policeman.

Slowing It Down

The rock steady style became official, as it were, in 1966, when Alton Ellis's huge hit 'Rock Steady' was the first record to use the term as a title, but his lyric was merely offering instruction for a dance that had already existed for a couple of years. Sound system operators looking for a change of pace amid ska's relentless vigour had been promoting "Midnight Hour" sessions when, at the appointed time, they'd spin 60 minutes of blues, soul or slow ska to give the dancers a breather, during which time the fashionable cool-down moves were merely to sway in time to the beat.

Naturally, record producers were quick to pick up on this and started to record tracks specifically

> "ASK ANY JAMAICAN MUSICIAN AND THEY'LL TELL YOU THE ROCK STEADY DAYS WERE THE BEST DAYS OF JAMAICAN MUSIC."
>
> *Derrick Harriot*

LEADING EXPONENTS

Duke Reid

The Paragons

The Heptones

Slim Smith

The Wailers

The Melodians

Alton Ellis

Phillis Dillon

ROCK STEADY

The rock steady sound is more laid-back then that of ska. A simple drum beat, sparse guitar style and a lazy bass groove are combined at a slow tempo to characterize the sound.

for it, a move which was responsible for several enormous changes in Jamaican musical style. The slower, more soulful numbers allowed singers to be far more prominent, and it was during this era that so many of Jamaican music's biggest stars came to prominence: Ken Boothe, Slim Smith, John Holt, Delroy Wilson, Bob Andy, Pat Kelly, Alton Ellis, Marcia Griffiths, Hopeton Lewis and Phillis Dillon are all products of rock steady, as is what became known as the classic Jamaican three-part harmony style. Popular US group the Impressions, led by Curtis Mayfield, regularly toured Jamaica in the mid-1960s, and it was their singing structure that became the basis of the Jamaican three-part harmony style: all three voices sharing the lead, often alternating in the same verse (rather than using clearly defined lead and background singers) to create a fabulous depth of harmony and provide continual surprises for the listener. Bob Marley's Wailers slimmed down to a trio in 1966 and took their place alongside such other brilliant threesomes such as the Melodians, the Paragons, the Jamaicans, the Uniques, the Techniques, the Heptones and the Gaylads.

Defining The Sound

Musically the changes were just as significant, as record producers switched big bands with groups to back these singers, as much an economic measure as it was fear that the vocalists would get lost against the orchestras. The introduction of the electric bass and electric organ did much to facilitate this change and shaped the sounds that were to dominate Jamaican music for the next 20 years. It was true that rock steady was in the same 4/4 time as ska and similarly on the off-beat, just with its tempo slowed down, but the new bass guitars were much more imposing than the acoustic double bass. Instead of underlining the drumbeats, the guitars formed the foundation of the rhythm with their own syncopated patterns. While the kick drum emphasized this slowing down by sounding on the third beat only (known as "the one drop"), the guitar chopped out chords on the second and fourth beats. It may have been rock steady in the mid-1960s, but it was the obvious basis of the reggae that was to follow.

Although ska producers Prince Buster and Coxsone Dodd made some interesting rock steady records, and new faces Sonia Pottinger, Bunny Lee and Joe Gibbs produced some excellent tunes, this period really belonged to Duke Reid and his Trojan sound system. An R&B and soul fan, he'd produced some excellent Jamaican boogie and ska sides, but this was the style he truly connected with. Having assembled the best of Jamaica's new wave of musicians – including guitarist Lynn Taitt, drummer Drumbago, organist Winston Wright and saxman Tommy McCook – and overseeing most of the activity in his studio deep in downtown Kingston, Reid's Treasure Isle label was a rock steady byword. 'On The Beach' and 'The Tide Is High' (the Paragons), 'Queen Majesty' and 'You Don't Care' (the Techniques), 'Swing & Dine' and 'I Will Get Along' (the Melodians) are just six of the stream of classics that came out of there. These records were so technically well recorded and their arrangements so spot on that their rhythm tracks continue to be used by today's dancehall reggae producers.

Above

The Heptones (Leroy Sibbles, Barry Llewellyn and Earl Morgan) are one of the most important trios of the 1960s and 1970s. They played a key role in the transition between ska and rock steady with their exquisite three-part harmonies.

Left

Alton Ellis was one of the consummate vocalists of the rock steady era. Since then, he has gone on to record scores of reggae songs, and in 1984 was celebrated internationally for 25 years in show business.

Roots

ROOTS REGGAE IS PROBABLY THE BEST-KNOWN GENRE OF JAMAICAN MUSIC. THANKS TO ARTISTS SUCH AS BOB MARLEY AND BURNING SPEAR, IT ACHIEVED GENUINE WORLDWIDE SUCCESS. THROUGH THESE ARTISTS AND THEIR CAREFULLY ARTICULATED POLITICAL DISSENT, SOCIAL COMMENTARIES AND PRAISES TO JAH RASTAFARI, IT HAS BEEN ACCEPTED ACROSS THE WORLD AS ONE OF THE MOST POTENT PROTEST MUSICS.

> "ROOTS AND CULTURE WAS A NECESSITY, THE TIMES CALLED FOR A POSITIVE STANCE...."
>
> *Jimmy Cliff*

Above

The deejay Prince Far-I was known for his gruff voice and critiques aimed at the government of the time. His 'Under Heavy Manners' took a lyrical stance against new measures initiated towards violent crime.

LEADING EXPONENTS

Burning Spear
The Mighty Diamonds
Bob Marley
Big Youth
Augustus Pablo
Luciano
Black Uhuru
Culture
Lee Perry
Peter Tosh

ROOTS reggae grew up in Kingston's slums in the early 1970s, as the ghetto dwellers – or "sufferahs" as they called themselves – wanted to express their dissatisfaction at a government that, almost a decade after independence, had failed to deliver on its promises for a better life. If anything, ordinary people were worse off. Many were turning to Rastafarianism, if not going so far as to grow dreadlocks then at least following its principles as a way of surviving the harsh times as Jamaica's underclass. Rasta is a faith inspired by Marcus Garvey (1870–1940) who believed that black Caribbeans were the lost tribes of Israel, and that they should rid themselves of the oppressions of the west and return to the promised land, to Africa. Rasta espoused black self-help and self-respect, and it struck a particular chord with a people less than a century removed from the slave ships. And this being Jamaica, popular feeling soon found its way into popular song.

Finding A Voice

It was on the sound systems that the voices of protest first made themselves heard, as people could simply pick up the mic and chat about anything they wanted to, provided it was on the beat. This was a new breed of deejays, who felt the same pressures as their audiences and gave voice to them in a way the people could identify with. It was then that Big Youth, Prince Jazzbo, I-Roy and Prince Far-I built up huge followings and went on to have hits with tunes like 'Heavy Manners' (Prince Far-I), 'Natty Cultural Dread' (Big Youth) and 'Natty Passing Thru' (Prince Jazzbo). It did not take long for a new wave of producers to sit up and take notice, and who saw this new attitude as their chance to make an impact: Gussie Clarke, Augustus Pablo, Keith Hudson, Niney, Jack Ruby, Lee Perry and Yabby U all made their names producing roots reggae's first records.

Once it became obvious that there was a market for protest music, it broadened out and as Michael Manley's People's National Party, voted into office in 1972, was far more tolerant of Rastafari, reggae's whole tone changed. As part of the shift towards Rasta's ganja-fuelled spirituality, rhythms slowed, basslines became more pronounced, east-Africanisms began to creep in, dub versions sought to intimidate with the very weight of their presence, and lyrics pulled few punches as they told of society's ills and preached revolution.

The Main Man

Singers like Culture ('Two Sevens Clash'), the Mighty Diamonds ('Right Time'), the Abyssinians ('Satta Massa Gana'), Max Romeo ('War Inna Babylon') and the Congos ('Heart Of The Congos') made sure the roots era took Jamaican music all over the world, but none made a bigger impact than Bob Marley. First with Peter Tosh and Bunny Wailer as part of the Wailers, releasing albums like *Catch A Fire* and *Burning*, Marley showed he had all the sensibilities and charisma to take roots reggae to rock-star levels. In 1974 the Wailers split, going on to pursue international solo careers.

ROOTS

Roots is probably the "purest" form of reggae. Similar to rock steady in style, the lyrical content usually bears a Rastafarian or political influence, but the style also makes a sound basis for love ballads.

THE REGGAE INTRO ➡ 348   REGGAE PEOPLE A-Z ➡ 367   INSTRUMENTS A-Z ➡ 436   POP: 2-TONE ➡ 52   THE BLUES INTRO ➡ 154

Tosh's *Legalise It* remains a dope-smoker's anthem, and Wailer's *Blackheart Man* is one of roots reggae's best albums. Bob Marley's star burned brightest, though, and through albums such as *Exodus*, *Natty Dread* and *Kaya* he quickly became the biggest artist Jamaica has ever produced. He was an easily understood figurehead, and through his depth of purpose, virtuoso musicianship and close associations with high-grade marijuana, roots reggae found a place for itself in mainstream rock that Jamaican music had not achieved before or has since.

Roots Lives On

Roots'n'culture seemed to fade out at the end of the 1970s, as so many in Jamaica believed that 10 years of sufferation had made no difference at all and that it was time to have some fun. In the wider world, once Bob Marley died in 1981, the mainstream record industry seemed to lose interest as it couldn't see another obviously rock-friendly leader. However, during the 1990s, as reggae's pendulum swung the other way towards glorifying violence, misogyny, homophobia and general unpleasantness, the roots movement has undergone something of a revival through deeply spiritual artists like Luciano ('Where There Is Life'), Bushman ('Nyah Man Chant'), Tony Rebel ('If Jah'), Cocoa Tea ('One Way'), Morgan Heritage ('Protect Us Jah') and the Bobo deejays Sizzla ('Black Woman And Child'), Capleton ('More Fire') and Anthony B ('Real Revolutionary').

Below

Producer Lee Perry became an important part of the roots'n'culture movement. His single 'People Funny Boy' used a lazy, bass-driven beat, the first Jamaican pop record to signal the shift from upbeat ska to the languor of roots.

IN JAMAICA, NOTHING GETS THROWN AWAY. OIL DRUMS, FLOORBOARDS ... MORE OR LESS EVERYTHING HAS TO BE USED AGAIN AT LEAST ONCE, INCLUDING MUSIC. WHY THROW A TUNE AWAY JUST BECAUSE IT'S BEEN A HIT, WHEN THE SAME RHYTHM CAN BE REDRESSED WITH NEW LYRICS OR RADICALLY ALTERED INSTRUMENTATION TO LIVEN UP THE DANCEHALLS AGAIN? AND AGAIN. AND AGAIN.

Dub

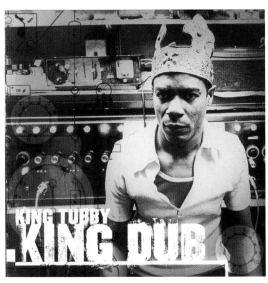

> "KING TUBBY TRULY UNDERSTOOD SOUND, IN A SCIENTIFIC SENSE. HE KNEW HOW THE CIRCUITS WORKED AND WHAT THE ELECTRONS DID. THAT'S WHY HE COULD DO WHAT HE DID."
> *Mikey Dread*

TO many outside reggae, this constant recycling smacks of musical laziness or creative bankruptcy. However, in the 1970s, as remixing became a greater and greater part of the Kingston studio culture, it evolved into dub, which was an art form in itself. In Jamaica, to "dub" a tune meant more than merely to remix it. Using echo and reverb, sound effects, frequency control and, most importantly, dexterous and inventive use of faders, dub masters such as King Tubby, Errol T, Mikey Dread, Scientist, King Jammy's, Jack Ruby and Niney could totally turn a tune round by remixing it. Dub is a world where every rhythm track has endless possibilities and what may have begun life as a smoochy love song could end up as a militant roots reggae stepper. It is a world where the studio itself becomes the most important instrument; where whole albums are devoted to different takes of the same track; and a world that inspired the likes of Arthur Baker and Fatboy Slim,

but for years was unique to reggae. Dub albums like *Garvey's Ghost* (dubs of Burning Spear's *Marcus Garvey*), Augustus Pablo's *King Tubby Meets Rockers Uptown*, the Joe Gibbs and Errol Thompson-mixed *African Dub Chapter Three* and Sly & Robbie's *Raiders Of The Lost Dub* are among the best examples of what dub is all about.

A Happy Accident

It all began by accident. In 1967, a disc cutter accidentally left the vocal track off a disc, and the sound system operator he was cutting for followed the correct cut of the tune (the Paragons' 'On The Beach') with an instrumental version; the crowd went wild because they had a unique cut of a song they could sing along to. Suddenly every sound man wanted instrumentals, and because so many of the bigger operators were also record producers, they began to record various takes featuring different lead instruments. As an abbreviation of "instrumental versions", these takes without the vocal became known simply as "versions", which in time became a verb, and to "version" a tune meant to remix it. The instrumental sides were

LEADING EXPONENTS

King Tubby
Mikey Dread
Scientist
Bobby Digital
King Jammy's
Lee Perry
Errol T
Denis Bovell

DUB

A dub track will usually have most of the vocals removed. The instruments are then taken out of the mix gradually and brought back in with heavy use of studio sound effects such as echo and reverb.

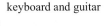
keyboard and guitar

bass

THE REGGAE INTRO ➡ 348   REGGAE PEOPLE A–Z ➡ 367   INSTRUMENTS A–Z ➡ 436   REGGAE: ROOTS ➡ 354   REGGAE: DANCEHALL ➡ 362

perfect for a sound system's deejay to toast over, and became even more exciting when the original vocals were mixed in and out, allowing the deejay to interact with important snatches of the song. From there, as technology allowed instruments to be faded out and brought back into the mix, the creation of Dub As We Know It was only a matter of time.

Dubby Brilliant

At the forefront of the 1970s dub developments, and still revered as the genius founding father of the style, was King Tubby, sound system owner, disc cutter, mixer and electronics wizard. Tubby took dub from simply being a hole in the mix in which deejays did their thing, to manipulating the elements of a tune with such imagination and precision he could unearth vibes buried within it that the original producer didn't even know existed. What set Tubby apart was his electronics skill. His sound system was known all over Jamaica as much for its tonal quality as its power, and as part of the controls he devised and constructed a series of electronic frequency filters so precise he could drop different instruments in and out of the records he played. He built his remixing reputation on this same equipment, and once he got a proper mixing desk he immediately rebuilt it to better suit his purpose, then added all manner of either home-made or radically customized outboard gear such as echo machines and sound-effects packages. Refusing to be limited by the scope of his studio, King Tubby

continually modified it, rewiring circuits on the spot in order to achieve the effect or sound he had in his head.

Understandably, King Tubby had Jamaica's top producers queuing for his services, and he formed the basis for dub's dynasty: Tubby ruled the 1970s; Mikey Dread and Scientist, both King Tubby's apprentices, were the kings of early 1980s dub; King Jammy's, who ruled the roost in the 1990s, was Tubby's engineer; and Bobby Digital, one of today's dub masters, was Jammy's engineer.

Remixing Old Favourites

Dancehall reggae, which took over from roots at the end of the 1970s, was made for dub – it was increasingly computerized, and was deejay-dominated. However, it was more of a return to the old ways of straight versioning rather than fiddling about with tunes to turn them into something else. It was dancehall in the 1980s that started the trend that still exists in reggae, whereby producers create rhythm tracks, and if one proves popular with the dancehall crowds they will get a host of different deejays and singers, each with their own lyrics, to record versions of it. Some of the more successful rhythms in songs like 'Boops', 'Punany', 'Sleng Teng', 'Stalag 17' and 'Playground' have been versioned literally hundreds of times.

Many see this way of doing things as stunting reggae's creativity, but the same thing was said about versioning when it first caught on 30 years ago – and what did that blossom into?

BRITAIN HAS HAD A THRIVING REGGAE SCENE FOR AS LONG AS THERE'S BEEN REGGAE. THERE WERE SOUND SYSTEMS IN LONDON IN THE 1950S, IMPORTING THE SAME AMERICAN R&B RECORDS AS THEIR KINGSTONIAN COUNTERPARTS, AND SKA WAS RECORDED IN THE UK FROM THE EARLY 1960S.

UK Reggae

Above

Aswad, meaning "black" in Arabic, are one of Britain's greatest roots outfits dating from the 1970s. Their unique sound comprises jazz, funk, soul and fusion layered over a rock steady reggae beat.

BUT while the British sound systems were a carbon copy of Jamaican rigs, the music made in the UK was always slightly different. Starting with Millie Small's 1964 release 'My Boy Lollipop' (which had a slightly faster tempo than regular ska because it was so cold in Britain), reggae recorded in the UK has always adapted to its environment.

In spite of Millie's success and a subsequent minor hit, 'King Of Kings' by UK-based Jamaican group Ezz Reco & the Launchers, the vibrant British ska scene was based almost entirely on Jamaican-originated music. Likewise, the reggae of the late 1960s. Modified to fit the market, only the smoothing strings were grafted on in the UK: the rhythm tracks and vocals were all made in Jamaica. It was only Dandy, Laurel Aitken and Tony Tribe who left a significant impression.

Made In Britain

British reggae came of age in the late 1970s, when it virtually polarized itself between a roots militancy and the most sentimental love songs. The roots'n'culture set consisted of Steel Pulse ('Handsworth Revolution'), Aswad ('Hulet'), Misty In Roots ('Wise And Foolish'), Tradition ('Moving On'), Black Slate ('Black Slate') and Matumbi ('Seven Seals'), all who focused on black life in Britain and its attendant injustices. They cut dub versions as heavy as anything Jamaican, but were all self-contained groups in the western pop music sense, practically

> "THERE WAS A SERIOUS IDENTITY CRISIS AMONG BLACK KIDS BORN IN ENGLAND ... WE NEEDED TO DOCUMENT WHAT WAS HAPPENING."
>
> *David Hinds*

unheard of in Jamaica. As a result, their music involved more inherent musicianship and although their songs had reggae rhythms, they were built around rock structures. Then there was dub poetry, spoken in Jamaican patois. Unlike toasting, in dub poetry the music was composed to fit the words rather than the other way round, and carried a sharper message. Jamaican ex-pat Linton Kwesi Johnson made London the centre for this art form with his beautifully rhymed but biting polemics with no-nonsense titles like 'Inglan Is A Bitch', 'All Wi Is Doin Is Defendin' ' and 'Di Great Insohreckshan'.

Lovers Rock: Indigenous Pop

At the other extreme was lovers rock, a wholly pop style that owed as much to Motown and Philly as it did to Jamaican reggae. The first indigenous British black pop music, it was made by and for born-in-the-UK children of Caribbean immigrants, black youngsters who wanted their own soundtrack but couldn't identify with the "back to Africa" vibe. As its name suggests, the music was concerned with that pop staple, "lurrrrve", and it made stars out of teenage singers Janet Kay, Carroll Thompson, Louisa Mark, Brown Sugar, Victor Romero Evans, Peter Hunningale and Trevor Walters. With the exception of Janet Kay's number two hit 'Silly Games' in 1979, its popularity went largely unnoticed until the late 1980s, when the sweet-voiced Maxi Priest had a string of pop reggae hits including covers of Robert Palmer's 'Some Guys Have All The Luck' and Cat Stevens' 'Wild World'.

Where reggae has made the most impression on British music recently is as a foundation for the urban styles jungle and UK garage, and UK artists such as So Solid Crew and Mis Teeq are always quick to cite their ragga roots.

LEADING EXPONENTS

Millie Small
Matumbi
Steel Pulse
Smiley Culture
Janet Kay
Apache Indian
Carroll Thompson
Laurel Aitken
Linton Kwesi Johnson

UK REGGAE

Much of UK reggae is based on roots reggae with a UK twist in the lyrics. The music is firmly Jamaican with the characteristic off beat and bass.

tune

keyboard

bass

THE REGGAE INTRO ➡ 348   REGGAE PEOPLE A–Z ➡ 367   INSTRUMENTS A–Z ➡ 436   POP: 2-TONE ➡ 52   REGGAE: SKA ➡ 350

Reggae Pop

JAMAICAN MUSIC HAS NEVER BEEN THAT FAR AWAY FROM MAINSTREAM BRITISH MUSIC SINCE MILLIE SMALL STORMED THE CHARTS IN 1964 WITH THE GALLOPING SKA OF 'MY BOY LOLLIPOP', BUT IT WAS NOT UNTIL THE END OF THAT DECADE THAT REGGAE BECAME A BONA FIDE PART OF POP.

HERALDED by Desmond Dekker's incredible success in 1969 with 'It Mek' and 'The Israelites', hardly a week went by until the end of 1972 when the Top 40 didn't feature at least one reggae record. With bouncy, upbeat tunes, Max Romeo ('Wet Dream'), Bob & Marcia ('Young, Gifted and Black'), Jimmy Cliff ('Wonderful World'), Nicky Thomas ('Love of the Common People'), Dave & Ansell Collins ('Double Barrel'), and the Pioneers ('Long Shot Kick The Bucket') all became an integral part of the British Saturday night soundtrack.

Right Atmosphere For Success

One of the reasons reggae did so well in Britain as the 1960s rolled into the 1970s was the sorry state of the singles charts. Bands like Marmalade, Herman's Hermits and the Tremeloes still clung on but were clearly part of a bygone era, prog rock was not exactly the most disco-friendly music and glam hadn't really kicked off. Soul and Motown were all over the pop charts and dominating the dancehalls, and reggae fitted alongside perfectly. Such was the demand for the music in the UK during this period that more reggae was sold in Britain than in Jamaica.

Kingston record producers reacted to this new market-place with alacrity, and pretty soon men like Joe Gibbs, Bunny Lee, Derrick Harriot and Lee Perry were adapting their output to accommodate it. They would up the tempo, and lyrics and accents were adjusted accordingly. The big change came about in response to BBC radio's reluctance to give reggae airplay because, it claimed, the music was "unsophisticated". Producers began to record vocals and rhythm tracks in Kingston, then send the tapes over to the UK to have lush string arrangements added, meaning songs like 'Young

Gifted & Black' or 'Black Pearl' were as good as any other pop music and, consequently, became massive hits.

Reggae Goes Pop

Of course, reggae did not disappear from the pop charts in the early 1970s, but it became a much less frequent visitor as tastes were changing on both sides of the Atlantic. In the UK, glam rock was taking over from soul and reggae as the dance music of choice, while in Jamaica the onset of roots meant fewer producers and artists were concerning themselves with an overseas pop market. But reggae that has been recorded in the UK or mixed with that market in mind has always maintained a presence, with artists including Matumbi, Maxi Priest, Shaggy, Apache Indian, Musical Youth and hardy perennials UB40, who continue to manage to translate reggae to a mainstream audience.

Jamaican music has had a great influence on the pop scene on both sides of the Atlantic. Beyond 10cc and the Police are the British 2-Tone bands – the Selector, the Specials, the Beat and Madness – all punkified ska revivalists, while in the US ska bands like Bim Skala Bim, Dancehall Crashers and the Toasters have taken 2-Tone as their model, removing it one stage further. And reggae hasn't been completely ignored by American pop fans – Eric Clapton covered Bob Marley's 'I Shot The Sheriff', and Johnny Nash topped the singles charts for four weeks in 1972 with his own composition 'I Can See Clearly Now', later covered by Jimmy Cliff.

Above
Reggae pop star Jimmy Cliff starred in the 1973 film The Harder They Come. *The movie is seen through the eyes of a country boy who is lured from his home by the bright lights and promise of the big city.*

> "I NEVER BELIEVED THE ENGLISH PEOPLE COULD LOVE REGGAE SO MUCH...."
> *Dave "Dave & Ansell Collins" Barker*

Left
Desmond Dekker's Jamaican accent presented a problem for some western fans of 'The Israelites'; the opening line "Wake up in the morning, slaving for bread sir" was often misheard, one common example being the somewhat less evocative "Wake up in the morning, baked beans for breakfast".

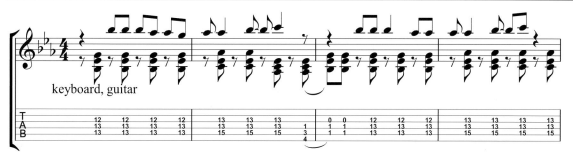

keyboard, guitar

REGGAE POP
Reggae pop is just that. Here the drums play a basic pop rhythm with the familiar reagge beat provided by the guitar and keyboards.

LEADING EXPONENTS
Nicky Thomas
Desmond Dekker
Bob & Marcia
Dave & Ansell Collins
The Pioneers
Max Romeo
Johnny Nash
Shaggy

THE REGGAE INTRO ➡ 348   REGGAE PEOPLE A-Z ➡ 367   INSTRUMENTS A-Z ➡ 436   THE POP INTRO ➡ 8   POP: 2-TONE ➡ 52

RAGGA (SHORT FOR "RAGAMUFFIN") IS THE TERM FOR LATER-MODEL DANCEHALL REGGAE ADOPTED BY THE SOUND SYSTEM CROWDS TO HIGHLIGHT THEIR EXISTENCE SOMEWHERE OUTSIDE POLITE JAMAICAN SOCIETY. RAGGA IS THE ALL-DIGITAL STYLE THAT CAME ABOUT IN THE MID-1980S, WHICH TOOK COMPUTERIZATION TO SUCH A DEGREE THAT, FOR THE FIRST TIME, REGGAE RHYTHMS WERE MADE WITH NO BASS LINE.

Ragga

> "WHEN I FIRST PLAY 'SLENG TENG' ON MY SOUND SYSTEM, THE WHOLE PLACE POP UP! FROM THEN IT WAS NINETY MINUTES OF PURE 'SLENG TENG'. LICK IT BACK!"
>
> *King Jammy's*

Above

Pre-eminent producer Bobby Digital helped shape the computerized phase of Jamaican music in the 1980s. An accomplished digital engineer, he has played a key part in many ragga stars' careers, including Shaggy's.

RAGGA was a harsher, more jagged sound that positively revelled in its sounding anything other than *ital* (that is, anything that remains in its natural state and is uncontaminated by the western world) and was perfect not only for the new wave of faster-talking, uncompromising deejays, but also seemed better-suited to the edgier mood of the inner cities at the time. Ragga completed the power shift away from artists who had, essentially, controlled things during the roots era, but were being edged out as dancehall took over.

Driven By Rhythm

Once ragga established itself in the second half of the 1980s, producers built rhythms themselves and then brought in artists to voice them, rather than building up a song around a singer's idea for a tune. It was a return to the way the likes of Duke Reid and Coxsone Dodd had done things in the ska days. This rhythm-driven situation led to vast numbers of different

versions of popular tunes, and instead of stifling creativity it resulted in an explosion of talent among deejays, as they had to try just that bit harder to make something special. It's difficult imagining any other era producing the likes of Bounty Killer

LEADING EXPONENTS

Sly & Robbie

Gregory Isaacs

Admiral Bailey

Tenor Saw

Gussie Clarke

King Jammy's

Bobby Digital

Chaka Demus & Pliers

RAGGA

Ragga bears many similarities with dancehall and will often feature a singer and a deejay countering each other's input.

THE REGGAE INTRO ➡ 348   REGGAE PEOPLE A-Z ➡ 367   INSTRUMENTS A-Z ➡ 436   HIP HOP: GANGSTA & HARDCORE ➡ 344

('My Xperience'), Elephant Man ('Log On'), Beenie Man ('Maestro'), Shabba Ranks ('Raw As Ever'), Buju Banton (' 'Til Shiloh') and Ninjaman ('Bounty Hunter').

Dancehall had been moving towards computerisation since 1984, as the Roots Radics Band, the Blood Fire Posse and Sly & Robbie were creating rhythms so automated and robotic in style they might as well have been fully digital. But the song that really sounded the starting pistol for this music to dominate the dancehalls was 'Under Mi Sleng Teng', sung by Wayne Smith and produced by King Jammy's, an established sound system operator (King Jammy's Super Power) and record producer with a broad adventurous streak. In 1985, while looking to do something different, he took pre-programmed rhythm from a cheap Casio keyboard (as opposed to using drum beats played in his studio), slowed it down and added chords, but nothing else – no conventional bass line. With Wayne Smith's vocal laid on top, the genre was born, and for the next five years Jammy's studios were the most important in Jamaica as he recorded ragga's original superstars. Singers Tenor Saw ('Ring the Alarm'), Sanchez and Pinchers ('Pinchers Meets Sanchez') made their names during this period, while Cocoa Tea and Frankie Paul adapted to the new style with Jammy's, as did Dennis Brown and Gregory Isaacs, while Jammy's equally high-calibre deejays included Admiral Bailey, Lieutenant Stitchie, Josey Wales and Major Worries.

Setting The Standard

As the 1980s moved into the 1990s, the relatively low cost of making ragga music meant the number of studios and producers in Jamaica multiplied hugely. Winston Riley – who had produced Dave & Ansell Collins' UK number one 'Double Barrel' nearly 20 years previously – emerged as one of Jammy's early challengers, producing top deejays Super Cat and Flourgon and one of the original digital roots singers, Admiral Tibet. In what was to become the common ragga practice of re-recording classic rhythms from rock steady and early reggae days, Riley re-made one of his old tunes from the Ansell Collins days, 'Stalag 17', and turned it into Tenor Saw's massive hit 'Ring The Alarm'. The rhythm then became a ragga standard as it was versioned literally hundreds of times – almost as many times as 'Under Mi Sleng Teng'.

Going International

It was the next generation of ragga stars, Shabba Ranks, Buju Banton, Ninjaman, Bounty Killer, Lady Saw, Cobra and Beenie Man, that took the style international. Perhaps unsurprisingly, the new wave of producers included several of Jammy's apprentices in its ranks: Bobby Digital

had been his engineer, while Steelie & Cleevie were his house musicians. Elsewhere, the top producers were Dave Kelly, Gussie Clarke, Fatis Burrell and Donovan Germaine, plus Sly & Robbie who were enjoying a resurgence, and between them they were widening ragga out from the common dancehall concerns of sex and violence to incorporate roots sentiments (Capleton, Sizzla and Anthony B), pop (Tiger, Buccaneer, Chaka Demus & Pliers, Ini Kamoze), lurrrrve (Beres Hammond, Freddie McGregor, Deborahe Glasgow) and the conscious singing of Garnett Silk, Everton Blender and Yami Bolo.

Today, acts like Goofy ('I Don't Give A Damn'), Red Rat ('Oh No … It's Red Rat') and Mr. Vegas ('Heads High') understand what international pop music wants. Bounty Killer and Lady Saw brought their own particular style to No Doubt's 2001 album *Rock Steady* and in doing so introduced themselves to a massive American audience. Elephant Man and the Scare Dem Crew brought an element of pure Kingston showbiz pizzazz to proceedings. And T.O.K. are ragga's original boy band, combining hardcore deejaying with sweet harmonizing. Surely it is only a matter of time before ragga becomes as big as roots reggae was.

Left
Buju Banton's 1992 release 'Boom Bye Bye', with its homophobic lyrics, caused his appearance at the Womad Festival to be cancelled. He has since made a comeback with releases such as ' 'Til Shiloh'.

Below
Deejay Chaka Demus and vocalist Pliers have had more commercial success with mainstream pop fans since joining forces in the early 1990s than either artist ever had in his solo career.

DANCEHALL REGGAE IS A VIVID EXAMPLE OF HOW THE MUSIC PERPETUALLY REINVENTS ITSELF TO REFRESH ITS REBEL SPIRIT AND TO KEEP ITSELF RELEVANT TO ITS PRIMARY AUDIENCE: DOWNTOWN KINGSTON (BOTH SPIRITUALLY AS WELL AS GEOGRAPHICALLY). IT BEGAN TO APPEAR ON THE SOUND SYSTEMS AT THE BEGINNING OF THE 1980S, WHEN ROOTS REGGAE HAD REACHED A WORLD STAGE THROUGH THE LIKES OF BOB MARLEY.

Dancehall

Above

Rhythm twins Sly & Robbie have produced some of the most innovative dancehall on their Taxi label, and sell their records to roots traditionalists as well as to a new generation of sound system followers.

DANCEHALL reggae intentionally opposed itself to what these international acts had become. Musically, it was little more than sparse, jagged rhythm tracks, often sounding deliberately computerized as it made the most of the advancing technology, and the first dancehall vocals were deejays toasting live on dub plates (special one-off acetates of songs, cut for sound system use only). In the dancehall. Because of its "one-off" nature, dancehall's popularity was always based on releases of singles rather than albums, a situation which remains the same today, although collections of singles by artists and producers do exist as compilation albums.

Returning To The People

The style got its name not only because of where it was born but because this was a form that, in its infancy, Jamaican radio would not touch, so its only outlet was the dancehall. This was

"I NEVER KNOW WHY THEY CALL IT SLACKNESS. I TALK ABOUT SEX, BUT IT'S JUST WHAT HAPPENS BEHIND CLOSED DOORS. WHAT I TALK IS REALITY."

Yellowman

an important development for a music that, for a few years, had been coming increasingly under the sway of the international record business as a bona fide branch of rock music. It was now returning to the traditions established 20 years previously by the likes of Coxsone Dodd, Prince Buster and Duke Reid, whereby it didn't have to conform to local radio's prescribed standards,

and so put the control back in the hands of the people it was made by and for. Not surprisingly, the first important dancehall producers were sound system operators. Henry "Junjo" Lawes, King Jammy's, Jack Scorpio and Bobby Digital owned, respectively, Volcano, King Jammy's Super Power, Scorpio and Heatwave, the biggest sets on the island, and had a bond with the audience that so many of roots reggae's producers hadn't enjoyed. Under these circumstances, left pretty much to its own devices, reggae once again evolved into an accurate representation of its public: as in the ska days, it was responding immediately to what the people wanted.

And the most public face of this public were the deejays. Deejays were the perfect manifestation of early dancehall's DIY ethic, as the original vibe was for anybody to get a turn on the mic in a dance and see how far their skills could take

DANCEHALL

Dancehall uses a lot of the same techniques as dub with the removal of instruments, often leaving just bass and drums or even just drums, for the vocalist to sing, or "toast", over.

hi hat

rimshot & bass drum

snare

THE REGGAE INTRO ➡ 348   REGGAE PEOPLE A-Z ➡ 367   INSTRUMENTS A-Z ➡ 436   THE DANCE INTRO ➡ 310   REGGAE: SKA ➡ 350

them. A decade of roots, with its protest lyrics, appeared to have made virtually no difference to conditions in Jamaica, so these deejays took a step back to when their job involved nothing more complicated than "bigging up" their sound system, commenting on the dancehall soap opera unfolding around them or scatalogically duelling with the music. A sense of humour returned to reggae, as deejays such as Michigan & Smiley, Lone Ranger, Burru Banton and General Echo preceded the almost surreal likes of Eek-A-Mouse and Yellowman.

The Yellow King Of Slackness

It was the latter, or King Yellow as he was known at the height of his popularity, who became the figurehead for a sub-genre of dancehall: slackness. It consisted of the best dancehall rhythms, topped off with "Carry On"-style nudge-nudge smutty lyrics, and it probably did most to define dancehall's initial concerns to the world still clinging to roots'n'culture. But although Yellowman's sex chat (and that of his rude-talking peers General Echo and Lone Ranger) was loudly condemned, when the music made it into the wider world, it was little more than a continuation of the apparent traditions in Caribbean song, in which bawdiness is an entirely valid subject matter. Anyway, appreciation of the opposite sex was what brought most people to the dancehall in the first place.

Rhythm Nation

On the more musical side, the most important session band in the early days of dancehall was the Roots Radics Band, who were a nucleus of the drum and bass combo of Style Scott

and Flabba Holt, augmented by guitarist Bingy Bunny. Horn sections had become a costly rarity, and the fact that this trio were seldom supplemented by anything other than a keyboard player is testament to dancehall's uncluttered sound. This band provided rhythms for a host of producers, often revisiting classic Studio One and Treasure Isle backing tracks, on which very little was changed except the tempo, particularly the old Slim Smith number 'Never Let Go'. Dancehall wasn't without singers either. New faces were coming up through the sound systems rather than studio auditions; Little John, Sammy Dread, Half Pint and Phillip Frazer all made their names in the style. Then there were established figures such as Gregory Isaacs, Barrington Levy, Al Campbell, Sugar Minott and Johnny Osbourne, who found dancehall suited them so perfectly that they went on to have their biggest hits in it. Even the old-time likes of John Holt and Bunny Wailer found new leases of life.

Around the mid-1980s, dancehall started to conquer the world. It was led by the duo of drummer Sly and bass player Robbie, who, after gaining an international reputation providing backing for and producing the likes of Grace Jones (*Warm Leatherette*), Bob Dylan (contributing to *Down In The Groove*) and Ian Dury (playing on *Lord Upminster*), returned to their reggae roots and started their label, Taxi. With this they had a string of mainstream hits, including Junior Delgado ('Fort Augustus' and 'Merry Go Round') the Tamlins, and Ini Kamoze ('Trouble You A Trouble Me'). But true to reggae's cyclical nature, as new technology was being eagerly absorbed, back on Kingston's sound systems something new was about to break.

Above

As an albino, Yellowman has faced all the odds during his career and come out on top. Albinos are usually shunned in Jamaica, so to have dance-hall crowds adopt him as their spiritual leader is a measure of his great success.

Left

Half Pint, with releases such as 'Money Man Skank', recorded by King Jammy's in the early 1980s, possessed all the energy, ebullience and style that exemplified dancehall at the time.

Bobo Dread Deejays

THE BOBO ASHANTI IS RASTA FOR THE TWENTY-FIRST CENTURY: MORE MILITANT AND LESS TOLERANT. WITH THEIR IDEOLOGICAL ATTACKS ON ROME, SOCIAL DEMOTION OF WOMEN AND CONDEMNATION OF HOMOSEXUALITY DEEJAYS LIKE CAPLETON AND ANTHONY B MAY SEEM WORLDS APART FROM THE HIPPY-ISH NOTIONS OF DREADLOCKS THAT WAS BOB MARLEY'S LEGACY. THERE'S ACTUALLY NOT MUCH DIFFERENCE.

Above

The deejay Sizzla, with his prolific output and scathing lyrics, is one of Bobo's most popular artists. Brought up in Kingston by devout Rasta parents, he built up his reputation on the Caveman Hi-Fi sound system.

UNLIKE roots reggae, which had a discernible musical style, Bobo music is defined purely by its content. The sounds of Bobo records are a spectrum of modern reggae – dancehall digital, spiritually acoustic or just plain reggae rhythm – it is the singer or deejay's message that sets it apart. It has taken up the mantle of Rastafari and uses Jamaican music to spread its word, and given that today's reggae has fragmented to such a degree, Bobo uses any aspect of the music to get its message across to what it sees as an increasingly wayward youth. As artists with existing careers convert to Bobo, so they bring with them their own styles as a method of giving thanks and praise. While it definitely has replaced the Marley-esque protest songs of the 1970s and 1980s, it has also added a twenty-first-century bent: the reggae business itself is now far more diverse, but essentially it remains the same chanting-down Babylon of its predecessor.

Bobo Ashanti dates from the 1950s, when Emmanuel Edwards established his Ethiopian International Congress Rasta camp in Kingston. He was trying to create a more committed version of the faith, drawing upon Garveyism, Ethiopian Christianity and Old Testament ideology to a create a communal living environment. This remains central to today's Bobo, as does a diet eschewing all meat, wheat and salt; fasting and prayer are frequent, and Bobo camps are as self-sufficient as possible.

> "WHEN WE SAY 'BURN FIRE' WE DON'T MEAN TAKE A MATCH AND LIGHT SOMEBODY, WE ARE SAYING 'GET RID OF THESE THINGS THAT ARE NO GOOD FOR HUMANITY'."
>
> *Anthony B*

Bobo dreads have always stood apart from the rest of Rasta with their red-, green- and gold-trimmed white robes and turbans rolled almost vertically around their dreadlocks, which are kept covered because Bobos believe that, from Bob Marley's time onwards, dreadlocks became a fashion statement rather than a show of devotion. To keep them under wraps this way keeps faith as a personal issue for the wearer.

Exciting And Uncompromising

Such refocusing of Rasta's appearance is a useful metaphor for the refocusing of its purpose. Modern Bobo believes Rasta has become part of mainstream life and no longer provides the strict guidance that, in its adherents' opinion, black people need to survive Babylon. Inside Bobo's uncompromising ways is exactly the same ideology as Rasta had in the 1970s when it first made a wide impact; all Bobo has done is put it back on track. Bobo believes that the world is descending into moral chaos – something it sees as best illustrated by the state of today's reggae and hip hop, with its apparently demeaning obsessions with sex and violence – and that desperate times call for desperate measures. Like Bobo's counterparts from 30 years ago, the music has the dancehall credibility to go with its hard-core spirituality, and tunes such as Anthony B's 'Fire 'Pon Rome and Repentance Time', Capleton's 'Pure Sodom' and 'Burn Dem Dreadie', and Sizzla's 'Attack' are exciting, uncompromising blasts that sweep the listener along.

Bobo will survive, but whether it grows to enjoy the status that regular Rasta did is another matter. Old dreads claim that any praise of Jah is better than none at all, while many ordinary people believe anything that kicks against the current encroaching nihilism is A Good Thing.

LEADING EXPONENTS

Sizzla
Capleton
Anthony B
Junior Reid
Fatis Burrell
Jah Cure
Norris Man
Determine

BOBO DREAD DEEJAYS

Bobo deejays differ from standard deejays in the lyrics they use, which tend to focus mainly on Rastafarian morals and ideals.

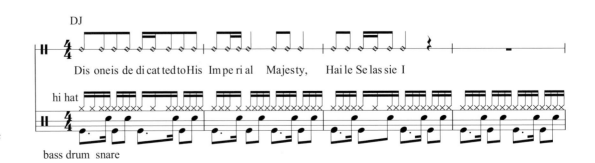

THE REGGAE INTRO ➡ 348   REGGAE PEOPLE A-Z ➡ 367   INSTRUMENTS A-Z ➡ 436   FOLK: POLITICAL FOLK & PROTEST SONGS ➡ 230

US Reggae

FOR MOST OF REGGAE'S LIFE THE TERMS "AMERICAN REGGAE" OR "REGGAE IN AMERICA", HAVE REMAINED OXYMORONS. A NUMBER OF POSSIBLE REASONS HAVE BEEN PROPOSED, RANGING FROM THE PLAUSIBLE TO THE PATENTLY ABSURD, AS TO WHY REGGAE HAS NEVER ENJOYED THE SAME SUCCESS IN THE US THAT IT FOUND IN THE UK, IN TERMS OF PROPORTIONATE RECORD SALES AND GENERAL ROCK-BIZ PROFILE.

SOME of the reasons given include: America already has a healthy black musical heritage and does not need or want any imports; there is not a sufficiently influential Jamaican community to give it a kick start; Americans are not able to dance to reggae's beats or understand the lyrics; or, during the roots era, any potential audience was totally baffled by the notion of sufferation – the righteous pursuit of the ultra-simple life in the name of Jah – as something to be aspired to. However, in spite of reggae never really making much of an impact on the American cultural mainstream, Jamaican music has seeped into the landscape on a number of levels as the result of it having been marketed there for 40 years.

The World's Fair

In 1964, the Jamaican government organized a ska delegation to the World's Fair in New York – Kingston musicians, vocalists Jimmy Cliff, Millie Small and Prince Buster, and former Jamaican Miss World Carol Crawford were sent to demonstrate the dance – to attempt to sell the music to US record companies. It nearly worked. Atlantic, Epic, ABC-Paramount and Capitol Records all put out ska albums the following year, but the only notable successes were Millie's 'My Boy Lollipop' and Prince Buster's '10 Commandments Of Man'. America never took to The Sound Of Young Jamaica as any sort of rival to Motown's Sound Of Young America.

Rock steady passed America by, and the next Jamaican style to have an impact was roots reggae. Coming at the end of the hippy era in the early 1970s, it offered an extension of the same peace'n'love, dope-smoking vibe, and found an audience on the US college circuit, which was far more open-minded than the rigidly formatted commercial radio stations.

Acts like Bob Marley and the Wailers, Burning Spear, the Mighty Diamonds, Big Youth, Culture, Steel Pulse and Linton Kwesi Johnson all did well among largely middle-class, young white audiences. It was one of Bob Marley's biggest disappointments that he was unable to reach black America who, at the time, simply didn't get what roots reggae was all about. Since his death in 1981, Marley has become something of a revolutionary icon in black America, but it's unlikely his records will be found in the same households as his picture.

Having An Impact

By dabbling in the same samples and presentation styles as hip hop of the day, in the early 1990s dancehall began to make headway in the US.

Rappers KRS-One, Public Enemy and Queen Latifah all flirted with the sound, and deejays Shabba Ranks (*Raw As Ever*) and Supercat (*Sweets For My Sweet*) appeared to open the door for a significant Jamaican invasion. But that fell apart in the Dancehall Is Homophobic shockwaves sent out by Banton's 1992 'Boom Bye Bye' single. Today, although Busta Rhymes plays up his Jamaican heritage and Lady Saw and Bounty Killer guested on No Doubt's 1992 debut *No Doubt*, reggae has yet to succeed on its own terms. When it does, Shaggy is likely to be the standard bearer; his success with 'Oh Carolina' and 'Boombastic' show he is entirely capable of maintaining a true dancehall attitude while lightening it up.

Above
Second to Bob Marley, Burning Spear has the biggest worldwide following of all reggae artists, and is one of only a few reggae stars to have made an impact in the US.

"TOO MANY ARTISTS GO OVERSEAS AND TRY TO COPY WHAT IS THERE. THAT'S NOT WHAT ANYBODY WANTS."
Bounty Killer

Queen Latifah

keyboard

hi hat

bass drum   snare

US REGGAE

Often reminiscent of soca, a modern fusion of calypso and Indian rhythms from the two main ethnic groups of Trinidad and Tobago. US reggae uses a similar off-beat pattern but on the keyboard, and with a very simple drum pattern.

LEADING EXPONENTS
Bounty Killer/No Doubt
Bob Marley
Busta Rhymes
Red Alert
Red Fox
Bobby Konders
Steel Pulse
Shabba Ranks
Shaggy

THE REGGAE INTRO ➡ 348   REGGAE PEOPLE A-Z ➡ 367   INSTRUMENTS A-Z ➡ 436   SOUL AND R&B: URBAN SOUL ➡ 229   REGGAE: ROOTS ➡ 354

IF THERE WAS ONE THING THAT SUMMED UP JAMAICAN MUSIC – ITS UNIQUENESS, ITS ABILITY TO ADAPT FROM ELSEWHERE, ITS INVENTIVENESS, ITS INFLUENCE ABROAD, ITS SOUND SYSTEM ROOTS AND ITS CONTINUING CLOSENESS TO ITS AUDIENCE – IT WOULD BE THE DEEJAY.

Deejays

BORN on the sound systems in the 1950s, the deejay's job was to vibe up the dance by "bigging up" his employer's sound system (the term "toasting" comes from this main part of the deejay's job), comment on what was going on around him, interact with the records, push liquor sales and announce the next dance, all while riding the rhythms. As a sound system operator, having the right records was one thing, but having the right *deejay* could be everything – when Prince Buster launched his Voice Of The People Sound System in 1958, he poached Coxsone Dodd's deejay Count Machuki, considered the best on the island. Buster maintains "It was so important to have the right deejay, that when Machuki join my new sound system, even though I was just a yout' everybody knew they had to take me seriously."

Creating Their Own Style

As with so much that is uniquely Jamaican, the idea of deejaying in this manner was originally appropriated from somewhere else – it was inspired by the jive-talking jocks on the southern black American radio stations that were picked up in Jamaica. These guys scatted around and over their records, turning the most mundane tunes into something exciting, which suited their Caribbean counterparts for two reasons: prior to a Jamaican recording industry, all but the biggest sound systems had pretty much the same imported US records as each other and an inventive deejay could customize them; and by speaking in their own style it was a handy way to put a Jamaican twang on American songs. It's hugely ironic that it was a Jamaican, Kool DJ Herc, who moved to New York with his sound system in 1967 and introduced toasting, which was quickly taken up by native New Yorkers and metamorphosed into rap.

Deejays found their way on to wax in the late-1960s when the acknowledged founding father was U-Roy, who toasted on top of old rock steady classics. He was followed by Dennis Alcapone, I-Roy and Dillinger. With their eloquent protests, deejays had something serious to say, and Big Youth, Tapper Zukie, Prince Far-I, I-Roy, Prince Jazzbo, U-Roy and Dr. Alimantado assumed griot status as they ushered in the roots'n'culture era. U-Roy's album *Version Galore* contains some of the first deejay songs to go on record, while Big Youth's *Screaming Target* LP and Prince Far-I's *Under Heavy Manners* are roots deejay classics.

Taking It Further

Dancehall reggae was all about deejays, and as they moved to centre stage, characters like Yellowman ('Mr Yellowman'), Eek-A-Mouse ('Wa Do Dem') and Michigan & Smiley ('Rub A Dub Style') proved to be hugely inventive. The 1990s generation of deejays brought MTV-style showmanship to their craft: Ninjaman, Supercat, Bounty Killer, Capleton, Buju Banton, Lady Saw, Beenie Man and Shabba Ranks, with his *Raw As Ever* album. Absorbing hip hop influences and keeping a hardcore dancehall base, they took deejaying to new levels. Their groundwork means today's rising stars – Elephant Man, T.O.K., Goofy, Mr. Vegas – have a much broader canvas to work on. Cultural toasting is currently enjoying a revival through Sizzla, Capleton, Anthony B and a righteous Buju Banton.

"DEEJAYS WERE CLOSEST TO THE PEOPLE BECAUSE THERE WASN'T ANY KIND OF ESTABLISHMENT CONTROL ON THE SOUND SYSTEMS."

Big Youth

Above

Deejay U-Roy developed a unique style in which he would fill in the spaces in a song when the singers weren't singing so people felt more involved, and would sing along to it. Later deejays would emulate his technique.

LEADING EXPONENTS

Big Youth
U-Roy
Shabba Ranks
Lady Saw
Bounty Killer
Tapper Zukie
Elephant Man
Yellowman
Josey Wales

DEEJAYS

The deejay has become an integral part of reggae, providing the crucial link between the music and the audience. This extract shows an example of some typical deejay-crowd banter.

THE REGGAE INTRO ➡ 348   REGGAE PEOPLE A-Z ➡ 367   INSTRUMENTS A-Z ➡ 436   REGGAE: ROOTS ➡ 354   REGGAE: DANCEHALL ➡ 362

Artists: Reggae

Entries appear in the following order: name, music style, year(s) of popularity, type of artist, country of origin

Abyssinians, The, Dub; Roots, 1960s-1990s, Artist, Jamaican
Aces, Rock Steady, 1990s, Artist, American
Admiral Bailey, Dancehall, 1980s-1990s, Artist, Jamaican
Admiral Tibbet, Ragga; Dancehall, 1980s-, Artist, Jamaican
Afari, Yasus, Dancehall; Dub, 1990s, Producer; Artist, Jamaican
African Disciples, Ragga, 1980s, Artist, Jamaican
African Head Charge, Dub, 1980s-1990s, Artist, British
Aitken, Laurel, Ska; Roots, 1950s-1990s, Artist, Jamaican
AKA, Ska, 1970s, Artist, American
Akabu, Dub, 1990s, Artist, American
Alcapone, Dennis, Deejays, 1970s-1990s, Artist, Jamaican
Alpha & Omega, Dub, 1980s-, Artist, British
Alpha Blondy, Reggae Pop, 1980s-, Artist, African
Alphonso, Rolando, Ska; Roots; Rock Steady, 1950s-1960s, Artist, Cuban
Andy, Bob, Rock Steady; Ska, 1960s-1990s, Artist, British
Andy, Horace, Roots; Dub, 1960-, Artist, Jamaican
Anthony B, Bobo Dread Deejays, 1990s-, Artist, Jamaican
Aswad, Roots, 1970s-1990s, Artist, British
Bad Manners, Ska, 1980s-, Artist, British
Banner, Spanner, Dancehall, 1990s-, Artist, Jamaican
Banton, Buju, Dancehall; Roots, 1990s-, Artist, Jamaican
Banton, Mega, Dancehall; Ragga, 1990s, Artist, Jamaican
Banton, Pato, Ragga, 1980s-, Artist; Producer, British
Basement 5, Dub, 1980s, Artist, British
Beenie Man, Dancehall; Ragga, 1980s-, Artist, Jamaican
Big Mountain, Reggae Pop, 1990s-, Artist, American
Big Youth, Deejays, 1970s-, Artist, Jamaican
Bim Skala Bim, Ska, 1980s-, Artist, American
BIX, Ska, 1970s, Artist, British
Black Uhuru, Dub; Roots, 1970s-, Artist, Jamaican
Blender, Everton, Dancehall; Roots, 1990s-, Artist, Jamaican
Bolo, Yami, Dancehall, 1990s-, Artist, Jamaican
Boom Shaka, US Reggae, 1980s-1990s, Artist, American
Boothe, Ken, Roots; Rock Steady, 1960s-1970s, Artist, Jamaican
Bounty Killer, Dancehall; Ragga, 1990s-, Artist, Jamaican
Bovell, Dennis, Dub, 1970s-1980s, Artist, British
Breeze, Jean "Binta", Dub, 1990s, Artist, Jamaican
Brevette, Lloyd, Ska, 1990s, Artist, American
Brissett, Bunny, UK Reggae, 1990s-, Artist, British
Broggs, Peter, US Reggae, 1980s-, Artist, American
Brown, Dennis, Dancehall; Ragga, 1970s-1990s, Artist, Jamaican
Brown, Glenn, Dub; Dancehall, 1960s-1990s, Artist; Songwriter, American
Bucaneer, Ragga, 1990s, Artist, Jamaican
Burning Spear, Dub; Roots, 1970s-1990s, Artist, Jamaican
Byles, Junior, Dub, 1970s-1990s, Artist, Jamaican
Campbell, Al, Reggae Pop; UK Reggae, 1990s-, Artist, British
Campbell, Cornell, Ska; Rock Steady, 1980s-, Artist, Jamaican
Capleton The Prophet, Bobo Dread Deejays; Dancehall; Roots; Ragga; Rock Steady, 1980s-, Artist, Jamaican
Carlos, Don, Roots, 1970s-, Artist, Jamaican
Chaplin, Charlie, Ragga, 1980s-1990s, Composer, British

Cherry Poppin' Daddies, Ska, 1990s-, Artist, American
Chuckleberry, Dancehall; Ragga; Deejays, 1990s, Artist, Jamaican
Clail, Gary, Dub, 1980s-1990s, Artist, British
Clarendonians, Rock Steady; Ska, 1990s-, Artist, Jamaican
Clarke, Johnny, Reggae Pop, 1970s-1990s, Artist, Jamaican
Cliff, Jimmy, Reggae Pop, 1960s-, Artist, Jamaican

Cobra, Ragga, 1980s-1990s, Artist, Jamaican
Cocoa Tea, Dancehall; Ragga, 1980s-, Artist, Jamaican
Collins, Dave & Ansell, Rock Steady, 1970s, Artist, Jamaican
Congos, The, Dub, 1970s; 1990s, Artist, Jamaican
Creation Rebel, Dub, 1980s-1990s, Artist, British
Crystal, Conrad, UK Reggae, 1990s, Artist, British
Culture, Roots, 1970s-, Artist, Jamaican
Curtis, Tony, Ragga, 1990s-, Artist, Jamaican
Cutty Ranks, Ragga; Dancehall, 1990s-, Producer, Jamaican
Da Bush Babees, Ragga, 1990s, Artist, Jamaican
Daddy Freddy, Dancehall; Ragga, 1990s-, Artist, Jamaican
Daley, Lloyd, Ska, 1960s-1970s, Artist, Jamaican
Dance Hall Crashers, Ska, 1990s-, Artist, American
Davis, Ronnie, Reggae Pop, 1990s, Artist, Jamaican
Dekker, Desmond, Ska; Rock Steady, 1960s-, Artist, Jamaican
Delgado, Junior, Dub, 1970s-1990s, Artist, Jamaican
Dillinger, Dancehall, 1970s-, Artist, Jamaican
DJ Faust, Deejays; US Reggae, 1990s, Artist; Producer, American
Dodd, Clement "Coxsone", Roots; Rock Steady; Ska, 1960s-1990s, Producer, Jamaican
Dread, Mikey, Deejays, 1970s-1990s, Artist, American
Drummond, Don, Ska; Rock Steady, 1960s, Artist, Jamaican
Dub Syndicate, Dub, 1980s-, Artist, British
Dunbar, Sly, Reggae Pop; Dancehall; Rock Steady, 1970s-1990s, Producer; Artist, Jamaican
Dunkley, Errol, Rock Steady, 1970s-, Artist, Jamaican
Eastwood, Clint, Dancehall, 1970s-1980s, Artist, Jamaican
Eccles, Clancy, Rock Steady; Ska, 1950s-1980s, Artist, Jamaican
Edwards, Rupie, Ska, 1980s, Artist, Jamaican
Eek-A-Mouse, Dancehall; Ragga, 1980s-, Artist, Jamaican
Ellis, Alton, Ska; Rock Steady, 1950s-, Artist, Jamaican
Ellis, Hortense, Rock Steady, 1970s, Artist, Jamaican
Ethiopians, The, Rock Steady, 1960s-1980s, Artist, Jamaican
Fearon, Clinton, Rock Steady; Ska, 1960s, Artist, Jamaican
Fraser, Dean, Dancehall, 1980s-, Artist, Jamaican
Gaylads, The, Rock Steady, 1960s-1970s, Artist, Jamaican
General Saint, Dancehall, 1980s, Artist, Jamaican
General Trees, Dancehall; Ragga; Deejays, 1980s-1990s, Artist, American
Gibbs, Joe, Dub, 1970s, Producer, Jamaican
Gladiators, Rock Steady; Ska, 1970s-, Artist, Jamaican
Gold, Brian & Tony, Ragga, 1980s-1990s, Artist, Jamaican
Goldfinger, Ska, 1990s-, Artist, American
Grant, Eddy, Reggae Pop, 1970s-, Artist; Producer, African
Grennan, Winston, Rock Steady; Ska, 1960s-, Artist, Jamaican
Griffiths, Marcia, Dancehall, 1960s-1990s, Artist, Jamaican
Half Pint, Dancehall; Roots; Reggae Pop, 1980s-, Artist; Composer, Jamaican
Hammond, Beres, Dancehall, 1970s-, Artist, Jamaican
Heptones, The, Rock Steady; Roots, 1960s-1990s, Artist, Jamaican

Hinds, Justin, Ska; Rock Steady, 1970s-1990s, Artist, Jamaican
Holt, John, Reggae Pop, 1960s-, Artist, Jamaican
Hudson, Keith, Dub, 1970s-1990s, Artist; Producer, Jamaican
Ijahman, Dub; Rock Steady; Ska, 1970s-1990s, Artist, Jamaican
Inner Circle, Reggae Pop, 1970s-, Artist, Jamaican
Irie, Tippa, Ragga; Dancehall, 1980s-, Artist, Jamaican-British
I-Roy, Dancehall; Ragga, 1970s-, Artist, Jamaican
Isaacs, Gregory, Reggae Pop, 1970s-, Artist, Jamaican
Itals, The, Roots, 1980s-1990s, Artist, Jamaican
Jamaicans, The, Rock Steady, 1960s-1970s, Artist, Jamaican
Jarrett, Winston, Rock Steady, 1970s-1990s, Artist, Jamaican
Jigsy King, Dancehall; Ragga, 1990s, Artist, Jamaican
Johnson, Linton Kwesi, Dub, 1970s-, Artist, Jamaican
Joi, Dub, 1990s, Artist, American
Jolly Boys, Ska, 1980s-1990s, Artist, Jamaican
Kamoze, Ini, Ragga, 1980s-1990s, Artist, American
King Jammy, Dub, 1970s-1980s, Artist, Jamaican
King Tubby, Dub, 1960s-1980s, Artist; Producer, Jamaican
King, Diana, Dancehall; Ragga; US Reggae, 1990s-, Artist, American
Laswell, Bill, Dub, 1970s-, Artist; Producer, American
LeBlanc, Keith, Dub, 1980s-1990s, Artist, British
Lee, Bunny, Roots; Dub, 1970s, Producer, Jamaican
Lee, Byron, Dancehall; Ska, 1960s-, Producer; Artist, Jamaican
Levy, Barrington, Dancehall, 1970s-1990s, Artist, Jamaican

Lieutenant Stitchie, Dancehall; Ragga, 1980s-1990s, Artist, Jamaican
Lodge, J. C., Dancehall; Reggae Pop, 1980s-1990s, Artist, American
Luciano, Dancehall; Roots, 1990s-, Artist, Jamaican
Macka B, Dancehall, 1980s-, Artist, British
Mad Cobra, Ragga; Dancehall, 1990s-, Artist, Jamaican
Mad Lion, Dancehall, 1960s-, Artist, American
Mad Professor, Dub, 1970s-, Artist; Producer, Jamaican
Madness, Ska, 1970s-, Artist, British
Manasseh, Dub, 1990s, Artist, British
Mandators, Dancehall, 1990s, Artist, Nigerian
Marley, Bob, Ska; Roots; Rock Steady, 1960s-1980s, Artist, Jamaican
Marley, Ziggy, Reggae Pop, 1980s-, Artist, Jamaican
McCook, Tommy, Ska, 1960s-1990s, Artist, American
McGregor, Freddie, Dancehall; Dub; Roots; 1960s-, Artist; Composer, Jamaican
McKay, Freddie, Rock Steady; Ska, 1960s-1980s, Artist, Jamaican
Mee, Michie, Dancehall; Ragga, 1990s, Artist, Canadian
Mellotones, Rock Steady, 1990s-, Artist, American
Melodians, The, 1960s-1970s; 1990s, Artist, American,
Melody Makers, Reggae Pop, 1990s, Artist, Jamaican
Michigan & Smiley, Dancehall, 1980s-1990s, Artist, Jamaican
Mighty Mighty Bosstones, The, Ska, 1980s-, Artist, American
Minott, Sugar, Dancehall; Ragga, 1970s-1990s, Artist, Jamaican
Mittoo, Jackie, Ska; Reggae Pop; Rock Steady, 1960s-1980s, Artist, Jamaican
Morgan Heritage, Dancehall; US Reggae, 1990s-, Artist, American

Mowatt, Judy, Roots, 1960s-, Artist, Jamaican
Murvin, Junior, Roots, 1960s-, Artist, Jamaican
Musical Youth, Reggae Pop; Ska, 1970s-1990s, Artist, British
Mutabaruka, Dub, 1980s-, Artist, Jamaican
Nash, Johnny, Reggae Pop, 1950s-1970s, Artist, American
New Age Steppers, The, Dub, 1980s-1990s, Artist, British
Niney The Observer, Dancehall; Dub, 1960s-1990s, Artist, Jamaican
Ninjaman, Dancehall; Ragga, 1970s-1990s, Artist, Jamaican
No Doubt, Ska, 1990s-, Artist, British
Operation Ivy, Ska, 1980s, Artist, American
Osbourne, Johnny, Dancehall, 1980s-1990s, Artist, Jamaican
Pablo, Augustus, Dub, 1970s-1990s, Artist; Producer, Jamaican
Papa San, Dancehall; Ragga, 1990s, Artist, American
Paradise, Ska, 1980s, Artist, American
Paragons, The, Rock Steady; Dub, 1960s-1980s, Artist, Jamaican
Partridge, Andy, Dub, 1980s-, Artist; Composer; Songwriter, British
Patra, Dancehall; Ragga, 1990s, Artist, Jamaican
Paul, Frankie, Dancehall, 1980s-, Artist, American
Penn, Dawn, Dancehall; Rock Steady, 1990s-, Artist, Jamaican
Perry, Lee "Scratch", Dub; Roots; Rock Steady, 1960s-, Artist; Producer, Jamaican
Pinchers, Dancehall; Ragga, 1980s-, Artist, American
Pioneers, The, Rock Steady; Roots, 1960s-1970s, Artist, Jamaican
Priest, Maxi, Dancehall; Reggae Pop; UK Reggae, 1980s-1990s, Artist, British
Prince Buster, Ska; Rock Steady, 1960s-1990s, Artist, Jamaican
Prince Fari, Dub; Deejays, 1970s-1980s, Artist, Jamaican
Prince Jazzbo, Dancehall; Ragga; Deejays, 1970s; 1990s-, Producer; Artist, American
Radics, Jack, Dancehall; Ragga, 1990s, Artist, American
Rancid, Ska, 1990s-, Artist, American
Ranks, Cutty, Dancehall; Ragga, 1990s-, Producer, Jamaican
Ranks, Nardo, Dancehall; Ragga, 1990s, Artist, Jamaican
Ranks, Shabba, Dancehall; Ragga, 1980s-1990s, Artist, Jamaican
Ras Michael, Roots; Dub, 1970s-1990s, Artist, Jamaican
Rayvon, Dancehall, 1990s-, Artist, American
Rebel, Tony, Dancehall; Ragga, 1990s-, Artist, American
Reel Big Fish, Ska, 1990s-, Artist, American
Reid, Duke, Ska; Roots, 1950s-1970s, Producer, Jamaica
Reid, Junior, Bobo Dread Deejays, 1980s-, Artist, Jamaican
Renegade Soundwave, Dub, 1980s-, Artist, British
Rico, Ska, 1960s-1990s, Artist, Jamaican
Riley, Jimmy, UK Reggae, 1970s-1990s, Artist, British
Rodriguez, Rico, Ska, 1990s, Artist, Jamaican
Roots Radics, Dub, 1980s-, Artist, Jamaican
Rootsman, Dub; UK Reggae, 1990s-, Artist, British
Sanchez, Reggae Pop; Ragga, 1980s-, Artist, Jamaican
Scientist, Dub, 1970s-, Artist; Producer, Jamaican
Shaggy, Dancehall; Ragga, 1990s-, Artist, American
Shankin's Pickle, Ska, 1990s, Artist, American
Sherwood, Adrian, Dub, 1980s-, Producer, British
Shinehead, Dancehall; Ragga, 1980s-1990s, Artist, British
Shirley, Roy, Rock Steady; Ska, 1960s-1980s, Artist; Composer, Jamaican
Sibbles, Leroy, Rock Steady; Roots, 1970s-1990s, Artist, Jamaican
Silk, Garnett, Roots; Ragga; Dancehall, 1980s-1990s, Artist, Jamaican
Silvertones, Rock Steady, 1970s-1990s, Artist, Jamaican
Sister Carol, Dancehall; Ragga, 1990s-, Artist, Jamaican
Sizzla, Bobo Dread Deejays, 1990s-, Artist, Jamaican
Skatalites, The, Ska; Rock Steady, 1960s-, Artist, Jamaican
Sly & Robbie, Dub; Roots; Dancehall, 1970s-, Artist, Jamaican
Smart, Leroy, Dancehall; Ragga, 1970s-1990s, Artist, Jamaican
Smiley Culture, Dancehall, 1980s, Artist, British
Smith, Slim, Ska, 1960s-1970s, Artist, Jamaican
Snow, Dancehall; Reggae Pop; Ragga, 1990s, Artist, Canadian
Spice, Mikey, Ragga, 1990s-, Artist, Jamaican
Spragga Benz, Dancehall; Ragga, 1990s-, Artist, Jamaican
Steel Pulse, Reggae Pop; Roots, 1970s-1990s, Artist, British
Steelie & Cleevie, Dancehall; Roots, 1980s-1990s, Artist, Jamaican
Sublime, Ska, 1980s-, Artist, American
Suicide Machines, The, Ska, 1990s-, Artist, American
Suns Of Arca, Dub, 1970s-, Artist, British

Super Cat, Dancehall; Ragga, 1980s-1990s, Artist, Jamaican
Tamlins, The, UK Reggae, 1990s, Artist, British
Terror Fabulous, Dancehall; Ragga, 1990s, Artist, Jamaican
Third World, Reggae Pop, 1970s-, Artist, Jamaican
Thomas, Ruddy, UK Reggae, 1970s-1990s, Artist, British
Thompson, Linval, Dancehall; Dub, 1970s-1990s, Artist, American
Thunder, Shelley, Dancehall, 1980s-1990s, Artist, Jamaican
Tiger, Dancehall, 1970s-1990s, Artist, Jamaican
Toots & the Maytals, Rock Steady; Ska, 1960s-1990s, Artist, Jamaican
Tosh, Peter, Roots, 1960s-1980s, Artist, Jamaican

Tuff, Tony, UK Reggae, 1980s; 2000s-, Artist, British
UB40, Reggae Pop, 1980s-, Artist, British
U-Brown, Dancehall, 1970s-, Artist, Jamaican
Unity 2, Dancehall; Ragga, 1980s-1990s, Artist, Jamaican
Upsetters, The, Dub; Roots, 1960s-1980s, Artist, Jamaican
U-Roy, Roots; Dub, 1960s-, Artist, Jamaican
Viceroys, The, Dub, 1960s-1990s, Artist, Jamaican
Wailer, Bunny, Roots, 1970s-, Artist, Jamaican
Wailers, The, Rock Steady, 1960s-1990s, Artist, Jamaican
Wailing Souls, The, Dub; Roots, 1970s-, Artist, Jamaican
Wales, Josey, Ragga, 1980s-, Artist, Jamaican
Wilson, Delroy, Reggae Pop; Roots, 1960s-1990s, Artist, Jamaican
Yellowman, Dancehall; Ragga, 1980s-, Artist, Jamaican
Zephaniah, Benjamin, Dub, 1980s-1990s, Artist, Jamaican
Zukie, Tapper, Dub, 1970s-1990s, Artist, Jamaica

SKA ➡ 350 ROCK STEADY ➡ 352 ROOTS ➡ 354 DUB ➡ 356 UK REGGAE ➡ 358 REGGAE POP ➡ 359 RAGGA ➡ 360 DANCEHALL ➡ 362
BOBO DREAD DEEJAYS ➡ 364 US REGGAE ➡ 365 DEEJAYS ➡ 366

Soul And R&B

Above

*Ray Charles' Genius +
Soul = Jazz is mainly an
instrumental album, featuring
big band arrangements from
the Count Basie band.*

IN 1949, two apparently small events took place, which in hindsight were to have monumental significance for popular culture. The first of these saw *Billboard* magazine change the name of its "Race Records" chart to the more relevant and politically correct "Rhythm & Blues" chart, reflecting the success of the American dance music of the moment.

Meanwhile, a 19-year-old blind Georgia orphan called Ray Charles Robinson (he dropped the Robinson to avoid confusion with the legendary boxer Sugar Ray Robinson) released his first single 'Confession Blues'. By the mid-1950s, rhythm & blues had mutated into rock'n'roll, the ultimate crossover between black and white popular music, and in the form of R&B would remain the dominant label attached to pop music of Afro-American origin. By 1954, the visionary and eclectic Charles, with his arrangement for bluesman Guitar Slim's 'The Things That I Used To Do' and the irresistible fusion of jazz, blues and gospel on his own 'I Got A Woman' (later covered by Elvis Presley), had invented soul music – rock's spiritual, sensual Afro-American twin.

Soul is an innovative blend of musical styles: the Baptist hymn and the juke joint dance exhortation, the plantation field holler and the sophisticated jazz standard, the romantic vocal flights of doo-wop and the driving rhythms of small-band R&B, the gospel plea for deliverance and the altogether earthier blues lament. It rose to prominence through the innovations of two

> "IT WAS A SLANG THAT WOULD RELATE TO THE MAN ON THE STREET, PLUS IT HAD ITS OWN SOUND: THE MUSIC ON ONE-AND-THREE, THE DOWNBEAT, IN ANTICIPATION."
>
> *James Brown on 'Papa's Got A Brand New Bag'*

Right

*The Apollo Theatre in
Harlem, New York, played a
major part in the development
of black music. In 1934, the
theatre introduced its amateur
night, providing aspiring black
performers with a chance to
prove themselves. James Brown
launched his career at
the Apollo.*

further black male pioneers from the southern states. Mississippi gospel heart-throb Sam Cooke made a controversial move to secular pop in 1956. By 1957 his 'You Send Me' – a heart-melting mix of teen pop and Cooke's alternately tender and roaring gospel vocals – had gone to number one in the US and truly ignited the soul era. He continued to be one of pop's most loved crossover pioneers until his shocking death in 1964, at the hands of a motel manager who claimed she shot the singer in self-defence after he had allegedly raped another woman.

Georgia's James Brown released his first single, 'Please Please Please', in 1956, a record so vocally intense and rhythmically tough that it made a romantic plea to a woman sound like a hysterical scream from the very depths of sexual desperation and despair. Brown's prolific writing and recording schedule was sent into commercial overdrive by the most extreme live performances of the period, a theatrical and almost militarily precise singing and dancing spectacular that had a profound influence on Mick Jagger, Michael Jackson, Prince and every star since who has combined flamboyant sexual display, bravura dance moves and unstoppable physical

STYLES

The Classic Soul Era

Northern Soul

Funk Soul

Funk

Urban Soul

Contemporary R&B

THE SOUL & R&B STYLE

*Soul and R&B, in all its
guises, is heavily influenced
by the classic Motown sound.
With its strong bass and drum
lines, this is a formula which
has been successfully repeated
over the past four decades.*

SOUL AND R&B PEOPLE ➡ 382   INSTRUMENTS A-Z ➡ 436   THE POP INTRO ➡ 8   POP: ROCK'N'ROLL ➡ 16   THE BLUES INTRO ➡ 154

James Brown

energy with playful drama and driving rhythm. A recorded document of that show, 1962's *Live At The Apollo*, along with another Ray Charles innovation, *Modern Sounds In Country And Western Music* from the same year, established soul as an album-selling genre. James Brown, of course, was key in turning soul music into funk and disco, and through his ability to make African-derived rhythm into a complex but universally understood musical language, he had the most profound influence upon hip hop and all subsequent genres of dance music.

By late-1963, soul was so dominant in the American singles market that the black chart was abolished, for the first and only time, until early 1965. Over the next 30 years, the original soul impulse was taken in so many different directions that the term is now largely applied only to the 1960s/early 1970s Golden Era. Nevertheless, just as all white rock and pop eventually refers back to the blues, Elvis, the Beatles or Dylan, the black pop we now (rather ironically) call R&B owes its existence to the leaps of artistic faith made by Charles, Cooke and Brown.

THE STORY OF SOUL'S GOLDEN AGE IS LINKED WITH THE STORY OF TWO AMERICAN RECORD LABELS: BERRY GORDY'S MOTOWN AND JIM STEWART & ESTELLE AXTON'S STAX. THEY DISCOVERED ARTISTS, WROTE SONGS AND DEVELOPED RECORDING AND MARKETING METHODS THAT WOULD IRREVOCABLY CHANGE POPULAR MUSIC, AND HAVE A PROFOUND EFFECT ON THE PERCEPTION OF RACE ALL OVER WORLD.

The Classic Soul Era

Above

Originally just the Miracles, in 1967 the group became known as Smokey Robinson & the Miracles. They had a total of 25 Top 40 hits during the 1960s.

MOTOWN'S base in Detroit and Stax's in Memphis symbolized the Afro-American migration from south to north, and the differences in style and aspirations between those who left and those who stayed. Berry Gordy came from a Georgian farming family who had relocated to Detroit. He began writing songs in the mid-1950s, after stints as a boxer, soldier, jazz record shop assistant and car worker, and hit big with songs for former sparring partner Jackie Wilson, including big band R&B classic 'Reet Petite'. Gordy was persuaded to form his own record company in 1959 by singer/songwriter protégé Smokey Robinson, making his big breakthrough in 1961 with 'Shop Around', performed by Robinson's vocal group the Miracles. Gordy's tightly controlled methods were considered both revolutionary and controversial in later years. Artists were signed on salaries and ordered to perform the material that Gordy insisted upon. The house producers and composers – Robinson, Holland/Dozier/Holland, Ashford/Simpson, Whitfield/Strong – were all-important. The in-house band the Funk Brothers (pianist Joe Hunter, guitarist Dave Hamilton, drummer Benny Benjamin and the legendary James Jamerson on the most influential bass guitar in pop history) pioneered the all-important Motown sound but saw little in the way of financial recompense (a complaint subsequently echoed by many Motown artists) or recognition.

> "THE TEMPTATIONS COULD HAVE COME FROM CENTRAL CASTING. . .FIVE GREAT-LOOKING MEN, ALL OVER SIX FOOT TALL, AND THEY DID IT ALL."
>
> *Shelly Berger, manager*

LEADING EXPONENTS

Smokey Robinson & the
  Miracles
Aretha Franklin
Diana Ross & the
  Supremes
Otis Redding
Marvin Gaye
James Brown
Wilson Pickett
Marvin Gaye
Stevie Wonder
The Four Tops
The Temptations
Dionne Warwick
Solomon Burke
Bobby Womack
Al Green

Motown package tours were tightly choreographed and chaperoned, with the young stars given lessons in deportment and etiquette by Motown staffers.

The Hit Factory

Whatever the rights or wrongs of the set-up, the inexhaustible supply of Motown hits dominated the 1960s, in Europe as well as America. The unmistakable Motown blend of powerful R&B rhythm, highly sophisticated orchestral arrangements and poetic lyricism came to define the language of pop. The peerless parade of charismatic virtuoso gospel-derived vocal groups and solo artists beguiled white fans as much as black, and raised the level of artistry that pop could attain. The likes of Robinson, Diana Ross & the Supremes, Marvin Gaye, the Four Tops, the Temptations and Stevie Wonder fronted hit after hit, rising from pop ingénues to era-defining artists within the ten years of Motown's peak period. Although they may have signed to Motown in 1968, after its peak, the Jackson Five's debut single 'I Want You Back' was the label's fastest-selling record ever, and three of their subsequent five singles reached the number one spot in the US.

THE CLASSIC SOUL ERA

This bass pattern is typical of the classic Motown sound. Arranged in counterpoint to the tune, with a tight, hard-sounding drum accompaniment, it should be played at a fast tempo.

THE SOUL AND R&B INTRO ➡ 368   SOUL AND R&B PEOPLE A-Z ➡ 382   INSTRUMENTS A-Z ➡ 436   THE ROCK INTRO ➡ 74   THE BLUES INTRO ➡ 154

The Southern Melting Pot

1960 saw the formation of Stax, a label that, by signing a distribution deal with powerful New York jazz and R&B company Atlantic, would see their completely contrasting style of soul cross over to the rapidly growing rock audience. The Stax/Atlantic phenomenon was based upon a complete racial mix: raucous and untamed black gospel-raised vocalists such as the Stax label's Otis Redding, Sam & Dave, and Carla Thomas; plus Atlantic's Aretha Franklin, Ben E. King, Solomon Burke and Wilson Pickett, worked with multi-racial R&B bands Booker T & the MG's (from Memphis) and the Muscle Shoals rhythm section (the in-house band from the Muscle Shoals studio in Alabama), performing the songs and sounds of racially integrated backroom geniuses. They defined the sound envisioned by behind-the-scenes masters including producers Chips Moman and Billy Sherrill and composers Dan Penn, Spooner Oldham, Isaac Hayes and David Porter. If Stax/Atlantic's true reflection of the young southerners' rebuffal of segregation was challenging, then the music was incendiary: power-packed testimonies of love, sex, spiritual freedom and political protest matched with horn-driven proto-funk that gave a feeling of earthy, spontaneous, almost live authenticity, and contrasted perfectly with Motown's highly sophisticated studio symphonies.

Soul's Full Circle

While Motown and Stax/Atlantic dominated, the market inevitably became saturated with soul artists and records pouring from labels both major and independent. Many magnificent singles became lost amidst the deluge, but some non-Motown/Stax/Atlantic artists emerged to comparable acclaim and impact. James Brown continued to be known as "Soul Brother Number One", remaining soul's greatest live performer and developing the rhythmic innovation known as funk. Ohio singer/songwriter/guitarist Bobby Womack who was discovered in the early 1960s by Sam Cooke, saw his 'It's All Over Now' covered by the Rolling Stones, and had a slew of tough and bluesy R&B hits based around his rough, gruff vocals and hard rocking blues guitar. In complete contrast, New Jersey's Dionne Warwick forged the template for the perennial sophisticated soul diva in the mid-1960s, with her subtle and beautiful recordings of songs by Burt Bacharach & Hal David, most famously on the sweeping romantic dramas of 1964's 'Anyone Who Had A Heart' and 'Walk On By'.

As the integrationist hope of the 1960s faded into the pessimistic 1970s, Motown and Stax struggled to come to terms with changing trends and a loss of identity. Amidst the

coming dominance of funk and disco, the death of Otis Redding in a 1967 plane crash and the reinvention of Marvin Gaye and Stevie Wonder as social comment singer/songwriters, one last great soulman emerged. Arkansas vocalist Al Green, working out of Willie Mitchell's Hi studio label in Memphis, brought a new sexual intensity to romantic soul with his astonishing falsetto voice and a string of sensual hits produced between 1971 and 1974. In October of that year, a horrifying incident, in which a girlfriend poured boiling grits over the singer before shooting herself, prompted Green to reject his sex-symbol stardom and the promiscuous lifestyle it had led to. He reverted to gospel music and became the pastor of his own church, symbolizing a full circle for the Golden Age of soul.

Above

Otis Redding recorded 'Sittin' On the Dock Of The Bay' just three days before he died in a plane crash near Madison, Wisconsin, in 1967. It was number one for four weeks in 1968.

Above Left

Berry Gordy, the owner of Motown records, with Diana Ross. Following the defection of producers Holland/ Dozier/Holland in 1970, Gordy concentrated on promoting the solo career of Diana Ross.

Northern Soul

THIS ENDURING BRITISH CULT DANCE SCENE TAKES ITS NAME FROM THE POST-MOD DISCOS IN THE NORTH-WEST OF ENGLAND WHERE IT DEVELOPED, RATHER THAN THE GEOGRAPHICAL LOCATION OF THE MUSIC-MAKERS. LEGENDARY DISCO VENUES LIKE MANCHESTER'S TWISTED WHEEL, BLACKPOOL'S MECCA AND THE WIGAN CASINO, ARE STILL SPOKEN ABOUT IN REVERENTIAL TONES BY SOUL AND DANCE CONNOISSEURS.

Above

Geno Washington achieved chart success with the Ram Jam band during the 1960s. His album Geno's Back in 1976 took him back on the road and he continued to tour into the 1990s.

THE reason northern soul exists is because of the extraordinary amount of quality soul produced – and often initially ignored – in the Motown- and Stax-dominated 1960s soul Golden Age.

From Levi's Genes

The immediately recognizable northern soul sound derives directly from Motown, and specifically from one key record: the Four Tops' 1965 hit 'I Can't Help Myself (Sugar Pie, Honey Bunch)'. With its circular piano/guitar riff, pounding rhythm, dramatic orchestral arrangement, and masochistic, lovelorn lyric howled like a sermon by lead vocalist Levi Stubbs, this track saw Motown composer/producers Eddie and Brian Holland and Lamont Dozier taking jazz and classical complexity and making it into totally accessible dancefloor R&B, with hooklines to match. As one of Motown's defining peak moments, it had an immediate influence on fledgling soul artists and small labels all over America. But, with Motown so commercially dominant, the majority of these more modest and derivative soul recordings failed to get radio airplay and slipped into obscurity.

" ...UNTIL YOU'VE BEEN THERE I DON'T THINK ANY MERE WRITTEN WORD CAN FULLY CONVEY TO YOU THAT SPECIAL AND UNIQUE VIBRATION THAT GENERATES AMONGST THE BROTHERS AND SISTERS THERE."

Dave Godin, soul guru and the first to use the phrase "Northern Soul" in the Blues and Soul magazine in 1971

No-Hit Wonders

Meanwhile, England's loyal late-1960s mods, who had made

LEADING EXPONENTS

Holland/Dozier/Holland

The Four Tops

Edwin Starr

Jackie Wilson

The Impressions

Robert Knight

The Velvelettes

R. Dean Taylor

Dobie Gray

Ramsey Lewis Trio

NORTHERN SOUL

Northern soul comes in various guises. In this example, the piano and drums drive the rhythm with an almost rock-like groove.

Motown and melodic soul their dance music of choice, were demanding something more from DJs than the familiar big hits. Those DJs began to take more chances on obscure US imports, and the competition to find the most upfront, unheard new tunes took off, particularly around the north-west of England, in and around Manchester. But by 1968, soul was changing, taking on influences from funk, the blues & roots revival, and psychedelic rock, as typified by Norman Whitfield and Barrett Strong's productions for the Temptations including 'Cloud Nine' and 'Just My Imagination'. As they entered the 1970s the serious Twisted Wheel and Mecca dancers, who were now developing a post-mod dress code of longer hair, tight T-shirts or sweaters, and voluminous "Oxford Bag" pants, wanted their DJs to stick with light, uptempo grooves despite their increasing rarity. DJs like future Hi-NRG pioneer Ian Levine began to make trips to the US, often tracking down entire warehouses full of mid- to late-1960s soul singles that no one had bought. Played in the northern clubs, they sent the dancers wild and began a self-contained scene based not around artists or albums, but particular singles. This also meant that northern soul discovered a non-dancefloor foundation built around collecting rare records, with "failed" singles often fetching hundreds of pounds on the collectors' market.

The Fad That Wouldn't Die

The northern soul cult spread throughout Britain, to Scotland, the Midlands, and eventually London, reaching its peak in 1975 when two novelty groups, Ovation and Chosen Few, both from Wigan, reached the UK singles chart with records designed to exploit the hitherto underground scene. This caused a split between the 1960s diehards and those – particularly the DJs and patrons of the Wigan Casino – who put crossover pop such as 'A Lover's Concerto' by Toys and 'Love On A Mountain Top' and 'Everlasting Love' by Robert Knight into the mix. By the late-1970s, the Casino, Mecca and Twisted Wheel had closed down, and northern DJs such as Levine and Pete Waterman began mixing light soul with Europop, creating the gay disco of Hi-NRG and having a profound influence over all subsequent forms of British manufactured pop. Nevertheless, northern soul refused (and still refuses) to die, and new generations of DJs and

followers continue to emerge, sustaining regular clubs and one-off "all-nighters", fanzines, a plethora of CD compilations and digital radio shows.

Anthems And Tributes

Inevitably, the music associated with northern soul has gone on to encompass an ever-widening range of styles; aficionados are still arguing over what is or isn't true northern soul. Scene anthems range from the pure soul stomp of Edwin Starr's 'S.O.S. (Stop Her On Sight)' and the great Jackie Wilson's 'The Sweetest Feeling' to the plaintive orchestral social conscience ballads of Curtis Mayfield and his 1960s vocal group the Impressions; to the girl-group pop of the Velvelettes and the Chiffons; to the R&B of Sugar Pie De Santo and the Capitols; to the soul-jazz instrumentals as 'The In Crowd' by Ramsey Lewis; to records such as Evelyn King's 'Shame' and the O'Jays' 'I Love Music', which typify the northern soul/disco crossover of the scene-splitting late-1970s.

Apart from the obvious influence on gay disco and manufactured pop, northern soul directly inspired various 1980s British acts. Electro pop duo Soft Cell covered northern classics 'Tainted Love' and 'What'. Dexys Midnight Runners scored their first UK number one with 'Geno', a tribute to club performer Geno Washington. Joboxers had a short shot at fame with northern-inspired hits 'Boxer Beat' and 'Just Got Lucky'. And the 2-Tone bands took a little from the genre too, as is especially obvious on 'Embarrassment' by Madness.

Left
Gloria Jones recorded 'Tainted Love' (the song made famous by Soft Cell's cover version) in the mid-1960s, but moved to Britain to find work amid the northern soul craze. She joined the rock band T Rex in 1974 and became the girlfriend of singer Marc Bolan.

Below
The Four Tops formed in 1953 after an impromptu performance at a friend's birthday party. Band member Lawrence Payton died in 1997, and the Tops split after an amazing 44 years of performing together.

ROCK: PSYCHEDELIC ROCK ➡ 80   THE JAZZ INTRO ➡ 118   THE BLUES INTRO ➡ 154   THE CLASSICAL INTRO ➡ 250

SINCE THE DAWN OF THE JAZZ ERA, THE APPEAL OF POP MUSIC HAD BECOME INCREASINGLY INTERTWINED WITH THE DEMANDS OF THE DANCEFLOOR. AS 1960S ROCK AND SOUL BECAME EVER TOUGHER AND MORE ORIENTATED TOWARDS YOUTH & HEDONISM IT WAS ONLY A MATTER OF TIME BEFORE SOMEONE WOULD COME UP WITH THE ULTIMATE DANCE GROOVE.

Funk Soul

Above

Tracks on Aretha: Lady Soul *include 'Chain Of Fools' and '(You Make Me Feel Like) A Natural Woman', written by Gerry Goffin and Carole King.*

THAT someone was soul's greatest innovator, James Brown, who pioneered a music so orientated towards pure, African-derived rhythm that melody would finally be forced to take a back seat as backbeat took the wheel.

Funk as a term had been around since the turn of the twentieth century, when it applied specifically to the odours produced by the human body during and after sex. By the 1930s it was used to describe music with a dirty, lowdown feel, and by the 1950s it was an alternative name for hard bop, the post-bebop jazz with a straight-ahead, gospel- and swing-influenced rhythm, as typified by Milt Jackson and Horace Silver. But it was 1964 before funk formally twinned with soul, on James Brown's minor American hit single 'Out Of Sight'. The track had a familiar blues structure, but the hard-but-swinging, hip-grinding rhythm dominated, and was further developed by Brown on 1965's world-changing 'Papa's Got A Brand New Bag' and 1966's 'I Got You (I Feel Good)', by which time the entire JB band – horns, guitar, Brown's screeching staccato vocal – was surrendering melody to beat with a power and vibe as much African as Afro-American. Somewhat surprisingly however, Brown didn't apply the term funk to his new sound until 1967's flop single, the instrumental 'Funky Soul No. 1'.

As Brown's career progressed, funk began to dominate his oeuvre. As well as making his own genre-defining classics

> "HE WAS THE TRUE REPRESENTATIVE OF THE DREAM OF THE CROSSOVER BETWEEN ROCK AND SOUL AND FUNK AND PSYCHEDELIA."
>
> *Jim Irvin on Sly Stone*

Right

Sly & the Family Stone formed in 1967 and, unusually for the time, included male and female and black and white members.

LEADING EXPONENTS

James Brown

Fred Wesley & the JB's

Wilson Pickett

Aretha Franklin

Sly & the Family Stone

The Temptations/ Whitfield/Strong

The Isley Brothers

Isaac Hayes

Dr. John

The Meters

including 'Say It Loud – I'm Black And I'm Proud', 'Sex Machine' (arguably the first disco record) and 'Funky Drummer' (which became the most sampled track of the late-1980s/early-1990s when Clyde Stubblefield's drum break became ubiquitous on hip hop tracks of the period), Brown co-wrote, arranged and produced an enormous catalogue of funk classics for his "Funk Family". In some cases, tunes by the likes of Fred Wesley & the JB's, Maceo & the Macks, Bobby Byrd, Vicki Anderson, Lyn Collins and Marva Whitney are more treasured than Brown's own by the funk connoisseur.

Soul Greats Get Funky

Of course, other soul greats applied the same kind of rolling, undulating rhythms to their work. Atlantic Records soul singer Wilson "The Wicked" Pickett's 1965 anthem 'In The Midnight Hour' is a blueprint for strutting downtempo funk, and arguably the greatest soul singer of all, Memphis's Aretha Franklin, essayed a more subtle, gospel-edged funk sound on 1967 classics 'Respect' and 'Chain Of Fools' and 1971's 'Rock

FUNK SOUL

An approximation of the Norman Whitfield sound with rhythms similar to James Brown-style funk. Musically, however, there is more happening, with slick orchestral and vocal arrangements.

THE SOUL AND R&B INTRO ➡ 368   SOUL AND R&B PEOPLE A–Z ➡ 382   INSTRUMENTS A–Z ➡ 436   THE POP INTRO ➡ 8

Steady'. Funk/R&B crossovers like Eddie Floyd's 1966 'Knock On Wood' and Bob & Earl's 1969 'Harlem Shuffle' (originally recorded in 1964 and arranged by Barry White) also added to the burgeoning funk wave. The most sophisticated funk soul sounds came, predictably, from Motown and Stax alumni. Motown backroom boys Norman Whitfield and Barrett Strong began constructing tracks for the Temptations that blended funky wah-wah guitars, widescreen orchestration, and tough counter-cultural lyrical themes. From 1969's 'Cloud Nine' to 1973's 'Papa Was A Rollin' Stone', the formerly poppy vocal group became an object lesson in funk as artistically ambitious social commentary. Fellow Motown vocal group and R&B veterans the Isley Brothers left the Detroit label and released defiant funk affairs such as 'It's Your Thing' and 'Work To Do', as they built up to their funk/rock crossover peak. The same late-1960s/early 1970s period saw Stax writer/producer Isaac Hayes step into the limelight. His 1969 *Hot Buttered Soul* album invented a whole new seduction soul, transforming standards like 'Walk On By' into groaning, heavy breathing orchestral funk epics that inspired the likes of Barry White and Teddy Pendergrass. Of course, Hayes's 1971 soundtrack for the blaxploitation movie *Shaft*, with its intro of twitching hi-hats and chattering wah-wah guitar, is one of funk's most instantly recognizable motifs.

A Sly One

Meanwhile, Texan Sylvester Stewart – better known as Sly Stone – was approaching funky soul from a different angle. He was already a 24-year-old veteran artist, producer and DJ

on the San Francisco hippy rock scene before his inter-racial, multi-gender big band Sly & the Family Stone grabbed their first US hit with the exuberant 'Dance To The Music' in 1968. Sly & co. mixed funk, soul, big-band jazz, pop and psychedelic rock with brave abandon, making a string of era-defining US hits until 1971's extraordinary *There's A Riot Goin' On* album marked both his peak and his downfall. A dark, rambling yet powerful funk comment on the disillusion of the times, the album reached number one but also highlighted Stone's increasing emotional decline through drug addiction. Subsequent records became weaker until addiction, rehab and prison stretches rendered one of pop's greatest talents missing in action.

Swamp Funk

New Orleans, the birthplace of so much jazz and R&B, had its own unique take on the new sound. Dr. John (originally Malcolm Rebennack) was a white piano prodigy already steeped in bayou jazz and blues when he made 1968's *Gris Gris*, a unique mélange of voodoo mysticism, woozy psychedelia and laid-back funk virtuosity. His friends the Meters, led by Art Neville, responded with their 1969 self-titled instrumental album, which boiled funk down to subtly insistent syncopated beats and infectious "chicken scratch" guitar, a uniquely live-sounding style that reached its height on 1974's vocal *Rejuvenation* album.

Above

The Cry Baby wah-wah pedal. The wah-wah effect was originally intended to imitate the crying tone of a muted trumpet, but became an expressive tool in its own right when soloing or being used to create "wacka-wacka" funk rhythms.

Left

By 1976 the Temptations had seen so many line-up changes that only two of the original five members remained. In this year they recorded their final album for Motown – The Temptations Do The Temptations.

BY THE 1970S, THE NEW SOUND OF FUNK DOMINATED AFRO-AMERICAN MUSIC. JAZZERS SUCH AS MILES DAVIS AND HERBIE HANCOCK SCORED THEIR BIGGEST COMMERCIAL SUCCESSES BY INCORPORATING ITS HIP-GRINDING RHYTHMS INTO WHAT BECAME KNOWN AS FUSION OR JAZZ FUNK, WHILE SOUL ACTS ENJOYED A SECOND WAVE OF POPULARITY AS FUNK PROVIDED THE BRIDGE BETWEEN THE SOUL AND DISCO ERAS.

Funk

Above

The members of Funkadelic were initially part of George Clinton's funk band, Parliament. The album One Nation Under A Groove *proved their breakthrough and sold a million copies.*

FUELLED by Sly & the Family Stone's dark and druggy *There's A Riot Goin' On*, many of funk's themes were street-tough and angry, swapping soul's romance and hope for reportage on harsh ghetto realities. Other funk acts went in the opposite direction, using little more than chanted hooks and slogans to embellish their funky instrumental jams. Whichever way, the 1970s funk era remains one of the most vibrant periods in black music history, and those deep, dirty rhythms went on to provide sampling source material for hip hop's explosion in the late-1980s.

Funky Soul Men

"The Godfather Of Soul", James Brown, continued to develop the funk he'd invented throughout the 1970s and 1980s.

Although well-documented problems with drugs, women and the police led to an inevitable decline in his music's potency, classics such as 1975's 'Funky President' and 1976's disco-exploiting 'Get Up Offa

"JAMES HAS MORE FUNK IN HIS LITTLE FINGER THAN MOST PEOPLE HAVE IN THEIR LIFE."

Saxophone player Pee Wee Ellis on James Brown

Right

An all-round musical talent, Curtis Mayfield is a guitarist, singer, producer and songwriter. His movie soundtrack to Superfly *proved his greatest solo success, with the tracks 'Freddie's Dead' and 'Superfly' both selling millions in the US.*

That Thing' established him forever as the definitive funk artist. While Brown continued to throwdown, two other 1960s soul masters blended a mellower form of funk with socially concerned singer/songwriter elements. Former Motown child prodigy Stevie Wonder reached artistic peaks with the powerful fear-fuelled funk rock of 1973's 'Superstition' and the same year's *Innervisions*, an all-time-great LP mixing tough funk protest, sublime ballads and a jazzy spontaneity, despite Wonder playing almost everything himself. Meanwhile, Chicago's

Curtis Mayfield broke away from his 1960s vocal group the Impressions and fashioned a unique muse based upon his beautiful falsetto vocals and vivid lyrical pleas for social justice. This produced a funk masterpiece in 1972 with his soundtrack for blaxploitation movie *Superfly*. All this Sly Stone-influenced funk politics was defined by a classic 1972 single by Ohio's O'Jays. This Philadelphia Sound vocal group produced, in the extraordinary 'Backstabbers', an expression of desperate pop paranoia that matched Marvin Gaye's legendary 'I Heard It Through The Grapevine' in intensity and dread.

The Coming Of P-Funk

North Carolina's George Clinton had already been through 1950s doo-wop and 1960s soul with little success before his singular funk vision bore fruit in 1970. The debut album by his Funkadelic project took Sly Stone's psychedelic funk on an even weirder trip, mixing hard black rhythm with hallucinogenic guitar freak-outs and LSD-inspired sci-fi lyrics. By 1973, former James Brown cohorts Bootsy Collins (bass), Maceo

LEADING EXPONENTS

James Brown

Stevie Wonder

Curtis Mayfield

Parliament/Funkadelic

The Isley Brothers

War

The O'Jays

Earth, Wind & Fire

Kool & The Gang

Prince

FUNK

The funk of James Brown produced a very hard-edged sound. The guitar off-beat sounds almost Caribbean, with a repeated bass figure that recalls the ground bass style, or ostinato, used in early opera.

THE SOUL AND R&B INTRO ➡ 368   SOUL AND R&B PEOPLE A-Z ➡ 382   INSTRUMENTS A-Z ➡ 436   THE ROCK INTRO ➡ 74

Parker (sax) and Fred Wesley (trombone) had joined Clinton in his two parallel groups, Funkadelic and Parliament. The two outfits mixed and matched up to 35 members and played the greatest freak-out live shows of their day. They swapped between pounding low-tempo big band grooves and maverick acid funk excursions, carried Clinton's bizarre but meaningful vision of black freedom in a futuristic cosmic journey, and became one of America's biggest bands. 1971's *Maggot Brain* (Funkadelic), 1976's *Mothership Connection* (Parliament) and 1978's *One Nation Under A Groove* (Funkadelic again) represent the high points of Clinton & co.'s catalogue, which took in equally influential sets by Bootsy Collins's Rubber Band and, in the 1980s, by Clinton as a solo artist. That influence is particularly evident in 1980s keepers of the funk faith – especially soul-pop and sex-funk genius Prince, his Motown label rival Rick James, electro-funk exhibitionists Cameo, and the Gap Band, who scored disco success by boiling Clinton's big beat excursions down into hook-laden pop singles such as 1980's infectious 'Oops Upside Your Head' – as well as hip hop's west coast G-Funk of the 1990s.

Above

Kool & the Gang began life as a jazz quartet during the 1960s, but developed into an internationally successful funk band. Their enigmatic frontman, "J. T." Taylor stayed with the band until 1988, when he left to pursue a solo career.

Low Riders And High Rollers

Four remaining classic funk bands symbolize black American music's swift 1970s journey from rock and jazz-influenced bohemian innovation, through the much-parodied but well-loved period of sartorial flamboyance represented by Afro dos and outrageous flared jump-suits, to funk's eventual defeat and dilution at the hands of late-1970s disco crossover.

LA's War began as a back-up band for former Animal Eric Burdon before forging their own path with a heavily jazz- and rock-influenced form of funk complexity. Their finest moments veer from the dramatic protest of 1972's 'The World Is A Ghetto' to the irresistible street scene grooves of 1973's 'Me And Baby Brother' and 1976's gravel-voiced 'Low Rider'. But by 1978 their attempts to ride the disco wave floundered and obscurity beckoned. Faring rather better were hardy perennials the Isley Brothers, who, after having adapted to 1950s R&B, Motown pop, early funk, and even superb versions of folk rock protest song covers, encouraged brother Ernie to unleash his coruscating post-Hendrix electric guitar licks. The result was the benchmark *3 + 3* album in 1973, and

a prolific stream of small-band funk rock and ballad singles and albums. Again, the Isleys faltered over disco, but bounced back in 1983 with the 'Sexual Healing'-inspired boudoir soul of 'Between The Sheets'.

In the wake of P-Funk, horn-driven big bands from all over America mixed infectious chants with grooving jams. Two of those bands gradually changed tack and were two of disco's big winners. Maurice White's Earth, Wind & Fire blended Clinton's cosmic vision with White's own jazz arrangement virtuosity and, as their massively successful career progressed, increasingly sophisticated pop songcraft. Between 1973's *Head To The Sky* and 1981's *Raise!* they were black America's most globally successful act, mixing pop, big-band jazz, funk, soul, disco, unintentionally hilarious cosmic peace and love pretension, and an incredible theatrical live show. The 1980s advance of machine-driven dance music finally ended their triumphant run.

The less flamboyant but similarly adaptable Ohio big band Kool & the Gang hit with a more modest form of funk-to-disco transition. After a string of jam'n'chant successes culminating in 1976's 'Open Sesame' (as featured on the *Saturday Night Fever* soundtrack), they hired crooner James "J.T." Taylor and became disco pop hitmakers from 1979's 'Ladies Night' onwards, before those pesky machines rendered them unKool in the mid-1980s.

ALTHOUGH THE 1960S GOLDEN AGE ESTABLISHED SOUL AS THE FOUNDATION OF AFRO-AMERICAN POP, THE 1970S AND 1980S SAW SOUL'S SUPREMACY CHALLENGED AND ULTIMATELY ENDED BY, IN TURN, FUNK, DISCO, ELECTRO, DANCE-ROCK, HIP HOP AND HOUSE. IN HINDSIGHT, THE SOUL MUSIC OF THE 1980S WENT INTO A FORM OF STASIS, WAITING FOR A NEW STYLE OF SOUL TO REVIVE THE GENRE.

Urban Soul

Above

A seminal album of the era, What's Going On *addresses many political issues troubling America at the time, and captures the frustration and concern felt by Marvin Gaye and many of his fellow countrymen.*

NEVERTHELESS, soul, like rock'n'roll, will never die, and a few true soul voices continued to survive and adapt to the new market. Before looking at these 1980s urban soul artists, it's necessary to acknowledge the important performers who kept soul breathing during the funk- and disco-deluged 1970s.

Sweet Soul

Producer Thom Bell and songwriters Kenny Gamble and Leon Huff set up the Philadelphia International label in the late-1960s. By the mid-1970s, the trio had established the "Philly sound", a massively successful blend of gospel- or doo-wop-influenced vocals and heavily orchestrated black pop that heavily informed disco through the music of the O' Jays, Harold Melvin & the Blue Notes, the Three Degrees and the cast-of-thousands house band MFSB. Bell also co-wrote and produced for the three vocal groups who defined the mellifluous sound of sweet soul: the Delfonics, the Stylistics and the Spinners, who all produced a string of much-loved romantic hits in the early 1970s. Bell had no hand in Chicago's Chi-Lites, who mined an identical seam, reaching a peak of tear-stained male masochism on 1972's gorgeous 'Have You Seen Her?' An altogether more defiant gospel-derived take on sweet soul came from Atlanta's Gladys Knight & the Pips, a 1950s vocal group who had signed with Motown in the 1960s, fronted the first and funkier version of 'I Heard It Through The Grapevine' in 1967, and scored their

> "IF YOU GOT THE FEELING, YOU CAN SING SOUL. YOU JUST SING FROM THE HEART."
>
> *Otis Redding*

biggest Motown hit in 1972 with country composer Kris Kristofferson's 'Help Me Make It Through The Night'. The group became part of the Motown talent drain the following year, when they signed for Buddah and made the extraordinary 'Midnight Train To Georgia', a weepy ballad about heading back down south that showcased one of the toughest and most expressive voices in soul history.

The first solo sweet soul superstar arrived when Teddy Pendergrass, gravel-voiced lead singer of Melvin's Blue Notes,

LEADING EXPONENTS

Marvin Gaye
The Chi-Lites
The Stylistics
Teddy Pendergrass
Donny Hathaway
Luther Vandross
Anita Baker
Prince
Jam & Lewis
Alexander O'Neal
The S.O.S. Band
Sounds Of Blackness
Soul II Soul

URBAN SOUL

In this, an example of the British sound of Soul II Soul – rhythmic keyboard and bass lines combine with drum loops to form a breakbeat-style effect.

THE SOUL AND R&B INTRO ➡ 368   SOUL AND R&B PEOPLE A-Z ➡ 382   INSTRUMENTS A-Z ➡ 436   POP: DOO-WOP ➡ 20   THE JAZZ INTRO ➡ 118

went solo in 1976. His definitive take on boudoir soul seduction produced a string of US hit albums before a car crash in 1982 paralyzed him from the neck down. Undaunted, Pendergrass continued to record throughout the 1980s, duetting on 'Hold Me' with a pre-stardom Whitney Houston in 1984.

An even more tragic story concerns critically acclaimed Chicago vocalist Donny Hathaway. His virtuoso blends of soul balladry, subtle jazz and Latin grooves brought admiration but little commercial impact, aside from hit duets with former classmate Roberta Flack. In 1979 he fell to his death: a suicide brought about by depression over his faltering career, which seemed to symbolize the demise of soul in the disco era.

Marvellous Marvin

In the early 1970s, Marvin Gaye made his break from Motown's formula-pop and made music that stands among the greatest in any genre, defining soul's conscience on 1971's *What's Going On* and soul's sensuality on 1973's *Let's Get It On*. After a bitter break from Motown and a wilderness period in Belgium, Gaye returned in 1982 with the extraordinary *Midnight Love*, featuring a single, 'Sexual Healing', that proved that deep soul and the new technology could co-exist perfectly – as long as you happened to be one of the best singers on Earth. The glorious comeback was ended forever when the tortured Gaye was shot dead by his father in April 1984.

The King And Queen Of Sophisto-Soul

As disco and its beat-led offshoots dominated, it became obvious that the soul alternative lay in ignoring the dancefloor completely and producing a new kind of sweet soul for an adult audience. Cue chubby New Yorker Luther Vandross, who began his career as a session singer (including backing vox on David Bowie's blue-eyed soul excursion *Young Americans*) before taking centre stage by blending a voice like melting chocolate shot through with a subtle vulnerability, and clean, synthetic backdrops constructed by jazz bassist Marcus Miller. It was masochistic romantic yearning all the way for Luther, hitting heights on 1986's *Give Me The Reason*.

The same year saw jazzy soul siren Anita Baker seduce the world with the smoky sensuality of her *Rapture* album, which took adult soul into a level of glossy sophistication, some way away from the throaty gospel hollers of Aretha Franklin and Otis Redding.

The Minneapolis Sound

Flip back to the turn of the 1980s, and a Minneapolis all-singing, dancing, composing, arranging and instrument-playing prodigy called Prince Rogers Nelson. His backing band, the Time, includes in its number Jimmy Jam and Terry Lewis, who eventually left Prince to his approaching superstardom and became writer/producers.

While their former leader was effortlessly mixing soul with funk, rock, jazz and pop (and creating, along with Michael Jackson, the ultimate soul/pop crossover.) Jam and Lewis opened their Flyte Tyme studios and explored ways to fit their beloved soul and gospel with the electro-funk, groove-based opportunities that new synthesizer technology offered. The emphatic, funky and soulful 1980s hits they went on to create for Janet Jackson, The S.O.S Band, Alexander O'Neal, Change (whose former lead singer was Luther Vandross) and gospel choir Sounds Of Blackness built a bridge between the funk era and the swingbeat/R&B future.

The Coming Of Brit-Soul

Negotiating the same river from the direction of London, two new black British acts also sought ways to blend electro with soul melodicism. Carl McIntosh's Loose Ends fused 'Sexual Healing'-type synthetic soul with a tougher hip hop feel, hitting a commercial peak with the lovely 'Hangin' On A String', a transatlantic hit in 1985. This proved to be the harbinger of a sound that will be forever associated with loved-up London at the turn of the 1990s. Jazzie B (originally Beresford Romeo) and his Soul II Soul collective took the Loose Ends sound and doubled it, adding deep, much-imitated hip hop beats, bittersweet optimism and a sense of space borrowed from dub reggae. The 1989 hits 'Keep On Movin'' and 'Back To Life' effectively reminded America what it was missing by rejecting soul, and inspired R&B's self-consciously retro cousin, nu soul.

Far Left
Roberta Flack and Donny Hathaway studied music together at Howard University. Having already dueted together before, in 1973 she recorded his track 'Killing Me Softly'. It was a huge success and spent five weeks at the top of the charts.

Left
Anita Baker followed her Grammy Award-winning album Rapture *with a world tour. She went on to win two further Grammys in 1988 for her follow-up album* Giving You The Best That I Got.

JAZZ: LATIN JAZZ ➡ 148   DANCE: DISCO ➡ 314   THE GOSPEL INTRO ➡ 384

Contemporary R&B

ALTHOUGH CONTEMPORARY R&B PREFERS TO ALIGN ITSELF WITH ITS RUDER AND MORE STREET-CREDIBLE COUSINS IN HIP HOP, THE ROOTS OF ITS MAINSTREAM PRACTITIONERS LIE FIRMLY IN MANUFACTURED POP. IN A THROWBACK TO THE MOTOWN ERA, R&B HAS BECOME A GLOBAL PHENOMENON BY COMBINING PRODUCER-LED FACTORY FORMULA WITH A HIGH LEVEL OF MUSICAL INNOVATION AND ADVENTURE.

Above

The ambitious Sean Combs quickly made a name for himself in the music industry and formed his own record label, aptly named Bad Boy. He has courted controversy throughout his career; most famously through his feud with Death Row records.

> "IT'S HER AURA, HER WHOLE PERSONALITY, HER MUSIC AS WELL, IT DEFINITELY TOUCHES YOUR HEART."
>
> *Romeo of So Solid Crew on Ms Dynamite*

THIS balance of pop smarts and muso credibility has produced many of the twenty-first century's most vital artists, entrepreneurs and recordings, while simultaneously conforming to many of pop's most facile stereotypes, particularly when it comes to gender issues and the worship of money.

Boys To Men

When Boston boy band New Edition sacked their mentor Maurice Starr in 1984, their subsequent move into a tougher, funkier, hip hop-informed blend of dance pop and balladry set the contemporary R&B train in motion. Their audience grew with them, and when Bobby Brown quit the group in 1986 they simply hired replacement Johnny Gill and continued to impress. By 1989, Brown had become the new sound's first superstar with his *Don't Be Cruel* album, and the rest of the band had split. While Gill and Ralph Tresvant enjoyed successful solo careers, Michael Bivins, Ricky Bell and Ronnie Devoe formed Bell Biv Devoe, effectively manufacturing themselves toward further success. Bivins also discovered winsome vocal group Boyz II Men, and the R&B era was brought into being by hugely successful male vocal groups with the above, Jodeci, R. Kelly and Public Announcement all treading a clever line between increasingly graphic teen girl seduction, hip hop attitude and increasing musical sophistication.

The key producer/composer in this wave was Guy (and later BlackStreet) member Teddy Riley, who coined the term "New Jack Swing" in an infectious anthem for hip hop crew Wreckx-N-Effect. His sophisticated melanges of synthetic soul, pop, rap and P-Funk in productions for the likes of Guy, Keith Sweat and Heavy D made swingbeat a household term, turning US success into global recognition. With few exceptions, swing vocals were light, nasal and hugely indebted to Stevie Wonder, aiming squarely at a youthful black (and largely female) market that found hip hop just a little too hardcore.

LEADING EXPONENTS

New Edition
Bobby Brown
Guy
Craig David
En Vogue
TLC
Mary J. Blige
P. Diddy
D'Angelo
Erykah Badu
Destiny's Child
Ms Dynamite

CONTEMPORARY R&B

Late-1990s R&B dance music uses a lot of repeated bass lines, together with busy, arpeggiated keyboard lines and fairly simple drum programming.

THE SOUL AND R&B INTRO ➡ 368   SOUL AND R&B PEOPLE A-Z ➡ 382   INSTRUMENTS A-Z ➡ 436   THE POP INTRO ➡ 8

The Ladies In The House

But any universal black pop sound needs equal female input to thrive. Enter entirely male producers Denzil Foster and Thomas McElroy, who, at the end of the 1980s, decided to put together a girl group who could challenge swing's growing appeal with an altogether earthier take on the hip hop-inspired times. En Vogue were stylish, sassy and sang with gospel-derived maturity, providing the world with a new jack feminist Supremes on 1990 debut album *Born To Sing*. Pundits played with the term "New Jill Swing", as less vocally ferocious but equally feisty and entertaining girl groups such as SWV and TLC began to emerge. All this changed when a young ghetto New Yorker, Mary J. Blige, teamed up with on-the-make producer Sean "Puffy" Combs. Combs labelled Blige's debut *What's The 411?* album "hip hop soul", and Blige's strident vocals and "ghetto fabulous" style sold millions and made swingbeat a redundant term, but set the troubled diva on the road to alcohol and drug problems, a traumatic private life, and enduring superstardom. Combs, of course, went on to rename himself Puff Daddy and P. Diddy, mentor the likes of Biggie Smalls and Faith Evans, and become the embodiment of the obscenely rich, constantly bragging ghetto superstar, admired and reviled in equal measure.

The New Bohemians

Every cultural action provokes a reaction, and so it was with 1990s R&B. To balance the extravagant, cash-flaunting excesses of the R&B mainstream, a set of artists emerged touting a less style-conscious, more bohemian and organic form of black music, unashamedly in love with soul's classic past. The likes of Maxwell, Ben Harper, Macy Gray, Angie Stone, India Arie and former Fugee Lauryn Hill have all made key records in this vein. But the two crucial artists in what is often termed nu soul are both singular talents from America's southern states.

D'Angelo (originally Michael Archer) from Richmond, Virginia grabbed immediate acclaim with his 1995 debut album *Brown Sugar*, which blended hip hop beats and attitude, classic soul melodies and textures, jazzy technique, and vocals reminiscent of both Al Green and Marvin Gaye. The follow-up in 2000, *Voodoo*, was even more extraordinary, updating the dark, rambling jam feel of Sly & the Family Stone's seminal *There's A Riot Goin' On*. All that, and with the looks and six-pack to match, the world is truly his.

The female version emerged in 1997 from Atlanta, Georgia. Erykah Badu's debut, *Baduizm*, was both sexual and spiritual, a sparse soundscape of low-tempo funk rhythms, jazzy songcraft and Ms. Badu's smoky, Billie Holiday-esque voice singing lyrics soaked in love, religion and politics. Again, the visual anti-image was strong – shawls and bare legs,

Left
Mary J. Blige shot to stardom with her first album in 1992. She released her fifth album, No More Drama, *in 2001 and the title of the album and quality of the tracks reflect the personal and musical development Blige has achieved during her ten years in the business.*

headscarf atop a striking, almost regal face, as accusatory as it was beautiful. In 2000, *Mama's Gun* added rock to the mix with less success, but she'll undoubtedly return with something equal to that classic first set.

R&B's Destiny

The new century sees vocal trio Destiny's Child firmly established as brand leaders in R&B's rise to global popularity, with Beyoncé Knowles & co. fusing sex, money, feminism, vocal virtuosity, cutting-edge production and pure pop fizz into a seamless and irresistible whole. Credible British R&B stars have finally arrived, with Craig David and Ms Dynamite bringing in influences from UK garage and Jamaican reggae respectively. The team of Missy Elliott and Tim "Timbaland" Mosley continue to mix R&B and rap so thrillingly that their influence makes it increasingly difficult to tell where hip hop begins and R&B ends. But, despite the impact of all the artists mentioned, R&B remains a producers' medium, its sound shaped and dominated by the likes of Teddy Riley, LA & Babyface, Rodney Jerkins, P. Diddy, Jermaine Dupri, Timbaland and the Neptunes, who all have a loyal following regardless of which artist fronts the video. Ironically, a star who had successfully managed to splice the artist and producer roles, one R. Kelly, also came to symbolize the distasteful side of R&B's "macho loverman" syndrome when he was arrested in 2001 on charges of underage sex and possession of child pornography.

Far Left
Bobby Brown pioneered new jack swing during the 1980s. His hits continued into the 1990s, but by 1997 headlines about his bad-boy behaviour and marital problems with Whitney Houston took precedence over his music and his album flopped.

DANCE: UK GARAGE ➡ 331   THE HIP HOP INTRO ➡ 334   THE REGGAE INTRO ➡ 348

Artists: Soul And R&B

Entries appear in the following order: name, music style, year(s) of popularity, type of artist, country of origin

112, Urban Soul, 1990s–, Artist, American
2LW, Contemporary R&B, 1990s–, Artist, American
3T, Urban Soul, 1990s, Artist, American
52nd Street, Urban Soul, 1980s, Artist, British
Aaliyah, Contemporary R&B; Urban Soul, 1990s–, Artist, American
Abbott, Gregory, Urban Soul, 1980s–, Artist, American
Abdul, Paula, Urban Soul, 1980s–1990s, Artist, American
Acklin, Barbara, Northern Soul, 1960s–1970s, Artist, American
Adams, Johnny, The Classic Soul Era, 1950s–1990s, Artist, American
Adams, Oleta, Urban Soul, 1990s–, Artist, American
Alexander, Arthur, The Classic Soul Era, 1960s–1970s, Artist, American
Ali, Tatayana, Urban Soul; Contemporary R&B, 1990s–, Artist, American
All Day Long, The Classic Soul Era, 1950s, Artist, American
All-4-One, Contemporary R&B, 1990s–, Artist, American
Allen, Debbie, The Classic Soul Era, 1970s–1980s, Artist, American
Allen, Donna, Urban Soul, 1980s–1990s, Artist, American
Allure, Urban Soul, 1990s–, Artist, American
Alston, Shirley, The Classic Soul Era, 1950s–1970s, Artist; Songwriter, American
Always, Billy, Urban Soul, 1960s–1990s, Artist, American
Amerie, Contemporary R&B; Urban Soul, 2000s–, Artist, American
Anderson, Carl, The Classic Soul Era; Urban Soul, 1980s–1990s, Artist, American
Anderson, Ernestine, Northern Soul, 1940s–, Artist, American
Anderson, Kip, The Classic Soul Era, 1960s, Artist, American
Anderson, Roshell, Urban Soul, 1980s–1990s, Artist, American
Anderson, Sunshine, Contemporary R&B; Urban Soul, 2000s–, Artist, American
André, Peter, Contemporary R&B, 1990s, Artist, Australian
Andrews, Ruby, The Classic Soul Era, 1960s–1970s, Artist, American
Answered Questions, Urban Soul, 1990s, Artist, American
Aquarian Dream, Funk Soul, 1970s–1980s, Artist, American
Armstrong, Vanessa Bell, Urban Soul, 1980s–, Artist, American
Arnold, P. P., Urban Soul, 1960s–1980s, Artist, American
Arrington, Steve, The Classic Soul Era, 1980s, Artist, American
Artistics, The, Northern Soul, 1960s–1970s, Artist, American
Ashanti, Contemporary R&B; Urban Soul, 2000s–, Artist, American
Ashford & Simpson, Urban Soul, 1970s–1980s, Artist, American
Astors, The, The Classic Soul Era, 1960s, Artist, American
Atlantic Starr, Urban Soul; Funk Soul, 1970s–1990s, Artist, American
Aurra, Urban Soul, 1980s, Artist, American
Autographs, The, Northern Soul, 1960s–1970s, Artist, American
Avant, Contemporary R&B, 2000s–, Artist, American
Average White Band, Funk Soul, 1970s–1980s, Artist, British
B., Stevie, Urban Soul, 1980s–, Artist, American
B2K, Contemporary R&B, 2000s–, Artist, American
Baby Huey, The Classic Soul Era, 1960s, Artist, American
Babyface, Contemporary R&B, 1980s–, Producer, Artist, American
Badu, Erykah, Contemporary R&B, 1990s–, Artist, American
Bailey, Philip, Urban Soul, 1980s–, Artist, American
Bailey, Rene, Northern Soul, 1960s–1970s, Artist, American
Baker, Anita, Urban Soul, 1980s–1990s, Artist, American
Baker, LaVern, The Classic Soul Era, 1950s–1960s; 1980s–1990s, Artist, American
Ballard, Hank, Northern Soul, 1950s–1990s, Artist; Songwriter, American
Banks, Darrell, The Classic Soul Era, 1960s, Artist, American
Banks, Doug, Northern Soul, 1960s–1970s, Artist, American
Bar-Kays, The, The Classic Soul Era, 1960s–1990s, Artist, American
Barnes, J. J., Northern Soul; The Classic Soul Era, 1960s–1980s, Artist, American
Barnum, Eve, Northern Soul, 1960s–1970s, Artist, American
Barnum, H. B., The Classic Soul Era, 1950s–1960s, Producer; Artist, American
Bartley, Chris, The Classic Soul Era, 1960s, Artist, American
Bass, Fontella, Northern Soul, 1960s–1970s; 1990s–, Artist, American
Baylor, Helen, Urban Soul, 1990s–, Artist, American
Bell Biv Devoe, Urban Soul, 1980s–, Artist, American
Bell, Archie, The Classic Soul Era, 1960s–1970s, Artist; Songwriter, American
Bell, Ricky, Urban Soul, 2000s–, Artist, American
Bell, Thom, Urban Soul, 1950s–1990s, Producer; Artist, American
Bell, William, Northern Soul, 1960s–, Artist, American
Belle, Regina, Urban Soul, 1980s–, Artist, American
Belvin, Jesse, The Classic Soul Era, 1950s, Artist, American
Benet, Eric, Contemporary R&B; Urban Soul, 1990s–, Artist, American
Bennett, Lou, The Classic Soul Era, 1950s–1980s, Artist, American
Bilal, Contemporary R&B; Urban Soul, 1990s–, Artist, American
Black, Bill, The Classic Soul Era, 1950s–1960s, Artist, American
Blackstreet, Urban Soul, 1990s, Artist, American
Bland, Bobby "Blue", The Classic Soul Era, 1950s–, Artist, American
Blaque, Contemporary R&B, 1990s–, Artist, American
Blast, C. L., The Classic Soul Era, 1980s, Artist, American
Blige, Mary J., Contemporary R&B, 1990s–, Artist, American
Bloodstone, Funk Soul, 1970s–1990s, Artist, American
Blue Magic, Urban Soul, 1970s–1990s, Artist, American
Blues Brothers, The, The Classic Soul Era, 1970s–, Artist, American
Boneshakers, The, Urban Soul, 1990s, Artist, American
Booker T & the MGs, The Classic Soul Era, 1960s–1970s, Artist, American
Booker, James, The Classic Soul Era, 1950s–1980s, Artist, American
Bourbon Tabernacle Choir, The, Contemporary R&B, 1980s–1990s, Artist, American
Boyz II Men, Contemporary R&B; Urban Soul, 1980s–, Artist, American
Brandy, Urban Soul, 1990s–, Artist, American
Brass Construction, The Classic Soul Era, 1960s–1980s, Artist, American
Braxton, Toni, Contemporary R&B; Urban Soul, 1990s, Artist, American
Braxtons, The, Urban Soul, 1990s, Artist, American
Brazton, Tamar, Contemporary R&B, 1990s–, Artist, American
Brenda & the Tabulations, The Classic Soul Era, 1960s–1970s, Artist, American
Bridges, Alicia, The Classic Soul Era, 1970s–1980s, Artist, American
Bridges, Calvin, Contemporary R&B, 1980s–1990s, Artist, American
Brighter Side Of Darkness, The Classic Soul Era, 1970s, Artist, American
Bristol, Johnny, The Classic Soul Era, 1960s–1980s, Artist, American
Brother To Brother, Funk Soul, 1970s, Artist, American
Brothers Johnson, The, Funk Soul, 1970s–1990s, Artist, American
Brown, Bobby, Urban Soul, 1980s–, Artist, American
Brown, James, Funk; Funk Soul, 1950s–1980s, Artist, American
Brown, Jocelyn, Contemporary R&B, 1980s–, Artist, American
Brown, Maxine, Funk Soul, 1960s–1970s, Artist, American
Brown, Randy, The Classic Soul Era, 1970s–1980s, Artist, American
Brown, Ruth, The Classic Soul Era, 1940s–1960s, Artist, American
Brown, Shirley, Urban Soul, 1970s–, Artist, American
Brownmark, The Classic Soul Era, 1980s, Artist, American
Brownstone, Urban Soul, 1990s–, Artist, American
Bryant, Don, The Classic Soul Era, 1960s–1990s, Artist, American
Bryant, Leon, The Classic Soul Era, 1980s–1990s, Artist, American
Bryant, Sharon, The Classic Soul Era, 1980s, Artist, American
Bryson, Peabo, Urban Soul, 1970s–1990s, Artist, American
Buckshot LeFonque, Contemporary R&B, 1990s, Artist, American
Burch, Vernon, The Classic Soul Era, 1970s–1980s, Artist, American
Burke, Solomon, The Classic Soul Era, 1950s–, Artist, American
Butler, Billy, Northern Soul, 1960s–1970s, Artist, American
Butler, Jerry, Northern Soul, 1950s–1990s, Artist, American
By All Means, The Classic Soul Era, 1980s–1990s, Artist, American
Byrd, Bobby, Funk Soul, 1960s–1990s, Artist, American
Caldwell, Bobby, Urban Soul, 1970s–1990s, Artist, American
Callier, Terry, Northern Soul, 1960s–1970s, Artist; Songwriter, American
Cameo, Funk Soul; Urban Soul, 1970s–, Artist, American
Cameron, G. C., The Classic Soul Era, 1960s–1990s, Artist, American
Campbell, Cornell, The Classic Soul Era, 1980s–, Artist, Jamaican
Campbell, Tevin, Urban Soul, 1990s–, Artist, American
Cannon, Ace, The Classic Soul Era, 1960s–1990s, Artist, American
Cantrell, Blu, Contemporary R&B; Urban Soul, 2000s–, Artist, American
Capitols, The, Urban Soul, 1960s, Artist, American
Carey, Mariah, Contemporary R&B, 1990s–, Artist, American
Carlton, Carl, Funk Soul, 1960s–1990s, Artist, American
Carne, Jean, The Classic Soul Era, 1980s–1990s, Artist, American
Carr, Barbara, Northern Soul, 1960s–1970s, Artist, American
Carr, James, The Classic Soul Era, 1960s–1990s, Artist, American
Carrack, Paul, Urban Soul, 1970s–, Artist, British
Carter, Clarence, The Classic Soul Era, 1960s–1990s, Artist, American
Carter, Mel, The Classic Soul Era, 1960s–1970s, Artist, American
Cartouche, Urban Soul, 1990s, Artist, American
Chairmen Of The Board, The, The Classic Soul Era, 1960s–1970s, Artist, American
Chakachas, Funk Soul, 1960s–1970s, Artist, Belgian
Chambers Brothers, The, The Classic Soul Era, 1960s–1970s, Artist, American
Champaign, Urban Soul, 1980s–1990s, Artist, American
Chandler, Gene, Northern Soul, 1960s–1990s, Artist, American
Chantelles, The, Funk Soul, 1950s–1960s, Artist, American
Chapter 8, The Classic Soul Era, 1970s–1980s, Artist, American
Charles, Ray, The Classic Soul Era, 1950s–1980s, Artist, American
Chase, Lincoln, The Classic Soul Era, 1950s–1970s, Artist; Songwriter, American
Cherelle, Contemporary R&B; Urban Soul, 1980s–1990s, Artist, American
Cherry, Neneh, Urban Soul, 1980s–1990s, Artist, Swedish
Chestnutt, Cody, Contemporary R&B, 2000s–, Artist, American
Chicano, El, The Classic Soul Era, 1970s; 1990s, Artist, American
Chi-Lites, The, Urban Soul, 1960s–1990s, Artist, American
Chocolate Milk, Funk Soul, 1970s–1980s, Artist, American
Choice Four, The Classic Soul Era, 1970s, Artist, American
Christians, The, Urban Soul, 1980s–1990s, Artist, British
Clark, Chris, The Classic Soul Era; Northern Soul, 1960s–1980s, Artist, American
Clark, Dee, Northern Soul, 1950s–1980s, Artist, American
Clark, Mike, Funk Soul, 1970s–, Artist, American
Clarke, Tony, Northern Soul, 1960s, Artist; Songwriter, American
Clay, Otis, The Classic Soul Era, 1960s–1990s, Artist, American
Clayton, Willie, Northern Soul, 1960s–, Artist, American
Cleopatra, Urban Soul, 1990s–, Artist, British
Clifford, Linda, The Classic Soul Era, 1970s–1980s, Artist, American
Clinton, George, Funk Soul; Urban Soul, 1970s–1990s, Artist, American
Club Nouveau, Urban Soul, 1980s–1990s, Artist, American
Coffey, Dennis, Urban Soul, 1970s–1980s, Artist, American
Coko, Contemporary R&B, 1990s, Artist, American
Cole, Natalie, Urban Soul, 1970s–, Artist, American
Coleman, Durrell, The Classic Soul Era, 1980s, Artist, American
Collier, Mitty, Northern Soul, 1960s, Artist, American
Collins, Bootsy, Funk Soul, 1970s–, Artist, American
Commodores, The, Funk Soul; Urban Soul, 1970s–1990s, Artist, American
Conley, Arthur, The Classic Soul Era, 1960s, Artist, American
Continental Four, The, The Classic Soul Era, 1970s, Artist, American
Contours, The, The Classic Soul Era, 1960s–1980s, Artist, American
Controllers, The, Urban Soul, 1970s–1990s, Artist, American
Cooke, Sam, The Classic Soul Era, 1940s–1960s, Artist, American
Cool Notes, The, The Classic Soul Era, 1980s, Artist, British
Cooper, Michael, Urban Soul, 1980s–, Artist, American
Cortez, Dave "Baby", The Classic Soul Era, 1950s–1970s, Artist, American
Counts, The, Funk Soul, 1970s, Artist, American
Covay, Don, ClassicSoul, 1960s–, Artist, American
Cover Girls, The, Urban Soul, 1980s–1990s, Artist, American
Cox, Deborah, Contemporary R&B, 1990s–, Artist, American
Crawford, Randy, Urban Soul, 1970s–, Artist, American
Crown Heights Affair, Funk Soul, 1970s–1980s, Artist, American
Culture Club, The Classic Soul Era, 1980s–1990s, Artist, British
Curtis, King, The Classic Soul Era, 1950s–1970s, Artist, American
Cymande, Funk Soul, 1970s, Artist, West Indian
D'Angelo, Contemporary R&B, 1990s–, Artist, American
D'Arby, Terence Trent, Contemporary R&B, 1980s–1990s, Artist, American
David, Craig, Contemporary R&B, 1990s–, Artist, British
Davidson, Diane, The Classic Soul Era, 1970s–1980s, Artist; Songwriter, American
Davis, Carl, Northern Soul, 1960s–1970s, Artist, American
Davis, Tyrone, Urban Soul, 1960s–, Artist, American
Day, Otis, & the Knights, Contemporary R&B, 1980s, Artist, American
Dazz Band, Funk Soul, 1980s–, Artist, American
DeBarge, Urban Soul, 1980s, Artist, American
Defunkt, Funk Soul, 1980s–1990s, Artist, American
Déja, The Classic Soul Era, 1980s–1990s, Artist, American
Delfonics, The, Urban Soul, 1960s–1970s, Artist, American
Dells, The, Northern Soul, 1950s–1990s, Artist, American
Destiny's Child, Urban Soul, 1990s–, Artist, American
DeVaughan, William, Urban Soul, 1970s–1980s, Artist, American
Dorsey, Lee, The Classic Soul Era, 1960s–1980s, Artist, American
Dozier, Lamont, The Classic Soul Era, 1970s–, Producer; Composer; Songwriter; Artist, American
Dramatics, The, Urban Soul, 1970s–1990s, Artist, American
Drifters, The, The Classic Soul Era, 1950s–1990s, Artist, American
Dru Hill, Urban Soul, 1990s, Artist, American
Duke, Doris, The Classic Soul Era, 1960s–1980s, Artist, American
Duke, Douglas, The Classic Soul Era, 1950s, Artist, American
Duncan, Daryll, Urban Soul, 1980s, Artist, American
Dupree, Simon, Funk Soul, 1960s, Artist, American
Dyer, Ada, Urban Soul, 1980s–1990s, Artist, American
Dynamic Superiors, The, The Classic Soul Era, 1970s, Artist, American
Dyson, Ronnie, The Classic Soul Era, 1970s–1980s, Artist, American
Earth, Wind & Fire, Funk; Funk Soul; Urban Soul, 1970s–, Artist, American
Ebo, Vince, Urban Soul, 1990s, Artist, American
Ebonys, The, Funk Soul, 1970s, Artist, American
Edwards, Dennis, The Classic Soul Era; Urban Soul, 1970s–1980s, Artist, American
Edwards, John, Northern Soul, 1970s–1980s, Artist, American
Elbert, Donnie, The Classic Soul Era, 1950s–1970s, Artist, American
Elgins, The, The Classic Soul Era, 1960s, Artist, American
Ellis, Pee Wee, Funk Soul, 1960s–, Artist, American
Ellis, Shirley, The Classic Soul Era, 1960s, Artist, American
Emotions, The, Urban Soul, 1970s–1990s, Artist, American
En Vogue, Urban Soul, 1980s–, Artist, American
Enchantment, The Classic Soul Era, 1970s–1990s, Artist, American
Ertegun, Ahmet M., Funk Soul, 1950s–1960s, Producer, Turkish
Esquires, The, The Classic Soul Era, 1950s–1990s, Artist, American
Eternal, Urban Soul, 1990s–, Artist, British
Evans, Faith, Urban Soul, 1990s–, Artist, American
Everett, Betty, The Classic Soul Era, 1950s–1970s, Artist, American
Faith, Hope & Charity, The Classic Soul Era, 1970s, Artist, American
Falcon, The, The Classic Soul Era, 1950s–1960s, Artist, American
Fantastic Johnny C., The, The Classic Soul Era, 1960s, Artist, American
Farr, Gary, The Classic Soul Era, 1960s–1980s, Artist, British
Fine Young Cannibals, Contemporary R&B, 1980s–1990s, Artist, British
First Choice, Urban Soul, 1970s–1980s, Artist, American
Five Stairsteps, The, The Classic Soul Era, 1960s–1970s, Artist, American
Five Star, Urban Soul, 1980s, Artist, British
Flack, Roberta, Urban Soul, 1960s–, Artist, American
Flaming Ember, The Classic Soul Era, 1970s, Artist, American
Floaters, The, The Classic Soul Era, 1970s, Artist, American
Floetry, Contemporary R&B, 2000s–, Artist, British
Floyd, Eddie, The Classic Soul Era, 1960s–1970s, Artist, American
Force MD's, Urban Soul, 1980s–, Artist, American
Foundations, The, Funk Soul, 1960s, Artist, British
Four Tops, The, The Classic Soul Era, 1950s–1980s, Artist, American
Franklin, Aretha, The Classic Soul Era, 1950s–1990s, Artist, American
Franklin, Erma, Northern Soul, 1960s, Artist, American
Franklin, Rodney, Urban Soul; Funk Soul, 1970s–1990s, Artist, American
Fred, John, The Classic Soul Era, 1960s, Artist, American
Free Movement, The Classic Soul Era, 1970s, Artist, American
Freeman, Bobby, Northern Soul, 1950s–1960s, Artist, American
Freeman, Ernie, The Classic Soul Era, 1950s–1960s, Producer, American
Friends Of Distinction, The, Urban Soul, 1960s–1970s, Artist, American
Funk Brothers, The, The Classic Soul Era, 1960s–1970s, Artist, American
Fuzz, The, The Classic Soul Era, 1970s, Artist, American
Gabrielle, Contemporary R&B, 1990s–, Artist, British
Gaines, Rosie, Urban Soul, 1990s–, Artist, American
Galactic, Funk Soul, 1990s–, Artist, American
Gap Band, The, Funk Soul, 1970s–1990s, Artist, American
Garrett, Siedah, Urban Soul, 1980s–1990s, Artist, American
Gaye, Marvin, The Classic Soul Era; Urban Soul, 1950s–1980s, Artist, American
Gaye, Nona, Urban Soul, 1990s, Artist, American
G-Clefs, Contemporary R&B, 1990s, Artist, American
General Kane, Urban Soul, 1980s, Artist, American
George, Barbara, The Classic Soul Era, 1960s, Artist, American
Georgio, Urban Soul, 1980s–1990s, Artist, American
Gilstrap, Jim, Urban Soul, 1970s–1990s, Artist, American
Ginuwine, Contemporary R&B, 1990s–, Artist, American
Glass House, The, The Classic Soul Era, 1970s, Artist, American
Glenn, Garry, The Classic Soul Era, 1980s, Artist, American
Goffin, Gerry, Funk Soul, 1960s–1970s; 1990s, Artist; Songwriter, American
Gordy, Berry, Jr., The Classic Soul Era, 1960s–1980s, Producer, American
Graham, Larry, Urban Soul; Funk Soul, 1960s–1990s, Artist, American
Grant, David, Urban Soul, 1980s–1990s, Artist, British
Gray, Dobie, The Classic Soul Era, 1960s–1990s, Artist, American
Gray, Macy, Contemporary R&B, 1990s–, Artist, American
Greaves, R. B., The Classic Soul Era, 1960s–1970s, Artist, British
Green, Al, Urban Soul, 1960s–, Artist, American
Green, Garland, The Classic Soul Era, 1960s–1970s, Artist, American
Greyboy Allstars, The, Funk Soul; Urban Soul, 1990s, Artist, American
Griffin, Billy, The Classic Soul Era, 1970s–1980s, Artist, American
Griffin, Mary, Contemporary R&B, 1990s–, Artist, American
Grimes, Howard, The Classic Soul Era, 1970s, Artist, American
Groove Theory, Urban Soul, 1990s–, Artist, American
Guy, Urban Soul, 1980s–, Artist, American
Guy, Jasmine, Urban Soul, 1990s, Artist, American
Hall & Oates, The Classic Soul Era, 1970s–, Artist, American
Hammond, Beres, The Classic Soul Era, 1970s–, Artist, Jamaican
Harari, Funk Soul, 1970s, Artist, South African
Harris, Major, Northern Soul, 1970s; 1990s, Artist, American
Harris, Norman, The Classic Soul Era, 1970s, Producer; Artist, American
Hartman, Don, Urban Soul, 1970s–1990s, Artist, American
Haskins, Clarence "Fuzzy", Funk Soul, 1970s, Artist, American
Hathaway, Donny, Urban Soul, 1960s–1990s, Artist, American
Hawkins, Screamin' Jay, Funk Soul, 1950s–1990s, Artist, American
Hawkins, Tramaine, Urban Soul, 1970s–, Artist, American
Hayes, Isaac, Funk Soul, 1960s–, Artist; Songwriter, American
Haywood, Leon, Northern Soul, 1960s–1990s, Artist, American
Head, Roy, The Classic Soul Era, 1960s–1980s, Artist, American
Heaven & Earth, Urban Soul, 1980s–, Artist, American
Henderson, Willie, The Classic Soul Era, 1960s–1990s, Artist, American
Hendricks, James, The Classic Soul Era, 1960s–1970s, Artist, American
Hendryx, Nona, Urban Soul, 1970s–1990s, Artist, American
Hewett, Howard, Urban Soul, 1980s–, Artist, American
Hicks, Joe, The Classic Soul Era, 1960s–1970s, Artist, American
Hi-Five, Urban Soul, 1990s, Artist, American
Higgins, Chuck, The Classic Soul Era, 1950s–1960s, Artist, American
High Inergy, Urban Soul, 1970s–1980s, Artist, American
Hill, Lauryn, Contemporary R&B, 1990s–, Artist, American
Hill, Z. Z., The Classic Soul Era, 1960s–1980s, Artist, American
Hines, Gregory, Urban Soul, 1980s, Artist, American
Hinton, Eddie, The Classic Soul Era, 1970s–1990s, Artist, American
Holiday, Jimmy, Northern Soul, 1960s–1970s, Artist; Songwriter, American
Holland, Eddie, The Classic Soul Era, 1960s–1970s, Songwriter; Artist, American
Holland/Dozier/Holland, The Classic Soul Era, 1960s–1970s, Producer; Songwriter, American
Hollister, Dave, Urban Soul, 1990s–, Artist, American
Holloway, Contemporary R&B, 1990s, Artist, American
Holloway, Brenda, The Classic Soul Era, 1960s, Artist, American
Holloway, Loleatta, Northern Soul, 1970s–1990s, Artist, American
Holman, Eddie, The Classic Soul Era, 1950s–1970s, Artist, American
Holmes Brothers, The, The Classic Soul Era, 1980s–, Artist, American
Holt, Redd, Funk Soul, 1950s–1970s, Artist, American
Honey Cone, Urban Soul, 1970s, Artist, American
Honeyz, Urban Soul, 1990s–, Artist, British
Hot Chocolate, Funk Soul, 1970s, Artist, British
Houston, Cissy, Urban Soul, 1970s–1990s, Artist, American
Houston, Thelma, The Classic Soul Era; Urban Soul, 1960s–1990s, Artist, American
Houston, Whitney, Urban Soul, 1980s–, Artist, American
Howard, Adina, Urban Soul, 1990s, Artist, American
Howard, Miki, Urban Soul, 1980s–, Artist, American
Hudson, Al, Urban Soul, 1970s–1990s, Artist, American
Hues Corporation, Northern Soul, 1970s, Artist, American
Huff, Leon, Urban Soul, 1960s–1980s, Producer; Artist; Composer; Songwriter, American
Hugh, Grayson, Urban Soul, 1980s–1990s, Artist, American
Hughes, Jimmy, Northern Soul, 1960s–1970s, Artist, American
Hunter, Alfonzo, Urban Soul, 1990s, Artist, American
Hutch, Willie, Urban Soul, 1960s–1980s, Artist, American
Hutson, Leroy, Northern Soul, 1970s–1990s, Artist, American
Ides Of March, The Classic Soul Era, 1960s–1970s; 1990s–, Artist, American
Imagination, Urban Soul, 1980s–1990s, Artist, British
Imajin, Contemporary R&B, 1990s, Artist, American
Impressions, The, Northern Soul, 1950s–1970s, Artist, American
IMX, Urban Soul, 1990s–, Artist, American
Incredibles, The, The Classic Soul Era, 1960s, Artist, American
Independents, The, The Classic Soul Era, 1970s, Artist, American
India.Arie, Contemporary R&B; Urban Soul, 2000s–, Artist, American
Ingram, James, Urban Soul, 1970s–1990s, Artist, American
Ingram, Luther, The Classic Soul Era, 1970s–1980s, Artist, American
Ink Spots, The Classic Soul Era, 1930s–1960s, Artist, American
Instant Funk, Funk Soul, 1970s–1990s, Artist, American
Intrigues, The, The Classic Soul Era, 1960s–1970s, Artist, American
Intruders, The, Northern Soul, 1960s–1970s, Artist, American
Isley Brothers, The, The Classic Soul Era; Funk; Funk Soul, 1950s–, Artist, American
Jackson 5, The, The Classic Soul Era, 1960s–1980s, Artist, American
Jackson, Chuck, Urban Soul, 1960s–1990s, Artist, American
Jackson, Deon, The Classic Soul Era, 1960s, Artist, American
Jackson, Freddie, Urban Soul, 1980s–, Artist, American
Jackson, George, The Classic Soul Era, 1960s–, Artist, American
Jackson, J. J., The Classic Soul Era, 1960s–1970s, Artist, American
Jackson, Janet, Contemporary R&B, 1980s–, Artist, American
Jackson, Jermaine, Urban Soul, 1970s–1990s, Artist, American
Jackson, LaToya, Urban Soul, 1970s–, Artist, American
Jackson, Michael, The Classic Soul Era, 1970s–, Artist; Songwriter, American
Jackson, Millie, The Classic Soul Era; Urban Soul, 1970s–, Artist, American
Jackson, Paul Jr., Urban Soul, 1970s–, Artist, American
Jackson, Rebbie, Urban Soul, 1980s–1990s, Artist, American
Jackson, Walter, Northern Soul, 1960s–1970s, Artist, American
Jagged Edge, Contemporary R&B; Urban Soul, 1990s–, Artist, American
Jaheim, Contemporary R&B; Urban Soul, 2000s–, Artist, American
Jamaica Boys, The, Urban Soul, 1980s–1990s, Artist, Jamaican
James, Etta, The Classic Soul Era, 1950s–, Artist, American
James, Jimmy, Northern Soul, 1960s–1990s, Artist, Jamaican
Jasper, Chris, Urban Soul; Funk Soul, 1970s–, Artist, American
Jaye, Miles, Urban Soul, 1980s–1990s, Artist, American
JBs, The, Funk Soul, 1960s–1990s, Artist, American
Jean, Wyclef, Contemporary R&B, 1990s–, Artist, American
Jenkins, Tomi, The Classic Soul Era, 1980s, Artist, American
Jhene, Urban Soul, 2000s–, Artist, America
Jimmy Jam & Terry Lewis, Contemporary R&B; Urban Soul, 1990s–, Artist; Producer, American
Jodeci, Urban Soul, 1990s, Artist, American
Joe, Urban Soul, 1990s–, Artist, American
Johnson, Gloria, Northern Soul, 1960s–1980s, Artist, American
Johnson, Jesse, Funk Soul, 1980s–1990s, Artist, American
Johnson, Marv, The Classic Soul Era; Northern Soul, 1950s–1960s, Artist, American
Johnson, Ruby, The Classic Soul Era, 1960s, Artist, American
Johnson, Syl, Northern Soul, 1950s–, Artist, American
Jon B., Contemporary R&B; Urban Soul, 1990s–, Artist; Producer, American
Jones Girls, The, Urban Soul, 1970s–1990s, Artist, American
Jones, Doris, Urban Soul; Funk Soul, 1970s–1980s, Artist, American
Jones, Glenn, Urban Soul, 1980s–1990s, Artist, American
Jones, Gloria, Northern Soul, 1960s–1980s, Artist, American
Jones, Jill, Urban Soul, 1980s–, Artist; Songwriter, American
Jones, Linda, The Classic Soul Era, 1960s–1970s, Artist, American
Jones, Oran "Juice", Urban Soul, 1980s, Artist, American
Jones, Quincy, Urban Soul, 1950s–, Producer; Composer, American
Jones, Thelma, The Classic Soul Era, 1970s, Artist, American
Jordan, Montell, Contemporary R&B, 1990s–, Artist, American
Joseph, Margie, Urban Soul, 1970s–1980s, Artist, American
Junior, Funk Soul; Urban Soul, 1970s–1990s, Artist, British
Junior Walker & the All Stars, The Classic Soul Era, 1960s–1970s, Artist, American
Kashif, Funk Soul, 1980s–1990s, Artist, American
K-Ci & JoJo, Urban Soul; Contemporary R&B, 1990s–, Artist, American
Kelis, Contemporary R&B, 1990s–, Artist; Songwriter, American
Kelly, Paul, The Classic Soul Era, 1960s–1990s, Artist, American
Kelly, R., Urban Soul, 1990s–, Artist; Producer; Songwriter, British
Kemp, Jack, Urban Soul, 1980s, Artist, American
Kendricks, Eddie, The Classic Soul Era, 1960s–1980s, Artist, American
Keys, Alicia, Contemporary R&B; Urban Soul, 1990s–, Artist, American
Khan, Chaka, Urban Soul; Funk Soul, 1970s–, Artist, American
Kidjo, Angelique, The Classic Soul Era, 1980s–, Artist, African
Kina, Contemporary R&B; Urban Soul, 2000s–, Artist, American
King Floyd, Funk Soul, 1960s–1970s, Artist, American
King, Ben E., The Classic Soul Era, 1960s–, Artist, American
King, Bobby, The Classic Soul Era, 1970s–1990s, Artist, American

Gospel

THE first African slaves arrived in America in 1619 and brought their music with them. From then until the Civil War of 1861-65, the music both fascinated and frightened the white slave owners who would flock to see the black people celebrating their weekly "day off" in New Orleans's Congo Square.

At the same time, slave owners suppressed the drumming that they saw as a possible means of communication between tribal groups who might rebel. During this period, the evangelical aspect of western religion led to efforts to Christianize these heathen "children".

Throughout the nineteenth century the emphasis was placed heavily on the supposed sinful unworthiness of congregations. However, a reaction to this brought about the more moderate movement instigated in the 1870s by Dwight Lyman Moody, who abandoned the hell-and-damnation approach in favour of compassion and redemption. A stream of white religious songwriters appeared, too, headed by Moody and his associate Sankey, and including P. P. Bliss, D. W. Whittle and Henry Date. Influential to both these and to later black composers was the work of the eighteenth-century English hymnist Isaac Watts.

In both black and white traditions, although more so in the case of the black songwriters, congregations would be largely illiterate, leading to the practice of "lining out" songs – a technique whereby the leader sang each line so that the flock could sing it after him. This left room for the development of innovative, overlapping answers, and was the basis of the call-and-response style so prominent in gospel song.

In the wake of the Civil War and emancipation, America's black population was faced with the problem of integrating itself into the white mainstream society, instigating a process that culminated in the Civil Rights Movement of the 1960s. Education was a major issue, but many newly founded black academic institutions found it a struggle to remain afloat during the economic upheavals of the 1870s. In an attempt to generate money to support Nashville's Fisk University, the choirmaster and treasurer George Leonard White, aided by his black protégé, the singer and pianist Ella Sheppard, assembled the formally trained Fisk Jubilee Singers and took them on a fund-raising tour of North America. The success of this ploy led to other such institutions forming their own travelling choirs. None, however, approached the stature of the Fisk group, who also toured Europe to wide acclaim.

Simultaneously, in more humble venues, liberated and increasingly urbanized black singers were adapting the popular style of four-part harmony group singing known as the "barbershop quartet" to their own ends, working a unique musical alchemy upon it with their rhythmic approach and loosening up its hitherto tight format. Their initial undertakings in this idiom were probably interpretations of popular secular songs, but they soon expanded their repertoire to include new arrangements of much-loved hymns. These were the roots of a music that was to accompany the progress of black America throughout the upheavals of the twentieth century, developing through "jubilee", "quartet" and other styles into the sounds heard in black churches today.

> "EVERY TONE WAS A TESTIMONY AGAINST SLAVERY, AND A PRAYER TO GOD FOR DELIVERANCE FROM CHAINS."
>
> *Frederick Douglass, My Bondage and My Freedom*

Above

The Bible's New Testament served as a kind of solace from the suffering of the slaves. The spiritual 'Everybody talkin' 'bout heaven ain't goin' there,' became an anthem of devotion and gave the slaves hopeful hearts.

STYLES
Jubilee
Quartet
Barbershop
Spirituals
Gospel Funk
Gospel Rap
Sacred Steel

THE GOSPEL STYLE

Traditional gospel music followed the "call and response" pattern of work songs sung by the slaves in the cotton fields. The main vocalist – often a preacher – would sing, and his words would be repeated by the congregation or choir.

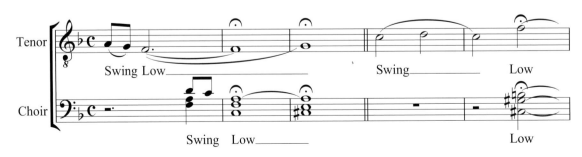

GOSPEL PEOPLE A-Z ➡ 391   INSTRUMENTS A-Z ➡ 436   BLUES: WORK SONGS ➡ 158   BLUES: RHYTHM & BLUES ➡ 173   FOLK: FOLK SONGS ➡ 226

A gospel choir

IN THE LATER YEARS OF THE NINETEENTH CENTURY, THE WORLD OF BLACK RELIGION WAS IN FERMENT. BREAKAWAY SECTS BEGAN TO FOUND THEIR OWN CHURCHES AND FOLLOWED THE DRIFT OF BLACK PEOPLE FROM THE COUNTRY TO THE CITIES, RESULTING IN THE MASS MIGRATIONS FROM SOUTHERN OPPRESSION TO A NEWER, BUT NOT ALWAYS EASIER LIFE IN THE INDUSTRIALIZED CITIES OF NORTH AMERICA.

Jubilee

Above

The principal objective of gospel music is to lift spirits and help people express their religion. During the Depression of the 1930s, many turned to religion and uplifting gospel music for relief from the hard times.

MANY of these churches were Pentecostal or "sanctified" in nature, and they rejected the stiffly formalized rituals of their Baptist or Methodist mother churches in favour of more extreme methods of worship, which could include haranguing sermons, speaking in tongues, dancing (known as "shouting") and the use of musical instruments. The active involvement of the congregation could induce fits of religious ecstasy during which the worshipper would "fall out", entering a trance-like state of exaltation. Perhaps the most influential of these new churches was C. H. Mason's Church Of God In Christ (COGIC), which began its life in Mississippi, but found its most fertile ground in the black ghettos of the north. Despite some fierce preaching, these churches projected a tone of joy and a basic message of "good news".

called the Norfolk Jazz & Jubilee Quartet recorded in New York. Their initial offerings were blues and popular songs, with a sprinkling of religious titles; by 1923, however, jubilee songs had come to dominate their repertoire. By the end of the 1920s, groups such as the Golden Leaf Quartet, the Pace Jubilee Singers and the Birmingham Jubilee Quartet were appearing regularly in record companies' "race" catalogues. They sang a cappella and introduced more daring and complicated arrangements built on a basic four-part harmony, sometimes utilizing stop-time or bringing forward the bass for novelty effect.

"NO ONE BUT THOSE WHO HAVE HAD THEIR SLUMBERS BROKEN BY THOSE SACRED SERENADES CAN REALIZE THEIR SWEETNESS AND POWER."

Daniel Alexander Payne, Recollections of Seventy Years (Nashville, 1888)

The 1920s And 1930s

In the early years of the new century, black music was very prominent in American life. Minstrelsy had given ground to ragtime, while blues had been noted and, along with jazz, was waiting in the wings. Both Scott Joplin and W. C. Handy had backgrounds in church music. Paralleling these developments was the innovation of sound recordings being made and sold as entertainment. In 1921, soon after Mamie Smith proved that a market existed among blacks, a group from Virginia

LEADING EXPONENTS

Fisk Jubilee Singers
Mamie Smith
Norfolk Jazz & Jubilee
  Quartet
Golden Leaf Quartet
Pace Jubilee Singers
Birmingham Jubilee
  Quartet
W. Henry Sherwood
C. A. Tindley
Thomas A. Dorsey
Roberta Martin
Mahalia Jackson
Golden Gate Quartet

JUBILEE

In jubilee, the traditional gospel melodies are enhanced by the close, adventurous harmonies of the barbershop quartet, characterized by unusual intervals and tag lines in accompanying voices.

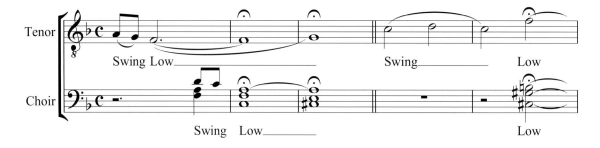

THE GOSPEL INTRO ➡ 384   GOSPEL PEOPLE A-Z ➡ 391   INSTRUMENTS A-Z ➡ 436   JAZZ: RAGTIME ➡ 122   BLUES: RHYTHM & BLUES ➡ 173

The financial crash of 1929, which ushered in the Great Depression, caused those recording companies that survived to restrict their activities, putting an end to many budding musical careers. However, religion provided solace for people who were hit hard by such desperate times and the popularity of "sanctified" material with the black audience ensured that it was well represented as the recording industry slowly regained its feet.

The earliest known black composer of religious songs was W. Henry Sherwood, a Baptist who, in 1893, produced a hymnal that found favour in black churches. Another famous collection, by the Methodist C. A. Tindley, followed in 1916. As the black diaspora spread across America, certain cities became famous in black society for their preachers and singers. COGIC was particularly strong in Chicago, and the quartets operating out of Birmingham, Alabama were to become the stuff of legend; even the largely Catholic New Orleans had its own "sanctified" tradition. In 1906, the Azusa Street Revival in Los Angeles saw the beginnings of Pentecostalism on the west coast.

Prior to 1932, Thomas A. Dorsey enjoyed considerable success in the arena of secular music. He employed his instrumental and vocal talents as "Georgia Tom", first leading a band supporting the blues singer "Ma" Rainey and later as half of a hokum duo with Tampa Red, which specialized in lightweight songs of a somewhat salacious nature. Although he had been raised in a religious family, Dorsey never had any problem with "the Devil's music", and even in his nineties he would sing a blues without a qualm. He had been writing religious songs since as early as 1921, and when his wife died he walked away from his secular success and dedicated himself to church music, deliberately marrying elements of jazz and blues to sacred songs. In the process, he became known as

the "father" of gospel and, in association with the entrepreneurial singer Sallie Martin, inaugurated the annual Gospel Singers' Convention and began to charge admission for concerts. The two also opened a highly successful publishing house, built around anthemic Dorsey compositions such as 'Peace In the Valley' and 'Precious Lord', and encouraged the early careers of great talents such as Mahalia Jackson and Roberta Martin.

In 1937 the most influential of all jubilee groups appeared in the form of the Golden Gate Quartet. In this period of secular, jazzy "rhythm groups", such as the Red Caps and the Mills Brothers, which spanned the war years and saw the advent of the first "independent" record companies, the Gates were as hip as any, with the possible exception of the instrumentally backed Blue Chips. They were to enjoy a career that mixed secular and sacred music, and saw them appearing in churches, nightclubs and even Hollywood movies.

Above

Considered the mother of the blues, Ma Rainey, born Gertrude Pridgett, toured the southern US performing blues, gospel and pop songs on the vaudeville circuit to great public acclaim.

Far Left

Pioneers of jubilee, the members of the Golden Gate Quartet developed a unique way of performing sacred hymns and enjoyed widespread acceptance outside the church.

Golden Age

THE PERIOD BETWEEN THE LATE-1940S AND THE MID-1960S IS DESCRIBED AS THE GOLDEN AGE OF GOSPEL MUSIC. DURING THIS TIME, ATTENTION WAS FOCUSED MAINLY, BUT NOT EXCLUSIVELY, ON THE QUARTETS THAT CRISSCROSSED AMERICA ON WHAT WAS KNOWN AS THE GOSPEL HIGHWAY, FILLING THE ROLE OF POP STARS FOR THE BLACK RELIGIOUS COMMUNITY OF THE TIMES.

"GOSPEL'S ROOTS IN THE HERITAGE OF SPIRITUALS, RING SHOUTS AND THE BLUES HAVE MADE IT THE WELLSPRING FROM WHICH OTHER AFRICAN-AMERICAN MUSICAL TRADITIONS HAVE FLOWED."

Richard Crawford, America's Musical Life, A History

Above

Singer/songwriter Sam Cooke (bottom) became one of the most popular and influential black singers to emerge in the late-1950s, blending gospel and secular themes that later provided the foundation for soul music.

LEADING EXPONENTS

The Soul Stirrers
The Harmonizing Four
The Pilgrim Travelers
Spirit Of Memphis
  Quartet
Five Blind Boys
  Of Mississippi
Sam Cooke
Five Blind Boys
  Of Alabama

THESE aggregations could have anything up to seven members, but the term "quartet" was used to describe both the groups and the style in which they sang, developed from the jubilee sounds of the 1920s and 1930s. The accent was still on performing a cappella, though a guitarist might form part of the group, and the range of vocal resources was explored to its limit. Both falsetto and bass were exploited for dramatic effect, and melisma was extended about as far as it could go. Non-musical effects such as grunts, exhortations, asides, hand-clapping, shouts and screams were brought in to augment the emotional arsenal. One of the greatest of all quartets, the Soul Stirrers, pioneered the use of the joint lead, in which two singers would vie with and encourage each other as they bounced a song between them across a background provided by the rest of the group. Performances were also extremely visual, with the formally attired groups weaving with choreographed, sweating exactitude around the microphone (if there was one), as the lead singers fell on their knees, wrung their hands, waved their arms, invaded the audience and even "fell out" under the impact of their own singing.

On the road, these groups sang commercially in churches and schoolhouses throughout America, finding their largest audiences in the bigger cities and the rural south. Personalities

GOLDEN AGE

With a strong beat and full chords, gospel piano playing draws on influences as diverse as W. C. Handy, Floyd Kramer and Ray Charles.

THE GOSPEL INTRO ➡ 384   GOSPEL PEOPLE A-Z ➡ 391   INSTRUMENTS A-Z ➡ 436   POP: FIFTIES POP SINGER/SONGWRITERS ➡ 14

emerged, inspiring their own followings, while fans avidly studied the movements of personnel between groups. Competition played a large part in generating interest, and "the programs", as gospel shows were known, would often advertise "battles" between eminent quartets. The groups and individual singers developed their own images and reputations; the Harmonizing Four were known for their more restrained reliance on hymns, while the Pilgrim Travelers were famous for songs about grey-haired mothers, alongside less-sentimental fare. The most admired singers were those who could deal with everything from a drawn-out rendition of the Lord's Prayer to the controlled hysteria of a "hard" quartet performance designed to "wreck the house". Some of the great men on the gospel circuit were: Silas Steele, who moved from the jubilee group The Blue Jay Singers to join with Wilbur "Little Ax" Broadnax in the celebrated Spirit Of Memphis Quartet; Rev. Rebert Harris and Paul Owens of the Soul Stirrers; Ira Tucker of the Dixie Hummingbirds and Julius Cheeks of the Sensational Nightingales. These men were famous not just for their amazing musical ability, but for the dedication and piety witnessed by their scorning of the secular arena and its considerable earthly rewards. Once upon a time the Norfolks and the Gates could get away with singing pop songs – but up until the late-1950s, any gospel singer "selling out" for popular acclaim risked ostracism and obloquy.

Sacred Moves Towards Secular

Reversing Rev. Dorsey's ploy, secular black music now began to plunder the churches. Gospel's biggest contribution to popular music was unfettered emotionalism; Ray Charles, often referred to as the originator of soul music, based his wailing and screaming on that of Archie Brownlee, the celebrated lead singer of the Five Blind Boys Of Mississippi, while James Brown extrapolated the drama of gospel into his famous, onstage "heart attacks". The shared lead would inspire soul duos such as Sam & Dave and James & Bobby Purify.

For every one of the nationally famous quartets, there were dozens of localized groups, many of whom never got to record. These were scouted regularly for new talent and some even became incubators, hatching new stars to fill gaps in the

ranks of their "parent" group. The most successful of these relationships was probably that between the Highway QCs and the Soul Stirrers, for whom they nurtured the outstanding talents of Sam Cooke and Johnnie Taylor.

Cooke, the good-looking, sweet-voiced gospel equivalent of a bobby-soxer's dream, with a huge following among teenage black girls, provoked consternation and condemnation when, lured by the material gains of popular music in comparison to gospel, he released 'Loveable' as a single under the pseudonym "Dale Cook" in 1957. A watershed had been reached. Before he made the transition to popular music, Cooke had already changed the face of the Soul Stirrers, and through them the quartet in general, by virtually relegating the group to a supporting role as he smoothed out their harmonies and refined his own crooning style of lead singing. Alongside this development, quartets witnessed a growing reliance on instrumentation and a marked fall from favour in the face of the soul onslaught. Many disbanded, while others continued to follow the gruelling cycle of the road, and some – notably the Five Blind Boys Of Alabama, who began life singing jubilee as the Happyland Singers in 1937 – still exist today. The Golden Age, however, was over.

Above

Organized by James B. Davis in the mid-1930s, the Dixie Hummingbirds became the grand masters of gospel quartet style.

Far Left

Mahalia Jackson's gospel singing contains the most heavily blues-based background of any of the major gospel singers of her time during the 1930s.

Modern Gospel

THE SPIRITUAL TRADITION GAVE RISE TO MANY GOSPEL STAPLES, THOUGH MANY OF THE EARLY "UNIVERSITY" SINGERS WHO PERFORMED THEM HAD RECEIVED A FORMAL EUROPEAN MUSICAL SCHOOLING. THE TRADITION REACHED A PEAK WITH THE SOLO CONCERT PERFORMANCES OF THE GREAT SINGER PAUL ROBESON AND THE FAMOUS CONTRALTO MARIAN ANDERSON – THE AMBASSADORS FOR BLACK AMERICA.

THE links between blues and gospel, developed by Rev. Dorsey, are illustrated in the work of "sanctified singers" such as Blind Willie Johnson and Joel "Blind Joe" Taggart. These artists of the 1920s and 1930s performed in a style that closely resembled the early blues singers, accompanying themselves on the guitar. Indeed, Taggart recorded a couple of blues under the nom du disque of "Joe Amos", while the famous blues singers Blind Lemon Jefferson and Charley Patton sang religious songs under the names of Deacon L. J. Bates and Elder J. J. Hadley. The style continued into the post-war years, with artists such as Rev. Utah Smith and Rev. Louis Overstreet using electrified instruments. Allied to these guitarists were Arizona Dranes, who supported her own lead vocals with a storming barrelhouse piano, and Washington Phillips, unique in his use of the dulceola.

In the period before the Second World War there was a fashion for recording preachers who would often end their sermons with a burst of song from their "congregation". Instruments such as trumpets and trombones, more readily associated with jazz, often backed these performances. Preaching on record continued after the war, its most famous exponent being Rev. C. L. Franklin, the father of Aretha and Erma, while the church founded by Daddy Grace became well known for its trombone-heavy brass bands.

"GOSPEL MUSIC WAS RESPONSIBLE FOR MUCH OF WHAT CAME TO BE CONSIDERED EMBLEMATIC IN AMERICAN CULTURE OF THE 1960S: FROM ROCK'N'ROLL'S BEAT... TO HYMN SINGING AT SIT-INS..."

Richard Crawford, America's Musical Life, A History

Above
The legendary singer Paul Robeson.

Right
Sister Rosetta Tharpe's distinct sound defied categorization.

LEADING EXPONENTS

Paul Robeson
Marian Anderson
Willie Johnson
Joel Taggart
Rev Utah Smith
Rev Louis Overstreet
Arizona Draines
Rev. C. L. Franklin
Sister Rosetta Tharpe
Rev. James Cleveland
Edwin Hawkins Singers
Willie Eason
Campbell Brothers
Katie Jackson

Men had not dominated the Golden Age exclusively; there were many mixed groups, such as the Roberta Martin Singers, and all-female line-ups such as those of the tragic Davis Sisters and the Clara Ward Singers. From the ranks of the last named came the magnificent Marion Williams who, along with Prof. Alex Bradford, "The Thunderbolt Of The Mid-West", rocked Europe in the early 1960s with the hit show *Black Nativity*. Prior to this event, the singer who made the biggest impact outside the USA was the genre's diva, Mahalia Jackson. The glittering, guitar-slinging Sister Rosetta Tharpe was also at her zenith during this period.

During the 1960s black culture developed a taste for church-based choirs. Energetically promoted by Rev. James Cleveland, it sparked the international hit 'Oh Happy Day' by the Edwin Hawkins Singers, and finds expression today in the massive choirs assembled for prestigious black religious events.

Since the 1960s the more "commercial" form of gospel has repeatedly followed the lead of popular black music, with groups performing disco, gospel funk, smooth soul ballads and most recently gospel rap, which may hark back in some way to the chanted narratives and social comment of the Golden Gate Quartet.

"Sacred steel" has developed in recent years. This springs from the musical tradition of the Keith and Jewel Dominions (churches), and centres on the use of the floor-mounted pedal-steel guitar, known as "the ironing board". Willie Eason, the Campbell Brothers and the vocalist Katie Jackson prove that there is still power and emotion to be found in gospel music.

MODERN GOSPEL

Modern gospel uses a style of rhythm piano that was created when syncopated rhythms played on snare drums were translated for use on the keyboard.

THE GOSPEL INTRO ➡ 384   GOSPEL PEOPLE A–Z ➡ 391   INSTRUMENTS A–Z ➡ 436   THE JAZZ INTRO ➡ 118   GOSPEL: GOLDEN AGE ➡ 388

Artists: Gospel

Entries appear in the following order: name, music style, year(s) of popularity, type of artist, country of origin

77's, The, Modern Gospel, 1980s–, Artist, American
A–1 Swift, Modern Gospel, 1990s, Artist, American
Abundant Life, Modern Gospel, 1990s, Artist, American
Abyssinian Baptist Gospel Choir, Jubilee; Golden Age, 1960s, Artist, American
Adams, Yolanda, Modern Gospel; Golden Age, 1980s–, Artist, American
Adoration–N–Prayze, Modern Gospel, 1990s, Artist, American
Alabama Sacred Harp Singers, Jubilee, 1940s, Artist, American
Allen and Allen, Modern Gospel; Golden Age, 1990s–, Artist, American
Allen, Rance, Golden Age; Modern Gospel, 1960s–, Artist, American
Allison, Margaret, Jubilee; Golden Age, 1940s–, Artist, American
Amada, Maia, Modern Gospel, 1990s, Artist, American
Amato, John, Modern Gospel, 1990s, Artist, American
Amazing Zion Travelers, Golden Age, 1990s, Artist, American
AME Zion National Mass Choir, Jubilee, 1990s, Artist, American
Amos, Daniel, Modern Gospel, 1970s–, Producer; Artist, American
Andrews, Inez, Jubilee; Modern Gospel; Golden Age, 1950s–1990s, Artist, American
Angelic Gospel Singers, Jubilee; Golden Age, 1940s–1990s, Artist, American

Angelic Voices of Faith, Modern Gospel, 1990s, Artist, American
Angelo & Veronica, Modern Gospel, 1990s, Artist, American
Anointed Pace Sisters, Modern Gospel, 1990s, Artist, American
Archer, Steve, Modern Gospel, 1980s, Artist, American
Armstrong, Vanessa Bell, Modern Gospel, 1980s–, Artist, American
Atlanta Centennial, Modern Gospel, 1990s, Artist, American
Audio Adrenaline, Modern Gospel, 1990s–, Artist, American
Babb, Dr. Morgan, Jubilee; Golden Age, 1970s, Artist, American
Bagwell, Wendy, Jubilee, 1970s–1990s, Artist, American
Bailey, Bob, Jubilee, 1980s, Artist, American
Bailey, Philip, Golden Age; Modern Gospel, 1980s–, Artist, American
Ball, E. C. & Orna, Jubilee, 1930s–1970s, Artist, American
Banks, Bishop Jeff, Golden Age, 1960s; 1980s–1990s, Artist, American
Banks, Willie, Jubilee; Golden Age, 1970s–1990s, Artist, American
Barnes & Brown, Golden Age, 1980s, Artist, American
Barnes, Luther, Modern Gospel; Golden Age, 1980s–, Artist, American
Barrett Sisters, The, Jubilee; Golden Age, 1960s–1990s, Artist, American
Baylor, Helen, Modern Gospel, 1990s–, Artist, American
BC & M Choir, Modern Gospel, 1990s, Artist, American
Beasley, Paul, Jubilee; Modern Gospel; Golden Age, 1980s–, Artist, American
Becker, Margaret, Modern Gospel, 1980s–1990s, Artist; Songwriter, American
Bell Jubilee Singers, Modern Gospel, 1990s–, Artist, American
Bell Sisters, The, Modern Gospel, 1990s, Artist, American
Bill Gaither Trio, Modern Gospel, 1990s–, Artist, American
Birmingham Jubilee Singers, Jubilee, 1920s–1930s, Artist, American
Black Movement, Modern Gospel, 1990s, Artist, American
Blackwood Brothers, The, Jubilee, 1930s–, Artist, American
Blackwood Singers, Modern Gospel, 1980s–1990s, Artist, American
Blair, Robert, Golden Age, 1960s–1990s, Artist, American
Bradford, Professor Alex, Golden Age; Jubilee, 1950s–1970s, Artist; Composer, American
Bridges, Modern Gospel, 1990s, Artist, American
Bright Star Male Chorus, Modern Gospel, 1990s–, Artist, American
Brinson, Christopher, Modern Gospel, 1990s, Producer, American
Broadnax, Wilmer, Golden Age, 1950s, Artist, American
Brooklyn All–Stars, Jubilee; Golden Age, 1950s–, Artist, American
Brooklyn Tabernacle Choir, Modern Gospel; Golden Age, 1970s, Artist, American
Brown, Janice, Modern Gospel, 1990s, Artist, American
Brown, Scott Wesley, Jubilee, 1980s–1990s, Artist, American
Brown's Ferry 4, Jubilee; Golden Age, 1950s–1960s, Artist, American
Brownlee, Archie, Jubilee; Golden Age, 1930s–1950s, Artist, American
Brunson, Professor Milton, Jubilee; Golden Age, 1940s–1990s, Artist, American
Brush Arbor, Jubilee, 1970s–1990s, Artist, American
Caesar, Shirley, Modern Gospel; Golden Age, 1970s–, Artist, American
Cage, Byron, Modern Gospel, 1990s, Artist, American
Campbell, Lamar, Modern Gospel, 1990s–, Artist, American
Canton Spirituals, The, Jubilee; Modern Gospel, 1980s–, Artist, American
Caravans, The, Golden Age; Jubilee, 1950s–1960s, Artist, American
Carman, Modern Gospel, 1970s–1990s, Artist, American
Carr, Sister Wynona, Jubilee, 1950s, Artist, American
Carroll, Bruce, Modern Gospel, 1990s, Artist; Songwriter, American
Carson, Martha, Jubilee, 1950s–1960s, Artist, American
Caston, Leonard, Golden Age, 1960s–1970s, Artist, American
Cathedrals, The, Jubilee , 1960s–, Artist, American
Chambers, James, Modern Gospel, 1980s, Artist, American
Chapman, Steven Curtis, Jubilee, 1980s–, Artist, American
Charioteers, The, Jubilee; Golden Age, 1940s–1950s, Artist, American
Charlie Daniels Band, The, Jubilee, 1970s–, Artist, American
Cheairs, Andrew, Modern Gospel, 1990s, Artist, American
Cheeks, Rev. Julius, Jubilee; Golden Age, 1950s–1960s, Artist, American
Chicago Mass Choir, Modern Gospel, 1990s–, Artist, American
Chosen Gospel Singers, Jubilee; Golden Age, 1950s, Artist, American
Chosen, The, Modern Gospel, 1990s, Artist, American
Christian, Al, Modern Gospel, 1990s, Artist, American
Christianaires, The, Jubilee; Modern Gospel, 1990s–, Artist, American
Chronicle, Jubilee, 1970s, Artist, American
Chuck Wagon Gang, Jubilee, 1940s–1990s, Artist, American
Church Of God And Saints Of Christ, Modern Gospel, 1990s, Artist, American
Clark Sisters, The, Modern Gospel, 1950s–1990s, Artist, American
Clark, Mildred, Modern Gospel, 1990s, Artist, American
Clark–Terrell, Twinkie, Modern Gospel, 1990s, Artist, American
CLC Youth Choir, Modern Gospel, 1990s, Artist, American
Cleveland, Rev. James, Golden Age; Jubilee; Modern Gospel, 1950s–1990s, Artist, American
Cluster Pluckers, The, Modern Gospel, 1990s, Artist, American
Coates, Dorothy Love, Golden Age; Jubilee, 1940s–1970s, Artist, American
Cobb, David, Modern Gospel, 1960s, Artist, American
Coley, Daryl, Modern Gospel; Golden Age, 1980s–, Artist, American
Commissioned, Modern Gospel, 1970s–, Artist, American
Condie, Richard, Jubilee, 1970s, Artist, American
Condran, Lee & Cindy, Jubilee, 1990s, Artist, American
Cone, Rev. Benjamin, Modern Gospel, 1990s–, Artist, American
Cooke Duet, Modern Gospel, 1990s, Artist, American
Cooke, Sam, Golden Age, 1950s–1960s, Artist, American
Cooling Waters, Modern Gospel, 1980s, Artist, American
Cooper, Marc, Modern Gospel, 1990s, Artist, American
Cosmopolitan Church Of Prayer, Golden Age, 1960s, Artist, American
Craig Brothers, Modern Gospel, 1990s, Artist, American
Cravens, Red, Jubilee, 1960s, Artist, American
Cross, Phil, Modern Gospel, 1990s, Artist, American
Crouch, Andraé, Modern Gospel, 1970s–1990s, Artist, American
Crouch, Sandra, Modern Gospel; Golden Age, 1970s–1990s, Artist, American
Daniels, Rev. Leo, Modern Gospel, 1990s, Artist, American
Daughters Of Zion, Modern Gospel, 1990s, Artist, American
Davis, Amos, Modern Gospel, 1990s, Artist, American
Davis, Clifton, Modern Gospel, 1990s, Artist, American
Davis, Louise, Golden Age, 1930s, Artist, American
Davis, Rev. Ernest Jr., Golden Age, 1990s, Producer, American
Davis, Rev. Gary, Golden Age; Jubilee, 1920s–1970s, Artist, American
DC Talk, Modern Gospel, 1980s–, Artist, American
Deep River Boys, Golden Age, 1940s–1950s, Artist, American
DeGarmo & Key, Modern Gospel, 1970s–1990s, Artist, American
Degrate, Don, Modern Gospel, 1990s, Artist, American
Derek & Diana, Modern Gospel, 1990s, Artist, American
Dillard, Ricky, Golden Age; Modern Gospel, 1990s–, Artist, American
Dixie Hummingbirds, The, Golden Age; Jubilee, 1930s–1990s, Artist, American
Dixon, Jessy, Jubilee; Golden Age; Modern Gospel, 1950s–1990s, Artist; Songwriter, American
Dobbin, Keith, Modern Gospel, 1990s, Artist, American
Dore, Lisa, Modern Gospel, 1990s, Artist, American
Dorsey, Rev. Thomas A., Jubilee, 1920s–1990s, Artist, American
Douglas, Rev. Isaac, Modern Gospel, 1990s, Artist, American
Draper, O'Landa, Golden Age, 1990s, Artist; Composer, American
Dupree, Leontine, Modern Gospel, 1990s, Artist, American
Dynamic Dixie Travelers, Modern Gospel, 1990s, Artist, American
Easter, Jeff & Sheri, Jubilee, 1980s–, Artist, American
Ellison, Tommy, Golden Age, 1990s–, Artist, American
English, Michael, Golden Age, 1990s–, Artist, American
Eternal, Modern Gospel, 1990s, Artist, British
Evans, Rev. Clay, Modern Gospel; Golden Age, 1990s–, Artist, American
Eveready's, The, Modern Gospel, 1990s–, Artist, American
Ewing, Rick, Modern Gospel, 1990s, Artist, American
Fairfield Four, The, Golden Age; Jubilee, 1950s–1960s; 1980s–1990s, Artist, American
Faith Instrumental, Modern Gospel, 1990s, Artist, American
Ferrell Jerome, Minister, Modern Gospel, 1980s–1990s, Artist, American
Fisk Jubilee Singers, Jubilee; Golden Age, 1900s–1960s, Artist, American
Five Blind Boys Of Alabama, The, Golden Age; Jubilee, 1940s–, Artist, American
Five Blind Boys Of Mississippi, The, Golden Age; Jubilee, 1930s–, Artist, American
Five Swinging Stars, Golden Age, 1990s, Artist, American
Florida A&M Choir, Modern Gospel, 1990s, Artist, American
Florida Boys, Jubilee, 1980s–, Artist, American
Florida Mass Choir, Golden Age, 1980s–1990s, Artist, American
Floyd, Mary, Modern Gospel, 1990s–, Artist, American
Fold, Charles, Modern Gospel, 1990s, Artist, American
Fountain, Clarence, Golden Age, 1990s–, Artist, American
Four Eagles, The, Modern Gospel, 1990s, Artist, American
Franklin, Aretha, Golden Age, 1950s–, Artist, American
Franklin, Kirk, Modern Gospel; Golden Age, 1990s–, Artist, American
Franklin, Rev. C. L., Golden Age, 1950s–1980s, Artist, American
Freedom Of Soul, Modern Gospel, 1990s, Artist, American
Friendly Temple Sanctuary Choir, Modern Gospel, 1990s, Artist, American
Full Gospel Baptist Mass Choir, Modern Gospel, 1990s, Artist, American
Futch Boys, The, Modern Gospel, 1990s, Artist, American
Gaither Vocal Band, Modern Gospel, 1990s–, Artist, American
Garmon, Terry, Modern Gospel, 1990s, Artist, American
Garner, Norris, Modern Gospel, 1990s, Artist, American
Gentlemen Of Gospel, Modern Gospel, 1990s, Artist, American
George, Cassieta, Golden Age, 1960s–1970s, Artist, American
Georgia Mass Choir, Modern Gospel, 1980s–1990s, Artist, American
Gideon, Modern Gospel, 1990s, Artist, American
Gold City, Jubilee, 1970s–, Artist, American
Golden Eagle Gospel Singers, Golden Age, 1930s–1940s, Artist, American
Golden Gate Quartet, Golden Age; Jubilee, 1930s–1970s, Artist, American
Golden Jubilees, Modern Gospel, 1990s, Artist, American
Goodman, Tanya, Modern Gospel, 1990s, Artist, American
Goodman, Vestal, Jubilee, 1990s–, Artist, American
Gospel Christian Singers, Jubilee, 1990s, Artist, American
Gospel Gangstas, Modern Gospel, 1990s, Artist, American
Gospel Harmonettes, The, Golden Age, 1990s, Artist, American
Gospel Hummingbirds, Jubilee, 1970s–1990s, Artist, American
Gospel Keynotes, The, Golden Age, 1990s, Artist, American
Gospel Music Workshop Of America, Jubilee; Golden Age, 1970s–1990s, Artist, American
Gospel Songbirds, Modern Gospel, 1990s, Artist, American
Gospelaires, The, Jubilee; Golden Age, 1960s, Artist, American
Grant, Amy, Modern Gospel, 1970s–, Artist, American
Greater Emmanuel Mass Choir, Modern Gospel, 1990s, Artist, American
Greater Victory Temple Choir, Modern Gospel, 1990s, Artist, American
Green, Al, Modern Gospel, 1960s, Artist, American
Green, Steve, Modern Gospel, 1980s–1990s, Artist, American
Grundy, Ricky, Golden Age, 1980s–1990s, Artist, American
Haddon, Deitick, Modern Gospel, 1990s–, Artist, American
Hall, Vera, Jubilee, 1940s–1950s, Artist, American
Hammond, Fred, Modern Gospel, 1990s–, Artist, American
Happy Goodman Family, The, Jubilee, 1940s–, Artist, American
Harlem Spiritual Ensemble, Modern Gospel, 1990s, Artist, American
Harmonizing Four, The, Golden Age; Jubilee, 1940s–1960s, Artist, American
Harris, Herman, Modern Gospel, 1990s, Artist, American
Harris, Larnelle, Modern Gospel; Golden Age, 1970s–1990s, Artist, American
Harris, R. H., Golden Age, 1940s–1950s, Artist, American
Hawkins, Edwin, Modern Gospel; Jubilee; Golden Age, 1960s–, Artist, American
Hawkins, Tramaine, Golden Age; Modern Gospel, 1970s–, Artist, American
Hawkins, Walter, Golden Age; Jubilee; Modern Gospel, 1960s–, Artist, American
Hayes, Mark, Modern Gospel, 1980s–1990s, Artist, American
Heavenly Gospel Singers, The, Golden Age, 1930s–1940s, Artist, American
Henry, Linda, Modern Gospel, 1990s, Artist, American
Hightower Brothers, Modern Gospel, 1960s, Artist, American
Highway QCs, The, Golden Age; Jubilee, 1940s–, Artist, American
Hines, Phoebe, Golden Age, 1990s, Artist, American
Holoman, Lola, Modern Gospel, 1990s, Artist, American
Homeland Quartet, Modern Gospel, 1990s–, Artist, American
Hoover, Greg, Modern Gospel, 1990s–, Artist, American
Horizon Family, Modern Gospel, 1990s, Artist, American
Howard Gospel Choir Of Howard, Modern Gospel, 1990s, Artist, American
Howard, Larry, Jubilee, 1980s–1990s, Artist, American
Howard, Walter, Modern Gospel, 1990s, Artist, American
Hudson, Lavine, Modern Gospel, 1990s, British,
Hudson, Rev. William III, Modern Gospel, 1990s, Artist, American
Hunt, Howard, Modern Gospel, 1990s, Artist, American
Hunter Brothers, The, Modern Gospel, 1990s, Artist, American
Institutional Radio Choir, Golden Age, 1980s–1990s, Artist, American
Invictas, The, Jubilee, 1960s, Artist, American
Irving, Rev. Fleetwood E., Modern Gospel, 1990s, Artist, American
J. C. Crew, Modern Gospel, 1990s, Artist, American
Jackson Southernaires, Modern Gospel; Jubilee; Golden Age, 1960s–, Artist, American
Jackson, Mahalia, Jubilee; Golden Age, 1920s–1960s, Artist, American
Jackson, Monica, Modern Gospel, 1990s, Artist, American
Jars Of Clay, Modern Gospel, 1990s–, Artist, American
Jefferson, Earnest, Modern Gospel, 1990s, Artist, American
Jenkins Brothers, Modern Gospel, 1990s, Artist, American
Jenkins, Juanita, Modern Gospel, 1990s, Artist, American
Johnson, Alvin, Modern Gospel, 1990s–, Artist, American
Johnson, C. J., Modern Gospel, 1990s–, Artist, American
Johnson, Mattie, Modern Gospel, 1970s, Artist, American
Johnson, Willie Neal, Jubilee; Golden Age, 1990s–, Artist, American
Jones, Bobby, Golden Age, 1980s–1990s, Artist, American
Jones, Rev. Paul, Modern Gospel, 1990s, Artist, American
Jordan, Frank, Jubilee, 2000s–, Artist, American
Keaggy, Phil, Modern Gospel, 1960s–, Artist, American
Kee, John P., & the New Life Community Choir, Modern Gospel, 1990s, Artist, American
Kindred, Modern Gospel, 1970s; 1990s, Artist, American
King's Men, The, Jubilee, 1950s–1980s, Artist, American
Kingdom Heirs, Jubilee, 1980s–, Artist, American
LA Mass Choir, Modern Gospel; Golden Age, 1980s–, Artist, American
La More, Modern Gospel, 1990s, Artist, American
Lewis, Crystal, Modern Gospel, 1990s–, Artist, American
Lexi, Modern Gospel, 1990s–, Artist, American

Ligon, Joe, Jubilee, 1950s–, Artist, American
Little Wayne, Modern Gospel, 1990s, Artist, American
Living Faith Mass Choir, Modern Gospel, 1990s, Artist, American
Lowery, Mark, Modern Gospel, 1990s, Artist, American
Luster, Darrell, Modern Gospel, 1990s, Artist, American
Lynch, Fred, Modern Gospel, 1990s, Artist, American
Madget, John, Modern Gospel, 1990s, Artist, American
Malloy, Donald, Jubilee; Modern Gospel; Golden Age, 1990s, Artist, American
Martin, Roberta, Jubilee; Golden Age, 1930s–1960s, Artist, American
Martin, Sallie, Golden Age; Jubilee, 1940s–1960s, Artist, American
May, Brother Joe, Golden Age; Jubilee, 1940s–1970s, Artist, American
McBride, Geoff, Modern Gospel, 1990s, Artist, American
McBride, Lannie Spann, Modern Gospel, 1990s, Artist, American
McCall, Toussaint, Golden Age, 1960s, Artist, American
McClurkin, Donnie, Golden Age; Modern Gospel, 1990s–, Artist, American
McDonald Sisters, The, Jubilee, 1990s, Artist, American
McElroy, Donna, Golden Age, 1980s–1990s, Artist, American
McFarland, Kim, Modern Gospel, 1990s, Artist, American
Meditation Singers, Jubilee; Golden Age, 1940s–1980s, Artist, American
Messengers, Modern Gospel, 1990s–, Artist, American
Mighty Clouds Of Joy, The, Golden Age; Jubilee, 1960s–1990s, Artist, American
Miller, Douglas, Golden Age, 1980s–, Artist, American
Mills, Walt, Modern Gospel, 1990s, Artist, American
Miner, Tim, Modern Gospel, 1990s, Artist, American
Mississippi Mass Choir, Modern Gospel; Jubilee, 1980s–, Artist, American
Mitchell, Kenneth, Modern Gospel, 1990s, Artist, American
Montclairs, The, Golden Age, 1970s, Artist, American
Montreal Jubilation Gospel Choir, Golden Age, 1980s–1990s, Artist, American
Moore, Anna, Modern Gospel, 1980s–1990s, Artist, American
Moore, Rev. James, Jubilee; Modern Gospel; Golden Age, 1970s–, Artist, American
Moore, Ron David, Modern Gospel, 1990s, Artist, American
Morgan, Bill, Jubilee, 1990s, Artist, American
Mormon Tabernacle Choir, Jubilee; Modern Gospel, 1940s–, Artist, American
Morton, Paul, Modern Gospel, 1990s–, Artist, American
Moss, Bill, Golden Age, 1960s–1990s, Artist, American
Mullins, Rich, Modern Gospel, 1980s–1990s, Artist, American
Music City Mass Choir, Modern Gospel, 1990s, Artist, American
Myles, Raymond Anthony, Golden Age, 1990s, Artist, American
Nation, Modern Gospel, 1990s, Artist, American
Netherton, Tom, Modern Gospel, 1970s–1990s, Artist, American
New Faith, Modern Gospel, 1990s, Artist, American
New Harmonizing Four, The, Golden Age, 2000s–, Artist, American
New King J, Modern Gospel, 1990s, Artist, American
Nicholas, Modern Gospel, 1980s–1990s, Artist, American
Nitro Praise, Modern Gospel, 1990s–, Artist, American
Norwood, Dorothy, Jubilee; Modern Gospel; Golden Age, 1940s–, Artist, American
NuJoi, Modern Gospel, 1990s, Artist, American
O'Neal Twins, The, Modern Gospel, 1990s, Artist, American
O'Neal, Edgar, Modern Gospel, 1990s, Artist, American
Oak Ridge Quartet, Jubilee, 1960s, Artist, American
Ohio National Baptist Mass Choir, Modern Gospel, 1990s, Artist, American
Oquin, Gregory, Modern Gospel, 1990s–, Artist, American
Original Gospel Harmonettes, The, Jubilee; Golden Age, 1950s–1970s, Artist, American
Original Soul Stirrers, The, Golden Age; Jubilee, 1990s, Artist, American
Overstreet, Rev. Louis, Jubilee, 1960s, Artist, American
Pace, Pastor Murphy, Modern Gospel, 1990s, Artist, American
Pace–Rhodes, Shun, Golden Age, 1970s–1990s, Artist, American
Palmer, Toby, Modern Gospel, 1990s, Artist, American
Paramount Singers, The, Jubilee; Golden Age, 1990s, Artist, American
Parham, Rev. Bruce, Modern Gospel, 1990s, Artist, American
Paris, Twila, Modern Gospel, 1980s–, Artist, American
Parker, Trenora, Modern Gospel, 1990s, Artist, American
Parsons, Squire, Jubilee, 1970s–, Artist, American
Paschal, Janet, Jubilee, 1980s–, Artist, American
Pattersonaires, The, Jubilee, 1980s, Artist, American
Patty, Sandi, Modern Gospel, 1970s–, Artist, American
Peacock, Charlie, Modern Gospel, 1970s–1990s, Artist, American
Pearson, Carlton, Jubilee; Modern Gospel, 1990s–, Artist, American
Peebles, Maggie Staton, Golden Age, 1950s, Artist, American
Perry Sisters, The, Modern Gospel, 1990s–, Artist, American
Peter's Rock Mass Choir, Modern Gospel, 1990s, Artist, American
Petra, Modern Gospel, 1970s–, Artist, American
Pilgrim Jubilee Singers, Golden Age; Jubilee, 1940s–1990s, Artist, American
Pilgrim Travelers, Golden Age; Jubilee, 1930s–1990s, Artist, American
Pittman, Willis, Modern Gospel, 1990s–, Artist, American
Pope, Sister Lucille, Golden Age, 1950s–1990s, Artist, American
Powell, Emmit, Modern Gospel, 1990s, Artist, American
Prince Dix, Modern Gospel, 1990s, Artist, American
Pringle, Keith, Golden Age, 1980s–1990s, Artist, American
Rambo, Dottie, Jubilee, 1940s–1950s, Artist, American
Ramey, Troy, Golden Age, 1980s–, Artist, American
Rance Allen Group, The, Golden Age; Modern Gospel, 1960s–1990s, Artist, American
Reagon, Beatrice Johnson, Golden Age, 1970s–1990s, Artist, American
Reagon, Toshie, Golden Age, 1980s–1990s, Artist; Composer; Songwriter, American
Reed's Temple Choir, Modern Gospel, 1990s, Artist, American
Reid, Michael, Modern Gospel, 1990s, Artist, American
Revived, Modern Gospel, 1990s, Artist, American
Rice, Rev. D. C., Golden Age, 1920s–1940s, Artist, American
Robeson, Paul, Jubilee, 1920s–1950s, Artist, American
Robinson, Faye, Modern Gospel, 1990s, Artist, American
Robinson, Roscoe, Modern Gospel, 1950s–1980s, Artist, American
Rogers, Kenton, Modern Gospel, 1990s, Artist, American
Roman–Smith, Lulu, Jubilee, 1980s–, Artist, American
Ross, John, Modern Gospel, 1990s, Artist, American
Salt Of the Earth, Modern Gospel, 1990s, Artist, American
San Quentin Mass Choir, Jubilee, 1990s, Artist, American
Scott, Lisa, Modern Gospel, 1990s, Artist, American
Second Chapter Of Acts, Jubilee, 1970s–1990s, Artist, American
Sensational Nightingales, The, Golden Age; Jubilee, 1940s–1990s, Artist, American
Sheppard, Johnson Holm, Modern Gospel, 1980s, Artist, American
Silver Leaf Quartet, Jubilee, 1920s–1930s, Artist, American
Sisters Of Glory, Modern Gospel, 1990s, Artist, American
Slim & the Supreme Angels, Modern Gospel, 1990s–, Artist, American
Smallwood, Richard, Jubilee; Modern Gospel; Golden Age, 1970s–, Artist, American
Smith, Kenny, Golden Age, 1990s, Artist, American

Smith, Michael W., Modern Gospel, 1970s–, Artist, American
Smith, Rev. Dan, Jubilee, 1960s–1970s, Artist, American
Smith, Willie May Ford, Golden Age; Jubilee, 1930s–1950s, Artist, American
Soul Mission, Modern Gospel, 1990s, Artist, American
Soul Stirrers, The, Golden Age; Jubilee, 1930s–1990s, Artist, American
Sounds Of Blackness, Modern Gospel, 1970s–, Artist, American
Southern California Community, Jubilee; Golden Age, 1990s, Artist, American
Southern Sons, The, Golden Age, 1940s–1950s, Artist, American
Speer Family, The, Jubilee, 1920s–1990s, Artist, American
St James, Rebecca, Modern Gospel, 1990s–, Artist, Australian
Staple Singers, The, Jubilee; Golden Age, 1950s–1990s, Artist, American
Starks, Derrick, Modern Gospel, 1990s–, Artist, American
Stars Of Faith, Golden Age; Jubilee, 1950s–1960s, Artist, American
Staten, Keith, Golden Age, 1990s, Artist, American
Staton, Candi, Modern Gospel, 1960s–, Artist, American
Steeles, The, Modern Gospel, 1980s–, Artist, American
Stonehill, Randy, Modern Gospel, 1970s–1990s, Artist, American
Story, Charly, Jubilee, 1990s, Artist, American
Straight Company, Modern Gospel, 1990s, Artist, American
Stryper, Modern Gospel, 1980s–1990s, Artist, American
Swan Silvertones, The, Golden Age; Jubilee, 1940s–1980s, Artist, American
Swanee Quintet, Jubilee, 1950s–1960s, Artist, American
Taff, Russ, Modern Gospel, 1980s–1990s, Artist, American
Take 6, Modern Gospel, 1980s–, Artist, American
Taylor, Spencer Jr., Modern Gospel, 1990s, Artist, American
Taylor, Steve, Modern Gospel, 1980s–1990s, Artist, American
Terry, Pat, Modern Gospel, 1970s–1980s, Artist, American
Tharpe, Sister Rosetta, Golden Age, 1930s–1960s, Artist, American
Thompson, Michael Earl, Modern Gospel, 1990s, Artist, American
Tonio K, Modern Gospel, 1970s–, Artist, American
Touch Of Faith, Modern Gospel, 1990s, Artist, American
Tramaine, Jubilee; Golden Age, 1980s, Artist, American
Tri–City Singers, The, Modern Gospel, 1990s, Artist, American
Trumpeteers, The, Jubilee; Golden Age, 1940s–1950s, Artist, American
Truthettes, Jubilee; Golden Age, 1970s–1990s, Artist, American
Tyson, Moses Jr., Modern Gospel, 1970s–, Artist, American
Utterbach, Clinton, Modern Gospel, 1980s–1990s, Artist, American
Vincent, Tony, Modern Gospel, 1990s, Artist, American
Voices Of Joy, Modern Gospel, 1990s, Artist, American
Voices Of Light, Golden Age, 1980s–1990s, Artist, American
Voices Of Unity, Modern Gospel, 1990s–, Artist, American
Voices Of Watts, Modern Gospel, 1990s, Artist, American
Voices Supreme, Modern Gospel, 1990s, Artist, American
Wagner, Bishop Norman L., Golden Age, 1990s, Artist, American
Walker, Albertina, Jubilee; Golden Age, 1960s–, Artist, American
Walker, Pastor Hezekiah, Modern Gospel, 1990s–, Artist, American
Walker, Perry, Modern Gospel, 1990s, Artist, American
Wallace, Kate, Modern Gospel, 1990s, Artist, American
Ward, Clara, Golden Age; Jubilee, 1950s–1970s, Artist, American
Washington, Ernestine, Golden Age; Jubilee, 1940s–1950s, Artist, American
Washington, Zozay, Modern Gospel, 1990s, Artist, American
Watkins, Harvey Jr, Modern Gospel, 1990s, Artist, American
Watson, Rob, Modern Gospel, 1990s, Artist, American
Watson, Wayne, Golden Age, 1980s–, Artist, American
Whitman, Walt, Golden Age, 1990s, Artist, American
Williams Brothers, The, Golden Age; Jubilee, 1960s–, Artist, American
Williams, Beau, Golden Age, 1980s–, Artist, American
Williams, Dewey, Golden Age, 1950s–1970s, Artist, American
Williams, Lionel, Modern Gospel, 1990s, Artist, American
Williams, Marion, Jubilee; Golden Age, 1950s–1990s, Artist, American
Williams, Rev. Boyd, Modern Gospel, 1990s, Artist, American
Williams, Ronald, Modern Gospel, 1990s–, Producer, American
Williams, Willie, Modern Gospel, 1980s–1990s, Artist, American
Wilson, Bryan, Modern Gospel, 1990s–, Artist, American
Wilson, Elder Roma, Jubilee, 1940s, Artist, American
Winans Phase 2, Modern Gospel, 1990s, Artist, American
Winans, Angie, Modern Gospel, 2000s–, Artist, American
Winans, BeBe & CeCe, Modern Gospel; Golden Age, 1980s–1990s, Artist, American
Winans, Mom & Pop, Modern Gospel, 1980s–1990s, Artist, American
Wings Over Jordan Choir, Jubilee, 1950s, Artist, American
Witness, Modern Gospel, 1980s–1990s, Artist, American
Woods, Rev. Maceo, Golden Age, 1960s–1980s, Artist, American
Wright, Marva, Modern Gospel, 1990s–, Artist, American
Wright, Orlando, Modern Gospel, 1990s, Artist, American
Wright, Rev. Timothy, Modern Gospel, 1980s–1990s, Artist, American
Zion Harmonizers, The, Modern Gospel, 1940s–1990s, Artist, American
Zion, Modern Gospel, 1990s, Artist, American

JUBILEE ➡ 386 GOLDEN AGE ➡ 388 MODERN GOSPEL ➡ 390

Electronic

Above

The 1975 album Another Green World *by Brian Eno is considered by many to be his most successful recording of experimental arrangements.*

UNLIKE rock music, electronic music is made partly or wholly using electronic equipment – tape machines, synthesizers, keyboards, sequencers, drum machines and computer programmes. Its origins can be found in the middle of the nineteenth century, when many of electronic music's theories and processes were conceived.

In 1863 German scientist Hermann Ludwig Ferdinand von Helmholtz published *On The Sensation of Tone As A Physiological Basis For The Theory Of Music*, which laid the foundations of modern acoustics and predicted the development of electrical means for creating sound and music. In 1877 Thomas Edison invented the phonograph, the precursor to the modern record turntable, which is still central to electronic music and DJ culture. In 1912 Luigi Russolo set up the futurist movement. Intent on representing the soul of the masses and the industrialized world, the first futurist concert took place in Milan, Italy, in 1914. The driving concepts behind futurism are still inherent in techno and electro, in which contemporary electronic styles try to define and capture the essence of the post-industrial world.

By the 1920s, Leon Theremin had developed the Theremin instrument, whose spooky, otherworldly sound was used in numerous Hollywood soundtracks. The rock band Led Zeppelin used it during the 1970s, and the instrument is still an essential part of modern music production. The Theremin was the inspiration for Robert Moog to develop his own instrument,

> "I CAN'T UNDERSTAND WHY PEOPLE ARE FRIGHTENED OF NEW IDEAS. I'M FRIGHTENED OF THE OLD ONES."
>
> *John Cage*

Right

John Cage's interest in experimental music led him to create a designer piano that made different sounds when altered. When objects were placed between the strings, the piano was transformed into a percussion orchestra.

the Moog synthesizer. First manufactured in 1964, it was one of the earliest electronic music synthesizers, and used most famously by US art-rock act the Doors. The 1920s also saw production of the avant garde *Ballet Mecanique* by American composer George Antheil, which featured both live and automated piano music, as well as the sound of doorbells and airplane propellers.

Orson Welles released his *War Of The Worlds* odyssey in 1938, and a decade later, Pierre Schaeffer and Jacques Poullin broadcast a "concert of noises" in 1948 which they christened musique concrète. Although electronic music won widespread support only with the advent of dance music and rave culture from the mid- to late-1980s, it was the sound collage and minimal work of John Cage and Karlheinz Stockhausen in the mid-twentieth century that provided the impetus for others to experiment with less familiar concepts and instruments.

In the 1960s, German bands Neu, Can and Faust, as well as seminal US outfit the Velvet Underground and psychedelic rockers Pink Floyd and Tangerine Dream, fused conventional rock instruments with sound effects, tapes and synthesizers, questioning and changing the nature of the "traditional" band. By the 1970s, Brian Eno had produced the first ambient music, and Jean Michel Jarre and Vangelis were writing epic compositions for synthesizers. Kraftwerk explored sampling, and their fusion of synthesized melodies and rigid electronic beats laid the foundation for techno and electro, while Terry Riley, Steve Reich and Philip Glass's minimalist works were precursors for ambient and new age music.

By the end of the decade, New York DJs and rappers merged street culture with sampling culture to create hip hop. Apart from affording the DJ a central role, hip hop's raw beats,

STYLES

Ambient

Krautrock

Electro

Trip Hop

New Age

THE ELECTRONIC STYLE

Synthesizers opened up a new universe of sounds. Here a simple motif (sequence) is modified by changing the brightness and decay of the sound.

Filter Frequency

Envelope decay

Synth

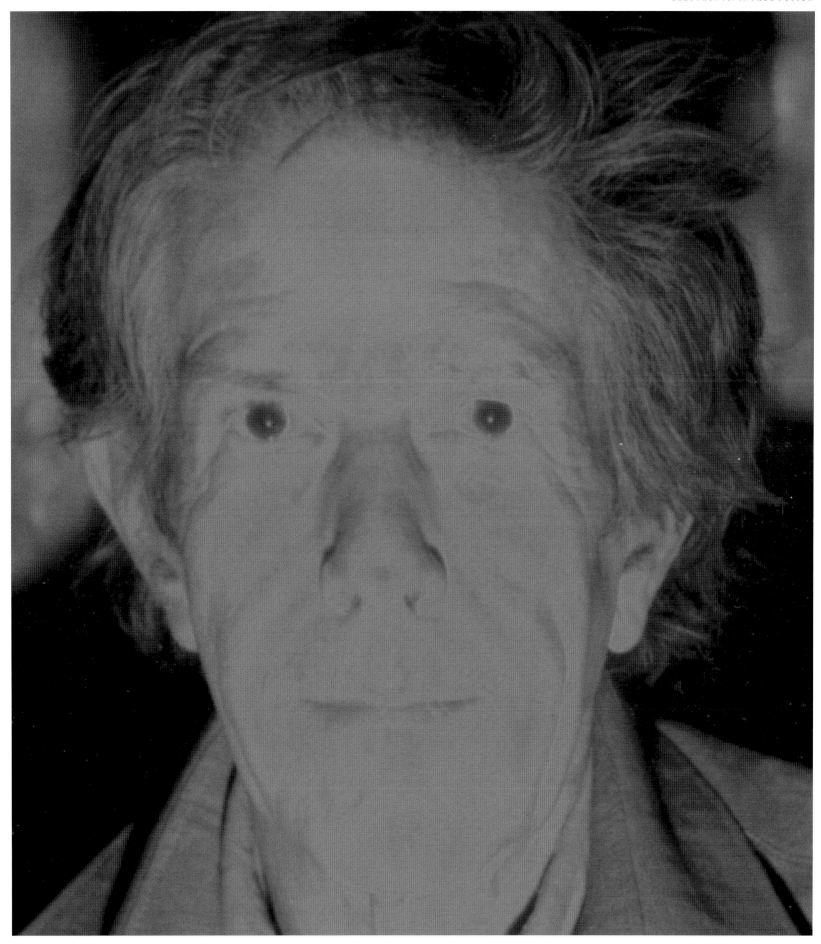

irreverent sampling ethic and confident lyrical outlook influenced the slow motion beats of trip hop and informed drum'n'bass, break beat and UK garage. The availability of sequencers and synthesizers also revolutionized British pop music, as a new wave of synth acts including Depeche Mode, Human League and Soft Cell stormed the charts. This was also the first time electronic music had entered the mainstream.

Electronic music also found a home in Detroit and Chicago in the mid-1980s and in Europe as the decade ended. Inspired by Ron Hardy and Frankie Knuckles' DJing in Chicago's Music Box club, producers, including Larry Heard and Phuture, started to make house music. House music also provided the basis for the techno sound that came from Detroit during the same period. The first wave of Detroit techno producers – Derrick May, Juan Atkins, Carl Craig and Kevin Saunderson – had all visited the Music Box in Chicago and were inspired to make their own version of this new instrumental electronic music.

House, hip hop, techno and electro all provided the basis for electronic music as it splintered into myriad categories and genres – with trance, progressive house, drum'n'bass, breaks, tech-house and UK garage all evolving from these electronic styles throughout the 1990s.

Electronic music also became intertwined in the fabric of popular music as the 1990s progressed. Acts like the Prodigy and the Chemical Brothers are now some of the biggest acts in the world, while the ambient soundscapes of Future Sound Of London, the Orb and Orbital have also proved popular for mass-market consumption. Pushing in the opposite direction, artists like Madonna have worked with innovative producers like Mirwais and William Orbit, assimilating their production style into crossover pop songs, and since the mid-1990s television commercials have often featured electronic music backing-tracks from underground artists like Aphex Twin.

It's no wonder, then, that electronic music is as broad a term as rock. Still fuelled by technological advances – the sophisticated software programmes and the MP3 and web possibilities which electronic artists were the first to embrace – this music keeps morphing, challenging the listener to guess what the next chapter will be.

Ambient

AMBIENT MUSIC HAS EXISTED SINCE THE LATE-NINETEENTH CENTURY. ALTHOUGH BRIAN ENO WAS THE FIRST ARTIST TO USE THE TERM "AMBIENT" TO DESCRIBE HIS MUSIC ON HIS 1978 ALBUM, MUSIC FOR AIRPORTS, COMPOSERS LIKE CLAUDE DEBUSSY AND ERIC SATIE, WITH THEIR NOTION OF COMPOSING PIECES TO COMPLEMENT LISTENING SURROUNDINGS, BROKE WITH MUSICAL CONVENTIONS AND EXPECTATIONS.

FRENCHMEN Erik Satie and Claude Debussy are often called the "fathers of modern music", and it's no idle claim. While Satie was writing musical pieces at the end of the 19th century that were based on the concept of setting a mood, his most significant works were composed around 1920. These were a series of pieces he called "furniture music", which Satie wanted both to be part of and include the surrounding noises. "Furniture music" laid the basis for what Brian Eno achieved with ambient music half a century later.

Similarly, Debussy's experiments with tone, texture and harmony in his orchestral works at the end of the 19th century and his early 20th century piano music would also play an important role in influencing the way composers – and later on, electronic producers – approached the composition of mood or ambient music.

Early Trendsetters

By the middle of the 20th century, experimental composer John Cage questioned accepted notions of percussion, tone and texture with '4' 33" '. As its title suggested, the piece was exactly four minutes and thirty three seconds long and consisted of silence. Cage's message was clear: any musical expression, silence included, was valid. Cage was followed by composers like Karlheinz Stockhausen, whose tape-based audio collages laid the basis for modern-day sampling, and the acknowledged founders of minimalism: Terry Riley, Steve Reich and Philip Glass

By the late-1960s this freethinking approach, combined with a growing drug culture, had also produced some of rock's most adventurous forays as bands like Pink Floyd and Tangerine Dream soundtracked rock music's first tentative flirtations with electronic sounds. Works like Pink Floyd's *Piper At The Gates Of Dawn* and *Set The Controls For The Heart Of The Sun*, released the same year man first walked on the moon, mapped out this new fusion, dubbed space rock. It heralded the beginning of synthesized sound's growing influence on contemporary music. It was only a matter of time before an artist made use of the technology in a mainstream manner, and Mike Oldfield's 1973 album, *Tubular Bells*, which did just that, was a huge success, selling millions worldwide.

Above
Mike Oldfield's innovative Tubular Bells *release in 1973 on Virgin Records has sold over 16 million copies worldwide and is regarded as one of the finest pieces of ambient music to date.*

> ## "IT'S EXACTLY WHAT YOU NEED IF YOU HAVE A BUSY AND STRESSFUL LIFE."
> *Mixmaster Morris*

Left
A contemporary of John Cage, Karlheinz Stockhausen was another pioneer of electronic music, with his tape-loop piece recordings amongst the first ever produced.

AMBIENT

The music of ambient composers often consists of slowly evolving textures over a simple repetitive pattern, which can induce a trance-like state of consciousness.

LEADING EXPONENTS

Brian Eno
The Orb
Air
John Cage
Mixmaster Morris
Aphex Twin
Orbital
Global Communications
Nightmares On Wax
Moby

Increased access to electronic equipment during the 1970s and 1980s allowed Brian Eno to fulfil his goal of making music that cultivated relaxation and "space to think". The advent of this technology also allowed German act Kraftwerk to pioneer their synth-based sound, a development that in turn influenced a whole range of 1980s synth producers, including Trevor Horn, Art Of Noise, Human League and Ultravox.

Acid House Changes The Rules

However, by the mid- to late-1980s, electronic music took a radical new departure. As acid house and Ecstasy culture exploded in the UK and Europe, it was clear that there was a need for a more relaxed accompaniment to the high-octane beats. Even at early acid house clubs, DJs like Alex Paterson, from ambient dub act the Orb, were in charge of providing a soothing musical antidote in a second room. Consequently, the late-1980s saw the release of classic ambient albums including the Orb's dubby *Adventures Beyond The Ultraworld* and Mixmaster Morris's pastoral work as Irresistible Force, as well as pop situationists KLF's groundbreaking *Chill Out*.

Ambient Branches Out

Rather than merely provide soft ear candy for tired ravers, ambient had spread its influence to house music – witness 808 State's classic late-1980s ambient house track 'Pacific State' – and had taken on world and dub influences. These ethnic ingredients were evident in the mish-mash of musical textures that defined early 1990s London clubs Whirly-gig and Megadog, as well as in the work of Banco De Gaia and Bedouin Ascent.

Indeed, ambient's relevance to electronic music cannot be understated during the early to mid-1990s. It can be measured by the number of benchmark albums released during this period. In the electronic field, Aphex Twin released the hypnotic *Selected Ambient Works Volume 1* and the darker *Polygon Window* album, while Sheffield label Warp started the *Artificial Intelligence* compilation series, introducing the subtle electronic nuances of Plaid, Autechre, Speedy J, Black Dog and B12 to a wide audience.

Orbital's *Yellow* and *Brown* albums documented ambient's influence on dance floor techno and Tom Middleton's Global Communications project debuted with the haunting textures

 DANCE: ACID ➡ 317   DANCE: TRANCE ➡ 321   DANCE: TECHNO ➡ 324 of the *76:14* album. Meanwhile, German producer Peter Namlook, along with Wagon Christ's *Phat Lab Nightmare* and the isolationist tones of Norway's Biosphere became the natural successor to John Cage and Steve Reich's minimalist legacy.

Ibiza Chills Out

Although ambient music's increased profile and popularity meant major labels saturated the market with a succession of pale imitations, there was no danger it would succumb to commercial forces.

Entwined in the original Balearic culture of Ibiza, pre- and post-club chill out sessions hosted by DJs like Lenny Ibizarre and Jon Sa Trincha had ensured tracks such as Sueño Latino's 'Sueño Latino', a version of 1970s German producer Manuel Gottsching's 'E2-E4', became as much the soundtrack to the White Island as high-octane house music.

By the mid-1990s, Ibiza bars and beaches like Café Del Mar, Salinas, Bora Bora and Calla Llonga were playing host to UK chill DJs like Chris Coco and Phil Mison, who were playing diverse but universally chilled DJ sets. At the time, it wasn't unusual to find Paper Moon's atmospheric deep house '51 Days' sitting alongside Ennio Morricone's film soundtracks and former bleep techno act Nightmares On Wax's atmospheric beats.

Chill Out On The Rise

Ambient had morphed into chill out and, although its name had changed, it still looked to the same concept of creating a mood to suit the listening environment. The other common bond between ambient and its mid- to late 1990s successor is that it still embraces a broad range of styles. From the wispy electronica of Warp act Boards Of Canada to Nightmares On Wax's soulful hip hop, Bent and Lemon Jelly's lush compositions, Zero 7's cinematic productions and Royksopp's pop-informed atmospherics, chill out assimilates a wide range of diverse musical sources. Its increased popularity was bolstered by the release of French duo Air's *Moon Safari* album, which fused dreamy 1960s pop with blissed-out electronic textures and former techno producer Moby's *Play* album, which sampled the mournful outpourings of old blues songs and set them to haunting ambient backing tracks. To date, *Play* has sold over 10 million copies worldwide, its sales spurred on by the use of every track in a multitude of television commercials.

Chill out also enjoys an increased following due to sociological concerns: most people who started clubbing in the early 1990s have by now reached their early thirties and have either reduced the frequency with which they go out or are married and have children. In this scenario, chill out is the perfect soundtrack to staying in. At the same time, this shouldn't detract from the fact that chill out has its own dedicated series of festivals and events (for example, The Big Chill) every year in the UK.

However, like ambient, chill has also attracted the attention of the corporate sector which has flooded the market with a succession of chill out compilations; the Ministry Of Sound's chill out albums have sold hundreds of thousands of units. Like most electronic forms, chill out music hasn't been watered down by mainstream attention. Indeed, recent years have seen producers like Blue States, Susumu Yokota and John Beltran explore folk, organic and lush techno soundscapes. It seems that, to paraphrase ambient guru Mixmaster Morris, chill knows "it's time to lie down for its rights".

Below
The Orb's 1992 chart-topping album, U. F. Orb, established the group as leading contributors to the growing interest in ambient electro.

Krautrock

KRAUTROCK, WHICH EMANATED FROM WEST GERMANY DURING THE LATE-1960S, FUSED THE VELVET UNDERGROUND'S WHITE NOISE EXPERIMENTS AND PINK FLOYD'S PSYCHEDELIC ROCK WITH THE FREE FORM JAZZ AESTHETIC AND FUNK-BASED RHYTHMS.

Above
Consisting of two former members of Kraftwerk, Neu's short existence as musicians during the 1970s did not prevent them from influencing such diverse artists as David Bowie and Sonic Youth.

AVOIDING the dull virtuosity of progressive rock and the sanitised R&B pop of the late-1960s, Krautrock's grand vision of reinventing the rock guitar as well as exploring the untapped possibilities of the electronic sound has seen it influence dance and electronic music as well as experimental rock.

The Krautrock Triumvirate

In the late-1960s, acts like Ash Ra Tempel, Amon Duul II and Cosmic Jokers were inspired by psychedelic rock and Cluster pioneered a hypnotic drone sound, but the most influential Krautrock bands were Neu, Can and Faust.

From the mid-1960s through to the early 1970s, Faust juxtaposed melodic songs like 'Jennifer' with screeching walls of noise, while Neu favoured a pulsating electronic sound as well as making blissful ambient passages. Michael Rother from Neu also explored a pure electronic sound on his Harmonia collaboration with Hans-Joachim Roedelius and Dieter Moebius from Cluster.

However, Can – who formed in the mid-1960s – were the most important Krautrock band. Consisting of bassist Holger Czukay, guitarist Michael Karoli, keyboardist Irmin Schmidt, drummer Jaki Leibezeit and vocalist Damo Suzuki, the band's free-form approach saw them jam for hours before translating their improvisations into arrangements. Holger Czukay said: "If you want to make something new, you shouldn't think too far beyond one certain idea," and this is evident on works like *Tago Mago*,

> ## "IF YOU WANT TO MAKE SOMETHING NEW, YOU SHOULDN'T THINK TOO FAR BEYOND ONE CERTAIN IDEA."
> *Holger Czukay*

Right
Pioneers of the exploratory sounds of post-psychedelia, Can's innovative sound would go on to influence the boom of technopop artists during the 1980s and 1990s.

Ege Bamyasi and *Future Days,* where the band fuses spacious, atmospheric textures with sparse, live funk rhythms.

Occupying the middle ground between guitar rock and the clean, synthesized techno sound, Krautrock, especially Can, is a fascinating paradox. Its proponents used guitars for purposes they weren't intended for – to emulate synthesized sounds – as well as gelling rock's often forgotten sense of rhythm with precise repetition, an aesthetic common to electronic rather than live music. Holger Czukay said: "Repetition is like a machine. Machines have a heart and soul, they are living beings. If you are aware of a machine's life then you are a master."

The wide range of artists and acts Can and their Krautrock contemporaries inspired straddles the rock and electronic worlds. Just as Krautrock kicked against the musical

LEADING EXPONENTS

Can
Neu
Faust
Julian Cope
Spacemen 3
Mouse On Mars
Kreidler
Kieron Hebden
Uwe Schmidt
Pole

KRAUTROCK

Tangerine Dream's album Phaedra is a kaleidoscope of evolving sounds and textures. Like much classical electronic music the timbre is as important as the pitch.

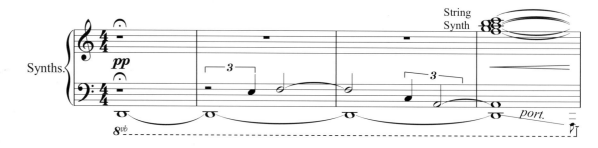

mediocrity of the late-1960s to early 1970s, so too did the punk era and post-punk acts it inspired in the following decade. Rallying against the spectre of progressive rock excess, the angular angst-funk of PiL and Gang Of Four, as well as the Fall's lyrical stream-of-consciousness and scratchy rhythm assault called to mind Can's juxtaposition of the free-flowing and the repetitive, albeit reinterpreted in an angry manner.

At the same time, the UK's burgeoning industrial scene, including Cabaret Voltaire and Throbbing Gristle, used Faust's experiments as a reference point, while trendsetter David Bowie's debt to Neu is clear on his seminal, electronic-tinged, *Low* and *Heroes* albums.

Spaced Out

By the 1980s, the Krautrock legacy was still strong amongst rock music's experimental proponents. Sonic Youth's free-form guitar work alluded to the German sound; there was a direct link between Cluster's drone sound and the hypno-rock of Loop; Julian Cope's frazzled acid rock made references to Krautrock's deranged sound; and, on a lighter note, the shoegazing indie style of Ride was shaped by Krautrock's wall of sound.

The 1980s act Spacemen 3 also embodied the Krautrock mentality. Their work was characterized by layers of feedback, pulsating hypno-rhythms and electronic textures, key components in the band's superb *Playing With Fire* album. Unlike Krautrock's LSD links, the album saw Spacemen singer Jason Pierce make a Faustian pact with heroin, only to be reborn as the ethereal electronic Spiritualised combo, whose *Laser Guided Melodies* album was one of the finest early 1990s works and heir to Neu's blissed-out, glacial electronic sound.

Electronic Heirs

By the 1990s, Krautrock influences were most notable in the electronic environment, exceptions being US guitar bands like Pavement and Mercury Rev, the Acid Mothers Temple, and Kieran Hebden's Fridge and Four Tet bands, which embraced the same freeform approach to composition and arrangement that Can pioneered.

The angular, difficult work of Tortoise, To Rococo Rot and Mouse On Mars gave way to Andy Votel and the Twisted Nerve label's skewed, lo-fi approach, while indietronica acts like Lali Puna, Dntel, Tarwater, Peaches, Kreidler and Schneider TM fused guitar elements with melodic, quirky and even sleazy electronic elements.

However, Germany is where the most apparent modern day heirs to Krautrock can be found. Uwe Schmidt has succeeded in reinventing Krautrock's legacy under a number of guises. Together with Burnt Friedmann as Flanger, he explores its free form, jazz-based rhythm approach, and as

Sieg Uber Die Sonne, Schmidt makes deep electronic music. Most famously, he has released a series of quirky, salsa-inspired cover versions of Kraftwerk under yet another incarnation, Señor Coconut.

For different reasons, the stripped-down electronic sound of the Scape label and its owner, Stefan "Pole" Betke is also an obvious Krautrock heir. Bearing similarities to the contemporary stripped-down, dub-influenced German techno sound, Betke's compositions lack the rhythm focus of 1960s Krautrock, but, together with like-minded producers Matmos, the jazz-inspired Jan Jelinek – who also records for Scape – and Russian act Fizzarum, he has inherited the Krautrock mantle.

Sparse yet immersive, mechanical yet warm these electronic glitch arrangements, so precise in their de- and re-construction of tiny slices of percussion and rhythm, are as much a revelation as Can's own work.

Below
Having released their debut album, Taking Drugs To Make Music To Take Drugs To *in 1986, Spacemen 3 was notorious for recording songs that lasted for upwards of 20 minutes at a time.*

ELECTRO IS CURRENTLY ENJOYING A HUGE RENAISSANCE. BUT, DESPITE THE CURRENT HYPE AND MAINSTREAM ACCEPTANCE OF THE MUSIC, IT HAS ALWAYS ENJOYED A STRONG CULT FOLLOWING. THIS IS DUE TO THE MUSIC'S MANY DIFFERENT STRANDS AND ITS CONSTANT NEED FOR REINVENTION.

Electro

Above

Considered the fathers of electronic body music, Front 242 create albums that contain dense percussion grooves, bass lines, growled vocals and exotic samples that enthral the listener.

AT its most basic level, electro differentiates itself from house and techno by the fact that it doesn't use a continuous 4/4 kick drum. Employing off-beat drums, as well as focusing more on rhythm elements like bass and percussion, DJ Dave Clarke neatly defines electro as being "held together by left-field spirit and no 4/4 beat programming".

Kraftwerk's Role

Although electro wasn't solely a product of the 1970s band Kraftwerk's pioneering synthesized sound, the German act's importance cannot be overestimated. By the early 1980s, Kraftwerk had influenced synth pop and new romantic acts

like Depeche Mode, Soft Cell, Visage, Human League, Heaven 17, John Foxx and Ultravox as well as maverick talents like '19' producer Paul Hardcastle, Gary Numan, Vince Clarke, Thomas Dolby, Trevor Horn and Art Of Noise.

While 1980s synth pop is playing an important role in the current electro revival, US producer Juan Atkins took inspiration from Kraftwerk's rigid beat structures and futurist sense of dislocation as well as from Afrika

> ## "YOU STILL HAVE TO LOOK TO THE PAST TO GO TO THE FUTURE."
>
> *Keith Tucker, ex-Aux 88*

LEADING EXPONENTS

Kraftwerk

Drexciya

Cybotron

Aux 88

Adult

Carl Finlow

I-F, Hacker & Kittin

Two Lone Swordsmen

Anthony Rother

ELECTRO

Much of Kraftwerk's music is based around a simple robotic sequence and electronic drums. This provides a backdrop for atmospheric washes and repetitive vocals.

Drms.

Synth

Bambaata's early 1980s fusion of the synth riffs of the Düsseldorf quartet's 'Trans Europe Express' and the hip hop beats on 'Planet Rock', to kick start Detroit's electro movement.

Detroit Electro

In particular, Juan Atkins' Cybotron and Model 500 projects as well as seminal acts like Underground Resistance, Aux 88 and Drexciya, were all influenced by Kraftwerk, but developed their own distinctive styles.

Not only was Atkins the first producer to coin the term "techno" for his sci-fi obsessed dance floor material, he also put out tracks like 'Clear' and 'Alleys Of Your Mind' as Cybotron, setting Detroit's influential electro scene in motion and realising the futurist agenda Kraftwerk hinted at. This electro funk sound was also realised by Keith Tucker's Aux 88 act, which released a number of seminal works before disbanding during the late-1990s.

Electro's sci-fi themes were also furthered by militant techno/electro act Underground Resistance, whose leader, "Mad" Mike Banks wears a balaclava and refuses to be photographed. The collective's exploration of deep techno and dance floor friendly electro funk was, and still is, riddled with outer-space references.

Meanwhile, mysterious act Drexciya turned electro's space fixation inside out, documenting the mythology of the lost city of Atlantis and the concept of an "inner space" on textured resonating releases like 'Deep Sea Dweller', 'Aquatic Invasion', 'The Journey Home' and 'Bubble Metropolis'. Like its techno sound, Detroit's electro innovations laid down a blueprint for others to follow.

Varied Strands

It would be too simplistic, however, to credit Kraftwerk and Detroit for being solely responsible for the vast contemporary electro scene, as throughout the 1970s and 1980s less well known acts also played a role. Funk bands like Parliament, Trouble Funk and Cameo, as well as composer John Carpenter's eerie film soundtracks to movies like *Halloween* were vital, while break dancing and B-Boy culture and the Miami bass sound of Luke Skkywalker and 2 Live Crew left a mark on electro music.

Of equal importance are the ebm (electronic body music) and Italo disco sounds. Using the 4/4 drum beat instead of electro's offbeat structures, ebm was pioneered by Nitzer Ebb and Front 242 during the 1980s, and its tough beats, brutal rhythms and oppressive tones still inform modern electro. Similarly, 1980s producers Giorgio Moroder, Patrick Cowley,

Left
Upon the 1995 release of Big Hit, *Nitzer Ebb had evolved from dominant sounds of technology-reliant blurbs to the live textures that are heard today.*

Below
Using the experimental explosion between electronic pop music and the German avant-garde, Kraftwerk became a dominant and influential force in electronic music's development.

While still a teenager, DJ Hell began mixing different genres of music from punk and new wave, to hip hop and house, until he found his niche in trance and hardcore.

Bobby O and Jellybean's electronic, high energy version of disco music; Italo Disco, also played a crucial role in the resurgence of electro in the latter part of the 1990s.

Leaders Of The New School

While the Detroit sound was revered, few producers outside the Motor City - with the exception of the Advent, DMX Krew, RAC and Carl Finlow - were making this complicated, intricate music. It seemed electro would remain a highly specialized sound.

However, in 1997, Dutch producer I-F released the classic 'Space Invaders Are Smoking Grass' track, a record that looked to Italo Disco as much as it did to the Detroit sound for inspiration. Together with like-minded producers Legowelt, the Clone label and Detroit's Adult, who were also influenced by androgynous new wave music, this dance floor sound found favour with techno DJs who could play their tracks without dropping the tempo. In the words of former Aux 88 front man Keith Tucker, Adult were "the architects of the revival".

In 1998, German DJ/producer DJ Hell set up the International Deejay Gigolos label. Although he released ebm-influenced work by David Caretta and Terence Fixmer as well as putting out material by some of Drexciya's offshoot projects, Hell also sought out a poppier, synth pop-flavoured variant of the Adult/I-F sound. Dubbed electroclash by New York club promoter Larry Tee, Hell's label brought glamour, style and accessibility to electro. Synth pop-influenced acts like Hacker & Miss Kittin sang about fame and decadence, while Tiga and Zombie Nation even made it into the mainstream charts. Unsurprisingly, electroclash came under major label scrutiny – Gigolos act Fischerspooner signed to Ministry Of Sound for

£2 million – and a whole slew of artists, labels and DJs started to discover, release and play electro.

Keep On Breakin'

Despite mainstream interest, electro has never been in a healthier state, evident in the increased variety of styles. Apart from the ongoing development of electroclash, fuelled by labels like City Rockers, White Leather and Bpitch, as well as club nights like Optimo in Glasgow and Erol Alkan's Trash night in London, many producers have veered away from this glitzy style. They are taking the music back underground and are looking to older influences again.

Anthony Rother, Scape One and Transparent Sound continue to explore the Kraftwerk/Detroit blueprint, albeit with polished, ultramodern production values, and DJ Hell recently announced that Gigolos will focus on a new rock-electro fusion.

Meanwhile, Detroit's booty bass sound keeps growing in popularity. A brutally raw, high-octane version of the expletive-filled Miami bass sound, it is the work of Motor City DJs Assault and Godfather, who have forged links with UK producers like Debasser and Andrea Parker. Similarly, maverick producer Andrew Weatherall and his studio partner Keith Tenniswood's work as Two Lone Swordsmen contrasts starkly with the glamour-obsessed electroclash sound.

Based on hyperspeed break beats, the duo's work and releases on their Rotters Golf Club and Control Tower labels take in techno, rave, drum'n'bass and house elements and have a dirty, edgy feel. It seems that not even the untimely demise of Drexciya's James Stinson in late 2002 can stop electro's forward march.

POP: NEW ROMANTICS & FUTURISM ➡ 50   DANCE: DISCO ➡ 314   DANCE: TECHNO ➡ 326

Trip Hop

JUNGLE AND UK GARAGE ARE OFTEN CITED AS THE ONLY REAL BRITISH CONTRIBUTIONS TO ELECTRONIC MUSIC. BUT THE SLOW MOTION BEATS OF TRIP HOP ARE ALSO STEEPED IN THE MULTI-CULTURAL SOUNDS OF UK MUSIC.

INFLUENCED by 1980s dub acts like On-U-Sound, Adrian Sherwood and African Headcharge and their own sound system backgrounds, Bristol based acts like Smith & Mighty and Massive Attack, as well as London outfits Pressure Drop and Renegade Soundwave, had been experimenting with the fusion of dub influences with hip hop and break beats since the mid-1980s.

Renegade Soundwave also released club-based, dub-influenced tracks like 'Biting My Nails,' and Massive Attack even drafted in dub pioneer the Mad Professor to do a dub version of their *Protection* album, called *No Protection*.

The dub ethic was also adopted by second wave Bristol producer Tricky, whose *Maxinquaye* album went to paranoid extremes – a mixture of dense, claustrophobic beats and ominous rapping.

It was Portishead, however, who brought the fusion of heavy basslines and dead-paced beats, as well as dub's sense of mournful spaciousness, to the wider public's attention. Captured on the duo's debut album, *Dummy*, Portishead's melancholic outpourings ensured that the album became a brooders' favourite without sanitizing blueprints explored by their predecessors.

The Mo'Wax Connection

In the US, producer DJ Shadow started to release his own haunting compositions. Unlike its progenitors, his 1994 'In/flux' release dispensed with the notion of vocals, especially the violent, misogynist gangster rhymes, breaking with the traditions of US hip hop and opting for barren, otherworldly instrumentals.

London DJ James Lavelle, who had already put out instrumental hip hop tracks on his Mo'Wax label, signed Shadow. Lavelle's label also put out the *Headz* compilation, which became a landmark release. Pre-empting the glut of compilations keen to cash in on the trip hop sound, Mo'Wax was also the first imprint to document the music's development from a narrow set of influences to a wide range of flavours,

Above
Considered by many critics to be their finest release, Portishead's 1994 album, Dummy, highlighted singer Beth Gibbons' haunting, soulful voice over hip hop/ trance beats and offbeat sampling.

> "I DON'T WANT TO BE PIGEON-HOLED. IT'S AN ATTITUDE THAT DESCRIBES WHAT I DO RATHER THAN A PARTICULAR STYLE".
> *James Lavelle, Mo'Wax*

Left
Tricky began collaborating with the teenage Martina during the early 1990s, while a member of Massive Attack. She launched her solo career in 1999.

LEADING EXPONENTS
Massive Attack
Portishead
DJ Shadow
Renegade Soundwave
Tricky
Coldcut
Thievery Corporation
Fila Brazilia
The Chemical Brothers
Kruder & Dorfmeister

TRIP HOP
Trip hop often uses "dotted rhythms" in which alternating heavy and light beats produce a lilting feel over the top of a constant, repetitive sound. Frequently the "drum" sounds are electronic or electronically manipulated.

THE ELECTRONIC INTRO ➡ 392   ELECTRONIC PEOPLE A–Z ➡ 407   INSTRUMENTS A–Z ➡ 436   WORLD: CARIBBEAN ➡ 288   DANCE: BIG BEAT ➡ 328

with contributions as diverse as Warp stalwarts Autechre's menacing 'Lowride' and US West Coast act Tranquility Bass's uplifting 'We Came In Peace'.

With Shadow's debut album, *Entroducing*, selling half a million copies, it looked like trip hop was set to follow an inclusive rather than an exclusive blueprint.

E Is For Eclectic

Trip hop's diverse approach was borne out by the individualistic approach other producers embraced. Washington DC act Thievery Corporation embraced dub and bossa flavours on their 1995 album *Sounds From The Thievery Hi-Fi*, Fila Brazilia looked to funk and jazz influences, Si Begg explored an unpredictable electronic sound, and Lamb's orchestral, vocal

Above

The world of dance music would not be the same without the contributions of DJ Shadow and his seminal release, IN/Flux, which is widely regarded as a revolutionary and groundbreaking electro record.

style, embodied on tracks like 'Gorecki', made clear that trip hop was flying in the face of purism and advocating a refreshing, eclectic agenda.

Unsurprisingly, this eclectic *modus operandi* influenced trip hop's most prominent DJs, with pioneering DJ/production/multimedia outfit Coldcut laying down the gauntlet with their aptly named *70 Minutes Of Madness* mix CD. Fusing the theme music from Dr. Who with Luke Slater's techno and Jhelisa's soulful 'Friendly Pressure' with the haunting jazz of Red Snapper's 'Hot Flush' and Masters At Work's Latino house, the mix was one of DJ culture's most important turning points.

Madness proved that adherence to a specific tempo, or indeed the 4/4 beat that had dominated club land, was no longer necessary and that with a degree of imagination and skill it was possible to pursue an eclectic musical agenda. This spirit was maintained by DJs like Jon Carter, Fatboy Slim, Midfield General and the Chemical Brothers (originally called the Dust Brothers), who, conscious of dance floor demands, imbued their sets and their production work, with faster, more club-friendly breaks and beats.

The Beats Get Bigger

Pioneered at the Chemicals' Heavenly Social Club and originally captured on the duo's Cocteau Twins sampling 'Song To The Siren' debut release, this new breed of eclectic DJ and clubbing experience superseded the dead paced beats that characterized trip hop, and the music was rechristened big beat.

Artists like Dirty Beatniks, Wiseguys, Propellerheads, Death In Vegas, Freestylers, Cut La Roc and Dub Pistols and labels like Skint and Wall Of Sound followed in this new direction. Big beat's uncomplicated, good time party aesthetic turned Fatboy Slim and the Chemical Brothers into dance music's biggest pop stars, but it also took trip hop out of the media glare, allowing some of the music's most innovative artists the space to blossom.

Trip Hop Makes A Comeback

As James Lavelle said on the release of his collaborative UNKLE album, *Psycence Fiction*, with DJ Shadow in 1998, "Big beat was such a blessing in disguise: finally trip hop can go and we can make a run for it!"

Despite Lavelle's detachment, trip hop's slow motion beats were revisited by Leftfield, who dedicated a sizeable chunk of their debut album, *Leftism*, to the dub-heavy rhythms and seismic dub basslines originally explored by Massive Attack and Smith & Mighty. Austrian act Kruder & Dorfmeister also brought trip hop back to the public's attention with the stoned grooves of their *K&D Sessions* album, which has become one of dance music's most popular releases.

True to electronic music's cyclical nature, trip hop had morphed into the new style of big beat before making a glorious comeback with these benchmark releases. Trip hop's legacy is still audible in the smoky grooves of chill out act Nightmares On Wax and in Zero 7's lush, down tempo compositions. It's unquestionable that trip hop left an indelible mark on electronic music.

New Age

NEW AGE MUSIC HAS BECOME THE MOST POPULAR FORM OF CONTEMPORARY ELECTRONIC MUSIC. UNLIKE THE OTHER VARIANTS, NEW AGE HAS BECOME POPULAR WITH A GLOBAL MAINSTREAM AUDIENCE, EVEN MORE SO THAN THE MOST COMMERCIAL STRAINS OF CONTEMPORARY CHILL OUT.

Synth Pioneers

The easiest way to explain its popularity is to look at where new age evolved from. Greek synth pioneer Vangelis contends "nothing's new, we didn't invent anything. It's just one particular moment where we take a piece of something and it belongs to us for just a little bit."

Some of new age music's initial reference points are similar to ambient music's background, particularly the epic, haunting synthesized sound-scapes of French artist Jean Michel Jarre, evident on *Oxygene* and *Equinoxe*; German act Tangerine Dream's spacey works like *Phaedra* and Mike Oldfield's *Tubular Bells*. Vangelis wrote the utopian soundtrack for cult sci-fi movie *Bladerunner*, which sowed the seeds for the fusion of the techno-futurist and spiritual enlightenment creed associated with new age.

New age also took inspiration from the neoclassical work of Eno collaborator Harold Budd's albums, *The Pavilion Of Dreams* and *Abandoned Cities*, and minimalists like Philip Glass, but, crucially, also looked to the healing music of Dr. Steve Halpern – especially his 'Spectrum Suite' work. Here, the origins of new age and ambient embark on separate journeys.

Above

The enormous popularity of Glastonbury, England's largest open-air summer festival, resulted in the 2003 event selling out in a record time of less than 24 hours.

Left

An accomplished pianist, Vangelis concentrates on producing soundtracks for such critically acclaimed films and projects as Chariots of Fire and Bladerunner.

ALTHOUGH similarities do exist between new age and ambient music – both styles were influenced by the same pioneers, and ambient, like new age, is often composed to evoke a sense of calm or well-being – these styles are, in many ways, radically different.

Unlike ambient, new age embraces a set of lifestyle choices, beliefs and philosophies and, though an electronic form, is more likely to take on classical, pop, folk and ethnic influences than modern chill out and ambient.

The other main difference is that whereas ambient is still a largely underground, specialist sound, new age has made the transition to a mainstream audience, and has become a ubiquitous part of popular contemporary music. An indication of the growing audience for this music is reflected by former Clannad singer Enya, who has sold over 10 million copies of her 1991 album, *Shepherd Moons*, worldwide.

> "I DON'T MAKE A DISTINCTION BETWEEN ELECTRONIC AND ACOUSTIC SOUNDS. SOUND IS SOUND AND WHETHER IT'S ACOUSTIC OR ELECTRONIC, IT'S STILL A NATURAL SOUND."
> *Vangelis*

Voice

la   la la   la   la   la   la

Synth.

NEW AGE

A style characterized by the timbre of electronic sound, new age often contains a quick moving, repetitive inner rhythmic feature (like an electronic heartbeat), sandwiched between a simple bass line and a vocal melody.

LEADING EXPONENTS

Vangelis
Tangerine Dream
Dr. Steve Halpern
Iasos
Enya
Yanni
Steve Roach
Michael Brook
Kitaro
David Lanz

THE ELECTRONIC INTRO ➡ 392   ELECTRONIC PEOPLE A-Z ➡ 407   INSTRUMENTS A-Z ➡ 436   THE EIGHTIES POP INTRO ➡ 44

Healing Music

While Eno's ambient concept was based on making music to think to as well as relax to, the message behind Halpern's work was to promote inner peace and well-being. He intended his music be used as an accompaniment to yoga, massage, meditation, and other healing arts practices. This is where new age is different from all other electronic music forms. Although, like other forms, it is often of an instrumental nature, one of its key drivers is its attendant lifestyle. The Californian new age movement was a gentle wake-up call from hippy excess and the post flower-power era, a west coast philosophy of enlightenment, self-awareness and healing. Eastern philosophies and practices have heavily influenced new age music, but, interestingly, new age has tried and mainly failed to assimilate ethnic musical sources.

Eighties Greed

As increased Western affluence became widespread in the 1980s, a commercialized, watered-down version of the Californian new agers' core values, as well as an increasingly bland version of new age music's soothing tones, became omnipresent in alternative book stores, health food stores and massage and meditation centres.

Fuelled by music industry greed as well as unscrupulous artists who, unlike most new age artists, embraced the fake lifestyle, ambient expert Mike Watson offers the following critique of new age music during this period: "New age is as much a religious movement as it is a musical style, and therein lies [sic] its limitations. During the 1980s, new age became a marketing tool for all kinds of instrumental music, regardless of whether or not it was associated with the lifestyle and its pot pourri of psychology, theology, charlatans and money-making opportunists."

The European New Age Movement

Despite this cynicism, Europe's new age movements told a very different story. Festivals, in particular the annual event at Glastonbury, had been a strong part of English rural life for centuries, and from the late-1960s onwards, the festival circuit was bolstered by the growing number of free spirits on the road. Glastonbury, allegedly the birthplace of King Arthur, was their natural home.

However, the new age travellers' preference for high octane rave and techno and the travelling sound systems Bedlam and Spiral Tribe were behind many early 1990s mass raves. Although demonized in the UK media, the new age phenomenon was supported by techno act the Shamen, who spoke of the impending utopian Age Of Aquarius and believed in techno-shamanism, whereby techno music would help clubbers transcend the woes of the world.

World Fusion

The 1980s also saw the advent of a number of innovative artists and inspirational works. Japanese producer Ryuichi Sakamoto – who fused Asian and European classical music with ethnic textures – penned the soundtrack to the film *Merry Christmas Mr. Lawrence*, while Vangelis continued his silver screen association, writing the unforgettable and uplifting score for *Chariots Of Fire*.

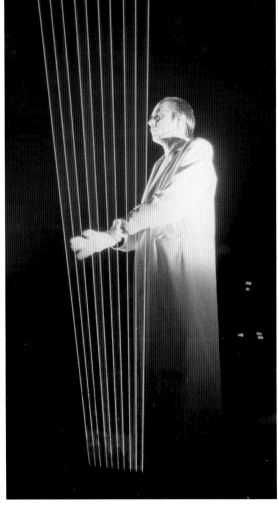

Vangelis also played a part in influencing Steve Roach, the US producer who took the new age synth legacy and reinterpreted it into warm, spacey electronics on his 1984 album, *Structures From Silence*, as well as fusing tribal percussion and Aboriginal sounds on his 1988 opus, *Dreamtime Return*. Michael Brook was another artist who debuted during the 1980s with the ethno-ambient *Hybrid* and who went on to work with Youssou N'Dour and the Pogues.

Although bland mainstream acts like Enigma and Deep Forest continued to exploit religious and ethnic motifs for the mass market throughout the 1990s, new age's future lies in cross-pollination. Incorporating Kitaro and Greek producer Yanni's poppy hybrids, David Lanz's orchestral accompaniments and piano works, George Winston's pastoral, folk-influenced work, Dead Can Dance's moving chants and Enya's ethereal Celtic sound, this hugely popular music is spreading its focus far and wide.

CLASSICAL: CONTEMPORARY ➡ 272   THE WORLD INTRO ➡ 276   WORLD: EAST ASIA ➡ 280   WORLD : EUROPE ➡ 304

Artists: Electronic

Entries appear in the following order: name, music style, year(s) of popularity, type of artist, country of origin

Ackerman, William, New Age, 1970s-, Artist, German
Acoustic Alchemy, New Age, 1980s-, Artist, British
Afrika Bambaata, Electro, 1980s-, Artist; Producer, American
Agent Provocateur, Trip Hop; Ambient, 1990s, Artist, British
Akasha, Trip Hop; Electro, 1990s, Artist, British
Aloof, The, Trip Hop; Electro, 1990s-, Artist, British
Alpha & Omega, Trip Hop; Ambient, 1980s-, Artist, British
Alpha, Trip Hop; Electro, 1990s-, Artist, British
Alternative Frequencies, Trip Hop; Electro, 1990s, Artist, British
Amon Düül, Krautrock, 1960s-1990s, Artist, German
Animals On Wheels, Trip Hop; Electro, 1990s, Artist, American
Appliance, Krautrock, 1990s-, Artist, British
Ariel, Jack, Trip Hop, 1990s, Artist, British
Arkenstone, David, New Age; Electro, 1980s-, Artist, American
Ash Ra Tempel, Krautrock, 1970s-, Artist, German
Attica Blues, Trip Hop; Electro, 1990s-, Artist, British
Aura, William, New Age, 1970s-1990s, Artist, American
Avatar, Trip Hop; Ambient, 1990s, Artist, British
B., Howie, Trip Hop, 1990s-, Producer, British
Babbitt, Milton, Electro, 1930s-1990s, Artist, American
Baby Mammoth, Trip Hop; Ambient, 1990s-, Artist, British
Baker, Arthur, Electro, 1980s-, Producer; Artist, American
Ball, Patrick, New Age, 1980s-, Artist, American
Beanfield, Trip Hop, 1990s-, Artist, German
Beaver and Krause, Electro, 1960s-1970s, Artist, American
BecVar, Bruce, New Age, 1980s-1990s, Artist; Composer, American
Behrman, David, New Age; Electro, 1950s-1990s, Composer, Austrian
Bentley Rhythm Ace, Trip Hop, 1990s-, Artist, British
Beta Band, The, Trip Hop, 1990s-, Artist, British
Björk, Trip Hop; Electro, 1970s; 1990s-, Artist, Icelandic
Blackalicious, Trip Hop, 1990s-, Artist, American
Bowery Electric, Trip Hop; Ambient, 1990s-, Artist, American
Brainticket, Krautrock, 1970s-1980s, Artist, German
Budd, Harold, Electro; Ambient, 1960s-, Artist, American
Burmer, Richard, New Age; Ambient; Electro, 1980s-1990s, Artist, American
Cage, John, Electro, 1930s-1990s, Composer, American
Can, Krautrock, 1960s-1990s, Artist, German
Carlos, Wendy, Electro, 1960s-, Artist, American
Chaquico, Craig, New Age, 1990s-, Artist; Songwriter, American
Chemical Brothers, The, Trip Hop; Electro, 1990s-, Artist, British
Ciani, Suzanne, New Age, 1980s-, Artist, American
Cibo Matto, Trip Hop, 1990s-, Artist, American
Cirrus, Trip Hop, 1990s-, Artist, American
Clement, Tim, New Age; Ambient; Electro, 1990s, Artist; Composer, Canadian
Cluster, Krautrock; Albient; Electro, 1970s-1990s, Artist, German
Coldcut, Trip Hop; Electro, 1980s-, Artist, British
Conrad, Tony, Krautrock, 1960s-1970s, Artist, American
Cook, Norman, Trip Hop, 1990s-, Producer, British
Coyote Oldman, New Age; Ambient, 1980s-1990s, Artist, American
Cybotron, Electro, 1980s-, Artist, American
Czukay, Holger, Electro, 1960s-, Artist, German
Dan The Automator, Trip Hop; Electro, 1990s-, Artist, American
Danna, Mychael, New Age; Ambient, 1990s, Artist; Composer, American
Davol, New Age, 1980s-1990s, Artist; Composer, American
Death In Vegas, Trip Hop; Electro, 1990s, Artist, British
DeeJay Punk-Roc, Trip Hop, 1990s-, Producer, American
DeMarinis, Paul, New Age; Electro, 1970s-1990s, Composer, American
Demby, Constance, Ambient; New Age, 1970s-, Artist, American
Deuter, Ambient; Electro; New Age, 1970s-, Artist; Composer, German
Dirty Beatniks, Trip Hop; Electro, 1990s-, Artist, British
DJ Food, Trip Hop, 1990s-, Artist, British
DJ Icey, Trip Hop, 1990s-, Artist; Producer, American
DJ Krush, Trip Hop; Electro, 1990s-, Artist; Producer, Japanese
DJ Shadow, Trip Hop; Electro, 1990s-, Artist; Producer, American
DJ Spooky, Trip Hop; Electro, 1990s-, Artist; Producer, American
DJ Vadim, Trip Hop; Electro; Ambient, 1990s-, Artist; Producer, Russian
DJ Wally, Trip Hop; Ambient; Electro, 1990s-, Artist; Producer, American
Dockstader, Tod, Electro; Ambient, 1960s-1970s, Composer, American
Douglas, Bill, New Age, 1980s-, Artist; Composer, Canadian
Dr Octagon, Trip Hop; Electro, 1990s-, Artist, American
Drome, Trip Hop; Ambient, 1990s, Artist, German
Dynamix II, Electro, 1980s-, Artist, American
Early Grey, Trip Hop, 1990s, Artist, British
Egyptian Lover, The, Electro, 1980s-1990s, Producer, American
Eno, Brian, Ambient; Electro, 1970s-, Producer; Artist, British
Eno, Roger, Ambient; Electro, 1980s-, Composer; Artist, British
Enya, New Age, 1980s-, Artist, Irish
Fatboy Slim, Trip Hop; Electro, 1990s-, Artist; Producer, British
Faust, Krautrock, 1970s-, Artist, German
Faze Action, Trip Hop; Ambient, 1990s-, Artist, British
Fila Brazilia, Trip Hop; Electro; Ambient, 1990s-, Artist, British
Finitribe, Krautrock, 1990s, Artist, British
Forest Mighty Black, A, Trip Hop; Electro; Ambient, 1990s-, Producer, German
Franke, Christopher, New Age; Electro, 1990s-, Artist; Composer, German
Freddy Fresh, Trip Hop; Electro, 1980s-, Artist; Producer, American
Freestyle, Electro, 1980s-1990s, Producer, American
Freestylers, Trip Hop; Electro, 1990s-, Artist, British
Froese, Edgar, Ambient; Electro, 1970s-1980s, Producer; Artist, German
Funki Porcini, Trip Hop; Electro; Ambient, 1990s-, Producer, British
Future Sound Of London, Trip Hop; Ambient, 1990s-, Artist, British
Gandalf, Ambient; Electro, 1960s-1990s, Composer; Artist, Austrian
Gerd, Trip Hop; Ambient, 1990s, Artist, Dutch
Göttsching, Manuel, Krautrock; Ambient, 1970s-1990s, Artist, German
Grandmaster Flash, Electro, 1980s-, Artist; Producer, West Indian
Gunshot, Trip Hop; Ambient, 1990s, Artist, British
Guru Guru, Krautrock, 1970s-, Artist, German
Gus Gus, Trip Hop; Electro, 1990s-, Artist, Icelandic
Haack, Bruce, Electro, 1960s-1980s, Producer; Artist, Canadian
Halpern, Steven, Ambient; Electro; New Age, 1970s-, Artist, American
Hamel, Peter Michael, New Age, 1970s-, Artist, German
Hancock, Herbie, Electro, 1960s-, Artist; Composer, American
Harmonia, Krautrock, 1970s, Artist, German
Harrison, Lou, New Age, 1940s-, Composer, American
Harriss, Don, New Age; Electro, 1980s-1990s, Artist; Composer, American
Hassell, Jon, Ambient; Techno; New Age, 1970s-, Artist; Composer, American
Headrillaz, Trip Hop, 1990s, Artist, British
Hedges, Michael, New Age, 1980s-, Artist, American
Heines, Danny, New Age, 1980s-1990s, Artist, American
Henry, Pierre, Electro, 1950s-1990s, Artist; Composer, French
Herbaliser, The, Trip Hop; Ambient; Electro, 1990s-, Artist, British
Highstein, Max, New Age, 1980s-1990s, Artist, American
HIM, Trip Hop, 1990s-, Producer, American
Hoenig, Michael, New Age; Electro, 1970s-1980s, Artist; Composer, German
Horky, Robert Julian, New Age; Ambient, 1980s, Artist; Composer, Austrian
Husikesque, Trip Hop, 1990s, Artist, American
I:Cube, Trip Hop, 1990s-, Artist, French
I-F, Electro, 1990s-, Artist; Producer, Dutch
Inkuyo, New Age, 1980s-, Artist, American
Isham, Mark, Ambient; New Age, 1980s-1990s, Artist, American
Jamiroquai, Trip Hop, 1990s-, Artist, British
Jarre, Jean-Michel, New Age; Electro, 1970s-, Artist; Producer; Composer, French
Jhelisa, Trip Hop, 1990s, Artist, American
Jobson, Eddie, New Age; Electro, 1980s, Artist, British
Jones, Michael, New Age, 1980s-1990s, Artist; Composer, Canadian
Jonkey, Chuck, New Age, 1980s-, Artist, American
Jonzun Crew, The, Electro, 1980s-1990s, Artist, American
Kater, Peter, New Age, 1980s-, Producer; Artist, German
Keane, Brian, New Age, 1970s-, Artist; Composer, American
Kelly, Georgia, New Age, 1970s-1990s, Artist, American
Khan, Al Gromer, New Age; Ambient, 1970s-, Artist, Bavarian
Kid Loco, Trip Hop; Ambient, 1990s-, Producer, French
Kindler, Steve, New Age, 1970s-1990s, Artist, American
Kingsley, Gershon, New Age; Ambient; Electro, 1960s, Producer, American
Kitajima, Osamu, New Age, 1960s-1990s, Artist; Composer, Japanese
Kitaro, New Age; Electro, 1970s-, Artist; Composer, Japanese
Koch, Berward, New Age, 1990s, Artist, German
Kraftwerk, Electro; Krautrock, 1970s-, Artist, German
Kruder & Dorfmeister, Trip Hop; Electro, 1990s, Artist, Austrian
La Dusseldorf, Krautrock; Electro, 1970s-1980s, Artist, German
La Funk Mob, Trip Hop; Electro, 1990s, Artist, French
Lanz, David, New Age, 1980s-, Artist, American
Laraaji, New Age; Ambient, 1980s-1990s, Artist; Composer, British
Laswell, Bill, Ambient; Electro, 1970s-, Producer; Artist, American
Lavelle, James, Trip Hop, 1990s-, Artist, British
Lee, Tim "Love", Trip Hop, 1990s-, Producer, British
Les Rhythmes Digitales, Trip Hop; Electro, 1990s-, Producer, French
Liebert, Ottmar, New Age, 1990s-, Artist, German
Lightwave, New Age; Ambient, 1990s-, Artist, German
Liquid Liquid, Electro, 1980s, Artist, American
Lo Fidelity Allstars, Trip Hop; Electro, 1990s-, Artist, British
Love Spirals Downwards, New Age, 1990s, Artist, American
Lucier, Alvin, Electro, 1950s-, Composer, American
Lycia, Ambient, 1980s-1990s, Artist, American
Lynch, Ray, New Age; Ambient, 1980s-1990s, Artist; Composer, American
Mannheim Steamroller, New Age; Electro, 1970s-, Artist, American
Mantronix, Electro, 1980s-1990s, Artist, American
Manuel Göttsching, Krautrock; Ambient, 1970s-1990s, Artist, German
Mark, Jon, New Age; Ambient, 1970s-1990s, Artist; Composer, British
Massive Attack, Trip Hop; Electro, 1990s-, Artist, British
Material, Ambient, 1980s-1990s, Artist, American
Maunu, Peter, New Age; Electro, 1990s, Composer, American
McDonald, Steven, New Age, 1980s-, Artist, New Zealander
Mekon, Trip Hop; Electro, 1990s-, Producer, American
Micus, Stephan, New Age, 1970s-, Artist; Composer, German
Midfield General, Trip Hop, 1990s-, Producer, British
Miller, Radhika, New Age, 1980s-1990s, Artist; Composer, American
Moebius, Krautrock; Ambient; Electro, 1970s-, Artist, German
Moloko, Trip Hop; Electro, 1990s-, Artist, British
Money Mark, Trip Hop; Electro, 1990s-, Artist; Producer, American
Monk & Canatella, Trip Hop; Ambient, 1990s-, Artist, American
Moraz, Patrick, Ambient, 1970s-1990s, Artist, Swiss
Moses, Harold, New Age, 1990s, Composer; Artist, American
Mr Scruff, Trip Hop; Ambient; Electro, 1990s-, Producer, British
Nakai, R. Carlos, New Age, 1980s-, Artist, American
Namlook, Pete, Ambient; Electro, 1990s-, Producer, German
Neu!, Krautrock, 1970s-1990s, Artist, German
Newcleus, Electro, 1980s, Artist, American
Nightmares On Wax, Trip Hop; Electro, 1990s-, Artist, British
Nightnoise, New Age, 1980s-1990s, Artist, Irish
O'Hearn, Patrick, New Age; Electro, 1970s-, Artist; Producer; Composer, American
Oldfield, Mike, New Age, 1970s-, Artist, British
Olive, Trip Hop; Ambient, 1990s-, Artist, British
Orton, Beth, Trip Hop, 1990s-, Artist; Songwriter, British
Palm Skin Productions, Trip Hop; Electro, 1990s-, Producer, American
Panamatic, Trip Hop, 1990s, Artist, British
Parrish, Man, Electro, 1980s-1990s, Producer, American
Pasero, Stevan, New Age, 1980s-1990s, Producer, American
Peanut Butter Wolf, Trip Hop, 1990s-, Artist; Producer, American
Penguin Café Orchestra, The, New Age, 1970s-1990s, Artist, American
Peterson, Gilles, Trip Hop, 1990s-, Artist, British
Planet Patrol, Electro, 1980s-1990s, Artist, American
Poets Of Thought, Trip Hop, 1990s, Artist, British
Popol Vuh, Krautrock; Ambient, 1970s-1990s, Artist, German
Portishead, Trip Hop; Electro, 1990s, Artist, British
Pretty Tony, Electro, 1980s-1990s, Producer, American
Propellerheads, Trip Hop; Electro, 1990s, Artist, British
Radigue, Eliane, New Age, 1960s-1990s, Composer, French
Ranking Joe, Trip Hop, 1970s-1990s, Artist, Jamaican
Reaves, Giles, New Age; Ambient, 1980s-, Artist; Composer, American
Red Snapper, Trip Hop; Electro, 1990s-2000s, Artist, British
Req, Trip Hop; Electro; Ambient, 1990s-, Producer, British
Rich, Robert, Ambient; Electro, 1980s-, Artist; Producer; Composer, American
Riley, Terry, Ambient, 1950s-, Artist, American
Roach, Steve, Ambient; Electro; New Age, 1970s-, Artist; Producer, American
ROC, Trip Hop, 1990s, Artist, British
Rockers Hi-Fi, Trip Hop; Electro; Ambient, 1990s-, Artist, British
Roedelius, Krautrock; Ambient, 1970s-, Artist, German
Rootless, Trip Hop, 1990s, Artist, British
Ruby, Trip Hop, 1990s-, Artist, American
Scala, Trip Hop; Ambient; Trip Hop, 1990s, Artist, British
Schnitzler, Conrad, Krautrock; Electro, 1970s-1990s, Artist, German
Schulze, Klaus, Krautrock; Electro, 1960s-1990s, Artist, German
Scott, Raymond, Electro, 1930s-1980s, Artist; Composer, American
Shantel, Trip Hop; Electro, 1990s-, Artist, German
Shrieve, Michael, New Age, 1970s-, Artist, American
Silver Apples, Electro, 1960s; 1990s, Artist, American
Singh, Talvin, Trip Hop; Electro, 1990s-, Artist; Producer, British
Skylab, Trip Hop; Electro, 1990s-, Artist, American
Slotek, Trip Hop, 1990s, Artist, American
Sneaker Pimps, Trip Hop; Electro, 1990s-, Artist, British
Software, New Age; Electro, 1980s-1990s, Artist, German
Solid Doctor, Trip Hop; Electro; Ambient, 1990s, Producer, British
Spaceways, Trip Hop; Ambient; Electro, 1990s, Artist, British
Stagg, Hilary, New Age, 1980s-, Artist, American
Stearns, Michael, New Age, 1980s-, Artist; Composer, American
Stockhausen, Karlheinz, Electro, 1950s-1990s, Composer, German
Story, Liz, New Age, 1980s-1990s, Artist, American
Story, Tim, New Age; Ambient, 1980s-, Artist, American
Suicide, Electro, 1970s-1980s, Artist, American
Sukia, Trip Hop; Electro, 1990s, Artist, American
Tangerine Dream, Krautrock; Ambient; Electro, 1960s-, Artist, German
Tenor, Jimmy, Electro; Ambient, 1990s-, Producer, Finnish
Tesh, John, New Age, 1980s-, Artist, American
Thievery Corporation, Trip Hop; Electro, 1990s-, Artist, American
Tingstad & Rumbel, New Age, 1980s-, Artist, American
Tobin, Amon, Trip Hop; Electro, 1990s-, Artist; Producer, Brazilian
Tosca, Trip Hop; Ambient, 1990s-, Artist, Austrian
Tranquility Bass, Trip Hop; Ambient; Electro, 1990s, Producer, American
Tri Atma, New Age, 1980s, Artist, German
Tricky, Trip Hop; Electro, 1990s-, Artist; Producer, British
Uncle Jamm's Army, Electro, 1980s, Artist, American
Union Wireless, Krautrock, 1990s, Artist, British
United Future Organization, Trip Hop, 1990s-, Artist, Japanese
UNKLE, Trip Hop; Ambient; Electro, 1990s, Artist, British
Vangelis, Ambient; Electro, 1970s-, Artist; Producer, Greek
Varese, Edgar, Electro, 1920s-1960s, Composer, French
Vibert, Luke, Trip Hop; Ambient, 1990s-, Producer, British,
Visit Venus, Trip Hop; Electro, 1990s, Artist, German
Wagon Christ, Trip Hop; Electro; Ambient, 1990s-, Producer, British
Watkins, Kit, New Age; Electro, 1980s-1990s, Artist, American
Wax Doctor, Trip Hop, 1990s, Artist; Producer, British
Winston, George, New Age, 1970s-, Composer; Artist, American
Winter, Paul, New Age, 1960s-, Artist; Producer, American
Wreckin' Crew, Electro, 1990s-, Artist, American
Wright, Danny, New Age, 1980s-, Artist, American
Yanni, New Age; Electro, 1980s-, Artist, Greek
Yas-Kaz, New Age, 1980s-1990s, Artist, Japanese
Zephaniah, Benjamin, Trip Hop, 1980s-1990s, Artist, Jamaican

INTRODUCTION

Soundtracks And Theatre

Above
A prolific yet unsophisticated composer, Irving Berlin never learnt to read music or play the piano properly. Despite this he wrote 900 songs, 19 musicals and 18 film scores.

THIS chapter encompasses styles that were, at least initially, designed to work in tandem with other forms of expression, deepening or enhancing their impact. The scores of musical theatre are woven into stories played out by the characters on stage. A film soundtrack is composed to interlock with the action on a cinema screen, while cabaret songs work in harmony with the theatrical components of a cabaret performance.

Of course, the above styles may be appreciated in solely musical terms, and recordings of works by the likes of Rodgers & Hammerstein, Ennio Morricone and Marlene Dietrich have sold well in their own right. But to gain a true understanding of musical theatre, film music and cabaret, we need to appreciate their roles as pieces in a creative jigsaw.

Although they work within different constraints, the artists in this section are every bit as skilled as those of "pure" musical genres. Indeed, the composers who presided over the golden age of musical theatre (the 1920s to the late-1950s) were among the twentieth century's most gifted musicians. Following Jerome Kern, who pioneered the use of music to explore the themes of a production, George Gershwin (*Of Thee I Sing*), Irving Berlin (*Annie Get Your Gun*) and others combined traditional European melodies with the sounds of African-America to breathe new vibrancy into the musical. Oscar Hammerstein, working at the same time, developed numbers that were geared towards the dramatic functions of the show. *Carousel*, one of Hammerstein's many collaborations with Richard Rodgers, moved towards the synergy of score and speech that characterized musicals in the second half of the twentieth century. Stephen Sondheim introduced melodic themes that were fragmented over an entire show, and the baton then passed over the Atlantic to Andrew Lloyd Webber (*Sunset Boulevard*), whose productions borrowed tricks of style and staging from rock music.

The 1930s witnessed the golden age of the movie soundtrack, and many of its leading lights were, like their counterparts in musical theatre, European émigrés. Men such as the Austrian-born Max Steiner introduced operatic leitmotifs that tied specific melodies to individual characters. In the 1940s the hugely influential modernist Bernard Herrmann took the latter process one step further in his score for *Citizen Kane*, tailoring music to fit particular scenes and emotions. He was followed in the 1960s by John Williams, the soundtrack's most popular exponent, and Ennio Morricone, its most prolific. Vangelis's work for *Chariots Of Fire* ushered in a wave of electronic scores in the 1980s, and one of the biggest recent influences has been the riotous music of Bollywood, clearly recognizable in films such as *Moulin Rouge* (2001).

A more intimate and subversive spirit of cross-fertilization prevailed during the birth of cabaret in late-nineteenth to early-twentieth century Paris. Venues such as Le Chat Noir provided liberating countercultural forums, where formidable actor/musicians such as Yvette Guilbert performed a heady mixture of song, comedy, theatre and political satire. Germany embraced cabaret with a passion during the inter-war years, with Marlene Dietrich introducing movie audiences to the smoky decadence of Berlin's *Kabaretten*. Although any political edge was lost, post-war American cabaret upheld traditions through the subtle skills and genuine charisma of stars such as Sylvia Syms.

> ## "I HAND HIM A LYRIC AND GET OUT OF HIS WAY."
> *Lyricist Oscar Hammerstein on working with composer Richard Rodgers*

Right
This 1955 film version of Oklahoma starred Shirley Jones as Laurey Williams and Gordon McRae as the cowboy vying for her affection.

STYLES
Musicals
Film Music &
  Soundtracks
Cabaret

THE SOUNDTRACK AND THEATRE STYLE

Music composed for film or the theatre is descriptive; it reflects the action of the performance. The score or soundtrack can, as shown here, be used to build dramatic tension.

SOUNDTRACKS AND THEATRE PEOPLE A-Z ➡ 417   INSTRUMENTS A-Z ➡ 436

FROM THE ECLECTIC MUSICAL MELTING POT OF RAGTIME, GILBERT & SULLIVAN, EARLY JAZZ, VIENNESE OPERETTA, BLACKFACE MINSTREL SHOWS AND AUTHENTIC DEEP- SOUTH BLUES EMERGED THE BROADWAY SHOW TUNE. "SHOW" AND "TUNE", OF COURSE, ARE THE ESSENTIAL INDICATORS OF MUSICAL STYLE.

Musicals

> ## "WHAT'S WRONG WITH LETTING 'EM TAP THEIR TOES A BIT? I'LL LET YOU KNOW WHEN STRAVINSKY HAS A HIT – GIVE ME SOME MELODY!"
>
> *Joe, the Broadway producer in Stephen Sondheim's musical* Merrily We Roll Along *about a Broadway writing team.*

Above

Actor and singer Paul Robeson leaving for Hollywood to begin his role in the 1932 revival of Show Boat. *He sang the popular tune 'Ol' Man River' and changed the lyrics to form a protest song. He later became a political activist.*

LEADING EXPONENTS

Jerome Kern

Rodgers & Hammerstein

Irving Berlin

George Gershwin

Kander & Ebb

Lerner & Loewe

Frank Loesser

Boublil & Schönberg

Stephen Sondheim

Andrew Lloyd Webber

THE music created for Broadway musicals – and, subsequently, for the musical form whatever its geographical origin – is conditioned by its theatrical and dramatic role within a show, as well as the need to have the audience humming the tunes as they leave the theatre.

The first generation of musical-theatre composers, who included George Gershwin, Irving Berlin, Jerome Kern and Richard Rodgers, were tunesmiths of the highest order. Many were Jewish émigrés. As young men they eagerly embraced the music of a different displaced community of an earlier generation, the African-American. Perhaps it was their distinctly melodic Jewish Cantor tradition, combined with the emerging music of the black ghetto, that was to create the unique, vibrant and soulful sounds of Broadway, represented by songs ranging from 'I Got Rhythm' and 'On Your Toes' to 'The Man I Love' and 'Smoke Gets In Your Eyes'. Whatever the reason, this generation gave birth to what is sometimes called the Golden Age of the musical, dating, roughly, from *Show Boat* in 1927 to *Gypsy* in 1959. The father of them all was Jerome Kern. When asked what Kern's place in American music was, Richard Rodgers replied, simply: "Jerome Kern is American music."

In Kern's *Show Boat*, part of the distinguishing purpose of the music was to explore the themes of the show. 'Ol' Man River' has a majestic simplicity, creating a sense of time passing that brings both change and continuity, while 'Life Upon The Wicked Stage' has a cheerful mischievousness, brilliantly capturing the "playful" character of showgirls. And if Kern gave musical theatre its first melodic voice, then it was his lyricist collaborator, Oscar Hammerstein, who gave musical theatre an understanding of its theatrical and dramatic role.

The Theatricality And Drama Of Musical Theatre

Although he was not a composer, Hammerstein brought theatricality and dramatic intent to the musical form. His music and songs, usually referred to as "numbers", are geared for theatrical presentation. There are dance numbers, production numbers (involving elaborate sets and costumes), closing numbers, and so on. The songs are often written for a specific time within the show. The "11 o'clock number" will have enough punch and energy to give the show a lift when, late in the second act, it might start to sag a little – the title song from Rodgers & Hammerstein's *Oklahoma!* and 'Sit Down, You're Rockin' The Boat', from Frank Loesser's *Guys and Dolls*, are examples.

Equally important is dramatic function. In *The King And I*, when the head wife of the king sings 'Something Wonderful' to the children's governess, Mrs. Anna, the song not only reveals the wife's feelings for her husband and a side of the king we have not seen; it also dampens Mrs. Anna's growing anger towards the king. Such songs may have life as cabaret songs outside the theatre, but to appreciate them fully they

MUSICALS

Musicals rely on simple but emotionally evocative melodies to create character and tell the story through song.

Oh   if I'd on-ly had a son   I would have gi-ven ev-ery thing I own

THE SOUNDTRACKS AND THEATRE INTRO ➡ 408   SOUNDTRACKS AND THEATRE PEOPLE A–Z ➡ 417   INSTRUMENTS A–Z ➡ 436

must be heard and seen within their theatrical and dramatic context. That is what musical theatre is all about.

As for how context might dictate musical style, the opening overture or song not only lays out the score's melodic themes; it also, more importantly, sets up audience expectations about a show's content through its style. Famously, Stephen Sondheim's bawdy vaudeville show, *A Funny Thing Happened On The Way To The Forum*, never worked until the uptempo 'Comedy Tonight' was introduced, replacing a charming but unimposing song that had previously opened the show. Another early number might include an expression of resolve or need (sometimes known as the "I-Want" song). In *Gypsy*, it is 'Some People', a driving, brassy number illustrating Rose's ambition; in *My Fair Lady*, it is 'Wouldn't It Be Loverley?', a gentle, graceful melody suggesting Eliza's longing for an easier life. The irony is that neither character achieves her wants, and in act two both melodies are dramatically reprised to haunt them. The overriding theme of the show is often revealed in what is known as the "utopian number": for example, 'Somewhere' (*West Side Story*) or 'Bali Hai' (*South Pacific*). This type of song can, however, be chilling if the theme is darker, a good example being 'Tomorrow

Belongs To Me' in *Cabaret*. What we are seeing here is the theatrical and dramatic context of the show dictating musical style rather than the other way around, as is the case in compilation musicals such as *Mamma Mia!*

Musical Theatrical And Dramatic Integration

Apart from the continuing influence of his own work, Oscar Hammerstein had a second important contribution to make to musical theatre: he was a theatrical and parental mentor to Stephen Sondheim. A lot is often said about the development of the "integrated musical", referring to how songs became increasingly integrated into the story so that they naturally arose out of the dialogue, or "book", of the show. *Oklahoma!* is usually cited as the most important milestone. However, Sondheim rightly points to the 'If I Loved You' section of *Carousel* (Rodgers & Hammerstein) as more seminal. There is no "number", as such. What you have is a scene in which speaking, underscoring and singing are so interconnected as to appear seamless. This was to become the direction of the musical in the later half of the last century. The score would no longer be integrated into the book of the show; the score would become the show.

Above

Gershwin completed his folk opera, Porgy and Bess, *in 1935. Although this was the composer's favourite and most ambitious composition, it did not receive due acclaim until after his death in 1937.*

Sondheim developed a form of the musical in which melodic themes were not just broken and separated within a scene, but sometimes fragmented across an entire act or show. When Barbra Streisand wanted to record 'Children Will Listen', from *Into The Woods*, the song had to be pasted together from various parts in the show. Integration was complete.

Another devotee of the work of Rodgers & Hammerstein, especially that of Richard Rodgers, is Andrew Lloyd Webber. Early in his career Lloyd Webber, like Kern before him, was embracing an emerging sound. This time, however, it was rock, not blues. And yet the sudden appearance of a waltz, a strong feature of Rodgers's music, in Lloyd Webber's "sung-through" rock operas – such as *Evita* – shows the continuing influence of an earlier tradition. Even later Lloyd Webber shows continue this mixture of styles, in which elements of a driving rock song (the title song from

Sunset Boulevard, for example) share the stage with an entrancing, lyrical ballad ('With One Look', again from *Sunset Boulevard*).

This takes us back to where the musical began, with an eclectic variety of influences and sounds. Does the musical have a singular and distinct sound? Perhaps not, but from Kern onwards, the musical has had some of the greatest and most original creators of theatrical melody – or "show tunes", as most composers would modestly call them. The best writers created their own unique style, from the bluesy voice of Kern and the bright, breezily hummable numbers of Irving Berlin, to the sublime waltzes of Rodgers and the rising lyrical ballads of Lloyd Webber. And if there is one influence above all others on musical theatre, it is the theatre itself. In more recent years, musicals such as *Chicago* and *Cabaret* (both by Kander & Ebb) and *Company* and *Assassins* (both by Sondheim) went so far as to turn the characters, situation and themes of their stories into individual song-and-dance routines in the form of a theatrical revue, so that the very style of the theatrical presentation became the main means of expressing a show's purpose and meaning. Such shows are written from a distinctly theatrical perspective, but as Sondheim put it, the most important lesson in writing musical theatre is to write "from the back of the stalls".

Film Music & Soundtracks

ORIGINATING AS A DEVICE TO MASK THE SOUND OF A WHIRRING PROJECTOR, FILM MUSIC HAS BECOME SO MUCH MORE THAN "MUSIC FROM THE MOVIES". BEFORE THE ADVENT OF VIDEO AND DVD, THE SOUNDTRACK WAS THE MOST ACCESSIBLE WAY TO RETURN TO A FAVOURITE MOVIE. IT HAS SINCE EVOLVED INTO A MULTI-MILLION DOLLAR INDUSTRY AND ONE OF THE MOST THRIVING FORMS OF MODER.N CLASSICAL MUSIC.

A SOUNDTRACK provides the musical underscore to a movie, conveying what words or visuals cannot. Because it is a component of the bigger picture, it is not specifically written to be heard in isolation, and typically constitutes a series of short cues. But if – for the sake of argument – the movie-going public has little interest in movie editing or cinematography, why are soundtracks so popular? Perhaps the answer can be traced back to the purpose of the soundtrack: to form an emotional connection between the viewer and the film. And because the scope of cinema is so broad, the soundtrack can be transporting in itself. From the sweeping plains of the Old West in Ennio Morricone's *The Good, The Bad And The Ugly*, to the galactic battlegrounds of John Williams's *Star Wars* space opera, the soundtrack crosses continent, genre and generation.

Pop Culture

It's no coincidence that all-time best-selling soundtrack albums such as *The Bodyguard* (17 million copies), *Saturday Night Fever* (15 million) and *Purple Rain* (13 million) exclusively featured songs by established recording artists. However, the soundtrack enthusiast has little interest in modern "songs from and inspired by" albums, and would rather hark back to the Middle European roots of film music. The 1930s were the Golden Age of film music, with Hollywood opening its doors to the likes of immigrants Erich Wolfgang Korngold (*The Adventures Of Robin Hood, Captain Blood*) and Max Steiner (*Gone With The Wind*), who provided melodramatic suites of romantic, sweeping score.

For *King Kong*, Steiner used leitmotifs, an operatic device that attributes a specific melody or tune to an individual character. However, much of that era's music was a "wall-to-wall" backdrop to the movie rather than an aid to the on-screen drama. In Russia, the classical composer Sergei Prokofiev was also bridging the celluloid musical gap between romanticism and modernism; instead of the composer scoring to cut the film, the director Sergei Eisenstein actually cut his films *Alexander Nevsky* and *Ivan The Terrible* to the composer's scores.

The antidote to the richly textured Hollywood wall of sound came in the form of Bernard Herrmann, who brought modernism to the cinema. Widely regarded as the most influential of all soundtrack composers, he made his mark with *Citizen Kane,* by writing music that was specific to scenes and emotions. Frequently dissonant,

Above

Regarded a musical genius, Ennio Morricone has been Oscar-nominated five times but has never won the coveted award.

"IT'S NOT SO MUCH ABOUT HEARING THE MUSIC IN THE CINEMA ...IT'S THAT YOU CAN FEEL IT."
Howard Shore

LEADING EXPONENTS
Erich Wolfgang Korngold
Max Steiner
Sergei Prokofiev
Ennio Morricone
John Williams
James Horner
Bernard Herrmann
Jerry Goldsmith
Hans Zimmer
Howard Shore
Alfred Newman

FILM MUSIC
Music in films is used to enhance and mirror the action, with rhythmic movement and melodic intervals used in this instance to create a feeling of something ominous approaching.

THE SOUNDTRACKS AND THEATRE INTRO ➡ 408   SOUNDTRACKS AND THEATRE PEOPLE A-Z ➡ 417   INSTRUMENTS A-Z ➡ 436

Above

John Williams; former conductor of the Boston Symphony Orchestra and film composer extraordinaire. Williams' talent for composing tunes which capture perfectly the mood of a film has won him five Oscars and made him America's most famous composer.

repetitive and avant-garde, his peerless, groundbreaking scores paved the way for the hypnotic, modern, "minimalist" work of Michael Nyman (*The Piano*) and Philip Glass (*Koyaanisqatsi*).

The Blockbuster Sound

If Herrmann was the most influential soundtrack composer, John Williams is the most popular and most decorated. Having begun scoring with jazzy romantic comedies (*John Goldfarb, Please Come Home* and *How To Steal A Million*) in the 1960s, he later plunged to the depths of terror with his seminal soundtrack to the film *Jaws*. His simple, two-note shark motif is still hummed at swimming pools and beaches worldwide and the director (and long-term collaborator with Williams) Steven Spielberg maintains that half of the movie's success can be attributed to the Oscar-winning score.

If *Jaws* was Williams' wake-up call to Hollywood, *Star Wars* marked his subsequent invasion and, indeed, defined the sound of the blockbuster. Drawing inspiration from the music of Sir William Walton, Wagner's *The Ring*, Korngold's *King's Row* and even Holst's *The Planets*, the *Star Wars* score not only won an Oscar; the two-disc soundtrack release became the biggest-selling non-pop album in history, and a disco version by Meco topped the US singles chart. The big orchestral sound was back in town, and was further shaped by Williams' work on *ET*, as well as the *Superman*, *Indiana Jones* and *Harry Potter* series. And with his jazzy score for the Spielberg film *Catch Me If You Can*, Williams has gone full circle, back to his lounge scores of the 1960s.

Williams frequently conducts his work at dedicated film music concerts around the globe, as does Jerry Goldsmith, another composer with a strong fan following. Goldsmith's movie career spans nearly 50 years, his greatest critical achievement being his demonic, Oscar-winning choral mass for *The Omen*. His acoustic score for *Planet Of The Apes*, populated with animal horns and tribal percussion, shows his willingness to experiment, while *Logan's Run* and *Gremlins* showcase his dabblings with electronica.

Right

Orson Welles' film debut at the age of 25 was in Citizen Kane, *a film which he also produced and directed. It is believed to be the world's most highly rated film due to its innovative techniques in photography, editing and sound.*

Unforgettably, his heroic anthem to *Star Trek: The Motion Picture* served as the title theme for seven seasons of *The Next Generation*, and as a motif in four of the movie sequels.

If John Williams is the most popular soundtrack composer, the Italian composer Ennio Morricone boasts the most prolific output, with more than 400 score credits to his names (he has also been credited as Leo Nichols and Dan Savio). Sergio Leone's *A Fistful Of Dollars* and its sequels took the Roman composer to the US in the late-1960s, although the Academy arguably robbed him of the 1986 Oscar for Best Original Score when they spurned his sumptuous work for *The Mission* in favour of Herbie Hancock's for *Round Midnight*.

CLASSICAL: 20TH CENTURY ➡ 268   CLASSICAL: CONTEMPORARY ➡ 272   THE ELECTRONIC INTRO ➡ 392

The Electronic Revolution

The *Star Wars* score was subsequently eclipsed in sales by Vangelis's synthetic soundtrack to the 1981 film *Chariots Of Fire*. In effect, this ushered in an era of pulsating electronic scores – led by Harold Faltermeyer (*Beverly Hills Cop*), Giorgio Moroder (*Midnight Express*) and Tangerine Dream (*Thief*) – that were cheaper to produce than symphonic works. The latter band, a German keyboard trio, gained infamy in soundtrack circles when they provided a replacement for Jerry Goldsmith's score for Ridley Scott's 1985 film, *Legend*, on its US release.

In the late-1980s and early 1990s, the former pop producer Hans Zimmer entered the synth arena with *The Power Of One* and went on to strike gold with his Oscar-winning score for Disney's *The Lion King*. He also founded Media Ventures, a collection of composers who, typically, produce brash, percussion-heavy scores for action movies such as *The Rock* and *Con Air*. With *Crimson Tide*, *Gladiator* and *Hannibal*,

Zimmer translated his music to a full orchestra, though he still overlays synthesizers in order to create a complementary hybrid of the two mediums.

The Return Of The Orchestra

Perhaps it was James Horner's 11 million-selling soundtrack for *Titanic* that turned the tide (pun intended) in the late-1990s, proving to the industry that an orchestral score could still top the charts. Now, with Howard Shore's epic *The Lord Of The Rings* saga continuing to notch up sales and garner Academy recognition, a new generation is discovering the majesty of the orchestra.

With even more independent labels releasing expanded versions of classic soundtracks, and many DVDs featuring isolated score tracks to allow you to watch (and listen to) the movie without the distraction of dialogue or sound effects, the twenty-first century is a good time to be a soundtrack collector.

Below

The film of Margaret Mitchell's epic love story, Gone With The Wind required a suitably stirring soundtrack. Max Steiner captured the anguish and romance perfectly in his score to the 1939 film.

Cabaret

CABARET THRIVED ON SENSUALITY, WIT AND AN INTIMACY BETWEEN PERFORMER AND AUDIENCE. ITS ESSENCE LIES IN INTIMATE, ESCAPIST VENUES, WHERE CHARISMATIC ARTISTS PERFORM WITH AD-HOC BACKING FROM PIANO, BRASS AND BASS. UNLIKE THE POPULARIST MUSIC HALL, CABARET WAS BORN FROM EXPERIMENTATION AND A DESIRE TO EXPLORE THE SPACE BETWEEN MASS ENTERTAINMENT AND THE AVANT-GARDE.

Above
A true cabaret star, Yvette Guilbert started singing at five and began modelling at 16. She performed at the Moulin Rouge and sang at Carnegie Hall, as well as starring in a number of films.

A French word that alluded to any business serving alcohol, "cabaret" acquired its modern definition in 1881, when Le Chat Noir opened its doors to the bohemian denizens of Paris's Montmartre district. At a time when newspapers were controlled by the ruling classes, Le Chat provided a democratic forum where artists could swap ideas and rub shoulders with aristocrats, ne'er-do-wells and inquisitive members of the bourgeoisie. Audiences were treated to a heady mixture of music, dance, poetry, satire and theatre. The biggest cabaret stars were the *diseuses,* multi-talented female performers who were as much actresses as they were singers, and who accompanied their songs with dramatic expressions and expansive gestures. Foremost among these was Yvette Guilbert, who delivered wry, topical chansons and re-worked French folk standards in a voice rich with gruff melancholia.

Spreading across Europe during the inter-war years, cabaret found a particularly grateful home in Berlin, where a dangerous menu of jazz, satire and pornography flourished. Visual display equalled vocal performance in importance, and the most pungent evocations of this era are on film: Josef von Sternberg's *The Blue Angel* and Bob Fosse's *Cabaret.* The former rocketed Marlene Dietrich to Hollywood stardom, but with her outlandish, half-sung and half-spoken vocals, the German was a relatively minor figure on the live cabaret circuit. More important were such seminal *diseuses* as Rosa Valetti, an oft-overlooked icon of the Roaring Twenties. Valetti was committed to cabaret as a socio-political tool, and roared out provocative political numbers such as 'The Red Melody' in formidable, iron-lunged fashion.

"DIVINE DECADENCE, DARLING!"
Sally Bowles, a principal character in Cabaret

Right
Previously a German cabaret performer, Marlene Dietrich was perfectly suited to her role in the film The Blue Angel. Her performance as Lola, an aloof and elegant temptress, lifted her from obscurity to sex-symbol status.

Post-War Accessibility

Despite the intentions of wistful 1960s commentators such as the singer/songwriter Jacques Brel, modern cabaret has been a shadow of its former self in political terms. In France, it retained a strong sense of sensuality, humour and audience interaction, as the likes of Edith Piaf and the sashaying American Josephine Baker enjoyed considerable popularity. In America, cabaret was reborn in the speakeasies of the Prohibition era and, surviving alongside the gambling halls of Las Vegas, cabaret clubs also enjoyed a glamorous association with vice, as dramatized in films such as *Cabaret* (1972). Performers began to incorporate gutsy torch songs, jazz numbers and Broadway tunes into their routines.

This period was epitomized by the British-born Mabel Mercer, the piano-playing Barbara Carroll, and Sylvia Syms, a New Yorker and protégée of Billie Holiday who took the night-spots of the Big Apple by storm during the 1960s and 1970s. Syms's husky-voiced renditions of jazz-tinged originals, as well as inspired covers of pop favourites such as 'You Don't Have To Say You Love Me', influenced artists from Tony Bennett to Frank Sinatra, who described her as "the world's greatest saloon singer". Combining heartfelt lyrical interpretation with spot-on timing and an acute sense of dramatic irony, Syms was a worthy, accessible successor to *diseuses* like Guilbert and Valetti.

LEADING EXPONENTS
Yvette Guilbert
Marlene Dietrich
Rosa Valetti
Sylvia Syms
Jacques Brel
Edith Piaf
Maurice Chevalier
Barbara Carroll
Mabel Mercer
Josephine Baker

CABARET
The swing rhythm and flattened third note of the scale in this melody help to create a style that is provocative and bawdy.

They call me lu-cious Lay-la, the brigh-test gi-rl in town.

Artists: Soundtracks and Theatre

Entries appear in the following order:
name, music style, year(s) of popularity,
type of artist, country of origin

101 Strings Orchestra, Film Music & Soundtracks, 1950s–, Artist, American
Adamson, Barry, Film Music & Soundtracks, 1980s–1990s, Composer; Artist, American
Akers, Karen, Musicals, 1980s–, Artist, American
Albert, Eddie, Film Music & Soundtracks, 1950s–1960s, Artist, American
Allen, Peter, Musicals; Cabaret; Film Music & Soundtracks, 1960s–1990s, Artist; Songwriter, Australia
Andrews, Julie, Musicals, 1950s–1990s, Artist, British
Astaire, Fred, Musicals, 1920s–1970s, Artist, American
Bacharach, Burt, Film Music & Soundtracks, 1960s–1990s, Producer; Composer; Songwriter; Artist, American
Badalamenti, Angelo, Film Music & Soundtracks, 1980s–1990s, Composer; Artist, American
Baker, Josephine, Cabaret, 1920s–1970s, Artist, American
Barber, Patricia, Cabaret, 1990s–, Artist, American
Barry, John, Film Music & Soundtracks, 1950s–, Composer, British
Bennett, Tony, Musicals, 1950s–, Artist, American
Berlin, Irving, Musicals, 1900s–1960s, Composer; Songwriter, American
Bernstein, Elmer, Film Music & Soundtracks; Musicals, 1950s–1990s, Composer, American
Bernstein, Leonard, Musicals, 1940s–1990s, Artist, American
Black, Don, Musicals; Film Music & Soundtracks, 1960s–1990s, Songwriter, American
Boston Pops Orchestra, Film Music & Soundtracks, 1920s–1990s, Artist, American
Brel, Jacques, Cabaret, 1950s–1970s, Songwriter, Belgian
Breuker, Willem, Film Music & Soundtracks, 1960s–, Artist; Composer, Dutch
Brightman, Sarah, Musicals, 1980s–, Artist, British
Buckley, Betty, Musicals, 1970s–, Artist, American
Budd, Roy, Film Music & Soundtracks, 1960s–1990s, Composer, British
Carmichael, Hoagy, Musicals, 1920s–1960s, Composer; Artist, American
Carroll, Barbara, Cabaret, 1940s–1990s, Artist, American
Channing, Carol, Musicals, 1940s–, Artist, American
Chevalier, Maurice, Cabaret; Musicals, 1920s–1960s, Artist, French
Conti, Bill, Film Music & Soundtracks, 1980s–1990s, Composer, American
Cook, Barbara, Musicals, 1950s–, Artist, American

Corigliano, John, Film Music & Soundtracks, 1960s–, Composer, American
Coward, Noel, Cabaret; Musicals, 1920s–1970s, Artist; Songwriter, British
Crawford, Michael, Musicals, 1980s–, Artist, British
Creamer, Henry, Musicals, 1910s–1920s, Songwriter, American
David, Mack, Film Music & Soundtracks, 1930s–1950s, Songwriter, American
Delarue, Georges, Film Music & Soundtracks; Musicals, 1960s–, Composer, French
Denisov, Edison, Film Music & Soundtracks, 1940s–1990s, Composer, Russian
Dietrich, Marlene, Cabaret, 1920s–1970s, Artist, German
Dietz, Howard, Musicals, 1920s–1960s, Songwriter, American
Dun, Tan, Film Music & Soundtracks, 1980s–, Composer; Producer, Chinese
Edelman, Randy, Film Music & Soundtracks, 1970s–1990s, Artist; Composer, American
Edwards, Gus, Musicals; Film Music & Soundtracks, 1900s–1930s, Artist, American
Egan, Seamus, Film music & Soundtracks, 1970s–1990s, Artist, Irish
Elfman, Danny, Film Music & Soundtracks, 1980s–, Producer; Composer, American
Ellington, Duke, Film Music & Soundtracks, 1920s–1970s, Artist; Composer, American
Eno, Brian, Film Music & Soundtracks, 1970s–, Composer; Producer; Artist; Songwriter,
Fain, Sammy, Musicals; Film Music & Soundtracks, 1920s–1970s, Artist, American
Feather, Lorraine, Film Music & Soundtracks, 1970s–, Artist, American
Ferguson, Jay, Film Music & Soundtracks, 1970s–1990s, Artist, American
Foster, David, Film Music & Soundtracks, 1980s–, Producer; Artist, Canadian
Gainsbourg, Serge, Cabaret, 1950s–1980s, Artist, French
Garland, Judy, Musicals, 1930s–1960s, Artist, American
Gershwin, George, Musicals, 1910s–1930s, Composer; Songwriter, American
Gershwin, Ira, Musicals, 1910s–1960s, Songwriter, American
Gilbert & Sullivan, Musicals, 1860s–1900s, Composer; Songwriter, British
Gilbert, William, Musicals, 1870s–1900s, Composer; Songwriter, British
Gold, Ernest, Film Music & Soundtracks, 1970s–1980s, Composer, Austrian
Goldsmith, Jerry, Film Music & Soundtracks, 1960s–, Composer, American
Gould, Morton, Film Music & Soundtracks, 1930s–1990s, Composer, American
Grusin, David, Film Music & Soundtracks, 1960s–, Producer; Composer, American
Hall, Adelaide, Cabaret, 1920s–1980s, Artist, American
Hamlisch, Marvin, Musicals; Film Music & Soundtracks, 1970s–1980s, Composer; Artist, American
Hammer, Jan, Film Music & Soundtracks, 1960s–, Artist, Czech
Hammerstein, Oscar II, Musicals, 1920s–1950s, Songwriter; Composer, American
Harbach, Otto, Musicals, 1910s–1930s, Composer; Songwriter, American

Harburg, E. Y. 'Yip', Musicals; Film Music & Soundtracks, 1930s–1970s, Composer; Songwriter, American
Hart, Lorenz, Musicals; Film Music & Soundtracks, 1920s–1930s, Artist, American
Hefti, Neal, Film Music & Soundtracks, 1940s–1990s, Artist; Composer, American
Herbert, Victor, Film Music & Soundtracks, 1880s–1920s, Composer; Songwriter, American
Herrmann, Barry, Film Music & Soundtracks, 1930s–1970s, Composer, American
Herrmann, Bernard, Film Music & Soundtracks, 1930s–1970s, Composer, American
Horner, James, Film Music & Soundtracks, 1980s–1990s, Producer; Composer, American
Isham, Mark, Film Music & Soundtracks, 1980s–1990s, Artist, American
Jarre, Maurice, Film Music & Soundtracks, 1950s–, Composer, French
John, Elton, Film Music & Soundtracks, 1960s–, Artist; Songwriter, British
Johnson, Betty, Cabaret, 1950s–1960s, Artist, American
Kamen, Michael, Film Music & Soundtracks, 1970s–1990s, Artist; Composer, American
Kancheli, Giya, Film Music & Soundtracks, 1950s–, Composer, Russian
Kaye, Stubby, Musicals, 1950s–1990s, Artist, American
Kern, Jerome, Musicals, 1920s–1940s, Composer, American

Knight, Peter, Musicals; Film Music & Soundtracks, 1920s–1970s, Artist, American
Korngold, Erich Wolfgang, Film Music & Soundtracks, 1920s–1950s, Composer, American
Lai, Francis, Film Music & Soundtracks, 1960s–1990s, Composer, French
Lawrence, Gertrude, Cabaret, 1920s–1950s, Artist, German
Layton, Turner, Musicals, 1900s–1920s, Composer; Songwriter, American
Legere, Phoebe, Cabaret, 1990s–, Artist, American

Legrand, Michel, Film Music & Soundtracks, 1950s–, Composer; Artist, French
Leonard, Patrick, Film Music & Soundtracks, 1990s, Producer, American
Lerner and Loewe, Musicals, 1940s–1960s, Artist, American
Loesser, Frank, Musicals, 1930s–1960s, Songwriter, American
Loewe, Frederick, Musicals, 1930s–1980s, Composer, Austrian
Mancini, Henry, Film Music & Soundtracks, 1950s–1970s, Composer; Artist, American
Martin, Mary, Musicals, 1930s–1960s, Artist, American
McDonald, Audra, Musicals, 1990s–, Artist, American
Melle, Gil, Film Music & Soundtracks, 1950s–1990s, Artist; Composer, American
Mercer, Mabel, Cabaret, 1940s–1980s, Artist, British
Minnelli, Liza, Musicals, 1960s–, Artist, American
Montenegro, Hugo, Film Music & Soundtracks, 1950s–1980s, Producer, American
Moroder, Giorgio, Film Music & Soundtracks, 1960s–, Producer; Composer; Artist, Italian
Morricone, Ennio, Film Music & Soundtracks, 1960s–, Composer, Italian
Newman, Alfred, Film Music & Soundtracks, 1930s–1960s, Composer, American
Newman, Randy, Film Music & Soundtracks, 1960s–, Composer; Artist, American
Newton–Howard, James, Film Music & Soundtracks, 1970s–1990s, Producer; Artist; Composer, American
Nicastro, Michelle, Film Music & Soundtracks, 1990s, Artist, American
Niehaus, Lennie, Film Music & Soundtracks, 1950s–1990s, Artist, American
North, Alex, Film Music & Soundtracks, 1950s–1990s, Composer, American
Partch, Harry, Film Music & Soundtracks, 1920s–1970s, Composer, American
Patinkin, Mandy, Musicals; Film Music & Soundtracks, 1980s–, Artist, American
Piaf, Edith, Cabaret, 1930s–1960s, Artist, French
Piazzolla, Astor, Film Music & Soundtracks, 1940s–1990s, Composer, Argentinean
Poledouris, Basil, Film Music & Soundtracks, 1980s–1990s, Composer, American
Post, Mike, Film Music & Soundtracks, 1970s–1990s, Artist; Composer, American
Rice, Tim, Musicals, 1960s–, Songwriter, British
Riddle, Nelson, Film Music & Soundtracks, 1950s–1980s, Artist, American
Rodgers & Hammerstein, Musicals, 1940s–1950s, Composer, American
Rodgers & Hart, Musicals, 1920s–1940s, Songwriter, American
Rodgers, Richard, Musicals, 1920s–1950s, Songwriter; Composer, American
Rota, Nino, Film Music & Soundtracks, 1950s–1960s, Composer, Italian
Rozsa, Miklos, Film Music & Soundtracks, 1930s–1990s, Composer, Hungarian
Sablon, Jean, Cabaret, 1930s–1940s, Artist, French
Sakamoto, Ryuichi, Film Music & Soundtracks, 1970s–, Artist; Composer, Japanese
Schifrin, Lalo, Film Music & Soundtracks, 1950s–, Composer; Artist, Argentinean

Sherman, Richard M., Musicals; Film Music & Soundtracks, 1960s–1970s, Composer; Songwriter, American
Sherman, Robert B., Musicals; Film Music & Soundtracks, 1960s–1970s, Songwriter, American
Shore, Howard, Film Music & Soundtracks, 1990s–, Artist, American
Short, Bobby, Cabaret, 1950s–, Artist, American
Shostakovich, Dmitri, Film Music & Soundtracks, 1930s–1970s, Composer, Russian
Silvestri, Alan, Film Music & Soundtracks, 1970s–1990s, Producer; Songwriter; Composer, American
Sinatra, Frank, Musicals, 1930s–1990s, Artist, American
Snow, Mark, Film Music & Soundtracks, 1990s, Producer, American
Sondheim, Stephen, Musicals, 1970s–, Artist, American
Stalling, Carl, Film Music & Soundtracks, 1930s–1960s, Composer, American
Steiner, Max, Film Music & Soundtracks, 1990s, Composer, Austrian
Streisand, Barbra, Musicals; Cabaret, 1960s–, Artist, American
Sullivan, Arthur, Musicals, 1870s–1900s, Composer; Songwriter, British
Syms, Sylvia, Cabaret, 1950s–1990s, Artist, American
Tangerine Dream, Film Music & Soundtracks, 1960s–, Artist, German
Tiomkin, Dimitri, Film Music & Soundtracks, 1940s–1960s, Composer; Artist, Russian
Vereen, Ben, Musicals, 1970s–, Artist, American
Waxman, Franz, Film Music & Soundtracks, 1940s–1960s, Composer, American
Webber, Andrew Lloyd, Musicals, 1960s–, Composer; Producer, British
Wilder, Alec, Musicals, 1940s–1960s, Composer; Songwriter, American
Williams, John, Film Music & Soundtracks, 1960s–, Composer, American
Willson, Meredith, Musicals; Film Music & Soundtracks, 1920s–1960s, Composer; Songwriters, American
Yellen, Jack, Musicals; Film Music & Soundtracks, 1900s–1940s, Songwriter, American
Youmans, Vincent, Musicals, 1920s–1930s, Composer; Songwriter, American
Zimmer, Hans, Film Music & Soundtracks, 1990s–, Producer; Composer, German

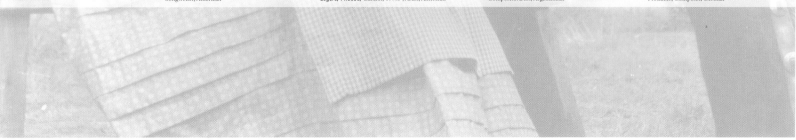

MUSICALS ➡ 410   FILM MUSIC & SOUNDTRACKS ➡ 413   CABARET ➡ 416

Popular And Novelty

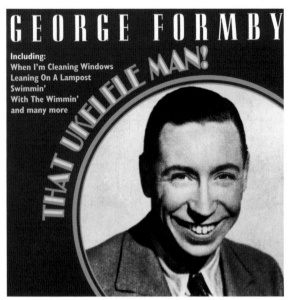

Above

Singing star George Formby, who made over 230 records.

ROCK, jazz, soul; each of these genres, while containing a multiplicity of various offshoots, is defined by some kind of unifying theme. But this miscellaneous section, as any record collector will know, is where everything else ends up. Most of the styles within this "genre" have little in common save the fact that they do not fit in comfortably anywhere else.

However, it would be wrong to assume that being difficult to classify makes these styles in some way inferior. Easy listening boasts artists as undeniably accomplished as Henry Mancini. Music hall stars like George Formby had the talent to cross over into successful cinema careers. The urbane complexity of Burt Bacharach's compositions ensure that lounge, too, does not lack genuine giants.

Nor would it be correct to say that the entrants in the miscellaneous section appeal solely to esoteric, niche tastes. Nostalgia artists like Vera Lynn voiced the hurts of entire nations. Christmas songs by everyone from Bing Crosby to Band Aid constitute some of the biggest sellers of all time. And children's songs pervade our musical consciousness: there are few of us, adults or kids, who cannot hum the theme tune to *The Muppet Show*.

The first entry focuses on contemporary Christian music: a fusion of the sacred and the secular, led by stars such as Larry Norman and Amy Grant, that seeks to enlighten its listeners as much as entertain them. Secondly, a look at novelty songs, which draw on a long-established link between comedy and music and revel in satire, silliness and topicality; a style whose history is strewn with the skeletons of one-hit wonders does have some longer-term success stories. The 1960s saw huge success for Allan Sherman, whose astute take-offs of folk and classical favourites drew on a rich tradition of Jewish-American humour. On the other side of the Atlantic, the vibrant London art college scene spawned the inimitable Bonzo Dog Doo Dah Band. Performing a mixture of traditional vaudeville songs, musical parodies and surreal rock compositions, the Bonzos achieved a cult following. Their legendary stage shows involved exploding robots, dancing dummies and other such silliness, and earned them a slot in the Beatles' 1967 film *Magical Mystery Tour*. The rise of the video in the 1980s afforded parodists like "Weird Al" Yankovic even more scope to lampoon the pop icons of the day, while Rolf Harris, a sometime television presenter, exploited an aura of affable eccentricity and survived into the twenty-first century, now playing regularly at rock festivals.

Sprouting from a bawdier fusion of humour and music was music hall, the favoured form of entertainment for the British working classes around the turn of the twentieth century. A broader, less politically motivated relation of

> "MUSIC IS ... A LABYRINTH WITH NO BEGINNING AND NO END, FULL OF NEW PATHS TO DISCOVER, WHERE MYSTERY REMAINS ETERNAL."
>
> *Pierre Boulez*

Right

The Bonzo Dog Doo Dah band launch Gorilla in 1967.

STYLES

- Contemporary Christian Music
- Novelty Songs
- Music Hall
- Children's Songs
- Christmas Songs
- Easy Listening
- Lounge Music
- Nostalgia

THE POPULAR AND NOVELTY STYLE

The common factor linking the popular musical styles is their accessibility. Simple, memorable words set to a basic but catchy tune ensure that a song is easy to sing along to and will appeal to a wide range of people.

with a li-ttle bit of this, and a li-ttle bit of that, put your han-dies in the air and clap clap clap!

POPULAR AND NOVELTY PEOPLE A–Z ➡ 435   INSTRUMENTS A–Z ➡ 436   THE POP INTRO ➡ 8   SOUNDTRACKS AND THEATRE: MUSICALS ➡ 410

Right

Popular stage entertainer Mistinguett was at one time the best-paid female entertainer in the world. She set the fashion for long, showy headdresses and gowns, which became part of the French music hall staple.

Below

Vera Lynn's strong, clear voice was a comfort to the troops and the home front during the Second World War. One comedian was prompted to say: "The war was started by Vera Lynn's agent!"

European cabaret, with the emphasis on accessible song-and-dance routines and innuendo, the style had a charismatic cockney queen in the shape of Marie Lloyd. At the French revues, costumed divas such as Mistinguett added an extra dimension of flamboyance and theatrical zest. And, while music hall's popularity faded when it was forced to compete with the arrival of radio and cinema, 1930s stars like the ukulele-strumming George Formby made sure its jovial spirit survived into the mass media age. Also in the singalong style of the music hall, although an altogether more subtle and intelligent version, were the gently satirical songs of witty duo Flanders & Swann. Their popular 1956 revue show *At The Drop Of A Hat* contained clever, catchy songs that invited the

audience to join in; some told of the foibles of everyday life – such as public transport and British weather – while others, like the 'Hippopotamus Song', were simply jolly (and sometimes slightly surreal) songs with universal appeal.

While music hall dates back more than a century, children's songs are as old as humanity itself. Lullabies and nursery rhymes have been passed down orally through the generations, and their spirit survives in the releases of artists such as mother-turned-musician Linda Arnold. Back in the 1960s, bands like the Beatles had blurred the distinction between adult and kid's pop with songs like 'Yellow Submarine'. But the most important distributors of children's music in the twentieth century were film musicals, via such stars as Julie Andrews and Elton John, and, most of all, television. The importance of the box is evident from the lasting impact of Jim Henson, whose Muppets treated kids the world over to a music hall-style mix of song, dance and humour run through with educational themes. On songs like Kermit the Frog's 'It's Not Easy Being Green', Henson even preached racial tolerance.

Left

Max Bygraves' big break came in 1951 when he was offered a role in the BBC comedy show Educating Archie, *which was based upon the unlikely premise of radio ventriloquism. He went on to become a hugely successful popular entertainer.*

but camper and more adventurous in its compass, lounge music is characterized by a swinging sense of eclecticism and a casual interest in far-away places and visions of the future. Burt Bacharach's kitsch, swinging melodies come under its banner, as does the output of Les Baxter, the godfather of exotica, who purloined the styles of Polynesia, Africa and Latin America. Baxter's adoption of early electronic instruments paved the way for another lounge offshoot named space-age pop, and his experimental mantle was taken up by Esquivel, a Mexican oddball whose willingness to tamper with tempos, styles and recording techniques produced some of the weirdest music of the 1960s.

Finally come the nostalgia performers, people whose music encapsulates key moments in the lives of great swathes of Americans and Britons. Al Jolson's jazz-inflected numbers evoke the arrival of talking pictures, while the songs and sly sexuality of Mae West provided an emblem of hope and hedonism for the victims of the American Depression. The essence of British sentiment during the Second World War, meanwhile, was never captured better than when Vera Lynn belted out 'We'll Meet Again'. In later years, in the UK, Max Bygraves turned nostalgia into his own cottage industry during the 1970s and 1980s via his TV show and numerous albums, such as *Singalongamax* (1972) and *Singalongawaryears* (1989).

Another style with ancient origins is the Christmas song, which also received an overhaul in the first half of the twentieth century, as the Yuletide period became increasingly commercialized. Festive profitability peaked in spectacular style with Bing Crosby's 'White Christmas', still the world's best-selling single, and the template for countless crooning imitators. Amid the snowdrift of clichés though, there were isolated pockets of inspiration. Phil Spector's production wizardry breathed new life into hoary old standards during the 1960s, while 'Fairytale of New York', the Pogues' defiantly un-slushy collaboration with Kirsty MacColl, gave the Christmas song a hefty kick up the behind in 1987.

A million miles away from the raucous barroom poetry of Shane McGowan is easy listening. The genteel sound of home entertainment throughout the 1950s and 1960s inherited the same focus on unobtrusive melody that characterized the Muzak that was piped into the offices of American corporations at around the same time. One of its first stars was the Anglo-Italian composer Mantovani, whose lush, string-led reinterpretations of popular songs defined a new style: light classical. The multi-talented Henry Mancini absorbed jazz and big band influences to create movie soundtracks whose graceful appeal lingered long after the closing credits, while the extroverted piano performances of Liberace proved that easy listening could thrive in a live environment. Other artists, including Perry Como and Patti Page in the 1950s and the Carpenters in the 1970s, introduced vocals to the mix with globally successful results. Overlapping with the accessible orchestrations of easy listening,

Below

Wheelchair-bound lyricist Michael Flanders (left) and composer/pianist Donald Swann first worked together at a school revue in 1939, before going on to form one of the greatest entertainment partnerships of all time.

Contemporary Christian Music

A PRODUCT OF THE SPIRITUAL SEARCHING OF THE 1960S, CONTEMPORARY CHRISTIAN MUSIC (CCM) HAS ALWAYS BEEN CONTROVERSIAL. COMBINING ROCK'N'ROLL WITH A BIBLE-BASED MESSAGE HAS SEEMED PROFANE TO SOME AND ARTISTICALLY INVALID TO OTHERS. DESPITE SUCH CRITICISMS, CCM HAS ATTRACTED MILLIONS OF LOYAL FANS AND GIVEN RISE TO A HOST OF GOLD- AND PLATINUM-SELLING ARTISTS.

Above

Larry Norman was inspired by Elvis Presley and brought rock'n'roll and religion together, forming a musical style that sought to enlighten its audience as much as entertain them.

THERE'S ambiguity as to what CCM actually is – some have asserted that the category applies only to artists who record for Christian-oriented labels or appeal to primarily Christian audiences. Then there's the question of what defines the subgenre musically. Just about every type of pop/rock musical form – including ska, hardcore punk and heavy metal – has been used by CCM artists to convey their message. Really, it is the lyrics that make a contemporary Christian song stand out from its secular counterpart. Whether drawing upon the Bible explicitly or tapping into a spiritual theme indirectly, CCM's intent is to express a believer's faith. Some CCM songs are modern-day hymns; others are commentaries on living the Christian life in everyday terms.

who combined an evangelistic fervour with an aggressive performing style. After achieving some success with the secular band People, Norman launched his solo career with 1969's *Upon This Rock*. Considered to be the first true CCM album, its key track was 'I Wish We'd All Been Ready', a dramatic depiction of Earth's final days. Norman's apocalyptic viewpoint was shared by many young Christians at the time. Other early Jesus music artists – among them Phil Keaggy, Randy Stonehill and the band Love Song – had a gently idealistic, almost otherworldly air about them. By the mid-1970s, such Christian record companies as Word, Myrrh, Sparrow and New Song were releasing albums by these and other artists to a growing fan base.

> "CHRISTIAN MUSIC HAS MATURED AND MOVED AWAY FROM THIS NEED TO SAY, 'WE HAVE IT ALL FIGURED OUT AND WE HAVE ALL THE ANSWERS'... BUT IT'S STILL ANCHORED TO THE HOPE OF THE GOSPEL."

Steven Curtis Chapman

Ragged, Rocking And Apocalyptic

Contemporary Christian music isn't a direct outgrowth of traditional gospel music. The true pioneers of the subgenre were the so-called "Jesus Freaks" of the late-1960s, many of whom had experimented with drugs and exotic religions prior to embracing Christianity. The music they made was often brash and ragged, drawing upon the acoustic folk and psychedelic rock elements of the time. The first well-known exponent of Jesus music (as CCM was called in its infancy) was Larry Norman, a California-based singer/songwriter

CCM Meets The Mainstream

Gradually, Jesus music began to resemble mainstream pop/ rock music and lose some of its rebellious, confrontational quality. The Christian music industry began to reach out beyond its core audience in the late-1970s, aided by the much-publicized conversions of Bob Dylan, Donna Summer

LEADING EXPONENTS

Steven Curtis Chapman
DC Talk
Amy Grant
Jars Of Clay
The Newsboys
Larry Norman
Petra
Sixpence None The Richer
Michael W. Smith
Third Day

CONTEMPORARY CHRISTIAN MUSIC

Contemporary Christian music often utilizes syncopated rhythms synonymous with secular pop, in combination with uplifting melodies in major keys and ascending phrases.

Praise the— Lord— in the high————— est!

THE POPULAR AND NOVELTY INTRO ➡ 418   POPULAR AND NOVELTY PEOPLE A–Z ➡ 435   INSTRUMENTS A–Z ➡ 436   THE POP INTRO ➡ 8

and other celebrities. True, there were still artists like Keith Green, who preached an uncompromising message and decried Christian music's growing commercialism. But it was the emergence of Amy Grant in 1977 that pointed the way CCM would follow in the coming decade. Her distinctive voice and stylish looks marked her as an artist with huge potential. She made good on her early promise in 1985, when her song 'Find A Way' became a mainstream Top 40 hit in the US.

The 1980s found CCM artists wrestling with the desire to connect with nonbelievers without sacrificing their integrity. Many of the better CCM acts of this era – including Mark Heard, Adam Again, Daniel Amos and the 77s – recorded creatively risky pop/rock works that transcended the limitations of the sub-genre. Still, those who moved away from upfront evangelism risked alienating their core audience. The most loved contemporary Christian hits of the 1980s were bold declarations of faith like Michael Card's 'El Shaddai' and Rich Mullins' 'Awesome God'. Bands like Petra (melodic hard rock) and Stryper (poppy heavy metal) kept their Christian content straight and simple. A definable contemporary Christian sound – trendy yet safe, lyrically devout without too much fire and brimstone – had taken shape by this time. Christian record companies and radio stations encouraged a degree of conformity. Some artists – most notably Steve Taylor and Leslie Phillips – felt constrained and left the CCM market, with varying success.

Above

Religious revellers at a Christian pop festival. There are a number of Christian music festivals, including Cornerstone in the US and Greenbelt in England.

The 'Kiss Me' Christian Content Controversy

Contemporary Christian music continued to expand throughout the 1990s. CCM stars like Amy Grant and Michael W. Smith made inroads into the mainstream market by avoiding explicit God references in hits like 'That's What Love Is For' and 'I Will Be Here For You'. Some artists managed to reach the platinum sales mark without appealing to non-Christians – Steven Curtis Chapman, DC Talk, the Newsboys and a few others built strong followings purely within the CCM world. Songwriting and production standards improved, as talented young artists who had grown up with the subgenre began recording. Among the outstanding newcomers were Jars of Clay (who scored a secular hit with 'Flood'), Rebecca St James (an Australian-born dance/pop evangelist) and Jaci Velasquez (successful in both the Latin and CCM markets).

Critics within the CCM industry noted that the three largest Christian record companies – Word, Sparrow and Provident – were all owned by secular entertainment conglomerates by the end of the 1990s. Concerns that

the subgenre was losing its sense of mission arose as well. When the Christian folk-pop band Sixpence None The Richer topped the international secular charts in 1999 with 'Kiss Me', it was hailed as a breakthrough for CCM as a whole. The Gospel Music Association, though, disqualified 'Kiss Me' from nomination for one of its Dove Awards (comparable to a Grammy) because of alleged lack of Christian content. This led such artists as singer/producer Charlie Peacock to suggest ending the awards entirely.

A New Wave Of Worship

As contemporary Christian music entered the twenty-first century, it was clear that it had evolved considerably from its origins in the 1960s counterculture. The maverick spirit of Larry Norman and his peers had been toned down and channeled into an increasingly formula-driven industry. Still, there were some indications that Christian music fans were looking for an alternative to CCM's emphasis on celebrity appeal. The year 2000 saw a renewed interest in worship music events, dedicated to praising the Lord rather than applauding an entertainer. OneDay, held in Memphis, Tennessee, drew 40,000 attendees. Such popular CCM artists as Michael W. Smith and Third Day released worship-oriented CDs in 2001 and 2002, confirming the trend's popularity.

It seems likely that contemporary Christian music will continue to veer between spiritually accented entertainment and back-to-basics revivalism for the foreseeable future. How great is its potential to keep expanding beyond its base audience of believers? Heaven only knows.

Left

Amy Grant (centre) grew up in Nashville and absorbed country and folk influences in addition to her religious inspiration, which may have aided her success as a crossover artist in the 1980s.

Novelty Songs

STRADDLING GENRES FROM POP TO ROCK, COUNTRY TO DANCE, NOVELTY SONGS TELL HUMOROUS STORIES USING SATIRE, WACKINESS OR A TOPICAL LINK WITH TELEVISION, FILM OR A POPULAR CRAZE. THOUGH OFTEN MUSICALLY DUBIOUS, THEY HAVE ENJOYED MASSIVE, BUT GENERALLY FLEETING, SUCCESS IN THE MODERN ERA.

Above
Weird Al's recording career took off when he began to send his parodies to Dr. Demento, the host of a radio show with a cult following, which specialized in novelty material.

MUSIC and comedy have been bedfellows since the days of music hall and vaudeville, when many singers doubled as comedians, incorporating burlesque and innuendo into their performances. The tradition was continued by Spike Jones' anarchic rock and classical parodies of the 1940s and 1950s (1942's 'Der Fuehrer's Face'), Tom Lehrer's twisted pop music satires of the 1950s and 1960s ('I Hold Your Hand in Mine' from 1953) and Ray Stevens' country crossovers in the 1960s and 1970s ('Bridget the Midget', 1971).

Sherman Conquers America

Perhaps the most successful musical humourist of the post-war years was Allan Sherman, a Jewish comedian who was the toast of America's radio waves during the early 1960s. Specializing in spot-on parodies of folk songs and popular hymns and classical works, his most famous hit was 'Hello Muddah, Hello Fadduh'. His first three LPs went to the top of the charts; legend has it that President Kennedy was overheard singing 'Sarah Jackman', Sherman's version of the French standard 'Frère Jacques'.

Since Sherman's star waned in the mid-1960s, there have been very few consistently successful novelty singers, but plenty of popular novelty songs. Some of these were light-hearted digressions by established American performers (Chuck Berry's 'My Ding-a-Ling' (1972) and Johnny Cash's 'A Boy Named Sue' (1979)) and unlikely celebrities (William Shatner's cover of 'Lucy In The Sky With Diamonds', 1968).

> "A LOT OF PEOPLE LOOK AT IT AS A BADGE OF HONOUR WHEN THEY GET A 'WEIRD AL' PARODY."
>
> *"Weird Al" Yankovic*

Right
Rolf Harris leaves for a tour of Bermuda in 1963, together with some of the props for his stage act: a wobble board (Harris's own invention) and a false limb, for his character Jake the Peg (with the extra leg).

A Long Line Of One-Hit Wonders

Britain has a particular thirst for silly one-offs: the comedian Benny Hill had a hit with 'Ernie (The Fastest Milkman In The West)' in 1971, as did actor Clive Dunn in the same year, with an eponymous spin-off from his *Grandad* series. The Tweets even coerced Britons into performing the actions to their 'Birdie Song' for much of 1981.

Links with non-musical popular culture often provided inspiration and publicity. Carl Douglas's 'Kung-Fu Fighting' ruthlessly exploited the 1970s enthusiasm for martial arts; The Firm topped the UK charts in 1987 with 'Star Trekkin', which was based around the sci-fi show; and Eric Idle hit the number one spot in 1991 with 'Always Look on the Bright Side of Life', from the film *Monty Python's Life Of Brian*.

Two notable exceptions transcended one-hit wonder status: Rolf Harris and "Weird Al" Yankovic. The latter was the king of parodic pop on both sides of the Atlantic throughout the 1980s and 1990s. His favourite target was Michael Jackson, whose 'Beat It' and 'Bad' he reworked in food-fixated style as 'Eat It' and 'I'm Fat'.

Harris's popularity is largely a result of an ironic appetite for lovable cheesiness. The Australian artist and TV personality made his musical debut in 1963 and has remained popular in the UK ever since. Harris performs gentle digs at antipodean stereotypes, like his 'Tie Me Kangaroo Down Sport', and cover versions of songs like Led Zeppelin's 'Stairway to Heaven'.

LEADING EXPONENTS

Allan Sherman
Johnny Cash
William Shatner
Carl Douglas
Spike Jone
Eric Idle
The Firm
"Weird Al" Yankovic
The Tweets
Rolf Harris

NOVELTY SONGS

In novelty music simple melodic phrases and accompaniments are backed with by a rhythmic hook that induces the audience to participate.

with a li-ttle bit of this, and a li-ttle bit of that, put your han-dies in the air and clap clap clap!

THE POPULAR AND NOVELTY INTRO ➡ 418   POPULAR AND NOVELTY PEOPLE A–Z ➡ 435   INSTRUMENTS A–Z ➡ 436   THE POP INTRO ➡ 8

Music Hall

DURING ITS GOLDEN YEARS, MUSIC HALL RIVALLED EUROPEAN CABARET AND AMERICAN VAUDEVILLE. BUT MUSIC HALL PERFORMERS WERE BAWDIER THAN THEIR CABARET COUNTERPARTS, INDULGING IN MORE BOISTEROUS BANTER WITH AUDIENCES THAN THEIR AMERICAN COUSINS. IT WAS SINGALONG FUN, SPRINKLED WITH LEWD HUMOUR.

THE term first entered common usage in 1848, when the Surrey Music Hall opened in London. It was followed over the next few decades by several other ornately designed venues, each capable of holding several hundred drinkers seated at tables. Musical entertainment was at first provided by the character singers who had become known in the taverns in and around London, and would take the eclectic form of ballads, black minstrel acts, extracts from popular operas and comedic routines.

Two Queens Of The Music Hall

Up until the 1880s, music hall was dominated by male performers, and the likes of Dan Leno and George Robey were top draws well into the twentieth century. But Leno and Robey were primarily comedians; the greatest British music hall singer was Marie Lloyd. A diminutive cockney extrovert who trod the boards from 1885 to 1922, Lloyd became known to her thousands of admirers as "The Queen of the Music Hall", or simply "Our Marie". While her cabaret counterparts like Yvette Guilbert railed against political injustice, she was content to employ her trademark repertoire of suggestive winks and gentle innuendo, and poke fun at the folk in the posh seats. Backed by a jaunty piano, she sang rousing, catchy numbers themed around the popular issues of the day. Many, like 'The Cock Linnet Song', better known as 'My Old Man Said Follow The Van', survive today as old-time favourites.

Meanwhile, on the other side of the English Channel, a more glamorous, cabaret-influenced version of music hall was thriving in the revues of Paris. The accent here was on theatrical style and elaborate costumes, and the master of both was Mistinguett. A spindly woman with much-adored legs and the instincts of a natural comedienne, "Le Miss" made her debut in 1895 in the fabled surrounds of the Moulin Rouge and became a regular onstage partner of her fellow French star, Maurice Chevalier. Her wistful signature tune, 'Mon Homme' ('My Man'), which she recorded in 1920, has become a standard for modern jazz and cabaret singers. This flamboyant scene was given a twenty-first-century spin in the 2001 film *Moulin Rouge*.

The Mass–Media Age

Performing in France from the 1920s until the 1970s, the American-born Josephine Baker ensured that Mistinguett's legacy did not die. But in Britain, the rise of radio and cinema ensured that live music hall was a fading force after the First World War. However, George Formby, whose father, George Formby Sr., had been one of the most successful music hall comedians of the Edwardian era, made the transition into the mass-media age with huge success. Formby's unorthodox ukulele playing, allied to goofy humour and chirpy Lancastrian tones, made him a nationwide star of stage, radio and film. The tuneful simplicity and saucy undertones of Formby's 'When I'm Cleaning Windows' typify a style that endures today in Britain's variety shows, pantomimes and working men's clubs.

"A LITTLE OF WHAT YOU FANCY DOES YOU GOOD."
From the Marie Lloyd song

Above

Despite her success, Marie Lloyd was always generous and supported the smaller performers' Music Hall Strike for better wages. Subsequently, the managers quietly excluded her from the first Royal Command Performance in 1912.

Left

A poster for Wilton's Grand Music Hall with a full programme of the show, which included comic songs and duets, ballads, serio-comic songs, quadrilles and "Ethiopian Entertainment".

MUSIC HALL

This example uses a swing rhythm that an actor would follow to give the impression of being slightly drunk, and a melodically simple tune, so that an audience can join in with the chorus.

LEADING EXPONENTS

Marie Lloyd
Harry Clifton
Dan Leno
George Robey
George Formby Sr.
Mistinguett
Maurice Chevalier
George Formby
Josephine Baker

Good eve - ning ev - 'ry bo - dy, my name is Cynth - ia Pew,

Children's Songs

CHILDREN'S SONGS HAVE EVOLVED FROM MOTHERS' LULLABIES TO TEACHERS' NURSERY RHYMES TO THE SINGALONG NUMBERS OF TV AND FILM. THROUGH ALL OF THEIR INCARNATIONS, THEY HAVE RETAINED THE SAME STYLISTIC VALUES: A MELODIC, UPBEAT MOOD; A CATCHY, EASILY REPEATABLE CHORUS; AND LYRICS THAT TELL A STORY.

Above

The children's songs on the Mary Poppins soundtrack included the Oscar-winning 'Chim Chim Cheree'.

MANY popular musicians have released child-friendly songs. The 1960s, in particular, saw a glut of light-hearted, escapist fantasies, such as Peter, Paul & Mary's 'Puff the Magic Dragon' (1963) and the Beatles' 'Yellow Submarine' (1966), both of which remain classroom favourites on both sides of the Atlantic. But, partly because pre-teens make up a small fraction of listening audiences and wield relatively little purchasing power, there have been few successful specialist children's musicians in the pop era.

The Dominance Of The Screen

Most new children's songs have come to prominence via movies and musicals, whether it is Julie Andrews' rendition of the nonsense classic 'Supercalifragilisticexpialidocious' in *Mary Poppins* (1964) or the sentimentality of Elton John's 'Can You Feel the Love Tonight' in *The Lion King* (1994). But, since television

> "I'VE GOT A DREAM TOO, BUT IT'S ABOUT SINGING AND DANCING AND MAKING PEOPLE HAPPY."
>
> *Kermit the Frog*

Right

Jim Henson's Muppets are popular with both children and adults. The songs performed in their shows and movies cover a wide range of musical styles and include a mixture of covers and original material.

schedules began to increasingly target youthful audiences in the 1950s, the small screen has been the most important arbiter of juvenile musical tastes. Once children have become attached to a TV programme's characters, they will inevitably be attracted to any musical spin-off. A string of shows, from *The Chipmunks* (late-1950s and 1960s) and *The Banana Splits* (1968–72) in America, to *Pinky and Perky* (late-1950s to 1970s), *Barney* (1992–present) and *Bob the Builder* (1999–present) in the UK, spawned popular songs. The latter's effort, 'Can We Fix It?', became the UK's best-selling single of 2000.

The Muppets

The most popular children's entertainer on television in the twentieth century was Jim Henson, whose menagerie of Muppets was the focus for both *Sesame Street* (1969–present) and *The Muppet Show* (1976–81). But his most high-profile

musical venture was a surprisingly poignant ballad performed by his best-loved Muppet, Kermit the Frog. 'It's Not Easy Being Green' had kids blubbing from Seattle to Sheffield; its anti-racist subtext made it that rarest of things: a children's song with a socio-political message.

Listen With Mother

But television was not the answer for all parents. Unhappy with the quality of music available for her children in the 1980s, Linda Arnold, a New Yorker with a background in folk and documentary music, started a record label named Ariel (after her daughter) and wrote, recorded and released *Make Believe*, in 1986. Six more albums followed, and she gained a fan base of mothers and children, making live appearances at zoos and museums. Dubbed "the Mary Poppins of Children's Music", her finest moment, 1994's *Lullaby Land*, which included original lullabies such as 'Teddy Bear King's Waltz' and perennials like 'Twinkle Twinkle Little Star', proved there was still life in the human race's most venerable musical form.

LEADING EXPONENTS

Peter, Paul & Mary

The Beatles

Jim Henson

Linda Arnold

Pamela Ballingham

Bob The Builder

The Banana Splits

Julie Andrews

Elton John

Barney

CHILDREN'S SONGS

Simple melodies in major keys, with a "one syllable to one note" pattern, and simple rhythms that are easy to remember, are intrinsic to children's music.

Walking up up the gar-den path, turn a-round and start to laugh

THE POPULAR AND NOVELTY INTRO ➡ 418   POPULAR AND NOVELTY PEOPLE A-Z ➡ 435   INSTRUMENTS A-Z ➡ 436   THE POP INTRO ➡ 8

Christmas Songs

BEING PERCHED AT THE TOP OF THE CHARTS ON 25 DECEMBER HAS REPRESENTED A PRESTIGIOUS ACHIEVEMENT FOR MUSICIANS SINCE THE DAWN OF THE POP ERA, WHILE THE SHOPPING FRENZY OF THE FESTIVE PERIOD MAKES IT ONE OF THE MOST POTENTIALLY PROFITABLE TIMES TO RELEASE A RECORD.

IT wasn't always that way: the original Yuletide songs were church carols that endure today. But Christmas music was changed immeasurably in the 1920s and 1930s when the commercialization of the period, particularly in America, saw Christian references increasingly give way to snowmen, sleigh-bells, and the Coca-Cola-sanctioned Santa Claus.

Idealistic nostalgia pieces such as Dick Smith & Felix Bernard's 'Winter Wonderland' (1934) and light-hearted ditties like Gene Autry's 'Rudolph The Red-Nosed Reindeer' (1949) reflected this shift and were covered countless times in the following decades. But the definitive example of this new, secular breed of Christmas song, and still the best-selling single of all time, is Bing Crosby's 'White Christmas'.

Written by the great composer Irving Berlin for the 1942 film *Holiday Inn*, this unmatched slice of seasonal schmaltz was first performed by Crosby on his radio show on Christmas Day, 1941. As the world's most popular entertainer poured his mellifluous baritone over a backing of strings, woodwind and festive chimes, there could be only one outcome: number one. The song repeated the feat every year for the next four years and has now sold in excess of 30 million copies around the world, a total that is highly unlikely to be matched.

Spector Spices Up The Formula

Once Crosby and Berlin had set the template for the Christmas classic, those who followed them ran the constant risk of falling into cliché. But, in 1963, the virtuoso producer Phil Spector consummately avoided that pitfall on his *A Christmas Gift For You* LP. With a string of standards from 'Santa Claus Is Coming To Town' to 'Silent Night', Spector added a twist with his Wall of Sound recording techniques and an exciting roster of predominantly black pop singers including the Ronettes, the Crystals and Darlene Love. Popular material, symphonic orchestration and soulful vocals were combined to sublime effect. Spector's Yuletide stock rose further in 1973 when he co-produced John Lennon and Yoko Ono's 'Merry Xmas (War is Over)', a rare example of a Christmas protest song.

Since then, festive charts have been dominated by jaunty novelty songs like Slade's 'Merry Christmas Everybody' (1973), charity efforts (Band Aid's 'Do They Know It's Christmas?', 1984), traditional revivals (numerous releases by Johnny Mathis), returns to Christian themes (Cliff Richard's 'Saviour's Day', 1990) and modern updates (Bruce Springsteen's 'Santa Claus Is Coming To Town' and the Backstreet Boys' *Christmas Album*, 1999). The Pogues' 'Fairytale Of New York', on the other hand, was completely unsentimental. Lines like "You scumbag, you maggot/You cheap lousy faggot/Happy Christmas your arse/I pray God it's our last" were worlds away from Crosby's restrained civility.

Above

The lavish arrangements of Phil Spector's A Christmas Gift For You *make it a feelgood seasonal treat.*

"IT ISN'T JUST THE BEST SONG I'VE EVER WRITTEN, IT'S THE BEST SONG ANYONE'S EVER WRITTEN".

Irving Berlin on 'White Christmas'

Above Left

Bing Crosby in Mark Sandrich's 1954 classic White Christmas. *Bing's early film career was eventually eclipsed by the runaway success of his 'White Christmas' single and he moved more towards television work.*

LEADING EXPONENTS

Bing Crosby
Phil Spector
Slade
Roy Wood with Wizzard
Johnny Mathis
Band Aid
Cliff Richard
Wham!
The Pogues featuring
  Kirsty MacColl
Backstreet Boys
John Lennon
  & Yoko Ono

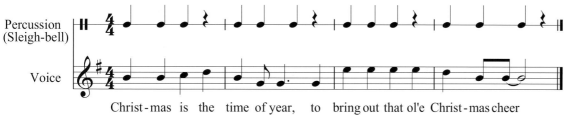

Percussion (Sleigh-bell)

Voice

Christ-mas is the time of year, to bring out that ol'e Christ-mas cheer

CHRISTMAS SONGS

Christmas hits have catchy melodies, quite often accompanied by sleigh-bell rhythms that are easy to sing along to.

Easy Listening

UNTIL IT WAS RECLAIMED WITH AN IRONIC WINK BY 1990S HIPSTERS, EASY LISTENING HAD BEEN HUGELY POPULAR, BUT RARELY COOL. WHILE THE TEENAGERS OF THE 1950S AND 1960S WERE GETTING OFF ON DANGEROUS ROCK'N'ROLL AND SUBVERSIVE R&B, THEIR PARENTS WERE SWEETLY COCOONED IN THE MUSIC OF MANTOVANI AND PERCY FAITH.

Above

Easy listening pioneer Percy Faith injured his hands in a fire at the age of 18, halting his promising career as a concert pianist.

EASY listening music never launched any rebellions; no riots raged to its syrupy strains. When Sam Mendes, the director of the 1999 movie *American Beauty*, wanted to emphasize the gulf between his two leads, he had Kevin Spacey rock out to Pink Floyd while Annette Bening daydreamed to the "champagne music" of Lawrence Welk.

Easy listening is unobtrusive, pacifying music built around pleasant, easily digestible melodies. Which is not to say it has no artistic value: within its wide borders can be found a rich spectrum of sounds, seasoned with influences from classical to pop to rock to jazz. Though often dismissed as hollow and uninspired, the genre has been distinguished by the work of some lavishly talented musicians, including such immortals as Henry Mancini and Burt Bacharach. Among its less publicized fans was one John Lennon, who admitted furtively indulging while Yoko Ono was away on business.

> "THE LIGHTER SIDE OF MUSIC HAS ALWAYS BEEN THROWN OUT AND NOT RECEIVED ITS PROPER DIGNITY."
>
> *Mantovani*

A Birthplace In Business

Beautiful music, mood music, elevator music, background music, light music, adult contemporary, light classical; all fall in some way beneath the umbrella of easy listening, as do the more sugary releases of Frank Sinatra, Dean Martin, Perry Como, Patti Page, Eva Cassidy and the Carpenters. Since it was concerned with the

LEADING EXPONENTS

Mantovani
Henry Mancini
Percy Faith
Liberace
Leroy Anderson
Lawrence Welk
Nelson Riddle
Jackie Gleason
Burt Bacharach
The Carpenters
Perry Como
Patti Page

EASY LISTENING

Liberated melodies with lush harmonies present a style that is gentle and unchallenging, as well as elegant and restful.

subtle influencing of mood, it also had much in common with movie music; many easy listening stars doubled as soundtrack composers.

But the genre's origins lie in commerce, and one of its fathers was not a musician but an American soldier. Brigadier General George Owen Squier patented the transmission of background music in the 1920s and his corporate intentions were implicit in the name he chose for it – "Muzak" – which combined "music" with "Kodak", the name of one of his favourite companies. Originally designed to soothe the nerves of workers making vertiginous journeys up the first skyscrapers, the modulated supply of watered-down classical, jazz and popular tunes soon became known as "elevator music".

Gradually increasing in tempo throughout a shift and regimented into a mood scale ranging from "gloomy-minus three" to "ecstatic-plus eight", Muzak became popular with company bosses, who believed it increased productivity and boosted morale. By the early 1970s, 47 of the world's 50 largest corporations were subscribers; Muzak was played in shopping malls and airport departure lounges, used as telephone hold music, and was even piped into Polaris submarines. Muzak's ability to influence, or "tint", human moods fascinated musicians like Brian Eno, who explored it in his *Discrete Music* LP (1975), generally acknowledged as one of the earliest examples of ambient music.

Others saw in Muzak sinister echoes of Aldous Huxley's dystopian *Brave New World*, in which citizens were fed a diet of "synthetic music" featuring "hyper-violin, super-cello, and oboe-surrogate". Detractors accused companies of using Muzak as an emotional sedative or a subliminal marketing tool. But the fact remains that it was popular with a large proportion of the millions of workers who were exposed to it from the 1920s onwards. A market for inoffensive, streamlined sounds was ready to be tapped.

The Maestro Of Light Classical

The people at the British Broadcasting Corporation were thinking much the same thing. In the 1920s, they introduced a new genre, light classical, in order to attract listeners who could later be nudged towards more "highbrow" music. The most notable light classicist, and a name synonymous with easy listening, was Annunzio Paolo Mantovani. Born in Venice but raised in England, the classically trained violinist was conducting the London Metropole Orchestra by the age of 20, went on to serve as Noel Coward's musical director during the 1940s and was a nationwide sensation in both America and Britain by the 1950s.

Heavily influenced by the Austrian violinist Fritz Kreisler, Mantovani reinvented classical music in a studio-produced

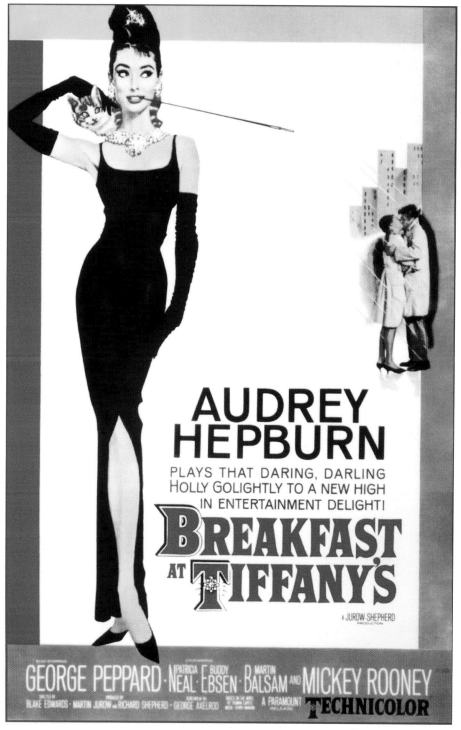

style whose hallmarks were "cathedralized" strings, close harmonies and echo-laden, overlapping sound. His output was divided between lush waltzes based on familiar tunes like 'Greensleeves', and original compositions such as 'Charmaine', a dreamy extravaganza of fluttering violins and woodwinds, that was a big American radio hit in 1951. Mantovani was one of the first popular artists to concentrate on albums rather than singles, topping the charts on both sides of the Atlantic and becoming the first musician to sell one million stereo records in the United States. "Perhaps 25 percent of

Above

Henry Mancini's 'Moon River' appears in various arrangements throughout Breakfast At Tiffany's. Audrey Hepburn even sings the song herself at one point.

Centre

Mantovani in 1953, leaving London for Amsterdam, where he was to conduct a Dutch orchestra.

Above

*The Carpenters' variety of
easy listening had a beautiful
clarity of sound – a
combination of Karen's clear
soprano, Richard's sparse
piano arrangements and
beautifully smooth studio
production techniques.*

the people like the classics, and about 25 percent like the Beatles," Mantovani later said. "I aim to please the 50 percent in the middle."

From The Screen To The Airwaves

Many of Mantovani's albums revisited romantic film themes of the day, as did the mood music of Jackie Gleason, but the undisputed master of cinematic easy listening was the composer/ conductor/arranger/multi-instrumentalist Henry Mancini. After cutting his teeth on jazz and the big band sound of the 1940s, the Clevelander soon graduated to scoring soundtracks for film and television. He developed an inspired knack for creating songs that escaped the confines of the movie or show they were written for and became memorable classics in their own right. They varied enormously in tone, from the killer rhythms of his jazz-inflected theme for *The Peter Gunn Show* (1959) to the bittersweet refrains of his most celebrated song, 1961's 'Moon River'.

The musical centrepiece of *Breakfast At Tiffany's* was inspired by the film's elfin star, Audrey Hepburn, and boasted sublime, dreamy lyrics by Johnny Mercer. But it is the elegant simplicity of Mancini's melodies that make it one of the most perfectly realized pop songs of the past 50 years, and proves that easy listening can be brushed with genius. Mancini's peers heartily agreed: *Breakfast At Tiffany's* alone won him two Oscars and five Grammys. His grand total for a 40-year career – four Oscars and 20 Grammys – remains unmatched by any popular artist.

A Bona Fide Showman

By the late-1960s, dedicated radio stations were pumping out what had then become known as "beautiful music", to devoted (mainly female) fans across America. The soft strings of conductor-composers like Mantovani, Mancini and Percy Faith dominated the schedules. But, in terms of charismatic showmanship, none of them could hold a candle to an incendiary pianist by the name of Wladziu Valentino Liberace.

Right

*Although an incredibly
popular performer – especially
with the ladies – Liberace
was panned by the critics for
his sentimental style. He
coined a phrase in response to
this, saying that he cried all
the way to the bank.*

A Polish-American from Milwaukee, Liberace was not just the most flamboyant figure in easy listening, but one of the biggest personalities in all of popular music. A child prodigy, he was playing solo piano with symphony orchestras by his teens, but rejected a concert career in favour of the glitzier New York club circuit. By the 1950s, he was a star, performing a mixture of light classical, lounge jazz and show

tunes while exuberantly clad in furs, sequins and gold lamé. Like many easy listening artists, he was never loved by the critics. But his audiences adored him, attending his concerts in droves well into the 1980s.

Enter The Vocalists

Largely because a lack of vocals was more conducive to its original status as "background music", the genre had been dominated by instrumentals.

Above

Stereolab are keen to address
descriptions of their sound
before the critics do, with
releases like 'John Cage
Bubblegum', Space Age
Bachelor Pad Music *and*
Transient Random Noise
Bursts With
Announcements.

But the laid-back vocal releases of Sinatra, Martin et al had always had plenty in common – debonair style, mellifluous tone – with the classic lounge and easy listening compositions and, in the 1970s, the beautiful music stations began to play more records by soft-edged pop acts like Barbra Streisand and the Carpenters.

The latter, a brother-sister duo from Connecticut, absorbed rock, folk, classical and pop influences to craft a melodic, commercial sound that was as popular with easy listeners as it was with chart followers. Like Mancini and Mantovani before him, Richard Carpenter was fond of lush, emotive arrangements. But the focus was his sister Karen's clean, resonant voice, showcased to seminal effect on a cover of Burt Bacharach's '(They Long to Be) Close To You' that was a hit around the world. The Carpenters' gentle-on-the-ear approach remains one of easy listening's most familiar touchstones. And the genre lives on in the output of both the deeply uncool, like Barry Manilow, and the knowingly trendy, like the Mancini-inspired Stereolab. It seems our appetite for hassle-free melody will never be sated.

Lounge Music

FOLLOWING ON FROM THE LUSH BOMBAST OF THE SWING ERA, AND ESTABLISHED BY A COLOURFUL GROUP OF AMERICAN ARTISTS IN THE 1950S AND 1960S, LOUNGE WAS EASY LISTENING'S QUIRKY KID BROTHER. IT WAS MORE PLAYFUL THAN ITS MORE POPULIST RELATIVE AND, WHEN VIEWED RETROSPECTIVELY, HAD A HIGH CAMP FACTOR.

Above

Prolific exotica pioneer Les Baxter also created the music for over 250 films and shows for television and radio, as well as composing and arranging pieces for the top swing bands of the 1940s and 1950s.

ALTHOUGH ostensibly laid-back and mellow, lounge artists like Les Baxter and Esquivel were not afraid to experiment with tempo and style and helped lounge mutate into new forms. Space-age pop made use of futuristic new instruments and exotica stole influences from Latin America, Africa and beyond with a magpie's zeal. This music was dilettantish rather than authentic, presenting snapshots of far-off countries or future worlds for an audience hungry for luxurious escapism.

Lounge music was later re-branded as cocktail music, martini music and lounge-core by the trendsetters who rediscovered it in the 1990s. To them, it evoked kitsch 1960s lifestyles pursued in bachelor pads stuffed with lava lamps and leopard-skin sofas. Whether this image was accurate or not was irrelevant: retro freaks descended in droves on second-hand record shops to unearth vintage LPs like *Equinox* (1967), by the Brazilian Sergio Mendes, and the entire back catalogue of the mighty Burt Bacharach.

> "IT SEEMS THAT MOST OF MY LIFE I HAVE HAD INCLINATIONS TOWARDS ... DIFFERENT, INTERESTING MUSIC. I NEVER LIKE TO DO PROSAIC."
>
> *Les Baxter*

A Musical Trip Around The World

One of the foremost lounge artists was Les Baxter, a pianist from Detroit who worked with some of the biggest bands of the swing era, but is best remembered as the most important pioneer of exotica, which gained considerable popularity in America during the 1950s. His compositions retained the backbone of strings and brass that characterized most popular music of the time.

But he also assimilated everything from the striking, four-octave range of the legendary Peruvian vocalist Yma Sumac to the steel guitars of Polynesia and Hawaii, whose tiki bars and hula dancing permeated American pop culture in the post-war years. African percussion was another influence: in 1951, Baxter recorded his seminal *Ritual of the Savage* LP, a

LEADING EXPONENTS

Les Baxter

Esquivel

Burt Bacharach

Sergio Mendes

Martin Denny

Arthur Lyman

Steve Allen

Earl Grant

Funki Porcini

Mike Flowers

LOUNGE MUSIC

Sophisticated melodies made up of small music cells based on large intervals and interrupted by rests create the character of lounge music.

THE POPULAR AND NOVELTY INTRO ➡ 418   POPULAR AND NOVELTY PEOPLE A–Z ➡ 435   INSTRUMENTS A–Z ➡ 436   POP: BRIT POP ➡ 62

musical travelogue replete with recorded jungle noises and bird calls. The album remains a classic of exotica – its lead track, 'Quiet Village', was covered with great success by another renowned lounger, Martin Denny, in 1959, and it also inspired Denny's bandmate Arthur Lyman, who had a hit with 'Yellow Bird' in 1961.

Back in 1948, Baxter had also experimented with a theremin, one of the world's first electronic instruments, combining its eerie, otherwordly sound with a choir, rhythm section, cello and French horn. The result, an LP titled *Music Out of the Moon*, was the progenitor of space-age pop, a future-fixated relation of lounge that exploited the possibilities afforded by the stereo format and nascent electronic instrumentation.

A Burst Of Latin Lunacy

A prime mover in both space-age pop and exotica was Esquivel, a bona fide lounge eccentric who created some of the strangest music of the late-1950s and 1960s. Much of the Mexican's output was based on the big band format and shot through with exaggerated Latin American rhythms, from cha-cha to mambo, but he also employed the theremin and an arsenal of other outlandish instruments, including Chinese bells, early electronic keyboards and the ondioline, a vacuum tube instrument that emits a reedy, vibrato sound. His surreal sense of humour extended to having his vocalists sing comic-book injections like "Pow!" and "Boink!".

His most infamous recording was 1962's *Latin-Esque*, the first album recorded with full stereo separation: two orchestras performing in separate studios whom he conducted using headphones. He divided opinions during the 1950s and 1960s: some critics were turned off by his wild clashing of styles and tempos and occasional disregard for tonal beauty. Others became great fans, and Esquivel ended his career as a stalwart of the Las Vegas circuit and a favourite with Frank Sinatra and REM.

Revival Of A Master Songwriter

The popularity of Esquivel and his cohorts declined after the 1970s, but enjoyed a revival in the 1990s, inspiring British electronic artists such as Funki Porcini and receiving a more tongue-in-cheek reworking by Mike Flowers, who achieved UK chart success with a lounge-style cover of Oasis's 'Wonderwall' in 1996. And it was this exposure, along with appearances in the Austin Powers films, that helped to renew interest in another 1960s star – Burt Bacharach – who would come to embody lounge for a new generation of listeners.

Of course, it would be an injustice to one of the twentieth century's greatest musicians to describe the Kansas City-born Bacharach as solely a lounge artist. Since the early 1950s he has written hits for the Carpenters, toured with cabaret star Marlene Dietrich, composed Oscar-winning music for *Butch Cassidy & The Sundance Kid* and released a string of classic collaborations with Dionne Warwick.

Left

Esquivel's bizarre use of instrumentation and innovative arrangements were designed to exploit the new stereo equipment. Futuristic as the music sounded, it dated quickly, but became a kitsch favourite in the 1970s.

Bacharach's sophisticated yet light melodies have something in common with those of easy listening titans like Henry Mancini. But his twinkling versatility, which has taken in jazz, bossa nova, soul, Brazilian grooves and pure pop, is even truer to the playful eclecticism of lounge. Today, such tracks as 1965's 'Make It Easy On Yourself', which he wrote for the Walker Brothers, exude a breezy, kitsch panache that makes Bacharach, among many other things, a quintessential lounge hero.

Above

Burt Bacharach, with guest stars Mireille Mathieu, Juliet Prowse and Dusty Springfield, on a 1970 television show. Springfield is considered to be one of the best interpreters of Bacharach's songs, along with Dionne Warwick.

JAZZ: SWING ➡ 128   JAZZ: LATIN JAZZ ➡ 148   WORLD: LATIN & SOUTH AMERICA ➡ 300

ALTHOUGH IT GENERALLY REFERS TO MUSIC RECORDED UP TO THE END OF THE SECOND WORLD WAR, NOSTALGIA IS NOT A GENRE IN THE SENSE THAT THE ARTISTS SHARE INHERENT CHARACTERISTICS OR SENSIBILITIES. INSTEAD THEY HAVE A SPECIAL RESONANCE, AN ABILITY TO CONJURE UP FEELINGS AND MEMORIES OF A SPECIFIC ERA.

Nostalgia

Above

Al Jolson, shown here in the first talking picture The Jazz Singer, *was an energetic performer with an electric stage presence. No one could follow his act, and as a result he was always last on the bill.*

> "I BELIEVE IN CENSORSHIP. I MADE A FORTUNE OUT OF IT."

Mae West

Right

A brilliant comic actress ahead of her time, Mae West's sexually charged performances and wicked sense of humour horrified the authorities but endeared her to audiences. Some of her phrases have now come into common usage.

LEADING EXPONENTS

Al Jolson

Mae West

Vera Lynn

George Formby

Edith Piaf

Marie Lloyd

Noel Coward

Ethel Merman

Jeanette MacDonald

Nelson Eddy

Max Bygraves

SOME of them stood for harrowing times: Mae West epitomized the defiance of the Depression years and Vera Lynn defined British sentiment during the Second World War. Some harked back to evocative periods; though he began his career after the war, the British crooner Max Bygraves enjoyed success with his *Singalongwaryears* LPs in the 1990s. Other artists evoked exciting artistic periods or distinctive styles. Marie Lloyd was the quintessential music hall performer in Britain at the turn of the twentieth century. Nelson Eddy and Jeanette McDonald bestrode the Hollywood musicals of the 1930s to the 1950s. Noel Coward's wordplay virtually defined English urbanity in the mid-twentieth century and Al Jolson will forever be synonymous with the advent of talking pictures.

The Lithuanian-born Jolson began his career on the vaudeville circuit and his command of song, dance and comedy had made him America's first superstar by the early 1920s. Often performing minstrel-style, he borrowed heavily from early jazz and ragtime. Jolson sealed his status as "The World's Greatest Entertainer" in 1927 when he starred in *The Jazz Singer*, ushering in the era of movie sound with the immortal, ad-libbed words "You ain't heard nothing yet". The film also saw him perform his signature tune, 'My Mammy', which remains a standard of the talkie era.

As America wallowed in the Depression during the late-1920s and early 1930s, Mae West, another vaudeville favourite turned movie star and recording artist, flouted the puritan mood with a welcome spark of glamour, wit and winking sexuality. At a time of tight censorship, the Brooklyn sexpot's weapon of choice was the double entendre: among her song titles were 'Easy Rider' and 'I Like A Guy What Takes His Time'. But West's sultry, suggestive delivery is best exemplified by 'Come Up And See Me Some Time', a lascivious classic that was a huge influence on Marilyn Monroe.

The Soldiers' Solace

Vera Lynn captured the mood on the other side of the Atlantic. If one voice encapsulated the pain and romance of the Second World War for Britons, it was Lynn's. Making her solo debut in 1940, the east Londoner was the country's favourite singer during the wartime years and the link between lonely servicemen and their sweethearts back home. Lynn hosted a BBC programme, *Sincerely Yours*, in which she read out personal messages and trilled bittersweet ballads themed around long distance love. Her plangent vocals were most famously employed on 'We'll Meet Again', a string-backed paean to post-war reunion that she first performed in 1939 and reprised in the 1942 film of the same name. Lynn's career continued long after hostilities ended. She had several hits in the US in 1948–54, and was the first British artist to top the US charts with 'Auf Wiederseh'n Sweetheart' in 1952. Her inspirational legacy was recognized in 1976 when she was made a Dame of the British Empire.

NOSTALGIA

Nostalgia often incorporates chromatic patterns and a "one note to one syllable" control, to offer dream-like reassurance.

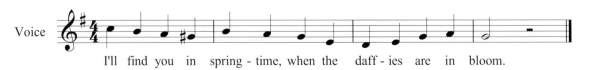

Voice

I'll find you in spring - time, when the daff - ies are in bloom.

THE POPULAR AND NOVELTY INTRO ➡ 418   POPULAR AND NOVELTY PEOPLE A-Z ➡ 435   INSTRUMENTS A-Z ➡ 436

Artists: Popular And Novelty

Entries appear in the following order: name, music style, year(s) of popularity, type of artist, country of origin

2 Live Jews, Novelty Songs, 1990s, Artist, American
101 Strings Orchestra, Easy Listening, 1950s–, Artist, American
Adam Again, Contemporary Christian Music, 1980s, Artist, American
Adler, Jerry, Easy Listening, 1990s, Artist, American
Ahbez, Eden, Lounge Music, 1940s–1960s, Artist, American
Allen, Steve, Lounge Music, 1950s–1990s, Artist, American
Alpert, Herb, Easy Listening, 1960s–, Artist, American
Amis, John, Easy Listening, 1990s, Artist, American
Ames, Nancy, Novelty Songs, 1960s, Artist, American
Amos, Daniel, Contemporary Christian Music, 1980s–, Artist, American
Anderson, Leroy, Easy Listening, 1940s–1960s, Composer, American
Andrews, Julie, Children's Songs, 1960s–, Artist, British
Angrave, Scott, Novelty Songs, 1990s, Artist, American
Arnold, Linda, Children's Songs, 1980s–1990s, Artist, American
Arvedon, David, Novelty Songs, 1960s–1970s, Artist, American
Ashton, Susan, Contemporary Christian Music, 1990s, Artist, American
Autry, Gene, Christmas Songs, 1940s–1950s, Artist, American
Bacharach, Burt, Easy Listening; Lounge Music, 1960s–1990s, Composer, American
Backstreet Boys, Christmas Songs, 1990s–2000s, Artist, American
Baker, Josephine, Music Hall, 1920s–1970s, Artist, American
Ballingham, Pamela, Children's Songs, 1980s–1990s, Artist, American
Band Aid, Christmas Songs, 1980s, Artist, British
Barnes & Barnes, Novelty Songs, 1980s–1990s, Artist, American
Barney, Children's Songs, 1990s–, Animation, American
Baxter, Les, Lounge Music, 1940s–1970s, Artist; Composer, American
Beatles, The, Children's Songs, 1960s, Artist, British
Becker, Margaret, Contemporary Christian Music, 1980s–1990s, Artist, American
Bell, Benny, Novelty Songs, 1970s, Artist, American
Benzedrine Monks Of Santa Demo, The, Novelty Songs, 1990s, Artist, American
Berlin, Irving, Christmas Songs, 1940s–50s, Composer, American
Bernard, Felix, Christmas Songs, 1930s, Artist, American
Berry, Chuck, Novelty Songs, 1950s–, Artist, American
Bessette, Mimi, Children's Songs, 1990s, Artist, American
Black, Stanley, Easy Listening, Composer, British
Black Happy, Contemporary Christian Music; Novelty Songs, 1990s, Artist, American
Blackman, Honor, Novelty Songs, 1960s, Artist, British
Bob The Builder, Childrens' Songs, 1990s–, Animation, British
Bollock Brothers, The, Novelty Songs, 1980s–, Artist, British
Boltz, Ray, Contemporary Christian Music, 1980s–, Artist, American
Bongos, Bass & Bob, Novelty Songs, 1980s, Artist, American
Bonzo Dog Doo Dah Band, Novelty Songs, 1960s, Artist, British
Boone, Debby, Contemporary Christian Music, 1970s–1990s, Artist, American
Boston Pops Orchestra, Easy Listening, 1920s–1990s, Artist, American
Brooks, Mel, Novelty Songs, 1950s–1970s, Artist, American
Brown, Julie, Novelty Songs, 1980s, Artist, American
Buchanan & Goodman, Novelty Songs, 1950s, Artist, American
Buckner & Garcia, Novelty Songs, 1980s, Artist, American
Bygraves, Max, Nostalgia, 1970s–1980s, Artist, British
Cabot, Sebastian, Novelty Songs, 1960s, Artist, British
California Raisins, Novelty Songs; 1980s–1990s, Christmas Songs, Animation, American
Cambridge Singers, The, Christmas Songs, 1980s–, Artist, British
Camp, Steve, Contemporary Christian Music, 1980s–1990s, Artist, American
Canadian Brass, Easy Listening, 1970s–, Artist, Canadian
Cantinflas, Novelty Songs, 1990s, Artist, Mexican
Card, Michael, Contemporary Christian Music, 1980s, Artist, American
Carlisle, Bob, Contemporary Christian Music, 1990s–, Artist, American
Carman, Contemporary Christian Music, 1970s–1990s, Artist, American
Carpenters, The, Easy Listening, 1970s, Artist, American
Carroll, David, Lounge Music, 1950s, Artist, American
Case, Russ, Lounge Music, 1960s, Artist, American
Cash, Johnny, Novelty Songs, 1970s, Artist, American
Cassidy, Eva, Easy Listening, 1990s, Artist, American
Chacksfield, Frank, Easy Listening; Novelty Songs, 1950s–1970s, Artist, British
Chapin, Tom, Children's Songs, 1970s–, Artist, American
Chapman, Steven Curtis, Contemporary Christian Music, 1980s–, Artist, American
Chas & Dave, Novelty Songs, 1970s–, Artist, British
Chevalier, Maurice, Music Hall, 1920s–1960s, Artist, French
Chipmunks, The, Novelty Songs, 1950s–1990s, Animation, American
Cincinnati Pops Orchestra, Easy Listening, 1970s–1990s, Artist, American
Clark, Louis, Easy Listening, 1970s–1980s, Artist, British
Clay, Cassius, Novelty Songs, 1960s, Artist, American
Clayderman, Richard, Easy Listening, 1960s–, Artist, French
Clifton, Harry, Music Hall, 1890s, Artist, British
Clinton, Roger, Novelty Songs, 1990s, Artist, American
Clooney, Rosemary, Christmas Songs, 1940s–1990s, Artist, American
Combustible Edison, Lounge Music, 1990s, Artist, American
Como, Perry, Easy Listening, 1950s, Artist, American
Connif, Ray, Easy Listening, 1950s–, Artist, American
Cortese, Dom, Easy Listening, 1960s–1990s, Artist, Italian
Costanzo, Jack, Lounge Music, 1940s–1970s, Artist, American
Coward, Noel, Nostalgia, 1920s–1970s, Artist, British
Crosby, Bing, Christmas Songs; Nostalgia, 1940s–1950s, Artist, American
Crouch, Andraé, Contemporary Christian Music, 1970s–1990s, Artist, American
Cugat, Xavier, Easy Listening, 1930s–1960s, Artist, Spanish
Dalida, Easy Listening, 1950s–1980s, Artist, French
dc Talk, Contemporary Christian Music, 1980s–, Artist, American
Dead Milkmen, The, Novelty Songs, 1980s–1990s, Artist, American
Dee, Lenny, Lounge Music, 1950s–1970s, Artist, American
Denny, Martin, Lounge Music, 1950s–1980s, Artist, American
Detergents, The, Novelty Songs, 1960s, Artist, American
Dickens, Little Jimmy, Novelty Songs, 1940s–1960s, Artist, American
Dietrich, Marlene, Nostalgia, 1920s–1970s, Artist, German
Disney, Children's Songs, 1930s–, Artist, American
Doan, John, Christmas Songs, 1980s–1990s, Artist, American
Douglas, Carl, Novelty Songs, 1970s, Artist, Jamaican
Dr. Demento, Novelty Songs, 1970s–, Artist, American
Dr. Seuss, Children's Songs, 1990s, Artist, British
Dr. West's Medicine Show & Junk Band, Novelty Songs, 1960s, Artist, American
Dread Zeppelin, Novelty Songs, 1980s–, Artist, American
Dunn, Clive, Novelty Songs, 1970s, Artist, British
Durante, Jimmy, Nostalgia, 1920s–1960s, Artist, American
Eddy, Nelson, Nostalgia, 1930s–1960s, Artist, American
Elgart, Les, Lounge Music, 1940s–1990s, Artist, American
Elmo & Patsy, Novelty Songs, 1980s, Artist, American
English, Michael, Contemporary Christian Music, 1990s–, Artist, American
Eno, Brian, Easy Listening, 1970s–, Artist, American
Esquivel, Lounge Music, 1950s–1960s, Artist, Mexican
Fabian, Tony, Easy Listening, 1990s–, Artist, Brazilian
Fairey Band, Easy Listening, 1990s, Artist, British
Faith, Percy, Easy Listening, 1950s–1970s, Composer, Canadian
Fantastic Strings, Easy Listening, 1990s, Artist, American
Feller, Dick, Novelty Songs, 1970s–1980s, Artist, American
Ferrante, Arthur, Lounge Music, 1950s–1990s, Artist, American
Fiedler, Arthur, Easy Listening, 1950s–1970s, Artist, American
Firm, The, Novelty Songs, 1980s, Artist, British
Fischer, Larry "Wild Man", Novelty Songs, 1960s–1980s, Artist, American
Fisher, Harvey Sid, Novelty Songs, 1990s, Artist, American
Flanders, Michael, Novelty Songs, 1940s, Artist, British
Formby, George, Music Hall, 1930s, Artist, British
Formby Sr., George, Music Hall, 1890s–1900s, Artist, British
Freberg, Stan, Novelty Songs, 1950s–1960s, Artist, American
Frenchy, Lounge Music, 1990s–, Artist, American
Frogs, The, Novelty Songs, 1980s–, Artist, American
Funki Porcini, Lounge Music, 1990s–, Artist, British
Gagnon, André, Christmas Songs, 1960s, Artist, Canadian
Gaillard, Slim, Novelty Songs, 1930s–1950s; 1980s, Artist, American
Gaither, Bill, Contemporary Christian Music, 1970s–, Artist, American
Gentle People, The, Lounge Music, 1990s–, Artist, American
Gilbert, Francois, Easy Listening, 2000–, Artist, Spanish
Gilberto, Astrud, Easy Listening, 1960s–1990s, Artist, Brazilian
Glazer, Tom, Children's Songs; Novelty Songs, 1940s–1960s, Artist, American
Gleason, Jackie, Easy Listening, 1950s–1960s, Artist, American
Godwin, Pat, Children's Songs; Christmas Songs; Novelty Songs, 1990s, Artist, American
Gold, Marty, Lounge Music, 1960s, Artist, American
Goober & the Peas, Novelty Songs, 1990s, Artist, American
Goodman, Dickie, Novelty Songs, 1960s–1970s, Artist, American
Goons, The, Novelty Songs, 1950s, Artist, British
Gordon, Barry, Christmas Songs, 1950s, Artist, American
Gorelick, Kenny, Easy Listening, 1980s–, Artist, American
Grant, Amy, Contemporary Christian Music, 1980s–, Artist, American
Grant, Earl, Lounge Music, 1950s–1960s, Artist, American
Green, Keith, Contemporary Christian Music, 1970s–1980s, Artist, American
Green Jelly, Novelty Songs, 1990s–, Artist, American
Grenadine, Lounge Music, 1990s–, Artist, American
Haack, Bruce, Lounge Music, 1960s–1980s, Artist; Producer, Canadian
Hampton String Quarted, Easy Listening, 1980s–1990s, Artist, American
Harmonicats, The, Easy Listening, 1950s, Artist, American
Harris, Rolf, Novelty Songs, 1960s–, Artist, Australian
Heard, Mark, Contemporary Christian Music, 1980s, Artist, American
Henson, Jim, Children's Songs, 1960s–1990s, Composer, American
Henley, Vic, Novelty Songs, 1990s, Artist, American
Hickman, Jay, Novelty Songs, 1990s, Artist, American
Hill, Benny, Novelty Songs, 1970s, Artist, British
Hoosier Hot Shots, Novelty Songs, 1930s–1960s, Artist, American
Hope, Bob, Nostalgia, 1930s–1970s, Artist, American
Hyman, Dick, Lounge Music, 1940s–, Artist, American
Idle, Eric, Novelty Songs, 1990s, Artist, British
Jankowski, Horts, Easy Listening, 1960s–1990s, Artist, German
Jars Of Clay, Contemporary Christian Music, 1990s–, Artist, American
Jenkins, Ella, Children's Songs, 1950s–1990s, Artist, American
John, Elton, Children's Songs, 1990s, Artist, British
Jolson, Al, Nostalgia, 1910s–1940s, Artist, American
Jones, Spike, Novelty Songs, 1930s–1960s, Artist, American
Jurgens, Dick, Easy Listening, 1930s–1970s, Artist, American
Kaempfert, Bert, Easy Listening, 1950s–1979s, Composer, German
Katz, Mickey, Novelty Songs, 1920s–1970s, Artist, American
Kaye, Danny, Nostalgia, 1930s–1980s, Artist, American
Keaggy, Phil, Contemporary Christian Music, 1960s–, Artist, American
Kee, John P., Contemporary Christian Music, 1980s–, Artist, American
Kenney, Ed, Novelty Songs, 1990s, Artist, Hawaiian
Kentucky House Painters, 1990s, Artist, American
Kid Dave, Novelty Songs, 1990s, Artist, American
Killer Pussy, Novelty Songs, 1990s, Artist, American
King Uszniewicz & his Usniewicztones, Novelty Songs, 1970s, Artist, American
Kingsley, Gershon, Lounge Music, 1960s, Artist, American
Klein, Mark, Novelty Songs, 1990s, Artist, American
Kostelanetz, Andre, Easy Listening, 1940s–1970s, Composer, Russian
Kunzel, Erich, Easy Listening, 1980s–, Artist, American
Kweskin, Jim, Novelty Songs, 1960s–1970s, Artist, American
Lanz, David, Christmas Songs, 1990s, Artist, American
Last, James, Easy Listening, 1970s–, Composer, German
Lawrence, Eddie "The Old Philosopher", Novelty Songs, 1950s, Artist, American
League Of Decency, Christmas Songs, 1990s, Artist, American
Lehrer, Tom, Novelty Songs, 1950s–1960s, Artist, American
Lennon, John, Christmas Songs, 1970s, Artist, British
Leno, Dan, Music Hall, 1880s–1900s, Artist, British
LeFevre, Raymond, Easy Listening, 1990s, Artist, French
Liberace, Easy Listening, 1940s–1970s, Artist, American
Light, Enoch, Easy Listening, 1920s–1970s, Producer, American
Living Strings, Easy Listening, 1960s–1970s, Artist, Various
Lloyd, Marie, Music Hall, 1880s–1920s, Artist, British
Lombardo, Guy, Easy Listening, 1920s–1970s, Artist, Canadian
Lorber, Alan, Easy Listening, 1960s, Artist, American
Louis L'Amour, Novelty Songs, 1990s, Artist, American
Love Song, Contemporary Christian Music, 1960s–1970s, Artist, American
Love Unlimited Orchestra, 1970s–1980s, Artist, American
Lyman, Arthur, Lounge Music, 1950s–1960s, Artist, American
Lynn, Vera, Nostalgia, 1930s–1970s, Artist, British
MacColl, Kirsty, Christmas Songs, 1980s–1990s, Artist, British
MacDonald, Jeanette, Nostalgia, 1920s–1950s, Artist, American
Mancini, Henry, Easy Listening; Lounge Music, 1950s–1990s, Artist; Composer, American
Manilow, Barry, Easy Listening, 1970s–, Artist, American
Mansfield, Jayne, Novelty Songs, 1950s–1960s, Artist, American
Mantovani, Easy Listening, 1950s–1960s, Composer, Anglo–Italian
Markham, Pigmeat, Novelty Songs, 1960s, Artist, American
Martin, Dean, Easy Listening, 1940s–1980s, Artist, American
Martin, Juan, Easy Listening, 1970s–, Artist, Spanish
Martin, Mary, Nostalgia, 1930s–1960s, Artist, American
Marx, Groucho, Nostalgia, 1940s–1950s, Artist, American
Mathis, Johnny, Christmas Songs, 1950s–, Artist, American
Mauriat, Paul, Easy Listening, 1960s–, Composer, French
Maxwell, Robert, Lounge Music, 1970s, Artist, American
May, Billy, Easy Listening, 1940s–1970s, Artist, Composer, American
McGrew, Steve, Novelty Songs, 1990s–, Artist, American
Meco, Easy Listening, 1970s–1980s, Producer, American
Mendes, Sergio, Lounge Music, 1960s–, Artist, Brazilian
Merman, Ethel, Nostalgia, 1930s–1960s, Artist, American
Midas, John, Novelty Songs, 1990s, Artist, American
Mister Rogers, Children's Songs, 1950s–1990s, Artist, American
Mistinguett, Music Hall, 1890s–1920s, Artist, French
Mojo Nixon, Novelty Songs, 1980s–1990s, Artist, American
Moog Cookbook, The, Lounge Music, 1990s–, Artist, American
Moore, Geoff, Contemporary Christian Music, 1980s–1990s, Artist, American
Mossman, Sterling, Novelty Songs, 1990s, Artist, Hawaiian
Mrs. Miller, Novelty Songs, 1960s, Artist, American
Mullins, Rich, Contemporary Christian Music, 1980s–1990s, Artist, American
Müller, Werner, Easy Listening, 1970s–1980s, Artist, German
Muppets, The, Children's Songs, 1970s–1990s, Artist, American
Napoleon XIV, Novelty Songs, 1960s, Artist, American
National Philharmonic Orchestra, Easy Listening, 1940s–, Artist, American
Nervous Norvus, Novelty Songs, 1950s, Artist, American
Newsboys, Contemporary Christian Music, 1980s–1990s, Artist, American
Nimoy, Leonard, Novelty Songs, 1960s–1980s, Artist, American
Norman, Jessye, Christmas Songs, 1960s–, Artist, American
Norman, Larry, Contemporary Christian Music, 1960s–1970s, Artist, American
North Star Orchestra, Christmas Songs, 1990s, Artist, American
NRBQ, Novelty Songs, 1960s–, Artist, American
Nutty Squirrels, 1960s, Animation, American
Omartian, Michael, Contemporary Christian Music, 1970s–1990s, Artist, American
Ono, Yoko, Christmas Songs, 1970s, Artist, Japanese
Page, Patti, Children's Songs; Easy Listening, 1950s–, Artist, American
Palance, Jack, Novelty Songs, 1970s, Artist, American
Pamela, Lucia, Novelty Songs, 1960s, Artist, American
Pandit, Korla, Lounge Music, 1950s–1990s, Artist, Indian
Parachute Express, Children's Songs, 1980s–1990s, Artist, American
Paramor, Norrie, Easy Listening, 1950s–1970s, Producer, British
Patty, Sandi, Contemporary Christian Music, 1970s–, Artist, American
Paz, Suni, Children's Songs, 1960s–, Artist, Latin American
Peacock, Charlie, Contemporary Christian Music, 1990s, Artist, American
Peel, David, Novelty Songs, 1960s–1990s, Artist, American
Perrey, Jean–Jacques, Lounge Music, 1960s, Artist, French
Peter, Paul & Mary, Children's Songs, 1960s–1990s, Artist, American
Peters, Red, Novelty Songs, 1990s, Artist, American
Petra, Contemporary Christian Music, 1980s, Artist, American
Phillips, Leslie, Contemporary Christian Music, 1980s, Artist, American
Piaf, Edith, Nostalgia, 1930s–1960s, Artist, French
Pickett, Bobby "Boris", Novelty Songs, 1960s, Artist, American
Pierce, Larry, Novelty Songs, 1990s, Artist, American
Pogues, The, The Christmas Songs, 1980s–1990s, Artist, Irish
Poindexter, Buster, Novelty Songs, 1980s–1990s, Artist, American
Powell, Dick, Nostalgia, 1930s–1950s, Artist, American
Prater, Ollie Joe, Novelty Songs, 1990s, Artist, American
Raffi, Children's Songs, 1970s–1990s, Artist, Canadian
Rainer, Carl, Novelty Songs, 1950s–1970s, Artist, American
Ren & Stimpy, Children's Songs; Christmas Songs; Novelty Songs, 1990s, Animation, American
Rene, Henri, Lounge Music, 1950s, Producer; Artist, German
Rey, Albino, Lounge Music, 1940s–1980s, Artist, American
Richard, Cliff, Christmas Songs, 1960s–, Artist, British
Riddle, Nelson, Easy Listening, 1950s–1980s, Artist, American
Ritchie, Jim, Novelty Songs, 1990s, Artist, American
Rivers, Bob, Novelty Songs, 1990s–, Artist, American
Robey, George, Music Hall, 1880s–1900s, Artist, British
Robison, Carson, Novelty Songs, 1920s–1950s, Artist, American
Roper, Skid, Novelty Songs, 1980s–1990s, Artist, American
Royal Guardsmen, The, Novelty Songs, 1960s, Artist, American
Royal Philharmonic Orchestra, Easy Listening, 1970s, Artist, British
Santo & Johnny, Easy Listening, 1950s–1970s, Artist, American
Sarducci, Father Guido, Novelty Songs, 1980s, Artist, American
Scott, Raymond, Lounge Music; Novelty Songs, 1930s–1980s, Artist; Composer, American
Screaming Santas, Christmas Songs; Novelty Songs, 1990s, Artist, American
Sedlar, James, Easy Listening, 1960s, Artist, American
Sellers, Peter, Novelty Songs, 1950s–1970s, Artist, British
Sesame Street, Children's Songs, 1970s–, Animation, American
Seville, David, Novelty Songs, 1950s–1960s, Artist, American
Sha Na Na, Novelty Songs, 1960s–, Artist, American
Shaggs, The, Novelty Songs, 1960s–1970s, Artist, British
Sharon, Lois & Bram, Children's Songs, Artist, Canadian
Shatner, William, Novelty Songs, 1990s–, Artist, American
Shaw, Robert, Easy Listening, 1950s–, Artist, American
Sherman, Allan, Novelty Songs, 1960s, Artist, American
Sigue Sigue Sputnik, Novelty Songs, 1980s–, Artist, British
Simpsons, The, Novelty Songs, 1990s–, Animation, American
Sinatra, Frank, Easy Listening, 1950s–1990s, Artist, American
Sixpence None The Richer, Contemporary Christian Music, 1990s–, Artist, American
Slade, Christmas Songs, 1970s, Artist, British
Slatkin, Felix, Lounge Music, 1970s, Artist, American
Slim & Slam, Novelty Songs, 1930s–1940s, Artist, American
Smith, Dick, Christmas Songs, 1930s, Artist, American
Smith, Michael W., Contemporary Christian Music, 1970s–, Artist, American
Smurfs, The, Children's Songs; Christmas Songs, 1980s–1990s, Animation, American
Soulful Strings, Christmas Songs, 1960s, Artist, American
Sounds Of Blackness, Contemporary Christian Music, 1970s–, Artist, American
Spector, Phil, Christmas Songs, 1960s–1970s, Producer, American
Spinal Tap, Novelty Songs, 1980s–1990s, Artist, British
Springer, Jerry, Novelty Songs, 1990s, Artist, American
St James, Rebecca, Contemporary Christian Music, 1990s–, Artist, Australian–American
Stanshall, Vivian, Novelty Songs, 1960s–1980s, Artist, British
Stereolab, Easy Listening, 1990s–, Artist, British
Stevens, Ray, Novelty Songs, 1960s–, Artist, American
Stonehill, Randy, Contemporary Christian Music, 1960s–1970s, Artist, American
Stryper, Contemporary Christian Music, 1980s, Artist, American
Sturr, Jimmy, Easy Listening, 1960s–, Artist, American
Stuttering John, Novelty Songs, 1990s, Artist, American
Sumac, Yma, Lounge Music, 1950s–1980s, Artist, Peruvian
Swann, Donald, Novelty Songs, 1940s, Composer, Artist, British
Swayne, Steve, Novelty Songs, 1990s, Artist, American
Tappet Brothers, Novelty Songs, 1990s, Artist, American
Taylor, Steve, Contemporary Christian Music, 1980s–1990s, Artist, American
Teicher, Louis, Lounge Music, 1950s–1990s, Artist, American
Tenuta, Judy, Novelty Songs, 1980s–1990s, Artist, American
Texas Chainsaw Orchestra, 1990s, Artist, American
Thackeray Jake, Novelty Songs Songs, 1960s–2000s, Artist; Songwriter, British
Third Day, Contemporary Christian Music, 1990s–, Artist, American
Thomas, Marlo, Children's Songs, 1970s–1980s, Artist, American
Thomas, Peter, Lounge Music, 1960s, Artist, German
Thompson, Bob, Lounge Music, 1970s–1990s, Artist, American
Three Suns, The, Lounge Music, 1940s–1950s, Artist, American
Tiny Tim, Novelty Songs, 1960s–1990s, Artist, American
Top Dog, Christmas Songs; Novelty Songs, 1990s, Artist, American
Trenet, Charles, Nostalgia, 1930s–1970s, Artist, French
Troccoli, Kathy, Contemporary Christian Music, 1980s–, Artist, American
Trucker Wally, Novelty Songs, 1990s, Artist, American
Tucker, Sophie, Nostalgia, 1910s–1960s, Artist, American
Tweets, The, Novelty Songs, 1980s, Artist, British
Yankovic, Frankie, Easy Listening, 1940s–1990s, Artist, American
Yankovic, "Weird Al", Novelty Songs, 1980s–1990s, Artist, American
Vallée, Rudy, Nostalgia, 1920s–1960s, Artist, American
Van Dyke, Dick, Children's Songs, 1960s, Artist, American
Vaughn, Billy, Easy Listening, 1950s–1970s, Artist, American
Velasquez, Jaci, Contemporary Christian Music, 1990s–, Artist, Latin American
Venus Envy, Novelty Songs, 1980s–1990s, Artist, American
Verne, Larry, Novelty Songs, 1960s, Artist, American
Wanderley, Walter, Lounge Music, 1960s–1980s, Artist, Brazilian
Welk, Lawrence, Easy Listening, 1950s–1980s, Artist, American
West, Mae, Nostalgia, 1920s–1970s, Artist, American
Weston, Paul, Easy Listening, 1940s–1960s, Artist, American
Weymes, Ted, Nostalgia, 1920s–1940s, Artist; Composer, American
Wham!, Christmas Songs, 1980s, Artist, British
White, Ron, Novelty Songs, 1990s, Artist, American
Williams, Roger, Easy Listening, 1950s–1990s, Artist, American
Willis, Wesley, Novelty Songs, 1990s–, Artist, American
Winans, The, Contemporary Christian Music, 1980s–, Artist, American
Winans, Vicki, Contemporary Christian Music, 1980s–1990s, Artist, American
Winston, George, Christmas Songs, 1970s–, Artist, American
Wirtz, Billy C., Novelty Songs, 1980s–, Artist, American
Wood, Roy, Christmas Songs, 1970s, Artist, British
Wooley, Sheb, Novelty Songs, 1940s–1970s, Artist, American
Wright, Steve, Novelty Songs, 1970s, Artist, British
Zacherly, John, Novelty Songs, 1960s, Artist, American

CONTEMPORARY CHRISTIAN MUSIC ➡ 422 NOVELTY SONGS ➡ 424 MUSIC HALL ➡ 425 CHILDREN'S SONGS ➡ 426 CHRISTMAS SONGS ➡ 427
EASY LISTENING ➡ 428 LOUNGE MUSIC ➡ 432 NOSTALGIA ➡ 434

Instruments

PERCUSSION INSTRUMENTS

BASS DRUM

The dominant feature of every military band is its big bass drum. Throughout the history of percussion instruments, this drum has been the mainstay of time-keeping, whether it is used for a marching army or in a late-twentieth century heavy metal band.

Early versions of the bass drum (it was certainly known in Asia around 3500 BC) were often gigantic constructions, although the world's largest bass drum record is claimed by one with a diameter of over 3 metres: built for Disneyland by Remo of Hollywood. Both sides of the drum have heads, so the marching player can strike the heads with felt-covered drumsticks with alternate hands. The resulting boom has great power, but the drum is not really suited to rapid notes or drumrolls.

In an orchestra, the bass drum is usually held in a tilting position on a stand that can be adjusted for a better angle of attack. A smaller bass drum – struck by a foot pedal – is a staple of the drum kit (ideal as an advertisement hoarding, like Ringo Starr's Ludwig bass drum for the Beatles). In the late 1960s and early 1970s there was a vogue for using a double bass drum kit inspired by Cream's Ginger Baker.

CASTANETS

Castanets are closely associated with the musical and dance traditions of Spain, but they are by no means unique to the Iberian peninsula. Clappers were played as far back as Sumerian times, and the Egyptians fashioned wood, bone and ivory into forearms and hands that worked like castanets.

Castanets are disc-shaped pieces of wood hollowed out on one side with a loop of cord holding each pair together. Although the word castanet derives from *castaña*, the Spanish for 'chestnut', they are most frequently made from other woods, including walnut and ebony.

In performance, the loop is placed round the thumb or middle finger, so the two halves can be snapped together by the palm and fingers.

Flamenco dance virtuosos like Antonio Gades and Cristina Hoyos have the ability to manipulate the castanets with spellbinding speed and breathtaking dexterity to complement the rhythm of their footwork. In the orchestra, for ease of use, the castanets are mounted on the end of a stick and held apart by elastic.

CONGAS

The rhythm sections of Latin American bands are enhanced by a range of propulsive percussion instruments, of which the largest are the congas, the single-headed drums that found their way from Africa to Cuba and beyond.

The congas – also known as tumba drums – have an upright barrel shape: the body of the drum is made of hard wood or fibreglass, open at the bottom and supported by four legs. A vellum or calfskin head is held tight on to the body below the actual level of the drumhead, giving the player unencumbered access to all parts of the head. As with the tabla, the skill lies in using all parts of the hand, including the flat palm and the fingertips.

Generally used in pairs with different pitches, the congas are frequently complemented in Latin American line-ups by:

- Timbales: a pair of high-pitched metal-shelled drums, played with sticks and mounted on a stand with a cowbell.
- Bongos: two small bucket-shaped wooden drums, joined by a metal bar and played with the thumb and fingers.

CYMBALS

We know that the clashing of "loud" and "well-tuned" cymbals were familiar to the writers of the Psalms, but their origins are unclear: certainly they were first used in the East, possibly in Assyria or Turkey, from where they reached the orchestras of Western Europe during the eighteenth century.

Cymbals are concave plates of brass or bronze, held at the centre – either by leather handles or a pole – so that the edges of the metal can vibrate. Their manufacture remains a craft full of closely guarded secrets and tradition: the present-day Zildjian cymbal company is descended from a long line of Turkish cymbal-makers.

There are now hundreds of varieties to select from, particularly for use on a drum kit, including:

- The crash: a bright cymbal with a fast crescendo.
- The sizzle: with half a dozen rivets set loosely in the cymbal.
- The ride: a ringing cymbal for driving the rhythm along.
- The hi-hat: two smaller cymbals clashed together by pedal action.

For alternative effects the cymbals can be played with drum sticks, timpani sticks or wire brushes – or even recorded backwards, as the Beatles did on 'Strawberry Fields Forever'.

DRUM KIT

The drum kit is so much a part of contemporary music that it's easy to forget it's a relatively recent invention, even though the separate elements that make it up often date to antiquity. In the 1900s, a need emerged for a way of playing various percussion instruments, ideally while sitting down; this need was driven in the main, though not exclusively, by jazz drummers.

The resulting set-up was first known as "traps" (short for contraption – a term still used by some players) and was common by the 1920s in Dixieland and dance bands. By the 1950s the basic combination of instruments and implements had stabilized:

- Bass drum (smaller than in military bands), struck by a floor-pedal beater.
- Snare drum.
- Different sized tom-toms and cymbals mounted either on the drum or a floor stand.
- Hi-hat cymbal (two cymbals clashed together by a foot pedal).

Drummers can explore endless variations: double bass drums (Billy Cobham once used three!), additional instruments like wood blocks, and also a customized mix of drum heads, cymbal shapes or stick weights, so each drummer creates a blend of sounds that becomes his or her signature.

GONG

The gong has played an important role in the theatre and in religious ceremonies – particularly in the Far East and Central Asia, where it is believed to have originated; in Malaysia gongs were long considered a valuable part of any dowry.

Essentially a large round dish of metal with an upturned edge, often with a raised boss at its centre, the gong is hit with a padded drumstick or beater, the heavier the better to build its crescendo of sound. In the classical orchestra, the instrument – about 100 cm in diameter, with a hammered surface and suspended from a frame – is technically called the "tam-tam".

Gongs feature large in the gamelan music of Indonesia; more recently new-age practitioners of "gong therapy" have used them. Twentieth-century composers also sought to expand its sound range by instructing the percussionist to play the gong with a violin bow (Kryzstof Penderecki) or lower it into water (John Cage).

MARACAS

The hustling, shaking sound of the maracas is an essential part of Cuban music (the rumba and the mambo), although rattles go back to the Egyptians and beyond, in fact predating the drum. Many civilizations believed that the rattle's sound can ward off evil spirits or win over benevolent deities.

The sound of the maracas is multi-textured, but the technology is straightforward: a pair of round or egg-shaped containers, made from gourds, wood or plastic, mounted on the end of sticks, filled with anything from beans or pebbles to buttons or lead shot to provide the necessary sizzle. Various techniques are available, including twirling both maracas to create a kind of drumroll, banging one maraca into an open hand, or flicking the shot into the top side of the maracas before letting it fall back to the bottom for a double shuffle.

Bo Diddley's right-hand man, maracas player Jerome Green, was an essential component of the distinctively syncopated sound of Diddley's singles in the 1950s. Mick Jagger was a fan of both men and was rarely without his maracas during early Rolling Stones' performances.

SNARE DRUM

The insistent rhythm of the snare drum has accompanied war, work and play since antiquity. The Romans marched to its beat, Elizabethan revellers danced to the pipe and tabor and in the days before field telephones, military messages were transmitted via drum calls. In the twentieth century the snare (or side) drum became an essential part of the standard drum kit, and provided the off-beat drive of rock'n'roll.

In its simplest form the snare drum is a small, cylindrical drum covered with parchment. What gives the drum its distinctive sound is the snare: a strip of metal wires, nylon or gut stretched across the bottom of the drum. When the drummer strikes the top skin, the snare vibrates and the high-pitched rattle is able to slice through the loudest of bands and the fiercest of battles.

The military snare drum is hung over the drummer's shoulder, with the drumhead at an angle for ease of access; rolls, flams and paradiddles support the brass or bagpipes. In jazz and rock the rim shot, a smart crack with the stick simultaneously hitting the metal rim and the drumhead, is a frequent device.

STEEL DRUMS

The steel drum or steelpan is a relatively recent addition to the ranks of percussion instruments. It wasfirst created in Trinidad in the 1930s and 40s, when a plentiful supply of 45-gallon oil drums was available; and it was found that they could be sliced in half, turned upside down and tuned.

Creating a finished steel drum involves cutting the pans to size, sinking down the main pan with a sledge-hammer, defining the areas for up to 30 different notes with compass, chalk, hammer and punch, and then hammering each note back up to form a low dome. Each note is carefully tuned – usually by ear. Finally the drum is tempered and painted, or electroplated, ready for players to use sticks with rubber tips.

A complete range of drums form families, either called after choir voices (treble, alto, bass) or traditional instruments (guitar, cello) supported by a rhythm section. The steel orchestra, particularly in the major West Indian carnivals, can require anywhere up to 100 performers, producing a significantly uplifting volume of sound.

TABLA

It is said that the tabla – the double drums that have been a primary instrument in the classical music of northern India, Bangladesh and Pakistan since the end of the eighteenth century – have the power to talk at the hands of a skilled player. Certainly many people consider that the tabla represents the pinnacle of percussive ability.

The tabla consists of two individual drums, each with its own character. The lower is the bayan – or bhaya – usually positioned to the musician's left (the word *bayan* in fact means "left"), which has a copper shell, somewhat like a kettledrum, and a double-skinned head attached to the drum body by laces. The distinctive off-centre black spot, a patch made from a concoction using flour, iron filings, tamarind juice and other secret ingredients, lies under the fingertips. The smaller drum, the tabla, has a wooden body; its black patch is in the middle of the head.

The two drums lie on cushions, and players, sitting cross-legged, with the drums between their knees, use all parts of the hand – the heel, fingertips, knuckles and nails – to bring out all the expressive quality of the drums.

TAMBOURINE

The tambourine is one of the oldest – but one of the most underrated – of all instruments. The version used today has changed little from that used thousands of years ago by the ancient Greeks (which they called the "timpnon"). Egyptian friezes show tambourines in the hands of women celebrating sacred ceremonies.

Although its construction is simple – a shallow, round wooden frame or hoop, sometimes with a single, taut, parchment head, and circular metal discs set in pairs into the hoop – the tambourine's bright, fluttering jingle can lift a piece of music on its own. The player can shake the tambourine for a constant, rhythmic pulse, use the finger pads to provide a sharp tap, or strike the tambourine on to a knee, leg or open hand; the thumb trill involves moistening the thumb and running it round the edge of the tambourine.

The tambourine has proved particularly versatile throughout its life: as appropriate to the religious rites of antiquity as it is in folk dancing

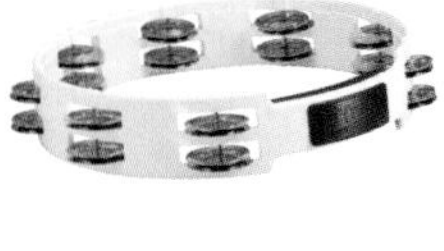

(particularly in Spain), marching band, who borrowed the instrument from Turkish military music, in rock and pop line-ups, and through generations of Salvation Army bands.

TIMPANI

The shape of their copper cauldrons suggests the term "kettledrums"; the Italian name "timpani", referring to the drumhead, is from the word for a membrane of the ear. Bowl-shaped drums appear in Babylonian drawings, but they first entered Western consciousness when Crusaders brought back examples mounted on horses, camels or carriages.

The essence of the timpani is the fact they can be tuned. Originally this was achieved – with difficulty – by a network of laces, before the introduction of tension screws set round the collar. The problem was that each drum could only play one note at one time, limiting the range or demanding serried ranks of drums. Various people (including Leonardo da Vinci and Adolphe Sax) tried inventing systems, but only the arrival of pedal tuning in the 1880s finally solved the problem. Now pedals change tunings in a second or two and allow a glissando effect where the note is deliberately allowed to slide up or down.

Their great dynamism and colour, and an ability to create special effects – storms, gunfire in Sergey Prokofiev's *Peter and the Wolf*, a beating heart in Piotr Ilyich Tchaikovsky's *Romeo and Juliet* – has made timpani central to the percussion section.

TUBULAR BELLS

The sound of a bell can carry for miles, celebrating weddings or warning of attack. Since the great foundry cast bells are weighed in tons, they are less than practical for concert use – hence the invention of the tubular bells by John Hampton of Coventry in the 1880s.

The tubular bells (known in the US as "chimes") are a portable, efficient way of reproducing the bell sound, although they can never reproduce the sheer power of a genuine belfry. The most common version uses 18 narrow tubes, of the same width but different lengths to produce an octave and a half of individual chromatic notes. They are hung on a frame, damped by a foot-operated pedal to stop the sound and struck by a wooden mallet or a drumstick at the top of the tube.

Other instruments that composers and arrangers can turn to for bell sounds include:

- Handbells, played by teams of ringers.
- Traditional sleigh bells.
- The cowbell, often mounted on top of a drum kit.
- The triangle, which although a single steel rod, has a clear ringing tone with the ability to cut through the largest of orchestras or bands.

VIBRAPHONE

The vibraphone, or vibes, took the metal of the glockenspiel – a small xylophone with metal bars – and added metal resonators underneath the bars, kept in motion by an electric motor to provide a quivering, breathy edge to the sound. Originally called the vibraharp, it was invented in the early twentieth century; dance and jazz bands were quick to pick up on its potential.

The glockenspiel ("bell-play" in German), struck with metal beaters, was a relatively simple instrument, and could be carried in marching bands mounted on a rod, when it was known as the bell-lyra. The vibraphone added luscious layers of sophistication: the speed of the vibrations could be varied and a sustain pedal controlled the length of the notes. Another incarnation is the tubaphone, which has metal tubes rather than bars, creating a softer sound.

The jazz world has produced the largest crop of virtuoso vibraphone players, most using a pair of mallets per hand, allowing them to play chords.

WASHBOARD

A staple instrument in zydeco music (black American dance music, also featuring guitar and accordian) and the skiffle bands of the late 1950s, the washboard is one of the most widely used of the instruments that produce their sound by scraping. It is a form of rhythm-making that goes way back. It is also an example of inventive recycling for musical purposes, since the washboard was adapted directly from the domestic corrugated metal board once used in washing clothes.

The washboard as an instrument is based on the same principle as the guiro, a Latin American instrument that uses a stick scraped along the serrated notches carved into a wood block or gourd, except that the washboard creates its sound from the contact between metal and metal – players place thimbles on the ends of their fingers to produce a harder-edged, more rasping sound than the gentler guiro.

Over the years musical washboards have become increasingly elaborate constructions, worn over the shoulder and round the player's neck like an apron and involving Edward Scissorhands-style industrial gloves tipped with metal talons.

XYLOPHONE

The wood on wood sound of the xylophone (*xylo* from the Greek for "wood"), produces a dry, choppy sound that has its roots in much ethnic music: the gamelan orchestras of Indonesia use bamboo, African native instruments used wooden bars set in frames and before that simple logs.

The tuned wooden bars (ideally Honduras rosewood, although some are now synthetic) are the same overall size, but with different-sized recesses underneath to create the pitch of individual notes. Layout of the three to four octaves of notes is as the piano keyboard, with the "black" notes raised from the "white" notes. There is no sustain on a xylophone, so players compensate by relying on a tremolando or trill technique; a range of beaters can also brighten or mellow the notes.

The xylophone's role as a concert instrument is primarily due to the Polish player Michael Josef Gusikov, who performed throughout Europe in the 1830s; the instrument enjoyed a vogue for the next 100 years, and was particularly popular during the early days of the gramophone and radio.

BRASS INSTRUMENTS

BUGLE

Best known in its military guise, the bugle is one of the simplest of brass instruments in terms of construction, but it is very difficult to play. The single tube of metal has no valves to help create different notes, so players have to do all the work by changing their embouchure – a combination of the tightness of the lips and the amount of air pushed through them.

Although simple tube trumpets date back to the Roman "tuba", the bugle was a development from circular hunting horns and the usually straight posthorns used by mail-coaches to announce the arrival of the post from the fifteenth century onwards. A coiled horn emerged during the Seven Years' War of the mid-eighteenth century as an army signalling device. By 1800 the English bugle had stabilized as a single loop of copper or brass with a bell at the front, trumpet-style; following the Crimean War the double-loop form was standard.

Because of the restricted range of notes available, bugles were rarely heard outside the context of the army, although orchestral composers did use them to add a whiff of the battlefield. A keyed bugle was patented in 1810, but was shortly replaced by the cornet and the flugelhorn.

CORNET

Many people find it difficult to distinguish between the cornet, stalwart of the brass band, and the trumpet, since at first sight the cornet looks like a squat, fat trumpet. Although they share much in common, the essential difference lies in the conical shape of the cornet's body.

Although it works like a trumpet, the conical bore is more like that of a horn, and as a result the cornet possesses a tone which is sweeter, less piercing and more expressive than the trumpet. A deeper mouthpiece also allows players greater versatility: the cornet is a solo instrument of great agility, handling fast, complex runs with nonchalance.

The cornet emerged in the early 1800s as a valved variation on the German posthorn, and even briefly threatened to drive the trumpet out of the symphonic orchestra (an idea strongly supported by playwright George Bernard Shaw). In the nineteenth century, it emerged in the ranks of the brass bands, but it also proved to be a popular solo instrument in early jazz orchestras. The cornet's cousin, the flugelhorn, was a valved bugle that likewise never quite achieved symphonic status (although Ralph Vaughan Williams gave it a prominent role in his Ninth Symphony).

FRENCH HORN

The circular shape of the horn is a visual guide to its lineage as a technologically advanced descendant of the traditional hunting horn. The French horn – the name used in English since the 1600s – could more accurately be called the German horn, since that was the true centre of its development.

The distinctive characteristics of the French horn are its constantly growing conical tube ending in a widely flared bell, and a funnel-shaped mouthpiece, both of which contribute to its mellow tone. Much of the history of the horn revolves around players' attempts to control its tuning, using a hand in the bell to change natural notes by a semitone, or relying on sets of cumbersome crooks until the arrival and acceptance of valves during the nineteenth century.

Even with the use of valves, horn players still rely on stopping the bell with a hand to control tuning, helping to create the horn's distant-sounding tone. The sheer playing difficulty has resulted in few concertos for the instrument; orchestral composers rely on at least two pairs working in tandem. Applications in jazz or rock music tend to be found less frequently.

SOUSAPHONE

A common misconception about the all-American sousaphone is that the instrument was invented from scratch by the March King, John Philip Sousa. In reality Sousa, who was in charge of the US Marine Band in the 1890s, asked Philadelphia instrument makers J.W. Pepper to modify an instrument called the helicon; the company named the final result in his honour.

The helicon was a circular bass tuba created in Vienna in the 1840s; the sousaphone added a detachable bell pointing straight up on early versions, and later in a forward direction. In fact there is no technical need for the bell, now often made of fibreglass: it has a purely decorative role. The player stands inside the circular tubing, which sits coiled like a metal boa constrictor over one shoulder and under the other.

Adjusted and reshaped to improve the ease of carrying such a heavy bass instrument, the sousaphone is particularly suited for the American marching band. It was also a regular part of Dixieland bands, adding some beef to the bass part in the rhythm section. It is rarely seen in Europe.

THE SAXOPHONE FAMILY

Musicologists say, with justification, that the saxophone is a wind instrument because it combines a clarinet mouthpiece and an oboe-like body. But the instrument has always been a slightly uneasy hybrid because of its brass construction – and now sits as comfortably in a brass section as the trumpet or trombone.

In the 1840s Adolphe Sax, the prolific Belgian-born, Paris-based instrument maker, was seeking a way to fill a gap between the clarinet and tenor brass instruments. Using recent improvements in woodwind key construction he developed the instrument, including the upturned bell of the bass clarinet, and began supplying it to military bands. Eventually some classical composers saw its potential (Ravel included sax parts in *Boléro*) but it was the jazz- and dance-band worlds which took it to new heights.

Of the 14 members of the family. the most commonly used – apart from the tenor are:

- B-flat soprano: usually in its straight version, capable of a strident or other-worldly sound.
- E-flat alto: a creamy tone, often delivered with a soulful feel.
- E-flat baritone: plenty of growling punch in the lower register.

TENOR SAXOPHONE

The B-flat tenor saxophone is by far the best known of the saxophone family. After a sluggish start, where its appearance was limited to military bands, a move indoors ensured that its distinctive timbre would create some of the best popular music of the twentieth century – from rock'n'roll to funk, soul to jazz, for which it became a universal icon. When the tenor sax was adopted by the jazz world it was imbued with the dangerous allure the electric guitar held for a different generation.

A tenor sax can deliver both the emotional immediacy and the lack of precision in tuning and note placing which horrified many classical composers and attracted jazz performers. The mouth's direct contact with the instrument allows the saxophonist to communicate as if through speech patterns, bringing his or her personality into direct connection with the audience.

The technique of circular breathing – where the player breathes in through their nose and out through the mouth and instrument simultaneously, using the cheeks like bellows – is challenging but allows long fluid lines of improvization.

TROMBONE

The noble sound of the trombone (although Sir Thomas Beecham dubbed it "a quaint and ancient drainage system") has changed remarkably little since its appearance in the fifteenth century, other than the later addition of a flared bell. It is the only naturally chromatic brass instrument: the slide actually predated the valves trumpeters and horn players use by some four centuries.

Every note on the trombone is played by one of the seven positions of the detachable slide – valve trombones do exist, but purists believe it creates a significant loss of tone. The glissando slide up or down the scale is a unique – and sometimes deliberately comic – effect, but what is perceived of as the trombone's exaggerated expressiveness has limited the classical solo repertory.

The trombone is available in a range of choral voices, including a soprano version, but by far the most common is the tenor, followed by the bass. A late entrant to orchestral music – towards the end of the eighteenth century – it forms the heart of orchestral brass. It was quickly adopted by jazz line-ups (even handling the difficulties of be-bop) and has become an essential ingredient in soul, funk and rock horn sections.

TRUMPET

When Tutankhamen's tomb was re-opened, two metal trumpets were discovered: proof that the trumpet has, for at least 3,000 years, been an instrument of great pomp. Court trumpeters were held in high esteem through to the 1600s. The instrument experienced a decline in popularity during the Classical era but began to rise again in the twentieth century. The instrument really found its *raison d'être*, however, with the arrival of jazz.

Common to all trumpets is a cylindrical metal bore, flared at the end. In the same way as other brass instruments, the trumpet's brilliant flourish is produced through air being vibrated by the player's embouchure – like blowing a raspberry, except putting the tongue behind the front teeth. Until the fifteenth century different notes could only be produced by tightening the embouchure, but thereafter additional loops, crooks, slides and valves were gradually added to the trumpet.

Following various tunings, the B-flat trumpet had become the norm by 1900. The three valves are pushed down to divert the air into separate loops; played in combination they can create every regular note, but high ones are still difficult. A plastic or wooden mute, placed in the bell of the trumpet, technically deadens the sound, but produces a haunting, plaintive sound.

WOODWIND INSTRUMENTS

BAGPIPE

Somewhere, perhaps in Mesopotamia, about 7,000 years ago, a shepherd may well have looked at a goat skin and some hollow bones and had an idea for a new musical instrument: the bagpipe. In the early Christian era, the instrument spread from the Middle East eastward into India and westward to Europe. By the seventeenth century bagpipes were being played in European courts, but by the eighteenth century they were declining to become a minority folk instrument. In countries as diverse as Albania, Spain, Scotland and Ireland, the bagpipe is rightly valued as a living part of the culture.

BASSOON

The bassoon is known for its twin characteristics – as the "clown", for its comic effects, or the "gentleman", for its eloquent, lyrical capacities. Its early development is thought to have followed the reconstruction of the shawm, a strident-sounding instrument often played in outdoor ceremonies during the Middle Ages and the Renaissance. Similarities in design and use also suggest the curtal or dulcian was the true forerunner of the bassoon.

It was used in Henry Purcell's 1691 score *The History of Dioclesian* and the English musicologist James Talbot identified "a bassoon in four joynts" around 1695. The four-key version made by the Denners of Nuremberg was the eighteenth-century standard, and Carl Almenräder's 15-key bassoon met nineteenth-century demands for louder, more reliable, instruments. Two types now commonly used are made by the Heckel family and the Buffet-Crampon firm.

The bassoon has a smoother and less reedy sound than the oboe and is the true bass of the woodwind group. The size of this bass instrument poses special problems. The nine-foot-long tube has to be doubled back on itself and the finger-holes bored obliquely to be reached by the player's fingers. Böhm's key innovations did not work well for the bassoon, and its resultant system is exceptionally difficult to play. With a reed made by bending double a shaped strip of cane, the bassoon's sound is one of the orchestra's primary colours.

CLARINET

The clarinet's predecessor was a small single-reeded mock trumpet called a chalumeau. It is not certain, but the invention of the clarinet is ascribed to Johann Christoph Denner of Nuremburg in the early 1700s. With its strong upper register, it found a place in military bands, but was not regularly used in the orchestra until around 1800. The clarinet is usually made of African blackwood. To play it, you blow, gripping the mouthpiece, reed down, between your lips or lower lip and upper teeth.

The clarinet has an acoustical feature that sets it apart: if you blow harder, or "overblow", on other woodwinds the pitch goes up an octave, but on a clarinet it goes up an octave and a fifth. The clarinet's separate registers produce a range of characteristic timbres (sounds) – rich and oily in the lowest register, slightly pale in the middle, clear and singing in the higher and shrill at the top.

There are two distinct key systems:

- Albert system: developed by Eugène Albert of Brussels, this is a modernisation of Iwan Müller's 13-key system of around 1812. Used in German-speaking countries.
- Böhm system: patented by Klosé and Buffet (Paris, 1844), it incorporates much of Böhm's 1832 flute fingering system. It brings many technical advantages and is standard in most countries.

DIDGERIDOO

The is probably the best-known instrument of Australia and is played by the Aboriginals of that country. At least 40 aboriginal names for it are known, from the north of Western Australia through the Arnhem Land peninsula to northern Queensland. Aboriginals trace the birth of the didgeridoo (also spelt didjeridu) to their ancestral Dreamtime, although some research suggests its origin might have been as recent as 1,000 years ago.

A type of drone pipe or straight wooden trumpet, the didgeridoo is an unstopped hollowed piece of bamboo or wood about four or five feet long, with a bore of two inches or more and a mouth-piece made of wax or hardened gum. Bamboo didgeridoos are traditionally hollowed out with a fire stick or hot coals. The yidaki is a hardwood version particular to Arnhem Land. Although traditional instrument-making techniques continue, they have also been made out of salvaged materials such as exhaust pipes.

The player blows into the instrument trumpet-fashion; the sound can vary from a continuous fundamental drone to a sharp "toot". Using a process of circular breathing, with the cheeks being used much like bellows, players can set up remarkable continuous drones. Traditionally, the didgeridoo accompanies clicking sticks, singing and dancing, primarily in more "open" ceremonies such as clan songs. Boys learn to play from an early age and talented players are recognized and held in high esteem by their community.

FLUTE

To have heard some of the earliest flute music, you would have had to be sitting in a cave 45,000 years ago, where a Neanderthal musician in Slovenia is thought to have fashioned such an instrument from the leg bone of a bear. The flute was known in ancient Greece by the second century BC, but it was not until around 1100 that it began to be used in Europe. King Henry VIII, a keen musician, had a good collection of them.

The sound is made when the flautist blows a stream of air against the edge of a hole in the side of the flute, causing the air enclosed in the instrument to vibrate. It was Theobald Böhm, a Munich flute player and inventor, who made the modern instrument possible. His definitive 1847 design incorporated an ingenious system of keys and levers. Before keys, fingerholes had to be placed where the player could reach them; with keys they could be positioned to achieve the best possible note. A modern flute is made of wood, or more commonly (since the twentieth century) of metal such as silver; and it is 67 cm (26.5 in) long.

KAZOO

A kazoo is one of a family of instruments called mirlitons. They have in common a membrane which is vibrated by sound waves produced either by the player's voice or by an instrument. The distinctive sound produced has a buzzing quality, and the kazoo is the best-known member of the mirliton family. This has a membrane set into the wall of a short tube into which the player makes vocal noises. Many pop and jazz musicians have used kazoos in their music.

An even simpler homemade version has probably been tried by every child using tissue paper and a comb. Less well-known is the fact that certain flutes contain mirlitons, for example the Chinese ti, and that some African xylophones have mirliton resonators to give a slight rasping, rattling tone to the notes. Using the same principle, African mirlitons can even be found with a vibrating membrane made from spiders' webs.

MOUTH ORGAN

The arrival of the Chinese sheng in Europe in the eighteenth century encouraged a great deal of experimentation with free-reed instruments in the early nineteenth century. One of the most popular was produced by Friedrich Buschmann of Berlin in 1821; this was the *Mundäoline*, now known as the mouth organ or harmonica.

From the early twentieth century, the instrument was adopted by folk and blues musicians, particularly in the US. Blues players gave it the name "harp" and could create powerful effects by altering the shape of the mouth, making the instrument shriek and moan or even imitate a rhythmic train.

Inside the mouth organ, free metal reeds are set in slots in a small, metal-enclosed wooden frame. The notes are sounded by alternately blowing and sucking through two parallel rows of wind channels. The reeds are positioned so they respond to alternate directions of wind flow. The tongue covers channels not required. In chromatic (12-note scale) models, a finger-operated stop alternates between two sets of reeds tuned a semitone apart. They can range from two to four octaves in compass, and bass models are also played.

OBOE

The word "oboe" comes from the French *hautbois*, meaning "high (or loud) wood". Its origins can be found in the shawm.

The orchestral oboe proper really came about during the mid-seventeenth century with the refinements of the French court musician, Jean Hotteterre, and others (it is worth noting that today, all orchestral instruments tune to the oboe). Having lost its former coarseness, it could be played indoors with stringed instruments and by the middle of the eighteenth century it was firmly established. Further improvements based on Theobald Böhm's key technologies have given the modern oboe one of the most complex key systems. The main types of oboe are:

- Treble or soprano oboe: the principal member of the family, pitched in C.
- Oboe d'amore : the alto oboe, pitched in A. So called for the warmth of its sound and much used in J. S. Bach's time.
- Cor anglais or English horn: neither English nor a horn, it is a tenor oboe pitched in F with a richer, more throaty tone.
- Baritone oboe: possibly originating in the seventeenth century, this is pitched in C an octave below the soprano.

PANPIPES

According to Greek legend, when Pan pursued the mountain-nymph Syrinx to the river's edge, she was transformed into reeds which he then fashioned into the Pan's pipes or Syrinx. The panpipes was also known in many other parts of the world, including China, Egypt and Oceania. In parts of Europe, for example the Pyrénées, it has been mainly a shepherd's instrument. In Romania, by contrast, the 15- to 29-pipe instrument called a nai is played in virtuoso professional folk groups. Panpipes are at their most haunting when heard in South American folk ensembles, whose melodies evoke the mystery and atmosphere of snow-capped mountains. They are still popular in many parts of that continent, such as Chile, Argentina, Bolivia, Paraguay and Peru.

The panpipes consist of cane pipes of different lengths, tied in a row or held together by other means and generally closed at the bottom. Metal, clay or wood versions are also made. The sound is produced when the player holds the pipe end to their mouth, blowing across the hole. Each pipe gives a different note. Although usually hand-held, the largest of the South American siku can exceed 2 m (6.5 ft) and has to be rested on the ground.

PICCOLO

This instrument's full name – *Flauto Piccolo*, Italian for "small flute" – says it all. It is the highest-pitched woodwind instrument to be found in orchestras and military bands, and its orchestral use dates from around the end of the eighteenth century, when it replaced the flageolet (also called at that time "flauto piccolo"). As with the flute, the player holds the instrument sideways and blows across the edge of a hole in the side of the instrument, finding just the right angle to make the sound. The sound has a high-pitched and shrill quality and can be heard above the range of other orchestral instruments.

Half the size of the standard flute, the piccolo has a conical or cylindrical bore and is a transverse (horizontally played) instrument. As with the ordinary concert flute, it is fitted with a key system developed by Theobald Böhm and the fingering is exactly the same. To make it easier for players of both instruments, piccolo music is written so that it looks the same, but the piccolo's notes are actually an octave higher than as written on the page.

RECORDER

The recorder has a long history in Western music, probably dating back to the fourteenth century, when it appears to have been a development from an earlier kindred instrument. In 1619 Michael Praetorius listed seven members of the recorder family in his *Syntagmatis Musici Tomus Secundus*. Its chief repertory comes from the Renaissance and Baroque periods, when it was very popular. Many composers, including J. S. Bach and George Frideric Handel, included recorder parts in their works, but its clear piping sound fell out of favour during the late eighteenth century.

The recorder was revived in 1919 by the English instrument maker Arnold Dolmetsch. Since this time the design of recorders has followed the early eighteenth-century Baroque style. They are made in four main sizes: descant (or soprano), treble (or alto), tenor and bass, although great bass, double bass and sporanino instruments are also made. They are traditionally made of wood, occasionally of ivory, although thousands are now made for schools using plastic.

The recorder has a beak-like mouthpiece at the top end of the instrument with a whistle-like aperture that provides the edge that makes the air vibrate when blown. The cylindrical body has holes that can be covered by seven fingers at the front and one thumb at the back to make different notes.

STRINGED INSTRUMENTS

ACOUSTIC GUITAR

Throughout its history, the guitar has – perhaps more than any other instrument – managed to bridge the gap between the often disconnected worlds of classical, folk and popular music. Its roots go back to Babylonian times, when reliefs reveal a plucked, guitar-like instrument; by the 1500s it was prevalent in Spain, and is still sometimes called the Spanish guitar.

Medieval versions – like the lute – sometimes sported rounded backs and paired strings: the 12-string guitar still exists (as heard on the Byrds' 'Mr Tambourine Man'). The standardized modern acoustic guitar has a flat back and sound board with a pronounced curved "waist" to the body.

The acoustic guitar remained relatively unchanged until the twentieth century, when additions included steel strings for greater attack in dance-band settings, where it took over from the banjo. This marked the beginning of the guitar's rise to a major role in popular music, leading directly to the development of the semi-acoustic and fully electric versions.

AEOLIAN HARP

The aeolian harp is one of the rare instruments that does not require a human player. Even more significantly, there is no automatic or mechanical replacement for the performer, as there is in the player piano, for example. All that the aeolian harp requires is the wind to activate its other-worldly sound – it takes its name from Aeolus, the Greek god of the winds.

The harp's origins are somewhat obscure, although it was certainly in use from the end of the sixteenth century. In construction it is not unlike the dulcimer: a box-like rectangular frame, about a metre long, with a range of strings made of gut laid across it. Each of these strings is tuned in unison (in other words, all to the same note) and the instrument is positioned at a suitable location to catch the wind. The current of air vibrates the strings to produce a soft humming sound; the stronger the wind the more harmonic overtones come into play, creating disembodied chords.

There have been efforts to modify the harp's simplicity by tuning the strings to a chord, but it is generally accepted that the purest form is the best. Some organs attempt to imitate its soft sound with a stop called the Aeolina or Aeoline.

BALALAIKA

The triangular shape of the balalaika is universally recognized, but few people are aware of the importance of its role in Eastern European music; the balalaika is the Russian guitar. Lute-like predecessors were known from as early as the twelfth century, but it was a Russian nobleman called Vasily Andreyev, a virtuoso balalaika performer, who improved, modified and standardized the traditional instrument in the late 1800s.

Andreyev's basic balalaika is characterized by the familiar shape: three strings and a fretted neck. The most common version is the "prima balalaika", which unusually has two of the three strings tuned to the same note: despite this apparent restriction the instrument has a surprisingly large range. In addition the top two strings are set much closer together, allowing the bottom string to be plucked hard by the left-hand thumb, creating the typical strumming effect.

Another of Andreyev's innovations was the creation of a balalaika family in a choice of sizes – from piccolo to contrabass. This range means that entire balalaika orchestras can be created using the one instrument, often backed up by the bayan (a Russian accordion), tambourines and various flutes and pipes.

BANJO

In 1688 the physician and naturalist Hans Sloane came across an instrument in Jamaica which he noted down as the "strum-strum". This was probably an early banjo, which had come to the Americas along with the shiploads of slaves transported from north-west Africa.

The banjo's most distinguishing features are its circular vellum or skin – a bit like a snare drum head – and long neck; a standard issue banjo has five strings, usually made of steel, although any number from four to nine are known. One string carries the melody, while the rest are ripe for finger-picking. The instrument's dry tone has a percussive, penetrating power and so it proved useful in adding volume and crispness in unamplified bands.

After the banjo's arrival in the New World, it accompanied spirituals, and thence became a regular ingredient in the Black Minstrel (and white pseudo-Minstrel) movement. In turn this led to its involvement in traditional Dixieland jazz; in the 1940s Bill Monroe introduced it to bluegrass music, from where it found its way into the 1970s country rock sound. The banjo also features in the music of countries such as Malawi and Morocco.

CELLO

Through performers like Jacqueline du Pré and Paul Tortelier, the cello has created a position for itself within the orchestral string family as an emotional vehicle, less brilliant and showy than the violin, less mysterious than the viola, more heart-rending than the double bass.

The full name of the cello is "violoncello", a small violone or bass viol. However its original name "basso di viola di braccio" meaning "bass arm viol" suggests that its roots lie more closely with the violin. The current tuning and size of the cello were pretty well fixed by the end of the seventeenth century, and the instrument established itself through continuous work in the Baroque period, asserting dominance over its closest challenger, the bass viol.

Surprisingly, despite its expressiveness, which appealed greatly to the Romantic movement, solo cello works were relatively infrequent until the arrival of the great soloists of the twentieth century – such as Pablo Casals and YoYo Ma – encouraged a cluster of works from the likes of Edward Elgar and Shostakovich. By contrast, Brazilian composer Villa-Lobos uses eight cellos and no other instruments to support a soprano voice in his 'Cantilena' from *Bachianas Brasileiras No. 5*.

DOUBLE BASS

The double bass was for a long time no more than a reinforcement at the foot of orchestral string arrangements, often merely echoing the cello part. It was rarely given a chance to shine by classical composers, but thanks to jazz the double bass found its voice with a vengeance, and was free to come out of the twilight into the limelight – even helping to kick off rock'n'roll on early Elvis tracks like 'That's All Right (Mama)'.

Of all the orchestral string instruments, the double bass is the most closely related to the viol, as a direct descendant of the sixteenth-century violone – a heritage revealed in its steeply sloping shoulders. The bass viol carried six strings; over time the number of strings dropped to four, although some modern double basses have a fifth string for rumbling low work. The double bass is available in a number of sizes: for orchestral work the three-quarter size is more common than the awkward full-size version.

Lower metal strings on the bass are not far off the consistency of steel hawsers, and bass players' fingers are usually topped off by calluses. In jazz settings the bass is generally plucked rather than bowed, whereas in orchestral settings it is the other way around. Jazz players are sometimes amplified to compete with the volume of the other instruments.

HARP

The harp is an instrument of great antiquity, appearing with frequency in the art and literature of the ancient Egyptians, Greeks, Hebrews and Celts – and during the medieval period. Common to all are an open frame, either curved or a two-sided angle – later enclosed by a fore-pillar – which contains strings vibrated by plucking.

The orchestral harp dates from the 1840s, a complex (and expensive) development of the simple frame harp. Expanding its range has been a challenge throughout its history, since all the strings are tuned to one scale – C flat major on today's harp. Awkward systems of hooks were tried out before a pedal system was developed in Bavaria and France. Seven pedals and a pin mechanism take the pitch of one set of strings up a semitone or tone.

The most commonly used harp techniques are the arpeggio – the notes of a chord rippled quickly and successively – and the glissando, the sweeping up and down of the strings that has unfortunately become a musical cliché. Harpists can in fact perform music as complex as that for the piano, although they can only play eight rather than 10 notes at one time, since the little finger is not used.

LUTE

A strong visual reminder of medieval music, the lute was a predominant instrument between the fifteenth and seventeenth centuries. It lost out to the guitar as the most used of the portable plucked instruments: the guitar proved more brilliant and versatile, but the musical world was deprived of the shimmering subtlety and persuasive charm that had made lutenists hypnotic performers.

Probably of Middle Eastern origin, derived from the Arab 'ud (which is still in use today), the lute gained wide coverage in Europe, from the French luth to the Romanian quitara – it was this European version that sported the body shape of a pear sliced in half. Other elements which set it apart from the guitar included the lack of a bridge, an ornate rose soundhole and the peg-box head at the top of the neck.

The lute contained a number of variations on the theme, including the large, double-necked arch-lute and the longer-necked theorbo.

Lute music was not read from classical musical notation but employed "tablature", a graphic representation that indicated the frets to be used. Within the music, the lute player – plucking with his or her fingers and in direct touch with the strings – had room to explore beautiful, gentle improvizations, either as a solo performer or accompanying dance or song.

MANDOLIN

The mandolin has some of the aspects of the guitar, violin and the lute – but unlike the lute it experienced a revival in the twentieth century in country and bluegrass.

The mandolin received an unexpected boost in public awareness thanks to the best-selling novel *Captain Corelli's Mandolin* by Louis de Bernières, himself a mandolin enthusiast. The instrument's name, derived from the Italian diminutive for an almond, refers to the shape of its body, which is often constructed from rosewood and inlaid with tortoiseshell.

Descended from the mandola, a fifteenth-century lute, the mandolin, or mandoline, has frets and a bridge like a guitar, but its strings are set in pairs tuned to the same note. The main technique involves playing these with a rapid tremolo, using a plectrum, to achieve a strongly percussive sound. Given the instrument's relatively small size, great dexterity is also required because the frets are so close to one another.

The mandolin has long been a popular instrument in southern Italy for serenaders – in Mozart's *Don Giovanni*, the Don serenades Elvira's maid on the mandolin in 'Deh, vieni alla finestra' – and featured in mandolin orchestras through to the beginning of the twentieth century. Bill Monroe, the father of bluegrass music, gave it another lease of life when he introduced the instrument to American country music in the 1940s.

SITAR

To Western ears the sitar became the quintessential sound of Indian music following its somewhat faddish promotion by the Beatles (through their collaboration with Ravi Shankar), the Rolling Stones and Traffic in the late 1960s – though its haunting sound has been a central part of Indian classical music for centuries.

Developed in the thirteenth century, the bulb-like body of the sitar, with something of the lute about it, is balanced by a thick fingerboard and extended neck. There are two sets of strings: four strings which play the melody line along with two or three drones, and a separate group of a dozen or more "sympathetic" strings which resonate in performance. A set of brass frets are both movable and curved, producing the instrument's distinctive bending, portamento sound.

Played in the lotus position, the sitar forms part of the classical Indian group, including the tabla, sarangi (a cello-like instrument) and shahnai (a relation of the oboe). Together they work around the complex improvised patterns of the raga, still alien to Western audiences: at the Concert for Bangladesh in 1971, Ravi Shankar received a rapturous ovation after several minutes, only to explain that he had in fact just been tuning up.

UKULELE

The ukulele, identified so closely with Hawaii, arrived on the island literally out of the blue, on a boat that arrived in Honolulu one day in 1879. One of the passengers produced a "braguinha" (a small Portuguese guitar) and the locals were smitten, adopting the instrument and calling it after a Polynesian word for a jumping flea – maybe referring to the movements of the player's fingers.

The tiny body of the braguinha was slightly enlarged – though not by much – and was strung with gut rather than steel. The native koa, an acacia, provided wood for the body. The versatile, and portable, ukulele was promoted by the Hawaiian royal family (one of whom wrote the classic 'Aloha Oe'), and then unleashed in the US after Hawaii took a stand at a San Francisco exposition in 1915. As things from the South Pacific came into vogue following the Second World War, the instrument enjoyed another burst of popularity, particularly led by Arthur Godfrey, who performed on a cheap plastic version. British audiences associate the ukulele with the toothy, winsome George 'When I'm Cleaning Windows' Formby, although he most often used a banjulele, a cross between the banjo and the ukulele.

VIOL

Partly because of the similarity of the names involved, viols are often assumed to be a variation of the orchestral string family. In fact, the viol family is a completely separate range of instruments (and indeed the first of the two to develop a distinctive identity) which were among the most important in Renaissance and early Baroque music.

The significant characteristics of the viol family, which probably originated in North Africa and reached Europe via Spain, are their completely flat back, sloping shoulders and fretted neck. Most viols have six gut strings – difficult to tune – and were always played in an upright position gripped between the knees.

The viol was particularly popular in England and France in the 1600s – households might own a chest of viols in different sizes, from treble to bass, and whole families played together. Charles I had his own consort, as did Oliver Cromwell. However the viol had effectively disappeared by the time the classical orchestra was established, and it was only in the 1890s that the instrument maker Arnold Dolmetsch promoted its revival.

VIOLA

The viola has been described as the Cinderella of the string section, frequently ignored and derided as something of a makeweight. However, its rich, mellow sound is a treat for the cognoscenti, who appreciate its value as a gastronome might savour a particularly exquisite truffle – indeed, woody and nutty are adjectives often applied to its tone.

Of all the strings, it is the one that bears the Italian name for the whole family – but by the end of the sixteenth century it had specifically come to mean the alto partner of the violin, tuned a fifth below its showier cousin. To correspond to that drop in pitch, it should be half as long again as the violin, making playing under the chin impractical; a compromise was reached, but even so the size of the instrument makes it difficult to hold.

Just as the double bass originally tended to echo the cello line, the viola had much the same role, shadowing the violins or even the bass; there are still few concertos or sonatas for the viola – which is something of a shame when you learn that many great composers were violists, including Mozart and J. S. Bach.

VIOLIN

The violin is perhaps the most familiar part of the classical orchestra and it is surprising that despite the scrolled head and horsehair bow that hark back to ages past, it is still the dominant orchestral instrument as well as a major force in folk, county and ethnic music.

Although there have been modifications to the instrument over the centuries, the violin of the 1600s is to all intents and purposes the same used today, including the f-shaped sound holes, the polished body with separate front and back, and the wooden tuning pegs. A straight and adjustable bow, the use of metal strings and the addition of a chin-rest were all in place by the nineteenth century.

Virtuosos such as Paganini delighted in the violin's instant and agile response, exploiting its armoury of techniques, including pronounced vibrato, staccato and pizzicato and more arcane techniques like striking the strings with the wood of the bow ("con legno") or bowing tight up to the bridge to create a harsher tone ("sul ponticello").

KEYBOARD INSTRUMENTS

ZITHER

The zither is part of a group of instruments which are linked by the fact that sets of strings run parallel to their main body, and that – unlike the lute, lyre or harp – they can still be played even without a resonating device. In the concept's least advanced state, native instruments exist which are little more than a stick carrying strings along its length.

Closely identified with the Alpine region of Europe – particularly the Austrian Tyrol – the zither is a closed wooden box which has anything from 30 to 40 strings lying across its surface. A number of these strings are placed over frets and can be stopped by the thumb of the left hand, while the right plucks the strings with a plectrum to pick out melodies or chords. In performance, the zither is usually placed on a table or on the knees of the performer.

Because the construction of the zither resembles keyboard instruments such as the harpsichord, it is sometimes seen as a relative of theirs. Other variants include:

- The dulcimer: struck by small wooden beaters, and popular in Hungarian and Romanian folk music.
- The cimbalom: a concert version of the dulcimer used for orchestral purposes.

CLAVICHORD

The clavichord affirms its place as the earliest of the string keyboard instruments in its very name, taken from the Latin for, simply, key and string. Chronologically older than the virginal and spinet – it is first mentioned in the 1400s – the clavichord differs from both since its strings were not plucked, and from the piano because they were not hit by hammers. Instead, small brass blades known as tangents would strike the strings from underneath.

The tangent would lift, strike and then hold the string in position, acting like a guitarist's or violinist's finger to determine the length of the vibrating string. This lessened the power of the instrument. What the clavichord lacked in volume it made up for in its response to the player's touch: the harder the key was pressed, the louder the note. After striking the string the player could also move the key up and down while the string continued to vibrate, creating a vibrato effect called "bebung".

Co-existing with the harpsichord from the sixteenth century onwards, the clavichord was popular for solo recitals throughout Europe, but particularly in Germany, where it continued to be played until the early nineteenth century. Arnold Dolmetsch championed its twentieth-century revival, as he did for many early instruments.

GRAND PIANO

The development of the early pianoforte into the magnificent grand piano was made possible by a number of innovations and inventions that together brought the kind of power and projection that could happily compete with the sound levels of a full orchestra or a jazz rhythm section.

A single cast-iron frame – perfected in the US – brought stability and the opportunity for more accurate tuning and better tension on the strings. The French manufacturer Érard provided the "double escapement" action, allowing for fast repetition of the same note. And laying the long bass strings over the shorter high strings ("over-stringing") helped to redeploy the stress. All of these elements came together in the 1859 patent by Steinway for an iron-framed, overstrung, double-escapement grand piano.

The modern concert grand is a beautiful, impressive object and an engineering triumph: with over 10,000 parts, including those three pedals that still puzzle many a piano player – the left one mutes, the right sustains by letting all the strings resonate, and the one in the middle sustains only those notes originally held down.

HARMONIUM

The humble harmonium was patented by the French company Debain in the 1840s. Its volume was limited, the number of stops few and its versatility minimal, but with the outlay of relatively little cost – and skill – a small church could acquire an organ sound; eventually heavy-weight composers such as Berlioz and Richard Strauss came to admire its qualities.

Two foot pedals were pressed up and down in turn, blowing air across the pipes; the air was transferred to a reservoir before passing through to the pipes, but the "expression" stop gave the player the option of directly controlling the airflow with their feet, thus gaining some small compensation against their organist colleagues (the French sometimes called it the "orgue expressif"). An alternative system, particularly common in America, sucked the air into the instrument to produce a softer tone.

The harmonium scored highly for its portability and convenience: at its peak 15,000 a year were being produced in the US for the chapel market. The instrument was also an attractive piece of home entertainment – a kind of aural Playstation – since it was easy to play and often used numbered buttons to produce the chords.

HARPSICHORD

The harpsichord took the plucked-string concept of the virginal and spinet to new heights. The earliest example still in existence dates from the 1520s, when Italy was the major centre, but the instrument continued to develop through to the early 1800s: French harpsichords of the seventeenth and eighteenth centuries were especially graceful and elegantly decorated.

The jack-and-plectrum technique remained essentially the same as its predecessors; however the strings ran at right angles to the keyboard or manual (of which there might be two), and the strings were set in courses of two or more. Yet the harpsichord still suffered from the problem of quick decay: once a string had been plucked the note would fade too swiftly. To compensate, performers and composers added all manner of trills and other ornamentation. And to deal with the lack of dynamics, various attempts – some using a Venetian blind system – were made to boost the volume.

Whereas the clavichord was seen primarily as a solo instrument, the harpsichord was particularly effective and important in ensemble work, providing the continuo for voices or other instruments (usually improvised from an annotated bass line).

ORGAN

Way before virginals, clavichords and spinets were dreamt of, the organ was already in its mature stage of development. Simple versions existed before the Christian era, and by the tenth century the organ was advanced enough to feature a double manual (or keyboard) and hundreds of pipes, providing the powerful swell of church music that accompanied the growth of Christianity.

At their most essential, organs are a set of pipes, sounded by air released from a windchest and controlled by valves operated by keys or foot pedals – there is power, but no touch sensitivity. The pipes fall into two distinct categories:

- Reed Flue: sounded whenever air strikes the top lip (like a panpipes).
- Reed: where the air is vibrated by a metal tongue.

From medieval times onwards the motto of the organ was "bigger and better", multiple manuals (including the great, swell, choir and solo) and a vast array of organ stops imitating different instruments and voices. When the French organ-maker Aristide Cavaillé-Col added the surge of electricity the volume continued to rise (a power responded to by composers like Charles-Marie Widor and Cesar Franck), up to the massive auditorium organ in Atlantic City, New Jersey, reckoned to be as loud as two dozen brass bands.

PIANO ACCORDION

The piano accordion, effectively an outsize mouth organ with bellows and a keyboard, emerged in the early nineteenth century as a Viennese invention; its roots go back 5,000 years to the cheng, a Chinese instrument which used bamboo pipes, a gourd and a windchamber to achieve a similar effect.

The principle of the accordion is relatively simple; by moving the bellows in and out with the left hand, air is forced through the various reeds. The left hand also presses pre-set chord buttons, while the right hand picks out the melody. The squeezebox was briefly on the verge of becoming accepted as an orchestral instrument (Tchaikovsky incorporated it in his Suite No. 2 in C Major), but the accordion's main role has always been as an extremely portable way of providing rich accompaniment to folk songs and dances.

In fact the most striking aspect of the instrument is its universality, from the cafés of France to the pubs of Galway and the klezmer bands of eastern Europe. The accordion adds an essential element to the sounds of the tango, merengue and polka, and features widely in country and cajun music.

PIANOFORTE

The title of father of the modern piano is generally credited to Bartolomeo Cristofori, who was the keeper of instruments at the court of the Florentine Medici family. Like others at the time he wanted to find a way to combine the ability of the clavichord to use crescendo and diminuendo with the brilliance and relative power of the harpsichord.

After a number of prototypes Cristofori produced his "gravicembalo col piano e forte", or harpsichord with loud and soft, in 1709, creating an action that allowed a leather hammer to hit a string (from underneath), be caught to prevent it rebounding on to the string, and finally damp the string. The idea, though, did not initially catch on – Cristofori only made a score of pianos – until German manufacturers like Gottfried Silbermann began improving the hammer action in the 1720s.

The development of the affordable square piano increased its popularity, and by the end of the eighteenth century the English Broadwood company had adopted the sustain pedal. By the time Broadwood sent Beethoven a pianoforte in 1818, the groundwork was set for the arrival of the metal frame and the innovations that created the modern grand piano in the nineteenth century.

UPRIGHT PIANO

From honky-tonk bars to the low point of piano-smashing contests of the 1970s, the upright has been seen as the poor cousin of the grand. It can never recreate the power and tone of a grand, but its compact shape brought music into the heart of hundreds of thousands of homes at the end of the nineteenth century.

The upright piano was developed in the 1800s from what previously had been grand pianos with the strings and soundboard placed up against a wall – constructions too tall to be practical. However, two amendments made all the difference: the Austrian Matthias Müller and the American John Hawkins realised independently that if the strings started from near ground level the height would be drastically reduced – further improved by using a diagonal layout for the strings. Robert Wornum of London added the final touch in the 1830s with a tape-check action, preventing the hammer rebounding on to the strings, and still in use today.

Although the placement against a wall could lead to a lack of resonance, with the added disadvantage of the player having his or her back to the audience, or fellow musicians, the upright proved convenient and immensely popular – a vogue enhanced by the arrival in the late nineteenth century of the automated player piano, which meant that no musical skill was required for families at home to enjoy performances by the great players of the day.

VIRGINAL

One of the oldest of the string keyboard instruments, the virginal dates from as early as the 1460s and marks the beginning of the harpsichord family. Its generally oblong case was often highly decorated, particularly the back of the lid, which might display an intricately painted landscape on being lifted up, revealing a small three- to four-octave keyboard with strings running parallel – the particular characteristic of the virginal.

The instrument was played on a table or laid across the performer's lap. To produce its clear, articulate and brilliant sound, the strings were plucked: as a key was pressed down, its jack would be raised, simultaneously lifting a damper clear and pushing a plectrum against the string, which could vibrate until the player took his – or more likely her – finger off the key.

Playing the virginal was considered part of the skills of an educated young woman (hence the instrument's name, according to some sources) and was particularly important in English music of the early seventeenth century. The concept was developed into the spinet – which frequently had a wing-shaped body more like a grand piano, strings set at 45 degrees to the keyboard and a fuller tone.

ELECTRONIC INSTRUMENTS

BASS GUITAR

In 1951, guitar maker Leo Fender launched the first commercially available electric bass guitar, the Fender Precision. Compared to the cumbersome and often difficult-to-hear acoustic double bass, Fender offered an instrument that had many advantages. Not only was it louder because it was amplified – and more portable – it allowed for more precise intonation because the neck was fretted. Country-and-western players were among the first to adopt the Precision, and during the 1950s and 1960s the bass guitar became established as a mainstay of all styles of modern music making. Four strings tuned E, A, D and G are usual, although a few models with five or more strings are made.

The design principles of the Fender bass guitars have stood the test of time remarkably well: a solid body, larger machine-heads to cope with heavier strings, one or two electro-magnetic pickups, and a bolt-on neck. Fender went on to introduce the Jazz Bass in 1960 and other less successful models. Apart from notable exceptions such as the Rickenbacker 4001S (1964) and the Gibson Thunderbird IV (1964), the electric basses of other big guitar companies never gained the broad acceptance of the Fenders. From the 1970s' specialist bass makers such as Ampeg, Alembic and Wal began to cater for more discer-ning players.

The Fender-based style of construction went unchallenged until Ned Steinberger brought out his radical innovation in the early 1980s: a bass guitar with no headstock and a tiny body. He did this by using reinforced epoxy resin (claimed to be stronger and lighter than steel) instead of wood, and by putting the tuning mechanisms at the other end of the body.

ELECTRIC GUITAR

If one instrument can claim to be the twentieth century's greatest, then the electric guitar is probably it. When the early pioneers, Adolph Rickenbacker, George Beauchamp and Paul Barth, experimented with electro-magnetic pickups to amplify the sound of a guitar in the 1930s, none could have foreseen what an impact this innovation would have on all styles of popular music.

In the mid 1930s, Charlie Christian was one of the first to see the potential as a soloist of playing a guitar that could be heard properly in a jazz band. He played an early Electric Spanish' ES-150 guitar made by Gibson. For generations of jazz players, the mellow clarity of the electric-acoustic guitar became a traditional and characteristic sound.

Early rock'n'roll records, such as Bill Haley and the Comets' 1954 hit 'Rock Around the Clock' kick-started the electric guitar's mass appeal. Rock'n'rollers like Chuck Berry exploited the chugging rhythmic capability of semi-acoustic instruments from the late 1950s into the 1960s. From the early 1960s, countless groups, led by the Beatles and the Rolling Stones, based their music around the electric guitar.

The advent in the late 1960s of very loud blues-influenced rock music saw the flowering of the solid electric guitar, led by the hugely influential Jimi Hendrix playing a Fender Stratocaster. The popularity of electric guitars was renewed in the 1990s with the success of groups like Nirvana and Oasis.

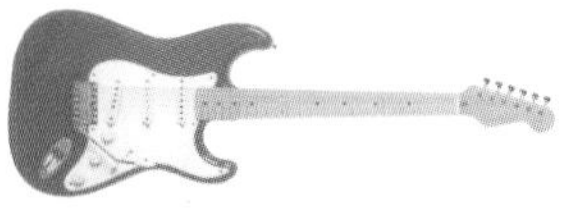

ELECTRIC ORGAN

The electric organ emerged in the early twentieth century, originally designed as an economical and compact substitute for the larger pipe organ. During its history, makers have employed various techniques for producing tones: vibrating reeds, spinning tone wheels, oscillator circuits and digital samplers. Notable early examples include the French *Orgue des Ondes* ("Wave Organ"), developed in the late 1920s by Edouard Coupleux and Armand Givelet, the "Radio Organ of a Trillion Tones" and the Rangertone of the early 1930s.

The most well-known is the Hammond organ, patented by its American inventor Laurens Hammond in 1934. Featuring two keyboards and a set of foot pedals, it produces its unmistakable sound through a set of rotary generators, using drawbars to produce a great variety of tone colours. The Hammond swirling through a Leslie rotating speaker cabinet was at the heart of much black American music from the 1960s onwards, especially gospel, jazz, blues and funk.

By the 1960s valves in electric organs had given way to transistors, which were superseded in turn by microcircuits in the 1970s. Instead of originating notes internally, the latest types play digitally-stored samples, allowing players to imitate almost any other instrument.

ELECTRIC PIANO

The electric piano can sound smooth and mellow, hard and funky, or anywhere in between. Its popularity peaked in the 1970s and declined during the 1980s, only to find a new generation of fans in the worlds of acid-jazz, hip-hop, and garage. Although the Yamaha CP70 electric grand became widely accepted and a new generation of digital pianos has emerged, for many players there were only two main makes to choose from: the Fender Rhodes or the Wurlitzer.

FENDER RHODES

Most influential in the 1970s, the 'Rhodes' helped define the sound of jazz-funk and jazz-fusion, and was played by many soul, funk and disco artists.

Harold Rhodes developed his Army Air Corps Piano from old bits salvaged from B-17 bombers. Using no electrics at all, he achieved a compact portable piano by using aluminium pipes instead of strings. In the late 1950s, Rhodes collaborated with guitar maker Leo Fender to make the 32-note Piano Bass model, made famous by Ray Manzarek of The Doors. The famous 72-note Suitcase model, introduced in 1965, was the first one with the unique "real" Rhodes sound.

WURLITZER

Frequently more at home in a guitar-based rock or pop band, the "Wurly" has enjoyed great success from the early 1960s onwards.

The Wurlitzer's development started when the Everett piano company experimented with B. F. Meissner's ideas about electro-magnetic pickups. The giant American jukebox and theatre organ manufacturer, Wurlitzer, then applied this pickup technology to make an amplifiable piano in which hammers strike metal reeds and the Wurlitzer electric piano was born. The popular EP200 model was first made in the early 1960s.

SAMPLER AND DRUM MACHINE

As with the latest synthesizers, a sampler uses digital technology to make sounds. The difference is that, instead of generating an original synthetic sound, it actually "plays" a mini digital recording of a sound. This could be anything – a voice, a drum beat or even a milk bottle being dropped! In the late 1970s, a pioneering sampling musical instrument such as the Fairlight CMI was as expensive as a Ferrari sports car. By the mid 1990s, samplers were no more expensive than regular synthesizers. In the future, it is likely that dedicated hardware samplers will be forsaken for more versatile personal computers that can do the same thing.

Many people use samples from CDs or download them from the Internet. Others prefer to make their own, using the sampler to make a digital recording of the sound they want (often from other people's records). Either way, the sample can then be played musically by connecting a keyboard to the sampler.

Drum machines have changed the approach to providing rhythm in music. There are two types: the type that produces a continuous beat to a pre-set pattern, and those that are played in "real time" using sticks. A key example of the first type is Roland's TR-606 Drumatix, introduced in 1981, which inspired a generation of dance-music mixers and audiences. Roger Linn's LinnDrum, launched in 1986, is an influential instrument of the second type. It makes sampled drum sounds when special pads are hit.

SYNTHESIZER

The synthesizer has come a long way since the world's first one – the American RCA Mk I, made in 1951, whose bulk occupied a laboratory. To play it, composers such as Milton Babbitt (a fan of Mk II) had to tap in punched-tape instructions – there was no keyboard. Synthesizers became available commercially during the mid-1960s when two innovators, Donald Buchla and Robert Moog, each brought out their own designs. Robert Moog's Moog, with its new voltage-controlled oscillator, was the more influential and was played by top rock keyboard players such as Keith Emerson.

A conventional synthesizer is a keyboard instrument that generates a wide variety of sounds purely electronically, using no mechanical parts at all. With many models providing pre-programmed sounds as well as the capability of altering every aspect of a sound (e.g. pitch, timbre, attack and delay), the synthesizer player can imitate a range of instruments or invent entirely new squeaks, warbles or rumbles.

Analogue synthesizers are now regarded as classics and are collected for the unique quality of their sounds. From the late 1970s, these gave way to a new generation that used digital microcomputers, for example the Fairlight CMI (which plays sampled sounds and Yamaha's FM (frequency modulation) models.

OTHER INSTRUMENTS

THE VOICE

The human voice is our primeval musical instrument, with our earliest ancestors finding expression through their voices before thought was ever given to other sources of sound. Vocal music has been sung from the beginnings of recorded history; the Sumerians sang in their temples 5,000 years ago. In the West, traditions of singing have evolved from the plainchant of the middle ages, through seventeenth-century opera to today's various music styles. Rather than survey the vast history of vocal music, this section considers some of the ususual uses to which the voice has been put.

How to Read Music

Reading music is not a prerequisite of being musical, in just the same way that being able to read is not necessary before learning to speak. However, learning to read music becomes more relevant once an individual's fundamental musical abilities have been developed, and in turn the ability to read notation will help develop those abilities further.

This section is going to demonstrate *how* to read music through practical exercises that will familiarize would-be musicians with the basics of music notation.

Pulse and Time

The most natural **pulse** is the heart beat. At times it beats faster, the pace can change, as in music. This pace, or speed is called **tempo**.

Exercise
To practice keeping time with a musical pulse or beat. Imagine you are walking and clap in time with each step. You should have no trouble keeping a regular musical beat.

Music is often linked to movement, which is why musicians group beats in relation to patterns of movement. For example, a **march** is in two-time because the movement of marching involves two parts; the first part is that you move your left foot and the second, you move your right.

The movement of the feet is also important in dance (which is nearly always accompanied by music). A **waltz,** for example, is in three-time because the movement of the waltz involves three parts; the left foot moves, then the right and for the third movement, the left foot moves again, to bring both feet together. (This pattern is then repeated on the other side.)

Music can also be in four-time. Most popular music is in four. Although music can also be in other times, two-time, three-time and four-time are the most common. The first thing to remember is that the first beat in any time, is the strongest. It is possible to work out the time of any music, by identifying the pulse and the first beat.

Exercise
Clap in time to music that you hear, and simultaneously listen out for the first beat. With practice, it will be eventually possible to distinguish which time the music is in.

In two-time, imagine marching. With each left foot-beat, say out loud "one", and with each right foot beat say out loud "two". Do this at the same time as clapping the pulse. Make sure that your pulse is as even as possible and maintain the tempo.

[Ex.1]

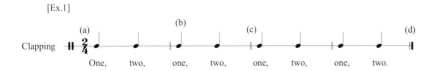

Clapping
One, two, one, two, one, two, one, two.

Musical **notes** Ex.1 (b) that look like the eight notes in this example, are one beat long and are called <u>crotchets</u>.

At the end of each first and second beat the vertical line – called the **bar-line** [Ex.1 (c)] – is used to mark the place before a new first beat is established. What lies between these bar-lines are the <u>bars</u>. A **double bar-line** [Ex.1 (d)] is used to mark the end of the music.

To signify the time of the music, the **time signature** [Ex.1 (a)] is used. The top number of the time signature gives the number of beats per <u>bar</u>, in this case **2**. The bottom number indicates the length of the beat. In this case the **4** actually represents a <u>crotchet</u> beat. Therefore in "two-four time", there are two <u>crotchet</u> beats in each bar.

Rhythm

Rhythm in music is like rhythm in speech. Listen to speech and you will hear a pattern of syllables, each one taking a certain length of time. The natural rhythm of speech does not require a musical pulse but rhythm in music does.

Exercise
The words "mummy" and "daddy" have two syllables. Imagine marching, but this time instead of saying "left", say "mummy" and instead of saying "right", say "daddy". Try to get the second syllable of each word in the middle of the pulse or beat that you are clapping. If this is done correctly, you should hear two even syllables to every beat. Now try four syllables to every beat using the word "honeysuckle". Alternating these words whilst keeping the pulse going by clapping, could give the variation "mummy, honeysuckle, daddy, honeysuckle".

[Ex.2]

Voice

Mu - mmy, ho - ney - su - ckle, Da - ddy, ho - ney - su - ckle.

Musical notes [Ex.2 (a)] that notate "mummy" and "daddy" in this example are half a beat long and are called <u>quavers</u>. The musical notes Ex.2 (b) that notate "honeysuckle" are quarter of a beat long and are called <u>semiquavers</u>.

By using a **dot** like a full stop at the end of any note, the value of that note is increased by 50%. So if we put a dot after a <u>crotchet</u>, the value of the note becomes one and a half. Musicians use dotted <u>crotchets</u> in **compound time**. As beats, they can be split easily in to three quavers. This gives a different feel to the time.

ALTERNATIVE TERMINOLOGY

Although most musical terms are universal, there are some which have alternative names, the most common of which are given opposite.

Breve:	Double-whole note (double-note rest)
Semi-breve:	Whole note (whole-note rest)
Minim:	Half note (half-note rest)
Crotchet:	Quarter note (quarter-note rest)
Quaver:	Eighth note (eighth-note rest)
Semi-quaver:	Sixteenth note (sixteenth-note rest)
Bar:	Measure

Exercise

Repeat the three syllable word "Birmingham" with each pulse or beat that you are clapping. If this is done correctly, you should hear three even syllables to every beat. After repeating the word three times, finish with the two syllable word "city", so that the third part of that beat is left silent.

[Ex.3]

The **time signature** [Ex.3 (a)] is now in "six-eight time" which means that there are six quavers in each bar. The quavers are grouped in threes which splits the bar into two **dotted** crotchet **beats**. The quaver **rest** Ex.3 (b) is written instead of a note as the music is silent at this point and in the last bar too, where there are two **dotted** crotchets [Ex.3 (c)].

Pitch

A scream is a sound that is referred to as being "high" in pitch. Musicians have developed a way to measure just how high or low a musical note is. Depending upon your age and gender, the pitch of your voice could be high or low.

Exercise

A good way to practice pitch is to sing. Getting started from scratch can often be difficult but a useful exercise is to sing back a musical note or sequence of notes that you might hear, for example something on the radio or television.

Five lines are all that are needed to notate pitch. These five lines are called a **staff** or **stave** [Ex.4 (a)]. Writing notes on and between each line, including notes above and below the staff with extra lines attached called **ledger lines** [Ex.4 (c)], allows a great range of notes to be shown.

At the beginning of the staff, a symbol is given to indicate a higher "female voice range" of notes, called the **treble clef** [Ex.4 (b)], or a lower "male voice range", called the **bass clef** [Ex.5 (a)]. It is possible to notate all audible musical pitch using this system, and by simultaneously noting rhythm, music can be written down. Scientists and musicians developed a system that arranged a series of individual musical pitches in an order. The pitches all have one thing in common and that is that the distance or musical **interval** between each of them is the same. These pitches, known as **chromatic** steps, are grouped in twelves for a particular reason. This is because of the **octave**. The octave is an interval between two pitches, where the upper note is double the frequency of the lower. This means that they sound the same but that one is higher than the other.

Exercise

The best way to check out this system is on a piano. On a piano, the chromatic series is laid out in front of you. Start from the lowest note and gradually work your way to the top. What you will be playing is a chromatic scale. A **scale** is the name of a series of notes that keeps to a specific pattern. From the twelve notes of the chromatic scale, other scales have been created. **Major** and **minor** scales are very common and both consist of eight notes. Some of the intervals between the notes in these scales are different from each another. This interval content characterizes the scale and on a very basic level, the major scale is said to sound "happy" and the minor scale "sad".

Using a piano keyboard, find a pair of black notes as close to the middle of the keyboard as possible. In between is a white note and the white note to the left of it is called **middle C**. Play a series of eight ascending white notes only, in a row, starting with middle C. Do this with a pulse and hold each note for two beats of the pulse. What you are playing is the scale in the **key** of C major.

[Ex.4]

The notes of this scale that last for two counts are called minims. The letters of the alphabet "A B C D E F G" are used in music to label the pitch of notes and when practiced, become as familiar as words themselves. The final **chord** [Ex.4 (d)] is made up of semibreves which are held for a count of four. Try playing this chord, which has been added at the end of the scale. Use the first, third and fifth notes of the scale and play them all at the same time. Chords form the basis of **harmony**, the name given to chord progressions in musical arrangements that accompany the tune or **melody**.

It is possible to play the major scale starting from anywhere on the keyboard. To keep the same interval content as that of the scale of C major, starting anywhere else will inevitably involve the use of black notes. This is when three musical symbols called sharps, flats and naturals may become involved. Sharps and flats present themselves in the **key signature** [Ex.5 (b)] and each one alters a given note by one chromatic step.

Exercise

Start with locating the G below middle C (the third white note down from middle C). Play a descending series of eight notes, to a pulse and hold each note for three counts. However, incorporate one black note. Instead of playing the second white note, play the black note.

[Ex. 5]

You may have noticed that some of the three beat notes have had to be split as they occur on the bar-line. By means of a musical **tie** [Ex.5 (c)], the tied notes sound as one continuous three beat note.

Melody and Harmony

If you were to "hum along" to a song, you would be performing a series of musical pitches in a rhythmic pattern. This expression of a line of single musical notes is known as the tune or **melody**. What accompanies a given melody may vary in style but the progression of chords that form the basis of this accompaniment, is referred to as the **harmony**.

Further Reading

POP

Brend, Mark, *American Troubadors: Groundbreaking Singer-Songwriters of the 60s*, Backbeat Books, San Francisco, 2001

Buskin, Richard, *Inside Tracks: A First-Hand History of Popular Music from the World's Greatest Record Producers and Engineers*, Avon, 1999

Carr, Roy, and Farren, Mick, *Elvis: The Complete Illustrated Record*, Eel Pie, London, 1982

Cooper, Kim, *Bubblegum Music is the Naked Truth*, Feral House, 2001

Escott, Colin, with Hawkins, Martin, *Good Rockin' Tonight: Sun Records and the Birth of Rock 'n' Roll*, St. Martin's Press, New York, 1992

Fong-Torres, Ben, *The Hits Just Keep On Coming: The History of Top 40 Radio*, Backbeat Books, San Francisco, 2001

Fox, Ted, *In the Groove*, St. Martins Press, New York, 1986

Kozinn, Allan, *The Beatles*, Phaidon, London, 1995

Larkin, Colin, *Encyclopedia of Popular Music*, Virgin Publishing, London, 2002

Larkin, Colin, *The Guinness Who's Who of Sixties Music*, Guinness Publishing, London, 1992

Lewisohn, Mark, *The Complete Beatles Chronicle*, Harmony Books, New York, 1992

Logan, Nick, and Woffinden, Bob (eds.), *The Illustrated New Musical Express Encyclopedia of Rock*, Hamlyn, London, 1976

Marcic, Dorothy, *Respect: Women and Popular Music*, Texere, New York, 2002

Marcus, Greil, *Mystery Train: Images of America in Rock'n'Roll Music*, E P Dutton, 1975

Morath, Max, and Feinstein, Michael, *The Npr Curious Listener's Guide to Popular Standards*, Perigee, New York, 2002

Mulholland, Garry, *This Is Uncool: The 500 Greatest Singles Since Punk and Disco*, Cassell, London, 2002

Olsen, Eric et al, *The Encyclopedia of Record Producers*, Billboard, New York, 1999

Pascall, Jeremy, *The Golden Years of Rock & Roll*, Phoebus Publishing, New York, 1974

Ramsey, Guthrie P., *Race Music: Black Cultures from Bebop to Hip-Hop*, University of California Press, Berkeley, 2003

Smith, Joe, *Off the Record: An Oral History of Popular Music*, Warner Books, 1988

Swern, Phil, and Greenfield, Shaun, *30 Years of Number Ones*, BBC Books, London, 1990

Thompson, David, *Pop*, Collectors Guide Publishing, 2000

Unterberger, Richie, *The Rough Guide to Music USA*, Rough Guides, London, 1999

Whitburn, Joel, *Billboard Top 1000 Singles 1955–2000*, Hal Leonard Publishing, Milwaukee, 2001

White, Charles, *The Life and Times of Little Richard*, Harmony Books, 1984

Wolfe, Tom, *The Kandy-Kolored Tangerine-Flake Streamline Baby*, Simon & Schuster, New York, 1965

ROCK

Asbjornsen, Dag Erik, *Scented Gardens of the Mind: A Comprehensive Guide to the Golden Era of Progressive Rock: 1968–1980*, Borderline Productions, New York, 2001

Azerrad, Michael, *Our Band Could Be Your Life: Scenes from the American India Underground 1981–1991*, Little Brown & Company, New York, 2001

Billboard Guide to American Rock and Roll, Billboard Books, New York, 1997

Blush, Steven, *American Hardcore: A Tribal History*, Feral House, 2001

Bogdanov, Vladimir (ed.), et al, *All Music Guide to Rock*, Backbeat, London, 2002

Christe, Ian, *The Sound of the Beast: The Complete Headbanging History of Heavy Metal*, William Morrow, New York, 2003

Cohn, Nik, *Awopbopaloobopalopbamboom: The Golden Age of Rock*, Grove Press, New York, 2003

Cole, Richard, and Trubo, Richard, *Stairway to Heaven: Led Zeppelin Uncensored*, HarperEntertainment, New York, 2000

Ellinham, Mark, *The Rough Guide to Rock*, Rough Guides, London, 1996

Gassen, Timothy, *The Knights Of Fuzz*, Borderline Productions, Columbia, 1996

George-Warren, Holly, et al, *The Rolling Stone Encyclopedia of Rock & Roll*, Fireside, New York, 2001

Graff, Gary, and Durchholz, Daniel, *MusicHound Rock: The Essential Album Guide*, Gale, 1998

Harrison, Hank, *Kurt Cobain, Beyond Nirvana: The Legacy of Kurt Cobain*, The Archives Press, 1994

Ingham, Chris, *The Book Of Metal*, Carlton Books, London, 2002

Jeffries, Neil (ed.), *The "Kerrang!" Direktory of Heavy Metal: The Indispensible Guide to Rock Warriors and Headbangin' Heroes*, Virgin Books, London, 1993

Juno, Andrea, *Angry Women In Rock*, Juno Books, 2003

Larkin, Colin, *The Virgin Encyclopedia of Heavy Rock*, Virgin Books, London, 1999

Larkin, Colin, *The Virgin Illustrated Encyclopedia of Rock*, Virgin Books, London, 1999

McIver, Joel, *Nu-Metal: The Next Generation Of Rock And Punk*, Omnibus Press, London, 2002

McNeil, Legs and McGain, Gillian (eds.), *Please Kill Me: The Uncensored Oral History of Punk*, Penguin USA, New York, 1997

Moynihan, Michael and Soderlind, Didrik, *Lords Of Chaos: The Bloody Rise Of The Satanic Underground*, Feral House, 2003

Porter, Dick, *Rapcore: The Nu-Metal Rap Fusion*, Plexus Publishing, New Jersey, 2002

Reynolds, Simon, *The Sex Revolts: Gender, Rebellion and Rock'n'roll*, Harvard University Press, Harvard, 1995

Spicer, Al, *The Rough Guide to Rock (100 Essential CDs)*, Rough Guides, London, 1999

Strong, Martin .C., *The Great Metal Discography*, Mojo Books, London, 2002

Strong, Martin C., *The Great Rock Discography*, Canongate Publications, Edinburgh, 2002

JAZZ

Blesh, Rubi and Janis, Harriet, *They All Played Ragtime*, Oak Publishers, 1950

Carr, Ian, *Miles Davis*, HarperCollins, New York, 1999 (new edition)

Carr, Ian, *The Rough Guide to Jazz*, Rough Guides, London, 2000

Castro, Roy, *Bossa Nova: The Story of the Brazilian Music that Seduced The World*, A Cappella, Chicago, 2000

Dance, Stanley, *The World of Swing*, Da Capo Press, Maryland, 1974

Deffaa, Chip, *Traditionalists & Revivalists in Jazz*, Scarecrow Press, Maryland, 1993

Giddins, Gary, *Celebrating Bird: The Triumph Of Charlie Parker*, Beechtree Books, New York, 1987

Gillespie, Dizzy and Fraser, Al, *To Be Or Not To Bop: Memoirs, The Autobiography Of Dizzy Gillespie*, Doubleday, New York, 1979

Gitler, Ira, *Jazz Masters Of The Forties*, Da Capo Press, Maryland, 1966

Goggin, Jim and Clute, Peter, *The Great Jazz Revival: A Pictorial Celebration of Traditional Jazz*, Donna Ewald Publishing, 1994

Goldberg, Joe, *Jazz Masters Of The Fifties*, Da Capo Press, Maryland, 1965

Hasse, John Edward (ed.), *Jazz: The First Century*, William Morrow, New York, 2000

Jost, Ekkehard, *Free Jazz*, Da Capo Press, Maryland, 1994

Kirchner, Bill (ed.), *The Oxford Companion To Jazz*, Oxford University Press, Oxford, 2000

Leymarie, Isabelle, *Cuban Fire: The Saga of Salsa and Latin Jazz*, Continuum International Publishing Group, New York, 2002

Lincoln Collier, James, *The Making Of Jazz: A Comprehensive History*, Houghton Mifflin Company, Boston, 1978

Mathieson, Kenny, *Cookin': Hard Bop and Soul Jazz, 1954-65*, Canongate Books Ltd, Edinburgh, 2002

Mezzrow, Mezz and Wolfe, Bernard, *Really The Blues*, Doubleday, New York, 1946

Milkowski, Bill, *Swing It! An Annotated History Of Jive*, Billboard Books, New York, 2001

Milkowski, Bill, *Jaco: Jaco Pastorius*, Backbeat, London, 1998

Pessanha, Ricardo and McGowan, Chris, *The Brazilian Sound: Samba, Bossa Nova and the Popular Music of Brazil*, Temple University Press, 1998

Roberts, John Storm, *The Latin Tinge*, Oxford University Press, Philadelphia, 1998

Rosenthal, David H., *Hard Bop: Jazz and Black Music, 1955–1965*, Oxford University Press Inc., New York, 1994

Schuller, Gunther, *The Swing Era*, Oxford University Press, Oxford, 1989

Sheridan, Chris (ed.), *Dis Here: A Bio-discography of Julian "Cannonball" Adderley (Discographies)*, Greenwood Press, Westport, 2000

Sudhalter, Richard M., *Lost Chords: White Musicians And Their Contributions To Jazz, 1915–1945*, Oxford University Press, Oxford, 1999

Tingen, Paul, *Miles Beyond: The Electric Explorations of Miles Davis, 1967-1991*, Billboard Books, 2001

Waldo, Terry, *This Is Ragtime*, Da Capo Press, Maryland, 1976

BLUES

Bascom, William R. and Herskovits, Melville J., *Continuity And Change In African Cultures*, University of Chicago Press, Chicago, 1962

Bogdanov, Vladimir (ed.), *All Music Guide to the Blues: The Definitive Guide to the Blues*, Backbeat, London, 2003

Charters, Samuel B., *The Blues Makers*, Da Capo Press, Maryland, 1991

Charters, Samuel B., *The Country Blues*, Da Capo Press, Maryland, 1959

Charters, Samuel, *Sweet As The Showers Of Rain*, Oak Publications, 1977

Chilton, John, *Let The Good Times Roll: The Story of Louis Jordan & His Music*, University of Michigan Press, 1997

Cuscuna, Michael and Lourie, Charlie, *The Blue Note Years*, Rizzoli, New York, 1995

Dixon, Willie, with Snowden, Don, *I Am The Blues: The Willie Dixon Story*, Da Capo Press, Maryland, 1989

Erlewine, Michael et al (ed.), *All Music Guide To The Blues*, Backbeat, London, 1996

Ferris, William, *Blues From The Delta*, Anchor Press/Doubleday, New York, 1978

Gillet, Charlie, *The Sound of the City*, Da Capo Press, Maryland, 1996

Knight, Richard, *The Blues Highway: New Orleans to Chicago*, Trailblazer Publications, London, 2001

McStravick, Summer and Roos, John, (eds.), *Blues-rock Explosion: From The Allman Brothers To The Yardbirds*, Old Goat Publishing, California, 2002

Newman, Richard, *Blues Breaker: John Mayall And The Story Of The Blues*, Sanctuary Publishing, London, 1995

Oakley, Giles, *The Devil's Music: A History of the Blues*, Da Capo Press, Maryland, 1997

Oliver, Paul, *The Story of the Blues: The Making of a Black Music*, Pimlico, London, 1997

Palmer, Robert, *Deep Blues*, Viking Press, 1981

Rosalsky, Mitch, *Encyclopedia Of Rhythm And Blues And Doo Wop Vocal Groups*, Scarecrow Press, Maryland, 2000

Rowe, Mike, *Chicago Blues: The City And The Music*, Da Capo Press, Maryland, 1973

Schumacher, Michael, *Crossroads: The Life And Music Of Eric Clapton*, Citadel Press, Sacramento, 2003

Shaw, Arnold, *Honkers and Shouters: The Golden Years of Rhythm and Blues*, Macmillan, London, 1978

Southern, Eileen, *The Music Of Black Americans: A History*, Norton, New York, 1983

Ward, Greg, *The Rough Guide To The Blues*, Rough Guides, London, 2000

Wyman, Bill, *Bill Wyman's Blues Odyssey: A Journey To Music's Heart And Soul*, Dorling Kindersley, London, 2001

COUNTRY

Bane, Michael, *The Outlaws: Revolution in Country Music*, Country Music Magazine/Doubleday/Dolphin, New York, 1978

Country Music Magazine (bi-monthly magazine), Nashville, Tennessee

From Where I Stand: The Black Experience In Country Music (annotated CD collection) Country Music Foundation/Warner Bros. Records, 1998

Gaillard, Frye, *Watermelon Wine: The Spirit of Country Music*, St. Martin's, New York, 1978

Grissim, John, *Country Music: White Man's Blues*, Paperback Library, New York, 1970

Hagan, Chet, *The Grand Ole Opry*, Henry Holt, New York, 1989

Kingsbury, Paul, and Axelrod, Alan, (ed.), *Country: The Music and the Musicians*, Country Music Foundation/Abbeville Press, New York, 1988

Kingsbury, Paul, *Country On Compact Disc: The Essential Guide to the Music*, ed., The Country Music Foundation/Grove Press, New York, 1993

Kingsbury, Paul, *The Grand Ole Opry History of Country Music*, Villard, New York, 1995

Malone, Bill C., *Country Music U.S.A.*, University of Texas Press, Austin, Texas, 1985

Millard, Bob, *Country Music: 70 Years of America's Favorite Music*, HarperPerennial, New York, 1993

Oermann, Robert K., *America's Music: The Roots of Country*, Turner, Atlanta, 1996

Rosenberg, Neil V., *Bluegrass: A History*, University of Illinois Press, Urbana and Chicago, Illinois, 1985

Watt, Sharon, (ed.), *Bluegrass Unlimited* (monthly magazine), Warrenton, Virginia, 2003

Whitburn, Joel, *Joel Whitburn's Top Country Singles*, Billboard/Record Research, Inc., Menomonee Falls, Wisconsin, 1994–2002

FOLK

Cantwell, Robert, *When We Were Good: The Folk Revival*, Harvard University Press, Harvard, 1996

Clancy, Liam, *Liam Clancy: Memoirs of an Irish Troubadour*, Virgin Books, London, 2003

Cohen, Ronald (ed.), *Alan Lomax: Selected Writings, 1934–1997*, Routledge, New York, 2003

Gray, Michael, *Song and Dance Man III: The Art of Bob Dylan*, Continuum International Publishing Group, New York, 1999

Griffith, Nanci, and Jackson, Joe, *Nanci Griffith's Other Voices: A Personal History of Folk Music (Come From the Heart)*, Amber Waves, Maidstone, 1998

Guthrie, Woody, *Bound For Glory*, Peter Smith Publisher Inc., 1985

Harper, Colin, *Dazzling Stranger: Bert Jansch and the British Folk and Blues Revival*, Bloomsbury, London, 2001

O'Brien, Karen, *Shadows and Light: Joni Mitchell: The Definitive Biography*, Virgin Books, London, 2002

Reuss, Richard A., and Reuss, JoAnne C., *American Folk Music and Left Wing Politics 1927–1957*, Scarecrow Press, Maryland, 2000

Sawyers, June Skinner, *The Complete Guide to Celtic Music: From the Highland Bagpipe and Riverdance to U2 and Enya*, Aurum Press, London, 2000

Seeger, Pete, and Schwartz, Jo Metcalf (ed.), *The Incompleat Folksinger*, University of Nebraska Press, Lincoln, 1995

Stambler, Irwin, and Stambler, Lyndon, *Folk and Blues: The Encyclopedia*, St Martin's Press, New York, 2001

Unterberger, Richie, *Turn! Turn! Turn!: The 60s Folk-Rock Revolution*, Backbeat UK, London, 2002

Vallely, Fintan, *Companion to Irish Traditional Music*, Cork University Press, Cork, 1999

Wall, Geoff, and Hinton, Brian, *Ashley Jennings: The Guv'nor & The Rise of Folk Rock*, Helter Skelter Publishing, London, 2002

Whittaker, Adrian, *Be Glad: An Incredible String Band Compendium*, Helter Skelter Publishing, London, 2003

CLASSICAL

Arnold, Denis, *The New Grove Italian Baroque Masters: Monteverdi, Frescobaldi, Cavalli, Corellis, A. Scarlatti, D. Scarlatti, Vivaldi* (The New Grove Composer Biography Series), Macmillan Reference Books, 1984

Atlas, Allan W., *Renaissance Music* (Norton Introduction to Music), W. W. Norton, 1998

Boyd, Malcolm, *Bach*, (Master Musicians Series), Oxford University Press Inc, USA, 2000

Brown, A. Peter, *The Symphonic Repertoire: The Second Golden Age of the Viennese Symphony: Brahms. Bruckner, Dvorak, Mahler and Selected Contemporaries*, Indiana University Press, 2002

Cage, John, *Silence: Lectures and Writings*, Wesleyan University Press, USA, 1973

Crocker, Richard, and Hiley, David, (eds.), *The Early Middle Ages to 1300* (The New Oxford History of Music), Oxford University Press, Oxford, 1990
Debussy, Claude, Busoni, Ferruccio, and Ives, Charles, *Three Classics in the Aesthetic of Music*, Dover Publications, New York, 1962
Grout, Donald J., and Palisca, Claude V., *A History of Western Music*, W. W. Norton & Co., 1960
Marrocco, W. Thomas, and Sandon, Nicholas (eds.), *Medieval Music* (Oxford Anthology of Music), Oxford University Press, Oxford, 1977
Perle, George, *Serial Composition and Atonality: Introduction to the Music of Schoenberg, Berg and Webern*, University of California Press, 1978
Potter, Keith, *Four Musical Minimalists: La Monte Young, Terry Riley, Steve Reich, Philip Glass*, Cambridge University Press, 2000
Reese, Gustave, *New Grove High Renaissance Masters: Josquin, Palestrina, Lassus,*
Rifkin, Joshua, et al., *The New Grove North European Baroque Masters: Schutz, Froberger, Buxtehude, Purcell, Telemann* (The New Grove Composer Biography Series), Macmillan Reference Books, 1985
Robbins Landon, H. C., *Essays of Viennese Classical Style: Gluck, Haydn, Mozart, Beethoven*, Barrie & Jenkins, 1970
Robbins Landon, H.C., *Handel and His World*, Little, Brown & Co. (T), 1984
Rosen, Charles, *The Classical Style: Haydn, Mozart, Beethoven*, Faber and Faber Ltd, 1971
Sadie, Stanley (ed.), The Billboard Illustrated Encyclopedia of Classical Music, 2000
Sadie, Stanley (ed.), The Billboard Encyclopedia of Classical Music, 2003
Staines, Joe (ed.), *The Rough Guide to Classical Music*, Rough Guides, 2001
Temperley, Nicholas et al., *The New Grove Early Romantic Masters 1: Chopin, Schumann, Liszt* (The New Grove Composer Biography Series), Macmillan Reference Books, 1985
Tyrrell, John, et al., *The New Grove Turn of the Century Masters: Janacek, Mahler, Strauss, Sibelius* (The New Grove Composer Biography Series), Macmillan Reference Books, 1985
Warrack, John, et al., *The New Grove Early Romantic Masters 2: Weber, Berlioz, Mendelssohn* (The New Grove Composer Biography Series), Macmillan Reference Books, 1985
Yudkin, Jeremy, *Music in Medieval Europe*, Prentice Hall, 1988

WORLD

Ancelet. Barry Jean, *Cajun and Creole Music Makers*, University Press of Mississippi, Mississippi, 1999
Blumenthal, Howard J., *The World Music CD Listener's Guide*, Billboard Books, New York, 1998
Bohlman, Philip V., *World Music: A Very Short Introduction*, Oxford Paperbacks, Oxford, 2002
Broughton, Simon (ed.), *World Music 100 Essential CDs: The Rough Guide*, Rough Guides, London, 2000
Eyre, Banning, *In Griot Time: An American Guitarist in Mali*, Serpent's Tail, London, 2002
FRoots magazine
Hart, Mickey, and Kostyal, Karen, *Songcatchers: In Search of the World's Music*, National Geographic Books, 2003
McGowan, Chris, and Pessanha, Ricardo, *The Brazilian Sound: Samba, Bossa Nova and the Popular Music of Brazil*, Temple University Press, Philadelphia, 1998
Shankar, Ravi, *Raga Mala: The Autobiography of Ravi Shankar*, Welcome Rain Publishers, New York, 2001
Olsen, Dale A., and Sheehy, Daniel (eds.), *The Garland Handbook of Latin American Music*, Garland Science, New York, 2000
Potter, John, *The Power of Okinawa: Roots Music from the Ryukyus*, SU Press, Selinsgrove, 2001
Songlines magazine
Schnabel, Tom, *Rhythm Planet: The Great World Music Makers*, Rizzoli Publications, New York, 1998
Stone, Ruth, *The Garland Handbook of African Music*, Garland Science, New York, 1999
The Rough Guide To World Music (2nd edition, Vols. 1 & 2), Rough Guides, London, 2000
Veal, Michael, *Fela: The Life and Times of an African Musical Icon*, Temple University Press, Philadelphia, 2000

DANCE

Barr, Tim, *Rough Guide to Techno*, Rough Guide, London, 2000
Belle-Fortune, Brian, et al, *All Crew Muss Big Up: Some Journeys Through Jungle, Drum and Bass Culture*, London, 1999
Bidder, Sean, *Pump Up The Volume*, Channel 4 Books, London, 2001
Bidder, Sean, *Rough Guide to House*, Rough Guides, London, 1999
Brewser, Bill, and Broughton, Frank, *Last Night a DJ Saved My Life*, Headline, London, 1999
Collin, Matthew and Godfrey, John, *Altered State: The Story of Ecstasy Culture and Acid House* Serpent's Tail, London, 1998
DJ magazine, 1993–2003
Garratt, Sheryl, *Adventures In Wonderland: a Decade of Club Culture*, Headline, London, 1999)
James, Martin, *State Of Bass: Jungle – the Story so Far*, Boxtree, London, 1997)
Larkin, Colin (ed.), *The Virgin Encyclopedia of Dance Music* Virgin Books, London, 1999
Reynolds, Simon, *Energy Flash: A Journey Through Rave Music and Club Culture*, Picador, London, 1997
Reynolds, Simon, *Generation Ecstasy: into the World of Techno and Rave Culture*, Routledge, London, 1999
Shapiro, Peter, *Rough Guide to Drum N' Bass*, Rough Guides, London, 1999
Thornton, Sarah, *Club Cultures: Music, Media and Subcultural Capital*, Polity Press, London, 1995

HIP HOP

Chalfont, Henry and Prigoff, James, *Spraycan Art* Thames and Hudson, London, 1991
Fricke, Jim, Ahearn Charlie, Nelson, George *Yes, Yes, Y'all: The Experience Music Project Oral History of Hip Hop: The First Decade*, Perseus Press, London, 2002
George, Nelson, *Hip Hop America*, Penguin, London, 2000
Krims, Adam, Rap Music and the Poetics of Identity Cambridge University Press, Cambridge, 2000
Lee, Spike (foreword), D. Chuck, Yusuf Jah, *Fight The Power: Rap, Race & Reality*, Payback Press, Edinburgh, 1999
Light, Alan, *The Vibe History Of Hip Hop*, Plexus, London, 1999
Ogg, Alex, and Upshal, David, *The Hip Hop Years*, Channel 4 Books, London, 1999
Perkins, William Eric (ed.), *Droppin' Science: Critical Essays on Rap Music and Hip Hop Culture*, Temple University Press, Philadelphia, 1996
Ro, Ronin, *Have Gun Will Travel: The Spectacular Rise Of Death Row Records*, Quartet Books, London, 1998
Rose, Tricia, *Black Noise: Rap Music and Black Culture in Contemporary America*, Wesleyan University Press, Middletown, 1994
Shapiro, Peter, *The Rough Guide To Hip Hop*, Rough Guides, London, 2001
Stancell, Steven, *Rap Whoz Who: The World Of Rap Music*, Schirmer Books, New York, 2001
Toop, David, *The Rap Attack 3: African Jive To New York Hip Hop*, Serpent's Tail, London, 1999)
Westbrook, Alonzo, *The Hip Hoptionary: The Dictionary Of Hip Hop Terminology*, Harlem Moon, New York, 2002

REGGAE

Barrett, Leonard, *Rastafarians,* Beacon Press, Boston, 1997
Barrow, Steve and Dalton, Peter, *The Rough Guide To Reggae*, Rough Guides, London, 1997
Bradley, Lloyd and Morris, Dennis, *Reggae: The Story Of Jamaican Music*, BBC Books, London, 2002
Bradley, Lloyd, Bass Culture: *When Reggae Was King*, Penguin, London, 2001
Davis, Stephen, Bob Marley: *Conquering Lion Of Reggae*, Plexus, London, 1993
De Koningh, Michael, Cane-Honeysett, Laurence, *Young, Gifted and Black: the Story of Trojan Records,* Sanctuary Publishing, London, 2003
Gunst, Laurie, *Born Fi Dead: A Journey Through The Jamaican Posse Underground*, Payback Press, Edinburgh, 1999
Katz, David, *People Funny Boy: The Genius of Lee 'Scratch' Perry,* Payback Press, London, 2000
Katz, David, *Solid Foundation: An Oral History of Reggae*, Bloomsbury, London, 2003
Larkin, Colin, *The Virgin Encyclopedia Of Reggae*, Virgin Books, London, 1998
Morrow, Chris, *Stir It Up: Reggae Cover Art*, Thames & Hudson, London, 1999
O'Brien-Chang, Kevin and Chen, Wayne, *Reggae Routes: The Story Of Jamaican Music*, Temple University Press, Philadelphia, 1998
Potash, Chris (ed.) *Reggae, Rasta, Revolution: Jamaican Music from Ska to Dub*, Books With Attitude, Schirmer Books, 1997
Salewicz, Chris and Boot, Adrian, *Bob Marley: Songs Of Freedom*, Bloomsbury, London, 1995
Salewicz, Chris and Boot, Adrian, *Reggae Explosion*, Virgin Books, London,.2001

SOUL AND R&B

Abbott, Kingsley (ed.), *Calling Out Around the World: A Motown Reader*, Helter Skelter Publishing, London, 2000
Franklin, Aretha, and Ritz, David, *Aretha: From These Roots*, Villard Books, New York, 1998
Guralnick, Peter, *Sweet Soul Music – Rhythm and Blues and the Southern Dream of Freedom*, Mojo Books, London, 2002
Hildebrand, Lee, *Stars of Soul, Rhythm and Blues: Top Recording Artists and Show Stopping Performers, from Memphis and Motown to Now*, Billboard Books, New York, 1994
Hirshey, Gerri, *Nowhere to Run: The Story of Soul Music*, Macmillan, 1994
Lydon, Michael, *Ray Charles: Man and Music*, Payback Press, Edinburgh, 1999
Marsh, Dave, *For the Record: Sam and Dave*, Avon Books, New York, 1998
Marsh, Dave, *George Clinton and P-Funk (For the Record)*, Avon Books, New York, 1998
Nathan, David, *Soulful Divas*, Billboard Books, New York, 1999
Pruter, Robert, *Chicago Soul*, University of Illinois Press, Chicago, 1992
Ritz, David, *Divided Soul: The Life of Marvin Gaye*, Da Capo Press, Maryland, 1991
Shapiro, Peter, *The Rough Guide to Soul Music*, Rough Guides, London, 2000
Slutsky, Allen, *Standing in the Shadows of Motown*, Hal Leonard Corporation, 1991
Taylor, Marc, *A Touch of Classical Soul: Soul Singers of the Early 1970s*, Partners Publishing Group, 1999
Vincent, Ricky, *Funk: Music, People and Rhythm of the One*, St Martin's Press, New York, 1996

GOSPEL

Boyer, Horace Clarence, et al, *The Golden Age Of Gospel*, University of Illinois Press, Chicago, 2000
Broughton, Viv, *Black Gospel: Illustrated History of Gospel*, Blandford Press, Poole, 1985
Cusic, Don, *The Sound of Light: A History of Gospel and Christian Music*, Hal Leonard Publishing, Miami, 2002
Goff, James R. Jr., *Close Harmony: A History of Southern Gospel*, The University of North Carolina Press, 2002
Heilbut, Tony, *The Gospel Sound*, Limelight Editions, New York, 1973
Lornell, Kip, *Happy In the Service Of The Lord*, University of Illinois Press, Chicago, 1988
Moore, Allan (ed.), *The Cambridge Companion to Blues and Gospel Music*, Cambridge University Press, Cambridge, 2003
Oliver, P., *The New Grove Gospel, Blues and Jazz*, Grove Publications, London, 1987
Ward, Andrew, *Dark Midnight When I Rise: The Story of the Fisk Jubilee Singers*, HarperCollins, New York, 2001
Weldon Johnson, James, et al, *The Books of American Negro Spirituals*, Da Capo Press, Maryland, 2003
Williams, Doug, et al, *Still Standing Tall: The Story of Gospel Music's Williams Brothers*, Billboard Books, New York, 1999
Wolff, Daniel, *You Send Me: The Life and Times of Sam Cooke*, Virgin Books, New York, 1995
Young Alan, *The Pilgrim Jubilees*, University Press of Mississippi, Mississippi, 2002
Young, Alan, *Woke Me Up This Morning: Black Gopsel Singers and the Gospel Life*, University Press of Mississippi, Mississippi, 1997

ELECTRONIC

Barr, Tim, *The Mini Rough Guide To Techno Music*, Rough Guides, London, 2000
Bogdanov, Vladimir (ed.), *All Music Gude to Electronica: The Definitive Guide to Electronic Music*, Backbeat Books, San Francisco, 2001
Duckworth, William, *Talking Music: Conversations with John Cage, Philip Glass, Laurie Anderson, and Five generations of American Experimental Composers*, Da Capo Press, Maryland, 1999
Eno, Brian (foreword), Nyman, Michael, *Experimental Music: Cage and Beyond*, Cambridge University Press, Cambridge, 1999
Eno, Brian, *A Year with Swollen Appendices: the Diary of Brian Eno*, Faber and Faber, London, 1995
Holmes, Thomas B., *Electronic and Experimental Music*, Routledge, London, 2002
Kettlewell, Ben, *Electronic Music Pioneers*, Artistpro.com, California, 2001
McKay, George, *Glastonbury: A Very English Fair*, Orion, London, 2000
Nicholls, David (ed.), *The Cambridge Companion to John Cage*, Cambridge University Press, Cambridge, 2002
Prendergast, Mark, *The Ambient Century*, Bloomsbury, London, 2000
Rule, Greg, *Electro Shock! The Groundbreakers of Electronica*, Backbeat Books, San Francisco, 1999
Sicko, Dan, *Techno Rebels: The Renegades of Electronic Funk*, Billboard Books, New York, 1999
Smith Brindle, Reginald, *The New Music: The Avant-Garde Since 1945*, Oxford University Press, Oxford, 1987
Toop, David, *Ocean of Sound: Aether Talk, Ambient Sound and Imaginary Worlds*, Serpent's Tail, London, 2001
Werkhoven, Henk N. *International Guide To New Age Music: A Comprehensive Guide to the Vast and Varied Artists and Recordings of New Age Music*, Billboard Books, New York, 1998

SOUNDTRACKS AND FILM MUSIC

Appignanesi, Lisa, *Cabaret*, Random House USA Inc, New York, 1984
Bernstein, Charles H., *Film Music and Everything Else*, Turnstyle Music, 2000
Burlingame, Jon, *Sound & Vision: 60 Years of Motion Picture Soundtracks*, Billboard Books, New York, 2000
Citron, Stephen, *The Musical From The Inside Out*, Hodder and Stoughton General, London, 1991
Deutsch, Didier C. (ed.), *VideoHound's Soundtracks*, Visible Ink Press, Michigan, 1998
Flinn. Denny Martin, *Musical! A Grand Tour*, Wadsworth, 1997
Freedland, Michael, *Irving Berlin*, W. H. Allen, London, 1974
Green, Stanley, *Broadway Musicals, Show by Show*, Hal Leonard, 1997
Herman, Jerry, *Showtune: A Memoir*, Viking/Allen Lane, London
Isherwood, Christopher, *The Berlin Novels*, Vintage, London, 1993
Karlin, Fred, *Listening to Movies: The Film Lover's Guide to Film Music*, Wadsworth, 1994
Kislan, Richard, *The Musical: A Look at American Musical Theatre*, Applause Theatre Book Publishers, New York, 1995
Rona, Jeff, *The Reel World*, Backbeat UK, London, 2001
Schelle, Michael, *The Score: Interviews with Film Composers*, Silman-James Press, New York, 1999
Tonks, Paul, *Film Music: Pocket Essentials*, Pocket Essentials, London, 2001
Zadan, Craig, *Sondheim and Co.*, Collier-Mac, 1975

POPULAR AND NOVELTY

Alfonso, Barry, *Billboard Guide to Contemporary Christian Music*, Billboard Books, New York, 2002
Baker, Paul, *Contemporary Christian Music*, Crossway Books, Wheaton, 1985
Gillies, Midge, *Marie Lloyd: The One and Only*, Weidenfeld & Nicholson, London, 1999
Howard, Jay R. and Streck, John M., *Apostles of Rock*, University of Kentucky Press, Kentucky, 1999
Hudd, Roy, *Music Hall*, Methuen, London, 1976
Jones, Dylan, *Easy! The Lexicon of Lounge*, Pavilion Books, London, 1997
Knopper, Steve (ed.), *MusicHound Lounge: The Essential Album Guide to Martini Music and Easy Listening*, Omnibus Press, London, 2000
Menendez, Albert J., *Christmas Songs Made in America: Favorite Hoilday Melodies and the Stories of Their Origins*, Cumberland House Publishing, Nashville, 1999
Otfinoski, Steve, *The Golden Age of Novelty Songs*, Billboard, New York, 2000
Peacock, Charlie, *Crossroads*, Broadman and Holman, Nashville, 1999
Powell, Mark Allan, *Encyclopedia of Contemporary Christian Music*, Hendrickson Publishers, Massachusetts, 2002
The Big Book of Nostalgia, Hal Leonard Publishing, Milwaukee, 1999
Warner Brothers, *Best of Children's Favourites: 200 Great Songs and Instrumentals*, Warner Brothers Publications, Miami, 1987
Warner Brothers, *Wacky, Weird & Wonderful Novelty Songs*, Warner Brothers Publications, Miami, 2000
Zinsser, William Knowlton, *Easy to Remember: The Great American Songwriters and Their Songs*, David R. Godine, Boston, 2001

Picture Credits

Arbiter Group plc: 31 (b), 70 (l), 130 (l), 196 (tl), 302 (tl), 406 (tl), 436 (cr), 437 (cl), 438 (bl); Fender Musical Instruments Inc. 74 (tl), 142 (l), 206 (r), 439; Millennium Products 107 (tr).

ArenaPal.com: Jak Kilby: 296 (r)

C.F. Martin & Co., Inc., Nazareth, PA USA: 225 (bl)

Chris Stock: 436 (bc)

Foundry Arts: 16 (l), 20 (l), 26 (l), 28 (l), 34 (l), 40 (l), 44 (l), 46 (l), 48 (l), 58 (l), 80 (l), 86 (l), 87 (l), 92 (t), 97 (tr), 101 (r), 104 (l), 109 (tr), 110 (l), 118, 124 (l), 128 (l), 142 (r), 154 (tl), 157 (b), 158 (l), 161 (l), 172 (tl), 174 (l), 175 (tl), 182 (l), 199 (tr), 209, 213 (r), 224 (tl), 233 (tr), 236, 245 (tr), 248 (c), 249 (br), 255 (br), 258 (tl), 260 (tl), 261 (tr), 266 (tl), 268 (tl), 278 (tl), 293 (tl), 296 (tl), 300 (tr), 314 (tl), 318 (tl), 320 (tl), 328 (tl), 329 (tr), 342 (tl), 344 (tl), 356 (tl), 359 (tr), 365 (tr), 368 (tl), 374 (tl), 375 (tr), 376 (tl), 378 (tl), 392, 395 (tr), 403 (tr), 418, 427 (tr)

Kobal Collection Ltd: DISPATFILM/GEMMA/TUPAN: 150 (l); Film Four/Lafayette Films: 344 (br), 347 (br)

Mary Evans Picture Library: 120 (t), 201 (bl), 222, Thomas Gilmor: 190 (br)

Nimbus Records: Robin Broadbank: 287

Ragga **Magazine:** 352 (tl)

With grateful thanks to **Redferns** and the following list of photographers: Richie Aaron: (Country): 4, 44 (r), 76 (r), 365 (br), 367 (br); Glenn A Baker Archives: 24 (l), 31 (t), 38 (l), 43, 47, 50 (l), 74 (bl), 80 (r), 90 (r), 122 (r), 152 (c), 164, 183, 187, 188, 190 (tl), 192, 193, 210 (all), 211, 240, 302 (br), 309 (br), 354, 371, 373, 382 (tr), 411, 417 (l), 421 (br), 428 (tl); Michael Ochs Archives: (pop): 5, (Blues): 5, (Folk): 5, (Soul): 5, 9, 13 (t), 14 (b), 15, 16 (r), 17, 18 (t), 19, 20 (r), 21, 24 (r), 26 (r), 27, 28 (r), 29, 32 (l), 33 (b), 36 (r), 41, 42 (all), 74 (tr), 82 (l), 83, 109 (bl), 117, 121 (tr), 122 (l), 123, 125, 134 (tl), 135, 137 (r), 153 (tl & bl), 155, 159 (tr), 165, 166 (b), 167 (l), 170 (r), 173 (all), 174 (l), 175 (bl), 177, 180 (c), 181 (c), 181 (br), 181 (tr), 184, 186 (r), 191, 194, 195 (br), 198, 199 (cl), 200, 201 (tl), 203, 212 (tr), 223, 224 (br), 228, 231 (br), 237 (tr), 248 (cr), 248 (bl), 249 (l), 297, 301, 304 (tl), 369, 370 (all), 374 (tr),

378 (tr), 386 (br), 387, 388 (tl), 391 (b), 405 (tl), 412 (tl), 413, 432 (all), 444 (tr), Bob Baker: 141, 153 (c); Dick Barnatt: 76 (l); Paul Bergen: 57, 64 (l), 67, 147, 178 (r), 215 (tr), 313, 381, 402; Chuck Boyd: 79, 81; Carey Brandon: 68 (l); Henrietta Butler: (Classical): 5, 6 (bl), 251, 280 (r); William P. Gottlieb/ Library of Congress: 120 (b), 121 (bl), 152 (bl), 230 (tl); Fin Costello: 49, 50 (r), 52 (l), 78 (l), 82 (r), 93 (tr), 94 (tl), 97 (b), 107 (bl), 108 (r), 237 (bl), 299 (bl), 314 (tr), 332 (tr); Nigel Crane: 115, 276 (tl); Geoff Dann: 176 (l); Grant Davis: 46 (r), 60 (r), 61; Frank Debaeker: 138 (tl); DeltaHaze Corporation: 160; Phil Dent: 225 (br), 249 (c); Ian Dickson: 88 (r), 91, 243 (l), 422 (br); Kieran Doherty: 62 (l); Debbie Doss: 39; Jill Douglas: 304 (r); Rico D' Rozario: 148 (r), 153 (tr); David Warner Ellis: 85; James Emmett: 217; Brigitte Engl: 98 (l), 215 (l), 280 (tl); JM International: 68 (r); Erica Echenberg: 113 (r), 319 (tr); Max Jones Files: (Jazz): 5, 119, 124 (r), 126 (all), 127, 128 (r), 130 (r), 151, 152 (tr), 390 (all); Tabatha Fireman: 350 (tl); Patrick Ford: 58 (r), 62 (r), 103 (bl), 246, 360 (tl), 372 (tl); Fotex: 356 (r); Colin Fuller: 132 (br); Gems: 11 (t), 22 (r), 195 (t), 208, 226 (tl), 230 (tr), 235 (all); Suzi Gibbons: 51, 103 (tr), 283 (b); Steve Gillett: 238, 249 (tr), 293 (b); Harry Goodwin: 18 (b), 310, 333 (br); William Gottlieb: 133, 149; Beth Gwinn: 213 (l), 218 (r), 221 (br); Tim Hall: 54 (l), 279, 288 (tl), 290 (r), 308 (tl); Olivia Hemingway: 144 (r); Richie Howell: 234; Clive Hunte: 99 (l); Mick Hutson: 92 (l), 95 (all), 98 (r), 104 (r), 108 (l), 112 (tl), 114 (all), 247 (tr), 320 (r); Salifu Idriss: 364; Benedict Johnson: 69; K&K: 96 (bc), 172 (br); Max Scheler/K&K Studios: 25; Simon King: 312 (t & bl); John Kirk: 362 (br); Robert Knight: 176 (r); Elliott Landy: 284 (r); Martin Langer: 395 (bl); Michel Linssen: (Rock): 5, 7 (l), 60 (l), 64 (r), 66 (r), 75, 99 (tr), 111 (c), 326 (r), 423; Jon Lusk: 294 (tl), 305, 306 (all), 307; Hayley Madden: 102, 294 (r), 309 (tl); Gered Mankowitz: 10 (t), 84 (l), 96 (tl); Marc Marnie: 300 (tr); Sue Moore: 100; Keith Morris: 38 (r), 48 (r), 84 (r), 86 (r), 243 (r), 372 (r), 382 (bl); Leon Morris: 291, 317 (r); Stuart Mostyn: 66 (l); Tim Motion: 286 (tr), 308 (cr); Charlie Murphy: 278 (b), 309 (tr); Odile Noel: 290 (tl); Jan Olofsson: 205; Roberta Parkin: 289; Dave Peabody: 232 ; Martin Philbey: (Dance): 5, 7 (br), 311; Andrew Putler: 138 (r), 282, 299 (t), 353 ; Christina Radish: 71; RB: 32 (r), 33 (l), 35, 40 (r), 157 (t), 180 (tl), 202: David Redfern: (Gospel): 5, (Popular and Novelty): 5, 34 (r), 55, 129, 132 (tl), 134 (br), 136, 137 (l), 140 (all), 146 (all), 150 (r), 162, 180 (br), 182 (r), 189, 204 (tl), 206 (tl), 214, 231 (tl), 233 (l), 239 (tr), 242 (tl), 244, 288 (r), 303, 375 (b), 385, 388 (r), 389, 391 (tr & l), 419: Ebet Roberts: (World): 5, 53, 78 (r), 89, 90 (l), 93 (bl), 105, 106, 110 (r), 112 (br), 113 (l), 166 (l), 185, 196 (br), 207, 216, 219, 245 (l), 277, 281, 308 (br), 315: Redferns: 70 (r), 139; Rick Richards: 22 (tl), 23; Steve Richards: 94 (br); Simon Ritter: 65, 247 (bl); John Rodgers: 37; Kerstin Rodgers: 101 (l); S&G: 45; S&G Press Agency: 30 (r); Donna Santisi: 59, 87 (b); Philippe Schneider: 148 (l); Pankaj Shah: 276 (br), 284 (tl), 285; Brian Shuel: 226 (r), 239 (l), 242 (br), 248 (tr); Nicky J. Sims: 56 (r), 145, 218 (tl), 283 (t), 286 (tl), 292, 324 (tl); Colin Streater: 144 (l); Jon Super: 111 (tr), 321 (tr), 329 (l), 333 (c); Gai Terrell: 225 (t); Virginia Turbett: 52 (r); Colin Turner: 229 ; Toby Wates: 143, 431; Des Willie: 63, 73 (b), 361, 367 (tr); Bob Willoughby: 12, 131, 171; Val Wilmer: 10 (b), 30 (l), 36 (l); Jon Wilton: 8; Geo Johnston Wright: 394; Charlyn Zlotnik: 204 (br)

Retna UK: Jenny Lewis: 316 (tl); Êneil Massey: 330 (tl)

With grateful thanks to **S.I.N.** and the following list of photographers: Peter Anderson: (Reggae): 5, 6 (tr), 338, 340 (br), 347 (bc), 363; Andrew Catlin: 339 (tl); David Corio: 337, 341, 347 (cl), 347 (tr), 349, 351, 352 (r), 355, 359 (bc), 367 (c), 376 (br), 383; Melanie Cox: 325 (tr), 330 (br), 331 (br); Joe Dilworth: 398 (br); Steve Double: 312 (br), 318 (b), 323 (tr), 326 (tl), 331 (tr), 333 (l), 342 (r), 360 (r), 362 (br), 380 (tl), 403 (bl); Eye and Eye/Jack Barron: 358, 367 (tl); Greg Freeman: 380 (br); Martyn Goodacre: 321 (b), 322 (br), 343, 346 (tl), 396; Colin Hawkins: 317 (tl), 323 (cl), 324 (r); Jane Houghton: 399; Dee Johnston: 316 (br), 322 (tr), 327 (tr), 332 (tl); Jouko Lehtola: 346 (r); Hayley Madden: 405 (tr), 407; Anna Meuer: 377, 400 (r), 401, 406 (b); Phil Nicholls: 340 (tl), 347 (tl); Peter Noble: (Electronic): 5, 393; Alessio Pizzicannella: 327 (cl), 328 (br), 397, 398 (tl); Ronni Randall: 400 (tl); Leo Regan: 345; Paul Stanley: (Hip Hop): 5, 319 (b), 335, 444 (bl); Roy Tee: 379; Kim Tonelli: 325 (br), 332 (b); Alison Turner: 339 (tr); Andy Willsher: 404

Sylvia Pitcher Photo Library: 154 (r), 156, 159 (bl), 161 (bl), 163 (tr), 167 (tr), 168, 169 (all), 180 (bl), 180 (tr), 181 (cl), 186 (tl); The Weston Collection: 158 (r); Tony Mottram: 179; Brian Smith: 163 (l), 178 (l)

Topham Picturepoint: (Soundtracks and Theatre): 5, 11 (b), 13 (b), 14 (t), 77, 88 (l), 116, 170 (tl), 197, 212 (tl), 227, 250 (all), 252, 253 (t), 255 (t), 256, 257 (t), 258 (r), 260 (r), 261 (bl), 262 (r), 263, 265, 268 (tr), 270 (tl), 271, 272 (tr), 274, 275, 336 (r), 348, 350 (tr), 367 (bl), 368 (br), 384, 386 (tl), 409, 410, 414 (all), 415, 416 (all), 417 (c), 420 (bl), 421 (tl), 422 (tl), 424 (all), 425 (all), 426 (tl), 427 (tl), 429, 430 (all), 433, 434 (all); AP: 412 (b), 417 (r); Clive Barda/PAL: 262 (tl), 267 (l); Marco Borggreve/PAL: 259; Lebrecht Music Collection: 264 (tl); Fritz Curson/PAL: 272 (tl); The British Library/HIP: 257 (b); Museum of London/HIP: 253 (b); Robert Millard/PAL: 273; PA: 54 (r), 241, 269, 295, 309 (c), 420 (tr), 426 (r), 428 (r), 435 (br); Linda Rich/PAL: 270 (br); UPPA Ltd: 56 (l), 254, 264 (tr), 267 (br), 408; Image Works: 334; Richard Lucas/The Image Works: 336 (tl); Syracuse Newspapers/The Image Works: 298

Urbanimage.tv: Tim Barrow: 357

Yamaha-Kemble Music (UK) Ltd: 266 (c), 437 (tr), 437 (r), 437 (b), 437 (bl), 438 (c), 438 (br)

Biographies

FOREWORD: Sir George Martin

Sir George Martin has produced more than 700 recordings in a 50-year career which has encompassed a wide range of musical genres - jazz, rock, classical, comedy and film soundtracks, including an unprecedented 30 number one Beatles and post-Beatles hits. Martin is arguably the most influential and prolific record producer in history. He has worked with artists like Stan Getz and Judy Garland, establishing himself as a jazz, classical and light music producer, and produced a string of hit comedy records with Peter Ustinov and the Goons, before in 1960, as head of Parlophone, the Temperance Seven gave him his first number one hit. But it was the 1960s which saw him make his greatest impression, with the emergence of the Beatles. In 1963, Martin spent a record-breaking 37 weeks at the number one spot, as the producer of the Beatles and other artists. Martin produced almost every Beatles single and album during their career. In the '70s and '80s, he produced albums by the Mahavishnu Orchestra, America, Jeff Beck, Neil Sedaka, Jimmy Webb, Cheap Trick and Kenny Rogers. He was knighted in 1996, and received a Lifetime Achievement Award at the Grammys the same year. A year later, Martin produced his 30th number one hit in the UK, Elton John's 'Candle in the Wind 1997', a charity single recorded after Diana, Princess of Wales' death, that became the bestselling single of all time and, in Martin's words, "...probably my last single. It's not a bad one to go out on."

GENERAL EDITOR: Paul Du Noyer

Paul Du Noyer has written about music for over 20 years. He began his career as a reporter on the *NME*, went on to edit *Q* magazine, launched *Mojo* and is now associate editor of *Word*. With hundreds of interviews to his credit he's been face to face with Madonna, Bruce Springsteen and David Bowie, as well as every Liverpool legend from Billy Fury to the La's. He has also collaborated with Paul McCartney on three World Tour magazines. His books include *We All Shine On*, about the songs of John Lennon, and *Liverpool: Wondrous Place*, a history of his home town's music scene.

CONSULTANT EDITORS

Ian Anderson (Folk): Ian is the founder and editor of the renowned folk music magazine, *fROOTS*, radio presenter, occasional record producer, semi-retired musician and completely retired festival and tour organizer.

Geoff Brown (Pop; Gospel; Soul And R&B): Geoff is a writer on popular music at *Mojo* magazine. Following about a year as a professional drummer with the Jimmy Brown Sound, Geoff spent several years with *Melody Maker* and *Black Music* magazine. He is currently production editor for *Mojo* magazine His most recent book was *Otis Redding: Try a Little Tenderness*.

Richard Buskin (Pop; Rock; Popular And Novelty): Used to be senior editor and bureau chief of *Performance*, as well as a researcher and on-screen music expert for the BBC (also see below).

Paul Kingsbury (Country): Paul Kingsbury is a freelance writer and former director of special projects at the Country Music Hall of Fame and Museum in Nashville, Tennessee, and was the editor for the Hall of Fame's press and its *Journal of Country Music*. Books he has written and edited include *The Grand Ole Opry History of Country Music*, *The Encyclopedia of Country Music* and *Country: The Music and the Musicians*.

Chrissie Murray (Jazz): Chrissie Murray is a freelance journalist and former jazz consultant to London's Capital Radio. She has worked as a record-plugger/press officer for Charly/Affinity Records. She was co-founder/launch editor of the ground-breaking magazine *The Wire* and was relaunch editor of *Jazzwise* magazine. She is currently an associate editor of *Jazz At Ronnie Scott's* (the revered jazz club's house magazine) and freelances for *JazzUK*.

Michael Paoletta (Dance): Michael Paoletta is the Dance/Electronic Music Editor and Album Reviews Editor of *Billboard* magazine in New York. Prior to joining Billboard in 1998, Paoletta was a freelance journalist. His byline has appeared in numerous publications, including *Vibe*, *Spin*, *the Advocate*, *Paper*, *Detour*, and *Time Out New York*.

Stanley Sadie (Classical): Stanley was the music critic for *The Times* for 17 years, editor of *The Musical Times* for 20 years and music consultant of the television series, *Man and Music*. Since 1970 he has been the editor of *The New Grove Dictionary of Music*, the standard classical reference work for over 20 years. He is renowned throughout the world as an educator and expert of integrity and is generally regarded as a premier authority on classical music. He was appointed CBE in 1982. He was the general editor for the *Billboard Illustrated Encyclopedia of Classical Music*.

Philip Van Vleck (Blues; World; Hip Hop; Reggae): Currently the pop music critic for the Durham Herald-Sun newspaper (Durham, NC), Philip Van Vleck also covers world music, blues, jazz and world jazz for *Billboard* magazine, and is a regular contributor to College Music Journal's *New Music Monthly* magazine, *Dirty Linen* magazine, and BMGmusic.com. In addition to his music journalism, he holds a Ph.D. from Duke University and teaches in the history department at North Carolina State University in Raleigh.

John Wilson (Soundtracks And Theatre): John is a conductor, arranger and scholar and is recognized internationally as an expert in the specialist fields of light music and music for screen. He has restored a number of classic film scores and he recently took on the enormous task of reconstructing the orchestrations of all the major MGM Musicals. He is based in the UK.

AUTHORS

Barry Alfonso (Contemporary Christian Music): Based in the US, Barry is a freelance writer, having recently authored *The Billboard Guide to Contemporary Christian Music*. He lived and worked in Nashville and has had songs recorded by Trisha Yearwood, Pam Tillis and Kathy Mattea.

Bob Allen (Country): Bob Allen has spent the last quarter century as a country music journalist, historian and critic. He is former Nashville editor for, and has been a regular contributor to, the popular Nashville-based fan magazine, *Country Music Magazine,* since 1977. His writing on country music has appeared in *Esquire, Rolling Stone,* the *Washington Post*, the *Atlanta Journal,* and the *Baltimore Sun*. Allen is the author of *The Life And Times Of A Honky Tonk Legend*, the (unauthorized) biography of singer George Jones, and he has contributed to various historical and reference books on country music in recent years. He resides in Eldersburg, Maryland.

Julian Beecroft (Classical): Julian Beecroft studied music at the Guildhall School of Music and Drama, specializing in composition. After graduating, he worked at the same institution for several years as, among other things, a lecturer in twentieth century music history. During this period he was also a composer and performer in various experimental music ensembles. In the past, he has written for the music journal *Tempo* and as a sub-editor for *Musical Opinion* magazine.

Lloyd Bradley (Hip Hop; Reggae): Lloyd Bradley is a classically trained chef and toured the USA as a member of ParliamentFunkadelic. As a teenager he was sucked into the nether world of north London sound systems and owned and operated the Dark Star rig in the late-1970s. For the last twenty years he has written about music for *Mojo*, *Q*, the *Guardian*, *NME* and *Blender*, amongst others. He is the author of *Bass Culture: When Reggae Was King*, *Reggae: The Story Of Jamaican Music* and was Associate Producer of the BBC2 series of the same name.

Keith Briggs (Gospel): Since 1983 Keith Briggs has been the reviews editor of the magazine *Blues And Rhythm: The Gospel Truth*. He has also contributed articles to this and other specialist publications as well as compiling and/or writing the notes for several hundred CDs.

Richard Brophy (Electronic): Seduced by early nineties dance music, Irish journalist Richard Brophy wrote for Dublin fanzine *Club Dub*, before becoming the dance music correspondent for Irish music magazine *Hot Press*. By the mid- to late-1990s, he was writing for UK dance magazines *Jockey Slut* and *DJ* magazine as well as contributing articles to newspapers like the *Irish Times* and the *Evening Herald*. In 1998, Brophy saw the potential of reaching dance music's worldwide audience via the Internet and set up the pioneering website, Etronik – *www.etronik.com*.

Richard Buskin (50s and 60s Pop; Rock): A *New York Times* best-selling author, Richard Buskin has been a full-time freelance journalist specializing in the fields of popular music, film, television, and cultural affairs for the past twenty years. Having written for numerous music and film magazines around the world, he has also authored more than a dozen pop culture books. Among the most recent are *Inside Tracks: A First-Hand History of Popular Music from the World's Greatest Record Producers and Engineers* and *Sheryl Crow: No Fool to This Game*. A native of London, England, he lives in Chicago with his wife and daughter.

Leila Cobo (World; Latin): A native of Colombia, Leila Cobo is *Billboard Magazine*'s Latin/Caribbean Bureau Chief, and the first woman to hold that post for the magazine. Ms. Cobo is considered one of the leading experts in Latin music in the country and is regularly interviewed and onsulted by outlets such as CNN, VH1, the BBC, Reuters, the *Los Angeles Times*, the *Washington Post* and *USA Today*.

Cliff Douse (Jazz, Blues): Cliff Douse has written hundreds of articles and columns during the past ten years for many of the UK's foremost music and computer magazines including *Guitarist*, *Guitar Techniques*, *Total Guitar*, *Computer Music*, *Future Music*, *Rhythm* and *Mac Format*. He is also the author and co-author of several music books published by *IMP*, *Music Sales*, *Music Maker* and *Thunder Bay*. He is currently the editor of *Guitarist Icons* magazine (a quarterly special issue of *Guitarist* magazine) and is working on a number of new books and music software projects.

David Hutcheon (World): David Hutcheon first discovered the joys of world music when he accidentally married a member of the Cambodia National Ballet in a Chinese restaurant in Newcastle in 1990. Oddly, prestigious publications such as *Time Out*, the *Sunday Times*, *Mojo* and *The Times* like his unorthodox approach and continue to commission him.

Colin Irwin (Folk): London-based music journalist Colin Irwin has been writing about folk music for 25 years. He joined *Melody Maker* in the mid-1970s, eventually becoming assistant editor. He was editor of the weekly pop magazine *Number One* before turning to freelance writing and has presented several BBC series on folk music, both on radio and television. He's also a regular contributor to UK magazines *Mojo* and *fROOTS*, has written for *The Times*, the *Guardian* and the *Independent* and also wrote The *Name Of The Game*, a biography of ABBA.

Nick Joy (Soundtracks): Nick Joy has contributed countless CD reviews to soundtrack magazines such as *Film Score Monthly* and *Music from the Movies*. In the last four years he has also interviewed a number of the genre's leading composers, including Howard Shore, Ennio Morricone, Elmer Bernstein, Craig Armstrong, Michael Nyman, David Arnold and Gabriel Yared.

Dave Ling (Rock): Dave Ling has been a music journalist for more than two decades, with work published in *Sounds*, *Kerrang!*, *Metal Hammer*, *RAW* and *Frontiers* magazines, plus various websites. In November 1998, Dave was among the co-founders of *Classic Rock* magazine, a publication that was recently acknowledged as the fastest growing music title in the UK. He also edits *Subterranea*, a monthly extreme music supplement to *Metal Hammer* magazine.

Carl Loben (Dance): Once the drummer in a couple of no-mark indie bands, Carl Loben was soon seduced by the acid house sounds he first encountered at the Glastonbury festival in the late-1980s. An early UK convert, he started writing about the emerging dance scene in the music weekly *Melody Maker* as well as in more specialist dance publications. In the mid-1990s he became wholeheartedly immersed in the nascent London drum & bass scene and he settled into his current day job as features editor of the widely-respected *DJ* magazine.

Bill Milkowski (Jazz; Blues): Bill Milkowski is a New York-based music writer whose work has appeared in several magazines over the past 25 years, including *Down Beat*, *Jazz Times*, *Jazziz*, *Guitar Player*, *Guitar World*, *Bass Player* and *Modern Drummer*. He is also the author of *JACO: The Extraordinary and Tragic Life of Jaco Pastorius* (Back Beat Books) and *Swing It! An Annotated History of Jive* (Billboard Books).

Garry Mulholland (70s, 80s, 90s, 00s Pop; Soul And R&B): Garry is a music writer based in London, and has contributed features and interviews on pop, rock, dance and black music to *NME*, *Select*, the *Guardian*, the *Sunday Times*, the *Independent* and *Time Out*. His first book *This is Uncool: The 500 Greatest Singles Since Punk and Disco* was published by Cassell Illustrated in 2002.

Steve Nallon (Musicals): Steve Nallon is a writer, broadcaster, performer and theatre director. His work on musical theatre includes contributions to the magazine *Musical Stages*, the BBC series *Soul Music* and the book for the musical *Like Love*. He is also a contributor to *The New Statesman* and *Screenwriter*. Steve has been a visiting lecturer at the department of Drama and Theatre arts at the University of Birmingham since 1995, notably in the Broadway musical, Greek theatre, stand-up comedy, screenwriting and film studies. As a theatre director Steve specializes in new writing.

Douglas J Noble (Rock): Douglas J Noble is a musician, guitar instructor and freelance music journalist based in Edinburgh. He has written books on Jimi Hendrix and Peter Green as well as a guitar tuition book – *The Right Way To Play Guitar* – and has contributed to several books on the electric guitar. He is the Music Director of *UniVibes*, the international Jimi Hendrix magazine, and is an examiner for Rock School/Trinity College of Music. He has contributed to over a dozen music magazines, interviewed many of the world's top guitarists and is the tablature editor for *The Guitar Magazine*. He also has a degree in psychology and diplomas in classical guitar.

Ed Potton (00s Pop; Soundtracks And Theatre; Popular And Novelty): Ed works as a writer and editor. A regular contributor of articles on music, film and literature to *The Times*, he has also written for *Elle*, the *Independent on Sunday*, *Muzik* and the BBC, and is co-author of *Into the Woods: the Definitive Story of the Blair Witch Project*. He has been an associate producer for Channel 4 television and a broadcast journalist for BBC radio. He has lectured at the University of Bournemouth and the Chelsea College of Art. Travel, Billy Wilder films and Stevie Wonder's *Songs in the Key of Life* are among his favourite things. He lives in London.

Index